INVESTIGATE
the Big Ideas of
History!

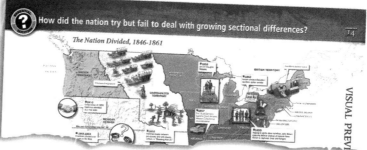

? How did the nation try but fail to deal with growing sectional differences?

The Nation Divided, 1846-1861

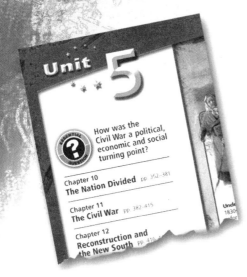

Unit 5

? How was the Civil War a political, economic and social turning point?

Chapter 10
The Nation Divided pp. 352–381

Chapter 11
The Civil War pp. 382–415

Chapter 12
Reconstruction and the New South pp. 416–...

Essential Questions for every unit, chapter, and section will lead you on an inquiry-based exploration of our nation's history.

THINK LIKE A HISTORIAN ACTIVITY

Divide into three groups to build an answer to the unit question: How was the Civil War a political, economic, and social turning point?

One group should use the Think Like a Historian documents to describe the Civil War's political effects. Another group should use the documents to describe the economic effects of the war. The last group should cover the war's social effects. After each group has had time to prepare a presentation, it should report its findings to the rest of the class in the format of a documentary news program.

Historian's Apprentice Activity Pack

Using primary and secondary sources, the **Historian's Apprentice Activity Pack** activities allow you to "roll-up-your-sleeves" and explore **Essential Questions** firsthand.

Each folder focuses on an Essential Question:

- How is the rule of law in the Constitution of the United States rooted in the past?

- How can a nation be united and divided at the same time?

- Was Reconstruction a success or failure?

- How did industrialization affect the United States?

- What major influences have helped shape American society and culture?

- How has the United States tried to remain safe and to defend democracy?

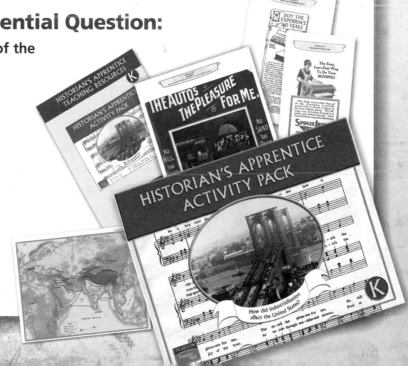

HISTORIAN'S APPRENTICE ACTIVITY PACK

Prentice Hall

AMERICA

HISTORY OF OUR NATION

Beginnings Through 1877

James West Davidson

PEARSON

Upper Saddle River, New Jersey • Boston, Massachusetts • Glenview, Illinois • Parsippany, New Jersey • Shoreview, Minnesota

THE LANDING OF THE PILGRIMS :1620   MABELLE L HOLMES

Acknowledgments appear on page T704, which constitutes an extension of this copyright page.

Copyright © 2009 by Pearson Education, Inc. All rights reserved. Printed in the United States of America. This publication is protected by copyright, and permission should be obtained from the publisher prior to any prohibited reproduction, storage in a retrieval system, or transmission in any form or by any means, electronic, mechanical, photocopying, recording, or likewise. For information regarding permission(s), write to Pearson School Rights and Permissions Department, One Lake Street, Upper Saddle River, New Jersey 07458.

Discovery School® is a registered trademark of Discovery Communications, Inc.
MapMaster® is a registered trademark of Pearson Education, Inc.

Prentice Hall® and **Pearson Prentice Hall**™ are
trademarks, in the U.S. and/or in other countries,
of Pearson Education, Inc., or its affiliate(s).

PEARSON

13-digit ISBN 978-0-13-365245-1
10-digit ISBN 0-13-365245-9

2 3 4 5 6 7 8 9 10   11 10 09 08 07

Author

James West Davidson

Dr. James Davidson is coauthor of *After the Fact: The Art of Historical Detection* and *Nation of Nations: A Narrative History of the American Republic.* Dr. Davidson has taught at both the college and high school levels. He has also consulted on curriculum design for American history courses. Dr. Davidson is an avid canoeist and hiker. His published works on these subjects include *Great Heart,* the true story of a 1903 canoe trip in the Canadian wilderness.

Senior Program Consultants

Albert M. Camarillo

Dr. Albert Camarillo received his Ph.D. in U.S. history from the University of California at Los Angeles. He has been teaching history at Stanford University since 1975. Dr. Camarillo has published six books, including *Chicanos in a Changing Society: From Mexican Pueblos to American Barrios* and *California: A History of Mexican Americans.* His awards for research and writing include a National Endowment for the Humanities Fellowship and a Rockefeller Foundation Fellowship. Dr. Camarillo is the Miriam and Peter Haas Centennial Professor in Public Service.

Diane Hart

Diane Hart is a writer and consultant in history and social studies. She earned bachelor's and master's degrees in history from Stanford University and was a Woodrow Wilson Fellow. As a former teacher at the elementary, secondary, and college levels, Ms. Hart remains deeply involved in social studies education through her active participation in both the National and California Councils for the Social Studies. She has written a number of textbooks for middle school students.

Senior Reading Consultants

Kate Kinsella

Kate Kinsella, Ed.D., is a faculty member in the Department of Secondary Education at San Francisco State University. A specialist in secondary language acquisition and adolescent literacy, she teaches coursework addressing language and literacy development across the secondary curricula. Dr. Kinsella earned her M.A. in TESOL from San Francisco State University and her Ed.D. in Second Language Acquisition from the University of San Francisco.

Kevin Feldman

Kevin Feldman, Ed.D., is the Director of Reading and Early Intervention with the Sonoma County Office of Education (SCOE) and an independent educational consultant. At the SCOE, he develops, organizes, and monitors programs related to K–12 literacy. Dr. Feldman has an M.A. from the University of California, Riverside, in Special Education, Learning Disabilities, and Instructional Design. He earned his Ed.D. in Curriculum and Instruction from the University of San Francisco.

Academic Reviewers

William R. Childs, Ph.D.
Associate Professor of History
Ohio State University
Columbus, Ohio

Theodore DeLaney, Ph.D.
Associate Professor of History
Washington and Lee University
Lexington, Virginia

Wanda A. Hendricks, Ph.D.
Associate Professor of History
University of South Carolina
Columbia, South Carolina

Emma Lapsansky, Ph.D.
Professor of History
Haverford College
Haverford, Pennsylvania

Brendan McConville, Ph.D.
Professor of History
Boston University
Boston, Massachusetts

Gordon Newby, Ph.D.
Chair, Department of Middle Eastern
    and South Asian Studies
Emory University
Atlanta, Georgia

Judy A. Ridner, Ph.D.
Assistant Professor of History
Muhlenberg College
Allentown, Pennsylvania

Teacher Reviewers

Peggy Althof
Social Studies Facilitation, K–12
D-11 Public Schools
Colorado Springs, Colorado

Lon Van Bronkhorst
K–12 Social Studies Curriculum Supervisor
Grand Rapids Public Schools
Grand Rapids, Michigan

Katherine A. Deforge
Chair, Social Studies Department
Marcellus Central Schools
Marcellus, New York

Roceal N. Duke
District of Columbia Public Schools
Washington, D.C.

Dee Ann Holt
Chair, Social Studies Department
Horace Mann Arts and Science
    Magnet Middle School
Little Rock, Arkansas

Deborah J. Miller
Detroit Public Schools
Detroit, Michigan

Carol Schneider
Curriculum Coordinator
Rock Point Community School
Rock Point, Arizona

Leigh Tanner, Ph.D.
Division of Instructional Support
Pittsburgh Public Schools
Pittsburgh, Pennsylvania

Partnership School Consultants

Melanie Alston
Hackensack Middle School
Hackensack, New Jersey

Matthew Facella
Hackensack Middle School
Hackensack, New Jersey

Karina Koepke
Hackensack Middle School
Hackensack, New Jersey

Richard Yannarelli
Principal
Hackensack Middle School
Hackensack, New Jersey

Content Consultants

Elizabeth Alexander
Social Studies Consultant
Fort Worth, Texas

Dianna Davis-Horine
Social Studies Consultant
Jacksonville, Florida

Michal Howden
Social Studies Consultant
Zionsville, Indiana

Kathy Lewis-Stewart
Social Studies Consultant
Fort Worth, Texas

Joseph Wieczorek
Social Studies Consultant
Nottingham, Maryland

Table of Contents

Explore the past through the power of technology.

MAP MASTER® Skills Activity	**Discovery School Video**	PRENTICE HALL **StudentEXPRESS™** Learn · Study · Succeed	**History _Interactive_** 
Develop geographic literacy through dynamic map skills instruction. Learn map skills, and interact with every map online and on CD-ROM.	Visit the times and places you are studying in American history with a high-impact video program created to enhance your experience of this textbook by our partner Discovery School.	Activate your learning with a suite of tools online and on CD-ROM: • Interactive Textbook • Reading and Notetaking Study Guide • Social Studies Skills Tutor • Web Resources	Launch into an interactive adventure online—using special graphics in this textbook as jumping-off points—to extend your understanding of American history.

Unit 1 Beginnings of American History.. 1

? Essential Question: How did the colonists, with strong roots in the past, develop their own way of life?

Surrender at Yorktown

Table of Contents

The signing of the Constitution

UNIT 3 The New Republic 276

 Essential Question: What problems might a new nation face?

**The Lewis and
Clark expedition**

Table of Contents

San Francisco, 1850s

The Civil War: African American soldiers

Special Features

History Reading Skills

Enhance your ability to read and understand textbooks through reading skills instruction.

THINK LIKE A HISTORIAN

Answer the Unit Essential Question by analyzing historical documents.

GEOGRAPHY AND HISTORY

Discover the role geography has played in American history.

HISTORIAN'S APPRENTICE ACTIVITY PACK

Complete the activity packs to answer essential questions about American history.

LIFE AT THE TIME

Learn more about how people lived at different places and times in history.

Literature

Experience American history through works of literature.

Links Across Time

Expand your understanding of American history by connecting the past and the present.

Skills for Life

Build skills that will help you analyze American history content.

● INFOGRAPHIC

Understand the significance of important historical events and developments.

Special Features *(continued)*

History *Interactive*

Launch into an interactive adventure to extend your understanding of American history.

Biography Quest

Search for answers to mysteries about key people in American history.

Discovery School Video

Watch American history unfold in exciting video stories for every chapter.

Quick View Video

Experience spectacular stories and get a quick overview of each chapter's main ideas with these high-interest videos. Review questions appear after each video segment.

Explore More Video

Visit times and places in American history and learn more about specific topics in each chapter with these high-impact videos.

Increase your understanding of American history by studying maps.

Illustrated Atlas of American History

Understand your world by comparing maps of the United States today with historical maps.

Special Features *(continued)*

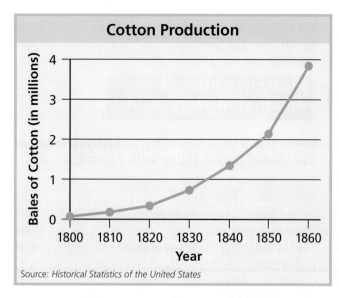

Cotton Production

Source: *Historical Statistics of the United States*

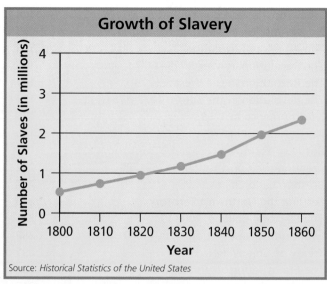

Growth of Slavery

Source: *Historical Statistics of the United States*

Timelines

Cause-and-Effect Charts

Political Cartoons

King Andrew the First

A king's crown

Trampling on rights

Reading Political Cartoons

Skills Activity

The national press ridiculed Jackson for his quick temper and steely will.

(a) Detect Points of View Name two negative images in the cartoon. Why do you think Jackson is shown stepping on the bank document?

(b) Distinguish Relevant Information Would this cartoon have the same impact in Britain if, instead of Jackson, it showed a British leader? Explain your answer.

In-Text Sources

Gain insights by examining documents, eyewitness accounts, and other sources.

Special Features (continued)

Primary Sources

Tools to help you along the way...

Taking Notes

In history, there's a lot to read about and a lot to understand. Taking good notes is one way to help you remember key ideas and to see the big picture. This program has two ways to help you.

You can keep your notes in the *Interactive Reading and Notetaking Study Guide*. Or you can go online to take your notes. Either way, you will be able to record what you are learning. And, by the end of the year, you'll have created a perfect study tool.

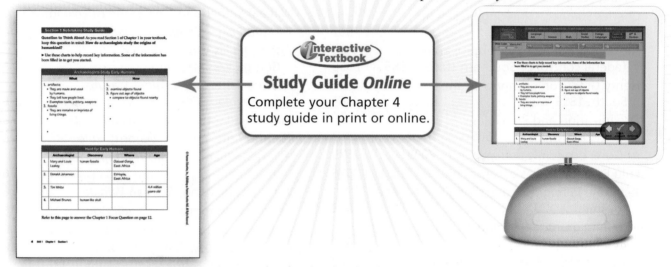

Study Guide *Online*

Complete your Chapter 4 study guide in print or online.

Monitor Your Progress

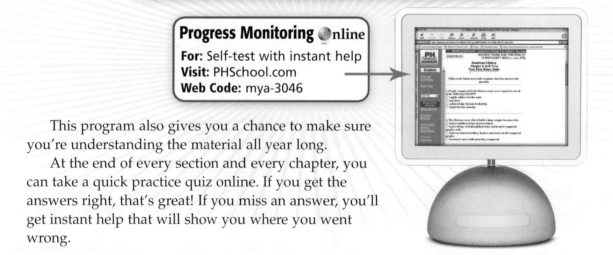

Progress Monitoring *Online*

For: Self-test with instant help
Visit: PHSchool.com
Web Code: mya-3046

This program also gives you a chance to make sure you're understanding the material all year long.

At the end of every section and every chapter, you can take a quick practice quiz online. If you get the answers right, that's great! If you miss an answer, you'll get instant help that will show you where you went wrong.

The Value of Primary Sources: A Note from James Davidson

An American colonist would have known what was meant if a friend insisted he had gotten his information "straight from the horse's mouth." The news was not second-hand or passed along; it came directly from the person involved. And for that reason it was valued.

James West Davidson
Author

Historians value primary sources for just that reason. Primary sources are those words or artifacts that come directly from the past times we study. They are not second-hand summaries. They get us as close to the original events as we are likely to get, years after a particular event happened. As close as the horse's mouth itself!

Try an experiment. The Great Awakening was a series of religious revivals in the colonies during the 1730s and 1740s. George Whitefield was a minister who led many of them. A secondary source—a historian, let's say—might describe the crowds who flocked from all over to hear Whitefield when he came to a city or town. Such a secondary account might emphasize how excited the colonists were to hear Whitefield.

Would you prefer hearing the historian's description? Or would it be better to listen to Nathan Cole, a Connecticut farmer who was there? Cole came all afire when he heard that Whitefield was going to speak only twelve miles from his farm.

"I was in my field at Work. I dropt my tool that I had in my hand and ran home and run through my house and bade my wife get ready quick to go and hear Mr. Whitefield preach at Middletown, and run to my pasture for my horse with all my might fearing that I should be too late to hear him. I…took my wife up and went forward as fast as I thought the horse could bear, and when my horse began to be out of breath, I would get down and put my wife on the Saddle and bid her ride as fast as she could and not Stop or Slack for me except I bad her, and so I would run until I was much out of breath.…"

Who wouldn't prefer the primary source? It takes us to the scene with a vividness that a secondary account would be hard pressed to match.

For this reason, my co-author Michael Stoff and I integrate primary sources throughout our narrative as we tell the story of American history. I encourage you to use this program to help your students approach primary sources as if they were detectives, whether the sources are the words in a letter or diary, legislative journals, or photographs or pictures created by people living at the time. Primary sources are our essential links to the past. They are our own personal time machine, in effect. By listening to voices "straight from the horse's mouth"—and by analyzing them carefully—we can travel to lands where no ordinary passport could take us.

James West Davidson
Author

Program Organization

America: History of Our Nation is designed to help middle school students of all abilities master core American history content. It presents a chronological history of the American experience from the earliest times to the present. The mission of the program is to forge a clear path for students to master the content, providing access for diverse learners and inspiring further exploration. Author James West Davidson offers a book that uses narrative, images, and primary sources as the key to unlocking the exciting story of our nation's history for all students.

Essential Questions

Essential Questions are thought-provoking questions that identify the "big ideas" of each chapter and unit of study, forming the foundation of student learning. The questions provide the framework that helps them organize and remember the facts. But the questions also help students recognize the broader concerns and implications of history— they move beyond rote memorization of dates and events. For example, instead of learning facts because they're going to be on a test, students learn about events to determine a cause-and-effect relationship.

These questions are meant to be thoughtfully considered and argued. An essential question strategy fosters effective inquiry. Since there is not a single correct answer, students need to think critically. They become investigators, asking questions and seeking information that will help them answer the essential question. They need to analyze and synthesize information to construct their response. The process of answering essential questions demands that students master the skills commonly tested on high-stakes exams: analysis, comparison, making arguments backed up by evidence, and synthesis.

America: History of Our Nation presents essential questions at the chapter and unit levels. Questions are scaffolded, with section focus questions acting as building blocks to help students answer the chapter-level essential questions. Taken together, the thinking students do about the chapter-level questions will help them answer the unit-level question.

You may ask, "Don't they need to know the facts before we ask these big questions?" They need some background knowledge, of course. The fallacy is to assume that good questions come after learning most of the facts. Inquiry works in both directions: You need some knowledge to ask and pursue good questions. But you also need

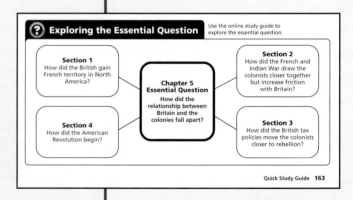

Exploring the Essential Question   Use the online study guide to explore the essential question.

Section 1
How did the British gain French territory in North America?

Chapter 5 Essential Question
How did the relationship between Britain and the colonies fall apart?

Section 2
How did the French and Indian War draw the colonists closer together but increase friction with Britain?

Section 4
How did the American Revolution begin?

Section 3
How did the British tax policies move the colonists closer to rebellion?

Quick Study Guide **163**

good questions to point toward new learning and a reason to learn the facts. Experts such as Grant Wiggins, author of *Understanding by Design,* and teachers who use this strategy find that the students are more involved and like the challenge of answering tough questions. History becomes more engaging. There is a clearer purpose to the work and the learning of information. And since an essential question can often be addressed from different perspectives, it encourages participation by students at all ability levels.

Finally, using this strategy helps students develop skills—research, recognition of bias, decision-making, and so on—that are essential for higher levels of schooling and which can be transferred to real-life situations. Questioning as we learn is a key component of critical thinking that will enable students to be life-long learners.

Dr. Grant Wiggins
Understanding by
Design Consultant,
President of
Authentic Education

Think Like a Historian

Tom Holt's book, *Thinking Historically: Narrative, Imagination, and Understanding,* makes the case that good history instruction should not just result in an understanding of historical events but also succeed in getting students to think like historians. Students should understand that the creation of history is driven by real people with different opinions, perspectives, backgrounds, and audiences. In *The Historian's Toolbox: A Student's Guide to the Theory and Craft of History,* Robert C. Williams argues, "History is not really an art, nor a science, but a craft. The craft of doing history—as opposed to reading history—involves a further intellectual process of research, writing, and revision." The Historian's Toolkit in this program is based on this premise (see pages HT 1–HT 25). It teaches students about the process of creating history—from asking a question, collecting and analyzing information, forming a hypothesis, writing an argument supporting a hypothesis, to publishing. The Historian's Toolkit also can be used as an introduction to the course, helping students to review basic social studies skills like reading a map, while developing their abilities to think like historians.

At the end of every unit, students are asked to apply their knowledge of the subject and use the steps historians follow in trying to make sense of events and issues in American history. The unit-level Think Like a Historian activity provides students with primary source material and asks them to use these sources to explore the Unit Essential Question. Through creative activities, students are required to use critical thinking skills to develop answers to the Essential Question. This brings into focus the "why" of history—helping students make meaning of what happened long ago, why it happened, and how it remains important to us today.

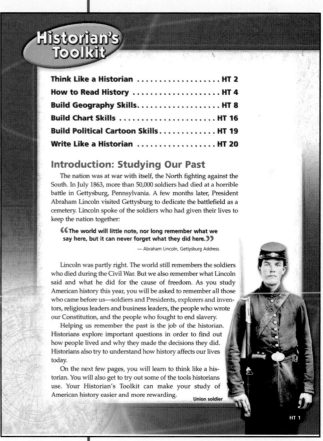

Program Organization

Explicit Reading and Vocabulary Instruction

Based on guidance from senior reading consultants Dr. Kate Kinsella and Dr. Kevin Feldman, this student book integrates explicit instruction in reading in the content area into the teaching of history. This instruction encompasses both the teaching of reading skills and the development of academic language, or vocabulary. This program embeds the development of solid reading skills in the student edition, giving students ample opportunity to learn, practice, and apply these skills. (For further information about how reading research is put into practice in this program, see page T18.)

Reading Skills Instruction Every chapter develops strategies for a specific reading skill, such as using clues to determine meaning. Each section begins by focusing on a specific aspect of the same skill, such as using word clues to determine meaning, building up to more complex mastery of the skill, such as using sentence clues and using paragraph clues. Students are directed to apply the skill as they read the section. Section and chapter assessments give students another opportunity to apply the skill.

Academic Language Instruction The program provides explicit instruction in academic vocabulary. By pre-teaching key social studies terms and high-use academic words, you enable students to comprehend what they read when they encounter these words in context. The high-use words are based on an academic word list derived from scholarly work on the needs of Grade 8 students. High-use words in the narrative are defined in the margins. These words reappear several times throughout the book so that students can develop fluency through repetition. To gain additional practice with these words, students can use the Vocabulary Builder Online before they read the chapter. Students will also preview the key social studies terms they will be taught in the chapter. Students have support for the during-reading stage of instruction as well. Key terms are highlighted and defined in context. Assessments at the chapter and section level give students additional practice with key terms.

Reading Skills Instruction

Chapter 12: Draw Conclusions From Sources

Evaluate credibility of sources and use details to draw conclusions

Skill Step for Section	Focus on Aspect of Skill
1. Assess evidence for a conclusion	Evaluate details to draw conclusion
2. Form an opinion based on evidence	Use details and evidence to form an opinion
3. State the meaning of evidence	Make statement in your own words
4. Draw logical conclusions	Develop conclusion based on details and logic

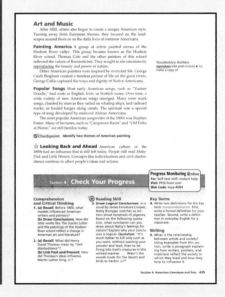

Different Ways of Accessing the Content

Since delivering essential content through a variety of media increases access for diverse learners, this student book provides multiple entry points for understanding the content. Visuals were designed to contribute directly to students' deeper understanding and retention of the content. Images, including photographs, timelines, charts and graphs, and illustrations, were chosen to support the main ideas of the narrative. The purpose of these visuals is reinforced through critical thinking questions. Skill instruction is provided at point-of-use to teach students to use visual information, such as reading a diagram. Maps require students to think critically, and the online interactive versions of these maps provide additional practice and an alternative way to interact with the content they support. An illustrated atlas shows relationships between geography and history.

Special features and activities allow for different ways of learning and inspire further exploration.

- **Visual Preview** gives students a visual introduction to the chapter, providing them with a timeline for a historical frame of reference and information to begin formulating answers to the Chapter Essential Question.

- **Geography and History** helps students picture how the content they are learning relates to geography.

- **Links Across Time** shows students how issues they learn about in history continue to have an impact today.

- **History Interactive** provides a bridge between the text and the online resources—allowing students to extend their learning through in-depth exploration on a critical topic of interest.

- **Biography Quest** highlights an interesting figure in history, asking students to find the answer to an intriguing question about that person through Internet research.

- **Literature** allows students to experience American history through works of literature.

- **Videos** take students to visit the times and places they study through high-impact stories.

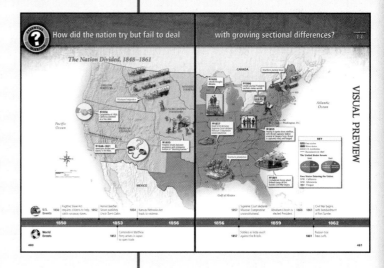

Program Organization

Primary Sources

This program was shaped by the idea of teaching history through history, using primary sources extensively throughout the student text as a vehicle for instruction. Speeches, letters, diaries, documents, political cartoons, and photographs provide windows for students into the thoughts and feelings of the people who lived history. Students learn how to think like a historian by using historical evidence—including primary and secondary sources—in the Historian's Toolkit. To engage students in the content, every section opens with a primary or secondary source dealing with events as they happened. Excerpts from primary sources are embedded into the narrative and special features to impart a flavor of the times—supporting the presentation of history as a well-told story. The Think Like a Historian activity at the end of the unit provides students with primary sources that they can apply as they explore and extend their understanding of the Unit Essential Question. Primary sources in the reference section grant students access to longer readings related to important content topics, allowing more practice with document-based assessment skills.

Writing

One of the goals of this program is to help students develop their writing skills through scaffolded writing instruction and practice. Students are introduced to the writing instruction provided in the program in the "Write Like a Historian" section of the Historian's Toolkit at the beginning of the student book. Each section offers a writing activity that prompts students to practice a fundamental skill needed to accomplish the more complex chapter-level writing assignment. Then, each chapter assessment provides students with an opportunity to use these skills to produce a specific type of writing assignment.

Chapter 8 Writing Sequence
Biographical Essay

Section	Section Assignment	Chapter Assignment
8.1	List questions to research about George Washington.	Write a biographical paragraph about either George Washington or John Adams. Include major events and personality traits, and determine which was his most important contribution to the new nation.
8.2	Create a timeline showing the most important events in Washington's life.	
8.3	Write a description of George Washington's personality using specific examples of actions he took as President.	
8.4	Find the principal events in the life of John Adams and write a thesis statement introducing a biographical essay about Adams.	

Skill Instruction

Every chapter provides a lesson in an essential social studies skill. Students will learn to master the skills needed to analyze history, such as learning to detect historical points of view and analyzing cause and effect. Within the student text, skills are consistently taught and practiced—allowing students to learn and apply skills within the context of history.

Assessments

This program provides assessments that monitor progress and prepare students for social studies tests. These assessments can review content, allow self-assessment, and foster critical thinking.

Content Review Students can increase their understanding of the material by using assessments to review content. Each chapter ends with a Quick Study Guide that restates the Chapter Essential Question and summarizes the main ideas of the chapter needed to answer the question. Students are encouraged to complete their Study Guide Online or use their *Interactive Reading and Notetaking Study Guide* for further review.

Self-Assessment Since it is vitally important for students to monitor their own progress toward content mastery, the program offers self-assessment tools at each level of instruction. As students read the narrative, Checkpoint questions appear after every major topic in the section. By answering the Checkpoint question, a student can find out whether he or she has learned the main idea before moving on to the next topic. Questions in the section and chapter assessments can also be used for self-assessment, and offer opportunities for students to apply skills in the context of the chapter content they learned. Progress Monitoring Online allows students to take a self-test for each section and chapter that provides instant feedback and offers suggestions for remediation for incorrect answers.

Critical Thinking Development This program offers unique multi-part scaffolded questions that help students build from comprehension to critical thinking. The first part of the question asks students to show they have basic comprehension of the content covered, using lower-order thinking skills from Bloom's taxonomy, such as recall or identify. The second part(s) of the question uses this basic comprehension of the content as a jumping-off point to help students transition to higher-order thinking skills, such as draw conclusions or make predictions. This scaffolding supports differentiated instruction by helping all students think critically.

Each chapter also challenges students to think like a historian with a Document-Based Assessment. Students read, evaluate, analyze, and interpret different reading passages and images that relate to a specific topic. They will use these primary and secondary sources to write an essay demonstrating their understanding of the topic in American history.

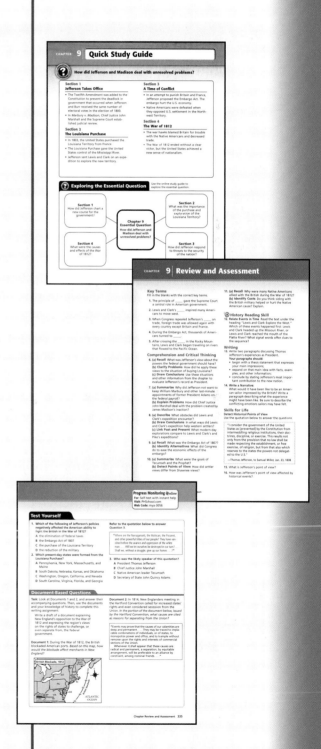

Program Organization

INSTRUCTIONAL TOOLS TO PLAN, TEACH, AND ASSESS

This program was designed to provide teachers with extensive support for instruction, offering tools to help plan, teach, and assess.

PLAN

- **Teacher's Edition** provides comprehensive planning support and professional development.

- **TeacherExpress™ CD-ROM** (powered by *LessonView*®), grants instant access to the electronic Teacher's Edition and teaching resources, creates customized lesson plans, and tracks progress of student understanding.

TEACH

STUDENT TOOLS

- **Student Edition** presents American history through a compelling narrative rich in primary sources.

- **Interactive Reading and Notetaking Study Guide** provides vocabulary practice, summaries of every section of the student text, and notetaking support. Available in On-level, Adapted, and Spanish versions.

- **Companion Web Site** grants instant access to a wealth of resources to support learning—chapter overviews, primary sources, biographies, Internet activities—as well as special interactive resources:

    1. **Vocabulary Builder Online** allows students to work with high-use academic vocabulary through interactive practice.

    2. **History Interactive** launches students into an interactive adventure, focusing on a specific topic to extend their understanding.

    3. **MapMaster™ Interactive** develops geographic literacy through dynamic map skills instruction, providing electronic access to every MapMaster® map in the student book.

    4. **Progress Monitoring Online** lets students assess their own understanding of content and get instant remediation.

    5. **Links Across Time** provides investigations into contemporary examples of issues that have endured over time.

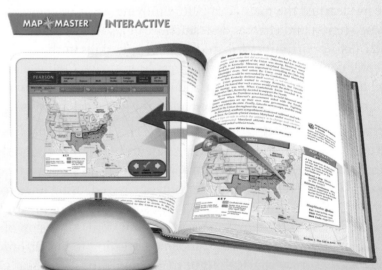

- **Student Express™ CD-ROM** is an interactive textbook with interactive glossaries, built-in activities, and instant feedback assessments. Electronic versions of the *Interactive Reading and Notetaking Study Guide,* as well as History Interactive, Vocabulary Builder, MapMaster™, and Progress Monitoring Online make this the most powerful student study tool available.

- **Social Studies Skills Tutor CD-ROM** helps students learn, practice, and apply social studies skills.
- **Exploring Primary Sources in U.S. History CD-ROM** offers interactive explorations of 100 primary sources.
- **Interactive Constitution CD-ROM** shows students that the Constitution affects their lives today and includes a law-making simulation.
- **Student Edition on Audio CD** offers the narrative of the entire book read aloud.
- **Spanish Guided Reading Audio CD** contains audio summaries of every section of the text read aloud in Spanish.

TEACHER TOOLS

- **Teacher's Edition** provides a step-by-step guide for instruction for every lesson.
- **Teaching Resources** provide extensive reading, vocabulary, and writing support, content review and enrichment, assessment, and lesson plans.
- **PresentationExpress™ CD-ROM** offers ready-made PowerPoint presentations with "talking points" and graphics for each section of the text.
- **Historian's Apprentice Activity Pack** explores questions about American history using reproducible primary sources and realia.
- **Color Transparencies** provide maps, graphs, fine art, History Interactive, and section lesson support.
- **Progress Monitoring Transparencies** provide on going content review to monitor student understanding.
- **Discovery School Video Program** on tape and DVD lets teachers show students the times and places they are studying through high-impact videos.

Explore More Video

Discovery School Video To learn more about Lewis and Clark, view the video.

Lewis and Clark: A Hard Journey At times during their travel up the Missouri River, members of the Lewis and Clark party had to carry their boats around rapids and falls. Here, Sacagawea, Clark, Lewis, and York examine the Great Falls in present-day Montana. **Critical Thinking: Apply Information** What other hazards did Lewis and Clark face on their river voyages?

In late October 1804, the expedition reached the territory of the Mandan people, in what is now North Dakota. Lewis and Clark

ASSESS

- **AYP Monitoring Assessments** provide a year-long assessment plan that helps identify student strengths and weaknesses, monitor progress, and prepare students for exams.
- *ExamView*® **Test Bank CD-ROM** allows teachers to quickly and easily generate tests.
- **MindPoint™ Quiz Show CD-ROM** is an interactive multi-media game that assesses student understanding, makes learning fun, and tracks student performance.
- **Assessment Rubrics** provide a variety of assessment rubrics to evaluate student performance.
- **Test Prep Workbook With Document-Based Assessment** prepares students for social studies activities.
- **Test-taking Strategies With Transparencies** helps students learn how to answer different types of standardized test questions.

Instructional Planning and Support

Successfully teaching American history is a challenge for teachers in today's dynamic and heterogeneous classrooms. This program helps teachers respond to students' needs and to enable all students to master the content.

Planning Effective Instruction

This program provides complete support for teachers to plan effective instruction. The principal teacher planning tools include the *AYP Monitoring Assessments*, the Teacher's Edition, and the TeacherExpress™ CD-ROM.

Initial Assessment At the beginning of the school year, teachers need to determine the level of students' reading and social studies skills. By conducting and evaluating an initial assessment, teachers will gain the information they need to modify instruction for individual students to ensure access for diverse learners. The "Screening Test" and "Diagnosing Readiness Tests" for initial assessment are in the *AYP Monitoring Assessments*.

Course Planning It is critical to lay out a long-range plan of instruction for the whole school year—a "master plan" for how to cover the social studies curriculum in the available class time. The Section Lesson Plan provides a model pacing guide to achieve this goal. Teachers will pace instruction based on the school calendar, class time periods, and analysis of the needs of their students.

TeacherExpress™ CD-ROM is the primary tool recommended for creating lesson plans. It enables teachers to align content with standards, address differentiated instruction, view teaching resources electronically, and link to teacher-generated resources. Integrating program resources helps teachers support learning and modify instruction. By designing lessons well, teachers will be able to teach the required content while addressing students' differing ability levels and interests. The TeacherExpress™ CD-ROM makes it easy to adapt lesson plans should revisions become necessary.

Daily Guidance for Instruction The building block for content and skills mastery directed at all students is the daily lesson. The Teacher's Edition helps guide daily instruction. The chapter planning guide provides professional development: History Background; Differentiated Instruction; and Concepts Across Time. The Section Lesson Plan previews each lesson, relates resources to the lesson, and identifies which resources to use with specific student populations.

This Teacher's Edition has step-by-step direct instruction available on what, how, and when to teach. This in-depth support for instruction begins with a review and preview for each section. It offers a complete plan for daily instruction that suggests specific strategies to improve student comprehension (see page T20–T25) and recommends the use of specific resources. A Vocabulary Builder on each section opener aids preteaching high-use academic words. The Teacher's Edition provides a clear road map for effective program implementation.

Research shows that virtually all students benefit from direct, systematic, and explicit instruction in reading informational text. The lesson plans in this Teacher's Edition follow the three stages of the instructional process: 1. instructional frontloading before reading; 2. guided instruction during reading; 3. reflection and study after reading. The comprehensive section instruction starts with "Prepare to Read," which front-loads reading and vocabulary instruction. "Teach" suggests ways for the teacher to model engaging with the text, use structured activities, and encourage student practice. In "Assess and Reteach," the lesson plan asks teachers to check for student understanding, provides extension activities, and makes recommendations for remediation. Lesson formats include the Teacher's Edition in print and an interactive Teacher's Edition on the TeacherExpress™ CD-ROM.

Accessing Professional Development

Teachers need to stay informed of current research on effective teaching methods and to keep pace with recent scholarship. This program helps teachers achieve these important goals. The Teacher's Edition offers professional development on instructional methodology and American history content in every chapter and section and at point-of-use in the lesson plan. Additional professional development is provided in the *Writing for Social Studies Assessment*.

Using Library Media Centers

Library media centers can be used to improve instruction and to complement the study of history. Teachers may want to begin each year with a class visit to their library media center, asking its staff to teach students how to use the center. Suggested activities throughout the Teacher's Edition, such as the Extend the Lesson Through Technology Research activities, call for the use of the library media center. Teachers may use *Assessment Rubrics* to help assess students' library research skills.

Working With Parents or Guardians

Home involvement has been shown to be effective in improving student performance. This program provides materials to support parent or guardian contact, such as letters that teachers can send home that explain what content is being covered and offer activities to be done at home. StudentExpress™ CD-ROM, which includes *Interactive Reading and Notetaking Study Guide* and links to the Companion Web site, is another excellent tool for parents or guardians who want to work with their children.

Instructional Planning and Support

Incorporating Outside Resources

Resources such as guest speakers, museum visits, and electronic field trips can effectively increase differentiated instruction. The following guidelines can help teachers integrate outside resources into a lesson.

- **Start with the content:** Identify a particular lesson in which the resource can be used to support the instruction. Explain in your lesson plan how the resource will help students understand the content.

- **Plan the timing:** For maximum effectiveness, plan your instruction so that students learn the content before they are introduced to the outside resource. It is less effective to visit a museum exhibit months after learning about the topic.

- **Explain the goal to students:** Explain to students exactly how the outside resource relates to what they are learning. Help students see how the experience will reinforce and extend their knowledge of the content.

- **Provide structure:** Provide students with structure for experience with an outside resource. Give students a guiding question to think about and tasks to accomplish. (The unit, chapter, or section focus questions in the Teacher's Edition would make excellent guiding questions.) Provide students with support appropriate for their individual needs.

- **Assess the learning:** Develop an assessment to show how the outside resource helped students master the content. This assessment could be part of a formal test, or it could be a performance or portfolio assessment with a specific rubric.

Ensuring Deeper Understanding

With a thorough examination of events and issues, students gain a new dimension to the way they perceive American history. Teachers can work towards this appreciation by focusing on deeper understandings and concepts in their instruction.

Essential Questions Using questions to guide them, students are better able to see how specific events and individuals fit into the broader themes of history. To help maintain their focus, students will find these questions on the unit, chapter and section openers. The Essential Question is posed on the Visual Preview to highlight the big idea of the chapter and again on the Quick Study Guide to help students draw together the main ideas of learning. A graphic organizer provides a visual connection of the questions, showing how the section questions support the chapter-level question. These Essential Questions guide notetaking in the *Interactive Reading and Notetaking Study Guide*, providing students with the knowledge to participate in a unit-end summary discussion.

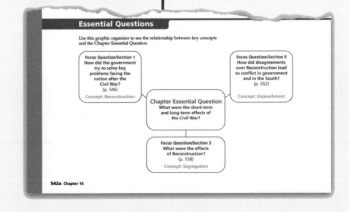

The Essential Questions are outlined in the graphic organizer on the chapter Professional Development page of the Teacher's Edition (see TE, p. 32a). Teachers can use these questions to direct their instruction. Teacher support material reinforces this organization. Color Transparencies offer graphic organizers and discussion prompts to be used as either a quick way to summarize the issues or as an opportunity for extended debate. The Historian's Apprentice Activity Pack allows students to further explore the issues with primary source materials.

Social Studies Concepts For history to have meaning for them, students need to develop an understanding of certain general ideas. For each chapter in the textbook, there is a specific lesson included in the Teaching Resources and referenced in the Teacher's Edition that helps build understanding of a concept associated with the content. These concepts include ideas like democracy, urbanization, and ethics.

Integrating Technology in the Classroom

Technology offers teachers and students a wide range of useful, creative, and motivating tools that provide access to history content and skills. Whether through viewing high-impact video about the Underground Railroad, practicing vocabulary online, or launching into a Biography Quest Internet adventure, technology provides new ways to connect with today's learners.

Reaching Today's Learners Audio, transparencies, video, CD-ROMs, interactive textbooks, and the Internet can help teachers reach more students. Technology enables all students to learn by effectively delivering instruction that:

- Motivates students to explore social studies topics in depth.

- Provides access to content through different learning styles: visual, auditory, and kinesthetic.

- Individualizes the pace of learning through tutorial and practice opportunities.

- Connects students to resources beyond the classroom.

Time-Saving Teacher Tools Technology can save time and connect teachers to a network of professional resources and educators who are collaborating and sharing ideas. Technology supports instruction and planning by offering:

- Time-saving electronic lesson plans.

- Instant access to teaching resources.

- Online links to professional development and networks of educators.

- Presentation software for daily lessons.

- Assessment tools to monitor progress.

Differentiated Instruction

Differentiated Instruction

The nation is more diverse than ever, and this diversity is a significant asset to the strength of our nation. Yet this diversity also places considerable stress on the educational system to effectively accommodate the range of learning needs found in today's classrooms. The goal of a comprehensive American history program should be to provide differentiated instruction of the curriculum for all students.

Success in Differentiated Instruction

Differentiated instruction happens when curriculum and instruction are provided in ways that allow all learners to participate and to succeed (Kinsella, et.al., 2002). Instruction should be designed so that all learners can master the essential understandings and skills needed to analyze history, even though they use different content, processes, and products to get there. To reach the goal, teachers focus instruction on the essential content, but provide multiple options for taking in this information. To adapt learning processes, teachers give students multiple options for making sense of the content and use a range of whole-class, group, and individual assignments. To adapt products, teachers conduct initial and ongoing assessments of student readiness and growth and allow multiple options for expression of what students know.

Reading and Vocabulary Instruction Integrating reading and vocabulary instructional strategies into the content lesson benefits virtually all students, helping them read and understand informational text. Textbooks should incorporate principles for creating student–considerate text into their design to further improve access.

Comprehension Strategies Teachers can increase access by incorporating strategies to improve student comprehension into their instruction for all students. Research-informed, classroom-tested strategies should be used consistently over the course of the whole year.
(See p. T20–T24.)

Modifying Instruction Teachers can also foster differentiated instruction by modifying instruction to meet individual needs. Less proficient students and English language learners benefit from a focus on learning and comprehension strategies, as well as vocabulary and reading fluency. Instruction for special needs students should incorporate adaptations and modifications. Advanced learners and gifted and talented students can explore topics in-depth.

Differentiated Instruction

Differentiated Instruction

L1 English Language Learners   **L1** Special Needs

Visualizing the Word Students should demonstrate their understanding of the words by finding pictures that illustrate them. For example, for the word *rigid*, students may show someone standing at attention. Pair students to exchange their pictures and have the partners check each other's understanding of the relationship of the image to the word. Review the material with students.

Research on Effective Reading Instruction

Why do many students have difficulty reading textbooks? How can we help students read to learn social studies? In the pages that follow, we examine the research on the challenge of reading textbooks; explain the direct, systematic, and explicit instruction needed to help students; and then show how Prentice Hall has responded to this research.

What Is Skillful Reading?

Recent research (Snow et al., 2002) suggests that skillful and strategic reading is a long-term developmental process in which "readers learn how to simultaneously extract and construct meaning through interaction with written language." In other words, successful readers know how to decode all types of words, read with fluency and expression, have well-developed vocabularies, and possess various comprehension strategies to understand and retain what is read, such as note taking and summarizing. Skillful readers also know how to initiate these abilities when the academic task demands it.

Why Do Many Students Lack Reading Skills?

Sadly, many secondary students do not have solid reading skills. In the early years, students read mainly engaging and accessible narratives, such as stories, poems, and junior biographies. But in the upper elementary years, they must read significantly more conceptually dense and challenging nonfiction, or expository texts. It is no accident that the infamous "Fourth-Grade Slump" (Chall and Jacobs, 2003; Hirsch, 2003)—a well-documented national trend of declining literacy after Grade Four—occurs during this time. Hirsch posits that after the primary grades, the much heralded achievement gap between socioeconomic groups (NAEP, 2004) is in fact a language gap.

Even students quite skilled in reading novels, short stories, and adolescent magazines typically come to middle school ill-equipped for the rigors of informational texts, or reading to learn. They tend to dive right into a social studies chapter as if reading a recreational story. They don't first preview the material to create a mental outline and establish a purpose in reading. They have not yet learned other basic strategies for comprehending nonfiction, such as reading a section more than once, taking notes as they read, and reading to answer specific questions.

Dr. Kate Kinsella
Senior Reading Consultant
Department of Secondary Education
San Francisco State University, CA

Dr. Kevin Feldman
Senior Reading Consultant
Director of Reading and Early Intervention
Sonoma County, CA

Differentiated Instruction

The Unique Demands of Textbooks

The differences between textbooks and the narratives students are used to reading are dramatic. The most distinctive challenges include:

1. **Conceptual content** Content-area textbooks are laden with new and largely unfamiliar and abstract concepts (such as human-environment interaction and states' rights).

2. **Vocabulary load** The unique vocabulary used in academic texts is often referred to as *academic language*. Academic language consists of high-use academic words, such as *classify* and *significant*, and discipline-specific vocabulary (or Key Terms), such as *capitalism* and *caucus*.

3. **Paragraph and organizational patterns** Academic texts are constructed using unfamiliar organizational patterns at both the paragraph and chapter levels, such as cause-effect, problem-solution, categorization, chain of events, or compare and contrast.

4. **Sentence structures** Because the purpose of textbooks is to communicate complex information as efficiently as possible, readers are likely to come across significantly more sophisticated sentence structure than when they read fictional texts.

Academic texts present such a significant challenge to most students that linguists and language researchers liken them to learning a foreign language (Schleppegrell, 2002). In other words, most secondary students are second-language learners: They are learning the academic language of informational texts.

The Need for Vocabulary Instruction

There is a clear consensus among literacy researchers that accelerating vocabulary growth is a vital and often neglected component of a comprehensive reading program (Baumann and Kameenui, 2004). Numerous studies have documented the strong and reciprocal relationship between vocabulary knowledge and reading comprehension. Research focused on school-age second-language learners similarly concludes that vocabulary knowledge is the single best predictor of their academic achievement across subject-matter domains. Therefore, educators need to make robust intentional vocabulary instruction a high priority. Intensive instruction should be focused on words related to central lesson concepts (or Key Terms) and high-use academic words. Academic word lists developed by researchers can help educators determine appropriate high-use academic words (Coxhead, 2000; Xue and Nation, 1984).

References

Baker, Scott, and Russell Gersten. "What We Know About Effective Instructional Practices for English Language Learners." *Exceptional Children*, 66 (2000): 454–470.

Baumann, J.F., and Kameenui, E.J. (2004), *Vocabulary Instruction: From Research to Practice.* New York: Guilford Press.

Chall, Jeanne S., and Jacobs, Vicki A. "Poor Children's Fourth-Grade Slump." *American Educator* (Spring 2003): 14.

Coxhead, Averil. "A New Academic Word List." *TESOL Quarterly* (Summer 2000): 213–238.

Feldman, Kevin, and Kinsella, Kate (2004), *Narrowing the Language Gap: The Case for Explicit Vocabulary Instruction.* New York: Scholastic Inc.

Hirsch, E.D., Jr. "Reading Comprehension Requires Knowledge—of Words and the World." *American Educator* (Spring 2003):10–29.

Kinsella, Kate, et al. *Teaching Guidebook for Universal Access.* Upper Saddle River, N.J.: Prentice Hall, 2002.

National Assessment of Educational Progress (NAEP) (2004). Group results for sex, region, and size of community. Washington D.C.: U.S. Government Printing Office.

Schleppegrell, M. "Linguistic Features of the Language of Schooling." *Linguistics and Education*, 12, no. 4 (2002): 431–459.

Snow, C., et al. "Reading for Understanding: Toward an R&D Program" in *Reading Comprehension.* Santa Monica, California: The Rand Corporation, 2002.

Xue, G., and Nation, I.S. P. "A University Word List." *Language Learning and Communication* (1984): 215–229.

Effective Reading Instruction

Research illustrates that virtually all students benefit from direct, systematic, and explicit instruction in reading informational texts (Baker and Gersten, 2000). There are three stages to the instructional process for content-area reading:

1. Before Reading: Preparation

2. During Reading: Constructing Meaning

3. After Reading: Reflection, Elaboration, and Study

Before Reading If teachers emphasize preparing students for the demands of a challenging text, or instructional frontloading, they ensure all students will have meaningful access to the content. Students can prepare to read by using strategies to build background knowledge and setting a purpose for reading (see pages T20–T21). Teachers can provide direct teaching of individual words by introducing the Key Terms and high-use academic words for the chapter that students will read (see page T21).

Explicitly teaching students strategies for actively engaging with the text is another crucial factor for success. Frontloading instruction is especially critical in mixed-ability classrooms with English language learners, students with special needs, and other students performing below grade level in terms of literacy.

During Reading In guided instruction, the teacher models approaches for how to actively engage with the text to gain meaning. The teacher guides students through the first reading of the text using passage reading strategies (see pages T22–T23), and then guides discussion about the content using participation strategies (see pages T24–T25). Finally, students record key information in a graphic organizer to build their knowledge of organizational patterns.

After Reading During the reflection and study phase, the teacher formally checks for student understanding, offers remediation if necessary, and provides activities that challenge students to apply content in a new way. To review the chapter, students of all ability levels recall content, analyze the reading as a whole, and study key vocabulary and information likely to be tested.

BEFORE READING: Preparation

Strategies:
- Visual Preview
- Prereading
- Reading Readiness: Anticipation Guide
- Reading Readiness: K-W-L Chart
- Pre-teach Key Vocabulary

DURING READING: Constructing Meaning

Strategies:
- Passage Reading
  - Oral Cloze
  - Choral Reading
  - Structured Silent Reading
- Paragraph Shrinking: Summarization
- ReQuest: Reciprocal Questioning
- Structured Discussion
  - Idea Wave
  - Numbered Heads
  - Think-Write-Pair-Share
  - Give One, Get One

AFTER READING: Reflection, Elaboration, and Study

Strategies:
- Structured Discussion
  - Idea Wave
  - Numbered Heads
  - Think-Write-Pair-Share
  - Give One, Get One

Differentiated Instruction

Putting Research Into Practice—Student Edition

Prentice Hall enlisted the assistance of Dr. Kate Kinsella and Dr. Kevin Feldman to ensure that the *America: History of Our Nation* program would provide the direct, systematic, and explicit instruction needed to foster student success in reading informational texts. To help students rise to the challenge of reading an informational text, reading and vocabulary instruction was embedded right into the student book.

Embedded Reading and Vocabulary Instruction in the Student Text

Before Reading: Preparation

- **Preview Content** with a primary source excerpt and a visual, giving students a frame of reference, as well as brief summaries of what they will learn and objectives for every section.
- **Why It Matters** introduces students to the section content.
- **Reading Skill** provides a section lesson about how to use the chapter reading skill.
- **Key Terms and People** are introduced up front.

During Reading: Constructing Meaning

- **Reading Skill** cues help students know how to read and understand the narrative.
- **High-Use Academic Words** are underlined and defined in the margin.
- **Key Terms** are defined in context, with terms and definitions called out in blue type.
- **Checkpoints** allow students to monitor their own understanding as they read.
- **Critical Thinking Questions** help students connect the content to images they see on the page.

After Reading: Reflection, Elaboration, and Study

- **Check Your Progress** revisits Key Terms, reviews the content, provides an opportunity to demonstrate mastery of the Reading Skill, and allows students to explore their understanding of the text through the Writing assignment.

Putting Research Into Practice—Teacher's Edition

This book offers teachers guidance in direct, systematic, and explicit reading instruction. The instructional sequence in the Teacher's Edition provides guidance in the use of effective strategies at each stage of the instructional process.

Reading and Vocabulary Instruction in the Teacher's Edition

Reading instruction in the student text is consistently supported in the Teacher's Edition. It provides ample cues for the teacher to instruct and engage learners.

Before Reading Professional Development before each chapter often provides background on reading and vocabulary instruction. Lesson plans always provide suggestions that help teachers integrate frontloading strategies into their teaching. Each section lesson starts with a Prepare to Read section. Build Background Knowledge activates prior knowledge. Set a Purpose prompts students to predict and anticipate content and motivates students to engage with the text. The Vocabulary Builder explains the meaning of high-use words students will need to comprehend the lesson.

During Reading In the "Teach" part of the lesson plan, teachers can use suggestions for getting students actively engaged in the text. Instruction clarifies high-use words and Key Terms, applies a reading strategy to the passage to promote text comprehension, and guides discussion to construct meaning. Independent Practice prompts students to reread and take notes in the graphic organizer provided to aid understanding. Monitor Progress checks students' notetaking and verifies students' prereading predictions.

After Reading After reading is completed, the lesson plan closes with specific strategies for the reflection and study phase. Assess Progress measures students' recall and understanding of content. Reteach provides suggestions for additional instruction if needed. Extend offers activities that allow students to explore content further.

Integrated Reading Resources

The *America: History of Our Nation* program provides instructional materials to support the reading instruction in the Teacher's Edition.

The *All-in-One Teaching Resources* offers reading and vocabulary instruction support, such as Reading Readiness Guides, History Reading Skill, and Word Knowledge Rating Forms.

Students can use the *Interactive Reading and Notetaking Study Guide* (On-level, Adapted, and Spanish versions) to preview content, take notes, monitor reading comprehension, and review content.

Tips for Helping Students Read Challenging Social Studies Text

- Prepare students by building background knowledge, setting a purpose for reading, and raising interesting questions

- Chunk the text into manageable sections and guide students in reading and re-reading each chunk using various comprehension strategies (e.g. Paragraph Shrinking)

- Structure focused discussions before, during, and after reading to ensure ALL students are grappling with key concepts and constructing meaning that they are able to express verbally and in writing

Differentiated Instruction

Instructional Strategies for Improving Student Comprehension

In response to today's environment of the NCLB legislation and testing reform, Prentice Hall asked Dr. Kate Kinsella and Dr. Kevin Feldman to provide specific strategies you can use to improve student comprehension. Their guidance informed the development of the *America: History of Our Nation* Teacher's Edition. The lesson plans in this Teacher's Edition incorporate the following instructional strategies.

Before Reading Strategies: Preparation

This program uses various research-based strategies designed to build background knowledge and help students set a purpose for reading including: Visual Preview, Prereading, and Reading Readiness Guides, and a K-W-L chart. It also prepares students by preteaching critical social studies and high-use words.

Visual Preview

Purpose: To assist students in grasping the Essential Question addressed in the chapter
How to Do It
1. Teach the main concept (e.g. compromise, immigration) that is associated with the question.

2. Help students connect the concept to the Essential Question by describing parallel examples for them. Have students give their own examples of the connection.

3. Lead a review of previous knowledge connected to the Essential Question.

4. Conduct the Visual Preview by helping students study the elements. Break down the various components and direct student attention to these elements. Ask students to analyze the map by reviewing the map key (color scheme, other features). Lead a discussion by asking two or three questions about the images associated with the Visual Preview. Have students review the timeline by identifying key events or dates.

5. Wrap up by establishing the Essential Question as a major reading purpose for the chapter.

Prereading

Purpose: To build background knowledge, provide an overview of topics, and acquaint students with the structure of the chapter
How to Do It

1. Distribute the Chapter Prereading Guide. Read the text chapter title aloud. Model how to use the What You Will Learn chart to pull out the topic, possible questions the chapter will address, how it relates to previous chapters, etc.

2. Read each heading and subheading, clarify the structure (e.g., cause-effect relationships) and frame the topics as questions to be answered as students read.

3. Briefly preview maps and pictures and discuss how they are related to the topics or questions.

4. Help students identify unfamiliar words and model ways to find clues to their meanings.

5. Guide students in reflecting on two or three key topics or questions the chapter will be addressing—what to look for as they read.

Reading Readiness: Anticipation Guide

Purpose: To focus students' attention on key concepts, and guide them to interact with ideas in the text

How to Do It

1. Distribute the Reading Readiness Guide. Read each statement aloud, and then ask students to react to the statements individually and in groups, marking their responses in the Before Reading column.

2. Use the worksheet as a springboard for discussing the section's key concepts as a class. Refrain from revealing the correct responses at this time, to avoid taking away the need for students to read the text.

3. Have students read the section in order to find evidence that confirms, disproves, or elaborates on each statement in the Reading Readiness Guide.

4. After students finish reading, have them return to the statements and mark the After Reading column on their worksheets. Have them locate information from the text that supports or disproves each statement.

5. Discuss what the class has learned and probe for any lingering confusion about key concepts.

Reading Readiness: K-W-L Chart

Purpose: To engage students before, during, and after reading

How to Do It

The K-W-L worksheet guides students to recall what they **K**now, determine what they **W**ant to learn, and identify what they **L**earn as they read.

1. Distribute the Reading Readiness Guide. Brainstorm with the group about what they already know about the topic. List students' ideas on the board.

2. Students then list pieces of information they already know and questions they want to answer in the first two columns of their worksheets.

3. As students read, have them note information that answers their questions or adds to what they know.

4. After reading, facilitate a class discussion about what the students have learned. Clarify misconceptions.

Critical Social Studies and High-Use Academic Words

Purpose: To teach students words that are essential to grasping the key concept as well as the terms often used in academic texts, beyond the content-specific Key Terms

How to Do It

1. Distribute the Word Knowledge Rating Form. Have students rate how well they know each word on their form. Tell them there is no penalty for a low rating.

2. Survey students' ratings to decide which words need the most instruction.

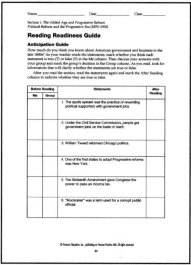

Differentiated Instruction

3. Provide a brief definition or sample sentence for each word. (See Vocabulary Builder in the Teacher's Edition at the beginning of each section.) Rephrase your explanation, leaving out the word and asking students to substitute it aloud.

4. Have students fill in the "Definition or Example" column of their Word Knowledge Rating Forms.

5. Point out each word in context as you read the chapter.

During Reading Strategies: Constructing Meaning

Teachers can guide students in active critical reading of the text in order to extract and construct meaning. This program utilizes a number of research-based strategies designed to ensure all students are actively engaged in thoughtful reading and re-reading of the text including: passage-reading strategies, paragraph shrinking, and reciprocal questioning.

Passage Reading: Oral Cloze

Purpose: To ensure all students have basic access to the text while engaged in actively reading along with the teacher

How to Do It

1. Choose a passage and direct students to "read aloud silently using their inner voices" as you read the passage aloud. Be sure students understand that reading is an active process, not simply a listening activity, and their job is to follow along—eyes riveted to each word, saying the words to themselves as you read aloud.

2. Tell students that you will be omitting an occasional word and they must chorally supply the word.

3. The first few times you use the Oral Cloze, demonstrate by telling the students in advance what word you will be leaving out, directing them to read the word at the right time. Practice this a few times until they have the feel for the procedure. Leave out fewer words as students become more familiar with the Oral Cloze and require less direction to remain focused as you read aloud.

Passage Reading: Choral Reading

Purpose: To have students actively read along with the teacher in a non-threatening atmosphere

How to Do It

1. Choose a relatively short passage.

2. Tell students that you will all read the text aloud at once. Direct students to "keep your voice with mine" as they read.

3. Read the passage slowly and clearly.

4. Have students read the text again silently.

Passage Reading: Structured Silent Reading

Purpose: To deepen comprehension via critical re-reading of a passage with an accountable task (e.g. identify the cause, analyze a historical figure)

How to Do It

1. Assign a section to read silently. Pose a question for the whole class to answer from their silent reading, such as the Checkpoint question at the end of the subsection.

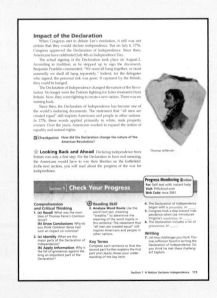

Model how one thinks while reading to find answers to a question. Do this by thinking aloud.

2. When students get used to reading to answer the Checkpoint question, pose more in-depth questions, progressing from factual recall to questions that stimulate interpretive or applied thinking.

3. Teach students to ask and answer their own questions as they read. To model this process, read a section aloud and tell students what you thought to answer your own questions as you read.

4. Have a brief class discussion to clarify unresolved questions, vocabulary, and key concepts.

Paragraph Shrinking: A Summarization Strategy

Purpose: To increase comprehension by learning how to summarize and paraphrase key information during reading

How to Do It

1. Pair struggling students with more proficient students and assign a small portion of the text.

2. Ask one member of each pair to identify the "who or what" the paragraph is about and tell the other. Have the other member identify important details about the "who or what" and tell his or her partner.

3. Ask the first member to summarize the paragraph in ten to fifteen words using the most important details. The second member of the pair monitors the number of words and says "Shrink it!" if the summary goes over fifteen words.

4. Have students record the "shrink" in their notebooks.

5. Have the partners reverse roles and continue reading.

6. Assign an additional section of the text for students to read and "shrink" for homework. Be sure to model this strategy and do a number of paragraphs in class before asking students to do this on their own.

ReQuest (Reciprocal Questioning)

Purpose: To ask and answer questions during reading to establish a purpose for reading and monitor comprehension

How to Do It

1. Prepare students to read by doing the section's Background Knowledge, Prepare to Read, and the Vocabulary Builder activities.

2. Begin reading a brief portion of the text aloud. Ask and answer your own questions about the text, progressing from recall to critical thinking questions.

3. After modeling this question and response pattern with a brief passage, ask students to read the next section of the text. Tell students that they will be taking turns asking you questions about what they read, and you will answer their questions, just as you modeled for them.

4. Ask students to read the next section. Inform them they will be answering your questions.

5. Continue to alternate between student-generated questions. As students become used to the strategy, they gradually assume more responsibility in the process.

6. When the students have read enough information to make predictions about the remainder of the assignment, stop the exchange of comprehension questions. Instead, ask prediction questions, such as, "What do you think will be discussed in the next section? Why do you think so?"

7. Have students read the remaining portion silently. Then lead a wrap-up discussion of the section.

During and After Reading Discussion Strategies

Structured discussion is at the very heart of reading comprehension and is the core vehicle for helping students to extract and construct meaning from text and other classroom experiences (simulations, video, etc.). The following strategies can be effectively used during and after reading to ensure all students are meaningfully engaged in historical discourse.

Idea Wave Discussion Strategy

Purpose: To actively engage students in structured whole-class discussions, especially for brainstorming and review

How to Do It

1. Pose a question or task.

2. Give students quiet time to consider what they know about the topic or question and record responses in their notes. It's often helpful to provide one or two ideas to jumpstart their thinking.

3. Prompt students to share with a partner to expand and improve their answers.

4. Provide an academic "sentence starter" to ensure students use key academic vocabulary in the discussion (e.g. "One cause of westward migration during the 1870's was _____."). Students copy the sentence starter and plug in one of the ideas from their written list.

5. Students practice their responses with their partner.

6. Call on students randomly (no hand raising) to share their ideas. Then invite two or three volunteers to share anything else that hasn't been shared as yet.

Numbered Heads Discussion Strategy

Purpose: To actively engage students in structured whole-class discussions, moving from groups of four to whole-class discussion

How to Do It

1. Seat students in groups of four and number off one through four. (If possible, combine established partners to form groups of four.)

2. After giving the discussion prompt, allow students to discuss possible responses for an established amount of time.

3. Remind students to pay close attention to the comments of each group member because you will be randomly selecting one student to represent the best thinking of the entire group.

4. Call a number (one through four), and ask all students with that number to raise their hands, ready to respond to the topic at hand in a teacher-directed, whole-class discussion.

5. Add comments, extend key ideas, ask follow-up questions, and make connections between individual comments to create a lively whole-class discussion.

6. Provide any summary comments required to ensure that all students understand critical points.

Think-Write-Pair-Share Discussion Strategy

Purpose: To engage students in brief class discussion using structured partners

How to Do It

1. **Think**—Students listen as you pose a question or a task related to the reading or classroom discussion. The level of questions should vary from lower-level literal to higher-order inferential or analytical.

2. **Write**—Provide quiet thinking or writing time for students to deal with the question and to go back to the text or review notes. Have students record their ideas in their notebooks.

3. **Pair-Share**—Cue students to find a partner and discuss their responses, noting similarities and differences. Teach students to encourage one another to clarify and justify responses.

4. Randomly call on students to share answers they have rehearsed with their partners.

5. Invite any volunteers to contribute additional ideas and points of view to the discussion after calling on a reasonable number of students randomly.

6. Direct students to revise their notes based on their partner and class discussions.

Give One, Get One Discussion Strategy

Purpose: To foster active student engagement in class discussion

How to Do It

1. Pose a thought-provoking question or a concrete task to the class.

2. Allow three to five minutes of quiet time for students to jot down a number of potential responses (e.g. reviewing key events, critical causes).

3. Ask students to place a check mark next to the two or three ideas that they perceive as their strongest and then draw a line after their final idea to separate their ideas from those that they will gather from classmates.

4. Give students a set amount of time (about eight to ten minutes) to get up from their seats and share ideas with classmates. After finding a partner, the two students exchange papers and first quietly read each other's ideas. They discuss the ideas briefly, then select one idea from their partner's list and add it to their own, making sure to accurately copy the idea alongside the partner's name. When one exchange is completed, students move on to interact with a new partner.

5. At the end of the exchange period, facilitate a unified class discussion. Call on a volunteer to share one new idea acquired from a conversation partner. The student whose idea has just been reported then shares the next idea, gleaned from a different conversation partner.

Differentiated Instruction

Strategies for Specific Student Populations

Differentiated instruction can be fostered through modifying instruction to address individual needs. To increase student achievement, teachers can use strategies for specific student populations to offer specialized support. Lesson plans in this Teacher's Edition provide strategies for diverse learners and suggest ancillary support such as the *Interactive Reading and Notetaking Study Guide.* The following pages provide general guidelines for modifying instruction for students with special needs, less proficient readers, English language learners, and gifted and talented students and advanced learners.

SPECIAL NEEDS STUDENTS

Students with special education needs are a highly heterogeneous group of learners, presenting unique cognitive, behavioral, social, and physical challenges. To help create a classroom culture that supports the participation and achievement of students with such challenges, set clear expectations and provide reasonable choices for all students. Lessons should be planned with individual adaptations and modifications. Offer instructional activities that foster the development of relationships among students and between students and teacher.

Preteach Preteaching helps prepare students for learning.

- Preteach critical social studies terms and high-use academic words using the Vocabulary Builder in the chapter and section openers.

- Provide preferred seating in the front of the class, face-to-face talk for students who read lips, interpreters, or space for a guide dog as necessary.

Teach Using a variety of approaches enhances lessons.

- Provide an overview of key ideas and concepts presented in the text using outlines, maps, or study guides, such as the *Adapted Interactive Reading and Notetaking Study Guide.*

- Present all ideas orally and visually, and when possible, incorporate tactile and kinesthetic experiences as well.

- Require students to demonstrate that they are listening and following along (e.g., taking notes, running a finger along the text).

- Incorporate active reading strategies (e.g., choral reading, paired reading) to assist students in maintaining attention.

- Provide adaptive materials as appropriate (e.g., enlarged print, Braille edition, captions for the video program, audiotapes, CD-ROMs).

- Incorporate the same comprehension and learning strategies over time to allow for mastery.

Differentiated Instruction

Assess Students need to know what is expected.

- Assess students' understanding by asking them to write questions about what they have learned, identify what they find unclear or confusing, or complete short quick writes of the key points.

- When having students work in groups or pairs, set up procedures that maintain each student's accountability (e.g., students each having to write, draw, or state a response).

- Make sure that you have adequately scaffolded tasks for special needs students and equipped them with writing instruction and practice that builds the prerequisite skills.

- When appropriate, have students self-manage and chart their academic performance, homework and assignment completion, and behavior.

- Provide outlines of what is to be done, with suggested dates and timelines for project completion.

> **Differentiated Instruction**
>
> **L1 English Language Learners**   **L1 Special Needs**
>
> **Visualizing the Word** Students should demonstrate their understanding of the words by finding pictures that illustrate them. For example, for the word *rigid*, students may show someone standing at attention. Pair students to exchange their pictures and have the partners check each other's understanding of the relationship of the image to the word. Review the material with students.

ENGLISH LANGUAGE LEARNERS

Students who are learning English are the fastest-growing segment of the school-age population. These students require frontloading, or preteaching, in order to grasp challenging literacy tasks, such as those encountered in a social studies textbook. Since English language learners may be approaching an assignment with impoverished background knowledge and weak English vocabulary, concentrate on activities that build strong conceptual and linguistic foundations, guide them through the text's organization, and model appropriate comprehension strategies. The following practices will support English language learners in making strides in their second-language literacy.

Preteach English language learners require extra preparation.

- Use Word Knowledge Rating Forms to determine understanding of essential words. Introduce these words in meaningful contexts, through simple sentences drawing on familiar issues, scenarios, and vocabulary. Ask students to write the definitions in their own words and then present the words when they occur within the reading.

- Utilize realia and visuals (e.g., photographs, objects, color transparencies) to make the concepts less abstract.

- Lead a quick text prereading, or "text tour," focusing student attention on illustrations, title and subtopics, and boldfaced words.

Teach Many of these techniques will benefit all learners.

- Get students physically involved with the page, using sticky notes or small pieces of cardboard to focus and guide their reading.

- Encourage students to read while listening to a recording of the same passage read aloud, such as on the *Student Edition on Audio CD*. Spanish-language speakers can also listen to section summaries on the *Spanish Guided Reading Audio CD*.

Differentiated Instruction

- Have students engage in repeated readings of the same brief passage to build word recognition, fluency, and reading rate.

- Praise students' efforts to experiment with new language in class, both in writing and in speaking.

Assess Students will demonstrate learning in different ways.
- Ask students to demonstrate their understanding by drawing upon different language skills: formal and informal writing assignments, posters, small group tasks, and oral presentations.

- Make sure students understand assessment criteria in advance. Distribute rubrics provided in the *Assessment Rubrics*. Whenever possible, provide models of student work to emulate, along with a nonmodel that fails to meet the specified assessment criteria.

LESS PROFICIENT READERS

Less proficient readers are individuals who begin the year one or more years below grade level yet do not qualify for special education services. They may or may not be English language learners. They may be underprepared for the academic challenges due to difficulties with attention and memory, learning strategies, or vocabulary and reading fluency. It is especially important to engage these students in challenging lessons while incorporating support or instructional scaffolding to increase their likelihood of success.

Preteach Preteaching helps build students' confidence.
- *For Difficulties With Attention and Memory*: Gain attention by requesting a simple physical response (e.g., "Everyone, eyes on me please."). Then keep the lesson pace brisk—a "perky, not pokey" pace is helpful.

- *For Difficulties With Learning Strategies*: Clarify the rationale for learning a new strategy in terms the students value. Directly teach any prerequisite skills needed to perform the strategy. Make strategies concrete by having students fill out the Anticipation Guide or K-W-L Chart provided in the section's Reading Readiness Guide.

- *For Difficulties With Vocabulary and Fluency*: Directly teach meanings of critical vocabulary required for full understanding of the lesson.

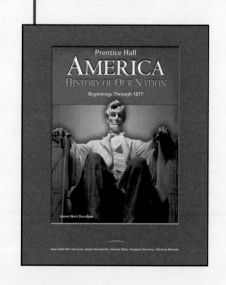

Teach Lessons have to address specific, different needs.
- *For Difficulties With Attention and Memory*: Emphasize connections between new and known information. Engage students in a collaborative "read/reflect/discuss/note" cycle, filling out a graphic organizer from the *Interactive Reading and Notetaking Study Guide*.

- *For Difficulties With Learning Strategies*: Explicitly model the use of the strategy, including a significant focus on thinking aloud during the execution of each step in the strategy. Discuss where else in or out of school students could use the strategy.

- *For Difficulties With Vocabulary and Fluency*: Intentionally revisit newly acquired vocabulary during discussion. Suggest that students use Vocabulary Builder Online.

Assess Assessment must accommodate special needs.

- *For Difficulties With Attention and Memory*: Ask students to reorganize, prioritize, and otherwise reflect on the key aspects of the lesson. Have them explain their graphic organizers to a partner. Monitor, and reteach as necessary.

- *For Difficulties With Learning Strategies*: Include explicit use of strategies taught as part of the quiz, report, project, and other formal assessments.

- *For Difficulties With Vocabulary and Fluency*: Randomly call on students to provide examples of the vocabulary word under examination.

GIFTED AND TALENTED STUDENTS/ADVANCED LEARNERS

Gifted and talented students and advanced learners need modified instruction to achieve their highest potential. They tend to understand complex concepts quickly, learn more rapidly and in greater depth, and may have interests that are different from their peers. Teachers can modify pacing and offer enrichment to allow for exploring topics in-depth, manipulating ideas in novel ways, and making connections to other disciplines.

Preteach These students may have extensive background.

- Before beginning a new unit, have students write about, verbalize, or draw what they know about the topic and present this information to peers.

- Ask students to brainstorm what they'd like to learn, and then work with them to create a plan for advanced study based on their interests.

Teach Activate students' ability to think creatively and see connections.

- Help students adjust the pace of their learning, speeding through concepts they master quickly or slowing down to study content in depth. The Teacher's Edition provides ideas for ways to extend content in the Extend part of the lesson plan.

- Challenge students to tackle more complex topics and offer them frequent opportunities to focus on abstract ideas. A starting point for this focus could be the Concept Lessons in the Teaching Resources.

- Provide opportunities for in-depth research on student-directed topics. Have students explore topics on the Internet under your direction.

- Encourage students to make connections between content they are learning and other disciplines, such as language arts, science, and math. For example, students might want to read fiction about the historical period they are studying in class.

Assess Assessment can take many forms.

- Have students be responsible for part of the assessment of their learning. Allow them to plan, design, and monitor the project or assignment.

- Encourage students to apply their understandings to new situations. Challenge them to take information and use it in novel ways.

Informing Instruction With Assessment

Assessment is a never-ending cycle. With the spotlight now on improving student performance and providing differentiated instruction, it is essential to use assessment to target goals, identify strategies to achieve results, monitor progress, and assess results to inform lesson planning.

Using AYP Monitoring Assessments

The key to success is using a variety of assessment tools coupled with data analysis and decision making. The *AYP Monitoring Assessments* in this program provide four types of assessments.

AYP Monitoring Assessments

Prentice Hall
AMERICA
HISTORY OF OUR NATION

Provide Differentiated Instruction Through Year-Long Progress Monitoring
• Screen reading skills for proper intervention
• Diagnose skills in social studies, critical thinking, and writing
• Provide direction for remediation
• Check progress towards content mastery with Benchmark and Outcome Tests

PEARSON

Types of Assessment	AYP Monitoring Assessments
Screening assessments are brief procedures used to identify at-risk students who are not ready to work at grade level.	Screening test identifies students who are reading 2–3 years below grade level.
Diagnostic assessments provide a more in-depth analysis of strengths and weaknesses that can help teachers make instructional decisions and plan intervention strategies.	Diagnostic tests focus on social studies skills, including subtests in geographic literacy, visual analysis, critical thinking and reading, as well as vocabulary and writing.
Progress-monitoring assessments (sometimes referred to as benchmark tests) provide an ongoing, longitudinal record of student achievement, detailing individual student progress toward meeting end-of-year and end-of-schooling, grade level, district, or state standards.	Benchmark tests assess progress toward mastery of social studies content, and offer remediation recommendations tied to specific program content for each question.
Summary assessments judge students' achievement at the end of a course of study. Large-scale assessments, such as state tests and standardized tests, can be used to determine whether individual students have met the expected standards and whether a school system has made adequate progress in improving its performance.	Outcome tests also test content mastery.

Ongoing Assessment

Ongoing assessment is a critical part of the assessment process. Used in conjunction with AYP monitoring tools—screeners, diagnostics, benchmark tests and summary assessments— it can help teachers monitor student progress and adjust instruction on a day-to-day basis.

Progress Monitoring

Progress Monitoring Transparencies in this program allow teachers to check student understanding of each section on a daily basis. They serve as a tool to track students' mastery of content.

Periodic Testing

Teachers should use periodic quizzes and tests to measure how students are progressing in what they can do and what they understand. Administered between benchmark tests, tests that assess students' analysis skill acquisition and content understanding also inform teacher planning. Assessments include multiple-choice, short answer, and written essays. This program offers printed tests in these formats in the Teaching Resources. *Test Prep With Document-Based Assessment* prepares students for document-based questions by evaluating, analyzing, and interpreting primary and secondary sources.

Portfolios

Portfolios are a form of assessment that contain samples of a student's work collected over time. They enable both the teacher and the student to evaluate progress. Many assignments in this program are appropriate for inclusion in a portfolio. Biography Quest, History Interactive, and other Internet activities can offer evidence of student understanding. The research activity in the Extend the Lesson Through Technology Research can also show content mastery, as well as demonstrate library media center and information literacy skills. The unit-level Think Like a Historian activity and the Historian's Apprentice Activity Pack both provide materials to enhance student portfolios.

Using Rubrics to Assess Writing

Social studies teachers help build students' writing skills throughout the year and monitor progress through written assessments. This program offers writing assessments that build in levels of complexity. Students practice basic skills through writing prompts in the section assessment. They use these skills to tackle more complex scaffolded assignments in the chapter assessment. Professional development and suggestions for improving student writing are found in *Writing for Social Studies Assessment*.

Sample Contents of a Portfolio

Written work
- short paragraphs
- compositions
- short stories
- journals

Audio and video cassettes of oral presentations

Quizzes and tests

Individual student projects

Artwork

Technology projects and Web research

Storyboards

Evidence of student reflection on his or her own writing

Section 2 **Check Your Progress**

Progress Monitoring Online
For: Self-test with instant help
Visit: PHSchool.com
Web Code: mya-3052

Comprehension and Critical Thinking
1. (a) **Recall** Why was New Orleans important to the United States? (b) **Identify Benefits** What was the significance of the Louisiana Purchase?
2. (a) **Identify** Who was Sacagawea, and how was she important to the success of the Lewis and Clark expedition? (b) **Compare and Contrast** How was Pike's expedition similar to that of Lewis and Clark's? How was it different?

Reading Skill
3. **Distinguish Events in Sequence** Describe how the sequence of Lewis and Clark's expedition related to that of Zebulon Pike.

Key Terms
4. Draw a table with two rows and two columns. In the first column, list the key terms from this section: expedition, continental divide. In the next column, write the definition of each word.

Writing
5. Use this section and the following items to write a thesis statement about the life of Meriwether Lewis. **Items:** Born in 1774; Virginian; family friend of Jefferson; in 1792 asked by Jefferson to lead exploration of the Northwest; with Clark led expedition through Louisiana Territory; was appointed governor of Louisiana Territory in 1808; died mysteriously in 1809.

Section 2 The Louisiana Purchase 319

Rubrics are a critical component of an assessment system. They provide structure that helps teachers make expectations clear, and an equitable way to assess student performance. Rubrics allow students to assess their own work. *Assessment Rubrics* include reproducible rubrics for students and instructions for teacher rubric use.

Encouraging Self-Assessment

Students should use the following checks on understanding of skills and concepts to evaluate their own progress before moving on to the next topic:

- **Caption Questions** enhance critical thinking skills and maximize the effectiveness of art, graphics, maps, and narrative.

- **Reading Checkpoints** reinforce and confirm students' understanding.

- **Scaffolded Check Your Progress** questions ease students into the review, then challenge them with more advanced questions.

- **Comprehensive Chapter Review and Assessment** enable students to check their understanding and prepare for test-taking success.

- **Progress Monitoring Online** lets students assess their understanding of content and get instant remediation.

Using Assessment Technology

Technology can ease the assessment process for teachers. Products with this program generate tests, calculate test results, and analyze assessment data.

Test Generators This program's *ExamView®* Test Bank CD-ROM allows teachers to easily create tests from banks of thousands of questions, which can be sorted by difficulty levels to provide leveled quizzes and tests. The questions provide text page numbers for content to foster remediation.

Student-Centered Tools The use of technology can make assessment more engaging for students. MindPoint® Quiz Show CD-ROM is an interactive multimedia game that assesses student understanding, makes learning fun, and tracks student performance. Progress Monitoring Online helps students assess their own development toward mastery of the content.

Progress Monitoring Online
For: Self-test with instant help
Visit: PHSchool.com
Web Code: mwa-2033

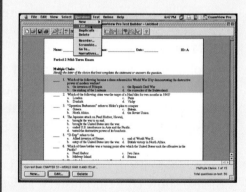

ILLUSTRATED ATLAS
OF AMERICAN HISTORY

Table of Contents

Introduction

This illustrated atlas contains dramatic maps and vibrant pictures and graphs to bring your study of American history to life. You can use these pages to compare regions or to make connections between past and present. The atlas has been placed at the front of your textbook, so you will have it as a ready reference throughout the year.

Get up-to-date information about any country in the world. Use the World Desk Reference Online to learn about the world today, practice critical thinking skills, and get updated statistics and data.

UNITED STATES
POLITICAL

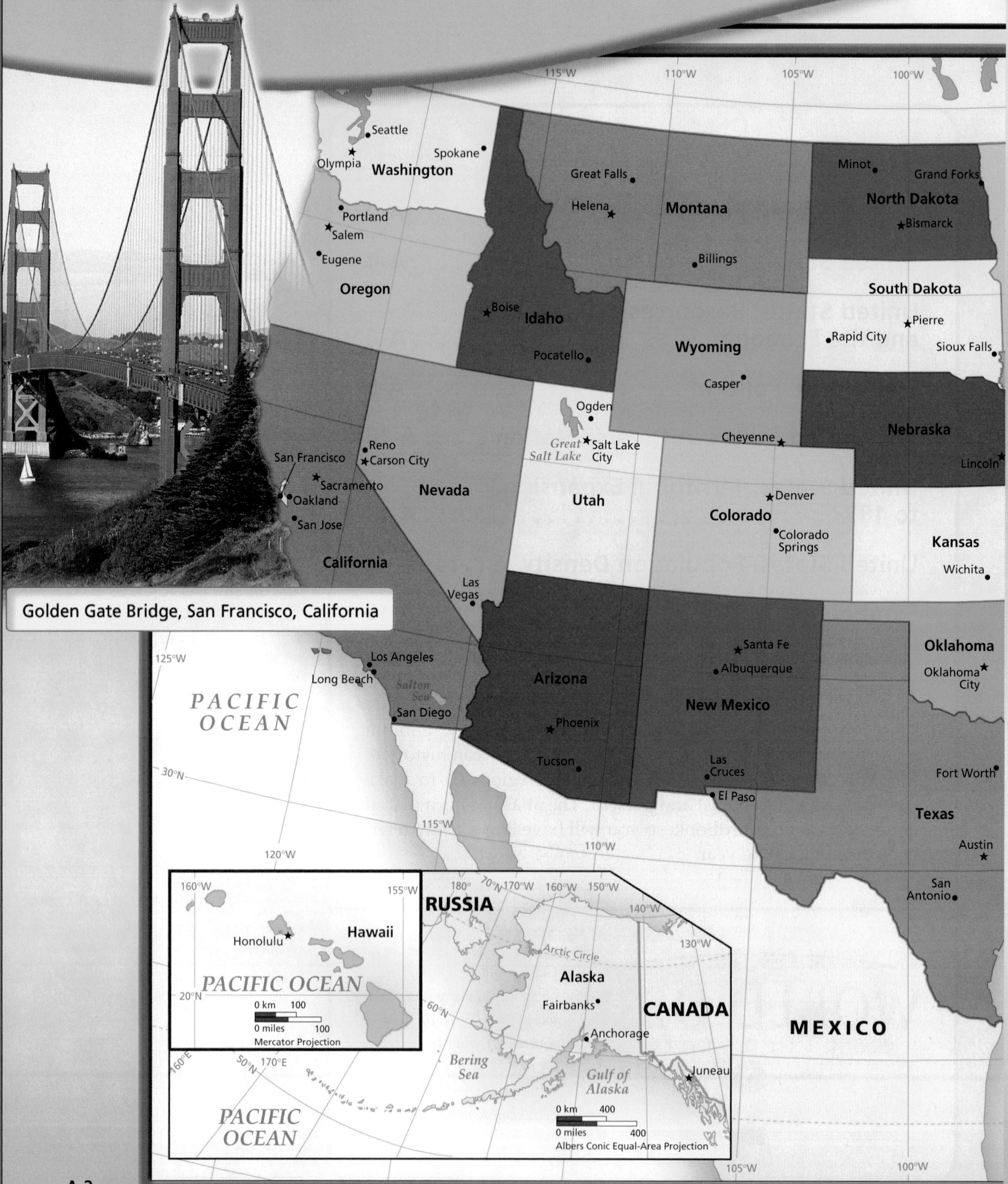

Golden Gate Bridge, San Francisco, California

115°W 110°W 105°W 100°W

Seattle
Olympia Spokane
Washington
Great Falls
Helena ★ **Montana**
Portland
Salem
Eugene
Oregon
Billings
Boise ★ **Idaho**
Pocatello
Minot Grand Forks
North Dakota
★Bismarck
South Dakota
★Pierre
Rapid City
Sioux Falls
Wyoming
Casper
Ogden
Great Salt Lake ★Salt Lake City
Cheyenne ★
Nebraska
Lincoln
Reno
Carson City
San Francisco
Sacramento
Oakland
San Jose
Nevada
Utah
★Denver
Colorado Springs
Colorado
Kansas
Wichita
California
Las Vegas
125°W
Los Angeles
Long Beach
Salton Sea
San Diego
PACIFIC OCEAN
30°N
120°W
115°W
110°W
Arizona
Phoenix ★
Tucson
Santa Fe ★
Albuquerque
New Mexico
Las Cruces
El Paso
Oklahoma
Oklahoma City ★
Fort Worth
Texas
Austin ★
San Antonio
105°W 100°W

160°W 155°W 180° 70°N 170°W 160°W 150°W
Honolulu ★ **Hawaii**
PACIFIC OCEAN
20°N
0 km   100
0 miles 100
Mercator Projection
160°E 170°E
50°N

RUSSIA
Arctic Circle
140°W
Alaska
Fairbanks
60°N
CANADA
130°W
Anchorage
Bering Sea
Gulf of Alaska
Juneau
MEXICO
PACIFIC OCEAN
0 km   400
0 miles 400
Albers Conic Equal-Area Projection

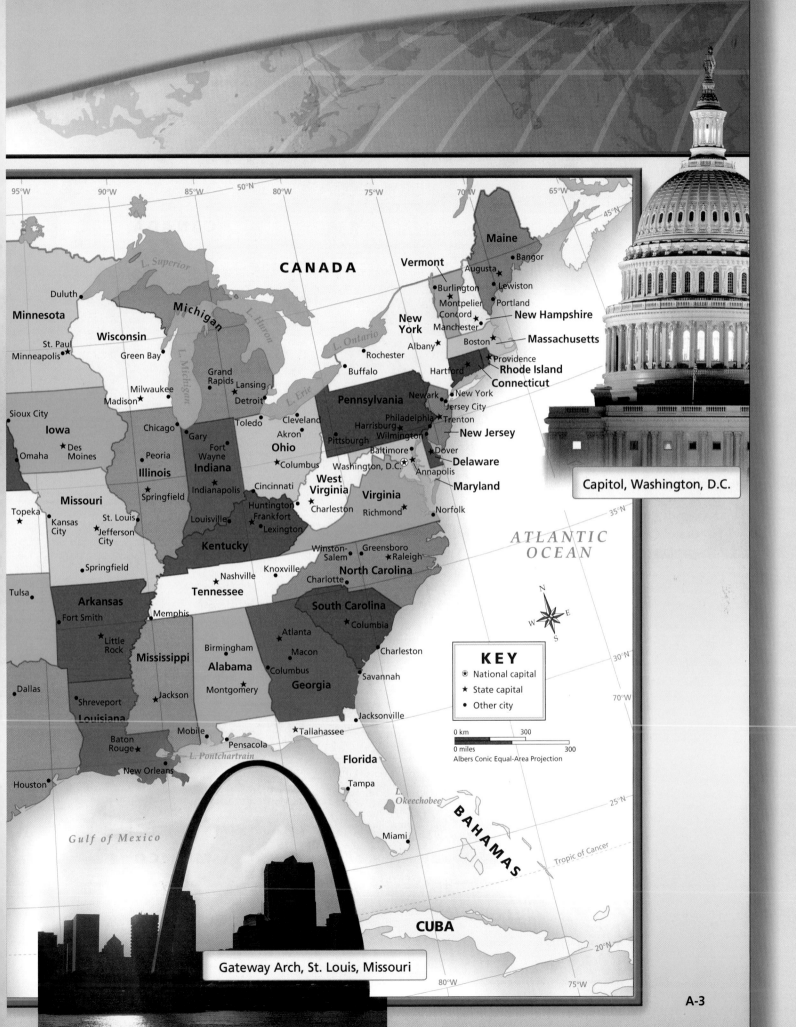

95°W 90°W 85°W 50°N 80°W 75°W 70°W 65°W 45°N

CANADA

Duluth

Minnesota

St. Paul
Minneapolis
★

Green Bay

Wisconsin

Milwaukee
Madison ★

L. Superior

Michigan

L. Michigan

L. Huron

Grand
Rapids
Lansing

Detroit

L. Erie

L. Ontario

Maine

Vermont

Augusta
Bangor

Burlington
Montpelier
Concord
Manchester

Lewiston
Portland

New Hampshire

Albany ★
Rochester
Boston ★
Massachusetts

Buffalo
Hartford
Providence
Rhode Island
Connecticut

**New
York**

Sioux City

Iowa

Omaha
Des
Moines
★

Chicago
Gary
Fort
Wayne

Illinois
Peoria

Springfield

Indiana
Indianapolis
★

Toledo
Cleveland
Akron

Ohio
Columbus ★

Cincinnati

Pennsylvania
Harrisburg ★
Pittsburgh

Philadelphia
Newark
New York
Jersey City
Trenton
New Jersey
Wilmington
Dover
Delaware

Missouri

Topeka
★

Kansas
City

St. Louis
Jefferson
City ★

Springfield

Louisville

Huntington
Frankfort ★
Lexington

Kentucky

**West
Virginia**
Charleston

Baltimore
Washington, D.C. ⊛
Annapolis
Maryland

Virginia
Richmond ★
Norfolk

**ATLANTIC
OCEAN**

35°N

Tulsa

Arkansas

Fort Smith

Little
Rock ★

Memphis

Nashville ★

Tennessee

Knoxville

Winston-
Salem
Greensboro
★ Raleigh

Charlotte

North Carolina

Mississippi

Birmingham

Alabama
Columbus
Montgomery ★

Atlanta
★

Macon

Georgia

South Carolina
★ Columbia

Charleston

Savannah

KEY
⊛ National capital
★ State capital
• Other city

30°N

70°W

Dallas

Shreveport
Jackson ●

Louisiana

Baton
Rouge ★

Mobile
Pensacola

★ Tallahassee

Jacksonville

0 km 300
0 miles 300
Albers Conic Equal-Area Projection

Houston

New Orleans

L. Pontchartrain

Florida
Tampa

*L.
Okeechobee*

BAHAMAS

25°N

Gulf of Mexico

Miami

Tropic of Cancer

CUBA

20°N

80°W 75°W

Capitol, Washington, D.C.

Gateway Arch, St. Louis, Missouri

UNITED STATES
PHYSICAL

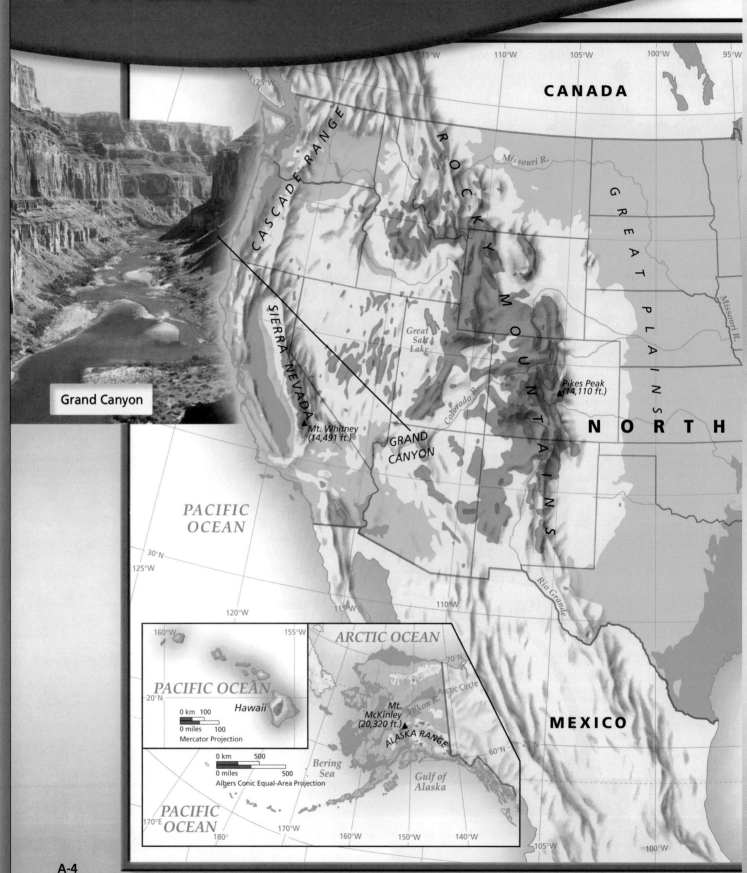

Grand Canyon

CANADA

Missouri R.

ROCKY

GREAT

CASCADE RANGE

Great Salt Lake

PLAINS

SIERRA NEVADA

Pikes Peak (14,110 ft.)

Colorado R.

Mt. Whitney (14,491 ft.)

GRAND CANYON

MOUNTAINS

NORTH

PACIFIC OCEAN

30°N

125°W

Missouri R.

115°W

120°W

115°W

110°W

Rio Grande

ARCTIC OCEAN

160°W   155°W

PACIFIC OCEAN

Hawaii

20°N

0 km   100
0 miles   100
Mercator Projection

70°N

Arctic Circle

Mt. McKinley (20,320 ft.)

Yukon R.

ALASKA RANGE

60°N

MEXICO

0 km   500
0 miles   500
Albers Conic Equal-Area Projection

Bering Sea

Gulf of Alaska

PACIFIC OCEAN

170°E

170°W

180°

160°W

150°W

140°W

105°W

100°W

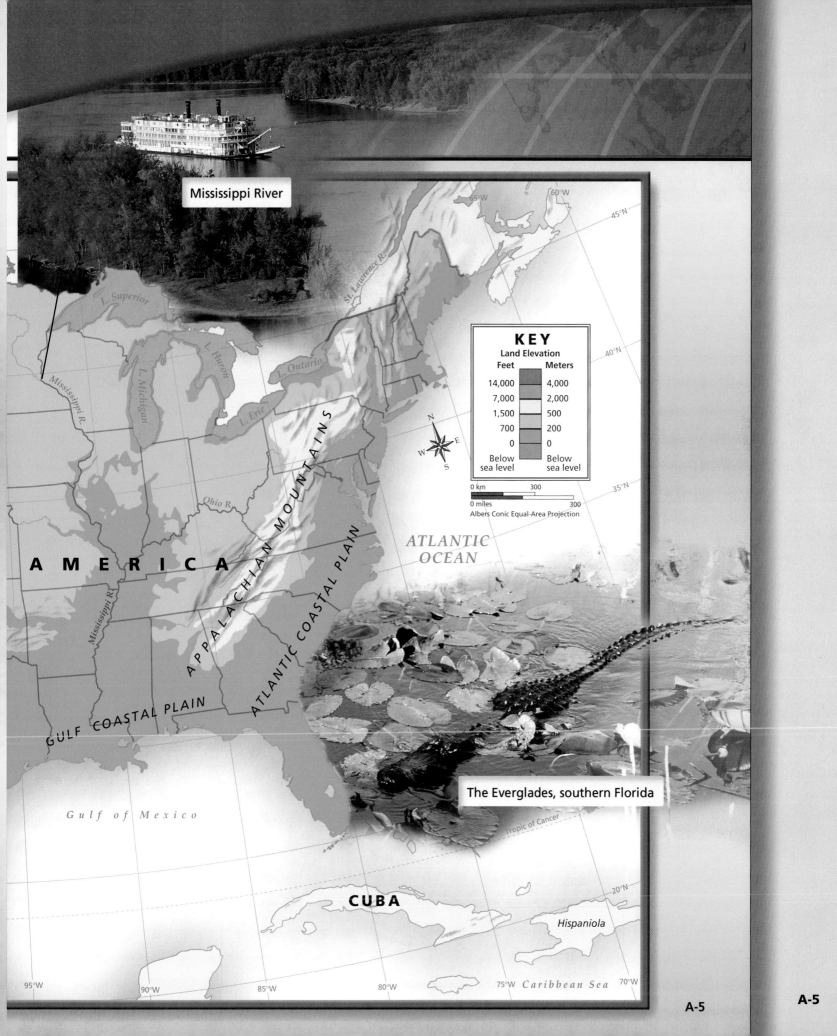

Mississippi River

KEY

Land Elevation

Feet	Meters
14,000	4,000
7,000	2,000
1,500	500
700	200
0	0
Below sea level	Below sea level

0 km — 300
0 miles — 300
Albers Conic Equal-Area Projection

N
W E
S

ATLANTIC
OCEAN

A M E R I C A

APPALACHIAN MOUNTAINS

ATLANTIC COASTAL PLAIN

GULF COASTAL PLAIN

L. Superior
L. Michigan
L. Huron
L. Ontario
L. Erie
St. Lawrence R.

Mississippi R.

Ohio R.

Mississippi R.

The Everglades, southern Florida

Gulf of Mexico

Tropic of Cancer

CUBA

Hispaniola

Caribbean Sea

95°W 90°W 85°W 80°W 75°W 70°W

65°W 60°W

45°N

40°N

35°N

20°N

UNITED STATES
RESOURCES & THE ECONOMY

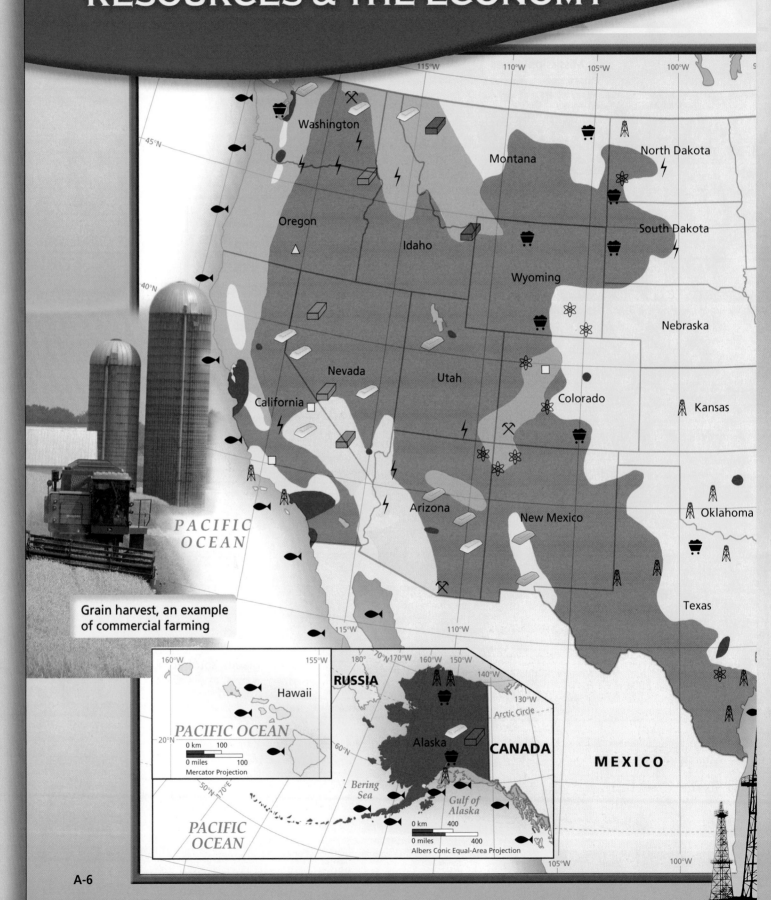

Grain harvest, an example of commercial farming

CANADA

Minnesota
Wisconsin
Iowa
Missouri
Illinois
Indiana
Ohio
Michigan
L. Superior
L. Huron
L. Michigan
L. Erie
L. Ontario
New York
Vermont
Maine
New Hampshire
Massachusetts
Rhode Island
Connecticut
Pennsylvania
New Jersey
Delaware
Maryland
West Virginia
Virginia
Kentucky
Tennessee
Arkansas
North Carolina
South Carolina
Georgia
Alabama
Mississippi
Louisiana
Florida
Gulf of Mexico

ATLANTIC OCEAN

0 km   300
0 miles   300
Albers Conic Equal-Area Projection

N W E S

95°W 90°W 85°W 50°N 80°W 75°W 70°W 65°W

20°N

75°W

Medical research, a key service industry in the U.S. economy

Oil wells pump petroleum, an important natural resource

KEY

Hunting and gathering	Iron
Forestry	Copper
Livestock raising	Bauxite
Commercial farming	Gold
Manufacturing and trade	Silver
Commercial fishing	Phosphates
Little or no activity	Uranium
Coal	Lead
Petroleum	Nickel
Hydroelectric power	Tungsten

THE WORLD: POLITICAL

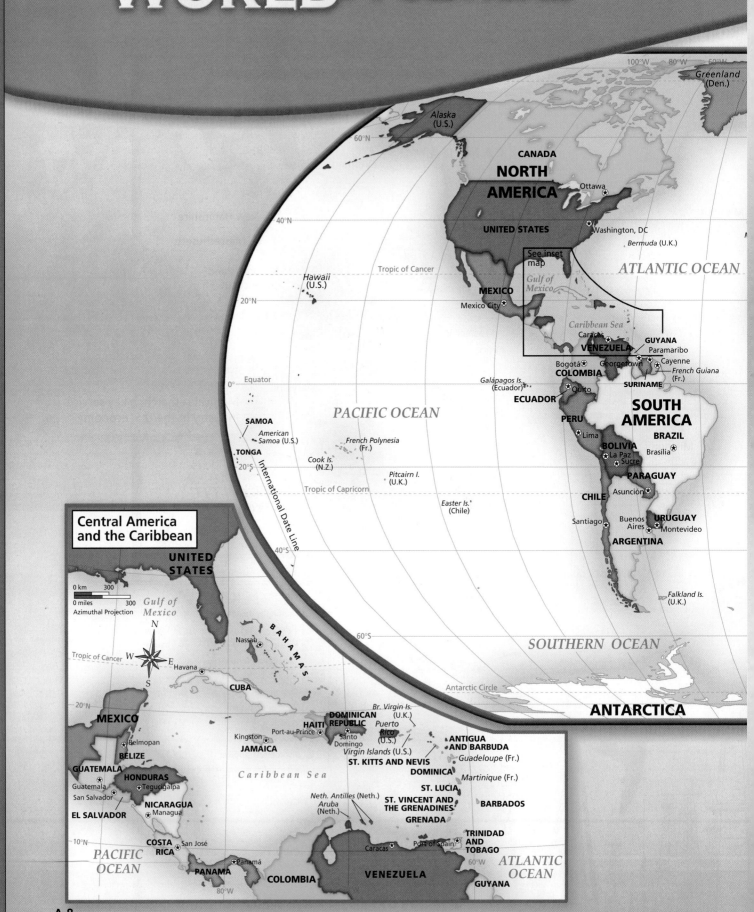

Greenland (Den.)

Alaska (U.S.)

60°N

CANADA

NORTH AMERICA

Ottawa ✪

40°N

UNITED STATES

Washington, DC ✪

Bermuda (U.K.)

ATLANTIC OCEAN

See inset map

Tropic of Cancer

Gulf of Mexico

Hawaii (U.S.)

20°N

MEXICO

Mexico City ✪

Caribbean Sea

Caracas ✪

GUYANA

VENEZUELA

Paramaribo ✪

Cayenne ✪

Bogotá ✪

Georgetown ✪

French Guiana (Fr.)

COLOMBIA

SURINAME

Galápagos Is. (Ecuador)

0° Equator

✪ Quito

ECUADOR

SOUTH AMERICA

PACIFIC OCEAN

PERU

BRAZIL

SAMOA

American Samoa (U.S.)

✪ Lima

BOLIVIA

Brasília ✪

French Polynesia (Fr.)

La Paz ✪ Sucre

TONGA

Cook Is. (N.Z.)

20°S

Pitcairn I. (U.K.)

PARAGUAY

Asunción ✪

CHILE

Tropic of Capricorn

Easter Is. (Chile)

Santiago ✪

Buenos Aires ✪

URUGUAY

Montevideo ✪

ARGENTINA

International Date Line

40°S

Falkland Is. (U.K.)

60°S

SOUTHERN OCEAN

Antarctic Circle

ANTARCTICA

Central America and the Caribbean

0 km 300

0 miles 300

Azimuthal Projection

UNITED STATES

Gulf of Mexico

N

W ⊕ E

S

Tropic of Cancer

Nassau ✪

BAHAMAS

60°S

Havana ✪

CUBA

20°N

MEXICO

DOMINICAN REPUBLIC

Br. Virgin Is. (U.K.)

HAITI

Puerto Rico (U.S.)

ANTIGUA AND BARBUDA

Kingston ✪

Port-au-Prince ✪

Santo Domingo ✪

✪ Belmopan

JAMAICA

Virgin Islands (U.S.)

Guadeloupe (Fr.)

BELIZE

ST. KITTS AND NEVIS

DOMINICA

GUATEMALA

Guatemala ✪

HONDURAS

✪ Tegucigalpa

Caribbean Sea

Martinique (Fr.)

ST. LUCIA

San Salvador ✪

Neth. Antilles (Neth.)

ST. VINCENT AND THE GRENADINES

BARBADOS

NICARAGUA

✪ Managua

Aruba (Neth.)

EL SALVADOR

GRENADA

10°N

COSTA RICA

San José ✪

TRINIDAD AND TOBAGO

PACIFIC OCEAN

Caracas ✪

Port of Spain ✪

ATLANTIC OCEAN

PANAMA

✪ Panamá

COLOMBIA

VENEZUELA

80°W

60°W

GUYANA

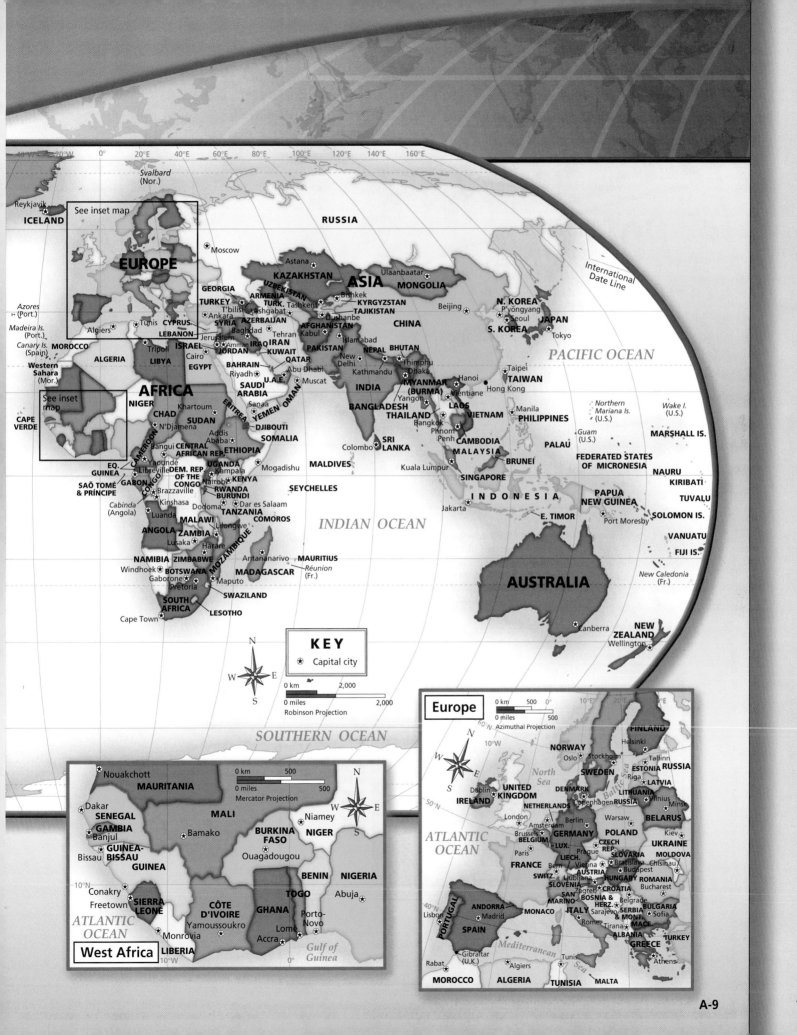

10°W 20°W 0° 20°E 40°E 60°E 80°E 100°E 120°E 140°E 160°E

Svalbard
(Nor.)

Reykjavik
ICELAND

See inset map

EUROPE

★ Moscow

RUSSIA

★ Astana

KAZAKHSTAN

ASIA

Ulaanbaatar ★

MONGOLIA

International Date Line

GEORGIA
TURKEY
UZBEKISTAN
ARMENIA
TURK. Tashkent ★
Bishkek ★
KYRGYZSTAN
TAJIKISTAN
Dushanbe ★

Beijing ★

N. KOREA
P'yŏngyang ★
Seoul ★
S. KOREA
JAPAN
Tokyo ★

Azores
Is. (Port.)

★ Tunis
CYPRUS
LEBANON
Ankara ★
T'bilisi ★
Ashgabat ★
AFGHANISTAN
Kabul ★
Islamabad ★

CHINA

Taipei
TAIWAN

PACIFIC OCEAN

Algiers ★

Madeira Is.
(Port.)

SYRIA
AZERBAIJAN
Baghdad ★
Tehran ★
IRAN

PAKISTAN

New Delhi ★

NEPAL
Kathmandu ★

BHUTAN
Thimphu ★

Hanoi ★
Hong Kong

Canary Is.
(Spain)

MOROCCO
Tripoli ★
ISRAEL
Jerusalem ★
Amman ★
JORDAN
IRAQ
KUWAIT
Riyadh ★
QATAR
Abu Dhabi ★

Dhaka ★
MYANMAR (BURMA)

Vientiane ★
LAOS

Western Sahara (Mor.)

ALGERIA
LIBYA
Cairo ★
EGYPT
BAHRAIN
U.A.E.
SAUDI ARABIA
Muscat ★
OMAN

INDIA
Yangon ★

Bangkok ★
THAILAND

AFRICA

Khartoum ★

BANGLADESH

VIETNAM
PHILIPPINES

Manila ★

Northern Mariana Is. (U.S.)

Wake I. (U.S.)

CAPE VERDE

See inset map

NIGER
CHAD
SUDAN
N'Djamena ★
Sanaa ★
YEMEN
ERITREA
DJIBOUTI
SOMALIA

Addis Ababa ★
ETHIOPIA

Colombo ★
SRI LANKA

MALDIVES

Kuala Lumpur ★

CAMBODIA
Phnom Penh ★
MALAYSIA
BRUNEI

Guam (U.S.)

PALAU

FEDERATED STATES OF MICRONESIA

MARSHALL IS.

NAURU

Bangui ★
CENTRAL AFRICAN REP.
Yaoundé ★
CAMEROON
EQ. GUINEA
Libreville ★
UGANDA
Kampala ★
Nairobi ★
KENYA
Mogadishu ★

SEYCHELLES

SINGAPORE

I N D O N E S I A

Jakarta ★

KIRIBATI

TUVALU

SAŌ TOMÉ & PRÍNCIPE
GABON
DEM. REP. OF THE CONGO
Brazzaville ★
RWANDA
BURUNDI
Dodoma ★

INDIAN OCEAN

PAPUA NEW GUINEA

Port Moresby ★

SOLOMON IS.

VANUATU

CONGO
Kinshasa ★
Cabinda (Angola)
Luanda ★
Dar es Salaam ★
TANZANIA
COMOROS

E. TIMOR

New Caledonia (Fr.)

FIJI IS.

ANGOLA
MALAWI
Lilongwe ★
ZAMBIA
Lusaka ★

NAMIBIA
ZIMBABWE
Harare ★
MOZAMBIQUE
Antananarivo ★
MAURITIUS
Réunion (Fr.)

Windhoek ★
BOTSWANA
Gaborone ★
Pretoria ★
MADAGASCAR
Maputo ★

AUSTRALIA

SOUTH AFRICA
SWAZILAND
LESOTHO

Cape Town ★

Canberra ★

NEW ZEALAND
Wellington ★

KEY

★ Capital city

N
W ✦ E
S

0 km   2,000
0 miles   2,000
Robinson Projection

SOUTHERN OCEAN

West Africa inset

Europe

0 km   500   0°
0 miles   500
Azimuthal Projection

60°N

FINLAND

10°E 20°E 30°E

N
W ✦ E
S

10°W

NORWAY
Oslo ★
Stockholm ★
Helsinki ★

North Sea

SWEDEN

Tallinn ★
ESTONIA
RUSSIA
Riga ★
LATVIA

50°N

Dublin ★
IRELAND
UNITED KINGDOM

DENMARK
Copenhagen ★
LITHUANIA
RUSSIA
Vilnius ★
Minsk ★

ATLANTIC OCEAN

London ★
NETHERLANDS
Amsterdam ★
Berlin ★
Warsaw ★
BELARUS
Kiev ★

BELGIUM
Brussels ★
GERMANY
POLAND
UKRAINE

Paris ★
LUX.
Prague ★
CZECH REP.
SLOVAKIA
Chisinau ★
MOLDOVA

FRANCE
Bern ★
LIECH.
Vienna ★
Bratislava ★
SWITZ.
AUSTRIA
HUNGARY
ROMANIA
Budapest ★
Bucharest ★

Ljubljana ★
SLOVENIA
Zagreb ★
CROATIA
Belgrade ★
SERBIA & MONT.
BULGARIA
Sofia ★

40°N

PORTUGAL
ANDORRA
Madrid ★
MONACO
SAN MARINO
BOSNIA & HERZ.
Sarajevo ★
MACE.
Tirana ★
ITALY
Rome ★
ALBANIA
GREECE
TURKEY

Lisbon ★
SPAIN
Gibraltar (U.K.)
Rabat ★
Mediterranean Sea
Algiers ★
Tunis ★
Athens ★

MOROCCO
ALGERIA
TUNISIA
MALTA

West Africa inset

Nouakchott ★
MAURITANIA

0 km   500
0 miles   500
Mercator Projection

Dakar ★
SENEGAL
MALI
Niamey ★

N
W ✦ E
S

GAMBIA
Banjul ★
Bamako ★
BURKINA FASO
NIGER

GUINEA-BISSAU
Bissau ★
Ouagadougou ★

GUINEA
BENIN
NIGERIA

10°N

Conakry ★
Freetown ★
SIERRA LEONE
CÔTE D'IVOIRE
GHANA
TOGO
Abuja ★

ATLANTIC OCEAN

Yamoussoukro ★
Lomé ★
Porto-Novo ★

Monrovia ★
Accra ★
LIBERIA
Gulf of Guinea

West Africa

10°W 0°

POLLING PLACE

投票站 CASILLA ELECTORAL
投票所 LUGAR NG BOTOHAN
투표소 PHÒNG PHIẾU

Sign at a California polling place

CANADA

ASIA

UNITED

Asian Migration

According to the 2000 census, 10.2 million Asian Americans make up 3.6 percent of the total U.S. population. Asian immigrants include people from China, Japan, Korea, the Philippines, as well as those from countries in Southeast Asia and South Asia.

0 km — 3,000
0 miles — 3,000
Mercator Projection

PACIFIC OCEAN

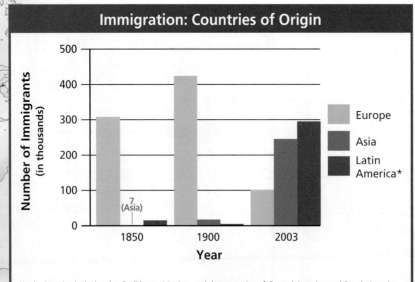

Immigration: Countries of Origin

Number of Immigrants (in thousands)

500
400
300
200
100
0

7 (Asia)

1850   1900   2003
Year

- Europe
- Asia
- Latin America*

*Latin America includes the Caribbean, Mexico, and the countries of Central America and South America.

Sources: *Historical Statistics of the United States* and *Statistical Yearbook of the Immigration and Naturalization Service*

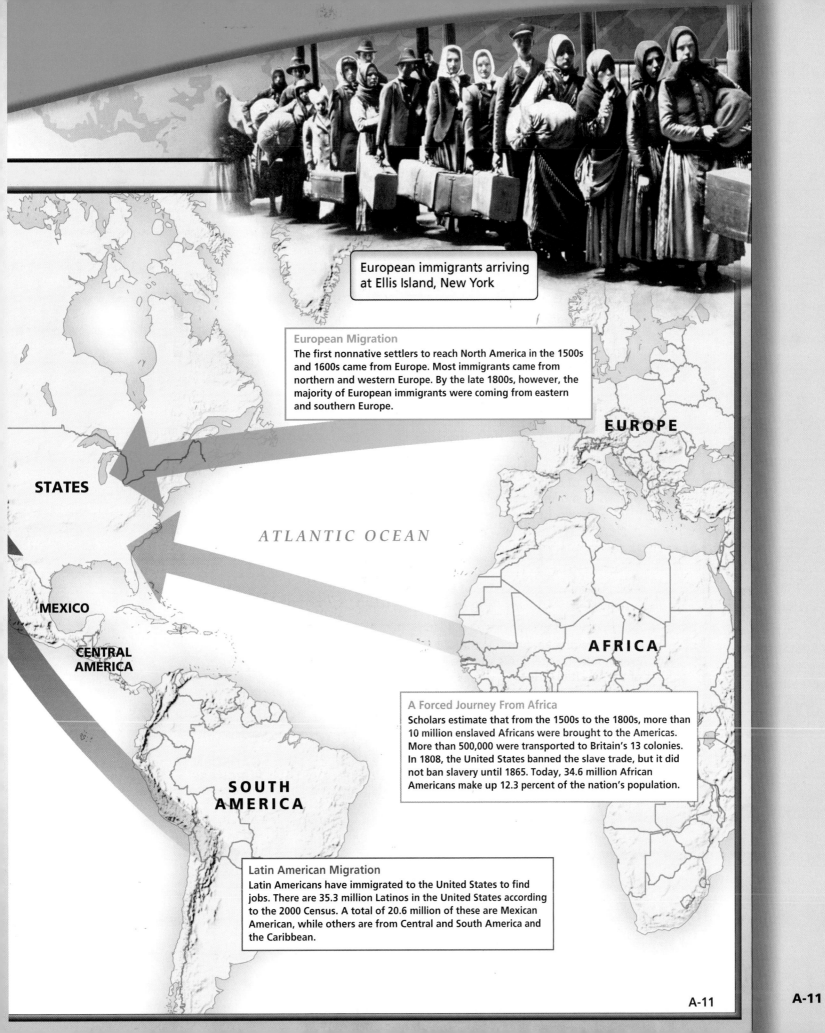

European immigrants arriving at Ellis Island, New York

European Migration

The first nonnative settlers to reach North America in the 1500s and 1600s came from Europe. Most immigrants came from northern and western Europe. By the late 1800s, however, the majority of European immigrants were coming from eastern and southern Europe.

EUROPE

STATES

ATLANTIC OCEAN

MEXICO

CENTRAL AMERICA

AFRICA

A Forced Journey From Africa

Scholars estimate that from the 1500s to the 1800s, more than 10 million enslaved Africans were brought to the Americas. More than 500,000 were transported to Britain's 13 colonies. In 1808, the United States banned the slave trade, but it did not ban slavery until 1865. Today, 34.6 million African Americans make up 12.3 percent of the nation's population.

SOUTH AMERICA

Latin American Migration

Latin Americans have immigrated to the United States to find jobs. There are 35.3 million Latinos in the United States according to the 2000 Census. A total of 20.6 million of these are Mexican American, while others are from Central and South America and the Caribbean.

UNITED STATES
TERRITORIAL EXPANSION
TO 1853

Mandan Village, like the one visited by Lewis and Clark during their exploration of the Louisiana Territory

A covered wagon, the mode of transportation for people moving west in the 1800s

PACIFIC OCEAN

The Alamo, site of a key battle in the war for Texas independence; Texas became part of the Mexican Cession

OREGON COUNTRY
(Agreement with Britain, 1846)

(Ceded by Britain, 1818)

LOUISIANA PURCHASE
(Purchased from France, 1803)

MEXICAN CESSION
(Treaty of Guadalupe-Hidalgo, 1848)

TEXAS ANNEXATION
(Annexed by Congress, 1845)

GADSDEN PURCHASE
(Purchased from Mexico, 1853)

MEXICO

A-12

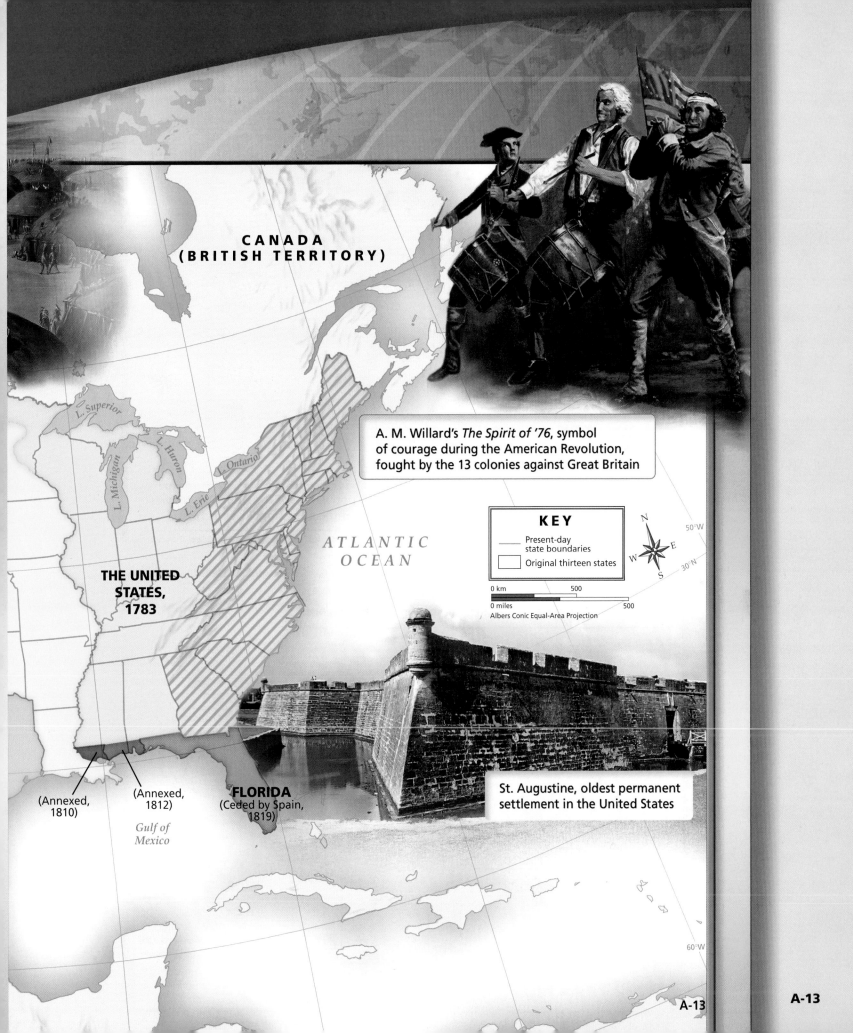

CANADA
(BRITISH TERRITORY)

L. Superior

L. Michigan

L. Huron

L. Ontario

L. Erie

THE UNITED
STATES,
1783

ATLANTIC
OCEAN

A. M. Willard's *The Spirit of '76*, symbol
of courage during the American Revolution,
fought by the 13 colonies against Great Britain

KEY

Present-day
state boundaries

Original thirteen states

0 km   500

0 miles   500

Albers Conic Equal-Area Projection

50°W

30°N

(Annexed,
1810)

(Annexed,
1812)

FLORIDA
(Ceded by Spain,
1819)

St. Augustine, oldest permanent
settlement in the United States

*Gulf of
Mexico*

60°W

UNITED STATES
POPULATION DENSITY

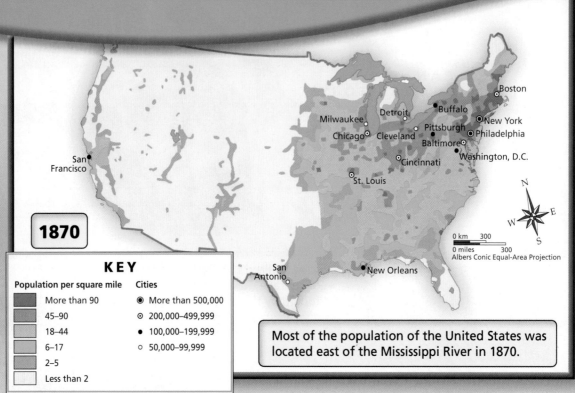

1870

KEY

Population per square mile

■	More than 90
■	45–90
■	18–44
■	6–17
■	2–5
□	Less than 2

Cities

◉ More than 500,000

⊙ 200,000–499,999

● 100,000–199,999

○ 50,000–99,999

Most of the population of the United States was located east of the Mississippi River in 1870.

By 1960, the Midwest and the West had become more populated. A number of large cities had grown in these regions.

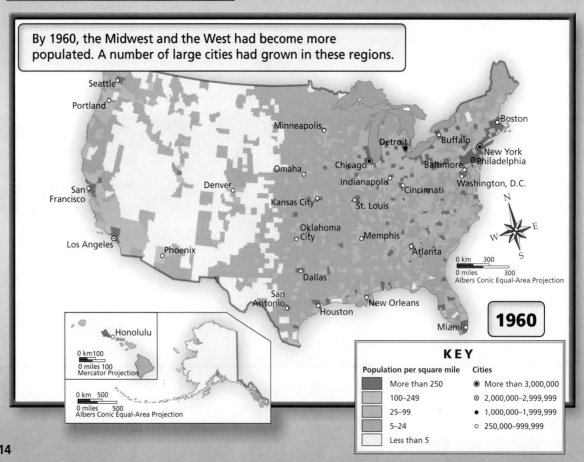

1960

KEY

Population per square mile

■	More than 250
■	100–249
■	25–99
■	5–24
□	Less than 5

Cities

◉ More than 3,000,000

⊙ 2,000,000–2,999,999

● 1,000,000–1,999,999

○ 250,000–999,999

In the 1880s, Anaheim, California, outside of Los Angeles was rural. By the twenty-first century Los Angeles, as well as surrounding cities like Anaheim, were modern bustling cities connected by freeways.

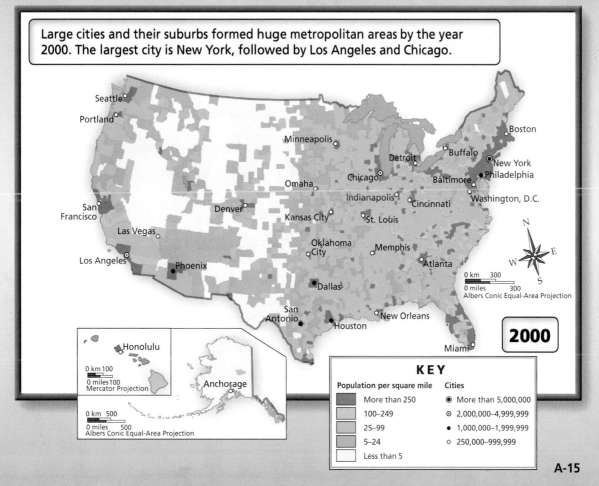

Large cities and their suburbs formed huge metropolitan areas by the year 2000. The largest city is New York, followed by Los Angeles and Chicago.

Seattle
Portland
Minneapolis
Detroit
Buffalo
Boston
New York
Chicago
Baltimore
Philadelphia
Omaha
Indianapolis
Cincinnati
Washington, D.C.
San Francisco
Denver
Kansas City
St. Louis
Las Vegas
Oklahoma City
Memphis
Los Angeles
Atlanta
Phoenix
Dallas
San Antonio
Houston
New Orleans
Miami

0 km 300
0 miles 300
Albers Conic Equal-Area Projection

2000

Honolulu

0 km 100
0 miles 100
Mercator Projection

Anchorage

0 km 500
0 miles 500
Albers Conic Equal-Area Projection

KEY

Population per square mile		Cities	
	More than 250	◉	More than 5,000,000
	100–249	◎	2,000,000–4,999,999
	25–99	●	1,000,000–1,999,999
	5–24	○	250,000–999,999
	Less than 5		

SYMBOLS OF OUR NATION

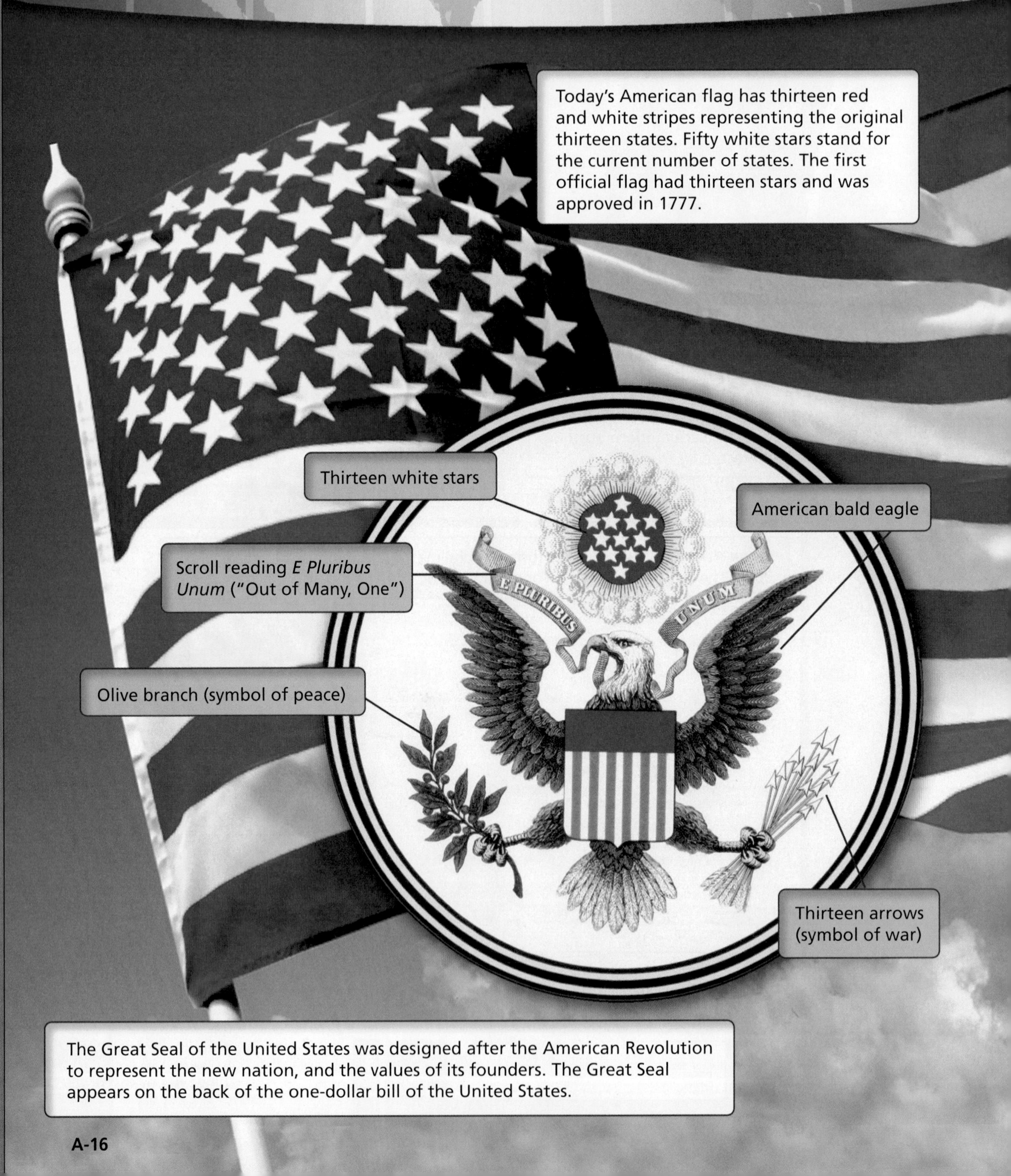

Today's American flag has thirteen red and white stripes representing the original thirteen states. Fifty white stars stand for the current number of states. The first official flag had thirteen stars and was approved in 1777.

Thirteen white stars

American bald eagle

Scroll reading *E Pluribus Unum* ("Out of Many, One")

Olive branch (symbol of peace)

Thirteen arrows (symbol of war)

The Great Seal of the United States was designed after the American Revolution to represent the new nation, and the values of its founders. The Great Seal appears on the back of the one-dollar bill of the United States.

Historian's Toolkit

Introduction: Studying Our Past

The nation was at war with itself, the North fighting against the South. In July 1863, more than 50,000 soldiers had died at a horrible battle in Gettysburg, Pennsylvania. A few months later, President Abraham Lincoln visited Gettysburg to dedicate the battlefield as a cemetery. Lincoln spoke of the soldiers who had given their lives to keep the nation together:

❝The world will little note, nor long remember what we say here, but it can never forget what they did here.❞

—Abraham Lincoln, Gettysburg Address

Lincoln was partly right. The world still remembers the soldiers who died during the Civil War. But we also remember what Lincoln said and what he did for the cause of freedom. As you study American history this year, you will be asked to remember all those who came before us—soldiers and Presidents, explorers and inventors, religious leaders and business leaders, the people who wrote our Constitution, and the people who fought to end slavery.

Helping us remember the past is the job of the historian. Historians explore important questions in order to find out how people lived and why they made the decisions they did. Historians also try to understand how history affects our lives today.

On the next few pages, you will learn to think like a historian. You will also get to try out some of the tools historians use. Your Historian's Toolkit can make your study of American history easier and more rewarding.

Union soldier

HT 1

Introduction

Objective
- Learn why studying history helps us understand current and future events.

Prepare to Read

Build Background Knowledge   L2

Call students' attention to the name of this handbook: Historian's Toolkit. Ask: **What do you think you will find in this section of the textbook?** (*Answers will vary but should reflect an understanding that they will find tools that will help them learn and understand history.*)

Instruction   L2

Read Introduction: Studying Our Past with the class.

Write the following two quotations on the board or display them on an overhead projector.

*"*History is a guide to navigation in perilous times. History is who we are and why we are the way we are.*"*
—David McCullough

*"*Those who cannot learn from history are doomed to repeat it.*"*
—George Santayana

Have students discuss what each of these people might have meant. (*Answers will vary but should include some understanding of why history is important.*)

Ask: **In what ways do these historians agree with each other about the importance of remembering the past?** (*Possible answer: They both see value in the study of history and that what came before has an impact on what is happening now.*)

Independent Practice

Write the following quotation from Aristotle on the board: "If you would understand anything, observe its beginning and its development."

Have students rewrite the quotation in their own words.

Monitor Progress

Circulate and check that students' work reflects the meaning of the quotation.

Objectives

■ Learn the difference between primary and secondary sources.

■ Learn the steps historians take to understand historical events.

Build Background Knowledge   L2

Ask students to think about what sources they would use if they wanted to write a history of their community.

Ask: **What would be some important sources of information?** (*Possible answers: interviews of older inhabitants, historical pictures, documents such as deeds and surveys, other histories, newspaper articles, old maps*) Jot these answers on the board.

Ask: **Why do you think you would need more than one source?** (*Different sources provide different kinds of information. Two people might remember things differently.*)

Historical Evidence

Historians use many types of evidence to learn about the past. This evidence can be divided into primary sources and secondary sources.

Primary Sources A primary source is firsthand information about people or events. Primary sources include official documents, such as laws and public speeches, as well as eyewitness accounts, such as diaries, letters, and autobiographies. Primary sources may also include visual evidence, such as news photographs or videotapes.

Another type of primary source is an artifact. This is an item left behind by people in the past. This might take the form of a statue, a tool, or an everyday object.

Primary sources are valuable because they are created at the time when an event occurs. But this does not necessarily make them "true." Primary sources are created by people, and they may reflect the points of view of the people who created them. The person might not have been aware of certain facts, might have been trying to impress someone, or may even have been lying. So primary sources must be evaluated carefully and considered in relation to other sources on the subject.

Secondary Sources Historians also use secondary sources. These are sources created by someone who did not actually witness events. This textbook, for example, is a secondary source. The authors gathered information from many sources to reach an understanding of what happened and why it happened. Then, they wrote their interpretation of the events. Other secondary sources include news articles and biographies.

Types of Historical Sources

Type of Source	Description	Examples

Primary Sources	• Provide direct evidence about an event
	• Have a limited viewpoint
	• May be reliable or unreliable
	• Include objects left behind by people
		• Official documents
		• Letters and diaries
		• Speeches and interviews
		• Autobiographies
		• Photographs
		• Artifacts
		  • Tools and weapons
		  • Statues and other art

Secondary Sources	• Consist of secondhand information about an event • Use primary sources to create a broader picture • May be reliable or unreliable	• History books • Biographies • Encyclopedias and other reference works • Internet Web sites

Using Historical Sources

Everyone who wants to know about history starts by asking questions. You might be familiar with the types of questions found in your textbook or asked by your teacher. But historians ask questions the way a detective would. Each answer is a clue that leads to another question. The questions and answers bring the historian to an understanding of events in the past.

Consider this situation. Patricia was going through some very old books she found in her great-grandmother's trunk in the attic. Between the pages of one book, she found an old letter on thin, yellowing paper. A copy of the letter is shown here at right.

While reading the letter, Patricia asked herself many questions. Some of her questions are shown at right. Trying to find the answers to the questions is the same sort of thinking that historians use to find out about the past.

June 12, 1849

Dear Sean,

Everyone was happy to get your last letter. After surviving such a long, difficult journey, it must have been wonderful to arrive at last in New York.

Things in our village are not as bad as when you left. But many children and old people are still starving, and too many people have no place to live. You were wise to go to America.

Please tell me more about your plans. After traveling for so long, why would you want to begin a new journey? Where is this place called California? And why are you so sure you can get rich there?

I miss you. I only hope I live long enough to join you someday.

Your loving brother,
Michael

Where did Sean come from? Why was the trip so hard?

What has happened to cause these problems?

How does Sean plan to get rich?

Patricia may follow several steps to find the answers to her questions.

- **Start with what is known.** Patricia knows that her ancestors came to the United States from Ireland many years ago. She thinks this letter might explain why.
- **Read and observe.** Patricia can look for further information in primary and secondary sources. She might look at a map to see where Ireland is and how far it is from New York to California.
- **Speculate.** To help get started, Patricia might make some guesses, called hypotheses, about the answers to her questions.

- **Evaluate evidence.** As Patricia finds more information, she will test her hypotheses against the information that turns up. She can always change her hypotheses as she learns more.
- **Draw conclusions.** Patricia states what she believes are the final answers to her questions.

To start her search, though, Patricia will need to practice her skills of reading like a historian and using maps. The information on the following pages will help you review some of these skills.

Have students read Think Like a Historian: Historical Evidence and Using Historical Sources using the Choral Reading method (TE, p. T22).

Have students refer to the sources of information about the history of their community that are listed on the board. Discuss with them which of these sources would be considered primary sources and which would be considered secondary sources.

Ask: **Which sources would be most reliable, and which might be less reliable?** (*Answers will vary, but should reflect an understanding of the reliability and validity of the various sources.*)

Independent Practice

Pair students and have them come up with a list of reasons why no two historians' accounts will be exactly the same.

Monitor Progress

Have students share their answers with the class. Answers should reflect an understanding that different people would gather different information and choose different ways of telling the story.

Objectives

- Learn how to read informational, nonfiction text with a critical eye.
- Learn how to evaluate the credibility of an informational text.

Build Background Knowledge `L2`

Ask students to identify sources from which they get information about the world around them. Write student answers on the board. (*Possible answers: newspaper stories, editorials, encyclopedias, atlases, Internet, magazines, documentaries, news broadcasts, textbooks*) Tell students that they must actively evaluate the information in most of the nonfiction they read.

Historian's Toolkit — # How to Read History

Read Informational Texts

Reading a magazine, an Internet page, or a textbook is not the same as reading a novel. The purpose of reading nonfiction texts is to acquire new information. On page HT 7, you'll read about some ⊙ **Reading Skills** that you'll practice as you read this textbook. Here, we'll focus on a few skills that will help you read nonfiction with a more critical eye.

Analyze the Author's Purpose

Different types of materials are written with different purposes in mind. For example, a textbook is written to teach students information about a subject. The purpose of a technical manual is to teach someone how to use something, such as a computer. A newspaper editorial might be written to persuade the reader to accept a particular point of view. An author's purpose influences how the material is presented. Sometimes, an author states his or her purpose directly. More often, the purpose is only suggested, and you must use clues to identify the author's purpose.

Distinguish Between Facts and Opinions

Active reading enables you to distinguish between facts and opinions when reading informational texts. Facts can be proved or disproved, but opinions reflect someone's own point of view.

Because newspaper editorials usually offer opinions on current events and issues, you should watch for bias and faulty logic when reading them. For example, the newspaper editorial at right shows factual statements in blue and opinions in red. Highly charged words are underlined. They reveal the writer's bias.

> More than 5,000 people voted last week in favor of building a new shopping center, but the opposition won out. The margin of victory is irrelevant. Those radical voters who opposed the center are obviously self-serving elitists who do not care about anyone but themselves.
>
> This month's unemployment figure for our area is 10 percent, which represents an increase of about 5 percent over the figure for this time last year. These figures mean that unemployment is worsening. But the people who voted against the mall probably do not care about creating new jobs.

Identify Evidence

Before you accept a writer's conclusion, you need to make sure that the writer has based the conclusion on enough evidence and on the right kind of evidence. A writer may present a series of facts to support a claim, but the facts may not tell the whole story. For example, the writer of the newspaper editorial on the previous page claims that the new shopping center would create more jobs. But what evidence is offered? Is it possible that the shopping center might have put many small local stores out of business? This would decrease employment rather than increase it.

Evaluate Credibility

Whenever you read informational texts, you need to assess the credibility of the writer. In other words, you have to decide whether the writer is believable. This is especially true of sites you may visit on the Internet. All Internet sources are not equally reliable. Here are some questions to ask yourself when evaluating the credibility of a Web site:

☐ Is the Web site created by a respected organization, a discussion group, or an individual?

☐ Does the Web site creator include his or her name as well as credentials and the sources he or she used to write the material?

☐ Is the information on the site balanced or biased?

☐ Can you verify the information using two other sources?

☐ Is there a date telling when the Web site was created or last updated?

Have students read How to Read History: Read Informational Texts using the Structured Silent Reading strategy (TE, p. T22).

As students read, they should consider the relative value and reliability of each of the sources of information listed on the board. Have students discuss ways they could determine the value of each item as a source of information.

To help students grasp the difference between fact and opinion, put a series of factual statements on the board and have students offer suggestions for changing the statement into an opinion. For example: The sun is shining brightly.—The sun is shining too brightly. Many people supported the right of women to vote.—Many people gladly supported the right of women to vote. Ask: **What clues helped you to draw your conclusions?** (*Underline the words students identify as those that suggest an opinion.*)

Independent Practice

Have each student write two factual statements and two statements of opinion.

Monitor Progress

Circulate and check students' work.

Objectives

- Learn special skills needed to read and understand history texts.
- Learn how this textbook helps students understand important vocabulary.

Build Background Knowledge

L2

Have a discussion with students about their experiences using a textbook. Which subjects require the most reading? What textbooks have they found easiest to use? Have they ever had problems reading and understanding the contents of a textbook? What do they think makes textbooks difficult?

Build Vocabulary

One of the most important tools in reading informational texts is to make sure you understand the key vocabulary used by the writer. This textbook helps you with two types of vocabulary—key terms and high-use academic words. Key Terms are words that you need to understand to read about a particular historical event or development. High-use academic words are words that will help you read any textbook.

Key Terms and High-Use Academic Words

Reading Skill

Identify Propositions The study of history often takes you inside important debates over ideas and actions. People propose their ideas and then give reasons to support those ideas. Identifying those propositions will help you to understand the beliefs and experiences of people in an earlier time. One way to identify propositions is to ask yourself what problems people had and how they proposed solving those problems.

Key Terms and People

constitution   Daniel Shays
executive
economic
depression

Government by the States

As the Continental Congress began moving toward independence in 1776, leaders in the individual states began creating governments. Eleven of the 13 states wrote new constitutions to support their governments. A constitution is a document stating the rules under which a government will operate. The other two states—Rhode Island and Connecticut—kept using their colonial charters. However, they removed all references to the British king.

Writing State Constitutions In writing state constitutions, Americans were well aware of the problems that had led to the Revolution. Colonists had been unhappy with governors appointed by the British Crown. Thus, the new constitutions minimized the powers of state governors. Instead, they gave most of the power to state legislatures elected by the people.

204   Chapter 7   Creating the Constitution

① Key social studies terms for each section are introduced in the section opener.

② Notice that they are always shown in blue type within the text narrative. Their definitions are also in blue.

Reading Skill

Identify Propositions The study of history often takes you inside important debates over ideas and actions. People propose their ideas and then give reasons to support those ideas. Identifying those propositions will help you to understand the beliefs and experiences of people in an earlier time. One way to identify propositions is to ask yourself what problems people had and how they proposed solving those problems.

Key Terms and People

constitution   Daniel Shays
executive
economic
depression

Government by the States

As the Continental Congress began moving toward independence in 1776, leaders in the individual states began creating governments. Eleven of the 13 states wrote new constitutions to support their governments. A constitution is a document stating the rules under which a government will operate. The other two states—Rhode Island and Connecticut—kept using their colonial charters. However, they removed all references to the British king.

Writing State Constitutions In writing state constitutions, Americans were well aware of the problems that had led to the Revolution. Colonists had been unhappy with governors appointed by the British Crown. Thus, the new constitutions minimized the powers of state governors. Instead, they gave most of the power to state legislatures elected by the people.

204   Chapter 7   Creating the Constitution

Protecting Rights The Declaration of Independence listed ways that Britain had violated the rights of colonists. To prevent such abuses, states sought to protect individual rights. Virginia was the first state to include a bill of rights in its constitution. Virginia's list included freedom of the press and the right to trial by jury, and it also barred "cruel and unusual punishments." The final clause guaranteed freedom of religion:

"That religion, or the duty which we owe to our Creator, and the manner of discharging it, can be directed only by reason and conviction, not by force or violence; and therefore all men are equally entitled to the free exercise of religion, according to the dictates of conscience."
—Virginia Bill of Rights, 1776

Vocabulary Builder

individual (in duh vu oo uhl)
adj. of, for, or by a single person or thing

Protecting Rights
Virginia included a bill of rights in its constitution. The Virginia bill of rights became a model for other states and, later, for the national Constitution. Critical Thinking: Link Past and Present Which protections in the Virginia bill of

③ High-use words are underlined in the text and defined in the margin. You can practice these words at **Vocabulary Builder Online.**

Reading Skills

The History Reading Skills described on this page are important in helping you read and understand the information in this book. Each section teaches a reading skill and gives you a chance to practice the skill as you read. As you learn to use these skills, you will find that you can apply them to other books you read.

Clarify Meaning You can better understand what you read by using summaries and outlines and by taking notes to help identify main ideas and supporting details. **Chapters 1, 2.**

Compare and Contrast When you compare, you examine the similarities between things. When you contrast, you look at the differences. **Chapter 3.**

Use Context Learn to use context clues to help you understand the meaning of unfamiliar words and words with more than one meaning. **Chapter 4.**

Word Analysis Discover how to analyze words to determine their meanings. **Chapters 6, 8.**

Understand Sequence A sequence is the order in which a series of events occurs. Noting the sequence of important events can help you understand and remember the events. **Chapters 9, 15.**

Analyze Cause and Effect Every event in history has causes and creates effects. You will learn how to identify causes, which are what make events happen, and effects, which are what happen as a result of an event. **Chapters 10, 14.**

Draw Conclusions You will learn how to use details from primary and secondary sources to draw conclusions. **Chapters 5, 12.**

Evaluate Information As you read history, it is important to evaluate how writers' support their propositions, or the ideas they put forth. To do so, it is important to know how to identify and explain central issues and frame good research questions. **Chapters 7, 11, 13, 16, Epilogue.**

Instruction

Have students read How to Read History: Build Vocabulary and Reading Skills.

Explain the difference between the Key Terms and the High-Use Academic Words in their textbook.

Have students identify the History Reading Skills and then turn to the chapters referenced in the Student Edition to see how each skill is taught. Discuss with students why these skills are important in order to understand a history textbook.

Independent Practice

Have students pick one chapter in the textbook and identify all of the places where reading and vocabulary are taught in that chapter.

Monitor Progress

Circulate and quiz individual students. Have them point to the appropriate places in their textbook.

Objectives

- Recognize the connection between geography and history.
- Learn the five themes of geography.

Build Background Knowledge

L2

Students may not have a clear understanding of what geography is and how it can affect history. Write a simple definition on the board: *Geography is a study of where people, places, and things are located and how they relate to each other.* Tell students that the word *geography* comes from a Greek word meaning "writing about" or "describing" Earth.

MAP ★ MASTER®

CONTENTS

Go Online PHSchool.com — The maps in this textbook can be found online at **PHSchool.com**, along with map-skills practice.

Geography and History

Historical information is not presented only in written sources. Maps are often a key to understanding what happened and why.

Do you remember when Patricia was asking questions about the letter she found? (See page HT 3.) In addition to using primary and secondary sources, Patricia could have used maps to locate Ireland and to trace Sean's route from New York to California.

In order to get the most out of maps as sources, you need to make sure that your geography map skills are strong. On the next few pages, you can review some of the basic tools historians use to understand maps and geography.

The pictures above show two different geographical regions of the United States. The Midwest (above, left) has fertile plains suitable for farming. The rocky coasts of New England (right) are home to a large fishing industry.

Five Themes of Geography

Studying the history and geography of the United States is a huge task. You can make that task easier by thinking of geography in terms of five themes. The five themes below are tools you can use to organize geographic information and to answer questions about the influence of geography and human history.

Location

1 The exact location of a country or city is expressed in terms of longitude and latitude. Relative location defines where a place is in relation to other places. For example, the exact location of the city of Chicago, Illinois, is 42° north (latitude) and 88° west (longitude). Its relative location could be described as "on the shore of Lake Michigan" or "821 miles north of New Orleans."

Place

2 Location answers the question, "Where is it?" Place answers the question, "What is it like there?" You can identify a place by such features as its landforms, its climate, its plants and animals, or the people who live there. Much of the history of the southeastern United States was shaped by the fact that it had a mild climate and fertile land suitable for large-scale farming of crops such as cotton.

Regions

3 Regions are areas that share common features. Regions may be defined by geography or culture. For example, New York is one of the Middle Atlantic states because it is located on the Atlantic Ocean. In colonial days, it was one of the Middle Colonies. And in the early 1800s, New York was one of the "free states" because slavery was banned there.

Movement

4 Much of history has to do with the movement of people, goods, and ideas from place to place. In Patricia's letter, we saw two examples of movement: the movement of immigrants to the United States from other countries and the movement of Americans from the East to the West. Both played a key role in the history and growth of the United States.

Interaction

5 Human-environment interaction has two parts. The first part has to do with the way an environment affects people. For example, people in the desert of the American Southwest developed very different ways of life from those living in the rich farmlands of California. The second part of interaction concerns the way people affect their environment. People mined silver in Nevada and harnessed the power of falling water in North Carolina. In each case, they changed their environment.

> *Practice* **Geography Skills**
>
> Look at the photographs on page HT 8 and read the caption. How do these pictures illustrate the themes of place, region, and interaction?

Instruction [L2]

Have students read Geography and History and Five Themes of Geography using the Paragraph Shrinking strategy (TE, p. T23).

Have students name the five themes that geographers use to organize information, and then brainstorm for examples of each. (*Examples may vary but should illustrate an understanding of each theme. Possible answers: Location—the United States is in the Western Hemisphere; place—the climate of Florida is warm most of the year; regions—a physical region of the United States is the Rocky Mountains; movement—there are people in our community who were not born here; interaction—there are roads and buildings built by people.*)

Independent Practice

Ask students to write a description of the geography of where they live in terms of the five themes.

Monitor Progress

As students write, check to see that they are giving appropriate answers. Provide help when needed.

Practice Geography Skills

Possible answers: Their physical characteristics set the Midwest and New England apart from other places. Each of these regions shares common geographical features. Farming and fishing are two examples of human-environment interaction.

Objective

- Recognize the advantages and disadvantages of using globes as a source of information.
- Understand map projections.

Build Background Knowledge   **L2**

Have students look at a map in the classroom. Ask them to identify the kinds of information they can get from it. (*Answers will vary depending on the map but should include that students can determine the shape of landmasses, exact location, and relative location.*)

Instruction   **L2**

Have students read Build Geography Skills: Globes and Map Projections, using the Choral Reading strategy (TE p. T22).

Ask: **What are the advantages of a globe?** (*Globes show areas, directions, and distances more accurately than maps.*) **What are the disadvantages?** (*Globes are inconvenient to carry around.*) **What are two kinds of map projections?** (*Mercator and Robinson*) **How are they different?** (*Mercator accurately shows direction and shape of landmasses. It distorts distance and size. Robinson shows correct shape and size, but it does not show direction as well. It also distorts the size of the North and South poles.*)

Practice Geography Skills

Answer: Advantage: It is easy to determine direction and distance. Disadvantage: Globes are awkward and not manageable in a large size. A map can show a small area in greater detail.

Globes

A globe is a model of Earth. It shows the actual shape, size, and location of each landmass and body of water.

Globes divide Earth into lines of latitude and longitude. Latitude measures distance north or south of the Equator, which is an imaginary line around the widest part of Earth. Longitude measures distance east or west of the Prime Meridian, which is an imaginary line running from the North Pole to the South Pole. The diagram below shows how lines of longitude and latitude form a grid pattern on a globe.

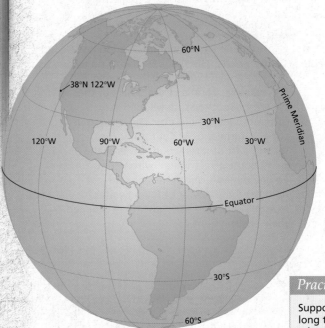

Using lines of latitude and longitude, you can locate any place on Earth. The location of 38° north latitude and 122° west longitude is written as 38° N/122° W. Only one place on Earth has this location: the city of San Francisco, California.

Practice **Geography Skills**

Suppose that you wanted to plan a long trip. What would be some advantages and disadvantages of using a globe?

Map Projections

Globes are accurate, but they are not easy to carry around, and they are not useful for showing smaller areas of Earth in detail. So mapmakers had to develop methods to show the curved Earth on a flat surface. These methods are known as map projections. All map projections distort Earth in some way. Below are two common types of map projections.

Mercator Projection

In the 1500s, ocean travelers relied on the Mercator projection, named after mapmaker Gerardus Mercator. The Mercator projection accurately shows direction and the shape of Earth's landmasses. However, it distorts distance and size.

Robinson Projection

The Robinson projection shows the correct shape and size of landmasses for most parts of the world. However, it does not show directions as well as a Mercator projection does. It also distorts the size of the North Pole and South Pole.

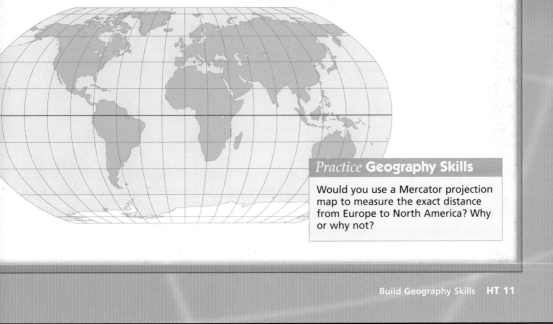

Practice **Geography Skills**

Would you use a Mercator projection map to measure the exact distance from Europe to North America? Why or why not?

Independent Practice

Provide several globes for students to study and compare to a flat map. Ask them to determine the relative size of Greenland on the globe to its relative size on a flat map. (*On a globe it is much smaller, about the same size as Mexico.*)

Monitor Progress

Circulate and see whether students are coming to reasonable conclusions.

Practice Geography Skills

Answer: No, because it distorts distance.

Objective

■ Learn how to use the elements of a map.

Build Background Knowledge L2

Have students examine the classroom map. Have volunteers identify all the parts of the map that give them information. These may include the title of the map, the compass rose, labels, key, scale bar, place names, colors, lines, etc.

Historian's Toolkit — Build Geography Skills

How to Use a Map

Mapmakers provide several clues to help in understanding the information on a map. Maps provide different clues, depending on their purpose or scale. However, most maps have several clues in common.

Locator
Many maps are shown with locator maps or globes. They show where on Earth the area of the map is located.

Title
Maps have titles. The title tells you the subject of the map.

Key
Often a map has a key, or legend. The key shows the meaning of the symbols and colors used on the map.

Compass rose
Many maps show direction by displaying a compass rose with the directions north, east, south, and west. The letters N, E, S, and W are placed to indicate these directions.

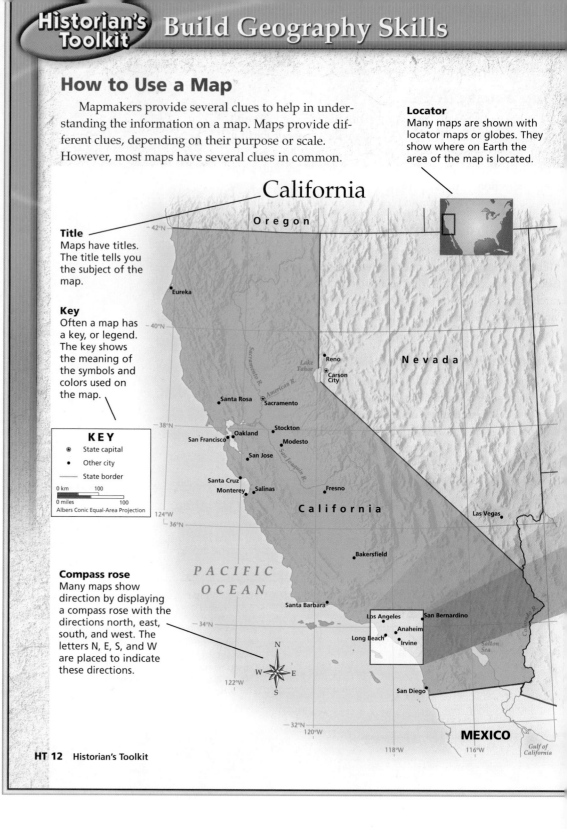

California

KEY
⊛ State capital
• Other city
— State border

0 km 100
0 miles 100
Albers Conic Equal-Area Projection

Maps of Different Scales

Maps are drawn to different scales, depending on their purpose. Here are three maps drawn to very different scales. Keep in mind that maps showing large areas have smaller scales. Maps showing small areas have larger scales.

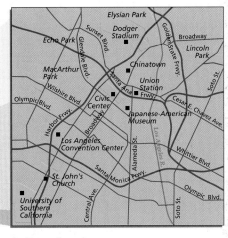

▲ **Downtown Los Angeles**

Find the gray square on the map of Greater Los Angeles. This square represents the area shown on the map above. This map moves you closer into the center of Los Angeles. Like a zoom on a computer or a camera, this map shows a smaller area, but in greater detail. It has the largest scale. You can use this map to explore downtown Los Angeles.

KEY
- ■ Point of interest
- ▢ Park

0 km ▭ 2
0 mile ▭ 2
Albers Conic Equal-Area Projection

▲ **Greater Los Angeles**

Find the light gray square on the main map of California (left). This square represents the area shown on the map above. It shows Los Angeles in relation to nearby cities, towns, and the Pacific Ocean. It also shows some features near the city, such as the airport and major roadways.

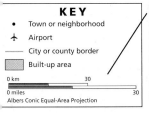

KEY
- • Town or neighborhood
- ✈ Airport
- — City or county border
- ▢ Built-up area

0 km ▭ 30
0 miles ▭ 30
Albers Conic Equal-Area Projection

Scale bar

A scale bar helps you find the actual distances between points shown on the map. Most scale bars show distances in both miles and kilometers.

Practice Geography Skills

- What part of a map explains the colors used on the map?
- How does the scale bar change depending on the scale of the map?

Instruction　L2

Have students read How to Use a Map to themselves and study the illustrations and captions on the page.

Ask: **What information does each of the elements provide?** (*Title tells subject of map; locator shows where the area of the map is located; compass rose shows direction; key shows meaning of symbols and colors; scale shows actual distances.*)

Have students calculate the distance between Sacramento and Los Angeles using the scale. (*about 350 miles, or about 560 km*)

Ask: **What direction would you go if traveling from Bakersfield to San Francisco?** (*northwest*)

Ask: **What are the scales used in the two maps of Los Angeles?** (*Greater Los Angeles: 0 to 30 miles and km; Downtown Los Angeles: 0 to 2 miles and km*)

Independent Practice

Have students choose another map in their textbook and find each of these elements on that map.

Monitor Progress

Call on individuals to share their information with the class and to explain how each element helps them understand the map they are looking at.

Practice Geography Skills

- the key
- As the area shown on the map gets smaller, the scale gets larger; as the scale gets larger, the scale bar represents a shorter distance.

Objectives

■ Learn the difference between political and physical maps.

■ Learn how to read special-purpose maps.

Build Background Knowledge
L2

Tell students that on the next four pages they will be learning about the different kinds of maps they will see as they study history. Have them look over these pages, paying attention to the keys, the visuals, and the headings. Write the following headings on the board: Political Maps; Physical Maps; Special-Purpose Maps. Under each heading, make a list of what students think they already know about that type of map. Use the Idea Wave participation strategy (TE, p. T24) to help generate a list.

Instruction
L2

Read Political Maps using the Structured Silent Reading strategy (TE, p. T22).

After students read, ask: **What is the main purpose of a political map?** (*to show political divisions between countries or states*) **What does the map on this page show?** (*the United States in 1790*)

Have students compare this political map with the map of the present-day United States on pages A2–A3. Ask: **How has this part of the United States changed?** (*Answer: There are more states now; territory claimed by Virginia and other states in 1790 is now part of other states.*) **How can you tell?** (*The borders and colors indicate the divisions between states.*)

Practice Geography Skills

• Possible answers: New York, New Jersey, Maryland, Delaware

• Spain, Britain

Political Maps

Historians use many different types of maps. On the next four pages, you will see four maps that relate to American history. Each map shows a different area in a different way and for a different purpose.

One of the most familiar types of map is the political map. Political maps show political divisions, such as borders between countries or states. Colors on a political map help make the differences clear. Political maps also show the location of cities. This map shows the United States in 1790, at the time George Washington was President.

KEY
- United States
- U.S. Territory

Practice Geography Skills

• Identify two states that bordered Pennsylvania.

• Which European nations controlled territory bordering the United States?

This early flag shows 13 stripes and 13 stars. There is one star and one stripe for each state.

Physical Maps

Physical maps show the major physical features of a region, such as seas, rivers, and mountains. The larger the scale of a physical map, the more detail it can show. For example, the map below shows the rivers that run through the American Southwest. If you compare this map to the physical map in the Atlas at the front of this textbook, you will notice that there are several rivers shown on this map that are not shown on the Atlas map.

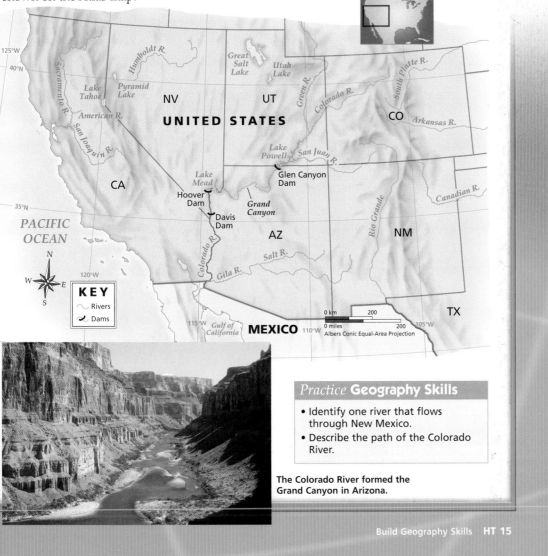

The Colorado River formed the Grand Canyon in Arizona.

Practice **Geography Skills**

- Identify one river that flows through New Mexico.
- Describe the path of the Colorado River.

Instruction

L2

Have a volunteer read Special-Purpose Maps: Battle Map.

Ask: **What information is shown on the map on this page?** (*battles and troop movements leading up to the Battle of Gettysburg*)

Ask: **How can you tell the troop movements?** (*Different color arrows show the paths of Confederate and Union troops.*)

Have students suggest the kinds of information that would be best shown on a special-purpose movement map. (*Possible answers: trade routes, routes followed by armies or by settlers, the movement of ideas and goods over time*)

Special-Purpose Maps
Battle Maps

In addition to political maps and physical maps, there are different types of special-purpose maps. These range from road maps to weather maps to election maps. Some special-purpose maps use arrows to show the movement of people and goods from place to place. The map below shows the battles and troop movements that led up to the Battle of Gettysburg in July 1863.

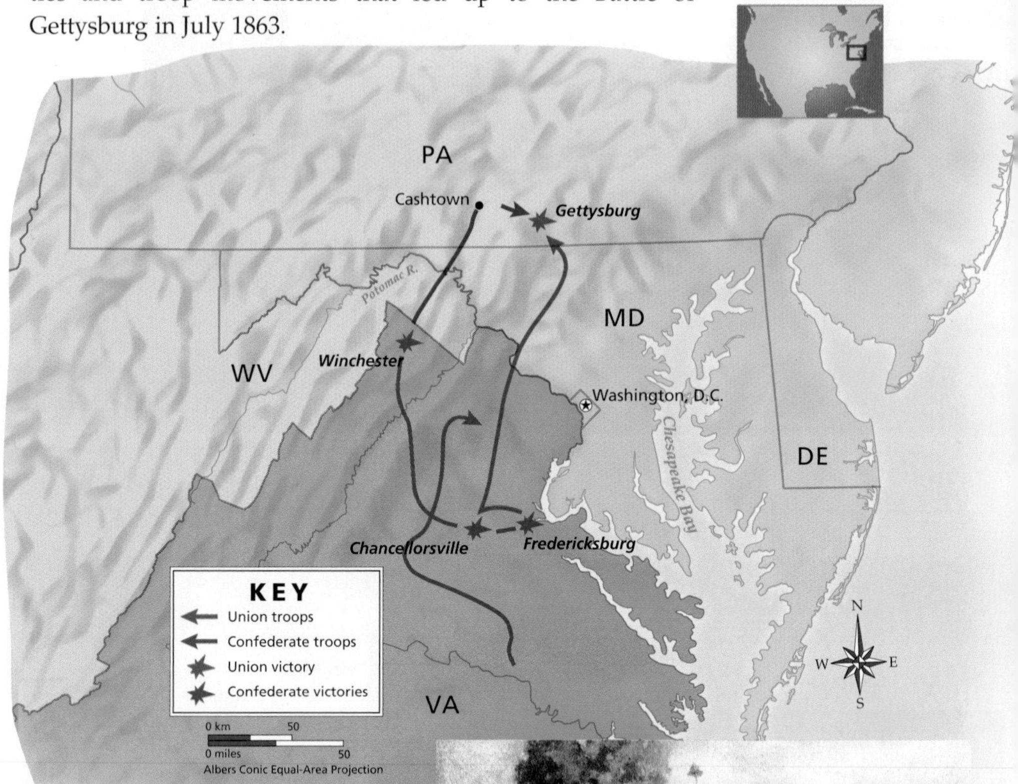

KEY
- Union troops
- Confederate troops
- Union victory
- Confederate victories

0 km 50
0 miles 50
Albers Conic Equal-Area Projection

Practice **Geography Skills**

- Identify one Confederate victory shown on the map above.
- In what direction did Confederate troops travel to get to Gettysburg?

The Battle of Gettysburg

Practice Geography Skills

- Possible answers: Winchester, Fredericksburg, Chancellorsville
- north and the east

Election Maps

Have you ever seen a newspaper or watched television during a presidential election? If you have, then you have probably seen an election map. Election maps show all of the states voting in the election. Different colors are used to show which candidates won the vote in which states. The map below shows the election of 1912, when three major candidates were running for President.

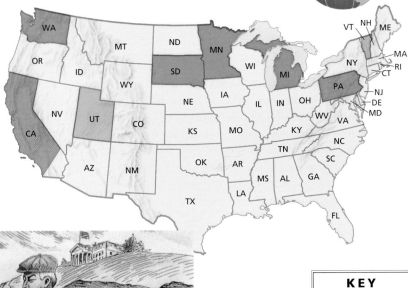

KEY
- Theodore Roosevelt
- William Taft
- Woodrow Wilson

Practice Geography Skills

- Which candidate won in California? In Illinois?
- How many states did Taft win?

Cartoon showing Wilson, Taft, and Roosevelt running for President in 1912

Objectives
- Learn various ways information can be presented visually.
- Learn to obtain information from these visual sources.
- Compare different types of charts and graphs.

Build Background Knowledge L2

Have students scan their textbook to find all the ways information is presented. (*text, maps, charts, graphs, pictures, timelines*) Conduct an Idea Wave (TE, p. T24) and write student responses on the board.

Instruction L2

Have students read Build Chart Skills: Read Visual Information, using the Paragraph Shrinking strategy (TE, p. T23).

Ask students to describe a timeline in their own words. (*Answers will vary but should show an understanding that a timeline is a visual representation of a period of time showing events that occurred during that period in chronological, or time, order.*)

Ask: **Which event happened first on this timeline?** (*Famine strikes Ireland.*) **Which U.S. and world events happened in the same year?** (*Slavery leads to violence in Kansas; Japan opens ports to foreign ships.*)

Historian's Toolkit — Build Chart Skills

Read Visual Information

In this textbook, the information you need to know is presented in written form. Often, however, key information is also summarized in chart form. Charts organize facts and ideas in a visual way that makes them easier to understand.

The next four pages review some of the basic types of visuals you will find in this textbook. Building your ability to analyze visuals will help you get the most out of the information provided.

Timelines

Every chapter in this textbook begins with a timeline. You have used timelines before, but the ones in this book have a few special features. Most of them are made up of two parts:

- **U.S. Events** This is the main part of the timeline. It shows the events that are described in that chapter that took place within the United States.
- **World Events** This part of the timeline shows events that took place in other parts of the world during the same time period. These events are often included because they related to what was going on in the United States.

Timelines make it easier to understand the sequence of events over time. The timelines in this textbook will help you explain how major events are related to one another in time.

> ### Practice **Chart Skills**
> - How many years after gold was discovered in California was gold discovered in Australia?
> - Which world event was probably related to one of the U.S. events?

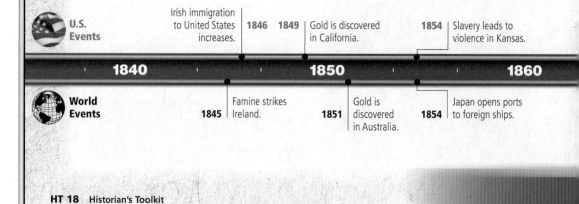

| U.S. Events | Irish immigration to United States increases. | 1846 | 1849 | Gold is discovered in California. | 1854 | Slavery leads to violence in Kansas. |

1840 · · **1850** · · **1860**

| World Events | | 1845 | Famine strikes Ireland. | 1851 | Gold is discovered in Australia. | 1854 | Japan opens ports to foreign ships. |

Practice Chart Skills
- 2 years
- Famine in Ireland led to an increase in Irish immigration to the United States.

Build Chart Skills

Tables

Tables provide a simple way to organize a large amount of information graphically. A table is arranged in a grid pattern. Columns run vertically, from top to bottom. Rows run horizontally, from left to right.

This sample table summarizes some basic facts about four major wars you will learn about this year. The four wars are listed in the column at the far left, at the beginning of each row. The categories of information given about each war are listed at the top of each column.

Tables can be very large. You may have seen computer spreadsheets that include dozens of columns and rows. Yet, all tables follow the same basic grid pattern shown below.

Four American Wars

War	Dates	Opponents	Results
American Revolution	1775–1781	American colonists vs. Britain	• Colonists win. • United States wins independence.
War of 1812	1812–1814	United States vs. Britain	• No clear winner emerges. • Increased sense of national pride felt.
Mexican-American War	1846–1848	United States vs. Mexico	• United States wins. • United States gains new territory in the West.
Civil War	1861–1865	North vs. South	• North wins. • Union is preserved. • Slavery ends.

Practice Chart Skills

- What were the results of the Mexican-American War?
- In which two wars did Americans fight the same opponent?

Instruction

Have students look at the table on this page.

Ask: **How is the table organized?** (*The names of the wars are listed at the start of each row and the categories of information are at the top of each column.*)

Discuss the advantages of this organization. (*simple, easy to read*)

Independent Practice

Have students locate a table in their textbook. Remind them that the Table of Contents is a helpful tool for finding special elements in their book. Tell students to describe the information provided in the table.

Monitor Progress

Check students' work to make sure they understand what information is presented in the table.

Practice Chart Skills

- The United States won and gained new territory in the West.
- American Revolution and War of 1812

Instruction

Have students read Pie Charts and Line Graphs and Bar Graphs using the Structured Silent Reading strategy (TE, p. T22) and study the chart and graphs on the page.

After students read, ask: **What is the purpose of a pie chart?** (*to show how a whole is divided into parts*) Have them study the pie chart and compare the portions within the circle. Ask: **Which wedge in the pie chart is the biggest?** (*whites*) **Which is the smallest?** (*free blacks*)

Point out that the line graph and bar graph both present the same information. Ask: **Which type of graph might be more useful for showing trends over time?** (*line graph*) **Which type might be more useful for making comparisons between years?** (*bar graph*)

Independent Practice

Have students pick one of the graphs on the page and write a sentence or two describing a conclusion that can be drawn from that graph.

Monitor Progress

Check students' work to make sure they are drawing appropriate conclusions. Circulate and offer assistance as needed.

Pie Charts

Some charts and graphs in this book show statistical information, that is, information based on exact numbers. Pie charts show statistical information in terms of percentages. The circle, or pie, represents 100 percent of a group. Each wedge of the pie represents one subgroup of the whole. The bigger the wedge is, the larger the group. This pie chart shows how the population of southern states was divided in the year 1850, when slavery was still legal in the South.

Population of the South, 1850

- 2.5% Free blacks
- 64.4% Whites
- 33.1% Enslaved African Americans

Line Graphs and Bar Graphs

Line graphs and bar graphs show statistical information as it changes over time. The horizontal, or side to side, axis usually tells you the time period covered by the graph. The vertical, or up and down, axis tells you what is being measured. By lining up the points on the graph with the horizontal and vertical axes, you can see how many or how much of something there was at a given time.

On a line graph, the points are connected. On a bar graph, each year is represented by a bar. The line graph (below left) and the bar graph (below right) show the same information: the number of patents, or licenses for new inventions, issued by the U.S. government.

Practice **Chart Skills**

- What percentage of southern society in 1850 was made up of enslaved African Americans?
- About how many patents were issued in 1860? In 1880?

U.S. Patents, 1860–1900

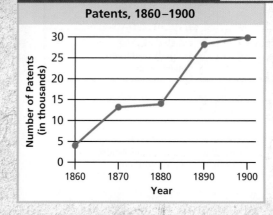

Patents, 1860–1900

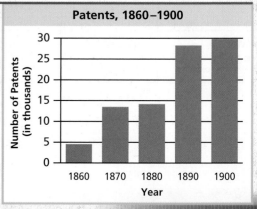

Patents, 1860–1900

Practice Chart Skills

- 33.1%
- nearly 5,000; nearly 15,000

Build Political Cartoon Skills

This textbook also includes a number of political cartoons. Political cartoons are drawings that comment on events and issues through both visual imagery and words. Cartoonists often use symbols and exaggeration to make their points. Learning to analyze cartoons can help you better understand viewpoints on current and historical events.

The first step in analyzing a political cartoon is to identify common symbols. A symbol is an object that represents something besides itself. For example, an eagle or the figure of Uncle Sam may be used to represent the United States. Sometimes, symbols are labeled to make their meaning clear.

Look at the details in the drawing. (In this textbook, we help you focus on certain details by calling them out.) Also, look at the words being spoken by the people in the cartoon. Finally, use both words and pictures to identify the main point the cartoonist is making.

The cartoon below comments on one of the main responsibilities of American citizens: voting.

Practice Chart Skills

- Why is the pan labeled "Non-Voters" lower than the pan labeled "Voters"? What does this mean?
- What is the cartoonist's view of people who do not vote?

The cartoon starts with one person who decides not to vote.

The label shows what the scale symbolizes.

L2

Instruction

Have students read Build Political Cartoon Skills and study the cartoon.

Ask students if there are any comic strips they enjoy reading. Point out that political cartoons are similar in some ways to comic strips, but they aim to express a point of view, rather than simply tell a story. Remind students that the political cartoonist's purpose is to sway the reader's opinion.

Independent Practice

Ask students to bring in a current political cartoon from the editorial section of a newspaper, or distribute copies of an appropriate cartoon. Ask students to analyze the cartoon using the steps outlined here. Have them write a brief paragraph explaining the cartoon.

Monitor Progress

If students bring in their own cartoons, make sure that the one they select is on a familiar issue. Circulate and offer assistance in interpreting the cartoon as needed.

Practice Chart Skills

- It weighs more on the scale. Nonvoters outnumbered voters.
- They have a significant impact on the outcome of an election.

Objectives

- Learn the purpose and unique elements of four types of writing.
- Use a systematic approach to write expository, narrative, research, and persuasive essays.

Build Background Knowledge L2

As a group, brainstorm for all the ways that people use writing to communicate. Start with these examples: labeling a folder, writing an e-mail. Use the Idea Wave strategy (TE, p. T24), and write students' responses on the board. Tell them that people often write to express ideas or share information.

Instruction L2

Read the steps for writing expository essays with students.

Tell students that the graphic organizer example on the Student Edition page is for a problem-solution essay. They might use a Venn diagram for a compare and contrast essay and a flowchart for a cause-and-effect essay.

Model how to create a topic sentence from the information in the graphic organizer. (*Sample topic sentence: The main problem with the Articles of Confederation was that they did not provide for a central authority.*)

Create a brief outline showing how you will organize the paragraphs in your essay.

Independent Practice

Tell students to plan an expository essay based on a recent current event. Have them brainstorm for ideas with a partner, then choose which type of expository essay best suits their topic (cause and effect, compare and contrast, or problem-solution). Have students create a graphic organizer to plan their writing.

Monitor Progress

Check graphic organizers and offer help when needed.

Historian's Toolkit Write Like a Historian

You have learned how to use historians' tools to learn about the past. The next step is to write about what you have discovered. Historians share their findings in a variety of ways, including expository essays, narratives, research papers, and persuasive essays or speeches. You will have a chance to practice each type through end-of-section and end-of-chapter writing activities.

Expository Essays

An expository essay is a piece of writing that explains something in detail.

1 Select and Narrow Your Topic

Define exactly what you want your essay to do. Do you want to describe a process? Compare and contrast two ideas? Explain the causes and effects of a historical event or development? Explore possible solutions to a problem? You cannot plan your essay until you know what you are trying to do in it.

2 Gather Evidence

Create a graphic organizer that identifies details to include in your essay, such as the one shown below.

3 Write a First Draft

Write a topic sentence, and then organize the essay based on what you are trying to do. If your essay describes a process, write about the steps of the process in order. If your essay explores solutions to a problem, state the problem, and then describe different possible solutions.

4 Revise and Proofread

Make sure that all the details support your topic sentence.

Problem	Suggested Solutions	Evaluation of Solution
The Articles of Confederation left the nation weak because they did not provide for a central authority.	Leave the Articles alone, and persuade other countries and Americans to respect the new nation.	Not practical—what would make more established governments and local rebels accept a weak authority?
	Get rid of the Articles, and create an entirely new plan.	Possible, but it would be a huge task to start all over again.

If you were writing a problem-solution essay, you might create a chart like this to help you organize your ideas.

Research Papers

Research papers present information that you have found about a topic.

1 Select and Narrow Your Topic

Choose a topic that interests you. Make sure that your topic is not too broad. For example, instead of writing a report on Native Americans, you might write a report about the Cherokees who were forced to move west in 1837 on a journey known as the Trail of Tears.

2 Acquire Information

Locate several sources of information about the topic from the library or on the Internet. Be sure to evaluate the source. Is it reliable? How does the information compare to what you have found in other sources?

For each resource, create a source index card. Then, take notes using an index card for each detail or subtopic. On the card, note which source the information was taken from. Use quotation marks when you copy exact words from a source.

3 Make an Outline

Use an outline to decide how to organize your research paper. Sort your index cards in the same order.

4 Write a First Draft

Write an introduction, a body, and a conclusion. If you are preparing your first draft by hand, leave plenty of space between lines so you can go back and add details that you may have left out.

5 Revise and Proofread

Be sure to include transition words between sentences and paragraphs. Here are some examples:

- To describe a process: *first, next, then*
- To show a contrast: *however, although, despite*
- To point out a reason: *since, because, if*
- To signal a conclusion: *therefore, as a result, so*

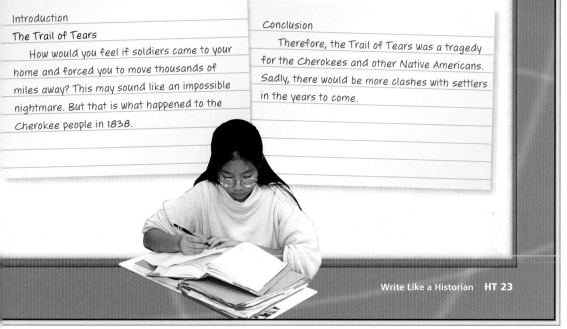

Introduction

The Trail of Tears

How would you feel if soldiers came to your home and forced you to move thousands of miles away? This may sound like an impossible nightmare. But that is what happened to the Cherokee people in 1838.

Conclusion

Therefore, the Trail of Tears was a tragedy for the Cherokees and other Native Americans. Sadly, there would be more clashes with settlers in the years to come.

Instruction

L2

Tell students that research papers present information that has been gathered from a variety of sources, which they can find in a Library Media Center, on a specific topic.

Discuss the steps listed in the Student Edition and why each is important.

Take a topic and model narrowing the topic. For example, start with History of the United States and have students begin to suggest ways to limit the scope (*Examples: history of California; history of California during the Gold Rush; life in the mining towns*)

Have students brainstorm for a list of resources. (*Possible answers: Internet, encyclopedia, atlas, magazines, newspapers, reference books*) Discuss these different types of materials. Ask: **How would you find these materials in the Library Media Center?** (*Possible answers: use the search engine for the Internet, ask the reference librarian*)

Independent Practice

Pair students and have them follow Step 1 to choose a topic. Then have them predict the effectiveness of the various resources on the list for gathering the necessary information.

Monitor Progress

Have students volunteer their topic and the list of resources they think will be most useful. Review and have the class evaluate the choices.

Instruction ⬛L2

Tell students that a narrative essay tells a story about the writer's experiences. Discuss the steps listed in the Student Edition.

To model a narrative essay for students, choose an event in your own life (or invent one) such as visiting friends in another city. Write your topic on the board and model how to list details (what the trip was like, what you did while you were there, what your friends are like). Cross out the least interesting details.

Think aloud as you form your topic into a sentence that conveys the main idea of your essay. Tell students that you would next flesh out the details into a colorful story.

Independent Practice

Tell students to follow similar steps in preparation for writing a narrative essay about a recent positive experience. Depending on student ability levels, you may wish to pair students to brainstorm for ideas.

Instruction ⬛L2

Tell students that the purpose of a persuasive essay is to convince other people to accept your point of view. However, you must use solid, reliable evidence and arguments to make your points.

Model the thought process by pointing out how you might present an argument about a school-related topic, such as why the cafeteria should or should not serve junk food or why students should or should not be allowed to have cell phones in school. List pros and cons on the board.

Independent Practice

Tell students to choose one side of the argument you have modeled and write a persuasive essay on the topic. They should add any of their own ideas.

Monitor Progress

Check students' work as you circulate around the class. Offer help to students who are having difficulty.

Historian's Toolkit — Write Like a Historian

Narrative Essays

History is like a story. It has characters, both leaders and everyday people. It has a setting where events take place. It even has a plot, in which events unfold, conflicts arise, and resolutions occur.

❶ Select and Narrow Your Topic

In this textbook, you will be asked to write narratives about the past. You might be asked to imagine a setting and describe how it affects what is happening. You might be asked to take the point of view of one of history's characters. Or you might be asked to explain the conflict or resolution of a historical situation. First, you must understand what you are being asked to do or who you are asked to be.

❷ Gather Details

Brainstorm a list of details you would like to include in your narrative.

❸ Write a First Draft

Start by writing a simple opening sentence that conveys the main idea of your essay. Continue by writing a colorful story that has interesting details. Write a conclusion that sums up the main points.

❹ Revise and Proofread

Check to make sure you have not begun too many sentences with the word *I*. Replace general words with more colorful ones.

Persuasive Essays

A persuasive essay is a piece of writing that supports a position or opinion.

❶ Select and Narrow Your Topic

Choose a historical topic that has at least two sides or two interpretations. Choose a side. Decide which argument will best persuade your audience to agree with your point of view.

❷ Gather Evidence

Create a chart that states your position at the top, and then lists the pros and cons for your position in two columns below. Predict and address the strongest arguments against your viewpoint.

❸ Write a First Draft

Write a strong thesis statement that clearly states your position. Continue by presenting the strongest arguments in favor of your position and acknowledging and refuting opposing arguments.

❹ Revise and Proofread

Check to make sure you have made a logical argument and that you have not oversimplified the argument.

Explore With Essential Questions

There are many types of questions in your textbook. Checkpoint Questions help you check your understanding of a small section of your reading. The questions in Check Your Progress at the end of each section help you practice the information and skills you have gained while reading the whole section. Likewise the questions at the end of the chapter help you make sure you have mastered the skills and content in the chapter.

There is another type of question in this textbook that may be even more important than the others. They are called Essential Questions. You will find them at the beginning of each unit and each chapter. They are also the basis of the Think Like a Historian feature at the end of each unit.

Essential questions are important because they can really make you think. They don't have a right answer. They often make you think of other questions. But they are important because they get to the heart of the matter. As you think about them, you will come to deep understanding.

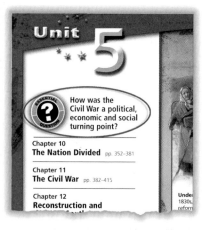

▲ The Essential Question for the unit is introduced on the unit opener.

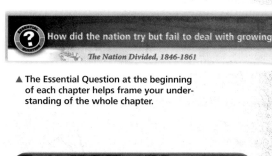

How did the nation try but fail to deal with growing

The Nation Divided, 1846–1861

▲ The Essential Question at the beginning of each chapter helps frame your understanding of the whole chapter.

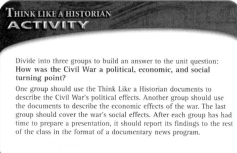

THINK LIKE A HISTORIAN
ACTIVITY

Divide into three groups to build an answer to the unit question: How was the Civil War a political, economic, and social turning point?

One group should use the Think Like a Historian documents to describe the Civil War's political effects. Another group should use the documents to describe the economic effects of the war. The last group should cover the war's social effects. After each group has had time to prepare a presentation, it should report its findings to the rest of the class in the format of a documentary news program.

▲ At the end of every unit you complete an activity that will help you show your understanding.

Objectives

■ Recognize questions that deepen understanding of the information.

Build Background Knowledge   `L2`

Define the idea of an *open-ended question* with students. Explain that they can have many answers to such a question, depending on their perspective and information available. An example would be "Why is there poverty?" Have the class brainstorm together to write a few sample questions.

Instruction   `L2`

Have students read Explore with Essential Questions. **What is the purpose of the Checkpoint Question?** (*check their understanding of the information*)

What is the aim of the Check Your Progress questions? (*give students practice of the information and skills in the section*)

What are Essential Questions? (*questions that lead to other questions and don't necessarily have one right answer*)

Discuss with students the reasons they will find these different types of questions. (*The questions involve different levels of thinking. Some are probing for basic comprehension, some want application of information, and the essential question encourages critical thinking about the material.*)

Independent Practice

Have students read the sample Unit Essential Question on the Student Page. Have them work in groups of 3 or 4 to discuss why this question could not be answered in just a few words.

Monitor Progress

Have students share their answers with the class. Check to see that they have arrived at reasonable conclusions.

Unit 1

Why It Matters

The United States is a culturally diverse nation. Americans trace their roots to nearly every continent on earth and every country in the world. We also share a distinctly American culture that has strong roots in the past and has been enriched over time by the cultural backgrounds of all Americans.

- Learning about the beginnings of American history gives us a common past and experience. This commonality complements our cultural diversity.

- This unit discusses the early civilizations and cultures of the Americas, placing them in a global historical context. It examines European exploration and colonization of the Americas, focusing on the colonies in North America and aspects of the European heritage that formed the basis of life and government in the colonies, and the foundations upon which were built many institutions of American society.

Unit Essential Question

How did the colonists develop their own way of life with strong roots in the past?

Think Like a Historian

- To preview this unit, have students review the content on these pages of the Student Edition. Ask: **What will you be learning about in this unit?** (*European exploration, European colonies in the Americas, life in the English colonies*)

- Write the Unit Focus Question on the board. Using the Idea Wave strategy (TE, p. T24), have students brainstorm answers to the question. Ask them to think about the challenges of ruling a colony from overseas. (*difficult to apply laws and respond to problems quickly*)

- Record students' answers on a flip chart. Keep a copy of them. Once students have completed their responses, tell them that they will be learning about the beginnings of American history. Tell students that you will return to this question at the end of the unit and review their responses for additions or changes. (*See Think Like a Historian, p. 127.*)

Unit 1

ESSENTIAL QUESTION

How did the colonists, with strong roots in the past, develop their own way of life?

Across the Atlantic Sailing three small ships across the Atlantic in uncharted waters, Christopher Columbus opened the Americas to regular contact with the people of Europe.

1492

Slave Trade By the late 1600s, a steady stream of ships carried enslaved Africans to the Americas. Most enslaved Africans were forced to work on plantations in the West Indies and in South America. Slavery grew in North America after the plantations system took hold in the South.

LATE 1600s

Unit 1

- Preview the primary sources in Think Like a Historian on pp. 130–133. You may wish to introduce and discuss these documents to enrich chapter content.

Home Involvement

A summary of the early American history content students will be studying and suggested activities adults at home can do with their child are available in reproducible outline in the Teacher Resource Kit.

All in One Teaching Resources, Unit 1, Letter Home, Chapters 1, 2, 3, 4

Beginnings of American History

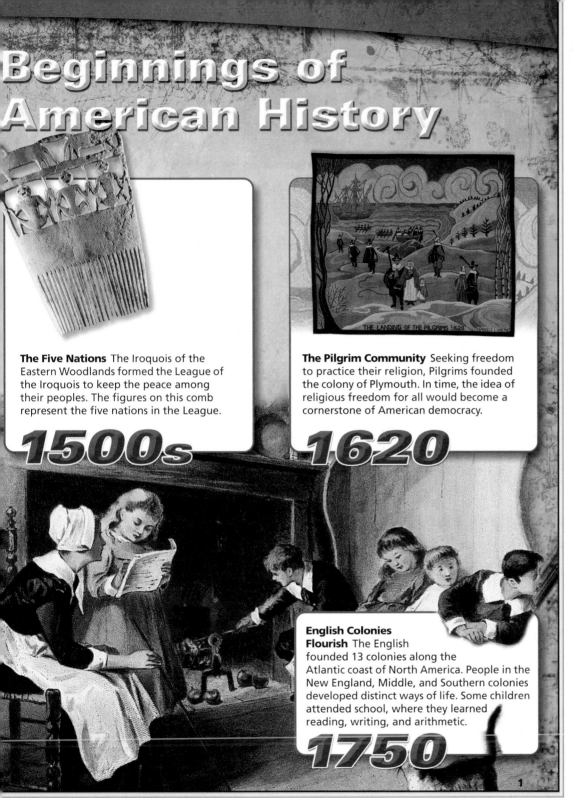

The Five Nations The Iroquois of the Eastern Woodlands formed the League of the Iroquois to keep the peace among their peoples. The figures on this comb represent the five nations in the League.

1500s

The Pilgrim Community Seeking freedom to practice their religion, Pilgrims founded the colony of Plymouth. In time, the idea of religious freedom for all would become a cornerstone of American democracy.

1620

English Colonies Flourish The English founded 13 colonies along the Atlantic coast of North America. People in the New England, Middle, and Southern colonies developed distinct ways of life. Some children attended school, where they learned reading, writing, and arithmetic.

1750

1

Unit Skills

■ Skills for Life

Identify Main Ideas and Supporting Details
Chapter 1, p. 28

Understand Sequence
Chapter 2, p. 58

Read a Primary Source
Chapter 3, p. 94

Compare and Contrast
Chapter 4, p. 126

■ Reading Skills

Clarify Meaning
Chapter 1, p. 3

Clarify Meaning
Chapter 2, p. 33

Compare and Contrast
Chapter 3, p. 63

Use Context
Chapter 4, p. 99

■ Writing Workshop *Online*

Historical Overview
Web Code: mve-4000

■ Think Like a Historian

Students complete an activity in which they use primary sources to explore the Essential Question.
pp. 130–133.

 eTeach

Read the essay on eTeach for further ideas on Efficient and Effective Use of the Textbook.
Visit: PHSchool.com
Web Code: mvf-0101

DK World Desk Reference

Use the resources on the DK World Desk Reference for further information about the United States.
Visit: PHSchool.com
Web Code: mve-0102

History Background

Victims of Enclosure During the 1600s and 1700s, many English farmers were victims of the enclosure movement, in which wealthy landowners fenced off or enclosed what had previously been common land. The enclosure movement forced many small farmers and farm workers off the land. Many of these landless people moved into cities where they formed a supply of cheap labor that was readily exploited by newly forming industries, such as mills. Some displaced people looked to North America, which seemed to have limitless, available land.

Professional Development

History Background

Cultures and Cultural Influences

The roots of the American people extend to other continents and peoples, and to the cultures and civilizations they created. The first people in the Americas were Asians. They arrived tens of thousands of years ago, long before people kept records, and so it is not known whether they arrived by land or sea. They gradually spread across North America and South America. In time some descendants of these first people built civilizations in Central and South America. First, the Mayas, then the Aztecs and the Incas flourished. Scholars have found evidence of Mayan and Aztec ideas among some groups of people farther north. Traders and migrating people carried goods and beliefs from Central America to the early peoples of North America.

Many distinct cultures developed in North America. The Hohokams developed irrigation techniques in present-day Arizona. The Anasazi irrigated fields in the southwest. To the east, cultures known as Mound Builders constructed earthen mounds for burial and religious purposes. By the 1400s various culture areas had developed in North America. Geography shaped Native American cultures in the different regions. Climate and natural resources influenced which crops people grew and which animals they hunted. They also affected their clothing and shelter. Native American groups shared some basic ideas. A deep respect for the earth was universal.

Native Americans were isolated from people on other continents. Yet events and ideas on far-off continents would soon change Native American cultures forever. People in Europe, Africa, and Asia had much contact with each other through trade, exchanging not only goods but ideas and influences. Africans and Asians had forged close links over time, but the rebirth of learning during the Renaissance inspired Europeans to look outward. The ideas and traditions that Europeans would bring with them to America would take firm root. These traditions included Judeo-Christian values and Greek and Roman ideas about democracy that would influence the development of American society and government. It would become part of the roots of the American people.

Essential Questions

Use this graphic organizer to see the relationship between key concepts and the Chapter Essential Question.

Focus Question/Section 1
How did early civilizations develop in the Americas?
(p. 6)

Concept: Civilization

Focus Question/Section 2
How did geography influence the development of cultures in North America?
(p. 10)

Concept: Culture

Chapter Essential Question
How did different cultures and traditions develop around the world?

Focus Question/Section 4
What major influences shaped European civilization?
(p. 22)

Concept: Continuity

Focus Question/Section 3
How did trade link Europe, Africa, and Asia?
(p. 16)

Concept: Trade

Differentiated Instruction

High-Use Academic Words

This textbook contains several unique ways to help your students build their vocabulary. **Key Terms** are introduced in the section opener and highlighted in blue within the narrative text. **High-Use Academic Words** are underlined and defined where they are used in the narrative text.

Learning New Words

High-Use Academic Words have been identified by experts as words that students are likely to encounter when reading any textbook. The ones highlighted in this book have been identified as appropriate for students in eighth grade. When students can comprehend and use this type of academic vocabulary, they will become better readers in any subject area.

Research shows that the best way to learn unfamiliar words is by encountering them in familiar contexts. A vocabulary chart found in the wrap at the beginning of each section lists the words to preteach for that section. You can give students help with these words by offering them the

Sample History sentences, which use the high-use word in the context of history topics studied earlier this year or in previous years.

Some high-use academic words are also everyday words. You can give students further help with these words by providing sample sentences from everyday life. For example, one high-use word from this chapter is *participate*. If students are unfamiliar with this word, write this sentence on the board: *The boy joined the theater club so he could participate in the school musical show.* Read the sentence aloud. Ask students to restate the sentence in their own words.

Research also suggests that students will best learn new words by frequent encounters with them. For this reason, this text continues to use the high-use words after they are introduced. You may even notice that a word is highlighted a second time later in the book. This was done to reinforce the vocabulary that students will continue to use throughout their academic careers.

Concepts Across Time

Have students develop an understanding of the enduring concepts of history by connecting these ideas.

Concept: Civilization

Civilizations share some basic features. Have students compare the early civilizations in the Americas. Ask: **In what ways were the cities of the Mayan, Aztec, and Inca civilizations alike?** (*Possible responses: All three civilizations had large cities; the planning of Mayan cities and the Aztec capital of Tenochtitlán was elaborate; Mayan and Aztec cities had many temples in addition to other buildings; Tenochtitlán and the Inca capital of Cuzco were linked to other places by roadways.*) Ask: **What are some other similarities of the early civilizations in the Americas?** (*Possible responses: They had empires; they believed in many gods; they used engineering to improve farming: the Aztecs built floating platforms for raising crops; the Incas built walls to hold soil in their fields and canals to carry water.*) Use these questions when discussing Three Civilizations in Section 1.

Concept: Trade

Trade networks linked the people of Asia, Africa, and Europe. Have students explore how trade influenced the development of cultures. Ask: **What ideas and influences did trade among Asians, Africans, and Europeans help spread?** (*Answers will vary, but should include religious beliefs of Islam and Christianity; advances in learning such as the use of the decimal; advances in technology such as the magnetic compass; languages.*) Use these questions when discussing trade in Section 3.

Concept: Continuity

Have students link ideas that influenced the democratic government of the United States to ancient Greece and Rome. Ask: **What basic idea of American government came from ancient Greece?** (*that the people should have the power to govern*) Ask: **How is our government like the government of the Roman Republic?** (*We elect people to represent and make decisions for us in government, just as citizens in the Roman Republic did.*) Use these questions when discussing Greek and Roman Traditions in Section 4.

Section 1 The Earliest Americans

⏱ *1.5 periods, .75 block*

Objectives

Students will

1. Understand how people may have first reached the Americas.
2. Find out how people learned to farm.
3. Explore the civilizations of the Mayas, Aztecs, and Incas.

Differentiated Instruction Key

L1 Basic to Average
L2 All Students
L3 Average to Advanced

AR Advanced Readers
ELL English Language Learners
GT Gifted and Talented
LPR Less Proficient Readers
SN Special Needs

Prepare to Read

Build Background Knowledge
Preview the section and discuss the arrival of the first people in the Americas.

Set a Purpose for Reading
Have students begin to fill out the Reading Readiness Guide.

Preview Key Terms
Preview the section's Key Terms.

Instructional Resources

 Teaching Resources, Unit 1
L2 Chapter Prereading Guide, p. 4
L2 History Reading Skill Worksheet, p. 14
L2 Word Knowledge Rating Form, p. 15
L2 Reading Readiness Guide, p. 16

Teacher's Edition
L2 Vocabulary Builder, pp. 5, 7

Differentiated Instruction

💿 **Guided Reading Audio CD**
Spanish ELL, LPR, SN

Teach

Instruction
The First Americans
Explore how people first came to the Americas and learned to farm.

Three Civilizations
Discuss the early civilizations of the Mayas, the Aztecs, and the Incas.

Instructional Resources

📖 **Interactive Reading and Notetaking Study Guide**
L2 Chapter 1, Section 1

Color Transparencies
L2 Early Civilizations in the Americas

Discovery School Video
L2 Tenochititlán and the Aztecs

Differentiated Instruction

📖 **Interactive Reading and Notetaking Study Guide, Adapted Version (English/ Spanish)**
L1 Chapter 1, Section 1 ELL, LPR, SN

Teacher's Edition
L1 Listen/Speak–Ask/Answer, p. 6 ELL, LPR, SN
L3 Write a Report, p. 8 AR
L3 Create a Diorama, p. 8 GT

Assess and Reteach

Assess Progress
Evaluate student comprehension with Check Your Progress and Section Quiz.

Reteach
Assign the Interactive Reading and Notetaking Study Guide to help struggling students.

Extend
Extend the lesson by having students research how archaeologists uncovered evidence of the Aztec city of Tenochtitlán.

Instructional Resources

📖 **Interactive Reading and Notetaking Study Guide**
L2 Chapter 1, Section 1

 Teaching Resources, Unit 1
L2 Reading Readiness Guide, p. 16
L2 Section Quiz, p. 24

Progress Monitoring Transparencies
L2 Chapter 1, Section 1

Differentiated Instruction

Teacher's Edition
L1 Checkpoints, TE pp. 7, 9

💿 **SE on Audio CD**
L1 Chapter 1, Section 1

Internet Resources
PHSchool.com

Section 2 Cultures of North America *1 period, .5 block*

Objectives

Students will

1. Learn about the earliest peoples of North America.
2. Discover what different groups of Native Americans had in common.
3. Explore the impact of geography on Native American cultures.

Differentiated Instruction Key

L1 Basic to Average
L2 All Students
L3 Average to Advanced

AR Advanced Readers
ELL English Language Learners
GT Gifted and Talented
LPR Less Proficient Readers
SN Special Needs

Prepare to Read

Build Background Knowledge
Preview the section and discuss what a culture is.

Set a Purpose for Reading
Have students begin to fill out the Reading Readiness Guide.

Preview Key Terms
Preview the section's Key Terms.

Instructional Resources

All in One Teaching Resources, Unit 1
L2 Reading Readiness Guide, p. 17

Teacher's Edition
L2 Vocabulary Builder, p. 11

Differentiated Instruction

🔊 Guided Reading Audio CD
Spanish **ELL, LPR, SN**

Teach

Instruction
First Cultures of North America
Identify early cultures that developed in the Southwest and the Mississippi Valley.

Ways of Life
Discuss basic features shared by the varied cultures of North America.

Native Americans of North America
Analyze how culture groups of North America adapted their ways of life to their environment.

Instructional Resources

📖 Interactive Reading and Notetaking Study Guide
L2 Chapter 1, Section 2

All in One Teaching Resources, Unit 1
L2 The Iroquois Constitution, p. 20
L2 Concept Lesson, p. 23
L2 Concept Organizer, p. 6

Differentiated Instruction

📖 Interactive Reading and Notetaking Study Guide, Adapted Version (English/Spanish)
L1 Chapter 1, Section 2 **ELL, LPR, SN**

Teacher's Edition
L3 Summarize a Scholarly Article, p. 10 **AR**
L3 Create a Poster, p. 10 **GT**
L1 Create a Picture Dictionary, p. 12 **ELL, SN**
L1 Create a Chart, p. 14 **LPR**

Assess and Reteach

Assess Progress
Evaluate student comprehension with Check Your Progress and Section Quiz.

Reteach
Assign the Study Guide to help students.

Extend
Extend the lesson by having students identify shared beliefs in Native American songs, folk tales, and oral histories.

Instructional Resources

📖 Interactive Reading and Notetaking Study Guide
L2 Chapter 1, Section 2

All in One Teaching Resources, Unit 1
L2 Reading Readiness Guide, p. 17
L2 Section Quiz, p. 25

Progress Monitoring Transparencies
L2 Chapter 1, Section 2

Differentiated Instruction

Teacher's Edition
L1 Checkpoints, TE pp. 11, 15

🔊 SE on Audio CD
L1 Chapter 1, Section 2

Section 3 Trade Networks of Asia and Africa *1 period, .5 block*

Objectives

Students will

1. Learn about the role played by Muslims in world trade.
2. Discover how great trading states rose in East and West Africa.
3. Find out how China dominated an important trade route across Asia.

Differentiated Instruction Key

L1 Basic to Average   **AR** Advanced Readers
L2 All Students   **ELL** English Language Learners
L3 Average to Advanced   **GT** Gifted and Talented
    LPR Less Proficient Readers
    SN Special Needs

Prepare to Read

Build Background Knowledge
Preview the section and explore the origin of goods valued by American consumers.

Set a Purpose for Reading
Have students begin to fill out the Reading Readiness Guide.

Preview Key Terms
Preview the section's Key Terms.

Instructional Resources

All in One Teaching Resources, Unit 1
L2 Reading Readiness Guide, p. 18

Teacher's Edition
L2 Vocabulary Builder, p. 17

Differentiated Instruction

Guided Reading Audio CD
Spanish **ELL, LPR, SN**

Teach

Instruction
The Muslim Link in Trade
Learn how Muslims linked trade on three continents.

The African Link in Trade
Identify trade networks in East and West Africa.

The East Asian Link in Trade
Analyze why China dominated the trade routes linking East Asia to the Middle East.

Instructional Resources

Interactive Reading and Notetaking Study Guide
L2 Chapter 1, Section 3

All in One Teaching Resources, Unit 1
L2 Marco Polo, p. 21

Color Transparencies
L2 Global Trade in the Fifteenth Century

Differentiated Instruction

Interactive Reading and Notetaking Study Guide, Adapted Version (English/Spanish)
L1 Chapter 1, Section 3 **ELL, LPR, SN**

Teacher's Edition
L1 Restate with Synonyms, p. 16 **ELL, LPR, SN**
L3 Research an Oral Report, p. 18 **AR**
L3 Make a Diagram and Model, p. 18 **GT**

Assess and Reteach

Assess Progress
Evaluate student comprehension with Check Your Progress and Section Quiz.

Reteach
Assign the Interactive Reading and Notetaking Study Guide to help struggling students.

Extend
Extend the lesson by having students do research to prepare a news report on Zheng He's expeditions.

Instructional Resources

Interactive Reading and Notetaking Study Guide
L2 Chapter 1, Section 3

All in One Teaching Resources, Unit 1
L2 Reading Readiness Guide, p. 18
L2 Section Quiz, p. 26

Progress Monitoring Transparencies
L2 Chapter 1, Section 3

Differentiated Instruction

Teacher's Edition
L1 Checkpoints, TE pp. 17, 18, 19

SE on Audio CD
L1 Chapter 1, Section 3

Internet Resources
PHSchool.com

Section 4 The European Heritage *1.5 periods, .75 block*

Objectives

Students will

1. Understand the importance of the Judeo-Christian tradition.
2. Learn how Greece and Rome shaped ideas about government and law.
3. Discover the impact of the Crusades and the Renaissance on Europe.
4. Find out why Europeans began to look beyond their borders.

Differentiated Instruction Key

L1 Basic to Average
L2 All Students
L3 Average to Advanced

AR Advanced Readers
ELL English Language Learners
GT Gifted and Talented
LPR Less Proficient Readers
SN Special Needs

Prepare to Read

Build Background Knowledge
Preview the section and discuss the concept of heritage.

Set a Purpose for Reading
Have students begin to fill out the Reading Readiness Guide.

Preview Key Terms
Preview the section's Key Terms.

Instructional Resources

All in One Teaching Resources, Unit 1
L2 Reading Readiness Guide, p. 19

Teacher's Edition
L2 Vocabulary Builder, p. 23

Differentiated Instruction

Guided Reading Audio CD
Spanish **ELL, LPR, SN**

Teach

Instruction
The Judeo-Christian Tradition
Understand that the Jewish and Christian religions became the foundation of European religious beliefs.

Greek and Roman Traditions
Discuss the impact of Greek and Roman ideas on modern democratic government.

New Horizons
Analyze how the Crusades and the Renaissance encouraged Europeans to look outward.

An Age of Exploration Begins
Identify the Portuguese as leading the way in European exploration.

Instructional Resources

Interactive Reading and Notetaking Study Guide
L2 Chapter 1, Section 4
All in One Teaching Resources, Unit 1
L2 Skills for Life Worksheet, p. 22

Color Transparencies
L2 Religion, Trade and Exploration

Differentiated Instruction

Interactive Reading and Notetaking Study Guide, Adapted Version (English/ Spanish)
L1 Chapter 1, Section 4 **ELL, LPR, SN**

Teacher's Edition
L1 Vocabulary Development, p. 22 **ELL, SN**
L1 Reading Aids, p. 24 **LPR**
L1 Create an Annotated Timeline, p. 26 **ELL, LPR, SN**

Assess and Reteach

Assess Progress
Assign Check Your Progress and Section Quiz.

Reteach
Assign the Study Guide to help students.

Extend
Extend the lesson by having students write a diary entry about rounding the tip of Africa with Vasco da Gama.

Instructional Resources

Interactive Reading and Notetaking Study Guide
L2 Chapter 1, Section 4
All in One Teaching Resources, Unit 1
L2 Reading Readiness Guide, p. 19
L2 Word Knowledge Rating Form, p. 15
L2 Section Quiz, p. 27
L2 Chapter Test, p. 31

Progress Monitoring Transparencies
L2 Chapter 1, Section 4

Differentiated Instruction

Teacher's Edition
L1 Checkpoints, TE pp. 23, 25, 26, 27
All in One Teaching Resources, Unit 1
L1 Chapter Test, p. 28

SE on Audio CD
L1 Chapter 1, Section 4

Social Studies Skills Tutor CD-ROM
Identifying Main Ideas

Use the following research activities to help students deepen their understanding of the Chapter Essential Question: **How did different cultures and traditions develop around the world?** Students should use library or Internet resources. The Web Codes provided offer access to Internet resources students can use to complete each activity. Use the appropriate four-point rubric in Assessment Rubrics to evaluate the activity.

 Assessment Rubrics

Create a Multimedia Presentation about an Early Civilization

Have students work as a group to create a multimedia presentation about one of the early civilizations that developed in the Americas. Students may focus on the Mayas, the Aztecs, or the Incas. Ask students to use both graphics and text to present information about the society, government, religion, economy, arts, and achievements of the civilization. Have students share their multimedia presentation with the class. Use this activity when studying Three Civilizations in Section 1.

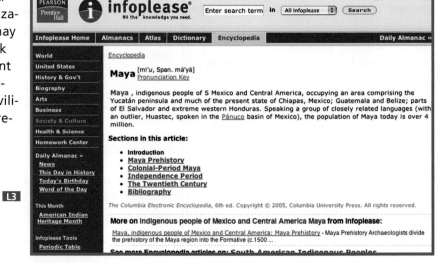

 Group research activity AR, GT ▪ **L3**

Go Online
PHSchool.com **Web Code:** mve-0103

Write Placards about Native American Dwellings

Go Online
PHSchool.com **Web Code:** mve-0104

Tell students that museum exhibits usually include not only visual displays but written text that provides information about the objects shown. Have students write placards for an exhibit on Native American dwellings that displays these shelters: igloo, adobe apartment house, tepee, longhouse. For each dwelling students should explain the geographic region in which it was found, the materials used to build it, and how it illustrates adaptation to the environment. Have students present their placards after the class reads Native Americans of North America in Section 2.

 Individual research activity ELL, LPR, SN ▪ **L1**

Write a Journal Entry about Trade on the Silk Road

Ask students to use the Web site to learn more about travel and trade on the Silk Road. Have students write a two-paragraph journal entry that shows familiarity with the route and its termini, modes of transportation used, and goods carried by traders. Invite students to read their journal entries to the rest of the class. Use this activity when studying The East Asian Link in Trade in Section 3.

 Individual research activity AR **L3**

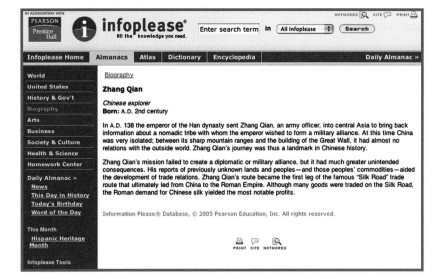

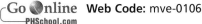 **Web Code:** mve-0105

Create a Roots of the American People Timeline

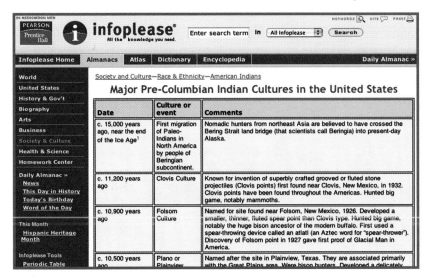

 Web Code: mve-0106

Have students create their own roots of the American people timelines that show these events: First people arrive in the Americas (about 30,000 years ago), Mound Builders build first cities in North America (about 3,000 years ago), Romans set up representative democracy (2,500 years ago), Judeo-Christian teachings spread (about 2,000 years ago), Renaissance begins in Europe (1300s), Aztecs and Incas create great civilizations (1400s), Native American cultures well-established in North America (1500). Tell students to conduct research to decide on an icon, or representative image, to accompany each event on the timeline. Ask students to explain their timelines and choice of icons to the class. Use this activity as a wrap-up at the end of the chapter.

 Group research activity ELL, LPR **L1**

Extend the Lesson Through Technology Research

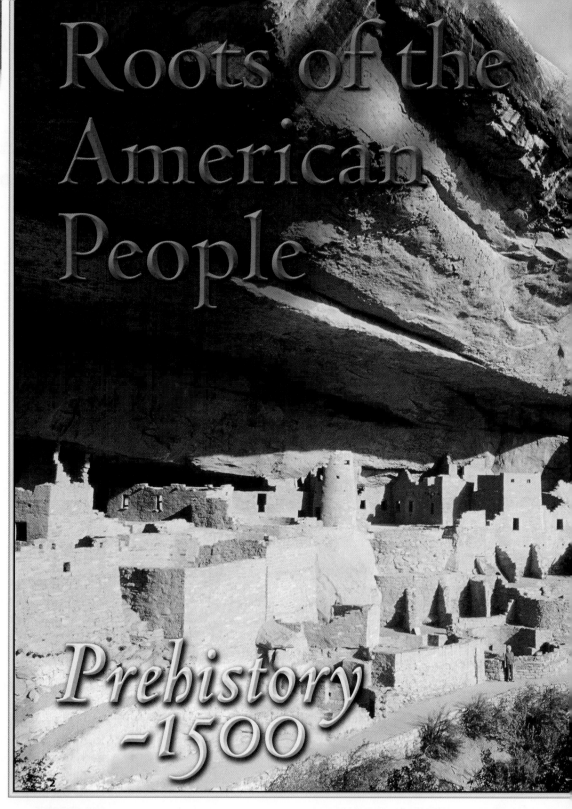

Roots of the American People

Prehistory –1500

Why It Matters

In this chapter, students will learn about earliest Americans.

Even thousands of years ago, people were already forging global trade links that are in place today. Native American groups spread across North America. Asians sailed along the east coast of Africa. Europeans journeyed to Asia, and Arab people followed trade routes to Africa. In time, explorers would bring European ideas and traditions to the Americas. Today we live in a truly global age. People can fly from the United States to Asia in less than one day. News from Africa is broadcast worldwide within hours. Sending an e-mail to someone in Russia takes seconds.

The cultures of Native Americans in North America reflected the land and climate of the regions in which they lived. Geography influences how people in different regions of the United States today live, work, and play.

Chapter Essential Question

How did different cultures and traditions develop around the world?

Think Like a Historian

- To preview this chapter, have students review the content on pp. 2–3 of the Student Edition. Ask: **What will you be learning about in this chapter?** *(early people in the Americas; what people in Africa, Asia, and Europe were doing at the same time; how different cultures became acquainted with one another through trade; European ideas and traditions that were brought to the Americas)*

- Have students study the image of the Cliff Palace on these pages. Then ask students to name some of the advantages of communal living in the 1100s. *(Responses will vary, but could include that the community would have been well protected from the elements; people might have shared responsibilities, as well as food and a social network; and defense would have been easier.)*

- Have students read the section summaries and the quote from Alan Taylor and predict what this chapter is going to be about. *(Students should recognize that Africans, Europeans, and Native Americans borrowed elements from one another to create new cultures.)*

Bibliography

For the Teacher

Alcock, Antony. *A Short History of Europe: From the Greeks and Romans to the Present Day.* Palgrave/Macmillan, 2002.

Fagan, Brian. *The Great Journey: The Peopling of America.* University Press of Florida, 2004.

For the Student

L1 Wood, Marion. *The World of Native Americans.* Peter Bedrick Books, 1997.

L2 Harris, Nathaniel. *Democracy.* Raintree, 2001.

L3 Bowker, John W. *World Religions.* Dorling Kindersley, 1997.

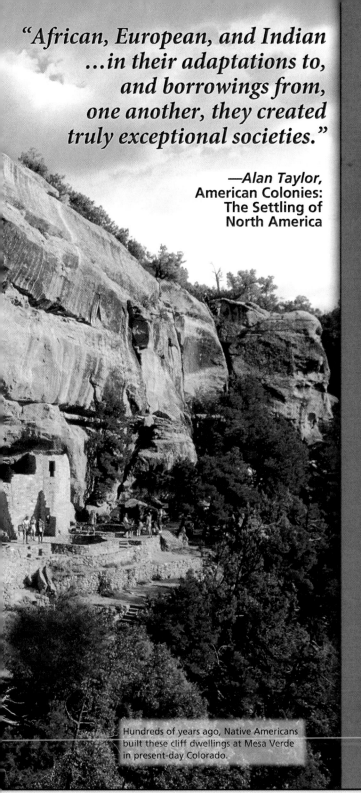

"African, European, and Indian ...in their adaptations to, and borrowings from, one another, they created truly exceptional societies."

—Alan Taylor,
American Colonies:
The Settling of
North America

Hundreds of years ago, Native Americans built these cliff dwellings at Mesa Verde in present-day Colorado.

CHAPTER 1

What You Will Learn

Section 1
THE EARLIEST AMERICANS
Early people spread across the Americas and eventually built great civilizations.

Section 2
CULTURES OF NORTH AMERICA
Peoples of North America developed a wide variety of cultures.

Section 3
TRADE NETWORKS OF ASIA AND AFRICA
A complex trade network linked Africa, Asia, and Europe.

Section 4
THE EUROPEAN HERITAGE
Traditions that came to the Americas from Europe included Judaism, Christianity, and Greek and Roman ideas about government.

Reading Skill

Read Actively In this chapter, you will practice active reading by taking notes and using review questions to identify main ideas and supporting details.

3

History Background

Cliff Dwellings at Mesa Verde Visitors to Mesa Verde National Park in southwestern Colorado can view hundreds of cliff dwellings built by the Anasazi peoples in the period 1150–1200. The Anasazi constructed the houses under cliffs and facing south-southwest to take advantage of the sun's heat during the winter. The largest of the dwellings is Cliff Palace, shown here. With more than 200 rooms, it gave shelter to as many as 250 people. Most of the other cliff dwellings were smaller, with just one to five rooms. About 5,000 people may have lived at Mesa Verde at its peak. In the late 1200s, however, a drought forced the Anasazi to abandon the site. Many relocated farther south, in present-day New Mexico and Arizona.

Prepare to Read

Use the following for reading skill support.

All in One Teaching Resources, Unit 1, Chapter Prereading Guide, p. 4; History Reading Skill, p. 14

History Reading Skill, *Online*
Web code: mve-3000

Differentiated Instruction

The following Teacher's Edition strategies are suitable for students of varying abilities.

L3 **Advanced Readers,** pp. 8, 10, 18 AR

L1 **English Language Learners,** pp. 5, 6, 12, 16, 20, 22, 26 ELL

L3 **Gifted and Talented,** pp. 8, 10, 18 GT

L1 **Less Proficient Readers,** pp. 6, 14, 16, 24, 26 LPR

L1 **Special Needs,** pp. 5, 6, 12, 16, 22, 24, 26 SN

Chapter Resources

Teaching Resources, Unit 1
Chapter Prereading Guide, p. 4
Word Knowledge Rating Form, p. 15
History Reading Skill, p. 14
Skills for Life Worksheet, p. 22
Chapter Tests A/B (L1/L2), pp. 28, 31
Letter Home (English/Spanish), pp. 7, 8

Spanish Support
L1 **Interactive Reading and Notetaking Study Guide, Spanish,** Adapted Version
L1 **Guided Reading Audio CD,** Spanish

Media and Technology
L1 SE on Audio CD
L2 Social Studies Skills Tutor CD-ROM

Quick View Video
View the chapter video for a quick preview of the main ideas.

Visual Preview

? **How did different traditions and customs develop around the world?**

Build Background Knowledge [L2]

Define the terms "tradition" and "custom." Bring out the idea that people living together develop patterns of behavior and common beliefs, which are handed down over a period of time. Lead a structured discussion about why these social patterns develop. (See TE p. T24 for more on structured discussion.) Give students an example of a tradition to which they can relate. For example, after winning an important football game, a coach takes his team out for ice cream. The following week, the team has another win, and the coach takes them out again for ice cream. This begins the tradition of the coach taking the football team out for a celebration after each win. Have students give examples of traditions from their own lives.

Instruction [L2]

For background information on conducting a lesson for the Visual Preview, see TE p. T20.

- Write the Essential Question on the board. Ask students why they think traditions vary in different parts of the world. Use the Idea Wave strategy (TE p. T24) to lead a structured discussion of what people need in order to survive. *(food, shelter, clothes)* Ask: **Do you think your food, clothing, and shelter are the same as someone living in Asia? Or as someone living in another state? Why or why not?** *(Student answers should discuss the impact of geography, values, and beliefs.)* Discuss how traditions and customs develop, based on the needs of people. Ask: **Why would people develop different traditions around the world?** *(Possible answers: People have different natural resources to work with and different experiences in working together.)*

- Have students look at the map title, *"The World, ca. 1500."* Explain that "ca." is an abbreviation for the Latin word *circa,* and it is used before a date to indicate that it is an approximate or estimated date.

? **How did different cultures and traditio**

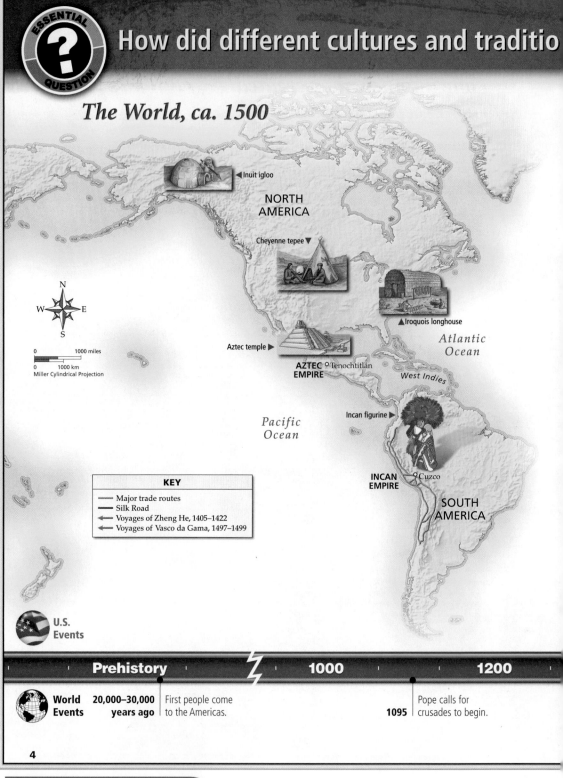

The World, ca. 1500

Inuit igloo

NORTH AMERICA

Cheyenne tepee ▼

▲ Iroquois longhouse

Aztec temple ▶

Atlantic Ocean

AZTEC ○ Tenochtitlán
EMPIRE

West Indies

Pacific Ocean

Incan figurine ▶

INCAN ○ Cuzco
EMPIRE

SOUTH AMERICA

KEY
— Major trade routes
— Silk Road
◀— Voyages of Zheng He, 1405–1422
◀— Voyages of Vasco da Gama, 1497–1499

U.S. Events

| Prehistory | 1000 | 1200 |

World Events | 20,000–30,000 years ago | First people come to the Americas. | 1095 | Pope calls for crusades to begin.

4

History Background

Impact of Trading The trade route known as the Silk Road was used for more than 1,000 years and was an important channel of contact between civilizations. New goods were introduced in both directions.

Products such as gunpowder and porcelain moved westward, while merchants brought muslin, glass, and new foods into China. Technology such as papermaking and the use of windmills was taken east. Religions such as Buddhism and Islam spread peacefully as traders and missionaries moved along the road. The traditions and cultures of many people were affected by the exposure to new ideas, religions, merchandise, and technology.

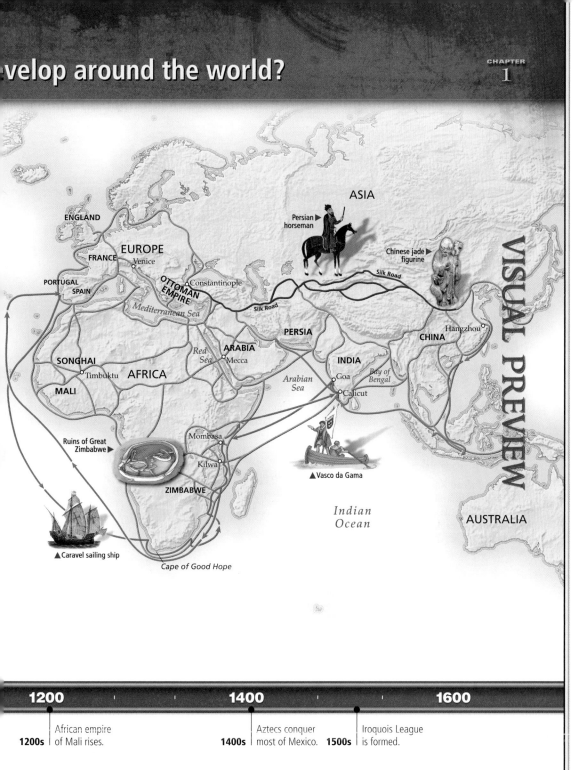

ASIA

ENGLAND

EUROPE
FRANCE
Venice

PORTUGAL
SPAIN

OTTOMAN EMPIRE
Constantinople

Mediterranean Sea

Silk Road

Persian ► horseman

Chinese jade ► figurine

Silk Road

Hangzhou

CHINA

PERSIA

ARABIA
Red Sea
Mecca

INDIA
Goa
Bay of Bengal
Calicut

SONGHAI
Timbuktu
AFRICA

Arabian Sea

MALI

Ruins of Great Zimbabwe ►

Mombasa

Kilwa

▲ Vasco da Gama

ZIMBABWE

Indian Ocean

AUSTRALIA

▲ Caravel sailing ship

Cape of Good Hope

VISUAL PREVIEW

1200	1400	1600

1200s African empire of Mali rises.

1400s Aztecs conquer most of Mexico.

1500s Iroquois League is formed.

5

Instruction (continued)

- Using the map key, ask students to identify the blue lines. *(voyages of Vasco da Gama)* Ask: **When did Zheng He complete his voyages?** *(1405-1422)* **What areas did the Silk Road travel through?** *(Ottoman Empire, Arabia, Persia, China)*

- Have students identify which continents had most of the trade routes at this time. *(Europe, Africa, Asia)* Ask: **Why do you think is so?** *(Possible answers: the ships needed to stay close to land, more people lived in these regions)*

- Draw the students' attention to the dwellings in North America. Ask why they think there are different types shown. *(Responses may include comments on available materials and climate.)*

- Call students' attention to the break in the timeline. Explain that this jagged line indicates a long span of years. Ask students to identify the first event given on the timeline. *(First people come to the Americas.)* **What is the time span for the remaining events given on the timeline?** *(1095 to 1500s)*

- Have students rewrite the Essential Question in simple terms in their notes: **How did people develop different traditions and customs?** You may also post this question in a prominent place in the classroom and leave it there while discussing the chapter. Tell students to use the section focus questions as a guide to answering the Essential Question as they read the chapter.

- Tell students that as they complete the Notetaking Study Guide for this chapter, they will be building the answer to the Essential Question.

📖 **Interactive Reading and Notetaking Study Guide,** Chapter 1, (Adapted Version also available.)

Vocabulary Builder

Preview the Vocabulary Have students preview the vocabulary in the chapter and rate how well they know each word on the Word Knowledge Rating Form. Collect the sheets and explain that they will have a chance to go over the forms later.

All in One Teaching Resources, Unit 1, Word Knowledge Rating Form, p. 15

Monitor Progress Students should demonstrate their understanding of the words by finding pictures that illustrate them. For example, for the word *currency*, students may show a dollar bill. Pair students to exchange their pictures and have the partners check understanding of the relationship of the image to the word. Review the material with the students.

Review and Preview

Students have completed the Chapter Prereading Guide. Now they will learn about the first people in the Americas, how they learned to farm, and the civilizations they built.

How did early civilizations develop in the Americas?

Before you begin the lesson for the day, write the Section Focus Question on the board. (*Lesson focus: Early American farming communities grew into cities, and as cities developed, civilizations arose. The Mayas, Aztecs, and Incas built major civilizations in Central and South America.*)

Prepare to Read

Build Background Knowledge   **L2**

Before students open their books to this section, read aloud the first sentence in Background Knowledge: "Tens of thousands of years ago, no humans lived in North or South America." Then ask: **Where do you think the first people in the Americas came from, and how did they get here?** (*Students may hypothesize that the first people came to the Americas from one of the other continents, particularly Asia or Europe; they may suggest that they came by boat or by a land route that no longer exists.*) Use the Idea Wave participation strategy (TE, p. T24) to encourage brainstorming.

Set a Purpose   **L2**

■ Read each statement in the Reading Readiness Guide aloud. Ask students to mark the statements as True or False.

   All in One Teaching Resources, Unit 1, Reading Readiness Guide, p. 16

■ Have students discuss the statements in pairs or groups of four, then mark their worksheets again. Use the Numbered Heads strategy (TE, p. T24) to call on students to share their group's perspectives. The students will return to these worksheets later.

SECTION 1

Ancient Pyramid Found

❝When they first saw us digging there, the local people just couldn't believe there was a pyramid. . . . It was only when the slopes and shapes of the pyramid, the floors with altars were found, that they finally believed us. ❞

—Archaeologist Jesus Sanchez, describing discovery near Mexico City, 2006

◄ Mayan pyramid in Mexico

The Earliest Americans

Objectives
- Understand how people may have first reached the Americas.
- Find out how people learned to farm.
- Explore the civilizations of the Mayas, Aztecs, and Incas.

⟳ Reading Skill

Preview Before Reading The first step in active reading is to preview the text. Read the Objectives, Reading Skill, and Key Terms. Scan all the headings and side-margin notes. Read the captions and look at the illustrations. Finally, read the questions that appear at the section's end.

Key Terms

glacier   surplus
irrigation   civilization

Why It Matters Tens of thousands of years ago, no humans lived in North America or South America.

❷ Section Focus Question: How did early civilizations develop in the Americas?

The First Americans

Scientists have various ideas about how people came to the Americas. Some think that people may have come from Asia in large canoes. However, most think that the first humans arrived by land.

The Land-Bridge Theory Between 10,000 and 100,000 years ago, much of the world was covered by glaciers, or thick sheets of ice. As more and more of the world's water froze, the level of the oceans dropped. Areas that once were covered by shallow water became dry land. One of these areas stretched between Siberia and Alaska. It became a bridge of land many miles wide. The area now lies under a narrow waterway called the Bering Strait.

The land bridge may have appeared and disappeared several times. However, many scientists believe that people first came to North America between 20,000 and 30,000 years ago. They were hunters, possibly following the coast of Siberia as they hunted prehistoric mammals such as the woolly mammoth. Over thousands of years, hunting bands moved over the land. They eventually spread across North America and South America.

Other Theories Not everyone agrees with the land-bridge theory. Some scientists think that people may first have crossed the arctic waters by boat and traveled southward along the Pacific coast. This idea is known as the coastal-route theory.

6 Chapter 1 Roots of the American People

Differentiated Instruction

L1 English Language Learners   **L1** Less Proficient Readers   **L1** Special Needs

Listen/Speak–Ask/Answer To provide listening and speaking practice, encourage students to read parts of the section aloud. When they are comfortable, they can tape-record their reading. Then, have pairs of students work together to question each other about what they have read. Students should switch roles frequently so that each partner has a chance to ask and answer a number of questions. This questioning session also can be taped. Review tapes with students.

Many Native Americans also dispute both the land-bridge theory and the coastal-route theory. Each group has its own tradition explaining how they settled in the lands they did. These traditions appear in their creation stories.

Learning to Farm For centuries, early humans could fill most of their needs by hunting. Game animals provided food, furs for clothing, and bones for tools.

In time, many of the larger animals began to disappear. <u>Deprived</u> of their main source of food, hunters had to change their ways of life. In many places, hunters became gatherers. They traveled from place to place, searching for wild plants and small game.

Some 8,000 years ago, gatherers in Mexico began growing food plants, including squash and lima beans. The discovery of farming transformed life. No longer did families have to wander in search of food. In dry regions, farmers developed methods of irrigation. Irrigation is a method to water crops by channeling water from rivers or streams. Farmers also learned how to raise animals such as cattle, pigs, and llamas.

With a more dependable food supply, the population grew more rapidly. Once Native Americans produced surplus, or extra, food, they traded with others. Some farming communities grew into cities. The cities became centers of government and religious life.

Vocabulary Builder
deprive (dee PRĪV) *v.* to take away

 Preview Before Reading
Preview the matter on the following pages under the heading "Three Civilizations." What do the subheadings, images, and captions tell you?

✓**Checkpoint** How do scientists think people first reached the Americas?

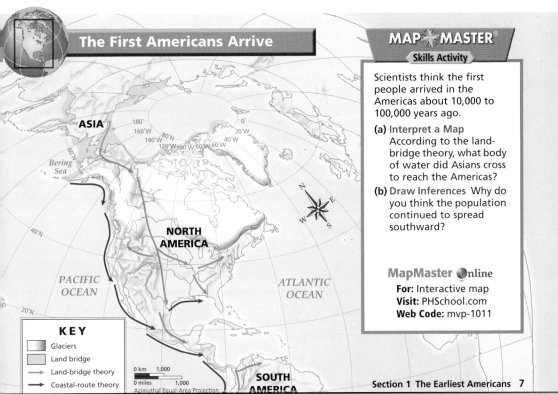

The First Americans Arrive

MAP★MASTER®
Skills Activity

Scientists think the first people arrived in the Americas about 10,000 to 100,000 years ago.

(a) Interpret a Map According to the land-bridge theory, what body of water did Asians cross to reach the Americas?

(b) Draw Inferences Why do you think the population continued to spread southward?

MapMaster ⬤nline
For: Interactive map
Visit: PHSchool.com
Web Code: mvp-1011

KEY
- Glaciers
- Land bridge
- → Land-bridge theory
- → Coastal-route theory

0 km 1,000
0 miles 1,000
Azimuthal Equal-Area Projection

Vocabulary Builder

Use the information below to teach students this section's high-use words.

High-Use Word	Definition and Sample Sentence
deprive, p. 7	*v.* to take away People who were enslaved were **deprived** of their freedom.
reside, p. 8	*v.* to live; to make one's home in The people who **reside** in a city or state make up its population.

Teach

The First Americans
p. 6

Instruction

- **Vocabulary Builder** Before teaching this section, preteach the High-Use Words **deprive** and **reside** before reading, using the strategy on TE p. T21.
  Key Terms Create a three-column See It–Remember It chart on the Key Terms. Have students write the terms in the first column, find and copy the definitions in the second column, and use the terms in sentences in the third column. Monitor their work and provide assistance as needed.

- Read The First Americans with students using the Structured Silent Reading strategy (TE, p. T22).

- Ask: **How did the ways of life of the earliest Americans change over time?** (*In addition to hunting, early people began growing food plants.*)

- Discuss how farming led to the growth of cities. Emphasize that because people no longer had to travel in search of food, they could build settlements.

Independent Practice
Have students begin to fill in the Study Guide for this section.

Monitor Progress

As students fill in the Notetaking Study Guide, circulate to make sure they understand how the first people came to the Americas and learned to farm. Provide assistance as needed.

Answers

✓**Checkpoint** Most scientists believe that the first people arrived by land.

⟳ **Reading Skill** The subheadings, images, and captions tell that the Mayas, Aztecs, and Incas built civilizations.

MAP★MASTER
Skills Activity **(a)** Bering Sea **(b)** Possible answers: They moved into unpopulated areas; they looked for a warmer climate; they followed animals in the hunt.

Explore More Video

Discovery School Video

Show the video *Tenochtitlán and the Aztecs* to tell the story of the rise and decline of Aztec civilization and to explain the role religion played in the lives of the Aztecs and the peoples in their empire.

Three Civilizations

p. 8

Instruction [L2]

■ Have students read Three Civilizations. Remind students to look for details to answer the Section Focus Question.

■ Ask: **What marked the rise of civilizations in the Americas?** (*the development of cities*)

■ Ask: **What are some basic features of advanced civilizations in the Americas?** (*large cities, development of arts and science, system of government, written language, religious beliefs, transportation networks, and engineering for construction, agriculture, and water supply*)

■ Display the transparency to review the civilizations of the Maya, Aztec, and Inca.

Color Transparencies, Early Civilizations in The Americas

Independent Practice

Have students complete the Study Guide for this section.

📖 **Interactive Reading and Notetaking Study Guide,** Chapter 1, Section 1 (Adapted Version also available.)

Monitor Progress

■ As students fill in the Notetaking Study Guide, circulate to make sure they understand the development and features of the Mayan, Aztec, and Inca civilizations.

■ Tell students to fill in the last column of the Reading Readiness guide. Probe for what they learned that confirms or invalidates each statement.

All in One Teaching Resources, Unit 1, Reading Readiness Guide, p. 16

Answer

Draw Conclusions The layout of the city has been carefully planned with roadways to make transportation to the mainland easy.

Explore More Video
To learn more about the Aztec Empire, view the video.

Tenochtitlán The Aztecs built their capital city of Tenochtitlán on a group of islands in the middle of a lake. The center of the city was dominated by a huge temple (inset). *Critical Thinking: Draw Conclusions How does this picture support the idea that the Aztec society was highly organized?*

Vocabulary Builder
reside (ree zīp) **v.** to live; to make one's home in

Three Civilizations

With the development of cities came the beginnings of civilization. A **civilization** is an advanced culture in which people have developed cities, science, and industries. Over the centuries, several civilizations rose and declined in the Americas. The largest were the civilizations of the Mayas, the Aztecs, and the Incas.

Mayas Between A.D. 250 and A.D. 900, the Mayas built cities in what is now Mexico and Central America. These splendid cities contained large public plazas lined with pyramids, temples, ball courts, and palaces.

The Mayas did more, however. They developed arts, a system of government, and a written language. They also observed the stars. From their study of the heavens, they created the most accurate calendar known until modern times. They also carved stories of their past and their gods into the stones of their buildings.

Around A.D. 900, the Mayas began to abandon their cities. Why this happened remains a mystery. Disease or overpopulation may have caused the decline. Although the Mayan civilization is gone, the Mayan language still forms the root of more than 20 languages of Central America.

Aztecs As Mayan civilization declined, a new civilization was on the rise. The Aztecs built a great capital city, Tenochtitlán (tay noch tee TLAHN), on the site of present-day Mexico City. It was built on a series of islands in a large lake. The city was connected to the mainland by stone roadways. In many parts of Tenochtitlán, farmers raised crops on floating platforms. More than 200,000 people resided in Tenochtitlán at its height, making it perhaps the largest city in the world at that time.

8 Chapter 1 Roots of the American People

Differentiated Instruction

[L3] Advanced Readers

Write a Report Tell students to imagine that they are returning from the far reaches of the Incan empire. Have students research and write a report to deliver to the emperor. Remind students to focus their research on the Incan way of life. Tell students to include details about Incan culture.

[L3] Gifted and Talented

Create a Diorama Tell groups of students to use the library or Internet to find illustrations of Tenochtitlán. Using the illustrations as a guide, groups should create a diorama of the city as it looked in 1500. Tell students to include these features: causeways, canals, floating platforms, markets, temples, and a palace.

The center of the city was a sacred place with dozens of temples that honored the Aztec gods. This was appropriate because religion dominated Aztec life. To the Aztecs, prosperity depended on the good will of the gods. Like a number of other ancient peoples, the Aztecs practiced human sacrifice as an offering to their gods.

During the 1400s, Aztec armies brought half of modern-day Mexico under their control. The Aztecs proved to be effective but harsh rulers. Conquered tribes were forced to send treasure, food, and prisoners to the Aztec capital. The Aztecs forced the people they conquered to pay high taxes. Resentful subjects would eventually turn on the Aztecs when the empire most needed allies.

Incas In the 1400s, the largest empire was not in Europe or Asia. It was in South America. The vast empire of the Incas stretched down the coast of South America along the Andes, across the Atacama desert, and reached the fringes of the Amazon rain forest.

At the center of the empire was the Inca capital, Cuzco (KOOS koh). Cuzco was linked to other cities and towns by a great network of roads. A Spaniard who traveled the main Inca highway called it "the finest road to be seen in the world."

The Incas constructed buildings of huge stones carefully shaped to fit together. Their engineers built walls to hold soil in their fields, canals to carry water, and bridges over deep canyons. The Incas produced fine weavings and metalwork. Inca rulers wore gold and silver jewelry, and their palaces contained plates of gold.

☑Checkpoint   **Where were the Aztec and Inca civilizations located?**

⭐ **Looking Back and Ahead** Most Native Americans did not live in large cities like Tenochtitlán or Cuzco. In the next section, you will learn about the ways of life of people north of Mexico.

Figure of an Inca ruler or priest

Section 1 | **Check Your Progress**

Progress Monitoring Online
For: Self-test with instant help
Visit: PHSchool.com
Web Code: mva-1011

Comprehension and Critical Thinking
1. **(a) List** Name one skill that people had to learn in order to grow crops.
(b) Identify Benefits What benefits could farmers get from learning to raise animals?

2. **(a) Define** What is a civilization?
(b) Apply Information How did the Mayas and Aztecs fit that definition?

Reading Skill
3. **Preview Before Reading** Preview Section 2. Read its headings, study its images and captions, and review its questions. Tell what you think Section 2 will be about. Use the headings to identify the text organization. How can you use this information to plan your reading?

Key Terms
Answer the following questions in complete sentences that show your understanding of the key terms.

4. How did the growth of glaciers affect water levels in the ocean?
5. Why was learning about irrigation important for farmers?
6. What are the advantages of having a surplus of crops?

Writing
7. Outline a paragraph in response to the following question: How did early civilizations use industry and science to improve their way of life? Then, list four or five supporting details. Next, write a concluding sentence.

Section 1 The Earliest Americans   9

Assess Progress   L2
Have students complete Check Your Progress. Administer the Section Quiz.

All in One **Teaching Resources, Unit 1,** Section Quiz, p. 24

Reteach   L1
If students need more instruction, have them read this section in the Interactive Reading and Notetaking Study Guide and complete the accompanying question.

Interactive Reading and Notetaking Study Guide, Chapter 1, Section 1 (Adapted Version also available.)

Extend   L3
Have students use the Internet to learn how archaeologists discovered that the Aztec city of Tenochtitlán was located on the site of present-day Mexico City. Tell students to focus on artifacts and other physical evidence archaeologists uncovered. Students may share their findings with the class in an oral report. Encourage students to include images in their report. Provide students with Web Code below.

Extend Online
For: Extend Online
Visit: PHSchool.com
Web Code: mvd-0107

Progress Monitoring Online
Students may check their comprehension of this section by completing the Progress Monitoring Online graphic organizer and self-quiz.

Answer

☑Checkpoint The Aztec civilization was in Central America, and the Inca civilization was in South America.

Section 1 Check Your Progress

1. **(a)** how to plant and irrigate crops
(b) Possible answers: They would not have to move around to hunt animals; some animals could be used for transportation.

2. **(a)** an advanced culture in which people have developed science and industries
(b) The Mayas observed the stars and studied the heavens and used their knowledge to create a very accurate calendar; the Aztecs used science to improve their farming. They planted crops on floating platforms. They built roads to allow access to their capital city, which was one of the largest cities in the world at its peak.

3. Possible answer: Section 2 will be about the Mayan, Aztec, and Inca civilizations; I can compare and contrast features of the three civilizations as I read.

4. Water levels fell as glaciers grew.

5. Farmers could bring water from rivers and streams to irrigate crops and did not have to wait for rain to water them.

6. Possible responses: Surplus crops can be traded for other things you want or need; you can feed more people; some people can live in cities and do work other than farming.

7. Answers will vary, but should include specific details from the text, such as the detail about how the Mayas used their observations of the heavens to make a calendar.

Chapter 1 Section 1 **9**

Review and Preview

Students have read about the civilizations that developed in Central and South America. Now they will learn about the cultures that emerged in North America.

Section Focus Question

How did geography influence the development of cultures in North America?

Before you begin the lesson for the day, write the Section Focus Question on the board. (*Lesson focus: Groups of Native Americans adapted their ways of life to the land and climate in the regions in which they lived.*)

Prepare to Read

Build Background Knowledge L2

Write *What is a culture?* on the board. Ask students to volunteer words or phrases that describe American culture today. Record their responses on the board. Then ask students to identify aspects of other cultures they know of or have studied. Also list these on the board. With students, categorize the aspects of American and other cultures to discover common elements, such as food, clothing, shelter, customs, religion, economy, arts, and government. List these elements on the board under the question *What is a culture?*

Set a Purpose L2

■ Read each statement in the Reading Readiness Guide aloud. Ask students to mark each statement True or False.

   All in One Teaching Resources, Unit 1, Reading Readiness Guide, p. 17

■ Have students discuss the statements in pairs or groups of four, then mark their worksheets again. Use the Numbered Heads participation strategy (TE, p. T24) to call on students to share their group's perspectives. The students will return to these worksheets later.

SECTION **2**

Preserving Native American Culture

❝ By encouraging a greater focus on native language programs, we are not only striving to preserve the identity of the nation's tribes, but we're encouraging greater academic performance among Native American students as well. ❞

—Congresswoman Heather Wilson, on the Esther Martinez Native American Languages Preservation Act of 2006

◀ Recreation of a Native American village

Cultures of North America

Objectives
- Learn about the earliest peoples of North America.
- Discover what different groups of Native Americans had in common.
- Explore the impact of geography on Native American cultures.

Reading Skill

Apply Prior Knowledge You can prepare for reading by building on and connecting to what you already know. This can be information from an earlier section, chapter, or other reading. It can also be prior knowledge from your own life experience. Applying this knowledge while you are reading helps you interact with and engage in the text. This, in turn, will help you understand and remember what you have read.

Key Terms

culture   adobe
culture area   clan
kayak   sachem
potlatch

Why It Matters As the Mayas, Aztecs, and Incas built civilizations in Central America and South America, diverse cultures developed to the north.

❓ **Section Focus Question: How did geography influence the development of cultures in North America?**

First Cultures of North America

In North America, as elsewhere, groups of people developed unique cultures, or ways of life. Around 3,000 years ago, various groups began to emerge in an area stretching from the Appalachian Mountains to the Mississippi Valley. We call these people Mound Builders because they constructed large piles of earth. Many mounds were burial places, but some served as foundations for public buildings. One group of Mound Builders, the Mississippians, built the first cities in North America. As many as 40,000 people may have lived in the largest Mississippian city, Cahokia, in present-day Illinois.

A far different culture, which we call the Anasazi, emerged in southern Utah, Colorado, northern Arizona, and New Mexico. They built large cliff dwellings, probably to defend against attacks by outsiders such as the Navajos or even the Aztecs. Their largest community housed about 1,000 people. The Anasazis were skilled in making baskets, pottery, and jewelry. They also engaged in trade. Mysteriously, by 1300, the Anasazis had abandoned their cliff dwellings.

10 Chapter 1 Roots of American People

Differentiated Instruction

L3 Advanced Readers

Summarize a Scholarly Article Have students choose one of the cultures discussed in this section. Tell them to find a scholarly article about the group. Students should read the article, make an outline to use as the basis of a critical review about the value of the article.

L3 Gifted and Talented

Create a Poster Have students work as a group to plan a poster about Native American artifacts. Artifacts help archaeologists learn how ancient peoples lived. Tell students to research and show the following on their poster: drawings of artifacts from different periods, and a brief description of each artifact and its function.

From about 300 B.C. to A.D. 1450, highly skilled farmers called the Hohokam dug irrigation canals in the deserts of present-day Arizona. Trade brought them in contact with people who lived on the Gulf of California. The Hohokam traded for seashells, which they used to create jewelry and religious objects.

☑Checkpoint **For what purposes were mounds built?**

Ways of Life

Scholars classify Native Americans into several culture areas, regions in which groups of people have a similar way of life. Though these cultures were very different from one another, many shared some basic traits.

Meeting Basic Needs Early Native American societies developed a variety of ways to meet their needs. In many areas, women collected roots, wild seeds, nuts, acorns, and berries. Men hunted for game and fished. Wild game was plentiful in regions like the Pacific Coast and the Eastern Woodlands.

In many culture areas, agriculture allowed people to grow and store food. Native Americans learned to grow crops suited to the climate in which they lived. They used pointed sticks for digging. Bones or shells served as hoes. Some used fertilizer, such as dead fish, to make the soil more productive. Where Native Americans lived by farming, their population was much larger than in nonfarming areas.

Trade was a common activity in all the North American cultures. In some areas, items such as seashells or beads were used as currency. Shells, flint for making fires, copper, and salt were all important trade items.

Shared Beliefs Many Native Americans felt a close relationship to the natural world. They believed that spirits dwelled in nature and that these spirits were part of their daily lives.

Traditions reflected these beliefs. For example, the Indians of the Southeast held the Green Corn Ceremony in late summer. The ritual, which could last for more than a week, was a form of natural and spiritual renewal at the end of the growing season. The Pueblo Indians revered spirits known as kachinas. To teach their children about these benevolent spirits, the Pueblos carved kachina dolls.

Native Americans also had a strong oral tradition. Storytellers memorized history and beliefs and then recited them. In this way, their tradition was passed on from generation to generation.

☑Checkpoint **How did North American cultures meet their needs?**

Vocabulary Builder
currency (KUH rehn see) *n.* items used as money

Native American Farmers
Early farmers made and used stone tools such as the digging stick and axe shown to the left. **Critical Thinking: *Clarify Problems*** *Based on this picture, what difficulties might these farmers face?*

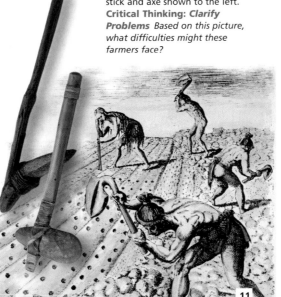

11

Instruction L2

■ **Vocabulary Builder** Before teaching this section, preteach the High-Use Words **currency** and **distinct** before reading, using the strategy on TE p. T21. **Key Terms** Have students continue filling in the See It–Remember It chart for the Key Terms in this chapter.

■ Have students read First Cultures of North America and Culture and Life using the Choral Reading strategy (TE, p. T22).

■ Ask students to name an achievement of the Mound Builder, Anasazi, and Hohokam cultures. (*Mound Builders built the first cities in North America; the Anasazi built cliff dwellings; and the Hohokam dug canals.*)

Independent Practice
Have students begin to fill in the Study Guide for this section.

Monitor Progress

As students fill in the Notetaking Study Guide, circulate to make sure they understand basic features that the cultures of North America shared. Provide assistance as needed.

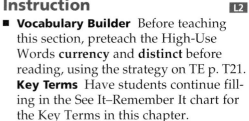

Vocabulary Builder

Use the information below to teach students this section's high-use words.

High-Use Word	Definition and Sample Sentence
currency, p. 11	*n.* items used as money The dollar is the basic unit off **currency** in the United States.
distinct, p. 12	*adj.* clearly different in quality There are **distinct** differences between the climate of Alaska and the climate of Florida.

Answers

☑Checkpoint Mounds were burial places and also served as foundations for public buildings.

Clarify Problems Possible response: farming was labor intensive work.

☑Checkpoint North American cultures met their needs by hunting, gathering, farming, and trading with each other.

Native Americans of North America

p. 12

Instruction

- Have students read Native Americans of North America. Remind them to look for details to answer the Section Focus Question.

- Ask: **What challenges did the Arctic ice and the desert of the Southwest present for Native Americans living there?** (*Native Americans in the Arctic had to hunt, fish, and gather foods because it was too cold for farming; some farming was possible in the Southwest, but Native Americans there had to collect and store rain water for dry times.*)

- Ask: **How were Native Americans in the Northwest able to establish permanent settlements without farming?** (*The forests and rivers of the Northwest supported many kinds of animals and fish and foods that could be gathered, such as roots and berries.*)

- Discuss the kinds of houses Native Americans in the Far West built. Lead students to draw conclusions about how land and climate of the region varied based on what they have learned about housing there. (*The land and climate varied; where people dug pit houses, there were probably few trees and the climate may have been rather hot; where people build cone-shaped houses covered with bark, the climate was probably mild to warm and there were trees; where people made homes of wooden planks, there were likely many trees and the climate was cooler generally.*)

- To help students better understand the concept of *culture,* which is important to the understanding of this section, use the Concept Lesson about Culture. Provide students with copies of the Concept Organizer.

    All in One Teaching Resources, Unit 1, Concept Lesson, p. 23; Concept Organizer, p. 6

Answer

Reading Skill Possible responses include: Many people live in separate parts of the same building; people often live on different levels above and below each other; there is usually a main entrance to the building and individual entrances inside to the different apartments, or living spaces. Students should apply these ideas to Pueblo life.

Vocabulary Builder
<u>distinct</u> (dihs TIHNKT) *adj.* clearly different in quality

Native Americans of North America

Well before 10,000 B.C., Native Americans had spread across the North American continent. They had adapted to the various climates and living conditions of the lands in which they settled. By A.D. 1500, when the first Europeans reached the Americas, the Native Americans living in North America were a richly diverse group of people with <u>distinct</u> ways of life.

Far North The people of the Arctic lived in a vast and harsh land, some of it covered with ice all year long. The people survived on fish, shellfish, and birds. They also hunted marine mammals, such as whales, seals, and walruses, from kayaks, small boats made from skins. In the summer, they fished on the rivers and hunted caribou.

South of the Arctic lay the dense forests of the subarctic region. With a climate too cold for farming, subarctic peoples relied on animals and plants of the forest for food. Most hunted caribou, moose, bear, and smaller animals.

Northwest Many Native Americans lived in the region of the Pacific Northwest, the land that stretches from southern Alaska to northern California. Deer and bears roamed forests rich with roots and berries. Rivers swarmed with salmon. With so much food available, people here were able to live in large, permanent settlements even though they were not farmers.

In many societies of the Northwest, high-ranking people practiced a custom called the potlatch. A potlatch was a ceremony at which the hosts showered their guests with gifts such as woven cloth, baskets, canoes, and furs. A family's status was judged by how much wealth it could give away.

Far West The people of the Far West lived in different geographic regions. Winters could be very cold in the forests and grasslands of the north. On the other hand, southern parts could be desertlike. In California, with its warm summers and mild winters, food was abundant. People there ate small game, fish, and berries.

Housing differed, depending on the area. Some Native Americans lived in pit houses, which were dug into the ground. Others lived in cone-shaped houses covered with bark. In the north, houses were made of wooden planks.

Southwest The area that is now Arizona, New Mexico, and the southern parts of Utah and Colorado was dry most of the year. But in late July and August, thunderstorms drenched the desert. All the groups in this area did some farming, although certain groups also followed and hunted animals. Farming peoples had to learn to collect and store the rain for the dry times.

The Pueblo people such as the Hopis and Zunis had stable towns that lasted for hundreds of years. To protect themselves from attack, they built large apartment houses made of adobe, or sun-dried brick.

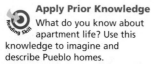 **Apply Prior Knowledge** What do you know about apartment life? Use this knowledge to imagine and describe Pueblo homes.

Differentiated Instruction

L1 English Language Learners   **L1 Special Needs**

Create a Picture Dictionary Visual images of unfamiliar words may help students grasp difficult concepts. Direct students to compile a picture dictionary of words associated with Native American cultures. For each picture entry, have students include a label and brief caption that uses the word in a sentence. Have students begin with words such as *mound, cliff dwelling, pottery, currency, kachina,* and *ceremony* and then add words such as *kayak, potlatch, adobe, clan,* and *sachem.* By illustrating and using these words, students will gain a better understanding of their meanings. The picture dictionary can be made part of a class reference library.

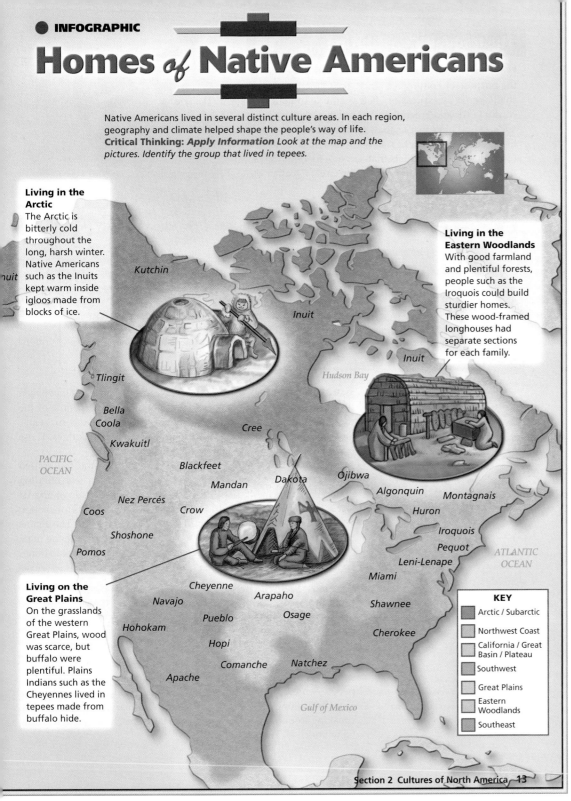

● **INFOGRAPHIC**

Homes *of* Native Americans

Native Americans lived in several distinct culture areas. In each region, geography and climate helped shape the people's way of life.
Critical Thinking: *Apply Information* Look at the map and the pictures. Identify the group that lived in tepees.

Living in the Arctic
The Arctic is bitterly cold throughout the long, harsh winter. Native Americans such as the Inuits kept warm inside igloos made from blocks of ice.

Living in the Eastern Woodlands
With good farmland and plentiful forests, people such as the Iroquois could build sturdier homes. These wood-framed longhouses had separate sections for each family.

Living on the Great Plains
On the grasslands of the western Great Plains, wood was scarce, but buffalo were plentiful. Plains Indians such as the Cheyennes lived in tepees made from buffalo hide.

Kutchin
Inuit
Inuit
Hudson Bay
Tlingit
Bella Coola
Cree
Kwakuitl
PACIFIC OCEAN
Blackfeet
Mandan
Dakota
Ojibwa
Algonquin
Montagnais
Nez Percés
Crow
Huron
Coos
Iroquois
Shoshone
Pequot
Pomos
Leni-Lenape
ATLANTIC OCEAN
Miami
Cheyenne
Arapaho
Navajo
Osage
Shawnee
Hohokam
Pueblo
Hopi
Cherokee
Comanche
Natchez
Apache
Gulf of Mexico

KEY
■ Arctic / Subarctic
□ Northwest Coast
□ California / Great Basin / Plateau
□ Southwest
□ Great Plains
□ Eastern Woodlands
■ Southeast

Seeing the Main Idea

The images on this page can be used to illustrate how geography influenced the development of cultures in North America. Ask: **How did the dwellings of Native Americans in the Arctic, the Great Plains, and the Eastern Woodlands reflect the local environment?** (*The Arctic was very cold, and Native Americans there built homes out of blocks of ice; wood was scarce on the Great Plains, but buffalo were plentiful, and Native Americans there used buffalo hides to build tepees to live in; in the Eastern Woodlands, Native Americans built sturdy houses out of wood from the abundant trees there.*) Ask: **In which culture areas did Native Americans probably not depend on the sea for food?** Explain. (*Native Americans in the Southwest and Great Plains did not have lands that bordered the ocean.*)

History Background

Distinct Ways of Life The Navajos, or Diné as they call themselves, were influenced by Pueblo ways. However, they never built villages. They would sometimes gather their shelters, known as hogans, into small family groups of mothers and married daughters, but this was as close as they came to village living. More often, Navajo hogans and their summer dwellings of brush were widely scattered.

Answer

Apply Information The Cheyennes lived in tepees.

Instruction (continued)

- After students complete the Skills Activity assign the worksheet The Iroquois Constitution to further explore the source.

  AllinOne Teaching Resources, Unit 1, The Iroquois Constitution, p. 20

- Students may have misconceptions about the roles of women in Native American cultures. Use the details provided in this section about the influence of women in Iroquois society to address these impressions. Point out that Native American women had many important roles, including guardians of the home and even rulers and warriors.

Independent Practice

Have students complete the Study Guide for this section.

Interactive Reading and Notetaking Study Guide, Chapter 1, Section 2 (Adapted Version also available.)

Monitor Progress

- As students fill in the Notetaking Study Guide, circulate to make sure they understand how Native Americans adapted their ways of life to the environment.

- Tell students to fill in the last column of the Reading Readiness guide. Probe for what they learned that confirms or invalidates each statement.

  AllinOne Teaching Resources, Unit 1, Reading Readiness Guide, p. 17

- To further assess student understanding, use the Progress Monitoring Transparency.

Progress Monitoring Transparencies, Chapter 1, Section 2

Answers

Reading Primary Sources (a) Possible responses: The selection shows that Native Americans recognize that the natural world helps them meet their needs; their message of thanks reflects their attitude that nature offers gifts, but does not belong to people; **(b)** Answers will vary, but should include that a set ritual helped emphasize the formal or official nature of the League, the seriousness of its business, and the responsibility shared by its members.

The Iroquois Constitution

"Whenever the Confederate Lords shall assemble for the purpose of holding a council, the Onondaga Lords shall open it by expressing their gratitude to their cousin Lords and greeting them, and they shall make an address and offer thanks to the earth where men dwell, to the streams of water . . . to the forest trees for their usefulness, to the animals that serve as food and give their pelts for clothing . . . and to the Great Creator who dwells in the heavens above."

—Iroquois Constitution

The figures on this Seneca comb represent the five Iroquois nations.

Reading Primary Sources
Skills Activity

The constitution of the Iroquois League was at first a spoken rather than a written document. The excerpt above describes how members of the Iroquois League were to begin a meeting.

(a) Apply Information What attitude toward nature does this selection reflect?

(b) Draw Conclusions Why do you think members of the Iroquois League wanted to begin each meeting with a set ritual?

Great Plains The Great Plains is a vast region stretching between the Mississippi River and the Rocky Mountains. The people of the eastern Plains lived mainly by farming. Women planted corn, beans, and squash in river valleys. Many people lived in earth lodges. These buildings had log frames and were covered with soil.

Much of the western Great Plains was too dry and too matted with grass to be farmed. The treeless land provided few building materials. In the west, some people lived in tepees made of animal skins. Other Plains people dug round pits near their fields for shelter.

Hunting parties followed buffalo across the plains. The Plains people depended on the buffalo for many things. They ate the meat and used the hides to make tepees, robes, and shields. Buffalo bones were made into tools.

Eastern Woodlands Hundreds of years ago, most of what is now the eastern United States was covered by forests of maples, birches, pines, and beeches. The earliest woodlands people lived by hunting, fishing, and foraging for nuts and berries. By about A.D. 1000, a number of woodlands people had taken up farming.

Two groups dominated the Eastern Woodlands. One group spoke Algonquian (al GOHN kee un) languages. The Algonquian people were scattered through southern Canada, the Great Lakes area, and along the Atlantic coast to Virginia. The other groups, speaking Iroquoian (IHR uh kwoy an) languages, lived in what is now New York.

Differentiated Instruction

L1 Less Proficient Readers

Create a Chart Have students create a two-column chart to organize information about Native American culture areas. Have them write the names of the seven culture areas in the left-hand column: *Far North, Northwest, Far West,* and so on. Then have them write facts about the ways of life of Native Americans in each area in the right-hand column. Students may use the chart as a study aid for reviewing material about Native American cultures.

The Iroquois were made up of five distinct nations. Each nation was made up of **clans**, or groups of families that were related to one another. Because membership in a clan was passed from a mother to her children, women had great influence in Iroquois society. They owned all the property that belonged to a clan. Women also chose the clan's **sachem**, or tribal chief.

During the 1500s, the five Iroquois nations went through a period of constant warfare. Finally, Iroquois leaders convinced their people to make peace. They formed a union called the League of the Iroquois. It established a council to make laws to keep the peace. Each tribe was still free to deal with its own affairs.

Southeast The climate in the Southeast was mild, but the summers were steamy and hot. The land and climate supported farming. People such as the Cherokees and Creeks built houses on wooden frames, covered with straw mats. They then plastered the houses with mud clay to keep the interiors cool and dry.

The Natchez people of the Gulf Coast created a complex society. At the top stood the ruler, called the Great Sun, and the nobles. At the bottom were commoners, known as Stinkards. By law, all nobles—including the Great Sun himself—had to marry Stinkards. In this way, membership in each class kept changing.

Cherokee mask

✓**Checkpoint** In what culture areas was hunting the main way of life?

⭐ **Looking Back and Ahead** In this section, you learned about Native American cultures. In the next sections, you will explore cultures that developed on the other side of the world.

Section 2 | Check Your Progress

Progress Monitoring Online
For: Self-test with instant help
Visit: PHSchool.com
Web Code: mva-1012

Comprehension and Critical Thinking
1. (a) Recall What role did nature play in many Native American religious beliefs?
(b) Draw Inferences How does that emphasis on nature reflect the everyday life of the people?

2. (a) Identify Identify two culture areas where farming was the main way of life.
(b) Analyze Cause and Effect Why do you think farming did not develop extensively in the Arctic and the subarctic regions?

Reading Skill
3. Apply Prior Knowledge Reread the first paragraph under the heading "Native Americans of North America." How is your culture group different from others? How is it the same? Use this knowledge to describe how Native American cultures were the same and different.

Key Terms
Fill in the blank in each question with a key term from this section.

4. The _____ of a people includes its customs, beliefs, and ways of making a living.
5. The _____ provided leadership in Iroquois communities.
6. Members of the same _____ shared a common ancestor.

Writing
7. Create a chart that shows how three different groups of Native Americans adapted to the regions in which they lived. Use the following column headings: Region, Way of Life, Diet, Shelter.

Section 2 Check Your Progress

1. (a) Native Americans believed that there were spirits in nature and these spirits played a part in their daily lives.
(b) Native Americans lived close to nature and used things from the environment to meet their needs.

2. (a) Eastern Woodlands and Southeast
(b) Some of the land in the Arctic was covered with ice all year long, and the climate in the subarctic was too cold for farming.

3. Answers will vary, but should include specific ways of life that make students' culture groups different from others, such as customs, food, music, and religious beliefs, and the observation that their culture group has the same basic needs for food, clothing, and shelter as other groups. Students should demonstrate an understanding that Native American cultures had the same basic needs and shared some general beliefs about nature but met their needs in different ways depending on the region in which they lived.

4. culture
5. sachem
6. clan
7. Students' charts should include specific details from the section about the regions, ways of life, diet, and shelter of different Native American peoples.

Assess and Reteach

Assess Progress [L2]
Have students complete Check Your Progress. Administer the Section Quiz.

All in One Teaching Resources, Unit 1, Section Quiz, p. 25

Reteach [L1]
If students need more instruction, have them read this section in the Interactive Reading and Notetaking Study Guide and complete the accompanying question.

Interactive Reading and Notetaking Study Guide, Chapter 1, Section 2 (Adapted Version also available.)

Extend [L3]
To extend the lesson, have students research and read songs, folk tales, or oral histories of two different Native American groups. You may wish to provide materials for classroom use. Tell students to look for examples of shared beliefs in the works. Suggest that students create a comparison-contrast chart to record notes. Then, have students share their findings and conclusions with the rest of the class.

Progress Monitoring Online
Students may check their comprehension of this section by completing the Progress Monitoring Online graphic organizer and self-quiz.

Answer
✓**Checkpoint** Far North

Review and Preview

Students have learned about Native American cultures in North America and their interaction through trade. Now they will learn about cultures on the continents of Europe, Africa, and Asia and how they were linked through trade.

Section Focus Question

How did trade link Europe, Africa, and Asia?

Before you begin the lesson for the day, write the Section Focus Question on the board. (*Lesson focus: Europeans, Africans, and Asians exchanged goods, ideas, and influences through trade.*)

Prepare to Read

Build Background Knowledge L2

On the board, write the word *goods*. Ask students to suggest specific goods that American consumers value highly. Record student responses on the board. Next, have students identify imported goods in the list on the board. Ask: **What countries do you know that produce these goods for American markets?** List the countries next to the corresponding product names. Then, have students categorize the countries by the continents on which they are located. Allow use of a map if necessary.

Set a Purpose L2

■ Form students into pairs or groups of four. Distribute the Reading Readiness Guide. Ask students to fill in the first two columns of the chart.

All in One Teaching Resources, Unit 1, Reading Readiness Guide, p. 18

■ Use the Numbered Heads participation strategy (TE, p. T24) to call on students to share one piece of information they already know and one piece of information they want to know. The students will return to these worksheets later.

The Wealth of Timbuktu

❝ The inhabitants are very rich. . . . Grain and animals are abundant, so that the consumption of milk and butter is considerable. But salt is in very short supply because it is carried here from Tegaza, some 500 miles from Timbuktu. . . . The royal court is magnificent and very well organized. . . . This king makes war only upon neighboring enemies and upon those who do not want to pay him tribute. ❞

—Hassan ibn Muhammad, *The Description of Africa*, 1526

◀ City of Timbuktu in West Africa

Trade Networks of Asia and Africa

Objectives

• Learn about the role played by Muslims in world trade.

• Discover how great trading states rose in East Africa and West Africa.

• Find out how China dominated an important trade route across Asia.

Reading Skill

Ask Questions Asking questions when you read will help you organize your reading plan and get involved with the text. You can use your questions, for example, to set a reading purpose— answering the questions. Two ways to generate questions are to restate headings and to study the review questions at the end of the section.

Key Terms and People

Muhammad
Mansa Musa
navigation
Zheng He

Why It Matters While Native Americans were developing diverse cultures and civilizations, other civilizations thrived in Europe, Africa, and Asia.

❓ Section Focus Question: How did trade link Europe, Africa, and Asia?

The Muslim Link in Trade

From earliest times, trade linked groups who lived at great distances from one another. As trade developed, merchants established regular trade routes. These merchants carried their culture with them as they traveled.

By the 1500s, a complex trade network linked Europe, Africa, and Asia. Much of this trade passed through the Arabian Peninsula in the Middle East. Ships from China and India brought their cargoes of spices, silks, and gems to ports on the Red Sea. The precious cargoes were then taken overland to markets throughout the Middle East.

Rise of Islam The growth in trade was also linked to the rise of the religion of Islam. Islam emerged on the Arabian Peninsula in the 600s. Its founder was the prophet Muhammad. Muhammad taught that there is one true God. Followers of Islam, called Muslims, believed that the Quran (ku RAHN), the sacred book of Islam, contained the exact word of God as revealed to Muhammad.

Islam was transmitted rapidly through conquest and trade. Arab armies swept across North Africa and into Spain. Muslim merchants also spread their religion far into Africa, and from Persia to India. Millions of people across three continents became Muslims.

16 Chapter 1 Roots of the American People

Differentiated Instruction

L1 English Language Learners   **L1 Less Proficient Readers**   **L1 Special Needs**

Restate with Synonyms Unfamiliar words pose recurring difficulties for some students. Restating sentences and substituting familiar synonyms can aid comprehension. Pair students and provide the partners with a thesaurus. Tell each partner to read a subsection silently. They should pause after each paragraph and

together make a list of any unfamiliar words (excluding specialized vocabulary). Together, partners can look up each word in the thesaurus and find a familiar synonym. Then, they can substitute synonyms for unfamiliar words and reread the paragraph.

Advances in Learning Arab scholars made remarkable contributions to mathematics, medicine, and astronomy. They helped develop algebra and later passed it along to Europe. Arab astronomers measured the size of Earth, supporting the Greek belief that Earth was a <u>sphere</u>. Arabs also made important advances in technology. They built ships with large, triangular sails that allowed captains to use the wind even if it changed direction.

☑Checkpoint How did Islam spread?

The African Link in Trade

Africa has a long history of trade, going back as far as 3100 B.C., when the great civilization of Egypt arose. Egyptian traders sailed throughout the eastern Mediterranean Sea and the Red Sea to bring home cedar logs, silver, and horses. Following routes south from Egypt, they traded for ivory, spices, copper, and cattle.

East African Trade Centers About A.D. 1000, trade centers began to appear in eastern Africa. The most powerful was Zimbabwe (zim BAH bway), which became the center of a flourishing empire in the 1400s. Zimbabwe lay on the trade route between the east coast and the interior of Africa. Traders passing through Zimbabwe had to pay taxes on their goods.

Trade brought prosperity to a number of cities along the east coast of Africa. Kilwa, the chief trading center, attracted merchant ships from as far away as China. Kilwa traders did a brisk trade with the African interior, exchanging cloth, pottery, and manufactured goods for gold, ivory, and furs. An active slave trade also developed between East Africa and Asia across the Indian Ocean.

Vocabulary Builder
<u>sphere</u> (sfeer) *n.* rounded shape

 Ask Questions
Preview the headings on the next two pages. Turn them into questions that you would expect to find the answers to as you read.

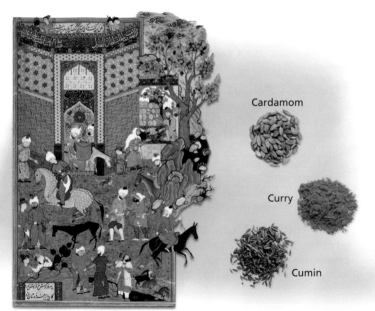

Cardamom

Curry

Cumin

Merchants in the Middle East

At outdoor bazaars, Muslim merchants bought and sold goods from around the world. Probably the most valuable goods sold at this Persian bazaar were spices from Southeast Asia, such as the ones shown here. **Critical Thinking:** *Link Past and Present How is this bazaar similar to a modern shopping area? How is it different?*

Instruction L2

- **Vocabulary Builder** Before teaching this section, preteach the High-Use Words **sphere** and **alternative** before reading, using the strategy on TE p. T21. **Key Terms** Have students continue filling in the See It–Remember It chart for the Key Terms in this chapter.

- Have students read The Muslim Link and The African Link using the Paragraph Shrinking strategy (TE, p. T23).

- Ask: **What does it mean to say that merchants "carried their culture with them as they traveled"?** (*The languages used by merchants, their customs and religious beliefs, their ideas in areas such as art and science were part of their cultures.*)

- Ask: **How did the trade network linking the Middle East and West Africa benefit people in both regions?** (*people in the Middle East wanted gold from West Africa, and people in West Africa needed salt from the desert.*)

Independent Practice

Have students begin to fill in the Study Guide for this section.

📖 **Interactive Reading and Notetaking Study Guide,** Chapter 1, Section 3 (Adapted Version also available.)

Monitor Progress

As students fill in the Notetaking Study Guide, circulate to make sure they understand the trade networks of Africa and Asia. Provide assistance as needed.

Answers

☑Checkpoint through conquest and trade

⟳ Reading Skill Responses should be questions about the headings.

Link Past and Present Possible responses: It is similar to a modern shopping area because it is full of buyers and sellers doing business; it is different because sellers don't have their own shops, and people are riding animals.

Vocabulary Builder

Use the information below to teach students this section's high-use words.

High-Use Word	Definition and Sample Sentence
sphere, p. 17	*n.* rounded shape Some early people believed Earth was flat rather than shaped like a **sphere**.
alternative, p. 19	*adj.* providing a choice between two or among more than two things When large animals began to disappear in ancient times, humans needed to find **alternative** food supplies.

The East Asian Link in Trade

p. 18

Instruction L2

- Have students read The East Asian Link. Remind them to look for details to answer the Section Focus Question.

- Ask: **What are two reasons for China's domination of trade routes between East Asia and the Middle East?** (*Chinese advances in navigation such as the magnetic compass and the link provided by the Silk Road help explain Chinese domination of trade routes between East Asia and the Middle East.*)

- Ask: **What Chinese goods did people in Europe and the Middle East value?** (*silk, pottery, bronze goods*) **What goods did the Chinese want to obtain through trade?** (*spices, gems, medicinal herbs, ivory*)

- Assign the worksheet Marco Polo to explore the development of Europe's interest in trading with China.

  All in One Teaching Resources, Unit 1, Marco Polo, p. 21

Independent Practice

Have students complete the Study Guide for this section.

Interactive Reading and Notetaking Study Guide, Chapter 1, Section 3 (Adapted Version also available.)

Monitor Progress

- As students fill in the Notetaking Study Guide, circulate to make sure they understand China's importance as a world trader. Provide assistance as needed.

- Tell students to fill in the last column of the Reading Readiness guide. Ask them to evaluate if what they learned was what they had expected to learn.

  All in One Teaching Resources, Unit 1, Reading Readiness Guide, p. 18

Answers

Biography Quest Mansa Musa's hajj weakened the Egyptian economy by flooding it with gold, which caused the money to decrease in value.

Checkpoint Ghana, Mali, Songhai

Biography Quest

Mansa Musa
1280?–1337

Every Muslim must make a *hajj*, or pilgrimage, to the holy city of Mecca. Mansa Musa's hajj became famous. His escort included 80 camels, each carrying 300 pounds of gold. Thousands of servants and officials accompanied the emperor across the Sahara.

Word of the emperor's hajj reached Europe. A Portuguese mapmaker described Mansa Musa as "the richest and most noble king in all the land."

Biography Quest Online

How did Mansa Musa's hajj affect the Egyptian economy?

For: The answer to the question about Mansa Musa

Visit: PHSchool.com

Web Code: mvd-1013

West African Trade Centers Trade networks also linked the Middle East and West Africa. Desert nomads guided caravans, or groups of camels and their cargo, across the vast Sahara, the largest desert in the world.

Ghana was the first major center of trade in West Africa. The kingdom was located between the sources of salt in the desert and the gold fields farther south. By the ninth century, the demand for gold had grown in the Middle East. On the other hand, people in West Africa needed salt in their diet to prevent dehydration in the hot tropical climate. As the trade in gold and salt increased, the rulers of Ghana became rich.

Shifting trade routes and disruptions caused by war gradually led Ghana to weaken. In the 1200s, the kingdom was absorbed into the empire of Mali. Mali reached its height under the Muslim ruler Mansa Musa. As Mali prospered, its great city of Timbuktu became a center of learning. Merchants from Mali traded throughout the region for kola nuts, food, and, of course, gold.

In the 1400s, Mali had a number of weak rulers. When nomads captured Timbuktu in 1433, the empire had been in decline for some time. It would soon be replaced by Songhai.

The rulers of Songhai captured Timbuktu in 1468. Songhai rulers restored the city as a center of Islamic learning. Trade across the Sahara expanded, which brought wealth to the Songhai Empire. Salt, gold, and captives for sale as slaves passed through Songhai on the way to Muslim markets in the north.

Checkpoint What trading kingdoms arose in West Africa?

The East Asian Link in Trade

As early as 221 B.C., a strong ruler had unified China into a single empire. Later rulers added to the empire until it covered a large part of the continent of Asia. Highways, canals, and a postal system linked China together.

As China's empire expanded, so did its trade. China established trade links with India, Korea, Japan, the Middle East, and Africa. China's trade centers grew into cities. By the 1200s, Hangzhou (HAN JOW) was one of the world's largest cities.

World Traders China had a higher level of technology than any other civilization of the time. Around 1050, the Chinese invented printing with movable type. This was about 400 years before this technology was developed in Europe.

Differentiated Instruction

L3 Advanced Readers

Research an Oral Report Have students research the development of the magnetic compass by the Chinese and its impact on navigation. Students should relate when the compass was invented and used by the Chinese, and when it passed to other cultures. Have students report their findings to the class.

L3 Gifted and Talented

Make a Diagram and Model Challenge students to explain how the magnetic compass worked and why it was a navigational break-through. Students should diagram the parts of the compass and indicate their functions. If possible, provide materials to make a working compass. Have students share their work with the class.

The Chinese made great advances in navigation. **Navigation** is the science of locating the position and plotting the course of ships. The Chinese invented the magnetic compass, which made it possible for ships to sail out of sight of land and still find their way home.

By the 1300s Chinese ships were sailing trade routes that stretched from Japan to East Africa. The Chinese explorer Zheng He made several voyages with a fleet of more than 300 giant ships. The fleet visited 30 nations throughout Asia and Africa, trading silks and pottery for spices, gems, medicinal herbs, and ivory.

Spice Trade and the Silk Road Chinese silks, bronze goods, pottery, and spices flowed west from China along a route known as the Silk Road. The Silk Road was one of the great trade routes of ancient times. It was not really a single road but a series of routes that stretched about 5,000 miles from Xi'an (SHE AHN) in China to Persia.

Merchants on the Silk Road brought silk and other goods from China across Asia for sale in Middle Eastern and European markets. Along the way they traded in the Middle East for products like cloves, nutmeg, and peppercorns from the Spice Islands in Southeast Asia. The Silk Road declined in importance when <u>alternative</u> sea routes were discovered.

This Chinese figurine is made of jade, a precious trade item.

Vocabulary Builder
<u>alternative</u> (awl TUR nuh tiv) *adj.* providing a choice between two or among more than two things

✓**Checkpoint** What was the Silk Road?

⭐ **Looking Back and Ahead** The trade links between Asia and Africa developed at a time when much of Europe was isolated. In the next section, you will learn about the development of Europe. You will also see how Europe began to look toward the riches of Asia.

Section 3 | Check Your Progress

Progress Monitoring Online
For: Self-test with instant help
Visit: PHSchool.com
Web Code: mva-1013

Comprehension and Critical Thinking

1. (a) Recall What role did the Muslim world play in trade?
(b) Interpret Maps Locate the Arabian Peninsula on a world map. Why was its location ideal for a trading center?

2. (a) Recall Why were gold and salt important in West African trade?
(b) Contrast How did trade in East Africa differ from trade in West Africa?

Reading Skill

3. Ask Questions Look at the questions you asked, and look at the section review questions. Did the reading answer those questions? How did previewing help you set purposes and increase your understanding?

Key Terms

4. Write two definitions for the key term navigation—one a formal definition for a teacher, the other an informal definition for a younger child.

Writing

5. Consider the following thesis statement: The trading network between Asia, Africa, and Europe began a useful exchange of ideas and products. Write one or two paragraphs to develop that thesis.

Section 3 Check Your Progress

1. (a) The Muslim world linked traders in Africa, Asia, and Europe.
(b) The Arabian Peninsula is in the Middle East, between Europe, Asia, and Africa; it was a crossroads for traders from all three continents.

2. (a) People in West Africa needed salt in their diet to protect against dehydration; gold was in demand in the Middle East; salt from the desert to the north was traded for gold from gold fields to the south of West African kingdoms such as Ghana.
(b) Trade in East Africa was with Asia across the Indian Ocean and with the African interior; trade in West Africa was with Muslim markets in the north and Middle East.

3. Answers will vary, but should demonstrate an understanding that previewing and then setting a purpose for reading by asking questions increase comprehension.

Assess and Reteach

Assess Progress ⬛L2

Have students complete Check Your Progress. Administer the Section Quiz.

⬛ **Teaching Resources,** Section Quiz, p. 26

To further assess student understanding, use the Progress Monitoring Transparency.

Progress Monitoring Transparencies, Chapter 1, Section 3

Reteach ⬛L1

If students need more instruction, have them read this section in the Interactive Reading and Notetaking Study Guide and complete the accompanying question.

📖 **Interactive Reading and Notetaking Study Guide,** Chapter 1, Section 3 (Adapted Version also available.)

Extend ⬛L3

To extend the lesson, have students use the Internet to learn more about the expeditions of Zheng He and their effect on trade. Students should use their research to prepare a script for a TV news report. Provide students with the Web Code below.

Extend Online
For: Help in starting the Extend activity
Visit: www.PHSchool.com
Web Code: mve-0108

Progress Monitoring Online

Students may check their comprehension of this section by completing the Progress Monitoring Online graphic organizer and self-quiz.

Answer

✓**Checkpoint** a series of trade routes stretching about 5,000 miles from China to Persia

4. Possible responses: Navigation is the science of locating the position and planning the course of ships; navigation is the way ships figure out how they will get where they want to go.

5. Students should support the thesis statement by citing specific details from the text that illustrate how the trading network began an exchange of ideas and influences.

Global Trade in the Fifteenth Century

Build Background Knowledge [L2]

Draw a large circle on the board to represent the globe. Around its circumference write Europe, Africa, and Asia and connect these labels with arrows pointing in both directions. Have students volunteer facts they learned in Section 3 about the trade network that linked the three continents. Use the Idea Wave strategy (TE p. T24) to elicit responses. Write students' ideas inside the circle.

Instruction [L2]

- Show the **History Interactive Transparency Global Trade in the Fifteenth Century.** Read the text and examine the map with students. On the map have students point to the names of the continents that were part of the global trading network, trace the trade routes that linked the continents, and identify the items traded and the bodies of water traders crossed.

Color Transparencies, Global Trade in the Fifteenth Century

- Ask: **Why weren't the Americas part of the global trading network of the fifteenth century?** (*People in fifteenth century Europe, Africa, and Asia did not know that the continents of North and South America existed.*)

- Have students locate the Silk Road on the map. Observe that the Silk Road was actually a network of roads, as shown on the map. Ask: **What places did the Silk Road connect?** (*China and Persia*)

- Direct students' attention to the other visuals. Ask: **What continent or continents were sources of the trade goods shown?** (*Spice from Asia, others from Africa*) **What goods were traded for these goods?** (*Salt and gold were traded for each other; ivory was probably traded for spices, silk, and other goods from Asia.*)

Global Trade in the Fifteenth Century

For centuries, merchants and traders used land and sea routes to travel between Europe, Africa, and Asia. Before the first European voyages to the Americas, a global trading network linked the major civilizations of three continents. Gold and salt moved east from Africa while silk and spices moved west from China and India. Use the map below to trace the patterns of global trade.

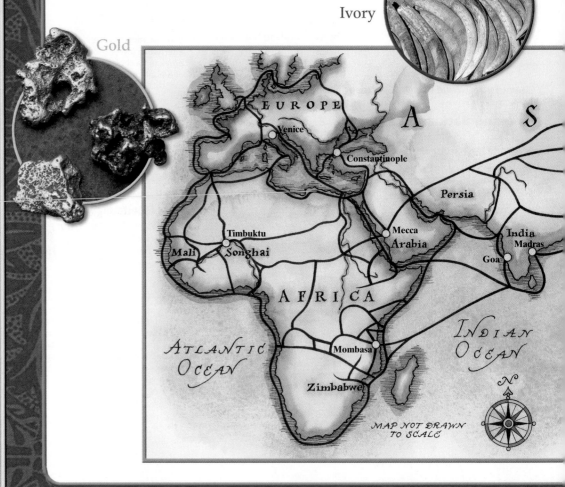

Differentiated Instruction

L1 English Language Learners

Understanding Global Trade To help students understand the development of global trade networks, ask them to think of items from other countries that may be difficult to find in the United States. Suggest that students consider foods and items of clothing that usually are not found in markets or stores here. Have students compile a list of these items. Then, ask: **What are these items used for? How might they be helpful to people in this country?** Have students share their responses with the class.

Gold, Salt, and Ivory

Trade centers in East and West Africa saw heavy traffic in gold, salt, and ivory. African gold was highly valued in the Middle East.

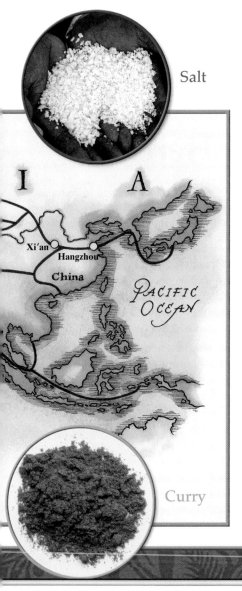

Salt

I   A

Xi'an
Hangzhou
China

PACIFIC OCEAN

Curry

Understand Effects:
The Network Expands

When Christopher Columbus sailed west from Spain in 1492, he opened up a new era in global trade. Prior to Columbus's voyage, the Americas were isolated from the flow of goods and ideas that connected Europe, Africa, and Asia. After 1492, the old trade networks expanded across an ocean to a new world of resources.

▲ Trade flourished throughout Asia. Ships from China and India unloaded their cargoes in Arabian ports for overland transport to African or European markets.

Analyze GEOGRAPHY AND HISTORY

Worldwide trade allowed for the exchange of goods and ideas across continents. Write a paragraph describing how West African gold might travel to China.

Geography and History **21**

Independent Practice

To help students expand their understanding of global trade in the fifteenth century, have them complete the History Interactive activity online.

Extend ●nline
For: Help with the History Interactive
Visit: PHSchool.com
Web Code: mvp-0109

Monitor Progress

Ask students to complete the Analyze Geography and History activity. Circulate to make sure individuals understand trade networks in the fifteenth century. Provide assistance as needed.

Writing Rubrics Share this rubric with students.

Score 1 Ideas unclear, organization poor.
Score 2 Paragraph has few details in support of its conclusion about trade between Africa and Asia, fails to explain clearly the role of the Middle East in such trade.
Score 3 Paragraph accurately explains the transit of West African gold to China, identifies the role of the Middle East in the trade between Africa and China.
Score 4 Paragraph is comprehensive and detailed with clear organization and supporting arguments, shows creativity.

History Background

Camel Caravans Merchant caravans in the 1400s traveled great distances in all kinds of weather over rough ground. Fresh supplies of food and water were not always available. The camel was a valuable business asset in these conditions. It was uniquely suited to travel on the trade routes of Asia and Africa. The camel's wide, soft feet enabled it to travel through sand or snow; its double rows of eyelashes, its ear hair, and its nostrils that closed protected its sensory organs from wind-blown objects; its hump stored fat; and its coat provided warmth in the winter.

Answer

Analyze **GEOGRAPHY AND HISTORY**

Paragraph should demonstrate an understanding of the importance of the Middle East in trade among Asia, Africa, and Europe.

Review and Preview

Students have learned how trade influenced the civilizations of Africa and Asia. Now they will read about the development of civilization in Europe.

Section Focus Question

What major influences shaped European civilization?

Before you begin the lesson for the day, write the Section Focus Question on the board. (*Lesson focus: Judeo-Christian traditions and Greek and Roman ideas influenced European civilization; the Crusades and Renaissance led Europe to look beyond its borders.*)

Prepare to Read

Build Background Knowledge **L2**

Direct students' attention to the section title The European Heritage. Explore the concept of heritage with students. Ask: **What is our American heritage?** Then use the Idea Wave participation strategy (TE, p. T24) to encourage students to brainstorm aspects of our common heritage as Americans. Record students' ideas on the board.

Set a Purpose **L2**

■ Read each statement in the Reading Readiness Guide aloud. Ask students to mark the statements as True or False.

All in One Teaching Resources, Unit 1, Reading Readiness Guide, p. 19

■ Have students discuss the statements in pairs or groups of four, then mark their worksheets again. Use the Numbered Heads participation strategy (TE, p. T24) to call on students to share their group's perspectives. The students will return to these worksheets later.

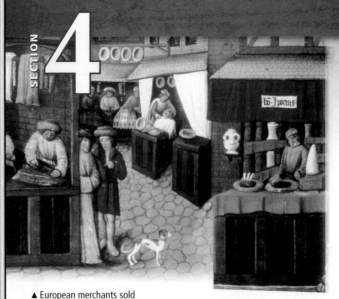

▲ European merchants sold goods from Africa and Asia.

Cinnamon, Pearls, and Gold

❝ [I] landed and showed them a variety of merchandise, with the view of finding out whether such things were to be found in their country. This merchandise included cinnamon, cloves, seepearls, gold, and many other things, but it was evident that they had no knowledge whatever of such articles. ❞

—Vasco de Gama, *Round Africa to India*, 1497–1498

The European Heritage

Objectives

- Understand the importance of the Judeo-Christian tradition.
- Learn how Greece and Rome shaped ideas about government and law.
- Discover the impact of the Crusades and the Renaissance on Europe.
- Find out why Europeans began to look beyond their borders.

🔍 Reading Skill

Use Graphics to Construct Meaning

Textbooks include information beyond the main text that can be useful to your understanding. Nontext material includes maps, charts, and photos. These materials often have accompanying text such as captions or titles. Use this material to gain understanding as you read.

Key Terms and People

monotheism	feudalism
Jesus	Martin Luther
salvation	Henry the
direct democracy	Navigator
republic	Vasco da Gama

Why It Matters Through migration and trade, Europeans, Africans, and Asians exchanged goods, inventions, and ideas.

❓ **Section Focus Question: What major influences shaped European civilization?**

The Judeo-Christian Tradition

European beliefs and values were shaped by two religions of the ancient Middle East: Judaism and Christianity. The influence of these two religions is known as the Judeo-Christian tradition.

Judaism Around 1700 B.C. a system of beliefs called Judaism arose among the Israelites, a nomadic people of the Middle East. Judaism was the first major world religion to teach monotheism, the idea that there is only one God.

The Israelites credited Moses with bringing God's laws to them. Those laws included the Ten Commandments, a set of religious and moral rules. Jews believed that every Jew must obey the Ten Commandments and other religious and moral laws.

Other early religions regarded rulers as gods. Judaism held that even the most powerful ruler had to obey God's laws. This belief formed the basis for the later view that no person, no matter how powerful or wealthy, is above the law.

22 Chapter 1 Roots of the American People

Differentiated Instruction

L1 English Language Learners **L1 Special Needs**

Vocabulary Development Have students make a list of Key Terms and High-Use Words and their definitions. Then have them create flashcards with the word on one side and its definition on the other. Pair students and have partners quiz each other on the definitions of the words using the flash cards.

Christianity About 2,000 years ago, a Jewish teacher named Jesus of Nazareth began to preach in the region around the Sea of Galilee. Jesus attracted a following. Many believed that he was the Messiah, the Savior chosen by God.

The Gospels, which recount the life of Jesus, tell how crowds flocked to hear Jesus teach and perform miracles. Local officials, however, saw Jesus as a political threat. The Roman rulers of Jerusalem arrested, tried, and crucified Jesus. Followers of Jesus said that he rose from the dead three days later.

The life and teachings of Jesus inspired a new religion, Christianity. Christianity is based on the belief that Jesus was indeed the Messiah, sent by God to save the world. Christians teach that Jesus was, in fact, God in human form.

The teachings of Jesus emphasized love, mercy, and forgiveness. Jesus also taught that all people have an equal chance for salvation, or everlasting life. These beliefs appealed to many people, especially the poor and oppressed. This helped Christianity spread from the Middle East across Europe.

As Christianity spread, the Romans at first viewed it as a threat. Christians were subject to arrest and death. Later, emperors accepted Christianity and made it the official religion of the Roman Empire. As a result, it eventually became the dominant religion of all of Europe.

☑**Checkpoint** What does Christianity teach about Jesus?

The Ten Commandments

❝[I.] I am the Lord your God, who brought you out of the land of Egypt, out of the house of bondage. You shall have no other gods before me. . . .
[III.] You shall not take the name of the Lord your God in vain; . . .
[V.] Honor your father and your mother, that your days may be long in the land which the Lord your God gives you.
[VI.] You shall not kill. . . .
[VIII.] You shall not steal.❞

—Book of Exodus, Revised Standard Version

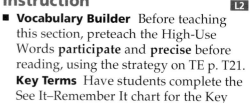

Painting showing Moses with the Ten Commandments

Reading Primary Sources
Skills Activity

According to the Bible, God gave the Ten Commandments to the Hebrew leader Moses. Five of the Commandments are given above.

(a) Apply Information How does this selection reflect the Judeo-Christian idea of monotheism?

(b) Draw Conclusions How do the Ten Commandments say we should treat other people?

Section 4 The European Heritage **23**

Vocabulary Builder

Use the information below to teach students this section's high-use words.

High-Use Word	Definition and Sample Sentence
participate, p. 24	*v.* to take part in Adult American citizens have the right to **participate** in elections.
precise, p. 27	*adj.* exact; accurate Early settlers were able to create **precise** calendars based on the sun.

Use Graphics to Construct Meaning
Preview the pictures in this section. What do they suggest to you about the content of the text?

Teach

The Judeo-Christian Tradition

p. 22

Instruction   L2

- **Vocabulary Builder** Before teaching this section, preteach the High-Use Words **participate** and **precise** before reading, using the strategy on TE p. T21. **Key Terms** Have students complete the See It–Remember It chart for the Key Terms in this chapter.

- Have students read The Judeo-Christian Tradition using the Oral Cloze strategy (TE, p. T22).

- Ask: **What is the connection between Judaism and Christianity?** (*Jesus, whose life and teachings inspired Christianity, was Jewish; Christianity embraced many Jewish beliefs.*)

Independent Practice

Have students begin to fill in the Study Guide for this section.

📖 **Interactive Reading and Notetaking Study Guide,** Chapter 1, Section 4 (Adapted Version also available.)

Monitor Progress

As students fill in the Notetaking Study Guide, circulate to make sure they understand how Judaism and Christianity were connected and came to influence Europeans. Provide assistance as needed.

Answers

Reading Skill Possible response: The pictures suggest that the text is going to make a link between past and present.

☑**Checkpoint** Christianity teaches that Jesus is the Messiah, the Savior, God in human form.

Reading Primary Sources **(a)** The speaker identifies himself as "the Lord your God" and says that people will have no other gods. **(b)** Possible response: The Ten Commandments say we should treat others with respect and kindness.

Greek and Roman Traditions

p. 24

Instruction
L2

- Have students read Greek and Roman Traditions. Remind them to look for details to answer the Section Focus Question.

- Have students contrast Athenian and Roman ideas about democratic government. (*Athenian democracy was a direct democracy in which an assembly of ordinary citizens made decisions. In the Roman republic, people chose representatives to govern.*)

- Discuss with students the connection between education and democracy. Ask: **Why is education important in a democracy?** (*Possible answer: Citizens in a democracy are responsible for the outcomes of government and need to be knowledgeable and informed so that they can analyze problems and make decisions.*)

Independent Practice

Have students continue filling in the Study Guide for this section.

 Interactive Reading and Notetaking Study Guide, Chapter 1, Section 4 (Adapted Version also available.)

Monitor Progress

As students fill in the Notetaking Study Guide, circulate to make sure they understand the contributions of Greek and Roman traditions to the European heritage. Provide assistance as needed.

Greek and Roman Traditions

Judaism and Christianity shaped European religious and moral thinking. At the same time, the ancient civilizations of Greece and Rome shaped European political traditions. Greek and Roman ideas would later deeply influence the Founders of the United States.

Athenian Democracy In the fifth century B.C., the Greek city-state of Athens experienced a sudden explosion of learning and creativity. Perhaps its most remarkable achievement was the birth of democracy.

Athens was a direct democracy. Direct democracy is a form of government in which an assembly of ordinary citizens makes decisions. This differs from the modern American form of government, in which citizens elect representatives to make laws. Any adult male citizen could <u>participate</u> in the Athenian Assembly. The Athenian leader Pericles described the Athenian idea of democracy:

> **❝**Our constitution is named a democracy, because it is in the hands not of the few but of the many. . . . We decide or debate, carefully and in person, all matters of policy.**❞**
> —Pericles, from *The History of the Peloponnesian War* (Thucydides)

Still, Athenian democracy had limitations. Women, slaves, and foreign-born people could not participate in government.

Athenians believed that a democracy depended on well-rounded, educated citizens. In Athenian schools, boys studied many areas of knowledge, from history and grammar to poetry and music. Because Athenian citizens were expected to voice their opinions in the Assembly, schools also trained students in public speaking.

Roman Government and Law While democracy was developing in ancient Greece, a few small villages in central Italy were growing into the city of Rome. Over time, the Romans developed new traditions in law and government.

Vocabulary Builder
<u>participate</u> (pahr TIHS uh payt)
v. to take part

Education in Athens
This Greek vase painting shows an Athenian school. At the center, a teacher checks a student's writing tablet. **Critical Thinking: Interpret Art** *Identify one other subject that the students at this school are learning.*

24

L1 Less Proficient Readers   **L1 Special Needs**

Reading Aids Suggest to students that they use a ruler to help them keep their place as they read, line to line, down a page of text. Have students mark unfamiliar words or phrases (such as *code of laws*) with sticky notes. Periodically check students' progress and help them understand vocabulary they have marked as well as difficult passages.

Answer
Interpret Art Music is depicted.

Links Across Time

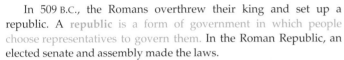

Republican Government

509 B.C. The Roman Republic was established. The elected Senate became the chief governing and law-making body of Rome.

1787 The Founders of the United States admired the Roman Republic. When they wrote the Constitution, they gave lawmaking power to an elected Congress similar to the Roman Senate. But they divided Congress into two separate houses, the Senate and the House of Representatives.

Link to Today Online

Congress Today Today, as in the past, the men and women of Congress make laws that affect the lives of all Americans.

For: Congress in the news
Visit: PHSchool.com
Web Code: mvc-1014

> **2004** Congress gathers to hear the President speak.

In 509 B.C., the Romans overthrew their king and set up a republic. A **republic** is a form of government in which people choose representatives to govern them. In the Roman Republic, an elected senate and assembly made the laws.

Rome's code of laws defined the rights of citizens. According to the code, everybody was equal under the law. People accused of crimes were considered innocent until proven guilty. These principles form the framework of the American system of justice.

Long years of civil war led to the collapse of the Roman republic. In 27 B.C., a noble named Octavian declared himself emperor. The Roman Empire would last for almost 500 years. During this time, Roman ideas about law and government spread over a wide area.

✓**Checkpoint** **How did citizens participate in Greek and Roman government?**

New Horizons

After a period of decline, the Roman Empire fell to invaders in A.D. 476. Europe fragmented into many small states. The 1,000-year period after the fall of Rome is known as the Middle Ages.

The Middle Ages By the ninth century, feudalism had arisen in Europe. **Feudalism** is a system in which a ruler grants parts of his land to lords. In exchange, lords owed the king military service and financial assistance. In turn, lords granted land to lesser lords.

Section 4 The European Heritage **25**

New Horizons
p. 25

Instruction

- Have students read New Horizons. Remind them to look for causes and effects.

- Discuss with students the causes and effects of the Crusades. See that students understand that many events have unintended effects. (*Europeans left their homes to fight in the Crusades. Europeans failed to win control of the Holy Land but the Crusades helped them look beyond their own world: they came into closer contact with the more advanced Muslim civilization; they learned about technology that could be used for navigation.*)

- Display the transparency to explore connections among religion, trade, and exploration.

Color Transparencies, Religion, Trade, and Exploration

- Ask: **What ideas and advances influenced European thought and learning during the Renaissance?** (*ideas from ancient Greece and Rome; advances in science; inventions, such as the printing press*)

Independent Practice

Have students continue filling in the Study Guide for this section.

📖 **Interactive Reading and Notetaking Study Guide,** Chapter 1, Section 4 (Adapted Version also available.)

Monitor Progress

As students fill in the Notetaking Study Guide, circulate to make sure they understand the changing European view of the world from the Crusades through the Renaissance. Provide assistance as needed.

History Background

Direct Democracy Direct democracy survives in the United States in the centuries-old institution of the New England town meeting. Town voters gather to consider town and school budgets and to discuss issues affecting the town. Many towns in New England have found that the demands of modern life have resulted in declining attendance at town meetings. Yet town meetings have kept pace with contemporary times, with attendees discussing such issues as genetically engineered food and nuclear power. In Vermont, the first Tuesday in March is Town Meeting Day, as it has been for centuries.

Answer

✓**Checkpoint** Any adult male citizen could take part in government in Athens by making decisions in their Assembly; Romans took part in government by electing representatives in the senate.

An Age of Exploration Begins

p. 27

Instruction   L2

- Have students read An Age of Exploration Begins. Remind them to look for details that answer the Section Focus Question.

- Ask: **Why was Portuguese prince Henry called Henry the Navigator?** (*He set up a center for exploration at Sagres where crews could learn about navigation and mapmaking.*)

- Ask: **Why did Portuguese sailors sail south along the coast of West Africa?** (*They were looking for a direct sea route to Asia so they could bypass other merchants and increase their profits from the spice trade.*)

Independent Practice

Have students complete the Study Guide for this section.

Interactive Reading and Notetaking Study Guide, Chapter 1, Section 4 (Adapted Version also available.)

Monitor Progress

- As students fill in the Notetaking Study Guide, circulate to make sure they understand Portugal's early domination of the age of exploration. Provide assistance as needed.

- Tell students to fill in the last column of the Reading Readiness Guide. Probe for what they learned that confirms or invalidates each statement.

- Have students go back to their Word Knowledge Raiting Form. Rerate their word knowledge and complete the last column with a definition or example.

All in One Teaching Resources, Unit 1, Reading Readiness Guide, p. 19; Word Knowledge Rating Form, p. 15

Answers

Make Predictions As books became more widely available, more people would learn to read and would become educated, and learning would spread.

✓**Checkpoint** a rebirth of learning in Europe that began in the 1300s

Copying a Manuscript
In Europe during the Middle Ages, learning was in the hands of the Church. Monks like this one spent hours and hours each day carefully copying books by hand. **Critical Thinking:** *Make Predictions How might the invention of mechanical printing affect learning in Europe?*

The Roman Catholic Church had great power in the Middle Ages. Daily life revolved around the rituals of the Catholic Church. The Catholic Church was also the center of learning. Outside of members of the clergy, few people, even among the nobility, were able to read and write.

The Crusades In 1095, the leader of the Roman Catholic Church, Pope Urban II, declared a crusade, or holy war. Its object was to win back control of the region known as the Holy Land, the land where Jesus had lived and taught. There were nine crusades over the next 200 years. In the end, they failed to win permanent control of the Holy Land.

Still, the Crusades had important long-term effects. They put Europeans in closer contact with the more advanced Muslim civilization. Europeans were attracted by the rich goods they saw in the Holy Land. They tasted strange foods and spices, such as oranges, pepper, and ginger. They also learned about advanced technology used for navigation. In time, the Crusades would help inspire Europeans to look overseas for trade.

The Renaissance Beginning in the 1300s, there was a rebirth of learning that is known as the Renaissance. European scholars rediscovered the classical texts of ancient Greece and Rome. Artists reflected a new interest in subjects that had influenced ancient thinkers.

Science and invention flourished. One invention, in particular, had a great impact on society. In the mid-fifteenth century, Johann Gutenberg invented a printing press. Using movable type, the printing press enabled a printer to produce a large number of identical books in a short time. As books became more available, the ability to read became more widespread.

During the late Middle Ages, powerful nation-states emerged in Europe. Italian cities had long controlled trade on the Mediterranean. The new nations—Spain, Portugal, France, and England—would shift the important trade routes to the Atlantic Ocean.

The Reformation Since the late Roman Empire, most Europeans had belonged to the Roman Catholic Church. Not all were happy with Catholicism, however. In 1517, a German monk named Martin Luther demanded that the Roman Catholic Church reform.

When his demands were rejected, Luther rebelled against the Catholic Church authority. Followers of Luther were called Protestants, because they were protesting certain Catholic Church practices. The movement Luther led is called the Protestant Reformation. Over time, Luther's movement split, and many Protestant churches emerged. The Reformation also plunged Europe into a long series of wars between Catholic and Protestant forces.

✓**Checkpoint** What was the Renaissance?

Differentiated Instruction

L1 English Language Learners   **L1 Less Proficient Readers**   **L1 Special Needs**

Create an Annotated Timeline Have students work in groups to create annotated timelines that present the information in the subsections New Horizons and An Age of Exploration Begins. Tell students to plot events and their dates in chronological order on a timeline spanning the time frame 400–1600. For each event, students should write a note that briefly describes the significance of the event in the development of European civilization. Post the timeline so the whole class can use it as a study aid.

An Age of Exploration Begins

The Renaissance, the rise of nations, and the expansion of trade set the stage for an era of exploration. The person who provided the leadership for this new era was a brother of the king of Portugal, known to history as Prince Henry the Navigator. A deeply religious man, Henry hoped not only to expand Portuguese power but also to spread Christianity to new lands.

In the 1400s, Henry set up a center for exploration at Sagres (SAH greesh) in southern Portugal. He brought mathematicians, geographers, and sea captains to this center to teach his crews everything they needed to know about navigation and mapmaking.

At Sagres, sailors learned how to use the magnetic compass to find their direction at sea. They also learned how to use an instrument called the astrolabe to determine their <u>precise</u> latitude, or distance from the equator.

Using their new skills, Portuguese sailors began sailing southward along the western coast of Africa. By 1498, the Portuguese sailor Vasco da Gama passed the southern tip of Africa and continued north and east to India. Da Gama's course became an important trade route and helped boost Portuguese wealth and power. Later, Portuguese sailors pressed on to the East Indies, the source of trade in spices.

☑**Checkpoint** What was Prince Henry's goal?

⭐ **Looking Back and Ahead** By the time Vasco da Gama reached India, Prince Henry was long dead. However, his work opened the way for European sailors to reach far-flung corners of the globe. In the next chapter, you will see how these sailors linked the long-separated worlds of the east and west.

> **Vocabulary Builder**
> <u>precise</u> (pree sĭs) *adj.* exact; accurate

Section 4 | Check Your Progress

> **Progress Monitoring ⬤nline**
> **For:** Self-test with instant help
> **Visit:** PHSchool.com
> **Web Code:** mva-1014

Comprehension and Critical Thinking

1. (a) Recall What role did citizens play in Athens?
(b) Contrast How did Athenian democracy differ from the Roman Republic?

2. (a) Recall How did Europeans make greater contact with the outside world?
(b) Identify Benefits How might Europeans of that time benefit from increased trade?

Reading Skill

3. Use Graphics to Construct Meaning How did previewing visual material in this section help you read more actively? How did this material add detail to your understanding of European civilization?

Key Terms

Answer the following questions in complete sentences that show your understanding of the key terms.
4. How did monotheism differ from other early beliefs?

5. Why were nobles important in feudalism?
6. How are leaders chosen in a republic?

Writing

7. Some of the events covered in this section include the Crusades, feudalism, and the Renaissance. What do you think life was like in Europe before these events happened? How did life in Europe change after these events? Answer the questions in one or two paragraphs.

Assess Progress

Have students complete Check Your Progress. Administer the Section Quiz.

📑 **Teaching Resources, Unit 1,** Section Quiz, p. 27

To further assess student understanding, use the Progress Monitoring Transparency.

Progress Monitoring Transparencies, Chapter 1, Section 4

Reteach   L1

If students need more instruction, have them read this section in the Interactive Reading and Notetaking Study Guide and complete the accompanying question.

📖 **Interactive Reading and Notetaking Study Guide,** Chapter 1, Section 4 (Adapted Version also available.)

Extend

Have students write a diary entry from the point of view of a sailor on Vasco da Gama's voyage around the tip of Africa. In their diary entries students should express their hopes and fears about the voyage.

Progress Monitoring Online

Students may check their comprehension of this section by completing the Progress Monitoring Online graphic organizer and self-quiz.

Answer

☑**Checkpoint** to expand Portuguese power and spread Christianity to new lands

---

Section 4 Check Your Progress

1. (a) Citizens made decisions in the Athenian Assembly
(b) Athenian citizens participated directly in their democratic government; Romans elected representatives to govern them.

2. (a) through the Crusades, and through trade
(b) new goods and ideas

3. Answers will vary, but should mention that previewing the visuals raised questions that helped students read actively to find answers; possible responses: the visuals offered details about traditions described in the text and illustrated the influences that shaped European civilization.

4. It taught that there was only one God, not many gods.

5. In return for grants of land, they provided military service and financial assistance to the king.

6. They are elected by citizens.

7. Students' paragraphs should demonstrate an understanding of the significance of the events in the development of European civilization and provide accurate supporting details from the text of this section.

Objective

Identifying main ideas and supporting details saves time and helps students understand and remember the most important information in their reading. This skills lesson will teach students how to locate main ideas and the facts, reasons, examples, and other details that support them.

Identify Main Ideas and Supporting Details

Instruction   L2

1. Write the steps to identify main ideas and supporting details on the board and ask the class to read the steps aloud.

2. Write *Main Idea and Supporting Details* on the board. Ask students where they would look to find the main idea of a paragraph, and list their responses under *Main Idea.* (*first sentence; then other parts of the paragraph*) Ask students to name kinds of details that are used to support main ideas and list their responses under *Supporting Details.* (*facts, reasons, explanations, examples, descriptions*)

3. Practice the skill by following the steps on p. 28 as a class. Model each step to identify main ideas and supporting details. (*1. (a) The first sentence (b) The first sentence 2. Possible responses: Native Americans met their needs for food, clothing, and shelter in various ways; Native Americans showed respect for nature in their activities. 3. Possible responses: Some groups depended on the sea for food; they adapted their ways of life to the natural world. 4. (a) They are examples of the variety of ways Native Americans met their basic needs. (b) They describe how Native Americans showed respect for the natural world.*)

Monitor Progress

Ask students to do the Apply the Skills activity. Then assign the Skills for Life worksheet. As students complete the worksheet, circulate to make sure individuals are applying the skill steps effectively. Provide assistance as needed.

All in One Teaching Resources, Unit 1, Skills for Life Worksheet, p. 22

History books are full of information. Although you cannot remember every fact, you can learn to identify the main ideas and note the details that explain and support them. The following passage is a description such as you might find in a textbook.

> Native Americans developed a variety of ways to meet their basic needs for food, clothing, and shelter. In some culture areas, tribes hunted animals and gathered the nuts and fruits that grew in the wild. Other tribes depended on the sea for food. They made boats out of animal skins or carved canoes out of trees. From their boats and canoes, they speared fish or hunted marine animals such as seals, walruses, and whales.
>
> Whether hunting, fishing, farming, or gathering wild plants, Native Americans had a great respect for the natural world. Their prayers and ceremonies were designed to maintain a balance between people and the forces of nature. They believed that they must adapt their ways to the natural world in order to survive and prosper.

Learn the Skill

Use these steps to learn how to identify main ideas and supporting details.

1 **Find the main idea.** The main idea is what the passage is about. Often, the main idea is stated in the first sentence of a paragraph. However, it can occur in other parts of a paragraph as well.

2 **Restate the main idea.** To be sure you understand the ideas expressed in the paragraph, restate the main idea in your own words.

3 **Look for details.** Details might include facts, reasons, explanations, examples, and descriptions that tell more about the main idea.

4 **Make connections.** Note how the details support and expand the main idea.

Practice the Skill

Answer the following questions based on the paragraph above.

1 **Find the main idea.** (a) What is the main-idea sentence in the first paragraph? (b) What is the main-idea sentence in the second paragraph?

2 **Restate the main idea.** Restate the main idea of each paragraph in your own words.

3 **Look for details.** Identify a detail that supports the main idea in each paragraph.

4 **Make connections.** (a) How do the details in the first paragraph help explain its main idea? (b) How do the details in the second paragraph help explain its main idea?

Apply the Skill

See the Review and Assessment at the end of this chapter.

Reteach   L1

If students need more instruction, use the Social Studies Skills Tutor to reteach this skill.

Social Studies Skills Tutor CD-ROM
Identifying Main Ideas

How did different cultures and traditions develop around the world?

Section 1
The Earliest Americans

- Most scientists believe that early people came to the Americas from Asia by way of a land bridge.
- As people learned to farm, they formed permanent settlements.
- The Mayas, Aztecs, and Incas built civilizations in Central America and South America.

Section 2
Cultures of North America

- The Mound Builders were among the earliest cultures of North America.
- People of North America developed varied ways of life, depending upon the environments in which they lived.
- The League of the Iroquois created a pact between warring nations in the Eastern Woodlands.

Section 3
Trade Networks of Asia and Africa

- The Muslim world linked Asia to Africa and Europe through trade.
- Various trading states emerged in both East Africa and West Africa.
- China dominated East Asian trade along the Silk Road.

Section 4
The European Heritage

- Judaism and Christianity formed the foundation for European religious beliefs.
- Greece and Rome shaped ideas about democratic government.
- After the Middle Ages, Europeans began to look beyond their boundaries.

Exploring the Essential Question

Use the online study guide to explore the essential question.

Section 1
How did early civilizations develop in the Americas?

Section 4
What major influences shaped European civilization?

Chapter 1 Essential Question
How did different cultures and traditions develop around the world?

Section 2
How did geography influence the development of cultures in North America?

Section 3
How did trade link Europe, Africa, and Asia?

Chapter 1

Essential Question

Remind Students of the Chapter Essential Question: **How did different cultures and traditions develop around the world?** Have them review the bulleted statements and the Visual Preview at the beginning of the chapter to help them answer this question.

To bolster students' retention, at this time they should complete the Study Guide in print or online. Remind students that they should also continue note taking for the Unit and Chapter Focus Questions.

 Interactive Reading and Notetaking Study Guide, Unit 1, Chapter 1 (Adapted Version also available.)

Study Guide *Online,* Chapter 1

Chapter Challenge

To wrap up this chapter, students should apply the knowledge they have gained to answer this question. **What would have happened if the Renaissance had not taken place in Europe?** *(Answers will vary, but should demonstrate an understanding that the Renaissance led to exploration and colonization of the Americas by encouraging European nation-states to look outward and thus ultimately helped Judeo-Christian and Greek and Roman traditions take hold in North America.)*

Assessment at a Glance

Formal Assessment

Chapter Tests A/B (L1/L2)

AYP Monitoring Assessment

Test Prep Workbook With Document-Based Assessment

Test-Taking Strategies With Transparencies

Performance Assessment

Group/Individual Activities, TE pp. 2g, 2h

Teacher's Edition, pp. 9, 15, 19, 27

Assessment Rubrics

Assessment Through Technology

ExamView CD-ROM

MindPoint CD-ROM

Progress Monitoring Transparencies

Progress Monitoring Online

Chapter 1
Review and Assessment

Key Terms

1. Students' definitions and illustrations should demonstrate the correct understanding of the words. Tables should be correctly configured.

Comprehension and Critical Thinking

2. **(a)** A land bridge between Asia and North America was formed by lower sea levels during an Ice Age. People used the land bridge to migrate from Asia to the Americas. **(b)** There are no written records of the event.

3. **(a)** They used armies to conquer other people. **(b)** The Aztecs built monumental architecture, cities, and roads. **(c)** The Aztec religion included human sacrifice; the Aztecs forced conquered people to pay taxes and give them treasure, food, and prisoners.

4. **(a)** To keep the peace **(b)** fighting with the other nations; peace **(c)** Possible responses: The nations of the League benefited from the common laws that kept peace but kept their freedom to deal with their own affairs.

5. **(a)** Overland **(b)** By caravans on the Silk Road and over land in the Middle East and East Africa and by merchant ships sailing to East African ports such as Kilwa **(c)** Sentences will vary, but mention the value of the trade to Asians and Africans, and the cultural exchange that resulted.

6. **(a)** Democracy, republic, equality under the law for all citizens **(b)** Our government is a representative democracy in which the people elect representatives to make laws in our Congress.

7. **(a)** A holy war started by the Roman Catholic Church to win control of the Holy Land from Muslims **(b)** Europeans came into contact with Muslim civilization, became interested in goods from the Middle East, and learned about advances in technology used for navigation. **(c)** Answers may vary, but should mention that although Europeans were not able to maintain control of the Middle East, they learned new skills and ideas that affected European civilization.

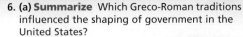

Key Terms

1. Draw a table with eight rows and three columns. In the first column, list the following key terms: glacier, irrigate, culture, clan, navigation, monotheism, direct democracy, republic. In the next column, write the definition of each word. In the last column, make a small illustration that shows the meaning of the word.

Comprehension and Critical Thinking

2. **(a) Recall** Describe the land-bridge theory that scientists have developed to explain how people first came to the Americas.
   (b) Clarify Problems Some scholars have different ideas about how people first came to the Americas. Why do you think we are not sure about this event?

3. **(a) Describe** How did the Aztecs build a large empire?
   (b) Compare What features did the Aztec civilization have in common with civilization of the Incas?
   (c) Contrast How did the civilization of the Aztecs differ from other societies of North America?

4. **(a) Recall** What was the purpose of the League of the Iroquois?
   (b) Identify Costs and Benefits What did each Iroquois Nation give up by joining the League? What did they gain?
   (c) Draw Conclusions Why do you think the Iroquois League succeeded?

5. **(a) Describe** How did trade goods move between West Africa and the Middle East?
   (b) Apply Information Describe two ways that goods from China might have reached the trading states of East Africa.
   (c) Make Generalizations Based on your reading, write a one-sentence generalization about the importance of trade routes in Asia and Africa.

6. **(a) Summarize** Which Greco-Roman traditions influenced the shaping of government in the United States?
   (b) Link Past and Present How do these Greco-Roman ideas directly impact political life in the United States today?

7. **(a) Define** What were the Crusades?
   (b) Analyze Cause and Effect What were the long-range effects of the Crusades?
   (c) Draw Conclusions Do you think the Crusades were a failure or a success? Explain.

History Reading Skill

8. **Read Actively** Apply what you learned about active reading to the next chapter. Preview the headings and prereading material. Scan the graphic material. Generate two questions to help you guide your reading.

Writing

9. Write a paragraph on the following topic: Historical events led to increasing contacts between people in different parts of the world. **Your paragraph should:**
   - begin with a thesis statement that explains the critical events and ideas that started the move toward increasing contacts;
   - support these events or ideas with facts and examples.

10. **Write a Narrative:**
    You are a sailor who studied with the navigator Prince Henry. Write a paragraph explaining why you attended Prince Henry's school, what you learned, and your goals after leaving the school.

Skills for Life

Identify the Main Idea
Reread the text following the subheading "Far West" in Section 2, then answer the following questions.

11. What is the main-idea sentence of each paragraph?

12. Summarize the main idea of the two paragraphs in your own words.

13. What details support the main-idea sentence of the first paragraph?

History Reading Skill

8. Possible response: Why did Europeans travel to the Americas? How did Native American groups live in North America?

Writing

9. Paragraph should show an understanding of cause and effect, with appropriate supporting details. Possible thesis: The expansion of trade led to increased exploration and contact between people in different parts of the world.

10. Answers may vary but paragraphs should be written in the first person, and should have period appropriate content.

Chapter 1
Review and Assessment

Test Yourself

1. Native American religious beliefs were based on

   A the Ten Commandments.

   B the Quran.

   C reverence for nature.

   D the teachings of the Mound Builders.

2. The Roman Senate was most similar to

   A the Athenian assembly.

   B the U.S. Congress.

   C the feudal system.

   D the Aztec government.

Refer to the map at right to answer Question 3.

3. What do the three civilizations shown on the map have in common?

   A They were all located in South America.

   B They all traded with the Iroquois.

   C They all disappeared for unknown reasons.

   D They were all very organized societies.

Early Civilizations in the Americas

NORTH AMERICA

ATLANTIC OCEAN

Tenochtitlán

Tikal

Caribbean Sea

PACIFIC OCEAN

SOUTH AMERICA

Cuzco

KEY

Aztec

Maya

Inca

0 km 2,000

0 miles 2,000

Lambert Azimuthal Equal-Area Projection

Document-Based Questions

Task: Look at Documents 1 and 2, and answer their accompanying questions. Then, use the documents and your knowledge of history to complete the following writing assignment:

Write a paragraph describing the influence of geography on the Tlingit society.

Document 1: This photograph shows the land where the people of the Pacific Northwest, such as the Tlingit and Nootka, lived. *Based on this picture, what resources did the Pacific Northwest people have for building homes and finding food?*

Document 2: In this excerpt from an oral history, a Tlingit boy describes the traditional life of his people. *Why did the Tlingit expect young people to work?*

"Land ownership is one of the biggest laws in the Tlingit culture. You did not fish or hunt on somebody else's land without their permission. If you did and you were caught, your equipment would be broken and you would have to leave. . . .

The Tlingit people subsisted in seasonal rounds. . . . They hunted black and brown bear with spear and deadfall. For wolf, coyote, and fox they used snares. They used traps to get mink, weasel, and land otter. With bow and arrow, they hunted the mountain goat. They fished Halibut, King salmon, Silver salmon, and Humpy salmon. . . .

The jobs of young children long ago depended on the mental and physical capabilities. They had to do whatever they could. They had to pick berries, gather roots and plants, and clean fish. The older they got the harder the tasks became. This is how they learned."

Chapter Review and Assessment **31**

Test Yourself

1. C

2. B

3. D

Document-Based Questions
Answers

Document 1 The forest provided opportunities for hunting and wood for building. The waterways provided opportunities for fishing.

Document 2 so that they would gradually learn the skills and discipline the Tlingit needed to survive

Writing Rubric: Write a Paragraph

Share this rubric with students before they begin writing.

Score 1 Paragraph does not address assigned topic and is poorly organized.

Score 2 Details, arguments, and organization are often unclear or incorrect.

Score 3 Paragraph has organization suited to the topic, some appropriate details, and some original analysis.

Score 4 Paragraph has clear organization suited to topic, many appropriate details, and original analysis and ideas.

For a more complete four-point rubric, see the Writing Rubrics in the Teaching Resources.

All in One **Teaching Resources, Unit 1,** p. 138

Skills for Life

11. first sentence in each paragraph

12. The land and climate in different parts of the Far West varied; houses differed from region to region.

13. There were forests and grasslands in the north; southern parts could be desert-like.

Europe Looks Outward (1000–1720)

History Background

The Significance of European Exploration of the Americas

In the 1400s and 1500s, sea routes brought European ships south along the West African coast and around the Cape of Good Hope at the southern tip of Africa before sailing across the Indian Ocean to Asia. Believing he could reach Asia by sailing west, Christopher Columbus gained the support of the Spanish monarchy for an expedition across the Atlantic. Instead of finding a new route to Asia, Columbus landed in the Americas.

Over the next 300 years, various European governments sponsored exploration of the Americas. The new exchange of ideas and goods between the Europeans and Native Americans, called the Columbian Exchange, affected both Europe and the Americas significantly. In fact, European exploration and new trade routes that were established transformed much of the world. A new, global economy linked old worlds with new worlds.

Spain made the earliest European claims in the Americas, gaining control of much of Central and South America. Spanish rule in the new lands was often brutal, and included the forced labor of Native Americans in mines and on large plantations. When labor became scarce, the Spanish colonies began importing enslaved West Africans to the Americas. These early actions laid groundwork for what later became the American South's dependence on slave labor on its plantations, which led, in turn, to the American Civil War.

Other European countries competed for influence in the Americas by financing more expeditions with two main goals: finding a northwest passage to Asia and claiming lands for the establishment of colonies. Multiple attempts to find a northwest passage failed, but Portugal, England, France, and the Netherlands in particular were successful in establishing colonies in North America. Today, many cities, bodies of water, and other landmarks in the United States bear the names from these nations' explorations.

The impact on Native Americans by contact with Europeans was enormous. Trading with European partners at times made tensions worse among the Native American groups. New diseases introduced by Europeans and brutal treatment by their conquerors depleted Native populations. An influx of European colonists pushed many Native Americans off their lands.

Essential Questions

Use this graphic organizer to see the relationship between key concepts and the Chapter Essential Question.

Focus Question/Section 1
How did the search for a water route to Asia affect both Europe and the Americas?
(p. 36)

Concept: Economic Growth

Focus Question/Section 2
How did Spain establish an empire in the Americas?
(p. 44)

Concept: Power

Chapter Essential Question
What were the causes and effects of European exploration of the Americas?

Focus Question/Section 4
What impact did the establishment of French and Dutch colonies in North America have on Native Americans?
(p. 53)

Concept: Alliance

Focus Question/Section 3
How did conflicts in Europe spur exploration in North America?
(p. 49)

Concept: Conflict

$500

$500

COLORED BILL STRAP

STEEL-STRONG
TRADE MARK
NO SLIPPAGE
U.S. PAT. OFF.

Differentiated Instruction

Paraphrasing/Scaffolding Language

Learning to rephrase Students will encounter open-ended questions and writing prompts in the Student Edition and ancillaries as well as in standardized tests. Paraphrasing the question or writing task is an important first step for students to complete prior to formulating their responses. Rephrasing helps students better understand what is being asked of them; it also helps you make certain that students understand what is being asked of them. Model the paraphrasing step when students encounter open-ended writing tasks.

Task: Compare the differences between Native Americans' interactions with the Spanish and the French colonists.

Paraphrase: What was life like for Native Americans who came into contact with the Spanish colonists? Which elements were similar for Native Americans interacting with the French? Which were different?

Breaking Down the Task After students have paraphrased a short-answer question or writing prompt, remind them to break down the task into smaller steps. This will help them think through the tasks and formulate complete responses. Use the following steps to model scaffolding a response:

1. Make a list or a chart of the information asked about.
2. Review the information gathered and decide how it relates/applies to the task.
3. Write a topic sentence and supporting sentences that provide a complete response to the prompt.

Concepts Across Time

Have students develop an understanding of the enduring concepts of history by connecting these ideas.

Concept: Economic Growth

Students learning about the voyages of European explorers should consider the role of new knowledge and innovations in economic growth. New knowledge about the Americas inspired further exploration and settlement of the new lands and the rise of a thriving transatlantic trade. More recently, the development of the computer chip has revolutionized communication and spurred new industries. Ask: **Why did the Europeans decide to continue exploring the Americas when it was clear that it was not Asia?** (*They wanted to develop economic opportunities for themselves.*) Ask: **What new industry did the introduction of cocoa help create in Europe?** (*The chocolate industry*) Use these questions when discussing the Columbian Exchange in Section 1.

Concept: Conflict

Students learning about how conflicts in Europe affected competition in the Americas should consider the long-ranging impact of these conflicts. For example, Martin Luther's break with the Roman Catholic Church resulted in the formation of hundreds of new Protestant denominations that continue to gain converts throughout the world today. Ask: **What was the source of conflict between Spain and England before the defeat of the Spanish Armada?** (*Their leaders had differences over religion, which worsened problems over other issues.*) Ask: **How did France and England take advantage of the defeat of the Spanish Armada?** (*Both countries increased exploration when the Spanish were no longer able to control the seas.*) Use these questions when discussing Conflicts in Europe in Section 3.

Concept: Alliance

Students learning about the alliances that Europeans made with the Native Americans should consider the ways that migration affects people in the areas to which the migrants are traveling. New alliances sometimes had disastrous effects on other groups which were not part of the alliance. Ask: **How did Native American life change as a result of alliances made with new settlers in North America?** (*Relationships among Native American groups were altered, and many new diseases were introduced.*) Ask: **How were the alliances made by early settlers in North America similar to or different from alliances made between groups or countries today?** (*In both instances, the new alliances brought agreements that benefited both parties. However, some alliances between nations today involve both benefits and sacrifices for both parties.*) Use these questions when discussing The Impact on Native Americans in Section 4.

Section 1 The Age of Exploration 🕐 *1.5 periods, .75 block*

Objectives

Students will

1. Explain what happened to the Vikings who explored Newfoundland.
2. Describe the voyages of Christopher Columbus.
3. Describe the expeditions of such Spanish explorers as Vasco Núñez de Balboa and Ferdinand Magellan.
4. Explain the importance of the Columbian Exchange.

Differentiated Instruction Key

- **L1** Basic to Average
- **L2** All Students
- **L3** Average to Advanced
- **AR** Advanced Readers
- **ELL** English Language Learners
- **GT** Gifted and Talented
- **LPR** Less Proficient Readers
- **SN** Special Needs

Prepare to Read	Instructional Resources	Differentiated Instruction
Build Background Knowledge Discuss students' impressions of European explorers. **Set a Purpose for Reading** Have students begin to fill out the Reading Readiness Guide. **Preview Key Terms** Preview the section's Key Terms.	**All in One Teaching Resources, Unit 1** **L2** Chapter Prereading Guide, p. 4 **L2** History Reading Skill Worksheet, p. 41 **L2** Word Knowledge Rating Form, p. 42 **L2** Reading Readiness Guide, p. 43 **Teacher's Edition** **L2** Vocabulary Builder, pp. 35, 37	💿 Guided Reading Audio CD Spanish **ELL, LPR, SN**

Teach	Instructional Resources	Differentiated Instruction
Instruction **First Visitors from Europe** Discuss the voyages to North America by the Vikings and by Christopher Columbus. **The Continuing Search for Asia** Discuss more attempts by Europeans to find a water route to Asia across the Atlantic Ocean. **The Columbian Exchange** Discuss the exchange of goods and ideas across the Atlantic as a result of European exploration of the Americas.	📖 **Interactive Reading and Notetaking Study Guide** **L2** Chapter 2, Section 1 **All in One Teaching Resources, Unit 1** **L2** Journal of Christopher Columbus, p. 47 **L2** Christopher Columbus, p. 48 **Color Transparencies** **L2** European Exploration, 1492–1609	📖 **Interactive Reading and Notetaking Study Guide, Adapted Version (English/ Spanish)** **L1** Chapter 2, Section 1 **ELL, LPR, SN** **Teacher's Edition** **L3** Write an Interview, p. 36 **AR, GT** **L1** Reading a Map, p. 38 **ELL, LPR** **L1** Understanding the Exchange, p. 40 **ELL**

Assess and Reteach	Instructional Resources	Differentiated Instruction
Assess Progress Evaluate student comprehension with Check Your Progress and Section Quiz. **Reteach** Assign the Interactive Reading and Notetaking Study Guide to help struggling students. **Extend** Extend the lesson by having students map Christopher Columbus's voyages.	📖 **Interactive Reading and Notetaking Study Guide** **L2** Chapter 2, Section 1 **All in One Teaching Resources, Unit 1** **L2** Reading Readiness Guide, p. 43 **L2** Section Quiz, p. 53 **Progress Monitoring Transparencies** **L2** Chapter 2, Section 1	**Teacher's Edition** **L1** Checkpoints, TE pp. 39, 40, 41 💿 SE on Audio CD **L1** Chapter 2, Section 1 **Internet Resources** PHSchool.com

Objectives

Students will

1. Describe how the Spanish were able to defeat the empires of the Aztecs and the Incas.
2. Identify Spanish explorations in areas that later became part of the United States.
3. Explain how society was organized in Spain's empire in the Americas.

Differentiated Instruction Key

L1 Basic to Average

L2 All Students

L3 Average to Advanced

AR Advanced Readers

ELL English Language Learners

GT Gifted and Talented

LPR Less Proficient Readers

SN Special Needs

Prepare to Read

Build Background Knowledge
Ask students to make predictions about the effects of the Columbian Exchange.

Set a Purpose for Reading
Have students begin to fill out the Reading Readiness Guide.

Preview Key Terms
Preview the section's Key Terms.

Instructional Resources

All in One Teaching Resources, Unit 1

L2 Reading Readiness Guide, p. 44

Teacher's Edition

L2 Vocabulary Builder, p. 45

Differentiated Instruction

Guided Reading Audio CD
Spanish **ELL, LPR, SN**

Teach

Instruction
Spanish Conquistadors
Discuss the Spanish conquest of empires in the Americas.

Spanish Explorers in North America
Discuss the first Spanish explorers who traveled in what is now the United States.

Colonizing Spanish America
Discuss how society was organized in Spain's empire in the Americas.

Instructional Resources

Interactive Reading and Notetaking Study Guide

L2 Chapter 2, Section 2

Color Transparencies

L2 The *Encomienda* System

Discovery School Video

L2 Spanish Exploration in the Americas

Differentiated Instruction

Interactive Reading and Notetaking Study Guide, Adapted Version (English/Spanish)

L1 Chapter 2, Section 2 **ELL, LPR, SN**

Teacher's Edition

L1 Study Aid, p. 44 **LPR, SN**

L3 Write a Newspaper Article, p. 46 **AR, GT**

Assess and Reteach

Assess Progress
Evaluate student comprehension with Check Your Progress and Section Quiz.

Reteach
Assign the Interactive Reading and Notetaking Study Guide to help struggling students.

Extend
Extend the lesson by having students research and make a poster about a Spanish empire in the Americas.

Instructional Resources

Interactive Reading and Notetaking Study Guide

L2 Chapter 2, Section 2

All in One Teaching Resources, Unit 1

L2 Reading Readiness Guide, p. 44

L2 Section Quiz, p. 54

Progress Monitoring Transparencies

L2 Chapter 2, Section 2

Differentiated Instruction

Teacher's Edition

L1 Checkpoints, TE pp. 45, 47, 48

SE on Audio CD

L1 Chapter 2, Section 2

Section 2 Lesson Plan

Objectives

Students will

1. Describe the religious and economic conflicts in Europe during the Reformation.
2. Explain why European powers continued to search for a new route to Asia.
3. Describe the outcome of the search by explorers John Cabot and Henry Hudson for a northwest passage around the Americas.

Differentiated Instruction Key

- **L1** Basic to Average
- **L2** All Students
- **L3** Average to Advanced
- **AR** Advanced Readers
- **ELL** English Language Learners
- **GT** Gifted and Talented
- **LPR** Less Proficient Readers
- **SN** Special Needs

Prepare to Read

Build Background Knowledge
Discuss students' impressions of conflict among nations.

Set a Purpose for Reading
Have students begin to fill out the Reading Readiness Guide.

Preview Key Terms
Preview the section's Key Terms.

Instructional Resources

All in One Teaching Resources, Unit 1
- **L2** Reading Readiness Guide, p. 45

Teacher's Edition
- **L2** Vocabulary Builder, p. 49

Differentiated Instruction

💿 **Guided Reading Audio CD**
Spanish ELL, LPR, SN

Teach

Instruction
Conflicts in Europe
Discuss how religious and economic differences created conflict among European countries and changed the balance of power.

Asia Continues to Beckon
Discuss the last serious attempts to find a northwest passage to Asia.

Instructional Resources

📖 **Interactive Reading and Notetaking Study Guide**
- **L2** Chapter 2, Section 3

All in One Teaching Resources, Unit 1
- **L2** The Protestant Reformation, p. 49

Color Transparencies
- **L2** The Trade Cycle Between a Home Land and its Colonies

Differentiated Instruction

📖 **Interactive Reading and Notetaking Study Guide, Adapted Version (English/ Spanish)**
- **L1** Chapter 2, Section 3 ELL, LPR, SN

Teacher's Edition
- **L1** Understanding Economics, p. 50 ELL, LPR, SN

Assess and Reteach

Assess Progress
Evaluate student comprehension with Check Your Progress and Section Quiz.

Reteach
Assign the Interactive Reading and Notetaking Study Guide to help struggling students.

Extend
Extend the lesson by having students paraphrase a portion of Martin Luther's 95 Theses.

Instructional Resources

📖 **Interactive Reading and Notetaking Study Guide**
- **L2** Chapter 2, Section 3

All in One Teaching Resources, Unit 1
- **L2** Reading Readiness Guide, p. 45
- **L2** Section Quiz, p. 55

Progress Monitoring Transparencies
- **L2** Chapter 2, Section 3

Differentiated Instruction

Teacher's Edition
- **L1** Checkpoints, TE pp. 51, 52

💿 **SE on Audio CD**
- **L1** Chapter 2, Section 3

Internet Resources
PHSchool.com

Objectives

Students will

1. Describe how the French colony of New France spread into the interior of North America.

2. Explain how the Dutch established a thriving colony along the Hudson River.

3. Explain the influence of these settlements on the Native Americans of the region.

Differentiated Instruction Key

L1 Basic to Average
L2 All Students
L3 Average to Advanced

AR Advanced Readers
ELL English Language Learners
GT Gifted and Talented
LPR Less Proficient Readers
SN Special Needs

Prepare to Read

Build Background Knowledge
Discuss students' recollections of Europeans' reasons for exploring the Americas.

Set a Purpose for Reading
Have students begin to fill out the Reading Readiness Guide.

Preview Key Terms
Preview the section's Key Terms.

Instructional Resources

All in One Teaching Resources, Unit 1
L2 Reading Readiness Guide, p. 46

Teacher's Edition
L2 Vocabulary Builder, p. 53

Differentiated Instruction

Guided Reading Audio CD
Spanish ELL, LPR, SN

Teach

Instruction
New France
Discuss French settlements in North America.

New Netherland
Discuss Dutch settlements in North America.

The Impact on Native Americans
Discuss the impact of European settlements on Native Americans in North America.

Instructional Resources

Interactive Reading and Notetaking Study Guide
L2 Chapter 2, Section 4

All in One Teaching Resources, Unit 1
L2 Concept Lesson, p. 52
L2 Concept Organizer, p. 6
L2 Dutch Colonization, 1609–1664, p. 50
L2 Skills for Life Worksheet, p. 51

Differentiated Instruction

Interactive Reading and Notetaking Study Guide, Adapted Version (English/Spanish)
L1 Chapter 2, Section 4 ELL, LPR, SN

Teacher's Edition
L3 Write a Letter, p. 54 AR, GT
L1 Writing Advertisements, p. 56 ELL
L3 Writing Advertisements, p. 56 GT

Assess and Reteach

Assess Progress
Assign Check Your Progress and Section Quiz.

Reteach
Assign the Interactive Reading and Notetaking Study Guide to help struggling students.

Extend
Extend the lesson by having students create a flowchart of the fur trade.

Instructional Resources

Interactive Reading and Notetaking Study Guide
L2 Chapter 2, Section 4

All in One Teaching Resources, Unit 1
L2 Reading Readiness Guide, p. 46
L2 Word Knowledge Rating Form, p. 42
L2 Section Quiz, p. 56
L2 Chapter Test, p. 60

Progress Monitoring Transparencies
L2 Chapter 2, Section 4

Differentiated Instruction

Teacher's Edition
L1 Checkpoints, TE pp. 55, 56, 57

All in One Teaching Resources, Unit 1
L1 Chapter Test, p. 57

SE on Audio CD
L1 Chapter 2, Section 4

Social Studies Skills Tutor CD-ROM
Sequencing

Use the following research activities to help students deepen their understanding of the Chapter Essential Question: **What were the causes and effects of European exploration of the Americas?** Students should use library or Internet resources to complete each activity. Use the appropriate four-point rubric in Assessment Rubrics to evaluate the activity.

 Assessment Rubrics

Write an Illustrated Biography

Have students research one of the European voyagers who explored the Americas, such as Christopher Columbus, Ferdinand Magellan, or Juan Ponce de León. Then have students write a short, illustrated biography. Tell students to include in their biographies information about how that person became an explorer, any personal information about his life, or whether he may have had difficulty gaining funding from particular nations. Have students share their biographies with the class. Then collect the biographies and keep them in an accessible place in the classroom as a reference material. Use this activity after students have completed Section 4.

 Individual research activity

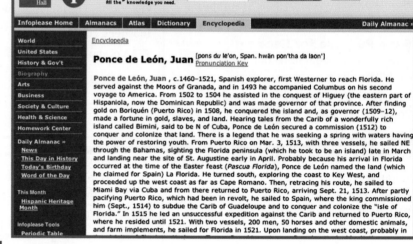

Go Online PHSchool.com **Web Code:** mve-0110

Make a Map of the Modern Caribbean

Have students research the impact today of colonization on the islands of the Caribbean. Tell students to create a map of the Caribbean islands with color codes that indicate whether an island is part of one or more independent countries, such as Cuba and Haiti, or still governed by a European country. Have students use specific color codes to indicate which countries govern which islands. Invite interested students to add information to the map, such as when an independent country gained its independence and from whom it gained it. Use this activity after students have completed Section 3.

 Individual research activity

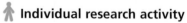

Go Online PHSchool.com **Web Code:** mvd-0111

Create a Timeline of Aztec Civilization

Have students create a timeline showing the rise of the Aztec Civilization and its later conquest by the Spanish conquistadors. Ask students to place six to eight major events on their timeline with a sentence detailing the significance of each event. Have students compare their timelines to check their work. Use the timeline when studying Spanish Conquistadors in Section 2.

 Group research activity LPR, SN **L1**

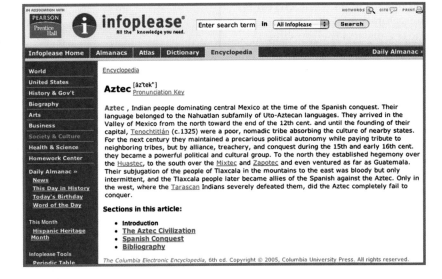

Go Online **Web Code:** mvd-0112

Deliver a Newscast About the End of the Search for a Northwest Passage

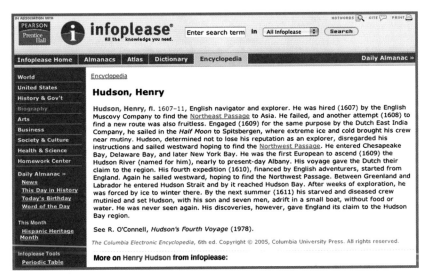

Have students work in groups to prepare a newscast and analysis about Henry Hudson's final, failed voyage and the end of serious attempts to find a northwest passage. One student might be the news anchor; others might be guest analysts; still others might assume responsibility for showing maps and other images. Groups can present their newscasts after the class has read Asia Continues to Beckon in Section 3.

 Group research activity AR, GT **L3**

Go Online **Web Code:** mve-0113

Chapter 2

Why It Matters

In this chapter, students will focus on European exploration of the Atlantic and Pacific oceans and the growing European interest in the Americas.

New technologies that allowed Europeans to sail farther brought great changes to people in Europe and the Americas, just as developing technology significantly affects our lives today in ways we can't always predict. We do not know for certain, for example, how future space exploration may affect our lives.

Competition for new lands in the Americas created and worsened tensions among European nations. Economic competition among nations continues today, often feeding rivalries and tensions.

The exploration and settlement of the Americas laid the foundations for the eventual development of the United States.

Chapter Essential Question

What were the causes and effects of European exploration of the Americas?

Think Like a Historian

- To preview this chapter, have students review the content on these pages of the Student Edition. Ask: **What will you be learning about in this chapter?** *(European exploration of the Americas)*

- Have students study the photo of the monument figures of Portuguese explorers. Ask: **By the way they are depicted, how do you think Europeans remember these explorers?** *(Students should see that since the explorers are depicted as brave, noble, and forward-looking, Europeans most likely remember them in a positive way.)*

- Ask students to identify the items held by the explorers. Have a volunteer read aloud the quote from Columbus. Then ask students if they think that the European explorers were motivated more by greed, glory, or some other factors. *(Explorers are holding a ship's replica, a sword, navigational tools, and an artist's brush and palette. Answers will vary.)*

Europe Looks Outward

With its long coastline facing the Atlantic Ocean, Portugal funded many journeys of exploration during the 1500s. This monument in Lisbon, Portugal, pays tribute to brave Portuguese explorers.

32

1000–1720

Bibliography

For the Teacher

Thomas, Hugh. *The Slave Trade: The Story of the Atlantic Slave Trade, 1440–1870.* Simon and Schuster, 1999.

William, Glyn. *Voyages of Delusion: The Quest for the Northwest Passage.* Yale University Press, 2003.

Wood, Michael. *Conquistadors.* University of California Press, 2002.

For the Student

L1 Dreher, Diane Sansevere. *Explorers Who Got Lost.* Tor, 1992.

L2 Hayes, Derek. *America Discovered: A Historical Atlas of Exploration.* Douglas & McIntyre, 2004.

L3 Dugard, Martin. *The Last Voyage of Christopher Columbus.* Little, Brown, 2005.

"*This is so beautiful a place... there are trees and herbs here which would be of great value in Spain...Should I meet with gold or spices in great quantity, I shall remain till I collect as much as possible.*"

—Journal of Christopher Columbus,
October 19, 1492

CHAPTER 2

What You Will Learn

Section 1
THE AGE OF EXPLORATION
The search for a water route to Asia led to the European discovery of two continents and the exchange of resources between the Eastern and the Western hemispheres.

Section 2
SPAIN'S EMPIRE IN THE AMERICAS
The Spanish established an extensive empire in the Americas and created a colonial society with a rigid class structure.

Section 3
EUROPEANS COMPETE IN NORTH AMERICA
European economic and religious conflicts quickly spilled over into North America, leading France, Holland, and England to finance explorations there.

Section 4
FRANCE AND THE NETHERLANDS IN NORTH AMERICA
Prosperous French and Dutch colonies in North America often interacted with Native Americans.

🔑 Reading Skill
Identify Main Ideas and Details In this chapter, you will learn to locate the most important ideas in a text, and the details that support them.

33

History Background

Portugal's Explorers Although Christopher Columbus initially sought support from Portugal for his exploration of the Atlantic, it was Portugal's rival, Spain, that elected to sponsor his voyage. When word of Columbus's discoveries reached Spain, rulers there sought the help of the current pope, Alexander VI, to lay claim to the new lands. The pope decreed that Spain would control all newly discovered and undiscovered land west of a north-south line of demarcation approximately 320 miles west of the Cape Verde islands. Portugal then entered into negotiations with Spain, and the two countries agreed in the 1494 Treaty of Tordesillas to move the line approximately 800 miles farther west. As a result of the new agreement, Portugal explored and settled what is today Brazil.

Prepare to Read

Use the following for reading skill support.

All in One Teaching Resources, Unit 1, Chapter Prereading Guide, p. 4; History Reading Skill, p. 41

History Reading Skill, *Online*
Web code: mve-3000

Differentiated Instruction

The following Teacher's Edition strategies are suitable for students of varying abilities.

- **L3 Advanced Readers,** pp. 36, 46, 54 AR
- **L1 English Language Learners,** pp. 35, 38, 40, 50, 56 ELL
- **L3 Gifted and Talented,** pp. 36, 46, 54, 56 GT
- **L1 Less Proficient Readers,** pp. 35, 38, 42, 44, 50 LPR
- **L1 Special Needs,** pp. 35, 42, 44, 50 SN

Chapter Resources

Teaching Resources, Unit 1
Chapter Prereading Guide, p. 4
Word Knowledge Rating Form, p. 42
History Reading Skill, p. 41
Skills for Life Worksheet, p. 51
Chapter Tests A/B (L1/L2), pp. 57, 60
Letter Home (English/Spanish), pp. 34, 35

Spanish Support
- **L1 Interactive Reading and Notetaking Study Guide, Spanish,** Adapted Version
- **L1 Guided Reading Audio CD,** Spanish

Media and Technology
- **L1 SE on Audio CD**
- **L2 Social Studies Skills Tutor CD-ROM**
ExamView Test Bank CD-ROM

DISCOVERY SCHOOL

Quick View Video
View the chapter video for a quick preview of the main ideas.

Visual Preview

? **What were the causes and effects of European exploration of the Americas?**

Build Background Knowledge L2

In Chapter 1, students read about the rise of civilizations in the Americas, Asia, and Africa and how trade helped link people together. Lead a structured discussion about the factors that influenced the development of trade. (See TE p. T24 for more on structured discussion.) Have students think of times when they have been in a competitive situation. How did they respond? *(Possible answers: worked hard, trained, teamed with others)*

As they saw in the chapter opener and on these pages, European nations began to explore and compete for empires. Have students predict what might happen as a result of this competition.

Instruction L2

- For background information on conducting a lesson for the Visual Preview, see TE p. T20.

- Write the Chapter Essential Question on the board. Draw a graphic organizer on the board for cause-and-effect. Ask students to recall a cause-and-effect situation from their own lives and share it with the class. Use the Think-Write-Pair-Share strategy on p. T25 to encourage participation and write their responses on the board. *(Answers will vary, but one example might be that when they did not complete their homework, they were grounded.)*

- Have students look at the map. Ask: **Which European countries explored North America?** *(Spain, Netherlands, England, and France)*

- Ask students what they think the arrows in the middle of the map represent. *(the flow of items from one area of the world to the other)*

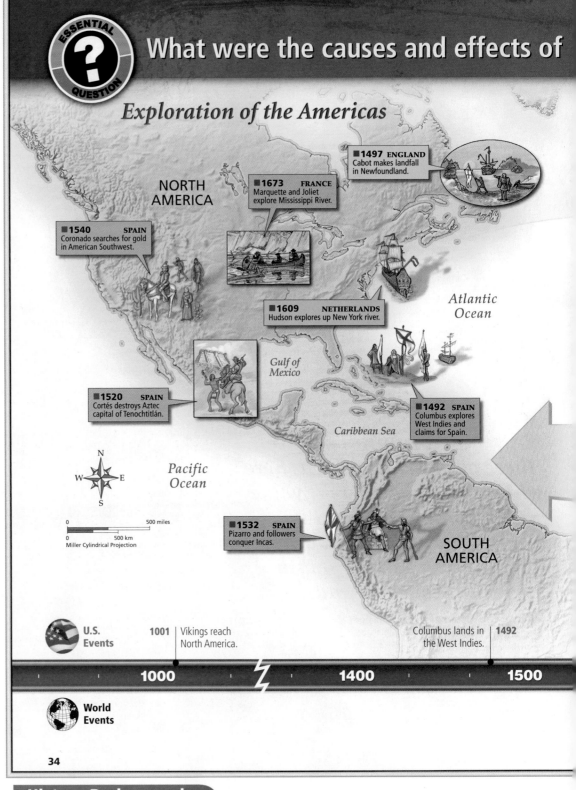

What were the causes and effects of

Exploration of the Americas

■1497 ENGLAND Cabot makes landfall in Newfoundland.

■1673 FRANCE Marquette and Joliet explore Mississippi River.

■1540 SPAIN Coronado searches for gold in American Southwest.

■1609 NETHERLANDS Hudson explores up New York river.

■1520 SPAIN Cortés destroys Aztec capital of Tenochtitlán.

■1492 SPAIN Columbus explores West Indies and claims for Spain.

■1532 SPAIN Pizarro and followers conquer Incas.

NORTH AMERICA

SOUTH AMERICA

Atlantic Ocean

Gulf of Mexico

Caribbean Sea

Pacific Ocean

0   500 miles
0   500 km
Miller Cylindrical Projection

U.S. Events

1001 | Vikings reach North America.

Columbus lands in the West Indies. | 1492

World Events

1000   1400   1500

34

History Background

Geography As students saw on the Chapter 1 Visual Preview, early trade routes followed coastlines or crossed land. In the late 1400s, however, maritime developments opened the possibilities of exploration. As more reliable navigational tools (discussed on p. 27) became available, sailors were able to travel greater distances, no longer bound to keeping land in sight.

Shipbuilders redesigned ships, adding masts and rearranging sails. Ships became larger, more maneuverable, faster, and more seaworthy. As sailors gained more experience and traveled farther, mapmakers gathered more information about landfalls and ocean currents, allowing them to produce better maps. These developments made it possible to cross the Atlantic.

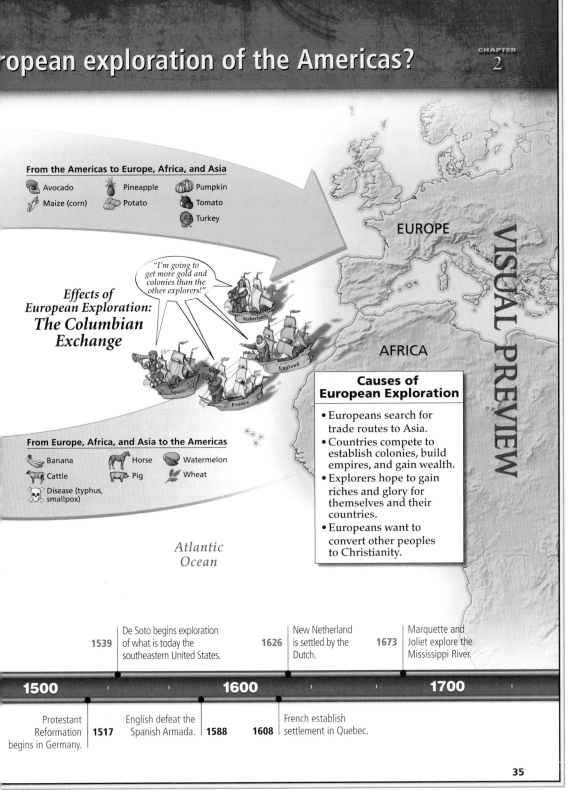

From the Americas to Europe, Africa, and Asia

- Avocado
- Maize (corn)
- Pineapple
- Potato
- Pumpkin
- Tomato
- Turkey

"I'm going to get more gold and colonies than the other explorers!"

Netherlands
England
Spain
France

Effects of European Exploration:
The Columbian Exchange

From Europe, Africa, and Asia to the Americas

- Banana
- Cattle
- Disease (typhus, smallpox)
- Horse
- Pig
- Watermelon
- Wheat

EUROPE

AFRICA

VISUAL PREVIEW

Atlantic Ocean

Causes of European Exploration

- Europeans search for trade routes to Asia.
- Countries compete to establish colonies, build empires, and gain wealth.
- Explorers hope to gain riches and glory for themselves and their countries.
- Europeans want to convert other peoples to Christianity.

1539 De Soto begins exploration of what is today the southeastern United States.	**1626** New Netherland is settled by the Dutch.	**1673** Marquette and Joliet explore the Mississippi River.	

1500   **1600**   **1700**

Protestant Reformation begins in Germany. **1517**   English defeat the Spanish Armada. **1588**   **1608** French establish settlement in Quebec.

35

Instruction (continued)

- Have students examine the timeline. Ask them to recall what the jagged break in the timeline represents. *(a long period of time)* Ask: **What is the span of time represented on the timeline?** *(1000-1700)* **Name two regions that were explored during these years.** *(North America, West Indies, southeastern United States, New Netherland, Mississippi River)*

- Have students look at the graphic of men in a canoe on the map of North America. Ask students to identify who the explorers are and what nation they represent. *(Marquette and Joliet, France)* Pair students and have them select two graphics to analyze, using the Think-Write-Pair-Share strategy (TE p. T25). Have students share their work with the class.

- Have students rewrite the Essential Question in simple terms in their notes. **Why did Europeans explore the Americas and what happened as a result?** You may also post this question in a prominent place in the classroom and leave it there while discussing the chapter. Tell students to use the section focus questions as a guide to answering the Essential Question as they read the chapter.

- Tell students that as they complete the Notetaking Study Guide for this chapter, they will be building the answer to the Chapter Essential Question.

Interactive Reading and Notetaking Study Guide, Chapter 2, (Adapted Version also available.)

Vocabulary Builder

Preview the Vocabulary Have students preview the vocabulary in the chapter and rate how well they know each word on the Word Knowledge Rating Form. Collect the sheets and explain that they will have a chance to go over the forms later.

All in One Teaching Resources, Unit 1, Word Knowledge Rating Form, p. 42

Monitor Progress Have students create a line drawing or a cartoon for these words to illustrate that they know what each word means. Review these images with the students. Have them then use the words in their own sentences. Ask volunteers to read their sentences aloud.

Review and Preview

Students have learned about the Renaissance and the beginnings of the Age of Exploration in Europe. Now they will focus on how the Europeans began exploring the Americas and Asia and the effects of the new contacts they made.

Section Focus Question

How did the search for a water route to Asia affect both Europe and the Americas?

Before you begin the lesson for the day, write the Section Focus Question on the board. (*Lesson Focus: The search for a water route to Asia brought Europeans to the Americas and led to the Columbian Exchange.*)

Prepare to Read

Build Background Knowledge   L2

Ask students what they know about the first European explorers. Encourage students to explain what challenges these explorers faced and what mistaken beliefs they had to overcome to reach distant continents. Use the Idea Wave strategy (TE, p. T24) to elicit responses. After they state what they already know, address any misconceptions that students may have about the topic. Remind them to confirm or revise their statements after they read the section.

Set a Purpose   L2

■ Read each statement in the Reading Readiness Guide aloud. Ask students to mark the statements True or False.

All in One Teaching Resources, Unit 1, Reading Readiness Guide, p. 43

■ Have students discuss the statements in pairs or groups of four, then mark their worksheets again. Use the Numbered Heads participation strategy (TE, p. T24) to call on students to share their group's perspectives. The students will return to these worksheets later.

SECTION 1

Columbus Opened the Door

❝ He opened the door to European settlement of the Americas—and all the devastation, innovation, and reinvention that came with it. ❞

—Christine Gibson, *Christopher Columbus, Hero or Villian*, in AmericanHeritage.com, October, 2005

◄ Columbus claims West Indies island for Spain.

The Age of Exploration

Objectives
- Explain what happened to the Vikings who explored Newfoundland.
- Describe the voyages of Christopher Columbus.
- Describe the expeditions of such Spanish explorers as Vasco Núñez de Balboa and Ferdinand Magellan.
- Explain the importance of the Columbian Exchange.

🔁 Reading Skill

Identify Stated Main Ideas Each section in this textbook begins with a paragraph headed **Why It Matters** that presents information you learned earlier and highlights the importance of what you will learn in this section. Then, throughout each section, important ideas are organized by major red headings that look like this: **First Visitors From Europe.**

Key Terms and People

Christopher Columbus
Vasco Núñez de Balboa
Ferdinand Magellan
strait
circumnavigate

Why It Matters The Crusades and the Renaissance led Europeans to look beyond their borders. Trade with Africa and Asia expanded, and an era of exploration began. As European sailors searched for shorter and easier routes to the riches of Asia, they came into contact with the people of the Americas.

❓ **Section Focus Question: How did the search for a water route to Asia affect both Europe and the Americas?**

First Visitors From Europe

If you had been in school 50 years ago and your teacher asked "Who discovered America?" you would probably have answered, "Christopher Columbus." But was Columbus really the first?

In a previous chapter, you have read that ancestors of today's Native Americans crossed into the Americas from Asia thousands of years ago. There are also many theories about people from Europe, Asia, and Africa who may have visited the Americas prior to Columbus.

So far, we only have evidence of the arrival of a European people known as the Vikings. The Vikings were a seagoing people who originally lived in the part of northern Europe known as Scandinavia.

In 1963, scientists found the remains of an early Viking settlement in Newfoundland. The findings supported the truth of old Viking stories. According to one story, a Viking named Leif Erikson and 35 others sailed from a colony on Greenland, in 1001, to investigate reports of land farther west. They explored the region and spent the winter in a place they named Vinland.

Differentiated Instruction

L3 Advanced Readers   **L3 Gifted and Talented**

Write an Interview Have students research the life of Christopher Columbus. Then pair students and have them use their research findings to write questions they would ask Columbus in an interview. Make sure that the questions focus on exploration, such as, "Why did you want to explore other lands?" and "To what places did you sail?" Then have students present their interviews to the class, with one student asking the questions and the other student answering as Columbus might.

The Voyages of Columbus Vinland existed only in <u>myths</u> for the next 500 years. Whether Christopher Columbus ever heard the stories is not known. However, Columbus believed he could reach Asia and the East by sailing west across the Atlantic Ocean. He never suspected that a huge landmass was blocking the way.

Christopher Columbus grew up near Genoa, an important port on the west coast of Italy. In the 1470s, he settled in Portugal, which was Europe's leading seafaring nation. Columbus sailed on Portuguese ships, studied maps and charts, and learned about the world beyond Europe. From all this he developed his idea for a voyage to Asia.

Portugal's king showed little interest in Columbus's plan. The king hoped to reach Asia by following the route Bartholomeu Dias and other Portuguese explorers were pioneering around southern Africa. He also believed the world was larger than Columbus had calculated. Thus, in his view, the voyage would be much longer than Columbus expected. For these reasons, Portugal refused to finance such a trip.

Columbus did not give up. He moved to Spain and set his plan before King Ferdinand and Queen Isabella. They liked Columbus's plan. But it took six years before they finally agreed to provide ships for the voyage.

Setting Sail In August 1492, about 90 men—most of them Spaniards—prepared to make the voyage. Columbus's ships—the *Niña*, the *Pinta*, and the *Santa Maria*—were tiny, between 55 and 90 feet long. Sailing with the wind, they covered up to 170 miles per day.

Columbus predicted that they would reach Asia in 21 days. After a month at sea, there was no sight of land. The crew became restless and spoke of mutiny, or soldiers and sailors rebelling against their officers. Columbus held firm against the threat.

Finally, on October 12, a sailor spotted land. Coming ashore in a small boat, Columbus claimed the island for Spain. Curious islanders soon gathered on the beach. Believing he was in the Asian islands known as the Indies, Columbus called these people Indians. The next day he wrote in his journal, "I intend to go see if I can find the island of Japan."

Columbus then sailed southwest to a large island. At first he thought it was Japan. Actually, Columbus was on the island of Cuba. His guides next pointed Columbus west to the island of Hispaniola. Columbus set sail to return to Spain in January 1493.

Vocabulary Builder
myth (mihth) *n.* traditional story of unknown authorship

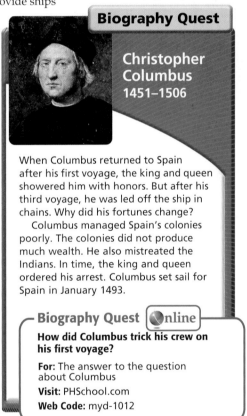

Biography Quest

Christopher Columbus
1451–1506

When Columbus returned to Spain after his first voyage, the king and queen showered him with honors. But after his third voyage, he was led off the ship in chains. Why did his fortunes change?

Columbus managed Spain's colonies poorly. The colonies did not produce much wealth. He also mistreated the Indians. In time, the king and queen ordered his arrest. Columbus set sail for Spain in January 1493.

Biography Quest **Online**

How did Columbus trick his crew on his first voyage?

For: The answer to the question about Columbus
Visit: PHSchool.com
Web Code: myd-1012

First Visitors from Europe
p. 36

Instruction L2

- **Vocabulary Builder** Before teaching this section, preteach the High-Use Words **myth** and **negative** before reading, using the strategy on TE p. T21. **Key Terms** Following the instructions on p. 7, have students create a See It–Remember It chart for the Key Terms in this chapter.

- Have students read First Visitors From Europe using the ReQuest strategy (TE, p. T37).

- Ask students: **Why did Columbus try to sail west across the Atlantic Ocean?** (*He hoped to find a water route to Asia.*)

- After you have completed this discussion, assign the worksheet Journal of Christopher Columbus. After students have completed the worksheet, discuss reasons why Columbus was confused about where he was when he found land. (*Columbus believed he had sailed to Asia and did not know that he had arrived on a completely different continent.*)

All in One Teaching Resources, Unit 1, Journal of Christopher Columbus, p. 47

- Ask: **Why do you think coastal European countries such as Spain, England, and the Netherlands sent explorers to North America, but inland countries did not?** (*Coastal countries may have already had fleets of ships, probably for fishing.*)

Use the information below to teach students this section's high-use words.

High-Use Word	Definition and Sample Sentence
myth, p. 37	*n.* traditional story of unknown authorship The ancient Greeks developed many **myths** to explain the world around them.
negative, p. 41	*adj.* opposite to something regarded as positive The arrival of Europeans in the Americas had some **negative** results for the Native Americans.

Answer

Biography Quest Columbus kept a second travel log, showing a lesser distance traveled to quiet the crew's anxiety about the distance from home.

Instruction (continued)

- Display the History Interactive transparency European Exploration 1492–1609 to show students the travels of European explorers during the fifteenth through seventeenth centuries.

Color Transparencies, European Exploration 1492–1609

- After you have completed this discussion, assign the worksheet on the biography of Christopher Columbus to further understand his life. After students have completed the worksheet, ask: **How did Columbus come to live in Portugal?** (*He was shipwrecked after departing from Genoa, Italy, and decided to remain in Portugal to live.*)

All in One Teaching Resources, Unit 1, Christopher Columbus, p. 48

Independent Practice

Have students begin to fill in the Study Guide for this section.

Interactive Reading and Notetaking Study Guide, Chapter 2, Section 1 (Adapted Version also available.)

Monitor Progress

As students fill in the Notetaking Study Guide, circulate to make sure that they understand the reasons why Europeans began to seek a sea route to Asia. If students do not have a good understanding, have them reread the section. Provide assistance as needed.

Answers

Draw Conclusions Possible answer: Explorers used routes that had already been proven to be successful in order to increase their chances of success.

Reading Skill Columbus believed he could reach Asia by sailing west across the Atlantic Ocean, and he was a skilled sailor.

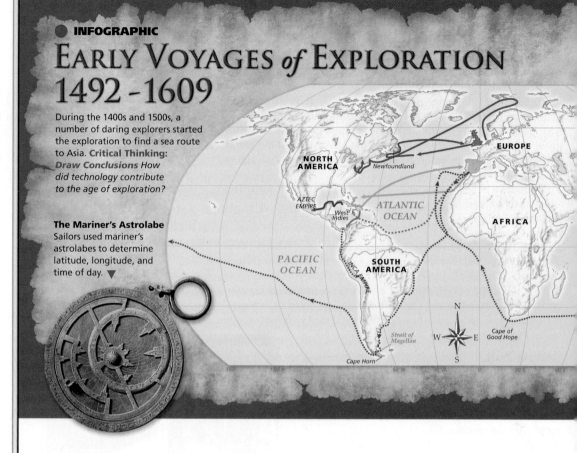

INFOGRAPHIC

EARLY VOYAGES *of* EXPLORATION 1492-1609

During the 1400s and 1500s, a number of daring explorers started the exploration to find a sea route to Asia. **Critical Thinking: *Draw Conclusions*** How did technology contribute to the age of exploration?

The Mariner's Astrolabe Sailors used mariner's astrolabes to determine latitude, longitude, and time of day. ▼

Identify Stated Main Ideas What important idea from the first paragraph following the subheading "Spain Backs More Voyages" is discussed throughout the passage?

Spain Backs More Voyages In Spain, Columbus reported that there were huge amounts of gold in the land he referred to as the West Indies. The grateful monarchs made him governor of all he had claimed for Spain.

In September 1493, he sailed again for the West Indies. This time he commanded 17 ships filled with 1,500 soldiers, settlers, and priests. The Spanish planned to colonize and rule the land they thought was the West Indies. They also intended to convert the people there to Christianity.

On this second voyage, Columbus discovered other islands, including Puerto Rico. He found that the men he had left behind on Hispaniola had been killed by Indians. Not discouraged, Columbus built another settlement nearby and enslaved the local Indians to dig for gold. Within a few months, 12 of his ships returned to Spain, with gold, trinkets, and a number of captives.

On his third expedition in 1498, Columbus reached the northern coast of South America and decided it was the Asian mainland. Spain permitted him to try to prove his claims in a fourth voyage, in 1502.

38 Chapter 2 Europe Looks Outward

Differentiated Instruction

L1 English Language Learners   L1 Less Proficient Readers

Reading a Map Pair students and ask them to choose two of the voyages depicted on the map on pp. 38–39. For each trip, have students trace the route with their finger. Then, identify the continents and countries the explorer sailed to, in the order he saw them. Have students write a detailed description that identifies the route of each of the two voyages they have chosen. Remind students that many of the countries identified on today's maps did not have the same names or boundaries at the time of the explorers' voyages. Encourage students to use the maps in the front of their textbooks to identify places using the names that they have today.

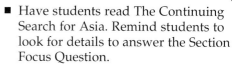

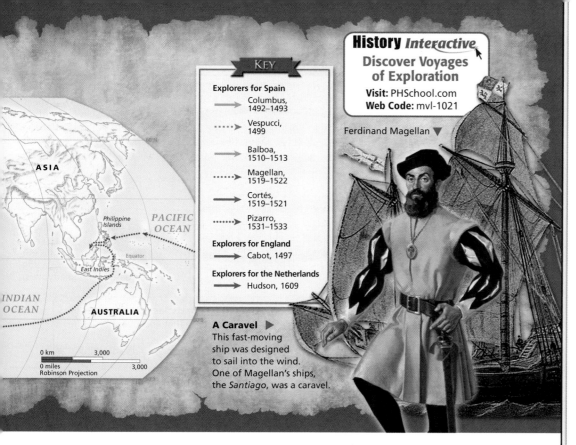

KEY

Explorers for Spain

→ Columbus, 1492–1493

┄┄► Vespucci, 1499

→ Balboa, 1510–1513

┄┄► Magellan, 1519–1522

→ Cortés, 1519–1521

┄┄► Pizarro, 1531–1533

Explorers for England

→ Cabot, 1497

Explorers for the Netherlands

→ Hudson, 1609

History *Interactive*

Discover Voyages of Exploration

Visit: PHSchool.com
Web Code: mvl-1021

Ferdinand Magellan ▼

A Caravel ►
This fast-moving ship was designed to sail into the wind. One of Magellan's ships, the *Santiago*, was a caravel.

0 km 3,000
0 miles 3,000
Robinson Projection

He returned to Spain two years later with his beliefs unchanged. Columbus died in 1506, still convinced that he had reached Asia.

☑ **Checkpoint** **Why were Spain's monarchs interested in the proposal Columbus made to them?**

The Continuing Search for Asia

Many explorers followed the route charted by Columbus. Another Italian explorer, Amerigo Vespucci, made two trips to the new lands. His trips convinced Vespucci that the lands he saw were not part of Asia. Upon his return to Europe, he wrote a letter describing a "new world . . . more densely peopled and full of animals than our Europe or Asia or Africa." A German mapmaker labeled the region "the land of Amerigo" on his maps. The name was soon shortened to "America."

Meanwhile, the Spanish continued to explore and colonize. In 1510, Vasco Núñez de Balboa, a Spanish colonist, explored the Caribbean coast of what is now Panama. Hacking his way across the jungle, he became the first European to set eyes on the Pacific Ocean.

Instruction L2

- Have students read The Continuing Search for Asia. Remind students to look for details to answer the Section Focus Question.

- Ask students: **How did America get its name?** (*A German mapmaker named the land after the explorer Amerigo Vespucci, and the name was shortened to America.*)

- Discuss with students the difficulties that Magellan and his sailors faced as the fleet exited the Strait of Magellan. (*They had no idea how far they would have to travel to reach land or how much food and other supplies they would need to have.*)

Independent Practice

Have students continue to fill in the Study Guide for this section.

📖 **Interactive Reading and Notetaking Study Guide,** Chapter 2, Section 1 (Adapted Version also available.)

Monitor Progress

As students fill in the Notetaking Study Guide, circulate to make sure that they understand the challenges the European explorers faced during their journeys. If students do not have a good understanding, have them reread the section. Provide assistance as needed.

History Background

Ferdinand Magellan Ferdinand Magellan, a native of Portugal, sailed for both the Portuguese and the Spanish governments during his lifetime. In his early career, Magellan enlisted in the Portuguese fleet and fought battles off the African and Indian coasts to help secure Portuguese supremacy of the sea. After returning from fighting in Morocco, he requested a raise in pay from the Portuguese king, who refused. After a second refusal, he offered his services to King Charles of Spain, who sent Magellan on a mission to claim the Spice Islands for that country. It was on this voyage that some of his crew became the first people to circumnavigate the globe.

Answer

☑ **Checkpoint** They were eager for the wealth promised by trade.

The Columbian Exchange

p. 41

Instruction

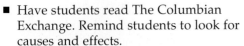

- Have students read The Columbian Exchange. Remind students to look for causes and effects.

- Have students define the Columbian Exchange between the Eastern and Western Hemispheres. Ask: **What crops were taken from the Americas to the Eastern Hemisphere?** (*Maize, potato, sweet potato, beans, peanut, squash, pumpkin, pineapple, tomato, cocoa, peppers, avocado, and turkeys*)

- Discuss with students the negative impact of European diseases on the Native American population. See that students understand that many events have unintended consequences. (*Europeans came to the Americas looking for a route to Asia and ended up exposing Native Americans to deadly diseases.*)

Independent Practice

Have students complete the Study Guide for this section.

Interactive Reading and Notetaking Study Guide, Chapter 2, Section 1 (Adapted Version also available.)

Monitor Progress

As students fill in the Notetaking Study Guide, circulate to make sure that they understand the Columbian Exchange. Provide assistance as needed.

Tell students to fill in the last column of the Reading Readiness Guide. Probe for what they learned that confirms or invalidates each statement.

All in One Teaching Resources, Unit 1, Reading Readiness Guide, p. 43

Answers

Reading Charts (a) Sheep, horses, chickens, pigs, and goats **(b)** Students will probably say that Europeans benefited the most because many Native Americans died of European diseases.

✓Checkpoint Balboa became the first European to see the Pacific Ocean. Magellan's sailors were the first to circumnavigate Earth.

The Columbian Exchange

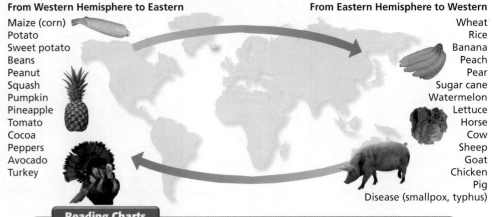

From Western Hemisphere to Eastern

Maize (corn)
Potato
Sweet potato
Beans
Peanut
Squash
Pumpkin
Pineapple
Tomato
Cocoa
Peppers
Avocado
Turkey

From Eastern Hemisphere to Western

Wheat
Rice
Banana
Peach
Pear
Sugar cane
Watermelon
Lettuce
Horse
Cow
Sheep
Goat
Chicken
Pig
Disease (smallpox, typhus)

Reading Charts
Skills Activity

The Columbian Exchange brought many European, Asian, and African goods to the Americas. At the same time, American crops and livestock were distributed to the rest of the world.

(a) Interpret Charts Identify two kinds of farm animals that Europeans brought to the Americas.

(b) Identify Benefits Who do you think benefited most from the Columbian Exchange? Explain.

The discovery that another ocean lay west of the Americas did not end the search for a water route to Asia. In September 1519, Portuguese explorer Ferdinand Magellan set out to find an Atlantic-Pacific passage.

For more than a year, the small fleet slowly moved down the South American coast looking for a strait, a narrow passage that connects two large bodies of water. As it pushed farther south than earlier expeditions, it encountered penguins and other animals that no European had ever seen before. Finally, near the southern tip of present-day Argentina, Magellan found a narrow passage. After 38 days of battling winds, tides, and currents, his ships exited what today is called the Strait of Magellan. They now entered the large ocean Balboa had seen nine or ten years earlier. Although Magellan did not realize it, Asia was still thousands of miles away.

Magellan finally reached the Philippine Islands. There, he and several others were killed in a battle with Filipinos. The survivors fled in two of the ships. One ship finally reached Spain, in September 1522. Three years after they had begun, the 18 men aboard became first to circumnavigate, or travel around, the entire Earth.

✓Checkpoint What were the contributions of Balboa and Magellan as explorers?

Differentiated Instruction

L1 English Language Learners

Understanding the Exchange To help students understand why the Columbian Exchange was important, ask them to use the Idea Wave strategy (TE, p. T24) to brainstorm about items from their native countries that may be difficult to find in the United States. Have students compile a list of these items. Then ask: **What are these items used for? How might they be helpful to people in this country?** Have students share their responses with the class.

The Columbian Exchange

These early Spanish voyages set the stage for a great exchange between the Western and the Eastern hemispheres. The next century began what is now known as the Columbian Exchange, a transfer of people, products, and ideas between the hemispheres.

Many of the changes brought about by the Columbian Exchange were positive. Europeans introduced cows, hogs, and other domestic animals to the Western Hemisphere. Many food plants, such as wheat and oats, also arrived on the ships that brought the Europeans.

The exchange also had <u>negative</u> effects on the Americas. Europeans brought germs to which Native Americans had no immunity, or natural resistance. Smallpox, chickenpox, measles, and other contagious diseases killed Native Americans by the thousands.

The impact of the Americas on Europe was no less important. Europeans in the Americas found plants and animals they had never seen before either. For example, the Americas introduced llamas, turkeys, squirrels, and muskrats to the rest of the world. More important, however, were the crops that Native Americans taught the Europeans to cultivate. Today, plants that once were found only in the Americas account for nearly one third of the world's food supply.

Vocabulary Builder
<u>negative</u> (NEHG ah tihv) *adj.* opposite to something regarded as positive

✓**Checkpoint** What impact did the Columbian Exchange have on Europe?

☆ **Looking Back and Ahead** The voyages of Columbus marked the beginning of a new historical era. The foothold he established in the Caribbean would expand into a vast empire. By 1600, Spain would control much of North and South America and would be one of the world's richest nations.

Section 1 | **Check Your Progress**

Progress Monitoring ⬤nline
For: Self-test with instant help
Visit: PHSchool.com
Web Code: mva-1021

Comprehension and Critical Thinking

1. (a) Recall Who were the Vikings?
(b) Apply Information What problems might there be with using Viking myths as historical sources?

2. (a) Recall What is the Columbian Exchange?
(b) Support a Point of View Did the Columbian Exchange bring more changes to the Americas or to Europe? Explain your view.

⟳ Reading Skill
3. Identify Stated Main Ideas Read the text under the heading "The Columbian Exchange." Identify the stated main idea and explain how the paragraphs support that idea.

Key Terms
Fill in the blanks with the correct key terms.
4. Magellan's ships sailed through a _____ in order to reach the Pacific Ocean.
5. The few survivors of Magellan's crew were the first to _____ Earth.

Writing
6. Create a timeline showing early explorations in the Americas. Choose three entries that you think are most significant. For each choice, write one or two sentences explaining why you made that choice.

Assess Progress L2

Have students complete Check Your Progress. Administer the Section Quiz.

All in One Teaching Resources, Unit 1, Section Quiz, p. 53

To further assess student understanding, use the Progress Monitoring Transparency.

Progress Monitoring Transparencies, Chapter 2, Section 1

Reteach L1

If students need more instruction, have them read this section in the Interactive Reading and Notetaking Study Guide and complete the accompanying question.

📖 **Interactive Reading and Notetaking Study Guide,** Chapter 2, Section 1 (Adapted Version also available.)

Extend L3

Have students complete the History Interactive activity online.

Extend ⬤nline
For: Help with the History Interactive
Visit: PHSchool.com
Web Code: mvp-0114

Progress Monitoring Online

Students may check their comprehension of this section by completing the Progress Monitoring Online graphic organizer and self-quiz.

Section 1 Check Your Progress

1. (a) Explorers from Scandinavia who preceded Columbus to the Americas **(b)** Myths or legends are not able to be proved.

2. (a) The transfer of people, products, and ideas between the Western and Eastern hemispheres after Columbus's arrival in the Western Hemisphere

(b) The Columbian Exchange brought more changes to Europe because many different kinds of crops and animals were introduced to Europe.

3. "The next century began what is now known as the Columbian Exchange, a transfer of people, products, and ideas between the hemispheres." The next paragraphs describe this transfer in detail.

4. strait

5. circumnavigate

6. Students should point out significant entries on their timelines and explain their importance.

Answer

✓**Checkpoint** New people, products, and ideas were introduced in Europe.

Danger at Sea
p. 42

Build Background Knowledge L2

Ask students to suppose that they are going hiking in a large forest. They have no map to guide them. Have students use the Idea Wave strategy (TE, p. T24) to brainstorm for what they might need to bring with them during the hike. Then have them make a list of the dangers they might encounter along the way.

Instruction L2

- Read Danger at Sea with the students. Ask: **Why were Europeans unaware of what they might find on their voyages of discovery?** (*They were sailing into uncharted territory.*)

- Discuss some of the dangers of sea travel. (*Storms could sink ships, sailors might become lost, pirates might attack ships, crews could run out of supplies.*)

- Ask: **Do you think the benefits of these voyages would have outweighed the dangers? Why or why not?** (*Students may suggest that discovering new lands was worth the dangers of sea travel because a country could gain new goods and great wealth. Students may also suggest that a successful country would not need to subject its people to the dangers of sea travel.*)

Monitor Progress

Ask students to complete the Analyze Life at the Time activity. Circulate to make sure that individuals understand the dangers of sea travel during European voyages of discovery. Provide assistance as needed.

LIFE AT THE TIME

Danger at Sea

When Europeans began to make voyages of discovery, they had no idea what they would find. Some of the dangers that they feared did not really exist. Other dangers were all too real. But the more they traveled, the more their views of the world changed.

◀ **Fearsome Sea Monsters**

Popular tales warned that the oceans were filled with dragons, sea serpents, and other monsters. Happily, these dangers turned out to be imaginary.

▲ **Storms at Sea**

One real danger was bad weather. A violent storm could send a ship and its whole crew to the bottom of the ocean.

Differentiated Instruction

L1 Less Proficient Readers   **L1** Special Needs

Organizing Information To help students organize and understand the information in this feature, have them create a chart that lists in a separate row each of the dangers identified in the text. Next to each danger, have students write its consequences. Then have students work in pairs to think about how each danger might be prevented. Post the charts so that students may refer to them when completing the Life at the Time activity.

▼ Getting Lost

Another real fear was that a ship might get lost in the vast, endless ocean. Fortunately, improved navigational tools, like the sextant and more accurate maps, made this danger less likely.

Sextant

▼ Starvation

Running low on supplies at sea meant disaster. One Spanish sailor described what happened when his ship ran out of food.

"We . . . ate only old biscuit reduced to powder, full of grubs and stinking from the dirt which rats had made on it. We drank water that was yellow and stinking."

—Antonio Pigafetta, *Journal*

Piracy ▲

When ships began to carry treasure to Europe, a new danger emerged: piracy. Pirates would attack merchant ships, steal the cargo, and often, murder the crew. Some pirates, such as Captain Kidd (shown above), became legendary for their boldness.

Analyze LIFE AT THE TIME

Imagine you are a European sailor about to go on an ocean voyage. Write a letter explaining your view of the world and why you are going on the voyage in spite of the dangers.

Writing Rubrics Share this rubric with students.

Score 1 Letter is poorly written, ideas not clearly stated, does not address topic.
Score 2 Letter is somewhat well written, ideas not fully developed, some details irrelevant.
Score 3 Letter is well written, ideas clearly stated, opinions well supported.
Score 4 Letter is very well written, ideas are well developed and supported, with a strong conclusion.

History Background

Captain Kidd Captain William Kidd did not begin his sea career as a pirate. When piracy became a problem for English merchant ships on their way to the colonies, Kidd was hired by the colonial governor of New York to help stop it. He was also hired as a privateer—someone who legally captures other countries' ships—against the French. When Kidd failed to capture any French ships, he decided to become a pirate himself. He captured several ships and their treasures before returning to New York to find himself wanted for piracy. Although he attempted to persuade the New York governor of his innocence, he was sent to trial in England, found guilty of piracy, and hanged.

Answer

Analyze LIFE AT THE TIME Students' letters will differ, but they should demonstrate an understanding of the dangers of sea travel—legends of sea monsters and risks of storms, getting lost, starvation, and piracy—and the reasons why voyages of discovery were important.

Review and Preview

Students have learned about new contacts between peoples of the Eastern and Western hemispheres during the Age of Exploration. Now students will focus on Spain's early success at establishing colonies in the Americas.

Section Focus Question

How did Spain establish an empire in the Americas?

Before you begin the lesson for the day, write the Section Focus Question on the board. (*Lesson Focus: Spanish conquistadors took control of land in the Americas, and then Spain created a formal system to rule over the new lands.*)

Prepare to Read

Build Background Knowledge L2

Remind students about what they have learned about the Columbian Exchange. Ask students to look at the illustration and caption on p. 45 to predict one outcome of the Columbian Exchange. Tell them they will review their predictions and correct them as needed after they have read the section.

Set a Purpose L2

■ Read each statement in the Reading Readiness Guide aloud. Ask students to mark the statements True or False.

All in One Teaching Resources, Unit 1, Reading Readiness Guide, p. 44

■ Have students discuss the statements in pairs or groups of four, then mark their worksheets again. Use the Numbered Heads participation strategy (TE, p. T24) to call on students to share their group's perspectives. The students will return to these worksheets later.

◀ Hernando de Soto

The Indians Fear Us

❝ The Indians of the coast, because of some fears of us, have abandoned all the country, so that for thirty leagues not a man of them has halted. ❞

—Hernando de Soto, Spanish explorer and conqueror, report on expedition to Florida, 1539

Spain's Empire in the Americas

Objectives

• Describe how the Spanish were able to defeat the empires of the Aztecs and Incas.

• Identify Spanish explorations in areas that later became part of the United States.

• Explain how society was organized in Spain's empire in the Americas.

🔄 Reading Skill

Identify Supporting Details Text includes details to support a main idea. These details might be examples, reasons, facts, or descriptions. They enable readers to understand a main idea by helping them to picture it, to make sense of its argument or to believe its accuracy. As you read Section 2, look for details that support the main ideas.

Key Terms and People

conquistador	Bartolomé de Las
Hernando Cortés	Casas
Moctezuma	mission
plantation	*peninsular*
encomienda	

Why It Matters Even though Columbus never realized that he had reached a region previously unknown to Europeans, his voyages gave Spain a head start on its European rivals in colonizing the Americas.

❓ **Section Focus Question: How did Spain establish an empire in the Americas?**

Spanish Conquistadors

By the early 1500s, the Spanish had a firm foothold in the Americas. From Spain's island colonies in the Caribbean, soldier-adventurers called **conquistadors** set out to explore and conquer a world unknown to them. They hoped for riches and glory for themselves and for Spain.

Cortés and Pizarro In 1519, conquistador Hernando Cortés sailed from Cuba to Mexico with more than 500 soldiers. The first Native Americans he met presented him with gifts of gold.

On November 8, 1519, Cortés marched into the Aztec capital city of Tenochtitlán. As the Spaniards moved closer to Tenochtitlán, many Native Americans joined them. Conquered by the Aztecs, they hated the Aztec's brutal rule.

The Aztec leader Moctezuma (mokt uh ZOO muh) (also spelled *Montezuma*) met with Cortés and tried to get him to leave by offering him gold. The gold had the opposite effect. Cortés took Moctezuma hostage and claimed all of Mexico for Spain. However, the Aztecs soon rebelled and forced the Spaniards to flee.

44 Chapter 2 Europe Looks Outward

Differentiated Instruction

L1 Less Proficient Readers   **L1 Special Needs**

Study Aid To help students remember details about the Spanish conquistadors, have them create a graphic organizer showing the relationships among the various groups identified in the text, such as the Spanish, the Incas, and the Aztecs. Students should provide details about each of these groups in their graphic organizers.

About a year later, Cortés returned with a larger force, recaptured Tenochtitlán, and then destroyed it. In its place he built Mexico City, the capital of the Spanish colony of New Spain.

Cortés used the same methods to subdue the Aztecs in Mexico that another conquistador, Francisco Pizarro, used in South America. Pizarro landed on the coast of Peru in 1531 to search for the Incas, who were said to have much gold. In September 1532, he led about 170 soldiers through the jungle into the heart of the Inca Empire. Pizarro then took the Inca ruler Atahualpa (ah tuh WAHL puh) prisoner. Although the Inca people paid a huge ransom to free their ruler, Pizarro executed him anyway. By November 1533, the Spanish had defeated the leaderless Incas and captured their capital city of Cuzco.

Why the Spanish Were Victorious How could a few hundred Spanish soldiers defeat Native American armies many times their size? Several <u>factors</u> explain the Spaniards' success. First among these was technology. The Indians' weapons simply were no match for the armor, muskets, and cannons of the Europeans. In addition, many of the Spaniards rode horses, which the Native Americans had never before seen. Finally, the Native Americans were divided among themselves. In Peru, a civil war had just ended. In Mexico, many Native Americans hated the Aztecs.

✓**Checkpoint** Why were a few Spanish conquistadors able to defeat the larger armies of the Aztecs and Incas?

Vocabulary Builder
<u>factor</u> (FAK tor) **n.** important element of something

Spanish Conquistadors
The Spanish soldiers were outnumbered by the Aztecs and the Incas, yet they were able to easily defeat these empires.
Critical Thinking: Explain Problems *Some Native Americans sided with the Spanish against the Aztecs and the Incas. What problems might this have caused between the groups after the battle?*

Section 2 Spain's Empire in the Americas **45**

Vocabulary Builder

Use the information below to teach students this section's high-use words.

High-Use Word	Definition and Sample Sentence
factor, p. 45	*n.* important element of something A major **factor** in pushing Spain to explore a sea route to Asia was the control of the land route by Italy.
rigid, p. 48	*adj.* not bending; not flexible European feudalism was a **rigid** social system that prevented people from rising in society.

Teach

Spanish Conquistadors
p. 44

Instruction L2

- **High-Use Words** Before teaching this section, preteach the High-Use Words **factor** and **rigid** before reading, using the strategy on TE p. T21.
  Key Terms Have students continue filling in the See It–Remember It chart for the Key Terms in this chapter.

- Have students read Spanish Conquistadors using the Structured Silent Reading strategy (TE, p. T22).

- Ask students: **Why did some Native Americans join the Spanish against the Aztecs?** (*The ruling Aztecs treated them unfairly.*)

- Discuss the ways that technology contributed to the Spanish victories over larger armies of Native Americans. (*The more advanced technology of the Spanish meant that they had significantly better weapons than the Native Americans.*)

Independent Practice
Have students begin to fill in the Study Guide for this section.

📖 **Interactive Reading and Notetaking Study Guide,** Chapter 2, Section 2 (Adapted Version also available.)

Monitor Progress

As students fill in the Notetaking Study Guide, circulate to make sure that they understand how the conquistadors helped Spain gain territory in the Americas. Provide assistance as needed.

 Explore More Video

Discovery School Video
Show the video *Spanish Exploration in the Americas* to tell the story of Aztec life before the arrival of the Spanish.

Answers

✓**Checkpoint** The Spanish had much better weapons than the Native Americans, as well as horses, and the Native American groups were very divided.

Explain Problems Answers may differ, but students may say that some Native Americans may have been treated badly by the Aztecs and/or the Incas.

Chapter 2 **45**

Spanish Explorers in North America

Instruction **L2**

- Have students read Spanish Explorers in North America. Remind students to look for the sequence of events.

- Ask: **Why did Spanish explorers travel to North America?** (*They hoped to find gold.*)

- Discuss with students the role that information played in the Spanish exploration of the Americas. See that students understand that information, misinformation, and a need for more information played a large role in this exploration. (*The Spanish were motivated to explore by stories about cities of gold, but they suffered greatly when they tried to explore new lands about which they did not have much knowledge.*)

Independent Practice

Have students continue to fill in the Study Guide for this section.

📖 **Interactive Reading and Notetaking Study Guide,** Chapter 2, Section 2 (Adapted Version also available.)

Monitor Progress

As students fill in the Notetaking Study Guide, circulate to make sure that they understand the reasons why the Spanish began exploring North America. If students do not have a good understanding, have them reread the section. Provide assistance as needed.

Answers

MAP MASTER Skills Activity **(a)** Ponce de León–Puerto Rico, the Southeastern United States from Florida to Louisiana; Cabeza de Vaca/Estevanico–western Florida, Texas, Mexico, and New Mexico; De Soto–southeastern United States from the Carolinas to Oklahoma; Coronado–New Mexico, Texas, Arizona, and Kansas **(b)** the southern United States

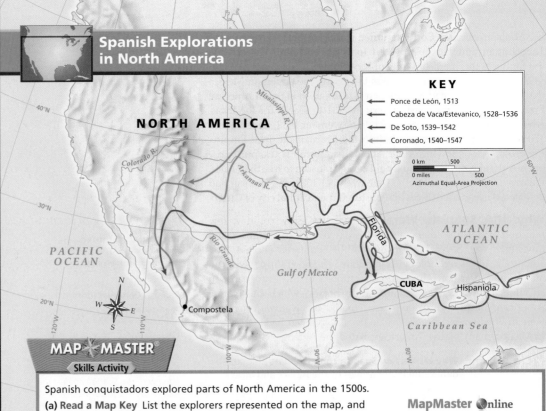

Spanish Explorations in North America

KEY
- ← Ponce de León, 1513
- ← Cabeza de Vaca/Estevanico, 1528–1536
- ← De Soto, 1539–1542
- ← Coronado, 1540–1547

0 km 500
0 miles 500
Azimuthal Equal-Area Projection

NORTH AMERICA

PACIFIC OCEAN · Compostela · Gulf of Mexico · ATLANTIC OCEAN · CUBA · Hispaniola · Caribbean Sea · Florida

Colorado R. · Rio Grande · Arkansas R. · Mississippi R.

MAP MASTER®
Skills Activity

Spanish conquistadors explored parts of North America in the 1500s.

(a) Read a Map Key List the explorers represented on the map, and briefly describe the area each one explored.

(b) Link Past and Present Based on this map, in what areas of the present-day United States would you expect to find Latino influence strongest?

MapMaster Online

For: Interactive map
Visit: PHSchool.com
Web Code: mvp-1022

Spanish Explorers in North America

The Spanish did not limit themselves to the exploration of what we now call Latin America. In 1513, Juan Ponce de León sailed north from Puerto Rico to investigate reports of a large island. He found beautiful flowers there, so he named the place *La Florida.* Ponce de León became the first Spaniard to set foot in what is now the United States.

Exploration along Florida's west coast began in 1528, when about 400 Spaniards landed near the present-day city of St. Petersburg. Finding none of the gold they had hoped for, they marched into northern Florida. There, under attack by Native Americans, they built five crude boats and set out to sea. About 80 survivors led by Álvar Núñez Cabeza de Vaca eventually landed at present-day Galveston Island on the Texas coast.

Starvation and disease reduced their number to 15 before Indians enslaved them. Finally, only four—including Cabeza de Vaca and Estevanico, an African slave—remained alive. After six years in

Differentiated Instruction

L3 Advanced Readers   **L3 Gifted and Talented**

Write a Newspaper Article Have students learn more about Spanish exploration of North America and the challenges that explorers faced. Have students write a story about one of the expeditions for a newspaper. Tell them that their story should be directed toward either a Spanish or a Native American audience. Remind students to use the five W's: who, what, where, when, and why. Have students share their articles with the class.

captivity, they escaped and spent two more years finding their way to Mexico City. In 1536, eight years after landing in Florida, the four survivors of the 400-man expedition returned to Spanish lands.

In Mexico City, the men related stories they had heard from Native Americans about seven great cities filled with gold far to the north. Officials asked the survivors to head an expedition to find these cities. However, only Estevanico was willing to go. In 1539, he led a group into what is now western New Mexico. When Estevanico was killed by Indians, the others returned to Mexico City.

The conquistador Francisco Coronado (koh roh NAH doh) set out with about 1,100 Spaniards and Native Americans to find the golden city. Although he never found the city, he did explore much of what is now New Mexico, Arizona, Texas, and Kansas.

While Coronado was trekking through the southwest, Hernando de Soto was searching for riches in today's southeastern United States. De Soto traveled as far north as the Carolinas and as far west as Oklahoma. He died in what is now Louisiana, in 1542, having found the Mississippi River but no cities of gold.

Native Americans received harsh treatment from Spaniards.

✅**Checkpoint** What regions in the present-day United States did Spaniards explore?

Colonizing Spanish America

At first, Spain let the conquistadors govern the lands they had conquered. However, this was not successful. In order to control its new empire, Spain created a formal system of government to rule its colonies.

Harsh Life for Native Americans Within Spain's vast empire, there was little place for Native Americans except as a source of labor. Government officials granted settlers huge tracts of land to start mines, ranches, and plantations—large farms worked by laborers who live on the property. To help Spanish colonists find needed workers, the Spanish government granted *encomiendas* (ehn KOH mee ehn dahz). These were land grants that included the right to demand labor or taxes from Native Americans. The Spanish forced Native Americans to work in the gold and silver mines. Many died when the tunnels caved in. Some Spaniards protested this cruel treatment. The priest Bartolomé de Las Casas traveled through New Spain working for reform. Largely due to Las Casas's efforts, the government of Spain ordered reform of the *encomienda* system in the mid-1500s.

Like other Europeans in the Americas, the Spanish believed they had a duty to convert Native Americans to Christianity. They set up missions, religious settlements, run by Catholic priests and friars. San Francisco, San Diego, San Antonio, and a number of other U.S. cities got their start as Spanish missions in the 1700s.

History Background

Bartolomé de Las Casas Las Casas himself received an *encomienda* as a reward for joining several expeditions in the Americas. After helping take control of Cuba in 1513, he received a land grant which included the right to demand work from local Native Americans. However, a year later he gave up his *encomienda* and began working to improve conditions for Native Americans. In his work *Historia de las Indias*, published after his death, Las Casas described domination, oppression, and injustice as sins for which Spain would one day be divinely punished.

Colonizing Spanish America

p. 47

Instruction

- Have students read Colonizing Spanish America. Remind students to look for details that answer the reading checkpoint question.

- Ask: **How did *encomiendas* affect life in the Spanish colonies?** (*They not only gave Spanish colonists the right to claim land but also the power to force Native Americans to work the land and pay taxes.*)

- Ask: **Why did the Spanish begin bringing enslaved Africans to the Americas?** (*The death toll among Native Americans was so high that there were not enough workers in the colonies.*)

- Discuss how the rigid social system helped Spain maintain control over the colonies. (*The most powerful people in the colonies were the people who had been born in Spain, so Spanish interests were always represented by the people in power.*)

- Display the transparency The *Encomienda* System to show students the details of Spanish colonization in North America.

Color Transparencies, The *Encomienda* System

Independent Practice

Have students complete the Study Guide for this section.

📖 **Interactive Reading and Notetaking Study Guide,** Chapter 2, Section 2 (Adapted Version also available.)

Monitor Progress

- As students fill in the Notetaking Study Guide, circulate to make sure that they understand Spanish colonization of North America. If students do not have a good understanding, have them reread the section. Provide assistance as needed.

- Tell students to fill in the last column of the Reading Readiness Guide. Probe for what they learned that confirms or invalidates each statement.

All in One **Teaching Resources, Unit 1,** Reading Readiness Guide, p. 44

Answer

✅**Checkpoint** the Southeast and the Southwest

Assess and Reteach

Assess Progress `L2`

Have students complete Check Your Progress. Administer the Section Quiz.

All in One Teaching Resources, Unit 1, Section Quiz, p. 54

To further assess student understanding, use the Progress Monitoring Transparency.

Progress Monitoring Transparencies, Chapter 2, Section 2

Reteach `L1`

If students need more instruction, have them read this section in the Interactive Reading and Notetaking Study Guide and complete the accompanying question.

Interactive Reading and Notetaking Study Guide, Chapter 2, Section 2 (Adapted Version also available.)

Extend `L3`

Have students conduct research to find out more about the Aztecs, Incas, or other Native American empires. Ask students to create an illustrated brochure about one of them, including such information as the empire's location, its size, and details about its people. Have volunteers share their brochures with the class.

Progress Monitoring Online

Students may check their comprehension of this section by completing the Progress Monitoring Online graphic organizer and self-quiz.

Answers

Reading Skill Almost all government officials came from the *peninsulares* class, people who were born in Spain. Next were Creoles, colonists born in America of two Spanish parents.

✓Checkpoint They were forced to pay taxes or work in often dangerous conditions.

Section 2 Check Your Progress

1. (a) The Southeastern and Southwestern areas
(b) They defeated the empires that existed and gathered information about the lands to take back to Spain.

2. (a) He convinced Spain to reform the *encomienda* system.
(b) Possible answer: Their lives were

The Trade in Humans As the death toll for Native Americans continued to rise, Spanish colonists looked across the Atlantic Ocean for a new source of labor.

In 1517, Spain brought about 4,000 Africans to the Caribbean islands and forced them to work there. By the middle of the 1500s, the Spaniards were shipping about 2,000 enslaved Africans each year to Hispaniola alone. You will read about the growing slave trade in another chapter.

Society in the Spanish Colonies A rigid social system based on birthplace and ethnic group developed in the Spanish colonies. At the top of the social structure were the *peninsulares,* Spanish colonists who had been born in Spain. Almost all government officials came from this class. Colonists born in America of two Spanish parents were called *Creoles.* Generally, Creoles also held important positions. Many of the wealthiest merchants and plantation owners were Creoles.

People of mixed parentage were lower on the social ladder. *Mestizos,* people of Spanish and Indian heritage, could achieve economic success as ranchers, farmers, or merchants. But entrance into the upper levels of society was impossible for them. Below mestizos were *mulattos*—people of Spanish and African heritage. Native Americans and African Americans were held at the bottom of society. This rigid class system helped Spain keep control of its empire in the Americas for more than 300 years.

Vocabulary Builder
rigid (RIH jihd) *adj.* not bending; not flexible

 Identifying Supporting Details Identify two details in these two paragraphs that support the following main idea: *Spain created a formal system of government in America to rule the vast regions it claimed.* Explain how the details support the main idea.

✓Checkpoint How were Native Americans treated under the *encomienda* system?

⭐ **Looking Back and Ahead** The resentment and tensions caused by the rigid class system eventually provided the seeds for revolutions in the early 1800s that ended Spain's American empire.

Section 2 | Check Your Progress

Progress Monitoring Online
For: Self-test with instant help
Visit: PHSchool.com
Web Code: mva-1022

Comprehension and Critical Thinking

1. (a) Identify What parts of the North American continent did Spanish conquistadors explore?
(b) Apply Information How did the conquistadors help establish the Spanish Empire in the Americas?

2. (a) Identify What was the lasting accomplishment of Bartolomé de Las Casas?
(b) Summarize How would you describe the lives of Native Americans in New Spain?

Reading Skill

3. Identify Supporting Details Read the text following the subheading "Society in the Spanish Colonies." Identify three details that support its main idea: A rigid social system, based on birthplace and ethnic group, developed in Spain's colonies over time. Explain how the details support the main idea.

Key Terms

4. Write two definitions for each of the following key terms: conquistador, plantation, mission, *peninsular.* First, write a formal definition for your teacher. Second, write a casual definition in everyday English for a classmate.

Writing

5. (a) Prepare an outline you would use to write an essay describing the effects of Spanish colonization in the Americas.
(b) Then, write several sentences describing the views of Bartolomé de Las Casas and a conquistador about Spanish rule in the Americas.

---

probably miserable because they were forced to work in dangerous conditions.

3. Government officials came from the *peninsulares* class; Creoles held many important positions in government; *mulattos* had very little power. These details explain how rigidly the class system worked.

4. Conquistador: a Spanish soldier-adventurer; someone who explored and conquered the Americas for Spain; plantation: large farm worked by laborers who lived on the property; big farm with one owner and many workers; mission: religious settlement; an outpost of priests and friars; *peninsulares*: Spanish colonists born in Spain; the highest of the social classes in the Spanish colonies

5. (a) Student outlines should describe accurately the section content relating to Spanish colonization in the Americas.
(b) Sentences should indicate that de Las Casas wanted to treat the Native Americans fairly and conquistadors wanted to conquer them.

Blood-Thirsty Adversaries

" . . . Aldermen of this great City waited . . . to stand by and support her Majesty at this critical Juncture . . . when her invaluable Life, the true Protestant Religion, and all the Privileges of free-born Englishmen are threatened by an open Attack from our bigoted and blood-thirsty Adversaries the Spaniards. "

—*The English Mercurie*, on the approach of the Spanish Armada, 1588

◄ English warships engage the invading Spanish Armada.

Europeans Compete in North America

Objectives

- Describe the religious and economic conflicts in Europe during the Reformation.
- Explain why European powers continued to search for a new route to Asia.
- Describe the outcome of the search by explorers John Cabot and Henry Hudson for a northwest passage around the Americas.

Reading Skill

Identify Implied Main Ideas Sometimes a portion of text does not state the main idea directly. However, the text still has a main idea. This idea is implied, or suggested, by the many details contained in the text. You can identify this idea by reading all the details and developing an idea that fits all of them. State the idea to yourself in a sentence, then reread the text and confirm that the details do support it.

Key Terms and People

mercantilism   northwest passage
John Cabot   Henry Hudson

Why It Matters Spain's empire in the Americas increased Spain's wealth and power. As a result, the rulers of other European countries grew jealous. The Protestant Reformation was another source of tension. After the Roman Catholic Church rejected Martin Luther's demands for reform, Luther and other protesters formed new Protestant churches. The Protestant Reformation plunged Europe into a long series of wars between Catholic and Protestant forces.

❷ **Section Focus Question: How did conflicts in Europe spur exploration in North America?**

Conflicts in Europe

As the appeal of the Reformation increased, the split between the Catholics and the Protestants increased religious and economic tensions between countries in Europe.

Religious Conflicts By 1530, the rulers of Sweden, Denmark, and several European states had split with the Roman Catholic Church and set up Protestant churches in their countries. Elsewhere in Europe, the teachings and writings of Swiss thinker John Calvin had a great influence on the development of Protestant churches in France, Switzerland, Scotland, and the Netherlands.

English Protestants found a supporter in King Henry VIII. Henry was married to Catherine of Aragon, the daughter of King Ferdinand and Queen Isabella of Spain. When Catherine did not produce a male heir to the English throne, Henry sought to divorce her and remarry.

Section 3 Europeans Compete in North America **49**

Review and Preview

Students have learned about Spanish exploration and colonization of the Americas. Now they will focus on the conflicts among European countries for control of North America.

Section Focus Question

How did conflicts in Europe spur exploration in North America?
Before you begin the lesson for the day, write the Section Focus Question on the board. (*Lesson Focus: Because of conflict spurred by religious and economic differences, European countries began competing for the best trade routes and control of lands in North America.*)

Prepare to Read

Build Background Knowledge   L2

Tell students that in this section they will learn about how conflict in Europe increased interest in North American lands. Have students use the Think-Pair-Share strategy (TE, p. T25) to list issues that cause conflict among countries today. Ask students to think about how these differences affect different parts of the world. Tell them that the issues that were important in the sixteenth century were causing conflicts in Europe that impacted many parts of the world.

Set a Purpose   L2

■ Read each statement in the Reading Readiness Guide aloud. Ask students to mark the statements True or False.

All in One Teaching Resources, Unit 1, Reading Readiness Guide, p. 45

■ Have students discuss the statements in pairs or groups of four, then mark their worksheets again. Use the Numbered Heads participation strategy (TE, p. T24) to call on students to share their group's perspectives. The students will return to these worksheets later.

Vocabulary Builder

Use the information below to teach students this section's high-use words.

High-Use Word	Definition and Sample Sentence
restore, p. 50	*v.* to give back something taken away Roman senators hoped to **restore** a republic by assassinating Julius Caesar.
province, p. 51	*n.* territorial district of a country Quebec and Alberta are **provinces** of Canada.

Conflicts in Europe

p. 49

Instruction

L2

■ **Vocabulary Builder** Before teaching this section, preteach the High-Use Words **restore** and **province**, using the strategy on TE p. T21.
Key Terms Have students continue filling in the See It–Remember It chart for the Key Terms in this chapter.

■ Have students read Conflicts in Europe using the Paragraph Shrinking strategy (TE, p. T23).

■ After you have completed this discussion, assign the worksheet The Protestant Reformation to explore debates on the issue. After students have completed the worksheet, ask students: **How did the Renaissance help lead to the Reformation?** (*The Renaissance led to the development of new ideas, including new ideas about religion.*)

All in One Teaching Resources, Unit 1, The Protestant Reformation, p. 49

■ Display the transparency The Trade Cycle Between a Home Land and its Colonies to show students the details of mercantilism.

Color Transparencies, The Trade Cycle Between a Home Land and its Colonies

Independent Practice

Have students begin to fill in the Study Guide for this section.

Monitor Progress

As students fill in the Notetaking Study Guide, circulate to make sure that they understand the religious and economic conflicts occurring in Europe during this time. If students do not have a good understanding, have them reread the section. Provide assistance as needed.

Answers

Identify Economic Benefits and Costs The home country risked not being sent any gold or silver from its colonies.

 Reading Skill Religious conflicts were only some of the many changes in Europe during this period.

Mercantilism
European leaders of the time believed that the purpose of colonies was to benefit the home country. This belief was part of an economic theory known as mercantilism. According to this theory, a nation became strong by building up its gold and silver supply. One way to do this was to take gold and silver from colonies and send it to the royal treasury. **Critical Thinking:** *Identify Economic Benefits and Costs* What risks did the home country take in relying on colonies to support its economy?

Raw Materials
Such as:
• Gold
• Cotton
• Timber

Colonies
Can trade only with the home country

Home Country
Trades to acquire wealth

Manufactured Goods
Such as:
• Clothing
• Furniture

Identify Implied Main Ideas
What is the implied main idea of the text you have read so far in this section?

Vocabulary Builder
restore (ree STOR) *v.* to give back something taken away

Because Catholic law does not permit divorce, Henry asked the pope to annul, or cancel, his marriage. This had occurred before. Popes had annulled royal marriages. The pope's refusal to grant the annulment caused Henry to break with the Roman Catholic Church in 1533. He set up a Protestant church and named it the Church of England.

Economic Conflicts Religious tensions created by the Reformation inflamed rivalries that already existed among the nations of Europe. Wars were common and alliances often shifted. This uncertainty made European rulers believe they could not depend on one another to protect their country's security.

For example, Spain was unwilling to depend on Italian or Portuguese traders. As a result, the Spanish monarchs eagerly supported Columbus's search for a new route to Asia. The Spanish thought that if they could start colonies there, goods from those colonies would make Spain wealthy and powerful. Most importantly, the Spanish hoped Asian colonies would provide gold. Nearly every European nation sought gold to pay for its wars and help strengthen its armies. In fact, Spain required one fifth of all gold that Spaniards found to be sent to the king. This requirement was part of a system widely followed at the time, called mercantilism (MER kuhn tihl ihz uhm). The system of mercantilism held that colonies existed to make the home country wealthy and powerful.

The Spanish Armada England's King Henry VIII died in 1547. He was succeeded by his son Edward, who ruled only a short time before he died, too. The throne then passed to Mary I, who made plans to restore the Roman Catholic Church in England. However, Mary died in 1558 and Elizabeth I, a Protestant, took the throne.

Differentiated Instruction

L1 English Language Learners   **L1 Less Proficient Readers**   **L1 Special Needs**

Understanding Economics Students may need further explanation to understand the term *mercantilism*. Give students the following example: Suppose that your neighborhood has a surplus of lemons. Under mercantilism, you would buy the lemons from the other children cheaply. Then you would use the lemons to make lemonade, which you would then sell back to them at a higher price than that for which you paid for the lemons. You would also make rules so that the other children would not be able to sell lemons to anyone else except you, buy lemonade from anyone else other than you, or make their own lemonade.

The rule of the Protestant Queen Elizabeth I renewed the rivalry with Roman Catholic Spain. Spain's King Phillip II hoped to make England a Catholic nation again. Relations were also strained by English raids on Spanish ships at sea. Many of these ships carried gold from the Americas. The Spanish also resented English assistance to rebels trying to win independence in the Spanish <u>province</u> of Holland.

In 1588, Phillip assembled a fleet of 130 warships known as the Spanish Armada. Phillip hoped to force Elizabeth from the throne. A fleet of English ships met the Spanish off the coast of France. The smaller and faster English ships sank many of the Spanish ships. Barely half of the Spanish Armada returned to Spain.

The defeat of the Spanish Armada changed the balance of power in Europe. Spain was weakened and so was its control of the seas. This enabled countries like England and France to found colonies in the Americas. Europe's religious and economic conflicts were not settled by the defeat of the Armada, however. As England and France founded colonies, these conflicts spread to the Americas.

✓**Checkpoint** How did economic concerns among European nations lead to conflicts?

Asia Continues to Beckon

Columbus's return from his first voyage interested another Italian explorer, John Cabot. Cabot decided that a more northern route to Asia would be shorter and easier.

The Northern Voyages Neither Spain nor Portugal had any interest in Cabot's ideas. However, the English were interested enough to finance a voyage of exploration. Cabot left England with one ship, in May 1497. He crossed the North Atlantic and explored the region around Newfoundland. On a second voyage in 1498, Cabot may have explored the North American coast as far south as Chesapeake Bay. However, we cannot be sure. His ships disappeared without a trace.

Europeans soon realized that the lands Cabot had reached were not Asia, but a land they had never seen. England, France, and Holland all financed voyages of exploration to North America. These voyages focused on finding a northwest passage, a sea route from the Atlantic to the Pacific that passed through or around North America.

In 1524, another Italian explorer, Giovanni da Verrazano (vehr rah TSAH noh), searched for such a passage for King Francis I of France. Verrazano explored the Atlantic coastal region from North Carolina to Newfoundland. In doing so, he discovered the mouth of the Hudson River and New York Bay. French explorer Jacques Cartier (kar tee YAY) made three trips to North America for France. In searching for a northwest passage, he discovered the St. Lawrence River and explored it as far as present-day Montreal.

Section 3 Europeans Compete in North America 51

Vocabulary Builder
<u>province</u> (PRAHV ahns)
n. territorial district of a country

Queen Elizabeth I

Instruction L2

- Have students read Asia Continues to Beckon. Remind students to look for details that answer the Section Focus Question.

- Ask: **Why was finding a northwest passage so important?** (*It would give European traders another, faster, way to reach Asia.*)

- Discuss with students the difficulties that Henry Hudson and his crew may have faced in the Arctic Ocean. (*He would have faced extremely cold temperatures, running into ice, and lack of food sources on the land nearby.*)

Independent Practice

Have students complete the Study Guide for this section.

📖 **Interactive Reading and Notetaking Study Guide,** Chapter 2, Section 3 (Adapted Version also available.)

Monitor Progress

- As students fill in the Notetaking Study Guide, circulate to make sure that they understand the reasons for the attempts to find a northwest passage. If students do not have a good understanding, have them reread the section. Provide assistance as needed.

- Tell students to fill in the last column of the Reading Readiness Guide. Probe for what they learned that confirms or invalidates each statement.

All in One Teaching Resources, Unit 1, Reading Readiness Guide, p. 45

History Background

The Drake Passage Although the Dutch did not find a northwest passage to Asia, they did discover a new route to the Pacific. In 1615, Dutch explorer Willem Schouten set off to find a route to the Pacific that did not go through the Strait of Magellan. As he rounded the southernmost tip of South America, he named it Cape Horn, for the city in which he was born. He discovered a new passage around the southern end of the Tierra del Fuego islands. The passage is now known as the Drake Passage, named for sixteenth-century British explorer Sir Francis Drake. Although the Drake Passage was longer than the Strait of Magellan, it was easier to navigate.

Answer

✓**Checkpoint** Because European nations needed gold and goods from colonies to gain the wealth needed to strengthen their armies, they began competing for control of ocean trading routes and the Americas.

Assess and Reteach

Assess Progress `L2`

Have students complete Check Your Progress. Administer the Section Quiz.

All in One Teaching Resources, Unit 1, Section Quiz, p. 55

To further assess student understanding, use the Progress Monitoring Transparency.

Progress Monitoring Transparencies, Chapter 2, Section 3

Reteach `L1`

If students need more instruction, have them read this section in the Interactive Reading and Notetaking Study Guide and complete the accompanying question.

📖 **Interactive Reading and Notetaking Study Guide,** Chapter 2, Section 3 (Adapted Version also available.)

Extend `L3`

Have students conduct research to find out more about Martin Luther's challenge to the Roman Catholic Church. Have students create a paraphrase of a portion of Luther's "95 Theses" and post it in the classroom.

> **Extend ⦿nline**
> **For:** Information about Martin Luther and his 95 Theses
> **Visit:** PHSchool.com
> **Web Code:** mve-0115

Progress Monitoring Online

Students may check their comprehension of this section by completing the Progress Monitoring Online graphic organizer and self-quiz.

Answer

☑**Checkpoint** Explorers realized that North America was not Asia, but a land no one had ever seen before. They wanted to find the route to Asia for a shorter trade route.

Section 3 Check Your Progress

1. (a) Many countries broke with the Roman Catholic Church. The split between Protestants and Catholics increased religious and economic tensions among the countries.

With his son and a few loyal crew members, Henry Hudson was set adrift, by mutineers, in Hudson Bay. They died a lonely death somewhere on the bay.

English explorer Henry Hudson made four voyages in search of a northwest passage. Two voyages in the Arctic Ocean, during 1607 and 1608, were unsuccessful, and Hudson's English backers gave up on him. However, the Dutch grew interested in his activities and financed a third expedition in 1609. Crossing the Atlantic, Hudson reached what is now New York and explored up the river that today bears his name.

Hudson's discoveries on his third voyage convinced the English to sponsor a fourth voyage in 1610. Hudson again sailed into the Arctic, looking for a passage to the Pacific. He reached as far as Hudson Bay, which also is named for him, before the icy waters forced a halt to the voyage. In the spring of 1611, Hudson's crew, unhappy about spending the winter in this harsh land, grew desperate. They mutinied and set the explorer, his teenage son, and seven loyal crew members adrift in a small boat. The mutineers returned to England. Like John Cabot, Hudson was never heard from again.

☑**Checkpoint** Why did explorers continue to look for routes to Asia?

⭐ **Looking Back and Ahead** Hudson's last voyage marked the end of serious efforts to find a northwest passage. Europe's attention shifted to the lands that the voyagers had explored. In these lands, explorers reported, were vast amounts of timber, fish, and other resources. Europeans began to think of North America not as an obstacle blocking their way to Asia but as a land to be exploited for profit.

> **Progress Monitoring ⦿nline**
> **For:** Self-test with instant help
> **Visit:** PHSchool.com
> **Web Code:** mva-1023

Section 3 | Check Your Progress

Comprehension and Critical Thinking

1. (a) Recall How did the Reformation lead to religious conflict in Europe?
(b) Apply Information Why do you think the religious tensions that developed during the Reformation among European nations spread to the Americas?

2. (a) Summarize How did the defeat of the Spanish Armada change the political balance of power among European countries?

(b) Analyze Cause and Effect How did the shift in the political balance of power affect the exploration of North America?

🔵 **Reading Skill**

3. Identify Implied Main Ideas Find the implied main idea of the text under the heading "Asia Continues to Beckon." Then, combine this main idea with the main idea you identified under the heading "Conflicts in Europe" to state a single main idea for both of these portions of text.

Key Terms

Complete each of the following sentences so that the second part further explains the first part and clearly shows your understanding of the key term.

4. Spain's economy was based on the system of mercantilism, under which _____.

5. European explorers searched for a northwest passage, _____.

Writing

6. Why do you think Spain and Portugal refused to support John Cabot's proposed voyage? Write a paragraph explaining your views.

(b) Possible answer: Europeans were colonizing the Americas. They brought their religious beliefs with them.

2. (a) The defeat weakened Spain and strengthened England and France.
(b) England and France began exploring North America.

3. European explorers were still more interested in finding a route to Asia than in North America. Conflicts in Europe led European governments to continue financing their own explorations across the Atlantic and Pacific Oceans.

4. the home country became richer by controlling the trade of the colonies.

5. a route through or around North America to the Pacific Ocean.

6. Students' paragraphs should present a clear idea supported by details from the text.

Settlement of New France

❝Acting upon the information which has been given us by those who have returned from New France, respecting the good quality and fertility of the lands of that country, and the disposition of the people to accept the knowledge of God, We have resolved to continue the settlement previously undertaken there. . . .❞

—Proclamation by the King of France to continue settling New France, 1608

◄ Settlement of Quebec in New France, 1608

France and the Netherlands in North America

Objectives
- Describe how the French colony of New France spread into the interior of North America.
- Explain how the Dutch established a thriving colony along the Hudson River.
- Explain the influence of these settlements on the Native Americans of the region.

🔄 Reading Skill

Combine Main Ideas to Construct Meaning Several main ideas are developed in each section in this textbook. Use the red heads to identify the bigger main ideas. The blue heads introduce text that further develops the main ideas. As you read Section 4, identify the main ideas and the ways in which the information helps you to understand these ideas.

Key Terms and People

Samuel de Champlain
coureur de bois

Jacques Marquette
alliance

Why It Matters European countries competed for the best trade routes and for control of lands in North America. In the early 1600s, England, France, and the Netherlands sent explorers to North America and staked claims to land there.

❓ **Section Focus Question: What impact did the establishment of French and Dutch colonies in North America have on Native Americans?**

New France

The French began to settle colonies in the early 1600s. In 1603, Samuel de Champlain made the first of 11 voyages to explore and map the lands along the St. Lawrence River. In 1608, Champlain established a settlement on the banks of the St. Lawrence, which he named Quebec. From this base he ventured east, in 1609, and explored the large lake on the border of present-day Vermont and New York that bears his name. His activities gave the French an influence in the region that lasted 150 years.

Life in New France New France, as the French colony was called, developed in quite different ways than New Spain. As you know, the Spanish sought gold, silver, and other precious minerals. The French, on the other hand, profited from fish and furs. The Spanish forced Native Americans into harsh labor. The French traded with Native Americans for the animal skins so highly valued in Europe. Beaver skins sent to Europe and made into hats were a profitable item.

Section 4 France and the Netherlands in North America **53**

Vocabulary Builder

Use the information below to teach students this section's high-use words.

High-Use Word	Definition and Sample Sentence
decline, p. 54	*v.* to lessen in force, health, strength, or value England's defeat of Spain's navy in 1588 signaled the **decline** of Spain's power.
motive, p. 55	*n.* inner drive that causes a person to do something Most Spanish soldiers' **motive** for coming to the Americans was to gain wealth.

Section 4
Step-by-Step Instruction

Review and Preview

Students have learned about conflicts in Europe that increased competition for lands in North America. Now students will focus on attempts by France and the Netherlands to explore and colonize North America.

Section Focus Question

What impact did the establishment of French and Dutch colonies in North America have on Native Americans?

Before you begin the lesson for the day, write the Section Focus Question on the board. (*Lesson Focus: The trade with Europeans increased tensions between Native American groups, and Native Americans suffered from diseases carried by the Europeans.*)

Prepare to Read

Build Background Knowledge ▪L2

Tell students that in this section they will learn about exploration of North America by the French and the Dutch. Ask students to recall why other European countries began exploring North America. Then ask them to predict how the decision by more European nations to explore and colonize North America might affect those other European nations and the Native Americans in North America. Use the Idea Wave strategy (TE, p. T24) to elicit responses. As students read, ask them to monitor the accuracy of their predictions.

Set a Purpose ▪L2

- Form students into pairs or groups of four. Distribute the Reading Readiness Guide. Ask students to fill in the first two columns of the chart.

  All in One Teaching Resources, Unit 1, Reading Readiness Guide, p. 46

- Use the Numbered Heads participation strategy (TE, p. T24) to call on students to share one piece of information that they already know and one piece if information they want to know. The students will return to these worksheets later.

Teach

New France

p. 53

Instruction

L2

- **Vocabulary Builder** Before teaching this section, preteach the High-Use Words **decline** and **motivate**, using the strategy on TE p. T21.
  Key Terms Have students complete the See It–Remember It chart for the Key Terms in this chapter.

- Have students read New France using the Oral Cloze strategy (TE, p. T22).

- Ask: **What effect did Samuel de Champlain's exploration of the St. Lawrence River have on the area?** (*It helped France establish influence in the area for the next 150 years.*)

- Have students compare and contrast Spanish and French interactions with Native Americans. (*The Spanish forced Native Americans into hard labor, but the French traded with them as partners.*)

- To help students better understand the concept of *alliance*, which is important in the understanding of this section, use the Concept Lesson Alliance. Provide students with copies of the Concept Organizer.

  All in One Teaching Resources, Unit 1, Concept Lesson, p. 52; Concept Organizer, p. 6

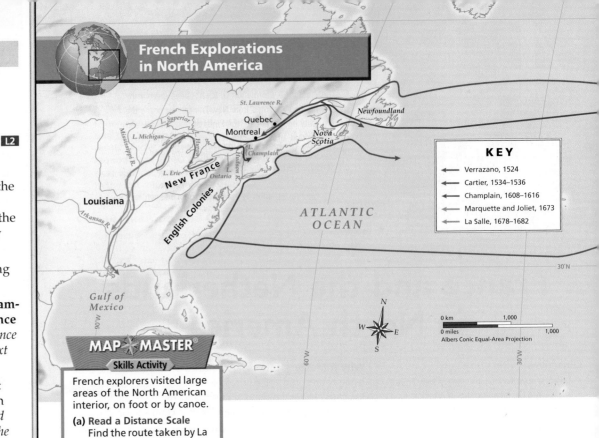

French Explorations in North America

KEY

→ Verrazano, 1524
→ Cartier, 1534–1536
→ Champlain, 1608–1616
→ Marquette and Joliet, 1673
→ La Salle, 1678–1682

MAP★MASTER®

Skills Activity

French explorers visited large areas of the North American interior, on foot or by canoe.

(a) Read a Distance Scale Find the route taken by La Salle. About how many miles did he travel from Montreal to the mouth of the Mississippi River?

(b) Make Predictions What kinds of rivalries do you think the French explorations started?

MapMaster ●nline

For: Interactive map
Visit: PHSchool.com
Web Code: mvp-1024

Vocabulary Builder
<u>decline</u> (dee KLĪN) **v.** to lessen in force, health, strength, or value

This pattern was set during Champlain's first days in the Americas. He established the colony's first settlement—a trading post—in what is today Nova Scotia, in 1604. As he continued to explore the region, he convinced local Indians to bring pelts to the trading posts established by the French. Trading posts such as Quebec City and Montreal became busy centers of commerce.

Brave employees of the fur companies paddled large canoes into the wilderness to find and acquire pelts from Native Americans. *Coureurs de bois*, the French term for "runners of the woods," were independent traders who lived among the Indians. Many of them married Indian women and started families.

Not until the late 1600s did French colonists begin to farm in large numbers. One reason for this change was that the market for furs in Europe was in <u>decline</u>. Another reason was the disruption that Indian wars brought to the fur trade. Still another was the 3,000 French settlers—including many single young women—that King Louis XIV sent to New France in the 1660s. After the new settlers arrived, the population began to expand. New France had about 5,000 colonists by 1672.

54 Chapter 2 Europe Looks Outward

Differentiated Instruction

L3 Advanced Readers   **L3 Gifted and Talented**

Write a Letter Have students learn more about the fur trade in North America and the challenges fur traders faced. Then, have students use what they learned to write a letter from the perspective of a French fur trader to a government official back in France explaining any problems he may be facing. Have students share their letters with the class.

Answers

MAP★MASTER
Skills Activity **(a)** about 2,000 miles **(b)** Possible answer: rivalries with the English and Spanish colonies

Exploring the Mississippi The same economic and religious <u>motives</u> that established New France also inspired its expansion. By 1670, French missionary Jacques Marquette had founded two missions along the Great Lakes, in present-day Michigan. Meanwhile, French traders explored the Great Lakes area looking for new sources of furs.

In 1673, Father Marquette and Louis Joliet, a French Canadian trader, paddled their canoes along the shores of Lake Michigan to what is now Green Bay, Wisconsin. They made their way west until they reached the Mississippi River. For the next month they followed the river downstream, thinking that it might be the long-sought northwest passage. In July, the group reached the Mississippi's junction with the Arkansas River. Convinced that the Mississippi flowed into the Gulf of Mexico and not into the Pacific Ocean, they returned home.

Although Marquette and Joliet did not find a northwest passage, they provided the French with a water route into the heart of North America. The river's exploration was completed in 1682 by René Robert Cavelier, also known as La Salle. Reaching the river's mouth at the Gulf of Mexico, La Salle claimed the entire Mississippi Valley for France. He named the region Louisiana, in honor of King Louis XIV.

✓**Checkpoint** **What was the goal of the voyage of Marquette and Joliet on the Mississippi?**

Vocabulary Builder
motive (MOH tihv) **n.** inner drive that causes a person to do something

 Combine Main Ideas to Construct Meaning Identify three main ideas from the paragraphs following the subheading "Life in New France." Then, state the big idea of these paragraphs.

Exploring the Mississippi
This drawing shows Father Marquette and Louis Joliet traveling the unknown waters of the Mississippi River. **Critical Thinking:** *Draw Conclusions How would settling the Mississippi Valley benefit New France?*

55

Independent Practice
Have students begin to fill in the Study Guide for this section.

📖 **Interactive Reading and Notetaking Study Guide,** Chapter 2, Section 4 (Adapted Version also available.)

Monitor Progress

As students fill in the Notetaking Study Guide, circulate to make sure students understand French interests and the development of New France. If students do not have a good understanding, have them reread the section. Provide assistance as needed.

History Background

French Settlement The development of a system for granting land holdings, called the seigneurial system, began to develop in French parts of Canada and Acadia by the middle of the 1600s. Under the system, seigneurs who were granted land plots were obligated to bring in new settlers and provide them with services such as roads or a mill to use for grinding grain. In exchange, the new inhabitants received large plots of land and had to make payments of dues to the seigneur. In contrast with the Spanish system of *encomiendas*, the inhabitants of the land had more freedom and greater rights, including the right to will the land to their children.

Answers

↻ **Reading Skill** Answers will vary, but should show students' understanding of the main ideas of the paragraphs.

Draw Conclusions Possible answer: The Mississippi River could be used exclusively by the French for trade.

✓**Checkpoint** They wanted to find a northwest passage.

New Netherland
The Impact on Native Americans

pp. 56–57

Instruction L2

- Have students read New Netherland and The Impact on Native Americans. Remind students to look for details that answer the Section Focus Question.

- Have students complete the worksheet Dutch Colonization, 1609–1664.

All in One Teaching Resources, Unit 1, Dutch Colonization, 1609–1664, p. 50

- Ask: **Why did the English take control of New Amsterdam?** (*The Dutch colonists prevented English settlers from moving west.*)

- Discuss with students how competition for limited resources can cause conflict. Ask students to identify limited resources discussed in the section and the impact of competition over them. (*A decline in fur-bearing animals from trapping weakened the Native Americans' food supply; Europeans' use of land for farming pushed Native American groups into new lands and into conflict with other Native American groups.*)

Independent Practice

Have students complete the Study Guide for this section.

Monitor Progress

- As students fill in the Notetaking Study Guide, circulate to make sure that they understand the impact of European settlement on Native Americans. Provide assistance as needed.

- Tell students to fill in the last column of the Reading Readiness Guide. Ask them to evaluate if what they learned is what they had expected to learn.

- Have students go back to their Word Knowledge Rating Form. Rerate their word knowledge and complete the last column with a definition or example.

All in One Teaching Resources, Unit 1, Reading Readiness Guide, p. 46; Word Knowledge Rating Form, p. 42

Answer

Checkpoint To trade furs with Native Americans.

Links Across Time

Wall Street

Late 1600s Built in 1653, a wall at the lower end of Manhattan protected Dutch settlers from outside attacks. Gradually, the path by the wall became an important place for merchants and traders.

1792 The New York Stock Exchange began in lower Manhattan where a group of New York businessmen met daily to buy and sell stocks. Today, Wall Street is part of the thriving commerce of New York City.

Link to Today Online

Wall Street Today How has the role of Wall Street changed in today's financial market? Go online to find out more about Wall Street today.

For: Wall Street in the news
Visit: PHSchool.com
Web Code: mvc-1024

New Netherland

Dutch land claims in North America were based on Henry Hudson's exploration of the Hudson River. In 1610, Dutch traders arrived in the Hudson River valley and began a busy trade with Native Americans. The trade was so profitable that the Dutch West India Company decided to establish a permanent colony in what the Dutch called New Netherland.

In 1624, about 300 settlers arrived from the Netherlands. Most of them settled at Fort Orange, a fur-trading post that was later renamed Albany. In 1626, another group settled at the mouth of the Hudson River. The colony's governor, Peter Minuit, purchased the island from nearby Indians. The colonists named their new home New Amsterdam. The town grew steadily as new colonists arrived. By 1653, it had a population of about 800.

New Netherland was a barrier to the English. It kept English settlers from moving westward. In 1664, English forces seized New Netherland. The new territory was renamed New York, after the king's brother, the Duke of York.

Checkpoint Why did the Dutch establish settlements along the Hudson River?

Differentiated Instruction

L1 English Language Learners   **L3 Gifted and Talented**

Writing Advertisements Tell students that colonies advertised in Europe for traders and settlers. Ask students to work in pairs or small groups to prepare an advertisement that the Dutch East India Company might have used to recruit people to come to North America. Tell students to use the information they know about North America in the advertisement.

Remind students that some prospective trappers or settlers may not understand the English language or may be illiterate. Tell students that the advertisements should be written simply and clearly with appealing visuals. Have students present their advertisements to the class.

The Impact on Native Americans

As you have read, Native Americans provided fur pelts to French and Dutch traders. The Europeans gave Native Americans manufactured goods, such as cloth, iron pots and tools, and guns. Ultimately, however, the fur trade had a grave effect on Native Americans.

The French and the Dutch each made alliances with Native American peoples. An **alliance** is an agreement between parties that benefits them both. Long before the Hurons became trading partners with the French, the Iroquois and the Hurons were enemies. The Hurons became partners with the French, and the Dutch had an agreement with the Iroquois. The Iroquois, using guns from the Dutch, began to attack the Hurons. The attacks were devastating to the Hurons.

Even worse were the diseases caused by contact with Europeans. Furthermore, the overtrapping of animals weakened the food chain on which Native Americans depended. As the fur-bearing animals disappeared, the Native Americans' value to the colonists decreased. Instead, Native American land became more valuable to the colonists.

Dutch traders with Iroquois

Checkpoint How did the French and Dutch settlements affect Native Americans?

Looking Back and Ahead England did not stand by as France and Holland carved out colonies in North America. As English colonies spread over the Atlantic shores of North America, their competition with New France and New Netherland grew.

Section 4 | Check Your Progress

Progress Monitoring Online
For: Self-test with instant help
Visit: PHSchool.com
Web Code: mva-1024

Comprehension and Critical Thinking

1. **(a) Describe** How did the colonists in New France support themselves?
   (b) Compare and Contrast How did the economic activities of New France compare with those of New Spain?
2. **(a) Identify** Name two Dutch settlements in the Americas.
   (b) Apply Information How did the geographic location of these settlements contribute to their success?

Reading Skill

3. **Combine Main Ideas to Construct Meaning** What is the big idea of Section 4? What smaller main ideas work together to support this big idea?

Key Terms

Answer the following questions in complete sentences that show your understanding of the key terms.

4. Who were the *coureurs de bois,* and how did they contribute to the economic success of New France?
5. What were the consequences of the Dutch alliance with the Iroquois for the Hurons?

Writing

6. In Section 2, you read about Bartolomé de Las Casas's observations concerning relations between the Spaniards and the Native Americans. Write similar eyewitness accounts of relations between Native Americans and **(a)** the French and **(b)** the Dutch in the Americas.

Assess and Reteach

Assess Progress L2

Have students complete Check Your Progress. Administer the Section Quiz.

All in One Teaching Resources, Unit 1, Section Quiz, p. 56

To further assess student understanding, use the Progress Monitoring Transparency.

Progress Monitoring Transparencies, Chapter 2, Section 4

Reteach L1

If students need more instruction, have them read this section in the Interactive Reading and Notetaking Study Guide and complete the accompanying question.

Extend L3

Have students conduct research to find out more about the North American fur trade. Have them make a flow chart depicting the trade, including how the furs were obtained, and by whom, how the furs were traded to Europeans, and where they were then resold. Display their flowcharts in the classroom.

Progress Monitoring Online

Students may check their comprehension of this section by completing the Progress Monitoring Online graphic organizer and self-quiz.

Section 4 Check Your Progress

1. **(a)** By fur trading, then by farming **(b)** The economic activities of New France centered around furs and fish and trading with Native Americans, while New Spain focused on searching for gold, silver, and precious minerals.
2. **(a)** New Amsterdam and Fort Orange **(b)** Their locations along rivers made transporting people and goods easier.
3. Answers will vary, but should reflect students' understanding that European interest in and settlement of North America grew, having significant effects on both the Europeans and the Native Americans.
4. They were independent traders who lived among the Native Americans. They found and acquired the fur pelts from the Native Americans.
5. The alliance increased tensions with the Iroquois, rivals of the Huron.
6. Students' accounts should present a clear understanding of the impact of these relations on both the French and the Dutch with Native Americans.

Answer

Checkpoint The French and Dutch settlements provided new goods through trading, such as cloth and iron pots, but also increased tensions among Native American groups and introduced new diseases that killed many Native Americans.

Skills for Life

Objective

Understanding sequence can help students recognize the significance of the order in which major historical events occurred. Reading a timeline can also help students see the order in which multiple events happened.

Understand Sequence

Instruction `L2`

1. Write the steps to identify main ideas and supporting details on the board and ask the class to read the steps aloud.

2. Have students look at the timeline. Discuss with them how the timeline shows events in order. Help them see that the timeline also gives an idea of the amount of time between events. Point out that the organization of a timeline could help show sequence even without including the exact dates.

3. Practice the skill by following the steps on p. 58 as a class. Model each step to understand sequence. (**1. (a)** *1492* **(b)** *1673* **2.** *50 years* **3.** *Answers will vary, but should include events that fall in the period shown by the timeline.* **4.** *The timeline includes events such as the English defeat of the Spanish Armada and other conflicts among the nations exploring the Americas.*)

Monitor Progress

Ask students to do the Apply the Skills activity. Then assign the Skills for Life worksheet. As students complete the worksheet, circulate to make sure individuals are applying the skill steps effectively. Provide assistance as needed.

All in One Teaching Resources, Unit 1, Skills for Life Worksheet, p. 51

Reteach `L1`

If students need more instruction, use the Social Studies Skills Tutor to reteach this skill.

Social Studies Skills Tutor CD-ROM Sequencing

Skills for Life — Understand Sequence

When you study history, you generally read about events in the sequence, or order, in which they happened. One way to understand the sequence of historical events is by creating a timeline. A timeline identifies major events and the dates that each took place. You should read a horizontal timeline from left to right. Reading a timeline helps you judge how events could be related in time.

Exploring the Americas

1497: Cabot sails to North America for England.

1524: Verrazano explores along the Atlantic coast for France.

1664: The English take New York from the Dutch.

1450 · 1500 · 1550 · 1600 · 1650 · 1700

1492: Columbus sails to islands in the Caribbean Sea for Spain.

1519–1522: Magellan's crew circumnavigates the globe for Spain.

1588: The English navy defeats the Spanish Armada.

1609: Sailing for the Dutch, Hudson reaches New York.

1673: Marquette and Joliet explore the Mississippi River for France.

Learn the Skill
Use these steps to understand sequence.

1. **Identify the time period covered in the timeline.** Look for the beginning date and the ending date.

2. **Figure out the intervals between each date on the timeline.** Timelines are always divided into time periods of equal length, such as 10, 50, or 100 years.

3. **Add additional events.** Include other important historical events on the timeline, based on your reading of the text.

4. **Draw conclusions.** Use the timeline to draw conclusions about the events that took place during a particular period in history. Framing questions based on the timeline can help you draw sound conclusions.

Practice the Skill
Answer the following questions about the timeline on this page.

1. **Identify the time period covered in the timeline.** (a) What is the date of the first event? (b) What is the date of the last event?

2. **Figure out the intervals between each date on the timeline.** How many years are there between each major date on the timeline?

3. **Add additional events.** What other events might you add to this timeline? Why?

4. **Draw conclusions.** How does the timeline show conflict among European nations during this period?

Apply the Skill
See the Review and Assessment at the end of this chapter.

What were the causes and effects of European exploration of the Americas?

Section 1
The Age of Exploration

- The Vikings set up a colony in Newfoundland.
- Christopher Columbus, seeking a sea route to Asia, reached the West Indies in 1492 instead.
- European explorers continued to explore and colonize the Americas.
- The Columbian Exchange resulted in the transfer of products, people, and ideas between Europe and the Americas.

Section 2
Spain's Empire in the Americas

- Spanish conquistadors conquered Native American civilizations in the Americas.
- As the Spanish Empire grew, Native American workers were harshly treated.
- A strict class system developed in Spain's American colonies.

Section 3
Europeans Compete in North America

- During the Reformation, the authority of the Roman Catholic Church was challenged.
- The defeat of the Spanish Armada undermined Spanish control of the seas.
- European explorers continued to seek a northwest passage to Asia.

Section 4
France and the Netherlands in North America

- Colonists in New France established a fur trade with Native Americans.
- The Dutch established permanent settlements in what is now the northeastern United States.
- The French and Dutch settlements had a negative impact on Native American life.

(?) Exploring the Essential Question

Use the online study guide to explore the essential question.

Section 1
How did the search for a water route to Asia affect both Europe and the Americas?

Section 2
How did Spain establish an empire in the Americas?

Chapter 2 Essential Question
What were the causes and effects of European exploration of the Americas?

Section 4
What impact did the establishment of French and Dutch colonies in North America have on Native Americans?

Section 3
How did conflicts in Europe spur exploration in North America?

Quick Study Guide **59**

Essential Question

Remind students of the Chapter Essential Question: **What were the causes and effects of European exploration of the Americas?** Have them review the bulleted statements and the Visual Preview at the beginning of the chatpter to help them answer this question.

To bolster students' retention, at this time they should complete the Study Guide in print or online. Remind students that they should also continue notetaking for the Unit and Chapter Focus Questions.

📖 **Interactive Reading and Notetaking Study Guide,** Unit 1, Chapter 2 (Adapted Version also available.)

 Study Guide *Online,* Chapter 2

Chapter Challenge

To wrap up this chapter, students should apply the knowledge they have gained to answer this question: **Would you consider European governments who sponsored explorations of the Atlantic successful even though they did not find a direct trading route to Asia?** (*Answers will vary, but should reflect an understanding that the knowledge European explorers gained about new lands benefited their home countries greatly.*)

Assessment at a Glance

Formal Assessment
   Chapter Tests A/B (L1/L2)
   AYP Monitoring Assessment
   Test Prep Workbook With Document-Based Assessment
   Test-Taking Strategies With Transparencies

Performance Assessment
   Group/Individual Activities, TE pp. 32g, 32h
   Teacher's Edition, pp. 41, 48, 52, 57
   Assessment Rubrics

Assessment Through Technology
   ExamView CD-ROM
   MindPoint CD-ROM
   Progress Monitoring Transparencies
   Progress Monitoring Online

Key Terms

1. who set out to explore and conquer a new world.

2. or land grants that allowed Spanish settlers the right to demand labor or taxes from Native Americans.

3. in which the nations' colonies would send valuable goods back to the home nation.

4. or group of other people or nations working together for the same goals.

Comprehension and Critical Thinking

5. **(a)** Balboa crossed Panama and was the first European to see the Pacific Ocean; Magellan found a strait near the southern tip of present-day Argentina and sailed into the Pacific. **(b)** Answers may vary, but students may say that these achievements encouraged more exploration.

6. **(a)** The Europeans brought crops such as wheat, rice, and sugar cane, as well as fruits, vegetables, animals, and, unfortunately, diseases to the Americas. The Native Americans sent vegetables such as maize, potatoes, beans, and peanuts, as well as animals such as turkeys to Europe. **(b)** Answers may vary, but students should be able to mention items traded with other countries, such as oil from the Middle East, or electronics and cars from Japan. Cultural exchanges occur when students attend international universities, for example.

7. **(a)** It created a formal system of government. **(b)** Possible answers: The priests appear to be teaching the Native Americans how to pray; the Native Americans appear to be participating in a ceremony at the mission.

8. **(a)** by trading with them, exposing them to foreign diseases, and providing new goods, such as cloth and guns **(b)** England may have been concerned that French wealth and power would grow.

9. **(a)** Countries used gold to pay for wars and strengthen armies. **(b)** Mercantilism encouraged the establishment and growth of the colonies.

Key Terms

Complete each of the following sentences so that the second part further explains the first part and clearly shows your understanding of the key term.

1. Hernando Cortés and Francisco Pizarro were Spanish conquistadors_____.

2. Because Spain's empire in the Americas needed workers, the government issued *encomiendas*_____.

3. In the 1500s and 1600s, many European nations practiced mercantilism_____.

4. During a time of war, it may help to form an alliance_____.

Comprehension and Critical Thinking

5. **(a) Recall** What discoveries did Balboa and Magellan make on their voyages?
   (b) Apply Information How did the achievements of those explorers change the way in which people viewed their world?

6. **(a) Identify** What were some of the products exchanged between Europe and the Americas as a result of the Columbian Exchange?
   (b) Link Past and Present What kinds of cultural and economic exchanges occur between nations today?

7. **(a) Recall** How did the Spanish government bring order to new Spanish settlements being developed in Spanish colonies?
   (b) Apply Information How does the image below show how religion was used to bring order to the settlements?

---

8. **(a) List** List three ways that French and Dutch colonists affected the lives of Native Americans.
   (b) Explain Problems Why do you think England felt it was a problem when they learned of the presence of French settlements in the valleys of the Ohio and the Mississippi rivers?

9. **(a) Recall** What role did gold play in the economy of Europe during the 1500s?
   (b) Identify Costs How did mercantilism affect the growth of colonies in the Americas?

History Reading Skill

10. **Identify Main Ideas and Details** Identify the main idea of Section 2. Find details to support the main idea.

Writing

11. **Write two paragraphs:**
    Discuss the causes and effects of European exploration in the Americas.
    Your paragraphs should:
    • begin with a thesis statement that expresses a main idea about the beginning of European exploration in the Americas;
    • support the main idea with facts, examples, and other information about the era;
    • use chronological order as much as possible.

12. **Write a Persuasive Speech:**
    The year is 1510. You are an adventurer eager to continue the attempt to find a route to Asia. Prepare a speech you will give to persuade a monarch that spending money on this voyage is a wise decision.

Skills for Life
Understand Sequence
Use the chapter timeline on pages 34–35 to answer the following questions.

13. What time period is covered in the timeline?

14. Into what time intervals is the timeline divided?

15. **(a)** When did the French establish Quebec?
    (b) How many years later did Marquette and Joliet explore the Mississippi?

16. What additional events might you add to the timeline? Why?

17. What trend does this timeline show? Explain.

History Reading Skill

10. Main idea: The Spanish created a large empire in the Americas and established a colonial society with a rigid class structure. Details: The explorers Cortés and Pizarro claimed land in the Americas and conquered many of the native peoples living there. Spanish explorers believed that cities of gold could be found in the area that is today the United States. The *encomienda* system made life harsh for Native Americans. Bartolomé de Las Casas spoke out against this system.

Writing

11. Possible thesis statement: European nations, of which Spain was the first, sent explorers west across the Atlantic Ocean in search of a new trade route to Asia. Possible effects or supporting examples: Instead of finding a new trade route to Asia, explorers landed in the Americas where they began

Chapter 2
Review and Assessment

Test Yourself

1. **Which of the following people was the first Spaniard to set foot in what is now the United States?**

   A Christopher Columbus

   B Juan Ponce de León

   C Francisco Pizarro

   D Francisco Coronado

2. **How did Europe's attitude toward North America change after Henry Hudson's last voyage?**

   A Efforts to find a northwest passage continued.

   B French and Dutch fur traders set up more trading posts.

   C Efforts began to profit from the lands explored.

   D Most countries no longer gained from the system of mercantilism.

3. **In return for the fur pelts, what goods did the Europeans trade with Native Americans?**

   A tobacco

   B food crops

   C cloth and tools

   D pots and silk

4. **Unlike the Spaniards, French claims in North America were largely for**

   A settling farm communities.

   B economic gains.

   C establishing fur trade posts.

   D establishing lumber trade posts.

Document-Based Questions

Task: Look at Documents 1 and 2, and answer their accompanying questions. Then, use the documents and your knowledge of history to complete the following writing assignment:

Write a two-paragraph essay describing positive and negative effects of the Columbian Exchange.

Document 1: The Columbian Exchange involved hundreds of items that enriched people's lives. But one item was deadly—European disease. Bernal Díaz del Castillo, who traveled with Hernando Cortés, describes the scene in the Aztec capital of Tenochtitlán in 1521. *What conditions did the Spanish encounter in Tenochtitlán?*

"All the houses and stockades in the lake were full of corpses. . . . It was the same in the streets and courts. . . . We could not walk without treading on the bodies and heads of dead Indians. . . . . Indeed, the stench was so bad that no one could endure it . . . and even Cortés was ill from the odors which assailed his nostrils."

Document 2: The arrival of Columbus set off a tragic chain of events for the people of the Americas. Study the graph to see how the population of central Mexico declined after the European arrival. *What happened to the population between 1500 and 1560?*

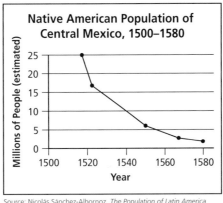

Native American Population of Central Mexico, 1500–1580

Millions of People (estimated) vs. Year

Source: Nicolás Sánchez-Albornoz, *The Population of Latin America*

Test Yourself

1. B

2. C

3. C

4. C

Document-Based Questions
Answers

Document 1 Many people had died and unburied bodies remained on the streets and in houses. The smell was terrible.

Document 2 The population decreased by more than 20 million.

Rubric: Write an Essay

Share this rubric with students before they begin writing.

Score 1 Ideas unclear, organization poor.

Score 2 Essay has few details in support of the positive or negative effects of the Columbian Exchange, fails to identify pros and cons accurately.

Score 3 Essay accurately describes positive and negative effects of the Columbian Exchange, has clear organization, and some supporting arguments.

Score 4 Essay is comprehensive and detailed with clear organization and supporting arguments, shows creativity.

conquering Native Americans and establishing colonies. In time, the Columbian Exchange trade network was established.

12. Students' speeches should include the following possible reasons that a monarch should support the voyage: finding a route west to Asia would greatly increase that country's wealth through extensive trade. New colonies, which would send goods back to the home country, and new, unknown riches in the discovered lands would further enrich the home country.

For a more complete four-point rubric, see the Writing Rubrics in the Teaching Resources.

All in One Teaching Resources, Unit 1, p. 138

Skills for Life

13. 1000–1700

14. 100 years, with a symbol showing a break in the timeline

15. **(a)** 1608 **(b)** 65

16. Answers will vary, but should include events that happened in the time period covered by the chapter.

17. This timeline shows increased European involvement in North America as more countries began exploring and starting settlements toward the end of the period covered by the timeline.

Colonies Take Root (1587–1752)

History Background

Colonizing North America

In the 1400s and 1500s, European nations were competing against one another to claim new lands that would bring them wealth. The development of capitalist and mercantilist economies, which stressed profiting from the exportation of goods, amplified the need to explore new lands. Having colonies in regions rich with natural resources would supply countries with raw materials for their exports and provide companies with an arena for investment.

The English colonies developed out of these economic policies. However, once England controlled land overseas, many people began moving to the colonies for social and political, rather than economic, reasons. Surviving in a new world was a challenge. Colonists learned to use the resources of their local regions to make a living. Those resources in turn shaped the colonial economies. For example, the fertile soil and long growing season found in the Southern Colonies led to the development of a plantation economy, which led to the growth of slavery.

Colonies also began to establish unique cultural traditions that would resurface in the development of the United States as a nation. Colonists set up forms of representative government to establish order and ensure the survival and success of their colonies. Because many early colonists had migrated for religious reasons, various policies toward religious practices were implemented—some allowing more freedom of religion than others. This foreshadowed a key question that would be raised when the United States formed its own government, and a question that remains quite relevant today: should church and state be connected or separate?

Essential Questions

Use this graphic organizer to see the relationship between key concepts and the Chapter Essential Question.

Focus Question/Section 1
How did the English set up their first colonies?
(p. 66)

Concept: Self-Government

Focus Question/Section 2
How did religious beliefs and dissent influence the New England Colonies?
(p. 71)

Concept: Rights

Chapter Essential Question
How did the English start colonies with distinct qualities in North America?

Focus Question/Section 5
How did the Spanish establish colonies on the borderlands?
(p. 90)

Concept: Influence

Focus Question/Section 4
What factors influenced the development of the Southern Colonies?
(p. 84)

Concept: Region

Focus Question/Section 3
How did the diverse Middle Colonies develop and thrive?
(p. 77)

Concept: Mercantilism

Differentiated Instruction

Sharing Key Concepts

Explain Concepts Ask each student to explain one key concept, high use word, or key term on a note card. Then have students form two concentric circles. Students on the inside circle should pair with the student facing them on the outside circle. Each pair should explain their concepts or words to each other using their cards. The two students can also ask each other questions to make sure they both understand the concept, word, or term.

Repeat the Process Students then trade cards and the outside circle moves clockwise one person. Repeat the process until students wind up with their original cards.

Concepts Across Time

Have students develop an understanding of the enduring concepts of history by connecting these ideas.

Concept: Rights
Remind students that issues regarding the consideration of individual rights of citizens date back to the Roman Republic. Ask: **What kind of rights did citizens have in the Roman Republic?** (*Everybody was equal under the law. People accused of crimes were considered innocent until proven guilty.*) Explain to students that many of the earliest settlers of the English colonies had come to North America seeking certain rights, such as the right of religious freedom. Use this question when discussing The Plymouth Colony in Section 1.

Concept: Mercantilism
Have students compare trade networks in the Middle Colonies and ancient Africa. Ask: **How did the trade system of the Middle Colonies resemble the trade networks of ancient Africa?** (*Possible answer: Goods made in one region using the resources local to that area were sold to people in other, far-away regions. This benefited both sides: bringing profit to those who made the goods and introducing exotic items to those who purchased them. England dominated trade networks in the colonies just as the Muslims dominated in ancient Africa. The furs and agricultural items produced in the Middle Colonies were largely acquired for and sold to sponsoring companies in England.*) Use this question when discussing Growth and Change in Section 3.

Concept: Region
The unique features of the Southern region heavily influenced the development of the colonies that developed there. Ask: **How was the development of the regional economy in the Southern Colonies similar to the development of early North American civilizations after the Ice Age?** (*Possible answer: In the Southern Colonies, the economy developed distinctly, based on the natural resources and climate of the region. The fertile soil and long growing season were ideal for agriculture. Similarly, early humans were able to survive by making use of the resources and climate in the areas where they lived.*) Use this question when discussing Geography of the Southern Colonies in Section 4.

Section 1 The First English Settlements *1.5 periods, .75 block*

Objectives

Students will

1. Explain why England wanted to establish colonies in North America.
2. Describe the experience of the settlers who founded the first permanent English colony in Jamestown.
3. Explain how the Pilgrims managed to survive their first years in the Plymouth Colony.

Differentiated Instruction Key

- **L1** Basic to Average
- **L2** All Students
- **L3** Average to Advanced

- **AR** Advanced Readers
- **ELL** English Language Learners
- **GT** Gifted and Talented
- **LPR** Less Proficient Readers
- **SN** Special Needs

Prepare to Read

Build Background Knowledge
Preview the section and have students predict what they will learn about the first English settlements.

Set a Purpose for Reading
Have students begin to fill out the Reading Readiness Guide.

Preview Key Terms
Preview the section's Key Terms.

Instructional Resources

All in One Teaching Resources, Unit 1
- **L2** Chapter Prereading Guide, p. 4
- **L2** History Reading Skill, p. 71
- **L2** Word Knowledge Rating Form, p. 72
- **L2** Reading Readiness Guide, p. 73

Teacher's Edition
- **L2** Vocabulary Builder, pp. 65, 67

Differentiated Instruction

Guided Reading Audio CD
Spanish ELL, LPR, SN

Teach

Instruction
England Seeks Colonies
Discuss the reasons why England sought colonies in North America.

Founding Jamestown
Evaluate self-government in the Jamestown colony.

Jamestown Prospers
Analyze the effect of tobacco on the Jamestown economy.

The Plymouth Colony
Discuss the establishment of the Plymouth Colony and the Mayflower Compact.

Instructional Resources

Interactive Reading and Notetaking Study Guide
- **L2** Chapter 3, Section 1

All in One Teaching Resources, Unit 1
- **L2** Proceedings of the Virginia Assembly, 1619, p. 78
- **L2** Concept Lesson, p. 85
- **L2** Concept Organizer, p. 6

Discovery School Video
- **L2** Jamestown

Differentiated Instruction

Interactive Reading and Notetaking Study Guide, Adapted Version (English/Spanish)
- **L1** Chapter 3, Section 1 ELL, LPR, SN

Teacher's Edition
- **L1** Make Flashcards, p. 66 ELL, LPR, SN
- **L3** Plan an Expedition, p. 68 AR, GT

All in One Teaching Resources, Unit 1
- **L3** Your Voyage to the Americas, p. 80

Assess and Reteach

Assess Progress
Evaluate student comprehension with Check Your Progress and Section Quiz.

Reteach
Assign the Interactive Reading and Notetaking Study Guide to help struggling students.

Extend
Extend the section by having students create a plan for a new colony.

Instructional Resources

Interactive Reading and Notetaking Study Guide
- **L2** Chapter 3, Section 1

All in One Teaching Resources, Unit 1
- **L2** Reading Readiness Guide, p. 73
- **L2** Section Quiz, p. 86

Progress Monitoring Transparencies
- **L2** Chapter 3, Section 1

Differentiated Instruction

Teacher's Edition
- **L1** Checkpoints, TE pp. 66, 68, 69, 70

SE on Audio CD
- **L1** Chapter 3, Section 1

Section 2 The New England Colonies *1 period, .5 block*

Objectives

Students will

1. Describe the geography and climate of the New England Colonies.

2. Describe the Puritan settlement in Massachusetts.

3. Identify the new settlements that developed in New England as a result of Puritan religious practices.

4. Explain the changes that took place in the New England Colonies in the 1600s.

Differentiated Instruction Key

L1 Basic to Average   **AR** Advanced Readers
L2 All Students   **ELL** English Language Learners
L3 Average to Advanced   **GT** Gifted and Talented
    LPR Less Proficient Readers
    SN Special Needs

Prepare to Read

Build Background Knowledge
Preview the section and have students discuss why the English continued to settle in North America.

Set a Purpose for Reading
Have students begin to fill out the Reading Readiness Guide.

Preview Key Terms
Preview the section's Key Terms.

Instructional Resources

All in One Teaching Resources, Unit 1
L2 Reading Readiness Guide, p. 74

Teacher's Edition
L2 Vocabulary Builder, p. 71

Differentiated Instruction

🔘 **Guided Reading Audio CD**
Spanish ELL, LPR, SN

Teach

Instruction
Geography of New England
Explore the land and climate of the northeastern region of the United States.

Puritans in Massachusetts Bay
Discuss the colony established by Puritans.

New Colonies
Analyze the role of religion in the establishment of new colonies.

Growth and Change
Describe daily life, government, and conflict in the colonies during the late 1600s.

Instructional Resources

📖 **Interactive Reading and Notetaking Study Guide**
L2 Chapter 3, Section 2
All in One Teaching Resources, Unit 1
L2 *To My Dear and Loving Husband*, p. 79

Color Transparencies
L2 The Salem Witch Trials

Discovery School Video
L2 Colonies Take Root

Differentiated Instruction

📖 **Interactive Reading and Notetaking Study Guide, Adapted Version (English/Spanish)**
L1 Chapter 3, Section 2 ELL, LPR, SN

Teacher's Edition
L1 Write a Descriptive Paragraph, p. 72 ELL, LPR
L3 Write a Descriptive Paragraph, p. 72 AR, GT
L3 Write a Defense, p. 74 AR, GT

Assess and Reteach

Assess Progress
Evaluate student comprehension with Check Your Progress and Section Quiz.

Reteach
Assign the Interactive Reading and Notetaking Study Guide to help struggling students.

Extend
Extend the section by having students write and perform a skit about the life of a New England colony leader.

Instructional Resources

📖 **Interactive Reading and Notetaking Study Guide**
L2 Chapter 3, Section 2
All in One Teaching Resources, Unit 1
L2 Reading Readiness Guide, p. 74
L2 Section Quiz, p. 87

Progress Monitoring Transparencies
L2 Chapter 3, Section 2

Differentiated Instruction

Teacher's Edition
L1 Checkpoints, TE pp. 71, 72, 73, 75, 76

🔘 **SE on Audio CD**
L1 Chapter 3, Section 2

Internet Resources
PHSchool.com

Section 3 The Middle Colonies

 1.5 periods, .75 block

Objectives

Students will

1. Describe the geography and climate of the Middle Colonies.
2. Describe the early history of New York and New Jersey.
3. Explain how Pennsylvania and Delaware were founded.
4. Explain how the Middle Colonies changed in the 1600s and early 1700s.

Differentiated Instruction Key

L1 Basic to Average	**AR** Advanced Readers
L2 All Students	**ELL** English Language Learners
L3 Average to Advanced	**GT** Gifted and Talented
	LPR Less Proficient Readers
	SN Special Needs

Prepare to Read

Build Background Knowledge
Preview the section and discuss the Middle Colonies.

Set a Purpose for Reading
Have students begin to fill out the Reading Readiness Guide.

Preview Key Terms
Preview the section's Key Terms.

Instructional Resources

All in One Teaching Resources, Unit 1
L2 Reading Readiness Guide, p. 75

Teacher's Edition
L2 Vocabulary Builder, p. 77

Differentiated Instruction

Guided Reading Audio CD
Spanish ELL, LPR, SN

Teach

Instruction
Geography of the Middle Colonies
Discuss the land and climate of the Middle Colonies.

New York and New Jersey
Identify significant events in the history of New York and New Jersey.

Pennsylvania and Delaware
Describe William Penn's effect on the development of Pennsylvania and Delaware.

Growth and Change
Analyze the changes that occurred in the Middle Colonies in the 1600s and early 1700s.

Instructional Resources

Interactive Reading and Notetaking Study Guide
L2 Chapter 3, Section 3

All in One Teaching Resources, Unit 1
L2 Colonial Population Growth, p. 82

Color Transparencies
L2 Penn's Treaty With the Indians

Discovery School Video
L2 Life in the Colonies

Differentiated Instruction

Interactive Reading and Notetaking Study Guide, Adapted Version (English/Spanish)
L1 Chapter 3, Section 3 ELL, LPR, SN

Teacher's Edition
L3 Write an Interview, p. 78 AR, GT
L3 Write a Fact Sheet, p. 80 AR, GT
L1 Organizing Information, p. 82 ELL, SN

Assess and Reteach

Assess Progress
Evaluate student comprehension with Check Your Progress and Section Quiz.

Reteach
Assign the Interactive Reading and Notetaking Study Guide to help struggling students.

Extend
Extend the section by having students write a short report comparing and contrasting the populations and economies of the Middle Colonies.

Instructional Resources

Interactive Reading and Notetaking Study Guide
L2 Chapter 3, Section 3

All in One Teaching Resources, Unit 1
L2 Reading Readiness Guide, p. 75
L2 Section Quiz, p. 88

Progress Monitoring Transparencies
L2 Chapter 3, Section 3

Differentiated Instruction

Teacher's Edition
L1 Checkpoints, TE pp. 77, 78, 80, 81

SE on Audio CD
L1 Chapter 3, Section 3

Internet Resources
PHSchool.com

Section 4 The Southern Colonies *1 period, .5 block*

Objectives

Students will

1. Describe the geography and climate of the Southern Colonies.
2. Describe the early history of Virginia.
3. Explain how Maryland, the Carolinas, and Georgia were founded.
4. Identify the factors that produced the Tidewater and backcountry ways of life.

Differentiated Instruction Key

L1	Basic to Average	**AR**	Advanced Readers
L2	All Students	**ELL**	English Language Learners
L3	Average to Advanced	**GT**	Gifted and Talented
		LPR	Less Proficient Readers
		SN	Special Needs

Prepare to Read

Build Background Knowledge
Preview the section and have students make a prediction about life in the Southern Colonies.

Set a Purpose for Reading
Have students begin to fill out the Reading Readiness Guide.

Preview Key Terms
Preview the section's Key Terms.

Instructional Resources

All in One **Teaching Resources, Unit 1**
L2 Reading Readiness Guide, p. 76

Teacher's Edition
L2 Vocabulary Builder, p. 85

Differentiated Instruction

⦿ **Guided Reading Audio CD**
Spanish ELL, LPR, SN

Teach

Instruction
Geography of the Southern Colonies
Identify the unique geographic qualities of the Southern Colonies.

Virginia Grows
Relate economy to geography. Ask what conflicts arose over the economy and geography of Virginia.

Religious Toleration in Maryland
Describe the various factors that influenced the growth of Maryland.

Colonies in the Carolinas and Georgia
Discuss the reasons why the Carolina and Georgia colonies were founded.

Change in the Southern Colonies
Compare the cultures of people living along the coast to the culture of inland people.

Instructional Resources

📖 **Interactive Reading and Notetaking Study Guide**
L2 Chapter 3, Section 4

Color Transparencies
L2 Climate and Agriculture in the 13 Colonies

Differentiated Instruction

📖 **Interactive Reading and Notetaking Study Guide, Adapted Version (English/Spanish)**
L1 Chapter 3, Section 4 ELL, LPR, SN

Teacher's Edition
L1 Make a Timeline, p. 84 LPR, SN
L1 Evaluate Learning, p. 86 ELL, LPR, SN
L1 Gaining Comprehension, p. 88 LPR

Assess and Reteach

Assess Progress
Evaluate student comprehension with Check Your Progress and Section Quiz.

Reteach
Assign the Interactive Reading and Notetaking Study Guide to help struggling students.

Extend
Extend the section by having students write a colonist's journal entry.

Instructional Resources

📖 **Interactive Reading and Notetaking Study Guide**
L2 Chapter 3, Section 4

All in One **Teaching Resources, Unit 1**
L2 Reading Readiness Guide, p. 76
L2 Section Quiz, p. 89

Progress Monitoring Transparencies
L2 Chapter 3, Section 4

Differentiated Instruction

Teacher's Edition
L1 Checkpoints, TE pp. 84, 85, 86, 87, 89

⦿ **SE on Audio CD**
L1 Chapter 3, Section 4

Section 5 Lesson Plan

Objectives

Students will

1. Describe Spain's colony in Florida.

2. Explain how Spain established settlements throughout much of North America.

3. Describe the significance of the Spanish missions.

Differentiated Instruction Key

L1 Basic to Average
L2 All Students
L3 Average to Advanced

AR Advanced Readers
ELL English Language Learners
GT Gifted and Talented
LPR Less Proficient Readers
SN Special Needs

Prepare to Read

Build Background Knowledge
Preview the section and discuss students' impressions of a Spanish presence in North America.

Set a Purpose for Reading
Have students begin to fill out the Reading Readiness Guide.

Preview Key Terms
Preview the section's Key Terms.

Instructional Resources

All in One Teaching Resources, Unit 1
L2 Reading Readiness Guide, p. 77

Teacher's Edition
L2 Vocabulary Builder, p. 91

Differentiated Instruction

Guided Reading Audio CD
Spanish ELL, LPR, SN

Teach

Instruction
Spanish Florida
Discuss Spanish settlements along the borderlands.

Settling the Spanish Borderlands
Analyze the influence of Spanish missions in the borderlands.

Life in Spanish Missions
Explain why missions arose in Spanish colonies, and describe life in a mission.

Instructional Resources

Interactive Reading and Notetaking Study Guide
L2 Chapter 3, Section 5

All in One Teaching Resources, Unit 1
L2 Junípero Serra, p. 83
L2 Skills for Life Worksheet, p. 84

Color Transparencies
L2 A Mission: Then and Now

Differentiated Instruction

Interactive Reading and Notetaking Study Guide, Adapted Version (English/Spanish)
L1 Chapter 3, Section 5 ELL, LPR, SN

Teacher's Edition
L1 Exploring the Main Idea, p. 90 ELL, LPR, SN
L3 Build a Model, p. 92 AR, GT

Assess and Reteach

Assess Progress
Evaluate student comprehension with Check Your Progress and Section Quiz.

Reteach
Assign the Interactive Reading and Notetaking Study Guide to help struggling students.

Extend
Extend the section by having students complete the History Interactive activity.

Instructional Resources

Interactive Reading and Notetaking Study Guide
L2 Chapter 3, Section 5

All in One Teaching Resources, Unit 1
L2 Word Knowledge Rating Form, p. 72
L2 Reading Readiness Guide, p. 77
L2 Section Quiz, p. 90
L2 Chapter Test, p. 94

Progress Monitoring Transparencies
L2 Chapter 3, Section 5

Differentiated Instruction

Teacher's Edition
L1 Checkpoints, TE pp. 90, 93

All in One Teaching Resources, Unit 1
L1 Chapter Test, p. 91

SE on Audio CD
L1 Chapter 3, Section 5

Social Studies Skills Tutor CD-ROM
Analyzing Primary and Secondary Sources

Internet Resources
PHSchool.com

Use the following research activities to help students deepen their understanding of the Chapter Essential Question: **How did the English start colonies with distinct qualities in North America?** Students should use library or Internet resources. The Web Codes provided offer access to Internet resources students can use to complete each activity. Use the appropriate four-point rubric in Assessment Rubrics to evaluate the activity.

 Assessment Rubrics

Write a Biography

Have students conduct research individually to write a biography of John Smith. Have them write a bulleted list of fast facts describing events and accomplishments in Smith's life prior to 1607 that help explain his success as a leader of Jamestown. Have students illustrate their lists by depicting one key event or accomplishment. Post students' lists on the bulletin board. Use this activity when studying Founding Jamestown in Section 1.

 Individual research activity   L2

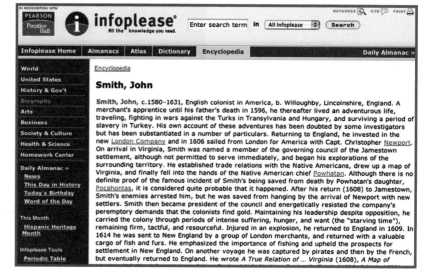

Go Online **Web Code:** mve-0116
PHSchool.com

Create a Design for a Colonial Settlement

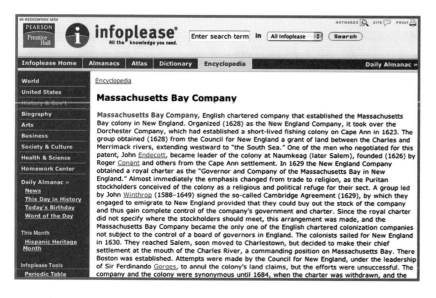

Go Online **Web Code:** mvd-0117
PHSchool.com

Tell students that Plimoth Plantation, which recreates the Plymouth Colony, is a popular tourist attraction today. Have students work in groups to design a similar attraction for another colonial settlement, such as the Massachusetts Bay Colony, with appropriate buildings and events. Use this activity as a wrap-up at the end of the chapter.

 Group research activity AR, GT   L3

Chapter 3

Colonies Take Root

1587–1752

Why It Matters

In this chapter, students will learn about the first English colonies in North America.

Many English settlers sought opportunity and freedoms in North America that they did not find in their homeland. One of the freedoms these settlers wanted was the freedom to practice their religion.

Religious freedom continues to be an important right in the United States, and is protected by law.

Englishmen who settled in the colonies also had political opportunities. They had the right to vote, and many took part in elected government.

The U.S. Senate and House of Representatives are part of a legacy started by colonial lawmaking bodies. Local, county, and state legislatures are part of this legacy as well.

People come to the United States every year, seeking opportunity and more freedom.

Chapter Essential Question

How did the English start colonies with distinct qualities in North America?

Think Like a Historian

- To preview this chapter, have students review the content on these pages of the Student Edition. Ask: **What will you be learning about in this chapter?** (*about English colonies in North America*)

- Have students study the painting of the Pilgrims giving thanks at Plymouth on this page. Ask: **Why do you think more men than women arrived to settle the colony?** (*Settling a colony was hard work and there may have been a need to fight as well.*)

- Have students read the section summaries and the quotation. Ask: **Why do you think belief in God was such an important element in colonial life?** (*Students' responses will vary, but should include the idea that many of the colonies were founded by people who had suffered religious intolerance, and colonists often felt that they survived harsh conditions through divine intervention.*)

Bibliography

For the Teacher

Middleton, Richard. *Colonial America: A History, 1565–1776.* Blackwell Publishers, 2002.

For the Student

L1 Rossi, Ann. *Cultures Collide: Native Americans and Europeans, 1492–1700.* National Geographic, 2004.

L2 Pobst, Sandy. *Virginia, 1607–1776.* National Geographic, 2005.

L3 Edwards, Judith. *Jamestown, John Smith, and Pocahontas in American History.* Enslow Publishers, 2002.

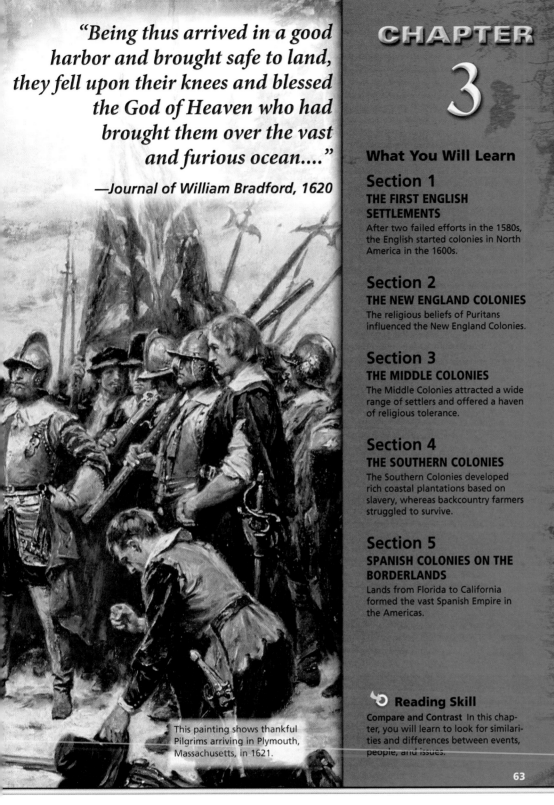

"Being thus arrived in a good harbor and brought safe to land, they fell upon their knees and blessed the God of Heaven who had brought them over the vast and furious ocean...."

—Journal of William Bradford, 1620

This painting shows thankful Pilgrims arriving in Plymouth, Massachusetts, in 1621.

CHAPTER 3

What You Will Learn

Section 1
THE FIRST ENGLISH SETTLEMENTS
After two failed efforts in the 1580s, the English started colonies in North America in the 1600s.

Section 2
THE NEW ENGLAND COLONIES
The religious beliefs of Puritans influenced the New England Colonies.

Section 3
THE MIDDLE COLONIES
The Middle Colonies attracted a wide range of settlers and offered a haven of religious tolerance.

Section 4
THE SOUTHERN COLONIES
The Southern Colonies developed rich coastal plantations based on slavery, whereas backcountry farmers struggled to survive.

Section 5
SPANISH COLONIES ON THE BORDERLANDS
Lands from Florida to California formed the vast Spanish Empire in the Americas.

Reading Skill
Compare and Contrast In this chapter, you will learn to look for similarities and differences between events, people, and issues.

63

History Background

Carver and the Pilgrims John Carver, an English Separatist merchant living in Holland, helped arrange the voyage that would bring some of his fellow Separatists to the New World. After hiring and provisioning the *Mayflower,* Carver and other Separatists, now known as Pilgrims, set sail with a group of soldiers and adventurers to North America. Although most of the Pilgrims were English, some were from Belgium and one was from Poland. It is believed that Carver decided the *Mayflower* should anchor at Plymouth, Massachusetts. Carver went on to become the first governor of the Plymouth Colony.

Prepare to Read

Use the following for reading skill support.

All in One Teaching Resources, Unit 1, Chapter Prereading Guide, p. 4; History Reading Skill, p. 71

History Reading Skill, *Online*
Web code: mve-3000

Differentiated Instruction

The following Teacher Edition strategies are suitable for students of varying abilities.

- **L3** **Advanced Readers,** pp. 68, 72, 74, 78, 80, 92 AR
- **L1** **English Language Learners,** pp. 65, 66, 72, 82, 86, 90 ELL
- **L3** **Gifted and Talented,** pp. 68, 72, 74, 78, 80, 92 GT
- **L1** **Less Proficient Readers,** pp. 66, 72, 84, 86, 88, 90 LPR
- **L1** **Special Needs,** pp. 65, 66, 82, 84, 86, 90 SN

Chapter Resources

Teaching Resources, Unit 1
Chapter Prereading Guide, p. 4
Word Knowledge Rating Form, p. 72
History Reading Skill Worksheet, p. 71
Skills for Life Worksheet, p. 84
Chapter Tests A/B (L1/L2), pp. 91, 94
Letter Home (English/Spanish), pp. 63, 64

Spanish Support
L1 **Interactive Reading and Notetaking Study Guide, Spanish,** Adapted Version
L1 **Guided Reading Audio CD,** Spanish

Media and Technology
L1 SE on Audio CD
L2 Social Studies Skills Tutor CD-ROM
ExamView **Test Bank CD-ROM**

Quick View Video
View the chapter video for a quick preview of the main ideas.

Visual Preview

? **How did the English start colonies with distinct qualities in North America?**

Build Background Knowledge   **L2**

In Chapter 2, students read about the effects of exploration in North America by several European countries. Lead a structured discussion about the development of colonies. (See TE p. T24 for more on structured discussion.) Have students suppose that they were on a plane that made an emergency landing in an inaccessible, undeveloped forest, and that it would take a few days to be rescued. What would be the first needs that would have to be taken care of? (*Possible answers: Where would they live? What would they do for food and water? Who would be in charge?*) Ask students to consider what the first settlers would need to do to survive when they arrived in North America. What challenges would they face?

Instruction   **L2**

- For background information on conducting a lesson for the Visual Preview, see TE p. T20.

- Write the Chapter Essential Question on the board. Discuss the phrase "distinct qualities." Define "distinct." (*clearly different and separate*) Have students think about what makes their city or town distinct from another nearby city or town. Use the Numbered Heads strategy (TE p. T24) to encourage participation. (*Students might say the number of people who live there, or the type of school, or the local businesses such as stores, factories, and farms*) Ask students to predict why colonies might form distinctive characteristics as they develop. (*Possible answers: location, natural resources available, background of people who found it*)

- Discuss how the various parts of the country today are known for different crops, industries, businesses, and so on. (*Responses will vary, but students should note that even today differences in climate, location, and natural resources make the regions of the country different.*)

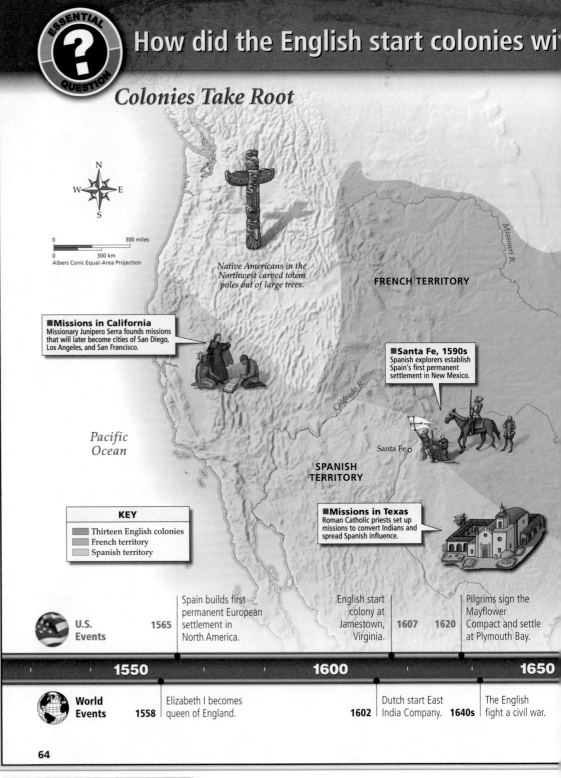

? ESSENTIAL QUESTION

How did the English start colonies wit

Colonies Take Root

N W E S

0 ——— 300 miles
0 ——— 300 km
Albers Conic Equal-Area Projection

Native Americans in the Northwest carved totem poles out of large trees.

FRENCH TERRITORY

■ **Missions in California**
Missionary Junipero Serra founds missions that will later become cities of San Diego, Los Angeles, and San Francisco.

■ **Santa Fe, 1590s**
Spanish explorers establish Spain's first permanent settlement in New Mexico.

Pacific Ocean

Santa Fe ○

SPANISH TERRITORY

■ **Missions in Texas**
Roman Catholic priests set up missions to convert Indians and spread Spanish influence.

KEY	
▮	Thirteen English colonies
▮	French territory
▮	Spanish territory

Missouri R.
Colorado R.

U.S. Events — 1565 Spain builds first permanent European settlement in North America. — 1607 English start colony at Jamestown, Virginia. 1620 Pilgrims sign the Mayflower Compact and settle at Plymouth Bay.

1550 ———— **1600** ———— **1650**

World Events — 1558 Elizabeth I becomes queen of England. 1602 Dutch start East India Company. 1640s The English fight a civil war.

64

History Background

Government Of the thirteen colonies, Pennsylvania is distinct for representing a collaboration of beliefs and people. Other colonies were established for a specific reason—religious freedom, economic gain, or as a haven from political persecution. Penn's colony was known for its religious tolerance, ethnic diversity, and peaceful relations with Native Americans.

Even its government departed from that of other colonies. Under its first constitution, the Frame of Government, Pennsylvania had the most liberal government in the colonies. In 1701, Penn signed the Charter of Liberties, establishing a unicameral assembly, the only one in the colonies. Penn also established schools that were open to all Philadelphia's children, their religious or economic status notwithstanding.

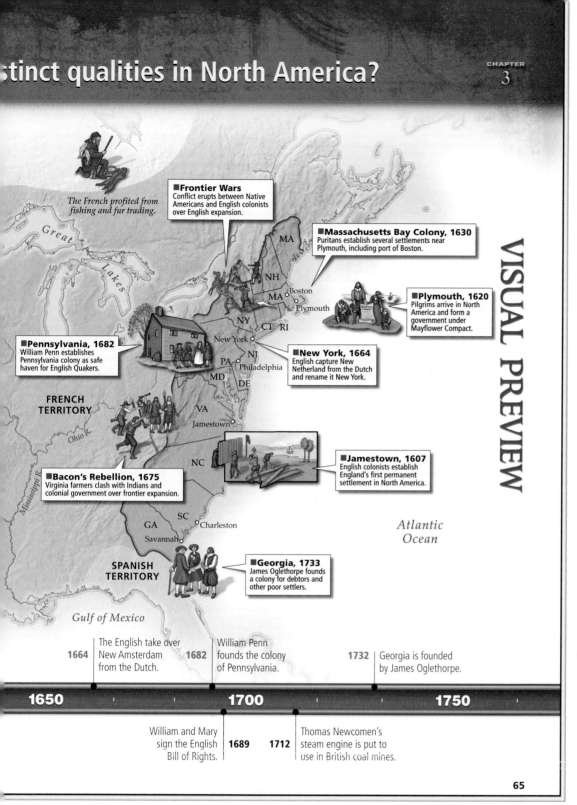

The French profited from fishing and fur trading.

■Frontier Wars
Conflict erupts between Native Americans and English colonists over English expansion.

■Massachusetts Bay Colony, 1630
Puritans establish several settlements near Plymouth, including port of Boston.

■Plymouth, 1620
Pilgrims arrive in North America and form a government under Mayflower Compact.

■Pennsylvania, 1682
William Penn establishes Pennsylvania colony as safe haven for English Quakers.

■New York, 1664
English capture New Netherland from the Dutch and rename it New York.

FRENCH TERRITORY

■Bacon's Rebellion, 1675
Virginia farmers clash with Indians and colonial government over frontier expansion.

■Jamestown, 1607
English colonists establish England's first permanent settlement in North America.

Atlantic Ocean

SPANISH TERRITORY

■Georgia, 1733
James Oglethorpe founds a colony for debtors and other poor settlers.

Gulf of Mexico

Great Lakes
Ohio R.
Mississippi R.
MA
NH
MA Boston
Plymouth
NY CT RI
New York
NJ
PA Philadelphia
MD DE
VA
Jamestown
NC
SC Charleston
GA
Savannah

VISUAL PREVIEW

| 1664 | The English take over New Amsterdam from the Dutch. | 1682 | William Penn founds the colony of Pennsylvania. | 1732 | Georgia is founded by James Oglethorpe. |

1650 **1700** **1750**

| | William and Mary sign the English Bill of Rights. | 1689 | 1712 | Thomas Newcomen's steam engine is put to use in British coal mines. |

65

Instruction (continued)

- Have students study the map on these pages. Ask: **What does the shaded green area represent?** (*13 English colonies*) **Where do you find Spanish territory?** (*southwest and southeast*) **Who seems to control the largest territory?** (*French*)

- Have students study the timeline. Ask: **Who established the first permanent European settlement in North America?** (*Spain*) **Name two colonies established during the years shown on the timeline.** (*Jamestown, Virginia; Plymouth Bay; New Amsterdam; Pennsylvania; Georgia*)

- Ask students to look at the graphics and read the captions on the map. **When was Pennsylvania established and why?** (*1682, as safe haven for English Quakers*) Pair students to analyze the captions and discuss the information with their partner using the Think-Write-Pair-Share strategy. (TE p. T25) Write the timeline of U.S. events on the board. Have students add information they learned from the captions to the timeline.

- Have students rewrite the Essential Question in their notes in simple terms. **How did English colonies grow and become so different from each other?** You may also post this in a prominent place in the classroom and leave it there while discussing the chapter. Tell students to use the section focus questions as a guide to answering the Essential Question as they read the chapter.

- Tell students that as they complete the Notetaking Study Guide for this chapter, they will be building the answer to the Chapter Essential Question.

Interactive Reading and Notetaking Study Guide, Chapter 3, (Adapted Version also available.)

Vocabulary Builder

Preview the Vocabulary Have students preview the vocabulary in the chapter and rate how well they know each word on the Word Knowledge Rating Form. Collect the sheets and explain that they will have a chance to go over the forms later.

All in One Teaching Resources, Unit 1, Word Knowledge Rating Form, p. 72

Monitor Progress Students should demonstrate their understanding of the words by finding pictures in books or magazines that illustrate their meanings. For example, for the word *restrict*, students may show a dog on a leash. Pair students to exchange their pictures and have the partners check understanding of the relationship of the image to the word. Review the material with students.

Review and Preview

Students have learned of Spanish colonization of North America during the 1500s and how conflict between nations spurred other European countries to colonize the continent. Here they will discover why England established these colonies and the success of their efforts.

Section Focus Question

How did the English set up their first colonies?

Before you begin the lesson for the day, write the Section Focus Question on the board. (*Lesson focus: The English government cooperated with private companies, sending various groups to establish colonies in North America.*)

Prepare to Read

Build Background Knowledge **L2**

This section describes England's earliest efforts to establish colonies in North America. Ask students to list all the reasons someone might move to a new, previously unexplored land. Use the Give One, Get One strategy (TE, p. T25) to elicit responses. (*Possible responses include: for freedom, for opportunity, for financial gain, to escape trouble, to find out about new people and places*)

Set a Purpose **L2**

■ Read each statement in the Reading Readiness Guide aloud. Ask students to mark the statements True or False.

  All in One **Teaching Resources, Unit 1,** Reading Readiness Guide, p. 73

■ Have students discuss the statements in pairs or groups of four, then mark the worksheets again. Use the Numbered Heads participation strategy (TE, p. T24) to call on students to share their group's perspectives. The students will return to these worksheets later.

Answer

☑Checkpoint It hoped to get new customers and raw materials for industry.

Moldy Rotten Peas

❝The allowance in those times for a man was only eight ounces of meal and half a pint of peas for a day, the one and the other moldy, rotten, full of cobwebs and maggots . . ., which forced many to flee for relief to the [Native Americans] . . . and others . . . to filch.❞

—General Assembly of Virginia, describing colonists' hardships, 1624

◄ Recreation of English settlement at Jamestown, Virginia

The First English Settlements

Objectives

• Explain why England wanted to establish colonies in North America.

• Describe the experience of the settlers who founded the first permanent English colony in Jamestown.

• Explain how the Pilgrims managed to survive their first years in the Plymouth Colony.

🔵 Reading Skill

Identify Contrasts As you read about early English settlements in North America, think how each of these settlements was unique. How was each different from the other early settlements? For example, you might look at the purpose of the settlements, the conditions each endured, and the types of settlers who came.

Key Terms and People

charter	pilgrim
John Smith	Squanto
representative government	

Why It Matters As Spain, France, and Holland sought colonies in the Americas, England entered the competition, too. The English established colonies on the east coast of North America.

❓ **Section Focus Question: How did the English set up their first colonies?**

England Seeks Colonies

Like most of Europe in the age of exploration, England was a monarchy. However, in England, the power of the king or queen was limited by law and by a lawmaking body called Parliament.

Ever since the 1200s, English law had limited the king's power to punish people without trial. The law guaranteed the right to trial by jury. Other provisions limited the king's power to impose new taxes. The king could set new taxes only with Parliament's consent. Still, the king's powers were much greater than those of Parliament.

England began to establish colonies in North America in the late 1500s. Colonies would provide new markets for English products and important raw materials for English industries.

Two of the earliest English efforts to establish colonies took place during the 1580s. Both were set up on a small island off the coast of what today is North Carolina. The first colony at Roanoke Island was established in 1585, but it was abandoned a year later. The second colony is one of the great mysteries of American history. It was set up in 1587. The next year, England found itself at war with Spain. No ship was able to visit the Roanoke colony until 1590. By then, the colony was abandoned. It had disappeared without a trace.

☑Checkpoint What benefits did England hope to get from establishing colonies?

Differentiated Instruction

L1 **English Language Learners** **L1** **Less Proficient Readers** **L1** **Special Needs**

Make Flashcards To make sure that students do not misinterpret the content of this section because they are skipping unfamiliar words, have them make a list of the Key Terms and High-Use Words. Then have them create flashcards with each word on one side and its definition on the other. Pair students with a partner and have them quiz each other on the definitions of the words using the flashcards.

Founding Jamestown

In 1607, a group of wealthy people pooled their resources and made a new attempt to establish an English colony in North America. Eager to gain a share of the wealth of the Americas, they formed the Virginia Company of London. Some of the founders hoped to discover gold or silver. Others expected the colonists to trade with the Indians for furs, which could then be sold in Europe at a profit. Lumber also could be cut from North America's vast forests. Farmers could plant vineyards to grow grapes or mulberry trees to produce silk. England needed all of these products.

England's King James I backed the project. The king granted the merchants a charter to establish a colony called Virginia. A charter is a document issued by a government that grants specific rights to a person or company. It gave the Virginia Company authority over a large portion of North America's Atlantic coastline.

The first colonists arrived in Virginia in the spring of 1607. About 100 men sailed into Chesapeake Bay and built a fort they called Jamestown. It would prove to be England's first permanent settlement in North America.

Jamestown barely survived its first year. It was located on a swampy peninsula where insects thrived in warm weather. During the first summer, many colonists caught diseases, such as malaria, and died.

The colony had another serious problem. Many of the colonists had no intention of doing the hard farmwork needed to grow crops. Those men who came to the colony were not farmers. They were skilled in other trades. They spent their time looking for gold, expecting to get the food they needed from the Native Americans. The colonists found no gold. The local people, led by a chief named Powhatan, supplied some food to the colony. But it was not enough. By the spring of 1608, only 38 of the original colonists were still alive.

John Smith Takes Charge Conditions in Jamestown were extremely bad, in part because the colony was poorly led. Then, in the fall of 1608, John Smith was sent out from London to lead the colony. Smith lost no time taking command. He drew up tough, new rules. The most important rule was "He who works not, eats not."

Under Smith's firm leadership, the Jamestown colonists cut timber, put up new

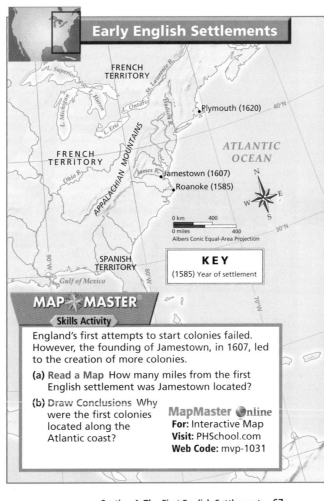

Early English Settlements

FRENCH TERRITORY

FRENCH TERRITORY

APPALACHIAN MOUNTAINS

L. Superior
L. Michigan
L. Huron
L. Ontario
L. Erie
St. Lawrence R.
Hudson R.
Ohio R.
James R.

Plymouth (1620) — 40°N

ATLANTIC OCEAN

Jamestown (1607)
Roanoke (1585)

0 km 400
0 miles 400
Albers Conic Equal-Area Projection

30°N

SPANISH TERRITORY

Gulf of Mexico

KEY
(1585) Year of settlement

90°W 80°W 70°W

MAP★MASTER
Skills Activity

England's first attempts to start colonies failed. However, the founding of Jamestown, in 1607, led to the creation of more colonies.

(a) Read a Map How many miles from the first English settlement was Jamestown located?

(b) Draw Conclusions Why were the first colonies located along the Atlantic coast?

MapMaster Online
For: Interactive Map
Visit: PHSchool.com
Web Code: mvp-1031

Instruction L2

- **Vocabulary Builder** Before teaching this lesson, preteach the High-Use Words **establish** and **sustain** using the strategy on TE p. T21.

  Key Terms Following the instruction on p. 7, have students create a See It–Remember It chart for the Key Terms in this chapter.

- Read England Seeks Colonies and Founding Jamestown with students using the Oral Cloze strategy (TE, p. T22)

- Ask: **What reasons did England have for establishing colonies?** (*England sought new markets for its products and a supply of raw materials for its industries.*)

- Ask: **What was the effect of John Smith's leadership on Jamestown** (*He drew up new rules demanding everyone work for the colony. The colony became more established during his year as leader.*)

Independent Practice

Have students continue to fill in the Study Guide for this section.

📖 **Interactive Reading and Notetaking Study Guide,** Chapter 3, Section 1 (Adapted Version also available.)

Monitor Progress

As students fill in the Notetaking Study Guide, circulate to make sure that they understand the importance of the struggles faced by early English settlers. Provide assistance as needed.

Vocabulary Builder

Use the information below to teach students this section's high-use words.

High-Use Word	Definition and Sample Sentence
establish, p. 67	*v.* to set up, found People worked together to **establish** a colony.
sustain, p. 68	*v.* to support, to keep going The colonists were unable at first to grow enough food to **sustain** themselves.

Answers

MAP★MASTER Skills Activity **(a)** about 125 miles **(b)** The coast provided a convenient source of food and transportation

Jamestown Prospers

p. 68

Instruction ▐L2▌

- Have students read Jamestown Prospers. Remind students to look for the sequence of events.

- Ask: **Why do you think the Virginia Company gave settlers the right to self-government?** (*Possible answer: Company leaders in England realized they were too far away to make day-to-day decisions about governing the colony.*)

- Have students complete the worksheet Proceedings of the Virginia Assembly, 1619. Discuss the historical importance of the principles established by the House of Burgesses. (*The House of Burgesses established principles of self-government that later found their way into the Constitution.*)

  All in One Teaching Resources, Unit 1, Proceedings of the Virginia Assembly, 1619, p. 78

Independent Practice

Have students continue to fill in the Study Guide for this section.

Interactive Reading and Notetaking Study Guide, Chapter 3, Section 1 (Adapted Version also available.)

Monitor Progress

As students fill in the Notetaking Study Guide, circulate to make sure that they understand the importance of the changes that led to Jamestown's prosperity. Provide assistance as needed.

🌐 Explore More Video

Discovery School Video

Show the *Jamestown* video to tell the story of the founding of Jamestown and the struggles of that colony in its early years.

Answers

☑Checkpoint Jamestown setters initially struggled due to a poor location, laziness, a harsh winter, a lack of skills, and poor leadership.

Link Past and Present Similarities: Members are elected. Members meet together to make laws. Differences: Members would not meet in a church. Today there are many more lawmakers.

---

buildings, and planted crops. Meanwhile, hundreds of new colonists arrived. They included the first English women to settle in Jamestown. To get more food, Smith raided Native American villages. This angered Powhatan, who feared the English intended "to invade my people and possess my country."

The "Starving Time" In the fall of 1609, John Smith returned to England after being injured in an explosion. With Smith gone, conditions in Jamestown quickly worsened. So did relations with the Native Americans. Powhatan decided the time had come to drive the English away. First, he refused to supply them with food. The English settlers quickly ran out of food. The terrible winter of 1609–1610 is called the "starving time." By the spring of 1610, only 60 colonists were still alive.

☑Checkpoint Why did settlers in Jamestown have difficulties at first?

Jamestown Prospers

During the hard times, the Virginia Company did not give up. It continued to send new colonists and offered free land to keep old colonists from leaving. Most important, it sent new leaders from England to restore order in the colony.

These measures would not have succeeded if the colonists had not found a dependable source of income to sustain the colony. What they found was tobacco, a crop native to the Americas. By the 1580s, smoking tobacco had become popular in several European countries, including England.

Vocabulary Builder
sustain (suh STAYN) **v.** to support; to keep going

Explore More Video
To learn more about the Jamestown Colony, view the video.

The House of Burgesses On July 30, 1619, the 22 elected members of the House of Burgesses first met together at the Jamestown church. That hot day marked the beginning of representative government in what is now the United States. *Critical Thinking: Link Past and Present How would a lawmaking body today be similar? What differences would you expect to see?*

68 Chapter 3 Colonies Take Root

The governor calls the meeting to order.

Soldiers stand guard.

The secretary records what is said at the meeting.

Differentiated Instruction

▐L3▌ **Advanced Readers**   ▐L3▌ **Gifted and Talented**

Plan an Expedition Have students find out more about the events and issues leading to the eventual success of the Plymouth Colony. Ask them to plan their own expedition to set up a colony in North America.

All in One Teaching Resources, Unit 1, Your Voyage to the Americas, p. 80

Farmers in Jamestown and nearby settlements in Virginia began planting tobacco in 1612. By the early 1620s, Virginia farmers were selling all the tobacco they could grow. Their success drew new colonists from England.

The House of Burgesses During these years, Virginia developed a tradition of representative government—the form of government in which voters elect people to make laws for them. In 1619, Virginia's lawmaking body, the House of Burgesses, was elected and met for the first time. The House of Burgesses could pass laws and set taxes. However, it shared power with Virginia's appointed governor, who could veto its acts. The House of Burgesses marked the start of representative government in North America.

Africans Come to Virginia In the summer of 1619, a Dutch ship arrived in Virginia from the West Indies. On board were 20 Africans, who had been captured and taken from their homeland. The Africans were sold to the Virginia colonists as slaves. However, that did not necessarily mean they would be enslaved for the rest of their lives. In the early days of the colony, enslaved people had a chance to earn their freedom after working a certain number of years. Some enslaved Africans were able to do this. Permanent slavery for Africans was not established in Virginia until the last part of the 1600s.

☑ **Checkpoint** What were the responsibilities of the House of Burgesses?

The Plymouth Colony

In England during the 1500s, people could be punished for their religious beliefs. In the 1530s, when King Henry VIII declared himself head of the Church of England, everyone was expected to follow the ways of the Church of England.

About the time Jamestown was founded, a group of people in eastern England left their homes and settled in the Netherlands. They wanted to separate from the Church of England and practice Christianity in their own way. These people, called Separatists, were often persecuted or treated badly because of their religion.

Between 1607 and 1609, several groups of Separatists settled in the Netherlands. Although they were allowed to worship as they pleased, they still were not happy. In 1620, one group of Separatists decided to leave the Netherlands and settle in Virginia. They are the people we know today as the Pilgrims. A pilgrim is a person who takes a religious journey.

The Mayflower Compact In September 1620, about 100 Pilgrims sailed for Virginia aboard a ship called the *Mayflower*. After a long voyage, they arrived safely in North America. However, storms had blown them off course, and they landed far to the north in what today is Massachusetts. They called their new home Plymouth, after a port city in England.

African American artist Romare Bearden presents the forced journey enslaved Africans made to the Americas in his painting *Roots Odyssey*.

Identify Contrasts
How were the Pilgrims' reasons for coming to America different from those of the Jamestown settlers?

History Background

The House of Burgesses After the Jamestown Colony struggled to succeed in its early years, King James I sent Sir Thomas Dale to act as governor. To establish order, Dale controlled almost every aspect of the settlers' lives under martial law. Each woman, man, and child was assigned a military rank, and was punished severely for failing to perform his or her assigned duties. Dale's "Laws Divine, Moral, and Martial" did in fact bring order to the colony, but they also discouraged new colonists from settling there. When George Yeardley took over the position of governor in 1618, he helped establish the House of Burgesses, setting the course for self-government in the English colonies.

The Plymouth Colony
p. 69

Instruction

- Have students read The Plymouth Colony. Remind students to look for causes and effects.

- Ask students to suggest reasons why the Pilgrims had to come all the way to North America to practice their religion. (*King Henry VIII had made it illegal to disobey the ways of the Church of England.*)

- To help students better understand the concept of *self-government*, which is important to the understanding of this section, use the Concept Lesson Self-Government. Provide students with copies of the Concept Organizer.

  All in One **Teaching Resources, Unit 1,** Concept Lesson, p. 85; Concept Organizer, p. 6

- Discuss the Pilgrims' establishment of self-government. Ask: **Why was it important for the colony to have a government?** (*Possible answer: to keep order; to ensure religious freedom; to provide leaders with guidelines*)

Independent Practice

Have students complete the Study Guide for this section.

📖 **Interactive Reading and Notetaking Study Guide,** Chapter 3, Section 1 (Adapted Version also available.)

Monitor Progress

- As students complete the Notetaking Study Guide, circulate to make sure students understand the importance of the Mayflower Compact. Provide assistance as needed.

- Tell students to fill in the last column of the Reading Readiness Guide. Probe for what they learned that confirms or invalidates each statement.

  All in One **Teaching Resources, Unit 1,** Reading Readiness Guide, p. 73

Answers

☑ **Checkpoint** to pass laws and to set taxes

🔵 **Reading Skill** They wanted to separate from the Church of England and be free to practice Christianity in their own way.

Assess and Reteach

Assess Progress
L2

Have students complete Check Your Progress. Administer the Section Quiz.

All in One Teaching Resources, Unit 1, Section Quiz, p. 86

To further assess student understanding, use the Progress Monitoring Transparency.

Progress Monitoring Transparencies, Chapter 3, Section 1

Reteach
L1

If students need more instruction, have them read this section in the Interactive Reading and Notetaking Study Guide and complete the accompanying question.

Interactive Reading and Notetaking Study Guide, Chapter 3, Section 1 (Adapted Version also available.)

Extend
L3

Have students work in small groups to create a plan for establishing a new colony. Each member of the group may be assigned a particular aspect of colonization, including political, social, economic, and geographic. Have them draw upon their knowledge of the successes and failures of early English colonies when developing their plans. Have groups present their plans to the class.

Progress Monitoring Online

Students may check their comprehension of this section by completing the Progress Monitoring Online graphic organizer and self-quiz.

Answer

✓**Checkpoint** It was the first document in which Americans claimed the right to self-government.

Squanto

Because they had landed outside Virginia, the Pilgrims believed they were not bound by the rules of the Virginia Company. But they needed rules of some sort. Before going ashore, 41 adult men signed the Mayflower Compact. It called for a government that would make and follow "just and equal laws." Officeholders would be elected by the colony's adult males.

Thus, a year after the creation of Virginia's House of Burgesses, the Pilgrims had taken a second step toward self-government in the Americas. The Mayflower Compact was the first document in which American colonists claimed a right to govern themselves.

The First Thanksgiving The Pilgrims had a very difficult first winter in Plymouth. They had arrived too late to plant crops and did not have enough food. During the winter of 1620–1621, half the colonists died from hunger or disease.

Conditions improved in the spring of 1621. As had happened at Jamestown, help from local Native Americans sustained the Pilgrims. A local chief gave the Pilgrims some food. Another Native American, named Squanto, brought the Pilgrims seeds of native plants—corn, beans, and pumpkins—and showed them how to plant them. He also taught the settlers how to catch eels from nearby rivers.

In the fall of 1621, the Pilgrims set aside a day to give thanks for their good fortune. Today's Thanksgiving holiday celebrates that occasion.

✓**Checkpoint** Why was the Mayflower Compact important?

⭐ **Looking Back and Ahead** The early settlers faced many challenges before they were able to claim success. In the next section, you will read how English settlers established additional colonies in New England.

Section 1 | Check Your Progress

Progress Monitoring Online
For: Self-test with instant help
Visit: PHSchool.com
Web Code: mva-1031

Comprehension and Critical Thinking

1. (a) Recall What actions did John Smith take to help Jamestown?
(b) Identify Alternatives What other methods do you think Smith could have used to save the colony?

2. (a) Identify Who were the Pilgrims?
(b) Analyze Cause and Effect How did the Pilgrims' experiences in England affect the government they established in the Plymouth Colony?

Reading Skill

3. Identify Contrasts How did the government of the Jamestown settlers differ from that of the Plymouth settlers?

Key Terms

Fill in the blanks with the correct key terms.

4. The English king gave the merchants of the Virginia Company a ____ to establish a colony called Virginia.

5. English colonies in North America established a form of ____ based on elections.

Writing

6. Imagine that you are preparing a news report about the founding of Jamestown Colony. Make notes providing background information about this development. Your notes should include the economic benefits of colonialism and the particular details about how Jamestown Colony was founded.

70 Chapter 3 Colonies Take Root

Section 1 Check Your Progress

1. (a) John Smith developed tough rules, including one that required people to work if they wanted to eat.
(b) Possible answers: Smith could have asked Native Americans to teach them to survive and developed friendly trade relationships with them.

2. (a) People who came to North America to separate from the Church of England.

(b) They established self-government to prevent persecution from their leaders.

3. The Plymouth settlers self-governed. The House of Burgesses was beholden to the king.

4. charter

5. representative government

6. Students' notes should include economic benefits and complete details about how Jamestown was founded.

God Has Preserved Me

❝In [sixteen] sixty-one, my house was burnt, . . . and it was a most violent fire. . . . It pleased God to stir up the hearts of my loving friends to help me to the carrying on of another. . . . Thus God has all along preserved and kept me all my days.❞

—John Dane, recalling his life in New England, 1670

◄ Boston, Massachusetts, in the 1660s

The New England Colonies

Objectives

- Describe the geography and climate of the New England Colonies.
- Describe the Puritan settlement in Massachusetts.
- Identify the new settlements that developed in New England as a result of Puritan religious practices.
- Explain the changes that took place in the New England Colonies in the 1600s.

🅞 Reading Skill

Make Comparisons Despite differences, the New England colonies were alike in many ways. Look for these similarities in this section. For example, how was the climate similar in various colonies? You might also look at the shared reasons colonists had for coming to North America and at the ways that similar government structures evolved throughout New England.

Key Terms and People

John Winthrop
toleration
Roger Williams
Anne Hutchinson

Thomas Hooker
John Wheelright
town meeting
Metacom

Why It Matters Religious beliefs led the Pilgrims to move to North America and establish Plymouth Colony. Religion played a key role in other colonies that were established in New England.

🅞 **Section Focus Question: How did religious beliefs and dissent influence the New England Colonies?**

Geography of New England

New England is in the northeastern corner of the United States. Massachusetts, Connecticut, and Rhode Island make up southern New England. New Hampshire, Vermont, and Maine make up the northern part.

Much of New England is made up of hills and low mountains. Large areas are covered by forests. The soil is thin and rocky, which makes farming difficult. There are narrow plains located along the Atlantic coast. The Connecticut River, the region's longest river, flows from New Hampshire and Vermont through Massachusetts and Connecticut before reaching the sea. Just off New England's long, jagged coastline are some of the richest fishing grounds in the world.

Winters in New England tend to be long and snowy. Summers are shorter and warm. This helped the early colonists in the region, who caught fewer diseases and lived longer than the colonists in Virginia.

☑**Checkpoint** Why would colonists in New England have turned to fishing rather than to farming?

Section 2 The New England Colonies **71**

Vocabulary Builder

Use the information below to teach students this section's high-use words.

High-Use Word	Definition and Sample Sentence
specify, p. 73	*v.* to point out in detail The government will **specify** the exact procedures for registering land.
restrict, p. 75	*v.* to place limitations on something or somebody Some laws **restrict** undesirable activities.

Section 2
Step-by-Step Instruction

Review and Preview

Students have read about how early colonies were established. They will now explore the role religion played in settling the New England Colonies.

Section Focus Question

How did religious beliefs and dissent influence the New England Colonies?

Before you begin the lesson for the day, write the Section Focus Question on the board. (*Lesson focus: Disputes over religious freedom inspired people to leave England and influenced the governments that were established.*)

Prepare to Read

Build Background Knowledge L2

Remind students that they have read about the first English colonies founded at Jamestown and Plymouth. Ask students why they think English colonists continued to come to North America to start other colonies. Use the Idea Wave strategy (TE, p. T24) to help students brainstorm. (*Possible answers: to seek religious freedom, to begin a new way of life, to gain wealth*)

Set a Purpose L2

- Form students into pairs or groups of four. Distribute the Reading Readiness Guide. Ask students to fill in the first two columns of the chart.

  All in One Teaching Resources, Unit 1, Reading Readiness Guide, p. 74

- Use the Numbered Heads participation strategy (TE, p. T24) to call on students to share one piece of information they already know and one piece they want to know. The students will return to these worksheets later.

Answer

☑**Checkpoint** Fish were abundant in the ocean and rivers. Thin, rocky soil made farming too difficult.

Chapter 3 Section 2 **71**

Teach

Geography of New England

p. 71

Instruction

L2

- **Vocabulary Builder** Before teaching this lesson, preteach the High-Use Words **specify** and **restrict** using the strategy on TE p. 65.

  Key Terms Have students continue filling in the See It–Remember It chart for the Key Terms in this chapter.

- Have students read Geography of New England using the Paragraph Shrinking strategy (p. T23).

- Ask students to identify good conditions and bad conditions in New England. (*good: thick forests and miles of freshwater rivers and coastline rich with fish; bad: rocky, hilly land with thin soil*)

Independent Practice

Have students begin to fill in the Study Guide for this section.

📖 **Interactive Reading and Notetaking Study Guide,** Chapter 3, Section 2 (Adapted Version also available.)

Monitor Progress

As students fill in the Notetaking Study Guide, circulate to make sure students understand the importance to the Puritans of upholding religious ideals. If students do not seem to have a good understanding, have them reread the section. Provide assistance as needed.

Answers

🔵 **Reading Skill** Both the Pilgrims and the Puritans left England for religious freedom.

Draw Conclusions Today's court system uses a jury of peers and includes various provisions to protect the rights of the accused.

Puritans in Massachusetts Bay

Similar to the Pilgrims, a group known as the Puritans had disagreements with the Church of England. Rather than split off from the established church, they wanted to reform, or change, it. In the early 1600s, the Puritans were influential in England. Many were important professionals such as merchants, landowners, or lawyers.

The 1620s brought hard times for England's Puritans. King Charles I opposed their movement and persecuted them. Hundreds of Puritan ministers were forced to give up their positions.

The Puritans Leave England A number of Puritans eventually decided to leave England and make the hazardous voyage to North America. In 1630, about 900 Puritans set off in 11 ships. They had formed the Massachusetts Bay Company, which received a charter to establish settlements in what are now Massachusetts and New Hampshire. The Puritans were led by John Winthrop, a respected landowner and lawyer.

In founding their own colony, Puritan leaders believed that their way of life would provide an example to others. As Winthrop said in a sermon during their voyage:

❝Now the only way . . . is . . . to walk humbly with our God. . . . We must consider that we shall be as a City upon a Hill. The eyes of all people are upon us.❞

—John Winthrop, "A Model of Christian Charity," 1630

Make Comparisons
Compare the reasons that England's Puritans went to North America with the reasons that the Pilgrims left England. How are they similar?

● **INFOGRAPHIC**

SALEM WITCH Trials

Today, the Salem witch trials show how quickly false accusations can be accepted as true. **Critical Thinking: Draw Conclusions** Do you think this kind of judgment is possible today? Explain.

The Accusers
Clergymen such as Cotton Mather of Boston helped to feed the hysteria by asserting that the Devil was luring Salem's people into witchcraft.

▼ **On Trial**
In 1692, hysteria about witches swept through Salem, Massachusetts. A special court tried dozens of women and men accused of witchcraft.

72 Chapter 3 Colonies Take Root

Differentiated Instruction

L1 English Language Learners	**L1** Less Proficient Readers
L3 Advanced Readers	**L3** Gifted and Talented

Write a Descriptive Paragraph Pair L1 and L3 students. Ask pairs to work together to prepare a description of the settlement of the Plymouth Colony, including the reasons the Pilgrims migrated and the struggles they faced. Students should include their personal feelings and opinions regarding the establishment of the colony, based on their backgrounds and experiences. Partners should practice presenting their paragraphs to the class, with the L3 student acting as coach.

The Massachusetts Bay Colony The Puritans established several settlements in their colony. The main town was Boston, which was located on an excellent harbor. By 1643, about 20,000 people lived in the Massachusetts Bay Colony.

By the mid-1630s, Massachusetts Bay had an elected assembly, the General Court. Each town sent representatives to the assembly. But voting was limited to adult male members of the Puritan church. Both the General Court and the colony's governor were elected each year.

The Puritans had founded their colony so they could worship as they chose. However, they did not give non-Puritans the same right. The Puritans did not believe in religious toleration—recognition that other people have the right to different opinions.

☑ **Checkpoint** Why did the Puritans go to North America?

New Colonies

Disagreements about religion led to the founding of other colonies in New England. A key dispute involved Roger Williams, minister of a church in the town of Salem. Williams believed the Puritans should split entirely from the Church of England. He also criticized colonists who had seized Native American lands. Williams specified that colonists should pay Native Americans for their land.

Williams was forced to leave Massachusetts Bay in 1635. He moved south, to what today is Rhode Island, where he bought land from Native Americans. In 1636, he founded the town of Providence.

Vocabulary Builder
specify (SPEHS ah fī) **v.** to point out in detail

The Accused
An accused woman is strapped to a dunking stool, a common form of punishment.

Section 2 The New England Colonies **73**

Instruction L2

- Have students read Puritans in Massachusetts Bay. Remind students to make comparisons among colonies.

- Have students complete the worksheet *To My Dear and Loving Husband*. Ask: **What does this poem suggest about the women in the Massachusetts Bay Colony?** (*Possible answer: The poem suggests that the women were devoted and loyal to their husbands.*)

All in One **Teaching Resources, Unit 1,** *To My Dear and Loving Husband*, p. 79

- Remind students that the Puritans came to New England to escape persecution, then persecuted others in Salem. Ask: **Why do you think the Puritans did not offer the same rights to everyone?** (*They believed that their religion was the only correct religion.*)

- Display the transparency The Salem Witch Trials. Have students discuss the injustices of the trials.

Color Transparencies, The Salem Witch Trials

Independent Practice

Have students continue to fill in the Study Guide for this section.

📖 **Interactive Reading and Notetaking Study Guide,** Chapter 3, Section 2 (Adapted Version also available.)

Monitor Progress

As students fill in the Notetaking Study Guide, circulate to make sure that students understand how Puritan beliefs influenced the government they designed. If students do not seem to have a good understanding, have them reread the section. Provide assistance as needed.

History Background

Puritan Beliefs Puritans had challenged the Church of England to reform since the 1500s. In fact, the name *puritan* refers to their desire to *purify* the church and society. Puritans believed that there were two kinds of people: those who declared repentance for their wrongdoings and those who did not. Puritans believed that people were basically bad. As such, they lived by strict standards of behavior in order to make up for their sins. Common Puritan disciplines included hard work and staying away from gambling, drinking, and swearing.

Answer

☑ **Checkpoint** to build a colony based on their religious beliefs and serve as a model to others

New Colonies

p. 73

Instruction

L2

- Have students read New Colonies. Remind students to make comparisons among colonies.

- Ask: **Why were settlers in Rhode Island free to worship as they saw fit?** (*Rhode Island did not have an established church.*)

- Ask: **Why did Thomas Hooker leave Massachusetts for Connecticut?** (*He disagreed with the Puritan leaders in Massachusetts.*)

Independent Practice

Have students continue to fill in the Study Guide for this section.

Interactive Reading and Notetaking Study Guide, Chapter 3, Section 2 (Adapted Version also available.)

Monitor Progress

As students fill in the Notetaking Study Guide, circulate to make sure students understand the importance of conflicts over religious beliefs in the establishment of new colonies. If students do not seem to have a good understanding, have them reread the section. Provide assistance as needed.

Answers

MAP MASTER **Skills Activity** **(a)** Maine, New Hampshire, and the area claimed by New York and New Hampshire **(b)** lumber, fish, whales, and iron

---

The New England Colonies

▶ Fishing for cod off the New England coast

▲ New England farm

St. Lawrence R.

Maine (part of MA)

45°N

Connecticut R.

New Hampshire

Falmouth

Area claimed by New York and New Hampshire

New York

Portsmouth

Newburyport

▼ Monument to the Pilgrim landing at Plymouth

Salem

Massachusetts

Boston

ATLANTIC OCEAN

Plymouth

Connecticut

Pennsylvania

New Haven

Newport

New Jersey

Rhode Island

◀ Anne Hutchinson

40°N

75°W

70°W

N
W   E
S

KEY

Cattle		Lumber	
Fish		Rum	
Furs		Ships	
Grain		Whales	
Iron			

0 km   100
0 miles   100
Albers Conic Equal-Area Projection

MAP MASTER
Skills Activity

The New England Colonies had a great variety of resources. Seas, forests, and farms provided a good living to colonists.

(a) **Read a Map** In which area was fur trade important?

(b) **Evaluate Information** What resources were available to settlers along the Atlantic coast?

MapMaster Online

For: Interactive map
Visit: PHSchool.com
Web Code: mvp-1032

Differentiated Instruction

L3 **Advanced Readers**   **L3** **Gifted and Talented**

Write a Defense Have students perform additional research on one of the four colonial leaders who faced conflict with their colonies: Roger Williams, Anne Hutchinson, Thomas Hooker, and John Wheelright. Have students write a legal defense for the position held by the leader and present it to the class. Students should include specific details that occurred in the struggle of their selected leader.

In 1644, the colonists in Rhode Island received a charter from the king to govern themselves. In doing so, they made an important contribution to religious toleration. They decided that Rhode Island would have no established, or official, church. People of all faiths could worship as they saw fit. Among the people who found religious freedom in Rhode Island were followers of the Jewish faith.

Anne Hutchinson's Dissent A Boston woman, Anne Hutchinson, questioned some of the Puritan teachings. She was put on trial in 1638 and was expelled from Massachusetts. Hutchinson established a settlement on an island that is now a part of Rhode Island. In 1642, she traveled farther south, into what is today New York State.

Settling Connecticut Thomas Hooker, a minister, disagreed with the Puritan leaders. He left Massachusetts with about 100 followers in 1636 and settled in what today is Connecticut. There, he founded the town of Hartford. Hundreds of Puritans followed, and soon Connecticut had several new settlements.

In 1639, the colonists drew up the Fundamental Orders of Connecticut, which established a new government with an elected legislature and governor. In 1662, Connecticut received an official charter from the king granting it self-government.

John Wheelright also was forced to leave Massachusetts. He got into trouble because he agreed with some of Anne Hutchinson's views. In 1638, Wheelright and some followers moved to New Hampshire, where they founded the town of Exeter. For a time, Massachusetts tried to control New Hampshire. Finally, in 1680, a charter from the king made New Hampshire a separate colony.

✓Checkpoint **Why did Roger Williams and Anne Hutchinson leave the Massachusetts Bay Colony?**

Growth and Change

The Puritans believed that towns and churches should manage their own affairs. They also believed that people should work hard and live in strong and stable families.

Each Puritan town governed itself by setting up a town meeting—an assembly of townspeople that decides local issues. Membership in town meetings was <u>restricted</u> to male heads of households. Town meetings set local taxes and elected people to run the towns. Town meetings also gave New Englanders an opportunity to speak their minds. This early experience encouraged the growth of democratic ideas. New England became a region of towns and villages where neighbors knew one another and participated together in government.

New England families earned their livelihoods in many different ways. Farmers grew crops, but they also made leather goods and other products. Fishers caught cod and other fish that were shipped to customers in Europe. A shipbuilding industry provided many jobs. By the 1660s, more than 300 ships from New England were fishing off the coast or moving products across the Atlantic Ocean.

Vocabulary Builder
<u>restrict</u> (ree STRIHKT) **v.** to place limitations on something or somebody

---

History Background

Population and Economic Growth By 1730, there were over half a million people living in England's original 13 colonies. Massachusetts was among the most populous, with about 114,000 people. Fifty years later, the population of Massachusetts had more than doubled, to 260,000. As the population grew in the colonies, so did the economies. And as the economy grew, new social classes developed. Members of merchant families held social and political as well as economic power.

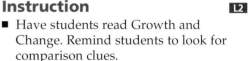

Growth and Change
p. 75

Instruction
L2

■ Have students read Growth and Change. Remind students to look for comparison clues.

■ Ask: **How was New England's environment closely related to its economy?** (*Forest products were used in shipbuilding. Fishing and whaling were big industries.*)

■ Discuss the conflicts that arose during the 1670s. Have students suggest reasons why there were so many conflicts with Native American groups. (*Answers will vary, but may include: Native Americans were frustrated by losing their land, their people, and their resources. Native Americans fought to retain what little they had left. Native Americans wanted to keep the colonists from moving further west.*)

Independent Practice
Have students complete the Study Guide for this section.

📖 **Interactive Reading and Notetaking Study Guide,** Chapter 3, Section 2 (Adapted Version also available.)

Monitor Progress

■ As students complete the Notetaking Study Guide, circulate to make sure students understand the importance of the changes that began to take place in New England Colonies. Provide assistance as needed.

■ Tell students to fill in the last column of the Reading Readiness Guide. Ask them to evaluate if what they learned was what they expected to learn.

All in One **Teaching Resources, Unit 1,** Reading Readiness Guide, p. 74

Answers
✓Checkpoint They did not agree with some of the Puritan teachings.

Assess and Reteach

Assess Progress L2

Have students complete Check Your Progress. Administer the Section Quiz.

All in One Teaching Resources, Unit 1, Section Quiz, p. 87

To further assess student understanding, use the Progress Monitoring Transparency.

Progress Monitoring Transparencies, Chapter 3, Section 2

Reteach L1

If students need more instruction, have them read this section in the Interactive Reading and Notetaking Study Guide and complete the accompanying question.

Interactive Reading and Notetaking Study Guide, Chapter 3, Section 2 (Adapted Version also available.)

Extend L3

Have students use the Internet to learn more about the life of one of the key Puritan leaders in colonial New England. After students have conducted research individually, form them into small groups to create a skit that illustrates what they learned.

Extend Online
For: Help in starting Extend activity
Visit: PHSchool.com
Web Code: mve-0118

Progress Monitoring Online

Students may check their comprehension of this section by completing the Progress Monitoring Online graphic organizer and self-quiz.

Answer

✓Checkpoint He wanted to stop Puritan expansion.

Section 2 Check Your Progress

1. (a) New England is hilly and rocky with rich forests and much coastland. It has cold, snowy winters and short, warm summers.
(b) Colonists fished and whaled in the waters and built ships from the lumber.

2. (a) to build a colony based on their religious beliefs and serve as a model to others
(b) Many people were forced to leave and started their own colonies.

3. Just as the English government had, the Puritans made it illegal to question their religious practices.

4. Possible answers: Toleration is the recognition that other people might have different opinions. Toleration is respecting other peoples' point of view, even if you don't agree with them. A town meeting is an assembly of townspeople that decides local issues. At town meetings, people talk about and solve local problems.

5. Concept webs should be completed accurately, with appropriate secondary ovals connected to the main oval.

Metacom, known to the English as "King Philip"

King Philip's War By the 1670s, the Native American population was decreasing, mainly because large numbers of Native Americans had died from diseases that they caught from Europeans. By 1670, there were only 12,000 Native Americans in New England, one tenth of their population 100 years earlier.

In 1675, a major conflict erupted. Opponents of the English were led by Metacom, the chief of the Wampanoag, who was also known by his English name, King Philip. His goal was to stop Puritan expansion. Other Native American groups, from Maine to Rhode Island, joined the war, some siding with the settlers. The fighting lasted a year and cost thousands of lives. Metacom and his allies destroyed 12 English towns. The uprising ended in 1676 when Metacom was captured and killed. The war's end left the English colonies free to expand.

Puritan Influence Declines By the 1670s, the outlook of New Englanders was changing. There was a new generation of people born in North America. The new generation had lost some of their parents' religious fervor, as people concentrated on running farms and businesses. In growing towns like Boston, successful merchants were becoming the new community leaders. The English colonies of New England were doing well. But the stern religious rules of the original founders now had less influence over the people who lived there.

✓Checkpoint **Why did Metacom declare war on the English colonists?**

⭐ **Looking Back and Ahead** As English colonies spread through New England, other colonies were being established to the west and south.

Section 2 | Check Your Progress

Progress Monitoring Online
For: Self-test with instant help
Visit: PHSchool.com
Web Code: mva-1032

Comprehension and Critical Thinking

1. (a) Summarize What was the geography and climate of New England?
(b) Identify Economic Costs How did geography affect the New England economy?

2. (a) Recall Why did Puritans establish the Massachusetts Bay Colony?

(b) Analyze Cause and Effect How did the lack of religious toleration affect politics in the Massachusetts Bay Colony?

Reading Skill

3. Make Comparisons Compare the way the English government treated the Puritans with the way the Puritans treated Anne Hutchinson. How are they similar?

Key Terms

4. Write two definitions for each key term: toleration, town meeting. First, write a formal definition for your teacher. Second, write a casual definition in everyday English for a classmate.

Writing

5. Create a concept web. Label the main oval "Religion." Then, add entries that show how religion played a major role in the settling of the New England Colonies. Add as many secondary ovals as necessary.

A Diverse Colony
"On the island of Manhattan, . . . there may well be four or five hundred men of different sects and nations: the Director General told me that there were men of eighteen different languages."

—Father Isaac Jogues, describing the Dutch settlement of New Amsterdam, 1646

◄ Dutch settlement of New Amsterdam, 1670s

The Middle Colonies

Objectives
- Describe the geography and climate of the Middle Colonies.
- Describe the early history of New York and New Jersey.
- Explain how Pennsylvania and Delaware were founded.
- Explain how the Middle Colonies changed in the 1600s and early 1700s.

Reading Skill

Identify Signal Words Signal words help readers spot comparisons and contrasts. For example, when we say, "Kentucky is warm. New York is *also* warm," the word *also* suggests that the two states and climates are similar. If the text reads, "Kentucky is warm. *Instead,* New York is cool," the word *instead* suggests that the two states and climates are different. Look for comparison and contrast signal words as you read this section.

Key Terms and People
proprietary colony   William Penn
royal colony   backcountry

Why It Matters While the New England colonies were growing, important developments were taking place in the region south of New England, known as the Middle Colonies.

? Section Focus Question: How did the diverse Middle Colonies develop and thrive?

Geography of the Middle Colonies

Four states made up the Middle Colonies: New York, Pennsylvania, New Jersey, and Delaware. New York, now the largest of these states, also is the farthest north. The scenic Hudson River flows south through eastern New York before reaching the sea at New York City. Long Island, the easternmost piece of New York, extends into the Atlantic Ocean for more than 100 miles. Today, New York City is the most populous city in the country.

Pennsylvania is the region's second-largest state. The southeastern section is a lowland. Philadelphia, Pennsylvania's largest city, is located there, on the Delaware River.

Most of New Jersey is a lowland along the Atlantic coast. Delaware, the region's smallest state, is on the coast directly south of New Jersey.

Middle Colony farmers had an easier time than farmers in New England. The climate was warmer, with a longer growing season. The fertile soil was well suited for crops like wheat, fruits, and vegetables.

✓**Checkpoint** What conditions in the Middle Colonies favored farming?

Section 3 The Middle Colonies **77**

Vocabulary Builder

Use the information below to teach students this section's high-use words.

High-Use Word	Definition and Sample Sentence
fundamental, p. 78	*adj.* most important part Religious freedom was a **fundamental** goal of many settlers in colonial America.
accumulate, p. 81	*v.* to increase in amount over time A person who invests wisely may **accumulate** great wealth.

Section 3
Step-by-Step Instruction

Review and Preview

Students have learned that the New England colonies grew from conflict over religious beliefs. Now students will focus on the reasons for the growth of the Middle Colonies.

Section Focus Question

How did the diverse Middle Colonies develop and thrive?

Before you begin the lesson for the day, write the Section Focus Question on the board. (*Lesson focus: Settlers made use of local resources to develop their culture and economy.*)

Prepare to Read

Build Background Knowledge   L2

Remind students that the strict religious beliefs of New England settlers strongly influenced their daily life and government. Have students brainstorm ideas about how leaders with more tolerant beliefs might govern. Have students also consider life in colonies whose settlers had interests that were largely economic. Use the Idea Wave strategy (TE, p. T24) to elicit responses.

Set a Purpose   L2

■ Read each statement in the Reading Readiness Guide aloud. Ask students to mark the statements True or False.

    All in One Teaching Resources, Unit 1, Reading Readiness Guide, p. 75

■ Have students discuss the statements in pairs or groups of four, then mark the worksheets again. Use the Numbered Heads participation strategy (TE, p. T24) to call on students to share their group's perspectives. The students will return to these worksheets later.

Answers

✓**Checkpoint** The climate was warm and soil was fertile.

Teach

Geography of the Middle Colonies

New York and New Jersey

pp. 77–78

Instruction

- **Vocabulary Builder** Before teaching this lesson, preteach the High-Use Words **fundamental** and **accumulate** using the strategy on TE p. T21.

  Key Terms Have students continue filling in the See It–Remember It chart for the Key Terms in this chapter.

- Read Geography of the Middle Colonies and New York and New Jersey with students using the Choral Reading strategy (TE, p. T22).

- Ask: **How might settlers in the Middle Colonies use these resources to build an economy?** (*Answers should indicate students' knowledge of the resources: freshwater rivers and ample coastline, long growing seasons and fertile soil*)

- Ask students why the English wanted to and were able to take over New Netherland. (*The Dutch had made it a thriving fur trade center. There were far more English settlers living there than Dutch settlers.*)

Independent Practice

Have students begin to fill in the Study Guide for this section.

> **Interactive Reading and Notetaking Study Guide,** Chapter 3, Section 3 (Adapted Version also available.)

Monitor Progress

As students fill in the Notetaking Study Guide, circulate to make sure students understand the·importance of trade in the new colonies. If students do not seem to have a good understanding, have them reread the section. Provide assistance as needed.

Answer

☑**Checkpoint** It was split off from New York after England took New Netherland from the Dutch.

New York and New Jersey

New York began as the Dutch colony of New Netherland. By 1660, it was an economic success. Farmers in the Hudson River valley were prosperous. The colony was the base for a profitable fur trade between the Dutch and Native Americans. The Dutch also made money trading with merchants in the British colonies. This trade violated Britain's mercantile laws and angered the government.

One of New Netherland's major problems was its small Dutch population. Many of the colonists came from Sweden, France, and Portugal. There also were some English Puritans who had settled on Long Island. These people often were hostile to Dutch rule.

Tension also existed between England and the Netherlands. New Netherland separated England's northern colonies from its colonies farther south. Furthermore, England and Holland were rivals at trade.

New Netherland Becomes New York In 1664, England's King Charles II granted the right to all the Dutch lands in North America to his brother James. All that James had to do was conquer the territory. James sent a few warships to do the job, and the Dutch surrendered immediately. The colony was renamed New York, after James, the Duke of York. New Amsterdam, its capital, became New York City. The colony grew slowly. At the end of the 1600s, New York City was still a village on the southern end of Manhattan.

New Jersey New Jersey was established in 1665, when part of southern New York was split off to form a new colony. Like New York and several other English colonies, New Jersey at first was a proprietary colony—a colony created by a grant of land from a monarch to an individual or family. In 1702, New Jersey received a new charter as a royal colony—a colony controlled directly by the English king. New York had become a royal colony in 1685.

☑**Checkpoint** How did New Jersey become a separate colony?

Pennsylvania and Delaware

In the 1640s and 1650s, the Quakers were one of a number of new religious groups in England. Their ideas set them apart from most groups, including the Puritans.

The Quakers believed that all people had a direct link, or "inner light," with God. Groups of Quakers, therefore, did not need ministers. Another <u>fundamental</u> Quaker belief was that all people were equal in God's eyes. Thus, they were among the first in England to speak out against slavery. Women were considered equal to men in spiritual matters and often were leaders in Quaker meetings.

By the 1660s, there were thousands of Quakers in England. Many of them refused to pay taxes to support the Church of England. Because of their views, they often suffered from persecution. One Quaker leader was William Penn, a wealthy man who personally knew King Charles II. Penn wanted to find a place for Quakers to live

James, Duke of York

Vocabulary Builder
<u>fundamental</u> (fuhn duh MEHN tahl)
adj. most important part

Differentiated Instruction

L3 Advanced Readers **L3** Gifted and Talented

Write an Interview Have students research a colony of their choice—New York, New Jersey, or Pennsylvania. Then, pair students and have them use their research to write questions they would ask a colonist in an interview. Make sure that the questions focus on life specific to that colony, such as, "Why did you decide to move to the colonies?" and "What do you do for a living?" Then, have students present their interviews to the class, with one student asking the questions and the other student answering as the colonist might.

where they would be safe from persecution. He used his connections to get a charter from the king for a new colony in North America. In 1681, he received an area almost as large as England itself, mainly in what is now Pennsylvania.

Penn's "Holy Experiment" Penn arrived in his colony in 1682. For his capital, Penn established a city named Philadelphia, which means "City of Brotherly Love." To attract settlers, he printed pamphlets in several languages and distributed them in England and on the European continent. Soon, new settlers began arriving from many places—England, Scotland, Wales, and Ireland. Still others came from Germany, Holland, and Switzerland.

Penn considered his colony to be a "holy experiment." His goal was to create a colony in which people from different religious backgrounds could live peacefully. In 1682, Penn wrote his Frame of Government for Pennsylvania. It granted the colony an elected assembly. It also provided for freedom of religion.

Penn tried to deal fairly with Native Americans. He did not allow colonists to settle on land until the Native Americans sold it to them. Relations between settlers and Native Americans in Pennsylvania were far from perfect. However, during Penn's lifetime they were much better in Pennsylvania than in other colonies.

Delaware: A Separate Colony People from Sweden were the first European settlers in Delaware. The Dutch took control of the territory in the 1650s, but they lost it to the English when they lost New York.

Penn's charter for Pennsylvania included Delaware. Because Delaware settlers did not want to send delegates to a distant assembly in Philadelphia, Penn gave the area its own representative assembly. In 1704, Delaware became a separate colony.

✓**Checkpoint** Why did Penn call Pennsylvania "a holy experiment"?

Growth and Change

By the early 1700s, more than 20,000 colonists lived in Pennsylvania. Fertile soil and hard work made its farms productive. Farmers grew more than they could use and sold the balance. The top cash crop, wheat, was sold to customers in New England and abroad. Because of all its wheat, Pennsylvania was called America's breadbasket. New Jersey also produced large amounts of wheat.

Manufacturing was just beginning in the Middle Colonies during the 1700s. The largest manufacturers produced iron, flour, and paper. Meanwhile, artisans in towns worked as shoemakers, carpenters, masons, weavers, and in many other trades. Among the most important artisans were coopers, who made the barrels used to ship and store flour and other foods.

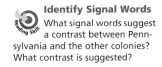

Identify Signal Words
What signal words suggest a contrast between Pennsylvania and the other colonies? What contrast is suggested?

William Penn and other leading Quakers make a peace treaty with Native Americans.

Instruction   L2

■ Have students read Pennsylvania and Delaware. Remind students to look for comparison clues.

■ Ask: **What was William Penn's policy about who was welcome to settle in Pennsylvania?** Have students provide support for their answers. (*Penn welcomed all those who believed in one God, as evidenced in his multilingual pamphlets and his Frame of Government.*) Discuss whether Penn's policy allowed religious freedom. (*Some students may point out that, at the time, it was more freedom than was granted by other colonies. Others may state that it is restrictive because it excludes those who don't believe in one God.*)

■ Display the transparency Penn's Treaty With the Indians to discuss the relations between the Pennsylvania colony and the Indians, and how that relationship compared with those in other colonies.

Color Transparencies, Penn's Treaty With the Indians

Independent Practice

Have students continue to fill in the Study Guide for this section.

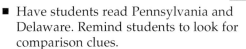 **Interactive Reading and Notetaking Study Guide,** Chapter 3, Section 3 (Adapted Version also available.)

Monitor Progress

As students fill in the Notetaking Study Guide, circulate to make sure students understand the significance of Penn's idea for a "holy experiment." Provide assistance as needed.

History Background

William Penn William Penn was born in England in 1644. He got his first taste of Quakerism on a trip to Ireland when he was 11 years old. Penn officially joined the "Society of Friends" at the age of 22. Back in England, Penn publicly proclaimed his new beliefs. He wrote many books about his religious ideas. Several times his outspokenness led to his arrest. Penn wrote his most famous book, *No Cross, No Crown,* during one of his times in prison.

In 1670, Penn inherited his father's fortune. He began spending time in the English court where he befriended future King James I. Penn used this connection a decade later to secure land for his "holy experiment."

Answers

🔵 **Reading Skill** *However* is a signal word. It suggests that the relationship between Native Americans and settlers were better in Pennsylvania than in other colonies.

✓**Checkpoint** Possible answer: He considered his plan unique and ordained by God.

Growth and Change

p. 80

Instruction L2

- Have students read Growth and Change. Remind students to look for ways the Middle Colonies are similar to the New England colonies.

- Have students consider the complementary nature of the industries developing in the New England and Middle Colonies. Ask them to draw conclusions about the economic effects on the regions. (*The colonies became interdependent, trading with each other.*)

- Have students complete the worksheet Colonial Population Growth. Ask: **How many more colonists lived in New York in 1700 than in 1650?** (*15,000*)

  All in One Teaching Resources, Unit 1, Colonial Population Growth, p. 82

Independent Practice

Have students complete the Study Guide for this section.

Interactive Reading and Notetaking Study Guide, Chapter 3, Section 3 (Adapted Version also available.)

Monitor Progress

- As students complete the Notetaking Study Guide, circulate to make sure students understand the importance of agriculture and manufacturing in the Middle Colonies. Provide assistance as needed.

- Tell students to fill in the last column of the Reading Readiness Guide. Probe for what they learned that confirms or invalidates each statement.

  All in One Teaching Resources, Unit 1, Reading Readiness Guide, p. 75

Answers

MAP MASTER Skills Activity (a) Delaware, Hudson, and Susquehanna (b) Possible answer: They provided food and transportation.

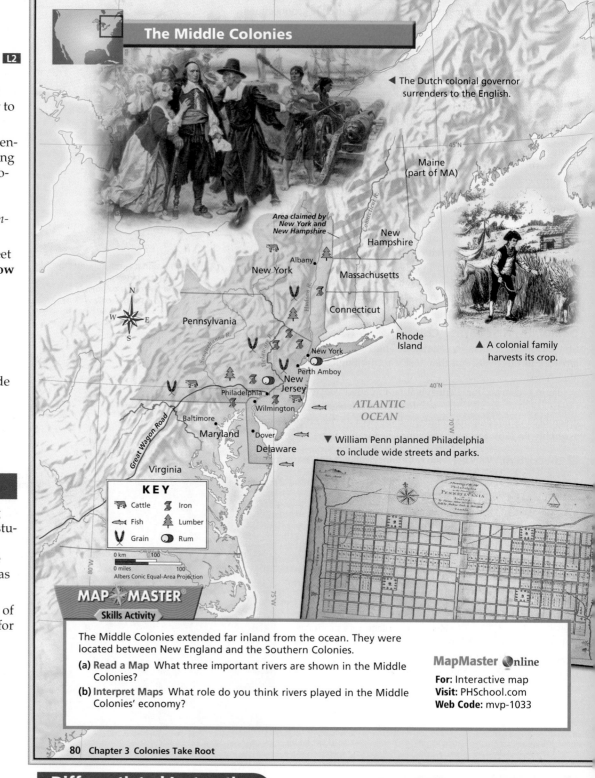

The Middle Colonies

◄ The Dutch colonial governor surrenders to the English.

▲ A colonial family harvests its crop.

▼ William Penn planned Philadelphia to include wide streets and parks.

KEY

- 🐄 Cattle
- 🗡 Iron
- 🐟 Fish
- 🌲 Lumber
- V Grain
- ◐ Rum

0 km 100
0 miles 100
Albers Conic Equal-Area Projection

MAP★MASTER®
Skills Activity

The Middle Colonies extended far inland from the ocean. They were located between New England and the Southern Colonies.

(a) Read a Map What three important rivers are shown in the Middle Colonies?

(b) Interpret Maps What role do you think rivers played in the Middle Colonies' economy?

MapMaster Online

For: Interactive map
Visit: PHSchool.com
Web Code: mvp-1033

Differentiated Instruction

L3 Advanced Readers   **L3 Gifted and Talented**

Write an Essay Have students choose one of the states that were once part of the Middle Colonies to research current religious and ethnic diversity. Have students write an essay comparing and contrasting the diversity of the state today with that of colonial times. Allow time to have them present their findings to the class.

The Backcountry The western section of Pennsylvania was part of a region called the backcountry. The backcountry was a frontier region extending through several colonies, from Pennsylvania to Georgia.

Many of the people who settled in the backcountry were not English. Thousands were Scotch-Irish. Originally from Scotland, they had settled in Ireland before coming to North America. Large numbers of German immigrants began arriving early in the 1700s. The word these German newcomers used to describe themselves was *Deutsch,* for "German." Americans thought they were saying "Dutch." As a result, German immigrants in Pennsylvania were called the Pennsylvania Dutch.

By the middle of the 1700s, many settlers were pushing south and west along a route that led from Pennsylvania to Georgia. Because they often traveled in covered wagons, the route was called the Great Wagon Road. These backcountry settlers often fought with Native Americans.

Diverse and Thriving Colonies By 1750, the non-English immigrants had made the Middle Colonies the most diverse part of English North America. Philadelphia and New York were <u>accumulating</u> people at such a rate that they had become the largest cities and busiest ports in the colonies. All of the colonies had thriving economies.

Vocabulary Builder
<u>accumulate</u> (uh KYOOM yoo layt)
v. to increase in amount over time

☑Checkpoint **How was Pennsylvania a breadbasket?**

☆ **Looking Back and Ahead** Both the New England and Middle Colonies had many small family farms. In the next section, you will read that parts of the Southern Colonies developed a plantation economy that was far different.

Section 3 | **Check Your Progress**

Progress Monitoring Online
For: Self-test with instant help
Visit: PHSchool.com
Web Code: mva-1033

Comprehension and Critical Thinking
1. (a) Recall What was the geography and climate of the Middle Colonies?
(b) Identify Economic Benefits What advantages did the geography and climate give to people living in the Middle Colonies?

2. (a) Summarize What were William Penn's goals for his colony?
(b) Compare How did Penn's "holy experiment" differ from the Puritans' "city on a hill"?

Reading Skill
3. Identify Signal Words What word in the sentence that follows suggests a comparison? What similarity is being identified? **Sentence:** Both Pennsylvania and New Jersey produced a lot of wheat.

Key Terms
Answer the following questions in complete sentences that show your understanding of the key terms.
4. How was New Jersey different after it became a royal colony in 1702?

5. Why did settlers and Native Americans clash in the backcountry?

Writing
6. Imagine that you are a Pennsylvania farmer. Write a letter to a fellow farmer in New England telling him about your life in your new home. Then, write a letter that the New England farmer might send back describing his life in New England.

Section 3 Check Your Progress

1. (a) It had rivers and coastline, fertile soil, and long growing seasons.
(b) They used the rivers for trade and transport and the land for farming.

2. (a) to create a colony in which people from different religious backgrounds could live peacefully
(b) Penn sought cooperation between religions; the Puritans were not as tolerant.

3. *Both*; a similarity in agricultural products

4. Possible response: As a royal colony, New Jersey was controlled directly by the king, not a private company or family.

5. The backcountry was a frontier that seemed welcome to new immigrants.

6. Letters should accurately describe life in Pennsylvania and New England.

Assess and Reteach

Assess Progress [L2]

Have students complete Check Your Progress. Administer the Section Quiz.

All in One **Teaching Resources,** Section Quiz, p. 88

To further assess student understanding, use the Progress Monitoring Transparency.

Progress Monitoring Transparencies, Chapter 3, Section 3

Reteach [L1]

If students need more instruction, have them read this section in the Interactive Reading and Notetaking Study Guide and complete the accompanying question.

📖 **Interactive Reading and Notetaking Study Guide,** Chapter 3, Section 3 (Adapted Version also available.)

Extend [L3]

Have students write a short report comparing and contrasting the populations and economies of the four Middle Colonies.

Extend Online
For: Help in starting Extend activity
Visit: PHSchool.com
Web Code: mvd-0119

Progress Monitoring Online

Students may check their comprehension of this section by completing the Progress Monitoring Online graphic organizer and self-quiz.

Answer

☑Checkpoint It produced wheat, from which flour for bread is made.

Landscapes of the 13 Colonies

Build Background Knowledge L2

Remind students that people moved to the colonies for different reasons and with varying abilities. Ask them to recall some of the reasons colonists came to North America. (*religious freedom, opportunity, profit*) Have students discuss what they know about the various challenges the land and climate of the 13 colonies presented to settlers.

Instruction L2

- Have students read the text and examine the visuals in this section. Discuss the three colonial areas designated on the map. Have students use the map key to relate the regions shown in the three photographs to their locations on the map.

- Have students point to each region on the map as you list the area's physical characteristics. (*New England is hilly and rocky, with forests, good fishing, and long winters. The Middle Colonies were good for farming, particularly wheat. Farmers in the Tidewater region grew rice and sugar.*)

- Ask: **Why do you think plantations did not develop in the Middle Colonies?** (*Possible answer: The crops grown in the Middle Colonies did not require as much land and labor as did those grown in the Southern Colonies.*)

Monitor Progress

Ask students to complete the Analyze Geography and History activity. Circulate to make sure that individuals understand the relationship between each region's resources and the industries that developed. Provide assistance as needed.

Landscapes of the 13 Colonies

The physical geography of the 13 British colonies differed widely from region to region. While farmers in New England had difficulty planting crops in thin and rocky soil, farmers in the Middle and Southern colonies had better luck with more fertile soil and warmer climates.

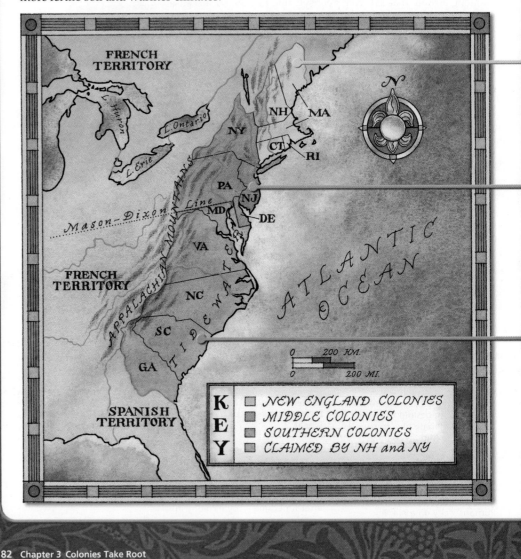

FRENCH TERRITORY

L. Huron

L. Ontario

L. Erie

NH   MA

NY

CT

RI

PA

NJ

MD

DE

Mason-Dixon Line

APPALACHIAN MOUNTAINS

VA

FRENCH TERRITORY

NC

SC

TIDEWATER

GA

ATLANTIC OCEAN

N

SPANISH TERRITORY

0   200 KM.
0   200 MI.

KEY
- NEW ENGLAND COLONIES
- MIDDLE COLONIES
- SOUTHERN COLONIES
- CLAIMED BY NH and NY

Differentiated Instruction

L1 English Language Learners   **L1** Special Needs

Organizing Information To help students organize and understand the information in this feature, have them create a chart that lists the characteristics of each region.

Then have students work in pairs to add a column that identifies ways that colonists adapted to the geographic conditions of each region.

Three Regions

Although farming was an important economic activity throughout the colonies, poor soil forced people in New England to concentrate on the sea for economic survival. For the colonists to the south, better geography yielded more favorable soils and longer growing seasons.

▲ **New England** farmers had to break up rocks in the soil to clear land for crops. Because this was difficult work with only a small chance for financial success, many New Englanders relied upon fishing off the New England coast to provide for their families.

◄ Farmers in the **Middle Colonies** of Pennsylvania and New Jersey had an easier time growing crops. Better soil and a warmer climate in this region rendered huge wheat fields that gave Pennsylvania the nickname America's breadbasket.

◄ The **Southern Colonies** shared a lowland area called the Tidewater. Farmers there grew crops such as sugar, tobacco, and rice (pictured left). These crops thrived in the region's hot, humid environment. Because the Tidewater crops were grown on great stretches of land and required a great deal of labor, large farms, called plantations, developed in the South.

Understand Effects:
Slavery in the Southern Colonies

Because the climate of the Southern Colonies supported long growing seasons, plantation owners purchased enslaved people and used their labor to harvest rice and sugar crops. As the plantation system grew to dominate the economy of the Southern Colonies, slavery spread throughout the region.

Analyze GEOGRAPHY AND HISTORY

Colonists in each of the three major regions of the 13 colonies learned to adapt to their environments. Write a paragraph describing how physical geography affected the output of food in the colonies.

Writing Rubric Share this rubric with students before they write their paragraphs.

Write a Paragraph

Score 1 Statements are incomplete.

Score 2 Statements are inaccurate or vague.

Score 3 Paragraph is logical and uses effective transitions.

Score 4 Paragraph is comprehensive and has detailed information.

History Background

Slavery North American slavery in the English Colonies began in Virginia in 1619. Although originally from Africa, most of the enslaved people brought to work Southern plantations were brought in from the Caribbean (then called the British West Indies) where they had toiled on sugar farms. At the time, wealthy plantation owners relied heavily on the labor of indentured servants—people who worked in the colony in exchange for passage to the new world. It was not until the 1660s that slave labor became more widely used in the area.

Answer

Analyze **GEOGRAPHY AND HISTORY**

Possible answer: Since the soil in New England was poor, fish was a main food source. Better soil and a warmer climate in the Middle Colonies allowed wheat to grow, which could be used to produce bread. The hot, humid climate of the Southern Colonies made rice an important food product.

Review and Preview

Students have read about England's New England and Middle Colonies. They will now learn about the challenges faced by colonists in the South.

Section Focus Question

What factors influenced the development of the Southern Colonies?

Before you begin the lesson for the day, write the Section Focus Question on the board. (*Lesson focus: The Southern Colonies capitalized upon the area's fertile soil and long growing season.*)

Prepare to Read

Build Background Knowledge L2

Remind students of the struggles colonists faced in New England and in the Middle Colonies. (*Possible answers: poor location choices, conflict with the Dutch, conflict among themselves, conflict with Native Americans*) Ask students to consider why colonists settled in the South. Use the Idea Wave strategy (TE, p. T24) to help students brainstorm. (*Possible answers: The other areas were getting crowded, the climate was milder.*)

Set a Purpose L2

■ Read each statement in the Reading Readiness Guide aloud. Ask students to mark the statements True or False.

All in One **Teaching Resources, Unit 1,** Reading Readiness Guide, p. 76

■ Have students discuss the statements in pairs or groups of four, then mark the worksheets again. Use the Numbered Heads participation strategy (TE, p. T24) to call on students to share their group's perspectives. The students will return to these worksheets later.

Answer

☑Checkpoint The climate provided a long growing season that farmers used to raise tobacco and rice. Both of these crops required many workers in the field.

▲ Virginia planters feast as their slaves harvest tobacco.

Persons of the Worst Character

❝These overseers are indeed for the most part persons of the worst character. . . . They pay no regard to . . . the lodging of the field negroes. Their huts, which ought to be well covered, and the place dry where they take their little repose, are often open sheds, built in damp places; so that, when the poor creatures return tired from the toils of the field, they contract many disorders. ❞

—Olaudah Equiano, *The Interesting Narrative of the Life of Olaudah Equiano*

The Southern Colonies

Objectives

- Describe the geography and climate of the Southern Colonies.
- Describe the early history of Virginia.
- Explain how Maryland, the Carolinas, and Georgia were founded.
- Identify the factors that produced the Tidewater and backcountry ways of life.

🔁 Reading Skill

Compare and Contrast As you read about the Southern Colonies in this section, think about how they are the same and different from one another. What physical features do they share? What human features? In what ways are the communities and places different? Comparing and contrasting will help you better understand the colonies.

Key Terms and People

Nathaniel Bacon   debtor
Lord Baltimore   plantation
James Oglethorpe

Why It Matters The New England and Middle Colonies had much in common. But the two regions also differed because of local geographic conditions and other factors.

❓ **Section Focus Question: What factors influenced the development of the Southern Colonies?**

Geography of the Southern Colonies

During the 1760s, Charles Mason and Jeremiah Dixon were hired to settle a boundary dispute between Maryland and Pennsylvania. They conducted a survey—a careful measuring of an area with scientific instruments using the techniques of mathematics—that took four years to complete. The boundary they drew is known as the Mason-Dixon line. This line on a map marked much more than the boundary between two colonies. After the American Revolution, it was the dividing line between the northern states where slavery was abolished and the southern states where slavery persisted.

Five colonies were located south of the Mason-Dixon line: Maryland, Virginia, North Carolina, South Carolina, and Georgia. They shared a coastal area called the Tidewater, a flat lowland that includes many swampy areas. On its west, the Tidewater blends into a region of rolling hills called the Piedmont.

The climate of these states is warm and humid. Hot summers provide a long growing season that colonial farmers used to raise crops such as tobacco and rice. Both crops required many workers in the fields and thus were partly responsible for helping to spur the early development of slavery.

☑Checkpoint What conditions favored the development of a plantation economy?

Differentiated Instruction

L1 **Less Proficient Readers**   L1 **Special Needs**

Make a Timeline Using the information on p. 85, have students track changes in the Virginia population during the 1600s by filling in a timeline. Students should place dated entries for Native Americans on the top of the timeline and entries for settlers on the bottom. Then have students work in pairs to make two generalizations based on the information in their timelines.

Virginia Grows

Virginia's population grew gradually during the 1600s. New settlers arriving from Europe made up for the fact that disease and difficult living conditions kept the death rate high. After 1650, the death rate fell, and the population increased more quickly. In 1640, about 10,000 settlers lived in Virginia. By 1670, the number had reached 40,000.

The makeup of Virginia's population also changed. By the 1670s, there were more children because fewer were dying at a young age. The percentage of women in the population rose as well.

Conflicts With Native Americans As Virginia's white population grew, the Native American population shrank. Disease and violence took their toll. In 1607, there had been about 8,000 Native Americans in Virginia. By 1675, only about 2,000 Native Americans were left.

Farmers took over more land to plant tobacco. This led to trouble with the Native Americans. There were two violent confrontations—one in 1622 and the other in 1644. Although the Native Americans killed hundreds of colonists, they were defeated both times. After 1644, the Native Americans living near the coast had to accept English rule.

Bacon's Rebellion There was more trouble to come. Beginning in the 1660s, wealthy Virginia tobacco planters bought most of the good farmland near the coast. That left no land for poorer colonists who wanted to start their own farms. Most of these colonists were young men who were forced to work the land for wealthier farmers. The young men also were angry because without property, they could not vote.

Many poor colonists moved inland to find good farmland. Fighting broke out with Native Americans, and people were killed on both sides. Farmers on the frontier demanded that the governor take strong measures against the Native Americans. However, the governor hesitated. He hoped to avoid an all-out war with the Native Americans, partly because he benefited from his fur trade with them.

Nathaniel Bacon became the leader of the frontier settlers. In 1675, he organized a force of 1,000 westerners and began attacking and killing Native Americans. The governor declared that Bacon and his men were rebels. Bacon reacted by attacking Jamestown, burning it to the ground, and forcing the governor to run away.

The revolt, known as Bacon's Rebellion, collapsed when Bacon became sick and died. The governor hanged 23 of Bacon's followers. Still, he could not stop English settlers from moving onto Native American lands.

☑**Checkpoint** What was the main cause of Bacon's Rebellion?

Bacon's Rebellion
Nathaniel Bacon (center) is shown here taking part in the burning of Jamestown during his 1675 rebellion. **Critical Thinking: Explain Problems** *How did the interests of frontier settlers differ from those of colonists in towns and on plantations?*

Section 4 The Southern Colonies **85**

Vocabulary Builder

Use the information below to teach students this section's high-use words.

High-Use Word	Definition and Sample Sentence
proprietor, p. 86	*n.* owner of a business or a colony Lord Baltimore was the **proprietor** of Maryland in colonial times.
contrast, p. 89	*n.* difference shown between things when compared The lives of women and men in colonial times Provided many **contrasts**.

Religious Toleration in Maryland

p. 86

Instruction

L2

- Have students read Religious Toleration in Maryland. Remind students to look for causes and effects.

- Ask: **What was Calvert's aim in settling Maryland?** (*He wanted to provide Catholics with a safe colony.*)

- Have students discuss the fears that arose with tensions between the Protestants and Catholics living in Maryland. (*Catholics began to fear that they would lose their rights.*) Ask: **How did the Acts of Toleration seek to address colonists' fears?** (*It welcomed all Christians, including Catholics, and gave adult male Christians the right to vote and hold office.*)

Independent Practice

Have students continue to fill in the Study Guide for this section.

Interactive Reading and Notetaking Study Guide, Chapter 3, Section 4 (Adapted Version also available.)

Monitor Progress

As students fill in the Notetaking Study Guide, circulate to make sure students understand the importance of conflicts that arose due to Virginia's rapid population growth. If students do not seem to have a good understanding, have them reread the section. Provide assistance as needed.

Answers

MAP MASTER **Skills Activity** **(a)** in the Tidewater region of Maryland, Virginia, and North Carolina; **(b)** As port cities, they offered easy access inland and overseas by water.

Reading Skill Virginia's conflicts arose between rich and poor and colonists and Native Americans due to land shortages. Maryland's conflicts arose between Protestants and Catholics for religious reasons.

Checkpoint adult, male Christians

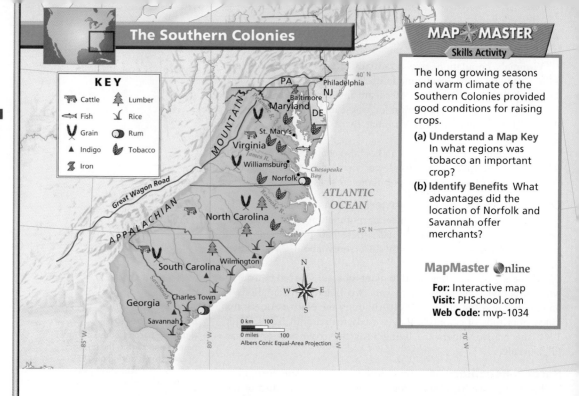

The Southern Colonies

KEY

- Cattle
- Fish
- Grain
- Indigo
- Iron
- Lumber
- Rice
- Rum
- Tobacco

MAP MASTER
Skills Activity

The long growing seasons and warm climate of the Southern Colonies provided good conditions for raising crops.

(a) Understand a Map Key In what regions was tobacco an important crop?

(b) Identify Benefits What advantages did the location of Norfolk and Savannah offer merchants?

MapMaster Online

For: Interactive map
Visit: PHSchool.com
Web Code: mvp-1034

Vocabulary Builder
proprietor (proh PRĪ ah tor) **n.** owner of a business or a colony

Compare and Contrast
Compare and contrast the population growth, agriculture, and political tensions of Maryland with those of Virginia.

Religious Toleration in Maryland

In 1632, King Charles I granted a charter for a new colony to George Calvert, an English Catholic. Catholics suffered great discrimination in England. Calvert aimed to set up a colony where Catholics could live safely. His colony, Maryland, lay across Chesapeake Bay from Virginia.

The first settlers included both Catholics and Protestants. They grew tobacco and harvested the sea life of Chesapeake Bay. When George Calvert died, his son, Cecil Calvert, Lord Baltimore, became proprietor. As the charter required, there was a representative assembly similar to the House of Burgesses in Virginia.

Soon there was tension between Protestants and Catholics. Fearing that Catholics might lose their rights, Lord Baltimore got the assembly to pass the Act of Toleration in 1649. It welcomed all Christians and gave adult male Christians the right to vote and hold office. Although the Toleration Act did not protect people who were not Christian, it was still an important step toward religious toleration in North America.

Checkpoint Who benefited from Maryland's toleration?

Colonies in the Carolinas and Georgia

By the 1660s, a few settlers from Virginia had moved south beyond the colony's borders. In 1663, King Charles II granted a charter for a new colony to be established there, in the area called Carolina.

Differentiated Instruction

L1 English Language Learner   **L1** Less Proficient Readers   **L1** Special Needs

Evaluate Learning Give students a page protector to put over their text. Have students reread Religious Toleration in Maryland and mark each sentence with a "?" if they are uncertain about its content, a "*" if they understand the sentence, or a "!" if they find the information interesting or new.

Review any sentences that students have marked with a question mark. Then, pair students to compare the sentences they found interesting or new.

The northern part of Carolina developed slowly. It lacked harbors and rivers on which ships could travel easily. Settlers lived on small farms, raising and exporting tobacco. Some produced lumber for shipbuilding.

The southern part of Carolina grew more quickly. Sugar grew well in the swampy lowlands. Many planters came from Barbados in the West Indies. They brought enslaved people to grow sugar. Soon the colonists were using slave labor to grow another crop, rice. It became the area's most important crop.

As rice production spread, Carolina's main city, Charles Town (today's Charleston), eventually became the biggest city in the Southern Colonies. By then, Carolina had become two colonies: North Carolina and South Carolina.

Georgia The last of England's 13 colonies, Georgia was founded for two reasons. First, the English feared that Spain was about to expand its Florida colony northward. An English colony south of Carolina would keep the Spanish bottled up in Florida. Second, a group of wealthy Englishmen led by James Oglethorpe wanted a colony where there would be protection for English debtors— people who owe money. Under English laws, the government could imprison debtors until they paid what they owed.

Georgia's founders wanted Georgia to be a colony of small farms, not large plantations. Therefore, slavery was banned. However, this restriction was unpopular with settlers and did not last. By the 1750s, slavery was legal in Georgia.

☑ Checkpoint **Why did Oglethorpe and the other founders establish the colony of Georgia?**

Change in the Southern Colonies

During the 1700s, the Southern Colonies developed two distinct ways of life. People along the coast lived very differently from people who settled inland on the frontier.

The Tidewater Region The most important feature of life along the coast in the Southern Colonies was the plantation, a large farm especially in a hot country where crops such as cotton, sugar, and rice are grown. This led to an economy dominated by plantations in the Tidewater region. The plantation system began in Virginia and Maryland when settlers started growing tobacco. It spread southward when planters found other crops they could export profitably to Europe.

Biography Quest

James Oglethorpe
1696–1785

James Oglethorpe was a fighter. A soldier since the age of 16, he fought in many winning battles. Later, as a member of England's Parliament, he fought against slavery and other injustices.

In 1728, a friend of Oglethorpe's died of smallpox while in jail for debt. Oglethorpe organized a committee to investigate conditions in debtors' prisons. Four years later, he founded Georgia as a place where debtors could start a new life.

Biography Quest   **Online**

Why did Georgia colonists later rebel against Oglethorpe?

For: The answer to the question about Oglethorpe

Visit: PHSchool.com

Web Code: mvd-1034

Colonies in the Carolinas and Georgia

p. 86

Instruction L2

- Have students read Colonies in the Carolinas and Georgia. Remind students to look for the sequence of events.

- Ask: **How did the development of northern Carolina compare to southern Carolina?** (*Northern Carolina developed slower than southern Carolina.*)

- Ask: **Why was Georgia founded as a colony?** (*The English feared that the Spanish were about to expand the Florida colony northward, and a group of wealthy English settlers wanted a colony where there would be protection for English debtors.*)

Independent Practice

Have students complete the Study Guide for this section.

📖 **Interactive Reading and Notetaking Study Guide,** Chapter 3, Section 4 (Adapted Version also available.)

Monitor Progress

As students fill in the Notetaking Study Guide, circulate to make sure students understand the role of religion in the Maryland Colony. Provide assistance as needed.

Answers

Biography Quest The colonists did not like Oglethorpe's strict management of the colony.

☑ Checkpoint to protect English land claims from the Spanish and to give English debtors a place to live

Change in the Southern Colonies

p. 87

Instruction L2

- Have students read Change in the Southern Colonies. Remind students to look for comparison clues.

- Ask students to describe the Tidewater region. (*The Tidewater economy was dominated by sugar, rice, and tobacco plantations. Large farms producing labor-intensive cash crops led to the rise in southern slavery. A few people were very wealthy, the rest were poor and worked for the plantation owners.*) Then have students describe life in the backcountry. (*Poor families lived in shacks on small farms they did not usually own. The people did not feel represented by the colonial government.*)

- Show the transparency Climate and Agriculture in the 13 Colonies. Have students compare the Southern Colonies to New England and the Middle Colonies.

Color Transparencies, Climate and Agriculture in the 13 Colonies

Independent Practice

Have students complete the Study Guide for this section.

Interactive Reading and Notetaking Study Guide, Chapter 3, Section 4 (Adapted Version also available.)

Monitor Progress

- As students complete the Notetaking Study Guide, circulate to make sure students understand the difference between life in the Tidewater and backcountry regions. Provide assistance as needed.

- Tell students to fill in the last column of the Reading Readiness Guide. Probe for what they learned that confirms or invalidates each statement.

All in One Teaching Resources, Unit 1, Reading Readiness Guide, p. 76

Answer

Reading Charts (a) Possible answer: Pennsylvania and Maryland **(b)** 11 colonies

Founding of the 13 Colonies

Colony / Date Founded	Leader(s)	Reason(s) Founded
New England Colonies		
■ Massachusetts Plymouth / 1620 Massachusetts Bay / 1630	William Bradford John Winthrop	Religious freedom Religious freedom
■ New Hampshire / 1622	Ferdinando Gorges John Mason	Profit from trade and fishing
■ Connecticut / 1636	Thomas Hooker	Expand trade; religious and political freedom
■ Rhode Island / 1636	Roger Williams	Religious freedom
Middle Colonies		
■ New York / 1624	Peter Minuit	Expand trade
■ Delaware / 1638	Swedish settlers	Expand trade
■ New Jersey / 1664	John Berkeley George Carteret	Expand trade; religious and political freedom
■ Pennsylvania / 1682	William Penn	Profit from land sales; religious and political freedom
Southern Colonies		
■ Virginia / 1607	John Smith	Trade and farming
Maryland / 1634	Lord Baltimore	Profit from land sales; religious and political freedom
■ The Carolinas / 1663 North Carolina / 1712 South Carolina / 1719	Group of eight proprietors	Trade and farming
■ Georgia / 1733	James Oglethorpe	Profit; home for debtors; buffer against Spanish Florida

Reading Charts
Skills Activity

By 1733, England had established 13 colonies on the Atlantic coast of North America. These colonies were founded for a variety of reasons.

(a) Interpret a Chart Identify one Middle Colony and one Southern Colony founded for religious reasons.

(b) Understand Sequence How many English colonies were there by 1700?

The Tidewater region in South Carolina and Georgia was well suited for rice. However, rice-growing required large numbers of workers laboring in hot, humid, unhealthy conditions. This was one reason rice-farming helped promote the spread of slavery. In time, the enslaved population outnumbered the free population of South Carolina.

Differentiated Instruction

L1 Less Proficient Readers

Gaining Comprehension Suggest to students that they use a ruler to help them keep their place as they read, line by line, down a page. Have students mark unfamiliar words or phrases with a sticky note, or jot down questions that occur as they are reading. Periodically provide assistance to the students to clarify these issues.

The plantation system did not just create a society of slaveholders and enslaved people in the Tidewater. It also divided the white community into a small group of wealthy people and a much larger group with little or no property, most of whom were poor and lived in the backcountry South.

The Backcountry The backcountry was cut off from the coast by poor roads and long distances. Families usually lived on isolated farms. They often did not legally own the land they farmed. Many families lived in simple one-room shacks. Few families had servants or enslaved people to help them with their work. Women and girls worked in the fields with the men and boys.

In the backcountry, people cared less about rank. Life in the backcountry provided a sharp <u>contrast</u> to life near the coast. As a result, backcountry people believed that the colonial governments on the coast did not care about them. They thought that colonial government cared only about protecting the wealth of the Tidewater plantation owners.

Vocabulary Builder
<u>contrast</u> (KAHN trast) ***n.*** difference shown between things when compared

✓**Checkpoint** How did people live in the backcountry?

☆ **Looking Back and Ahead** As you have seen, the English colonies developed along distinct regional lines. But Spain, too, was competing for influence in North America. It had started its own colonies long before the English arrived.

Section 4 | **Check Your Progress**

Progress Monitoring ⬤nline
For: Self-test with instant help
Visit: PHSchool.com
Web Code: mva-1034

Comprehension and Critical Thinking

1. (a) Summarize How did the geography of the Southern Colonies affect the kinds of crops that were grown there?
(b) Draw Conclusions Why did the struggle for rich farmland affect the colonists in Virginia?

2. (a) Recall Why did Lord Baltimore want Maryland's Act of Toleration?
(b) Compare How would you compare the motives of Lord Baltimore in founding the colony of Maryland with those of James Oglethorpe in founding Georgia?

🔁 **Reading Skill**

3. Compare and Contrast Compare and contrast the Tidewater and the backcountry regions of the Southern Colonies.

Key Terms

Read each sentence. If the sentence is true, write YES. If the sentence is not true, write NO and explain why.
4. Debtors could not be imprisoned under English law.
5. There were many plantations where crops such as wheat, fruits, and vegetables were grown.

Writing

6. List the different groups of people living in the Southern Colonies between 1620 and the 1700s. Write two or three sentences about each group.

Assess Progress L2

Have students complete Check Your Progress. Administer the Section Quiz.

All in One Teaching Resources, Unit 1, Section Quiz, p. 89

To further assess student understanding, use the Progress Monitoring Transparency.

Progress Monitoring Transparencies, Chapter 3, Section 4

Reteach L1

If students need more instruction, have them read this section in the Interactive Reading and Notetaking Study Guide and complete the accompanying question.

📖 **Interactive Reading and Notetaking Study Guide,** Chapter 3, Section 4 (Adapted Version also available.)

Extend L3

Have students suppose that they are English colonists who have just arrived in the Virginia Colony. Have them write a journal entry identifying who they are, why they came to the colony, and what their life is like.

Progress Monitoring Online

Students may check their comprehension of this section by completing the Progress Monitoring Online graphic organizer and self-quiz.

Answer

✓**Checkpoint** on small, isolated farmland that they usually did not own

---

Section 4 Check Your Progress

1. (a) The warm, humid climate provided a long growing season that farmers used to raise tobacco, rice, as well as other crops.
(b) It led to conflicts between poor colonists and Native Americans over land; it led to hostility between poor farmers and wealthy plantation owners.

2. (a) There was tension between Protestants and Catholics, and he was afraid Catholics might lose their rights.

(b) Both colonies were founded to protect groups of people. Lord Baltimore founded Maryland so that Catholics could practice their religion freely. Oglethorpe founded Georgia as a land of small farms and a place where English debtors would be protected from imprisonment.

3. The Tidewater was the region along the coast; the backcountry was cut off from the coast by poor roads and long distances. People in the Tidewater lived on large plantations owned by slaveholders. In contrast, the people in the backcountry were poor, did not own their land, and were not divided according to social rank.

4. No. Debtors were people who owed money and could be put in jail.

5. No. Crops, such as rice, sugar, and cotton were grown on plantations.

6. Lists should be accurate and contain two or three sentences explaining each group.

Review and Preview

Students have read about English settlements in North America. Now they will learn about Spanish colonization.

Prepare to Read

Build Background Knowledge **L2**

Remind students that the English were actually following Spain's lead by exploring and settling North America. Ask them to predict how the Spanish reacted to the English colonies. (*Possible answers: The Spanish did not worry because the English settlements were so far away. The Spanish became concerned that the English would also try to move onto Spanish land claims.*)

Set a Purpose **L2**

■ Read each statement in the Reading Readiness Guide aloud. Ask students to mark the statements True or False.

   All in One **Teaching Resources, Unit 1,** Reading Readiness Guide, p. 77

■ Have students discuss the statements in pairs or groups of four, then mark the worksheets again. Use the Numbered Heads participation strategy (TE, p. T24) to call on students to share their group's perspectives. The students will return to these worksheets later.

Answer

✓ Checkpoint to protect the area from France

SECTION 5

Baptisms and Conquests

❝I have baptized here in these new conquests . . . about four thousand five hundreds souls, and could have baptized twelve or fifteen thousand if we had not suspended further baptisms until our Lord should bring us missionary fathers to aid us.❞

   —Father Eusebio Kino, describing missionary activity in present-day Arizona, late 1600s

◄ Spain's empire extended from Florida (left) to the present-day Southwest.

Spanish Colonies on the Borderlands

Objectives
- Describe Spain's colony in Florida.
- Explain how Spain established settlements throughout much of North America.
- Describe the significance of the Spanish missions.

🔄 Reading Skill

Compare and Contrast Across Sections The colonies discussed in Sections 1 through 4 were settled primarily by people from the British Isles. Section 5 discusses Spain's colonies in North America. Recall information from Sections 1 through 4 in order to compare and contrast the English colonies with those of Spain. Examine the text in Section 5 to ask: How are these similar to or different from the colonies discussed in Sections 1 through 4?

Key Terms and People

borderland   presidio
Junípero Serra   pueblo

Why It Matters While France and England were building colonies in North America, Spain's colonies in the Americas were already hundreds of years old. Some of Spain's colonies bordered lands where French and English settlers were moving. The people of these colonies would influence each other for many years to come.

❓ Section Focus Question: How did the Spanish establish colonies on the borderlands?

Spanish Florida

Spanish explorers reached Florida early in the 1500s. In 1565, fearing that France might take over the area, Spain built a fort called St. Augustine in northern Florida. It was the first permanent European settlement in what is now the United States.

As English colonies spread southward, Spanish control was threatened. To weaken the English colonies, in 1693, the Spanish announced that enslaved Africans who escaped to Florida would be protected. They would be given land if they helped to defend the colony. During the 1700s, hundreds of enslaved African Americans fled to Florida.

Spain's Florida colony grew slowly. By 1763, there were only three major Spanish settlements there. All were centered around forts, and all were in the north. The Spanish had little control over the rest of Florida.

✓ Checkpoint Why did the Spanish colonize Florida?

Differentiated Instruction

L1 English Language Learners   **L1** Less Proficient Readers   **L1** Special Needs

Exploring the Main Idea Students may use the map on p. 91 to learn about the Spanish settlements in North America. Review map features with students. Ask them to identify the meaning of each of the symbols used in the key, then have students find the symbols on the map. Pair students and have them ask each other questions about the map contents.

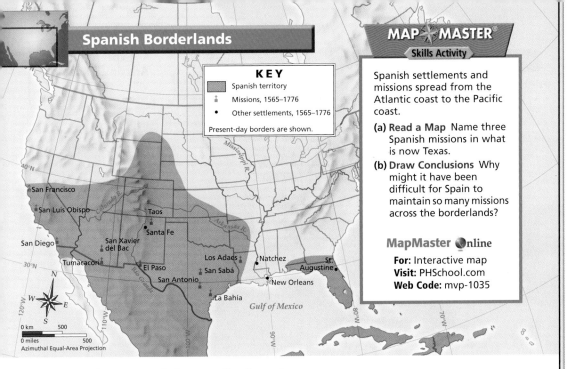

Spanish Borderlands

KEY

	Spanish territory
	Missions, 1565–1776
●	Other settlements, 1565–1776

Present-day borders are shown.

Azimuthal Equal-Area Projection

MAP MASTER®
Skills Activity

Spanish settlements and missions spread from the Atlantic coast to the Pacific coast.

(a) Read a Map Name three Spanish missions in what is now Texas.

(b) Draw Conclusions Why might it have been difficult for Spain to maintain so many missions across the borderlands?

MapMaster ●nline

For: Interactive map
Visit: PHSchool.com
Web Code: mvp-1035

Settling the Spanish Borderlands

Spain's most important colonies were in Mexico and South America. Its territories north of Mexico were called the borderlands, meaning lands along a frontier. The main <u>function</u> of the Spanish borderlands was to protect Mexico from other European powers.

The borderlands began in the east with Florida. Farther west, they included most of Texas, New Mexico, Arizona, Colorado, Utah, Nevada, and California. This vast area differs greatly from place to place with humid lowlands in Texas and deserts and mountains in New Mexico, Arizona, and Utah. Colorado has highlands and mountains, while California has deserts in its southeast corner.

Juan de Oñate in New Mexico The first Spanish explorers did not start permanent settlements. Then, in 1598, Juan de Oñate (WAN day ohn YAH tay) led an expedition into New Mexico. He aimed to find gold, <u>convert</u> Native Americans to Christianity, and establish a permanent colony. Oñate never found gold, but in 1598 he established Spain's first permanent settlement in the region at Santa Fe.

Oñate brought more than 300 horses. At their settlements, the Spanish used Native Americans to look after the horses. When some Native Americans ran away from the Spanish, they spread the skill of horseback riding from one Native American group to another. This skill forever changed the lives of the Native Americans of the region.

The Native Americans suffered under Spanish rule. In 1680, several groups in New Mexico rebelled and drove the Spanish from the region. After that defeat, the Spanish did not return for more than 10 years.

Vocabulary Builder

function (FUHNK shuhn) **n.** purpose; proper use; official duty

Vocabulary Builder

<u>convert</u> (kuhn VERT) **v.** to change from one religion to another

Section 5 Spanish Colonies on the Borderlands **91**

Vocabulary Builder

Use the information below to teach students this section's high-use words.

High-Use Word	Definition and Sample Sentence
function, p. 91	*n.* purpose; proper use The **function** of government is to serve the people.
convert, p. 91	*v.* to change from one religion to another European missionaries sought to **convert** Native Americans to Christianity.

Teach

Spanish Florida
Settling the Spanish Borderlands

pp. 90–91

Instruction   L2

- **Vocabulary Builder** Before teaching this lesson, preteach the High-Use Words **function** and **convert,** using the strategy on TE p. 64.

  Key Terms Have students complete the See It–Remember It chart for the Key Terms in this chapter.

- Have students read Spanish Florida and Settling the Spanish Borderlands, using the Oral Cloze strategy (TE, p. T22).

- Ask: **Why do you think the Florida colony grew so slowly?** (*Possible answer: Its main purpose was protection, so soldiers were drawn there, not settlers. It was too far from other Spanish settlements.*)

- Have students complete the worksheet Junípero Serra. Discuss the importance of Serra's missions to the Spanish. (*They helped strengthen Spanish control in California.*)

  All in One Teaching Resources, Unit 1, Junípero Serra, p. 83

Independent Practice

Have students begin to fill in the Study Guide for this section.

  Interactive Reading and Notetaking Study Guide, Chapter 3, Section 5 (Adapted Version also available.)

Monitor Progress

As students fill in the Notetaking Study Guide, circulate to make sure students understand why Spain began to settle the borderlands. Provide assistance as needed.

Answers

 MAP MASTER Skills Activity **(a)** Possible answers: El Paso, La Bahía, San Antonio, Los Adaes, and San Sabá **(b)** They were spread out, making it difficult to protect and support them.

Life in Spanish Missions

p. 93

Instruction L2

- Have students read Life in Spanish Missions. Remind students to look for causes and effects.
- Ask: **What caused the death of thousands of Native Americans?** (*poor living conditions and European diseases*)
- Display the History Interactive transparency Spanish Missions. Have students discuss the questions.

Color Transparencies, A Mission: Then and Now

Independent Practice

Have students complete the Study Guide for this section.

 Interactive Reading and Notetaking Study Guide, Chapter 3, Section 5 (Adapted Version also available.)

Monitor Progress

- As students complete the Notetaking Study Guide, circulate to make sure students understand the different types of Spanish settlements. Provide assistance as needed.
- Tell students to fill in the last column of the Reading Readiness Guide. Probe for what they learned that confirms or invalidates each statement.
- Have students go back to their Word Knowledge Rating Form. Rerate their word knowledge and complete the last column with an example.

All in One Teaching Resources, Unit 1, Reading Readiness Guide, p. 77; Word Knowledge Rating Form, p. 72

Answers

Draw Conclusions Possible answer: They show examples of early architecture and building materials, which give some idea of the culture of the people who lived there.

Reading Skill Unlike the English in the Southern Colonies and New England, the Spanish set up missions to spread their religion to the Native Americans.

A Mission: Then and Now

A Mission: Then and Now
The Tumacácori Mission in southern Arizona was founded in 1691 and rebuilt in 1800. It looks much as it did when Henry Cheever Pratt portrayed it in 1855 (at left). The mission is now a National Historical Park. **Critical Thinking: *Draw Conclusions*** *Why are abandoned missions like this one considered important to the history of the U.S. Southwest?*

Compare and Contrast Across Sections
Compare and contrast the role of religion in the Spanish settlements with that in the Southern Colonies and New England.

Missions in Texas and Arizona Roman Catholic missionaries played a key role in colonizing the borderlands. To win Native Americans to Christianity, they established missions—religious settlements that aim to spread a religion into a new area. At the missions, priests taught about Catholicism and made Native Americans work by set rules. The missionary who led the way in spreading Spanish influence in what today is Arizona and Texas was Father Eusebio Francisco Kino.

At first, the Spanish had little success. The only early mission that took root in Texas was about 150 miles north of the Rio Grande. Although the mission failed to convert many Native Americans, it did attract Spanish colonists. This mission became the city of San Antonio.

Missions Along the California Coast Spain's California missions were especially important. Spain began colonizing California in 1769. A missionary named Junípero Serra (hoo NEE peh roh SEHR rah) played an important role in that effort. His first mission, just north of today's Mexican-American border, eventually became the city of San Diego. Serra later established other missions, including those located in what is now San Francisco and Los Angeles. Altogether, the Spanish founded almost 20 missions in California between 1769 and 1800.

Presidios and Pueblos Along with missionaries, Spain sent soldiers. They set up presidios—military posts—to defend the missions.

Differentiated Instruction

L3 Advanced Readers   **L3 Gifted and Talented**

Build a Model Have students work in three small groups. Assign each group one type of Spanish settlement. (*mission, presidio, or pueblo*) Ask each group to create a detailed model of their assigned settlement type using their textbook, literary resources or the Internet. Display models in the classroom.

The Spanish also established what they called pueblos—civilian towns. The pueblos were centers of farming and trade. In the middle of the town was a plaza, or public square. Here, townspeople and farmers came to do business or to worship at the church. Church, shops, and homes lined the four sides of the plaza.

☑ **Checkpoint** What role did missionaries play in Spain's expanding North American empire?

Life in Spanish Missions

Thousands of Native Americans labored at Spanish missions. They farmed, built churches, and learned a wide range of crafts. The Native Americans were not overworked by Spanish standards of the time. They worked from five to eight hours per day and five or six days per week. They did not work on Sundays or religious holidays.

However, the Native Americans did not have control over their lives. The missionaries punished them harshly if the Native Americans violated mission rules. Native Americans were imprisoned and often kept in shackles or whipped while tied to whipping posts.

Native Americans often rebelled against such treatment. Meanwhile, their population fell as thousands died because of poor living conditions and European diseases.

☑ **Checkpoint** Why did some Native Americans rebel against rules set by missionaries?

⭐ **Looking Back and Ahead** Spain had now built a vast empire in the Americas. But the 13 English colonies were destined to grow, too. New frictions would develop within the English Empire as it grew.

Section 5 | Check Your Progress

Progress Monitoring Online
For: Self-test with instant help
Visit: PHSchool.com
Web Code: mva-1035

Comprehension and Critical Thinking

1. (a) **Identify** Where is Saint Augustine located?
   (b) **Draw Conclusions** Why do you think the colony failed to attract settlers?

2. (a) **Summarize** Why were the borderlands important to Spain?
   (b) **Apply Information** How did the importance of the borderlands influence the way Spain ruled this region?

3. (a) **Recall** How did Junípero Serra help establish Spain's presence in the Americas?
   (b) **Link Past and Present** In what way have the early Spanish missions influenced today's Americans?

🔄 **Reading Skill**
4. **Compare and Contrast Across Sections** Compare and contrast the experiences of Native Americans in Spanish settlements and in English colonies.

Key Terms
5. Draw a table with two rows and three columns. In the first column, list the following key terms from this section: presidio, pueblo. In the next column, write a definition of each word. In the last column, make a small illustration that shows the meaning of each word.

Writing
6. Review the table you created in Vocabulary Builder. Add a column to the table. Write two or three sentences for each key term. Explain how it relates to the settlement of Spanish colonies in the Americas.

Assess Progress L2

Have students complete Check Your Progress. Administer the Section Quiz.

All in One Teaching Resources, Unit 1, Section Quiz, p. 90

To further assess student understanding, use the Progress Monitoring Transparency.

Progress Monitoring Transparencies, Chapter 3, Section 5

Reteach L1

If students need more instruction, have them read this section in the Interactive Reading and Notetaking Study Guide and complete the accompanying question.

📖 **Interactive Reading and Notetaking Study Guide,** Chapter 3, Section 5 (Adapted Version also available.)

Extend L3

To help students expand their understanding of Spanish Missions, have them complete the History Interactive activity online.

Extend Online
For: History Interactive activity
Visit: PHSchool.com
Web Code: mvp-0120

Progress Monitoring Online

Students may check their comprehension of this section by completing the Progress Monitoring Online graphic organizer and self-quiz.

Section 5 Check Your Progress

1. (a) Florida
   (b) Possible answers: It was far from Spain. It was too close to English settlements.

2. (a) Spain used the land to protect Mexico from other European powers.
   (b) To maintain control of this important area, Spain established missions and military posts there.

3. (a) His first mission eventually became San Diego.
   (b) Some of these missions, such as San Antonio, San Diego, San Francisco, and Los Angeles, are now major American cities.

4. The Spanish made Native Americans workers in their colonies. The English pushed Native Americans off their land to build colonies.

5. Tables should accurately define and illustrate the terms.

6. Sentences should explain how the key terms in the table relate to Spanish colonies in the Americas.

Answers

☑ **Checkpoint** Their missions became major cities throughout the Southwest.

☑ **Checkpoint** They wanted to be in control of their own lives.

Skills for Life

Objective

A primary source provides firsthand information of an event, person, or period of time. Learning to read primary sources can give students greater, more personal insight into the motives and ideas of people from the past.

Read a Primary Source

Instruction L2

1. Write the steps to read a primary source on the board and ask the class to read the steps aloud.

2. Using the Numbered Heads strategy (TE, p. T24) have students suggest reasons why reading primary sources is important when studying history. (*Possible answers: Students can form their own opinions of important events. Primary sources are useful when doing historical research.*)

3. Practice the skill by following the steps on p. 94 as a class. Model each step to read a primary source. (*1. (a)* John Smith; *(b)* 1608 *2.* John Smith wrote this to describe his capture by Native Americans and his rescue by Pocahontas. *3.* He refers to them as savages and barbarians. *4.* Possible answer: No, because this source only shows Smith's opinion of historical events.)

Monitor Progress

Ask students to do the Apply the Skill activity. Then assign the Skills for Life Worksheet. As students complete the worksheet, circulate to make sure individuals are applying the skill steps effectively. Provide assistance as needed.

All in One Teaching Resources, Unit 1, Skills for Life Worksheet, p. 84

Reteach L1

If students need more instruction, use the Social Studies Skills Tutor to reteach this skill.

⊙ Social Studies Skills Tutor CD-ROM Analyzing Primary and Secondary Sources

---

Skills for Life — Read a Primary Source

Historians use primary sources to find out information about the past from people who lived during that period. A primary source is firsthand information about people or historical events. The following primary source describes events that took place near the Jamestown Colony in 1608.

> This selection is from John Smith's book *A Generall Historie of Virginia, New-England, and the Summer Isles*, published in 1624. It describes his capture by Native Americans and his rescue by Pocahontas, the daughter of the Indian chief Powhatan. Using the writing style of this period of history, Smith refers to himself in the third person, using "he" or "him" instead of "I" or "me."
>
> **Primary Source**
>
> ". . . Finding he was beset with 200 savages, two of them he slew still defending himself with the aid of a savage, his guide, . . . yet he was shot in his thigh a little, and had many arrows that stuck in his clothese; but no great hurt, til at last they took him prisoner.
>
> Six or seven weeks those barbarians kept him prisoner, . . . yet he . . . diverted them from surprising the fort . . . [gained] his own liberty, and got himself and his company such estimation among them that those savages admired him more than their own *quiyouckosuchs* [gods]. . . .
>
> 1608   At last they brought him to . . . Powhatan, their emperor. . . . Having feasted him after their best barbarous manner they could, a long consultation was held, but the conclusion was: two great stones were brought before Powhatan; then as many as could laid hands on him, dragged him to them, and thereon laid his head, and being ready with their clubs to beat out his brains, Pocahontas, the king's dearest daughter, . . . got his head in her arms, and laid her own upon his to save him from death."

Learn the Skill
Use these steps to read a primary source.

1. **Identify the source.** Ask questions that help you identify the writer or speaker.

2. **Identify the author's purpose for writing.** Often, eyewitnesses might want to inform or persuade the reader to share their views.

3. **Recognize the author's point of view.** Distinguish between facts and the author's opinion.

4. **Evaluate whether the source is reliable.** Consider who wrote the primary source and the information presented. Compare this information with what you know about the subject.

Practice the Skill
Answer the following questions about the primary source on this page.

1. **Identify the source.** (a) Who wrote this excerpt? (b) When did the events occur?

2. **Identify the author's purpose for writing.** Why did the author write this source?

3. **Recognize the author's point of view.** What is the author's opinion of Native Americans?

4. **Evaluate whether the source is reliable.** Is this a reliable source for learning about the history of the Jamestown Colony? Explain.

Apply the Skill
See the Review and Assessment at the end of this chapter.

94 Chapter 3 Colonies Take Root

Quick Study Guide

How did the English start colonies with distinct qualities in North America?

Section 1
The First English Settlements

- The English colony at Jamestown is founded in 1607.
- English Pilgrims seeking religious freedom settled the Plymouth Colony.

Section 2
The New England Colonies

- Puritans seeking religious freedom settled the Massachusetts Bay Colony in 1630.
- People unhappy with the Puritans' religious intolerance founded Rhode Island, Connecticut, and New Hampshire.

Section 3
The Middle Colonies

- After the English takeover, New Netherlands was renamed New York.
- Pennsylvania was founded in 1681 by a Quaker, William Penn.

Section 4
The Southern Colonies

- Maryland was founded as a colony where Catholics could worship freely.
- Large plantations marked the Tidewater region, and small farms dominated the backcountry.

Section 5
Spanish Colonies on the Borderlands

- Spain had large colonies in the Caribbean, Mexico, and South America.
- Spanish missions sought to convert Native Americans to Christianity.
- Spain established presidios and pueblos throughout the borderlands.

? Exploring the Essential Question

Use the online study guide to explore the essential question.

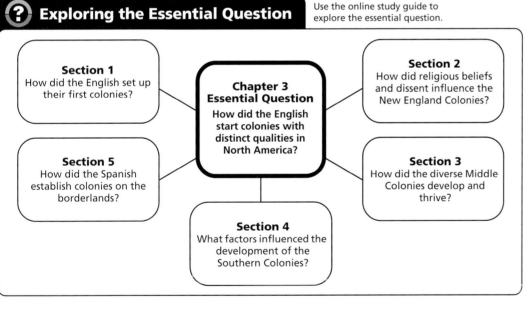

Essential Question

Remind students of the Chapter Essential Question: **How did the English start colonies with distinct qualities in North America?** Have them review the bulleted statements and the Visual Preview at the beginning of the chapter to help them answer this question.

To bolster students' retention at this time, they should complete the Study Guide in print or online. Remind students that they should also continue notetaking for the Unit and Chapter Focus Questions.

Interactive Reading and Notetaking Study Guide, Unit 1, Chapter 3 (Adapted Version also available.)

 Study Guide *Online,* Chapter 3

Chapter Challenge

To wrap up this chapter, students should apply the knowledge they have gained to answer this question: **What two groups of people were negatively affected by European settlement in North America? Explain.** (*Possible answer: Native Americans and Africans were negatively affected by European settlement in North America. Native Americans lost land, and thousands died from European diseases. Many Africans were enslaved and brought to North America to work plantations.*)

Assessment at a Glance

Formal Assessment
  Chapter Tests A/B (L1/L2)
  AYP Monitoring Assessment
  Test Prep Workbook With Document-Based Assessment
  Test-Taking Strategies With Transparencies

Performance Assessment
  Group/Individual Activities, TE p. 62h
  Teacher's Edition, pp. 70, 76, 81, 89, 93
  Assessment Rubrics

Assessment Through Technology
  ExamView CD-ROM
  MindPoint CD-ROM
  Progress Monitoring Transparencies
  Progress Monitoring Online

Key Terms

1. The charter enabled merchants to establish the colony of Virginia.

2. Because they didn't believe that other people could practice their own religions, some left the settlement and founded new colonies elsewhere.

3. The backcountry was settled by Scotch-Irish and Germans, or Pennsylvania Dutch.

4. Town meetings set local taxes and elected people to run the towns.

5. New Jersey was controlled directly by the English king.

Comprehension and Critical Thinking

6. **(a)** A document signed by the Pilgrims on board the *Mayflower*. **(b)** It called for a government of "just and equal laws" and emphasized the right of colonists to govern themselves.

7. **(a)** They were both English religious groups who established colonies in the New World. **(b)** They were both religious groups who were persecuted for their beliefs. Pilgrims were separatists who wanted to worship in their own way; Puritans wanted to reform the English Church, not separate from it. **(c)** They couldn't because Puritans did not believe in religious toleration for non-Puritans.

8. **(a)** Possible answer: The painting shows that Penn's dealings with Native Americans were friendly. **(b)** The colonists in Pennsylvania had a much better relationship with the Native Americans than did the Puritans in Massachusetts.

9. **(a)** In the Tidewater region, crops were grown on plantations. In the backcountry, crops were grown on isolated farms. **(b)** A plantation farmer in the Tidewater would be more likely to support the Virginia government, which would probably pass laws to protect his economic interests.

History Reading Skill

10. Answers will vary according to choice of colonies, but should demonstrate accurate knowledge of the features of the selected colonies as well as an ability to compare and contrast.

Key Terms

Answer the following questions in complete sentences that show your understanding of the key terms.

1. How did the charter of the Virginia Company help the colonization of the Americas?

2. What problems resulted because Puritans did not believe in religious toleration?

3. What groups settled in the backcountry?

4. How did town meetings affect the governing of New England colonies?

5. Why was New Jersey a royal colony?

Comprehension and Critical Thinking

6. **(a) Recall** What was the Mayflower Compact? **(b) Apply Information** Why do you think the Mayflower Compact is an important part of our country's history?

7. **(a) Identify** Who were the Puritans and the Pilgrims? **(b) Compare and Contrast** How would you compare and contrast the Pilgrims and Puritans? **(c) Synthesize** Do you think Puritans and Pilgrims would worship together in America? Explain.

8. **(a) Summarize** How does the Edward Hicks painting below show the nature of William Penn's dealings with Native Americans? **(b) Contrast** How would you contrast the way colonists in Pennsylvania and in Massachusetts got along with Native Americans?

9. **(a) Identify** How was land farmed in the Tidewater region and in the Virginia backcountry? **(b) Draw Conclusions** Would a farmer living in the Tidewater or in the backcountry be more likely to support the Virginia government? Explain.

History Reading Skill

10. **Compare and Contrast** Choose any two colonies from among those discussed in Chapter 3. Make a list of three important features of the colonies. Then, compare and contrast these features in the two colonies you have chosen.

Writing

11. **Write two paragraphs on the following topic:** Describe the factors that led to the establishment of English and Spanish colonies in the Americas.

12. **Write a Dialogue:** Write a conversation that Roger Williams might have had with William Penn. Include issues about how their colonies were settled.

Skills for Life

Read a Primary Source

Use the primary source below by William Bradford, governor of the Plymouth Colony, to answer the questions that follow.

> [1621] "[What] was most sad and lamentable was that in two or three months' time, half of their company died, . . . being infected with the scurvy and other diseases. . . . [I]n the time of most distress, there were but six or seven sound persons who . . . spared no pains night or day, but with abundance of toil and hazard to their own health fetched them wood, made them fires . . . made their beds . . . and all this willingly . . . without any grudging in the least."
>
> —from the book *Of Plymouth Plantation, 1620–1647*, by William Bradford

13. Who wrote these observations?

14. Why did the author write this source?

15. How does the author show his feeling about the people who cared for the sick colonists?

16. Do you think the author gives an accurate view of the events? Why?

Writing

11. Students' paragraphs should contain a solid thesis statement and details that support the main idea. Possible thesis: *England and Spain colonized the Americas for both economic and religious reasons.* Possible details: *Many English settlers came to the Americas for religious freedom; many Spanish settlers came to the Americas to convert Native Americans to Christianity.*

12. Students' dialogues should address key issues. Possible details: *Rhode Island was settled by Puritans, Pennsylvania was settled by Quakers; both colonies allowed for religious freedom.*

For a complete Four-Point rubric, see the writing rubrics in the Teaching Resources.

All in One **Teaching Resources, Unit 1,** p. 138

Chapter 3
Review and Assessment

Test Yourself

1. **Which of the following established the right of American colonists to govern themselves?**

   A mercantilism

   B pueblo

   C proprietary colony

   D Mayflower Compact

2. **The followers of Nathaniel Bacon**

   A supported the governor of Virginia.

   B had a profitable fur trade with the Native Americans.

   C were poor farmers seeking good farmland.

   D were fully represented in the House of Burgesses.

3. **What geographical feature helped New England colonists?**

   A long growing seasons

   B mountains

   C natural harbors

   D fertile soil

Refer to the passage below to answer Question 4.

> Roger Williams said that "God Land will be as great a God with us English as God Gold was with the Spanish."

4. **Which event can be judged as a result of English colonists' push for land in the Americas?**

   A Spanish expeditions to find gold

   B King Philip's War

   C the election of the House of Burgesses

   D John Smith's return to England

Document-Based Questions

Task: Look at Documents 1 and 2, and answer their accompanying questions. Then, use the documents and your knowledge of history to complete this writing assignment:

> Write a short essay explaining why these two documents were important in the development of democratic government in America.

Document 1: The Ordinance for Virginia, dated July 24, 1619, called for the creation of an assembly chosen by and made up of colonists. The House of Burgesses, as the assembly is known, marked the beginning of representative government in America. *What powers did the Burgesses have?*

> "And this General Assembly shall have free Power . . . to make, ordain, and enact such general Laws and Orders, for the Behoof [good] of the said Colony, and the good government thereof. . . ."

Document 2: In 1620, the Pilgrims arrived in America. While still aboard the *Mayflower,* they drew up and signed the Mayflower Compact. *What powers did the Mayflower Compact give the Plymouth settlers?*

> "We . . . combine ourselves together into a civil Body Politick, . . . [to] enact, constitute, and frame, such just and equal Laws, Ordinances, Acts, Constitutions and Offices, from time to time, as shall be thought most meet and convenient for the general Good of the Colony; unto which we promise all due Submission and Obedience."

Test Yourself
1. **D**
2. **C**
3. **C**
4. **B**

Document-Based Questions
Answers

Document 1 The Burgesses had the power to make, ordain, and enact laws.

Document 2 The Mayflower Compact gave settlers the power to enact, constitute, and frame laws for the good of the colony.

Rubric: Write an Essay

Share the rubric with students before they begin writing.

Score 1 Ideas unclear, organization poor.

Score 2 Essay has few details that help explain the importance of the Burgesses Ordinance for Virginia and the Mayflower Compact.

Score 3 Essay accurately describes the importance of the Ordinance for Virginia and the Mayflower Compact. (*Both the Ordinance for Virginia and the Mayflower Compact gave American colonists the right to govern themselves.*)

Score 4 Essay is comprehensive and detailed with clear organization and supporting details.

Skills for Life

13. William Bradford

14. Possible answer: He wanted to describe for others the details of life in the Plymouth Colony.

15. Possible answer: He speaks highly of them for continuing to help run the colony without complaining.

16. Possible answer: It seems accurate because, although it contains Bradford's opinion of events, he does not seem to exaggerate.

Life in the Colonies (1650–1750)

History Background

The Development of Ways of Life in the Colonies

The English colonists who settled in North America faced uncertainty and danger in an unfamiliar wilderness. As they persevered, they began to build communities and towns. European ideas about social class, race, individual rights, and government deeply influenced the colonists.

The class divisions in the colonies reflected European heritage. Colonial society was divided into an elite class, a middle class, and the servant classes. Members of each class were easily identifiable. However, these categories of class were much more flexible than in Europe, where aristocrats could point to a heritage of class distinctions. In the Americas, movement between classes, while not common, was certainly a possibility. English precedent encouraged the colonists to assert rights propounded first in the Magna Carta and expanded in the following centuries to include the English Bill of Rights.

Gentler class distinctions and guarantees of rights in the colonies did not apply in matters of race. Free Africans in the English colonies were not permitted full rights of citizenship. They were denied the vote, and were not allowed to serve on juries. Enslaved Africans who survived the harrowing Middle Passage confronted enormous challenges as slavery in the Americas came to apply exclusively to captured Africans and people of African descent. Various forms of slavery have existed throughout human history and continue in parts of the world today. Lifelong slavery that extended down through the generations made the institution exceptionally harsh in North America.

As the colonies prospered and developed their own cultural identity, the rising colonial merchant class affected Europe. Colonial demands for political rights undermined traditional notions of social class. Scholars began applying reason to scientific, political, and social issues. This new commitment to rigorous thinking, known as the Enlightenment, inspired ideas that would undermine the power of monarchies throughout Europe. Belief in the divine right of kings was supplanted by new ideas about natural rights. These ideas flourished in North America, where colonists were developing a distinctively American political and cultural identity.

Essential Questions

Use this graphic organizer to see the relationship between key concepts and the Chapter Essential Question.

Focus Question/Section 1
How did English ideas about government and trade affect the colonies?
(p. 102)
Concept: Rights

Focus Question/Section 2
What were the characteristics of colonial society?
(p. 107)
Concept: Colony

Chapter Essential Question
How did colonial life take shape?

Focus Question/Section 4
How did ideas about religion and government influence colonial life?
(p. 118)
Concept: Enlightenment

Focus Question/Section 3
How did slavery develop in the colonies and affect colonial life?
(p. 113)
Concept: Slavery

Differentiated Instruction

Idea Wave Strategy

Spontaneous Responses to Questions In this chapter students will use the Idea Wave engagement strategy to develop and share their responses to questions. This strategy allows students to be spontaneous in their thinking and to hear a broad range of possible responses to a prompt. Because students offer ideas rapidly, the process offers many of the effects of a good brainstorming session. Students do not engage in the critical self-reflection that can limit creative thinking. Once a variety of ideas are shared, students can begin to evaluate the responses.

Analyzing Responses Remind students that it is a good idea to try to elaborate on interesting or unusual responses. Below are sample language strategies to help students achieve this goal.

Which response made you think about _____ in a new way? Why?

How are the responses given by _____ and _____ similar or different?

What more could we say about _____?

Concepts Across Time

Have students develop an understanding of the enduring concepts of history by connecting these ideas.

Concept: Rights

Students studying the development of rights should recall that the American colonies developed forms of self-government to establish order and ensure their success. These forms of self-government also offered settlers rights. Ask: **What English roots are present in the colonists' idea of rights?** (*Possible answer: The Magna Carta and the English Bill of Rights limited the power of the king and protected the rights of the people.*) Use this question when discussing the Colonial Self-Government on p. 104 of Section 1.

Concept: Slavery

Students learning about the Atlantic slave trade should recall earlier contact between Europeans and Africans. Ask: **Before Columbus' voyage, how did Europeans travel to Asia?** (*They sailed around the tip of Africa.*) Ask: **What contact did Europeans and Africans have?** (*They traded goods such as gold and salt.*) Ask: **How did European colonizing of the Americas lead to an agricultural economy based on slave labor?** (*The development of new land for large plantation farming required more workers, and colonists used enslaved people to do the work.*) Use these questions when discussing The Atlantic Slave Trade on p. 113 of Section 3.

Concept: Enlightenment

Students studying the ideas of the Enlightenment should recall the impact of the English Bill of Rights on the rights of English citizens. Ask: **How did the English Bill of Rights extend the power of English citizens?** (*It restated many traditional rights guaranteed by the Magna Carta and restricted the right of the king to raise taxes or form an army without the consent of Parliament.*) Ask: **What do these restrictions reveal about the limits to the power of kings?** (*They indicate that the power of kings is limited by the need to gain the consent of the people.*) Use this question when discussing the Enlightenment on p. 122 of Section 4.

Section 1 Governing the Colonies *1.5 periods, .75 block*

Objectives

Students will

1. Explain how English political traditions influenced the 13 colonies.
2. Describe the responsibilities of early colonial governments.
3. Identify John Peter Zenger's role in establishing freedom of the press.
4. Understand how the Navigation Acts affected the colonies' economy.

Differentiated Instruction Key

L1	Basic to Average	AR	Advanced Readers
L2	All Students	ELL	English Language Learners
L3	Average to Advanced	GT	Gifted and Talented
		LPR	Less Proficient Readers
		SN	Special Needs

Prepare to Read

Build Background Knowledge
Discuss students' previous knowledge of Europeans' reasons for establishing colonies in North America.

Set a Purpose for Reading
Have students begin to fill out the Reading Readiness Guide.

Preview Key Terms
Preview the section's Key Terms.

Instructional Resources

All in One Teaching Resources, Unit 1
- **L2** Chapter Prereading Guide, p. 4
- **L2** History Reading Skill, p. 104
- **L2** Word Knowledge Rating Form, p. 105
- **L2** Reading Readiness Guide, p. 106

Teacher's Edition
- **L2** Vocabulary Builder, pp. 101, 103

Differentiated Instruction

🔊 **Guided Reading Audio CD**

Spanish ELL, LPR, SN

Teach

Instruction
The English Parliamentary Tradition
Discuss rights guaranteed in the Magna Carta and English Bill of Rights.

Colonial Self-Government
Discuss the development of self-government in the colonies.

Freedom of the Press
Discuss how the trial of John Peter Zenger helped establish the principle of freedom of the press in the colonies.

Regulating Trade
Discuss the impact of the Navigation Acts on the colonies' economies.

Instructional Resources

📖 **Interactive Reading and Notetaking Study Guide**
- **L2** Chapter 4, Section 1

All in One Teaching Resources, Unit 1
- **L2** Concept Lesson, p. 114
- **L2** Concept Organizer, p. 6

Color Transparencies
The English Bill of Rights

Differentiated Instruction

📖 **Interactive Reading and Notetaking Study Guide, Adapted Version (English/Spanish)**
- **L1** Chapter 4, Section 1

Teacher's Edition
- **L3** Read a Primary Source, p. 102 AR
- **L1** Study Aid, p. 104 LPR, SN

All in One Teaching Resources, Unit 1
- **L1** English Bill of Rights, p. 110

Assess and Reteach

Assess Progress
Evaluate student comprehension with Check Your Progress and Section Quiz.

Reteach
Assign the Interactive Reading and Notetaking Study Guide to help struggling students.

Extend
Extend the lesson by having students research and summarize the Zenger case.

Instructional Resources

📖 **Interactive Reading and Notetaking Study Guide**
- **L2** Chapter 4, Section 1

All in One Teaching Resources, Unit 1
- **L2** Reading Readiness Guide, p. 106
- **L2** Section Quiz, p. 115

Progress Monitoring Transparencies
- **L2** Chapter 4, Section 1

Differentiated Instruction

Teacher's Edition
- **L1** Checkpoints, TE pp. 104, 105, 106

🔊 **SE on Audio CD**
- **L1** Chapter 4, Section 1

Internet Resources
PHSchool.com

Section 2 Colonial Society

 1 period, .5 block

Objectives

Students will

1. Learn about life on a colonial farm.
2. Describe the roles of men, women, and children in colonial America.
3. List the class differences that existed in colonial society.

Differentiated Instruction Key

- **L1** Basic to Average
- **L2** All Students
- **L3** Average to Advanced

- **AR** Advanced Readers
- **ELL** English Language Learners
- **GT** Gifted and Talented
- **LPR** Less Proficient Readers
- **SN** Special Needs

Prepare to Read

Build Background Knowledge
Ask students to preview the section and predict what they will learn about colonial societies.

Set a Purpose for Reading
Have students begin to fill out the Reading Readiness Guide.

Preview Key Terms
Preview the section's Key Terms.

Instructional Resources

All in One Teaching Resources, Unit 1
- **L2** Reading Readiness Guide, p. 107

Teacher's Edition
- **L2** Vocabulary Builder, p. 107

Differentiated Instruction

- Guided Reading Audio CD
  Spanish **ELL, LPR, SN**

Teach

Instruction
The Family in Colonial Times
Discuss the family structures and ways of life common on colonial farms.

Men, Women, and Children
Discuss the clearly defined roles of men, women, and children in the colonies.

Social Classes
Discuss the division of colonial society into distinct social classes.

Instructional Resources

Interactive Reading and Notetaking Study Guide
- **L2** Chapter 4, Section 2

Color Transparencies
History Interactive: Colonial Women

Differentiated Instruction

Interactive Reading and Notetaking Study Guide, Adapted Version (English/Spanish)
- **L1** Chapter 4, Section 2

Teacher's Edition
- **L1** Making Flashcards, p. 108 **ELL, LPR, SN**
- **L3** Describing Social Classes, p. 110 **AR, GT**

Assess and Reteach

Assess Progress
Evaluate student comprehension with Check Your Progress and Section Quiz.

Reteach
Assign the Interactive Reading and Notetaking Study Guide to help struggling students.

Extend
Extend the lesson by having students complete the History Interactive about the lives of colonial women.

Instructional Resources

Interactive Reading and Notetaking Study Guide
- **L2** Chapter 4, Section 2

All in One Teaching Resources, Unit 1
- **L2** Reading Readiness Guide, p. 107
- **L2** Section Quiz, p. 116

Progress Monitoring Transparencies
- **L2** Chapter 4, Section 2

Differentiated Instruction

Teacher's Edition
- **L1** Checkpoints, TE pp. 108, 110, 112

- SE on Audio CD
- **L1** Chapter 4, Section 2

Internet Resources
PHSchool.com

Section 3 Slavery in the Colonies 🕐 *1 period, .5 block*

Objectives

Students will

1. Describe the conditions under which enslaved Africans came to the Americas.
2. Explain why slavery became part of the colonial economy.
3. Identify the restrictions placed on enslaved Africans in the colonies.
4. Describe how African culture influenced American culture.

Differentiated Instruction Key

L1 Basic to Average   **AR** Advanced Readers
L2 All Students   **ELL** English Language Learners
L3 Average to Advanced **GT** Gifted and Talented
                           LPR Less Proficient Readers
                           SN Special Needs

Prepare to Read

Build Background Knowledge
Discuss students' prior knowledge of slavery in the Americas.

Set a Purpose for Reading
Have students begin to fill out the Reading Readiness Guide.

Preview Key Terms
Preview the section's Key Terms.

Instructional Resources

All in One Teaching Resources, Unit 1
L2 Reading Readiness Guide, p. 108

Teacher's Edition
L2 Vocabulary Builder, p. 113

Differentiated Instruction

🔊 **Guided Reading Audio CD**
Spanish ELL, LPR, SN

Teach

Instruction
The Atlantic Slave Trade
Discuss the Middle Passage and the development of triangular trade routes.

Slavery in the Colonies
Discuss factors that made slavery in the colonies harsh and attempts to resist it.

African Cultural Influences
Discuss ways that African cultural influences brought by enslaved Africans impact American culture today.

Instructional Resources

📖 **Interactive Reading and Notetaking Study Guide**
L2 Chapter 4, Section 3

All in One Teaching Resources, Unit 1
L2 The Middle Passage, p. 111
L2 Slave Codes, p. 112

Color Transparencies
The Atlantic Slave Trade

Discovery School Video
L2 Life of Enslaved Africans

Differentiated Instruction

📖 **Interactive Reading and Notetaking Study Guide, Adapted Version (English/Spanish)**
L1 Chapter 4, Section 3

Teacher's Edition
L3 Give a Biographical Presentation, p. 114 AR, GT
L1 Unfamiliar Words, p.116 ELL, LPR, SN

Assess and Reteach

Assess Progress
Evaluate student comprehension with Check Your Progress and Section Quiz.

Reteach
Assign the Interactive Reading and Notetaking Study Guide to help struggling students.

Extend
Extend the lesson by having students paraphrase passages from Olaudah Equiano's autobiography.

Instructional Resources

📖 **Interactive Reading and Notetaking Study Guide**
L2 Chapter 4, Section 3

All in One Teaching Resources, Unit 1
L2 Reading Readiness Guide, p. 108
L2 Section Quiz, p. 117

Progress Monitoring Transparencies
L2 Chapter 4, Section 3

Differentiated Instruction

Teacher's Edition
L1 Checkpoints, TE pp. 115, 116, 117

🔊 **SE on Audio CD**
L1 Chapter 4, Section 3

Internet Resources
PHSchool.com

Section 4 The Spread of New Ideas *1.5 periods, .75 block*

Objectives

Students will

1. Describe the education colonial children received.
2. Summarize the development of poetry and literature in colonial America.
3. Explain how the Great Awakening affected the colonies.
4. Explain how the colonies were affected by the spread of new ideas.

Differentiated Instruction Key

L1	Basic to Average	**AR**	Advanced Readers
L2	All Students	**ELL**	English Language Learners
L3	Average to Advanced	**GT**	Gifted and Talented
		LPR	Less Proficient Readers
		SN	Special Needs

Prepare to Read

Build Background Knowledge
Have students preview the chapter to predict what they will learn.

Set a Purpose for Reading
Have students begin to fill out the Reading Readiness Guide.

Preview Key Terms
Preview the section's Key Terms.

Instructional Resources

All in One Teaching Resources, Unit 1
L2 Reading Readiness Guide, p. 109

Teacher's Edition
L2 Vocabulary Builder, p. 119

Differentiated Instruction

◎ Guided Reading Audio CD
Spanish ELL, LPR, SN

Teach

Instruction
The Importance of Education
Discuss the organization and curriculum of colonial schools.

Roots of American Literature
Discuss the development of a unique literature in colonial America.

The Great Awakening
Discuss the impact of the Great Awakening and its impact on religious tolerance and the spread of democratic ideas.

The Enlightenment
Discuss the development of new ideas about rights and government.

Instructional Resources

📖 Interactive Reading and Notetaking Study Guide
L2 Chapter 4, Section 4

All in One Teaching Resources, Unit 1
L2 Skills for Life Worksheet, p. 113

Differentiated Instruction

📖 Interactive Reading and Notetaking Study Guide, Adapted Version (English/Spanish)

L1 Chapter 4, Section 4

Teacher's Edition
L1 Comprehension Aids, p. 118 LPR, SN
L3 Creating an Introductory Pamphlet, p. 120 AR, GT
L1 Gaining Comprehension, p. 122 ELL, LPR, SN

Assess and Reteach

Assess Progress
Evaluate student comprehension with Check Your Progress and Section Quiz.

Reteach
Assign the Interactive Reading and Notetaking Study Guide to help struggling students.

Extend
Have students write about rights from the point of view of a colonist studying the Enlightenment.

Think Like a Historian
Using information from primary sources and the chapters in this unit, revisit the unit essential question.

Instructional Resources

📖 Interactive Reading and Notetaking Study Guide
L2 Chapter 4, Section 4

All in One Teaching Resources, Unit 1
L2 Reading Readiness Guide, p. 109
L2 Word Knowledge Rating Form, p. 105
L2 Section Quiz, p. 118
L2 Chapter Test, p. 122

Progress Monitoring Transparencies
L2 Chapter 4, Section 4

Color Transparencies
L2 Think Like a Historian

Differentiated Instruction

Teacher's Edition
L1 Checkpoints, TE pp. 120, 122, 123

◎ SE on Audio CD
L1 Chapter 4, Section 4

All in One Teaching Resources, Unit 1
L1 Chapter Test, p. 119

◎ Social Studies Skills Tutor CD-ROM
Compare and Contrast

Help students deepen their understanding of the Chapter Essential Question: **How did colonial life take shape?** Students should use library or Internet resources. The Web codes provided offer access to Internet resources students can use to complete each activity. Use the appropriate four-point rubric in Assessment Rubrics to evaluate the activity.

 Assessment Rubrics

Write an Illustrated Biography

Have students research one of the great Enlightenment thinkers who influenced American colonists, such as John Locke or Montesquieu. Have students write a short illustrated biography. Have students share their biographies with the class. Biographies should include an overview of the subject's contributions to the Enlightenment, and basic information about the thinker's personal history and educational background. Then collect the biographies and keep them in an accessible place in the classroom as reference material. Use this activity after students have completed Section 4.

 Individual research activity　L2

 Web Code: mve-0121

Hold a Mock Trial

Have students hold a mock libel trial of John Peter Zenger. Assign each student a role in the trial (Zenger, lawyers, judge, court reporter, jury member, etc.). All students should research the case to prepare for their roles. They may use the information in the Student Edition as a starting point. After performing the trial, hold a class discussion to assess the process and the outcome of the trial. Use this activity after students have completed Section 1.

 Group research activity　L2

 Web Code: mve-0122

Make an Informational Poster About the Atlantic Slave Trade

Have students use the Web site to research the impact of the Atlantic slave trade on West Africa. Then have them create a poster about this trade. Suggest that they include information about and images of the communities of specific groups in West Africa affected by the trade as well as its impact on that region. Remind students that when a community loses people, it also loses the unique skills and talents they may have. Ask students to look for skills people in West Africa may have developed in their communities. Use the posters when studying Section 3.

 Individual research activity ELL, LPR, SN   `L1`

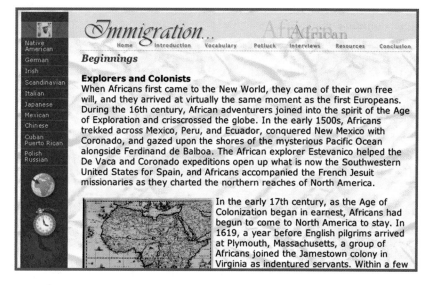

 Web Code: mve-0123

Plan a Tour of a Colonial Town

Organize students into small groups. Have them research life in a colonial town, such as Williamsburg, Virginia. Once students have researched the town, have them use words and images to make a tri-fold brochure describing the places and inhabitants of the town. Use this activity after students have completed Section 4.

 Group research activity AR, GT   `L3`

Go Online PHSchool.com **Web Code:** mve-0124

Extend the Lesson Through Technology Research

Chapter 4

Why It Matters

In this chapter, students will focus on life in the English colonies, the impact of slavery, and the Enlightenment.

Although colonial society was divided into distinct classes, colonists had greater opportunity to change social class in America than they had in Europe. Belief in the colonies as lands of new opportunities carried over to the United States after its founding and continues to draw immigrants seeking better lives to our shores.

The introduction of slavery in the colonies left a bitter legacy. Divisions over slavery led the country to Civil War and the segregation that followed, and racism remains a complex issue today.

Even as the colonists imported enslaved Africans, they were embracing the ideas of Enlightenment thinkers such as Locke and Montesquieu. Enlightenment ideas inspired the Revolution, the Constitution, and the end of slavery, and remain vital to American democracy today.

Chapter Essential Question

How did colonial life take shape?

Think Like a Historian

- To preview this chapter, have students review the content on these pages of the Student Edition. Ask: **What will you be learning about in this chapter?** *(about what life in the colonies was like)*

- Have students read the quote. Ask: **How can you tell from this quote that life in the colonies differed from life in England?** *(Because the writer is from New England and notes that a colonist here may control his own work and own his own land; he could start with nothing, work hard, and become rich.)*

- Have students look at the picture of the needlework. Ask: **How can you infer that the people shown in this needlework are wealthy colonists?** *(Student responses will vary, but students will recognize that the colonists depicted here are wearing fine clothes, are in an idealized setting showing large houses and beautiful vegetation, and are relaxing not working.)*

Life in the Colonies

1650-1750

98

Bibliography

For the Teacher

Berlin, Ira. *Many Thousands Gone: The First Two Centuries of Slavery in North America.* Harvard, 1998.

Castillo, Susan P. Gordon S. *The Literatures of Colonial America: An Anthology.* Blackwell, 2000.

Kramnick, Isaac, ed. *The Portable Enlightenment Reader.* Penguin, 1995.

For the Student

L1 Fleming, Candace. *Ben Franklin's Autobiography: Being a True Account of the Good Gentleman's Life.* Atheneum, 2003.

L2 Earle, Alice Morse. *Home Life in Colonial Days.* Berkshire, 1993.

L3 Horton, James Oliver and Lois E. Horton. *Slavery and the Making of America.* Oxford, 2004.

> "...Here every man may be master of his own labour and land...and if he have nothing but his hands he may set up his trade, and by industry grow rich."
>
> —New England colonial farmer

This needlework depicts the fine clothing and refined manners of wealthy colonists. Most members of colonial society did not enjoy such an elegant lifestyle.

CHAPTER 4

What You Will Learn

Section 1
GOVERNING THE COLONIES
English ideas about government, individual rights, and trade deeply affected colonial life.

Section 2
COLONIAL SOCIETY
Although colonial society was divided into different social and economic classes, it was far less rigid than European society of the time.

Section 3
SLAVERY IN THE COLONIES
By the 1700s, slavery had become a part of American life, serving the economic interests of both northern traders and southern planters.

Section 4
THE SPREAD OF NEW IDEAS
Religion played a key role in colonial life, while the European Enlightenment influenced scientific and political thought.

↻ Reading Skill
Determine Meaning From Context
In this chapter, you will practice using context and word clues to understand unfamiliar passages in a text.

99

History Background

Social Class Most members of colonial society were not members of the elite classes. Class distinctions developed in ancient times. Aristotle argued that society ought to have three classes: the rich, the poor, and a large middle class. In feudal Europe, class divisions had been highly organized from the serfs at the bottom to the nobility at the top.

Rigid class distinctions began to disintegrate in European societies with the rise of mercantilism and the new wealth it brought to merchants and manufacturers. These newly wealthy classes began demanding a share of political power. Some Enlightenment thinkers argued that social equality would be advantageous economically since people were forced to compete on equal terms.

Prepare to Read

Use the following for reading skill support.

All in One **Teaching Resources, Unit 1,** Chapter Prereading Guide, p. 4; History Reading Skill, p. 41

History Reading Skill, *Online*
Web code: mve-3000

Differentiated Instruction

The following Teacher Edition strategies are suitable for students of varying abilities.

L3 **Advanced Readers,** pp. 102, 110, 114, 120 AR

L1 **English Language Learners,** pp. 101, 108, 116, 122, 124 ELL

L3 **Gifted and Talented,** pp. 110, 114, 120 GT

L1 **Less Proficient Readers,** pp. 101, 104, 108, 116, 118, 122, 124 LPR

L1 **Special Needs,** pp. 101, 104, 108, 116, 118, 122 SN

Chapter Resources

Discovery SCHOOL

Quick View Video
View the chapter video for a quick preview of the main ideas.

How did colonial life take shape?

Visual Preview

How did colonial life take shape?

Build Background Knowledge `L2`

In Chapter 3, students read how English colonies took root in North America. Lead a structured discussion about how colonists created a new life for themselves. (See TE p. T24 for more on structured discussion.) Remind students that colonial life evolved, or developed, over time. Colonists based their society on the way they had lived in their parent country, but adapted it to fit their new surroundings. Ask students to think about how they would react if they entered a new school. How would they adapt to the new environment? *(Possible answer: They would act the way they did in their former school, then see how things were done differently in the new school and try to fit in.)* Tell students that the colonists faced a similar situation in America.

Instruction `L2`

- For background information on conducting a lesson for the Visual Preview, see TE p. T20.

- Write the Chapter Essential Question on the board. Ask: **What influenced how people lived in the colonies?** *(Possible answers: the physical environment, living with people from diverse backgrounds, laws and traditions from the parent country)* Use the Idea Wave strategy (TE p. T24) to encourage participation.

- Ask students to study the timeline. **What years of colonial life are represented on the timeline?** *(1647-1750)* **What happened in 1647?** *(Massachusetts required large towns to have public schools.)* **What concern is found on three of the dates on this timeline?** *(slavery)*

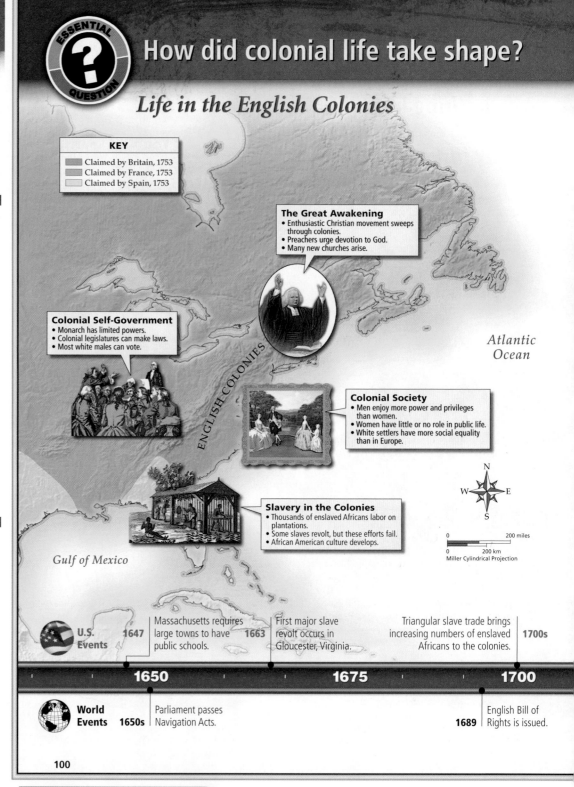

How did colonial life take shape?

Life in the English Colonies

KEY
- Claimed by Britain, 1753
- Claimed by France, 1753
- Claimed by Spain, 1753

The Great Awakening
- Enthusiastic Christian movement sweeps through colonies.
- Preachers urge devotion to God.
- Many new churches arise.

Colonial Self-Government
- Monarch has limited powers.
- Colonial legislatures can make laws.
- Most white males can vote.

Colonial Society
- Men enjoy more power and privileges than women.
- Women have little or no role in public life.
- White settlers have more social equality than in Europe.

Slavery in the Colonies
- Thousands of enslaved Africans labor on plantations.
- Some slaves revolt, but these efforts fail.
- African American culture develops.

Atlantic Ocean

Gulf of Mexico

ENGLISH COLONIES

0   200 miles
0   200 km
Miller Cylindrical Projection

U.S. Events 1647 Massachusetts requires large towns to have public schools. 1663 First major slave revolt occurs in Gloucester, Virginia. Triangular slave trade brings increasing numbers of enslaved Africans to the colonies. 1700s

1650   1675   1700

World Events 1650s Parliament passes Navigation Acts. 1689 English Bill of Rights is issued.

100

History Background

Geography Colonial America developed at a very rapid pace. In 1700, there were about 230,000 Europeans and 20,000 Africans settled in British North America. By 1750, there were approximately 900,000 Europeans and 240,000 Africans. New England's growth was generally from natural reproduction, while in the Mid-Atlantic region, the growth was largely due to immigration. In the South, almost 40 percent of the population was enslaved.

The population of the colonies in the late 1700s was remarkably young: approximately 50 percent of the population at any given time was under 16 years old.

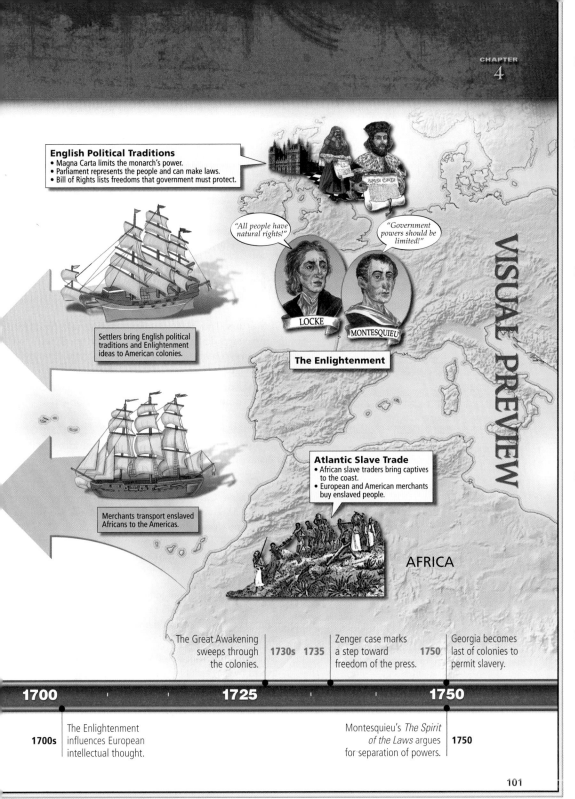

English Political Traditions
- Magna Carta limits the monarch's power.
- Parliament represents the people and can make laws.
- Bill of Rights lists freedoms that government must protect.

"All people have natural rights!"

"Government powers should be limited!"

LOCKE

MONTESQUIEU

The Enlightenment

Settlers bring English political traditions and Enlightenment ideas to American colonies.

Atlantic Slave Trade
- African slave traders bring captives to the coast.
- European and American merchants buy enslaved people.

Merchants transport enslaved Africans to the Americas.

AFRICA

VISUAL PREVIEW

	1730s	1735		1750	
The Great Awakening sweeps through the colonies.			Zenger case marks a step toward freedom of the press.		Georgia becomes last of colonies to permit slavery.

1700

1725

1750

| **1700s** | The Enlightenment influences European intellectual thought. | | Montesquieu's *The Spirit of the Laws* argues for separation of powers. | **1750** |

101

Instruction (continued)

- Have students examine the map. **What does the green shaded area show?** *(land claimed by Britain)* **What year of colonial development does this map represent?** *(1753)*

- Direct student attention to the arrows on the map. Ask: **What did the colonists and merchants bring from Europe? From Africa?** *(From Europe, colonists brought English political traditions and the ideas of the Enlightenment that guaranteed basic freedoms. From Africa, merchants brought slaves.)*

- Ask students to read the captions on the map. **What happened to enslaved Africans when they got to America?** *(They worked on plantations.)* Organize students into small groups, and have each group analyze one caption and make connections between what came from Europe and Africa and how it affected colonial life. On the board, write the terms "Political Traditions, Enlightenment, Slave Trade." Debrief the student groups, using arrows to show connections between these titles and colonial life.

- Have students rewrite the Essential Question in simple terms in their notes. **How did life in the colonies develop?** You may also post this question in a prominent place in the classroom and leave it there while discussing the chapter. Tell students to use the section focus questions as a guide to answering the Essential Question as they read the chapter.

- Tell students that as they complete the Notetaking Study Guide for this chapter, they will be building the answer to the Chapter Essential Question.

📖 **Interactive Reading and Notetaking Study Guide,** Chapter 4, (Adapted Version also available.)

Vocabulary Builder

Preview the Vocabulary Have students preview the vocabulary in the chapter and rate how well they know each word on the Word Knowledge Rating Form. Collect the sheets and explain that they will have a chance to go over the forms later.

All in One Teaching Resources, Unit 1, Word Knowledge Rating Form, p. 105

Monitor Progress Students should demonstrate their understanding of the words by drawing pictures that illustrate them. For example, for the word *domestic*, students may draw a person washing dishes. Pair students to exchange their pictures and have the partners check understanding of the relationship of the drawing to the word. Review the material with the students.

Review and Preview

Students have learned about the growth of the English colonies in North America. Now they will learn about the ways that the colonies were governed.

Section Focus Question

How did English ideas about government and trade affect the colonies?

Before you begin the lesson for the day, write the Section Focus Question on the board. (*Lesson focus: The colonists enjoyed the traditional political rights of English citizens, but under the theory of mercantilism trade policies were structured to benefit the parent country.*)

Prepare to Read

Build Background Knowledge   **L2**

Ask students to recall from earlier chapters what they have learned about Europeans' motives for exploring the Americas and establish colonies there. Use the Idea Wave participation strategy (TE, p. T24) to elicit responses and write students' answers on the board. Ask students to predict how these motives will influence the development of the colonies. Tell students that they will review their predictions and correct them as needed after they have read the section.

Set a Purpose   **L2**

■ Read each statement in the Reading Readiness Guide aloud. Ask students to mark the statements True or False.

   All in One Teaching Resources, Unit 1,
   Reading Readiness Guide, p. 106

■ Have students discuss the statements in pairs or groups of four, then mark the worksheets again. Use the Numbered Heads participation strategy (TE, p. T24) to call on students to share their group's perspectives. The students will return to these worksheets later.

An Assembly Yearly Chosen

"For the well governing of this province . . . , there shall be an assembly yearly chosen, by the freemen thereof, to consist of four persons out of each country . . . [to] prepare bills in order to pass into laws; impeach criminals, and redress grievances."

—William Penn, on the governing of Pennsylvania, 1710

◀ William Penn (right) receives the charter for Pennsylvania from King Charles II.

Governing the Colonies

Objectives

- Explain how English political traditions influenced the 13 colonies.
- Describe the responsibilities of early colonial governments.
- Identify John Peter Zenger's role in establishing freedom of the press.
- Understand how the Navigation Acts affected the colonies' economy.

🎯 Reading Skill

Use Word Clues to Analyze Meaning
When you encounter an unfamiliar word, look for clues within the word itself. For example, to understand the term *notable*, the familiar word *note* is helpful. If *note* means "to notice or remember," then *notable* may mean "worth remembering or noticing." Also, consider whether the word seems to be a verb, an adjective, or a noun.

Key Terms

legislature	freedom of the
bill of rights	press
habeas corpus	libel

Why It Matters The New England, the Middle, and the Southern colonies developed in some unique ways. But they were all English colonies, and they therefore shared a common English heritage.

❓ **Section Focus Question: How did English ideas about government and trade affect the colonies?**

The English Parliamentary Tradition

The English colonists brought with them the idea that they had political rights. This idea was rooted in English history.

Magna Carta In 1215, English nobles forced King John to sign the Magna Carta, the Latin name meaning "great charter." The Magna Carta was the first document to place restrictions on an English ruler's power. It limited the monarch's right to levy taxes without consulting the nobles. It also protected the right to own private property and guaranteed the right to trial by jury:

"31. Neither we nor our [officials] shall take, for our castles or for any other work of ours, wood which is not ours, against the will of the owner of that wood. . . .

39. No free man shall be taken or imprisoned . . . except by the lawful judgment of his peers, or by the law of the land."

—Magna Carta

The rights listed in the Magna Carta were at first limited to nobles. Over time, the rights were extended to all English citizens.

102 Chapter 4 Life in the Colonies

Differentiated Instruction

L3 Advanced Readers

Read a Primary Source Have students complete the worksheet English Bill of Rights to understand how the power of the monarch was limited in England. Have students share their findings with the class.

   All in One Teaching Resources, Unit 1,
   English Bill of Rights, p. 110

Parliament Under the Magna Carta, nobles formed a Great Council to advise the king. This body developed into the English Parliament (PAHR luh mehnt). Parliament was a two-house legislature. A **legislature** is a group of people who have the power to make laws. The House of Lords was made up of nobles, most of whom inherited their titles. Members of the House of Commons were elected. Only a few rich men and landowners had the right to vote for the House of Commons.

Parliament's greatest power was the right to approve new taxes. No monarch could raise taxes without the consent of Parliament. This "power of the purse" gave Parliament a degree of control over the monarch.

In the 1640s, power struggles between King Charles I and Parliament led to the English Civil War. Parliamentary forces eventually won the war, executed the king, and briefly ruled England. In 1660, the monarchy was restored. Still, Parliament <u>retained</u> its traditional rights.

English Bill of Rights An event in 1688 further boosted parliamentary power. Parliament removed King James II from the throne and invited his daughter Mary and her husband William to rule England. This event was called the Glorious Revolution. In 1689, King William and Queen Mary signed the English Bill of Rights. A **bill of rights** is a written list of freedoms that a government promises to protect.

> **Vocabulary Builder**
> **retain** (ree TAYN) **v.** to keep

English Bill of Rights

These selections from the English Bill of Rights deal with the powers of Parliament:

4. **"**That levying money for or to the use of the crown . . . without grant of Parliament . . . is illegal; . . .

6. That the raising or keeping a standing army within the kingdom in time of peace, unless it be with the consent of Parliament, is against the law; . . .

8. That election of members of Parliament ought to be free;

9. That the freedom of speech and debates or proceedings in Parliament ought not to be impeached [challenged] or questioned in any court or place out of Parliament.**"**

—English Bill of Rights

William and Mary

Reading Primary Sources
Skills Activity

The English Bill of Rights was issued under William and Mary in 1689. It guaranteed the powers of Parliament and the basic rights of English citizens.

(a) Interpret a Primary Source
Summarize item 4 in your own words.

(b) Draw Conclusions Why do you think Parliament included item 9 in the Bill of Rights?

Vocabulary Builder

Use the information below to teach students this section's high-use words.

High-Use Word	Definition and Sample Sentence
retain, p. 103	*v.* to keep The British government **retained** final say in colonial affairs.
levy, p. 104	*v.* to impose (a tax, for example); to force to be paid In the federal government, Congress holds the power to **levy** taxes.

Teach

The English Parliamentary Tradition
p. 102

Instruction ▪ L2

- **Vocabulary Builder** Before teaching this lesson, preteach the High-Use Words **retain** and **levy,** using the strategy on TE p. T21.

  Key Terms Following the instruction on p. 7, have students create a See It–Remember It chart for the Key Terms in this chapter.

- To help students better understand the concept of *rights,* use the Concept Lesson Rights. Provide students with copies of the Concept Organizer.

  All in One Teaching Resources, Unit 1, Concept Organizer, p. 6; Concept Lesson, p. 114

- Read The English Parliamentary Tradition with students using the ReQuest participation strategy (TE, p. T23).

- Ask: **What did the Magna Carta do that had never been done before?** (*It set limits on the power of the king.*)

- Have students discuss the importance of the English Civil War and the Glorious Revolution. Display the transparency The English Bill of Rights.

Color Transparencies, The English Bill of Rights

Independent Practice
Have students begin to fill in the Study Guide for this section.

📖 **Interactive Reading and Notetaking Study Guide,** Chapter 4, Section 1 (Adapted Version also available.)

Monitor Progress

As students fill in the Notetaking Study Guide, circulate to make sure students understand the importance of the expansion of rights under the English parliamentary system. Provide assistance as needed.

Answers
Reading Primary Sources (a) Item 4 states that the king cannot raise taxes without Parliament's approval. **(b)** Parliament wanted to make sure it could criticize the king's actions without fear of royal punishment.

Colonial Self-Government

p. 104

Instruction L2

- Have students read Colonial Self-Government. Remind students to look for details to answer the Section Focus Question.

- Ask: **How was lawmaking in Pennsylvania different from that in other colonies before 1701?** (*Before 1701, the governor and a council made all of the laws in Pennsylvania, while in the other colonies, legislatures of elected delegates made laws.*)

- Discuss with students how life might have been different if the colonists elected the governor and both legislative houses. (*Possible responses: Colonists would have had comprehensive control of the colonial government with less English interference.*)

Independent Practice

Have students continue to fill in the Study Guide for this section.

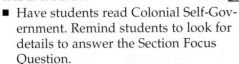 **Interactive Reading and Notetaking Study Guide,** Chapter 4, Section 1 (Adapted Version also available.)

Monitor Progress

As students fill in the Notetaking Study Guide, circulate to make sure students understand the importance of colonial self-government. If students do not seem to have a good understanding, have them reread the section. Provide assistance as needed.

Answers

☑Checkpoint The monarch needed Parliament's permission to raise taxes or an army. Parliament was allowed to meet regularly.

☑Checkpoint More than half of the white males were permitted to vote, but women, Native Americans, and African Americans could not vote.

Vocabulary Builder
levy (LEHV ee) **v.** to impose (a tax, for example); to force to be paid

The English Bill of Rights restated many of the rights granted by the Magna Carta, such as trial by jury. It upheld habeas corpus, the principle that a person cannot be held in prison without being charged with a specific crime. Finally, the Bill of Rights required that Parliament meet regularly and declared that no monarch could levy taxes or raise an army without the consent of Parliament.

☑Checkpoint **How was the power of English monarchs limited?**

Colonial Self-Government

The legal rights that Englishmen had won over the centuries led the colonists to expect a voice in their government. The ideas of limited monarchy and representative government were dear to them. In their new land, colonists wanted to take part in governing themselves.

Colonial Legislatures As you have read, from 1619 the Virginia Company allowed the House of Burgesses to make laws for the Jamestown Colony. The House of Burgesses became the first legislature in English North America. Massachusetts colonists also set up a legislature called the General Court in 1629. Five years later, Massachusetts colonists gained the right to elect delegates to the General Court.

On the other hand, the English government gave William Penn outright ownership of Pennsylvania. The governor and a large council made laws that an assembly could only approve or reject. But the Pennsylvania colonists wanted to draw up laws themselves. In 1701, they forced Penn to agree that only the General Assembly could make laws. The king could overturn laws passed by the General Assembly, but neither Penn nor his council had any part in lawmaking.

By 1760, every British colony in North America had a legislature of some kind. However, the legislatures still clashed at times with the colonial governors appointed by the king.

The Right to Vote In many ways, the colonies offered settlers greater political rights than they would have had in England. From 50 to 75 percent of white males in the American colonies could vote. This was a far greater percentage than in England.

Still, the right to vote did not extend to everyone in the colonies. English women—even those who owned property—could not vote in any colony. Neither could the Native Americans who still lived on land claimed by the colonists. Finally, no Africans, whether free or enslaved, could vote.

☑Checkpoint **Which groups of people were permitted to vote in colonial elections? Which were not permitted to vote?**

Links Across Time

Making State Laws

1619 The House of Burgesses became the first colonial legislature. For the next 155 years, the Burgesses helped govern the affairs of the Virginia Colony.

1776 After the United States declared independence from Britain, Virginia replaced the House of Burgesses with the General Assembly. The other states also set up state legislatures to make laws.

Link to Today ⊕nline

State Legislatures Today There are 50 separate state legislatures operating in the United States. What issues do these lawmakers face?

For: State legislatures in the news
Visit: PHSchool.com
Web Code: mvc-1041

Differentiated Instruction

L1 Less Proficient Readers

Study Aid To help students remember how the colonies were governed, help students create a graphic organizer showing the structure of a colonial government.

L1 Special Needs

Students' graphic organizers should indicate whether the English rulers or the American colonists elected or appointed each part of the government.

There are two Sorts of Monarchies; an absolute and a limited one. In the first, the Liberty of the Press can never be maintained . . .

Penalty for Criticism
British authorities burned John Peter Zenger's *Journal* newspaper publications as a punishment for criticizing the governor. **Critical Thinking:** *Link Past and Present* How did the jury's verdict in Zenger's trial help to pave the way for freedom of the press in the United States?

Freedom of the Press

The colonists expected to enjoy the traditional rights of English subjects. A notable court case in 1735 helped establish another important right. This was freedom of the press, the right of journalists to publish the truth without restriction or penalty.

John Peter Zenger, publisher of the *New York Weekly Journal,* was arrested for printing a series of articles that criticized the governor. Zenger was charged with libel, or the publishing of statements that damage a person's reputation. Under modern American law, statements must be untrue in order to be considered libel. However, English law at the time punished writings that criticized the government—even if the statements were true.

At Zenger's trial, Zenger's lawyer, Andrew Hamilton, admitted that Zenger had printed the statements against the governor. However, Hamilton argued that the articles Zenger published were based on fact and, therefore, should not be considered libel. Hamilton told the jury:

> ❝By your verdict, you will have laid a noble foundation for securing to ourselves, our descendants, and our neighbors, the liberty both of exposing and opposing tyrannical power by speaking and writing truth.❞
>
> —Andrew Hamilton, in A Brief Narrative of the Case and Trial of John Peter Zenger

The jurors agreed. They found that Zenger was not guilty of libel.

The Zenger case later helped establish a fundamental principle. A democracy depends on well-informed citizens. Therefore, the press has a right and responsibility to keep the public informed of the truth. Today, freedom of the press is recognized as a basic American liberty.

Use Word Clues to Analyze Meaning
Use the familiar base word part *tyrant* as a clue to the meaning of *tyrannical*.

☑**Checkpoint** Why was the Zenger case important?

Freedom of the Press Regulating Trade

pp. 105–106

Instruction

- Have students read Freedom of the Press and Regulating Trade, using the Choral Reading Strategy (p. T22). Remind students to look for comparison and contrast.

- Ask: **Why was Zenger found not guilty of libel?** (*He was found not guilty because what he published was true.*)

- Discuss why Zenger was tried even though he did not write the controversial pieces. (*As the printer, he was responsible for the journal's contents and he refused to identify the writers.*)

- Review the Navigation Acts. Discuss why mercantilism was bound to lead to conflict between the parent country and its colonies. (*The theory that colonies exist to serve the parent country put colonists at an economic disadvantage.*)

Independent Practice

Have students complete the Study Guide for this section.

Monitor Progress

- As students complete the Notetaking Study Guide, circulate to make sure students understand the importance of Freedom of the Press and the Navigation Acts. Provide assistance as needed.

- Tell students to fill in the last column of the Reading Readiness Guide. Probe for what they learned that confirms or invalidates each statement.

  All in One Teaching Resources, Unit 1, Reading Readiness Guide, p. 106

Answers

Link Past and Present It established the rights of people in the press to publish truthful information without fear of prosecution.

🔵 **Reading Skill** Possible answer: A *tyrant* is an oppressive ruler, so tyrannical means oppressive or ruthless.

☑**Checkpoint** The trial established the principle that the press has both the right and the responsibility to inform the public of the truth.

Assess and Reteach

Assess Progress `L2`

Have students complete Check Your Progress. Administer the Section Quiz.

All in One Teaching Resources, Unit 1, Section Quiz, p. 115

To further assess student understanding, use the Progress Monitoring Transparency.

Progress Monitoring Transparencies, Chapter 4, Section 1

Reteach `L1`

If students need more instruction, have them read this section in the Interactive Reading and Notetaking Study Guide and complete the accompanying question.

Interactive Reading and Notetaking Study Guide, Chapter 4, Section 1 (Adapted Version also available.)

Extend `L3`

Explain that there have been a number of important court cases that have helped define freedom of the press since the Zenger case. Have students research one such case, *New York Times* v. *Sullivan*. Ask students to summarize the case in their own words and then write a few sentences explaining their reaction to the Supreme Court's decision.

> **Extend Online**
> **For:** Help in starting Extend activity
> **Visit:** PHSchool.com
> **Web Code:** mve-0125

Progress Monitoring Online

Students may check their comprehension of this section by completing the Progress Monitoring Online graphic organizer and self-quiz.

Answer

Checkpoint The colonists believed the acts hurt them economically.

Section 1 Check Your Progress

1. (a) By 1688, English citizens had won the rights to a trial by jury and to own private property. The king's power to raise taxes was also limited by Parliament.
(b) Possible answer: The colonists living in North America believed they were

---

Regulating Trade

As you have read, under the theory of mercantilism, colonies existed in order to serve the economic needs of their parent country. They were a source of raw materials and a place to sell the home country's goods.

In 1651, the English Parliament passed the first of several Navigation Acts to support mercantilism. By these laws: (1) Shipments from Europe to English colonies had to go through England first. (2) Any imports to England from the colonies had to come in ships built and owned by British subjects. (3) The colonies could sell key products, such as tobacco and sugar, only to England. This helped create jobs for English workers.

In many ways, the Navigation Acts benefited the colonies. Colonial traders had a sure market for their goods in England. Also, the law contributed to a booming shipbuilding industry in New England.

Still, as colonial trade expanded, many colonists came to resent the Navigation Acts. In their view, the laws favored English merchants. Colonists felt that they could make more money if they were free to sell to foreign markets themselves. Some colonists got around the Navigation Acts by smuggling—that is, by importing and exporting goods illegally.

A Boston merchant counts up the profits from shipping.

Checkpoint Why did many colonists resent the Navigation Acts?

⭐ **Looking Back and Ahead** As the 13 colonies grew, colonists established lawmaking bodies and developed the economy. In the early days, England's monarchy and Parliament influenced the decisions the colonies made. Yet, the colonies were far from England, and colonists were developing their own ideas. In the next section, you will look at the structure of colonial society.

Section 1 | Check Your Progress

> **Progress Monitoring Online**
> **For:** Self-test with instant help
> **Visit:** PHSchool.com
> **Web Code:** mva-1041

Comprehension and Critical Thinking

1. (a) Identify What political rights had England's citizens won by 1688?
(b) Apply Information Why do you think those living in the 13 colonies believed they were entitled to those rights?

2. (a) Recall What were the Navigation Acts?
(b) Identify Economic Costs and Benefits How did the Navigation Acts affect the colonial economy?

Reading Skill

3. Use Word Clues to Analyze Meaning Use its part of speech to help you analyze the meaning of *boomed* in this sentence: As a result of a law that allowed colonists to build their own ships, the shipbuilding industry in New England *boomed*.

Key Terms

Complete each of the following sentences so that the second part further explains the first part and clearly shows your understanding of the key term.

4. Based on English traditions, colonial *legislatures* _____.
5. The English Bill of Rights protected the rights of individuals, including *habeas corpus*, _____.
6. John Peter Zenger was accused of *libel*, _____.

Writing

7. List at least two examples from colonial society to support this main idea: English colonists believed they should have the same freedoms as English citizens.

---

entitled to these rights because they were governed by the English government and were English citizens.

2. (a) These were a series of acts that restricted colonial trade so that the colony would benefit the parent country.
(b) It ensured a market for goods shipped from North America and contributed to the growth of New England's shipbuilding industry.

3. The word is used as a verb, and the context indicates it means *grew rapidly*.

4. passed laws

5. a procedure which protects people against unjust detention

6. or printing statements that unjustly harm another person's reputation

7. Colonists wanted the right to vote, input into lawmaking, and representation in the Parliament or a local legislature.

▲ A colonial farm

Colonial Society

A Cold North Wind

❝Wednesday. A fine clear morning with a cold north wind. My heart is burnt with anger and discontent, want of every necessary thing in life and in constant fear of gaping creditors consumes my strength and wastes my days. The horror of these things, . . . like to so many horse leeches, preys upon my vitals.❞

—Diary of Mary Cooper, Long Island, New York, 1769

Objectives

- Learn about life on a colonial farm.
- Describe the roles of men, women, and children in colonial America.
- List the class differences that existed in colonial society.

 **Reading Skill**

Use Sentence Clues to Analyze Meaning To find a word's meaning, you may examine other words within the same sentence for clues. For example, you may find familiar descriptive words near the unfamiliar word or find details that suggest a possible meaning. Ask: How is the unfamiliar word connected to a familiar word in the sentence? How is the word described?

Key Terms

extended family   middle class
apprentice   indentured servant
gentry

Why It Matters People in England's colonies enjoyed the traditional political rights of English citizens. This heritage, along with other shared characteristics, helped to create a unifying culture among the colonists.

❓ **Section Focus Question: What were the characteristics of colonial society?**

The Family in Colonial Times

The family played an important role in colonial America. Many people lived with their extended families. An **extended family** is a family that includes, in addition to the parents and their children, other members such as grandparents, aunts, uncles, and cousins.

On a Farm Most colonists lived on farms, where a large family was considered an advantage. Many hands were needed to operate a farm. Usually, farms were widely separated, often by dense forests. This made it necessary for families to be closely knit and self-sufficient. On a farm, each member of the family had many responsibilities. Family members helped plant, cultivate, and harvest crops. There were always fences to mend, animals to tend, and wood to chop.

By today's standards, farmhouses were not very comfortable. Most were made of wood and had few rooms. People sat on stools or benches and slept on planks. Some houses had mattresses of corncobs. There were few utensils, and they were crudely made. In the New England and the Middle colonies winters were cold, and the only source of heat in each house might be a fireplace in the kitchen room. On cold winter nights, the family might huddle around the fire telling stories and shelling nuts.

Section 2 Colonial Society 107

Review and Preview

Students have learned about the development of political and economic life in the English colonies. Now they will focus on how society in the colonies was organized.

Section Focus Question

What were the characteristics of colonial society?

Before you begin the lesson for the day, write the Section Focus Question on the board. (*Lesson focus: Colonists often lived in large extended families with clearly defined roles for men, women, and children, and distinct social classes.*)

Prepare to Read

Build Background Knowledge L2

Remind students that the colonists drew on English traditions as they built political institutions in the new colonies. Then ask students to preview the section by reading the headings and looking at the images. Ask students to predict what more they will learn about colonial society. Use the Numbered Heads participation strategy (TE, p. T24) to elicit responses.

Set a Purpose L2

■ Read each statement in the Reading Readiness Guide aloud. Ask students to mark the statements True or False.

All in One Teaching Resources, Unit 1, Reading Readiness Guide, p. 107

■ Have students discuss the statements in pairs or groups of four, then mark the worksheets again. Use the Numbered Heads participation strategy (TE, p. T24) to call on students to share their group's perspectives. The students will return to these worksheets later.

Vocabulary Builder

Use the information below to teach students this section's high-use words.

High-Use Word	Definition and Sample Sentence
domestic, p. 108	*adj.* having to do with the home or household; pertaining to a country's internal affairs The children busied themselves with **domestic** duties such as sweeping the floor and cooking dinner.
prospect, p. 110	*n.* expectation; something to look forward to happening The **prospect** of a brighter future drew many immigrants to America.

Teach

The Family in Colonial Times

p. 107

Instruction L2

- **Vocabulary Builder** Before teaching this lesson, preteach the High-Use Words **domestic** and **prospect** using the strategy on TE p. 101.

  Key Terms Following the instruction on p. 7, have students continue to fill in the See It–Remember It chart for the Key Terms in this chapter.

- Read The Family in Colonial Times with students using the Choral Reading participation strategy (TE, p. T22).

- Ask: **What challenges did families living on farms face?** (*They were often far from neighbors, and there was always work to do, such as tending crops, feeding animals, and making repairs.*)

- Discuss the ways in which family members on farms relied on each other. Ask students to compare and contrast family life then with family life today.

- Ask: **Would it be easier for a single person to live on a farm or in a town in colonial times? Why?** (*Living in a town would be easier because a farm would be difficult for one person to manage.*)

Independent Practice

Have students begin to fill in the Study Guide for this section.

Interactive Reading and Notetaking Study Guide, Chapter 4, Section 2 (Adapted Version also available.)

Monitor Progress

As students fill in the Notetaking Study Guide, circulate to make sure students understand the importance of the family in colonial times. If students do not seem to have a good understanding, have them reread the section. Provide assistance as needed.

Answer

☑Checkpoint Members of a large family could each perform some of the many tasks that had to be done on a large farm.

In a Town In the colonies' few cities and towns, it was easier for single people to sustain themselves. However, family ties were still held in the highest regard. In Puritan New England, single men and women were expected to live with a family as a servant or a boarder.

☑Checkpoint Why was a large family useful on a farm?

Men, Women, and Children

The lives of men and women differed. Even on the frontier, where families had to labor together to survive, men and women generally took on different roles. A North Carolina settler wrote:

> "Men are generally of all trades, and women the like within their spheres. . . . Men are generally carpenters, joiners, wheelwrights, coopers, butchers, tanners, shoemakers, tallow-chandlers, watermen, and what not; women soap-makers, starch-makers, dyers, etc. He or she that cannot do all these things, or has not slaves that can, over and above all the common occupations of both sexes, will have but a bad time of it."
>
> —John Urmstone, letter, July 7, 1711

A husband and father controlled a family's income and property. Other family members were expected to accept his authority. In addition to fulfilling their home duties, men represented their families in public life as voters and, sometimes, as officeholders.

Roles of Women In colonial America, most women were expected to marry men chosen by their parents. In choosing, parents considered a man's property, his religion, and their own family interests. Romantic love was not considered the most important reason for marriage. Furthermore, when a woman married, her property and any money she might earn became her husband's. A woman often bore her husband many children. She was expected to be his faithful helper in every way.

Besides childcare, a woman had many domestic responsibilities. She cooked, did the laundry, and spun yarn into cloth that she made into family clothing. Outside, she took care of the garden, milked the cows, tended the chickens, churned butter, and preserved food. If the family had money, she might have help from servants.

Sometimes, however, the line blurred between women's work and men's work. On the western frontier, a woman might help plow or pitch hay. If she lived in a town, she might keep a shop or an inn, or work as a baker, a printer, or even an undertaker. Her husband or sons might help make cloth, if needed.

Women had little or no role in public life. They could not hold office or vote. On the western and southern frontiers, however, the rules were sometimes bent. For example, Mary Musgrove Matthews, a woman of English and Creek ancestry, advised Georgia governor James Oglethorpe on Indian affairs.

Vocabulary Builder
domestic (doh MEHS tihk) *adj.* having to do with the home or household; pertaining to a country's internal affairs

---

Differentiated Instruction

L1 English Language Learners   **L1** Less Proficient Readers   **L1** Special Needs

Making Flashcards Have students make a list of the Key Terms and High-Use Words for this chapter. Then have them create flashcards with the word on one side and its definition on the other. Pair students with a partner, and have them quiz each other on the definitions of the words using the flashcards. Check their understanding as they continue to read the section.

● **INFOGRAPHIC**

COLONIAL WOMEN

Most women in colonial homes were required to handle a wide variety of tasks. In addition to domestic chores, women often worked in the fields along with the men. **Critical Thinking: *Compare and Contrast*** How might a woman's responsibilities differ if she lived in a town? *How might they be similar?*

History *Interactive*
Explore the Lives of Colonial Women
Visit: PHSchool.com
Web Code: mvl-1042

Running the Household
Women were responsible for running the household and caring for the children. Women were not permitted to vote and were not expected to take part in public affairs.

Preparing a Meal
In colonial times, preparing meals from scratch took a great deal of time and effort.

Making Clothes
Women's duties included making most of the clothes worn by their families. Among the gentry, women might wear fancier dresses sewed by professional seamstresses.

Milking the Cows ▶
Families that owned cows had fresh milk to use and sell.

Colonial butter churn ▶

109

History Background

Mary Musgrove Matthews, the daughter of an English trader and a Creek mother, played a key role in protecting Creek interests and maintaining peace in the Georgia frontier. She served as Oglethorpe's interpreter for 10 years, including during Oglethorpe's negotiations with Yamacraw chief Tomochichi. These negotiations led to the founding of Savannah.

Men, Women, and Children

p. 108

Instruction   L2

- Have students read Men, Women, and Children. Remind students to look for causes and effects.

- Read the letter from John Urmstone with students using the Choral Reading strategy (TE, p. T22). Ask: **What is the author's attitude toward work?** (*The author believes that hard work is necessary for the colonists to survive.*)

- Discuss the division of labor among men, women, and children in colonial times. Ask students to name examples of jobs performed by men (*carpentry, butchering meat, farming, representing the family publicly*), women (*childcare, cooking, laundry, and other tasks*) and young people (*household and farming chores*).

- Show the History Interactive Transparency Explore the Lives of Colonial Women. Ask: **What is one way that colonial women contributed to families' earnings?** (*by milking cows to sell the fresh milk*)

Color Transparencies, Explore the Lives of Colonial Women

Answer
Compare and Contrast Possible answer: She might sew or take in washing to earn money to buy milk, eggs, and other farm products instead of raising them herself. Many household chores such as cleaning and cooking would have been similar.

Seeing the Main Idea

Have students examine the image of children's dolls on this page. Ask: **What can you infer from the materials used to make dolls such as these?** (*The colonists used natural resources around them to make the things they needed or wanted.*)

Ask: **What can you infer from the costumes on the dolls?** (*The style of dress for women in colonial times reflected their social class and women's roles in society. The doll in the foreground is more elaborately dressed, and indicates a wealthier class.*)

Independent Practice

Have students continue to fill in the Study Guide for this section.

Interactive Reading and Notetaking Study Guide, Chapter 4, Section 2 (Adapted Version also available.)

Monitor Progress

As students fill in the Notetaking Study Guide, circulate to make sure students understand the importance of the division of labor in colonial times. If students do not seem to have a good understanding, have them reread the section. Provide assistance as needed.

Children's dolls were made from cornhusks or from more elaborate materials.

Vocabulary Builder
prospect (PRAHS pehkt)
n. expectation; something to look forward to happening

Young People If they survived infancy, colonial children had about seven years before they were required to work. In these years, they could pass the time playing. Children played many games that are still familiar. Marbles, hopscotch, leapfrog, and jump rope were all popular.

The toys colonial children played with were usually homemade. Girls enjoyed dolls made of cornhusks and scraps of cloth, while boys built houses of corncobs. Sometimes, a spinning top would be fashioned out of a bit of leftover wood and string. Children whose families were well-to-do had fine dolls and toy soldiers that were made in Europe.

By the age of seven, most children had work to do. They might do household or farm chores, or, if they were poor, they might become servants in other families. On farms, children were expected to fetch water and wood and to help in the kitchen and in the fields. Older children had greater responsibilities. Boys were expected to work the fields with their fathers, while girls labored beside their mothers learning how to run a house. Parents believed that tasks like these prepared children for adult life.

Boys who were learning trades, such as making shoes or building furniture, began as apprentices. An **apprentice** is someone who learns a trade by working for someone in that trade for a certain period of time. The apprentice would live in the home of a master artisan. At the end of his apprenticeship, the young man was prepared to work independently.

✓**Checkpoint** How did the jobs of boys and girls differ?

Social Classes

Many European colonists came to America hoping to build a better life than they could have in Europe. In England and other European countries, land was the main measure of wealth. Land in Europe, however, was in the hands of a relative few. America appeared to have land in abundance, offering immigrants the chance to own land. The possibility of owning land played a large part in the appeal of life in America.

In Europe, a person's prospects were determined by birth. Those who were born wealthy generally stayed wealthy. Those who were born poor had little opportunity to improve their station in life. By contrast, in colonial America there was more social equality among settlers—at least among white settlers. Still, there were many class distinctions.

The Gentry A group known as the gentry were the upper class of colonial society. The gentry included wealthy planters, merchants, ministers, royal officials, and successful lawyers. Prosperous artisans, like goldsmiths, were often considered gentry as well. The gentry were few in number, but they were the most powerful people. For example, in Virginia, some 50 plantation-owning families held most of the land and power.

Differentiated Instruction

L3 Advanced Readers   **L3 Gifted and Talented**

Describing Social Classes Using information from the text and additional research, have students write two paragraphs. The first paragraph should describe colonial life from the perspective of a member of the gentry. The second paragraph should describe colonial life from the perspective of a member of the lower class. After writing the paragraphs, have students share their work with the class. Then have students identify similarities and differences between the two experiences of colonial life.

Answer

✓**Checkpoint** Boys tended to do field work with men, and girls usually did housekeeping work alongside women. Boys sometimes also lived away from home as apprentices to learn a trade. Girls sometimes became servants in wealthy households.

In New York, wealthy Dutch estate owners lived in luxury. Their homes featured gold mirrors, clocks, richly carved furniture, and jewels. These things were far beyond the means of ordinary colonists.

Because many official jobs paid no salary, few but the gentry could afford to hold office. They felt that serving the community in public office was both their duty and their right, and most people agreed.

The Middle Class The great majority of colonists from Europe were what colonists called "the middling sort." Neither rich nor extremely poor, this middle class was made up of small planters, independent farmers, and artisans. Middle-class men could vote, and a few held office. This middle class was mostly white, but some of its members were of African descent. About 1 percent of African Americans were free during the colonial period.

The growth of the middle class gave the poor something to hope for and work for. The poor who were free might never be rich, but they could always maintain the hope that some day they would be middle class. In this way, the colonies were different from England and the rest of Europe. Not only could people move around the land, they could acquire property and move up the social scale.

Indentured Servants Lower on colonial America's social scale, and just above enslaved Africans, were farmhands and indentured servants. An indentured servant signed a contract to work from 4 to 10 years in the colonies for anyone who would pay for his or her ocean passage to the Americas. In the 1600s, most indentured servants came from England. In the 1700s, a growing number came from Ireland and Germany.

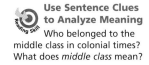 **Use Sentence Clues to Analyze Meaning** Who belonged to the middle class in colonial times? What does *middle class* mean?

Life Among the Gentry

The gentry lived a more comfortable life than most colonists. Servants attended to many of their needs. **Critical Thinking: Compare and Contrast** How do the comforts of the family in this picture compare to those of a middle-class family today?

Section 2 Colonial Society **111**

History Background

Social Class and Merchants Because the economies of the colonies grew by producing and exporting goods, merchants were among the highest social class. A merchant elite in Charleston, headed by three merchant families–the Pinckneys, Rutledges, and Lowndes–had social and political as well as economic power. In Virginia, which did not support a strong merchant class because of its focus on farming, those with the most political power were plantation farmers.

Social Classes

pp. 110–112

Instruction   L2

- Have students read Social Classes. Remind students to look for details to answer the Section Focus Question.

- Ask: **How were social classes in the Americas similar to and different from those in Europe?** (*Social classes existed and were important in both places, but in North America, there was more opportunity among white settlers to change classes.*)

- Discuss the system of indentured servitude with students. Ask: **Why might someone have chosen to become an indentured servant?** (*Possible answer: A poor person who wanted to start a new life in North America may have found that it was the only way to pay for the passage across the Atlantic Ocean. They were promised a land claim at the end of their term, so they would have the opportunity to begin anew and rise in wealth and social class.*)

Independent Practice

Have students complete the Study Guide for this section.

Interactive Reading and Notetaking Study Guide, Chapter 4, Section 2 (Adapted Version also available.)

Monitor Progress

- As students complete the Notetaking Study Guide, circulate to make sure students understand the importance of the protests in the colonies. Provide assistance as needed.

- Tell students to fill in the last column of the Reading Readiness Guide. Probe for what they learned that confirms or invalidates each statement.

All in One Teaching Resources, Unit 1, Reading Readiness Guide, p. 107

Answers

Reading Skill Small planters, independent farmers, and artisans belonged to the middle class. The term refers to people in the middle of the social and financial scales, those who are neither rich nor poor.

Compare and Contrast Possible answer: A middle class family today has access to many more technologies and goods that make their lives more comfortable, such as electricity and modern plumbing, but a middle class family today is unlikely to have servants as this family probably had.

Chapter 4 Section 2 **111**

Assess and Reteach

Assess Progress **L2**

Have students complete Check Your Progress. Administer the Section Quiz.

All in One Teaching Resources, Unit 1, Section Quiz, p. 116

To further assess student understanding, use the Progress Monitoring Transparency.

Progress Monitoring Transparencies, Chapter 4, Section 2

Reteach **L1**

If students need more instruction, have them read this section in the Interactive Reading and Notetaking Study Guide and complete the accompanying question.

 Interactive Reading and Notetaking Study Guide, Chapter 4, Section 2 (Adapted Version also available.)

Extend **L3**

To help students expand their understanding of the lives of colonial women, have them complete the History Interactive activity online.

Extend Online
For: History Interactive
Visit: PHSchool.com
Web Code: mvp-0126

Progress Monitoring Online

Students may check their comprehension of this section by completing the Progress Monitoring Online graphic organizer and self-quiz.

Answer

Checkpoint After completing a term as an indentured servant, one could build a successful farm, or one might be a merchant with a failing business who becomes an artisan.

Section 2 Check Your Progress

1. (a) Colonial children were expected to contribute to the work and train for the work they would do as adults.
(b) Today children work far less.

(c) Fewer children today live on farms, and labor saving devices are available to many people.

An indentured servant assists a colonial bricklayer.

During the time of service, indentured servants had few, if any, rights. They were bound to obey their masters, who could work them almost to death. Those who disobeyed or tried to run away risked being whipped or having time added to the service.

At the end of a term, an indentured servant received a set of clothes, tools, and 50 acres of land. About 1 indentured servant in 10 became a prosperous landowner. Another 1 in 10 became an artisan. The others either returned home to Europe or joined a class of landless, poor whites. The hardships they endured drove many poor whites to resent wealthy landowners.

Free African Americans Free people of African ancestry were never a large portion of the colonial population. By the time the first census was taken in 1790, there were nearly 60,000 free people of African ancestry, compared with more than 757,000 enslaved.

Free African Americans were allowed to own property, even in the South. This permitted them to become slaveholders. Some free blacks purchased relatives who were enslaved and set them free. Still, the lives of free African Americans were restricted. Most African American property owners were not allowed to vote or sit on juries.

☑ **Checkpoint** How might one become a member of the middle class?

⭐ **Looking Back and Ahead** Life in America offered more opportunities than did life in England. This was especially true for the poor and middle class. However, if indentured servants occupied the lowest level of white society in the English colonies, one group was even more disadvantaged. In the next section, you will look in detail at the enslaved Africans who were brought to America against their will.

Section 2 | **Check Your Progress**

Progress Monitoring Online
For: Self-test with instant help
Visit: PHSchool.com
Web Code: mva-1042

Comprehension and Critical Thinking

1. (a) Summarize Describe the responsibilities that children in colonial times were expected to meet.
(b) Link Past and Present How do these responsibilities differ from those of children today?
(c) Draw Conclusions How might you explain this difference?

2. (a) Recall Identify the social classes in colonial society.

(b) Apply Information Which two groups had the most privileges and opportunities? Which two groups had the least?

Reading Skill

3. Use Sentence Clues to Analyze Meaning Use sentence clues to analyze the meaning of *prospects* in the following sentence: In many countries, a person's *prospects* for success in life are determined by birth.

Key Terms

4. Write two definitions for each key term: extended family, apprentice, gentry, middle class, indentured servant. First, write a formal definition for your teacher. Second, write a casual definition for a classmate.

Writing

5. Write a paragraph describing the importance of work in colonial society.

---

2. (a) The gentry, the middle class, indentured servants, and free African Americans
(b) The gentry and middle class had the greatest privileges while the indentured servants and free African Americans had the least.

3. The sentence is describing the factors that allow a person to become successful, so *prospects* is likely a synonym for *chances.*

4. Definitions should show an understanding of the terms.

5. Answers will vary, but should explain that survival depended on work and that opportunity in colonial working life was uneven.

Those Who Shall Be Whipped

❝Be it enacted . . . that every . . . Negro or slave that shall be taken hereafter out of his master's plantation, without a ticket, or leave in writing, from his master or mistress . . . shall be whipped.❞

—South Carolina slave law, 1712

◄ Enslaved people were brought to the West African coast for shipment to the Americas.

Slavery in the Colonies

Objectives
- Describe the conditions under which enslaved Africans came to the Americas.
- Explain why slavery became part of the colonial economy.
- Identify the restrictions placed on enslaved Africans in the colonies.
- Describe how African culture influenced American culture.

🔵 Reading Skill

Use Paragraph Clues to Analyze Meaning When you encounter an unfamiliar word, read the nearby sentences for clues. You may find clues in examples or descriptions. Sometimes a nearby sentence includes a contrast clue to what the word *does not* mean.

Key Terms
triangular trade   slave code
racism

Why It Matters Spanish and Portuguese settlers were the first to bring Africans to the Americas as a source of slave labor. Slavery spread to the colonies of other European countries. Millions of Africans were transported to the colonies against their will.

❷ **Section Focus Question: How did slavery develop in the colonies and affect colonial life?**

The Atlantic Slave Trade

Some scholars estimate that more than 10 million enslaved Africans were transported to the Americas between the 1500s and the 1800s. The Spanish and Portuguese brought the first Africans to the Americas. The British, Dutch, and French also entered the slave trade. In time, English colonists—especially from New England—were actively shipping enslaved Africans across the Atlantic.

Slave traders set up posts along the West African coast. Africans who lived along the coast made raids into the interior, seeking captives to sell to the Europeans. Bound at the leg and neck, captives were forced to march as far as 300 miles to the coast. Half of these captives died along the way.

Middle Passage Once they arrived at the coasts, captives were traded for guns and other goods. They were then loaded onto slave ships and transported across the Atlantic on a brutal voyage that became known as the Middle Passage.

To increase their profits, some slave-ship captains crammed the maximum number of captives on board. As many as 350 people might be bound together in a tiny space below deck, without light or air. Other captains provided better conditions, in the hope that more captives would survive in good health and fetch a higher price.

Section 3 Slavery in the Colonies 113

Vocabulary Builder

Use the information below to teach students this section's high-use words.

High-Use Word	Definition and Sample Sentence
temporary, p. 115	*adj.* not permanent Indentured servants worked for planters for a limited number of years on a **temporary** basis.
revolt, p. 116	*v.* to rebel; to participate in an uprising Slave owners feared that angry slaves might **revolt** against their enslavement.

Review and Preview

Students have read about economic growth in the colonies. Now they will read about the development of slavery in the English colonies and its effect on colonial life.

Section Focus Question

How did slavery develop in the colonies and affect colonial life?

Before you begin the lesson for the day, write the Section Focus Question on the board. (*Lesson focus: Slavery started as a way to provide labor, especially on plantations. It became restricted to Africans; and developed into a system in which slaves and their descendents were bound for life.*)

Prepare to Read

Build Background Knowledge L2

Remind students that they read in Chapter 2 about the use of Africans as slaves by the Spanish. Ask them to recall why the Spanish began importing enslaved Africans (*There was a labor shortage in the Spanish colonies*). Then have students predict the reasons for the development of slavery in the English colonies. Address any misconceptions that students may have. Remind them to confirm or revise their predictions after they read the section. Use the Give One, Get One strategy (TE, p. T25) to encourage discussion.

Set a Purpose L2

- Form students into pairs or groups of four. Distribute the Reading Readiness Guide. Ask students to fill in the first two columns of the chart.

  All in One Teaching Resources, Unit 1, Reading Readiness Guide, p. 108

- Use the Numbered Heads participation strategy (TE, p. T24) to call on students to share one piece of information they already know and one piece they want to know. The students will return to these worksheets later.

Teach

The Atlantic Slave Trade
p. 113

Instruction   L2

- **Vocabulary Builder** Before teaching this lesson, preteach the High-Use Words **temporary** and **revolt,** using the strategy on TE p. 101.

  Key Terms Following the instruction on p. 7, have students continue to fill in the See It–Remember It chart for the Key Terms in this chapter.

- Read The Atlantic Slave Trade with students using the Oral Cloze strategy (TE, p. T22).

- Discuss the map of the Atlantic Slave Trade with students. Ask: **What percentage of Africans were destined for British America?** (*4.5 percent*)

- Have students complete the worksheet The Middle Passage. Ask: **Why did plantation owners use enslaved people to do their farmwork?** (*Slaves were not paid for their work. They did it to save money.*)

  All in One **Teaching Resources, Unit 1,** The Middle Passage, p. 111

- Show the transparency The Atlantic Slave Trade.

Color Transparencies, The Atlantic Slave Trade

Independent Practice

Have students begin to fill in the Study Guide for this section.

Monitor Progress

As students fill in the Notetaking Study Guide, circulate to make sure students understand the significance of the Middle Passage. Provide assistance as needed.

Answers

MAP MASTER Skills Activity **(a)** British slave trade was less extensive than that of the Spanish and Portuguese. **(b)** The slave trade probably hurt Africa because it caused disruption of African societies.

Reading Skill Possible answer: The sentences describe suffering that is so horrible it is difficult to image. *Inconceivable* probably means difficult to imagine.

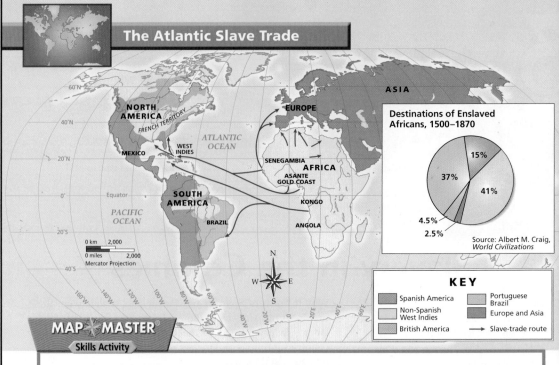

The Atlantic Slave Trade

Destinations of Enslaved Africans, 1500–1870

- 15%
- 37%
- 41%
- 4.5%
- 2.5%

Source: Albert M. Craig, *World Civilizations*

KEY

- Spanish America
- Non-Spanish West Indies
- British America
- Portuguese Brazil
- Europe and Asia
- → Slave-trade route

MAP MASTER®
Skills Activity

The slave trade linked the Americas with Europe and western Africa.

(a) **Evaluate Information** How did British trade in slaves compare to that of the Spanish and Portuguese?

(b) **Identify Costs** Did the slave trade help or hurt western Africa? Explain your reasoning.

MapMaster Online

For: Interactive map
Visit: PHSchool.com
Web Code: mvp-1043

Use Paragraph Clues to Analyze Meaning
Use the quoted paragraph's description and examples of *inconceivable* to analyze the word's meaning.

Olaudah Equiano told of being captured in western Africa when he was a boy. He later described the conditions aboard a slave ship:

"The closeness of the place, and the heat of the climate, added to the number in the ship, which was so crowded that each had scarcely room to turn himself, almost suffocated us. . . . The shrieks of the women, and the groans of the dying, rendered the whole a scene of horror almost inconceivable."

—The Interesting Narrative of the Life of Olaudah Equiano

As a result of such conditions, from 15 to 20 percent of enslaved Africans died or committed suicide during the Middle Passage.

Once slave ships reached the Americas, healthy men, women, and children were put on the auction block. They might be sold one by one or in groups. Family members were often separated at this stage. The vast majority of those sold ended up on plantations in the Spanish colonies, Brazil, or the Caribbean. (See the pie chart above.) But for some 500,000 enslaved Africans, their final destination was British North America.

114 Chapter 4 Life in the Colonies

Differentiated Instruction

L3 **Advanced Readers**   **L3** **Gifted and Talented**

Give a Biographical Presentation Have students read a biography of Olaudah Equiano, such as *The Kidnapped Prince: The Life of Olaudah Equiano* by Ann Cameron.

Then have students give a short presentation to the class about the Equiano's life and his efforts to end the slave trade.

Triangular Trade By about 1700, slave traders in the British colonies had developed a regular routine, known as the triangular trade. The triangular trade was a three-way trade between the colonies, the islands of the Caribbean, and Africa.

On the first leg of the three-leg voyage, ships from New England carried fish, lumber, and other goods to the Caribbean islands, or West Indies. There, Yankee traders bought sugar and molasses, a dark syrup made from sugar cane. The ships then sailed back to New England, where colonists used the molasses and sugar to make rum.

On the second leg, ships carried rum, guns, and other goods from New England to West Africa. There, merchants traded the goods for enslaved Africans. On the final leg, ships carried their human cargo to the West Indies for sale. With the profits from selling enslaved Africans, traders bought more molasses.

Many New England merchants grew wealthy from the triangular trade. In doing so, they often disobeyed the Navigation Acts, which required them to buy only from English colonies. Because demand for molasses was so high, traders also made purchases from other European colonies in the West Indies. They then smuggled their cargoes into New England.

☑ **Checkpoint** What was the Middle Passage?

Slavery in the Colonies

Slavery had existed since ancient times. However, in many cultures, slavery was not for life. In some early Christian societies, for example, slaves were freed if they became Christians. In many African societies, people captured in war were often enslaved for only a few years. Then, they were freed and became full members of the community. In the Americas, however, a harsher system of slavery developed over time.

Slavery Takes Root The first Africans who reached Jamestown may have been treated as servants. But by the late 1600s, ships were bringing growing numbers of enslaved Africans.

Why did slavery take root? One reason was the plantation system. The profits that could be made from tobacco and rice led planters to import thousands of enslaved Africans to work the fields. The southern economy came to depend on slavery.

Planters preferred slaves over servants. Indentured servants were <u>temporary</u>. Once their terms were over, they could go. Also, as conditions improved in England, fewer servants came to America.

Enslaved for Life As the need for cheap labor grew, colonies made slavery permanent. In 1639, Maryland passed a law stating that baptism did not lead to liberty. This meant people could be enslaved for life. In 1663, a Virginia court held that any child born to a slave was a slave too.

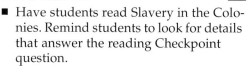

An advertisement for a colonial slave auction

Vocabulary Builder
temporary (TEM poh rehr ee)
adj. not permanent

History Background

Origin of Slave Trade in the English Colonies The slave trade in the English colonies had its roots in the early struggles of the Jamestown settlement in the colony of Virginia. After several years of hardship, Jamestown began to have some prosperity when it began farming tobacco as a cash crop for export in 1612. The trade in tobacco boomed over the next decade, but the small colony needed additional workers to maximize exports and profit. In 1619, a Dutch ship brought to Jamestown 20 captured Africans who would work in Virginia's tobacco fields. It was the first of many such shipments to North America during the following 200 years.

Slavery in the Colonies
p. 115

Instruction   L2

- Have students read Slavery in the Colonies. Remind students to look for details that answer the reading Checkpoint question.

- Discuss the unique character of slavery in the Americas. Ask: **How was slavery in the Americas different from other forms of slavery?** (*Slaves in the Americas were bound for life, their children were born as slaves, and slavery was linked to ideas about racial superiority.*)

- Discuss with students the advertisement for a colonial slave auction (p. 115). If necessary, read the text aloud to help students decipher the archaic script. Ask students to recall what they learned in Section 1 about English ideas about rights and freedoms since the Magna Carta. Then lead a discussion about the contrast between those ideas and the ideas about rights reflected in the advertisement. Use the Think-Write-Pair-Share strategy (TE, p. T25) to elicit responses.

- Assign the worksheet Slave Codes. Ask: **Why were there so many restrictions on the activities of slaves?** (*Owners feared that slaves would organize revolts.*)

  All in One **Teaching Resources, Unit 1,** Slave Codes, p. 112

Independent Practice
Have students continue to fill in the Study Guide for this section.

Interactive Reading and Notetaking Study Guide, Chapter 4, Section 3 (Adapted Version also available.)

Monitor Progress

As students fill in the Notetaking Study Guide, circulate to make sure students understand the importance of slavery's development in British America. If students do not seem to have a good understanding, have them reread the section. Provide assistance as needed.

Answer

☑ **Checkpoint** the brutal voyage that carried captured people across the Atlantic from the West African coast to slavery in the Americas

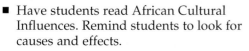

Explore More Video

Discovery School Video
Show the video *Life of Enslaved Africans* to tell the story of the Atlantic slave trade, the dangers of the Middle Passage, and the harsh treatment of slaves in the Americas.

African Cultural Influences

p. 117

Instruction L2

- Have students read African Cultural Influences. Remind students to look for causes and effects.

- Tell students that people captured in West Africa and sold into slavery came from many regions and spoke numerous languages. Ask: **What factors might lead Africans to develop a language such as Gullah?** (*They needed a way to communicate with each other and understand the instructions of the whites for whom they worked.*)

Independent Practice

Have students complete the Study Guide for this section.

Interactive Reading and Notetaking Study Guide, Chapter 4, Section 3 (Adapted Version also available.)

Monitor Progress

- As students complete the Notetaking Study Guide, circulate to make sure students understand the importance of African Cultural Influences. Provide assistance as needed.

- Tell students to fill in the last column of the Reading Readiness Guide. Ask them to evaluate if what they learned was what they had expected to learn.

All in One Teaching Resources, Unit 1, Reading Readiness Guide, p. 108

Answers

Draw Conclusions Cultivating these crops required many people to perform manual labor. Enslaved Africans were imported in increasing numbers to meet the need for labor on large plantations.

Checkpoint The slave codes were designed to restrict travel and communication among enslaved people. The codes were intended to prevent slave revolts.

Explore More Video
To learn more about slavery in the colonies, view the video.

Slave Labor Preparing tobacco was one of the tasks performed by enslaved workers at a Virginia plantation in the 1700s. *Critical Thinking: Draw Conclusions How did the cultivation of crops such as tobacco and rice encourage the growth of slavery in North America?*

Vocabulary Builder
revolt (ree VOHLT) **v.** to rebel; to participate in an uprising

Early on, there were attempts to stop slavery. In 1652, Rhode Island passed the first antislavery law. However, it did not survive long, because Rhode Island shippers made high profits from the slave trade. Georgia had a ban on slavery until the 1750s and then lifted it. Slavery became legal in all the colonies.

Not every African in America was a slave, but slavery came to be restricted to people of African descent. Thus, slavery was linked to racism. **Racism** is the belief that one race is superior or inferior to another. Most English colonists believed themselves superior to Africans. Also, some colonists believed that they were helping Africans by introducing them to Christianity and European ways.

Resistance to Slavery As the number of enslaved people grew, whites began to worry that they would <u>revolt</u>. The first serious slave revolt took place in 1663, in Gloucester, Virginia. The rebels were betrayed, probably by an indentured servant, and the uprising failed. Soon, other revolts occurred in Connecticut and Virginia.

Fearing more trouble, colonial authorities wrote **slave codes,** or strict laws that restricted the rights and activities of slaves. Under the codes, enslaved people could not meet in large numbers, own weapons, or leave a plantation without permission. It also became illegal to teach enslaved people to read and write. Masters who killed enslaved people could not be tried for murder. Slave codes gave masters more control over enslaved Africans. It also made it harder for escaped slaves to survive.

The new laws did not stop resistance. In 1739, an enslaved Angolan named Jemmy led a revolt in South Carolina. He and his followers killed more than 20 whites before they were defeated. Revolts continued to flare up until slavery itself ended in 1865.

Checkpoint What was the purpose of slave codes?

Differentiated Instruction

L1 English Language Learners   **L1 Less Proficient Readers**   **L1 Special Needs**

Unfamiliar Words Suggest to students that they use a ruler to help them keep their place on a page as they read. Have students mark unfamiliar words or phrases (such as *flare up* on this page) with sticky notes. Periodically review with students the words and phrases they have marked.

African Cultural Influences

The lives of enslaved Africans differed greatly from colony to colony. Only 10 percent of the enslaved population lived north of Maryland. In cities of the North, they were often hired out to work as blacksmiths or house servants. On small farms, they might work alongside the owner. Over time, they might buy their freedom.

Even in the South, the lives of enslaved Africans varied. On rice plantations in South Carolina, Africans saw few white colonists. As a result, more than any other enslaved Africans, these workers kept the customs of West Africa. They reproduced the African grass baskets used to sift rice. They spoke Gullah, a special dialect that was created on the west coast of Africa during slave times. This dialect blended English and several African languages. Even today, some residents of the coastal South speak Gullah.

Enslaved Africans in colonies, such as Virginia and Maryland, were less isolated from white society. Still, many African customs survived. Craftsworkers in cities used African styles to create fine quilts, furniture, carved walking sticks, and other objects. The rhythm of drums used for communication by Africans found its way into American music. The banjo came from Africa as well. African folk tales became a part of American culture.

✓Checkpoint **What cultural influences did Africans bring to America?**

⭐ **Looking Back and Ahead** In this section, we have seen how millions of Africans were transported to the colonies against their will. In the next section, we shall see how education and religion developed in colonial America.

African-style banjo from the 1700s

Section 3 | Check Your Progress

Progress Monitoring Online
For: Self-test with instant help
Visit: PHSchool.com
Web Code: mva-1043

Comprehension and Critical Thinking

1. (a) Recall Why did fewer indentured servants come to America in the 1700s?
(b) Analyze Cause and Effect How did the plantation system and the lack of indentured servants affect the status of Africans in America?

2. (a) Identify Why did the Gullah dialect appear in South Carolina?
(b) Compare and Contrast In general, how did the experience of enslaved Africans in the North differ from that of enslaved Africans in the South?

Reading Skill

3. Use Paragraph Clues to Analyze Meaning Some paragraphs give you examples and descriptions of unfamiliar words. Reread the second paragraph under the heading "African Cultural Influences." Use paragraph clues to explain the meaning of *dialect* in that context. Explain the clues you used.

Key Terms

Answer the following questions in complete sentences that show your understanding of the key terms.
4. What was triangular trade?

5. How did racism affect the status of Africans in America?
6. Why did white colonists create slave codes?

Writing

7. Create an outline for an essay that discusses the geographic and economic factors that resulted in some colonies using slave labor more than other colonies.

Section 3 Slavery in the Colonies **117**

Section 3 Check Your Progress

1. (a) Conditions in England were improving.
(b) These factors made their labor more valuable and increased efforts to control them legally through laws such as the slave codes.

2. (a) Enslaved people from different regions who spoke different languages needed a way to communicate with each other.
(b) Enslaved Africans in the South were much more likely to work on plantations and be enslaved for life, while slaves in the North typically worked in trades and had some opportunity to buy their freedom.

3. Possible answer: Dialect means a way of speaking that doesn't match any one language. Clues include that Gullah is a dialect and is a mixture of several languages.

4. Trade between North America, the Caribbean, and Africa in which certain goods were shipped between each of the points in exchange for other goods

5. Racism hurt the status of Africans in America because it helped Europeans justify to themselves the enslavement of Africans.

6. White colonists created slave codes to reduce the chances of slave revolts.

7. Answers will vary, but should address economic and geographical factors.

Section 4

Review and Preview

In the previous section, students learned how slavery developed and how it affected the colonies. In this section, students will read about the effect of new ideas in education, art, religion, and politics on life in the colonies.

Study Diligently

"Apply yourself, without delay, to the study of the law of nature. I would recommend to your perusal, Grotius, Puffendorf, Locke, Montesquieu, and Burlemaqui.... If you attend, diligently, to these [writers], you will not require any other."

—Alexander Hamilton, praising Enlightenment thinkers, 1775

◀ Harvard College, in Massachusetts, was the first college in the colonies.

Section Focus Question

How did ideas about religion and government influence colonial life?

Before you begin the lesson for the day, write the Section Focus Question on the board. (*Lesson focus: New ideas about religion and government strengthened democratic ideas among the colonists.*)

Prepare to Read

Build Background Knowledge   L2

Ask students to recall what they learned in Section 1 of this chapter about the development of rights in England from the Magna Carta to the English Bill of Rights. Then ask students to preview the section by reading the headings and looking at the images. Ask students to predict what they will learn about the spread of new ideas in the colonies. Use the Numbered Heads participation strategy (TE, p. T24) to elicit responses.

Set a Purpose   L2

■ Read each statement in the Reading Readiness Guide aloud. Ask students to mark the statements True or False.

   All in One Teaching Resources, Unit 1, Reading Readiness Guide, p. 109

■ Have students discuss the statements in pairs or groups of four, then mark the worksheets again. Use the Numbered Heads participation strategy (TE, p. T24) to call on students. The students will return to these worksheets later.

The Spread of New Ideas

Objectives

- Describe the education colonial children received.
- Summarize the development of poetry and literature in colonial America.
- Explain how the Great Awakening affected the colonies.
- Explain how the colonies were affected by the spread of new ideas.

🔊 Reading Skill

Use Context to Determine Meanings When the clues you have tried do not work, broaden the context. Where else might you have encountered this word? Do you remember it from films or books? Was it defined in previous sections? Can you find examples of it elsewhere? Finally, imagine yourself in a situation like the one in which the word appears.

Key Terms and People

public school	Jonathan Edwards
dame school	natural rights
Anne Bradstreet	divine right
Phillis Wheatley	separation of
Benjamin Franklin	powers

Why It Matters You have learned how English colonists shared certain cultural characteristics. In the 1700s, new ideas had a lasting impact on the colonists' thinking.

❓ Section Focus Question: How did ideas about religion and government influence colonial life?

The Importance of Education

To Puritans, education went hand in hand with religion. In early New England, everyone was expected to read the Bible.

Puritan Beginnings The Puritans passed laws to promote education. They required parents to teach their children and servants to read. Another law required every town with at least 50 families to start an elementary school. Every town with 100 families had to have a grammar school for older students.

These Massachusetts laws were the beginning of public schools in America. A **public school** is a school supported by taxes. Puritan schools were very different from the public schools of today, however. Puritan schools were run with both private and public money. In addition, Puritan education laws were not completely compulsory. Some towns paid a fine rather than set up a school. Laws that required all children to attend school did not begin until the late 1800s.

Colonial Schools Another difference between colonial schools and modern public schools is that colonial schools included instruction in religion. Most schools in the 1600s were under

Differentiated Instruction

L1 Less Proficient Readers   **L1 Special Needs**

Comprehension Aids Before reading the section, have students go through it and write down each heading to create an outline. As they read, have them jot down important words, concepts, people they want to remember, or questions they may have about the content under each heading. Check with students to see what questions they have. Encourage them to try to answer questions on their own before asking for help from you.

religious sponsorship. Schools in New Netherland (later New York) were run by the Dutch Reformed Church. Pennsylvania schools were run by the Quakers.

In addition to religion, colonial elementary schools taught basic skills such as reading, writing, and arithmetic. Many students learned lessons from a hornbook, a paddle-shaped board with a printed lesson on top, protected by a transparent piece of animal horn. The hornbook might have the ABCs, the Roman numerals, and the Lord's Prayer so that children could copy and memorize them. A reading book called the *New England Primer*, first published in the 1680s, became widely used.

In the South, people were separated by great distances, so there were few schools. Members of the gentry often hired private tutors to instruct their children. Children from poorer families often received no formal education at all.

Some colonial elementary schools admitted girls. Others taught them only in summers or when boys were not in school. Girls might also attend **dame schools**, schools that women opened in their homes to teach girls and boys to read and write.

Education for African Americans Most colonial schools were restricted to white children. However, in New York, an Anglican church group ran a school for free African Americans, as well as for Native Americans and poor whites.

Some Quaker and Anglican missionaries taught enslaved people to read. After slave codes in the South outlawed this, some enslaved people passed along their learning in secret. Still others taught themselves from stolen or borrowed books.

Colonial Education
Young children were often educated in dame schools, such as the one shown. **Critical Thinking: Evaluate Information** Look at the page from the New England Primer, *below. What kinds of lessons does it include?*

Now the Child being entred in his Letters and Spelling, let him learn thefe and fuch like Sentences by Heart, whereby he will be both inftructed in his Duty, and encouraged in his Learning.

The Dutiful Child's Promifes.

I Will fear GOD, and honour the KING.
I will honour my Father & Mother.
I will Obey my Superiours.
I will Submit to my Elders.
I will Love my Friends.
I will hate no Man.
I will forgive my Enemies, and pray to God for them.
I will as much as in me lies keep all God's Holy Commandments.

Hornbook ▶

▲ Page from the the *New England Primer*

119

Teach

The Importance of Education
p. 118

Instruction L2

- **Vocabulary Builder** Before teaching this lesson, preteach the High-Use Words **finance** and **reinforce**, using the strategy on TE p. 101.

  Key Terms Following the instruction on p. 7, have students complete the See It– Remember It chart for the Key Terms in this chapter.

- Read The Importance of Education with students using the Idea Wave participation strategy (TE, p. T24).

- Ask: **What effect have Puritan ideas about education had on the United States today?** (*The Puritans' commitment to education led to our modern system of public schools.*)

- Ask: **How did religion influence education in the colonies? Give at least two examples.** (*Most colonial schools were sponsored by religious groups. The Dutch Reformed Church operated schools in New York and Quakers operated schools in Pennsylvania.*)

Independent Practice
Have students begin to fill in the Study Guide for this section.

📖 **Interactive Reading and Notetaking Study Guide,** Chapter 4, Section 4 (Adapted Version also available.)

Monitor Progress

As students fill in the Notetaking Study Guide, circulate to make sure students understand the importance of education in the colonies. If students do not seem to have a good understanding, have them reread the section. Provide assistance as needed.

Vocabulary Builder

Use the information below to teach students this section's high-use words.

High-Use Word	Definition and Sample Sentence
finance, p. 120	*v.* to supply with money; to manage monetary situations People often seek a bank loan to **finance** the purchase of a home.
reinforce, p. 122	*v.* to make stronger; to strengthen; to make more effective The army **reinforced** its defenses in anticipation of an attack.

Answer
Evaluate Information Moral and religious lessons

Roots of American Literature

p. 120

Instruction L2

- Have students read Roots of American Literature. Remind students to look for details that answer the Section Focus Question.

- Ask: **About what subjects did Boston poet Anne Bradstreet write?** (*She wrote about life in Puritan New England.*)

- Ask: **What does the reading suggest about Benjamin Franklin's ability to influence public opinion in the colonies?** (*Possible answer: He was influential because he published well-known books and the colonies' most widely read newspaper.*)

Independent Practice

Have students continue to fill in the Study Guide for this section.

Interactive Reading and Notetaking Study Guide, Chapter 4, Section 4 (Adapted Version also available.)

Monitor Progress

As students fill in the Notetaking Study Guide, circulate to make sure students understand the importance of early American literature. If students do not seem to have a good understanding, have them reread the section. Provide assistance as needed.

Answers

☑**Checkpoint** Boys received more education than girls and studied a wider variety of subjects.

☑**Checkpoint** He published a newspaper, an almanac, and a popular autobiography.

Biography Quest Washington invited Phillis Wheatley to meet him in Cambridge, Massachusetts. They met and spent half an hour together.

120 Chapter 4

Vocabulary Builder
finance (fī nans) **v.** to supply with money; to manage monetary situations

Upper Levels After elementary school, some boys went on to grammar school. Grammar schools were similar to modern high schools. They prepared boys for college. Students learned Greek and Latin, as well as geography, mathematics, and English composition.

The first American colleges were founded largely to educate men for the ministry. The Puritan general council <u>financed</u> what became Harvard College. Opening in 1638, Harvard was the first college in the English colonies. In 1693, colonists in Virginia founded the College of William and Mary, the first college in the South.

☑**Checkpoint** How did education differ for girls and boys?

Roots of American Literature

The earliest forms of colonial literature were sermons and histories. Books such as John Smith's *General History of Virginia* and William Bradford's *Of Plymouth Plantation* provided lively accounts of life in the first colonies.

Poetry The first colonial poet was Anne Bradstreet. Her book *The Tenth Muse, Lately Sprung Up in America* was first published in 1650, in England. It was not published in Boston until after her death. Bradstreet's poems, such as "Upon the Burning of Our House" and "To My Dear and Loving Husband," expressed the joys and hardships of life in Puritan New England.

A later poet, Phillis Wheatley, was an enslaved African in Boston. Her first poem was published in the 1760s, when she was about 14. Her works were in a scholarly style that was then popular in Europe.

Ben Franklin Perhaps the best-loved colonial writer was Benjamin Franklin. At age 17, Ben moved from Boston to Philadelphia and started a newspaper, the *Pennsylvania Gazette*. It became the most widely read newspaper in the colonies.

Franklin's most popular work was *Poor Richard's Almanack,* published every year from 1733 to 1753. The *Almanack* was full of pithy sayings that usually had a moral. These included "Eat to live, not live to eat" and "God helps them who help themselves." Franklin also published a vivid autobiography.

Franklin was far more than a writer. He was a businessman, community leader, scientist, inventor, and diplomat. He founded a library and a fire department, made discoveries about electricity, and invented such useful items as bifocal eyeglasses and a stove. As you will see, he also became one of the founders of the United States.

☑**Checkpoint** How did Ben Franklin contribute to American literature?

Biography Quest

Phillis Wheatley
1753?–1784

When she was eight, Phillis Wheatley was captured by slave traders in Africa and sent to Boston. But she was luckier than most enslaved Africans. The family she worked for educated her and gave her time to write.

Wheatley won fame as a poet and later gained her freedom. Sadly, her last years were full of hardship. She is recognized today as America's first poet of African descent.

Biography Quest

How did Wheatley meet George Washington?

For: The answer to the question about Wheatley

Visit: PHSchool.com

Web Code: mvd-1044

Differentiated Instruction

L3 **Advanced Readers**   L3 **Gifted and Talented**

Creating an Introductory Pamphlet Have students research a writer from colonial America and create an informational pamphlet that might introduce the writer to a new audience. The pamphlet should include general information about the writer's life, as well as a list of suggested readings by the author that the student would recommend. Ask students to share their favorite quotation and explain their choice.

The Great Awakening

From the start, religion played a critical role in the 13 English colonies. In Plymouth and Massachusetts Bay, religious leaders set extensive rules on moral and religious matters. Even in colonies that were founded primarily for economic reasons, such as Jamestown, early laws required colonists to attend church regularly.

By the 1700s, rules on religion had become less strict in many of the colonies. The Puritan tradition gradually declined in New England. Still, churches remained centers of faith and community life in all of the colonies.

Religious Revival An emotion-packed Christian movement swept through the colonies in the 1730s and 1740s. This period of religious revival is called the Great Awakening. The Great Awakening began as a reaction against what some Christians saw as a decline of religious zeal in the colonies. Leaders such as Massachusetts preacher Jonathan Edwards called on people to examine their lives and commit themselves to God. In a famous sermon, Edwards warned sinners what would happen to them after they died unless they changed their ways and sought forgiveness:

> ❝The God that holds you over the pit of hell, much as one holds a spider, or some loathesome insect, over a fire, abhors you, and is dreadfully provoked; his wrath towards you burns like fire; he looks upon you as worthy of nothing else, but to be cast into the fire.❞
> —Jonathan Edwards, Sinners in the Hands of an Angry God

Forceful preachers quickly spread the Great Awakening throughout the colonies. George Whitefield, an English minister, made several tours of the colonies. His listeners often wept with emotion. After a Whitefield visit to Philadelphia, Benjamin Franklin observed that "one could not walk thro' the Town in an Evening without Hearing Psalms sung in different Families of every Street."

Impact of the Great Awakening The Great Awakening led to the rise of many new churches. Methodists and Baptists, which had been small sects or groups, grew quickly. The Presbyterian, Dutch Reformed, and Congregationalist churches split between those who followed the new movement and those who did not. In time, the growth of new churches led to more tolerance of religious differences in the colonies.

 Use Context to Determine Meaning Use the clues in the surrounding sentences and your own knowledge about colonial life to determine the meaning of the word *extensive*.

Religious Awakening
Traveling preachers, such as English evangelist George Whitefield (below), provoked a broad religious revival in the 1730s and 1740s. **Critical Thinking: Draw Conclusions** *Why might the Great Awakening have unsettled many prominent church leaders of the time?*

History Background

Jonathan Edwards Jonathan Edwards was born in East Windsor, Conn., in 1703 and enrolled at Yale College at the age of 13. Following in his father's footsteps, Edwards studied divinity and became a pastor in New York before moving to Northampton, an influential pulpit in Massachusetts. His developing religious ideas caused conflicts with his own congregation, which dismissed him in 1750.

The Great Awakening
p. 121

Instruction

- Have students read The Great Awakening. Remind students to look for causes and effects.
- Ask: **What was the goal of the Great Awakening?** (*to revive religious feeling*)
- Ask: **How did the Great Awakening contribute to increased tolerance of religious differences in the colonies?** (*The number of churches with different kinds of services increased, and this diversity fostered toleration of differences.*)

Independent Practice

Have students continue to fill in the Study Guide for this section.

📖 **Interactive Reading and Notetaking Study Guide,** Chapter 4, Section 4 (Adapted Version also available.)

Monitor Progress

As students fill in the Notetaking Study Guide, circulate to make sure students understand the importance of the Great Awakening. If students do not seem to have a good understanding, have them reread the section. Provide assistance as needed.

Answers

Reading Skill The passage states that leaders set rules for moral and religious matters. They also made laws about education and other issues. *Extensive* means wide-ranging.

Draw Conclusions Possible answer: The Great Awakening probably upset prominent church leaders of the time because it led to the rise of many new churches and the rapid growth of smaller existing churches, changes which threatened the influence of major established churches.

The Enlightenment

p. 122

Instruction L2

- Have students read The Enlightenment. Remind students to look for details that answer the Section Focus Question.

- Ask: **What rights did people have under an absolute monarch?** (*only those given to them by the monarch*)

- Ask: **How did Locke's idea of natural rights challenge the power of the monarchy?** (*Natural rights were birthrights and could justify overthrowing a monarch who denied people's rights.*)

- Have students discuss how the separation of powers suggested by Montesquieu would protect the natural rights that Locke described. (*No one group would have enough power to violate people's rights.*)

Independent Practice

Have students complete the Study Guide for this section.

📖 **Interactive Reading and Notetaking Study Guide,** Chapter 4, Section 4 (Adapted Version also available.)

Monitor Progress

- As students complete the Notetaking Study Guide, circulate to make sure students understand the importance of Enlightenment ideas. Provide assistance as needed.

- Tell students to fill in the last column of the Reading Readiness Guide. Probe for what they learned that confirms or invalidates each statement.

- Have students go back to their Word Knowledge Rating Form. Rerate their word knowledge and complete the last column with an example.

All in One **Teaching Resources, Unit 1,** Reading Readiness Guide, p. 109; Word Knowledge Rating Form, p. 105

Answers

Reading Charts (a) Natural Rights (b) Locke's view; colonists had a yearning for self-government

✓**Checkpoint** The Great Awakening reinforced democratic ideas by encouraging people to make their own decisions about religion and politics.

Divine Right Versus Natural Rights

	Divine Right 👑	Natural Rights 👥
Where does the right to govern come from?	From God to the ruler	From the people
Where do people's rights come from?	From the ruler	From God to the people
What happens if a government violates people's rights?	People must obey ruler	People can change their government

Reading Charts
Skills Activity

Did the right to rule come from the will of God or from the people? The answer to this question would alter the course of history in nations around the world.

(a) **Read a Chart** Which column represents the views of John Locke?
(b) **Draw Conclusions** Which of those views would be most attractive to the American colonists? Explain.

Vocabulary Builder
<u>reinforce</u> (ree ihn FORS) *v.* to make stronger; to strengthen; to make more effective

The Great Awakening was one of the first national movements in the colonies. It <u>reinforced</u> democratic ideas. People thought that if they could decide on their own how to worship God, they could decide how to govern themselves.

✓**Checkpoint** **How did the Great Awakening affect American society?**

The Enlightenment

Starting in the late 1600s, a group of European thinkers came to believe that all problems could be solved by human reason. They ushered in a new intellectual movement that became known as the Enlightenment. Enlightenment thinkers looked for "natural laws" that governed politics, society, and economics. The Enlightenment reached its height in France in the mid-1700s. However, some of its key ideas came from an Englishman, John Locke.

Locke In 1690, Locke published *Two Treatises on Government*. In this influential work, Locke argued that people have certain **natural rights**, that is, rights that belong to every human being from birth. These rights include life, liberty, and property. According to Locke, these rights are inalienable, meaning that they cannot be taken away.

Locke challenged the idea of divine right. **Divine right** is the belief that monarchs get their authority to rule directly from God. According to this belief, any rights that people have come to them from the monarch. By contrast, Locke stated that natural rights came from God. He argued that people formed governments in order to protect their rights. They give up some individual freedoms but only to safeguard the rights of the community.

Differentiated Instruction

L1 English Language Learners   **L1** Less Proficient Readers   **L1** Special Needs

Gaining Comprehension Have students read the text of The Enlightenment as they listen to the Student edition on Audio CD. Create exit cards for the student to complete at the end of the recording. The cards will read "What I learned about _____." or "It made me feel _____." Review their responses. Students can be provided with a copy of the CD to work independently at home or in the school Resource Center.

Locke's reasoning led to a startling conclusion. Because government exists to protect the rights of the people, if a monarch violates those rights, the people have a right to overthrow the monarch. This idea would later shape the founding of the United States.

Montesquieu A French thinker, the Baron de Montesquieu (MON tehs kyoo), also influenced American ideas. In his 1748 book *The Spirit of the Laws,* Montesquieu argued that the powers of government should be clearly defined and limited. Furthermore, he favored separation of powers, or division of the power of government into separate branches. Separation of powers, he said, protects the rights of the people because it keeps any individual or group from gaining too much power.

Montesquieu suggested that government should be divided into three branches: a legislative branch to make laws, an executive branch to enforce the laws, and a judicial branch to make judgments based on the law. He wrote:

> **“**There would be an end to everything, were the same man or the same body . . . to exercise those three powers, that of enacting laws, that of executing the public resolutions, and of trying the causes of individuals.**”**
>
> —Baron de Montesquieu, *The Spirit of the Laws*

Montesquieu

As you will see, this division of power would become the basis of government in the United States.

✓**Checkpoint** What was the goal of Enlightenment thinkers?

⭐ **Looking Back and Ahead** By the 1770s, educated colonists had come to accept the idea that they were born with certain natural rights. As you will see in the next chapter, this belief would set the stage for conflict with the English king and Parliament.

Section 4 | **Check Your Progress**

Progress Monitoring Online
For: Self-test with instant help
Visit: PHSchool.com
Web Code: mva-1044

Comprehension and Critical Thinking

1. **(a) Recall** What role did religion play in colonial schools?
   (b) Support Generalizations Find at least two facts to support the following generalization: Education was important to the colonists.

2. **(a) Describe** What was the Great Awakening?

(b) Analyze Cause and Effect What was one effect of the Great Awakening?

🔄 **Reading Skill**

3. **Use Context to Determine Meaning** Reread the quotation by Jonathan Edwards in this section. Use context to determine the meaning of *abhors.* Explain the clues you used.

Key Terms

4. Write two definitions for each key term: public school, dame school, natural rights, separation of powers. First, write a formal definition for your teacher. Second, write a definition in everyday English for a classmate.

Writing

5. Write two to three closing sentences for an essay on the Enlightenment. Focus particularly on the impact of this movement.

Assess and Reteach

Assess Progress 　L2

Have students complete Check Your Progress. Administer the Section Quiz.

All in One Teaching Resources, Unit 1, Section Quiz, p. 118

To further assess student understanding, use the Progress Monitoring Transparency.

Progress Monitoring Transparencies, Chapter 4, Section 4

Reteach 　L1

If students need more instruction, have them read this section in the Interactive Reading and Notetaking Study Guide and complete the accompanying question.

📖 **Interactive Reading and Notetaking Study Guide,** Chapter 4, Section 4 (Adapted Version also available.)

Extend 　L3

Ask students to suppose that they are American colonists who have recently studied the ideas of the Enlightenment. Have them write an editorial explaining what they believe their rights are and what might cause them to seek independence from Britain. Have volunteers share their work with the class.

Progress Monitoring Online

Students may check their comprehension of this section by completing the Progress Monitoring Online graphic organizer and self-quiz.

Answer

✓**Checkpoint** They wanted to solve problems by applying reason to discover the "natural laws" that governed the universe.

Section 4 Check Your Progress

1. **(a)** Schools were sponsored by religious groups, and religion was taught.
   (b) Education was paid for by both public and private sources in Massachusetts, and schools from the elementary to the college level were opened.

2. **(a)** A period of religious revival in the 1730s and 1740s
   (b) Tolerance of religious differences increased.

3. *Abhors* means dislikes intensely. Clues include the comparison to "some loathesome insect" and the description of being "worthy" only of being "cast into the fire."

4. Possible answers: Public school: a school supported by taxes, or a school that the community supports; dame school: schools that women opened in their homes to teach girls and boys, or home schools for colonial children; natural rights: rights that belong to every

human from birth, or rights we have because we are human; separation of powers: the division of the government into separate branches, or dividing power to keep anyone from having too much of it.

5. Answers will vary, but should reflect an understanding that the Enlightenment encouraged people to govern themselves and demand certain rights.

"How I Became a Printer" from *The Autobiography of Benjamin Franklin*

Build Background Knowledge   **L2**

Reading an autobiography can help students understand individuals' reactions to historical issues and events. Review with students what they know about the development of freedom of the press in the colonies. Ask: **How did the Zenger case help establish freedom of the press in the colonies?** (*Possible answer: By establishing a standard for charges of libel, the Zenger case established the principle that the press has the right to tell the public the truth.*) Discuss with students why freedom of the press is such an important right. Use the Think-Write-Pair-Share strategy (TE, p. T25) to elicit responses.

Reading Skill

Remind students that people who write about their own lives often express their opinions as well as describe events. As students read, ask them to look for details that show Franklin's opinions, especially about the government.

Vocabulary *Builder*

Pronounce each word in the Vocabulary *Builder* list. Ask a student to read the definitions. Ask them to suggest synonyms for these vocabulary words. For example, what is a synonym for "tedious"? (*boring*)

Instruction   **L2**

- Using the Reciprocal Questioning strategy (TE, p. T23), read the first three paragraphs of "How I Became a Printer." Ask students to identify Franklin's earliest talents and interests. (*Possible answer: As a child, Franklin was a good reader and was interested in managing boats.*)

- Have students read the remaining paragraphs. Ask: **How did Benjamin Franklin get along with his brother James?** (*Possible answer: The brothers often argued, and Benjamin was unhappy being his brother's apprentice.*) Ask: **What did Benjamin Franklin learn as an apprentice?** (*Possible answer: He learned about printing and how to run a newspaper. He also learned that it was important to be able to express opinions freely in print.*)

 Literature

How I Became a Printer
by Benjamin Franklin

Prepare to Read

Introduction

It took Benjamin Franklin 17 years to finish his *Autobiography*, and it was not published until after his death. Today, it is recognized as a classic of early American literature. The book covers only the first 51 years of Franklin's long life, so it does not tell of his later role in the founding of the United States.

Reading Skill

Analyze Autobiographical Approach Writers of autobiographies often convey their attitudes and beliefs as they are conveying a story. As you read, look for clues about Franklin's attitude toward the government. Do you think Franklin approves of the Assembly's actions against James?

Vocabulary *Builder*

As you read this literature selection, look for the following underlined words:

chandler (CHAND ler) *n.* person who makes or sells candles, soap, and other items made from the fat of animals

tedious (TEE dee uhs) *adj.* boring

censure (SEHN sher) *v.* to condemn or criticize

admonish (ad MAHN ihsh) *v.* warn

Background

Tithing (TĪTH ing) is the practice of giving one tenth of one's earnings to the church annually. Here, Franklin jokingly implies that his father wished to follow this same tradition by giving the tenth of his children, Benjamin, rather than a tenth of his earnings.

I was put to the grammar-school at eight years of age, my father intending to devote me, as the tithe of his sons, to the service of the Church. My early readiness in learning to read (which must have been very early, as I do not remember when I could not read), and the opinion of all his friends, that I should certainly make a good scholar, encouraged him in this purpose of his. . . . But my father, in the mean time, from the view of the expense of a college education, which having so large a family he could not well afford . . . took me from the grammar-school, and sent me to a school for writing and arithmetic. . . . At ten years old I was taken home to assist my father in his business, which was that of tallow-<u>chandler</u> and soapboiler. . . . Accordingly, I was employed in cutting wick for the candles, filling the dipping mold and the molds for cast candles, attending the shop, going of errands etc.

I disliked the trade, and had a strong inclination for the sea, but my father declared against it. However, living near the water, I was much in and about it, learned early to swim well, and to manage boats; and when in a boat or a canoe with other boys, I was commonly allowed to govern, especially in any case of difficulty; and upon other occasions I was generally a leader among the boys. . . .

From a child I was fond of reading, and all the little money that came into my hands was ever laid out in books. . . .

This bookish inclination at length determined my father to make me a printer, though he had already one son (James) of that profession. In 1717 my brother James returned from England with a press and letters to set up his business in Boston. I . . . signed the indenture when I was yet but twelve years old. I was to serve as an apprentice

---

Differentiated Instruction

L1 English Language Learners   **L1** Less Proficient Readers

Understanding Sentences Provide a transparent page protector to place over the text. Have students read the literature selection. Ask students to mark each sentence with a **?** if they don't understand the sentence, a ***** if they understand the sentence, and a **!** (for wow) if they find the information new and interesting. Review any sentences students have with a question mark. Pair students to compare their "wow" sentences.

till I was twenty-one years of age, only I was to be allowed journeyman's wages during the last year. In a little time I made great proficiency in the business, and became a useful hand to my brother.

Though a brother, he considered himself as my master, and me as his apprentice, and accordingly, expected the same services from me as he would from another, while I thought he demeaned me too much in some he required of me, who from a brother expected more indulgence. Our disputes were often brought before our father, and I fancy I was either generally in the right, or else a better pleader, because the judgment was generally in my favor. But my brother was passionate, and had often beaten me, which I took extremely amiss; and thinking my apprenticeship very <u>tedious</u>, I was continually wishing for some opportunity of shortening it, which at length offered in a manner unexpected.

One of the pieces in our newspaper on some political point, which I have now forgotten, gave offense to the Assembly. He [James] was taken up, <u>censured</u>, and imprisoned for one month, by the speaker's warrant, I suppose, because he would not discover [reveal] his author. I too was taken up and examined before the council; but, though I did not give them any satisfaction, they contented themselves with <u>admonishing</u> me, and dismissed me. . . .

During my brother's confinement, which I resented a good deal, notwithstanding our private differences, I had the management of the paper; and I made bold to give our rulers some rubs in it, which my brother took very kindly. . . . My brother's discharge was accompanied with an order of the House (a very odd one), that "James Franklin should no longer print the paper called the New England Courant."

There was a consultation held in our printing-house among his friends, . . . it was finally concluded on as a better way, to let it be printed for the future under the name of BENJAMIN FRANKLIN; . . . the contrivance was that my old indenture should be returned to me, with full discharge on the back of it, to be shown on occasion, but to secure to him the benefit of my service, I was to sign new indentures for the remainder of the term, which were to be kept private. A very flimsy scheme it was; however, it was immediately executed, and the paper went on accordingly, under my name for several months.

From The Autobiography of Benjamin Franklin,
by Benjamin Franklin. © 2003. Yale University Press.

Ben Franklin (center)

 Analyze Autobiographical Approach

Throughout the story, Franklin conveys his feelings about his brother. When his brother is imprisoned, Franklin takes action by giving the Assembly "some rubs in." Do you think he does this more out of family loyalty or because he supports a free press?

☑ **Checkpoint** What plan did Franklin's brother approve to keep publishing the newspaper after his confinement?

Analyze LITERATURE

Benjamin Franklin disliked being his brother's apprentice. Imagine that you are Franklin. Write a letter to the *New England Courant* expressing your opinion about the fairness or unfairness of being made an apprentice at the age of 12.

If you liked this passage, you might want to read *The Printer's Apprentice* by Stephen Krensky, illustrated by Madeline Sorel. Yearling. 1996.

Literature **125**

History Background

The Supreme Court and Freedom of the Press The Bill of Rights guaranteed freedom of the press in the First Amendment. Yet the Supreme Court has continued to clarify and expand this right. In 1931, the court ruled against a state law banning the publication of all "malicious . . . and defamatory" newspapers in *Near v. Minnesota.* The ruling stated that imposing "prior restraints" on publications is illegal. The Supreme Court affirmed this position in the 1971 Pentagon Papers case when it allowed newspapers to publish classified documents about the Vietnam War. The court ruled that, unless it would cause direct harm, the government cannot prevent newspapers from publishing government documents.

Skills for Life

Objective

Comparing and contrasting information about two events, ideas, people, or other information can help students develop a better understanding of similarities and differences between two subjects.

Compare and Contrast

Instruction L2

1. Ask the class to read aloud the steps to formulate questions and write them on the board.

2. Have students review the information that follows the subheading "Roles of Women" on p. 108. Ask students to compare and contrast colonial women and American women today using the information in the passage. Note these similarities and differences on the board.

3. Practice the skill by following the steps on p. 126 as a class. Model each step to compare and contrast. (*1. Comparing and contrasting colonial women and American women today 2. Colonial women did not hold political office or vote, but American women today do 3. Both can have personal opinions about politics. 4. Possible answer: American women today play a more direct role in politics than colonial women did.*)

Monitor Progress

Ask students to do the Apply the Skill activity. Then assign the Analysis Skill Worksheet. As students complete the worksheet, circulate to make sure individuals are applying the skill steps effectively. Provide assistance as needed.

All in One Teaching Resources, Unit 1, Skills for Life Worksheet, p. 113

Reteach L1

If students need more instruction, use the Social Studies Skills Tutor to reteach this skill.

Social Studies Skills Tutor CD-ROM, Compare and Contrast

Skills for Life   Compare and Contrast

A Venn diagram is a graphic organizer that shows similarities and differences. You can use a Venn diagram to compare and contrast information about any two items, including time periods, historical events, people, and ideas. Aspects of the two items that are different appear outside the shared area where the circles intersect. Aspects that are similar are listed within the shared area.

Copy and complete the Venn diagram below to compare and contrast information about colonial women and women today. Use information that follows the subheading 'Role s of Women" in Chapter 4, Section 2, and your own knowledge about contemporary American women.

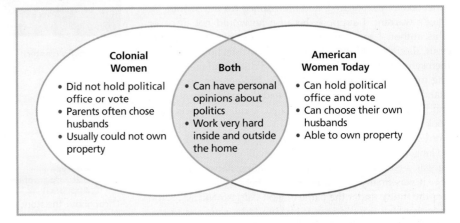

Learn the Skill
Use these steps to create a Venn diagram.

1. **Identify the subject.** Decide what items you will compare and contrast on the Venn diagram. Write a title summarizing the subject of the organizer.

2. **Identify the differences.** Write the differences between the items being compared in each circle under the appropriate heading.

3. **Identify the similarities.** Write the similarities between the items being compared in the intersecting circle under the heading "Both."

4. **Draw a conclusion about the subject.** Use the information on the Venn diagram to write a sentence summarizing the conclusions.

Practice the Skill
Answer the following questions about the Venn diagram on this page.

1. **Identify the subject.** What is a good title for the Venn diagram on this page?

2. **Identify the differences.** What is a difference between colonial woman and American women today?

3. **Identify the similarities.** What is a similarity between colonial women and American women today?

4. **Draw a conclusion about the subject.** Based on the information in the Venn diagram, what is one conclusion you can draw about colonial women and American women today?

Apply the Skill
See the Review and Assessment at the end of this chapter.

Quick Study Guide

How did colonial life take shape?

Section 1
Governing the Colonies

- The Magna Carta and English Bill of Rights guaranteed the rights of English citizens.
- By 1760, each of the 13 colonies had a legislature to make laws.
- The trial of John Peter Zenger helped establish the idea of freedom of the press.
- England passed the Navigation Acts to regulate colonial trade.

Section 2
Colonial Society

- In colonial society, men, women, and children had clearly defined roles.
- Colonial America offered poor and middle-class whites the opportunity to own land and improve their social status.

Section 3
Slavery in the Colonies

- More than 10 million Africans were transported to the Americas in the Atlantic slave trade.
- The plantation economy of the South became dependent on the labor of enslaved African Americans.
- Slave codes did not stop occasional slave revolts.

Section 4
The Spread of New Ideas

- Education during colonial times was influenced by religion.
- Colonial era literature included poetry, sermons, and popular writing.
- The Great Awakening of the 1730s and 1740s led to the rise of new churches.
- Enlightenment thinkers influenced ideas about government and natural rights.

(?) Exploring the Essential Question

Use the online study guide to explore the essential question.

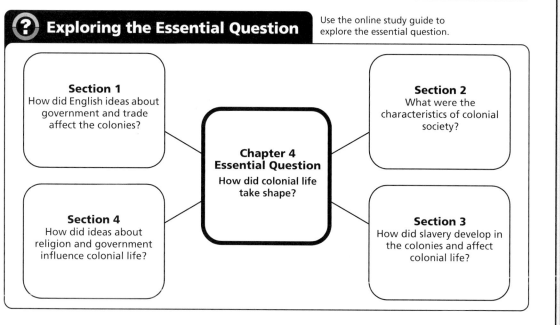

Section 1
How did English ideas about government and trade affect the colonies?

Section 2
What were the characteristics of colonial society?

Chapter 4 Essential Question
How did colonial life take shape?

Section 4
How did ideas about religion and government influence colonial life?

Section 3
How did slavery develop in the colonies and affect colonial life?

Quick Study Guide **127**

Think Like A Historian

Enrich Learning To enrich this unit, have students revisit the Unit Essential Question. Using information from the chapters in the unit and the primary sources on pp. 130–133, have students write a skit or short story showing the connection between the colonists and their past.

Think Like a Historian, pp. 130–133

Pressed for Time? If you do not have time to complete the activity, return to the essential question on the unit opener. Post the flip chart pages and ask students to review and revise the list. As a summary, display the Unit 1 Think Like a Historian transparencies

Color Transparencies, Think Like a Historian, Unit 1

Essential Question

Remind Students of the Chapter Essential Question. **How did colonial life take shape?** Have them review the bulleted statements and the Visual Preview at the beginning of the chapter to help them answer this question.

To bolster students' retention, at this time, they should complete the Study Guide in print or online. Remind students that they should also continue notetaking for the Unit and Chapter Essential Questions.

📖 **Interactive Reading and Notetaking Study Guide,** Chapter 4 (Adapted Version also available.)

Study Guide *Online,* Chapter 4

Chapter Challenge

To wrap up this chapter, students should apply the knowledge they have gained to answer this question: **How was colonial life influenced by ideas from other places?** (*Answers will vary but students should recognize that the colonists drew heavily on English cultural traditions as they developed a way of life in North America. Students may also point out that colonial life was also influenced by traditions from Africa brought to North America by enslaved Africans.*)

Assessment at a Glance

Formal Assessment
Chapter Tests A/B (L1/L2)

AYP Monitoring Assessment

Test Prep Workbook With Document-Based Assessment

Test-Taking Strategies With Transparencies

Performance Assessment
Group/Individual Activities, TE pp. 98g, 98h

Teacher's Edition, pp. 106, 112, 117, 123

Assessment Rubrics

Assessment Through Technology
ExamView CD-ROM

MindPoint CD-ROM

Progress Monitoring Transparencies

Progress Monitoring Online

Key Terms

1. groups of people who have the power to make laws.

2. a procedure by which judges protect people against unlawful arrest or detention.

3. then many members of the family could help perform the necessary work.

4. people who agreed to work for a certain period of time for a person who had paid their passage to North America.

5. that restricted the rights and activities of slaves.

Comprehension and Critical Thinking

6. **(a)** Trial by jury and habeas corpus **(b)** Most were either born in England or the children of English parents, and they were subject to English laws. **(c)** Americans today have all of these rights.

7. **(a)** Possible answers may include: descriptions of the enormous amount of difficult work, the modest amenities, and the closeness of families. **(b)** Both men and women had responsibilities for raising crops and tending animals. Women also were responsible for many tasks related to the care of children and the home.

8. **(a)** Gentry, middle class, indentured servants, free African Americans, enslaved people. **(b)** The poor in America had greater opportunity than in Europe to build wealth and social status over time. **(c)** Free African Americans could not participate as equal partners in political life because they could not vote or serve on juries.

9. **(a)** Trade between the colonies, the Caribbean, and West Africa in a variety of products, including enslaved people **(b)** Many New England merchants benefited from this trade because they were able to make great profits by avoiding the requirements of the Navigation Acts. **(c)** Enslaved Africans experienced the greatest hardship from this trade.

10. **(a)** Students in colonial schools learned basic subjects such as writing and arithmetic, and often learned about religion. **(b)** Answers will vary but should reflect knowledge of colonial schools.

Key Terms

Complete each of the following sentences so that the second part further explains the first part and clearly shows your understanding of the key term.

1. All colonies in British North America had legislatures, _____.

2. The English Bill of Rights guaranteed habeas corpus, _____.

3. On colonial farms, it was important to have an extended family because _____.

4. Many people came to the colonies from Europe as indentured servants, _____.

5. After a time, slave owners enforced slave codes _____.

Comprehension and Critical Thinking

6. **(a) Identify** What rights did the Magna Carta and the English Bill of Rights guarantee? **(b) Draw Conclusions** Why do you think colonists believed they were entitled to the rights guaranteed by the Magna Carta and the English Bill of Rights? **(c) Link Past and Present** Which of these rights do Americans still enjoy today?

7. **(a) Describe** What was life like on a colonial farm? **(b) Compare and Contrast** How were the responsibilities of men and women similar? How were they different?

8. **(a) Identify** What were the various classes into which colonial society was divided? **(b) Compare** In what ways were the poor better off in America than in Europe? **(c) Explain Problems** What were some of the limitations placed on free African Americans? Explain.

9. **(a) Recall** What was the triangular trade? **(b) Identify Benefits** Which groups benefited from this trade? **(c) Identify Costs** Which groups experienced hardships because of this trade?

10. **(a) Describe** What were colonial schools like? **(b) Frame Questions** List at least three questions you would ask a colonial school-age child.

History Reading Skill

11. **Determine Meaning From Context** Find an unfamiliar word in Chapter 4 and use context clues to analyze its meaning. Explain the clues you used.

Writing

12. Write two paragraphs summarizing how the ideas and customs that the colonists brought from England began to change once they left their homeland. Focus on the social and political changes.

   Your paragraphs should:
   - begin with a thesis statement that expresses a main idea;
   - include the ideas that the colonists brought from England;
   - list and discuss the changes that resulted in the colonists changing their views;
   - end by stating how the colonists changed.

13. **Write a Narrative:**
   You are a teacher in a colonial school. Name the colony in which you teach. Describe the school. How many students do you have? What are your goals for your students?

Skills for Life
Compare and Contrast
Review what you have learned about the lives of indentured servants and the lives of enslaved Africans in colonial America. Create a Venn diagram showing some of the similarities and differences. Then, answer the following questions.

14. Identify two differences between enslaved Africans and indentured servants.

15. What was one way in which the life of an indentured servant was similar to the life of an enslaved person?

16. Agree or disagree with the following conclusion: The life of an indentured servant was just as harsh as the life of an enslaved African. Give reasons for your answer.

History Reading Skill

11. Answers will vary, but should demonstrate application of the process called for in the question.

Writing

12. Possible answers: Enslaved Africans were bound permanently, but the service of indentured servants was limited by an agreement. Indentured servants freely entered into the arrangement, but enslaved Africans were usually captured by raiders.

13. Both were obligated to work for a particular person and were usually worked very hard.

For complete Four-Point rubrics, see the writing rubrics in the Teaching Resources.

All in One Teaching Resources, Unit 1, p. 13

Progress Monitoring nline
For: Self-test with instant help
Visit: PHSchool.com
Web Code: mva-1046

Chapter 4
Review and Assessment

Test Yourself

1. The colonies offered the right to vote to
   A Native Americans.
   B African Americans.
   C white male property owners.
   D any colonist born in England.

2. One reason that colonists disliked the Navigation Acts was that the laws
   A prevented colonial merchants from selling their goods in England.
   B led to a decline in the shipbuilding industry.
   C created manufacturing jobs in England.
   D cut colonial merchants off from profitable foreign markets.

3. What was one result of the Great Awakening in the 13 colonies?
   A It reinforced the principle of freedom of the press.
   B It led to the decline of the Puritan Church in New England.
   C It led to the formation of new churches.
   D It encouraged colonists to accept royal authority.

4. According to John Locke, natural rights
   A cannot be taken away.
   B are granted by the king or queen.
   C apply only to English citizens.
   D apply only to the gentry.

Document-Based Questions

Task: Look at Documents 1 and 2, and answer their accompanying questions. Then, use the documents and your knowledge of history to complete the following writing assignment:

Write an essay about the treatment of enslaved Africans on the journey to America. How does Document 1 support Equiano's statements about conditions during the journey?

Document 1: These diagrams show the loading plan of a slave ship during the Middle Passage from Africa to the Americas. *Based on this picture, describe the way enslaved Africans were treated on the journey.*

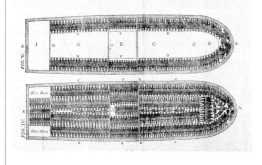

Document 2: Olaudah Equiano, an African who survived the voyage, wrote this description of his experiences. *What were two causes of suffering on the ship?*

"The closeness of the place and the heat of the climate, added to the number in the ship, which was so crowded that each had scarcely room to turn himself, almost suffocated us. . . . The air soon became unfit for respiration . . . and brought on a sickness among the slaves, of which many died. The shrieks of the women, and the groans of the dying, rendered the whole a scene of horror almost inconceivable. Happily perhaps for myself I was soon reduced so low here that it was thought necessary to keep me almost always on deck; and from my extreme youth I was not put in fetters. In this situation I expected every hour to share the fate of my companions, some of whom were almost daily brought upon deck at the point of death, which I began to hope would soon put an end to my miseries. Often did I think many of the inhabitants of the deep much more happy than myself; I envied them the freedom they enjoyed, and as often wished I could change my condition for theirs.

Every circumstance . . . served only to render my state more painful, and heighten my . . . opinion of the cruelty of the whites. One day they had taken a number of fishes, and when they had killed and satisfied themselves with as many as they thought fit . . . they tossed the remaining fish into the sea again, although we begged and prayed for some."

Test Yourself
1. C
2. D
3. C
4. A

Document-Based Questions
Answers

Document 1 Africans were packed into the ship very tightly and were treated poorly.

Document 2 The poor environment of the ships and the cruelty of the whites transporting them

Rubric: Write an Essay

Share rubric with students before they begin writing.

Score 1 Ideas unclear, organization poor.

Score 2 Essay has few details in support of stand taken, fails to answer questions completely.

Score 3 Essay accurately answers questions, points out crowded conditions on the ship, and the disease and death that could result from those conditions, has clear organization and some supporting arguments.

Score 4 Essay is comprehensive and detailed with clear organization and supporting arguments, shows creativity.

Skills for Life

14. Unlike enslaved Africans, indentured servants served for a limited time, and retained some legal rights.

15. Both were required to work without pay.

16. Possible answer: Indentured servitude was not as harsh as slavery, because the indentured servant could look forward to freedom.

Think Like a Historian

? **How did the colonists, with strong roots in the past, develop their own way of life?**

Build Background Knowledge `L2`

Discuss the roots of the early colonists. Bring out the idea that roots form the basis for development. Lead a structured discussion about the foundation of colonial life. (See TE p. T24 for more on structured discussion.) Give students the example of planting seeds and growing a flower; the type and color of the flower start with the seed. Other factors, such as soil, weather, and water will affect its growth. Using this analogy, have students preview the documents on these pages to list the roots of colonial life. What "seeds" or roots did they drawn upon? *(tradition from religions, Greek and Roman government, European political traditions)* What other factors influenced colonial way of life? *(Native Americans, slavery, geography)*

Instruction `L2`

■ Write the Unit Essential Question on the chalkboard. Have students put this question in their own words. *(Possible answer: What influenced the development of the colonies?)* Have students review the essential questions for chapters 1–4. Draw a web diagram on the chalkboard, showing how the chapter questions feed into the unit question. (See **Teaching Resources, Unit 1,** p. 3). Discuss how each chapter question helps answer the unit question.

■ Tell students that after they study the documents they will create a skit or short story using them to help answer this question.

Answers

Document 1: Religious freedom in many colonies influenced legislation, creating havens for those seeking refuge from persecution in Europe.

Document 2: They learned theories and models on constitutional government, human nature, and virtue.

? Unit **1** THINK LIKE A HISTORIAN

How did the colonists, with strong roots in the past, develop their own way of life?

DIRECTIONS: Analyze the following documents on the colonial period. Answer the questions that accompany each document or set of documents. You will use your answers to build an answer to the unit question: How did the colonists, with strong roots in the past, develop their own way of life?

HISTORIAN'S CHECKLIST

WHO produced the document?
WHERE was it made?
WHEN was it produced?
WHY was it made and for what audience?
WHAT is its viewpoint?
HOW does it connect to what I've learned?
WHY is the document important?

1 Religion

"No person or persons whatsoever within this province . . . professing to believe in Jesus Christ, shall from henceforth be in any way troubled, molested, or discountenanced for or in respect of his or her religion, nor in the free exercise thereof within this province . . . nor in any way compelled to the belief or exercise of any other religion against his or her consent."

—Maryland, Toleration Act, 1649

How did religion influence the colonies?

2 Ancient Greece and Rome

"Greek and Latin . . . literatures informed the educations . . . of 18th-century Americans, [but] few studies have fully attempted to describe and explore the formative role of the classics for the leaders of the American Revolution and the framers of the Constitution. . . . Historian Richard argues compellingly that the classics played a definitive role in the minds of figures such as Jefferson, Adams, Madison, Washington, and many others, providing not only theories of constitutional government, human nature, and virtue but even models for emulation"

—T.L. Cooksey, reviewing The Founders and the Classics: Greece, Rome, and the American Enlightenment *by Carl Richard*

What did 18th century Americans learn from ancient Greece and Rome?

130

Differentiated Instruction

`L1` **English Language Learners**   `L1` **Special Needs**

Determining Themes Review the definition of *theme.* Tell students that *theme* is the meaning, or message, of a story. It is the main, or central idea of the document or writing. When assigning a document, have students work in pairs to determine the theme of the document. Then, have them create a concept web diagram. Write the theme of their document in the center circle. Then, in the outer circles, have them write supporting statements based on the information in the unit. Remind them to use their Interactive Reading and Notetaking Study Guide to find facts to back up the theme. Use this web whesn completing the activity on p. 133.

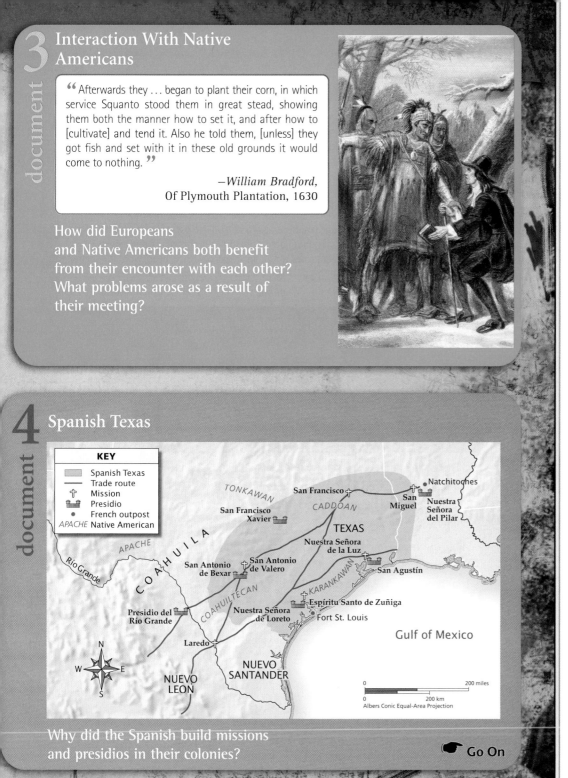

3 Interaction With Native Americans

document

"Afterwards they ... began to plant their corn, in which service Squanto stood them in great stead, showing them both the manner how to set it, and after how to [cultivate] and tend it. Also he told them, [unless] they got fish and set with it in these old grounds it would come to nothing."

—*William Bradford,*
Of Plymouth Plantation, 1630

How did Europeans and Native Americans both benefit from their encounter with each other? What problems arose as a result of their meeting?

4 Spanish Texas

document

KEY
Spanish Texas
— Trade route
✝ Mission
🏛 Presidio
• French outpost
APACHE Native American

TONKAWAN
CADDOAN
San Francisco ✝
• Natchitoches
San Miguel ✝
Nuestra Señora del Pilar 🏛
San Francisco Xavier 🏛
TEXAS
Nuestra Señora de la Luz ✝
COAHUILA
APACHE
Río Grande
San Antonio de Bexar 🏛
San Antonio ✝ de Valero
COAHUILTECAN
KARANKAWAN
San Agustín 🏛
Presidio del Río Grande 🏛
Nuestra Señora de Loreto ✝
Espíritu Santo de Zuñiga ✝
• Fort St. Louis
Gulf of Mexico
Laredo ✝
NUEVO LEON
NUEVO SANTANDER

N W E S

0   200 miles
0   200 km
Albers Conic Equal-Area Projection

Why did the Spanish build missions and presidios in their colonies?

👉 Go On

Instruction (continued)

■ If your students have examined these documents as enrichment to the chapters, you may have the class answer the Historian's Checklist questions as a review.

■ If you have not used these documents yet, students will need more time to work with these sources. For documents that present challenging reading, use the following steps.

1. As the students study the document, remind them to use the question associated with it as the focus question.

2. Have one student read the document aloud, breaking it into short segments. Then, as a class, work to paraphrase the document. For example, for Document 1, the first part could be summarized as "The assembly passed a law…"

3. Then, organize the class into groups. Using the Think-Write-Pair-Share strategy (TE p. T25), have each group answer the Historian's Checklist questions for one of the documents. If they need more information about the document, tell them to go back to the chapter to find out relevant information. Remind them to use the index or the Table of Contents to find which chapter covered the material. They may also use their Interactive Reading and Notetaking Study Guide to review.

4. Review the answers to the Historian's Checklist questions. Have students identify how each document helps answer the essential question. Ask them whether their document would fall in the category of "roots" or "way of life."

Answers

Document 3: Native Americans taught the colonists how to use local natural resources and cultivate crops. The colonists introduced the Native Americans to horses, advanced weapons, and knowledge of the broader world. However, Native Americans were victims of European diseases against which they had no immunity, and both Native Americans and colonists sometimes died as a result of disputes with one another.

Document 4: The Spanish were trying to establish Spanish culture and religion in their colonies in order to cement relations with the natives and expand their territories.

History Background

A New Identity Ideas about government and the rights of people evolved long before colonies existed in North America. The Code of Hammurabi was the first important attempt by a ruler to set down all the laws of the people. Although they were displayed for all to see, the rules were not applied equally to everyone: Punishment varied depending on who committed the crime. The Ten Commandments made it clear how people were to behave and applied to everyone. The Magna Carta established the precedent that no one is above the law. It was a synthesis of these ideas, and many other beliefs and philosophies, upon which colonists based their way of life.

Instruction (continued)

- Preview the documents and assign selections according to student abilities. You may organize students into groups to review the documents. For example, assign Document 3 to English language learners. Read the selection aloud to them and tell them to listen for the topic and the main idea as you read. Ask: **What is the topic?** (*Squanto helped colonists survive.*) Ask the students how they would feel in this situation if they were the colonists. (*Answers will vary, but students will either think that it was easy for the hungry colonists to accept expert help from Native Americans or that it might have been difficult for English natives to accept help from people who were so different from themselves.*)

- Assign Document 4 to students with less proficient reading skills. Ask: **What do you learn from the Key?** (*The map shows Spanish Texas and the trade routes, missions, and presidios established by the Spanish, French outposts, and Native American groups*) **What impact would the trade routes have on Native Americans?** (*Possible answer: There would be a great deal of contact with Spanish explorers and much cultural exchange and/or fighting.*)

- For Document 7, tell students that the style of printing in early America is different than much of printing they see today. Note that the lower case "s" looks like an "f". Have students read the document. Ask: **Why does this ad stress that the "negroes" were free from smallpox?** (*The sellers were guaranteeing the high quality of their "product."*)

- Assign Document 8 to advanced readers. Ask: **Who does Montesquieu think should have power? Why?** (*the people; he thinks they are well qualified for choosing representatives*) **How well would he think the colonists incorporated his ideas?** (*Answers may vary. Some may point out that although many white males could vote, women and enslaved people could not vote and had no representation.*)

Answers

Document 5: Colonists expected to have the right to own possessions, to vote, and to participate in the judicial process.

Document 6: Colonists began to govern themselves on the town level.

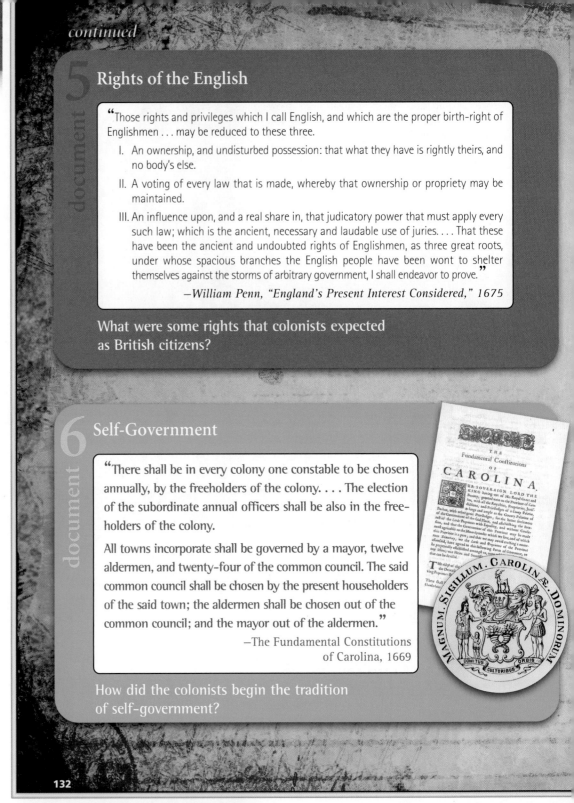

continued

document 5 — Rights of the English

"Those rights and privileges which I call English, and which are the proper birth-right of Englishmen . . . may be reduced to these three.

I. An ownership, and undisturbed possession: that what they have is rightly theirs, and no body's else.

II. A voting of every law that is made, whereby that ownership or propriety may be maintained.

III. An influence upon, and a real share in, that judicatory power that must apply every such law; which is the ancient, necessary and laudable use of juries. . . . That these have been the ancient and undoubted rights of Englishmen, as three great roots, under whose spacious branches the English people have been wont to shelter themselves against the storms of arbitrary government, I shall endeavor to prove."

—William Penn, "England's Present Interest Considered," 1675

What were some rights that colonists expected as British citizens?

document 6 — Self-Government

"There shall be in every colony one constable to be chosen annually, by the freeholders of the colony. . . . The election of the subordinate annual officers shall be also in the freeholders of the colony.

All towns incorporate shall be governed by a mayor, twelve aldermen, and twenty-four of the common council. The said common council shall be chosen by the present householders of the said town; the aldermen shall be chosen out of the common council; and the mayor out of the aldermen."

—The Fundamental Constitutions of Carolina, 1669

How did the colonists begin the tradition of self-government?

132

Differentiated Instruction

L3 Advanced Readers   **L3** Gifted and Talented

Emphasize Relevance Have students review the connections between the roots and colonial life. As they prepare their skit or short story, have them consider what colonial life might have been like without the influence of one or more of the roots discussed in the unit. What would colonial life be like if it were not based on religious ideals or ancient traditions? Have students use their answers to these questions to make their introductions and conclusions stronger.

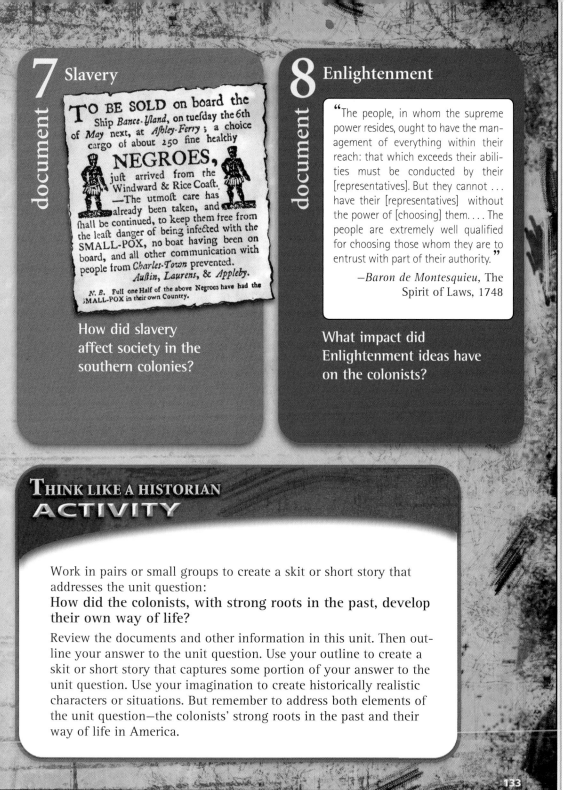

7 Slavery

document

TO BE SOLD on board the Ship *Bance-Island*, on tuesday the 6th of *May* next, at *Ashley-Ferry*; a choice cargo of about 250 fine healthy

NEGROES,

just arrived from the Windward & Rice Coast. —The utmost care has already been taken, and shall be continued, to keep them free from the least danger of being infected with the SMALL-POX, no boat having been on board, and all other communication with people from *Charles-Town* prevented.
Austin, Laurens, & Appleby.

N. B. Full one Half of the above Negroes have had the SMALL-POX in their own Country.

How did slavery affect society in the southern colonies?

8 Enlightenment

document

"The people, in whom the supreme power resides, ought to have the management of everything within their reach: that which exceeds their abilities must be conducted by their [representatives]. But they cannot . . . have their [representatives] without the power of [choosing] them. . . . The people are extremely well qualified for choosing those whom they are to entrust with part of their authority."

—*Baron de Montesquieu,* The Spirit of Laws, 1748

What impact did Enlightenment ideas have on the colonists?

THINK LIKE A HISTORIAN
ACTIVITY

Work in pairs or small groups to create a skit or short story that addresses the unit question:
How did the colonists, with strong roots in the past, develop their own way of life?

Review the documents and other information in this unit. Then outline your answer to the unit question. Use your outline to create a skit or short story that captures some portion of your answer to the unit question. Use your imagination to create historically realistic characters or situations. But remember to address both elements of the unit question—the colonists' strong roots in the past and their way of life in America.

-133-

Unit 2

Why It Matters

In this chapter, students will focus on the American Revolution and the establishment of the United States.

■ The fight for independence from Britain established the United States as the first modern country founded on democratic principles. Countries in many parts of the world have also adopted democratic governments.

■ The negotiations over the status of enslaved Africans during the drafting of the Constitution laid the groundwork for the American Civil War nearly 90 years later. The unresolved tensions between statements of freedom and legal enslavement were exacerbated as the new country grew and admitted more states. The Constitution remains our governing document today.

Unit Essential Question

How did the colonists break away from Britain and create a republican form of government?

Think Like a Historian

• To preview this unit, have students review the content and images on these pages of the Student Edition. Ask: **What will you be learning about in this unit?** (*the development of the United States*) Tell students that the country's founding documents continue to guide the nation today.

• Write the Unit Focus Question on the board. Using the Idea Wave strategy (TE, p. T24), have students brainstorm answers to the question. (*Answers may include the protests against British taxes, the armed revolution, the Declaration of Independence, and the Constitution.*)

• Record students' answers on a flip chart. Keep a copy of them. After students have completed their responses, tell them that they will be learning about the development of the new nation. Let them know that you will return to this

Unit 2

How did the colonists break away from Britain and create a republican form of government?

Declaration of Independence In unforgettable phrases, the Declaration expressed the conviction of American leaders that the colonies should be independent of the rule of Great Britain.

1776

Writing the Constitution All through t hot summer of 1787, delegates from the states debated the new shape of the U.S government. The Constitution created a framework for the government of the United States we enjoy today.

1787

134 Unit 2

same question at the end of the unit and review their responses for possible changes and additions. (*See Think Like a Historian, p. 271*)

• Preview the primary sources in Think Like a Historian on pages 272–275. You may wish to introduce and discuss these documents to enrich chapter content.

Home Involvement

A summary of the Forming a New Nation content that students will be studying and suggested activities that adults at home can do with their child are available in a reproducible outline in the Teacher Resources Kit.

All in One Teaching Resources, Unit 2, Letter Home, Chapters 5, 6, 7

Forming a New Nation

The Final Battle Trapped by American and French forces, the British were forced to surrender at the Battle of Yorktown. The British defeat marked the end of the fighting in the American Revolution.

1781

A Bill of Rights The Bill of Rights was intended to prevent the kind of abuses Americans had suffered under English rule. One of the rights protected was the right of the people peaceably to assemble.

1791

■ Think Like a Historian

Students complete an activity in which they use primary sources to explore the Essential Question.
pp. 272–275

History Background

John Trumbull The life of John Trumbull was deeply entwined with the American Revolution and early American politics. Trumbull's father was the only Royal Governor in the 13 colonies to support the American Revolution. Trumbull himself spent part of the Revolution on the staff of George Washington. Later in the war, the British government held Trumbull in prison in London, where he had gone to study painting. After the war, Trumbull became famous for painting historical scenes, such as *Yorktown: Surrender, 1781* (shown at the top of p. 135).

Eteach

Read the essay on eTeach for further ideas on Teaching Primary Sources.
Visit: PHSchool.com
Web Code: mvf-0128

DK World Desk Reference

Use the resources on the DK World Desk Reference for further information about the United States.
Visit: PHSchool.com
Web Code: mve-0129

History Background

The Growing Tensions Between Colonists and the British Government

In the middle of the eighteenth century, Britain and France were competing to expand their colonies in North America and for supremacy in other parts of the world. As a result of this competition, the two countries and many of their respective European allies became embroiled in a war fought in Europe, Africa, and Asia. In what is called the French and Indian War, the armies also clashed in North America over western territories, particularly in the Ohio River valley.

Britain managed to defeat French forces and its Native American allies, defeating French aspirations in North America. France ceded most of its North American claims to Britain and Spain at the end of the war. Britain's territory in North America grew immensely, but the British army almost immediately faced Pontiac's War, an unsuccessful campaign launched by an Ottawa chief to drive the British forts and settlements out of the Mississippi River valley. To quell the ongoing friction between the settlers and Native Americans, Britain barred settlements west of the Appalachian Mountains in the Proclamation of 1763.

Britain's victories had come at great financial cost. The British Parliament enacted new tax laws designed to make the colonists contribute to the costs of the wars and ongoing protection. These laws were met by boycotts, protests, and demands for repeal by the colonists. One consequence of the protests was an increasing unity among colonists as they fought against these new British policies. Incidents such as the Boston Tea Party and the Boston Massacre further strengthened both the colonists' outrage and their unity.

The colonists convened two Continental Congresses to voice their discontent and plan strategy for responding to British policies. The first open fighting between colonists and British troops broke out in April 1775, in Lexington and Concord, two Massachusetts towns in which Minutemen, the colonial militia, hastily assembled to prevent the British from seizing arms. The battle was a victory for the colonial forces, who inflicted heavy losses on the British using surprise attacks. Their determination and courage in the face of one of the world's most powerful armies inspired confidence in the ability of the Continental Army to confront the British.

Essential Questions

Use this graphic organizer to see the relationship between key concepts and the Chapter Essential Question.

Focus Question/Section 1
How did the British gain French territory in North America?
(p. 140)

Concept: Power

Focus Question/Section 2
How did the French and Indian War draw the colonists closer together but increase friction with Britain?
(p. 145)

Concept: Colony

Chapter Focus Question
How did the relationship between Britain and the colonies fall apart?

Focus Question/Section 4
How did the American Revolution begin?
(p. 156)

Concept: Protest

Focus Question/Section 3
How did British tax policies move the colonists closer to rebellion?
(p. 150)

Concept: Rights

Differentiated Instruction

Numbered Heads Strategy

Why Use This Strategy In this chapter, students will use the Numbered Heads engagement strategy to come up with and share their responses to questions. The Numbered Heads strategy allows students to become more confident of their individualized responses by sharing them with a smaller group before facing the whole class. Because students are then called on at random to speak for the group, they alternate taking on a leadership role, and all students are responsible for paying attention to the team's ideas.

Tips on Using This Strategy Remind students that it is a good idea to compare and contrast their responses with those of other teams. Below are sample strategies to help students achieve this goal:

Our answer was (similar to/different from) that team _____ because _____.

We agree with team _____ that _____.

Team _____ already mentioned _____, but I would like to add that _____.

Concepts Across Time

Have students develop an understanding of the enduring concepts of history by connecting these ideas.

Concept: Power

Students learning about the competition between France and Britain in North America should recall how European nations fought for control of the Western Hemisphere during the sixteenth and seventeenth centuries. The natural resources available in the colonies allowed the home country and its monarch to build both wealth and power. Ask: **Why did both France and Britain believe that their territories in North America were worth fighting over?** (*Possible answer: They wanted to control the territory so that they could enrich themselves by expanding settlements and trade.*) Use this question when discussing the Competing Empires in Section 1.

Concept: Protest

Remind students that although the events that led to the American Revolution are described in one chapter of the Student Edition, they took more than a decade to unfold and the outcome of the fighting was far from certain. Point out that advocating revolution and the overthrow of the government was a radical course that the colonists chose only after many years of attempted compromise and protests, some of which succeeded. Ask: **What kinds of protests by the colonists were successful? What kinds were unsuccessful?** (*Successful: boycotting British goods, a petition against the Stamp Act, making their own goods that they previously bought from Britain; Unsuccessful: Early complaints to Parliament, not complying with the Quartering Act by refusing to supply money to feed and house British soldiers, demanding the repeal of the Intolerable Acts and declaring that the colonies had a right to tax and govern themselves, the Olive Branch Petition, the Declaration of the Causes and Necessities of Taking Up Arms*) Ask students to discuss the reasons why some protests were successful and why some were not. Use these questions when discussing Section 4.

Section 1 **Trouble on the Frontier** *1.5 periods, .75 block*

Objectives

Students will

1. Identify the reasons why fighting broke out between France and Britain in North America.

2. Describe the early defeat of the British by the French at the beginning of the French and Indian War.

3. Explain how the British gained victory, and explain the results of the French and Indian War.

Differentiated Instruction Key

L1 Basic to Average

L2 All Students

L3 Average to Advanced

AR Advanced Readers

ELL English Language Learners

GT Gifted and Talented

LPR Less Proficient Readers

SN Special Needs

Prepare to Read

Build Background Knowledge
Discuss students' previous knowledge of European competition in the Americas.

Set a Purpose for Reading
Have students begin to fill out the Reading Readiness Guide.

Preview Key Terms
Preview the section's Key Terms.

Instructional Resources

All in One Teaching Resources, Unit 2

L2 Chapter Prereading Guide, p. 4

L2 History Reading Skill Worksheet, p. 14

L2 Word Knowledge Rating Form, p. 15

L2 Reading Readiness Guide, p. 16

Teacher's Edition

L2 Vocabulary Builder, pp. 139, 141

Differentiated Instruction

Guided Reading Audio CD

Spanish ELL, LPR, SN

Teach

Instruction
Competing Empires
Discuss how rival claims led to war in North America between Britain and France.

Early British Defeats
Discuss France's early victories in the French and Indian War and the effects of these victories on British attempts to ally with the Iroquois.

The British Turn the Tide
Discuss the eventual British victory and its effects on the North American colonies.

Instructional Resources

Interactive Reading and Notetaking Study Guide

L2 Chapter 5, Section 1

All in One Teaching Resources, Unit 2

L2 Concept Lesson, p. 23

L2 Concept Organizer, p. 6

Color Transparencies

L2 The French and Indian War

Differentiated Instruction

Interactive Reading and Notetaking Study Guide, Adapted Version (English/ Spanish)

L1 Chapter 5, Section 1 ELL, LPR, SN

Teacher's Edition

L1 Create a Flowchart, p. 140 ELL, LPR, SN

L3 Predicting, p. 142 AR, GT

Assess and Reteach

Assess Progress
Evaluate student comprehension with Check Your Progress and Section Quiz.

Reteach
Assign the Interactive Reading and Notetaking Study Guide to help struggling students.

Extend
Extend the lesson by having students research the Seven Years' War.

Instructional Resources

Interactive Reading and Notetaking Study Guide

L2 Chapter 5, Section 1

All in One Teaching Resources, Unit 2

L2 Reading Readiness Guide, p. 16

L2 Section Quiz, p. 24

Progress Monitoring Transparencies

L2 Chapter 5, Section 1

Differentiated Instruction

Teacher's Edition

L1 Checkpoints, TE pp. 142, 143, 144

SE on Audio CD

L1 Chapter 5, Section 1

Internet Resources

PHSchool.com

Section 2 The Colonists Resist Tighter Control

 1 period, .5 block

Objectives

Students will

1. Explain the conflict between Native Americans and British settlers in 1763.
2. Describe how the colonists responded to British tax laws.
3. Describe what happened during the Boston Massacre.

Differentiated Instruction Key

- **L1** Basic to Average
- **L2** All Students
- **L3** Average to Advanced
- **AR** Advanced Readers
- **ELL** English Language Learners
- **GT** Gifted and Talented
- **LPR** Less Proficient Readers
- **SN** Special Needs

Prepare to Read

Build Background Knowledge
Ask students to predict how the spread of Enlightenment ideas will affect the colonists' response to laws with which they disagree.

Set a Purpose for Reading
Have students begin to fill out the Reading Readiness Guide.

Preview Key Terms
Preview the section's Key Terms.

Instructional Resources

All in One Teaching Resources, Unit 2
- **L2** Reading Readiness Guide, p. 17

Teacher's Edition
- **L2** Vocabulary Builder, p. 145

Differentiated Instruction

- 🔊 **Guided Reading Audio CD**
  Spanish **ELL LPR SN**

Teach

Instruction
Conflict with Native Americans
Discuss the causes and effects of Pontiac's War.

British Rule Leads to Conflict
Discuss colonial discontent with British laws enacted to help pay the cost of the French and Indian War and defending the colonists.

The Stamp Act
Discuss the effect of the Stamp Act on relations between the colonists and the British government.

Protests Spread
Discuss the events that led to the Boston Massacre, and the effects of the massacre.

Instructional Resources

📖 **Interactive Reading and Notetaking Study Guide**
- **L2** Chapter 5, Section 2

All in One Teaching Resources, Unit 2
- **L2** Patrick Henry, p. 20

Discovery School Video
- **L2** Boston Massacre

Differentiated Instruction

📖 **Interactive Reading and Notetaking Study Guide, Adapted Version (English/Spanish)**
- **L1** Chapter 5, Section 2 **ELL LPR SN**

Teacher's Edition
- **L1** Describing, p. 146 **ELL LPR SN**
- **L1** Create a Media Campaign, p. 148 **LPR**
- **L3** Create a Media Campaign, p. 148 **GT**

Assess and Reteach

Assess Progress
Evaluate student comprehension with Check Your Progress and Section Quiz.

Reteach
Assign the Interactive Reading and Notetaking Study Guide to help struggling students.

Extend
Extend the lesson by having students research and write a paragraph about the Sons of Liberty and the Daughters of Liberty.

Instructional Resources

📖 **Interactive Reading and Notetaking Study Guide**
- **L2** Chapter 5, Section 2

All in One Teaching Resources, Unit 2
- **L2** Reading Readiness Guide, p. 17
- **L2** Section Quiz, p. 25

Progress Monitoring Transparencies
- **L2** Chapter 5, Section 2

Differentiated Instruction

Teacher's Edition
- **L1** Checkpoints, TE pp. 146, 147, 149

🔊 **SE on Audio CD**
- **L1** Chapter 5, Section 2

Internet Resources
PHSchool.com

Objectives

Students will

1. Identify the causes of the Boston Tea Party.
2. Explain how the colonists protested the Intolerable Acts.
3. Describe the events of April 19, 1775, at Lexington and Concord.

Differentiated Instruction Key

- **L1** Basic to Average
- **L2** All Students
- **L3** Average to Advanced
- **AR** Advanced Readers
- **ELL** English Language Learners
- **GT** Gifted and Talented
- **LPR** Less Proficient Readers
- **SN** Special Needs

Section 3 Lesson Plan

Prepare to Read	Instructional Resources	Differentiated Instruction
Build Background Knowledge Discuss students' predictions of how Britain may react to increasing unrest in its North American colonies. **Set a Purpose for Reading** Have students begin to fill out the Reading Readiness Guide. **Preview Key Terms** Preview the section's Key Terms.	**All in One** Teaching Resources, Unit 2 **L2** Reading Readiness Guide, p. 18 **Teacher's Edition** **L2** Vocabulary Builder, p. 151	💿 **Guided Reading Audio CD** Spanish ELL, LPR, SN

Teach	Instructional Resources	Differentiated Instruction
Instruction **A Dispute Over Tea** Discuss the protest against the Tea Act in which colonists dumped tea into Boston Harbor. **The Intolerable Acts** Discuss the impact of Britain's harsh response to the Boston Tea Party. **The Shot Heard Round the World** Discuss the events leading up to the first battle of the American Revolution.	📖 **Interactive Reading and Notetaking Study Guide** **L2** Chapter 5, Section 3 **Color Transparencies** **L2** Causes of the Revolution **L2** Protesting Taxes	📖 **Interactive Reading and Notetaking Study Guide, Adapted Version (English/Spanish)** **L1** Chapter 5, Section 3 ELL, LPR, SN **Teacher's Edition** **L1** Vocabulary Development, p. 150 ELL, LPR, SN **L1** Comparing Two Viewpoints, p. 152 LPR, SN

Assess and Reteach	Instructional Resources	Differentiated Instruction
Assess Progress Evaluate student comprehension with Check Your Progress and Section Quiz. **Reteach** Assign the Interactive Reading and Notetaking Study Guide to help struggling students. **Extend** Extend the lesson by having students prepare a news report about the Boston Tea Party.	📖 **Interactive Reading and Notetaking Study Guide** **L2** Chapter 5, Section 3 **All in One** Teaching Resources, Unit 2 **L2** Reading Readiness Guide, p. 18 **L2** Section Quiz, p. 26 **Progress Monitoring Transparencies** **L2** Chapter 5, Section 3	**Teacher's Edition** **L1** Checkpoints, TE pp. 151, 152, 153 💿 **SE on Audio CD** **L1** Chapter 5, Section 3 **Internet Resources** PHSchool.com

Section 4 The War Begins *1.5 periods, .75 block*

Objectives
Students will

1. Identify the issues facing the Second Continental Congress.
2. Describe the differences between Patriots and Loyalists.
3. Identify the Olive Branch Petition, and explain why it failed.
4. Explain the significance of the Battle at Bunker Hill.

Differentiated Instruction Key
L1 Basic to Average		**AR** Advanced Readers
L2 All Students		**ELL** English Language Learners
L3 Average to Advanced		**GT** Gifted and Talented
		LPR Less Proficient Readers
		SN Special Needs

Prepare to Read

Build Background Knowledge
Have students preview the chapter to predict how the conflict that began at Lexington and Concord will develop.

Set a Purpose for Reading
Have students begin to fill out the Reading Readiness Guide.

Preview Key Terms
Preview the section's Key Terms.

Instructional Resources
All in One Teaching Resources, Unit 2
- **L2** Reading Readiness Guide, p. 19

Teacher's Edition
- **L2** Vocabulary Builder, p. 157

Differentiated Instruction
- Guided Reading Audio CD
  Spanish ELL, LPR, SN

Teach

Instruction
The Second Continental Congress
Discuss the meeting that the colonists organized in response to the rising conflict between them and the British government.

Early Battles
Discuss the Battle of Bunker Hill and other early battles of the American Revolution, and their effects.

Instructional Resources
Interactive Reading and Notetaking Study Guide
- **L2** Chapter 5, Section 4

All in One Teaching Resources, Unit 2
- **L2** Revolution or Compromise?, p. 21
- **L2** Skills for Life Worksheet, p. 22

Differentiated Instruction
Interactive Reading and Notetaking Study Guide, Adapted Version (English/Spanish)
- **L1** Chapter 5, Section 4 ELL, LPR, SN

Teacher's Edition
- **L1** Outlining, p. 156 LPR, SN
- **L3** Explaining the Colonists' Point of View, p. 158 AR, GT
- **L1** Visualizing the Events, p. 160 ELL, LPR, SN

Assess and Reteach

Assess Progress
Evaluate student comprehension with Check Your Progress and Section Quiz.

Reteach
Assign the Interactive Reading and Notetaking Study Guide to help struggling students.

Extend
Extend the lesson by having students complete the History Interactive activity online.

Instructional Resources
Interactive Reading and Notetaking Study Guide
- **L2** Chapter 5, Section 4

All in One Teaching Resources, Unit 2
- **L2** Word Knowledge Rating Form, p. 15
- **L2** Reading Readiness Guide, p. 19
- **L2** Section Quiz, p. 27
- **L2** Chapter Test, p. 31

Progress Monitoring Transparencies
- **L2** Chapter 5, Section 4

Differentiated Instruction
Teacher's Edition
- **L1** Checkpoints, TE pp. 158, 161

All in One Teaching Resources, Unit 2
- **L1** Chapter Test, p. 28

- SE on Audio CD
- **L1** Chapter 5, Section 4

Extend the Lesson Through Technology Research

Help students deepen their understanding of the Chapter Essential Question: **How did the relationship between Britain and the colonies fall apart?** Students should use library or Internet resources. The Web codes provided offer access to Internet resources students can use to complete each activity. Use the appropriate four-point rubric in Assessment Rubrics to evaluate the activity.

📖 **Assessment Rubrics**

Write a Newscast

Have students work in small groups to conduct research about the battles of the French and Indian War. Have each group prepare a newscast about one of the battles, such as the battle at Fort Necessity. Use this activity after students have completed Section 1.

 Group research activity `L2`

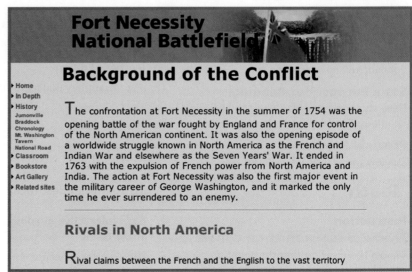

 Web Code: mve-0130

Conduct a Quiz Show

Arrange students into groups of three or four. Have each group conduct research on one of the laws passed by the British Parliament that affected the colonies from the end of the French and Indian War to the American Revolution, such as the Townshend Acts or the Tea Act. Ask each group to prepare questions and answers for a quiz show. Questions should focus on the purpose of each law or the responses or reactions from colonists. Ask one student to act as the host for each group. Rotate groups so the host asks the questions to students in a different group. Use this activity after students have completed Section 3.

 Group research activity `L2`

 Web Code: mvd-0131

Create an Editorial Cartoon about the Colonies in the 1770s

Have students use the Web site to research the use of political cartoons to influence public opinion in the colonies in the 1770s. Ask students to use what they have learned to create an original political cartoon that expresses a point of view about a person or an event from the period. Students should display their cartoons and offer brief explanations of the cartoons' symbols and meanings. Use the cartoons when studying Section 3.

 Individual research activity ELL, LPR, SN **L1**

 Go Online Web Code: mvd-0132
PHSchool.com

Hold a Debate

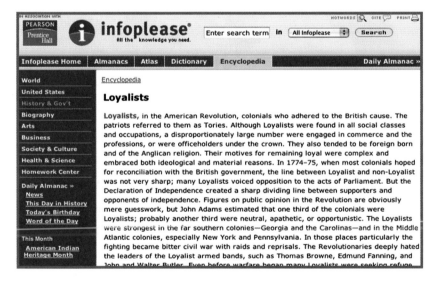

Organize students into two groups—Loyalists and Patriots. Have them do research to support why Americans should not seek independence (Loyalists) or should seek independence (Patriots). Then hold an in-class debate between the two groups. Each group should choose two or three students to present their argument. Use this activity after students have completed Section 4.

 Group research activity AR, GT **L3**

 Go Online Web Code: mvh-0133
PHSchool.com

Why It Matters

In this chapter, students will focus on how growing discontent with British policies led to open rebellion and eventually the desire for independence among a majority of colonists.

One of the colonists' complaints was that they had no voice in the British Parliament, but were bound by its laws. Today, elections in which people choose their government leaders make those leaders responsive to the desires of the people.

The early successes in the war against Britain, such as the ride of Paul Revere to warn the colonists in Lexington and Concord of approaching British troops, show the power that everyday people can have in uniting for the common good. Today, the participation of a nation's citizens in political and civic life is critical to the success of our communities and country.

Chapter Essential Question

How did the relationship between Britain and the colonies fall apart?

Think Like a Historian

- To preview this chapter have students review the content on these pages. Ask: **What will you be learning about in this chapter?** (about the tensions between Britain and the colonies that would lead to war)

- Have students read and then paraphrase the quotation. **How do the colonists feel towards King George?** (They are loyal and dutiful subjects.) **What is making them angry?** (the persecution and tyranny of his rule)

- Study the picture and read the caption. **Who do you think will win the battle? Why?** (Possible answer: The British will win the battle because they have horses and appear to have more troops than the colonists.)

The Road to Revolution

1745-1776

136

Bibliography

For the Teacher

Anderson, Fred. *Crucible of War: The Seven Years' War and the Fate of Empire in British North America, 1754–1766.* Vintage, 2001.

Ketchum, Robert. *Decisive Day: The Battle for Bunker Hill.* Owl Books, 1999.

Wood, Gordon S. *The American Revolution: A History.* Modern Library, 2003.

For the Student

L1 Brandt, Keith. *Paul Revere: Son of Liberty (Easy Biographies).* Sagebrush, 1999.

L2 Lavender, William. *Just Jane: A Daughter of England Caught in the Struggle of the American Revolution.* Gulliver, 2002.

L3 Irvin, Benjamin. *Samuel Adams: Son of Liberty, Father of Revolution (Oxford Portraits).* Oxford University Press, 2002.

"We profess to be his loyal and dutiful subjects.... Nevertheless, to the persecution and tyranny of his cruel ministry, we will not tamely submit."

—Massachusetts Provincial Congress, regarding King George III, 1775

Massachusetts colonists and British soldiers exchange fire across the green at Lexington, April 19, 1775.

CHAPTER 5

What You Will Learn

Section 1
TROUBLE ON THE FRONTIER
A struggle on the western frontier draws France and Britain into a worldwide struggle.

Section 2
THE COLONISTS RESIST TIGHTER CONTROL
Efforts to solve Britain's financial problems raise the anger of people in the colonies.

Section 3
FROM PROTEST TO REBELLION
By 1775, many Americans were so enraged by British tax policies that they were ready to break away from Britain.

Section 4
THE WAR BEGINS
In the first days of the war, both sides expected the struggle to be short. They never expected to fight for seven years.

🔍 Reading Skill
Draw Inferences and Conclusions
In this chapter, you will learn how to use details from primary and secondary sources to draw inferences and conclusions.

137

History Background

The Midnight Riders The famous midnight rider, Paul Revere, worked as a message carrier for Boston's Committee of Safety. He was instructed to warn colonists of the impending British attack. Two friends quietly rowed Revere across the Charles River past the large British warship, the *Somerset*, unnoticed.

Upon reaching the shore, Revere first set out to Lexington. He then rode on to Concord with fellow messengers William Dawes and Samuel Prescott. The trio ran into the British along the way. All escaped unharmed, but only Prescott was able to make it to Concord—Revere had his horse taken by the British and Dawes fell off his horse and ran away on foot. The riders' dedication to the Patriot cause reflected the growing sense of democratic ideals.

Prepare to Read

Use the following for reading skill support.

All in One Teaching Resources, Unit 2, Chapter Prereading Guide, p. 4; History Reading Skill, p. 14

History Reading Skill *Online*
Web code: mve-3000

Differentiated Instruction

The following Teacher's Edition strategies are suitable for students of varying abilities.

L3 Advanced Readers, pp. 142, 154, 158 AR

L1 English Language Learners, pp. 139, 140, 146, 150, 160 ELL

L3 Gifted and Talented, pp. 142, 148, 154, 158 GT

L1 Less Proficient Readers, pp. 139, 140, 146, 148, 150, 152, 156, 160 LPR

L1 Special Needs, p. 139, 140, 146, 150, 152, 156, 160 SN

Chapter Resources

Teaching Resources, Unit 2
Chapter Prereading Guide, p. 4
Word Knowledge Rating Form, p. 15
History Reading Skill, p. 14
Skills for Life Worksheet, p. 22
Chapter Tests A/B (L1/L2), pp. 28, 31
Letter Home (English/Spanish), pp. 7, 8

Spanish Support
L1 Interactive Reading and Notetaking Study Guide, Spanish, Adapted Version
L1 Guided Reading Audio CD, Spanish

Media and Technology
L1 SE on Audio CD
L2 Social Studies Skills Tutor CD-ROM
ExamView Test Bank CD-ROM

Discovery SCHOOL

Quick View Video
View the chapter video for a quick preview of the main ideas.

Chapter 5

Visual Preview

How did the relationship between Britain and the colonies fall apart?

Build Background Knowledge   L2

Have students think about how their experiences in school compare to those their parents had when they were in school. Lead a structured discussion (TE p. T24) about what is the same and what is different in schools. *(same: basic courses, pressure of tests, after school work, school activities; different: may have more diverse student body, new technology, new slang, clothing styles)* Remind students that life in the colonies was in some ways the same and some ways different from life in the parent country. Discuss how these new experiences might cause understanding or stress between the colonies and England.

Instruction   L2

- For background information on conducting a lesson for the Visual Preview, see TE p. T20.

- Write the Essential Question on the board. Ask students to recall what they know about the relationship between Britain and the colonies. Ask: **In what ways were the colonies dependent on Britain?** *(Britain provided defense against Native Americans; taxed the colonists; made laws; and traded with the colonists.)* Ask students to consider which of these matters colonists might want to do on their own. *(Colonists wanted to control their own laws, taxes, and trade.)*

- Have students look at the illustration on this page. Ask: **How did the king of England react to the colonial protests?** *(Possible answer: He warned the colonists to stop the protests.)* Ask: **What do you think he would do if the colonists did not stop protesting?** *(Possible answer: He would send the British sea power to punish them.)*

- Look at the list of acts. **Why did Parliament enact all the laws?** *(to pay for defending the colonists)*

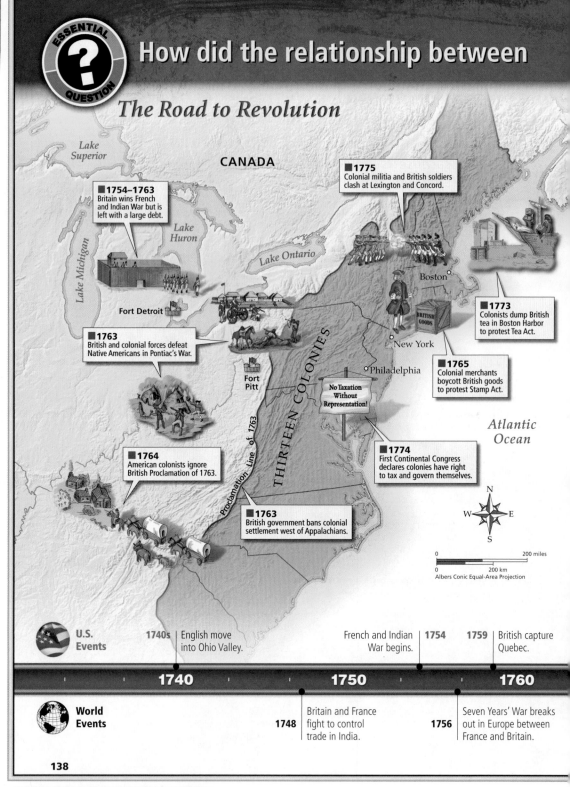

How did the relationship between

The Road to Revolution

1754–1763 Britain wins French and Indian War but is left with a large debt.

1775 Colonial militia and British soldiers clash at Lexington and Concord.

1763 British and colonial forces defeat Native Americans in Pontiac's War.

1773 Colonists dump British tea in Boston Harbor to protest Tea Act.

1765 Colonial merchants boycott British goods to protest Stamp Act.

1764 American colonists ignore British Proclamation of 1763.

1774 First Continental Congress declares colonies have right to tax and govern themselves.

1763 British government bans colonial settlement west of Appalachians.

No Taxation Without Representation!

U.S. Events	**1740s** English move into Ohio Valley.	French and Indian War begins. **1754**	**1759** British capture Quebec.

1740	**1750**	**1760**

World Events	**1748** Britain and France fight to control trade in India.	**1756** Seven Years' War breaks out in Europe between France and Britain.

138

History Background

Uncompromising Ruler King George III began his rule in 1760. He was determined to regain the powers lost by his immediate predecessors. He wanted to weaken the control by the Whig party and set out to choose his own ministers, dissolve the cabinet system, and have Parliament accept his authority. Although not trying to be tyrannical, he wanted to limit the power of the aristocracy.

His actions at home confirmed American fears that there was a plan by the king and his Parliament to deny colonists their liberty. His indignant reaction to colonial challenge of British rule, and his need to make an example of the colonists, made compromise unlikely.

Britain and the colonies fall apart?

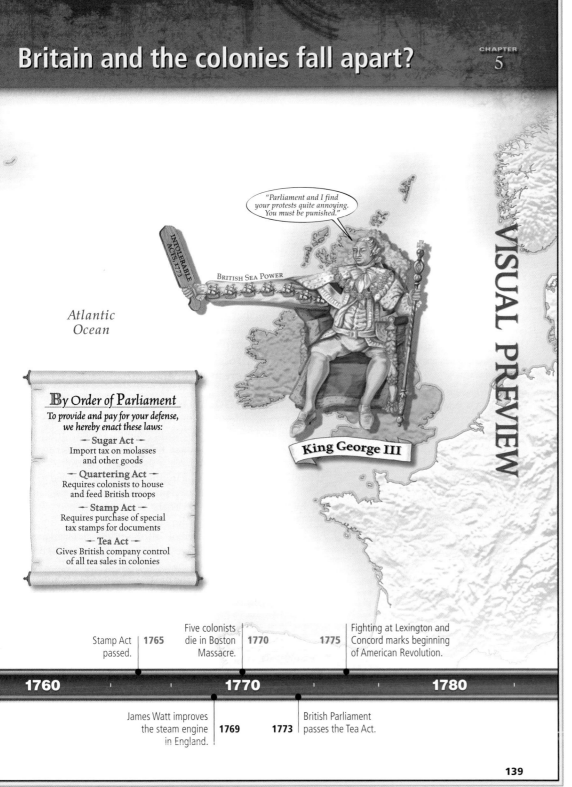

Instruction (continued)

- Have students examine the timeline. **What years are represented on the timeline?** *(1740–1780)* **When did the French and Indian War begin?** *(1754)* **When did the American Revolution begin?** *(1775)*

- Ask students to look at the graphics on the map of North America. **What two events occurred in 1763?** *(British and colonial forces defeated the French and the Native Americans, British government denied colonial settlement West of Appalachians.)* Pair students to write the dates and summaries of the events in order on a timeline. Draw a timeline on the board and have students give their answers. Ask: **How many of the events listed involve colonial protests against the British?** *(5)*

- Have students rewrite the Essential Question in simple terms in their notes. **Why did relations between Britain and the colonies change?** You may also post the question in a prominent place in the classroom and leave it there while discussing the chapter. Tell students to use the section focus question as a guide to answering the Essential Question as they read the chapter.

- Tell students that as they complete the Notetaking Study Guide for this chapter, they will be building the answer to the Essential Question.

Interactive Reading and Notetaking Study Guide, Chapter 5 (Adapted Version also available.)

Vocabulary Builder

Preview the Vocabulary Have students preview the vocabulary in the chapter and rate how well they know each word on the Word Knowledge Rating Form. Collect the sheets and explain that they will have a chance to go over the forms later.

All in One Teaching Resources, Unit 2, Word Knowledge Rating Form, p. 15

Monitor Progress Students should demonstrate their understanding of the words by finding pictures that illustrate them. For example, for the word *emotional*, students may show an athlete who has just won a championship. Pair students to exchange their pictures and have partners check understanding of the relationship of the image to the word. Review the material with students.

Review and Preview

Students have learned about the spread of new ideas about government in the colonies. Now they will focus on how competition between European countries in North America led colonists to begin considering new plans for self-government.

Section Focus Question

How did the British gain French territory in North America?

Before you begin the lesson for the day, write the Section Focus Question on the board. (*Lesson focus: The British gained control of French territory in North America with military victories during the French and Indian War.*)

Prepare to Read

Build Background Knowledge `L2`

Ask students to recall from earlier chapters what they have learned about competition between European countries for control of territories in North America. Write all accurate information on the board. Then ask students to preview the section by reading the headings and looking at the images. Ask students to predict what else they will learn about European competition for control of North America. Use the Numbered Heads strategy (TE, p. T24) to elicit responses.

Set a Purpose `L2`

- Read each statement in the Reading Readiness Guide aloud. Ask students to mark the statements True or False.

  All in One Teaching Resources, Unit 2, Reading Readiness Guide, p. 16

- Have students discuss the statements in pairs or in groups of four, then mark the worksheets again. Use the Numbered Heads participation strategy (TE, p. T24) to call on students to share their group's perspectives. The students will return to these worksheets later.

Four Bullets Through My Coat

" We were attacked by a body of French and Indians, whose number (I am certain) did not exceed 300 men. Ours consisted of about 1,300 well-armed troops, chiefly the English soldiers... I had four bullets through my coat, and two horses shot under me. "

—George Washington, reporting on the defeat of General Braddock's army, 1755

◀ Washington captures French Fort Duquesne, 1758.

Trouble on the Frontier

Objectives

- Identify the reasons why fighting broke out between France and Britain in North America.
- Describe the early defeat of the British by the French at the beginning of the French and Indian War.
- Explain how the British gained victory, and explain the results of the French and Indian War.

🎯 Reading Skill

Make Inferences When ideas are not actually stated, readers must infer these ideas by analyzing the details and evidence in the text. As you read about the choices and views of both the Americans and the British in colonial times, think about the inferences you can make from their actions.

Key Terms and People

George Washington   alliance
militia   cede

Why It Matters American colonists expanded their settlements. As they pushed further inland, they came into conflict with the French and Indians. In this power struggle, the future of much of North America was at stake.

❓ **Section Focus Question: How did the British gain French territory in North America?**

Competing Empires

By the middle of the 1700s, France and Britain each controlled large areas of North America which bordered on each other for thousands of miles. Each country feared the other and sought to increase the area it controlled. These ambitions collided on the frontier and eventually led to war.

Native Americans lived on most of the territory claimed by France and Britain. There were few French settlers. Therefore, they did not threaten to seize Native American lands. However, the need of British settlers for farmland led to conflict with the Native Americans. By the 1740s, British settlers were pushing into the Ohio River valley lands claimed by the French. The pressure soon led to trouble.

The French and Indian War Begins In 1753, the French began building forts to back their claim to the land between Lake Erie and the Ohio River. This news alarmed the Virginia Colony, which also claimed the Ohio River valley. The governor of Virginia decided to send soldiers to order the French to leave. He chose a 21-year-old surveyor in the Virginia militia, George Washington, as the leader. The **militia** is a force made up of civilians trained as soldiers but not part of the regular army. Washington made the dangerous journey, returning home to tell the governor that the French had rejected his warning.

140   Chapter 5 The Road to Revolution

Differentiated Instruction

`L1` **English Language Learners**   `L1` **Less Proficient Readers**   `L1` **Special Needs**

Create a Flowchart As students read, have them create a flowchart to organize the order of events that led to the outbreak of the French and Indian War. When they have finished, have students compare their charts with a partner before handing them in.

The next year, Washington traveled west again with orders to build a fort where the Allegheny and the Monongahela (muh non goh HEEL uh) rivers meet to form the Ohio River.

Washington arrived too late. The French were there already, building their own fort, which they called Fort Duquesne (du KANE). Washington marched south for about 50 miles and built a small fort of his own. He called it Fort Necessity.

Later, Washington's troops attacked and defeated a small French force. However, a larger French army arrived and forced Washington to surrender Fort Necessity. The French allowed Washington and his men to return home to Virginia with the message that they would never give up the Ohio River valley.

The Albany Congress Expecting war to break out soon, the British government called a meeting of colonial leaders. It took place in Albany, New York. The British wanted the colonies to agree to cooperate in defending themselves against the French. The British also invited the Iroquois tribes to the meeting. They hoped to form an alliance with the Iroquois against the French. An **alliance** is an agreement between nations or groups to help each other against other nations or groups.

The Iroquois refused to make an alliance, in part because they expected the French to defeat the British in a war. The colonial leaders tried to work out a plan to defend themselves. Benjamin Franklin of Pennsylvania believed the colonies had to succeed. To make that point, his newspaper, the *Philadelphia Gazette,* published a picture of a snake chopped into pieces with the warning "Join, or Die."

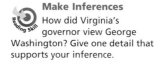

Make Inferences
How did Virginia's governor view George Washington? Give one detail that supports your inference.

Join, or Die

JOIN, or DIE.

Reading Political Cartoons
Skills Activity

Benjamin Franklin's 1754 cartoon was a plea for unity in defending the colonies during the French and Indian War.

(a) Distinguish Relevant Information Identify the eight sets of initials that label the eight pieces of the snake.

(b) Draw Conclusions What point is Franklin making about the importance of colonial unity?

Teach

Competing Empires
p. 140

Instruction L2

■ **Vocabulary Builder** Before teaching this lesson, preteach the High-Use Words **resolve** and **phase,** using the strategy on TE p. T21.

Key Terms Following the instructions on p. 7, have students create a See It–Remember It chart for the Key Terms in this chapter.

■ To help students better understand the concept of power, which is important to the understanding of this section and chapter, use the Concept Lesson Power. Provide students with copies of the Concept Organizer.

All in One Teaching Resources, Unit 2, Concept Lesson, p. 23; Concept Organizer, p. 6

■ Read Competing Empires with students using the Paragraph Shrinking strategy (TE, p. T23).

■ Discuss the Albany Plan of Union. Ask: **How would an alliance with the Iroquois have helped the British?** (*If the Iroquois joined the British in an alliance, then the French would have had to defend against two armies.*)

Independent Practice
Have students begin to fill in the Study Guide for this section.

Monitor Progress

As students fill in the Notetaking Study Guide, circulate to make sure students understand the importance of the Albany Congress. Provide assistance as needed.

Vocabulary Builder

Use the information below to teach students this section's high-use words.

High-Use Word	Definition and Sample Sentence
resolve, p. 143	*n.* strong determination to succeed in doing something The goal of gaining land for Spain strengthened Columbus's **resolve** to find a sea route to Asia.
phase, p. 143	*n.* stage of development Puritan ideas strongly influenced the early **phase** of colonial development.

Answers

Reading Skill He thought Washington was a capable leader because he sent him on an important mission even though Washington was only 23 years old.

Reading Political Cartoons (a) South Carolina, North Carolina, Virginia, Maryland, Pennsylvania, New Jersey, New York, New England **(b)** Possible answer: Without sticking together, the colonies would not survive.

Early British Defeats

p. 142

Instruction　L2

- Have students read Early British Defeats. Remind students to look for sequence of events.

- Ask: **How did the British defeats affect the chances of a British alliance with the Iroquois?** (*They made an alliance less likely because the Iroquois thought it was likely that the French would win the war against the British.*)

- Ask: **How would a French victory in the French and Indian War affect the British colonies and colonists in North America?** (*Possible answer: Britain would probably have to give up its colonies, and its colonists would either have to return to Britain, move to another of its colonies, or agree to live under French rule.*)

- Show students the transparency The French and Indian War.

Color Transparencies, The French and Indian War

Independent Practice

Have students continue to fill in the Study Guide for this section.

> **Interactive Reading and Notetaking Study Guide,** Chapter 5, Section 1 (Adapted Version also available.)

Monitor Progress

As students fill in the Notetaking Study Guide, circulate to make sure students understand the importance of the British military setbacks. If students do not seem to have a good understanding, have them reread the section. Provide assistance as needed.

Answers

☑Checkpoint The British also claimed the Ohio River valley.

MAP✦MASTER *Skills Activity* **(a)** Fort Frontenac and Fort Niagara **(b)** Capturing these two areas would give the British control of important naval routes and limit French power.

Franklin drew up a plan, called the Albany Plan of Union. It called for a council of representatives elected by the colonial assemblies. The council would have authority over western settlements, relations with Native Americans, and other urgent matters. It also could organize armies and collect taxes to pay its expenses.

The Albany Congress approved Franklin's plan, but the colonial assemblies rejected it. The colonies wanted to control their own taxes and armies. Franklin complained that "everyone cries, union is necessary," but they behave like "weak noodles" when the time comes to take action.

☑**Checkpoint** **Why were the British concerned about French activity in the Ohio River valley?**

Early British Defeats

Soon after Washington's return, the British government decided it had to push the French out of the Ohio River valley. In 1755, it sent General Edward Braddock to Virginia with orders to capture Fort Duquesne. Braddock arrived with a large force of regular British troops and Virginia militia. Colonel George Washington joined Braddock's force as a volunteer.

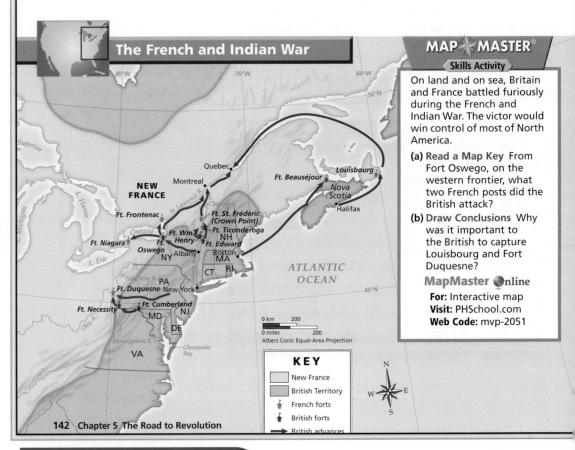

The French and Indian War

MAP✦MASTER®

Skills Activity

On land and on sea, Britain and France battled furiously during the French and Indian War. The victor would win control of most of North America.

(a) Read a Map Key From Fort Oswego, on the western frontier, what two French posts did the British attack?

(b) Draw Conclusions Why was it important to the British to capture Louisbourg and Fort Duquesne?

MapMaster ⬤nline

For: Interactive map
Visit: PHSchool.com
Web Code: mvp-2051

KEY
- New France
- British Territory
- French forts
- British forts
- British advances

142 Chapter 5 The Road to Revolution

Differentiated Instruction

L3 Advanced Readers

Predicting Have students work in pairs to select a major event from this chapter. Tell each pair to assume that the event chosen either had not occurred, or that it had a different outcome. For example, what if George Washington rather than Edward Braddock had been killed in the battle near

L3 Gifted and Talented

Fort Duquesne, or the French had won the French and Indian War? Have each pair give a brief presentation to the class in which they predict how subsequent events in American history might have been different.

Disaster at Fort Duquesne General Braddock understood military tactics used in Europe, where armies fought in formation on open fields. But he knew nothing about fighting in North America, where conditions were very different. Braddock did not respect colonial soldiers. He did not listen to warnings that soldiers marching down a narrow road through a dense forest in red uniforms were perfect targets for an enemy fighting from behind trees and bushes. When Benjamin Franklin warned him about the danger of ambushes, Braddock said they were no threat to his well-trained troops.

As Braddock's force neared Fort Duquesne in early July, it was ambushed by French troops and their Native American allies. More than half of Braddock's men were killed or wounded, with the general himself among the dead.

More British Defeats The British had other setbacks during 1755. An army led by the governor of Massachusetts failed to take Fort Niagara on Lake Ontario. Further east, an army of British colonists and Native Americans was ambushed and suffered heavy losses near Lake George. These defeats may have strengthened Iroquois leaders' <u>resolve</u> not to ally with Britain.

In May 1756, Britain declared war on France, marking the official beginning of the Seven Years' War between the two countries. Shortly thereafter, French troops led by General Louis de Montcalm captured and destroyed Britain's Fort Oswego on Lake Ontario. In 1757, Montcalm captured Fort William Henry on Lake George.

☑️**Checkpoint** **What fatal errors did General Edward Braddock make?**

The British Turn the Tide

The situation improved for Britain during 1757 when William Pitt became prime minister. Pitt sought top generals who had genuine military talent. He chose James Wolfe, who was only 30 years old when he became one of Britain's top generals.

With Pitt's generals in command, the war entered a new <u>phase</u>. In the summer of 1758, Britain scored its first major victory in the war. It captured the fort at Louisbourg. In the fall, the British took Fort Duquesne. The British renamed the post Fort Pitt, in William Pitt's honor. It later became the city of Pittsburgh.

These and other victories led the Iroquois to side with the British. More victories in 1759 set the stage for the British attack on Quebec and the key battle of the war.

Quebec, the capital of New France, was located on a high cliff, overlooking the St. Lawrence River. General Montcalm commanded the French defenders, and General Wolfe led the British attack. At first, the British made little progress. Then, at night, they found an unguarded trail that allowed them to climb the cliffs protecting the city without being discovered. In September 1757, approximately 4,000 British soldiers defeated 4,500 French soldiers on the plains in

General Edward Braddock

Vocabulary Builder
<u>resolve</u> (ree SAHLV) **n.** strong determination to succeed in doing something

Vocabulary Builder
<u>phase</u> (fayz) **n.** stage of development

History Background

Seven Years' War Most of the great powers of Europe fought in the Seven Years' War (1756–1763). Although alliances shifted, the war generally pitted France, Austria, Saxony, Sweden, and Russia against Prussia, Hanover, and Britain. In addition to North America, the countries also fought battles across Europe and in the West Indies, Africa, and India. Britain's victory over France, its main rival for colonies, gave it control of much of North America and India.

The British Turn the Tide
p. 143

Instruction [L2]

- Have students read The British Turn the Tide. Remind students to look for details to answer the Section Focus Question.

- Ask: **What lands did the British gain in the Treaty of Paris?** (*French Canada, Spanish Florida, and all French lands east of the Mississippi except New Orleans*)

- Ask: **How did the battle for Quebec affect the war?** (*It was a turning point for the British because the French could no longer defend the rest of their North American territory.*)

Independent Practice

Have students complete the Study Guide for this section.

📖 **Interactive Reading and Notetaking Study Guide,** Chapter 5, Section 1 (Adapted Version also available.)

Monitor Progress

- As students complete the Notetaking Study Guide, circulate to make sure students understand the importance of the British victory. Provide assistance as needed.

- Tell students to fill in the last column of the Reading Readiness Guide. Probe for what they learned that confirms or invalidates each statement.

  All in One **Teaching Resources, Unit 2,** Reading Readiness Guide, p. 16

Answer

☑️**Checkpoint** He tried to fight using tactics that worked in Europe and did not adapt to North American conditions.

Assess and Reteach

Assess Progress `L2`

Have students complete Check Your Progress. Administer the Section Quiz.

All in One Teaching Resources, Unit 2, Section Quiz, p. 24

To further assess student understanding, use the Progress Monitoring Transparency.

Progress Monitoring Transparencies, Chapter 5, Section 1

Reteach `L1`

If students need more instruction, have them read this section in the Interactive Reading and Notetaking Study Guide and complete the accompanying question.

Interactive Reading and Notetaking Study Guide, Chapter 5, Section 1 (Adapted Version also available.)

Extend `L3`

Explain to students that the French and Indian War was one part of the Seven Years' War between Britain and France. Have students research the Seven Years' War. Ask them to summarize in their own words the reasons for and the outcomes of the war, and then write a few sentences explaining its impact on Britain.

Extend Online

For: Help in starting Extend activity
Visit: PHSchool.com
Web Code: mve-0134

Progress Monitoring Online

Students may check their comprehension of this section by completing the Progress Monitoring Online graphic organizer and self-quiz.

Answer

☑Checkpoint The British defeated the French, who were no longer able to defend the rest of their North American territory.

Section 1 Check Your Progress

1. **(a)** The colonies could expand farther west after the war.
(b) Possible answer: Most probably wanted to help the British because they

---

The British attack Quebec.

front of the city. More than 2,000 soldiers were killed or wounded in the battle, including both Wolfe and Montcalm.

After losing Quebec, France could no longer defend the rest of its North American territory. Montreal, the other major French city in Canada, fell in 1760. In February 1763, Britain and France signed the Treaty of Paris. France lost almost all of its North American possessions. France ceded, or surrendered, French Canada to Great Britain. Great Britain also gained all other French territory east of the Mississippi, with the exception of New Orleans. Britain also received Spanish Florida. New Orleans, along with all French territory west of the Mississippi, went to Spain.

Native Americans also lost a great deal. Without French help, the Native Americans could not stop British settlers from moving on their lands.

☑**Checkpoint** **What was the outcome of the Battle of Quebec?**

⭐ **Looking Back and Ahead** The defeat of the French left the British in control of a vast area in North America. However, whatever sense of triumph British leaders felt at the war's outcome was soon replaced by a nagging realization. The victory had substituted one set of problems for another.

Section 1 | Check Your Progress

Progress Monitoring Online
For: Self-test with instant help
Visit: PHSchool.com
Web Code: mva-2051

Comprehension and Critical Thinking

1. **(a) Summarize** How did the French and Indian War affect the 13 colonies?
(b) Detect Points of View How did most colonists feel about helping the British? Explain.

2. **(a) Recall** How did the war go for the British before 1757? After 1757?
(b) Make Predictions How might the outcome influence relations between the British and the American colonists?

Reading Skill

3. **Make Inferences** Think about how the Iroquois felt about the Ohio River valley. Why do you think the Iroquois may have preferred to be neutral in the conflict between France and England? What can you infer about how the Iroquois felt about European conflicts in North America?

Key Terms

4. Write two definitions for each key term: militia, alliance. First, write a formal definition for your teacher. Second, write a definition in everyday English for a classmate.

Writing

5. Write two or three sentences identifying the problems facing the Albany Congress. Were these problems solved? Explain your answer in three or four sentences.

---

wanted to be safe from the French and their Native American allies.

2. **(a)** Before 1757, the British were losing many important battles, but after 1757 they began winning key battles.
(b) Answers will vary, but students should indicate that colonists might feel grateful to Britain for pushing back the French and Native Americans.

3. Possible answer: The Iroquois probably preferred to remain neutral because

they did not want to be on the losing side. They probably wanted only to protect their own interests and so did not care which of the European countries won the conflict.

4. Answers will vary, but students' definitions should be accurate.

5. Answers will vary, but students should show an understanding of the Albany Congress and the problems it faced.

▲ Colonial teapot protesting British tax stamps

A Burdensome Tax

"We have called this a burdensome tax, because the duties are so numerous and so high, and the embarrassments to business in this infant, sparsely settled country so great, that it would be totally impossible for the people to subsist under it."

—John Adams, speaking against the Stamp Act, 1765

The Colonists Resist Tighter Control

Objectives

- Explain the conflict between Native Americans and British settlers in 1763.
- Describe how the colonists responded to British tax laws.
- Describe what happened during the Boston Massacre.

Reading Skill

Support Inferences With Details Inferences must be based on information. This information may be details stated in the text. First, make the logical inference, then read the text and identify support for your inference. If you cannot support the inference, adjust it until the evidence will support it.

Key Terms and People

duty
boycott
petition

writ of assistance
John Adams
Samuel Adams

Why It Matters American colonists enjoyed a large degree of self-government. They were proud of their rights and loyal to the British monarch. But the French and Indian War strained this loyalty.

? Section Focus Question: How did the French and Indian War draw the colonists closer together but increase friction with Britain?

Conflict With Native Americans

By 1763, Britain controlled almost all of North America east of the Mississippi River. This enormous territory promised endless room for settlement. However, Native Americans living west of the Appalachian Mountains were desperately trying to keep their lands. Fighting between Native Americans and white settlers began as soon as the French and Indian War ended.

Pontiac's War In the last days of the French and Indian War, the leader of the Ottawa nation, Pontiac, formed an alliance of western Native Americans. In May 1763, Pontiac and his allies attacked British forts and settlements throughout the area. Nearly half a dozen western British forts were destroyed and at least 2,000 backcountry settlers were killed. British settlers reacted with equal viciousness. They killed Native Americans who had not attacked them.

The British finally defeated Pontiac's forces in early August at a battle near Fort Pitt. Pontiac continued to fight for another year, but by the fall of 1764, the war was over.

The Proclamation of 1763 Britain wanted to avoid further wars with Native Americans on the frontier. Therefore, the British government issued the Proclamation of 1763. It banned

Section 2 The Colonists Resist Tighter Control **145**

Review and Preview

Students have learned about the British victory over the French in the French and Indian War. Now they will focus on how the war affected the relationship between the colonists and the British government.

Section Focus Question

How did the French and Indian War draw the colonists closer together but increase friction with Britain?

Before you begin the lesson for the day, write the Section Focus Question on the board. (*Lesson focus: During the war, people from the colonies had greater contact with each other. Friction with Britain increased when Britain raised taxes on the colonists.*)

Prepare to Read

Build Background Knowledge   L2

Remind students that in Chapter 4 they read about new political ideas being spread in the colonies. Ask students how they think the colonists might react to British laws that they believed to be unfair. Use the Think-Write-Pair-Share strategy (TE, p. T25) to elicit responses.

Set a Purpose   L2

- Read each statement in the Reading Readiness Guide aloud. Ask students to mark the statements True or False.

  All in One Teaching Resources, Unit 2, Reading Readiness Guide, p. 17

- Have students discuss the statements in pairs or in groups of four, then mark the worksheets again. Use the Numbered Heads participation strategy (TE, p. T24) to call on students to share their group's perspectives. The students will return to these worksheets later.

Vocabulary Builder

Use the information below to teach students this section's high-use words.

High-Use Word	Definition and Sample Sentence
minimum, p. 146	*adj.* smallest quantity possible With the end of the French and Indian War, colonists expected a **minimum** rise in taxes to the British.
emotional, p. 147	*adj.* appealing to the emotions, or feelings, of people After the French and Indian War, colonial soldiers returned to an **emotional** homecoming.

Teach

Conflict with Native Americans

British Rule Leads to Conflict

pp. 145–146

Instruction L2

- **Vocabulary Builder** Before teaching this section, preteach the High-Use Words **minimum** and **emotional**, using the strategy on TE p. T21.

  Key Terms Have students continue filling in the See It–Remember It chart for the Key Terms in this chapter.

- Read Conflict with Native Americans and British Rule Leads to Conflict with students using the Give One, Get One strategy (TE, p. T25).

- Discuss Pontiac's War. Ask: **Why did Pontiac begin attacking British forts and settlements in the west?** (*He wanted to drive the British out of the lands west of the Appalachian Mountains.*)

- Ask: **How did the colonists start to think of themselves differently after the end of the French and Indian War?** (*They began to think of themselves as different from people living in Britain.*)

Independent Practice

Have students begin to fill in the Study Guide for this section.

📖 **Interactive Reading and Notetaking Study Guide,** Chapter 5, Section 2 (Adapted Version also available.)

Monitor Progress

As students fill in the Notetaking Study Guide, circulate to make sure students understand the importance of the differing perspectives of the colonists and the British government. Provide assistance as needed.

Answers

Reading Charts (a) Britain **(b)** Possible answer: The relations became more tense because Britain imposed new taxes on the colonies without any agreement from the colonists.

☑**Checkpoint** Colonial settlements were banned west of the Appalachian Mountains.

THE FRENCH AND INDIAN WAR

- France loses its North American possessions.
- Britain is left with a large debt.
- Colonists develop a sense of unity.
- Colonists begin settling in the Ohio River valley.
- Native Americans resist colonists settling in the Ohio River valley.

Reading Charts
Skills Activity

The struggle between France and Great Britain to establish an empire in the Americas ended in 1763. The results brought political, social, and economic change to North America.

(a) Read a Chart Which nation faced huge expenses after the war?

(b) Apply Information How do you think the war impacted relations between Britain and the colonies?

Vocabulary Builder
minimum (MIHN ah muhm)
adj. smallest quantity possible

colonial settlement west of a line drawn along the Appalachian Mountains. Settlers were told they had to move to a location east of that line.

The Proclamation of 1763 angered many colonists who believed they had the right to reside wherever they wanted. The proclamation was widely ignored and proved impossible for the British to enforce.

☑**Checkpoint** What were the terms of the Proclamation of 1763?

British Rule Leads to Conflict

The colonists were proud of their contribution toward winning the French and Indian War. Tens of thousands of men had served as soldiers, and many had died in the war. Massachusetts alone lost more than 1,500 men. The colonists expected Britain to be grateful for their assistance. At most, they expected only a minimum rise in taxes.

Although ties between the colonies had begun to grow before the war, the 13 colonies still were divided in many ways. But the people of those colonies also saw themselves as different from people living in Britain. In 1763, the colonists still considered themselves loyal British subjects. Increasingly, however, they identified more with one another than with Britain.

The British saw things differently. The French and Indian War left Britain deeply in debt. Furthermore, these expenses continued. The British government had to keep troops in North America to make sure France did not try to regain its lost territory and to protect settlers against Native American attacks. British leaders believed the colonists should pay part of the debt.

The Sugar Act The British effort to impose new taxes on the colonies began in 1764 when Parliament passed the Sugar Act, which put a duty—or import tax—on several products, including molasses. It also called for harsh punishment of smugglers. Colonial merchants, who sometimes traded in smuggled goods, protested.

Differentiated Instruction

L1 **English Language Learners**   L1 **Less Proficient Readers**   L1 **Special Needs**

Describing Ask students to describe in their own words the new laws mentioned in this section. Descriptions may be oral or written. Ask students to answer the following questions in their descriptions:

- What does the law state?
- Why did the British government believe that this law was necessary?
- What was the impact of this law on the colonists?

The Quartering Act One year later, Parliament passed the Quartering Act. The purpose of the Quartering Act was to save money. To enforce the Proclamation of 1763, Britain kept about 10,000 soldiers in the colonies. The act required colonists to quarter, or house, British troops and provide them with food and other supplies. The colonists protested angrily. Once again, the colonists complained that Parliament was violating their rights.

✓ **Checkpoint** Why did the British impose new taxes on the American colonists?

The Stamp Act

An even more unpopular law was the Stamp Act, passed by Parliament in early 1765. The Stamp Act required that all colonists buy special tax stamps for all kinds of products and activities. The stamps had to be placed on newspapers, wills, licenses, insurance policies, land titles, contracts, and other documents.

Protests against the Stamp Act were widespread. Virginia's House of Burgesses passed several resolutions declaring that it alone had the right to tax the people of Virginia. Patrick Henry, one of the youngest members of that body, made an <u>emotional</u> speech attacking the law. Henry ended his speech with a reference to the murder of Julius Caesar in ancient Rome. When Henry said that some good American would do the same to King George III, cries of treason were hurled against him. Henry replied, "If this be treason, make the most of it."

Other colonial assemblies followed Virginia's example. Merchants in New York, Boston, and Philadelphia organized a boycott—an organized campaign to refuse to buy certain products— of British goods. The protests spread to every colony.

In October, delegates from nine colonies met in New York for the Stamp Act Congress. They sent a petition—a written request to a government. Addressed to the king and Parliament, this petition demanded the end of both the Sugar Act and Stamp Act.

The protests worked. In 1766, Parliament repealed the Stamp Act. However, at the same time it passed the Declaratory Act, which said Parliament had total authority over the colonies. That set the stage for further trouble between Britain and her colonies.

✓ **Checkpoint** Why did colonists object to the Stamp Act?

Support Inferences With Details Use details from the text to support this inference: The British did not expect the colonists to react negatively to new policies after the French and Indian War.

Vocabulary Builder
emotional (ee MOH shuh nahl) **adj.** appealing to the emotions, or feelings, of people

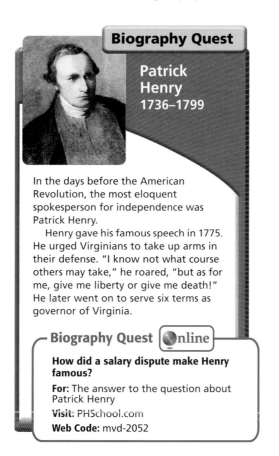

Biography Quest

Patrick Henry 1736–1799

In the days before the American Revolution, the most eloquent spokesperson for independence was Patrick Henry.

Henry gave his famous speech in 1775. He urged Virginians to take up arms in their defense. "I know not what course others may take," he roared, "but as for me, give me liberty or give me death!" He later went on to serve six terms as governor of Virginia.

Biography Quest 🔵 **Online**

How did a salary dispute make Henry famous?

For: The answer to the question about Patrick Henry

Visit: PHSchool.com

Web Code: mvd-2052

The Stamp Act

p. 147

Instruction

- Have students read The Stamp Act. Remind students to look for causes and effects.

- Ask: **How did colonists react to the Stamp Act?** (*There were widespread protests, boycotts, and petitions against the act.*)

- Have students complete the worksheet Patrick Henry to explore colonists' reaction to the Stamp Act. After students have completed the worksheet, ask: **How did the Stamp Act help draw the colonists closer together?** (*They united against an unpopular law and worked together to end the Stamp Act.*)

All in One Teaching Resources, Unit 2, Patrick Henry, p. 20

Independent Practice

Have students continue to fill in the Study Guide for this section.

📖 **Interactive Reading and Notetaking Study Guide,** Chapter 5, Section 2 (Adapted Version also available.)

Monitor Progress

As students fill in the Notetaking Study Guide, circulate to make sure students understand the importance of colonists' protests against unpopular laws. If students do not seem to have a good understanding, have them reread the section. Provide assistance as needed.

Answers

🔵 **Reading Skill** Possible answer: Since British troops would protect the colonists, Britain expected colonists to house and feed troops.

✓ **Checkpoint** to help pay the costs of the war and protecting the colonists

✓ **Checkpoint** They did not want to pay additional taxes on many additional products and services.

Biography Quest Henry earned his reputation as an eloquent speaker at a trial where tobacco farmers' salaries were reduced. Henry argued against repaying any owed monies and implied that the king of England was becoming a tyrant. Many people at the trial considered this treasonous.

History Background

Patrick Henry's Oratory Patrick Henry was 29 years old when he gave his 1765 speech to the Virginia House of Burgesses opposing the Stamp Act. The remarks to which the Student Edition refers were "Caesar had his Brutus, Charles the First his Cromwell"—references to two leaders and their assassins—"and George the Third may profit by their example. If this be treason make the most of it." Henry gave his most famous speech in 1775. When arguing for independence, he said, "I know not what course others may take, but as for me, give me liberty or give me death."

Explore More Video

Discovery School Video

Show the video *Boston Massacre* to tell the story of the events that led to the Boston Massacre and the aftermath of the incident.

Protests Spread

p. 148

Instruction $\boxed{\text{L2}}$

- Have students read Protests Spread. Remind students to look for sequence of events.

- Ask: **Why did Parliament keep the duty on tea when it repealed other taxes?** (*It wanted to assert its power to make laws in the colonies.*)

- Ask: **What effect did the Boston Massacre have on colonial resistance to British policies?** (*It helped strengthen the resistance by further uniting the colonists against the British government through groups like the Committees of Correspondence.*)

Independent Practice

Have students complete the Study Guide for this section.

Interactive Reading and Notetaking Study Guide, Chapter 5, Section 2 (Adapted Version also available.)

Monitor Progress

- As students complete the Notetaking Study Guide, circulate to make sure students understand the importance of protests in the colonies. Provide assistance as needed.

- Tell students to fill in the last column of the Reading Readiness Guide. Probe for what they learned that confirms or invalidates each statement.

All in One Teaching Resources, Unit 2, Reading Readiness Guide, p. 17

Answer

Detect Points of View Possible answer: The British soldiers look confused; the colonists look scared.

Explore More Video
To learn more about the Boston Massacre, view the video.

Massacre! An American view of the Boston Massacre shows an organized unit of British troops firing directly into a group of colonists. But, in fact, more than 400 colonists surrounded the troops, cursing them and throwing sticks, rocks, and ice at them. *Critical Thinking: Detect Points of View How does the artist show the tension at the scene of the Boston Massacre?*

Protests Spread

British officials sought a means of taxing the colonists in a way that would not anger them. Under the Townshend Acts of 1767, Britain would no longer tax products or activities inside the colonies. It would only tax products brought into the colonies.

Writs of Assistance The Townshend Acts set up a system to enforce the new import duties. To help customs officers find illegal goods, they were allowed to use writs of assistance—court orders that allowed officials to make searches without saying for what they were searching. Many colonists saw these writs and the searches they allowed as yet another violation of their rights.

Charles Townshend, the official in charge of the British treasury, also wanted to weaken the colonial assemblies. When the New York assembly refused to supply money to house and feed soldiers under the Quartering Act, Parliament suspended the assembly. The colonists again reacted by boycotting British goods.

The Boston Massacre Once again, the protests worked. The boycott hurt British merchants and manufacturers, who put pressure on Parliament. On March 5, 1770, Parliament repealed all the Townshend duties—except the one on tea. That tax was left in force to demonstrate Parliament's right to tax the colonies.

Differentiated Instruction

L1 Less Proficient Readers

Create a Media Campaign Organize students into small groups. Have the groups create a media campaign to try and persuade colonists either to support or oppose the new laws passed by Parliament, such as the Stamp Act or the Sugar Act. Assign a position, pro or con, for each group.

L3 Gifted and Talented

Have each group create a button, a print advertisement, and a one-minute announcement to communicate its viewpoint. Campaigns should take into account the reasons that Parliament passed these laws. Have students present their work to the class.

Parliament had not acted in time. On March 5, 1770, in Boston, an angry crowd of workers and sailors surrounded a small group of soldiers. They shouted at the soldiers and threw snowballs and rocks at them. The frightened soldiers fired into the crowd, killing five and wounding six. The first to fall for the cause of American independence was Crispus Attucks, an African American sailor.

Governor Thomas Hutchinson tried to calm things down by having the nine soldiers involved in the shooting arrested and tried for murder. John Adams, a well-known Massachusetts lawyer, defended them. Adams also was a leading defender of colonial rights against recent British policies. Yet, he took the unpopular case because he believed that in a free country every person accused of a crime had the right to a lawyer and a fair trial. Only two soldiers were convicted. Their punishment was having their thumbs branded.

Committees of Correspondence As tensions grew, colonial leaders saw the need to keep in closer contact with people in other colonies. After the Boston Massacre, Samuel Adams, a cousin of John Adams, established what he called a Committee of Correspondence. The aim was to keep colonists informed of British actions. Soon, committees were sprouting in other colonies. The committees wrote letters and pamphlets to spread the alarm whenever Britain tried to enforce unpopular acts of Parliament. In this way, the committees helped unite the colonists against Britain.

Samuel Adams

☑Checkpoint How did colonists react to the Townshend Acts?

⭐ **Looking Back and Ahead** When colonists heard that the Townshend Acts had been repealed, they were overjoyed. But the dispute over taxes was not settled. Before long, colonists would face other crises that would lead to armed resistance.

Section 2 | Check Your Progress

Progress Monitoring 🌐nline
For: Self-test with instant help
Visit: PHSchool.com
Web Code: mva-2052

Comprehension and Critical Thinking

1. **(a) Recall** What was the Proclamation of 1763?
   (b) Apply Information Why did the British feel the Proclamation was critical in their relationship with the Native Americans?

2. **(a) Describe** What happened during the Boston Massacre?
   (b) Detect Points of View Why do you think the colonists described this event as a "massacre"?

🔵 **Reading Skill**

3. **Support Inferences With Details** Read the text following the subheading "Committees of Correspondence." Give a detail from the text to support the following inference: The colonists believed that the strength of unity would help them.

Key Terms

Answer the following questions in complete sentences that show your understanding of the key terms.

4. How did the American boycott affect Great Britain economically?
5. What did the delegates to the Stamp Act Congress hope to achieve by sending a petition to the British king and Parliament?
6. Why did colonists object to writs of assistance?

Writing

7. As a member of Parliament, you vote against repealing the Stamp Act. Brainstorm one or two possible solutions that you think would work better.

Section 2 Check Your Progress

1. **(a)** a declaration issued by King George III stating that the colonists could not settle west of the Appalachian Mountains
   (b) The British hoped it would assure Native Americans that colonists would not settle on Native American land.

2. **(a)** British soldiers fired into a group of colonists.
   (b) Possible answer: because the victims were not armed with guns as the soldiers were

3. Possible answer: The committees wrote pamphlets and letters to spread news to other colonists about unpopular British laws.

4. It decreased the number of British imports.

5. They wanted Parliament to end the act.

6. They believed that the searches allowed under these writs were a violation of their rights.

7. Possible answers: Allow the colonists to propose their own ways to help pay the costs of the French and Indian War and for protection; reduce the number of documents covered by the Stamp Act

Review and Preview

Students have read about increasing tensions between colonists in North America and the British government. They will now read how the discontent turned into open rebellion against the British government.

Section Focus Question

How did British tax policies move the colonists closer to rebellion?

Before you begin the lesson for the day, write the Section Focus Question on the board. (*Lesson focus: Tax policies drove more colonists to openly question British authority in North America and begin to move toward demands for greater self-government.*)

Prepare to Read

Build Background Knowledge L2

In this section students will read about increasing rebellion by the colonists against the British government. Remind students that they have read about the harsh laws that Britain passed and that many colonists reacted angrily to the new laws. Ask students to consider how Britain might have reacted to even stronger resistance in the colonies. Use the Think-Write-Pair-Share strategy (TE, p. T25) to elicit responses.

Set a Purpose L2

- Form students into pairs or groups of four. Distribute the Reading Readiness Guide. Ask students to fill in the first two columns of the chart.

  All in One Teaching Resources, Unit 2, Reading Readiness Guide, p. 18

- Use the Numbered Heads participation strategy (TE, p. T24) to call on students to share one item of information they already know and one item they want to know. The students will return to these worksheets later.

SECTION 3

A Well-Regulated Militia

"*Resolved* unanimously, that a well-regulated militia, composed of . . . freemen, is the natural strength and only stable security of a free government, and that such a militia will relieve our mother country from any expense in our protection and defense."

—Maryland delegates' resolution, 1774, promoting colonial self-defense

◀ Colonial militiaman

From Protest to Rebellion

Objectives

- Identify the causes of the Boston Tea Party.
- Explain how the colonists protested the Intolerable Acts.
- Describe the events of April 19, 1775, at Lexington and Concord.

Reading Skill

Draw Logical Conclusions Reaching conclusions means analyzing what you have read and forming an opinion about what it means. As with inferences, you can add your own personal knowledge to the information to draw a conclusion. Always ask yourself: Does this conclusion make sense?

Key Terms

monopoly   minuteman
repeal

Why It Matters After the French and Indian War, friction with Britain increased when Britain imposed new taxes and regulations on the colonists. But the colonists' anger had stopped short of armed resistance to the British.

Section Focus Question: How did British tax policies move the colonists closer to rebellion?

A Dispute Over Tea

During the early 1770s, the protests in the colonies against British policies quieted down. However, that did not mean the colonists were satisfied with the British government. Although most of the Townshend duties had been repealed, the one on tea remained. Many colonists drank tea. With every cup they drank, they were paying a tax that Parliament had placed on them without their consent.

The Tea Act In 1773, the British Parliament passed the Tea Act. It was intended to help the British East India Company, one of Britain's most important companies. For many years, the company had made money growing tea in India and selling it in Britain and in the colonies. However, the colonial boycott of tea seriously hurt the company.

The Tea Act actually lowered the price of tea by allowing the East India Company to ship tea directly to the colonies. Prior to the Tea Act, the tea first had to be shipped to Britain. Frederick North, the prime minister of England, felt the colonists should not object to the Tea Act since the price of tea was lowered. However, some colonists reacted angrily to the part of the act that gave the East India

150 Chapter 5 The Root to Revolution

Differentiated Instruction

L1 English Language Learners   **L1 Less Proficient Readers**   **L1 Special Needs**

Vocabulary Development Have students make a list of the key terms and high-use words. Then have them create flashcards with the word on one side and its definition on the other. Pair students with a partner and have them quiz each other on the definitions of the words using the flashcards.

Company a monopoly on selling British tea in the colonies. A **monopoly** is total control of a market for a certain product.

The monopoly hurt colonial merchants. Many of them sold Dutch tea that was smuggled into the colonies. Now, they would not be able to compete with the lower-priced East India Company Tea. Many colonial leaders also argued that even though the price of tea was lowered, colonists still had to pay the tax on tea.

The Boston Tea Party A group of colonists called the Sons of Liberty soon organized in port cities to stop the East India Company tea from being unloaded. They threatened ship captains who were bringing in the tea and colonial tea merchants who said they would buy it. No tea was unloaded in New York, Philadelphia, or other ports. However, in Boston, Governor Thomas Hutchinson decided to make sure that the tea would be unloaded. He refused to give the arriving tea ships papers that would allow them to return to England. So, when the first tea ships from Britain arrived, Hutchinson ordered the cargo to be unloaded.

For more than two weeks, feelings were tense in Boston. Finally, on the night of December 16, 1773, a large crowd gathered in the harbor. Suddenly, a large group of men disguised as Native Americans boarded the tea ship. During the next three hours, they threw 342 cases of tea into the harbor. As the crowd cheered and shouted, the raiders destroyed 90,000 pounds of tea worth thousands of dollars.

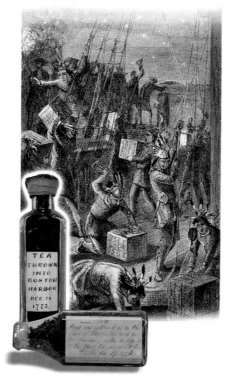

Boston Tea Party
Members of the Sons of Liberty protested the Tea Act by dumping chests of tea into Boston Harbor. **Critical Thinking:** *Apply Information Why do you think the colonists chose to disguise themselves as Native Americans?*

✓**Checkpoint** How did Boston colonists show their opposition to the Tea Act?

The Intolerable Acts

The Boston Tea Party outraged the British government. King George III called for tough action to make examples of the people of Boston and Massachusetts.

In response to the incident, Parliament passed four laws. These laws were so harsh that colonists called them the Intolerable Acts. The first act closed the port of Boston. Two others increased the powers of the royal governor, abolished the upper house of the Massachusetts legislature, and cut the powers of town meetings. Now, anyone accused of murdering a British colonial official could be tried in Britain, rather than in the colonies. Finally, a fourth law strengthened the 1765 Quartering Act.

Parliament also passed the Quebec Act, which set up a government for the territory taken from France in 1763. The Quebec Act claimed land between the Ohio and the Missouri rivers as part of Canada. Quebec's new boundaries took away the western lands claimed by several colonies and blocked colonists from moving west.

Vocabulary Builder
incident (IN suh dunt)
n. happening; occurrence

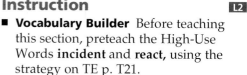

Teach

A Dispute Over Tea
p. 150

Instruction [L2]

- **Vocabulary Builder** Before teaching this section, preteach the High-Use Words **incident** and **react,** using the strategy on TE p. T21.

  Key Terms Have students continue filling in the See It–Remember It chart for the Key Terms in this chapter.

- Read A Dispute Over Tea with students using the Choral Reading strategy (TE, p. T22).

- Ask: **Why were the colonists opposed to the Tea Act even though it lowered prices for tea?** (*They disliked the fact that the Tea Act gave the East India Company a monopoly, which threatened many colonial merchants selling Dutch tea.*)

- Show students the transparency Protesting Taxes.

Color Transparencies, Protesting Taxes

Independent Practice
Have students begin to fill in the Study Guide for this section.

Monitor Progress

As students fill in the Notetaking Study Guide, circulate to make sure students understand the importance of the Boston Tea Party. Provide assistance as needed.

Vocabulary Builder

Use the information below to teach students this section's high-use words.

High-Use Word	Definition and Sample Sentence
incident, p. 151	*n.* happening; occurrence The Bacon's Rebellion **incident** revealed the different interests of frontier settlers and townspeople.
react, p. 152	*v.* to act in return The French **reacted** strongly to Washington's expedition into the Ohio River valley.

Answers

✓**Checkpoint** By threatening ship captains and merchants involved in the legitimate tea trade and by dumping tea into Boston Harbor

Apply Information Possible answer: They did not want anyone to know their identities.

The Intolerable Acts
The Shot Heard Round the World

pp. 151–152

Instruction

L2

- Have students read The Intolerable Acts and The Shot Heard Round the World. Remind students to look for causes and effects.

- Discuss the Intolerable Acts. Ask: **In what ways did the colonists show that they were angry about Britain's violation of their rights?** (*They sent support to Boston and organized the First Continental Congress.*)

- Show students the transparency Causes of the Revolution.

Color Transparencies, Causes of the Revolution

Independent Practice

Have students complete the Study Guide for this section.

📖 **Interactive Reading and Notetaking Study Guide,** Chapter 5, Section 3 (Adapted Version also available.)

Monitor Progress

- As students complete the Notetaking Study Guide, circulate to make sure students understand the importance of the battles at Lexington and Concord. Provide assistance as needed.

- Tell students to fill in the last column of the Reading Readiness Guide. Ask them if what they learned was what they had expected to learn.

All in One Teaching Resources, Unit 2, Reading Readiness Guide, p. 18

Answers

Explain Problems Possible answer: The colonists had been denied representation in Parliament, and so these laws had been passed without their being able to voice their opinions against them.

🕐 **Reading Skill** Possible answer: Most of the colonies agreed at this time that it was necessary for the British government to repeal the Intolerable Acts, but not that independence was the best solution.

☑**Checkpoint** It called on the British to repeal the Intolerable Acts and called for a boycott of British goods and the training of colonial militias.

152 Chapter 5

Causes of the Revolution

History *Interactive*
Discover the Events That Led to the Revolution
Visit: PHSchool.com
Web Code: mvl-2054

French and Indian War (1754–1763)

The Stamp Act (1765)

The Boston Tea Party (1773)

The Intolerable Acts (1774)

Roots of the Revolution
Relations between Great Britain and the colonies changed after the French and Indian War. Years of colonial protest against laws passed by Parliament gradually led to open revolt. **Critical Thinking: Explain Problems** *Why did colonists view these laws as attacks on their rights as British citizens?*

Outbreak of the Revolution

Vocabulary Builder
react (ree AKT) **v.** to act in return

🕐 **Draw Logical Conclusions**
What conclusion can you make about how the Congress felt about independence at this time?

Americans in all the colonies <u>reacted</u> by trying to help the people of Boston. Food and other supplies poured into Boston from throughout the colonies. Meanwhile, the Committee of Correspondence organized a meeting to discuss what to do next.

That meeting, known as the First Continental Congress, took place in Philadelphia in September and October 1774. Twelve of the 13 colonies sent delegates. Only Georgia did not send representatives. Among the delegates were John Adams and Samuel Adams from Massachusetts, John Jay of New York, and George Washington and Patrick Henry from Virginia.

The Congress demanded the **repeal**, or official end, of the Intolerable Acts and declared that the colonies had a right to tax and govern themselves. It also called for the training of militias to stand up to British troops if necessary. The Congress also called for a new boycott of British goods. It then voted to meet again in May 1775 if its demands were not met.

☑**Checkpoint** What did the First Continental Congress accomplish?

The Shot Heard Round the World

The British government had no intention of meeting the demands of the First Continental Congress. It chose, instead, to use force to restore its authority. Meanwhile, the colonists began to arm and form new militia units called **minutemen**—citizen soldiers who could be ready to fight at a minute's notice.

Differentiated Instruction

L1 Less Proficient Readers   **L1 Special Needs**

Comparing Two Viewpoints Have students work in pairs to compare the viewpoints of the colonists and the British government about two events: the Boston Tea Party and the passing of the Intolerable Acts. Have pairs make two separate two-column charts to explain each side's view of each of these events. Then have pairs share their charts with the class.

In April, General Thomas Gage, the new governor of Massachusetts, learned the minutemen were storing arms in Concord, about 20 miles from Boston. On April 18, 1775, he sent 700 troops to seize the arms and capture some important colonial leaders. As the troops set out, a signal sent by the Patriots appeared in the steeple of Boston's Old North Church. Two men, Paul Revere and William Dawes, then rode through the night to warn the minutemen.

Five miles from Concord in the town of Lexington, about 77 minutemen were waiting when the British arrived. The British commander ordered the minutemen to go home. They refused. Suddenly, a shot rang out. Nobody knows who fired it, but it turned out to be the first shot of the American Revolution—"the shot heard round the world." The British then opened fire, killing eight Americans.

A larger battle took place in nearby Concord. This time, 400 minutemen fought the British, killing three of them. As the British retreated toward Boston, about 4,000 Americans fired at them from behind trees and fences. By the time the British reached Boston, almost 300 of them had been killed or wounded.

✓**Checkpoint** What led to the conflict at Lexington and Concord?

⭐ **Looking Back and Ahead** News of the battles at Lexington and Concord traveled fast through the colonies. Many colonists saw their hopes of reaching an agreement with Britain fade. For many, the battles were proof that only war would decide the future of the 13 colonies.

Statue of a minuteman

Section 3 | **Check Your Progress**

Progress Monitoring ●nline
For: Self-test with instant help
Visit: PHSchool.com
Web Code: mva-2053

Comprehension and Critical Thinking

1. (a) Recall Why did Britain pass the Tea Act?
(b) Identify Alternatives What other ways, besides the Boston Tea Party, might colonists have protested the Tea Act?

2. (a) Summarize What were the Intolerable Acts?
(b) Apply Information How did the Intolerable Acts affect colonial unity?

3. (a) Describe How did the American Revolution begin?
(b) Draw Conclusions Why do you think the first shot fired at Lexington was called "the shot heard round the world"?

◉ Reading Skill
4. Draw Logical Conclusions Based on the battles of Lexington and Concord, what can you conclude about the colonists' advantage in fighting?

Key Terms
Fill in the blanks with the correct key terms.
5. The _____ were colonists who could prepare to fight in a very short time.
6. Because the East India Company had a _____ on selling British tea in the colonies, other countries could not sell their tea there.

7. The First Continental Congress provided for the training of _____ that could fight the British troops.

Writing
8. One of the decisions of the First Continental Congress was to boycott British goods. In a paragraph, identify the problem that Congress was trying to solve by boycotting British goods. Did the boycott solve the problem? Explain.

Section 3 Check Your Progress

1. (a) The Tea Act was supposed to help the East India Company by lowering the price of tea and giving the company a monopoly on selling tea in the colonies.
(b) Possible answer: They could have continued to boycott tea or sent a petition to Parliament to cancel the act.

2. (a) The first act closed the port of Boston; two others limited colonial self-government; the fourth act strengthened the 1765 Quartering Act.

(b) The acts unified the colonists and strengthened their sense of an identity that was different from the British.

3. (a) Minutemen attacked British soldiers sent to Concord to seize arms and arrest colonial leaders.

(b) because it was the beginning of the American Revolution, which set in motion events that would affect the entire world

4. Colonists used strategies such as ambush and surprise, and they were able to gather forces on short notice.

Assess Progress ▪L2▪

Have students complete Check Your Progress. Administer the Section Quiz.

🔲 **Teaching Resources, Unit 2,** Section Quiz, p. 26

To further assess student understanding, use the Progress Monitoring Transparency.

Progress Monitoring Transparencies, Chapter 5, Section 3

Reteach ▪L1▪

If students need more instruction, have them read this section in the Interactive Reading and Notetaking Study Guide and complete the accompanying question.

📖 **Interactive Reading and Notetaking Study Guide,** Chapter 5, Section 3 (Adapted Version also available.)

Extend ▪L3▪

Have students complete the History Interactive activity online.

Extend ●nline
For: Help with the History Interactive
Visit: PHSchool.com
Web Code: mve-0136

Progress Monitoring Online

Students may check their comprehension of this section by completing the Progress Monitoring Online graphic organizer and self-quiz.

Answer

✓**Checkpoint** The British tried to march to Concord to seize the minutemen's weapons and capture some important colonial leaders.

5. minutemen

6. monopoly

7. militias

8. Students' paragraphs will vary, but should reflect an understanding of the boycott on British goods and whether it solved the problem.

A Spirit of Protest

p. 154

Build Background Knowledge $\boxed{\text{L2}}$

Using the Idea Wave strategy (TE p. T24), have students identify points of disagreement between the colonists and the British government.

Instruction $\boxed{\text{L2}}$

- Read A Spirit of Protest with students. Ask: **In what ways did colonists protest British policies?** (*with boycotts, symbols, satires, and sometimes violence*)

- Ask a volunteer to read aloud the excerpt from "The Pen as a Weapon." Ask: **What effect is a play such as this likely to have on an audience of colonists?** (*Possible answer: By mocking British power, the play may help give the colonists the confidence to continue their defiance.*)

- Discuss the image of a tax collector on p. 155 being tarred and feathered. Ask: **Do you think an attack such as this would have helped or hurt the colonists' cause? Explain.** (*Students may suggest that such an attack might deter British officials from enforcing unpopular laws. Others may argue that such attacks would only have increased British determination to exert control over the colonists.*)

Monitor Progress

Ask students to complete the Analyze Life at the Time activity. Circulate to make sure individuals understand the spirit of protest in the colonies in the 1770s. Provide assistance as needed.

LIFE AT THE TIME

A Spirit of Protest

From the Stamp Act to the Boston Tea Party to the outbreak of fighting at Lexington and Concord, a spirit of protest steadily grew in the colonies. This defiant mood expressed itself in many ways.

A Warning of Danger

Benjamin Franklin was the first to use a serpent as a symbol of the colonies. (See Section 1.) By 1775, the serpent had become a rattlesnake, which stood for the idea that the colonists would ▼ fight back against tyranny.

DONT TREAD ON ME

Boycotting British Goods

Women took a leading role in refusing to buy British goods. In October 1774, a group of women in Edenton, North Carolina, signed a pledge. They promised "not to conform to the Pernicious Custom of Drinking Tea." Above, the women of Edenton pour away tea.

The Pen as a Weapon

Mercy Otis Warren of Boston wrote plays that made fun of the British. The plays were not acted in theaters but were circulated privately. In *The Blockheads*, Warren shows how the Patriots made fools of the ▼ British troops after Lexington and Concord. One British soldier says:

Mercy Otis Warren

"Ha, ha, ha,—yankee doodle forever. . . . We were sent here to ransack the country and hang up a parcel of leading fellows for the crows to pick, and awe all others into *peace* and *submission*—instead of this, in our first attempt, we were drove thro' the country, like a pack of *jackasses*."

—Mercy Otis Warren, *The Blockheads*

Differentiated Instruction

$\boxed{\text{L3}}$ Advanced Readers   **$\boxed{\text{L3}}$ Gifted and Talented**

Creating Artwork Have students review the issues discussed in the first three sections of this chapter that divided the colonists and the British government. Then have students design a symbol, write or act out a short, 2-minute satiric scene, or draw a political cartoon that expresses a point of view about one of the sources of conflict. When students are finished, have them share their work with the class and describe how the work they created expresses a point of view.

Violent Protests

The spirit of protest sometimes took a violent turn. The British cartoon below shows a tax official in Boston being tarred and feathered by members of the Sons of Liberty. Hot tar was poured over the body of the victim, who was then covered with chicken feathers. Tarring and feathering was not fatal, but it was painful and humiliating. In the background, colonists pour tea into Boston Harbor.

The first Liberty Tree was an elm in Boston, where dummies representing tax collectors were hanged. Patriots in many colonies raised Liberty Trees or Liberty Poles as symbols of protest.

In addition to being tarred and feathered, the unfortunate tax collector has tea poured down his throat.

Analyze LIFE AT THE TIME

Choose a person pictured on these pages. As that person, write a letter to a friend describing how you feel about the new mood of protest in the colonies.

Writing Rubrics Share this rubric with students.

Score 1 Does not address assigned topic, is poorly organized.
Score 2 Details and organization are often unclear or incorrect.
Score 3 Has organization suited to the topic, some appropriate ideas, some original ideas.
Score 4 Many appropriate details, original ideas, well-organized and developed.

History Background

Colonial Protests, British Backlash Seen through British eyes, the increasing mood of defiance among the colonists represented a fundamental and direct threat to the authority of the crown to govern the colonies. Rather than considering the colonists' specific complaints, King George III saw the protests as rebellion against his authority, which had to be crushed by force. In April 1774, at the House of Commons in London, Edmund Burke argued that the king's heavy-handed response was counter-productive: "Reflect how you [the king] are to govern a people who think they ought to be free, and think they are not. Your scheme yields no [tax] revenue; it yields nothing but discontent, disorder, disobedience; and such is the state of America . . . "

Answer

Analyze **LIFE AT THE TIME** Students' letters will vary, but they should demonstrate an understanding of the rising mood of protest among the colonists and express a reaction to this new mood.

Review and Preview

In the previous section, students learned how colonial discontent turned to open rebellion against the British government. In this section, students will read about efforts by the colonists to make peace and the early battles of the American Revolution.

Section Focus Question

How did the American Revolution begin?

Before you begin the lesson for the day, write the Section Focus Question on the board. (*Lesson focus: The American Revolution began when King George rejected the colonists' Olive Branch petition, and the Second Continental Congress voted to form an army.*)

Prepare to Read

Build Background Knowledge   L2

Ask students to recall the events that led to the battles at Lexington and Concord. Write all accurate information on the board, and address any misconceptions that students may have about the events that led to the battles. Then ask students to preview the section by looking at the illustrations on p. 160. Ask students to predict what more they will learn about the conflict between the colonists and the British government. Use the Give One, Get One strategy (TE, p. T25) to elicit responses.

Set a Purpose   L2

- Read each statement in the Reading Readiness Guide aloud. Ask students to mark the statements True or False.

  All in One Teaching Resources, Unit 2, Reading Readiness Guide, p. 19

- Have students discuss the statements in pairs or groups of four, then mark the worksheets again. Use the Numbered Heads participation strategy (TE, p. T24) to call on students to share their group's perspectives. The students will return to these worksheets later.

SECTION 4

▲ American soldiers prepare for British attack.

In the Heat of Action

"We were then very soon in the heat of action. Before we reached the summit of Bunker Hill, and while we were going over the Neck, we were in imminent danger from the cannon shot, which buzzed around us like hail."

—American Captain John Chester, describing the Battle of Bunker Hill, 1775

The War Begins

Objectives

- Identify the issues facing the Second Continental Congress.
- Describe the differences between Patriots and Loyalists.
- Identify the Olive Branch Petition, and explain why it failed.
- Explain the significance of the Battle of Bunker Hill.

⟳ Reading Skill

Identify Supporting Evidence Readers often draw conclusions without even realizing that they are doing so. However, like inferences, conclusions should be supported and challenged and the evidence identified. This ensures that your conclusions are logical and reliable. Remember, you may need to use evidence from prior reading to reach your conclusions.

Key Terms

blockade
mercenary

Why It Matters After the battles at Lexington and Concord, many colonists hoped that the British would give in quickly to the colonists' demands. The British did not. Instead, a long and difficult struggle lay ahead.

❓ Section Focus Question: How did the American Revolution begin?

The Second Continental Congress

Even after the battles of Lexington and Concord, most colonists still did not favor independence. At the same time, many of them were ready to use force, if necessary, to defend their rights against the British.

As the crisis with Britain deepened, the Second Continental Congress came together in Philadelphia in May 1775. The delegates included Thomas Jefferson, a young lawyer from Virginia; Boston merchant John Hancock; and Benjamin Franklin of Philadelphia.

The Congress, at first, was divided about what to do. A group of delegates from New England wanted to declare independence. A more moderate group from the Middle Colonies favored less drastic action. However, nearly all delegates felt they needed to prepare for war. The first step was to form an army.

The Congress chose George Washington as the commander of the newly formed Continental army. He had military experience and was well respected.

The Congress also took steps to pay for its army by printing paper money. The Second Continental Congress was starting to act like a government.

Differentiated Instruction

L1 Less Proficient Readers   **L1 Special Needs**

Outlining Have students create an outline of this section as they read. Tell them to use the headings in red as the main ideas and to number them using Roman numerals. Tell them to use the headings in blue as subheads, identifying them with capital letters. Have students write supporting details under each subhead, numbering them with Arabic numerals. After students have completed their outlines, have them share their work with a partner before handing it in.

Patriots Against Loyalists By 1775, a split was developing in the American colonies. Colonists who favored independence and were willing to fight for it took the name Patriots. Those who remained loyal to Britain and the king called themselves Loyalists. Most colonists were Patriots. However, as many as one third of the colonists may have had Loyalist sympathies.

The Loyalists came from every colony and all sections of the population. Everywhere, however, they were a minority. During 1774 and 1775, the Patriots took control of local governments.

The Loyalists included some people from the wealthiest families in the colonies. Many leading merchants and large landowners were Loyalists. They feared a rebellion would lead to a change in government and that they would lose their property. Government officials who owed their jobs and place in society to the British Crown often were Loyalists.

At the same time, many enslaved African Americans sided with the British, hoping to win their freedom. So did most Native Americans, who feared they would lose their lands if the colonists won independence.

During the Revolution, thousands of Loyalists fought on the British side. During and after the Revolutionary War, about 100,000 Loyalists left the country forever. Many settled in Canada.

Identify Supporting Evidence
Reading Skill Give evidence to support the conclusion that Loyalists strongly supported social order.

Lord Dunmore's Declaration

Lord Dunmore sent this declaration to the rebel Patriots in Virginia:

❝I do require every person capable of bearing arms to resort to His Majesty's standard, or be looked upon as traitors to His Majesty's Crown and government, and [be subject to] penalty . . . such as [loss] of life, confiscation of lands, etc. And I do hereby further declare all indentured servants, negroes, or others [in service to rebels] free that are able and willing to bear arms, they joining His Majesty's troops as soon as may be. . . .❞

—from Proclamation of Lord Dunmore, November 1775

Boys laughing at a Loyalist

Reading Primary Sources
Skills Activity

In 1775, Patriots had taken over Virginia. In desperation, Lord Dunmore, the Loyalist governor, issued a declaration against the rebel Patriots.

(a) Apply Information How does Lord Dunmore encourage indentured servants and black slaves to join the British army?

(b) Evaluate Arguments How could American Patriots accuse Lord Dunmore of being unfair?

Vocabulary Builder

Use the information below to teach students this section's high-use words.

High-Use Word	Definition and Sample Sentence
restore, p.158	*v.* to bring back to a normal state; to put back; to reestablish By the end of 1763, the French knew there was little opportunity to **restore** its empire in North America.
occupy, p. 158	*v.* take possession of When Washington traveled to the Ohio River valley to build a fort for Virginia, he found the French already **occupied** prime areas.

Teach

The Second Continental Congress
p. 156

Instruction

- **Vocabulary Builder** Before teaching this section, preteach the High-Use Words **restore** and **occupy**, using the strategy on TE p. T21.

  Key Terms Following the instruction on p. 7, have students complete the See It–Remember It chart for the Key Terms in this chapter.

- Read The Second Continental Congress with students using the Idea Wave strategy (TE, p. T24).

- Ask: **How did the Second Continental Congress respond to the battles at Lexington and Concord?** (*They formed a Continental army under the command of George Washington and sent the Olive Branch petition to the British king.*)

- Ask: **Who were the two groups in the debate over independence?** (*the Patriots who wanted independence and the Loyalists who were loyal to the king*)

- Point out that the outbreak of the Revolution was a time of great uncertainty for people living in and near the British colonies. Ask: **For what reasons did some people support the British government during the Revolution?** (*Some wealthy colonists feared losses of jobs and property, some enslaved African Americans hoped to win their freedom, and some Native Americans feared the loss of lands if the Patriots won.*)

- Ask: **What can you conclude about King George's attitude toward the colonists' complaints based on his refusal to answer the Olive Branch petition?** (*He was not interested in their point of view and believed that they did not have the right to oppose his policies with violent rebellion.*)

Answers

Reading Skill Possible answer: The Loyalists' support of the crown was based on the desire for continuity of property ownership.

Reading Primary Sources (a) They would gain their freedom when they joined the King's army. **(b)** Possible answer: They were upset that they would lose their servants and slaves.

Instruction (continued)

■ After you have completed this discussion, assign the worksheet Revolution or Compromise? to explore this issue further. After students have completed the worksheet, ask: **Why do you think there was disagreement between the Loyalists and the Patriots over how best to resolve matters with Britain?** (*Possible answers: Loyalists may have believed that it was still in their best interests to maintain ties with Britain; Patriots may have believed that they had made several efforts to improve relations with Britain, but that the time had come to sever ties and declare their independence.*)

All in One **Teaching Resources, Unit 2,** Revolution or Compromise?, p. 21

Independent Practice

Have students begin to fill in the Study Guide for this section.

Interactive Reading and Notetaking Study Guide, Chapter 5, Section 4 (Adapted Version also available.)

Seeing the Main Idea

Ethan Allen demanding the surrender of Fort Ticonderoga. Have students look at the image on p. 158 of Ethan Allen. Ask: **By looking at the painting, how can you tell that Ethan Allen surprised the British at Fort Ticonderoga?** (*Possible answers: the man answering the door appears to have been woken up; it appears to be night in the image; the woman answering the door appears to be in her night clothes.*)

Monitor Progress

As students fill in the Notetaking Study Guide, circulate to make sure students understand the importance of the Second Continental Congress. If students do not seem to have a good understanding, have them reread the section. Provide assistance as needed.

Answer

Checkpoint They passed resolutions that favored both negotiations and a tough stance against the British government.

Ethan Allen demanding the surrender of Fort Ticonderoga

Petitioning the King Even months after Lexington and Concord, many delegates at the Second Continental Congress hoped that peace could be <u>restored</u> between Britain and its American colonies. Two resolutions passed in July showed the uncertainty of Congress. The first resolution was called the Olive Branch Petition and was sent to King George. The petition stated that the colonists were loyal to the king. It asked George to stop the fighting so all disputes between the colonists and Britain could be solved peacefully. The petition got its name from the olive branch, a symbol of peace since ancient times.

The next day, the Congress passed a tougher statement called the Declaration of the Causes and Necessities of Taking Up Arms. Written in part by Thomas Jefferson, the document stated that the colonists were ready "to die freemen rather than to live as slaves."

The effort to make peace failed. King George did not bother to answer the Olive Branch Petition. Instead, he declared the colonies were "in open . . . rebellion." Parliament, meanwhile, voted to send 20,000 soldiers to the colonies to end the revolt.

An Important American Victory On May 10, 1775, the same day the Second Continental Congress began meeting, an important battle took place in northern New York. A daring band of colonists made a surprise attack on Fort Ticonderoga (ti kahn duh ROH guh).

The fort stood at the southern end of Lake Champlain and protected the water route to Canada. Leading the force was Ethan Allen, a blacksmith. Most of his followers came from the nearby Green Mountains of today's Vermont. Because of that, they were known as the Green Mountain Boys.

Allen's force of 83 men reached the fort by crossing the lake at night and surprising the British in the early morning. Only 42 British troops guarded the fort, and they surrendered almost immediately.

Fort Ticonderoga was important for two reasons. It controlled the main route between Canada and the Hudson River valley. It also held valuable weapons, especially cannons. The Americans needed the cannons to match the powerful British weapons. When the Green Mountain Boys took the fort, they seized several dozen cannons. Later, those cannons were moved to Boston, where George Washington used them to drive the British from the city.

Checkpoint **How did the divided loyalties of the colonists affect the Second Continental Congress?**

Early Battles

By June 1775, the British had 6,500 troops in Boston. The Americans had about 10,000 surrounding the city. About 1,600 of these troops <u>occupied</u> Breed's Hill overlooking the city. From this position, they could fire on British ships in Boston harbor. Nearby was Bunker Hill, also controlled by the Americans.

Differentiated Instruction

L3 **Advanced Readers**

Explaining the Colonists' Point of View Have students do additional research using the Internet, history books, or encyclopedias to find out more about the Olive Branch Petition. Then have stu-

L3 **Gifted and Talented**

dents write a persuasive letter from the delegates of the Second Continental Congress to King George III urging him to consider the petition. Have students read their letters aloud to the class.

Delivering the Cannons

From Fort Ticonderoga to Boston

The difficulty of dragging cannons from Fort Ticonderoga to Boston is evident in this painting of the event. **Critical Thinking: Apply Information** What does this effort indicate about the Continental army's military forces?

Battle of Bunker Hill The Americans surrounding Boston were farmers and workers, not trained soldiers. Nobody knew if they would stand and fight against tough British troops.

British General William Howe decided to attack straight up Breed's Hill. The American commander, Israel Putnam, knew his soldiers did not have much ammunition. The Americans waited until the British were only about 150 feet away. When they opened fire, hundreds of British soldiers fell dead and wounded.

The first British attack failed. So did the second. The third attack succeeded, only because the Americans ran out of ammunition and had to retreat. The British won the battle but at a terrible cost. More than 1000 were killed or wounded. American losses were about 400 killed or wounded. The Americans had proved they could fight and stand up to professional British soldiers.

The fighting, called the Battle of Bunker Hill, did not solve Britain's problem. Boston still was surrounded by American forces. In July 1775, George Washington arrived and took charge of the army.

Washington knew he had to build a regular army. Washington also needed powerful weapons to drive the British from Boston. He had the British cannons, which had been seized at Fort Ticonderoga, dragged on sleds across mountains and forests to Boston. That difficult 300-mile journey took three months.

In March, Washington placed the cannons on high ground overlooking Boston. The British could no longer defend the city. On March 17, 1776, they withdrew from Boston by sea and never returned.

Early Battles
p. 158

Instruction   L2

- Have students read Early Battles. Remind students to look for details to answer the Section Focus Question.

- Ask: **Why were Breed's Hill and Bunker Hill important positions to hold?** (*The hills overlooked Boston, and armies could fire on British ships in Boston harbor from these locations.*)

- Ask: **Why did the Americans lose the Battle of Bunker Hill?** (*They were forced to retreat when they ran out of ammunition.*)

- Ask: **How did the victory at Fort Ticonderoga help Washington's forces in Boston?** (*They used cannons seized during the battle at Ticonderoga to help drive the British out of Boston.*)

- Ask: **What do you think is one advantage and one disadvantage of using mercenaries during a war?** (*Possible answer: Mercenaries increase the size of your fighting force, but they may not be as loyal or fight as hard as the regular army.*)

Independent Practice

Have students complete the Study Guide for this section.

Interactive Reading and Notetaking Study Guide, Chapter 5, Section 4 (Adapted Version also available.)

History Background

Battle of Bunker Hill The Battle of Bunker Hill was the site of the famous command, "Don't fire until you see the whites of their eyes," which is generally attributed to Colonel William Prescott. Prescott is said to have delivered the order to anxious militia members as the British troops climbed Bunker Hill. British generals watching the first charge from nearby Copp's Hill were shocked to see their troops, which they considered the best in the world, driven back by the colonists.

Answer

Apply Information Possible answers: They were poorly organized; they did not have adequate forces; they did not have adequate equipment.

Instruction (continued)

- Ask: **Why do you think the colonists may have felt "a frenzy of revenge" after this battle?** (*Answers may vary, but students should cite the fact that colonists were able to more or less "hold their own" against the British for a while. This probably energized and encouraged them, deepening their resolve.*)

Monitor Progress

- As students complete the Notetaking Study Guide, circulate to make sure students understand the importance of the early battles of the Revolution. Provide assistance as needed.

- Tell students to fill in the last column of the Reading Readiness Guide. Probe for what they learned that confirms or invalidates each statement.

- Have students go back to their Word Knowledge Rating Form. Rerate their word knowledge and complete the last column with a definition or example.

 Teaching Resources, Unit 2, Reading Readiness Guide, p. 19; Word Knowledge Rating Form, p. 15

Answer

Understand Sequence Before: colonists built a fort on Breed's Hill from which to attack British ships; During: British soldiers took a position at the foot of Breed's Hill the day of the battle, eventually taking the colonists' position and winning the battle; After: although the British won the battle, the colonists surrounded Boston and took control of the city in March 1776.

The Battle of Bunker Hill

On June 16, 1775, the colonists occupied Bunker Hill and Breed's Hill, two high points near Charles Town, which was across the harbor from Boston. The battle that took place there the following morning fueled the colonists' determination to fight. After this battle, it is said that "a frenzy of revenge" gripped the colonists. **Critical Thinking:** *Understand Sequence Based on the information on this page and on your reading, describe the sequence of events before, during, and after the battle.*

▼ The Battle Begins
On the morning of June 17, British soldiers took position around the base of Breed's Hill. As shown in this painting, the British soldiers, wearing red coats, marched straight up the hill through tall grass and over fences.

William Howe ▶
British general at Bunker Hill

The Attack ▶
This painting shows the attack on Bunker Hill and the burning of Charles Town.

Israel Putnam ▶
American general at Bunker Hill

Differentiated Instruction

L1 English Language Learners **L1 Less Proficient Readers** **L1 Special Needs**

Visualizing the Events Discuss the illustrations on this page with students. Point out that this painting is the artist's re-creation of the event. Have students review the section to select and illustrate another event. Encourage interested students to conduct further research of the event for their illustrations. Have students write captions for their images and display them in the classroom.

Although the Americans won in Boston, Washington knew that the war was far from over. Britain still held most of the advantages. They had the most powerful navy in the world. They used it to transport troops and supplies and to blockade American ports. A **blockade** is the shutting off of a port by ships to keep people or supplies from moving in or out. The British also strengthened their army by hiring **mercenaries**—soldiers who serve another country for money.

Invading Canada While Washington was training one army outside Boston, two other American armies were moving north into Canada. One, led by Richard Montgomery, left from Fort Ticonderoga. The other, led by Benedict Arnold, moved north through Maine.

Arnold had a terrible journey through the Maine woods in winter. His troops were forced to boil candles, bark, and shoe leather for food. In late December 1775, the Americans attacked Quebec during a severe snowstorm. The attack was turned back. Montgomery was killed, and Arnold was wounded. The Americans stayed outside Quebec until May 1776, when the British landed new forces in Canada. Weakened by disease and hunger, the Americans withdrew, leaving Canada to the British.

✓**Checkpoint** What did the Battle of Bunker Hill show about the American and British forces?

⭐ **Looking Back and Ahead** After Bunker Hill, King George III was confident that he could soon restore order in the colonies. Meantime, colonists wondered what chance they had of defeating a well-armed, powerful nation such as Britain.

Section 4 | Check Your Progress

> **Progress Monitoring ◉nline**
> **For:** Self-test with instant help
> **Visit:** PHSchool.com
> **Web Code:** mva-2054

Comprehension and Critical Thinking

1. (a) Recall What were the major achievements of the Second Continental Congress?
(b) Apply Information How did the Second Continental Congress influence the conflict between the colonists and Britain?

2. (a) Recall What did the Patriots want?
(b) Apply Information Why do you think Loyalists were described as "having their heads in England . . . but their bodies in America"?

◉ Reading Skill

3. Identify Supporting Evidence Give evidence to support the conclusion that the war's momentum shifted after the Battle of Bunker Hill.

Key Terms

Read each sentence below. If the sentence is true, write YES. If the sentence is not true, write NO and explain why.
4. Countries set up **blockades** to help strengthen trade relations.
5. Most **mercenaries** are hired to fight for their own countries.

Writing

6. In a few sentences, describe how a Loyalist might have reacted to the Olive Branch Petition and to the Declaration of the Causes and Necessities of Taking Up Arms as possible solutions to the feud between Britain and the colonies. Then, write a brief response reflecting how a Patriot might have reacted to these documents as a solution to the feud.

Section 4 Check Your Progress

1. (a) They formed an army and recruited soldiers, chose a commander, printed paper money, petitioned the king to stop the fighting, and passed the Declaration of the Causes and Necessity of Taking Up Arms.
(b) It intensified the conflict because it provided for an expanded colonial military force, failed to make peace, and took a tough stand in support of war.

2. (a) The Patriots wanted independence from Britain.
(b) Because even though they lived in America, they thought of themselves as British.

3. Despite the loss, the Americans continued to fight for Boston and took control of it in March 1776.

4. No, because blockades prevent ships from entering or leaving ports, hurting trade.

Assess and Reteach

Assess Progress `L2`

Have students complete Check Your Progress. Administer the Section Quiz.

 Teaching Resources, Unit 2, Section Quiz, p. 27

To further assess student understanding, use the Progress Monitoring Transparency.

Progress Monitoring Transparencies, Chapter 5, Section 4

Reteach `L1`

If students need more instruction, have them read this section in the Interactive Reading and Notetaking Study Guide and complete the accompanying question.

📖 **Interactive Reading and Notetaking Study Guide,** Chapter 5, Section 4 (Adapted Version also available.)

Extend `L3`

Have students learn more about the Battle of Bunker Hill by researching the event online and in the library. Have them prepare a short news report describing the event and its effect. Have them present their work to the class. Provide students with the web code below.

> **Extend ◉nline**
> **For:** Help in starting the Extend activity
> **Visit:** PHSchool.com
> **Web Code:** mvp-0137

Progress Monitoring Online

Students may check their comprehension of this section by completing the Progress Monitoring Online graphic organizer and self-quiz.

Answer

✓**Checkpoint** The Americans lost the battle, but had proven that they could stand up to and fight the British.

5. No, mercenaries are hired to fight for another country.

6. Students may suggest that a Loyalist would react positively to the Olive Branch Petition, while finding the Declaration too confrontational. A Patriot might react less favorably to the petition and more favorably to the Declaration because it moved the colonies closer to independence.

Skills for Life

Objective

Formulating questions about a text can help students develop a more thorough understanding of what they read. As they consider the answers to their questions, students will think about the text in ways that connect their curiosity to the subject matter and make learning more meaningful.

Formulate Questions

Instruction [L2]

1. Ask the class to read the steps to formulate questions. Write the questions on the board.

2. Have students look at the excerpt. Ask them to identify passages that are either especially striking or confusing to them. Note these passages on the board.

3. Practice the skill by following the steps on p. 162 as a class. Model each step to formulate questions. (*1. He believes an armed revolution is necessary to protect the rights of the colonists. 2. (a) Possible answer: The tone of the passage is very passionate. (b) Possible answer: How does Henry describe the choice that colonists face during this crisis? 3. (a) Possible answer: because Henry's speech appeals to both reason and emotion (b) Possible answer: Is Henry's speech likely to persuade someone who disagrees with him to change his or her mind? 4. Patrick Henry and those who supported his views would have likely been punished as traitors and probably hanged.*)

Monitor Progress

Ask students to do the Apply the Skills activity. Then assign the Skill for Life worksheet. As students complete the worksheet, circulate to make sure individuals are applying the skill steps effectively. Provide assistance as needed.

All in One **Teaching Resources, Unit 2,** Skills for Life Worksheet, p. 22

Skills for Life — Formulate Questions

You can increase your understanding of history by asking questions about what you see and read. Formulating, or asking, questions helps you become a more effective learner. The better your questions, the more you will learn.

> Patrick Henry presented his views in this excerpt from a speech to the convention that gathered after the Virginia Assembly was suspended.
>
> **Primary Source**
>
> "Sir, we have done everything to avert the storm which is now coming on. We have petitioned; we have remonstrated; we have supplicated; we have prostrated ourselves before the throne. Our petitions have been slighted; our remonstrances have produced additional violence and insult; our supplications have been disregarded. . . .
>
> *There is no longer any room for hope.* If we wish to be free; if we mean to preserve inviolate those inestimable privileges for which we have been so long contending; . . . we must fight! I repeat it, sir, we must fight! An appeal to arms and to the God of hosts is all that is left us!
>
> —I know not what course others may take; but as for me,—give me liberty, or give me death!"
>
> —Patrick Henry, March 23, 1775

Learn the Skill
Use these steps to formulate questions.

1. **Examine the material.** Ask basic questions to summarize what you are reading. Formulate questions that begin with *who, what, when, where,* and *how much.*

2. **Think of analytical questions.** These are questions that reflect a thoughtful approach to the information. They might begin with *how* or *why.*

3. **Ask questions that evaluate.** These call for judgments and opinions based on evidence.

4. **Formulate hypothetical questions.** Hypothetical questions involve the word *if.* They suggest possible outcomes: *if this happens, would such and such occur?*

Practice the Skill
Answer the following questions about the primary source.

1. **Examine the material.** What is Patrick Henry's view of the American Revolution?

2. **Think of analytical questions.** (a) How would you describe the tone or feeling? (b) Formulate an analytical question.

3. **Ask questions that evaluate.** (a) Why is this primary source persuasive? Explain. (b) Formulate a question to evaluate the source.

4. **Formulate hypothetical questions.** If the British had won the Revolution, what do you think would have happened to Patrick Henry and those who supported his views?

Apply the Skill
See the Review and Assessment at the end of this chapter.

How did the relationship between Britain and the colonies fall apart?

Section 1
Trouble on the Frontier

- British settlers moved into lands claimed by the French in the Ohio River valley.
- After early British defeats at Fort Duquesne, Fort Niagara, and Lake George, France was defeated.
- Under the 1763 Treaty of Paris, Britain and Spain took control of almost all of France's North American possessions.

Section 2
The Colonists Resist Tighter Control

- To avoid conflict with Native Americans, Britain issued the Proclamation of 1763.
- After the end of the war, Britain strengthened its control over the American colonies by imposing a series of new taxes.
- Colonists protested Britain's actions by boycotting British goods.

Section 3
From Protest to Rebellion

- After Parliament passed the Tea Act, American colonists dumped cases of British tea into Boston Harbor.
- The Intolerable Acts further tightened Britain's control over the American colonies.
- The first major conflict between American colonists and British soldiers took place at Lexington and Concord on April 18, 1775.

Section 4
The War Begins

- The Second Continental Congress met in Philadelphia in May 1775 to deal with the deepening crisis with Great Britain.
- The British surrendered Fort Ticonderoga to a small American force led by Ethan Allen.
- When the Olive Branch Petition failed, the Continental Congress approved a more militant statement of purpose.
- Although the Patriots lost the Battle of Bunker Hill, George Washington finally drove the British from Boston.

(?) Exploring the Essential Question

Use the online study guide to explore the essential question.

Section 1
How did the British gain French territory in North America?

Section 2
How did the French and Indian War draw the colonists closer together but increase friction with Britain?

Chapter 5 Essential Question
How did the relationship between Britain and the colonies fall apart?

Section 4
How did the American Revolution begin?

Section 3
How did the British tax policies move the colonists closer to rebellion?

Chapter 5

Essential Question
Remind Students of the Chapter Essential Question: **How did the relationship between Britain and the colonies fall apart?** Have them review the bulleted statements and the Visual Preview at the beginning of the chapter to help them answer this question.

To bolster students' retention, at this time they should complete the Study Guide in print or online. Remind students that they should also continue notetaking for the Unit and Chapter Essential Questions.

Interactive Reading and Notetaking Study Guide, Chapter 5 (Adapted Version also available.)

 Study Guide *Online,* Chapter 5

Chapter Challenge
To wrap up this chapter, students should apply the knowledge they have gained to answer this question: **In what ways would the history of North America be different if King George III had responded favorably to the Olive Branch Petition?** (*Answers will vary, but students should recognize that the colonists and the British government might have worked out a compromise. Students may also suggest that the compromise only would have delayed the revolution.*)

Assessment at a Glance

Formal Assessment
    Chapter Tests A/B (L1/L2)
    AYP Monitoring Assessment
    Test Prep Workbook With Document-Based Assessment
    Test-Taking Strategies With Transparencies

Performance Assessment
    Group/Individual Activities, TE pp. 136g, 136h
    Teacher's Edition, pp. 144, 149, 153, 161
    Assessment Rubrics

Assessment Through Technology
    ExamView CD-ROM
    MindPoint CD-ROM
    Progress Monitoring Transparencies
    Progress Monitoring Online

Key Terms

1. The Iroquois thought that they were likely to gain an advantage by helping the British defeat the French.

2. The militia was transformed into an army during the Second Continental Congress.

3. Britain wanted to prevent supplies from reaching the colonists by blocking ships from entering or leaving American ports.

4. Parliament repealed the acts, but then passed the Declaratory Act.

Comprehension and Critical Thinking

5. **(a)** France lost most of its North American territory; Britain gained French Canada, French territory east of the Mississippi River except New Orleans; all French territory west of the Mississippi River went to Spain **(b)** Possible answer: Britain would have lost territory in North America, and France would have gained territory.

6. **(a)** A war fought against the British by a confederation of Native Americans led by the Ottawa chief, Pontiac **(b)** Possible answer: They came into continuing conflict as settlers moved west into Native American territory.

7. **(a)** Possible answers may include: It demanded a repeal of the Intolerable Acts; declared that colonists should govern and tax themselves; called for a boycott of British goods. **(b)** Possible answers may include: It formed the Continental army and named Washington as its commander; printed paper money to pay the army; sent the Olive Branch Petition to the British king **(c)** Both petitioned the British government while strengthening the unity of the colonies against Britain and the colonial armed forces. The Second Continental Congress went much further to establish the colonies as independent from Britain by, for example, forming an army, staffing it, and printing money.

8. **(a)** It asked King George to stop all fighting so that all disputes could be settled peaceably. **(b)** a statement that the colonists were ready to die as free men instead of living under harsh British rule **(c)** The king's rejection of the

Key Terms

Answer the following questions in complete sentences that show your understanding of the key terms.

1. Why did the British want to form an alliance with the Iroquois during the French and Indian War?

2. How did the role of the militia change after the battles of Lexington and Concord?

3. What did Britain hope to achieve by a blockade of American ports?

4. How did the English king react to the colonists' petition about the Sugar and Stamp Acts?

Comprehension and Critical Thinking

5. **(a) Identify** What were three results of the French and Indian War?
   (b) Make Predictions What would have happened if the French had won the French and Indian War?

6. **(a) Recall** What was Pontiac's War?
   (b) Draw Conclusions What happened to the relationship between Native Americans and colonists after the French and Indian War? Explain your answer.

7. **(a) Recall** What did the First Continental Congress do?
   (b) Recall What did the Second Continental Congress do?
   (c) Compare and Contrast Compare and contrast the achievements of the First and Second Continental Congress.

8. **(a) Recall** What were the terms of the Olive Branch Petition?
   (b) Identify What was the Declaration of the Causes and Necessities of Taking Up Arms?
   (c) Apply Information Given the terms of each document, why might British leaders have felt the colonists were sending mixed messages about independence?

9. **(a) Describe** How did colonists react to the Battle of Bunker Hill?
   (b) Make Predictions How do you think this reaction would help colonial forces during the war?

History Reading Skill

10. **Make Inferences and Draw Conclusions** Draw a conclusion about George Washington as a military leader. Use evidence from throughout this chapter to support your conclusion.

Writing

11. **Write two paragraphs on the following topic:** How did the French and Indian War affect the relationship between the 13 colonies and Britain?
   Your paragraphs should:
   • include a thesis statement that expresses your main idea;
   • develop that main idea with facts, examples, and other information;
   • conclude by describing the lasting impact of what happened.

12. **Write a Narrative:**
   Since 1766, you have been a colonial merchant living in Boston. Write a letter to a friend explaining why you feel it is important to serve on the correspondence committee in your town.

Skills for Life
Formulate Questions
Use the quotation below to answer the questions.

> "As to government matters, it is not in the power of Britain to do this continent justice; the business of it will soon be too weighty and intricate to be managed with any tolerable degree of convenience, by a power so distant from us, and so very ignorant of us; for if they cannot conquer us, they cannot govern us. . . .
> . . . Freedom has been hunted round the globe. . . . O receive the fugitive, and prepare in time an asylum for mankind."
>
> —Thomas Paine, *Common Sense,* January 1776

13. How does Thomas Paine feel about the American Revolution?

14. **(a)** Why does Thomas Paine compare "freedom" to a "fugitive"?
   (b) How would this comparison affect his readers?

Olive Branch Petition made a peaceful settlement less likely, and the Declaration showed that the colonists were prepared to fight the British.

9. **(a)** by gathering weapons, forming new militias, and replacing royal governments with colonial ones **(b)** It reflected a strong sense of colonial unity and support in the fight against the British.

History Reading Skill

10. **Make Inferences and Draw Conclusions** Possible response: Washington's decision to build Fort Necessity and his decision to bring captured British cannons to help capture Boston show that he was a resourceful and creative military leader.

Chapter 5
Review and Assessment

Test Yourself

1. How did the Battle at Bunker Hill affect the colonists?

   A They needed to train their militia.

   B They were proud of having stood their ground against the British soldiers.

   C They were proud of their victory.

   D They decided to call for a new commanding general.

Refer to the quotation below to answer Question 2.

> "Drive from the Ohio River any European foreigners, and do it in a way that will make them lose all taste for trying to return."

2. The result of this policy by the French government

   A ended relations between France and Spain.

   B increased tensions between France and Native Americans.

   C increased tensions between France and England.

   D pushed French colonists farther west.

Refer to the map below to answer Question 3.

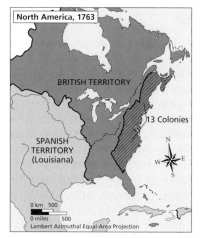

North America, 1763

BRITISH TERRITORY

13 Colonies

SPANISH TERRITORY (Louisiana)

0 km 500
0 miles 500
Lambert Azimuthal Equal-Area Projection

3. How did the boundaries after 1763 affect the British?

   A Britain could not expand farther west.

   B Britain gave up control of the 13 Colonies.

   C British colonists settled in Canada.

   D Britain offered to buy Louisiana from Spain.

Document-Based Questions

Task: Look at Documents 1 and 2, and answer their accompanying questions. Then, use the documents and your knowledge of history to complete this writing assignment:

> Use the evidence in the documents to write a two-paragraph essay explaining the causes and degree of colonial anger.

Document 1: Angered by the Stamp Act, in October 1765, representatives from nine colonies met in the Stamp Act Congress. Challenging Britain's right to tax the colonists, they issued a Declaration of Rights, excerpted below. *According to the delegates, why did Britain not have the right to tax the colonies?*

> "The members of this congress . . . make the following declarations. . . .
>   That His Majesty's . . . subjects in these colonies are entitled to all the . . . rights and privileges of his natural born subjects [in] Great Britain. . . .
>   That the people of these colonies are not . . . represented in the House of Commons in Great Britain. . . .
>   That the only representatives of the people of these colonies are persons chosen . . . by themselves; and that no taxes ever have been or can be constitutionally imposed on them but by their respective legislatures. . . ."

Document 2: Look at the 1774 engraving of the tarring and feathering of a British tax collector in the Life at the Time feature in this chapter. *The fury of the colonists surprised the British. Why do you think this was so?*

Test Yourself

1. B
2. C
3. C

Document-Based Questions
Answers

Document 1 The colonists should not be taxed without their consent or without representation.

Document 2 Possible answer: The British underestimated the extent to which the colonists valued their independence in America.

Rubric: Write an Essay

Share rubric with students before they begin writing.

Score 1 Shows a minimal understanding of the content; does not address all aspects of the task; shows minimal analytical abilities.

Score 2 Shows a limited understanding of the content; does not address all aspects of the task; shows limited analytical abilities.

Score 3 Shows a general understanding of the content (gives explanation of Stamp Act; gives causes for colonial anger); addresses all aspects of the task; shows good analytical abilities.

Score 4 Shows a clear understanding of the content and analytical abilities; supported with relevant details; good organization.

Writing

11. Students' paragraphs should have a thesis statement that clearly expresses the main idea. The main idea should be supported by facts or examples, and the conclusion should describe the lasting impact of the French and Indian War on the relationship between the 13 colonies and Britain.

12. Students' letters should be written from the point of view of a Patriot. Letters may contain reference to the growing tensions between the colonists and Britain and should mention that serving on the committee is a way of showing support to other colonists.

For a more complete four-point rubric, see the Writing Rubrics in the Teaching Resources.

All in One Teaching Resources, Unit 2, p. 123

Skills for Life

13. Possible answer: He feels that the American Revolution will succeed.

14. **(a)** Possible answer: He is suggesting that freedom has been hunted and captured like a fugitive. **(b)** Possible answer: It may have inspired them to fight for their freedom.

The American Revolution (1776–1783)

History Background

The Road to Independence

At its outset, the American Revolution was fought in protest over unfair colonial rule. However, as the Revolution progressed, so did the colonists' desire for independence. The colonists began to see the American Revolution as a war to protect and expand the ideas of rights and self-government that were drawn from the Enlightenment. The Declaration of Independence made their beliefs clear. Copies of the Declaration were distributed throught the colonies. Patriots greeted the news of independence with joyous—and sometimes rowdy—celebrations. In New York, colonists tore down a statue of King George III. In Boston, cannons fired for hours.

The fighting began in New England and steadily progressed toward the Middle States where the Continental army suffered grave losses. As the world looked on, it seemed as though the British would easily win. Yet American victories at Trenton and Princeton gave the Americans new hope, and the American victory at the battle of Saratoga ended the British threat to New England. These battles also convinced France to become an ally of the United States.

By 1778, the war had reached a stalemate in the North, and fighting shifted to the West, the South, and to the sea. Once again, Britain achieved several major victories, especially in the South. However, clever fighting by American militia and attacks on British vessels at sea ultimately led to an American victory. The last major battle of the American Revolution was the Battle of Yorktown. On October 19, 1781, the British surrendered their weapons. A British army played the tune "The World Turned Upside Down." In the Treaty of Paris, the British acknowledged the sovereignty of the United States. A new nation was born.

Essential Questions

Use this graphic organizer to see the relationship between key concepts and the Chapter Essential Question.

Focus Question/Section 1
Why did many colonists favor declaring independence?
(p. 170)

Concept: Enlightenment

Focus Question/Section 2
How were the early years of the war a critical time?
(p. 179)

Concept: Revolution

Chapter Essential Question
How did the American colonists gain their independence?

Focus Question/Section 4
How did the Americans win the war and make peace?
(p. 191)

Concept: Sovereignty

Focus Question/Section 3
How did the effects of the war widen?
(p. 186)

Concept: Independence

Differentiated Instruction

Test-Taking Tips

Improved Student Performance Provide students with these test-taking tips to apply when completing Section and Chapter Reviews, as well as standardized tests. Students' performance in tests improves when they apply simple test-taking tips such as these:

1. Read the directions slowly and carefully. Note important parts of the directions on scrap paper or underline them in the test booklet. Make sure you understand the directions before you begin the test.

2. Skip any questions to which you do not know the answers. Make a small mark next to the question and come back to it after you have completed the rest of the test. Doing this can keep you from wasting time and becoming frustrated while taking the test.

3. Begin a writing activity, such as an essay, by making a quick list of main points or a brief outline. A good place to start is with the items specified in the activity directions. That way you can be sure to include the required components.

Concepts Across Time

Have students develop an understanding of the enduring concepts of history by connecting these ideas.

Concept: Enlightenment

Ask students to recall how the Enlightenment affected life in Europe. (*Possible answers: New ideas about peoples' rights and government led to the weakening of the power of the Roman Catholic Church and kings. The use of reason and the scientific method led to advances in science and medicine.*) Before students read Section 1, have them predict how the Enlightenment affected the colonies. Then, after they have read the section, have them revise their predictions as needed. Use these questions when discussing the Declaration of Independence in Section 1.

Concept: Independence

Have students recall the definition of independence. (*freedom from outside rule or authority*) Explain to students that the colonists' desire for independence was unheard of at that time in history. Ask: **Why do you think the colonists were willing to risk their lives for independence?** (*Possible answer: They believed that life was not worth living if they were not free to rule themselves.*) Have students discuss whether the colonists had a right to declare independence. (*Possible answer: Yes, because the British government wasn't treating the colonists fairly.*) Use this question when discussing The War at Home in Section 3.

Concept: Sovereignty

Explain the definition of sovereignty. (*the authority of a state or country, free from outside interference*) Have students consider the responsibilities that come with sovereignty. Ask: **What challenges might the new republic face after winning its freedom?** (*Possible answers: It would have to set up a government. It would have to recover from the war. It would need a source of income.*) Use this question when discussing Making Peace with Britain in Section 4.

Section 1 A Nation Declares Independence *1.5 periods, .75 block*

Objectives

Students will

1. Find out how Thomas Paine stirred support for independence.

2. Understand the meaning and structure of the Declaration of Independence.

3. Learn how Congress finally agreed to separate from England.

Differentiated Instruction Key

L1 Basic to Average

L2 All Students

L3 Average to Advanced

AR Advanced Readers
ELL English Language Learners
GT Gifted and Talented
LPR Less Proficient Readers
SN Special Needs

Prepare to Read

Build Background Knowledge
Preview the section and have students predict what they will learn about the colonists' call for independence.

Set a Purpose for Reading
Have students begin to fill out the Reading Readiness Guide.

Preview Key Terms
Preview the section's key terms.

Instructional Resources

All in One Teaching Resources, Unit 2

L2 Chapter Prereading Guide, p. 4

L2 History Reading Skill, p. 41

L2 Word Knowledge Rating Form, p. 42

L2 Reading Readiness Guide, p. 43

Teacher's Edition

L2 Vocabulary Builder, pp. 169, 171

Differentiated Instruction

🎧 **Guided Reading Audio CD**

Spanish ELL, LPR, SN

Teach

Instruction
A Call for Independence
Discuss the impact of Thomas Paine's *Common Sense*.

The Declaration of Independence
Analyze the structure and meaning of the Declaration of Independence.

Impact of the Declaration
Identify the effects of the colonists' declaration.

Instructional Resources

📖 **Interactive Reading and Notetaking Study Guide**

L2 Chapter 6, Section 1

All in One Teaching Resources, Unit 2

L2 *Common Sense*, p. 47

L2 Concept Lesson, p. 53

L2 Concept Organizer, p. 6

Discovery School Video

L2 The Declaration of Independence, p. 174

Differentiated Instruction

📖 **Interactive Reading and Notetaking Study Guide, Adapted Version (English/ Spanish)**

L1 Chapter 6, Section 1

Teacher's Edition

L1 Study Aid, p. 170 ELL, LPR, SN

L3 Hold a Mock Trial, p. 172 AR, GT

All in One Teaching Resources, Unit 2

L3 King George III on Trial, p. 48

Assess and Reteach

Assess Progress
Evaluate student comprehension with Check Your Progress and Section Quiz.

Reteach
Assign the Interactive Reading and Notetaking Study Guide to help struggling students.

Extend
Extend the section by having students write a revolutionary editorial.

Instructional Resources

📖 **Interactive Reading and Notetaking Study Guide**

L2 Chapter 6, Section 1

All in One Teaching Resources, Unit 2

L2 Reading Readiness Guide, p. 43

L2 Section Quiz, p. 54

Progress Monitoring Transparencies

L2 Chapter 6, Section 1

Differentiated Instruction

Teacher's Edition

L1 Checkpoints, TE pp. 171, 172, 173

🎧 **SE on Audio CD**

L1 Chapter 6, Section 1

Section 2 A Critical Time *1 period, .5 block*

Objectives

Students will

1. Discover the results of fighting in the Middle States.
2. Understand why the Battle of Saratoga was a turning point in the American Revolution.
3. Learn how foreign nations and volunteers helped the Americans.

Differentiated Instruction Key

L1 Basic to Average
L2 All Students
L3 Average to Advanced

AR Advanced Readers
ELL English Language Learners
GT Gifted and Talented
LPR Less Proficient Readers
SN Special Needs

Prepare to Read

Build Background Knowledge
Preview the section and have students predict what they will learn about the battles of the American Revolution.

Set a Purpose for Reading
Have students begin to fill out the Reading Readiness Guide.

Preview Key Terms
Preview the section's Key Terms.

Instructional Resources

All in One Teaching Resources, Unit 2
L2 Reading Readiness Guide, p. 44

Teacher's Edition
L2 Vocabulary Builder, p. 179

Differentiated Instruction

🔊 Guided Reading Audio CD
Spanish ELL, LPR, SN

Teach

Instruction
Retreat from New York
Discuss the war in the Middle States.

Surprises for the British
Explain how George Washington changed the course of the war.

Saratoga: A Turning Point
Analyze the importance of the Battle of Saratoga.

Help from Overseas
Explain why European nations joined the war effort.

Valley Forge
Identify the significance of events at Valley Forge.

Instructional Resources

📖 Interactive Reading and Notetaking Study Guide
L2 Chapter 6, Section 2

Color Transparencies
L2 Revolutionary Soldier
L2 Turning Points of the Revolution

Differentiated Instruction

📖 Interactive Reading and Notetaking Study Guide, Adapted Version (English/Spanish)
L1 Chapter 6, Section 2

Teacher's Edition
L1 Make an Outline, p. 180 ELL, LPR, SN
L3 Make a Live Sequence of Events, p. 182 AR, GT

Assess and Reteach

Assess Progress
Evaluate student comprehension with Check Your Progress and Section Quiz.

Reteach
Assign the Interactive Reading and Notetaking Study Guide to help struggling students.

Extend
Extend the lesson by completing the History Interactive activity online.

Instructional Resources

📖 Interactive Reading and Notetaking Study Guide
L2 Chapter 6, Section 2

All in One Teaching Resources, Unit 2
L2 Reading Readiness Guide, p. 44
L2 Section Quiz, p. 55

Progress Monitoring Transparencies
L2 Chapter 6, Section 2

Differentiated Instruction

Teacher's Edition
L1 Checkpoints, TE pp. 180, 181, 183, 184

🔊 SE on Audio CD
L1 Chapter 6, Section 2

Internet Resources
PHSchool.com

Section 3 **The War Widens** *1 period, .5 block*

Objectives

Students will

1. Discover the role that African Americans played in the American Revolution.

2. Find out how the war affected women and other civilians.

3. Learn about the progress of the fighting on the western frontier and at sea.

Differentiated Instruction Key

L1 Basic to Average   **AR** Advanced Readers

L2 All Students   **ELL** English Language Learners

L3 Average to Advanced   **GT** Gifted and Talented

     LPR Less Proficient Readers

     SN Special Needs

Prepare to Read

Build Background Knowledge
Preview the section and have students predict what they will learn about the cultural and geographic expansion of the Revolution.

Set a Purpose for Reading
Have students begin to fill out the Reading Readiness Guide.

Preview Key Terms
Preview the section's Key Terms.

Instructional Resources

All in One Teaching Resources, Unit 2

L2 Reading Readiness Guide, p. 45

Teacher's Edition

L2 Vocabulary Builder, p. 187

Differentiated Instruction

🎧 **Guided Reading Audio CD**

Spanish ELL, LPR, SN

Teach

Instruction
African Americans in the War
Discuss the role of free and enslaved African Americans in the Revolution.

The War at Home
Analyze the impact of the Revolution on civilian life.

Fighting in the West
Explore the expansion of the fighting onto the western frontier.

The War at Sea
Identify the importance of the contribution of European nations to the colonists' victory.

Instructional Resources

📖 **Interactive Reading and Notetaking Study Guide**

L2 Chapter 6, Section 3

Color Transparencies

L2 The War Affects All Americans

Differentiated Instruction

📖 **Interactive Reading and Notetaking Study Guide, Adapted Version (English/ Spanish)**

L1 Chapter 6, Section 3

Teacher's Edition

L3 Write an Essay, p. 186 AR, GT

L1 Identifying Contributions, p. 188 ELL, LPR, SN

Assess and Reteach

Assess Progress
Evaluate student comprehension with Check Your Progress and Section Quiz.

Reteach
Assign the Interactive Reading and Notetaking Study Guide to help struggling students.

Extend
Extend the section by having students create a short news report.

Instructional Resources

📖 **Interactive Reading and Notetaking Study Guide**

L2 Chapter 6, Section 3

All in One Teaching Resources, Unit 2

L2 Reading Readiness Guide, p. 45

L2 Section Quiz, p. 56

Progress Monitoring Transparencies

L2 Chapter 6, Section 3

Differentiated Instruction

Teacher's Edition

L1 Checkpoints, TE, pp. 187, 188, 189, 190

🎧 **SE on Audio CD**

L1 Chapter 6, Section 3

Section 4 Winning Independence *1 period, .5 block*

Objectives

Students will

1. Find out how the Americans won the final battle of the Revolution.
2. Learn the terms of the peace treaty with England.
3. Explore the reasons that the Americans were victorious.
4. Examine the effects of the American Revolution.

Differentiated Instruction Key

L1 Basic to Average
L2 All Students
L3 Average to Advanced

AR Advanced Readers
ELL English Language Learners
GT Gifted and Talented
LPR Less Proficient Readers
SN Special Needs

Prepare to Read

Build Background Knowledge
Preview the section and have students predict what they will learn about how the American colonists defeated the British.

Set a Purpose for Reading
Have students begin to fill out the Reading Readiness Guide.

Preview Key Terms
Preview the section's Key Terms.

Instructional Resources

All in One Teaching Resources, Unit 2
L2 Reading Readiness Guide, p. 46

Teacher's Edition
L2 Vocabulary Builder, p. 191

Differentiated Instruction

Guided Reading Audio CD
Spanish ELL, LPR, SN

Teach

Instruction
Fighting Moves South
Analyze the effectiveness of the British strategy to move south.

Making Peace with Britain
Discuss the terms of the Treaty of Paris.

Impact of the Revolution
Identify the global effects of the Revolution.

Instructional Resources

Interactive Reading and Notetaking Study Guide
L2 Chapter 6, Section 4

All in One Teaching Resources, Unit 2
L2 The Battle of Yorktown, p. 50
L2 Refugees of the Revolution, p. 51
L2 Skills for Life Worksheet, p. 52

Differentiated Instruction

Interactive Reading and Notetaking Study Guide, Adapted Version (English/Spanish)
L1 Chapter 6, Section 4

Teacher's Edition
L1 Create a Timeline, p. 192 ELL, LPR, SN
L3 Write a Memo, p. 194 AR, GT

Assess and Reteach

Assess Progress
Assign Check Your Progress and Section Quiz.

Reteach
Assign the Study Guide to help students.

Extend
Extend the section by having students review the major battles of the Revolution from opposing points of view.

Instructional Resources

Interactive Reading and Notetaking Study Guide
L2 Chapter 6, Section 4

All in One Teaching Resources, Unit 2
L2 Word Knowledge Rating Form, p. 42
L2 Reading Readiness Guide, p. 46
L2 Section Quiz, p. 57
L2 Chapter Test, p. 61

Progress Monitoring Transparencies
L2 Chapter 6, Section 4

Differentiated Instruction

Teacher's Edition
L1 Checkpoints, TE pp. 192, 195

All in One Teaching Resources, Unit 2
L1 Chapter Test, p. 58

SE on Audio CD
L1 Chapter 6, Section 4

Use the following research activities to help students deepen their understanding of the Chapter Essential Question: **How did the American colonists gain their independence?** Students should use library or Internet resources. The Web Codes provided offer access to Internet resources students can use to complete each activity. Use the appropriate four-point rubric in Assessment Rubrics to evaluate the activity.

 Assessment Rubrics

Draft a Declaration of Rights

Have students thoroughly study the Declaration of Independence at the end of Section 1. Ask them to draft a modern declaration for a nation under unfriendly rule. Encourage students to include a Preamble, a list of grievances, and a declaration of rights similar to the structure of the American declaration. Have students present their document to the class. Use this activity after students have completed Section 1.

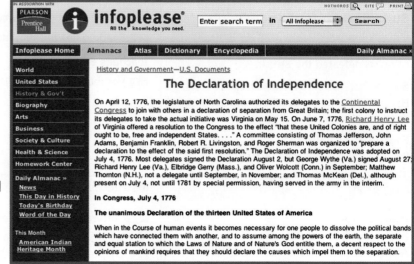

 Individual research activity AR, GT   **L3**

Go Online **Web Code:** mvd-0138
PHSchool.com

Hold a Debate

Organize students into two groups—Loyalists and Patriots. Have them research why Americans should not seek independence (Loyalists) or should seek independence (Patriots). Then hold an in-class debate between the two groups. Each group should choose two or three students to present their argument. Use this activity after students have completed Section 2.

 Group research activity AR, GT   **L3**

Go Online **Web Code:** mvh-0139
PHSchool.com

Map the Revolution

Organize the class into five groups. Assign each group one of the areas in which the American Revolution was fought: New England, the Middle States, the West, the South, and at sea. Have each group map the significant battles that took place in their assigned area. Students may use the Internet as well as the maps contained in Chapter 6 for reference. Remind students to make use of symbols and color to depict movements and events.

 Group research activity   L2

 Web Code: mvd-0140

Compare Revolutionary Movements

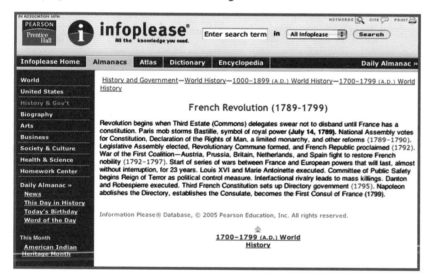

 Web Code: mve-0141

Just as the Declaration of Independence inspired the French Declaration of the Rights of Man and of the Citizen, the American Revolution inspired the French Revolution. Have students research a key aspect of the French Revolution (for example, its causes, early events, key battles, and its outcome) and compare it to that same aspect of the American Revolution. Then have students make a chart listing the similarities and differences between the two revolutions. Use this activity after students have completed Section 4.

 Individual research activity AR, GT   L3

Why It Matters

In this chapter, students will focus on the Declaration of Independence, and the course and outcome of the American Revolution.

The American War for Independence was the first time in the history of the world that a colony had successfully rebelled against its ruling country.

The Declaration of Independence is the most complete statement of the basic ideals behind the creation of the United States. Today, July 4—the date that Congress adopted the Declaration—is celebrated as Independence Day, the birthday of a new nation.

The American Revolution set an example for the overthrow of tyrannical governments, beginning with the demise of the French monarchy and continuing to our own day with the fight for free elections in South Africa and other countries.

Chapter Essential Question

How did the American colonists gain their independence?

Think Like a Historian

- To preview this chapter, have students review the content of these pages. Ask: **What will you be learning about in this chapter?** *(The fight for American independence from Britain)*

- Have students read and paraphrase the quotation. **What was the goal of the colonies?** *(to be free and independent)* **How would that be achieved?** *(All political ties to Great Britain would need to be ended.)*

- Have students study the picture, and ask them to describe the fighting. *(hand-to-hand combat; soldiers appear determined, fierce, scared; British seem to be retreating.)*

The American Revolution

1776–1783

166

Bibliography

For the Teacher

Martin, Joseph Plumb. *A Narrative of a Revolutionary Soldier.* Signet Classics, 2001.

McCullough, David. *1776.* Simon & Schuster, 2005.

Nash, Gary. *The Unknown American Revolution.* Viking, Adult, 2005.

For the Student

L1 Schanzer, Rosalyn. *George vs. George.* National Geographic Children's, 2004.

L2 Fish, Bruce and Becky Durost Fish. *Thomas Paine: Political Writer.* Chelsea House Publishers, 2000.

L3 Cox, Clinton. *Come All You Brave Soldiers: Blacks in the Revolutionary War.* Scholastic, 1999.

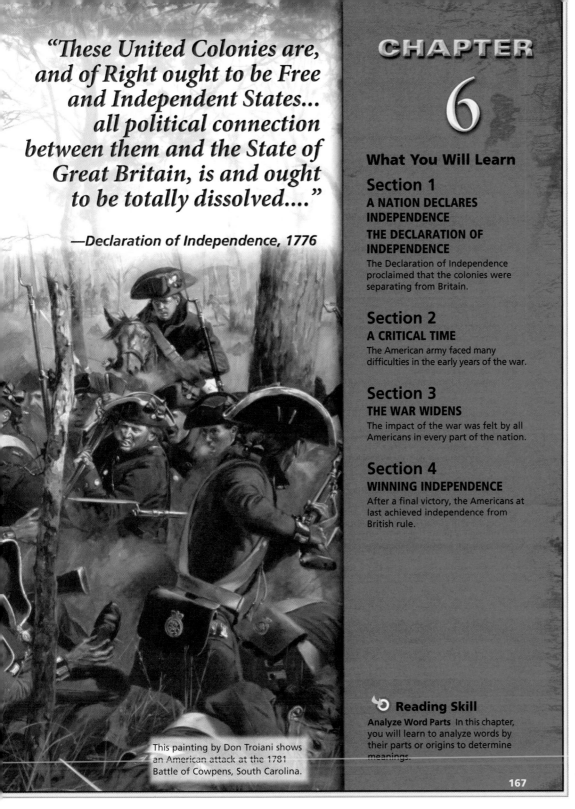

"These United Colonies are, and of Right ought to be Free and Independent States... all political connection between them and the State of Great Britain, is and ought to be totally dissolved...."

—Declaration of Independence, 1776

This painting by Don Troiani shows an American attack at the 1781 Battle of Cowpens, South Carolina.

CHAPTER 6

What You Will Learn

Section 1
A NATION DECLARES INDEPENDENCE
THE DECLARATION OF INDEPENDENCE
The Declaration of Independence proclaimed that the colonies were separating from Britain.

Section 2
A CRITICAL TIME
The American army faced many difficulties in the early years of the war.

Section 3
THE WAR WIDENS
The impact of the war was felt by all Americans in every part of the nation.

Section 4
WINNING INDEPENDENCE
After a final victory, the Americans at last achieved independence from British rule.

Reading Skill

Analyze Word Parts In this chapter, you will learn to analyze words by their parts or origins to determine meanings.

167

History Background

Surprising Victory "Cowpen" was the term for the pastureland widespread throughout South Carolina. This battlefield was some 500 yards square, a park-like setting cleared of undergrowth by grazing cattle.

Although both sides had approximately the same number of troops, the Continental forces, under the command of Daniel Morgan, used tactical surprise and natural resources to defeat the British. Of about 1,100 British troops involved, only about 260 escaped; the Americans took over 500 prisoners. The Patriots suffered only 73 casualties. One of the most brilliant American victories in the War, the defeat demoralized the British and was a psychological boost for the Patriots.

Prepare to Read

Use the following for reading skill support.

All in One Teaching Resources, Unit 2, Chapter Prereading Guide, p. 4; History Reading Skill, p. 41

History Reading Skill *Online*
Web code: mve-3000

Differentiated Instruction

The following Teacher's Edition strategies are suitable for students of varying abilities.

- **L3 Advanced Readers,** pp. 172, 182, 186, 194 AR
- **L1 English Language Learners,** pp. 169, 170, 180, 188, 192 ELL
- **L3 Gifted and Talented,** pp. 172, 182, 186, 194 GT
- **L1 Less Proficient Readers,** pp. 169, 170, 180, 188, 192 LPR
- **L1 Special Needs,** pp. 169, 170, 180, 188, 192 SN

Chapter Resources

Teaching Resources, Unit 2
Chapter Prereading Guide, p. 4
Word Knowledge Rating Form, p. 42
History Reading Skill, p. 41
Skills for Life Worksheet, p. 52
Chapter Tests A/B (L1/L2), pp. 58, 61
Letter Home (English/Spanish), pp. 34, 35

Spanish Support
- **L1 Interactive Reading and Notetaking Study Guide, Spanish,** Adapted Version
- **L1 Guided Reading Audio CD,** Spanish

Media and Technology
- **L1** SE on Audio CD
- **L2** Social Studies Skills Tutor CD-ROM
ExamView Test Bank CD-ROM

DISCOVERY SCHOOL

Quick View Video
View the chapter video for a quick preview of the main ideas.

Chapter 6

Visual Preview

? **How did American colonists gain their independence?**

Build Background Knowledge ⬜L2

Discuss with students the definition of *independence*. Have them understand that being independent means there is no outside rule or authority. Lead a structured review of why there was tension between the colonists and the British. (See TE p. T24.) Discuss why people often want to make rules for themselves. (*They feel someone else does not understand their needs and resent outside influence.*) Have students give examples of when they felt they should have been able to make their own decisions.

Instruction ⬜L2

- For background information on conducting a lesson for the Visual Preview, see TE p. T20.

- Write the Essential Question on the board. Use the Numbered Heads strategy (TE p. T24) to lead a structured review of the growing tensions between the colonists and the British. (*taxation; Intolerable Acts*) Ask: **Which protests led to fighting between the colonists and the British?** (*Boston Tea Party, Boston Massacre, Lexington and Concord*)

- Using the key, have students explain what the red stars mean. (*British victories*) **What do the blue lines and arrows mean?** (*the direction of American forces*) **Which countries helped the colonists?** (*France, Spain*)

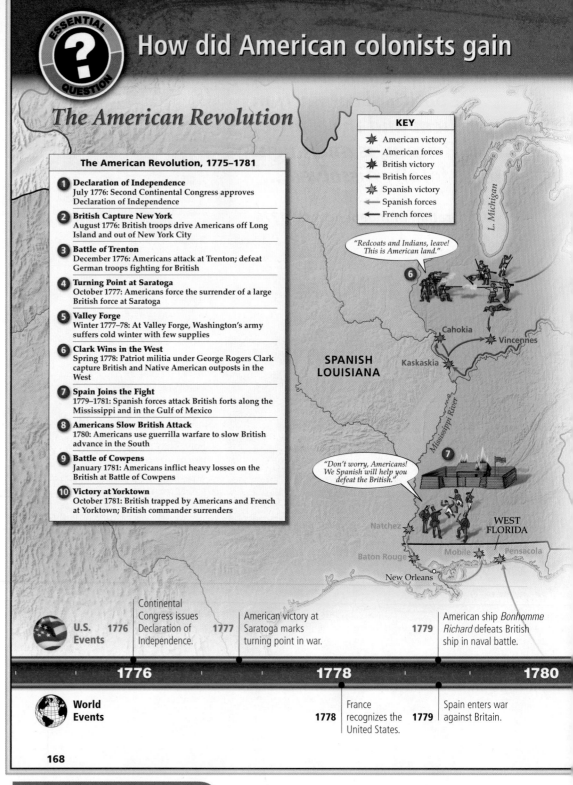

? How did American colonists gain

The American Revolution

KEY
- ✸ American victory
- ⬅ American forces
- ✸ British victory
- ⬅ British forces
- ✸ Spanish victory
- ⬅ Spanish forces
- ⬅ French forces

The American Revolution, 1775–1781

1. **Declaration of Independence**
   July 1776: Second Continental Congress approves Declaration of Independence

2. **British Capture New York**
   August 1776: British troops drive Americans off Long Island and out of New York City

3. **Battle of Trenton**
   December 1776: Americans attack at Trenton; defeat German troops fighting for British

4. **Turning Point at Saratoga**
   October 1777: Americans force the surrender of a large British force at Saratoga

5. **Valley Forge**
   Winter 1777–78: At Valley Forge, Washington's army suffers cold winter with few supplies

6. **Clark Wins in the West**
   Spring 1778: Patriot militia under George Rogers Clark capture British and Native American outposts in the West

7. **Spain Joins the Fight**
   1779–1781: Spanish forces attack British forts along the Mississippi and in the Gulf of Mexico

8. **Americans Slow British Attack**
   1780: Americans use guerrilla warfare to slow British advance in the South

9. **Battle of Cowpens**
   January 1781: Americans inflict heavy losses on the British at Battle of Cowpens

10. **Victory at Yorktown**
    October 1781: British trapped by Americans and French at Yorktown; British commander surrenders

"Redcoats and Indians, leave! This is American land."

L. Michigan

Cahokia — Vincennes

SPANISH LOUISIANA — Kaskaskia

Mississippi River

"Don't worry, Americans! We Spanish will help you defeat the British."

WEST FLORIDA

Natchez

Baton Rouge — Mobile — Pensacola

New Orleans

U.S. Events 1776 Continental Congress issues Declaration of Independence.

1777 American victory at Saratoga marks turning point in war.

1779 American ship *Bonhomme Richard* defeats British ship in naval battle.

1776 | **1778** | **1780**

World Events 1778 France recognizes the United States.

1779 Spain enters war against Britain.

168

History Background

Importance of Alliances Both France and Spain supported the Americans during the Revolution. They each had lost territory to the British during the French and Indian War and hoped to gain it back if the Americans won. French support came in the form of trade and, ultimately, a formal alliance and declaration of war against Britain.

The Spanish supported the colonists by providing ammunition and supplies for American forts in the west. They also attacked and took control of the Mississippi River towns of Natchez and Baton Rouge, and the Gulf towns of Mobile and Pensacola. French and Spanish support played a key role in the American victory.

CHAPTER
6

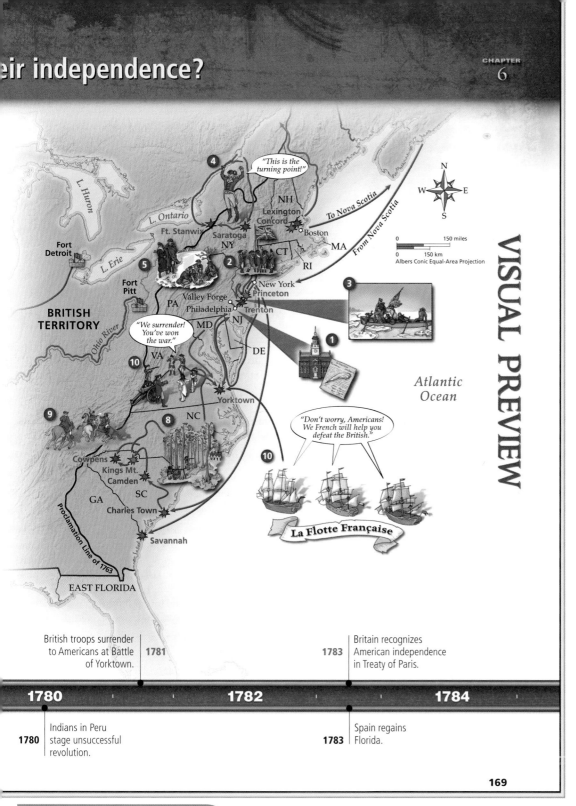

"This is the turning point!"

To Nova Scotia

From Nova Scotia

N
W — E
S

0   150 miles
0   150 km
Albers Conic Equal-Area Projection

L. Huron

L. Ontario

Ft. Stanwix

Saratoga
NY

Lexington
Concord

Boston

Fort
Detroit

L. Erie

CT

MA

RI

Fort
Pitt

New York

Princeton

BRITISH
TERRITORY

Valley Forge

Philadelphia

Trenton

"We surrender!
You've won
the war."

PA

MD

NJ

DE

Ohio River

VA

Yorktown

Atlantic
Ocean

"Don't worry, Americans!
We French will help you
defeat the British."

NC

Cowpens

Kings Mt.

Camden

GA

SC

Charles Town

La Flotte Française

Savannah

Proclamation Line of 1763

EAST FLORIDA

VISUAL PREVIEW

| British troops surrender to Americans at Battle of Yorktown. | **1781** | | **1783** | Britain recognizes American independence in Treaty of Paris. |

1780 | **1782** | **1784**

| **1780** | Indians in Peru stage unsuccessful revolution. | | **1783** | Spain regains Florida. |

169

Instruction (continued)

■ Have students review the timeline. Ask: **When did the Continental Congress declare independence?** *(1776)* **What does "Britain recognizes American independence" mean?** *(Britain acknowledges or accepts that America is independent.)* **How many years did it take Britain to recognize America's independence?** *(7 years)*

■ Have students review the graphics and the chart. Have them note the number on the chart and the location of the number on the map. Mark off different parts of the room and label them for regions of the country. (New England, Middle, Southern colonies; West) Using the Numbered Heads strategy (TE, p. T24), call on students to identify the number of an event and its location. Have students move to different parts of the room to show where the events occurred. Where did the largest number of events occur?

■ Have students rewrite the Essential Question in simple terms in their notes. **How did Americans win their freedom from Britain?** You may also post this question in a prominent place in the classroom and leave it there while discussing the chapter. Tell students to use the section focus questions as a guide to answering the Essential Question as they read the chapter.

■ Tell students that as they complete the Notetaking Study Guide for this chapter, they will be building the answer to the Chapter Essential Question.

Interactive Reading and Notetaking Study Guide, Chapter 6 (Adapted Version also available.)

Vocabulary Builder

Preview the Vocabulary Have students preview the vocabulary in the chapter and rate how well they know each word on the Word Knowledge Rating Form. Collect the sheets and explain that they will have a chance to go over the forms later.

All in One Teaching Resources, Unit 2, Word Knowledge Rating Form, p. 42

Monitor Progress Have students create a line drawing or cartoon for these words to illustrate the definition. These can be done in a fun way, but should demonstrate student understanding of the word. Review these images with students. Then, have students use the words in their own sentences.

Review and Preview

Students have read about the development of self-government in the colonies. Now they will learn why the colonists began to want independence.

Why did many colonists favor declaring independence?

Before you begin the lesson for the day, write the Section Focus Question on the board. (*Lesson focus: The colonists felt that the British government was treating them unfairly.*)

Prepare to Read

Build Background Knowledge **L2**

Ask students to recall from Chapter 3 what they learned about rights and self-government in the American colonies. Write each accurate recollection on the board. Then ask students to preview the section by reading the headings and looking at the images. Ask students to predict what more they will learn about self-government and rights in the colonies.

Set a Purpose **L2**

- Read each statement in the Reading Readiness Guide aloud. Ask students to mark the statements True or False.

  All in One Teaching Resources, Unit 2, Reading Readiness Guide, p. 43

- Have students discuss the statements in pairs or groups of four, then mark the worksheets again. Use the Numbered Heads participation strategy (TE, p. T24) to call on students to share their group's perspectives. The students will return to these worksheets later.

SECTION 1

Let Us Separate

"I could not join to day in the [prayers] of our worthy parson, for a reconciliation between our, no longer parent state, but tyrant state, and these colonies. —Let us separate, they are unworthy to be our brethren. Let us renounce them."

—Abigail Adams, letter to husband John Adams at the Continental Congress, 1775

◀ Benjamin Franklin, John Adams, and Thomas Jefferson reviewing the Declaration of Independence

A Nation Declares Independence

Objectives

- Find out how Thomas Paine stirred support for independence.
- Understand the meaning and structure of the Declaration of Independence.
- Learn how Congress finally agreed to separate from England.

Reading Skill

Analyze Word Roots Many English words have common word roots or parts. For example, the root *mot* means "move." That root appears in the words *motion, motor, promote,* and *demote.* Those words have different meanings, but all share some connection to movement. Learn to recognize familiar word roots and trace their origins.

Key Terms and People

Thomas Paine	preamble
Richard Henry Lee	grievance
resolution	

Why It Matters After King George rejected the Olive Branch Petition, thousands of British troops were sent to the colonies. As the fighting continued, American patriots called for independence.

❓ **Section Focus Question: Why did many colonists favor declaring independence?**

A Call for Independence

When the year 1776 began, few colonists could have predicted what lay ahead. Most colonists still hoped for a peaceful end to the quarrel with Britain.

Colonists Divided Both Patriots and Loyalists were in a minority at the start of 1776. Many colonists were in the middle, with no strong feelings about the dispute with Britain.

Even within the Continental Congress, support for independence was limited to about one third of the delegates. Patriots such as John Adams found it hard to win others to the cause of independence. Adams complained that Loyalists used the prospect of independence as a way to frighten people into giving up the struggle.

Common Sense In January 1776, a 50-page pamphlet titled *Common Sense* was published in Philadelphia. The pamphlet stimulated broad support for independence.

The author, Thomas Paine, called King George III a "royal brute." Paine ridiculed the very idea of rule by kings. Americans, he said, would be far better off if they governed themselves. (See Reading Primary Sources on the next page.)

170 Chapter 6 The American Revolution

Differentiated Instruction

L1 English Language Learners   **L1 Less Proficient Readers**   **L1 Special Needs**

Study Aid To help students track the development of revolutionary ideas and sentiments in the colonies, help them make a graphic organizer that shows the sequence of events discussed on pp. 170–171. Students should also be able to explain the different points of view of Patriots and Loyalists.

Paine's strong logic and powerful words inspired people in all the colonies. Some 500,000 copies of the pamphlet were sold between January and July of 1776. George Washington wrote, "*Common Sense* is working a powerful change in the minds of men."

Virginia's Resolution Paine's pamphlet increased support for independence within the Continental Congress. In May 1776, Virginia authorized its delegates to support independence. Soon after, Richard Henry Lee introduced a **resolution**, or formal statement of opinion, to Congress. The Virginia resolution proclaimed that "these United Colonies are, and of right ought to be, free and independent States."

Before voting on Lee's resolution, Congress appointed a committee to draw up a statement stating the reasons for separation from Britain. Thomas Jefferson, a 33-year-old delegate from Virginia, was given the task of composing the declaration. Highly educated but shy, Jefferson spoke little in Congress. However, he was known for his graceful writing style.

In the heat of the Philadelphia summer, Jefferson struggled to find the words that would convince Americans and the world of the rightness of independence. The result was masterful. John Adams and Benjamin Franklin, who were also on the committee, suggested only minor changes.

✔**Checkpoint** What proposal did Richard Henry Lee make to Congress?

Vocabulary Builder
logic (LAH jihk) **n.** reason; careful thought

Common Sense

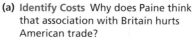

"I challenge the warmest advocate for reconciliation, to show a single advantage that this continent can reap, by being connected with Great Britain. I repeat the challenge, not a single advantage is derived. Our corn will fetch its price in any market in Europe, and our imported goods must be paid for, buy them where we will. . . . Whenever a war breaks out between England and any foreign power, the trade of America goes to ruin, because of her connection with Britain. . . . Every thing that is right or natural pleads for separation. The blood of the slain, the weeping voice of nature cries, 'TIS TIME TO PART."

—Thomas Paine, *Common Sense*

Thomas Paine

Reading Primary Sources
Skills Activity

In *Common Sense*, Thomas Paine gives political, military, and moral arguments for breaking away from Britain. In the excerpt above, Paine discusses some economic reasons.

(a) Identify Costs Why does Paine think that association with Britain hurts American trade?

(b) Make Inferences What do you think Paine means by "the blood of the slain"?

Section 1 A Nation Declares Independence 171

Vocabulary Builder

Use the information below to teach students this section's high-use words.

High-Use Word	Definition and Sample Sentence
logic, p. 171	*n.* reason; careful thought Thinkers of the Enlightenment believed in using **logic** to support their opinions.
violate, p. 172	*v.* fail to keep or observe; infringe on Colonial merchants who smuggled goods and avoided taxes **violated** British law.

Teach

A Call for Independence
p. 170

Instruction ▊L2

■ **Vocabulary Builder** Before teaching this section, preteach the High-Use Words **logic** and **violate**, using the strategy on TE p. T21.

Key Terms Following the instruction on p. 7, have students create a See It–Remember It chart for the Key Terms in this chapter.

■ Read A Call for Independence with students using the Oral Cloze participation strategy (TE, p. T22).

■ Ask: **Who was Thomas Paine?** (*He was a colonist who wrote a 50-page pamphlet outlining the need for colonial self-rule.*)

■ Have students complete the worksheet *Common Sense*.

▊All in One▊ **Teaching Resources, Unit 2,** *Common Sense,* p. 47

Independent Practice
Have students begin to fill in the Study Guide for this section.

📖 **Interactive Reading and Notetaking Study Guide,** Chapter 6, Section 1 (Adapted Version also available.)

Monitor Progress

As students fill in the Notetaking Study Guide, circulate to make sure students understand the importance of Paine's pamphlet to the revolutionary movement. Provide assistance as needed.

Answers

✔**Checkpoint** Richard Henry Lee proposed that they seek independence.

Reading Primary Sources (a) It keeps colonists from earning market prices on their exports. Also, colonial trade is cut off when English trade is cut off due to its conflicts with other nations. **(b)** Possible answer: Just as blood leaves the body of someone slain, the colonists must leave England.

The Declaration of Independence

Impact of the Declaration

pp. 172–173

Instruction `L2`

- Have students read The Declaration of Independence and Impact of the Declaration. Remind students to look for details that answer the Section Focus Question.

- To help students better understand the concept of *independence*, which is important to the understanding of this chapter, use the Concept Lesson about Independence. Provide students with copies of the Concept Organizer.

  All in One **Teaching Resources, Unit 2,** Concept Lesson, p. 53; Concept Organizer, p. 6

- To help students understand the importance of signing the Declaration of Independence, ask them to consider what the signers were risking individually and as a group. (*Individually they risked death. As a group, they risked war and, if they lost, possible imprisonment.*)

- Ask: **Who wrote the Declaration of Independence?** (*Thomas Jefferson*)

Independent Practice

Have students complete the Study Guide for this section.

Monitor Progress

- As students complete the Notetaking Study Guide, circulate to make sure students understand the structure and significance of the Declaration of Independence. Provide assistance as needed.

- Tell students to fill in the last column of the Reading Readiness Guide. Probe for what they learned that confirms or invalidates each statement.

  All in One **Teaching Resources, Unit 2,** Reading Readiness Guide, p. 43

Answers

Reading Skill *Respect* means "a view" or "attitude."

Checkpoint Possible answer: It says that everyone has certain inalienable rights.

Analyze Word Roots Determine the meaning of the word *respect*. The root *spec* means "see." Also read how the word is used in context.

Vocabulary Builder **violate** (VY uh layt) *v.* fail to keep or observe; infringe on

King George III

The Declaration of Independence

The Declaration of Independence is a brilliant piece of writing. Building on the ideas of the Enlightenment, it uses step-by-step logic to explain why the colonists wanted to break away from British rule. (See the Declaration of Independence following this section.)

The Declaration begins with a preamble, or introduction. It says that "a decent respect to the opinions of mankind" requires that Americans explain why they are breaking away from Britain.

Natural Rights Following the preamble, the Declaration has three main sections. The first section states some general ideas about society and government. "We hold these truths to be self-evident," or obvious to all. First among these truths is that "all men are created equal." Jefferson goes on to state that everyone is "endowed by their Creator with certain unalienable rights." This statement is based on John Locke's ideas about natural rights. (See Chapter 4.)

Like Locke, Jefferson goes on to state that governments are created in order to protect people's rights. And, like Locke, he concludes that, if a government violates those rights, the people have a right to abolish their government and create another.

List of Grievances Jefferson's next task was to prove that the British government had, in fact, violated the rights of the colonists. So the next section details a long list of specific grievances, or formal complaints, against King George III of England.

Many grievances accuse the king of ignoring rights that English citizens had enjoyed since the time of the Magna Carta. For example, the Magna Carta had established trial by jury as a basic right. The Declaration thus condemns the king "for depriving us, in many cases, of trial by jury." The Declaration also charges the king with "imposing taxes on us without our consent"—another violation of traditional English rights.

Time after time, says the Declaration, colonists have appealed to the king. But King George has ignored the petitions they sent. He must, therefore, be considered "unfit to be the ruler of a free people."

Dissolving the Bonds After stating the basic principle that the people have a right to abolish an unjust government and showing that the king has violated the rights of the colonists, the Declaration reaches a logical conclusion. It asserts that the colonies are "free and independent states . . . and that all political connection between them and the state of Great Britain is, and ought to be totally dissolved."

The document ends with a solemn pledge: "With a firm reliance on the protection of Divine Providence, we mutually pledge to each other our Lives, our Fortunes, and our sacred Honor." The serious tone shows that, to the Patriots, declaring independence was a serious and deeply felt step.

Checkpoint What does the Declaration of Independence say about people's rights?

Differentiated Instruction

L3 **Advanced Readers**   **L3** **Gifted and Talented**

Hold a Mock Trial Have students perform a mock trial in which they put King George III on trial for abusing the rights of American colonists. Assign each student a role in the trial (jury members, lawyers and witnesses for the defense, lawyers and witnesses for the plaintiff, etc.). After the trial, hold a class discussion about the outcome of the trial.

All in One **Teaching Resources, Unit 2,** King George III on Trial, p. 48

Impact of the Declaration

When Congress met to debate Lee's resolution, it still was not certain that they would declare independence. But on July 4, 1776, Congress approved the Declaration of Independence. Since then, Americans have celebrated July 4th as Independence Day.

The actual signing of the Declaration took place on August 2. According to tradition, as he stepped up to sign the document, Benjamin Franklin commented, "We must all hang together, or most assuredly we shall all hang separately." Indeed, for the delegates who signed, the personal risk was great. If captured by the British, they could be hanged.

The Declaration of Independence changed the nature of the Revolution. No longer were the Patriots fighting for fairer treatment from Britain. Now, they were fighting to create a new nation. There was no turning back.

Since then, the Declaration of Independence has become one of the world's enduring documents. The statement that "all men are created equal" still inspires Americans and people in other nations. In 1776, these words applied primarily to white, male property owners. Over the years, Americans worked to expand the notion of equality and natural rights.

☑**Checkpoint** How did the Declaration change the nature of the American Revolution?

⭐ **Looking Back and Ahead** Declaring independence from Britain was only a first step. For the Declaration to have real meaning, the Americans would have to win their liberties on the battlefield. In the next section, you will read about the progress of the war for independence.

Thomas Jefferson

Section 1 | Check Your Progress

Progress Monitoring 🌐nline
For: Self-test with instant help
Visit: PHSchool.com
Web Code: mva-2061

Comprehension and Critical Thinking

1. (a) Recall What was the main idea of Thomas Paine's *Common Sense*?
(b) Draw Conclusions Why do you think *Common Sense* had such an impact on colonists?

2. (a) Identify What are the major parts of the Declaration of Independence?
(b) Apply Information Why is the list of grievances against the king an important part of the Declaration?

🔄 Reading Skill

3. Analyze Word Roots Use the word root *spir*, meaning "breathe," to determine the meaning of the word *inspire* in this sentence: The statement that "all men are created equal" still *inspires* Americans and people in other nations.

Key Terms

Complete each sentence so that the second part further explains the first part and clearly shows your understanding of the key term.

4. The Declaration of Independence began with a preamble, or _____.
5. Congress took a step toward independence when Lee introduced Virginia's resolution, or _____.
6. The Declaration includes a list of grievances, or _____.

Writing

7. List two challenges you think Thomas Jefferson faced in writing the Declaration of Independence. Do you think he met these challenges? Explain.

The Declaration of Independence

By signing the Declaration of Independence, members of the Continental Congress sent a clear message to Britain that the American colonies were free and independent states. Starting with its preamble, the document spells out all the reasons the people of the United States have the right to break away from Britain. **Critical Thinking:** *Detect Points of View How would a Loyalist react to the Declaration of Independence?*

Explore More Video
To learn more about the roots of the Declaration of Independence, view the video.

Preamble
The document first lists the reasons for writing the Declaration.

Protection of Natural Rights
If a government fails to protect people's natural rights, the people have a right to reject it and create another.

Grievances Against the King
King George has violated colonists' rights and ignored their petitions.

Declaring Independence
Therefore, the colonies declare their independence from Great Britain.

★ In Congress, July 4, 1776

The Unanimous Declaration of the Thirteen United States of America

When in the Course of human events, it becomes necessary for one people to dissolve the political bands which have connected them with another, and to assume among the powers of the earth, the separate and equal station to which the Laws of Nature and of Nature's God entitle them, a decent respect to the opinions of mankind requires that they should declare the causes which impel them to the separation.

We hold these truths to be self-evident, that all men are created equal, that they are endowed by their Creator with certain unalienable Rights, that among these are Life, Liberty and the pursuit of Happiness. That to secure these rights, Governments are instituted among Men, deriving their just powers from the consent of the governed. That whenever any Form of Government becomes destructive of these ends, it is the Right of the People to alter or to abolish it, and to institute new Government, laying its foundation on such principles and organizing its powers in such form, as to them shall seem most likely to effect their Safety and Happiness. Prudence, indeed, will dictate that Governments long established should not be changed for light and transient causes; and

The Declaration of Independence has four parts: the Preamble, the Declaration of Natural Rights, the List of Grievances, and the Resolution of Independence. The Preamble states why the Declaration was written. The document will explain to the world the reasons why the colonists feel **impelled** to separate from Great Britain.

People set up governments to protect their basic rights. These rights are **unalienable**; they cannot be taken away. The purpose of government is to protect these natural rights. When a government does not protect the rights of the people, the people must change the government or create a new one. The colonists feel that the king's repeated **usurpations**, or unjust uses of power, are a form of **despotism**

accordingly all experience hath shown that mankind are more disposed to suffer, while evils are sufferable, than to right themselves by abolishing the forms to which they are accustomed. But when a long train of abuses and usurpations, pursuing invariably the same Object evinces a design to reduce them under absolute Despotism, it is their right, it is their duty, to throw off such Government, and to provide new Guards for their future security. Such has been the patient sufferance of these Colonies; and such is now the necessity which constrains them to alter their former Systems of Government. The history of the present King of Great Britain is a history of repeated injuries and usurpations, all having in direct object the establishment of an absolute Tyranny over these States. To prove this, let Facts be submitted to a candid world.

He has refused his Assent to Laws, the most wholesome and necessary for the public good.

He has forbidden his Governors to pass Laws of immediate and pressing importance, unless suspended in their operation till his Assent should be obtained; and when so suspended, he has utterly neglected to attend to them.

> The List of Grievances details the colonists' complaints against the British government, and King George III in particular. The colonists have no say in determining the laws that govern them and they feel King George's actions show little or no concern for the well being of the people.

He has refused to pass other Laws for the accommodation of large districts of people, unless those people would relinquish the right of Representation in the Legislature, a right inestimable to them and formidable to tyrants only.

> The colonists refuse to **relinquish**, or give up, the right to representation, which they feel is **inestimable**, or priceless.

He has called together legislative bodies at places unusual, uncomfortable, and distant from the depository of their public Records, for the sole purpose of fatiguing them into compliance with his measures.

He has dissolved Representative Houses repeatedly, for opposing with manly firmness his invasions on the rights of the people.

> The king has refused to allow new legislators to be elected. As a result, the colonies have not been able to protect themselves against foreign enemies and **convulsions**, or riots, within the colonies.

He has refused for a long time, after such dissolutions, to cause others to be elected; whereby the Legislative powers, incapable of Annihilation, have returned to the People at large for their exercise; the State remaining in the mean time exposed to all the dangers of invasion from without, and convulsions within.

> The king has tried to stop foreigners from coming to the colonies by refusing to pass naturalization laws. Laws for naturalization of foreigners are laws that set up the process for foreigners to become legal citizens.

He has endeavoured to prevent the population of these States; for that purpose obstructing the Laws for Naturalization of Foreigners; refusing to pass others to encourage their migrations hither, and raising the conditions of new Appropriations of Lands.

He has obstructed the Administration of Justice by refusing his Assent to Laws for establishing Judiciary powers.

> The king alone has decided a judge's **tenure**, or term. This grievance later would result in Article 3, Section 1, of the Constitution, which states that federal judges hold office for life.

He has made Judges dependent on his Will alone, for the tenure of their offices, and the amount and payment of their salaries.

He has erected a multitude of New Offices, and sent hither swarms of Officers to harass our people, and eat out their substance.

He has kept among us, in times of peace, Standing Armies without the Consent of our legislatures.

He has affected to render the Military independent of and superior to the Civil power.

He has combined with others to subject us to a jurisdiction foreign to our constitution, and unacknowledged by our laws; giving his Assent to their Acts of pretended Legislation:

For quartering large bodies of armed troops among us:

> Forced by the king, the colonists have been **quartering**, or lodging, troops in their homes. This grievance found its way into the Constitution in the Third Amendment.

For protecting them, by a mock Trial, from punishment for any Murders which they should commit on the Inhabitants of these States:

For cutting off our Trade with all parts of the world:

For imposing Taxes on us without our Consent:

For depriving us in many cases, of the benefit of Trial by Jury:

For transporting us beyond Seas to be tried for pretended offences:

For abolishing the free System of English Laws in a neighbouring Province, establishing therein an Arbitrary government, and enlarging its Boundaries so as to render it at once an example and fit instrument for introducing the same absolute rule into these Colonies:

> The king has taken away the rights of the people in a nearby province (Canada). The colonists feared he could do the same to the colonies if he so wished.

For taking away our Charters, abolishing our most valuable Laws, and altering fundamentally the Forms of our Governments:

For suspending our own Legislatures, and declaring themselves invested with power to legislate for us in all cases whatsoever.

He has abdicated Government here, by declaring us out of his Protection and waging War against us.

He has plundered our seas, ravaged our Coasts, burnt our towns, and destroyed the lives of our people.

He is at this time transporting large Armies of foreign Mercenaries to complete the works of death, desolation, and tyranny, already begun with circumstances of Cruelty and perfidy scarcely paralleled in the most barbarous ages, and totally unworthy the Head of a civilized nation.

> The king has hired foreign **mercenaries**, or soldiers, to bring death and destruction to the colonists. The head of a civilized country should never act with the cruelty and **perfidy**, or dishonesty, that the king has.

He has constrained our fellow Citizens taken Captive on the high Seas to bear Arms against their Country, to become the executioners of their friends and Brethren, or to fall themselves by their Hands.

He has excited domestic insurrections amongst us, and has endeavoured to bring on the inhabitants of our frontiers, the merciless Indian Savages whose known rule of warfare, is an undistinguished destruction of all ages, sexes and conditions.

> The colonists have tried repeatedly to petition the king to **redress,** or correct, these wrongs. Each time, they have been ignored by the king or punished by new laws. Because of the way he treats his subjects, the king is not fit to rule a free people.

In every stage of these Oppressions We have Petitioned for Redress in the most humble terms: Our repeated Petitions have been answered only by repeated injury. A Prince, whose character is thus marked by every act which may define a Tyrant, is unfit to be the ruler of a free People.

The colonists have appealed to the British people. They have asked their fellow British subjects to support them. However, like the king, the British people have ignored the colonists' requests.

The Resolution of Independence boldly asserts that the colonies are now "free and independent states." The colonists have proven the **rectitude**, or justness, of their cause. The Declaration concludes by stating that these new states have the power to wage war, establish alliances, and trade with other countries.

Nor have We been wanting in attentions to our British brethren. We have warned them from time to time of attempts by their legislature to extend an unwarrantable jurisdiction over us. We have reminded them of the circumstances of our emigration and settlement here. We have appealed to their native justice and magnanimity, and we have conjured them by the ties of our common kindred, to disavow these usurpations, which would inevitably interrupt our connections and correspondence. They too have been deaf to the voice of justice and of consanguinity. We must, therefore, acquiesce in the necessity, which denounces our Separation, and hold them, as we hold the rest of mankind, Enemies in War, in Peace Friends.

We, therefore, the Representatives of the United States of America, in General Congress, Assembled, appealing to the Supreme Judge of the world for the rectitude of our intentions, do, in the Name, and by Authority of the good People of these Colonies, solemnly publish and declare, That these United Colonies are, and of Right ought to be Free and Independent States; that they are Absolved from all Allegiance to the British Crown, and that all political connection between them and the State of Great Britain, is and ought to be totally dissolved; and that as Free and Independent States, they have full Power to levy War, conclude Peace, contract Alliances, establish Commerce, and to do all other Acts and Things which Independent States may of right do. And for the support of this Declaration, with a firm reliance on the protection of Divine Providence, we mutually pledge to each other our Lives, our Fortunes and our sacred Honor.

John Hancock, *President*
Charles Thomson, *Secretary*

Georgia
Button Gwinnett
Lyman Hall
George Walton

North Carolina
William Hooper
Joseph Hewes
John Penn

South Carolina
Edward Rutledge
Thomas Heyward, Jr.
Thomas Lynch, Jr.
Arthur Middleton

Maryland
Samuel Chase
William Paca
Thomas Stone
Charles Carroll

Virginia
George Wythe
Richard Henry Lee
Thomas Jefferson
Benjamin Harrison
Thomas Nelson, Jr.
Francis Lightfoot Lee
Carter Braxton

Pennsylvania
Robert Morris
Benjamin Rush
Benjamin Franklin
John Morton
George Clymer
James Smith
George Taylor
James Wilson
George Ross

Delaware
Caesar Rodney
George Read
Thomas McKean

New York
William Floyd
Philip Livingston
Francis Lewis
Lewis Morris

New Jersey
Richard Stockton
John Witherspoon
Francis Hopkinson
John Hart
Abraham Clark

New Hampshire
Josiah Bartlett
William Whipple
Matthew Thornton

Massachusetts
Samuel Adams
John Adams
Robert Treat Paine
Elbridge Gerry

Rhode Island
Stephen Hopkins
William Ellery

Connecticut
Samuel Huntington
William Williams
Oliver Wolcott
Roger Sherman

The Enemy Surrounded Them
❝O doleful! doleful! doleful!—Blood! Carnage! Fire! . . . Many battalions, of excellent men, went out into the woods on the right and left wing of the enemy;—Alas! numbers went never to return!—The enemy surrounded them. . . . Many, many we fear are lost.❞

—American soldier Philip Fithian, describing fighting in New York, 1776

◀ At Saratoga, American General Benedict Arnold won a key victory over the British.

A Critical Time

Objectives
- Discover the results of fighting in the Middle States.
- Understand why the Battle of Saratoga was a turning point in the American Revolution.
- Learn how foreign nations and volunteers helped the Americans.

🔁 Reading Skill

Apply the Meanings of Prefixes
Prefixes—word parts added to the beginning of words or word roots—can dramatically affect a word's meaning. Applying the meanings of common prefixes will help you define unfamiliar words. Piece together a likely meaning. Check how the word is used within the content of the surrounding text. If necessary, use a dictionary.

Key Terms and People

Nathan Hale
mercenary
alliance
Marquis de
  Lafayette

cavalry
Friedrich von
  Steuben

Why It Matters The thirteen colonies had proclaimed their independence. But this declaration would have lasting meaning only if Washington and his army of poorly trained troops could win victories over the powerful British army.

❷ Section Focus Question: How were the early years of the war a critical time?

Retreat From New York

In mid-1776, the heavy fighting shifted from New England to the Middle States. There, the Continental army suffered through the worst days of the war.

Attack and Retreat In June 1776, just as the Continental Congress was considering independence, a large British fleet arrived off New York. Sir William Howe, the British commander, gathered his forces on Staten Island, at the southern edge of New York harbor.

Washington expected Howe's attack. He already had led his forces south from Boston to Brooklyn on Long Island. However, his army was no match for the British. Howe had about 34,000 well-trained troops and 10,000 sailors, as well as ships to ferry them ashore. Washington had fewer than 20,000 poorly trained troops and no navy.

That summer saw a long series of battles and American retreats. In the Battle of Long Island, in August 1776, the British drove Washington's troops out of Brooklyn. The following month, Washington had to abandon New York City. The British pursued the Americans north to White Plains, then west and south across New Jersey.

Section 2 A Critical Time 179

Vocabulary Builder

Use the information below to teach students this section's high-use words.

High-Use Word	Definition and Sample Sentence
vital, p. 183	*adj.* necessary; of great importance Shipbuilding played a **vital** role in the New England economy.
transform, p. 183	*v.* to change from one thing or condition to another The battles of Lexington and Concord **transformed** the colonial struggle from a protest to a revolution.

Review and Preview

Students have read about the grievances the colonists had with British rule. Now they will learn how Americans won their independence.

Section Focus Question
How were the early years of the war a critical time?

Before you begin the lesson for the day, write the Section Focus Question on the board. (*Lesson focus: The Continental army faced hardships and defeat.*)

Prepare to Read

Build Background Knowledge   L2

Review with students the events that led up to the American Revolution. Then ask students to scan the headings and images to identify some of the major battles fought during the war. Ask them to make a prediction about the outcome of the Revolution. After they make a prediction about what they will learn, address any misconceptions. Remind students to confirm or revise their predictions after they read this section.

Set a Purpose   L2
- Read each statement in the Reading Readiness Guide aloud. Ask students to mark the statements True or False.

  All in One Teaching Resources, Unit 2, Reading Readiness Guide, p. 44

- Have students discuss the statements in pairs or groups of four, then mark the worksheets again. Use the Numbered Heads participation strategy (TE, p. T24) to call on students to share their group's perspectives. The students will return to these worksheets later.

Retreat from New York

p. 179

Instruction   L2

- **Vocabulary Builder** Before teaching this section, preteach the High-Use Words **vital** and **transform**, using the strategy on TE p. T21.

  Key Terms Have students continue filling in the See It–Remember It chart for the Key Terms in this chapter.

- Read Retreat from New York with students using the Structured Silent Reading strategy (TE, p. T22).

- Ask: **What was the result of fighting in New York?** (*The colonists were forced to retreat from New York into New Jersey.*)

- Discuss the reasons for repeated Continental army defeats. Have students contrast the British and American armies. (*The British had around 34,000 well-trained soldiers and a navy. The Americans had less than 20,000 soldiers who were poorly trained and had no navy.*)

Independent Practice

Have students begin to fill in the Study Guide for this section.

Interactive Reading and Notetaking Study Guide, Chapter 6, Section 2 (Adapted Version also available.)

Monitor Progress

As students fill in the Notetaking Study Guide, circulate to make sure students understand the impact of early defeat on the colonists. If students do not seem to have a good understanding, have them reread the section. Provide assistance as needed.

Answers

Checkpoint The colonists retreated and eventually abandoned New York City.

MAP MASTER Skills Activity (a) Lexington (b) They were able to sneak in reinforcements through the Chesapeake Bay and attack.

Nathan Hale During the fight for New York, Nathan Hale became an American legend. Hale was a Connecticut officer, and he volunteered for dangerous spy duty. His mission was to collect information about British battle plans on Long Island.

Caught behind British lines, Hale was tried and condemned to death. He was hanged the next morning. Later, it was reported that his last words had been, "I only regret that I have but one life to lose for my country."

Checkpoint What was the result of the Battle of Long Island?

Surprises for the British

Under relentless British pursuit, the Continental army kept retreating. In December, it crossed the Delaware River into Pennsylvania. The British now threatened Philadelphia. Patriot spirits were low. Many soldiers deserted. Others seemed ready to go home as soon as their terms of service ended.

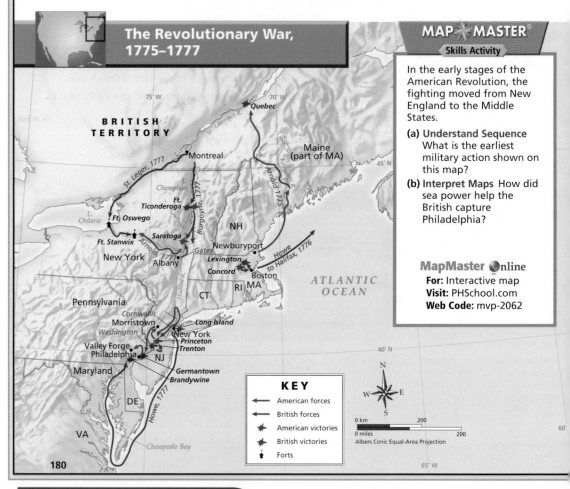

The Revolutionary War, 1775–1777

MAP MASTER®
Skills Activity

In the early stages of the American Revolution, the fighting moved from New England to the Middle States.

(a) **Understand Sequence** What is the earliest military action shown on this map?

(b) **Interpret Maps** How did sea power help the British capture Philadelphia?

MapMaster Online
For: Interactive map
Visit: PHSchool.com
Web Code: mvp-2062

KEY
- → American forces
- ← British forces
- ✶ American victories
- ✶ British victories
- ⚑ Forts

0 km 200
0 miles 200
Albers Conic Equal-Area Projection

180

Differentiated Instruction

L1 English Language Learners   **L1 Less Proficient Readers**   **L1 Special Needs**

Make an Outline Have students create an outline of the section as they read. Tell them to use the red heads as the main heads and number them with Roman numerals. Have them use the blue heads as subheads, noted with capital letters. Have students write supporting details under the subheads.

Thomas Paine had retreated with the army through New Jersey. To raise morale, he wrote another pamphlet, *The Crisis*. Paine urged Americans to support the army, despite hard times. He wrote:

"These are the times that try men's souls. The summer soldier and the sunshine patriot will, in this crisis, shrink from the service of his country; but he that stands it now deserves the love and thanks of man and woman."

—Thomas Paine, *The Crisis*

Washington had *The Crisis* read aloud to his troops. At the same time, he made plans for a bold attack.

Crossing the Delaware On Christmas night, 1776, Washington led 2,400 men across the river in small boats. Soldiers huddled in the boats as the spray from the river froze on their faces. So poorly supplied were the troops that some had no shoes. Once across the river, the soldiers marched in the swirling snow. To keep their feet from freezing, the soldiers bound them in rags.

On the far bank, the men trudged several miles with Washington urging them on. Early on December 26, they attacked Trenton from two sides, achieving complete surprise.

An American Victory The attack brought a ringing American victory. The soldiers in Trenton were Hessians (men from Hesse, a small German state). They were among thousands of German mercenaries who were fighting for the British. Mercenaries are soldiers who are paid to fight for a country other than their own. Washington's army captured almost a thousand Hessian mercenaries.

Pursued by the British, Washington used a clever trick to escape. His soldiers made camp near Trenton and lit campfires. After dark, most of the men packed up and quietly withdrew. The British did not discover the trick until daylight, when the main body of soldiers attacked and heavily damaged a British force near Princeton.

☑ **Checkpoint** How did Washington attack Trenton?

Saratoga: A Turning Point

British general John Burgoyne came up with a plan he hoped would quickly end the rebellion. His goal was to cut New England off from the rest of the states.

Washington at Trenton
During Washington's surprise attack on Trenton, the commander of the Hessian mercenaries was seriously wounded. In this picture, Washington orders his men to help the dying Hessian officer to his bed. **Critical Thinking: Apply Information** *Why was Washington able to win the battle at Trenton?*

Surprises for the British
p. 180

Instruction   L2

- Have students read Surprise for the British. Remind students to look for the sequence of events.

- Ask: **Why did Washington read The Crisis aloud to his troops?** (*Possible answer: He wanted to inspire his troops to continue the fight for independence.*)

- Ask students to explain George Washington's new strategy and its results. (*Washington led a sneak attack from two sides at Trenton. It was successful.*)

- Have students draw conclusions about why the victory was important for the Continental army. (*After so much defeat earlier in the year, victory lifted the spirits of the colonial troops.*)

Independent Practice

Have students complete the Study Guide for this section.

📖 **Interactive Reading and Notetaking Study Guide,** Chapter 6, Section 2 (Adapted Version also available.)

Monitor Progress

As students fill in the Notetaking Study Guide, circulate to make sure students understand how the war turned in the colonists' favor. If students do not seem to have a good understanding, have them reread the section. Provide assistance as needed.

History Background

A Quick Victory Early on December 26, the Americans surprised the Hessian troops guarding Trenton and took most of them prisoner. One American soldier summed up the battle in these words: "Hessian population of Trenton at 8 A.M.—1,408 men and 39 officers; Hessian population at 9 A.M.—0."

Answers

Apply Information He took the British by surprise.

☑ **Checkpoint** They crossed the Delaware, hiked through snow, and attacked the city on two sides by surprise.

Saratoga: A Turning Point

p. 181

Instruction ⬛L2

- Have students read Saratoga: A Turning Point. Remind students to keep track of the sequence of events.

- Ask: **What went wrong with General Burgoyne's plan?** (*Several things: The king sent the southern force to attack Philadelphia, American forces cut off the attack from the west, and Burgoyne was forced to lead the southern attack himself.*)

- Ask: **Why was the American victory at Saratoga such a turning point?** (*For several reasons: It ended the British threat to New England, it destroyed British hopes for an easy victory, and it showed European nations that the Americans had a chance of winning.*)

- Show the History Interactive transparency Revolutionary Soldier. Ask: **Why did it take colonial soldiers a long time to load their muskets?** (*Soldiers had to fill their muskets with gunpowder, then push down the ammunition with ramrods.*)

Color Transparencies, Revolutionary Soldier

Independent Practice

Have students complete the Study Guide for this section.

📖 **Interactive Reading and Notetaking Study Guide,** Chapter 6, Section 2 (Adapted Version also available.)

Monitor Progress

As students fill in the Notetaking Study Guide, circulate to make sure students understand the importance of the American victory at Saratoga. If students do not seem to have a good understanding, have them reread the section. Provide assistance as needed.

Answers

⊙ **Reading Skill** *Misguided* means "wrongly guided."

Clarify Problems Disadvantages include: a musket took a long time to reload and it required good marksmanship.

The British Plan Burgoyne's plan called for British forces to drive toward Albany, New York, from three directions. From Canada, an army of 8,000 would move south to capture the forts on Lake Champlain, Lake George, and the upper Hudson River. From the west, a smaller British force would drive through the Mohawk Valley toward Albany. And from the south, General Howe would lead a large army up the Hudson River from New York City.

Burgoyne's plan ran into trouble almost immediately. George III ordered Howe to move south from New York in a misguided attempt to attack Philadelphia. Not until November were Howe's forces ready to march north again. At the same time, American forces cut off the British troops coming through the Mohawk Valley.

An American Victory Burgoyne led the main British force from Canada in June. After recapturing Fort Ticonderoga, they slowly pushed south, dragging a large train of baggage carts through the woods. Supplies were running short.

Americans were rushing to block the British. By September, the American commander in New York, General Horatio Gates, had 6,000 men ready to fight. At the village of Saratoga, New York, the Americans surrounded the British. After suffering heavy casualties, Burgoyne surrendered on October 17, 1777.

⊙ **Apply the Meanings of Prefixes**
The prefix *mis-* means "badly" or "wrongly." What does the word *misguided* mean?

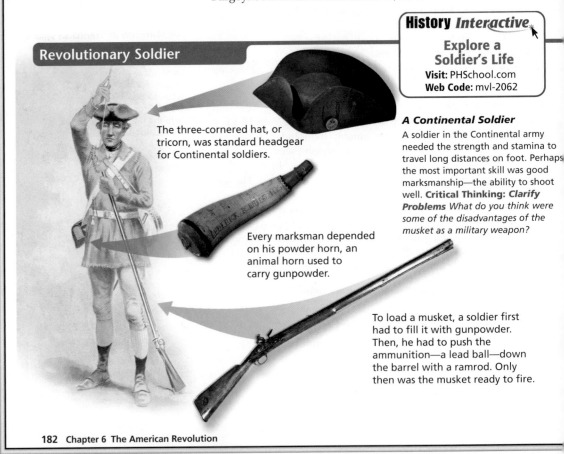

Revolutionary Soldier

The three-cornered hat, or tricorn, was standard headgear for Continental soldiers.

Every marksman depended on his powder horn, an animal horn used to carry gunpowder.

To load a musket, a soldier first had to fill it with gunpowder. Then, he had to push the ammunition—a lead ball—down the barrel with a ramrod. Only then was the musket ready to fire.

History Interactive

Explore a Soldier's Life
Visit: PHSchool.com
Web Code: mvl-2062

A Continental Soldier
A soldier in the Continental army needed the strength and stamina to travel long distances on foot. Perhaps the most important skill was good marksmanship—the ability to shoot well. **Critical Thinking:** *Clarify Problems What do you think were some of the disadvantages of the musket as a military weapon?*

182 Chapter 6 The American Revolution

Differentiated Instruction

⬛L3 **Advanced Readers**   ⬛L3 **Gifted and Talented**

Make a Live Sequence of Events To help students review the progress of the Revolution, have them work together in groups to list the sequence of events and their outcome from the beginning of the war to the Battle of Saratoga. Then have each group act out one event of the Revolution for the class.

Results of the Battle The Battle of Saratoga marked a major turning point in the war. The American victory ended the British threat to New England and destroyed British hopes of an easy victory. It also lifted Patriot spirits at a time when Washington's army was suffering defeats. Perhaps most important, the Battle of Saratoga helped convince Europeans that the Americans had a sound chance of winning.

☑ **Checkpoint** **List two results of the Battle of Saratoga.**

Help From Overseas

Soon after Saratoga, France agreed to openly support American independence. In February 1778, France officially formed an alliance with the United States. An alliance is a formal agreement between two powers to work together toward a common goal.

The French Alliance France was eager to weaken Britain. Even before Saratoga, the French had secretly supplied money and arms to the Americans. But the French did not want to take an open stand until it seemed the Americans might win. The Battle of Saratoga convinced the French government to help the struggling young nation. In February 1778, France became the first nation to sign a treaty with the United States.

France and its allies in the Netherlands and Spain also went to war with Britain. By carrying the fight to Europe and the Caribbean, the allies forced Britain to wage war on many fronts. This helped the American cause, because the British could spare fewer troops to fight in North America.

European Volunteers A number of Europeans volunteered to serve with the American forces. They were inspired by the American struggle for liberty.

A French noble, the Marquis de Lafayette (lah fay YET), became a high-ranking officer in Washington's army. He and Washington became close friends. When Lafayette was wounded in battle, Washington told a surgeon, "Treat him as though he were my son."

Volunteers from Poland also made <u>vital</u> contributions to the Patriot war effort. Thaddeus Kosciusko (kawsh CHUSH koh) was an engineer who took charge of building fortifications at West Point. Casimir Pulaski led and trained cavalry, or units of troops on horseback.

Baron von Steuben A German baron, Friedrich von Steuben (STOO buhn), helped train the Continental army. Steuben had served in the Prussian army, which was considered the best in Europe.

Before Steuben arrived in early 1778, American troops were often poorly trained and undisciplined. Steuben taught the soldiers how to march, how to improve their aim, and how to attack with bayonets. His methods helped to <u>transform</u> raw recruits into soldiers and shaped the Continental army into a more effective force.

☑ **Checkpoint** **How did France aid the Patriot cause?**

Medals commemorating the American-French alliance

Vocabulary Builder
vital (VĪ tuhl) **adj.** necessary; of great importance

Vocabulary Builder
transform (trans FORM) **v.** to change from one thing or condition to another

---

Instruction

- Have students read Help from Overseas and Valley Forge. Remind students to look for details that answer the Section Focus Question.

- Ask: **Why was European support so important to the colonists?** (*It helped them win the war by providing them with the necessary arms, ships, and reinforcements to defeat the British.*)

- Display the transparency Turning Points of the Revolution. Discuss the effect of each event.

Color Transparencies, Turning Points of the Revolution

- Ask: **How did women help the soldiers at Valley Forge?** (*Women collected food, medicine, warm clothes, and ammunition. Some tended the sick and wounded.*)

Independent Practice

Have students complete the Study Guide for this section.

📖 **Interactive Reading and Notetaking Study Guide,** Chapter 6, Section 2 (Adapted Version also available.)

Monitor Progress

- As students complete the Notetaking Study Guide, circulate to make sure students understand the significance of foreign aid to the Continental army. Provide assistance as needed.

- Tell students to fill in the last column of the Reading Readiness Guide. Probe for what they learned that confirms or denies each statement.

All in One Teaching Resources, Unit 2, Reading Readiness Guide, p. 44

History Background

The Continental Navy Established by the Second Continental Congress in 1775, the Continental navy supported the Continental army throughout the American Revolution. During the war, American ships attacked and captured many British merchant vessels. In 1784, the Continental navy was disbanded, and for the next 14 years American merchant ships fell prey to attacks by North Africa's Barbary pirates. In 1798, in an effort to cope with the attacks, Congress created the Department of the Navy.

Answers

☑ **Checkpoint** Results include: Saving New England, demoralizing Britain, and encouraging Europeans to support the colonists.

☑ **Checkpoint** At first, France secretly supplied money and arms to the colonists. After officially forming an alliance with the United States, France and its allies fought Britain in Europe and the Caribbean, which forced Britain to wage war on many fronts.

Assess and Reteach

Assess Progress L2

Have students complete Check Your Progress. Administer the Section Quiz.

All in One Teaching Resources, Unit 2, Section Quiz, p. 55

To further assess student understanding, use the Progress Monitoring Transparency.

Progress Monitoring Transparencies, Chapter 6, Section 2

Reteach L1

If students need more instruction, have them read this section in the Interactive Reading and Notetaking Study Guide and complete the accompanying question.

Interactive Reading and Notetaking Study Guide, Chapter 6, Section 2 (Adapted Version also available.)

Extend L3

Have students complete the History Interactive activity online.

> **Extend Online**
> **For:** Help with the History Interactive Extend activity.
> **Visit:** PHSchool.com
> **Web Code:** mvp-0142

Progress Monitoring Online

Students may check their comprehension of this section by completing the Progress Monitoring Online graphic organizer and self-quiz.

Answer

☑Checkpoint The soldiers were not sufficiently housed, clothed, or fed.

Section 2 Check Your Progress

1. (a) Washington's poorly equipped troops staged a surprise attack from two sides and won the battle, capturing a thousand soldiers. He then tricked the British by making them think that his soldiers were still in their camp, enabling his troops to escape.

Valley Forge

Washington's Continental army suffered through the cruel winter of 1777–1778 in a hastily built camp at Valley Forge in Pennsylvania. Meanwhile, some 22 miles away, British officers in Philadelphia danced the winter away in a merry round of parties and balls.

The 11,000 Continental soldiers were not sufficiently fed, clothed, or housed. Many lacked socks, shoes, and even trousers. Throughout the winter, they shivered in drafty huts. At any one time, about one soldier in four was sick with chills, fever, or worse.

Because food was so scarce, the soldiers mainly ate thin soup and dry bread patties. One private later recalled that he went without food for two days. He was so hungry he would have grabbed food away from anyone, even his best friend. Finally, he found half a pumpkin. He cooked it "upon a rock, the skin side up, by making a fire on it."

When Americans learned about conditions at Valley Forge, they sent help. Women collected food, medicine, warm clothes, and ammunition. Some women, including George Washington's wife, Martha, went to Valley Forge to tend the sick and wounded.

Despite its woes, the Continental army used that winter to gather its strength for the battles that lay ahead. Steuben's drills sharpened the soldiers' skills and discipline.

☑Checkpoint **Why was the winter at Valley Forge so difficult?**

Washington at Valley Forge

⭐ **Looking Back and Ahead** By the spring of 1778, the army at Valley Forge was ready to resume the fight. "The army grows stronger every day," wrote one New Jersey soldier. While soldiers drilled, Washington and his staff planned new campaigns against the British.

Section 2 | Check Your Progress

> **Progress Monitoring Online**
> **For:** Self-test with instant help
> **Visit:** PHSchool.com
> **Web Code:** mva-2062

Comprehension and Critical Thinking

1. (a) Recall What happened at Trenton in December 1776?
(b) Draw Inferences What did Washington's actions at the Battle of Trenton show about his character and leadership?

2. (a) List What were three important results of the American victory at Saratoga?
(b) Make Predictions What do you think would have happened if the Americans had lost the battle?

Reading Skill

3. Apply the Meanings of Prefixes The prefix *trans-* means "change." The word root *form* means "shape" or "structure." Use this information to explain the meaning of *transform* in this sentence: His methods helped to *transform* raw recruits into soldiers.

Key Terms

Read each sentence below. If the sentence is true, write YES. If the sentence is not true, write NO and explain why.

4. German mercenaries helped the British because they believed the king should rule the Americans.
5. After making an alliance with the Americans, France contributed money and arms to the Patriots.
6. The cavalry soldiers fired at the British soldiers from the ground before running away.

Writing

7. In order to gather enough soldiers to fight the battle in America, the British had to hire German mercenaries. List one strong argument for and one strong argument against this solution.

(b) He was a good leader, who was fearless and brave. He also was a clever military strategist.

2. (a) It ended British hopes of an early victory; it lifted Patriots' spirits; it convinced the Europeans that Americans had a chance of winning.
(b) America might have lost the war; Europeans would not have believed that the Americans could win.

3. Possible answer: to change; to improve the quality of

4. No. They helped because they were paid to do so.

5. Yes.

6. No. The cavalry fought on horseback.

7. Possible answers: For hiring mercenaries: the British needed more manpower. Against: mercenaries might not be loyal, might give up when attacked.

Valley Forge
by Maxwell Anderson

Introduction

Maxwell Anderson's play *Valley Forge* depicts the hardships faced by Washington's army in the winter of 1778. One problem the army faced was men trying to go home. Here, Washington hears the complaints of a soldier named Teague.

 Reading Skill

Analyze Dramatic Conflict An important element in any drama is conflict, when two characters want different things. As you read this scene, try to identify the source of the conflict between Washington and Teague.

Vocabulary *Builder*

As you read this literature selection, look for the following underlined words:

commissary (KAH muh sehr ee) *n.* food supplies

munitions (myoo NIH shuhns) *n.* weapons and ammunition

TEAGUE: I'm going hungry here and my woman's going hungry at home. You let me go home for the winter, and you won't have to feed me, and that relieves the <u>commissary</u>. I rustle some wild meat for the younguns and the old woman, and they don't starve and I don't starve. More'n that, everybody knows there's two or three thousand men gone home already for that same reason, and if they was here now they'd be chewing the bark off the second-growth birch like so many cottontails. I don't hold it against you and I don't hold it against anybody because I don't know who in thunder to hold it against, but there's nothing to eat here. . . .

WASHINGTON: Well, Master Teague, if they catch you they'll give you seventy-five lashes, and that's a good deal to take and live. On the other hand, you're quite right from your own angle, and if I were you I'd feel as you do. If you go home, and we all go home this winter, you won't need to bother about coming back in the spring. There'll be not fighting to come back to. General Howe will march out of Philadelphia and take over these states of ours. If he knew now how many have deserted, how many are sick, how many unfit for duty on account of the lack of food and clothes and <u>munitions</u>, he'd come back in force and wring our necks one by one, and the neck of our sickly little revolution along with us.

> From *America On Stage: Ten Great Plays of American History,*
> ed. Stanley Richards. Doubleday & Co., 1976.

Analyze LITERATURE

Do you think that Washington should permit Teague to go home without punishment? Write a paragraph explaining the reasons for your opinion.

 Analyze Dramatic Conflict

What does Teague want? What does Washington want? How are their wishes in conflict?

If you liked this excerpt and want to learn more about George Washington, you might want to read *George Washington and the Founding of a Nation* by Albert Marrin. Dutton Books, 2001.

Literature **185**

Valley Forge
Build Background Knowledge L2

Reading a dramatic interpretation of historical events can help students understand the feelings evoked during a certain time period. Review with students what they know about the winter spent by George Washington and his men at Valley Forge. Ask: **How did the winter at Valley Forge improve the outlook for the revolutionaries and their supporters?** (*Possible answers: Despite the rough conditions, soldiers used the time to train. Soldiers became more committed after going through a rough winter together. Supporters rallied around the troops, helping them get through the winter and improving morale.*) Discuss with students how they would have felt if they had been in that situation. Use the Idea Wave participation strategy to elicit responses (TE, p. T24).

Vocabulary *Builder*

Pronounce each word in the Vocabulary *Builder* list and have students repeat the word. Ask a student to read the definitions. Then ask students to write two sentences that correctly use each vocabulary word.

Instruction L2

- Using the Choral Reading participation strategy (TE, p. T22), read Teague's part from "Valley Forge." Ask students to describe his point of view of the situation. (*Teague felt that the army would be better off if soldiers were allowed to go home and spend time with their families and eat.*)

- Have students read Washington's response. Ask: **Do you think Washington's response inspired Teague to stay? Why or why not?** (*Possible answers: Yes, because Teague realized that the needs of the nation were more important than his personal needs for now. No, because Teague felt that his leader did not care about the sacrifices he and the other soldiers were making for the cause.*)

Monitor Progress

Have students complete the Analyze Literature activity. Circulate to be sure students understand how Washington inspired the troops to stay in the army. Provide assistance as needed.

Answers

 Reading Skill Teague wants to go home. Washington wants the troops to stay in the army. Teague is thinking only of himself and the short term. Washington is considering the needs of the Continental army and the long-term strategy for the Revolution.

Analyze LITERATURE Paragraphs should clearly give writer's point of view.

Writing Rubric Share this writing rubric with students.

Score 1 Statements are incomplete.
Score 2 Statements are inaccurate or vague.
Score 3 Paragraph is logical and supported with reasons.
Score 4 Paragraph is comprehensive and contains well-reasoned points.

Review and Preview

Students have learned about the early battles of the Revolution. Now they will learn how the war expanded to affect the lives of African Americans, women, and those living in the western frontier.

How did the effects of the war widen?

Before you begin the lesson for the day, write the Section Focus Question on the board. (*Lesson focus: More people became involved and battles were fought in the West and at sea.*)

Prepare to Read

Build Background Knowledge   **L2**

Remind students that the war affected all Americans. Ask them to consider how African Americans and women may have contributed during the war. Use the Idea Wave strategy (TE, p. T24) to elicit responses. (*Possible responses: They provided support and supplies to soldiers. They fought in the war themselves.*)

Set a Purpose   **L2**

- Form students into pairs or groups of four. Distribute the Reading Readiness Guide. Ask students to fill in the first two columns of the chart.

  All in One Teaching Resources, Unit 2, Reading Readiness Guide, p. 45

- Use the Numbered Heads participation strategy (TE, p. T24) to call on students to share one piece of information they already know and one piece they want to know. The students will return to these worksheets later.

Most Daring Conduct

❝Our situation was now truly critical—no possibility of retreating in case of defeat—and in full view of a town that had . . . six hundred men in it, troops, inhabitants and Indians. . . . We knew that nothing but the most daring conduct would insure success.❞

—George Rogers Clark, describing the battle against British and Indians at Vincennes, 1779

◀ Clark led his army through western wilderness.

The War Widens

Objectives
- Discover the role that African Americans played in the American Revolution.
- Find out how the war affected women and other civilians.
- Learn about the progress of the fighting on the western frontier and at sea.

🔄 Reading Skill

Analyze Word Roots Word roots can do more than help you define unfamiliar words. They can help you expand your vocabulary. As you read Section 3, use word roots to determine meanings. Then, list other words you know that come from the same word roots. Think about how they share meanings with the text words—and how the meanings differ. Notice the shades of meaning that can derive from a single word root.

Key Terms and People

enlist	Bernardo de
civilian	Gálvez
continental	John Paul Jones
George Rogers	privateer
Clark	

Why It Matters Many early battles of the American Revolution were fought in the Northeast. But the struggle for independence was waged on many fronts and affected Americans in all parts of the country.

❓ Section Focus Question: How did the effects of the war widen?

African Americans in the War

African Americans fought on both sides of the American Revolution. For them, the war meant both danger and opportunity.

Free and Slave From the beginning, free African Americans took part in the war. At least nine served as minutemen at Lexington and Concord. Peter Salem fought at Bunker Hill and Saratoga.

Enslaved people served as well. After fleeing his master in Rhode Island, Jehu Grant served in the American army for nine months. He later recalled:

❝When I saw liberty poles and the people all engaged for the support of freedom, I could not but like and be pleased with such thing. . . . The songs of liberty . . . thrilled through my heart.❞
—Jehu Grant, letter, December 1, 1836

The British offered freedom to enslaved people who deserted and joined the British. Many thousands did so. They served mainly in support roles as cooks, blacksmiths, and teamsters. However, some people who had formerly been enslaved fought for the British.

Differentiated Instruction

L3 Advanced Readers   **L3 Gifted and Talented**

Write an Essay Have students write a brief essay about the contributions of African Americans during the Revolution. Ask students to include their thoughts about

how these contributions affected the future role of African Americans in American society.

On the American side, Washington at first refused to accept African American soldiers. But the British offer of freedom to enslaved people made Washington change his policy. By the end of the war, some 7,000 African Americans had served on the American side, including 2,000 in the navy. African Americans also served in northern militias and state armies. Most southern states, however, refused to accept African American soldiers. Slave owners feared armed slave revolts.

Freedom Beckons During the Revolution, a number of northern states took steps to end slavery. For example, a Pennsylvania law of 1780 provided for a gradual end to slavery. It allowed slaveholders to keep their existing slaves but barred them from getting more.

☑**Checkpoint** **Why did some enslaved African Americans choose to fight for the British?**

The War at Home

Many men enlisted, or signed up for duty, in the military. After a set term, usually one year, they were free to leave. Thus, Washington had to struggle constantly to keep the ranks of his army filled.

Civilians, or people not in the military, also faced hardships. They were often subject to food shortages and military attack.

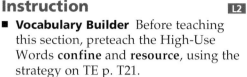

Analyze Word Roots
The word root *port* means "to carry." The prefix *sub-* means "under," and *sub-* becomes *sup-* when used before the letter *p*. Use these word parts to explain the meaning of *support*. List three other words that build on the root *port*.

Links Across Time

African American Soldiers

1777 Reversing his earlier policy, Washington permits free African Americans to enlist in the Continental army.

1863 During the last half of the Civil War, African Americans were allowed to join the Union army. Black and white soldiers served in separate units.

1948 President Harry Truman ended racial separation in the military. Two years later, black and white troops served side by side in the Korean War.

Link to Today ⬤nline

The Military Today In today's all-volunteer military, African Americans make up 21 percent of all military personnel.

For: U.S. military in the news
Visit: PHSchool.com
Web Code: mvc-2063

Section 3 The War Widens **187**

Vocabulary Builder

Use the information below to teach students this section's high-use words.

High-Use Word	Definition and Sample Sentence
confine, p. 188	*v.* to keep within certain limits Captives on slave ships were **confined** in small, crowded places.
resource, p. 188	*n.* supply of something to meet a particular need For New England shipbuilders, wood was a valuable **resource**.

The War at Home

p. 187

Instruction L2

- Have students read The War at Home. Remind students to look for details to answer the reading Checkpoint question.

- Ask: **What hardships did civilians face during the Revolution?** (*Civilians were often subject to food shortages and military attack.*)

- Have students compare and contrast the role of colonial women before and during the Revolution. (*Before the Revolution, women's roles were largely confined. During the Revolution, women had new opportunities. For example, some women took over their husbands' businesses.*)

- Display the transparency The War Affects All Americans. Discuss the impact of the Revolution on women and African Americans.

Color Transparencies, The War Affects All Americans

Independent Practice

Have students complete the Study Guide for this section.

Interactive Reading and Notetaking Study Guide, Chapter 6, Section 3 (Adapted Version also available.)

Monitor Progress

As students fill in the Notetaking Study Guide, circulate to make sure students understand how life changed in the United States during the Revolution. If students do not seem to have a good understanding, have them reread the section. Provide assistance as needed.

Answers

Evaluate Information Possible answers: Molly Pitcher symbolized the courage of Americans. She represents strength and patriotism.

☑Checkpoint Women tended farms, took over their husband's businesses, and took care of the wounded.

A Woman in Battle
When her husband was wounded at the Battle of Monmouth, Mary Ludwig Hays dropped her water bucket and took up his cannon. Her heroic actions made her a legendary American hero, known as Molly Pitcher. **Critical Thinking: Evaluate Information** *Why do you think Molly Pitcher has become a popular subject for American artists? What image of women does she represent?*

Vocabulary Builder
confine (kuhn FĪN) *v.* to keep within certain limits

Vocabulary Builder
resource (REE sors) *n.* supply of something to meet a particular need

Women As men went to war, women took over many of their duties. On farms, women planted crops and cared for livestock. In towns, women often ran their husbands' businesses.

Some women accompanied their husbands to military camps. In battles, they cared for the wounded. One woman, Deborah Sampson, joined the army, disguised as a man. Wounded in battle, Sampson tended her own wounds in order to keep her secret.

The added responsibilities of wartime gave many women a new confidence. At a time when women's roles were largely confined, the war opened up new opportunities for many women.

Financial Burdens Paying for the war was a difficult task. Congress had limited resources. With no power to tax, Congress had to plead with the states for money. However, the states had little money themselves.

To pay and supply troops, Congress printed continentals, or paper money. But the more money Congress printed, the less the money was worth. By the end of the war, paper money had lost almost all its value.

☑Checkpoint What roles did women play in the Revolution?

Fighting in the West

Throughout most of the American Revolution, attention was mainly focused on the 13 states along the Atlantic coast. However, skirmishes and battles occurred on the western frontier as well.

Native Americans Take Sides Americans tried to keep the Native Americans neutral. They offered payments to groups willing to remain at peace. Still, most Native American groups sided with Britain. They feared that an American victory would mean more settlers moving west or south onto Native American lands.

Differentiated Instruction

L1 English Language Learners **L1 Less Proficient Readers** **L1 Special Needs**

Identifying Contributions Students may have trouble keeping track of the contributions made by African Americans and women during the Revolution. Have students list the contributions of each group.

The turmoil of war hurt many Indian groups. Sometimes tribes split into warring factions when they could not agree which side to join. Thousands of Indians were driven west by raids. Sometimes whole villages picked up and moved to avoid the fighting. Other Native Americans responded by attacking white settlements.

A smallpox epidemic made matters even worse. The disease first spread among American soldiers in Quebec in 1775, and then along the east coast of the colonies. By 1779, it had reached New Orleans. Soon after, it spread to Native American groups all across North America. Smallpox deaths far outnumbered casualties during the American Revolution. By 1782, more than 130,000 whites and Indians had died from smallpox. In contrast, about 8,000 soldiers had died in battle during the same period.

Defending the Frontier

the frontier, Virginia sent George Rogers Clark

Mountains in 1778. Clark's forces easily captured two Mississippi River outposts, Kaskaskia and Cahokia.

Early in 1779, Clark and his men trudged across 200 miles, at times splashing through icy floodwaters up to their chests. Their midwinter attack on the fort at Vincennes caught the British by surprise. The British and their Native American allies surrendered.

Clark's victories allowed settlers to remain on the frontier. This strengthened the American claim on the Ohio Valley area.

Help From the Spanish

Spain governed Louisiana, the land west of the Mississippi stretching as far north as Canada. The Spanish were eager to get back Florida, which they had lost to Britain at the end of the French and Indian War.

Even before Spain declared war against Britain in 1779, Louisiana governor Bernardo de Gálvez began helping the Americans. He secretly provided money and munitions to George Rogers Clark and other Americans. He also gave American ships safe refuge in New Orleans harbor. From 1779 to 1781, Gálvez played a key role in Spanish attacks that captured British forts on the Mississippi River and the Gulf of Mexico. Financial help also came from the Spanish colony of Cuba.

✓ **Checkpoint** What was the result of the fighting in the West?

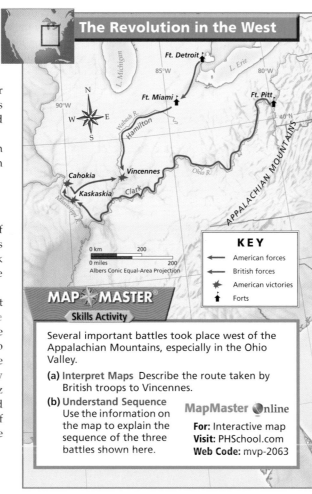

The Revolution in the West

KEY
← American forces
← British forces
⚔ American victories
↑ Forts

MAP✦MASTER®
Skills Activity

Several important battles took place west of the Appalachian Mountains, especially in the Ohio Valley.

(a) Interpret Maps Describe the route taken by British troops to Vincennes.

(b) Understand Sequence Use the information on the map to explain the sequence of the three battles shown here.

MapMaster ○nline
For: Interactive map
Visit: PHSchool.com
Web Code: mvp-2063

History Background

Women in the Revolution Many American women performed courageous deeds during the American Revolution. One daring Patriot was Sybil Ludington. Ludington was just 16 years old when on a chilly April night in 1777 she mounted her horse, Star, to gallop through the countryside and call the militia to report. The British were attacking, and there was no one to call the men to arms but Sybil.

Fighting in the West
The War at Sea
pp. 188–190

Instruction

- Have students read Fighting in the West and The War at Sea. Remind students to look for the sequence of events.

- Ask: **Why did most Native American groups side with Britain?** (*The Native Americans feared that an American victory would mean more settlers moving onto Native American lands.*)

- Have students discuss the contributions of George Rogers Clark to the American cause. (*Clark's military victories allowed settlers to remain on the frontier and strengthened American claims in the Ohio Valley.*)

- Ask: **Why did the Americans make hit-and-run attacks against British ships?** (*The American navy was smaller than the British navy and needed the advantage of surprise.*)

Independent Practice

Have students complete the Study Guide for this section.

📖 **Interactive Reading and Notetaking Study Guide,** Chapter 6, Section 3 (Adapted Version also available.)

Monitor Progress

- As students fill in the Notetaking Study Guide, circulate to make sure students understand the outcome of the fighting that took place on the western frontier. Provide assistance as needed.

- Tell students to fill in the last column of the Reading Readiness Guide. Ask them to evaluate if what they learned was what they had expected to learn.

All in One Teaching Resources, Unit 2, Reading Readiness Guide, p. 45

Answers

MAP✦MASTER Skills Activity **(a)** British troops came southwest from Fort Detroit to Fort Miami, then along the Wabash River to Vincennes. **(b)** Clark's men overtook Kaskaskia, then Cahokia, and then moved on to Vincennes for a final victory.

✓**Checkpoint** Possible answer: American settlers remained on the western frontier.

Assess and Reteach

Assess Progress `L2`

Have students complete Check Your Progress. Administer the Section Quiz.

 Teaching Resources, Section Quiz, p. 56

To further assess student understanding, use the Progress Monitoring Transparency.

Progress Monitoring Transparencies, Chapter 6, Section 3

Reteach `L1`

If students need more instruction, have them read this section in the Interactive Reading and Notetaking Study Guide and complete the accompanying question.

 Interactive Reading and Notetaking Study Guide, Chapter 6, Section 3 (Adapted Version also available.)

Extend `L3`

Have students create a short news report covering the widening of the Revolution into the West. Have each student present a portion of their news report for the class.

Progress Monitoring Online

Students may check their comprehension of this section by completing the Progress Monitoring Online graphic organizer and self-quiz.

Answer

✓**Checkpoint** They seized goods from British merchant ships, which forced Britain to spend resources protecting their ships.

Section 3 Check Your Progress

1. (a) Washington eventually allowed African Americans to fight for the American side because he felt threatened by Britain's offer to free slaves who fought with the British.
(b) They hoped to win rights.

2. (a) The Americans had a small navy while the British had a large fleet of

---

The War at Sea

Congress had voted to create a Continental navy as early as 1775. But American shipyards were able to build only a few warships. With only a small navy to go against the powerful British fleet, the Americans became skilled at making hit-and-run attacks on British shipping. Still, Britain dominated the seas. The British fleet blocked most ships from entering or leaving American ports.

The most famous naval battle took place off the coast of England in 1779. The American ship *Bonhomme Richard* (bon ohm ree CHARD), under the command of **John Paul Jones,** fought side by side with the larger British warship *Serapis*. Cannon and musket fire ripped the sails of both ships to shreds and blasted holes in their wooden sides. Though his ship was in tatters, Jones refused to give up. "I have not yet begun to fight," he vowed. Finally, with dozens of sailors dead on each side, the captain of the *Serapis* surrendered.

The navy had help from some 800 privateers that harassed British shipping. **Privateers** were armed civilian ships that had their government's permission to attack enemy ships and keep their goods. Operating like pirate ships, privateers seized cargoes of rum from the West Indies, wool from England, and furs from Canada. Such attacks forced Britain to spend valuable resources protecting merchant ships.

John Paul Jones

✓**Checkpoint** How did privateers help the American war effort?

⭐ **Looking Back and Ahead** Despite important battles at sea and in the west, the main war effort was concentrated in the colonies. In the next section, you will read about the final phase of the war.

Section 3 | Check Your Progress

Progress Monitoring Online
For: Self-test with instant help
Visit: PHSchool.com
Web Code: mva-2063

Comprehension and Critical Thinking

1. (a) Recall How did Washington's policy toward African American soldiers change? What was the reason for this change?
(b) Identify Benefits How did African Americans expect to benefit from serving in the military?

2. (a) Describe What challenges did the American navy face?
(b) Draw Conclusions Why do you think John Paul Jones is considered a great American hero?

Reading Skill

3. Analyze Word Roots The root *fid* means "faith." The prefix *con-* means "with." Use these word parts to determine the meaning of *confidence* in this sentence: The added responsibilities of wartime gave many women a new *confidence*.

Key Terms

4. Draw a table with four rows and three columns. In the first column, list the key terms from this section: enlist, civilian, continental, privateer. In the next column, write the definition of each word. In the last column, make a small illustration that shows the meaning of the word.

Writing

5. Identify the problems facing the Continental Congress during the war. Then, brainstorm one or two possible solutions.

---

ships. As a result, Americans used hit-and-run tactics against the British and relied on privateers, who operated like pirates and seized cargoes from enemy ships.
(b) Possible answer: Jones refused to give up during the battle between the *Bonhomme Richard* and the *Serapis*.

3. Possible answer: Women behaved with faith in themselves and their fellow countrymen when called upon to do so.

4. Enlist: to sign up for military duty. Civilian: a person not in the military. Continental: paper money. Privateer: an armed civilian ship that had the government's permission to attack enemy ships and keep the cargo.

5. Possible problems: lack of money, not enough troops or supplies available, morale when colonial troops lost battles. Students should offer possible solutions to the problems listed.

Lord Cornwallis's Catastrophe

"What we are to do after Lord Cornwallis's catastrophe, God Knows, or how anybody can think there is the least glimmering of hope for this nation surpasses my comprehension."

—Anthony Storer, letter to a British lord after the American victory at Yorktown, 1781

◄ General Washington looks on as the British surrender at Yorktown.

Winning Independence

Objectives

- Find out how the Americans won the final battle of the Revolution.
- Learn the terms of the peace treaty with England.
- Explore the reasons that the Americans were victorious.
- Examine the effects of the American Revolution.

Reading Skill

Apply the Meanings of the Prefix *re-*
Prefixes sometimes have more than one meaning. For example, the prefix *re-* can mean "again" or "anew," but it can also mean "back" or "backward." You must think about the surrounding words and context in which the word is used before deciding which meaning of the prefix to apply.

Key Terms and People

Charles Cornwallis   Nathanael Greene
guerrilla   traitor
Francis Marion

Why It Matters After the American victory at Saratoga, the British threat to New England had ended. The British next tried to win the war by invading and capturing the South. The attempt failed and the Americans won their independence.

❓ **Section Focus Question: How did the Americans win the war and make peace?**

Fighting Moves South

The British turned to the South late in 1778. Their aim was to capture some key cities, win over the local population, and then march north, acquiring one state after another.

British Advance At first, the plan seemed to work. British soldiers moved north from Florida to Georgia. In December 1778, the British took the city of Savannah. Within a month, they controlled most of Georgia.

Moving on to South Carolina, the British captured the main port, Charles Town, and then the rest of the state. The British commander, Lord Charles Cornwallis, then carried the war into North Carolina. It looked as if the British might be unstoppable.

To slow the British advance, Americans used guerrilla tactics. Guerrillas are fighters who work in small bands to make hit-and-run attacks. In South Carolina, Francis Marion led his men silently through the swamps. They attacked without warning, then escaped. Marion's guerrilla attacks were so efficient that he won the nickname the Swamp Fox. Other bands of guerrillas were also active.

Elsewhere in the South, Loyalist bands roamed the backcountry. They plundered and burned Patriot farms, killing men, women, and children. "If a stop cannot be put to these massacres," wrote one Continental general, "the country will be depopulated in a few months more."

Section 4 Winning Independence **191**

Vocabulary Builder

Use the information below to teach students this section's high-use words.

High-Use Word	Definition and Sample Sentence
fateful, p. 192	*adj.* having important consequences; decisive After the **fateful** Battle of Quebec, France agreed to give up most of its North American territory.
option, p. 192	*n.* choice; possible course of action A poor person who wanted to go to the colonies had the **option** of becoming an indentured servant.

Section 4
Step-by-Step Instruction

Review and Preview

Students have read about the beginning and the progression of the Revolution. Students will now learn about the Revolution's conclusion.

Section Focus Question

How did the Americans win the war and make peace?
Before you begin the lesson for the day, write the Section Focus Question on the board. (*Lesson focus: Brave militias, clever strategy, and European support combined for a colonial victory.*)

Prepare to Read

Build Background Knowledge   L2

Ask students to evaluate the American and the British armies. Ask: **Which army seems to have the better chance of winning the Revolution?** Have them explain their reasoning. Use the Idea Wave participation strategy to elicit responses (TE, p. T24). (*Possible answers: The Americans, because they are receiving help from Europeans. The British, because they have a larger army and navy than the Americans.*)

Set a Purpose

- Read each statement in the Reading Readiness Guide aloud. Ask students to mark the statements as True or False.

  All in One Teaching Resources, Unit 2, Reading Readiness Guide, p. 46

- Have students discuss the statements in pairs or groups of four, then mark the worksheets again. Use the Numbered Heads participation strategy (TE, p. T24) to call on students to share their group's perspectives. The students will return to these worksheets later.

Teach

Fighting Moves South
p. 191

Instruction
L2

- **Vocabulary Builder** Before teaching this section, preteach the High-Use Words **fateful** and **option**, using the strategy on TE p. T21.

  Key Terms Have students complete the See It–Remember It chart for the Key Terms in this chapter.

- Read Fighting Moves South with students using the Choral Reading strategy (TE, p. T22).

- Have students describe the Patriot strategy at the Battle of Cowpens. (*General Morgan put a small militia force in front, telling the men to fire three shots and then retreat. The British rushed forward, only to be met by charging calvary and a line of skilled riflemen.*)

- Ask: **Why did General Cornwallis move his main army to the Yorktown peninsula?** (*He thought that the British fleet could reinforce his position.*)

- Have students complete The Battle of Yorktown worksheet.

  All in One Teaching Resources, Unit 2, The Battle of Yorktown, p. 50

Independent Practice
Have students begin to fill in the Study Guide for this section.

Monitor Progress

As students fill in the Notetaking Study Guide, circulate to make sure students understand how the Americans won the final battles of the Revolution. Provide assistance as needed.

Answers

Biography Quest Benedict Arnold lived in exile from the United States in Canada and England.

Checkpoint American and French troops blocked his escape by land, and the French fleet blocked his escape by sea.

Biography Quest

Benedict Arnold
1741–1801

Why did Benedict Arnold betray the American army? Perhaps he was angry when Congress promoted several less experienced officers ahead of him. Arnold's wife also may have played a role. During the Revolution, Arnold married a woman whose family were strong Loyalists.

Whatever the reason, if you hear someone called a "Benedict Arnold," you know that person is seen as a traitor.

Biography Quest Online

What happened to Arnold after the American Revolution?

For: The answer to the question about Arnold
Visit: PHSchool.com
Web Code: mvd-2064

Vocabulary Builder
fateful (FAYT fuhl) *adj.* having important consequences; decisive

Vocabulary Builder
option (AHP shuhn) *n.* choice; possible course of action

Brighter Days Patriot fortunes began to improve in October 1780. Some 900 frontier fighters defeated a larger force of British troops and Loyalists atop Kings Mountain in South Carolina.

In December 1780, General Nathanael Greene took over command of the Continental army in the South. Greene split his small army in two. He led 1,200 men into eastern South Carolina, leaving General Daniel Morgan with 800 men in the west.

In January 1781, Morgan won a clear victory at the Battle of Cowpens. He put a small militia force in front, telling the men to fire three shots and then retreat. The British rushed forward, only to be met by charging cavalry and a line of skilled riflemen.

American Traitor Still, the British seemed to have the upper hand in the South. In addition to Cornwallis's forces, the British had troops under the command of an American traitor, Benedict Arnold. A **traitor** is a person who betrays his or her country or cause and helps the other side.

Early in the war, Arnold had fought bravely for the Patriots. But Arnold felt Congress undervalued him. He plotted to turn West Point, a key fort on the Hudson River in New York, over to the British. When the plot was discovered in September 1780, Arnold escaped. He and his Loyalist soldiers then staged a series of destructive raids in Virginia.

Final Battle Weakened by battles like Cowpens, Cornwallis headed to Virginia. That gave Greene an excellent opportunity. Over a five-month period, Patriot forces swept through the Deep South. By late summer, only Charles Town and Savannah remained in British hands.

Cornwallis then made a fateful mistake. He moved his main army to the Yorktown peninsula, a tongue of Virginia land poking into Chesapeake Bay. There, he thought, the British fleet could reinforce his position. But at the end of August, the French fleet arrived off Yorktown and chased off British ships.

At the same time, Washington rushed toward Virginia with American and French troops. Cornwallis found himself in a trap. American and French soldiers barred escape by land, while the French fleet blocked escape by sea. After three weeks, Cornwallis had no option but to surrender.

On October 19, 1781, the Americans and French lined up in two facing columns. The British marched glumly between the two columns and tossed their weapons into a large pile on the ground. The victory at Yorktown was the last major battle of the war.

✓Checkpoint How were Cornwallis and his troops trapped at Yorktown?

Differentiated Instruction

L1 English Language Learners   **L1 Less Proficient Readers**   **L1 Special Needs**

Create a Timeline Have students collaborate on a visual timeline of the American Revolution from the Declaration of Independence to the signing of the Treaty of Paris. Set aside a bulletin board in the classroom for the display. The timeline should show dates and locations of significant events throughout the war. Students can illustrate important people and events with drawings.

Making Peace With Britain

The news from Yorktown caused shockwaves in Britain. Although the king wanted to keep fighting, Parliament voted in favor of peace.

Peace talks began in Paris in 1782. The American delegation included Benjamin Franklin and John Adams. Britain was eager for peace, so the Americans got most of what they wanted.

Treaty of Paris The talks led to an agreement, the Treaty of Paris. Britain recognized the independence of the United States. The boundaries of the new nation were set at the Atlantic on the east, Canada on the north, the Mississippi River on the west, and Florida on the south. Florida itself was returned to Spain.

For its part, the United States agreed to "earnestly recommend" that the states restore rights and property taken from Loyalists during the war. However, most states ignored this pledge.

On April 15, 1783, Congress approved the treaty. The war was officially over. It had been almost exactly eight years since the "shot heard round the world" started the fighting at Lexington.

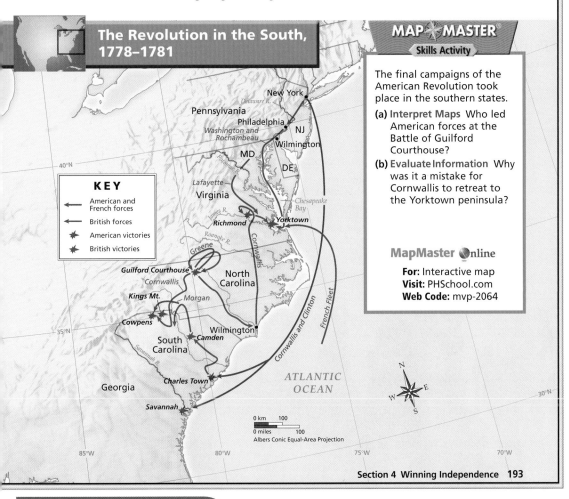

The Revolution in the South, 1778–1781

MAP★MASTER®
Skills Activity

The final campaigns of the American Revolution took place in the southern states.

(a) Interpret Maps Who led American forces at the Battle of Guilford Courthouse?

(b) Evaluate Information Why was it a mistake for Cornwallis to retreat to the Yorktown peninsula?

MapMaster ☽nline

For: Interactive map
Visit: PHSchool.com
Web Code: mvp-2064

KEY

← American and French forces
← British forces
✸ American victories
✸ British victories

New York
Delaware R.
Pennsylvania
Philadelphia
Washington and Rochambeau
NJ
Wilmington
MD
DE
Lafayette
Virginia
Chesapeake Bay
James R.
Richmond
Yorktown
Roanoke R.
Greene
Cornwallis
Guilford Courthouse
Cornwallis
North Carolina
Kings Mt.
Morgan
Cowpens
South Carolina
Camden
Wilmington
Savannah R.
Cornwallis and Clinton
French Fleet
ATLANTIC OCEAN
Charles Town
Georgia
Savannah

0 km 100
0 miles 100
Albers Conic Equal-Area Projection

Making Peace with Britain

p. 193

Instruction

- Have students read Making Peace with Britain. Remind students to track the sequence of events.

- Ask: **What was the Treaty of Paris?** (*the agreement between the United States and Britain ending the American Revolution.*) Ask: **What were its terms?** (*They included a British acknowledgement of the independence of the United States, a ceding of land to the new nation, and a U.S. promise to return land and property to Loyalists.*)

- Ask: **Why do you think many loyalists had already left the United States before the Tresty of Paris?** (*Possible answer: Loyalists had left because the British troops could no longer protect them in certain areas of the United States.*)

- Have students complete the Refugees of the Revolution worksheet.

All in One Teaching Resources, Unit 2, Refugees of the Revolution, p. 51

- Have students consider why it was important for Britain to acknowledge the states' independence. (*Possible answer: It placed the colonies on an equal footing with the well-established nation.*)

Independent Practice

Have students continue filling in the Study Guide for this section.

Monitor Progress

As students fill in the Notetaking Study Guide, circulate to make sure students understand the terms of the peace agreement with Britain. If students do not seem to have a good understanding, have them reread the section. Provide assistance as needed.

History Background

Britain's Dilemma Because they controlled the seas, the British could land and establish bases almost anywhere along the American coast. The navigable rivers that flowed into the Atlantic Ocean provided convenient invasion routes into the interior. To win the war, the British Army had to move away from these coastal bases and rivers. Yet when it did so, it opened its lines of communications and supply to constant attacks. British armies nearly always met defeat when they moved away from the areas where they could be supplied by ships from the homeland. These problems, a British colonel noted in 1777, had "absolutely prevented us this whole war from going fifteen miles from a navigable river."

Answers

MAP★MASTER Skills Activity **(a)** Greene **(b)** because the French fleet overtook his reinforcements

Impact of the Revolution

p. 195

Instruction
L2

- Have students read Impact of the Revolution. Remind students to look for answers to the Section Focus Question.

- Ask: **What was the immediate effect of the colonists' victory?** (*the creation of a new nation of 13 independent states*)

- Ask: **How did the Revolution affect other nations?** (*It inspired independence movements in France and countries in Latin America.*)

Independent Practice

Have students continue filling in the Study Guide for this section.

📖 **Interactive Reading and Notetaking Study Guide,** Chapter 6, Section 4 (Adapted Version also available.)

Monitor Progress

- As students complete the Notetaking Study Guide, circulate to make sure students understand the impact of the war. Provide assistance as needed.

- Tell students to fill in the last column of the Reading Readiness Guide. Probe for what they learned that confirms or invalidates each statement.

- Have students go back to their Word Knowledge Rating Form. Rerate their word knowledge and complete the last column with a definition or example.

All in One Teaching Resources, Unit 2, Reading Readiness Guide, p. 46; Word Knowledge Rating Form, p. 42

● INFOGRAPHIC

Why Did the Americans WIN?

Many factors contributed to the American victory. They fell into four main groups: geographic advantages, help from abroad, patriotic spirit, and skilled leadership. **Critical Thinking: Evaluate Information** *What do you think was the most important reason for the American victory?*

Geography

Americans, such as Francis Marion (pictured below), were on their home ground. They knew the forests, hills, and swamps. But British forces were far from their home country. They had to depend on longer supply lines, stretching across the Atlantic Ocean. ▼

Patriotic Spirit ▲

A key asset of the Americans was patriotism. Americans were fighting to create a new nation. Many soldiers stayed in the army for years, at great financial and personal sacrifice. Leaders such as Jefferson and Adams risked their lives and fortunes to champion independence.

Skilled Leadership ▶

Despite great odds, George Washington (left) never gave up. Although he faced criticism in Congress, his courage and knowledge won him broad support in the army. And though his troops suffered at Valley Forge, Washington led them through hardship to victory. ▼

◀ Help From Abroad

The Americans might never have won without help from Europe. Men such as Lafayette (right) and von Steuben (below) provided military leadership and support. Money from such countries as Spain and the Netherlands was also crucial. ▼

94

Differentiated Instruction

L3 **Advanced Readers**   L3 **Gifted and Talented**

Write a Memo Have students research Cornwallis' decision to retreat to Yorktown. Ask them to consider whether it would have been possible for Cornwallis to avoid defeat if he had made a different choice. Have students assume the role of an aide to Cornwallis and write a memo proposing an alternate strategy.

Answer

Evaluate Information Answers may vary, but students should give clear support for their reasons.

Washington's Farewell On December 4, 1783, Washington and his ranking officers were reunited for one last meal together at Fraunces Tavern in New York City. In parting, each man, in turn, embraced Washington. One officer wrote, "Such a scene of sorrow and weeping I had never before witnessed."

Washington wished to retire to his plantation. Soon, though, he would again be called to the aid of the nation he had helped create.

✓**Checkpoint** What was the Treaty of Paris?

Impact of the Revolution

The immediate effect of the American Revolution was to create a new nation of 13 independent states, linked by ties of custom and history. The long-term effects are still being felt today. The Declaration of Independence cemented ideas like equality and liberty in the American mind. Over time, those concepts have gained broader meanings.

The impact of American independence reached beyond the borders of the infant nation. In 1789, French citizens rebelled. Leaders of the French Revolution, including Lafayette, looked to the American example. They issued the Declaration of the Rights of Man and the Citizen, modeled in part on the Declaration of Independence. The American Revolution also inspired later independence movements in Latin America.

✓**Checkpoint** How did the American Revolution affect France?

⭐ **Looking Back and Ahead** The United States emerged from the American Revolution as a proud nation—but also weak and deeply in debt. In the next chapter, you will read how the new nation met the challenge of forming a democratic government.

Apply the Meaning of the Prefix re- The word root *belli* means "war." Apply a meaning of *re-* to determine the meaning of *rebelled*. Identify the prefix meaning that you applied.

Section 4 | **Check Your Progress**

Progress Monitoring Online
For: Self-test with instant help
Visit: PHSchool.com
Web Code: mva-2064

Comprehension and Critical Thinking
1. **(a) Recall** What military strategy defeated Cornwallis at Yorktown?
(b) Apply Information What was one important factor that contributed to the American victory at Yorktown?
2. **(a) Describe** What were the provisions of the Treaty of Paris?
(b) Identify Benefits Why was setting the nation's western border important economically to the new country?

Reading Skill
3. **Apply the Meanings of the Prefix re-** Read the text under the heading "Making Peace With Britain," and find at least two words that use the prefix *re-*. Apply the meanings of the prefix to define those words.

Key Terms
Answer the following questions in complete sentences that show your understanding of the key terms.
4. What advantages did guerrillas have against larger forces?

5. Why did Americans consider Benedict Arnold to be a traitor?

Writing
6. Once the Treaty of Paris was signed, the Americans had to address a new set of problems. Prepare a thesis statement for an essay about the challenges facing the new nation.

Section 4 Check Your Progress

1. **(a)** The American and French forces trapped Cornwallis and prevented his escape by land; the French fleet arrived off Yorktown and blocked his escape by sea.
(b) One important factor in the defeat was the help of the French forces.
2. **(a)** Britain recognized American independence and accepted American boundaries; also, Spain took East and West Florida from Britain. The United States agreed to recommend to states that Loyalists get back their rights and property.
(b) The Mississippi River, which was the western boundary, was very important for travel and trade.
3. Students should correctly define two of these words: recognized, recommend, reunited, and retire.
4. The guerillas could attack without warning and then escape.

Assess and Reteach

Assess Progress L2
Have students complete Check Your Progress. Administer the Section Quiz.

All in One **Teaching Resources, Unit 2,** Section Quiz, p. 57

To further assess student understanding, use the Progress Monitoring Transparency.

Progress Monitoring Transparencies, Chapter 6, Section 4

Reteach L1
If students need more instruction, have them read this section in the Interactive Reading and Notetaking Study Guide and complete the accompanying question.

📖 **Interactive Reading and Notetaking Study Guide,** Chapter 6, Section 4 (Adapted Version also available.)

Extend L3
To close this lesson, have students choose partners. One partner should take the point of view of the Americans and the other should take the point of view of the British. Have students take turns reviewing the final battles of the war from each side's point of view.

Progress Monitoring Online

Students may check their comprehension of this section by completing the Progress Monitoring Online graphic organizer and self-quiz.

Answers

✓Checkpoint The agreement in which Britain signed over its North American holdings to the Americans.

Reading Skill *Rebelled* means "fought to overthrow a government or ruling power." *Re* means "back" or "again."

✓Checkpoint It inspired France to undertake a revolutionary movement of its own.

5. because he plotted to turn West Point over to the British

6. Thesis statements should predict several problems that the United States would face.

Objective

Comparing maps can help students to synthesize historical information from multiple sources, understanding it in a new way. By learning to analyze and compare visual representations of changes that occur over time, students can better understand the effects of a historical event.

Compare Maps

Instruction   L2

1. Write the steps to comparing maps on the board and ask students to read the steps aloud.

2. Ask students what historical event these maps are about. (*the American Revolution*) Using what they have learned in the chapter, have students suggest the changes they are likely to see. (*changes in the boundaries in North America and changes in ownership of the land*)

3. Practice the skill by following the steps on p. 196 as a class. Model each step to comparing maps. (*1. (a) North America (b) 1763, 1783 2. (a) Land claimed by Britain (including the 13 colonies), Spain, France, and Russia (b) the color for disputed territory 3. (a) The United States came to exist by 1783. (b) Possible answer: Spain controlled New Spain and Louisiana, and Britain controlled Canada. 4. The Treaty of Paris reduced the amount of land claimed by Britain.*)

Monitor Progress

Have students do the Apply the Skill activity. Then assign the Skill for Life Worksheet. As students complete the worksheet, circulate to make sure individuals are applying the skill steps effectively. Provide assistance as needed.

All in One Teaching Resources, Unit 2,
Skills for Life Worksheet, p. 52

By comparing maps from different time periods, you can see how historical changes affected an area. The two maps below show North America before and after the Revolutionary War.

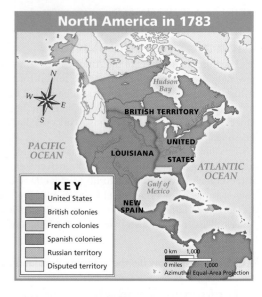

Learn the Skill
Use these steps to compare maps.

1. **Check the subject and area shown on each map.** What do the map titles and labels tell you? Is the same geographical area shown on each map?

2. **Study the map key.** Determine what symbols are used to present specific information that you can compare.

3. **Compare the maps.** Use the data on the maps to make comparisons and note changes over time.

4. **Interpret the maps.** Think over what you already know about this period from other sources. Draw conclusions or make predictions based on your own knowledge and the information on the maps.

Practice the Skill
Answer the following questions about the two maps on this page.

1. **Check the subject and area shown on each map.** (a) What area is shown on both maps? (b) What is the date of each map?

2. **Study the map key.** (a) What do the colors on the 1763 map key represent? (b) What color was added to the map key on the 1783 map?

3. **Compare the maps.** (a) What was the major difference between North America in 1763 and in 1783? (b) How was North America the same in 1763 and in 1783?

4. **Interpret the maps.** How did the 1783 Treaty of Paris affect the distribution of land in North America?

Apply the Skill
See the Review and Assessment at the end of this chapter.

196   Chapter 6 The American Revolution

How did American colonists gain their independence?

Section 1
A Nation Declares Independence

- Thomas Paine's pamphlet *Common Sense* convinced more Americans to support independence from Britain.
- The Declaration of Independence used Enlightenment ideas and careful logic to show why Americans wanted to be free of British rule.

Section 2
A Critical Time

- As fighting moved from New England to the Middle States, American troops faced many setbacks.
- The Battle of Saratoga was a turning point in the war.
- As a result of the American victory at Saratoga, France decided to aid the American cause.

Section 3
The War Widens

- African Americans fought on both sides of the Revolution, often in the hope of gaining freedom.
- As men went to war, women took on added responsibilities.
- Important battles took place on the western frontier and at sea.

Section 4
Winning Independence

- In the final stages of the war, fighting shifted to the South, ending in the British surrender at Yorktown.
- In the Treaty of Paris, Britain recognized American independence.
- The American Revolution and the Declaration of Independence have inspired people in other nations who sought freedom.

? Exploring the Essential Question

Use the online study guide to explore the essential question.

Section 1
Why did many colonists favor declaring independence?

Chapter 6 Essential Question
How did American colonists gain their independence?

Section 2
How were the early years of the war a critical time?

Section 4
How did the Americans win the war and make peace?

Section 3
How did the effects of the war widen?

Chapter 6

Essential Question

Remind students of the Chapter Essential Question: **How did American colonists gain their independence?** Have them review the bulleted statements and the Visual Preview at the beginning of the chapter to help them answer this question.

To bolster students' retention, at this time they should complete the Study Guide in print or online. Remind students that they should also continue notetaking for the Unit and Chapter Essential Questions.

Interactive Reading and Notetaking Study Guide, Unit 2, Chapter 6 (Adapted Version also available.)

Interactive Textbook Study Guide *Online,* Chapter 6

Chapter Challenge

To wrap up this chapter, students should apply the knowledge they have gained to answer this question: **How would American history have been different had Britain won the American Revolution?** (*Answers may vary slightly, but students should recognize that Americans might have remained under Britain's control, which might have meant that the United States could not exist. There might also have been a later war between the Americans and the British.*)

Assessment at a Glance

Formal Assessment

Chapter Tests A/B (L1/L2)

AYP Monitoring Assessment

Test Prep Workbook With Document-Based Assessment

Test-Taking Strategies With Transparencies

Performance Assessment

Group/Individual Activities, TE pp. 166g, 166h

Teacher's Edition, pp. 173, 184, 190, 195

Assessment Rubrics

Assessment Through Technology

ExamView **CD-ROM**

MindPoint CD-ROM

Progress Monitoring Transparencies

Progress Monitoring Online

Key Terms

1. continentals, or paper money

2. rights, and that if a government violates those rights, the people have a right to abolish their government and create another

3. alliances, or formal agrements to work together toward a common goal

4. privateers that attacked British merchant ships

5. cavalry, which fought on horseback

Comprehension and Critical Thinking

6. **(a)** The pamphlet inspired people in all the colonies to believe that they should rule themselves and increased their support for independence. **(b)** It explained the decisions to create a new nation and declare independence from Britain. **(c)** It probably made them more receptive to the ideas expressed in the Declaration.

7. **(a)** Possible answers: The war shifted from New England to the Middle States; Washington's army defeated the British at the Battle of Trenton on December 26, 1776. **(b)** It made them feel more confident about their ability to win the war.

8. **(a)** Possible answers: France became an ally of America after the Battle of Saratoga and signed a treaty that recognized the new country and agreed to give it military aid; France and its European allies went to war with Britain in Europe and the Caribbean, which weakened Britain's ability to fight in North America. **(b)** Possible answer: America would have had a much more difficult time winning the war.

9. **(a)** It didn't have the money to pay for the war and the states contributed very little money. Congress issued paper money that lost value and was almost worthless by the end of the war. **(b)** The new government could collect taxes.

10. **(a)** Their victories against Mississippi River outposts and against Fort Vincennes allowed settlers to stay on the frontier and made America's claim in the Ohio River Valley stronger. **(b)** Controlling the frontier and the Ohio River Valley meant the Unit-

Key Terms

Complete each of the following sentences so that the second part explains the first part and shows your understanding of the key term.

1. Congress decided to pay the soldiers and buy their food and equipment by printing continentals _____.

2. The Declaration of Independence declared that people have unalienable rights _____.

3. One of the reasons that America won the war was because of its French and Spanish alliances _____.

4. During the Revolution, the small American navy had help from privateers _____.

5. A Polish volunteer led the American cavalry _____.

Comprehension and Critical Thinking

6. **(a) Recall** Why was the publication of *Common Sense* so important?
   (b) Describe What was the political importance of the Declaration of Independence?
   (c) Draw Conclusions How do you think that *Common Sense* influenced people's reaction to the Declaration of Independence?

7. **(a) Review** How did the course of the war change from June to the end of December 1776?
   (b) Analyze Cause and Effect What effect do you think this change had on the Patriots?

8. **(a) Summarize** How did France help America during the Revolution?
   (b) Make Predictions What do you think might have happened if France had not come to the aid of America during the Revolution?

9. **(a) Summarize** What financial problems faced Congress during the Revolution?
   (b) Identify Alternatives What are some ways the new American government might avoid these same financial problems in the future?

10. **(a) Recall** How did the victories of the militia led by George Clark in the West benefit the frontier settlers?
    (b) Identify Benefits What were the economic benefits of these victories for the new nation?

History Reading Skill

11. **Analyze Word Parts** Choose a word that contains any of the word parts discussed in this chapter. Use the word part to define the word. Then, write a sentence that contains the word and clarifies its meaning.

Writing

12. **Write two paragraphs discussing the problem of winning support from other nations for the Patriot cause. Your paragraph should:**
    - include a thesis statement that expresses your main idea;
    - develop the main idea with facts, examples, and other information;
    - conclude by describing the lasting impact of what happened.

13. **Write a Dialogue:**
    It is May 1775. Your family is seriously divided over which course to take. Choose one of the following roles: a parent concerned about the safety of the children, a Loyalist supporter, a Patriot supporter. Write one page of conversation about the situation.

Skills for Life
Compare Maps
Use the maps in Sections 3 and 4 to answer the following questions.

14. **(a)** What areas are shown on both maps?
    (b) What is the date of the map in Section 4?

15. What information is provided in the map key for "The Revolution in the West" that is not included in the map key for "The Revolution in the South"?

16. Based on the information in the maps, how would you compare the success of the British troops in the South and the West?

ed States could farm more land and had access to an important trade route.

History Reading Skill

11. Answers will vary with word choice, but should reflect an understanding of how to use word parts to accurately define a word.

Writing

12. Possible thesis statement: In order to gain help from other countries, the

Americans had to convince the countries that the United States might win the Revolution. Possible examples: After the Battle of Saratoga, France openly supported the Americans. France and its allies in the Netherlands and Spain also went to war with Britain. Possible conclusion: If the Americans had not convinced other countries that they could win the Revolution, then they might not have received

Progress Monitoring Online

For: Self-test with instant help
Visit: PHSchool.com
Web Code: mva-2066

Test Yourself

1. Which statement best describes the effects of the American Revolution on women?

   A The political rights of women were reduced.

   B Women had to take on many new responsibilities.

   C Many women were forced to serve in the army.

   D The Declaration of Independence granted equal rights to women.

2. One effect of the Treaty of Paris was that Britain

   A gave up all its colonies in North America.

   B surrendered to the Patriots.

   C recognized American independence.

   D formed an alliance with the United States.

Refer to the map below to answer Question 3.

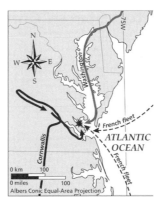

3. What battle is shown on the map?

   A Battle of Saratoga

   B Battle of Cowpens

   C Battle of Yorktown

   D Battle of Trenton

Document-Based Questions

Task: Look at Documents 1 and 2, and answer their accompanying questions. Then, use the documents and your knowledge of history to complete this writing assignment:

> Write an essay comparing the ways in which these two documents proclaim people's basic rights. How do they reflect the Enlightenment ideas of John Locke?

Document 1: This excerpt describes the basic principles behind the Declaration of Independence. *According to the Declaration, what basic rights do people have?*

> "We hold these truths to be self-evident, that all men are created equal, that they are endowed by their Creator with certain unalienable Rights, that among these are Life, Liberty, and the pursuit of Happiness. That to secure these rights, Governments are instituted among Men, deriving their just powers from the consent of the governed."
>
> —Declaration of Independence

Document 2: In 1789, on the eve of the French Revolution, the French Assembly issued the Declaration of the Rights of Man and the Citizen. As you can see from the excerpt below, this document was modeled in part on the American Declaration of Independence. *According to the Declaration of the Rights of Man and the Citizen, what is the aim of government?*

> "The representatives of the French people . . . have determined to set forth in a solemn declaration the natural, unalienable, and sacred rights of man.
>
> 1. Men are born and remain free and equal in rights. . . .
> 2. The aim of all political association is the preservation of the natural and imprescriptable rights of man. These rights are liberty, property, security, and resistance to oppression."
>
> —Declaration of the Rights of Man and the Citizen

Test Yourself

1. B

2. C

3. C

Document-Based Questions

Answers

Document 1 Life, liberty, and the pursuit of happiness

Document 2 To preserve the rights of man

Rubric: Write an Essay

Share this rubric with students.

Score 1 Ideas unclear, organization poor.

Score 2 Essay has few details in comparison of the documents, fails to answer how the documents reflect the ideas of John Locke.

Score 3 Essay accurately compares the two documents and answers how the documents reflect the ideas of John Locke, has clear organization.

Score 4 Essay is comprehensive and detailed with clear organization and supporting details.

---

help. Without this help, the Americans might have lost the war.

13. Students' dialogues should incorporate one of the suggested roles, and should be at least one page in length.

For more complete four-point rubrics, see the writing rubrics in Teaching Resources.

All in One **Teaching Resources, Unit 2,** p. 122

Skills for Life

14. **(a)** locations of American victories **(b)** 1778–1781

15. British victories, forts

16. The British were more successful in the South than in the West.

History Background

The Significance of the United States Constitution

In studying the roots of American government, students will learn about one of the most significant events in U.S. history—the creation of a new form of government under a written constitution.

After winning independence from Britain during the American Revolution, the leaders of the new United States faced the challenge of creating a government. The central dilemma was creating a national government with enough power to operate, yet enough limits on that power to prevent tyranny over the rights of states and individuals.

The first attempt at this resulted in the Articles of Confederation. However, the Articles were written while the experiences under British rule were

still fresh. Because of this, the government under the Articles was so restricted in its power that it could barely function.

The weaknesses of the government under the Articles of Confederation led to a call for reform. In 1787, delegates from the states met to revise the Articles at what became known as the Constitutional Convention. During the convention, the delegates decided to devise a new governmental framework. Through a series of compromises over issues such as representation in the legislature and slavery, they created a new written plan. This plan, the Constitution, provided for an authoritative, representative government while limiting its power over the states and individuals.

Not everyone thought the new Constitution did enough to protect basic rights. Some states would not ratify the new Constitution until it was amended by the addition of the Bill of Rights. These crucial first 10 amendments protected important individual rights and freedoms, such as free speech, freedom of religion, and freedom of the press.

The U.S. Constitution was the successful result of political thought, experimentation, and compromise. Not only did it eventually allow the fulfillment of most of the ideals of the Declaration of Independence, but over the last 200 years it has stood as a model for many new nations around the world.

Essential Questions

Use this graphic organizer to see the relationship between key concepts and the Chapter Essential Question.

Focus Question/Section 1
What were the major successes and failures of the government under the Articles of Confederation?
(p. 204)

Concept: Constitution

Focus Question/Section 2
What role did compromise play in the creation of the United States Constitution?
(p. 212)

Concept: Compromise

Chapter Essential Question
How did the United States Constitution overcome the weaknesses of the Articles of Confederation and provide for the organization of the new government?

Focus Question/Section 3
How did those in favor of the Constitution achieve its ratification?
(p. 218)

Concept: Values

Differentiated Instruction

Sharing Key Concepts

Ask each student to explain one key concept, key term, or high-use word on a note card. Then, have students form two concentric circles. Students on the inside circle should pair with the student facing them on the outside circle. Each pair should explain their concepts or words to each other using their cards. The two students can ask each other questions to make sure they both understand. Students then trade cards and the outside circle moves clockwise one person. Repeat the process until students end up with their original cards.

Concepts Across Time

Have students develop an understanding of the enduring concepts of history by connecting these ideas.

Concept: Constitution

As students learn about the adoption of constitutions, explain to them that all modern states need a set of rules and procedures to guide officials in their actions and to protect the rights of citizens. Discuss the reasons why a government needs a set of written rules. Ask: **Why might a written constitution provide greater protection for citizens' rights than ordinary laws and court decisions?** (*A constitution is a set of "super-rules" with which the actions of officials, legislatures, and courts must comply. It is harder to change a constitution than to change an ordinary law.*) Use this question when discussing state constitutions, the Articles of Confederation, and the writing of the Constitution in Sections 1 and 2.

Concept: Compromise

While students discuss the importance of compromise in writing the Constitution, have them recall what they learned about the debates among the colonists leading to the adoption of the Declaration of Independence. Remind them that delegates to the Second Continental Congress compromised by sending the Olive Branch Petition pledging loyalty to King George. Only after that effort failed did the Congress move to declare independence. Ask: **How was compromise important in broadening support among colonists for declaring independence?** (*It helped to convince many people that further peaceful petitions were useless and that the time had come to fight for independence.*) Use this question when discussing the Constitutional Convention in Section 2.

Concept: Values

As students learn how Americans struggled to write and then win approval for the Constitution, explain that the Constitution reflects many basic American values. Ask: **What American values were reflected in the Declaration of Independence?** (*The idea that all people have rights, that they have a right to govern themselves, that governments can be changed if they become oppressive.*) Ask: **What features of the Bill of Rights demonstrate those values?** (*The Bill of Rights protects essential rights and sets additional limits on the power of the central government and state governments.*) Use this question when discussing the ratification of the Constitution in Section 3.

Section 1 Governing a New Nation

 1.5 periods, .75 block

Objectives

Students will

1. Discuss the ideas that guided the new state governments.
2. Describe the government under the Articles of Confederation.
3. Explain the Ordinances of 1785 and 1787 and their importance to westward expansion.
4. Identify the problems created by a weak central government.

Differentiated Instruction Key

L1 Basic to Average		**AR**	Advanced Readers
L2 All Students		**ELL**	English Language Learners
L3 Average to Advanced		**GT**	Gifted and Talented
		LPR	Less Proficient Readers
		SN	Special Needs

Prepare to Read

Build Background Knowledge
Preview the section and brainstorm for challenges of a new government.

Set a Purpose for Reading
Students fill out the Reading Readiness Guide.

Preview Key Terms
Preview the section's Key Terms.

Instructional Resources

All in One Teaching Resources, Unit 2
- **L2** Chapter Prereading Guide, p. 4
- **L2** History Reading Skill, p. 70
- **L2** Reading Readiness Guide, p. 72
- **L2** Word Knowledge Rating Form, p. 71

Discovery School Video
- **L2** Creating the Constitution

Teacher's Edition
- **L2** Vocabulary Builder, pp. 203, 205

Differentiated Instruction

Guided Reading Audio CD
Spanish **ELL, LPR, SN**

Teach

Instruction
Government by the States
Discuss the purpose of the states' new constitutions.

The Articles of Confederation
Describe the government under the Articles of Confederation.

Settling the Western Lands
Explain the Ordinances of 1785 and 1787.

Growing Problems
Identify the problems that faced the United States because of a weak central government.

Instructional Resources

Interactive Reading and Notetaking Study Guide
- **L2** Chapter 7, Section 1

All in One Teaching Resources, Unit 2
- **L2** Concept Lesson, p. 80
- **L2** Concept Organizer, p. 6
- **L2** James Bowdoin's Account of Shays' Rebellion, p. 75

Color Transparencies
- **L2** Northwest Territory 1787

Differentiated Instruction

Interactive Reading and Notetaking Study Guide, Adapted Version (English/Spanish)
- **L1** Chapter 7, Section 1

Teacher's Edition
- **L1** Visualizing the Word, p. 203 **ELL, SN**
- **L1** Gaining Comprehension, p. 204 **LPR, SN**
- **L1** Reading and Vocabulary, p. 206 **ELL, LPR, SN**
- **L3** Explaining Shays' View, p. 208 **AR, GT**
- **L1** Reviewing Vocabulary, p. 210 **ELL, LPR**

Assess and Reteach

Assess Progress
Assign Check Your Progress and Section Quiz.

Reteach
Assign the Interactive Reading and Notetaking Study Guide to help struggling students.

Extend
Extend the lesson by having students research settlements in the Northwest Territory.

Instructional Resources

Interactive Reading and Notetaking Study Guide
- **L2** Chapter 7, Section 1

All in One Teaching Resources, Unit 2
- **L2** Reading Readiness Guide, p. 72
- **L2** Section Quiz, p. 81

Progress Monitoring Transparencies
- **L2** Chapter 7, Section 1

Differentiated Instruction

Teacher's Edition
- **L1** Checkpoints, TE pp. 205, 206, 207, 209

SE on Audio CD
- **L1** Chapter 7 **ELL, LPR, SN**

Internet Resources
PHSchool.com

Section 2 The Constitutional Convention

 1 period, .5 block

Objectives

Students will

1. Describe the proceedings of the Constitutional Convention.
2. Identify the specifics of the Virginia Plan.
3. Explain how the Great Compromise satisfied both large and small states.
4. Describe the disputes over slavery and the compromises that were reached.
5. Discuss the drafting of the new Constitution.

Differentiated Instruction Key

- **L1** Basic to Average
- **L2** All Students
- **L3** Average to Advanced
- **AR** Advanced Readers
- **ELL** English Language Learners
- **GT** Gifted and Talented
- **LPR** Less Proficient Readers
- **SN** Special Needs

Prepare to Read

Build Background Knowledge
Preview the section and discuss what students know about the United States Constitution.

Set a Purpose for Reading
Have students begin to fill out the Reading Readiness Guide.

Preview Key Terms
Preview the section's Key Terms.

Instructional Resources

All in One Teaching Resources, Unit 2
- **L2** Reading Readiness Guide, p. 73

Teacher's Edition
- **L2** Vocabulary Builder, p. 213

Differentiated Instruction

🔊 **Guided Reading Audio CD**
Spanish **ELL, LPR, SN**

Teach

Instruction
The Constitutional Convention Begins
Discuss the proceedings of the Constitutional Convention.

The Virginia Plan
Identify the specifics of the Virginia Plan.

The Great Compromise
Describe the compromise between the New Jersey Plan and the Virginia Plan.

Debates Over Slavery
Explain the Three-Fifths Compromise and problems between the North and South concerning slavery.

A New Constitution
Discuss the drafting of the new Constitution.

Instructional Resources

📖 **Interactive Reading and Notetaking Study Guide**
- **L2** Chapter 7, Section 2

All in One Teaching Resources, Unit 2
- **L2** The Great Compromise, p. 76

Discovery School Video
- **L2** Bill of Rights

Differentiated Instruction

📖 **Interactive Reading and Notetaking Study Guide, Adapted Version (English/Spanish)**
- **L1** Chapter 7, Section 2

Teacher's Edition
- **L3** Making a Timeline, p. 212 **AR, GT**
- **L1** Reading a Chart, p. 214 **ELL, LPR, SN**
- **L1** Building Vocabulary, p. 216 **ELL, SN**

All in One Teaching Resources, Unit 2
- **L1** The Articles of Confederation and the Constitution, p. 77

Assess and Reteach

Assess Progress
Evaluate student comprehension with Check Your Progress and Section Quiz.

Reteach
Assign the Interactive Reading and Notetaking Study Guide to help struggling students.

Extend
Extend the lesson by having students research the Constitutional Convention.

Instructional Resources

📖 **Interactive Reading and Notetaking Study Guide**
- **L2** Chapter 7, Section 2

All in One Teaching Resources, Unit 2
- **L2** Reading Readiness Guide, p. 73
- **L2** Section Quiz, p. 82

Progress Monitoring Transparencies
- **L2** Chapter 7, Section 2

Differentiated Instruction

Teacher's Edition
- **L1** Checkpoints, TE pp. 213, 214, 215, 217

🔊 **SE on Audio CD**
- **L1** Chapter 7 **ELL, LPR, SN**

Internet Resources
PHSchool.com

Section 3 Debating the Constitution

 1.5 periods, .75 block

Objectives

Students will

1. Compare the positions of the Federalists and the Antifederalists.
2. Discuss the debate over ratification.
3. Describe the Bill of Rights and how it protects the people.

Prepare to Read	Instructional Resources	Differentiated Instruction
Build Background Knowledge Preview the section and brainstorm reasons for the states to support or oppose the Constitution. **Set a Purpose for Reading** Have students begin to fill out the Reading Readiness Guide. **Preview Key Terms** Preview the section's Key Terms.	**All in One** Teaching Resources, Unit 2 **L2** Reading Readiness Guide, p. 74 **Teacher's Edition** **L2** Vocabulary Builder, p. 219	⊙ **Guided Reading Audio CD** **Spanish** ELL, LPR, SN

Teach	Instructional Resources	Differentiated Instruction
Instruction **Federalists Versus Antifederalists** Discuss why the Federalists supported the Constitution and why the Antifederalists were against the Constitution. **The Ratification Debate** Discuss how the states ratified the Constitution. **The Bill of Rights** Describe the Bill of Rights and how it protects the people.	📖 **Interactive Reading and Notetaking Study Guide** **L2** Chapter 7, Section 3 **All in One** Teaching Resources, Unit 2 **L2** James Madison's Speech Proposing the Bill of Rights, p. 78 **L2** Skills for Life Worksheet, p. 79 **Color Transparencies** **L2** The Federalist Papers ⊙ **Exploring Primary Sources in U.S. History CD-ROM** **L3** Objections to the Constitution	📖 **Interactive Reading and Notetaking Study Guide, Adapted Version (English/ Spanish)** **L1** Chapter 7, Section 3 ELL, LPR, SN **Teacher's Edition** **L1** Understanding Word Parts, p. 218 ELL, LPR, SN **L3** Exploring Primary Sources, p. 220 AR, GT

Assess and Reteach	Instructional Resources	Differentiated Instruction
Assess Progress Assign Check Your Progress and Section Quiz. **Reteach** Assign the Interactive Reading and Notetaking Study Guide to help struggling students. **Extend** Extend the lesson by having students research why Rhode Island was late in approving the Constitution.	📖 **Interactive Reading and Notetaking Study Guide** **L2** Chapter 7, Section 3 **All in One** Teaching Resources, Unit 2 **L2** Reading Readiness Guide, p. 74 **L2** Word Knowledge Rating Form, p. 71 **L2** Section Quiz, p. 83 **L2** Chapter Test, p. 87 **Progress Monitoring Transparencies** **L2** Chapter 7, Section 3	**Teacher's Edition** **L1** Checkpoints, TE pp. 219, 220, 221 **All in One** Teaching Resources, Unit 2 **L1** Chapter Test, p. 84 ⊙ **SE on Audio CD** **L1** Chapter 7 ELL, LPR, SN ⊙ **Social Studies Skills Tutor CD-ROM** Identifying Cause and Effect **Internet Resources** PHSchool.com

Use the following research activities to help students deepen their understanding of the Chapter Essential Question: **How did the United States Constitution overcome the weaknesses of the Articles of Confederation and provide for the organization of the new government?** Students should use library or Internet resources. The Web Codes provided offer access to Internet resources students can use to complete each activity. Use the appropriate four-point rubric in Assessment Rubrics to evaluate the activity.

 Assessment Rubrics

Make a Flowchart of the Causes and Effects of Shays' Rebellion

Have students research the details of Shays' Rebellion to find out the main causes and effects of this episode. Have students select the information they feel is important and order events in the form of a flowchart. The information should include the problems that led the farmers to rebel, the response of the Massachusetts government, and the overall effects of the rebellion on the Articles of Confederation. Post the flowcharts and summarize the importance of Shays' Rebellion. Use this activity when students study Shays' Rebellion in Section 1.

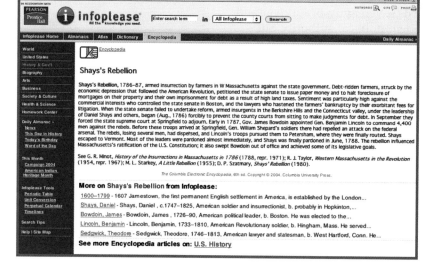

Individual research activity   L2

 **Web Code:** mye-0214

Compare the U.S. Constitution and the Declaration of Independence

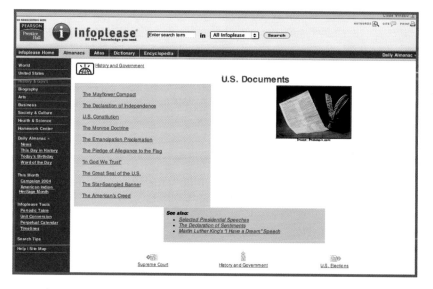

Have students print out a copy of the Declaration of Independence and Articles I and V of the U.S. Constitution from the Internet. Students should prepare by reading all the documents. Then, have students highlight or underline every instance in Articles I and V where they find evidence that the document carries out the ideals and goals of the Declaration. Then have students write a brief summary explaining whether or not these articles fulfill the ideals and goals of the Declaration of Independence. Use this activity after students have completed Section 3.

Individual research activity AR, GT   L3

 **Web Code:** mye-0215

Why It Matters

The Pledge of Allegiance refers to "one nation." This concept as we understand it today was unknown in 1787. The Articles of Confederation created "a firm league of friendship among the states." The states were like the United Nations member nations of today. The states sent delegates to the Congress and agreed to "assist each other" in the interests of "common defense" and "mutual welfare." However, each state retained its sovereignty, or supreme and independent political authority. Supporters of the Constitution had to persuade other delegates that stronger bonds were needed, and it was not an easy task. It took many years to turn the United States into a republic that was truly united with a shared national identity.

Chapter Essential Question

How did the United States Constitution overcome the weaknesses of the Articles of Confederation and provide for the organization of the new government?

Think Like a Historian

- To preview this chapter, have students review the content of these pages of the Student Edition. Ask: **What will you be learning about in this chapter?** *(the organization of the new government of the United States)*

- Ask a student to read the quotation aloud. Then, using the Section 1 summary as an aid, have students paraphrase the quotation. Ask: **According to Patrick Henry, what did the Convention need to do?** *(form a new government)*

- Have students look at the painting on these pages. Ask: **What seems to be happening at the Convention?** *(delegates are discussing issues)*

Creating the Constitution

1776–1790

200

Bibliography

For the Teacher

Jillson, Calvin C. *Constitution Making: Conflict and Consensus in the Federal Convention of 1787.* Algora Publishing, 2003.

For the Student

L1 Prolman, Marilyn. *Constitution.* Scholastic Library Publishing, 1995.

L2 Collier, James Lincoln and Christopher Collier. *Creating the Constitution: 1787.* Benchmark Books, 1998.

L3 Judson, Karen. *The Constitution of the United States.* Enslow Publishers, Inc., 1996.

"They were fully impressed with the necessity of forming a great consolidated government, instead of a confederation."

—Patrick Henry,
on the Constitutional Convention, 1788

Convention delegates sign the new Constitution in Philadelphia, 1787.

CHAPTER 7

What You Will Learn

Section 1
GOVERNING A NEW NATION
Weaknesses in the Articles of Confederation convinced leading Americans that the country needed a strong central government.

Section 2
THE CONSTITUTIONAL CONVENTION
After months of intense debate, delegates to the Constitutional Convention agreed on a new plan of government.

Section 3
DEBATING THE CONSTITUTION
The states approved the Constitution, but many of the states insisted that it also include a bill of rights.

Reading Skill

Analyze Propositions and Support In this chapter, you will learn how to identify and study arguments and research the evidence used to support them.

201

History Background

Convention Debates Although this portrait shows delegates in calm discussion, the Constitution was developed after a long and often bitter debate. For two months, the delegates argued over the structure and powers of a new federal government. A committee then was formed to review state constitutions, the Articles of Confederation, and the Convention's resolutions. Then Edmund Randolph of Virginia wrote a draft of the constitution, which was revised by the committee and presented to the delegates.

After 5 weeks of debate over the draft, another committee prepared a final version. On September 17, 1787, after several days of more changes, the Convention approved the Constitution. It was then up to the states to ratify it.

Prepare to Read

Use the following for reading skill support.

All in One Teaching Resources, Unit 2, Chapter Prereading Guide, p. 4; History Reading Skill, p. 70

History Reading Skill *Online*
Web code: mve-3000

Differentiated Instruction

The following Teacher Edition strategies are suitable for students of varying abilities.

L3 Advanced Readers, pp. 208, 212, 220 AR

L1 English Language Learners, pp. 203, 206, 210, 214, 216, 218 ELL

L3 Gifted and Talented, pp. 208, 212, 220 GT

L1 Less Proficient Readers, pp. 204, 206, 210, 214, 218 LPR

L1 Special Needs, pp. 203, 204, 206, 214, 216, 218 SN

Chapter Resources

Teaching Resources, Unit 2
Chapter Prereading Guide, p. 4
Word Knowledge Rating Form, p. 71
History Reading Skill, p. 70
Skills for Life Worksheet, p. 79
Chapter Tests A/B (L1/L2), pp. 84, 87
Letter Home (English/Spanish), pp. 64, 65

Spanish Support
L1 Interactive Reading and Notetaking Study Guide, Spanish, Adapted Version
L1 Guided Reading Audio CD, Spanish

Media and Technology
**L1 SE on Audio CD
**L2 Social Studies Skills Tutor CD-ROM
ExamView Test Bank CD-ROM

Discovery SCHOOL

Quick View Video
View the chapter video for a quick preview of the main ideas.

Visual Preview

(?) **How did the United States Constitution overcome the weaknesses of the Articles of Confederation and provide for the organization of the new government?**

Build Background Knowledge [L2]

Discuss the purpose of a constitution with the students. Lead a structured discussion about the need for written rules and a framework for the government. (See TE p. T24 for more on structured discussion.) A relevant example of this type of need would be a manual or rulebook for a sport. The guide would explain the goal of the game, how it is to be played, what is prohibited, etc. Help students give examples of other structured guidelines they have dealt with. (*student government, rules at home, rules at a job*)

Instruction [L2]

■ For background information on conducting a lesson for the Visual Preview, see TE p. T20.

■ Write the Essential Question on the board and explain what it means to organize a government. Use the Idea Wave strategy (p. T24) to lead a structured discussion about the functions of a government. Ask: **What is the job of the United States government?** (*to protect individual rights, make laws, defend the nation*)

■ Have students review the map. Ask: **What do the dates on the map indicate?** (*the year each state ratified the Constitution*) **Which state was the first to ratify the Constitution?** (*Delaware*)

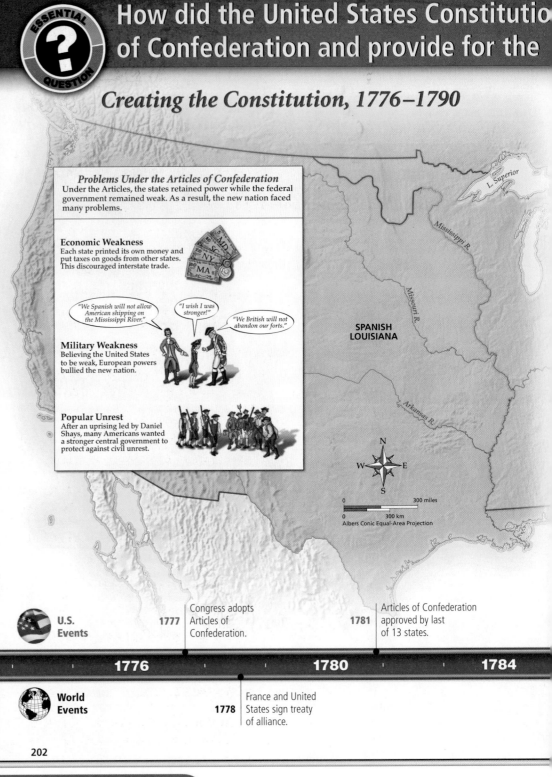

How did the United States Constitutio of Confederation and provide for the

ESSENTIAL QUESTION

Creating the Constitution, 1776–1790

Problems Under the Articles of Confederation
Under the Articles, the states retained power while the federal government remained weak. As a result, the new nation faced many problems.

Economic Weakness
Each state printed its own money and put taxes on goods from other states. This discouraged interstate trade.

"We Spanish will not allow American shipping on the Mississippi River."

"I wish I was stronger!"

"We British will not abandon our forts."

Military Weakness
Believing the United States to be weak, European powers bullied the new nation.

Popular Unrest
After an uprising led by Daniel Shays, many Americans wanted a stronger central government to protect against civil unrest.

SPANISH LOUISIANA

0 — 300 miles
0 — 300 km
Albers Conic Equal-Area Projection

U.S. Events **1777** Congress adopts Articles of Confederation. **1781** Articles of Confederation approved by last of 13 states.

| 1776 | 1780 | 1784 |

World Events **1778** France and United States sign treaty of alliance.

202

History Background

Post-war Issues Problems of adjusting to the conditions of independence overwhelmed the new republic. England, France, and Spain still harbored colonial ambitions in North America. Economic troubles mounted as Congress struggled to pay off war debts, prices dropped, and the money supply shrank. Merchants scrambled to find new markets and routes for profitable trade. Protective of their new self-rule, states did not work together on common issues of taxes, debt, and currency. Discontented citizens began to express their frustrations.

By 1786, most Americans agreed that the national government needed to be strengthened and restructured.

overcome the weaknesses of the Articles

organization of the new government?

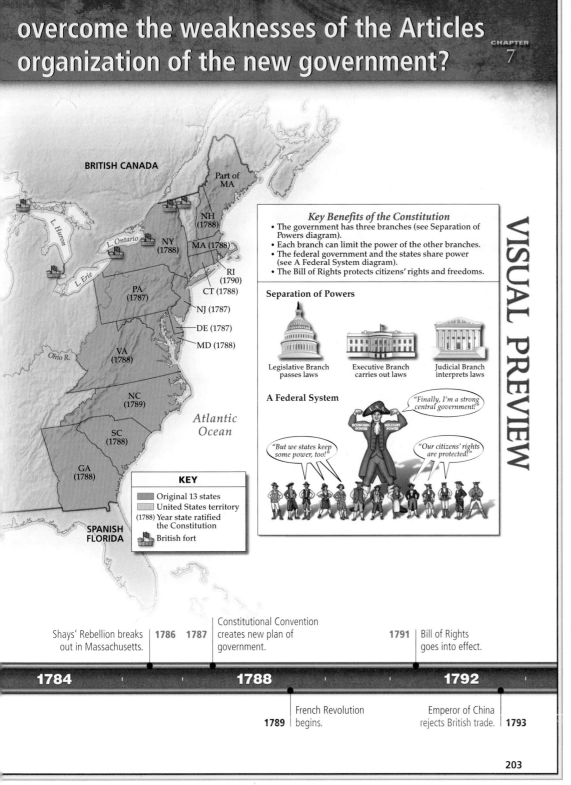

BRITISH CANADA

Part of MA

NH (1788)

NY (1788)

MA (1788)

RI (1790)

CT (1788)

NJ (1787)

DE (1787)

MD (1788)

PA (1787)

VA (1788)

NC (1789)

SC (1788)

GA (1788)

Atlantic Ocean

SPANISH FLORIDA

Key Benefits of the Constitution
- The government has three branches (see Separation of Powers diagram).
- Each branch can limit the power of the other branches.
- The federal government and the states share power (see A Federal System diagram).
- The Bill of Rights protects citizens' rights and freedoms.

Separation of Powers

Legislative Branch passes laws

Executive Branch carries out laws

Judicial Branch interprets laws

A Federal System

"Finally, I'm a strong central government!"

"But we states keep some power, too!"

"Our citizens' rights are protected!"

KEY
- Original 13 states
- United States territory
- (1788) Year state ratified the Constitution
- British fort

VISUAL PREVIEW

Shays' Rebellion breaks out in Massachusetts. | 1786 | 1787 | Constitutional Convention creates new plan of government. | 1791 | Bill of Rights goes into effect.

1784   **1788**   **1792**

1789 | French Revolution begins.

Emperor of China rejects British trade. | 1793

203

Instruction (continued)

- Have students review the timeline. Ask: **When did the Articles of Confederation go into effect?** (*1777*) **When was the new plan of government created?** (*1787*)

- Choose students to read the captions on p. 202 indicating the problems under the Articles of Confederation. Have other students do the same for the illustration on p. 203, showing how the U.S. government became stronger. Have students discuss the opinions and arguments from both sides.

- Have students rewrite the Essential Question in simple terms in their notes. **What was wrong with the Articles of Confederation and how did the new Constitution create a better government?** You may also post this question in a prominent place in the classroom and leave it there while discussing the chapter. Tell students to use the section focus questions as a guide to answering the Essential Question as they read the chapter.

- Tell students that as they complete the Notetaking Study Guide for this chapter, they will be building the answer to the Essential Question.

Interactive Reading and Notetaking Study Guide, Chapter 7 (Adapted Version also available.)

Vocabulary Builder

Preview the Vocabulary Have students preview the vocabulary in the chapter and rate how well they know each word on the Word Knowledge Rating Form. Collect the sheets and explain that they will have a chance to go over the forms later.

All in One Teaching Resources, Unit 2, Word Knowledge Rating Form, p. 71

Monitor Progress Have students demonstrate their understanding of the vocabulary terms by completing these activities:

- Have students describe the *emotions* they would feel if their favorite sports team won a championship.

- Ask students to make a two-panel drawing that shows the *contrast* between winter and summer.

Chapter 7 **203**

Review and Preview

Students have learned about the Articles of Confederation. Now they will read why Americans began to realize they needed a stronger government to meet the concerns of a new expanding nation.

Section Focus Question

What were the major successes and failures of the government under the Articles of Confederation?

Before you begin the lesson for the day, write the Section Focus Question on the board. (*Lesson focus: Successes—formed the framework of a government; established Congress. Failures—did not provide for a strong central government; did not provide for an executive or a system of national courts.*)

Prepare to Read

Build Background Knowledge **L2**

In this section, students will learn about some of the challenges the new government of the United States faced after the American Revolution. To start students thinking about this concept, have them suppose that they must set up many different booths for a school fair. Use the Idea Wave technique (TE, p. T24) to have them brainstorm for some of the challenges they might face if there is no committee in charge of the fair. How could they better organize the preparations for the fair?

Set a Purpose

- Form students into pairs or groups of four. Distribute the Reading Readiness Guide. Ask students to fill in the first two columns of the chart.

  All in One Teaching Resources, Unit 2, Reading Readiness Guide, p. 72

- Use the Numbered Heads strategy (TE, p. T24) to call on students to share one piece of information they already know and one piece of information they want to know. The students will return to these worksheets later.

Our Weak Federal Government
❝The weakness of our federal government . . . prevents the adoption of any measures that are requisite for us as a nation; it keeps us from paying our honest debts; it also throws out of our power all the profits of commerce, and this drains us of cash.❞

—Noah Webster, complaining about national government, 1786

◄ A variety of state currencies weakened the nation's economy.

Governing a New Nation

Objectives
- Discuss the ideas that guided the new state governments.
- Describe the government under the Articles of Confederation.
- Explain the Ordinances of 1785 and 1787 and their importance to westward expansion.
- Identify the problems created by a weak central government.

🔖 Reading Skill

Identify Propositions The study of history often takes you inside important debates over ideas and actions. People propose their ideas and then give reasons to support those ideas. Identifying those propositions will help you to understand the beliefs and experiences of people in an earlier time. One way to identify propositions is to ask yourself what problems people had and how they proposed solving those problems.

Key Terms and People

constitution
executive

economic depression
Daniel Shays

204 Chapter 7 Creating the Constitution

Why It Matters Leaders of the new American nation recalled how the king and Parliament in faraway England had exerted excessive power over colonial legislatures. Many Americans favored a republic in which the states had more power than the central government.

❓ **Section Focus Question: What were the major successes and failures of the government under the Articles of Confederation?**

Government by the States

As the Continental Congress began moving toward independence in 1776, leaders in the individual states began creating governments. Eleven of the 13 states wrote new constitutions to support their governments. A constitution is a document stating the rules under which a government will operate. The other two states—Rhode Island and Connecticut—kept using their colonial charters. However, they removed all references to the British king.

Writing State Constitutions In writing state constitutions, Americans were well aware of the problems that had led to the Revolution. Colonists had been unhappy with governors appointed by the British Crown. Thus, the new constitutions minimized the powers of state governors. Instead, they gave most of the power to state legislatures elected by the people.

Differentiated Instruction

L1 Less Proficient Readers   **L1 Special Needs**

Gaining Comprehension Have students read the text of Governing a New Nation as they listen to the Student Edition on Audio CD. Monitor student answers to Checkpoint questions to make sure they understand. Students can be provided with a copy of the CD to work independ-

dently at home or in the school Resource Center. When students have finished, ask them to share their answers to the Checkpoint questions with the class.

🔊 **SE on Audio CD,** Chapter 7, Section 1

The governor served as the state's executive. In a government, the executive is the person who runs the government and sees that the laws are carried out. Governors appointed key state officials, but usually the legislature had to approve the appointments.

The new constitutions allowed more people to vote than in colonial times. Nonetheless, all but a few states barred African Americans (including those who were free) from voting. New Jersey allowed some women to vote until 1807, but women could not vote in any other state. In order to vote, white males had to be 21 or older. In most states, they also had to own a certain amount of property.

Protecting Rights The Declaration of Independence listed ways that Britain had violated the rights of colonists. To prevent such abuses, states sought to protect <u>individual</u> rights. Virginia was the first state to include a bill of rights in its constitution. Virginia's list included freedom of the press and the right to trial by jury, and it also barred "cruel and unusual punishments." The final clause guaranteed freedom of religion:

> **"**That religion, or the duty which we owe to our Creator, and the manner of discharging it, can be directed only by reason and conviction, not by force or violence; and therefore all men are equally entitled to the free exercise of religion, according to the dictates of conscience.**"**
>
> —Virginia Bill of Rights, 1776

Many other states followed Virginia's lead. For example, the New York state constitution also included a bill of rights that guaranteed freedom of religion:

> **"**This convention doth further, in the name and by the authority of the good people of this State, ordain, determine, and declare, that the free exercise and enjoyment of religious profession and worship, without discrimination or preference, shall forever hereafter be allowed, within this State, to all mankind.**"**
>
> —New York Constitution of 1777

Massachusetts also included freedom of religion in its bill of rights. However, Massachusetts did retain its official church. Massachusetts's bill of rights declared that people have the freedom to worship as they please, so long as they did not disturb the public peace or interfere with other people's freedom of worship.

☑ **Checkpoint** Why did many state constitutions limit the power of state governors?

Vocabulary Builder
individual (in duh VIJ oo uhl)
adj. of, for, or by a single person or thing

Protecting Rights
Virginia included a bill of rights in its constitution. The Virginia bill of rights became a model for other states and, later, for the national Constitution. **Critical Thinking: Link Past and Present** *Which protections in the Virginia bill of rights are enjoyed by all Americans today?*

Virginia Bill of Rights

- Freedom of Religion
- Freedom of the Press
- Trial by Jury
- Limits on Searches
- Limits on Arrests
- No Cruel and Unusual Punishment

Government by the States

p. 204

Instruction

- **Vocabulary Builder** Before teaching this section, preteach the High-Use Words **individual** and **devise** using the strategy on TE p. T21.
  Key Terms Following the instructions on p. 7, have students create a See It–Remember It chart for the Key Terms in this chapter.

- To help students better comprehend the concept of a *constitution*, which is important to the understanding of this chapter, use the Concept Lesson, Constitution. Provide students with copies of the Concept Organizer.

  All in One Teaching Resources, Unit 2, Concept Lesson, p. 80, Concept Organizer, p. 6

- Read Government by the States with students using the Structured Silent Reading strategy (TE, p. T22).

- Discuss with students how the history of the United States as a British colony affected state constitutions. (*Because of their experience with tyrannical British rule, the writers of the new state constitutions minimized the power of the government while protecting individual rights.*)

- Ask: **How did the Virginia bill of rights limit the power of the government?** (*With these individual freedoms protected, the state government was limited in how it could interfere in the lives of its citizens.*)

Independent Practice

Have students begin filling in the study guide for this section.

Monitor Progress

As students fill in the Notetaking Study Guide, circulate to make sure that they understand the goals of the first state constitutions. Provide assistance as needed.

Answers

☑ **Checkpoint** because of bad experiences in the past under colonial governors

Link Past and Present Freedom of religion; Limits on searches; Trial by jury; Freedom of the press; No cruel and unusual punishment

---

Vocabulary Builder

Use the information below to teach students this section's high-use words.

High-Use Word	Definition and Sample Sentence
individual, p. 205	*adj.* of, for, or by a single person or thing The Declaration of Independence was based on the idea that **individuals** had natural rights and that England violated these rights.
devise, p. 206	*v.* to think up an idea for something and figure out how it will work Athens was the first city-state to **devise** a system of direct democracy.

The Articles of Confederation

p. 206

Instruction

- Have students read the Articles of Confederation. Remind them to look for details to answer the Section Focus Question.

- Ask: **What were the Articles of Confederation?** (*a document created during the Revolution defining the features of a central government for the United States*)

- Discuss with students the features and powers of the central government under the Articles. (*The central government was weak compared to the states and had only a one-branch legislature, called Congress, in which each state had one vote. Congress could make war and peace, coin money, and run the postal service. It could not tax, enforce its laws, or regulate trade.*)

Independent Practice

Have students continue filling in the study guide for this section.

Interactive Reading and Notetaking Study Guide, Chapter 7, Section 1 (Adapted Version also available.)

Monitor Progress

As students fill in the Notetaking Study Guide, circulate to be sure that they understand how the government was established by the Articles of Confederation. Provide assistance as needed.

Answers

Reading Skill They believed that the Articles of Confederation had been a failure. They proposed a stronger central government.

Checkpoint Congress could not regulate trade, could not tax, and had no way to enforce any laws it made. Only the states could exercise these powers.

The Articles of Confederation

While the states were writing their constitutions, the Continental Congress created a plan for the nation as a whole. It was called the Articles of Confederation. Congress adopted the Articles in 1777.

Form of Government Instead of having three branches of government like those of most states, the government under the Articles had just one branch—a one-house legislature, called Congress. There was no executive and no system of national courts.

Within Congress, all states would be equal and each had a single vote. Moreover, for the most important matters, nine states had to agree before a law could go into effect.

Limited Government The framers of the Articles of Confederation kept in mind their complaints against Britain. Parliament had passed laws the colonists considered unfair. The new states did not want to risk giving too much power to a central government far from the people. Thus, the Articles provided for a limited central government.

Under the Articles, most power remained in the hands of the states. Congress could not regulate trade or collect taxes. Instead, it had to ask the states for the money it needed.

Congress did have some powers under the Articles. It could deal with foreign nations and with Native Americans outside the 13 states. It could make laws, declare war, coin or borrow money, and run a postal service. However, the national government had no power to enforce the laws that it made. For that, it depended on the states.

Checkpoint How did the Articles of Confederation ensure the power of the states?

Settling the Western Lands

The Articles had to be approved by all 13 states. But some states would not give their approval until other states dropped their claims to vast areas of land west of the Appalachian Mountains. It took years to get all the states to give up their claims to western lands. In 1781, Virginia was the final state to agree. Only then did Maryland approve the Articles of Confederation, the final state to do so.

The western lands that the states had given up were turned over to the national government. They proved to be very valuable. Land was in great demand. It could be sold off, piece by piece, to private companies seeking to develop western settlements.

Land Ordinance of 1785 Congress had to <u>devise</u> a system for land sales and settlement. Under the Land Ordinance of 1785, surveyors were to divide public lands into townships, 6 miles on each side. This would result in a grid of squares. Within each township there would also be a grid, 1 mile on each side. These 36 sections would be sold for no less than $1 an acre.

Identify Propositions
What issues concerned the framers when they were drafting the Articles of Confederation? What did they propose in response?

Vocabulary Builder
<u>devise</u> (dee vīz) **v.** to think up an idea for something and figure out how it will work

---

Differentiated Instruction

L1 Less Proficient Readers   **L1 English Language Learners**   **L1 Special Needs**

Reading and Vocabulary Suggest to students that they use a ruler to help them keep their place as they read, line by line, down the page. Have students mark unfamiliar words or phrases (such as *surveyors*) with a sticky note, and periodically help them understand what they marked. Have students make a list of these words or phrases, along with their meanings, on the board.

Within each township, one section was set aside to support schools. This reflected the belief of the nation's leaders that democracy depended on education. Thomas Jefferson later wrote:

> **If a nation expects to be ignorant and free, in a state of civilization, it expects what never was and never will be.**
> —Thomas Jefferson, letter to Charles Yancey, 1816

Northwest Ordinance of 1787 Investors were eager to buy land in the Northwest Territory, north of the Ohio River. They pressed Congress to determine how this area would be governed. In response, Congress passed the Northwest Ordinance of 1787. It guaranteed basic rights for settlers and banned slavery there.

The Northwest Ordinance set a three-step process for admitting new states. When a territory was just starting to be settled, Congress would appoint a governor, a secretary, and three judges. Once the territory had 5,000 free adult male settlers, it could elect a legislature. When the free population reached 60,000, the territory could ask to become a state. In time, five states—Ohio, Indiana, Illinois, Michigan, and Wisconsin—were carved out of the Northwest Territory. (For more on the settling of the Northwest Territory, see the Geography and History feature.)

Checkpoint How did the two ordinances turn national land into private holdings?

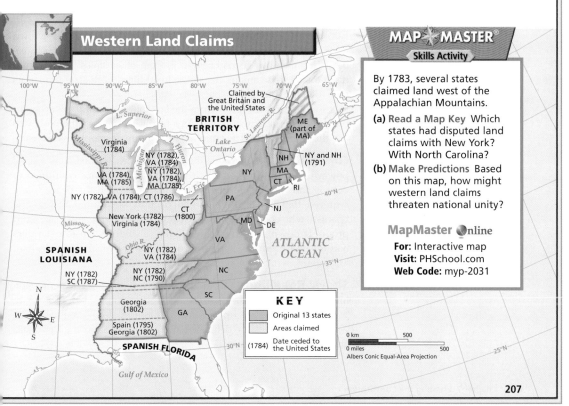

Western Land Claims

MAP MASTER
Skills Activity

By 1783, several states claimed land west of the Appalachian Mountains.

(a) Read a Map Key Which states had disputed land claims with New York? With North Carolina?

(b) Make Predictions Based on this map, how might western land claims threaten national unity?

MapMaster Online
For: Interactive map
Visit: PHSchool.com
Web Code: myp-2031

KEY
- Original 13 states
- Areas claimed
- (1784) Date ceded to the United States

207

Instruction L2

- Have students read Settling the Western Lands. Remind them to look for details that support the Section Focus Question.

- Before discussion begins, display transparency: Northwest Territory, 1787. Call on students to answer the questions.

Color Transparencies, Northwest Territory, 1787

- Ask: **What values did the Land Ordinance of 1785 and the Northwest Ordinance express?** (*a belief in the importance of education and the importance of settlement and expansion*)

- Tell students that, in addition to public township schools, there were several types of schools available in early America. Church schools tutored students in religious education. Dame schools, run for and by women, were designed to give girls a primary education. Home schools were prevalent in rural areas, where parents taught the basic 3 Rs as best they could. Wealthy families often sent their sons to boarding schools and hired private tutors for their daughters.

- Have students read Jefferson's quote. Ask: **Why was education so valued in America?** (*Possible answer: A democracy relies on educated citizens to participate in government.*)

Independent Practice

Have students continue filling in the study guide for this section.

Monitor Progress

As students fill in the Notetaking Study Guide, make sure that they understand how Americans began to settle west of the original 13 states from 1785 to 1787. Provide assistance as needed.

Answers

MAP MASTER Skills Activity **(a)** NH, VA, MA, CT, NC, SC; NY **(b)** states might fight wars over disputed lands

Checkpoint They divided public land into townships that could be purchased by private investors. Once a specified number of people resided in the purchased territory, it could apply to become a state.

History Background

Albany Plan of Union The Articles of Confederation were not the first attempt at creating a unified government. In the years leading up to the French and Indian War, colonial leaders felt the need to unite the colonies. In 1754, colonial representatives (as well as members of the Iroquois Nations) met in Albany, New York, to forge an agreement. Benjamin Franklin was the main author of the plan, called the Albany Plan of Union. However, the British did not support the plan, and the colonies feared the control of a central government, so the plan never went into effect. However, the plan held the seeds of many of the ideas that ended up in the Articles and, later, in the Constitution.

Growing Problems

p. 208

Instruction

L2

- Have students read Growing Problems. Remind them to look for information that answers the reading Checkpoint question.

- Ask: **What was the major problem with the Articles of Confederation?** (*It did not give the government enough power.*) Discuss how this affected the nation. (*The government could not regulate trade, so trade declined; could not raise taxes, so had little money; could not stand up to foreign nations; could not control popular unrest.*)

- Have students complete the primary source worksheet James Bowdoin's Account of Shays' Rebellion. Then, ask students to describe the circumstances and events of the passage in the worksheet.

    All in One Teaching Resources, Unit 2, James Bowdoin's Account of Shays' Rebellion, p. 75

- Ask: **How did Congress react to Shays' Rebellion?** (*Congress sent delegates to a convention to revise the Articles of Confederation.*)

Independent Practice

Have students complete the study guide for this section.

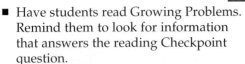 **Interactive Reading and Notetaking Study Guide,** Chapter 7, Section 1 (Adapted Version also available.)

Monitor Progress

As students complete the Notetaking Study Guide, circulate to make sure they understand the problems with the Articles of Confederation. Provide assistance as needed.

Have students fill in the last column of the Reading Readiness Guide. Ask them to evaluate whether what they learned was what they had expected to learn.

All in One Teaching Resources, Unit 2, Reading Readiness Guide, p. 72

Answer

Analyze Cause and Effect Declining prices made some farmers in Massachusetts unable to pay their taxes, so the state government was seizing their farms. Farmers became angry and some rebelled.

Shays' Rebellion
Abigail Adams called the leaders of Shays' Rebellion "ignorant, restless desperadoes without conscience or principles." However, many felt that the Massachusetts farmers had good reason for their anger. Here, farmers attack the Massachusetts statehouse.
Critical Thinking: *Analyze Cause and Effect*
What was the main cause of Shays' Rebellion?

Growing Problems

Under the Articles of Confederation, the United States had many successes. It waged a successful war for independence, negotiated a peace treaty with Britain, and set up rules for settling new territories. But the United States faced growing problems during the 1780s. Many Americans concluded that the Articles did not give the government enough power to solve these problems.

Economic Problems Under the Articles, each state set its own trade policy. Each state tried to help its own farmers and manufacturers by setting taxes on goods brought in from other states. This practice discouraged trade among the states. In addition, each state printed its own money, making trade between states harder.

Another problem grew from the fact that the central government did not have the power to tax. As a result, there was little money to run the government. The situation grew more desperate every year.

Foreign Affairs Because the United States seemed to be weak, powerful nations viewed it with scorn. British troops continued to occupy forts in the Northwest Territory, although the peace treaty required that the forts be turned over to the United States. The Spanish, who controlled New Orleans, refused to let Americans ship products down the Mississippi River. Therefore, western farmers had to send products along the rugged trails over the Appalachian Mountains, which was far more costly.

Shays' Rebellion In the mid-1780s, a severe economic depression hit the United States. An **economic depression** is a period when business activity slows, prices and wages drop, and unemployment rises. As the depression deepened, there was widespread despair and anger.

Differentiated Instruction

L3 Advanced Readers

Explaining Shays' View Have students do additional research using history books or encyclopedias to find out more about Daniel Shays and the rebellion he led. Then, have students use what they learned to write a letter from Daniel Shays to the

L3 Gifted and Talented

governor of Massachusetts explaining why the revolt occurred and what Shays thinks the government should do to solve the problem. Have students read their letters aloud to the class.

The depression hit farmers in Massachusetts especially hard. As crop prices declined, many were unable to pay their taxes. The state government then began seizing some farms and selling them in order to get the back taxes. Angry farmers demanded that the legislature stop the farm sales. They also demanded that the state issue more paper money to make it easier to get loans. Still, the legislators took no action.

In August 1786, a former Revolutionary War captain named Daniel Shays led an uprising of about 1,000 Massachusetts farmers. When the farmers tried to seize arms from a state warehouse, the state called out the militia. Shays and other leaders were arrested.

Although Shays' Rebellion fizzled, it had frightened some leading Americans. They believed that a stronger central government would protect against popular unrest. In response, Congress asked the states to send delegates to a convention in Philadelphia in 1787. Their task was to revise the Articles of Confederation.

✓ **Checkpoint** What did Shays' Rebellion demonstrate about the strength of the national government under the Articles of Confederation?

⭐ **Looking Back and Ahead** After 10 years of independence, some leading Americans had come to the conclusion that the Articles of Confederation needed improvement. The Philadelphia convention was called to revise the Articles. But were the Articles of Confederation worth saving? Or was an entirely new framework required? This decision would be one of the first issues that the delegates at the Philadelphia convention would confront.

Section 1 | Check Your Progress

Progress Monitoring Online
For: Self-test with instant help
Visit: PHSchool.com
Web Code: mya-2031

Comprehension and Critical Thinking

1. (a) **Recall** Why did the Continental Congress make the federal government weak when it drew up the Articles of Confederation?
   (b) **Explain Problems** Why did foreign powers treat the U.S. government under the Articles of Confederation with scorn?

2. (a) **Recall** Why was a section of public land set aside to support public schools under the Land Ordinance of 1785?
   (b) **Analyze Cause and Effect** How does education contribute to a successful democracy?

Reading Skill

3. **Identify Propositions** Reread the text following the heading "Land Ordinance of 1785." What belief did the nation's leaders have about education? What did they propose to further this belief?

Key Terms
Fill in the blanks with the correct key terms.

4. After the break with Britain, each of the states wrote a new _____, a framework for the state government.

5. The _____ is the person in a government responsible for carrying out the laws.

6. In the 1780s, when business slowed and unemployment rose, the nation entered a period of _____.

Writing

7. Identify two problems caused by the creation of a weak national government under the Articles of Confederation. Write a sentence about each problem, explaining why it was important that it be solved.

Assess Progress L2

Have students complete Check Your Progress. Administer the Section Quiz.

All in One Teaching Resources, Unit 2, Section Quiz, p. 81

To further evaluate student progress, use the Progress Monitoring Transparency.

Progress Monitoring Transparencies, Chapter 7, Section 1

Reteach L1

If students need more instruction, have them read this section in the Interactive Reading and Notetaking Study Guide and complete the accompanying questions.

📖 **Interactive Reading and Notetaking Study Guide,** Chapter 7, Section 1 (Adapted Version also available.)

Extend L3

Have students use the Internet to research settlement in the Northwest Territory. Tell students to use the information that they find to create a timeline of events that occurred in the Northwest Territory from 1787 to 1814.

Extend Online
For: Help in starting the Extend activity
Visit: PHSchool.com
Web Code: mye-0216

Progress Monitoring Online

Students may check their comprehension of this section by completing the Progress Monitoring Online graphic organizer and self-quiz.

Section 1 Check Your Progress

1. (a) The members did not want to set up a powerful central government that would cause a repeat of events that caused the American Revolution.
   (b) Foreign powers did not respect the weak central government.

2. (a) The nation's leaders believed that democracy depended on education.
   (b) Answers will vary. Possible answer: When people are educated, they are better equipped to participate in government and to understand what the government is doing.

3. They believed that democracy and education were closely linked, and proposed that every town set aside land for a public school.

4. constitution

5. executive

6. economic depression

7. Possible answer: Each state printed its own money and set its own trade policy. This made trade between states very difficult. The central government did not have the power to tax, so it had little money to run the government.

Answer

✓ **Checkpoint** The Articles of Confederation provided for a government that was too weak to keep popular unrest in check.

Settling the Northwest Territory

Build Background Knowledge L2

Discuss with students the difference between a territory and a state. Students have read that a territory is land that belongs to the United States but is not yet a state. In 1785, the government began selling the land in the Northwest Territory to private individuals. Ask: **How might the sale of land have benefited the federal government?** (*Possible answer: It would have increased the government's revenue.*)

Instruction L2

■ Have students read the text and examine the visuals in this section. Discuss the features of the grid pattern laid out under the Land Ordinance of 1785 and how it is still visible today.

■ Ask: **Why did people begin to settle in the Northwest Territory?** (*to establish a new life for themselves and their families*)

■ Use the *Northwest Territory* transparency. Ask: **Why do you think the territory was divided into grids?** (*Possible answer: It would have been easier to keep track of land sales and settlement.*)

Color Transparencies, Northwest Territory

■ Ask: **What was the impact of the Northwest Ordinance on slavery? on education?** (*It banned the spread of slavery in the Northwest Territory. It encouraged public education by setting aside land for schools.*)

■ Ask students to think about the benefits that a territory might gain from becoming a state. (*Students should note that a state may have had more influence in the government than a territory.*)

Settling the Northwest Territory

By the end of the American Revolution, the United States had acquired a vast territory west of the Appalachian Mountains. Congress passed two land ordinances, one in 1785 and another in 1787. The ordinances served as a framework for moving settlers into—and forming states out of—this Northwest Territory. The states of Ohio, Indiana, Illinois, Michigan, Wisconsin, and part of Minnesota were eventually carved out of the expanse.

■ NORTHWEST TERRITORY WITH PRESENT-DAY STATE BOUNDARIES

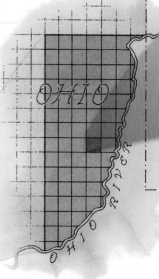

▲ **A New Organization**
The Land Ordinance of 1785 established a system for settling the Northwest Territory. Surveyors laid out a grid of lines spaced 6 miles apart. These lines marked off townships. Each township was divided into 36 sections, and these 1-mile square sections could be divided into smaller units for sale to farmers.

Differentiated Instruction

L1 English Language Learners   **L1** Less Proficient Readers

Reviewing Vocabulary Explain to students that an *ordinance* is a special statement by the government that has the power of law. It is related to another English word, *order,* meaning "to command." Have students write a sentence related to the content of this feature using the word *ordinance.* Write the different sentences on the board.

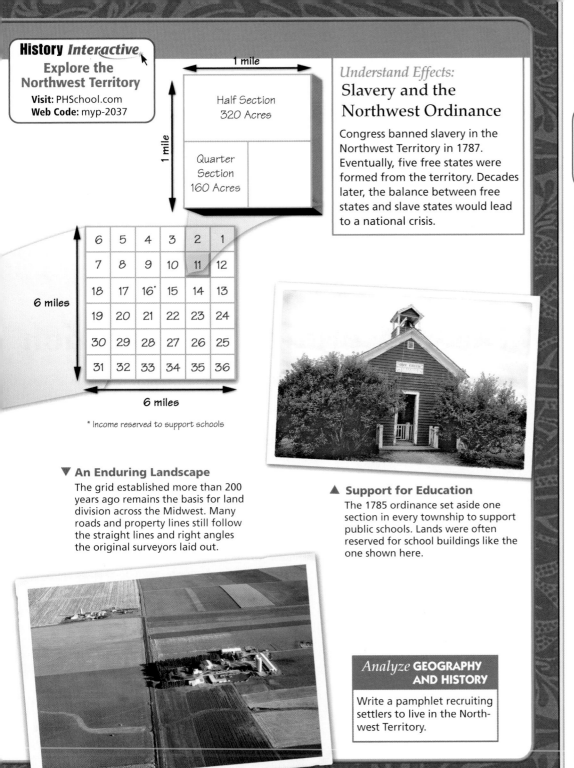

History Interactive
Explore the Northwest Territory
Visit: PHSchool.com
Web Code: myp-2037

1 mile

Half Section
320 Acres

Quarter
Section
160 Acres

1 mile

6	5	4	3	2	1
7	8	9	10	11	12
18	17	16*	15	14	13
19	20	21	22	23	24
30	29	28	27	26	25
31	32	33	34	35	36

6 miles

6 miles

* Income reserved to support schools

Understand Effects:
Slavery and the Northwest Ordinance

Congress banned slavery in the Northwest Territory in 1787. Eventually, five free states were formed from the territory. Decades later, the balance between free states and slave states would lead to a national crisis.

▼ An Enduring Landscape

The grid established more than 200 years ago remains the basis for land division across the Midwest. Many roads and property lines still follow the straight lines and right angles the original surveyors laid out.

▲ Support for Education

The 1785 ordinance set aside one section in every township to support public schools. Lands were often reserved for school buildings like the one shown here.

Analyze GEOGRAPHY AND HISTORY

Write a pamphlet recruiting settlers to live in the Northwest Territory.

Independent Practice

Have students complete the History Interactive activity online.

Extend Online
For: Help in starting the History Interactive Online activity
Visit: PHSchool.com
Web Code: myp-0237

Monitor Progress

Circulate to make sure students are doing the Analyze Geography and History exercise correctly.

Analyze GEOGRAPHY AND HISTORY

Pamphlets should highlight the reasons people would move to new lands.

Writing Rubric Share rubric with students.

Score 1 Material is confusing, poorly organized, few facts given.
Score 2 Material is organized and accurate.
Score 3 Material is accurate and visually appealing.
Score 4 Material is accurate, appealing, and creative.

History Background

The Western Reserve The city of Cleveland, in modern-day Ohio, was founded on land that belonged to Connecticut. Connecticut was one of the states that had had claims in the Northwest Territory, but had ceded most of those lands so that the Articles of Confederation could be adopted. However, it kept a part of its claim, known as the Western Reserve. In 1792, Connecticut granted 500,000 acres of this land to citizens whose property had been destroyed during the American Revolution. In 1795, the state sold the remainder to the Connecticut Land Company, which sent General Moses Cleaveland to the Western Reserve as a surveyor. One of the first permanent settlements in the Reserve, now the city of Cleveland, was named in the General's honor.

Review and Preview

Students have studied the challenges of government under the Articles of Confederation. Now they will learn how the delegates negotiated with each other to create a new Constitution.

Section Focus Question

What role did compromise play in the creation of the United States Constitution?

Before you begin the lesson for the day, write the Section Focus Question on the board. (*Lesson focus: Delegates of the Constitutional Convention compromised to come up with a plan for a strong central government.*)

Prepare to Read

Build Background Knowledge **L2**

In this section, students will learn about the ideas and compromises that went into writing the U.S. Constitution. After they state what they already know about the Constitution, address any misconceptions that students may have about the topic. Remind them to confirm or revise their statements after they read the section. Draw a concept web on the board. In the center oval write "U.S. Constitution." Ask students what they know about the Constitution. Use the Give One, Get One strategy (TE, p. T25) to elicit student ideas, then add relevant responses to the concept web.

Set a Purpose

■ Read each statement in the Reading Readiness Guide aloud. Ask students to mark the statements True or False.

All in One Teaching Resources, Unit 2, Reading Readiness Guide, p. 73

■ Have students discuss the statements in pairs or groups of four, then mark their worksheets again. Use the Numbered Heads strategy (TE, p. T24) to call on students to share their group's perspectives. The students will return to these worksheets later.

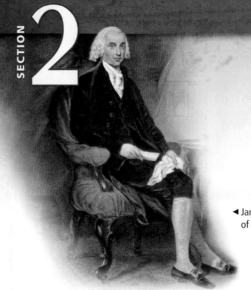

The Public Good

❝To secure the public good and private rights against a danger of such faction, and at the same time to preserve the spirit and the form of popular government, is then the great object to which our inquiries are directed.❞

—excerpt from *The Federalist* No. 10, promoting the Constitution, 1787–1788

◀ James Madison, author of several *Federalist Papers*

The Constitutional Convention

Objectives
• Describe the proceedings of the Constitutional Convention.
• Identify the specifics of the Virginia Plan.
• Explain how the Great Compromise satisfied both large and small states.
• Describe the disputes over slavery and the compromises that were reached.
• Discuss the drafting of the new Constitution.

⟳ Reading Skill

Identify Support for Propositions As you read about the propositions that people from history made to solve their problems and advance their ideas, look for supporting evidence. How did people try to convince those around them to support these propositions? What reasons did they give to explain their views? Identifying supporting evidence helps you understand and respond to propositions.

Key Terms and People

James Madison   James Wilson
judicial branch   compromise
Roger Sherman   Gouverneur Morris

Why It Matters The weaknesses of the Articles of Confederation prompted the states to call a meeting to revise the Articles. The Constitutional Convention in Philadelphia led to an entirely new framework of government.

❓ Section Focus Question: What role did compromise play in the creation of the United States Constitution?

The Constitutional Convention Begins

An air of mystery hung over Philadelphia in the summer of 1787. Every day, the nation's great leaders passed in and out of the statehouse. One Philadelphia resident, Susannah Dillwyn, wrote to her father, "There is now sitting in this city a grand convention, who are to form some new system of government or mend the old one."

Aims of the Convention In fact, members of the convention did not have the authority to "form some new system of government." Congress had called the meeting "for the sole and express purpose of revising the Articles of Confederation." However, many delegates argued that revising the Articles would not be enough.

Early on, the delegates voted to keep their debates secret. Despite the heat, windows remained tightly shut. Guards kept out members of the public. The delegates would be free to speak their minds—even if their discussions took the convention far beyond its original aims.

212 Chapter 7 Creating the Constitution

Differentiated Instruction

L3 Advanced Readers   **L3** Gifted and Talented

Making a Timeline Have students work in pairs to conduct research about the major documents from the beginning of colonial times to 1787 that helped shape the democratic tradition in America. Then have students create a timeline of these documents. Have students include a pertinent excerpt from each document on the timeline.

The Delegates In all, 55 delegates from 12 states took part in the convention. Only Rhode Island did not send any representatives.

Some delegates, such as George Washington and Ben Franklin, had been respected leaders of the Revolution. Washington was quickly voted president of the convention. Most delegates, however, were younger. Alexander Hamilton of New York was only 32. Another influential delegate was 36-year-old James Madison of Virginia. Madison took careful notes on the meetings. Published after his death, Madison's notes became a rich source of historical information.

✓ **Checkpoint** Why did delegates to the Constitutional Convention keep their debates secret?

The Virginia Plan

On the third day of the convention, Edmund Randolph of Virginia proposed a plan for a new, strong central government. James Madison was the principal author of this Virginia Plan. For the next month, debate focused on this proposal.

Three Branches of Government The Virginia Plan called for the central government to have three separate branches. Congress would continue to be the legislative branch. But two additional branches would be created. The executive branch would carry out the laws. The judicial branch would consist of a system of courts to interpret the law.

Many delegates believed that a strong executive was necessary to correct the weaknesses of the Articles of Confederation. But should the executive be one person or a group of people?

Birthplace of the United States
In 1787, delegates met in this room in Philadelphia's statehouse to debate a new plan of government. Today, the building is known as Independence Hall, in honor of another important event that took place there, the signing of the Declaration of Independence. **Critical Thinking:** *Draw Conclusions Why do you think many Americans today visit Independence Hall and other historic places?*

213

Instruction　L2

- **Vocabulary Builder** Before teaching this section, preteach the High-Use Words **contrast** and **emotion** using the strategy on TE, p. T21.

  Key Terms Have students continue to fill in the See It–Remember It chart.

- Read The Constitutional Convention Begins and The Virginia Plan using the Oral Cloze technique (TE, p. T22).

- Ask: **Who attended the Constitutional Convention?** (*55 delegates from 12 states*)

- Ask: **How did the Virginia Plan address the weaknesses of the Articles of Confederation?** (*It proposed three branches of government, including a strong executive.*)

Independent Practice

Have students begin filling in the study guide for this section. Briefly model the type of details to record.

📖 **Interactive Reading and Notetaking Study Guide,** Chapter 7, Section 2 (Adapted Version also available.)

Monitor Progress

As students begin work on the Notetaking Study Guide, circulate and make sure students understand the goals of the Constitutional Convention and the Virginia Plan. Provide assistance as needed.

Vocabulary Builder

Use the information below to teach students this section's high-use words.

High-Use Word	Definition and Sample Sentence
contrast, p. 214	*n.* difference In **contrast** with previous European explorers, Columbus sailed westward across the Atlantic Ocean.
emotion, p. 214	*n.* strong feeling about something or someone The people of Massachusetts reacted with **emotion** when they heard of the Boston Massacre.

Answers

✓**Checkpoint** They wanted to be able to freely speak their minds.

Draw Conclusions Responses will vary, but students should identify U.S. historical sites and demonstrate an understanding of their importance.

The Great Compromise

p. 214

Instruction L2

- Read The Great Compromise aloud with students. Remind students to look for details to answer the Section Focus Question.

- Discuss with students how the New Jersey Plan was different from the Virginia Plan. (*The New Jersey Plan benefited the smaller states.*)

- Ask: **What was the Great Compromise?** (*A blending of the Virginia and New Jersey Plans that set up a two-house legislature. Representation in the House of Representatives would be based on population and each state would have equal representation in the Senate.*)

- Assign The Great Compromise worksheet. Ask: **What features of both plans ended up in the Constitution?** (*Virginia Plan: two-house legislature and representation by population; New Jersey Plan: equal representation in one house*)

  All in One Teaching Resources, Unit 2, The Great Compromise, p. 76

- See the Differentiated Instruction note below. If students have completed The Articles of Confederation and the Constitution, ask **How did the Constitution reflect the decision reached in the Great Compromise?** (*It provided for the two-house legislature established in the Great Compromise.*)

Independent Practice

Have students continue filling in the study guide for this section.

  Interactive Reading and Notetaking Study Guide, Chapter 7, Section 2 (Adapted Version also available.)

Monitor Progress

As students work on the Notetaking Study Guide, circulate to make sure students understand the Great Compromise. Provide assistance as needed.

Answer

✓Checkpoint It called for three branches of government and representation based on state population.

James Wilson

Vocabulary Builder
<u>contrast</u> (KAHN trast) **n.** difference

Vocabulary Builder
<u>emotion</u> (ee MOH shuhn) **n.** strong feeling about something or someone

---

Randolph proposed that Congress appoint three people to serve jointly as chief executive. One person alone, he said, would never be able to win the people's confidence. Others objected. A single executive, they said, could act more quickly when urgent action was required. Eventually, the delegates voted to have one person, called the President, serve as executive.

A Two-House Legislature The Virginia Plan called for a change in the composition of Congress. Rather than a single legislative body, it would consist of two parts—a lower house and an upper house.

Delegates argued long and hard about methods of choosing members of the two houses. Some wanted state legislatures to elect both houses. Roger Sherman of Connecticut said the people "should have as little to do" with the selection process as possible because they can be misled.

On the other hand, James Wilson of Pennsylvania warned against shutting the people out of the process. According to Wilson, election of the legislature by the people was "not only the cornerstone, but the foundation of the fabric."

✓Checkpoint How was the national government organized under the Virginia Plan?

The Great Compromise

One part of the Virginia Plan nearly tore the convention apart. The plan called for representation based on population. The more people a state had, the more seats it would have in each house. Naturally, this idea drew support from big states like Virginia, Pennsylvania, and Massachusetts.

New Jersey Plan The smaller states strongly opposed this idea. They wanted each state to have the same number of votes in Congress, as was the case under the Articles of Confederation.

On June 15, William Paterson of New Jersey introduced a modified plan on behalf of the small states. This New Jersey Plan stood in sharp <u>contrast</u> to the Virginia Plan. It called for a single house of Congress, with equal representation for each state. The plan also expanded the powers of Congress to raise money and regulate commerce.

In the summer heat, delegates argued day after day over the great issues at stake. <u>Emotions</u> ran so high that some feared the convention would fail and the Union would break apart.

Terms of the Compromise Finally, Roger Sherman of Connecticut worked out a compromise that he hoped would satisfy both the large and small states. A compromise is an agreement in which each side gives up part of what it wants. On July 16, 1787, delegates narrowly voted to accept Sherman's proposals, which came to be known as the Great Compromise.

Differentiated Instruction

L1 Less Proficient Readers   **L1 Special Needs**   **L1 English Language Learners**

Reading a Chart Have students complete the worksheet The Articles of Confederation and the Constitution. Help students understand how the Constitution helped unify the nation by explaining that the Constitution combined the ideas of many of the nation's leaders and provided for a strong federal government.

  All in One Teaching Resources, Unit 2, The Articles of Confederation and the Constitution, p. 77

The key to Sherman's plan was a two-house Congress. To please the large states, the lower house, called the House of Representatives, was to be based on population. Bigger states would thus have more votes. Representatives would be chosen by a vote of the people to serve two-year terms. To please the small states, each state would have two seats in the upper house, or Senate. State legislatures would choose senators, who would serve six-year terms.

The Great Compromise was a vital step in creating a new Constitution. Now, small-state delegates were willing to support a strong central government.

✓ Checkpoint **What was the main difference between the Virginia Plan and the New Jersey Plan?**

Debates Over Slavery

Other issues also divided the delegates—none more so than the question of slavery. The issue touched off bitter debates between northerners and southerners.

Three-Fifths Compromise Southern delegates said that enslaved people should be counted in calculating how many representatives a state should have in Congress. Northern delegates said that because enslaved people could not vote, they should not be counted toward a state's representation.

Finally, Congress agreed to a plan called the Three-Fifths Compromise. Each enslaved person would be counted as three fifths of a free person. Thus, 500 enslaved people would count as 300 free people. The Three-Fifths Compromise was a gain for the South, which got more seats in the House. Northern delegates reluctantly agreed in order to keep the South in the Union.

The Three-Fifths Compromise was a blow to African Americans. It helped preserve slavery in the new Constitution by making a distinction between "free persons" and "all other persons." The compromise was finally overturned when slavery was banned in 1865.

Slave Trade Some northern delegates wanted to ban the buying and selling of people anywhere in the country. Southern delegates protested that a ban would ruin the South's economy.

Once again, a compromise was reached. Ships would be allowed to bring enslaved people into the country for a period of 20 years. After 1808, Congress could bar the importation of enslaved people. But the slave trade *within* the United States was not affected.

✓ Checkpoint **What was the Three-Fifths Compromise?**

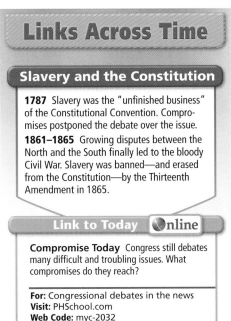

Links Across Time

Slavery and the Constitution

1787 Slavery was the "unfinished business" of the Constitutional Convention. Compromises postponed the debate over the issue.

1861–1865 Growing disputes between the North and the South finally led to the bloody Civil War. Slavery was banned—and erased from the Constitution—by the Thirteenth Amendment in 1865.

Link to Today ● Online

Compromise Today Congress still debates many difficult and troubling issues. What compromises do they reach?

For: Congressional debates in the news
Visit: PHSchool.com
Web Code: myc-2032

Identify Support for Propositions

Roger Sherman proposed a two-house Congress, hoping to satisfy both small and large states. What support did he give to show how this solution would meet the needs of all states?

Debates Over Slavery
p. 215

Instruction [L2]

- With students, read Debates Over Slavery. Have students look for details to answer the Section Focus Question.

- Ask: **What two compromises were made over the issue of slavery?** (*The Three-Fifths Compromise; the importation of enslaved people must end after 20 years but the internal slave trade could continue.*)

Independent Practice

Have students complete the study guide for this section.

📖 **Interactive Reading and Notetaking Study Guide,** Chapter 7, Section 2 (Adapted Version also available.)

Monitor Progress

- As students complete the Notetaking Study Guide, circulate to make sure they understand the importance of the debates over slavery. Provide assistance as needed.

Answers

↻ **Reading Skill** Sherman's solution allowed for representation based on population, which would benefit the large states, and equal representation, which would benefit the small states.

✓ Checkpoint The Virginia Plan called for a two-house legislature with more representation for larger states; the New Jersey Plan called for a one-house legislature with equal representation for all states.

✓ Checkpoint an agreement that for purposes of representation and taxation, each enslaved person would count as three fifths of a person

---

Signing the Constitution

p. 216

A New Constitution

p. 217

Instruction L2

- Have students read Signing the Constitution and A New Constitution. Remind them to look for details that answer the Section Focus Question.

- Have students look at the painting on this page. Ask: **How did the painter show the importance of the signing of the Constitution?** (*Possible answers: He portrays the signers as dignified men in a formal setting. The fact that he shows so many delegates demonstrates that the Constitution is a significant document.*)

- Ask: **Why did the artist paint George Washington standing in front of the delegates?** (*He was the president of the Constitutional Convention.*)

- Ask students who have completed the History Reading Skill worksheet to paraphrase the reasons why Benjamin Franklin thought everyone should sign the Constitution. (*Students' answers should reflect their reading of Franklin's speech.*)

Independent Practice

Have students complete the study guide for this section.

📖 **Interactive Reading and Notetaking Study Guide,** Chapter 7, Section 2 (Adapted Version also available.)

Monitor Progress

- As students complete the Notetaking Study Guide, make sure they understand the importance of the new Constitution. Provide assistance as needed.

- Have students fill in the last column of the Reading Readiness Guide. Probe for what they learned that confirms or invalidates each statement.

All in One Teaching Resources, Unit 2, Reading Readiness Guide, p. 73

Answer

Interpret Paintings Possible answer: Their faces are fully lit and facing forward, or they are standing.

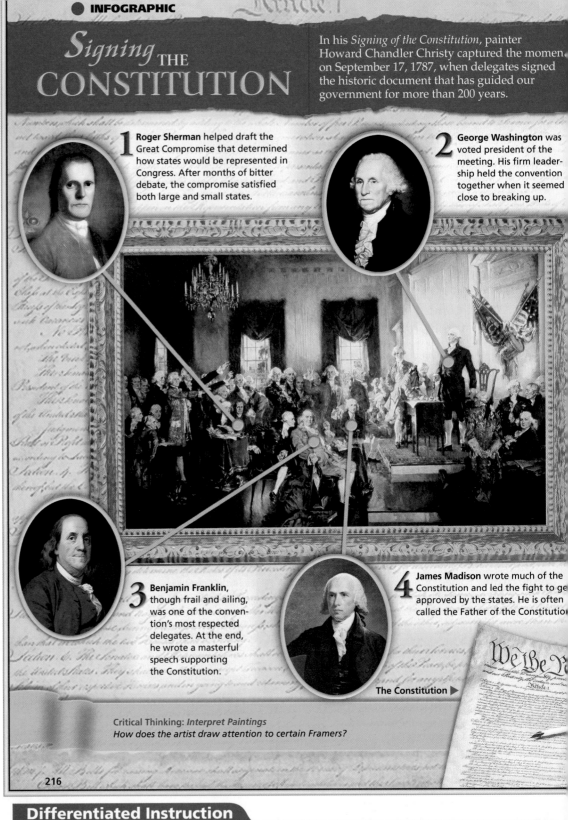

● **INFOGRAPHIC**

Signing THE CONSTITUTION

In his *Signing of the Constitution*, painter Howard Chandler Christy captured the moment on September 17, 1787, when delegates signed the historic document that has guided our government for more than 200 years.

1 **Roger Sherman** helped draft the Great Compromise that determined how states would be represented in Congress. After months of bitter debate, the compromise satisfied both large and small states.

2 **George Washington** was voted president of the meeting. His firm leadership held the convention together when it seemed close to breaking up.

3 **Benjamin Franklin,** though frail and ailing, was one of the convention's most respected delegates. At the end, he wrote a masterful speech supporting the Constitution.

4 **James Madison** wrote much of the Constitution and led the fight to get approved by the states. He is often called the Father of the Constitution.

The Constitution ▶

Critical Thinking: *Interpret Paintings*
How does the artist draw attention to certain Framers?

216

Differentiated Instruction

L1 English Language Learners   **L1** Special Needs

Building Vocabulary Have students make a list of all Key Terms and High-Use Words. Then, have them create flashcards with the word on one side and its definition on the other. Pair students with a partner and have them quiz each other on the definitions of the words using the flashcards.

A New Constitution

After many more weeks of debate, the delegates agreed on all the terms. A so-called Committee of Style was appointed to draw up the final wording of the new Constitution. Gouverneur Morris, a gifted writer, was largely responsible for writing the Preamble, or introduction.

The Preamble highlights a major difference between the Constitution and the Articles of Confederation. The Articles were a pact between separate states. By contrast, the Constitution opens with the words, "We the People of the United States, in order to form a more perfect union, . . . do ordain and establish this Constitution for the United States of America." The Constitution thus claims to take its authority from the people rather than from the states.

The aging Ben Franklin gave some final advice on the day of the signing. Because he was so ill, Franklin remained seated and another delegate read Franklin's speech. Like many other delegates, Franklin had some doubts about parts of the Constitution. Still, he said, "I agree to this Constitution with all its faults," and he urged others to do the same. At last, the delegates stepped forward to place their signatures on the document.

✓Checkpoint What is the significance of the Constitution's first phrase: "We the People of the United States"?

⭐ **Looking Back and Ahead** Once the Constitution had been signed, secrecy ended. Public debates began. These debates would stretch over 10 months. And, as the Constitution's supporters soon learned, the battle for approval would be hard-fought and bitter.

Section 2 | Check Your Progress

Progress Monitoring Online
For: Self-test with instant help
Visit: PHSchool.com
Web Code: mya-2032

Comprehension and Critical Thinking

1. (a) Summarize Summarize the arguments for and against having a single executive.
(b) Explain Problems What problems do you think might arise during a crisis if the executive power in the U.S. government was held by three people?

2. (a) Describe How was representation in Congress to be based, according to the terms of the Great Compromise?
(b) Apply Information Why did the small states decide to support a strong central government after the compromise?

Reading Skill

3. Identify Support for Propositions Reread the text following the heading "Slave Trade." What reason did southerners give to support their position against ending the slave trade?

Key Terms
Fill in the blanks with the correct key terms.
4. The Virginia Plan called for a _____, or system of courts to interpret the law.

5. Under a _____ between northern and southern states, Congress could bar slaves from being imported after 1808.

Writing

6. Choose one of the problems that the delegates at the Constitutional Convention had to solve. List several possible solutions for that problem, and then write a few sentences explaining the solution that the convention eventually chose. What were the advantages and disadvantages of this solution?

Assess Progress L2

Have students complete Check Your Progress. Administer the Section Quiz.

All in One Teaching Resources, Unit 2, Section Quiz, p. 82

To further evaluate student progress, use the Progress Monitoring Transparency.

Progress Monitoring Transparencies, Chapter 7, Section 2

Reteach L1

If students need more instruction, have them read this section in the Interactive Reading and Notetaking Study Guide and complete the accompanying questions.

📖 **Interactive Reading and Notetaking Study Guide,** Chapter 7, Section 2 (Adapted Version also available.)

Extend L3

Have students work in pairs. Ask them to use the Internet to research more information about the Constitutional Convention. Ask students to write questions that a reporter may have asked delegates just before the Constitutional Convention. Students should then play the role of one of the delegates and take turns answering each other's questions.

Extend Online
For: Help with this activity
Visit: PHSchool.com
Web Code: myd-0217

Progress Monitoring Online

Students may check their comprehension of this section by completing the Progress Monitoring Online graphic organizer and self-quiz.

Section 2 Check Your Progress

1. (a) Against—too much power for a single executive; For—a single executive could make decisions more efficiently
(b) Possible response: They might argue about a solution and not solve the crisis.

2. (a) Representation in the House of Representatives would be based on population; in the Senate each state would have equal representation.
(b) Because one house would have equal representation, the small states no longer feared that they would be controlled by the larger states.

3. They said that such a ban would ruin the South's economy.

4. judicial branch

5. compromise

6. Sentences should show an understanding of the problems.

Answer

✓Checkpoint It demonstrates that the government is based on the consent of the people.

Review and Preview

Students have learned about the compromises needed to create the Constitution. Now they will focus on the struggle for ratification and approval.

Section Focus Question

How did those in favor of the Constitution achieve its ratification?

Before you begin the lesson for the day, write the Section Focus Question on the board. (*Lesson focus: They published arguments supporting the Constitution in newspapers; they held conventions to debate the Constitution.*)

Prepare to Read

Build Background Knowledge   `L2`

Tell students that in this section they will read about the struggle for the states' approval of the Constitution. Ask students to preview the headings and visuals in the section and think about what they learned in Section 2. Have students brainstorm for a list of reasons that the states might have supported or opposed the Constitution. Use the Idea Wave technique (TE, p. T24) to elicit responses.

Set a Purpose

- Read each statement in the Reading Readiness Guide aloud. Ask students to mark the statements True or False.

    `All in One` **Teaching Resources, Unit 2,** Reading Readiness Guide, p. 74

- Have students discuss the statements in pairs or groups of four, then mark their worksheets again. Use the Numbered Heads strategy (TE, p. T24) to call on students to share their group's perspectives.

A Bill of Rights

❝A bill of rights is what the people are entitled to against every government on earth, general or particular; and what no just government should refuse or rest on inference.❞

—Thomas Jefferson, letter to James Madison, 1787

◀ The debate over the Constitution led to the Bill of Rights.

Debating the Constitution

Objectives

- Compare the positions of the Federalists and the Antifederalists.
- Discuss the debate over ratification.
- Describe the Bill of Rights and how it protects the people.

🕮 Reading Skill

Evaluate Support for Propositions When a person argues a proposition using reasons and support, listeners or readers must evaluate that support—that is, whether the evidence given really supports the proposition. As you read, ask yourself if the propositions are well supported and whether or not they convince you.

Key Terms and People

ratify
Alexander Hamilton
John Jay
George Mason

Why It Matters Americans debated whether or not to ratify, or approve, the Constitution. Many states insisted that a bill of rights be added. In the end, the Constitution was ratified and it included the Bill of Rights. The Constitution has successfully served as our framework of government for more than 200 years.

❓ Section Focus Question: How did those in favor of the Constitution achieve its ratification?

Federalists Versus Antifederalists

The convention had set a process for states to ratify, or approve, the Constitution. Each state was to hold a convention. The Constitution would go into effect once it was ratified by nine states.

The Federalist Position Supporters of the new Constitution called themselves Federalists because they favored a strong federal, or national, government. James Madison, Alexander Hamilton, and John Jay published the *Federalist Papers*, a series of 85 newspaper essays in support of the Constitution.

At the heart of the Federalist position was the need for a stronger central government. For the Union to last, they argued, the national government had to have powers denied to it under the Articles of Confederation, including the power to enforce laws. Hamilton wrote:

❝Government implies the power of making laws. It is essential to the idea of a law, that it be attended with . . . a penalty or punishment for disobedience. If there be no penalty . . . the resolutions or commands which pretend to be laws will, in fact, amount to nothing more than advice.❞

—Alexander Hamilton, *The Federalist* No. 15

218 Chapter 7 Creating the Constitution

Differentiated Instruction

`L1` **English Language Learners**   `L1` **Less Proficient Readers**   `L1` **Special Needs**

Understanding Word Parts Explain to students that *anti-* is a prefix, or word part that is added to the front of a word to change its meaning. Tell them that *anti-* means "against" or "opposite." When it is added to a word, such as *Federalist*, it makes a new word that means the opposite of the original. Explain that *-ist* is a

suffix, or word part added to the end of a word that creates a new word describing a person who does or believes something. So a Federal*ist* is someone who believes in the federal government. Have students search for other words with *anti-*, such as *antihero*, and with *-ist*, such as *motorist*. Ask them to share their findings with the class.

The Antifederalist Position Opponents of ratification were called Antifederalists. Leading Antifederalists, such as George Mason and Patrick Henry of Virginia, agreed that the Articles of Confederation were not strong enough. However, they felt the Constitutional Convention had gone too far.

Antifederalists were not all united in their reasons for opposing the Constitution. Some of their most frequent arguments included:

- **Weakening the States** Antifederalists argued that the Constitution dangerously weakened the state governments. They feared that a too-strong central government, like that of England, would wipe out state power and individual freedom. "There never was a government over a very extensive country without destroying the liberties of the people," warned Mason.

- **No Bill of Rights** Some Antifederalists pointed out that the proposed Constitution offered no protections for basic freedoms. Unlike the constitutions of many states, it had no bill of rights.

- **President or King?** Another objection was that the Constitution provided for a President who could be reelected again and again. Said Henry, "Your President may easily become a king."

 Checkpoint Why did Antifederalists believe that the Constitutional Convention had gone too far?

The Ratification Debate

The debate between Federalists and Antifederalists heated up as states held their ratification conventions. Without the approval of nine states, the Constitution would not go into effect.

Delaware acted first. Its convention unanimously approved the Constitution on December 7, 1787. Pennsylvania, New Jersey, Georgia, and Connecticut quickly followed.

Antifederalists hoped to win in Massachusetts. Opposition to the Constitution was strong in the rural areas from which Shays' Rebellion had drawn its strength. Only a major campaign by Constitution supporters won ratification by the state.

All eyes moved to Virginia. By then, Maryland and South Carolina had ratified, which made a total of eight state ratifications. Only one more was needed. But if large and powerful Virginia rejected the pact, New York and other remaining states might do so, too.

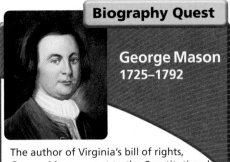

Biography Quest

George Mason
1725–1792

The author of Virginia's bill of rights, George Mason, went to the Constitutional Convention with hopes of forming "a wise and just government." But Mason quickly became dissatisfied. Though a slave owner himself, he favored an end to slavery and disliked the Three-Fifths Compromise. Mason was even more upset when the convention voted against his proposal to add a bill of rights. In the end, he refused to sign his name to the new Constitution.

Biography Quest **Online**

Why is Mason called "the father of the Bill of Rights"?

For: The answer to the question about Mason
Visit: PHSchool.com
Web Code: myd-2033

Evaluate Support for Propositions
How do Antifederalists support the proposition that the national government needed fewer powers?

Vocabulary Builder

Use the information below to teach students this section's high-use words.

High-Use Word	Definition and Sample Sentence
flexible, p. 221	*adj.* able to change The Puritans of Massachusetts found it difficult to be **flexible** on religious matters.
amendment, p. 221	*n.* addition or alteration to a document The Twenty-sixth **Amendment** allows citizens who are 18 years old to vote in state and national elections.

Teach

Federalists Versus Antifederalists
p. 218

Instruction

- **Vocabulary Builder** Before teaching this section, preteach the High-Use Words **flexible** and **amendment** using the strategy on TE p. T21.

  Key Terms Have students complete the See It–Remember It chart.

- Read Federalists Versus Antifederalists using the Paragraph Shrinking strategy (TE, p. 23).

- With students, compare and contrast the arguments of the Federalists and Antifederalists. Ask: **What was the basic position of each side?** (*Federalists supported the Constitution and a strong central government. Most Antifederalists were against the Constitution and feared the increased power of the central government.*)

- Ask: **Which side do you think made the strongest arguments, and why?** (*Answers will vary, but students should demonstrate an understanding of the two positions.*)

- Display the transparency The Federalist Papers. Discuss both Federalist and Antifederalist arguments.

Color Transparencies, The Federalist Papers

Independent Practice
Have students begin filling in the study guide for this section.

Monitor Progress

As students begin to fill in the Notetaking Study Guide, make sure they understand the Federalist and Antifederalist positions toward the Constitution. Provide assistance as needed.

Answers

Biography Quest George Mason strongly advocated the passage of the U.S. Bill of Rights, which was modeled largely on his Virginia Bill of Rights.

Checkpoint They argued that the meeting was called only to revise the Articles of Confederation.

Reading Skill Antifederalists feared a strong central government would limit state power and individual freedom.

The Ratification Debate
p. 219

The Bill of Rights
p. 220

Instruction L2

- With students, read The Ratification Debate and The Bill of Rights. Remind them to look for details that answer the Section Focus Question.

- Ask: **What was significant about the fact that all 13 states ratified the Constitution?** (*It meant that the union of the states would be preserved.*)

- Have students complete the worksheet James Madison's Speech Proposing the Bill of Rights. Ask: **Why was the Bill of Rights added to the Constitution?** (*to protect people against abuse by the federal government*)

All in One Teaching Resources, Unit 2, James Madison's Speech Proposing the Bill of Rights, p. 78

Independent Practice
Have students complete their work on the study guide for this section.

Monitor Progress

As students complete the Notetaking Study Guide, make sure they understand the debates over ratification and the objectives of the Bill of Rights. Provide assistance as needed.

Have students fill in the last column of the Reading Readiness Guide. Probe for what they learned that confirms or invalidates each statement.

Ask students to go back to their Word Knowledge Rating Form. Rerate their word knowledge and complete the last column with a definition or example.

All in One Teaching Resources, Unit 2, Reading Readiness Guide, p. 74; Word Knowledge Rating Form, p. 71

Answers
Reading Political Cartoons (a) the states; Delaware; New York, North Carolina, Rhode Island (b) It favored the Federalists because it supported ratification.

Checkpoint Virginia was a large and influential state. If it did not ratify the Constitution, other states might not, either, and the union could break apart.

220 Chapter 7

United We Stand . . .

United we stand—Divided we fall!

A hand reaches from the heavens to put Virginia in place.

New Hampshire was the ninth state to ratify, allowing the Constitution to go into effect.

Reading Political Cartoons
Skills Activity

The cartoon above appeared in an American newspaper in 1788—at a time when the states were debating whether or not to ratify the Constitution.

(a) **Identify Main Ideas** What do the pillars represent? Which pillar is first? What pillars are missing?

(b) **Detect Points of View** Do you think the cartoonist favored the Federalists or the Antifederalists?

Patrick Henry led the attack on the Constitution in Virginia. "There will be no checks, no real balances, in this government," he said. James Madison supported the Constitution and warned of the possible breakup of the Union. In the end, the Federalist view narrowly won out. Virginia's convention approved the Constitution by a vote of 89 to 79.

Meanwhile, in June 1788—while Virginia was still debating—New Hampshire became the ninth state to ratify. The Constitution could now go into effect. In time, New York and North Carolina followed. Finally, in May 1790, Rhode Island became the last of the original 13 states to ratify the Constitution.

On July 4, 1788, Philadelphia celebrated the ratification of the Constitution. A huge parade snaked along Market Street, led by soldiers who had served in the Revolution. Benjamin Rush, a Philadelphia doctor and strong supporter of the Constitution, wrote to a friend, "Tis done. We have become a nation."

Checkpoint Why was the vote in Virginia so important?

The Bill of Rights

Once the ninth state had ratified the Constitution, Congress took steps to prepare for a new government. George Washington was elected the first President, with John Adams as Vice President.

During the debate on the Constitution, many of the states had insisted that a bill of rights be added. This became one of the first tasks of the new Congress that met in March 1789.

220 Chapter 7 Creating the Constitution

Differentiated Instruction

L3 Gifted and Talented

Exploring Primary Sources Have students read George Mason's essay "Objections to the Constitution" from the Exploring Primary Sources in U.S. History CD-ROM. Using what they have learned in this section and from any necessary additional research—for example, they may

L3 Advanced Readers

read excerpts from the Federalist Papers—have students write a Federalist reply to Mason's essay that addresses each one of his points.

Primary Sources in U.S. History CD-ROM, Objections to the Constitution

The Framers had provided a way to amend the Constitution. They wanted to make the Constitution <u>flexible</u> enough to change. But they did not want changes made lightly. So, they made the process fairly difficult. (You will read more about the amendment process in the Citizenship Handbook.)

In 1789, the first Congress passed a series of <u>amendments</u>. By December 1791, three fourths of the states had ratified 10 amendments. These amendments are known as the Bill of Rights. The Bill of Rights aims to protect people against abuses by the federal government. Many of them came out of the colonists' struggle with Britain.

The First Amendment guarantees freedom of religion, speech, and the press. The Second Amendment deals with the right to bear arms. The Third Amendment bars Congress from forcing citizens to keep troops in their homes, as Britain had done.

The Fourth Amendment protects citizens from unreasonable searches of their homes or seizure of their property. Amendments Five through Eight protect citizens who are accused of crimes and are brought to trial. The last two amendments limit the powers of the federal government to those that are granted in the Constitution.

☑ **Checkpoint** Why did Congress move quickly to pass the Bill of Rights?

⭐ **Looking Back and Ahead** The delegates to the Constitutional Convention are often called the Framers because they framed, or shaped, our form of government. The Constitution they wrote established a republic that has thrived for more than 200 years. On the following pages, you will read the actual text of the Constitution and study its meaning in more detail.

Vocabulary Builder
<u>flexible</u> (FLEHKS ah bahl) *adj.* able to change

<u>amendment</u> (ah MEHND mehnt) *n.* addition or alteration to a document

Section 3 | Check Your Progress

Progress Monitoring Online
For: Self-test with instant help
Visit: PHSchool.com
Web Code: mya-2033

Comprehension and Critical Thinking

1. (a) Summarize In complete sentences, list three arguments of the Antifederalists against the Constitution.
(b) Draw Conclusions Why might the Antifederalists think the Constitution would reduce the power of the states?

2. (a) Recall Compare the attitudes of Patrick Henry and James Madison toward ratification.
(b) Apply Information How did the passage of the Bill of Rights help deal with Patrick Henry's concerns?

Reading Skill

3. Evaluate Support for Propositions Patrick Henry led the attack on the Constitution. "There will be no checks, no real balances, in this government," he said. Evaluate his supporting argument. Do you think it is an effective argument?

Key Terms

Answer the following question in a complete sentence that shows your understanding of the key term.
4. Why was it important that Virginia ratify the Constitution?

Writing

5. Write a paragraph discussing the Bill of Rights as the solution to a problem faced by the early U.S. government after the Constitution was ratified. Complete the following topic sentence, and then write four more sentences developing this idea with specific information. **Topic sentence:** In 1789, the first Congress passed 10 amendments to the Constitution, known as the Bill of Rights, in order to protect _____.

Assess Progress L2

Have students complete the section assessment. Administer the Section Quiz.

All in One Teaching Resources, Unit 2, Section Quiz, p. 83

To further evaluate student progress, use the Progress Monitoring Transparency.

Progress Monitoring Transparencies, Chapter 7, Section 3

Reteach L1

If students need more instruction, have them read this section in the Interactive Reading and Notetaking Study Guide and complete the accompanying questions.

Interactive Reading and Notetaking Study Guide, Chapter 7, Section 3 (Adapted Version also available.)

Extend L3

Have students use the Internet to find out the rights guaranteed under the first 10 amendments to the Constitution. Have them create a chart that summarizes their findings.

Extend Online
For: Help with this activity
Visit: ph.infoplease.com
Web Code: mye-0219

Progress Monitoring Online

Students may check their comprehension of this section by completing the Progress Monitoring Online graphic organizer and self-quiz.

Section 3 Check Your Progress

1. (a) Sentences should identify three of the following: the Convention exceeded its powers; the Constitution weakened state governments; it did not protect basic freedoms; it gave the President too much power; it reduced the political power of the public.
(b) Possible answer: The Constitution did not protect individual rights.

2. (a) Henry was against the Constitution and felt it would lead to tyranny; Madison supported it and thought the nation needed a strong government.
(b) Individual rights were protected.

3. Answers will vary. Many students will disagree, believing that the division of powers provides adequate checks and balances.

4. It was important that Virginia approve the Constitution because it was large and powerful.

5. individuals from government abuses; paragraphs will vary.

Answer

☑ **Checkpoint** to protect basic liberties

Objective

Analyzing cause and effect can help students understand the relationship between historical events and issues. Identifying the short-term and long-term impact of causes and effects can also help students evaluate the significance of these events and issues.

Analyze Cause and Effect

Instruction L2

1. Write the steps to analyze cause and effect on the board and ask the class to read the steps aloud.

2. Have students look at the chart. Ask them how the chart shows cause and effect. (*Causes are inside an arrow, which points to effects.*)

3. Practice the skill by following the steps on p. 222 as a class. Model each step to explain the chart. (*1.The Bill of Rights was added to the Constitution in 1791.* **2.** *(a) Accept any of the causes in the "Causes" box. (b) Possible answers: This was a short-term cause because it happened shortly before the Bill of Rights was added to the Constitution. This was a long-term cause because it began long before the Bill of Rights was added to the Constitution.* **3.** *(a) Accept either of the effects listed in the "Effects" box. (b) Possible answers: This is a short-term effect because it began to affect people as soon as the Bill of Rights was passed. This is a long-term effect because it has continued to be important for hundreds of years.* **4.** *Answers will vary, but should show students' understanding that specific issues and concerns during the colonial period led to later interest in protecting the rights of individuals.*)

Monitor Progress

Ask students to do the Apply the Skill activity. Then assign the Skills for Life Worksheet. As students complete the worksheet, circulate to make sure individuals are applying the skill steps effectively. Provide assistance as needed.

All in One Teaching Resources, Unit 2, Skills for Life Worksheet, p. 79

Major historical events have both causes and effects. Sometimes causes and effects are short term. They take place shortly before or after the major event. Causes and effects can also be long term. They build up over a period of time.

CAUSES

- King George III had limited colonists' liberty.
- America had fought a revolution to protect freedoms.
- Antifederalists wanted a specific list of rights that protected citizens' basic liberties.
- Some states refused to ratify the Constitution unless a bill of rights was added later.

BILL OF RIGHTS ADDED TO CONSTITUTION IN 1791

EFFECTS

- First 10 amendments identify and guarantee basic rights and freedoms.
- The federal government cannot take away rights spelled out in the Bill of Rights.

Learn the Skill

Use these steps to analyze cause-and-effect relationships.

1. **Read labels.** The labels on the chart tell which event is the focus of study and which statements are the causes and which are the effects.

2. **Identify causes.** Causal statements give reasons why an event occurred. Major events have both long- and short-term causes.

3. **Identify effects.** Effect statements tell what happened because of the events. Major events have both long- and short-term effects.

4. **Analyze cause-and-effect relationships.** Think about why certain causes led to the event and why the event in turn had the results it did.

Practice the Skill

Answer the following questions about cause and effect based on the chart above.

1. **Read labels.** To what event do the causes lead?

2. **Identify causes.** (a) What was one cause of the Bill of Rights? (b) Was this a long- or short-term cause? Explain.

3. **Identify effects.** (a) What was one effect of the Bill of Rights? (b) Was this a long- or short-term effect? Explain.

4. **Analyze cause-and-effect relationships.** How did colonial history lead to a concern about protecting citizens' rights?

Apply the Skill

See the Review and Assessment at the end of this chapter.

Reteach L1

If students need more instruction, use the Social Studies Skills Tutor to reteach this skill.

Social Studies Skills Tutor CD-ROM, Identifying Cause and Effect

Quick Study Guide

How did the United States Constitution overcome the weaknesses of the Articles of Confederation and provide for the organization of the new government?

Section 1
Governing a New Nation

- Many states added a bill of rights to their constitutions to protect individual freedoms.
- The Northwest Ordinance established a three-stage process for transforming a territory into a state.
- An increasing number of Americans came to believe that a stronger federal government was needed to deal with the country's pressing problems.

Section 2
The Constitutional Convention

- The Virginia Plan, calling for a strong central government with three branches, formed the basis of the U.S. Constitution.
- The Great Compromise set up a Congress with two houses, which pleased both the large and small states.

- As part of the compromise that won support for the Constitution, northern and southern delegates agreed that each enslaved person would count as three fifths of a free person.

Section 3
Debating the Constitution

- Federalists believed that three competing branches of government would keep any one part of the federal government from becoming too strong.
- Antifederalists were concerned that a strong federal government threatened states' rights and individual freedoms.
- A bill of rights was added to the Constitution to protect the people against abuses by the federal government.

? Exploring the Essential Question

Use the online study guide to explore the essential question.

Section 1
What were the major successes and failures of the government under the Articles of Confederation?

Chapter 7 Essential Question
How did the United States Constitution overcome the weaknesses of the Articles of Confederation and provide for the organization of the new government?

Section 2
What role did compromise play in the creation of the United States Constitution?

Section 3
How did those in favor of the Constitution achieve its ratification?

Chapter 7

Essential Question

Remind students of the Chapter Essential Question: **How did the United States Constitution overcome the weaknesses of the Articles of Confederation and provide for the organization of the new government?** Have them review the bulleted statements and the Visual Preview at the beginning of the chapter to help them answer this question.

To bolster students' retention, at this time they should complete the Study Guide in print or online. Remind students that they should also continue notetaking for the Unit and Chapter Essential Questions.

📖 **Interactive Reading and Notetaking Study Guide,** Chapter 7 (Adapted Version also available.)

 **Study Guide** *Online,* Chapter 7

Chapter Challenge

To wrap up this chapter, students should apply the knowledge they have gained to answer this question. **What might have happened if only nine states had ratified the Constitution?** (*Answers will vary, but should demonstrate an understanding of the threat to the ratification process and the consequences if some states had either set up as separate nations or continued as they had been under the Articles of Confederation.*)

Assessment at a Glance

Formal Assessment
- **Chapter Tests A/B (L1/L2)**
- **AYP Monitoring Assessment**
- **Test Prep Workbook With Document-Based Assessment**
- **Test-Taking Strategies With Transparencies**

Performance Assessment
- **Group/Individual Activities,** TE p. 200f
- **Teacher's Edition,** pp. 209, 217, 221
- **Assessment Rubrics**

Assessment Through Technology
- *ExamView* **CD-ROM**
- **MindPoint CD-ROM**
- **Progress Monitoring Transparencies**
- **Progress Monitoring Online**

Key Terms

Possible answers:

1. As crop prices declined, many farmers were unable to pay their taxes and the government seized their farms.

2. The courts interpret laws.

3. Each state held a convention to approve the Constitution.

Comprehension and Critical Thinking

4. **(a)** It did not have the powers to regulate trade, to tax, or to enforce the laws it passed. **(b)** It could not control what happened among the states or take much action because of the lack of money and the inability to enforce laws.

5. **(a)** When a territory began to be settled, Congress would appoint for it a governor, a secretary, and three judges. When there were 5,000 free adult male settlers in the territory, it could elect a legislature. When there were 60,000 free people in the territory, it could ask to become a state. **(b)** It gradually established a government.

6. **(a)** An economic depression caused farmers to lose money. The government was taking little action to help the farmers, so some farmers rebelled. **(b)** Possible response: He felt that the rebellion revealed the weaknesses of the central government under the Articles of Confederation.

7. **(a)** both—three branches of government; Virginia Plan—two legislative houses based on population; New Jersey Plan—one legislative house based on equal representation. **(b)** a one-house legislature. Possible answer: It did not take into account the size of each state when determining the number of representatives.

8. **(a)** Washington: president of convention; Madison: took notes; Sherman: proposed the Great Compromise; Morris: wrote Preamble **(b)** Answers will vary.

9. **(a)** basic freedoms such as freedom of religion, speech, and the press; it prevents Congress from forcing citizens to keep troops in their homes; it protects citizens who are accused of crimes and are brought to trial; and limits the powers of the federal government to only

---

Key Terms

Answer the questions in complete sentences that show your understanding of the key terms.

1. How did the economic depression of the mid-1780s impact farmers?

2. What is the role of the judicial branch in government?

3. What process did the Constitutional Convention set forth for states to ratify the Constitution?

Comprehension and Critical Thinking

4. **(a) Recall** Which powers did the Congress not have under the Articles of Confederation?
(b) Apply Information How did not having these powers make the national government weak?

5. **(a) Recall** List the three stages a territory had to go through to become a state under the Northwest Ordinance of 1787.
(b) Draw Conclusions How did this process help a territory prepare for statehood?

6. **(a) Describe** What were the causes of Shays' Rebellion of 1786?
(b) Detect Points of View Thomas Jefferson called Shays' Rebellion "a medicine necessary for the sound health of government." What do you think he meant?

7. **(a) Contrast** How did the New Jersey Plan differ from the Virginia Plan?
(b) Link Past and Present Which key part of the New Jersey Plan is not part of our Constitution today? Why not?

8. **(a) Recall** Describe one contribution made by each of the following to the writing and ratification of the Constitution: George Washington; James Madison; Roger Sherman; Gouverneur Morris.
(b) Evaluate Information Whose contribution do you think was most important? Give reasons for your answer.

9. **(a) Summarize** Which freedoms and rights are protected in the Bill of Rights?
(b) Draw Conclusions The Bill of Rights limited the powers of the federal government to those granted in the Constitution. Why do you think these limits were included?

History Reading Skill

10. **Analyze Propositions and Support** Reread the text under the heading "The Great Compromise." What did the Virginia Plan propose about representation in Congress? How did delegates from smaller states respond? What support did they give for their different responses? Evaluate that support.

Writing

11. **Write two paragraphs on the following topic:** Explain how the Constitution addressed weaknesses in the Articles of Confederation.
Your paragraphs should:
- include a thesis statement that expresses your main idea;
- develop that main idea with facts, examples, and other information;
- conclude by describing the lasting impact of what happened.

12. **Write a Narrative:**
You are a delegate who has just arrived in Philadelphia in May 1787. Write a letter home explaining your feelings about the upcoming convention.

Skills for Life

Analyze Cause and Effect
Use the information below to answer the questions that follow.

> **Cause:** In 1774, the British Parliament passes an act that forces American colonists to house British troops in their homes.
>
> **Event:** Bill of Rights, Third Amendment
>
> "No soldier shall, in time of peace, be quartered in any house without the consent of the owner; nor in time of war, but in a manner to be prescribed by law."

13. What right does the Third Amendment protect?

14. **(a)** What was one cause of the Third Amendment?
(b) Was this cause long term or short term? Explain.

15. How did the colonists' experiences under British rule influence their decision to change the Constitution?

---

those that are granted in the Constitution. **(b)** so that the central government would not usurp those rights that belonged to the states and to individuals

History Reading Skill

10. The Virginia Plan proposed a strong central government with three separate branches. Delegates from smaller states opposed this idea. They wanted each state to have one vote in Congress so they would all have equal representa-

tion. Student evaluations should show logical reasoning.

Writing

11. Paragraphs should list the problems of the central government under the Articles of Confederation. For example, the Congress could not regulate trade, collect taxes, or enforce laws. The essay should then explain how the Constitution gave more power to

Chapter 7
Review and Assessment

Test Yourself

1. The Great Compromise settled a dispute between
   A the North and the South.
   B Britain and the new United States.
   C the large states and the small states.
   D the President and Congress.

2. Antifederalists opposed the Constitution because it
   A did not give the President enough power.
   B weakened the state governments.
   C contained a bill of rights.
   D could not be amended.

Study the political cartoon below to answer Question 3. Consider how it is similar to and different from the cartoon in Section 3.

The FEDERAL EDIFICE.

3. What event is the creator of this political cartoon celebrating?
   A the approval of the Constitution
   B the abolition of the slave trade
   C the failure of Shays' Rebellion
   D the passage of the Northwest Ordinance

Document-Based Questions

Task: Look at Documents 1 and 2, and answer their accompanying questions. Then, use the documents and your knowledge of history to complete this writing assignment:

Write an essay explaining why the writers of the Constitution felt it was necessary to create a new plan of government.

Document 1: This excerpt from the Articles of Confederation defines the limitations on the powers of the national Congress. *According to this excerpt, what is Congress not allowed to do without the consent of the states?*

"The United States in Congress assembled shall never engage in a war . . . nor coin money, nor regulate the value thereof, nor [spend] the sums and expenses necessary for the defense and welfare of the United States . . . nor borrow money on the credit of the United States . . . nor agree upon the number of vessels of war, to be built or purchased, or the number of land or sea forces to be raised, nor appoint a commander in chief of the army or navy, unless nine States [agree] to the same. . . ."

Document 2: This excerpt from the Constitution defines some of the powers granted to Congress. *Why do you think the Framers of the Constitution gave Congress the power to set standards for weights and measures, rather than leaving it up to each state?*

"The Congress shall have power:
1. To lay and collect taxes . . . to pay the debts and provide for the common defense and general welfare of the United States. . . .
2. To borrow money on the credit of the United States. . . .
3. To coin money, regulate the value thereof, and of foreign coin, and for the standard of weights and measures. . . .
4. To declare war. . . .
5. To raise and support armies. . . .
6. To provide and maintain a navy."

Test Yourself

1. C
2. B
3. A

Document-Based Questions
Answers

Document 1 Under the Articles of Confederation, Congress could do little. It needed to have the consent of states to declare war; make, spend, or borrow money; supply the military or appoint a commander in chief of the military.

Document 2 Possible answer: to facilitate trade among states.

Rubric: Write an Essay
Share the rubric with students before they begin writing.

Score 1 Shows minimal analytic abilities, does not address assigned topic or misses the point.

Score 2 Does not address all aspects of the topic, lacks specific examples.

Score 3 Shows a general understanding of the Constitution's origins (*need to address the issues faced by the government under the Articles of Confederation; Congress could not run the government without some powers*), gives specific examples, answers document questions.

Score 4 Shows good analytical abilities, is well organized with many supporting details.

the government. One lasting effect is the Bill of Rights.

12. Letters should demonstrate an understanding of the issues faced by the Constitutional Convention.

For a more complete four-point rubric, see the Writing Rubric in the Teaching Resources.

All in One Teaching Resources, Unit 2, p. 123

Skills for Life

13. the right not to have soldiers move into their homes

14. **(a)** Parliament passed a law forcing colonists to house British soldiers.
    (b) short term because the revolution started two years later

15. They added the Bill of Rights to protect themselves against abuses of government like they experienced under British colonialism.

The Constitution of the United States: An Outline

Original Constitution

Preamble

Explore More Video
To learn more about the first 10 amendments to the Constitution, view the video.

The Constitution of the United States

A Note on the Text of the Constitution

The complete text of the Constitution, including amendments, appears on the pages that follow. Spelling, capitalization, and punctuation have been modernized, and headings have been added. Portions of the Constitution altered by later amendments or that no longer apply are printed in blue. Commentary appears in the outside column of each page.

The Preamble The Preamble describes the purpose of the government as set up by the Constitution. Americans expect their government to defend justice and liberty and provide peace and safety from foreign enemies.

Preamble

We the people of the United States, in order to form a more perfect union, establish justice, insure domestic tranquillity, provide for the common defense, promote the general welfare, and secure the blessings of liberty to ourselves and our posterity, do ordain and establish this Constitution for the United States of America.

Article I ★ Legislative Branch

Section 1 The Constitution gives Congress the power to make laws. Congress is divided into the Senate and the House of Representatives.

Section 1. A Two-House Legislature

All legislative powers herein granted shall be vested in a Congress of the United States, which shall consist of a Senate and House of Representatives.

Section 2. House of Representatives

1. Election of Members The House of Representatives shall be composed of members chosen every second year by the people of the several states, and the electors in each state shall have the qualifications requisite for electors of the most numerous branch of the state legislature.

2. Qualifications No person shall be a representative who shall not have attained to the age of twenty-five years, and been seven years a citizen of the United States, and who shall not, when elected, be an inhabitant of that state in which he shall be chosen.

3. Apportionment Representatives and direct taxes shall be apportioned among the several states which may be included within this Union, according to their respective numbers, which shall be determined by adding to the whole number of free persons, including those bound to service for a term of years and excluding Indians not taxed, three fifths of all other persons. The actual enumeration shall be made within three years after the first meeting of the Congress of the United States, and within every subsequent term of ten years, in such manner as they shall by law direct. The number of representatives shall not exceed one for every thirty thousand, but each state shall have at least one representative; and until such enumeration shall be made, the state of New Hampshire shall be entitled to choose three, Massachusetts eight, Rhode Island and Providence Plantations one, Connecticut five, New York six, New Jersey four, Pennsylvania eight, Delaware one, Maryland six, Virginia ten, North Carolina five, South Carolina five, and Georgia three.

4. Filling Vacancies When vacancies happen in the representation from any state, the executive authority thereof shall issue writs of election to fill such vacancies.

5. Officers; Impeachment The House of Representatives shall choose their Speaker and other officers; and shall have the sole power of impeachment.

Section 3. Senate

1. Composition; Term The Senate of the United States shall be composed of two senators from each state chosen by the legislature thereof, for six years, and each senator shall have one vote.

2. Classification; Filling Vacancies Immediately after they shall be assembled in consequence of the first election, they shall be divided as equally as may be into three classes. The seats of the senators of the first class shall be vacated at the expiration of the second year, of the second class at the expiration of the fourth year, and of the third class at the expiration of the sixth year, so that one third may be chosen every second year; and if vacancies happen by resignation, or otherwise, during the recess of the legislature of any State, the executive thereof may make temporary appointments until the next meeting of the legislature, which shall then fill such vacancies.

Clause 1 Electors refers to voters. Members of the House of Representatives are elected every two years. Any citizen allowed to vote for members of the larger house of the state legislature can also vote for members of the House.

Clause 3 The number of representatives each state elects is based on its population. An enumeration, or census, must be taken every 10 years to determine population. Today, the number of representatives in the House is fixed at 435. Clause 3 contains the Three-Fifths Compromise worked out at the Constitutional Convention. Persons bound to service meant indentured servants. All other persons meant slaves. All free people in a state were counted. However, only three fifths of the slaves were included in the population count. This three-fifths clause became meaningless when slaves were freed by the Thirteenth Amendment.

Clause 4 Executive authority means the governor of a state. If a member of the House leaves office before his or her term ends, the governor must call a special election to fill the seat.

Clause 5 The House elects a Speaker. Only the House has the power to impeach, or accuse, a federal official of wrongdoing.

Clause 2 Every two years, one third of the senators run for reelection. The Seventeenth Amendment changed the way of filling vacancies, or empty seats. Today, the governor of a state must choose a senator to fill a vacancy that occurs between elections.

3. Qualifications No person shall be a senator who shall not have attained to the age of thirty years, and been nine years a citizen of the United States, and who shall not, when elected, be an inhabitant of that state for which he shall be chosen.

4. President of the Senate The Vice President of the United States shall be president of the Senate, but shall have no vote, unless they be equally divided.

5. Other Officers The Senate shall choose their other officers, and also a president pro tempore, in the absence of the Vice President, or when he shall exercise the office of the President of the United States.

6. Impeachment Trials The Senate shall have the sole power to try all impeachments. When sitting for that purpose, they shall be on oath or affirmation. When the President of the United States is tried, the Chief Justice shall preside; and no person shall be convicted without the concurrence of two thirds of the members present.

7. Penalty on Conviction Judgment in cases of impeachment shall not extend further than to removal from office, and disqualification to hold and enjoy any office of honor, trust or profit under the United States: but the party convicted shall nevertheless be liable and subject to indictment, trial, judgment, and punishment, according to law.

Section 4. Elections and Meetings

1. Election of Congress The times, places, and manner of holding elections for senators and representatives, shall be prescribed in each state by the legislature thereof; but the Congress may at any time by law make or alter such regulations, except as to the places of choosing senators.

2. Sessions The Congress shall assemble at least once in every year, and such meeting shall be on the first Monday in December, unless they shall by law appoint a different day.

Section 5. Legislative Proceedings

1. Organization Each house shall be the judge of the elections, returns, and qualifications of its own members, and a majority of each shall constitute a quorum to do business; but a smaller number may adjourn from day to day, and may be authorized to compel the attendance of absent members, in such manner, and under such penalties, as each house may provide.

2. Rules Each house may determine the rules of its proceedings, punish its members for disorderly behavior, and with the concurrence of two thirds, expel a member.

3. Record Each house shall keep a journal of its proceedings, and from time to time publish the same, excepting such parts as may in their judgment require secrecy; and the yeas and nays of the members of either house on any question shall, at the desire of one fifth of those present, be entered on the journal.

4. Adjournment Neither house, during the session of Congress, shall, without the consent of the other, adjourn for more than three days, nor to any other place than that in which the two houses shall be sitting.

Section 6. Compensation, Immunities, and Disabilities of Members

1. Salaries; Immunities The senators and representatives shall receive a compensation for their services, to be ascertained by law, and paid out of the Treasury of the United States. They shall in all cases, except treason, felony, and breach of the peace, be privileged from arrest during their attendance at the session of their respective houses, and in going to and returning from the same; and for any speech or debate in either house, they shall not be questioned in any other place.

2. Restrictions on Other Employment No senator or representative shall, during the time for which he was elected, be appointed to any civil office under the authority of the United States, which shall have been created, or the emoluments whereof shall have been increased during such time; and no person holding any office under the United States shall be a member of either house during his continuance in office.

Section 7. Law-Making Process

1. Revenue Bills All bills for raising revenue shall originate in the House of Representatives; but the Senate may propose or concur with amendments as on other bills.

2. How a Bill Becomes Law; the Veto Every bill which shall have passed the House of Representatives and the Senate shall, before it become a law, be presented to the President of the United States; if he approve, he shall sign it, but if not, he shall return it, with his objections, to that house in which it shall have originated, who shall enter the objections at large on their journal, and proceed to reconsider it. If after such reconsideration two thirds of that house shall agree to pass the bill, it shall be sent, together with the objections, to the other house, by which it shall likewise be reconsidered, and if approved by two thirds of that house, it shall become a law. But in all such cases the votes of both houses shall be determined by yeas and nays, and the names of the persons voting for and against the bill shall be entered on the journal of each house respectively. If any bill shall not be returned by the President within ten days (Sundays excepted) after it shall have been presented to him, the same shall be a law, in like manner as if he had signed it, unless the Congress by their adjournment prevent its return, in which case it shall not be a law.

3. Resolutions Passed by Congress Every order, resolution, or vote to which the concurrence of the Senate and House of Representatives may be necessary (except on a question of adjournment) shall be presented to the President of the United States; and before the same shall take effect, shall be approved by him, or being disapproved by him, shall be repassed by two thirds of the Senate and House of Representatives, according to the rules and limitations prescribed in the case of a bill.

Clause 4 Neither house can adjourn, or stop meeting, for more than three days unless the other house approves. Both houses must meet in the same city.

Clause 1 Congress decides the salary for its members. While Congress is in session, a member is free from arrest in civil cases and cannot be sued for anything he or she says on the floor of Congress. This allows for freedom of debate. However, a member can be arrested for a criminal offense.

Clause 2 Emolument means salary. A member of Congress cannot hold another federal office during his or her term. A former member of Congress cannot hold an office created while he or she was in Congress. An official in another branch of government cannot serve at the same time in Congress.

Clause 1 Revenue is money raised by the government through taxes. Tax bills must be introduced in the House. The Senate, however, can make changes in tax bills.

Clause 2 A bill, or proposed law, that is passed by a majority of the House and Senate is sent to the President. If the President signs the bill, it becomes law.

A bill can also become law without the President's signature. The President can refuse to act on a bill. If Congress is in session at the time, the bill becomes law 10 days after the President receives it.

The President can veto, or reject, a bill by sending it back to the house where it was introduced. If the President refuses to act on a bill and Congress adjourns within 10 days, then the bill dies. This way of killing a bill without taking action is called the pocket veto.

Congress can override the President's veto if each house of Congress passes the bill again by a two-thirds vote.

Congress's power is expressed directly in the Constitution. Numbered from 1 to 18, these powers are also known as enumerated powers.

Clause 1 Duties are tariffs. Imposts are taxes in general. Excises are taxes on the production or sale of certain goods.

Clause 3 Only Congress has the power to regulate foreign and inter-state commerce. This allows a "common market" with a unified set of laws governing trade. This clause has also been interpreted as giving the federal government authority over Native American nations.

Clause 4 Naturalization is the process whereby a foreigner becomes a citizen. Bankruptcy is the condition in which a person or business cannot pay its debts.

Clause 5 Congressional power to coin money and set its value is one of the keys to creating a stable economy.

Clause 6 Counterfeiting is the making of imitation money. Securities are bonds. Congress can make laws to punish counterfeiters.

Clause 11 Only Congress can declare war. Declarations of war are granted at the request of the President. Letters of marque and reprisal were documents issued by a government allowing merchant ships to arm themselves and attack ships of an enemy nation. They are no longer issued.

Clauses 15, 16 The militia is a body of citizen soldiers. Each state has its own militia, today called the National Guard. Normally, the militia is under the command of a state's governor. However, it can be placed under the command of the President.

Portions of the Constitution altered by later amendments or that no longer apply are printed in blue.

Section 8. Powers of Congress

The Congress shall have power

1. To lay and collect taxes, duties, imposts, and excises, to pay the debts and provide for the common defense and general welfare of the United States; but all duties, imposts and excises shall be uniform throughout the United States;

2. To borrow money on the credit of the United States;

3. To regulate commerce with foreign nations, and among the several states, and with the Indian tribes;

4. To establish an uniform rule of naturalization, and uniform laws on the subject of bankruptcies throughout the United States;

5. To coin money, regulate the value thereof, and of foreign coin, and fix the standard of weights and measures;

6. To provide for the punishment of counterfeiting the securities and current coin of the United States;

7. To establish post offices and post roads;

8. To promote the progress of science and useful arts by securing for limited times to authors and inventors the exclusive right to their respective writings and discoveries;

9. To constitute tribunals inferior to the Supreme Court;

10. To define and punish piracies and felonies committed on the high seas and offenses against the law of nations;

11. To declare war, grant letters of marque and reprisal, and make rules concerning captures on land and water;

12. To raise and support armies, but no appropriation of money to that use shall be for a longer term than two years;

13. To provide and maintain a navy;

14. To make rules for the government and regulation of the land and naval forces;

15. To provide for calling forth the militia to execute the laws of the Union, suppress insurrections, and repel invasions;

16. To provide for organizing, arming, and disciplining the militia, and for governing such part of them as may be employed in the service of the United States, reserving to the states, respectively, the appointment of the officers, and the authority of training the militia according to the discipline prescribed by Congress;

17. To exercise exclusive legislation in all cases whatsoever, over such district (not exceeding ten miles square) as may, by cession of particular states, and the acceptance of Congress, become the seat of the government of the United States, and to exercise like authority over all places purchased by the consent of the legislature of the state in which the same shall be, for the erection of forts, magazines, arsenals, dock-yards, and other needful buildings; —and

18. To make all laws which shall be necessary and proper for carrying into execution the foregoing powers, and all other powers vested by this Constitution in the government of the United States, or in any department or officer thereof.

Section 9. Powers Denied to Congress

1. The Slave Trade The migration or importation of such persons as any of the states now existing shall think proper to admit, shall not be prohibited by the Congress prior to the year one thousand eight hundred and eight, but a tax or duty may be imposed on such importation, not exceeding ten dollars for each person.

2. Writ of Habeas Corpus The privilege of the writ of habeas corpus shall not be suspended, unless when in cases of rebellion or invasion the public safety may require it.

3. Bills of Attainder; Ex Post Facto Laws No bill of attainder or ex post facto law shall be passed.

4. Apportionment of Direct Taxes No capitation, or other direct, tax shall be laid, unless in proportion to the census or enumeration herein before directed to be taken.

5. Taxes on Exports No tax or duty shall be laid on articles exported from any state.

6. Special Preference for Trade No preference shall be given by any regulation of commerce or revenue to the ports of one state over those of another; nor shall vessels bound to, or from, one state, be obliged to enter, clear, or pay duties in another.

7. Spending No money shall be drawn from the Treasury, but in consequence of appropriations made by law; and a regular statement and account of the receipts and expenditures of all public money shall be published from time to time.

8. Titles of Nobility No title of nobility shall be granted by the United States; and no person holding any office of profit or trust under them, shall, without the consent of the Congress, accept of any present, emolument, office, or title, of any kind whatever, from any king, prince or foreign state.

Section 10. Powers Denied to the States

1. Unconditional Prohibitions No state shall enter into any treaty, alliance, or confederation; grant letters of marque and reprisal; coin money; emit bills of credit; make any thing but gold and silver coin a tender in payment of debts; pass any bill of attainder, ex post facto law, or law impairing the obligation of contracts, or grant any title of nobility.

2. Powers Conditionally Denied No state shall, without the consent of the Congress, lay any imposts or duties on imports or exports, except what may be absolutely necessary for executing its inspection laws; and the net produce of all duties and imposts, laid by any state on imports or exports, shall be for the use of the Treasury of the United States; and all such laws shall be subject to the revision and control of the Congress.

Clause 18 Clause 18 gives Congress the power to make laws as needed to carry out the first 17 clauses. It is sometimes called the elastic clause because it lets Congress stretch the meaning of its power.

Clause 1 "Such persons" means slaves. In 1808, as soon as Congress was permitted to abolish the slave trade, it did so.

Clause 2 A writ of habeas corpus is a court order requiring government officials to bring a prisoner to court and explain why he or she is being held. A writ of habeas corpus protects people from unlawful imprisonment. The government cannot suspend this right except in times of rebellion or invasion.

Clause 3 A bill of attainder is a law declaring that a person is guilty of a particular crime. An ex post facto law punishes an act which was not illegal when it was committed. Congress cannot pass a bill of attainder or ex post facto laws.

Clause 7 The federal government cannot spend money unless Congress appropriates it, or passes a law allowing it. The government must publish a statement showing how it spends public funds.

Clause 1 The writers of the Constitution did not want the states to act like separate nations, so they prohibited states from making treaties or coining money. Some powers denied to the federal government are also denied to the states.

Clauses 2, 3 Powers listed here are forbidden to the states, but Congress can pass laws that give these powers to the states.
Clause 2 forbids states from taxing imports and exports without the consent of Congress. States may charge inspection fees on goods entering the states. Any profits go to the United States Treasury.

Clause 3 forbids states from keeping an army or navy without the consent of Congress. States cannot make treaties or declare war unless an enemy invades or is about to invade.

Clauses 2, 3 Some writers of the Constitution were afraid to allow the people to elect the President directly. Therefore, the Constitutional Convention set up the electoral college. Clause 2 directs each state to choose electors, or delegates to the electoral college, to vote for President. A state's electoral vote is equal to the combined number of senators and representatives. Each state may decide how to choose its electors. Members of Congress and federal officeholders may not serve as electors. This much of the original electoral college system is still in effect.

Clause 3 Clause 3 called upon each elector to vote for two candidates. The candidate who received a majority of the electoral votes would become President. The runner-up would become Vice President. If no candidate won a majority, the House would choose the President. The Senate would choose the Vice President.

The election of 1800 showed a problem with the original electoral college system. Thomas Jefferson was the Republican candidate for President, and Aaron Burr was the Republican candidate for Vice President. In the electoral college, the vote ended in a tie. The election was finally decided in the House, where Jefferson was chosen President. The Twelfth Amendment changed the electoral college system so that this could not happen again.

Portions of the Constitution altered by later amendments or that no longer apply are printed in blue.

3. Other Denied Powers No state shall, without the consent of Congress, lay any duty of tonnage, keep troops, or ships of war in time of peace, enter into any agreement or compact with another state, or with a foreign power, or engage in war, unless actually invaded, or in such imminent danger as will not admit of delay.

Article II ★ Executive Branch

Section 1. President and Vice President

1. Chief Executive; Term The executive power shall be vested in a President of the United States of America. He shall hold his office during the term of four years, and, together with the Vice President, chosen for the same term, be elected as follows:

2. Electoral College Each state shall appoint, in such manner as the legislature thereof may direct, a number of electors, equal to the whole number of senators and representatives to which the state may be entitled in the Congress: but no senator or representative, or person holding an office of trust or profit under the United States, shall be appointed an elector.

3. Former Electoral Method The electors shall meet in their respective states, and vote by ballot for two persons, of whom one at least shall not be an inhabitant of the same state with themselves. And they shall make a list of all the persons voted for, and of the number of votes for each; which list they shall sign and certify, and transmit sealed to the seat of the government of the United States, directed to the president of the Senate. The president of the Senate shall, in the presence of the Senate and House of Representatives, open all the certificates, and the votes shall then be counted. The person having the greatest number of votes shall be the President, if such number be a majority of the whole number of Electors appointed; and if there be more than one who have such majority, and have an equal number of votes, then the House of Representatives shall immediately choose by ballot one of them for President; and if no person have a majority, then from the five highest on the list the said House shall in like manner choose the President. But in choosing the President, the votes shall be taken by states, the representation from each state having one vote; a quorum for this purpose shall consist of a member or members from two thirds of the states, and a majority of all the states shall be necessary to a choice. In every case, after the choice of the President, the person having the greatest number of votes of the electors shall be the Vice President. But if there should remain two or more who have equal votes, the Senate shall choose from them by ballot the Vice President.

4. Time of Elections The Congress may determine the time of choosing the electors, and the day on which they shall give their votes; which day shall be the same throughout the United States.

5. Qualifications for President No person except a natural-born citizen, or a citizen of the United States at the time of the adoption of this Constitution, shall be eligible to the office of President; neither shall any person be eligible to that office who shall not have attained to the age of thirty-five years, and been fourteen years a resident within the United States.

6. Presidential Succession In case of the removal of the President from office, or of his death, resignation, or inability to discharge the powers and duties of the said office, the same shall devolve on the Vice President, and the Congress may by law provide for the case of removal, death, resignation or inability, both of the President and Vice President, declaring what officer shall then act as President, and such officer shall act accordingly, until the disability be removed, or a President shall be elected.

7. Salary The President shall, at stated times, receive for his services, a compensation, which shall neither be increased nor diminished during the period for which he shall have been elected, and he shall not receive within that period any other emolument from the United States, or any of them.

8. Oath of Office Before he enter on the execution of his office, he shall take the following oath or affirmation:—"I do solemnly swear (or affirm) that I will faithfully execute the office of the President of the United States, and will to the best of my ability, preserve, protect, and defend the Constitution of the United States."

Section 2. Powers of the President

1. Military Powers The President shall be commander in chief of the army and navy of the United States, and of the militia of the several states, when called into the actual service of the United States; he may require the opinion, in writing, of the principal officer in each of the executive departments, upon any subject relating to the duties of their respective offices, and he shall have power to grant reprieves and pardons for offenses against the United States, except in cases of impeachment.

2. Treaties; Appointments He shall have power, by and with the advice and consent of the Senate, to make treaties, provided two thirds of the senators present concur; and he shall nominate, and by and with the advice and consent of the Senate, shall appoint ambassadors, other public ministers and consuls, judges of the Supreme Court, and all other officers of the United States, whose appointments are not herein otherwise provided for, and which shall be established by law: but the Congress may by law vest the appointment of such inferior officers, as they think proper, in the President alone, in the courts of law, or in the heads of departments.

3. Temporary Appointments The President shall have power to fill up all vacancies that may happen during the recess of the Senate, by granting commissions which shall expire at the end of their next session.

Clause 6 The powers of the President pass to the Vice President if the President leaves office or cannot discharge his or her duties. The Twenty-fifth Amendment replaced this clause.

Clause 7 The President is paid a salary. It cannot be raised or lowered during his or her term of office. The President is not allowed to hold any other federal or state position while in office.

Clause 1 The President is the head of the armed forces and the state militias when they are called into national service. So the military is under civilian, or nonmilitary, control. The President can get advice from the heads of executive departments. In most cases, the President has the power to grant reprieves and pardons. A reprieve suspends punishment ordered by law. A pardon prevents prosecution for a crime or overrides the judgment of a court.

Clause 2 The President has the power to make treaties with other nations. Under the system of checks and balances, all treaties must be approved by two thirds of the Senate.

The President has the power to appoint ambassadors to foreign countries and to appoint other high officials. The Senate must confirm, or approve, these appointments.

Section 3. Duties of the President

He shall from time to time give to the Congress information of the state of the Union, and recommend to their consideration such measures as he shall judge necessary and expedient; he may, on extraordinary occasions, convene both houses, or either of them, and in case of disagreement between them, with respect to the time of adjournment, he may adjourn them to such time as he shall think proper; he shall receive ambassadors and other public ministers; he shall take care that the laws be faithfully executed, and shall commission all the officers of the United States.

Section 4. Impeachment

The President, Vice President and all civil officers of the United States, shall be removed from office on impeachment for, and conviction of, treason, bribery, or other high crimes and misdemeanors.

Article III ★ Judicial Branch

Section 1. Courts, Terms of Office

The judicial power of the United States shall be vested in one Supreme Court, and in such inferior courts as the Congress may from time to time ordain and establish. The judges, both of the Supreme and inferior courts, shall hold their offices during good behavior, and shall, at stated times, receive for their services, a compensation, which shall not be diminished during their continuance in office.

Section 2. Jurisdiction

1. Scope of Judicial Power The judicial power shall extend to all cases, in law and equity, arising under this Constitution, the laws of the United States, and treaties made, or which shall be made, under their authority;— to all cases affecting ambassadors, other public ministers and consuls;—to all cases of admiralty and maritime jurisdiction;—to controversies to which the United States shall be a party;—to controversies between two or more states; between a state and citizens of another state; —between citizens of different states;—between citizens of the same state claiming lands under grants of different states, and between a state, or the citizens thereof, and foreign states, citizens, or subjects.

2. Supreme Court In all cases affecting ambassadors, other public ministers and consuls, and those in which a state shall be a party, the Supreme Court shall have original jurisdiction. In all the other cases before mentioned, the Supreme Court shall have appellate jurisdiction, both as to law and fact, with such exceptions, and under such regulations as the Congress shall make.

Section 4
Civil officers include federal judges and members of the Cabinet. High crimes are major crimes. Misdemeanors are lesser crimes. The President, Vice President, and others can be forced out of office if impeached and found guilty of certain crimes.

Clause 1 Jurisdiction refers to the right of a court to hear a case. Federal courts have jurisdiction over cases that involve the Constitution, federal laws, treaties, foreign ambassadors and diplomats, naval and maritime laws, disagreements between states or between citizens from different states, and disputes between a state or citizen and a foreign state or citizen.

Clause 2 Original jurisdiction means the power of a court to hear a case where it first arises. The Supreme Court has original jurisdiction over only a few cases, such as those involving foreign diplomats. More often, the Supreme Court acts as an appellate court. An appellate court does not decide guilt. It decides whether the lower court trial was properly conducted and reviews the lower court's decision.

Portions of the Constitution altered by later amendments or that no longer apply are printed in blue.

3. Trial by Jury The trial of all crimes, except in cases of impeachment, shall be by jury; and such trial shall be held in the state where the said crimes shall have been committed; but when not committed within any state, the trial shall be at such place or places as the Congress may by law have directed.

Section 3. Treason

1. Definition Treason against the United States shall consist only in levying war against them, or in adhering to their enemies, giving them aid and comfort. No person shall be convicted of treason unless on the testimony of two witnesses to the same overt act, or on confession in open court.

2. Punishment The Congress shall have power to declare the punishment of treason, but no attainder of treason shall work corruption of blood or forfeiture except during the life of the person attained.

Article IV ★ Relations Among the States

Section 1. Full Faith and Credit

Full faith and credit shall be given in each state to the public acts, records, and judicial proceedings of every other state. And the Congress may by general laws prescribe the manner in which such acts, records, and proceedings shall be proved, and the effect thereof.

Section 2. Privileges and Immunities of Citizens

1. Privileges The citizens of each state shall be entitled to all privileges and immunities of citizens in the several states.

2. Extradition A person charged in any state with treason, felony, or other crime, who shall flee from justice, and be found in another state, shall on demand of the executive authority of the state from which he fled, be delivered up, to be removed to the state having jurisdiction of the crime.

3. Fugitive Slaves No person held to service or labor in one state, under the laws thereof, escaping into another, shall in consequence of any law or regulation therein, be discharged from such service or labor, but shall be delivered up on claim of the party to whom such service or labor may be due.

Section 3. New States and Territories

1. New States New states may be admitted by the Congress into this Union; but no new states shall be formed or erected within the jurisdiction of any other state; nor any state be formed by the junction of two or more states, or parts of states, without the consent of the legislatures of the states concerned as well as of the Congress.

2. Federal Lands The Congress shall have power to dispose of and make all needful rules and regulations respecting the territory or other property belonging to the United States; and nothing in this Constitution shall be so construed as to prejudice any claims of the United States, or of any particular state.

Section 4. Protection Afforded to States by the Nation

The United States shall guarantee to every state in this Union a republican form of government, and shall protect each of them against invasion; and on application of the legislature, or of the executive (when the legislature cannot be convened) against domestic violence.

Section 4 In a <u>republic</u>, voters choose representatives to govern them. The federal government must protect the states from foreign invasion and from domestic, or internal, disorder if asked to do so by a state.

Article V ★ Provisions for Amendment

The Congress, whenever two thirds of both houses shall deem it necessary, shall propose amendments to this Constitution, or, on the application of the legislatures of two thirds of the several states, shall call a convention for proposing amendments, which, in either case, shall be valid to all intents and purposes, as part of this Constitution, when ratified by the legislatures of three fourths of the several states, or by conventions in three fourths thereof, as the one or the other mode of ratification may be proposed by the Congress; provided that no amendment which may be made prior to the year one thousand eight hundred and eight shall in any manner affect the first and fourth clauses in the ninth section of the first Article; and that no state, without its consent, shall be deprived of its equal suffrage in the Senate.

The Constitution can be <u>amended</u>, or changed, if necessary. An amendment can be proposed by (1) a two-thirds vote of both houses of Congress or (2) a national convention called by Congress at the request of two thirds of the state legislatures. (This second method has never been used.) An amendment must be <u>ratified</u>, or approved, by (1) three fourths of the state legislatures or (2) special conventions in three fourths of the states. Congress decides which method will be used.

Congress has proposed each of the 27 amendments to the Constitution by a vote of two-thirds in both houses. The only amendment ratified by constitutional conventions of the states was the Twenty-first Amendment. State legislatures have ratified all other amendments.

Article VI ★ National Debts, Supremacy of National Law, Oath

Section 1. Validity of Debts

All debts contracted and engagements entered into, before the adoption of this Constitution, shall be as valid against the United States under this Constitution, as under the Confederation.

Section 2. Supremacy of National Law

This Constitution, and the laws of the United States which shall be made in pursuance thereof, and all treaties made, or which shall be made, under the authority of the United States, shall be the supreme law of the land; and the judges in every state shall be bound thereby, anything in the constitution or laws of any state to the contrary notwithstanding.

Section 2 The "supremacy clause" in this section establishes the Constitution, federal laws, and treaties that the Senate has ratified as the <u>supreme</u>, or highest, law of the land. Thus, they outweigh state laws. A state judge must overturn a state law that conflicts with the Constitution or with a federal law.

Portions of the Constitution altered by later amendments or that no longer apply are printed in blue.

Section 3. Oaths of Office

The senators and representatives before mentioned, and the members of the several state legislatures, and all executive and judicial officers, both of the United States and of the several states, shall be bound by oath or affirmation, to support this Constitution; but no religious test shall ever be required as a qualification to any office or public trust under the United States.

Article VII ★ Ratification of Constitution

The ratification of the conventions of nine states shall be sufficient for the establishment of this Constitution between the states so ratifying the same.

Done in convention by the unanimous consent of the states present the seventeenth day of September, in the year of our Lord one thousand seven hundred and eighty-seven, and of the independence of the United States of America the twelfth. In Witness whereof, we have hereunto subscribed our names.

Article VII During 1787 and 1788, states held special conventions. By October 1788, the required nine states had ratified the United States Constitution.

Attest: William Jackson, SECRETARY
George Washington, PRESIDENT and deputy from Virginia

New Hampshire
John Langdon
Nicholas Gilman

Massachusetts
Nathaniel Gorham
Rufus King

Connecticut
William Samuel Johnson
Roger Sherman

New York
Alexander Hamilton

New Jersey
William Livingston
David Brearley
William Paterson
Jonathan Dayton

Pennsylvania
Benjamin Franklin
Thomas Mifflin
Robert Morris
George Clymer
Thomas Fitzsimons
Jared Ingersoll
James Wilson
Gouverneur Morris

Delaware
George Read
Gunning Bedford, Jr.
John Dickinson
Richard Bassett
Jacob Broom

Maryland
James McHenry
Dan of St. Thomas Jennifer
Daniel Carroll

Virginia
John Blair
James Madison, Jr.

North Carolina
William Blount
Richard Dobbs Spaight
Hugh Williamson

South Carolina
John Rutledge
Charles Cotesworth Pinckney
Charles Pinckney
Pierce Butler

Georgia
William Few
Abraham Baldwin

The Amendments Amendments are changes. The Constitution has been amended 27 times since it was ratified in 1788. The first 10 amendments are referred to as the Bill of Rights. These amendments give rights to the people and states, thus putting limits on the power of government.

First Amendment The First Amendment protects five basic rights: freedom of religion, speech, the press, assembly, and petition. Congress cannot set up an established, or official, church or religion for the nation. It cannot forbid the practice of religion, nor can it force the practice of religion.

Congress may not abridge, or limit, the freedom to speak and write freely. The government may not censor, or review, books and newspapers before they are printed. This amendment also protects the right to assemble, or hold public meetings. Petition means ask. Redress means to correct. Grievances are wrongs. The people have the right to ask the government for wrongs to be corrected.

Second Amendment Americans debate the exact meaning of the Second Amendment. Some believe that it guarantees the right of individuals to own firearms. Others argue that it guarantees the right of each state to maintain a militia. Gun control, or the passage of laws to regulate the ownership and use of firearms, is one of the most controversial issues today.

Third Amendment In colonial times, the British could quarter, or house, soldiers in private homes without permission of the owners. The Third Amendment prevents such abuses.

Portions of the Constitution altered by later amendments or that no longer apply are printed in blue.

Amendments

First Amendment ★

(1791) Freedom of Religion, Speech, Press, Assembly, and Petition

Congress shall make no law respecting an establishment of religion, or prohibiting the free exercise thereof; or abridging the freedom of speech, or of the press; or the right of the people peaceably to assemble, and to petition the government for a redress of grievances.

Second Amendment ★

(1791) Bearing Arms

A well-regulated militia being necessary to the security of a free state, the right of the people to keep and bear arms shall not be infringed.

Third Amendment ★

(1791) Quartering of Troops

No soldier shall, in time of peace, be quartered in any house, without the consent of the owner; nor in time of war, but in a manner to be prescribed by law.

Fourth Amendment ★

(1791) Searches and Seizures

The right of the people to be secure in their persons, houses, papers, and effects, against unreasonable searches and seizures, shall not be violated, and no warrants shall issue, but upon probable cause, supported by oath or affirmation, and particularly describing the place to be searched, and the persons or things to be seized.

Fifth Amendment ★

(1791) Criminal Proceedings; Due Process; Eminent Domain

No person shall be held to answer for a capital, or otherwise infamous, crime, unless on a presentment or indictment of a grand jury, except in cases arising in the land or naval forces, or in the militia, when in actual service in time of war or public danger; nor shall any person be subject for the same offense to be twice put in jeopardy of life and limb; nor shall be compelled, in any criminal case, to be a witness against himself; nor be deprived of life, liberty, or property, without due process of law; nor shall private property be taken for public use, without just compensation.

Sixth Amendment ★

(1791) Criminal Proceedings

In all criminal prosecutions, the accused shall enjoy the right to a speedy and public trial, by an impartial jury of the state and district wherein the crime shall have been committed, which district shall have been previously ascertained by law, and to be informed of the nature and cause of the accusation; to be confronted with the witnesses against him; to have compulsory process for obtaining witnesses in his favor, and to have the assistance of counsel for his defense.

Fourth Amendment This amendment protects Americans from unreasonable searches and seizures. Search and seizure are permitted only if a judge has issued a warrant, or written court order. A warrant is issued only if there is probable cause. This means an officer must show that it is probable, or likely, that the search will produce evidence of a crime.

Fifth Amendment This amendment protects the rights of the accused. Capital crimes are those that can be punished with death. Infamous crimes are those that can be punished with prison or loss of rights. The federal government must obtain an indictment, or formal accusation, from a grand jury to prosecute anyone for such crimes. A grand jury is a panel of between 12 and 23 citizens who decide if the government has enough evidence to justify a trial.

Double jeopardy is forbidden by this amendment. This means that a person cannot be tried twice for the same crime. However, if a court sets aside a conviction because of a legal error, the accused can be tried again. A person on trial cannot be forced to testify, or give evidence, against himself or herself. A person accused of a crime is entitled to due process of law, or a fair hearing or trial.

Finally, the government cannot seize private property for public use without paying the owner a fair price for it.

Sixth Amendment In criminal cases, the jury must be impartial, or not favor either side. The accused is guaranteed the right to a trial by jury. The trial must be speedy. If the government purposely postpones the trial so that it becomes hard for the person to get a fair hearing, the charge may be dismissed. The accused must be told the charges and be allowed to question all witnesses. Witnesses who can help the accused can be ordered to appear in court. The accused must be allowed a lawyer.

Seventh Amendment <u>Common law</u> refers to rules of law established by judges in past cases. This amendment guarantees the right to a jury trial in lawsuits where the sum of money at stake is more than $20. An appeals court can set aside a verdict only if legal errors made the trial unfair.

Eighth Amendment <u>Bail</u> is money that the accused leaves with the court as a pledge to appear for trial. If the accused does not appear, the court keeps the money. This amendment prevents the court from imposing bail or fines that are <u>excessive</u>, or too high. The amendment also forbids cruel and unusual punishments, such as physical torture.

Ninth Amendment The rights of the people are not limited to those listed in the Bill of Rights. In the Ninth Amendment, the government is prevented from claiming these are the only rights people have.

Tenth Amendment Powers not given to the federal government belong to the states. Powers reserved to the states are not listed in the Constitution.

Eleventh Amendment A private citizen from one state cannot sue the government of another state in federal court. However, a citizen can sue a state government in a state court.

Portions of the Constitution altered by later amendments or that no longer apply are printed in blue.

Seventh Amendment ★

(1791) Civil Trials

In suits at common law, where the value in controversy shall exceed twenty dollars, the right of trial by jury shall be preserved, and no fact tried by a jury shall be otherwise re-examined in any court of the United States, than according to the rules of the common law.

Eighth Amendment ★

(1791) Punishment for Crimes

Excessive bail shall not be required, nor excessive fines imposed, nor cruel and unusual punishments inflicted.

Ninth Amendment ★

(1791) Unenumerated Rights

The enumeration in the Constitution, of certain rights, shall not be construed to deny or disparage others retained by the people.

Tenth Amendment ★

(1791) Powers Reserved to the States

The powers not delegated to the United States by the Constitution, nor prohibited by it to the states, are reserved to the states respectively, or to the people.

Eleventh Amendment ★

(1795) Suits Against States

The judicial power of the United States shall not be construed to extend to any suit in law or equity, commenced or prosecuted against one of the United States by citizens of another state, or by citizens or subjects of any foreign state.

Twelfth Amendment ★

(1804) Election of President and Vice President

The electors shall meet in their respective states, and vote by ballot for President and Vice President, one of whom, at least, shall not be an inhabitant of the same state with themselves; they shall name in their ballots the person voted for as President, and in distinct ballots the person voted for as Vice President, and they shall make distinct lists of all persons voted for as President, and of all persons voted for as Vice President, and of the number of votes for each, which lists they shall sign and certify, and transmit sealed to the seat of the government of the United States, directed to the president of the Senate; the president of the Senate shall, in the presence of the Senate and the House of Representatives, open all the certificates and the votes shall then be counted;—the person having the greatest number of votes for President shall be the President, if such number be a majority of the whole number of electors appointed; and if no person have such a majority, then from the persons having the highest numbers not exceeding three on the list of those voted for as President, the House of Representatives shall choose immediately, by ballot, the President.

But in choosing the President, the votes shall be taken by states, the representation from each state having one vote; a quorum for this purpose shall consist of a member or members from two thirds of the states, and a majority of all states shall be necessary to a choice. And if the House of Representatives shall not choose a President whenever the right of choice shall devolve upon them, before the fourth day of March next following, then the Vice President, shall act as President, as in the case of death or other constitutional disability of the President—The person having the greatest number of votes as Vice President, shall be the Vice President, if such a number be a majority of the whole number of electors appointed, and if no person have a majority, then from the two highest numbers on the list, the Senate shall choose the Vice President; a quorum for the purpose shall consist of two thirds of the whole number of senators, and a majority of the whole number shall be necessary to a choice. But no person constitutionally ineligible to the office of President shall be eligible to that of Vice President of the United States.

Thirteenth Amendment ★

(1865) Slavery and Involuntary Servitude

Section 1. Outlawing Slavery Neither slavery nor involuntary servitude, except as a punishment for crime whereof the party shall have been duly convicted, shall exist within the United States, or any place subject to their jurisdiction.

Section 2. Enforcement Congress shall have power to enforce this article by appropriate legislation.

Twelfth Amendment This amendment changed the way the electoral college voted as outlined in Article II, Clause 3.

This amendment provides that each elector choose one candidate for President and one candidate for Vice President. If no candidate for President receives a majority of electoral votes, the House of Representatives chooses the President. If no candidate for Vice President receives a majority, the Senate elects the Vice President. The Vice President must be a person who is eligible to be President.

This system is still in use today. However, it is possible for a candidate to win the popular vote and lose in the electoral college. This happened in 1888 and in 2000.

Thirteenth Amendment The Emancipation Proclamation (1863) freed slaves only in areas controlled by the Confederacy. This amendment freed all slaves. It also forbids involuntary servitude, or labor done against one's will. However, it does not prevent prison wardens from making prisoners work. Congress can pass laws to carry out this amendment.

Fourteenth Amendment, Section 1
This amendment defines citizenship for the first time in the Constitution. It was intended to protect the rights of the freed slaves by guaranteeing all citizens "equal protection under the law."

Fourteenth Amendment, Section 2
This section replaced the three-fifths clause. It provides that representation in the House of Representatives is decided on the basis of the number of people in the state. It also provides that states which deny the vote to male citizens over age 21 will be punished by losing part of their representation in the House. This provision has never been enforced.

Fourteenth Amendment ★

(1868) Rights of Citizens

Section 1. Citizenship All persons born or naturalized in the United States, and subject to the jurisdiction thereof, are citizens of the United States and of the state wherein they reside. No state shall make or enforce any law which shall abridge the privileges or immunities of citizens of the United States; nor shall any state deprive any person of life, liberty, or property, without due process of law; nor deny to any person within its jurisdiction the equal protection of the laws.

Section 2. Apportionment of Representatives Representatives shall be apportioned among the several states according to their respective numbers, counting the whole number of persons in each state, excluding Indians not taxed. But when the right to vote at any election for the choice of electors for President and Vice President of the United States, representatives in Congress, the executive and judicial officers of a state, or the members of the legislature thereof, is denied to any of the male inhabitants of such state, being twenty-one years of age, and citizens of the United States, or in any way abridged, except for participation in rebellion, or other crime, the basis of representation therein shall be reduced in the proportion which the number of such male citizens shall bear to the whole number of male citizens twenty-one years of age in such state.

Section 3. Former Confederate Officials No person shall be a senator or representative in Congress, or elector of President and Vice President, or hold any office, civil or military, under the United States, or under any state, who having previously taken an oath, as a member of Congress, or as an officer of the United States, or as a member of any state legislature, or as an executive or judicial officer of any state, to support the Constitution of the United States, shall have engaged in insurrection or rebellion against the same, or given aid or comfort to the enemies thereof. But Congress may, by a vote of two thirds of each house, remove such disability.

Section 4. Public Debt The validity of the public debt of the United States, authorized by law, including debts incurred for payment of pensions and bounties for services in suppressing insurrection or rebellion, shall not be questioned. But neither the United States nor any state shall assume or pay any debt or obligation incurred in aid of insurrection or rebellion against the United States, or any claim for the loss of emancipation of any slave; but all such debts, obligations and claims shall be held illegal and void.

Section 5. Enforcement The Congress shall have power to enforce, by appropriate legislation, the provisions of this article.

Portions of the Constitution altered by later amendments or that no longer apply are printed in blue.

Fifteenth Amendment ★

(1870) Right to Vote—Race, Color, Servitude

Section 1. Extending the Right to Vote The right of citizens of the United States to vote shall not be denied or abridged by the United States or by any state on account of race, color, or previous condition of servitude.

Section 2. Enforcement The Congress shall have power to enforce this article by appropriate legislation.

Sixteenth Amendment ★

(1913) Income Tax

The Congress shall have power to lay and collect taxes on incomes, from whatever source derived, without apportionment among the several states, and without regard to any census or enumeration.

Seventeenth Amendment ★

(1913) Popular Election of Senators

Section 1. Method of Election The Senate of the United States shall be composed of two senators from each state, elected by the people thereof, for six years; and each senator shall have one vote. The electors in each state shall have the qualifications requisite for electors of the most numerous branch of the state legislatures.

Section 2. Vacancies When vacancies happen in the representation of any state in the Senate, the executive authority of such state shall issue writs of election to fill such vacancies: provided, that the legislature of any state may empower the executive thereof to make temporary appointments until the people fill the vacancies by election as the legislature may direct.

Section 3. Those Elected Under Previous Procedure This amendment shall not be so construed as to affect the election or term of any senator chosen before it becomes valid as part of the Constitution.

Fifteenth Amendment, Section 1
Previous condition of servitude refers to slavery. This amendment gave African Americans, both former slaves and free African Americans, the right to vote. In the late 1800s, southern states used grandfather clauses, literacy tests, and poll taxes to keep African Americans from voting.

Fifteenth Amendment, Section 2
Congress can pass laws to carry out this amendment. The Twenty-fourth Amendment barred the use of poll taxes in national elections. The Voting Rights Act of 1965 gave federal officials the power to register voters where there was voting discrimination.

Sixteenth Amendment Congress has the power to collect taxes on people's income. An income tax can be collected without regard to a state's population. This amendment changed Article 1, Section 9, Clause 4.

Seventeenth Amendment, Section 1
This amendment replaced Article 1, Section 2, Clause 1. Before it was adopted, state legislatures chose senators. This amendment provides that senators are directly elected by the people of each state.

Eighteenth Amendment ★

(1919) Prohibition of Alcoholic Beverages

Section 1. Ban on Alcohol After one year from the ratification of this article, the manufacture, sale, or transportation of intoxicating liquors within, the importation thereof into, or the exportation thereof from the United States and all territory subject to the jurisdiction thereof for beverage purposes is hereby prohibited.

Section 2. Enforcement The Congress and the several states shall have concurrent power to enforce this article by appropriate legislation.

Section 3. Method of Ratification This article shall be inoperative unless it shall have been ratified as an amendment to the Constitution by the legislatures of the several states, as provided in the Constitution, within seven years from the date of the submission hereof to the states by Congress.

> **Eighteenth Amendment** This amendment, known as Prohibition, banned the making, selling, or transporting of alcoholic beverages in the United States. Later, the Twenty-first Amendment repealed, or canceled, this amendment.

Nineteenth Amendment ★

(1920) Women's Suffrage

Section 1. The Right to Vote The right of citizens of the United States to vote shall not be denied or abridged by the United States or by any state on account of sex.

Section 2. Enforcement Congress shall have power to enforce this article by appropriate legislation.

> **Nineteenth Amendment** Neither the federal government nor state governments can deny the right to vote on account of sex. Thus, women won suffrage, or the right to vote. Before 1920, some states had allowed women to vote in state elections.

Twentieth Amendment ★

(1933) Presidential Terms; Sessions of Congress; Death or Disqualification of President-Elect

Section 1. Beginning of Terms The terms of the President and Vice President shall end at noon on the 20th day of January, and the terms of senators and representatives at noon on the 3rd day of January, of the years in which such terms would have ended if this article had not been ratified; and the terms of their successors shall then begin.

Section 2. Congressional Sessions The Congress shall assemble at least once in every year, and such meeting shall begin at noon on the 3rd day of January, unless they shall by law appoint a different day.

> **Twentieth Amendment, Section 1.** The date for the inauguration of the President was changed to January 20th, and the date for Congress to begin its term changed to January 3rd. Prior to this amendment, the beginning of term date was set in March. The outgoing officials with little or no influence on matters were not effective in office. Being so inactive, they were called "lame ducks."

> Portions of the Constitution altered by later amendments or that no longer apply are printed in blue.

Section 3. Presidential Succession If, at the time fixed for the beginning of the term of the President, the President-elect shall have died, the Vice President-elect shall become President. If a President shall not have been chosen before the time fixed for the beginning of his term, or if the President-elect shall have failed to qualify, the Vice President-elect shall act as President until a President shall have qualified; and the Congress may by law provide for the case wherein neither a President-elect nor a Vice President-elect shall have qualified, declaring who shall then act as President, or the manner in which one who is to act shall be selected, and such person shall act accordingly until a President or Vice President shall have qualified.

Section 4. Elections Decided by Congress The Congress may by law provide for the case of the death of any persons from whom the House of Representatives may choose a President whenever the right of choice shall have devolved upon them, and for the case of the death of any of the persons from whom the Senate may choose a Vice President whenever the right of choice shall have devolved upon them.

Section 5. Date of Implementation Sections 1 and 2 shall take effect on the 15th day of October following the ratification of this article.

Section 6. Ratification Period This article shall be inoperative unless it shall have been ratified as an amendment to the Constitution by the legislatures of three fourths of the several states within seven years from the date of its submission.

Twentieth Amendment, Section 3. If the President-elect dies before taking office, the Vice President-elect becomes President. If no President has been chosen by January 20 or if the elected candidate fails to qualify for office, the Vice President-elect acts as President, but only until a qualified President is chosen.

Finally, Congress has the power to choose a person to act as President if neither the President-elect nor the Vice President-elect is qualified to take office.

Twenty-first Amendment ★

(1933) Repeal of Prohibition

Section 1. Repeal The eighteenth article of amendment to the Constitution of the United States is hereby repealed.

Section 2. State Laws The transportation or importation into any state, territory, or possession of the United States for delivery or use therein of intoxicating liquors, in violation of the laws thereof, is hereby prohibited.

Section 3. Ratification Period This article shall be inoperative unless it shall have been ratified as an amendment to the Constitution by conventions in the several states, as provided in the Constitution, within seven years from the date of the submission hereof to the states by the Congress.

Twenty-first Amendment, Section 1 The Eighteenth Amendment is repealed, making it legal to make and sell alcoholic beverages. Prohibition ended December 5, 1933.

Twenty-second Amendment ★

(1951) Presidential Tenure

Section 1. Two-Term Limit No person shall be elected to the office of the President more than twice, and no person who has held the office of President, or acted as President, for more than two years of a term to which some other person was elected President shall be elected to the office of President more than once. But this article shall not apply to any person holding the office of President when this article was proposed by the Congress, and shall not prevent any person who may be holding the office of President, or acting as President, during the term within which this article becomes operative from holding the office of President or acting as President during the remainder of such term.

Section 2. Ratification Period This article shall be inoperative unless it shall have been ratified as an amendment to the Constitution by the legislatures of three fourths of the several states within seven years from the date of its submission to the state by the Congress.

Twenty-third Amendment ★

(1961) Presidential Electors for the District of Columbia

Section 1. Determining the Number of Electors The district constituting the seat of government of the United States shall appoint in such manner as the Congress may direct:

A number of electors of President and Vice President equal to the whole number of senators and representatives in Congress to which the district would be entitled if it were a state, but in no event more than the least populous state; they shall be in addition to those appointed by the states, but they shall be considered, for the purposes of the election of President and Vice President, to be electors appointed by a state; and they shall meet in the district and perform such duties as provided by the twelfth article of amendment.

Section 2. Enforcement The Congress shall have power to enforce this article by appropriate legislation.

Twenty-fourth Amendment ★

(1964) Right to Vote in Federal Elections—Tax Payment

Section 1. Poll Tax Banned The right of citizens of the United States to vote in any primary or other election for President or Vice President, for electors for President or Vice President, or for senator or representative in Congress, shall not be denied or abridged by the United States or any state by reason of failure to pay any poll tax or other tax.

Section 2. Enforcement The Congress shall have the power to enforce this article by appropriate legislation.

Twenty-fifth Amendment ★

(1967) Presidential Succession, Vice Presidential Vacancy, Presidential Inability

Section 1. President's Death or Resignation In case of the removal of the President from office or of his death or resignation, the Vice President shall become President.

Section 2. Vacancies in Vice Presidency Whenever there is a vacancy in the office of the Vice President, the President shall nominate a Vice President who shall take office upon confirmation by a majority vote of both houses of Congress.

Section 3. Disability of the President Whenever the President transmits to the President pro tempore of the Senate and the Speaker of the House of Representatives his written declaration that he is unable to discharge the powers and duties of his office, and until he transmits to them a written declaration to the contrary, such powers and duties shall be discharged by the Vice President as acting President.

Section 4. Vice President as Acting President Whenever the Vice President and a majority of either the principal officers of the executive departments or of such other body as Congress may by law provide, transmit to the President pro tempore of the Senate and the Speaker of the House of Representatives their written declaration that the President is unable to discharge the powers and duties of his office, the Vice President shall immediately assume the powers and duties of the office as acting President.

Thereafter, when the President transmits to the President pro tempore of the Senate and the Speaker of the House of Representatives his written declaration that no inability exists, he shall resume the powers and duties of his office unless the Vice President and a majority of either the principal officers of the executive department or of such other body as Congress may by law provide, transmit within four days to the President pro tempore of the Senate and the Speaker of the House of Representatives their written declaration that the President is unable to discharge the powers and duties of his office. Thereupon Congress shall decide the issue, assembling within forty-eight hours for that purpose if not in session. If the Congress, within twenty-one days after receipt of the latter written declaration, or, if Congress is not in session, within twenty-one days after Congress is required to assemble, determines by two-thirds vote of both Houses that the President is unable to discharge the powers and duties of his office, the Vice President shall continue to discharge the same as acting President; otherwise, the President shall resume the powers and duties of his office.

Twenty-fifth Amendment, Section 1
If the President dies or resigns, the Vice President becomes President. This section clarifies Article 2, Section 1, Clause 6.

Twenty-fifth Amendment, Section 3
If the President declares in writing that he or she is unable to perform the duties of office, the Vice President serves as acting President until the President recovers.

Twenty-fifth Amendment, Section 4
Two Presidents, Woodrow Wilson and Dwight Eisenhower, fell gravely ill while in office. The Constitution contained no provision for this kind of emergency. Section 3 provided that the President can inform Congress he or she is too sick to perform the duties of office. However, if the President is unconscious or refuses to admit to a disabling illness, Section 4 provides that the Vice President and Cabinet may declare the President disabled. The Vice President becomes the acting President until the President can return to the duties of office. In case of a disagreement between the President and the Vice President and Cabinet over the President's ability to perform the duties of office, Congress must decide the issue. A two-thirds vote of both houses is needed to find the President is disabled or unable to fulfill the duties of office.

Twenty-sixth Amendment ★

(1971) Right to Vote—Age

Twenty-sixth Amendment, Section 1
In 1970, Congress passed a law allowing 18-year-olds to vote. However, the Supreme Court decided that Congress could not set a minimum age for state elections.

Section 1. Lowering the Voting Age The right of citizens of the United States, who are eighteen years of age or older, to vote shall not be denied or abridged by the United States or by any state on account of age.

Section 2. Enforcement The Congress shall have the power to enforce this article by appropriate legislation.

Twenty-seventh Amendment ★

(1992) Congressional Pay

Twenty-seventh Amendment
If members of Congress vote themselves a pay increase, it cannot go into effect until after the next congressional election. This amendment was proposed in 1789. In 1992, Michigan became the thirty-eighth state to ratify it.

No law, varying the compensation for the services of the senators and representatives, shall take effect until an election of representatives shall have intervened.

Independence Hall room where the Constitution was signed

Portions of the Constitution altered by later amendments or that no longer apply are printed in blue.

History Background

Government and Citizenship

The privileges and responsibilities of being a citizen of the United States are established in the Constitution. The document was written using earlier civilizations, including the republic of ancient Rome, as models. It is also based on earlier documents, including the Magna Carta and the English Bill of Rights.

The Constitution consists of the Preamble, seven Articles, and the Amendments. Among other rights, it sets up the principles of popular sovereignty, limited government, a separation of powers, and a system of checks and balances. These provisions preserve individual rights and prevent the federal government from abusing its powers.

The three branches of government are key to preventing such abuses of power. The legislative branch, made up of the Senate and the House of Representatives, allows a large degree of public participation through political parties, elections, and interest groups. Although the executive branch allows less participation, it is nevertheless headed by an elected President and Vice President, each subject to election every four years. The judicial branch is the ultimate court in the land. Its decisions establish the constitutionality of the laws made by the legislative branch.

One of the most important strengths of the Constitution is its capacity to be amended. The first 10 amendments to the Constitution, the Bill of Rights, outline the fundamental rights of all citizens of the land. The Bill of Rights includes such rights as the freedom to practice religion and the freedom to speak openly.

A basic principle of federalism is the separation of powers between federal and state or local governments. For example, such services as fire protection and school regulation are reserved for state governments, while national defense is governed by federal lawmakers.

The citizens of the United States enjoy many freedoms. In exchange, they are obligated to obey laws, pay taxes, defend the nation, and serve on juries. In addition, there are other responsibilities that good citizens practice, including serving the community, voting in elections, and helping create a just society.

Essential Questions

Use this graphic organizer to see the relationship between key concepts and the Chapter Essential Questions.

Focus Question/Part 1
What were the ideas behind the Constitution?
Concept: Democracy

Focus Question/Part 2
What is the structure of the Constitution?
Concept: Constitution

Focus Question/Part 10
What are the rights and responsibilities of citizens?
Concept: Civil Rights

Citizenship Handbook Essential Question
How did the Constitution create a strong government with roots in history that allowed for change and met the needs of the people?

Focus Question/Part 3
What are the fundamental principles underlying the Constitution?
Concept: Federalism

Focus Question/Part 9
What are the powers of state and local governments?
Concept: States' Rights

Focus Question/Parts 7–8
How can the Constitution be amended to meet changing needs?
Concept: Change

Focus Question/Parts 4–6
What are the powers of each branch of government?
Concept: Checks and Balances

Differentiated Instruction

Scaffolding Tip

When asking students questions about the text, first ask questions with answers that can be clearly found in the text. Then ask more difficult questions that require students to make their own interpretations based on the easier questions. For example, you might ask students "What was John Locke's philosophy about the nature of people?" and "What was Montesquieu's concept of government?" After students have answered these questions, ask them, "How did the Constitution of the United States incorporate these ideas?"

Concepts Across Time

Have students develop an understanding of the enduring concepts of history by connecting these ideas.

Concept: Constitution

Ask students to recall the ideas of the Enlightenment. Ask: **How does the Constitution reflect a respect for human rights, a concept from the Enlightenment?** (*The Constitution spells out the rights of citizens. It keeps the federal government from growing too powerful and it gives all citizens a role in the governing process.*) Point out that the Enlightenment ideas that people are born with the ability to control their own affairs and have natural rights, and that balanced government is important, had a great influence on the Founders' thinking. Address this connection as students read Parts 1 and 3.

Concept: Checks and Balances

Ask students to recall their studies of the conflicts between the British colonies in America and England. Ask: **Why did the Founders work so carefully to impose checks and balances on the government of the young nation?** (*The Founders knew that a government could become too powerful, impinging on the rights of citizens.*) Explain that the events before the War of Independence had a direct effect on the drafting of the Constitution. Explain this cause-and-effect relationship when you study Parts 4–6 of the Citizenship Handbook.

Concept: States' Rights

Ask students to recall the main principles of feudalism. (*a system in which a ruler grants parts of his land to lords in exchange for military service and financial assistance*) Have them compare this system to the federalism established by the Constitution. Ask: **What were the similarities between a feudal lord and a state within the United States?** (*Both have governing rights over their immediate territory. Both the lords and the states had responsibilities to pay taxes and help defend the nation.*) Point out that feudalism and federalism help each society function smoothly. Explain this idea when students read Part 9.

Concept: Civil Rights

Have students recall the arguments between the Federalists and the Antifederalists. Ask: **What was one of the important concerns of the Antifederalists during the Constitutional Convention?** (*They feared that a national government could become so powerful that it would not need to respect the individual rights of citizens.*) Ask students to discuss the meaning of the word *rights* and to provide examples of basic rights that they believe are guaranteed by American citizenship. (*Answers should show understanding that citizens enjoy rights to life, liberty, and the pursuit of happiness.*) Explain that the concept of human rights began with the ideas of the Enlightenment in Europe many years before the Constitution was written. Discuss this topic when students read Part 10 of the Citizenship Handbook.

Citizenship Handbook *6 periods, 3 blocks*

Objectives

Students will

1. Explain how democratic thought and institutions were influenced by past political ideas.
2. Discuss the tradition of representation in colonial America.
3. List the three parts of the Constitution.
4. Explain how the Preamble defines the basic goals of the Constitution.
5. Identify the Articles of the Constitution.
6. Describe the seven principles of the Constitution.
7. Explain how individual rights are protected by the Constitution.
8. Discuss the powers of the legislative, executive, and judicial branches of the government.
9. Describe how to amend the Constitution.
10. Name the rights that the Bill of Rights protects.
11. Discuss the importance of the First Amendment to the Constitution.
12. Discuss the services that state governments provide.
13. Describe how local governments affect our daily lives.
14. Explain the rights of citizens.
15. Describe the responsibilities of citizenship.

Differentiated Instruction Key

- **L1** Basic to Average
- **L2** For All Students
- **L3** Average to Advanced
- **AR** Advanced Readers
- **ELL** English Language Learners
- **GT** Gifted and Talented
- **LPR** Less Proficient Readers
- **SN** Special Needs

Prepare to Read	Instructional Resources	Differentiated Instruction
Build Background Knowledge Discuss the reasons for writing the Constitution and its governing principles.		🔊 **Guided Reading Audio CD** **Spanish** ELL, LPR, SN

Teach	Instructional Resources	Differentiated Instruction
Instruction **Ideas Behind the Constitution** ■ Explain what American leaders learned from studying ancient Rome. ■ Identify the ideas of freedom from Great Britain and the Enlightenment that influenced the Framers of the Constitution. ■ Discuss the tradition of representation in colonial America.	📖 **Interactive Reading and Notetaking Study Guide** **L2** Citizenship Handbook **All in One Teaching Resources, Unit 2** **L2** The English Bill of Rights, 1689, p. 96	📖 **Interactive Reading and Notetaking Study Guide, Adapted Version (English/Spanish)** **L1** Citizenship Handbook ELL, LPR, SN **Teacher's Edition** **L3** Research, p. 252 AR, GT 🏴 **Historian's Apprentice Activity Pack**
Instruction **Structure of the Constitution** ■ List the three parts of the Constitution. ■ Identify the Articles of the Constitution.	📖 **Interactive Reading and Notetaking Study Guide** **L2** Citizenship Handbook	📖 **Interactive Reading and Notetaking Study Guide, Adapted Version (English/Spanish)** **L2** Citizenship Handbook ELL, LPR, SN **Teacher's Edition** **L1** Study Aid, p. 254 LPR

Citizenship Handbook Lesson Plan

Teach (continued)

Teach (continued)	Instructional Resources	Differentiated Instruction

Instruction
Principles of the Constitution

- Describe the seven principles of the Constitution.
- Discuss the ways in which the Constitution preserves individual rights.

Interactive Reading and Notetaking Study Guide

- **L2** Citizenship Handbook

Color Transparencies

- **L2** Separation of Powers
- **L2** Checks and Balances

Interactive Reading and Notetaking Study Guide, Adapted Version (English/Spanish)

- **L1** Citizenship Handbook ELL, LPR, SN

Teacher's Edition

- **L1** Reading a Chart, p. 256 ELL, LPR
- **All in One** Teaching Resources, Unit 2
- **L2** Checks and Balances, p. 97

Instruction
How the Federal Government Works

- Discuss how the legislative branch of government works.
- Describe how the executive branch of government works.
- Explain how the judicial branch of government works.

Interactive Reading and Notetaking Study Guide

- **L2** Citizenship Handbook
- **All in One** Teaching Resources, Unit 2
- **L2** Checks and Balances, p. 97
- **L2** How a Bill Becomes a Law, p. 98
- **L2** Shifting Electoral Votes, p. 99
- **L2** Sandra Day O'Connor, p. 101

Color Transparencies

- **L2** How a Bill Becomes a Law
- **L2** Federal Officeholders
- **L2** Federal Court System

Interactive Reading and Notetaking Study Guide, Adapted Version (English/Spanish)

- **L1** Citizenship Handbook ELL, LPR, SN

Teacher's Edition

- **L3** Lawmaking Simulation, p. 258 AR, GT
- **L1** Gaining Comprehension, p. 260 ELL, LPR, SN
- **L3** Research Court Cases, p. 262 AR, GT

Interactive Constitution CD-ROM

- **L3** Supreme Court Cases
- **L3** Lawmaking Simulation
- **All in One** Teaching Resources, Unit 2
- **L2** Checks and Balances, p. 97

Instruction
Amending the Constitution

- Discuss the process of amending the Constitution.
- Describe the Bill of Rights and other amendments.

The First Amendment

- Discuss the importance of the First Amendment to the Constitution.
- Describe the principles of freedom of religion, freedom of speech, freedom of the press, and the right to petition the government.

Interactive Reading and Notetaking Study Guide

- **L2** Citizenship Handbook
- **All in One** Teaching Resources, Unit 2
- **L2** The Bill of Rights, p. 102

Color Transparencies

- **L2** Amendment Process

Interactive Reading and Notetaking Study Guide, Adapted Version (English/Spanish)

- **L1** Citizenship Handbook ELL, LPR, SN

Teacher's Edition

- **L1** Vocabulary Development, p. 264 ELL, SN
- **L3** Conduct a Survey, p. 266 AR, GT

Teach (continued)	Instructional Resources	Differentiated Instruction
Instruction **State and Local Governments** ■ Discuss the role of state governments. ■ Describe the role of local governments.	📖 **Interactive Reading and Notetaking Study Guide** **L2** Citizenship Handbook **Color Transparencies** **L2** The Federal System **L2** Local Government	📖 **Interactive Reading and Notetaking Study Guide, Adapted Version (English/ Spanish)** **L1** Citizenship Handbook ELL, LPR, SN **Teacher's Edition** **L1** Gaining Comprehension, p. 268 LPR **All in One** Teaching Resources, Unit 2 **L1** Ratifying Amendments, p. 103
Instruction **Rights and Responsibilities of Citizenship** ■ Discuss the rights of citizens. ■ Describe the responsibilities of citizenship.	📖 **Interactive Reading and Notetaking Study Guide** **L2** Citizenship Handbook **All in One** Teaching Resources, Unit 2 **L2** George Mitchell, p. 104 **Color Transparencies** **L2** Naturalization Process **L2** Responsibilities of Citizenship	📖 **Interactive Reading and Notetaking Study Guide, Adapted Version (English/ Spanish)** **L1** Citizenship Handbook ELL, LPR, SN **Teacher's Edition** **L1** Citizenship in Other Countries, p. 270 ELL

Assess and Reteach	Instructional Resources	Differentiated Instruction
Assess Progress Evaluate student comprehension by assessing their skills and the chapter test. **Reteach** Have students review material in the section summaries. **Think Like a Historian** Using primary sources and information from the chapters in this unit, revisit the Unit Essential Question to check the concept comprehension.	📖 **Interactive Reading and Notetaking Study Guide** **L2** Citizenship Handbook **All in One** Teaching Resources, Unit 2 **L2** Chapter Test, p. 108 **Progress Monitoring Transparencies** **L2** Citizenship Handbook **Color Transparencies** **L2** Think Like a Historian, Unit 2	**All in One** Teaching Resources, Unit 2 **L1** Chapter Test, p. 105 **Teacher's Edition** **L1** Assessment, pp. 253, 255, 257, 259, 261, 263, 265, 267, 269, 271 💿 SE on Audio CD **L1** Citizenship Handbook ELL, LPR, SN

Use the following research activities to help students deepen their understanding of the Chapter Essential Question: **"How did the Constitution create a strong government with roots in history that allowed for change and met the needs of the people?"** Students should use library or Internet resources. The Web Codes provided offer access to Internet resources that students can use to complete each activity. Use the appropriate four-point rubric in Assessment Rubrics to evaluate the activity.

 Assessment Rubrics

Write a Letter

Have students get involved in the government process by researching the standing committees of the Senate and the House and writing a letter to the chairperson of one committee. Letters should either ask for information on a topic or state the student's opinion relevant to the committee of their choice. Ask students to share any response they receive. Use this activity with Part 4 of the Citizenship Handbook.

 Individual research activity

Go Online **Web Code:** mye-0290
PHSchool.com

Plan for World Press Freedom Day

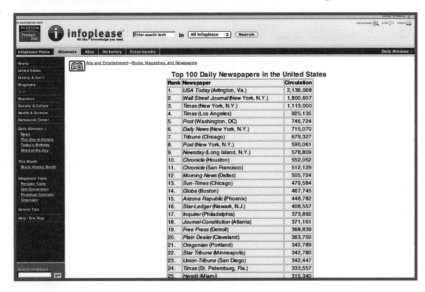

May 3 of every year is a celebration of the fundamental principles of press freedom. Have students research more about how freedom of the press is important throughout the world. Then have small groups brainstorm for activities to celebrate the day at your school. Have groups of interested students take charge of the event by making posters, organizing activities, and discussing the goals of the event with school administrators. After the event, evaluate the day's success. Use this activity with Part 8 of the Citizenship Handbook.

 Group research activity LPR, ELL

Go Online **Web Code:** mye-0291
PHSchool.com

CITIZENSHIP HANDBOOK

Table of Contents

Key Terms

Why It Matters

In 1850, Henry Clay declared, "The Constitution of the United States was made not merely for the generation that then existed, but for posterity—unlimited, undefined, endless, perpetual posterity." More so than any other political document, the Constitution shapes the lives of Americans today and probably will do so for generations to come.

Being a citizen of the United States involves rights, duties, and responsibilities. Fulfilling these responsibilities helps contribute to the common good. It is important for students to understand their civic responsibility to support the basic values that unite American society.

Citizenship Handbook Focus Question

How did the Constitution create a strong government with roots in history that allowed for change and met the needs of the people?

Think Like a Historian

- To preview this chapter, have students review the content on this page of the Student Edition. Ask: **What will you be learning about in this chapter?** (*American government and the Constitution*)

- Write the Chapter Focus Question on the board. Using the Idea Wave strategy (TE, p. T24), have students list ways our government today is shaped by the Constitution.

- Tell students that as they complete the Interactive Reading and Notetaking Study Guide for this chapter, they will be building the answer to this question.

Differentiated Instruction

The following Teacher's Edition strategies are suitable for students of varying abilities.

- **L3 Advanced Readers,** pp. 252, 258, 262, 266 AR
- **L1 English Language Learners,** pp. 256, 260, 264, 270 ELL
- **L3 Gifted and Talented,** pp. 252, 258, 262, 266 GT
- **L1 Less Proficient Readers,** pp. 254, 256, 260, 268 LPR
- **L1 Special Needs,** pp. 260, 264 SN

Ideas Behind the Constitution

Review and Preview

Students have learned about the foundations of American democratic institutions. Now they will focus on the significance of past political ideas in the framing of the Constitution of the United States.

Section Focus Question

What were the ideas behind the Constitution?

Build Background Knowledge L2

Have students recall the reasons American leaders decided to write the Constitution. (*The national government under the Articles of Confederation was unable to solve many of the country's problems; leaders wanted to establish a more effective national government.*) Ask students to describe the main ideas behind our form of government. (*republican government, justice, rights of individuals, limited power of government*) Now students can read about the origin of some of these ideas.

Instruction L2

■ Have students read Ideas Behind the Constitution. Begin the discussion by asking students to define republic. (*a government in which citizens rule themselves through elected representatives*)

■ Ask: **Which principle from the Magna Carta and the English Bill of Rights do you think is most important to the American system of government?** (*Answers will vary, but students should correctly identify one of these principles and give reasons why it is important to American government.*)

The delegates to the Constitutional Convention who gathered in Philadelphia were greatly influenced by past experiments with democracy and natural rights. As they debated the new document for American government, the Founders considered a variety of past political ideas.

Ancient Rome

Earlier in this textbook, you read about the ancient Roman Republic. The Framers of the United States Constitution looked to Rome as a model. Like the early Romans, they sought to create a lasting republic, or a government in which citizens rule themselves through elected representatives. American leaders also admired what they saw as the independent thinking and public service of Roman citizens. Romans, Americans said, had been willing to serve in public office out of devotion to the republic.

However, Americans also took the fate of Rome as a warning. The Roman Republic eventually collapsed and became a dictatorship, a government in which one person or a small group holds complete authority. American leaders believed that the Roman Republic faltered when citizens began to value luxury and comfort more than freedom and public service. The Framers of the Constitution wanted to avoid Rome's fate. They hoped to build a system in which informed, independent citizens played an active role in their own government.

Two Historic Documents

You also learned earlier about the following two important documents in British history: the Magna Carta, which British nobles forced King John to sign in 1215; and the Bill of Rights, which William and Mary issued in 1689 after the Glorious Revolution. These two documents created an English tradition of liberty, which the colonists brought to America.

The following principles found in the these two documents became part of the American system of government:

- Citizens have rights which the government must protect.
- Even the head of the government must obey the law.
- Taxes cannot be raised without the consent of the people.
- Elections should be held frequently.
- People accused of crimes have the right to trial by jury and the right of habeas corpus, meaning no person may be held in prison without being charged with a specific crime.
- People have the right to private property, or property owned by an individual.

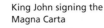

HISTORIAN'S APPRENTICE ACTIVITY PACK

To further explore the topics in this chapter, complete the activity in the Historian's Apprentice Activity Pack to answer this essential question:
How is the rule of law in the Constitution of the United States rooted in the past?

King John signing the Magna Carta

252

Differentiated Instruction

L3 Advanced Readers **L3** Gifted and Talented

Research Have students find out more about John Locke, Baron de Montesquieu, or another Enlightenment thinker. Then have students work in pairs to prepare questions as if they were to interview this thinker about his ideas. For example, what are his major ideas about government? Does he think these ideas are still important today? Have students speculate about what answers this thinker might have given.

Teachings of the Enlightenment

Many of the Framers were influenced by the works of European Enlightenment thinkers. In his book *Two Treatises on Government*, the English writer John Locke declared that every individual has natural rights to life, liberty, and property. Locke said government is an agreement between the ruler and the ruled. Further, he argued, if a ruler violates the people's natural rights, the people have a right to rebel.

The French thinker Baron de Montesquieu (MOHN tehs kyoo) suggested a concept known as separation of powers—the idea that powers of government must be clearly defined and divided into legislative, executive, and judicial branches. This concept was designed to keep one person or group from gaining too much power.

John Locke

Representative Traditions and the Declaration of Independence

Americans enjoyed a long tradition of representative government. The Virginia colonists set up the House of Burgesses, and the Pilgrims drafted the Mayflower Compact in 1620. The compact was the first document of self-government in North America.

Each of the 13 colonies had a written charter that identified the powers and limits of government granted by the British Crown. In addition to these traditions, the Framers of the Constitution drew on the grievances Thomas Jefferson had listed against George III in the Declaration of Independence. In writing the Constitution, they sought to prevent similar abuses in the new American government.

Baron de Montesquieu

Declaring Independence
Delegates sign the Declaration of Independence.

Assessment

1. Identify two principles of American government that came from the Magna Carta or the English Bill of Rights.

2. How did Montesquieu's ideas affect the crafting of the Constitution?

Ideas Behind the Constitution **253**

History Background

Influence of the Magna Carta The great influence of the Magna Carta can be seen in some of the actual language of the Constitution. For example, the Magna Carta states: "No freeman shall be taken, or imprisoned, or be [deprived of his land], or liberties, or free customs, or be outlawed, or exiled, or any otherwise destroyed; nor will we pass upon him, nor condemn him, but by lawful judgment of his peers, or by the law of the land." The Fifth Amendment to the Constitution states: "No person shall . . . be deprived of life, liberty, or property without due process of law." Today, the American government still recognizes the influence of the Magna Carta. On prominent display in the National Archives in Washington, D.C., is a copy of the Magna Carta from 1297.

Structure of the Constitution

Review and Preview

Students have completed the concept lesson discussing the idea of a constitution in Chapter 7. Now they will focus on how the Constitution of the United States is constructed.

Section Focus Question

What is the structure of the Constitution?

Build Background Knowledge   L2

This section explains how the Constitution is organized. Remind students that they have to think about organization and structure when they plan reports. Ask students to describe the different types of sections they might include in a report. (*introduction, main text, conclusion*)

Instruction   L2

- Have students read Structure of the Constitution and examine the visuals. Ask students to name the three main parts of the Constitution. (*Preamble, Articles, Amendments*) Ask students to briefly describe each section. (*The Preamble states the goals of the Constitution; the Articles describe the framework of American government; the Amendments make changes to the Constitution.*)

- Ask students to describe the main purpose of the first three Articles of the Constitution. (*They describe how the three branches of government work and the limits on the power of each branch.*) Ask: **Suppose you wanted to propose an amendment to the Constitution. In which Article would you look for information on this process?** (*Article V*)

The principles of the Constitution have guided the United States for more than 200 years. The Constitution is divided into three main parts: the Preamble, or opening statement; the Articles; and the Amendments. The Preamble begins with the words, "We the people of the United States." These words show that the authority of the government comes from its citizens. The Preamble then goes on to outline six basic goals for the new government. They are shown on the chart below.

Goals of the Preamble

Goals	What It Means to Us
■ To form a more perfect union	All states should work together as a unified nation.
■ To establish justice	Everyone should be treated equally and fairly under the law.
■ To ensure domestic tranquillity	The government has the responsibility to ensure peace and order at home.
■ To provide for the common defense	The government has the responsibility to protect its citizens against foreign attack.
■ To promote the general welfare	The government has the responsibility to promote the well-being of all its citizens.
■ To secure the blessings of liberty	The government should value and protect the rights of its citizens.

The Constitution

Articles

The main body of the Constitution is divided into seven sections called articles. Together, they establish the framework for American government. The first three articles describe the three branches of the national government: legislative, executive, and judicial. Article 1 establishes the powers and limits on Congress. Articles 2 and 3 do the same for the President and the courts.

Article 4 deals with relations between states. It requires states to honor one another's laws and also sets out a system for admitting new states. Article 5 provides a process to amend the Constitution. Article 6 states that the Constitution is the "supreme law of the land." States cannot make laws that violate the Constitution and federal laws prevail in all disputes. The final article, Article 7, sets up a procedure for the states to ratify the Constitution.

254 Citizenship Handbook

Differentiated Instruction

L1 Less Proficient Readers

Study Aid To help students remember what they learned in this section, have them create a table summarizing the three main parts of the Constitution: Preamble, Articles, Amendments. The table should list the name of the part of the Constitution in one column and a one-sentence summary of that part in the second column.

Amendments

The Amendments are formal changes that have been made to the Constitution. Some of these changes added new ideas to the document. Others repealed, or canceled, other parts of the Constitution.

In more than 200 years, only 27 changes have been made to the Constitution. The first 10 amendments, known as the Bill of Rights, were added in 1791. You will read more about the Bill of Rights later in this handbook.

Some later amendments had an immediate and powerful impact on American society. A few of them are illustrated below.

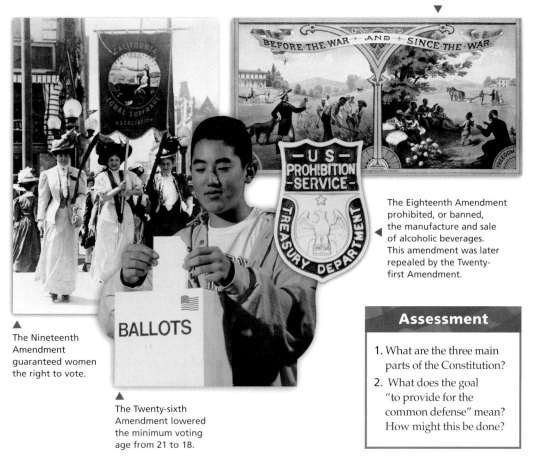

The Thirteenth Amendment ended slavery throughout the United States. ▼

The Eighteenth Amendment prohibited, or banned, the manufacture and sale of alcoholic beverages. This amendment was later repealed by the Twenty-first Amendment.

▲
The Nineteenth Amendment guaranteed women the right to vote.

▲
The Twenty-sixth Amendment lowered the minimum voting age from 21 to 18.

Assessment

1. What are the three main parts of the Constitution?

2. What does the goal "to provide for the common defense" mean? How might this be done?

Instruction (continued)

■ Ask: **Aside from the Bill of Rights, how many changes have been made to the Constitution?** (*17*) Using the photographs on p. 255 as a reference, ask students to name some of the rights citizens have gained through the later amendments. (*Women gained the right to vote. All citizens 18 and older gained the right to vote. The manufacture and sale of alcohol was prohibited; this was later repealed. Slavery was banned.*)

■ To help students better understand the process of amending the Constitution, direct them to the Eighteenth Amendment and the Twenty-first Amendment. Have students read the amendments. Then ask: **How did the Twenty-first Amendment affect the Eighteenth Amendment?** (*It repealed it.*) Ask: **Under the Twenty-first Amendment, who still has the power to ban the sale and use of alcohol?** (*the states*)

Monitor Progress

Have students share their answers to the Assessment questions in the Student Edition, p. 255. Correct any misunderstandings.

History Background

Providing for the Common Defense Born during the Revolution, the U.S. Army and Navy are the oldest branches of the armed services. The Marine Corps was established as a separate service in 1798. Marines operate on land, but their actions are linked to naval operations. They also guard U.S. naval stations and embassies in other countries. The army directed air operations until 1947, when the United States Air Force became a separate branch of the military. The U.S. Coast Guard was set up in 1790 to prevent smuggling and piracy. In 1915, it was combined with the Lifesaving Service and given its present name. In 2003, the Coast Guard was made part of the Department of Homeland Security.

Answers
Assessment

1. Preamble; Articles; Amendments

2. The government will protect the nation. It will have the power to form a military to accomplish this goal.

Principles of the Constitution

Review and Preview

Students have learned about the causes of the Revolutionary War and why colonists were unhappy with the rule of the English monarch. Now they will learn how the principles of the Constitution of the United States protected the individual rights of citizens.

Section Focus Question

What are the fundamental principles underlying the Constitution?

Build Background Knowledge   L2

Remind students that the Framers of the Constitution had all lived under King George III when the states were still British colonies. How might this experience have influenced their ideas about government? (*They learned the danger of allowing one person to have too much power.*) The Framers also lived under the Articles of Confederation. How might this have influenced their ideas? (*They learned that a government must have enough power to deal with its country's problems.*)

Instruction   L2

- Have students read the text and charts in this section. Ask: **What is popular sovereignty?** (*the principle that a government gets its authority from the people*) **Why was this an important new idea at the time the Constitution was written?** (*The Framers lived at a time when monarchs claimed their power came from God. Popular sovereignty gave people much more power over their government.*)

- Have students review Article I, Section 2 of the Constitution. Ask: **Which clause supports the idea of popular sovereignty?** (*Clause 1*)

The Constitution rests on seven basic principles. They are popular sovereignty, limited government, separation of powers, federalism, checks and balances, republicanism, and individual rights.

- **Popular Sovereignty** The Framers of the Constitution lived at a time when monarchs claimed that their power came from God. The Preamble, which begins "We the people," reflects a revolutionary new idea: a government gets its authority from the people. This principle, known as popular sovereignty, asserts that the people are the primary source of the government's authority.

- **Limited Government** The colonists believed that the British king had ruled them harshly. To avoid a repeat of this rule in their new government, the Framers made limited government a principle of the Constitution. In a limited government, the government has only the powers that the Constitution gives it. Equally important, every citizen of the United States—including the President—must obey the law.

- **Separation of Powers** To further limit the power of the government, the Framers provided for separation of powers. The Constitution divides the government into three branches, and each branch has its own duties. The chart below outlines the duties of each branch of government.

Separation of Powers

Legislative Branch (Congress)	**Executive Branch** (President)	**Judicial Branch** (Supreme Court and Other Federal Courts)
Passes Laws	**Carries Out Laws**	**Interprets Laws**
■ Can override President's veto	■ Proposes laws	■ Can declare laws unconstitutional
■ Approves treaties	■ Can veto laws	■ Can declare executive actions unconstitutional
■ Can impeach and remove President and other high officials	■ Negotiates foreign treaties	
■ Prints and coins money	■ Serves as commander in chief of armed forces	
■ Raises and supports armed forces	■ Appoints federal judges, ambassadors, and other high officials	
■ Can declare war	■ Can grant pardons to federal offenders	
■ Regulates foreign and interstate trade		

Differentiated Instruction

L1 English Language Learners   **L1 Less Proficient Readers**

Reading a Chart Have students complete the worksheet Checks and Balances. Help students understand that this chart gives details about how each branch of government can check, or limit, the powers of the other branches.

All in One Teaching Resources, Unit 2, Checks and Balances, p. 97

Checks and Balances

	Checks on the Executive Branch	Checks on the Judicial Branch
Legislative Branch (Congress makes laws) 	■ Can override President's veto ■ Confirms executive appointments ■ Ratifies treaties ■ Can declare war ■ Appropriates money ■ Can impeach and remove President	■ Creates lower federal courts ■ Can impeach and remove judges ■ Can propose amendments to overrule judicial decisions ■ Approves appointments of federal judges
	Checks on the Legislative Branch	**Checks on the Judicial Branch**
Executive Branch (President carries out laws) 	■ Can propose laws ■ Can veto laws ■ Can call special sessions of Congress ■ Makes appointments ■ Negotiates foreign treaties	■ Appoints federal judges ■ Can grant pardons to federal offenders
	Check on the Executive Branch	**Check on the Legislative Branch**
Judicial Branch (Supreme Court interprets laws) 	■ Can declare executive actions unconstitutional	■ Can declare acts of Congress unconstitutional

- **Checks and Balances** A system of checks and balances safeguards against abuse of power. Each branch of government has the power to check, or limit, the actions of the other two. This arrangement guarantees that no branch of government will become too powerful. The chart above describes the specific checks each branch has on the other two. The next six pages of this handbook will detail how each branch of government works.

- **Federalism** The Constitution also establishes the principle of federalism, or division of power between the federal government and the states. The Constitution grants specific powers to the federal government and other powers to the states. Powers that are not clearly given to the federal government belong to the states.

- **Republicanism** The Constitution provides for a republican form of government. Instead of direct participation in government, citizens elect representatives to carry out their will.

- **Individual Rights** The Constitution protects individual rights, such as freedom of speech, freedom of religion, and the right to trial by jury. You will learn more about the rights protected by the Constitution later in this handbook.

Assessment

1. How does the Constitution reflect the principle of separation of powers?

2. How can the judicial branch check the powers of the executive and legislative branches?

Principles of the Constitution **257**

How the Federal Government Works: The Legislative Branch

Review and Preview

Students have read that the first three Articles of the Constitution describe the branches of the government. Now they will learn how the legislative, executive, and judicial branches function.

What are the powers of each branch of government?

Build Background Knowledge   **L2**

Have students recall the three branches of government as defined in the first three Articles of the Constitution. (*legislative, executive, judicial*) Ask them to review the reason the Constitution divides the government into three branches. (*to prevent any one branch or person from gaining too much power*) This section describes the specific powers of each of the three branches of government.

Instruction   **L2**

- Have students read How the Federal Government Works: The Legislative Branch. Ask: **What is the main job of Congress?** (*to make laws*) **Into what two bodies is Congress divided?** (*House of Representatives and Senate*)

- Ask: **Aside from making laws, what are some important powers of Congress?** (*power to collect taxes, coin money, establish post offices, declare war*)

- Ask: **How many senators does each state have?** (2) **How many representatives does each state have?** (*depends on population*) **Does California have more representatives than Nevada? Why?** (*Yes, California has more representatives because it has a larger population.*)

The first and longest article of the Constitution deals with the legislative, or lawmaking, branch. Article 1 sets up the Congress to make the nation's laws. Congress is made up of two bodies: the House of Representatives and the Senate.

The Senate

The Senate is based on equal representation, with two senators for each state. Senators are elected to six-year terms. The Vice President of the United States is the president of the Senate. The Vice President presides over the Senate—casting a vote when there is a tie—but cannot take part in Senate debates.

The House of Representatives

The larger of the two bodies is the House of Representatives, which currently has 435 members. Representation in the House is based on population, with larger states having more representatives than smaller states. Every state has at least one representative. Representatives are elected by the people of their district for two-year terms. The leader of the House is called the Speaker. The Speaker, who is chosen by the representatives, regulates debates and controls the agenda.

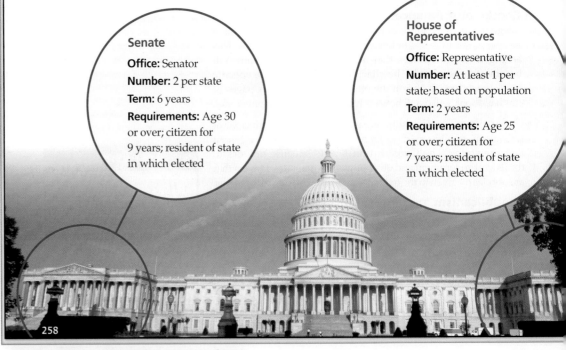

Senate

Office: Senator
Number: 2 per state
Term: 6 years
Requirements: Age 30 or over; citizen for 9 years; resident of state in which elected

House of Representatives

Office: Representative
Number: At least 1 per state; based on population
Term: 2 years
Requirements: Age 25 or over; citizen for 7 years; resident of state in which elected

258

Differentiated Instruction

L3 Advanced Readers   **L3** Gifted and Talented

Lawmaking Simulation Have students use the CD-ROM *Interactive Constitution* to explore the lawmaking process. Have them take the role of a new member of Congress in the lawmaking simulation feature on the CD-ROM. Students can be provided a copy of the CD to work inde-

pendently at home or in the school Resource Center. Ask students to share their experiences with the class. What about the lawmaking process did they find surprising?

🌐 **Interactive Constitution CD-ROM,** Lawmaking Simulation

How a Bill Becomes a Law

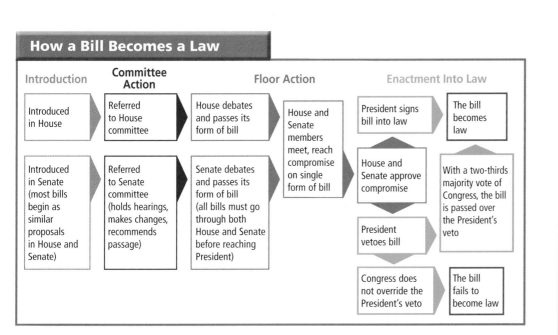

Introduction

- Introduced in House
- Introduced in Senate (most bills begin as similar proposals in House and Senate)

Committee Action

- Referred to House committee
- Referred to Senate committee (holds hearings, makes changes, recommends passage)

Floor Action

- House debates and passes its form of bill
- Senate debates and passes its form of bill (all bills must go through both House and Senate before reaching President)
- House and Senate members meet, reach compromise on single form of bill
- House and Senate approve compromise
- President vetoes bill
- Congress does not override the President's veto

Enactment Into Law

- President signs bill into law
- The bill becomes law
- With a two-thirds majority vote of Congress, the bill is passed over the President's veto
- The bill fails to become law

Powers of Congress

The most important power of Congress is the power to make the nation's laws. A **bill,** or proposal for a new law, may be introduced either in the House or the Senate. After debate and changes, the bill is voted on. If both houses vote to approve the bill, it then goes to the President to be signed. If the President signs the bill, it becomes a law. The President, however, has the power to **veto,** or reject, the bill. Congress may vote to **override,** or pass a law despite a presidential veto. A two-thirds vote is needed to override. (See flowchart above.)

Other powers of Congress are listed in Article 1, Section 8. These include the power to collect taxes, to coin money, to establish post offices, to fix standard weights and measures, and to declare war.

Congressional Committees

Much of the work in Congress is done through committees. Each committee deals with a specific topic. For example, if someone in Congress introduces a bill to improve the nation's railroad service, the bill would first go to the Transportation Committee for study. Other standing committees deal with such areas as defense, education, taxation, foreign affairs, agriculture, or science.

Assessment

1. What are the major differences between membership in the Senate and membership in the House?

2. How can Congress pass a bill over a presidential veto?

Instruction (continued)

- Have students complete the worksheet How a Bill Becomes a Law. Ask students to explain the purpose of a conference committee. (*to work out differences between bills that have passed the House and Senate*) Ask: **Why is it important to work out differences between bills that have passed the House and Senate?** (*Possible answer: If the House and Senate do not pass the same version of a bill, the bill cannot become law.*)

All in One Teaching Resources, Unit 2, How a Bill Becomes a Law, p. 98

- Have students read Article I, Section 7, Clause 2 of the Constitution. Ask: **Can the votes of senators and representatives be secret?** (*No, they are to be entered into official records.*) Ask: **Why do you think it is important that these votes be public?** (*Possible answer: In a democracy, it is important to know what elected representatives are voting for. If people do not like the way their elected officials are voting, they do not have to re-elect them.*)

- To reinforce students' understanding of the process of passing laws, display the transparency How a Bill Becomes a Law.

Color Transparencies, How a Bill Becomes a Law

Monitor Progress

Have students share their answers to the Assessment questions in the Student Edition, p. 259. Correct any misunderstandings.

History Background

How Many Representatives? Every ten years the United States Census Bureau conducts a census, counting not only the total number of people in the country, but also the number of people in each state. The census determines how many representatives each state will have in the House of Representatives. This process, known as "apportionment," has taken place every ten years since 1790. In 1790 the states with the largest populations, and therefore the largest number of representatives, were Virginia and Massachusetts. By 1900, New York and Pennsylvania had the most representatives. Since the 1970 census, California has had the largest number of representatives. California has 53 representatives today, the largest delegation of any state in U.S. history. Texas has the second highest total, with 32.

Answers

Assessment

1. Senators serve six-year terms; House members serve two-year terms. Senators represent their entire state; House members represent their district. Senators must be 30 years old or older; House members must be 25 or older.

2. Congress can override a veto with a two-thirds majority vote in both the House and Senate.

How the Federal Government Works: The Executive Branch

Instruction   L2

- Have students read How the Federal Government Works: The Executive Branch. Ask students to describe the main responsibilities of the executive branch. (*to carry out the law and run the affairs of national government*) Ask students to name some of the specific powers of the President. (*Possible answers: serve as commander in chief of armed forces, propose laws.*)

- Display the transparency Federal Officeholders. Have students compare how the President, Vice President, and other officeholders are selected and the requirements they must meet.

Color Transparencies, Federal Officeholders

- Ask: **How does the Twenty-second Amendment affect the President?** (*No President may be elected to more than two complete terms.*)

- Ask: **What determines how many electors each state has?** (*the number of senators and representatives the state has*) **How does this make states with large populations more influential than states with small populations in presidential elections?** (*States with large populations have more representatives in Congress, and therefore more electors.*)

- Have students review Article II, Section 1, Clause 2 of the Constitution. Ask: **Who may not be an elector?** (*members of Congress and federal officeholders*) **Why are they excluded?** (*Their jobs may depend on the vote.*)

Article 2 of the Constitution sets up an executive branch to carry out the laws and run the affairs of the national government. The President is the head of the executive branch. Other members include the Vice President, the Cabinet, and people in the many departments and agencies that help run the government.

Powers of the President

The Framers of the Constitution intended Congress to be the most powerful branch of government. Therefore, although the Constitution is very specific about the powers of the legislature, it offers few details about the powers of the President. (See the graphic organizer below.)

Beginning with George Washington, Presidents have often taken those actions they thought were necessary to carry out their job. Thus, they shaped the presidency to meet the nation's changing needs.

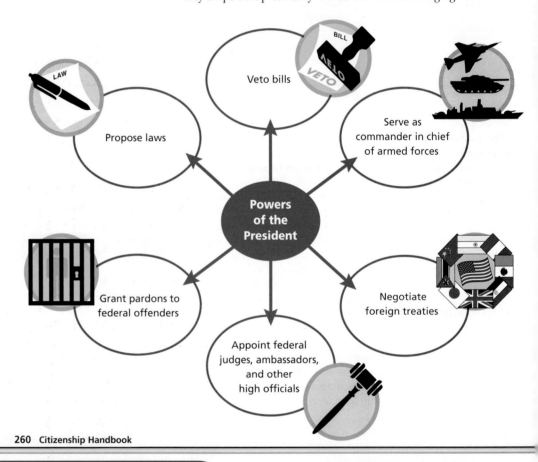

Propose laws · Veto bills · Serve as commander in chief of armed forces · Powers of the President · Grant pardons to federal offenders · Appoint federal judges, ambassadors, and other high officials · Negotiate foreign treaties

Differentiated Instruction

L1 English Language Learners   **L1 Less Proficient Readers**   **L1 Special Needs**

Gaining Comprehension Each President recites an oath when taking office, in accordance with Article II, Section 1 of the U.S. Constitution. Have students read Clause 8 on p. 235 and work with them to paraphrase it. Begin by defining difficult words such as *solemnly* and *execute*. Lead a discussion on what this oath means and why it is part of the Constitution. Finally, have students work in pairs to write down the meaning of the oath in their own words.

■ Have students look at the Electoral College map. Ask them to find the four states with the largest number of electoral votes. (*California, Texas, New York, Florida*) Ask: **What is the smallest number of electoral votes a state can have?** (*3*)

■ Have students complete the worksheet Shifting Electoral Votes. Tell students that to become President, a candidate must win a majority of the available 538 electoral votes. Ask students to figure out how many votes a candidate needs in order to be elected President. (*at least 270*)

All in One Teaching Resources, Unit 2, Shifting Electoral Votes, p. 99

The Electoral College, 2008

State	Electoral Votes
WA	(11)
MT	(3)
ND	(3)
MN	(10)
VT	(3)
NH	(4)
ME	(4)
OR	(7)
ID	(4)
SD	(3)
WI	(10)
MI	(17)
WV	(5)
NY	(31)
MA	(12)
WY	(3)
NE	(5)
IA	(7)
IL	(21)
IN	(11)
OH	(20)
PA	(21)
RI	(4)
NV	(5)
UT	(5)
CO	(9)
KS	(6)
MO	(11)
KY	(8)
VA	(13)
CT	(7)
CA	(55)
NJ	(15)
DE	(3)
AZ	(10)
NM	(5)
OK	(7)
AR	(6)
TN	(11)
NC	(15)
MD	(10)
MS	(6)
AL	(9)
GA	(15)
SC	(8)
TX	(34)
LA	(9)
FL	(27)
AK	(3)
HI	(4)

Key
(25) Indicates number of electoral votes for the state
Note: Washington, DC, has 3 electoral votes

Electing the President

The President is elected for a four-year term. As a result of the Twenty-second Amendment, adopted in 1951, no President may be elected to more than two complete terms.

The Framers set up a complex system for electing the President, known as the electoral college. When Americans vote for President, they do not vote directly for the candidate of their choice. Rather, they vote for a group of "electors" who are pledged to the candidate. The number of a state's electors depends on the number of its senators and representatives. (See the map above.)

A few weeks after Election Day, these electors meet in each state to cast their votes for President. In most states, the candidate with the majority of the popular vote receives all that state's electoral votes. The candidate who receives a majority of the electoral votes nationwide becomes President. Although electors are not required by federal law to vote for their pledged candidate, only a few have broken their pledges and voted for other candidates in past elections.

Monitor Progress

Have students share their answers to the Assessment questions in the Student Edition, p. 261. Correct any misunderstandings.

Assessment

1. Why do you think the Framers chose not to give the President the power to declare war?

2. How many electors does your state have?

History Background

The Two-Term Limit After serving as President from 1789 to 1797, George Washington decided not to run for a third term. Washington's decision set a precedent that lasted more than 140 years—during this time, no President served more than two terms in office. The precedent was broken in 1940, when Franklin Delano Roosevelt was elected to a third term as President.

Roosevelt was elected to a fourth term in 1944. After Roosevelt's death, Congress passed the Twenty-second Amendment, stating that a President can only be elected to two terms in office. Since the amendment was ratified in 1951, several members of Congress have proposed repealing it. These efforts have not gained broad support.

Answers
Assessment

1. Answers will vary, but could include the idea that the Framers did not want such an important power to be in the hands of just one person.

2. Students should find their state for the number.

How the Federal Government Works: The Judicial Branch

Instruction　L2

- Have students read How the Federal Government Works: The Judicial Branch. Ask students to identify the three levels of the federal court system. (*district court, appellate court, Supreme Court*)

- Ask students to define the term "appeal." (*to ask that a court decision be reviewed by a higher court*) Ask: **What happens when a district court decision is appealed?** (*It is reviewed by the appellate court to determine whether the lower court interpreted the law correctly.*)

- Have students read Article III, Section 2 of the Constitution. Ask: **Which clause gives the Supreme Court the power to hear appeals?** (*Clause 2: "In all the other cases . . . the Supreme Court shall have appellate jurisdiction. . . ."*) If students need help, explain that *jurisdiction* means the right to interpret or apply the law and direct them to the reference to appellate courts on p. 262.

- Display the transparency Federal Court System to review the two routes by which a case can reach the Supreme Court.

Color Transparencies, Federal Court System

The Constitution establishes a Supreme Court and authorizes Congress to establish any other courts that are needed. Under the Judiciary Act of 1789, Congress set up the system of federal courts that is still in place today.

Lower Courts

Most federal cases begin in district courts. Evidence is presented during trials, and a jury or a judge decides the facts of the case. A party that disagrees with the decision of the judge or jury may appeal it, that is, ask that the decision be reviewed by a higher court. The next level of court is the appellate court, or court of appeal. Appellate court judges review decisions of district courts to decide whether the lower court judges interpreted and applied the law correctly.

Court cases can be filed under federal or state jurisdiction. Jurisdiction is the power to hear and decide cases. Most cases are tried under state jurisdiction because they involve state laws. A case may be placed under federal jurisdiction if any of the following apply:

- The United States is either suing another party or being sued by another party.
- The case is based on the Constitution or on a federal law.
- The case involves disputes between different states.

Federal Court System

State Route	United States Supreme Court	Federal Route
State Supreme Court • Highest state court • Hears appeals of appellate court cases	• Nation's highest court • Reviews the decisions of lower courts • Decides cases involving U.S. Constitution and federal laws	**Court of Appeal** • Hears appeals of cases originating in U.S. district courts • Can review decisions by federal administrative agencies
Appellate Court • Hears appeals of trial court cases		**District Court** • Federal trial court • Handles civil and criminal cases
Trial Court • Handles civil and criminal cases		

Differentiated Instruction

L3 Advanced Readers

Research Court Cases Have students use the CD-ROM Interactive Constitution to research famous Supreme Court cases. Working in pairs, have students select one case from the list of cases on the CD-ROM. Have them read the information. Students can be provided a copy of the CD to work independently at home or in the school

L3 Gifted and Talented

Resource Center. Ask them to prepare a short oral presentation on the case. What was the case about? Why is it considered important? Do they agree with the Court's ruling? Why or why not?

Interactive Constitution CD-ROM, Supreme Court Cases

- Ask: **How many justices serve on the Supreme Court?** (*9*) **How are the justices chosen?** (*The President appoints justices; the Senate must approve the appointment.*) **How long does each justice serve?** (*for life*)

- Ask students to describe the Supreme Court's most important power. (*the power to interpret the Constitution*) Ask students to explain the meaning of "unconstitutional." (*something that is not legal under the Constitution*)

- Have students complete the Biography worksheet Sandra Day O'Connor. Ask: **Why did O'Connor often write her own opinions of Supreme Court cases?** (*She wanted to explain why she voted a certain way or present her interpretation of the ruling.*)

All in One Teaching Resources, Unit 2, Sandra Day O'Connor, p. 101

Monitor Progress

Have students share their answers to the Assessment questions in the Student Edition, p. 263. Correct any misunderstandings.

The Supreme Court
The nine members of the Supreme Court pose for their annual portrait. Chief Justice John G. Roberts, Jr., is seated, center.

The Supreme Court

At the top of the American judicial system is the Supreme Court. (See the chart on the facing page.) The Court is made up of a chief justice and eight associate justices. The President appoints the justices, but Congress must approve the appointments. Justices serve until they resign, retire, or die. However, like other federal officials, Supreme Court justices may be impeached and removed from office.

The main job of the Supreme Court is to serve as the nation's final court of appeal. It hears the cases that have been tried and appealed in lower federal and state courts. The Court hears and decides fewer than 100 cases each year.

Decisions rest on a majority vote of at least five justices. One justice then writes a majority opinion, a document that explains the constitutional reasons for the decision. A justice who voted against the majority may submit a dissenting opinion, explaining his or her reasons for disagreeing with the majority opinion.

There is no court of appeal beyond the Supreme Court. However, if another case dealing with the same issues comes up, the Supreme Court may sometimes reverse its own past decisions.

Judicial Review

The most important power of the Supreme Court is the power to decide what the Constitution means. At the beginning of the 1800s, the Court asserted the right to declare whether acts of the President or laws passed by Congress are unconstitutional, that is, not allowed under the Constitution. The landmark 1803 case of *Marbury* v. *Madison* established this power of judicial review for the Supreme Court.

Assessment

1. How does a case reach the United States Supreme Court?

2. What is judicial review?

History Background

A Traveling Court The white marble Supreme Court Building on Capitol Hill is a national landmark today, but the Court had several homes before settling in this building. The 1790 Supreme Court met in New York City, the nation's temporary capital. When the capital moved to Philadelphia, the Court moved with it, meeting in Philadelphia's Old City Hall from 1791 to 1799. In 1800, the Supreme Court moved to the nation's permanent capital, Washington, D.C., where Court sessions were held in the Capitol Building. While the building was still under construction, sessions sometimes had to be moved to private homes or taverns. The Court met in the Capitol until 1935, when it moved into the newly completed Supreme Court Building.

Answers
Assessment

1. A case must go before a district and appellate court before a Supreme Court hearing. It can also follow a second route—from trial court to appellate court to state supreme court and finally to the Supreme Court.

2. the power of the Supreme Court to determine whether acts of the President or laws passed by Congress are constitutional

Amending the Constitution

Review and Preview

Students have learned that the Constitution protects the rights of citizens. They will now read how the amendment process allows for changes to the Constitution. They will also read how the First Amendment addressed the grievances of the colonial experience.

Section Focus Question

How can the Constitution be amended to meet changing needs?

Build Background Knowledge **L2**

In Chapter 7, students read that the Bill of Rights was added to the Constitution in order to convince more people to support the new government. Now they will read about the process by which amendments are added to the Constitution. Before they read the section, ask students to speculate about whether they think the founders made it easy or difficult to change the Constitution. After they make their predictions, address any misconceptions that students may have about the topic. Remind them to confirm or revise their predictions after they read the section.

Instruction **L2**

■ Have students read Amending the Constitution, the section beginning on this page. Ask: **Where are the rules about amending the Constitution defined?** (*Article V of the Constitution*)

■ Direct students to read Article V of the Constitution. Ask: **Are there any limits on the kinds of amendments that can be added to the Constitution?** (*Yes, an amendment to the Constitution cannot take away a state's equal representation in the Senate.*)

Although the Framers were pleased with the government they had established through the Constitution, some were dissatisfied with the final document. For one thing, while establishing the powers of the state and federal governments, the document said nothing about the rights of the American people. In 1791, the new nation would do something about this omission when it added the Bill of Rights, the first 10 amendments to the Constitution.

This addition was possible because the founders had written a Constitution that allowed for change. The Constitution was flexible enough to be changed but not so flexible that it could be *easily* changed. Article 5 laid out the method for amending, or changing, the Constitution. The flowchart below shows the amendment process.

The Amendment Process

The Constitution can be changed in one of four ways. There are two different procedures for proposing amendments to the Constitution. There are also two different procedures for ratifying, or approving, amendments to the Constitution, the second step in the process.

Proposing an Amendment Congress can propose an amendment if both the House and Senate vote for a change to the Constitution. Each of the ConstitutionÕs 27 amendments has been proposed in this way.

The second way to propose an amendment begins at the state level. Currently, the legislatures of 34 states must call for a national convention. It is then up to the national convention to formally propose an amendment.

Ratifying an Amendment An amendment can be ratified through the action of state legislatures. Currently, the yes vote of 38 states is needed. Twenty-six of the 27 amendments to the Constitution have been ratified in this way.

An amendment can also be ratified through the action of state conventions rather than through state legislatures. Conventions, are special meetings that are called to address a specific issue. Only the Twenty-first Amendment was added through the process of state conventions.

The Amendment Process

Proposed by **CONGRESS** by two-thirds vote of each house	OR	Proposed by **NATIONAL CONVENTION** called by Congress at request of two thirds of state legislatures
Ratified by **LEGISLATURES** in three fourths of states	OR	Ratified by **CONVENTIONS** in three fourths of states

Differentiated Instruction

L1 **English Language Learners**   **L1** **Special Needs**

Vocabulary Development Have students review key terms *amendment* and *ratify* by making a list of these terms. Then have them create flashcards with the word on one side and its definition on the other. Pair students with a partner and have them quiz each other on the definitions of the words using the flashcards.

The Sixth Amendment
The right to trial by jury in a criminal case is guaranteed by the Sixth Amendment. It also ensures that a person accused of a crime has the right to be represented by a lawyer and to hear the testimony given by witnesses in the trial.

The Bill of Rights

The Preamble of the Constitution begins with the words, "We the People of the United States." However, the seven articles of the original document deal mostly with issues involving the structure and powers of the branches of government, not with the rights of individuals. The Bill of Rights, the name given to the first 10 amendments to the Constitution, addresses the freedoms guaranteed to citizens.

- *First Amendment:* freedom of religion, speech, and the press; right of petition and assembly (See the following page.)
- *Second Amendment:* right to bear arms
- *Third Amendment:* government cannot force people to quarter troops in their homes
- *Fourth Amendment:* protects against unreasonable search and seizure
- *Fifth Amendment:* rights of people accused of crimes
- *Sixth Amendment:* right to trial by jury in criminal cases
- *Seventh Amendment:* right to trial by jury in civil cases
- *Eighth Amendment:* forbids excessive bail and cruel or unusual punishment
- *Ninth Amendment:* people's rights are not limited to those listed in the Constitution
- *Tenth Amendment:* states or people have all powers not denied or given to federal government by the Constitution

Assessment

1. Which one of the four different two-step processes has most often been used to add amendments to the Constitution?

2. Why do you think the Founders added the Ninth Amendment to the Bill of Rights?

Amending the Constitution **265**

History Background

Changing the Constitution The Framers hoped that the specific requirements of Article V would make the Constitution very difficult, but not impossible, to change. History has shown that Article V was well designed to meet this goal. Since 1789, more than 10,000 constitutional amendments have been proposed; only 27 have made it through the long ratification process. Six amendments have been approved by Congress, but not ratified by the states. This happened most recently in 1978, when Congress approved an amendment that would have given the District of Columbia representation in the House and Senate, as if it were a state. Only 16 of the necessary 38 states approved this amendment.

The First Amendment

Instruction L2

- Have students read the text and look at the images. Ask them to identify the rights guaranteed in the First Amendment. (*freedom of religion, freedom of speech, freedom of the press, freedom of peaceful assembly and government petition*)

- Ask: **How did religious conflicts in colonial history influence the Framers?** (*The Framers wanted to avoid the kinds of disputes between church and state that took place in the colonies. When they wrote the First Amendment, they stated that government must remain neutral in questions of religion.*)

- Ask students to explain why dictators often shut down newspapers and jail critics of the government. (*Dictators' power depends on silencing public criticism.*) Ask: **How does the First Amendment protect against this danger?** (*by guaranteeing the right to speak without the fear of punishment and by protecting the press from censorship*)

Monitor Progress

Have students share their answers to the Assessment questions in the Student Edition, p. 267. Correct any misunderstandings.

The colonial past was very much on the minds of American leaders when they set out to write the Bill of Rights in the early 1790s. It is not surprising, therefore, that the colonial experience inspired the very first amendment to the Constitution.

First Amendment

Congress shall make no law respecting an establishment of religion, or prohibiting the free exercise thereof; or abridging the freedom of speech, or of the press; or the right of the people peaceably to assemble, and to petition the government for a redress of grievances.

Freedom of Religion
This painting by Norman Rockwell illustrates the principle of freedom of religion.

266

Freedom of Religion As you have learned, Pilgrims, Puritans, Quakers, and Catholics had come to North America because they wanted to practice their religion freely. Yet, colonial religious leaders such as Thomas Hooker, Roger Williams, and Anne Hutchinson were later driven from Massachusetts after clashing with community leaders over religious questions. The Founders wanted to avoid such church-versus-state disputes. Thus, the First Amendment affirms freedom of religion as a basic right. Americans are free to follow any religion or no religion, as they choose.

This part of the First Amendment was inspired by the Virginia Statute on Religious Freedom, written by Thomas Jefferson. Jefferson later spoke of a "wall of separation between Church and State." However, not everyone agrees on the nature of that separation. Some people believe that the First Amendment means that religion should play no role in government. Others argue that the Amendment merely says that Congress cannot establish an official, state-supported church or make any laws that interfere with freedom of worship.

Differentiated Instruction

L3 Advanced Readers   **L3 Gifted and Talented**

Conduct a Survey Have students work in small groups to conduct a survey on an important current issue. Ask each group to present its survey results to the class.

Encourage other students to discuss the conclusions that can be drawn from the survey results.

Freedom of the Press
American reporters do their jobs without fear of government interference.

Peaceful Assembly
These striking workers are exercising their right of peaceful assembly.

Freedom of Speech and Freedom of the Press Dictators understand that their power depends on silencing dissent, or disagreement. They will often shut down newspapers and jail people who criticize the government. By contrast, the First Amendment protects the right of Americans to speak without fear of punishment.

The First Amendment also protects the press from government censorship. Censorship is the power to review, change, or prevent the publication of news. Freedom of the press also means that journalists cannot be arrested for criticizing the government or public officials. (As you have read, this principle was established in the colonies by the case of John Peter Zenger.)

The Framers knew that a free flow of ideas is vital to a democratic government. Still, freedom of the press is not unlimited. The press has a responsibility to present the news fairly and accurately. Individuals may sue journalists for libel, or the publication of false and malicious information that damages a person's reputation.

Peaceful Assembly and Petition As you have read, King George III and Parliament ignored the colonists' petition protesting the Stamp Act. Such experiences had a powerful effect on the leaders who wrote the Bill of Rights. The First Amendment thus guarantees the right of Americans to assemble in peaceful protest. It also protects their right to petition the government for a change in policy.

Assessment

1. What does the First Amendment say about freedom of religion?
2. Identify two rights of a free press.

The First Amendment **267**

Answers
Assessment

1. Americans are free to follow any religion, or no religion, as they choose.

2. The government cannot censor the press, nor can it arrest journalists for criticizing the government or public officials.

State and Local Governments

Review and Preview

Students have learned that under the principle of federalism, there is a division of power between the federal government and the states. Students will now focus on the duties of the state and local governments.

Section Focus Question

What are the powers of state and local governments?

Build Background Knowledge   **L2**

Remind students that their own town and state have separate governments from the federal government in Washington, D.C. This section describes the main powers of state and local governments. Ask students to think about some of the jobs they associate with their state and local governments. (*running schools and libraries, building roads, running police and fire departments*)

Instruction   **L2**

- Have students read this section and study the diagram. Ask students to describe the principle of federalism. (*Some powers are assigned to the federal government, others to the states.*) Ask: **How are state governments similar to the federal government?** (*Both have constitutions that can be amended; both are divided into legislative, executive, and judicial branches.*)

- Based on the Venn diagram, have students identify two powers that the national government has which the states do not have. (*Students may choose any in the list that is specific for the National Government. Possible answers: regulate interstate and foreign trade, establish foreign policy, coin money*)

As you have learned, under the principle of federalism, the Constitution assigns some powers to the government in Washington, D.C., and other powers to the states. You have already read about the role of the federal government in our nation's life. Now you will learn about the role played by state and local governments.

State Governments

In general, the federal government deals with national issues. The states concern themselves with needs within each state.

State governments resemble the federal government in many ways. Each state has a constitution of its own, for example, and each state constitution can be amended. In addition, every state is divided into three branches of government. Each state has a legislature, a governor who serves as the chief executive, and a judiciary. But there are some differences between the state and federal governments. Nebraska, for instance, is the only state in the Union with a one-house legislature.

The Federal System

Powers of the National Government
- Regulate interstate and foreign trade
- Set standard weights and measures
- Create and maintain armed forces
- Make copyright and patent laws
- Establish postal offices
- Establish foreign policy
- Create federal courts
- Coin money
- Declare war
- Admit new states

Shared Powers
- Provide for public welfare
- Administer criminal justice
- Charter banks
- Raise taxes
- Borrow money

Powers Reserved to the States
- Create corporation law
- Regulate trade within state
- Maintain schools
- Establish local governments
- Make laws about marriage and divorce
- Conduct elections
- Provide for public safety

268 Citizenship Handbook

Differentiated Instruction

L1 **Less Proficient Readers**

Gaining Comprehension Remind students that state governments have the power to ratify or reject amendments to the Constitution. To reinforce their understanding of this process, assign the worksheet Ratifying Amendments. To make sure students understand the process, you may want to work through the worksheet questions as a class.

All in One **Teaching Resources, Unit 2,** Ratifying Amendments, p. 103

Local Government
City or town governments usually set up and fund fire departments.

State Services

Enforcing the law, protecting property, regulating business, building and maintaining highways, and operating state parks are just a few of the many tasks the state oversees. In addition, states supervise public education by setting standards and by funding school programs.

Local Governments

As we have seen, the Constitution carefully identifies the powers of state and federal governments. However, it says nothing about local government. Local governments administer smaller units, such as counties, cities, and towns.

Local governments have budgets just like the federal government and state government. Most of the money in their budgets is spent on education. Cities, towns, or school districts hire teachers and staff, buy books and supplies, and maintain school buildings. But local governments do not have sole control over the school system. They are required by law to meet the state's education standards.

Local government generally plays a more direct role in our lives than federal or state government does. For example, local governments hire people who interact with us on a regular basis, such as firefighters, police officers, and garbage collectors. In addition, local governments maintain local roads and hospitals, provide sewers and water, run libraries, oversee parks and recreational facilities, and conduct safety inspections of buildings.

Assessment

1. Name two powers the federal goverment and state governments share. Name two powers that are reserved to the states.

2. What permits local governments to function even though they are not mentioned in the Constitution? Explain your answer.

State and Local Governments **269**

Planning a State Budget Spending priorities of state and local governments relate closely to day-to-day demands of citizens. People want better schools, highways, and hospitals. Education accounts for more than one third of state and local government budgets.

Historically, taxation and spending by the federal government was independent and separate from state and local government. However, in the last 50 years, this pattern has changed. The states have turned to the federal government for assistance. And local governments have turned to their state governments for aid. These changes are reflected in the current revenue and spending patterns of state and local governments.

Rights and Responsibilities of Citizenship

Review and Preview

Students have learned of the constitutional protection of their individual rights. They will now explore the process of becoming a naturalized citizen and the responsibilities of citizenship.

Section Focus Question

What are the rights and responsibilities of citizens?

Build Background Knowledge `L2`

Students have read about many of the rights enjoyed by citizens. This section describes more of these rights, as well as some of the major responsibilities of citizenship. Ask students to think about some of the ways they can be good citizens. (*obeying laws, serving the community*)

Instruction `L2`

■ Have students read Rights and Responsibilities of Citizenship. Ask: **What is a naturalized citizen?** (*a person who has gone through the official legal process of becoming a citizen*) Ask: **What is the difference between the responsibilities and rights of natural-born citizens and naturalized citizens of the United States?** (*Naturalized citizens enjoy all of the same rights as natural-born citizens except the right to serve as President or Vice President.*)

■ Display the transparency Naturalization Process, which shows the process of becoming a citizen. Ask: **Why is a civics test part of the naturalization process?** (*Possible answer: New citizens should know their rights and responsibilities.*)

Color Transparencies, Naturalization Process

What is a citizen? A **citizen** is someone who is entitled to all the rights and privileges of a particular nation. Not everyone who lives in a certain nation is a citizen of that nation. On the other hand, some citizens live outside the nation to which they belong.

Becoming an American Citizen

To become a citizen of the United States, you must fulfill one of the following three requirements:

• You were born in the United States or have at least one parent who is a citizen of the United States.

• You were naturalized. **Naturalization** is the official legal process of becoming a citizen.

• You were 18 years old or younger when your parents were naturalized.

Each year, millions of people born in other countries and living in the United States become naturalized. To become a naturalized citizen, a person must live legally in the United States for at least five years. The person then applies for citizenship. He or she must take a citizenship examination and undergo a series of interviews. Finally, the applicant takes the citizenship oath before a judge, swearing to "support and defend the Constitution and laws of the United States."

A naturalized citizen enjoys every right of a natural-born citizen except one. Only natural-born citizens may serve as President or Vice President.

Naturalization
New citizens of the United States proudly take the citizenship oath.

270 Citizenship Handbook

Differentiated Instruction

`L1` English Language Learners

Citizenship in Other Countries Have English language learners make posters comparing the rights and responsibilities of citizens in their native countries with the rights and responsibilities of citizens of the United States. Encourage students to ask adults in their family about the rights and responsibilities they have or had as citizens in their native country. Ask students to present their finished posters to the class.

Rights of Citizens

As you have seen, the Bill of Rights guarantees certain rights to citizens. You have the right to worship as you please, the right to express your opinion, and the right to consult a lawyer if you are arrested. But the Ninth Amendment states that citizens' rights are not limited to those listed in the Constitution. Over the years, federal and state laws have identified other rights. For example, the Constitution does not mention education. But today, laws in every state guarantee that children have the right to an education.

Responsibilities of Citizens

In addition to rights, citizens have responsibilities. Some actions are required of every citizen. For example, all citizens *must*

- obey federal, state, and local laws;
- pay their fair share of taxes;
- serve on juries if called;
- defend the nation if called.

Citizens have other responsibilities that are not required by law. Good citizens *should*

- vote in federal, state, and local elections;
- stay informed on important issues;
- serve the community;
- help to create a just society.

Some citizens participate in the political process through interest groups. An **interest group** is an organization that represents the concerns of a particular group. The American Association of Retired Persons, the National Rifle Association, and the Sierra Club are examples of interest groups that try to influence lawmakers and raise public awareness of certain issues.

Young people, too, can get involved in the political process. For example, in one California community, poor children could not afford to pay for public transportation to school every day. Some students organized to solve this problem. Using their First Amendment rights, they collected signatures on petitions and held public rallies. As a result, the local transportation board took up the issue. Like thousands of other Americans, these students used their rights as citizens to voice their views and help their communities.

Registering to Vote
Before a U.S. citizen can vote, he or she must register.

Assessment

1. How does a person become an American citizen?

2. Identify three ways that Americans can participate in the political process.

Rights and Responsibilities of Citizenship **271**

Think Like A Historian

Enrich Learning To enrich this unit, have students revisit the Unit Essential Question. Using information from the chapters in the unit and the primary sources on pp. 272–275, have students demonstrate their understanding of this period by drawing political cartoons.

Think Like a Historian, pp. 272–275

Pressed for Time? If you do not have time to complete the activity, return to the essential question on the unit opener. Post the flip chart pages and ask students to review and revise the list. As a summary, display the Unit 2 Think Like a Historian transparencies.

Color Transparencies, Think Like a Historian, Unit 2

Instruction (continued)

- Have students turn to the Constitution. Ask them to read and summarize the Ninth Amendment to the Constitution. (*Americans have rights that are not stated in the Constitution.*) Ask: **What is one right federal or state laws have identified?** (*children's right to an education*)

- Ask students to identify responsibilities they have now and additional responsibilities they will have as adults. (*now: obeying the law, serving the community, being informed; adult: voting, defending the nation, serving on juries*)

- Display the transparency Responsibilities of Citizenship, which shows different responsibilities of good citizens. Discuss the importance of fulfilling these responsibilities.

Color Transparencies, Responsibilities of Citizenship

- Have students complete the Primary Source worksheet George Mitchell. Ask students to summarize what Mitchell says about "the rule of law." (*The rule of law is very important because it guarantees that everyone is equal before the law.*)

All in One Teaching Resources, Unit 2, George Mitchell, p. 104

Monitor Progress

Have students share their answers to the Assessment questions in the Student Edition, p. 271. Correct any misunderstandings.

Answers
Assessment

1. A person becomes an American citizen by being born in the United States or having at least one parent who is a citizen of the United States, by being naturalized, or by being 18 years old or younger when his or her parents are naturalized.

2. Possible answers: voting, staying informed on important issues, informing elected officials of their views, participating in interest groups, signing petitions, and holding peaceful public rallies

Unit 2

Think Like a Historian

❓ **How did the colonists break away from Britain and create a republican form of government?**

Build Background Knowledge **L2**

Discuss the difference between a "republican form of government" and a "monarchy." Lead a structured discussion about differences between these two types of government. (See TE p. T24 for more on structured discussion.) Have students consider if they prefer making their own decisions or if they would prefer having their parents making most of their decisions. Have students preview the documents on these pages to list possible reasons the colonists would want a republican form of government. *(growing colonial unity after French and Indian War; colonists want to make own decisions; George Washington's leadership; did not want to live under a monarchy; desire for "unalienable Rights")*

Instruction **L2**

■ Write the Essential Question on the board. Have students put this question into their own words. *(Possible answer: Why did the colonists want to be free and have their own government?)* Have students review the essential questions for Chapters 5–7. Draw a web diagram on the board, showing how the chapter questions connect to the unit question. (See **Teaching Resources, Unit 2,** p. 3.) Discuss how each chapter question helps answer the unit question.

■ Tell students that after they study the documents they will draw political cartoons on aspects of the unit question.

Answers

Document 1: After the war, Britain raised taxes to help pay for the war's cost. Also, Britain tried to keep the colonists from moving farther west.

Document 2: The colonists did not have any representatives in the British House of Commons.

Unit 2 — ESSENTIAL QUESTION — THINK LIKE A HISTORIAN

How did the colonists break away from Britain and create a republican form of government?

DIRECTIONS: Analyze the following documents from the years before, during and after the American Revolution. Answer the questions that accompany each document or set of documents. You will use your answers to build an answer to the unit question: How did the colonists break away from Britain and create a republican form of government?

HISTORIAN'S CHECKLIST

WHO produced the document?
WHERE was it made?
WHEN was it produced?
WHY was it made and for what audience?
WHAT is its viewpoint?
HOW does it connect to what I've learned?
WHY is the document important?

1 — document — Effects of the French and Indian War

THE FRENCH AND INDIAN WAR

- Colonists develop a sense of unity.
- Britain gains territory west of the Appalachians.
- To avoid war with Indians, Britain bans colonial settlement west of the Appalachians.
- War leaves Britain in debt.
- Britain raises taxes to pay for the war.

How did the French and Indian War lead to friction between American colonists and Britain?

2 — document — Americans Protest British Taxes

" . . . 3. That it is inseparably essential to the freedom of a people, and the undoubted right of Englishmen, that no taxes be imposed on them, but with their own consent, given personally, or by their representatives.

4. That the people of these colonies are not, and from their local circumstances cannot be, represented in the House of Commons in Great-Britain. "

—*Resolutions of the Stamp Act Congress, 1765*

Why did American colonists think that the Stamp Act was unfair?

Differentiated Instruction

L1 English Language Learners   **L1** Special Needs

Building Vocabulary Students may encounter several difficult or unfamiliar words as they read documents 2–5. Have pairs of students create a glossary of words they are having trouble with. Students can take turns looking up the words and read-ing the definitions in the glossary. Have students brainstorm for ways to capture the meaning of these documents in a political cartoon. Use this as preparation for the activity on p. 275.

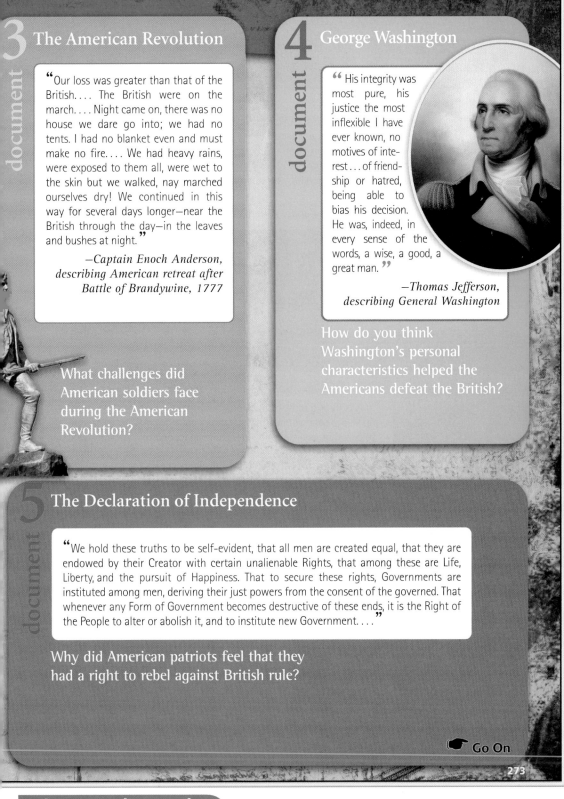

3 The American Revolution

document

"Our loss was greater than that of the British.... The British were on the march.... Night came on, there was no house we dare go into; we had no tents. I had no blanket even and must make no fire.... We had heavy rains, were exposed to them all, were wet to the skin but we walked, nay marched ourselves dry! We continued in this way for several days longer—near the British through the day—in the leaves and bushes at night."

—*Captain Enoch Anderson,
describing American retreat after
Battle of Brandywine, 1777*

What challenges did American soldiers face during the American Revolution?

4 George Washington

document

"His integrity was most pure, his justice the most inflexible I have ever known, no motives of interest...of friendship or hatred, being able to bias his decision. He was, indeed, in every sense of the words, a wise, a good, a great man."

—*Thomas Jefferson,
describing General Washington*

How do you think Washington's personal characteristics helped the Americans defeat the British?

5 The Declaration of Independence

document

"We hold these truths to be self-evident, that all men are created equal, that they are endowed by their Creator with certain unalienable Rights, that among these are Life, Liberty, and the pursuit of Happiness. That to secure these rights, Governments are instituted among men, deriving their just powers from the consent of the governed. That whenever any Form of Government becomes destructive of these ends, it is the Right of the People to alter or abolish it, and to institute new Government...."

Why did American patriots feel that they had a right to rebel against British rule?

☞ Go On

273

Instruction (continued)

- If your students have examined these documents as enrichment to the chapters, you may have the class answer the Historian's Checklist questions as a review.

- If you have not used these documents yet, students will need more time to work with these sources. For documents that present challenging reading, use the following steps:

1. As the students study the document, remind them to use the question associated with it as a focus question.

2. Have one student read the document aloud, breaking it into short segments. Then, as a class, work to paraphrase the document. For example, the first part of Document 2 could be summarized as "The colonists should not be taxed unless their rights are represented in Parliament."

3. Then, organize the class into groups. Using the Think-Write-Pair-Share strategy (TE p. T25), have each group answer the Historian's Checklist questions for one of the documents. If they need more information about the document, tell them to go back to the chapter to find out relevant information. Remind them to use the index or Table of Contents to find which chapter covered the material. They may also use their Interactive Reading and Note Taking Study Guide to review.

4. Review the answers to the Historian's Checklist. Have students identify how each document helps answer the essential question. Ask students whether their document provides a reason to "break away from Britain" or a reason to want a "republican form of government."

- Give students the Activity Rubric on p. 275 as a guide to their work.

History Background

Declaration of Independence The Committee of Five, led by Thomas Jefferson, drafted the resolution declaring the colonies independent from Britain on July 2, 1776. During the next two days, however, Congress debated the wording of the document, deleting several passages of this Declaration of Independence.

Jefferson expressed dismay about the deletions. Criticisms of English involvement in the slave trade and slavery were avoided. A clause that censured slavery was removed to please South Carolina and Georgia, both of which imported slaves. Members of Congress from the North also were unwilling to censure slavery, aware of those northern merchants who transported slaves.

Answers

Document 3: American soldiers sometimes had few supplies and were exposed to the weather.

Document 4: He instilled trust in his soldiers who were willing to serve under his command.

Document 5: They believed they had the right to rebel because Great Britain withheld from the colonists certain unalienable rights, including life, liberty, and the pursuit of happiness.

Instruction (continued)

- Preview the documents and assign selections according to student abilities. You may organize students into groups to review the documents. For example, assign Document 5 to English language learners. Read the selection aloud to them and tell them to listen for the topic and main idea as you read. Ask: **What is the topic?** (*that the United States should be free from Great Britain*) Ask students to explain what the title "Declaration of Independence" means. A key idea of this document is that people have the right, or guarantee, to "Life, Liberty, and the Pursuit of Happiness." Using the Idea Wave strategy (TE p. T24) with them, have students define these concepts.

- Assign Document 4 to students with less proficient reading skills. Help students define words such as *integrity, inflexible,* and *bias.* Then have them identify the characteristics described by Jefferson. Ask: **What was Jefferson's opinion of George Washington?** (*Possible answer: Jefferson liked Washington and thought highly of him.*)

- Assign Document 6 to more advanced readers. Ask: **What do students think the term "grand feu de joy" refers to?** (*Possible answer: firing cannon or rifles as part of a celebration*) **What aid do they think would be most required?** (*soldiers, arms, political support*)

Answers

Document 6: They provided soldiers, arms, and money to the Americans, who were happy to have their help.

Document 7: With their victory over the British at Yorktown, the Americans won the war. A formal peace treaty was signed two years later.

continued

6 Foreign Aid

document

"May 6, 1778. This day we fired a grand fue de joy on account of the news . . . which was that the Courts of France and Spain had declared the U States of America to be free and independent . . . and also to assist us in carrying on this just and necessary war. . . . In consequence of this intelligence, this day was set apart for a day of rejoicing throughout the whole army. Accordingly at ten o'clock A.M. a cannon was fired as a signal for the whole to parade."

—*Diary of George Ewing, American patriot and soldier*

How did the offer of French and Spanish assistance mark a turning point in the American war effort?

7 Yorktown

document

"This is to us a most glorious day, but to the English, one of bitter chagrin and disappointment. Preparations are now making to receive as captives that vindictive, haughty commander and that . . . army, who by their robberies and murders, have so long been a scourge to our brethren of the Southern states. . . . The captive troops are to march out with shouldered arms, colors cased and drums beating a British or German march, and to ground their arms at a place assigned for the purpose."

—*Journal of Dr. James Thacher, American soldier, October 19, 1781*

What was the lasting significance of the Battle of Yorktown?

274

Differentiated Instruction

L3 Advanced Readers   **L3 Gifted and Talented**

Research John Trumbull's Surrender at Yorktown Encourage students to research the American painter and how he went about creating the famous painting shown above. Students should prepare a brief outline of their findings, concentrating on the historical "liberties" he took while creating the painting. Students can apply this research to their political cartoons.

8 Shays' Rebellion

> "There are combustibles in every State, which a spark might set fire to.... That Great Britain will be an unconcerned Spectator of the present insurrections (if they continue) is not to be expected. That she is at this moment sowing the Seeds of jealousy and discontent among the various tribes of Indians.... We ought not therefore to sleep nor to slumber. Vigilance in watching, and vigour in acting, is, in my opinion, become indispensably necessary...."
>
> —*George Washington, in a letter to Henry Knox, 1786*

Why did Washington recommend "vigour in acting" against Shays' Rebellion?

9 A More Perfect Union

> "We the people of the United States, in order to form a more perfect union, establish justice, insure domestic tranquility, provide for the common defense, promote the general welfare, and secure the blessings of liberty to ourselves and our posterity, do ordain and establish this Constitution for the United States of America."
>
> —*The United States Constitution, September 17, 1787*

How was the new American government different from British colonial government?

THINK LIKE A HISTORIAN
ACTIVITY

Review the documents and other information to make political cartoons on the unit question:

How did the colonists break away from Britain and create a republican form of government?

Create a series of three or more political cartoons about the colonists' breakaway from Britain and their creation of a new republican form of government. Remember that political cartoons express a point of view about a situation. They also often use symbols or exaggeration to make a point. Hang your cartoons in your classroom. Be prepared to explain them to the class and to show how they help to answer the unit question.

275

Unit 3

Why It Matters

Under its new constitution, the United States grew stronger at home while striving to take its place in the world at large. It faced many challenges.

■ The need to draw the lines between federal and state power touched off bitter political struggles in the 1800s. States' rights are still in the news: Can U.S. environmental laws trump a state's laws? Should the federal government legislate student learning, or are decisions about education reserved to the states?

■ The Monroe Doctrine of 1823 announced a desire by the United States to limit European influence in the western hemisphere. In recent years the United States has warned against outside intervention in places like Cuba, Haiti, and Venezuela. It has also supported newfound democracies around the world.

Unit Essential Question

What problems might a new nation face?

Think Like a Historian

- To preview this unit, have students review the content on these pages of the Student Edition. Ask them: **What will you be learning about in this unit?** (*the founding and early years of the United States*)

- Write the Unit Focus Question on the board. Using the Idea Wave strategy (TE, p. T24), have students brainstorm answers to the question. Ask students to recall the difficulty of writing the Constitution and what challenges they think the nation could face after the Constitution was written.

- Record students' answers on a flip chart. Keep a copy of them. Let them know that you will return to this same question at the end of the unit and review their responses for possible additions or changes. (*See Think Like a Historian, p. 369.*)

Unit 3

ESSENTIAL QUESTION?

What problems might a new nation face?

George Washington After leading U.S. troops to victory against the British, Washington led the new nation as its first President. His actions set precedents that future Presidents would follow.

1789

Andrew Jackson A veteran of the War of 1812 and wars against Native Americans, Jackson was the first President from the West.

1828

- Preview the primary sources in Think Like a Historian on pp. 372–375. You may wish to introduce and use these documents to enrich chapter content.

Home Involvement

A summary of The New Republic content students will be studying and suggested activities adults at home can do with their child are available in a reproducible outline in the Teaching Resources.

All in One Teaching Resources, Unit 3, Letter Home, Chapters 8, 9, 10

The New Republic

Exploring the Louisiana Territory
President Thomas Jefferson acquired the Louisiana Territory and sent an expedition to explore lands west of the Mississippi River.

1803

War of 1812 In June 1812, the United States declared war on Great Britain. One reason for war was Britain's refusal to stop seizing U.S. Navy vessels and sailors.

1812

Trail of Tears Forced to move west to Indian Territory under harsh conditions, thousands of Native Americans lost their lives on what became known as the Trail of Tears.

1838

277

Unit Skills

■ Skills for Life

Distinguish Facts From Opinions
Chapter 8, p. 302

Detect Historical Points of View
Chapter 9, p. 332

Identify Bias
Chapter 10, p. 368

■ Reading Skills

Analyze Comparisons
Chapter 8, p. 279

Relate Events in Time
Chapter 9, p. 307

Analyze Cause and Effect
Chapter 10, p. 337

■ Writing Workshop *Online*

Narrative Essay: Biographical Essay
Web Code: mve-4000

■ Think Like a Historian

Students complete an activity in which they use primary sources to explore the Essential Question.
pp. 372–375

eTeach

Read the essay on eTeach for further ideas on Responding to the Needs of Diverse Learners.
Visit: PHSchool.com
Web Code: myf-0301

DK World Desk Reference

Use the resources on the DK World Desk Reference for further information about France and Great Britain today.
Visit: PHSchool.com
Web Code: mye-0302

History Background

Painting the West Charles Marion Russell's (1864–1926) painting *Lewis and Clark on the Lower Columbia,* shown on p. 277, depicts Lewis standing (at right) by the Native American woman Sacajawea as she addresses the Chinook Native Americans. Russell created this painting a century after Lewis and Clark reached the Columbia River in 1805. Russell was an American painter and sculptor famous for his scenes of the West, particularly scenes of cowboy life. His work is noted for its detail and authentic settings.

Launching a New Nation (1789–1800)

History Background

The New Republic Gets Its Bearings

With the election of George Washington as the nation's first President, the principles of a democratic republic made the transition from theory to practice. In its early years, the nation faced domestic and foreign challenges that raised issues threatening the unity established by the Framers. These issues are still in contention today: How much power should the federal government hold and how literally should the Constitution be interpreted?

In President Washington's cabinet, differing visions of government competed for the public's support. Secretary of the treasury Hamilton, a proponent of nationalism and a strong federal government, came up with a financial plan to provide the government with the funds to run itself, pay back the war debt, and establish a national bank. Jefferson, the secretary of state, believed a strong central government would infringe on people's and states' rights. He claimed that Hamilton's plan would allow the federal government to usurp powers not granted to it by the Constitution.

Supporters of Hamilton became known as the Federalists, and argued for a loose construction of the Constitution. Powers necessary to implement those specifically delineated in the Constitution were implied, the Federalists believed. Jefferson's supporters, the Republicans, believed the people and the states should receive any power not explicitly granted in the Constitution.

The election of 1796, making Federalist John Adams President and Jefferson Vice President, caused greater tension in the capital. It was clear by then that a bitter partisan split had developed in the nation's political life. Our familiar two-party system began in the conflicts of those years. The issues and ideologies surrounding the parties' rivalry have evolved considerably.

Federalists and Republicans would no doubt recognize another important legacy of the republic's early years. That is the idea that partisan conflicts can be addressed peacefully through civil means. Despite President Washington's entreaties against partisanship, Americans were learning that civil dispute could be an inevitable, and healthy, characteristic of the governing process.

Essential Questions

Use this graphic organizer to see the relationship between key concepts and the Chapter Essential Question.

Focus Question/Section 1
How did President Washington set the course for the new nation?
(p. 282)

Concept: Loose and Strict Construction

Focus Question/Section 2
How did two political parties emerge?
(p. 290)

Concept: Conflict

Chapter Essential Question
How did Americans respond to internal and external challenges?

Focus Question/Section 4
How did problems with France intensify the split between the Federalists and Republicans?
(p. 298)

Concept: States' Rights

Focus Question/Section 3
How did the actions of Britain and France affect the United States?
(p. 294)

Concept: Revolution

Differentiated Instruction

Numbered Heads Strategy

Why Use This Strategy In this chapter, students will use the Numbered Heads engagement strategy to come up with and share their responses to questions. Numbered Heads allows students to become more confident of their individual responses by sharing them with a smaller group before facing the whole class. Because students are then called on at random to speak for the group, they alternate taking on a leadership role, and all students are responsible for paying attention to the team's ideas.

Tips on Using This Strategy Remind students that it is a good idea to compare and contrast their responses with those of other teams. Below are sample language strategies to help students achieve this goal.

Our answer was (similar to/different from) that of team [blank] because [blank].

We agree with team [blank] that . . .

As team [blank] already mentioned, it seems like . . .

Team [blank] already mentioned . . ., but I would like to add that . . .

Concepts Across Time

Have students develop an understanding of the enduring concepts of history by connecting these ideas.

Concept: Loose and Strict Construction

Students learning about the importance of establishing a new government in accordance with the Constitution should recall that the Framers of the Constitution disagreed on the strength of the federal government. Ask: **How did Washington's administration demonstrate the clashing opinions of the Framers?** (*Leaders like Hamilton interpreted the Constitution loosely and supported a strong federal government. Leaders like Jefferson argued for a strict interpretation, saying that the Constitution granted the federal government limited powers for fear that it would become too strong.*) Use this question when discussing Hamilton's financial plan in Section 1.

Concept: Conflict

Students should recall the conflict between the 13 colonies and Britain before and during the American Revolution. Ask: **With the American Revolution having just ended, why might President Washington have resisted the development of factions?** (*Washington believed factions might weaken*

the new nation.) Use this question when discussing the birth of political parties in Section 2.

Concept: Revolution

Students learning about how the French Revolution affected the United States should recall that American colonists fought Britain for freedom and independence during the American Revolution. Ask: **How were the French and American revolutions different?** (*The French revolutionaries became violent and tyrannical, executing people who disagreed with them.*) Use these questions when discussing the French Revolution in Section 3.

Concept: States' Rights

Remind students that the Constitution did not make clear how disputes over the relative powers of federal and state governments should be settled. Ask: **How did people from Virginia and Kentucky seek to resolve such issues after Congress passed the Alien and Sedition Acts?** (*by having their state legislatures pass resolutions declaring the acts unconstitutional*) Use these questions when discussing states' rights in Section 4.

Section 1 Washington Takes Office *1.5 periods, .75 block*

Objectives

Students will

1. Discuss how the new government was organized during Washington's presidency.
2. Explain why the new nation faced an economic crisis.
3. Identify the three parts of Hamilton's financial plan.
4. Describe how Washington responded to the Whiskey Rebellion.

Differentiated Instruction Key

L1 Basic to Average
L2 All Students
L3 Average to Advanced

AR Advanced Readers
ELL English Language Learners
GT Gifted and Talented
LPR Less Proficient Readers
SN Special Needs

Prepare to Read	Instructional Resources	Differentiated Instruction

Build Background Knowledge
Preview the section and discuss why America needed a strong first President.

Set a Purpose for Reading
Have students begin to fill out the Reading Readiness Guide.

Preview Key Terms
Preview the section's key terms.

All in One Teaching Resources, Unit 3
L2 Chapter Prereading Guide, p. 5
L2 History Reading Skill, p. 15
L2 Word Knowledge Rating Form, p. 16
L2 Reading Readiness Guide, p. 17

Teacher's Edition
L2 Vocabulary Builder, pp. 281, 283

Guided Reading Audio CD
Spanish ELL, LPR, SN

Teach	Instructional Resources	Differentiated Instruction

Instruction
The First President
Describe the way Washington organized the new government.

The Nation's First Economic Crisis
Explain why the United States was in economic crisis during its early years.

Hamilton's Financial Plan
Identify the three parts of Hamilton's financial plan.

The Whiskey Rebellion
Discuss the reasons for protest over the whiskey tax.

Interactive Reading and Notetaking Study Guide
L2 Chapter 8, Section 1

All in One Teaching Resources, Unit 3
L2 Concept Lesson, p. 27
L2 Concept Organizer, p. 7
L2 Debating the National Bank, p. 21

Color Transparencies
L2 The United States in 1789
L2 Music of the 1800s
L2 Portrait of President Washington

Discovery School Video
L2 George Washington

Interactive Reading and Notetaking Study Guide, Adapted Version (English/Spanish)
L1 Chapter 8, Section 1

Teacher's Edition
L1 Visualizing the Word, p. 281 ELL, LPR, SN
L3 Oral History, p. 282 AR, GT
L1 Study Aid, p. 284 LPR
L1 Reviewing Vocabulary, p. 286 ELL, SN
L1 Creating Artwork, p. 288 ELL, LPR, SN

Assess and Reteach	Instructional Resources	Differentiated Instruction

Assess Progress
Evaluate student comprehension with Check Your Progress and Section Quiz.

Reteach
Assign the Interactive Reading and Notetaking Study Guide to help struggling students.

Extend
Extend the lesson by having students research and write a biography of Alexander Hamilton.

Interactive Reading and Notetaking Study Guide
L2 Chapter 8, Section 1

All in One Teaching Resources, Unit 3
L2 Reading Readiness Guide, p. 17
L2 Section Quiz, p. 28

Progress Monitoring Transparencies
L2 Chapter 8, Section 1

Teacher's Edition
L1 Checkpoints, TE pp. 284, 286, 287

SE on Audio CD
L1 Chapter 8 ELL, LPR, SN

Internet Resources
PHSchool.com

Section 2 The Birth of Political Parties *1 period, .5 block*

Objectives

Students will

1. Explain how early political parties emerged.
2. Compare the political views of the Republicans and the Federalists.
3. Discuss the result of the election of 1796.

Differentiated Instruction Key

L1 Basic to Average
L2 All Students
L3 Average to Advanced

AR Advanced Readers
ELL English Language Learners
GT Gifted and Talented
LPR Less Proficient Readers
SN Special Needs

Prepare to Read

Build Background Knowledge
Preview the section and have students make predictions about what they will learn.

Set a Purpose for Reading
Have students begin to fill out the Reading Readiness Guide.

Preview Key Terms
Preview the section's key terms.

Instructional Resources

All in One Teaching Resources, Unit 3
L2 Reading Readiness Guide, p. 18

Teacher's Edition
L2 Vocabulary Builder, p. 291

Differentiated Instruction

🎧 **Guided Reading Audio CD**
Spanish **ELL, LPR, SN**

Teach

Instruction
Political Parties Emerge
Explain how early political parties formed.

Republicans Against Federalists
Discuss the issues that divided the early political parties and their supporters.

The Election of 1796
Ask about how Republicans and Federalists differed in their political views, and discuss the result of the election of 1796.

Instructional Resources

📖 **Interactive Reading and Notetaking Study Guide**
L2 Chapter 8, Section 2

Differentiated Instruction

📖 **Interactive Reading and Notetaking Study Guide, Adapted Version (English/ Spanish)**
L1 Chapter 8, Section 2

Teacher's Edition
L3 Creating a Poster or Pamphlet, p. 290 **AR, GT**
L1 Reading a Chart, p. 292 **ELL, LPR, SN**

All in One Teaching Resources, Unit 3
L1 Presidential Elections, 1789–1800, p. 22

Assess and Reteach

Assess Progress
Evaluate student comprehension with Check Your Progress and Section Quiz.

Reteach
Assign the Interactive Reading and Notetaking Study Guide to help struggling students.

Extend
Extend the lesson by having students debate as Federalists and Republicans.

Instructional Resources

📖 **Interactive Reading and Notetaking Study Guide**
L2 Chapter 8, Section 2

All in One Teaching Resources, Unit 3
L2 Reading Readiness Guide, p. 18
L2 Section Quiz, p. 29

Progress Monitoring Transparencies
L2 Chapter 8, Section 2

Differentiated Instruction

Teacher's Edition
L1 Checkpoints, TE pp. 291, 293

🎧 **SE on Audio CD**
L1 Chapter 8 **ELL, LPR, SN**

Internet Resources
PHSchool.com

Section 3 Troubles at Home and Abroad

1 period, .5 block

Objectives

Students will

1. Discuss the conflicts with Native Americans in the Northwest Territory.
2. Describe how Americans reacted to the French Revolution.
3. Identify the main points of Washington's Farewell Address.
4. Summarize Washington's accomplishments as President.

Differentiated Instruction Key

L1 Basic to Average	**AR** Advanced Readers
L2 All Students	**ELL** English Language Learners
L3 Average to Advanced	**GT** Gifted and Talented
	LPR Less Proficient Readers
	SN Special Needs

Prepare to Read

Build Background Knowledge
Preview the section and have students make predictions about what they will learn.

Set a Purpose for Reading
Have students begin to fill out the Reading Readiness Guide.

Preview Key Terms
Preview the section's key terms.

Instructional Resources

All in One Teaching Resources, Unit 3
L2 Reading Readiness Guide, p. 19

Teacher's Edition
L2 Vocabulary Builder, p. 295

Differentiated Instruction

Guided Reading Audio CD
Spanish ELL, LPR, SN

Teach

Instruction
Conflicts in the Northwest Territory
Explain the conflicts that arose as a result of western settlement.

The French Revolution
Explore the conflicts with Native Americans and why the United States was divided over the French Revolution.

Washington Retires From Public Life
Discuss Washington's "Farewell Address."

Instructional Resources

Interactive Reading and Notetaking Study Guide
L2 Chapter 8, Section 3

Color Transparencies
L2 *Portrait of President Washington*

Differentiated Instruction

Interactive Reading and Notetaking Study Guide, Adapted Version (English/Spanish)
L1 Chapter 8, Section 3

Teacher's Edition
L1 Using Symbols When Reading, p. 294 ELL, LPR, SN
L3 Biography, p. 296 AR, GT

All in One Teaching Resources, Unit 3
L3 Martha Washington, p. 23

Assess and Reteach

Assess Progress
Evaluate student comprehension with Check Your Progress and Section Quiz.

Reteach
Assign the Interactive Reading and Notetaking Study Guide to help struggling students.

Extend
Extend the lesson by having students brainstorm for outcomes if history had been different.

Instructional Resources

Interactive Reading and Notetaking Study Guide
L2 Chapter 8, Section 3

All in One Teaching Resources, Unit 3
L2 Reading Readiness Guide, p. 19
L2 Section Quiz, p. 30

Progress Monitoring Transparencies
L2 Chapter 8, Section 3

Differentiated Instruction

Teacher's Edition
L1 Checkpoints, TE pp. 295, 296, 297

SE on Audio CD
L1 Chapter 8 ELL, LPR, SN

Section 4 The Presidency of John Adams

 1.5 periods, .75 block

Objectives

Students will

1. Discuss the reasons for tension between the United States and France.
2. Describe the main provisions of the Alien and Sedition acts.
3. Explain how controversy arose over states' rights.

Differentiated Instruction Key

L1 Basic to Average

L2 All Students

L3 Average to Advanced

AR Advanced Readers
ELL English Language Learners
GT Gifted and Talented
LPR Less Proficient Readers
SN Special Needs

Prepare to Read

Build Background Knowledge
Preview the section and have students make predictions about what they will learn.

Set a Purpose for Reading
Have students begin to fill out the Reading Readiness Guide.

Preview Key Terms
Preview the section's key terms.

Instructional Resources

All in One Teaching Resources, Unit 3

L2 Reading Readiness Guide, p. 20

Teacher's Edition

L2 Vocabulary Builder, p. 299

Differentiated Instruction

Guided Reading Audio CD
Spanish ELL, LPR, SN

Teach

Instruction
Troubles With France
Discuss how Adams avoided war with France.

The Alien and Sedition Acts
Explain how the Federalists reacted to potential threats to their power.

States' Rights
Consider why the Alien and Sedition acts were created. Explain why states found laws unconstitutional.

Instructional Resources

Interactive Reading and Notetaking Study Guide

L2 Chapter 8, Section 4

All in One Teaching Resources, Unit 3

L2 Debating the Alien Act, p. 24

L2 Skills for Life Worksheet, p. 26

Differentiated Instruction

Interactive Reading and Notetaking Study Guide, Adapted Version (English/Spanish)

L1 Chapter 8, Section 4

Teacher's Edition

L3 Group Activity, p. 298 AR, GT

L1 Reading a Chart, p. 300 ELL, LPR, SN

All in One Teaching Resources, Unit 3

L1 The Alien and Sedition Acts, p. 25

Assess and Reteach

Assess Progress
Evaluate student comprehension with Check Your Progress and Section Quiz.

Reteach
Assign the Interactive Reading and Notetaking Study Guide to help struggling students.

Extend
Extend the lesson by having students write newspaper articles from the perspective of either the Federalist or Republican party.

Instructional Resources

Interactive Reading and Notetaking Study Guide

L2 Chapter 8, Section 4

All in One Teaching Resources, Unit 3

L2 Reading Readiness Guide, p. 20

L2 Word Knowledge Rating Form, p. 16

L2 Section Quiz, p. 31

L2 Chapter Test, p. 35

Progress Monitoring Transparencies

L2 Chapter 8, Section 4

Differentiated Instruction

Teacher's Edition

L1 Checkpoints, TE pp. 299, 300, 301

All in One Teaching Resources, Unit 3

L1 Chapter Test, p. 32

SE on Audio CD

L1 Chapter 8 ELL, LPR, SN

Social Studies Skills Tutor CD-ROM
Distinguish Fact from Opinion

Extend the Lesson Through Technology Research

Use the following research activities to help students deepen their understanding of the Chapter Essential Question: **How did Americans respond to internal and external challenges?** Students should use library or Internet resources. The Web Codes provided offer access to Internet resources students can use to complete each activity. Use the appropriate four-point rubric in Assessment Rubrics to evaluate the activity.

 Assessment Rubrics

Write a Speech

Have students work in pairs to create two short speeches on the subject of states' rights. One speech will be from a Federalist perspective, and one will be from a Republican perspective. Speeches should address how much power the federal government should have to tax the states, create a national bank, and make laws. This activity will help students understand how each party interpreted the Constitution differently to support its own view. Have students present their speeches to the class. This activity works well with Sections 1, 2, and 4.

 Group research activity AR, GT

Go Online   **Web Code:** mye-0243
PHSchool.com

Write a Newscast

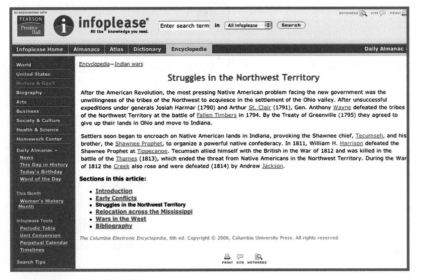

Have students work in small groups to conduct research about clashes between the British, Native Americans, and settlers in the Northwest Territory in the late 1700s. Have each group present a newscast about one of the leaders involved in the battles, such as General Wayne or Little Turtle; one of the battles; or the Treaty of Greenville. Use this activity with Conflicts in the Northwest Territory in Section 3.

 Group research activity AR, GT

Go Online   **Web Code:** mye-0244
PHSchool.com

Write an Opinion Statement

Have students work in small groups to conduct research about free speech or freedom of the press. Have each group write a one-page opinion statement about whether they think the Sedition Act opposed freedom of speech. Make sure students support their opinions with facts. Have students link past to present by stating whether they think it is important for news organizations to be allowed freedom of speech. If students disagree, have the group write statements supporting both sides. Use this activity when discussing the Sedition Act in Section 4.

 Group research activity　L2

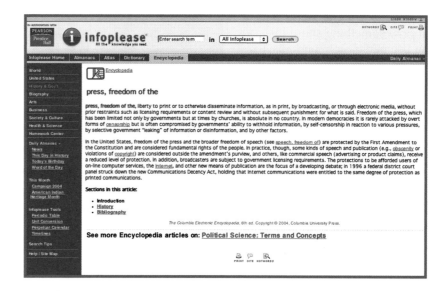

 Web Code: mye-0245

Conduct a Quiz Show

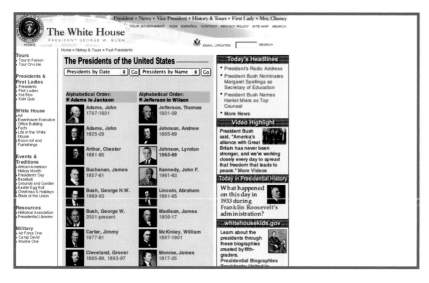

Divide students into groups. Each group should conduct research on the lives of Presidents Washington and Adams. Ask each group to prepare questions and answers for a quiz show. Questions should focus on the events that occurred during each man's presidency, such as the war between France and Britain and the XYZ Affair. Then, choose one student to act as the host for each group. Rotate groups so the host asks the questions to students in a different group. Use this activity as a wrap-up at the end of the chapter.

 Individual research activity　L2

 Web Code: mye-0246

Why It Matters

What if you really disagree with someone about how something should be done? You use persuasion, perhaps, to change minds. You get other neighbors who agree with you to join your cause. But how do you change something you disagree with on a state or national level? It seems obvious to us today: join a political party, or start your own. But that wasn't obvious when the first President took office. The idea of political parties that we take for granted today took time to grow and develop.

Chapter Essential Question

How did Americans respond to internal and external challenges?

Think Like a Historian

- To preview this chapter, have students review the content on these pages of the Student Edition. Ask: **What will you be learning about in this chapter?** *(the challenges the United States faced as a new nation)*

- Have students study the image of George Washington and read the quote from Henry Lee. Ask: **How do you think the people felt about George Washington?** *(George Washington was a popular President. The people respected him for leading them through the Revolutionary War.)*

- Have students read the section summaries and list some of the challenges facing Washington when he became the first president. *(Responses will vary but should include overseeing the creation of the government, creating political parties, and establishing relations with both Native Americans at home and the British abroad.)*

Launching a New Nation

In Trenton, New Jersey, girls throw flowers across Washington's path as the first American president travels to his inauguration.

1789–1800

278

Bibliography

For the Teacher

Ellis, Joseph J. *Founding Brothers: The Revolutionary Generation.* Vintage, 2002.

For the Student

L1 Schiel, Katy. *The Whiskey Rebellion: An Early Challenge to America's New Government (Life in the New American Nation).* Rosen Publishing Group, 2004.

L2 Plair, James B. *Three Score and Thirteen: A Study of the United States Constitution and the Federalist Papers.* Serendipity Press, 2002.

L3 Otfinoski, Steven. *Triumph and Terror: The French Revolution.* Facts on File, 1993.

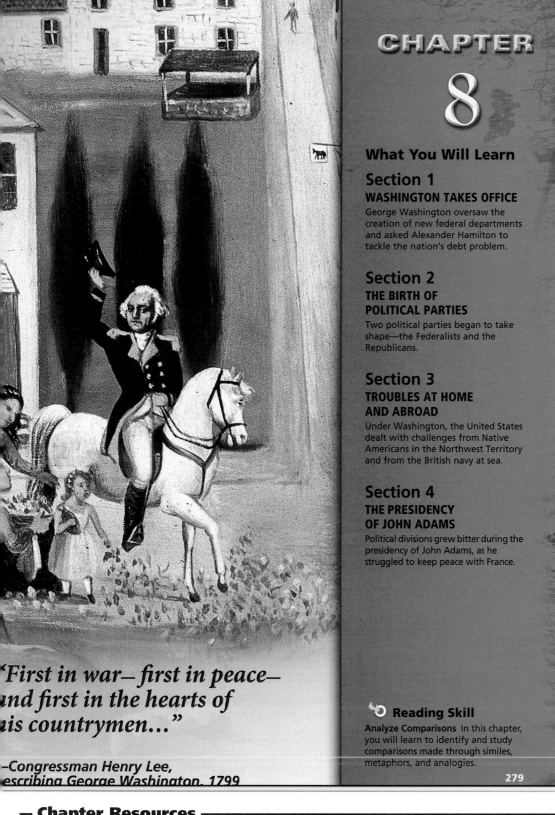

"First in war— first in peace—
and first in the hearts of
his countrymen..."

—Congressman Henry Lee,
describing George Washington, 1799

CHAPTER 8

What You Will Learn

Section 1
WASHINGTON TAKES OFFICE

George Washington oversaw the creation of new federal departments and asked Alexander Hamilton to tackle the nation's debt problem.

Section 2
THE BIRTH OF POLITICAL PARTIES

Two political parties began to take shape—the Federalists and the Republicans.

Section 3
TROUBLES AT HOME AND ABROAD

Under Washington, the United States dealt with challenges from Native Americans in the Northwest Territory and from the British navy at sea.

Section 4
THE PRESIDENCY OF JOHN ADAMS

Political divisions grew bitter during the presidency of John Adams, as he struggled to keep peace with France.

Reading Skill

Analyze Comparisons In this chapter, you will learn to identify and study comparisons made through similes, metaphors, and analogies.

279

History Background

A Different Kind of President Following the American Revolution, Washington retired to his home at Mount Vernon, with no intention of working in the public arena again. At Mount Vernon, he worked as a farmer. He also became president of the Potomac Company, which worked to improve navigation of the Potomac River. During this time, however, he continued to follow the country's affairs. In 1787, spurred by his desire to improve the Articles of Confederation, he left Mount Vernon for Philadelphia, and was elected president of the Constitutional Convention.

Prepare to Read

Use the following for reading skill support.

All in One Teaching Resources, Unit 3, Chapter Prereading Guide, p. 5; History Reading Skill, p. 15

History Reading Skill *Online*
Web code: mve-3000

Differentiated Instruction

The following Teacher Edition strategies are suitable for students of varying abilities.

L3 Advanced Readers, pp. 282, 290, 296, 298 AR

L1 English Language Learners, pp. 281, 286, 288, 292, 294, 300 ELL

L3 Gifted and Talented, pp. 282, 290, 296, 298 GT

L2 Less Proficient Readers, pp. 281, 284, 288, 292, 294, 300 LPR

L1 Special Needs, pp. 281, 286, 288, 292, 294, 300 SN

Chapter Resources

Teaching Resources, Unit 3
Chapter Prereading Guide, p. 5
Word Knowledge Rating Form, p. 16
History Reading Skill, p. 15
Skills for Life Worksheet, p. 26
Chapter Tests A/B (L1/L2), pp. 32, 35
Letter Home (English/Spanish), pp. 8, 9

Spanish Support
L1 Interactive Reading and Notetaking Study Guide, Spanish, Adapted Version
L1 Guided Reading Audio CD, Spanish

Media and Technology
L1 SE on Audio CD
L2 Social Studies Skills Tutor CD-ROM
ExamView Test Bank CD-ROM

DISCOVERY SCHOOL

Quick View Video
View the chapter video for a quick preview of the main ideas.

Chapter 8

Visual Preview

? **How did Americans respond to internal and external challenges?**

Build Background Knowledge [L2]

In Chapter 7, students read about the organization of the new government, and then reviewed key points of citizenship. Lead a structured discussion about the challenges America faced as a new nation. (TE p. T24) Discuss the idea of challenge and how people respond to decisions or hardships in life. What qualities do students think they need to have to overcome the difficulties they face? (*perseverance, compromise, diplomacy, seek help*) Have students provide examples about how they respond to challenges.

Instruction [L2]

■ For background information on conducting a lesson for the Visual Preview, see TE p. T20.

■ Write the Chapter Essential Question on the board. Explain the difference between "internal" and "external" challenges and the need to solve these if the nation is to survive. Use the Idea Wave strategy (TE p. T24) to review the challenges the nation faced after the Revolutionary War. Ask: **What problems did the nation face when it became independent?** (*creating an effective government, collecting taxes, Shays' Rebellion, gaining respect of other nations*) **Which of these were external?** (*respect of other nations*)

■ Have students study the map. Using the key, have students explain what the dark-green shaded area indicates. (*original 13 states*) **What foreign nations had forts near American territory?** (*Britain, Spain*) **Where were the lands given up by Indians in 1795?** (*pink area, between original 13 states and areas claimed by U.S.*)

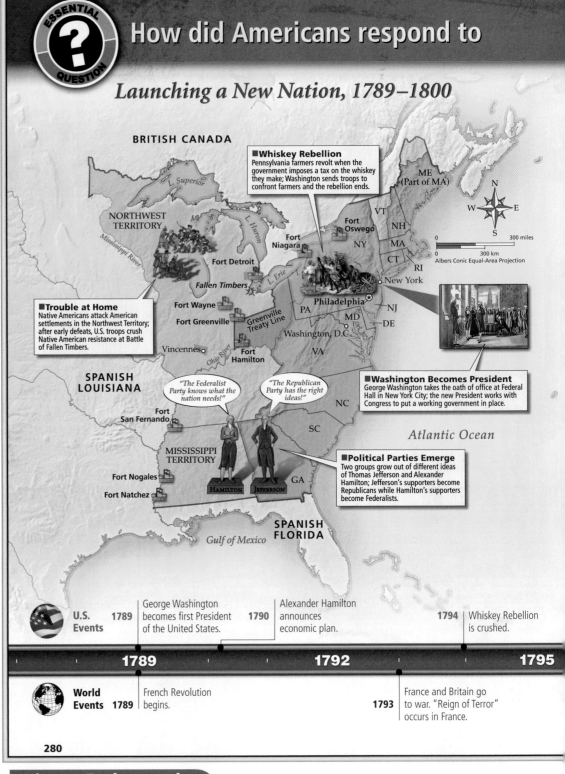

ESSENTIAL QUESTION

Launching a New Nation, 1789–1800

BRITISH CANADA

■Whiskey Rebellion
Pennsylvania farmers revolt when the government imposes a tax on the whiskey they make; Washington sends troops to confront farmers and the rebellion ends.

■Trouble at Home
Native Americans attack American settlements in the Northwest Territory; after early defeats, U.S. troops crush Native American resistance at Battle of Fallen Timbers.

■Washington Becomes President
George Washington takes the oath of office at Federal Hall in New York City; the new President works with Congress to put a working government in place.

"The Federalist Party knows what the nation needs!"

"The Republican Party has the right ideas!"

■Political Parties Emerge
Two groups grow out of different ideas of Thomas Jefferson and Alexander Hamilton; Jefferson's supporters become Republicans while Hamilton's supporters become Federalists.

Atlantic Ocean

SPANISH FLORIDA

Gulf of Mexico

0   300 miles
0   300 km
Albers Conic Equal-Area Projection

U.S. Events	1789	George Washington becomes first President of the United States.	
	1790	Alexander Hamilton announces economic plan.	
	1794	Whiskey Rebellion is crushed.	

1789 — **1792** — **1795**

World Events	1789	French Revolution begins.	
	1793	France and Britain go to war. "Reign of Terror" occurs in France.	

280

History Background

Leadership Winning independence did not guarantee a "United" States. It was in large part due to Washington's leadership that the former colonies were able to bond into a nation. His reputation for duty and sacrifice put him in high esteem. Americans trusted him. Loyalty to him could be transferred to allegiance to a central government.

Washington realized one of his jobs would be to cement the states into a cohesive body. He carefully chose his appointments, not only for their ability but also for the sectional support they would bring to the new government. Remaining above the factions of political parties, he used good judgment to limit partisan fighting and alleviate the anxieties of a new nation. He embodied the power and pride of a national government. Even in his own time, he was hailed as the "Father of Our Country."

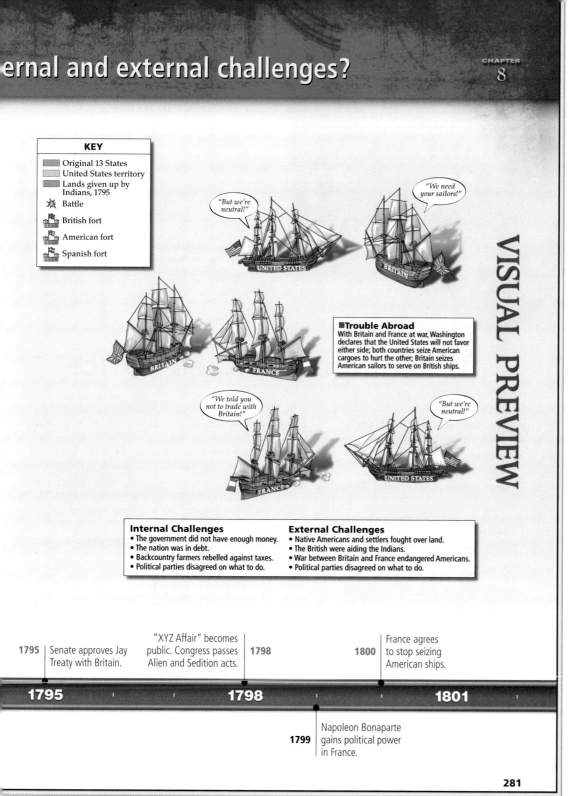

KEY

- Original 13 States
- United States territory
- Lands given up by Indians, 1795
- Battle
- British fort
- American fort
- Spanish fort

VISUAL PREVIEW

"But we're neutral!"

"We need your sailors!"

UNITED STATES

BRITAIN

BRITAIN

FRANCE

■Trouble Abroad
With Britain and France at war, Washington declares that the United States will not favor either side; both countries seize American cargoes to hurt the other; Britain seizes American sailors to serve on British ships.

"We told you not to trade with Britain!"

"But we're neutral!"

FRANCE

UNITED STATES

Internal Challenges
- The government did not have enough money.
- The nation was in debt.
- Backcountry farmers rebelled against taxes.
- Political parties disagreed on what to do.

External Challenges
- Native Americans and settlers fought over land.
- The British were aiding the Indians.
- War between Britain and France endangered Americans.
- Political parties disagreed on what to do.

| 1795 | Senate approves Jay Treaty with Britain. | "XYZ Affair" becomes public. Congress passes Alien and Sedition acts. | 1798 | | 1800 | France agrees to stop seizing American ships. |

1795　　　**1798**　　　**1801**

| | 1799 | Napoleon Bonaparte gains political power in France. |

281

Instruction (continued)

- Have students study the timeline. **When did George Washington become president?** *(1789)* **What major event occurred in France that same year?** *(French Revolution began.)* **Based on the timeline, what was the external challenge France posed to America?** *(France was seizing American ships.)*

- Call students' attention to the illustration of Washington becoming President. Explain the idea of a "working government." *(one that will solve problems and keep order)* Pair students to select a graphic to analyze. Using the Think-Write-Pair-Share strategy (TE p. T25), have students identify specific problems facing the new nation and the way in which each one was resolved. Then, as you review the issues with the class, write them on the board in two columns, under *internal* and *external*.

- Ask: **Which do you think were more of a threat to the development of the U.S.—the internal problems or the external?** *(Some students will say internal because a nation's citizens must stick together; others will say external because the young nation could still have been destroyed by strong European powers.)*

- Have students rewrite the Essential Question in simple terms in their notes: **What were the problems Americans faced and how were they solved?** You may also post this question in a prominent place in the classroom and leave it there while discussing the chapter. Tell students to use the section focus questions as a guide to answering the Essential Question as they read the chapter.

- Tell students that as they complete the Notetaking Study Guide for this chapter, they will be building the answer to the Chapter Essential Question.

📖 **Interactive Reading and Notetaking Study Guide,** Chapter 8 (Adapted Version also available.)

Vocabulary Builder

Preview the Vocabulary Have students preview the vocabulary in the chapter and rate how well they know each word on the Word Knowledge Rating Form. Collect the sheets and explain that they will have a chance to go over the forms later.

All in One Teaching Resources, Unit 3, Word Knowledge Rating Form, p. 16

Monitor Progress Pronounce each word and have students repeat the word after you. Ask a volunteer to read the definition. Students should demonstrate their understanding of the words by suggesting synonyms for each. For example, ask: **What is a synonym for *hostile*?** *(Resentful or acting in an angry way)*

Review and Preview

Students have learned about the compromises needed to create a new government. Now they will focus on the early challenges the nation faced.

Section Focus Question

How did President Washington set the course for the new nation?

Before you begin the lesson for the day, write the Section Focus Question on the board. (*Lesson focus: George Washington oversaw the creation of new federal departments and asked Alexander Hamilton to tackle the nation's debt problem.*)

Prepare to Read

Build Background Knowledge ▫L2▫

In this section, students will read about the challenges facing the new United States. Have students preview the headings and the visuals. Ask: **Why did the American people need a strong first President?** Use the Think-Write-Pair-Share strategy (TE, p. T25) to elicit responses. (*Students may suggest that the new nation needed an organized government and faced many challenges.*)

Set a Purpose ▫L2▫

■ Form students into pairs or groups of four. Distribute the Reading Readiness Guide. Ask students to fill in the first two columns of the chart.

　▫All in One▫ **Teaching Resources, Unit 3,** Reading Readiness Guide, p. 17

■ Use the Numbered Heads strategy (TE, p. T24) to call on students to share one piece of information they already know and one piece of information they want to know. The students will return to these worksheets later.

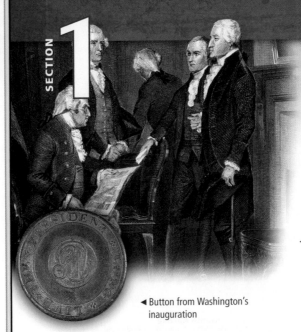

◄ Button from Washington's inauguration

The Sacred Fire of Liberty

❝The preservation of the sacred fire of liberty and the destiny of the republican model of government are . . . staked on the experiment entrusted to the hands of the American people.❞

—George Washington,
First Inaugural Address, 1789

◄ Advisers to President Washington (far right) included (from left) Henry Knox, Thomas Jefferson, Edmund Randolph, and Alexander Hamilton.

Washington Takes Office

Objectives

- Discuss how the new government was organized during Washington's presidency.
- Explain why the new nation faced an economic crisis.
- Identify the three parts of Hamilton's financial plan.
- Describe how Washington responded to the Whiskey Rebellion.

🎯 Reading Skill

Identify Similes Similes use the signal words *like* or *as* to connect two items being compared. The comparison helps the reader to imagine the description more fully. For example, "the gunfire echoed like thunder" creates a mental image of the sound of a battle. Look for similes as you read this section.

Key Terms

inauguration　　　speculator
precedent　　　　unconstitutional
bond　　　　　　tariff

Why It Matters In 1789, the American people had a new Constitution. They also had a new Congress and their first President. The United States was one fourth of its size today. All thirteen states were in the East. The nation's western border followed the Mississippi River. In the North, the Great Lakes formed much of the border separating the United States from British-controlled Canada. In the South, the United States bordered on Spanish-controlled Florida and Louisiana.

❓ Section Focus Question: How did President Washington set the course for the new nation?

The First President

In April of 1789, George Washington traveled from Virginia to the nation's capital, New York City, to begin his term as the first President of the United States. Washington's journey along bumpy roads took eight days. Large crowds lined the streets. As one newspaper reported, Americans greatly admired the tall, stately war hero:

❝Many persons in the crowd were heard to say they should now die contented—nothing being wanted to complete their happiness . . . but the sight of the savior of his country.❞

—*Gazette of the United States*, April 1789

Differentiated Instruction

▫L3▫ Advanced Readers　　　　▫L3▫ Gifted and Talented

Oral History After students have read the section, ask them to work in pairs to write an interview with George Washington in which they ask him about the main ideas in the section and he responds. Have the

students present their interviews to the class, with one student asking questions as the interviewer and the other student responding as George Washington.

Washington's **inauguration**—a ceremony in which the President takes the oath of office—was held on April 30, 1789. Despite all he had achieved, Washington was anxious. The country was divided on many issues. Washington understood how much the new nation depended on him. His actions would set a **precedent**—an example to be followed by others in the future.

The Executive Branch The Constitution of the United States provided only a general outline for organizing the government. When the President took office, the entire federal government was made up of little more than 75 post offices, a few clerks, and a tiny army of 672 soldiers.

The first job of the President and the Congress, therefore, was to put a working government in place. First, Congress passed laws to set up three departments for the executive branch: Treasury, State, and War. Each department was to be headed by a secretary nominated by the President. The President would also appoint an attorney general to advise him on legal matters.

Washington appointed four well-known men to take the new posts. He chose Alexander Hamilton to be secretary of the treasury. Hamilton was considered one of the country's outstanding leaders and an expert on economic affairs. Thomas Jefferson, the author of the Declaration of Independence, became secretary of state. His task was to manage relations with foreign countries. Henry Knox, a former general, was Washington's choice for secretary of war. Edmund Randolph, who had played an important role at the Constitutional Convention, became attorney general.

Washington soon began meeting regularly with these leaders as a group. Over time, this group became known as the Cabinet.

Explore More Video
To learn more about George Washington's presidency, view the video.

Washington's Inauguration
George Washington took the oath of office on a balcony of Federal Hall in New York City as well-wishers watched from the street below. *Critical Thinking: Link Past and Present* Who attended Washington's oath-taking? How would a modern-day President's inauguration be different?

Section 1 Washington Takes Office 283

Vocabulary Builder

Use the information below to teach students this section's high-use words.

High-Use Word	Definition and Sample Sentence
invest, p. 284	*v.* to purchase something with the hope that its value will grow Wealthy Americans **invested** in land, believing that they could sell it later for a profit.
impose, p. 285	*v.* to place a burden on something or someone Manufacturers wanted the government to **impose** a high tax on imports.

Teach

The First President
p. 282

Instruction

- **Vocabulary Builder** Before teaching this section, preteach the High-Use Words **invest** and **impose** using the strategy on TE p. T21.

  Key Terms Following the instructions on p. 7, have students create a See It–Remember It chart for the Key Terms in this chapter.

- Read The First President with students, using the Structured Silent Reading strategy (TE, p. T22).

- Display the transparency The United States in 1789. Ask students to discuss the challenges presented by the size and location of the original 13 states.

Color Transparencies, The United States in 1789

- Ask: **How was the first government organized?** (*It had an executive branch with departments of Treasury, State, and War, and a judiciary system.*)

Independent Practice
Have students begin filling in the study guide for this section.

Interactive Reading and Notetaking Study Guide, Chapter 8, Section 1 (Adapted Version also available.)

Monitor Progress

As students fill in the Notetaking Study Guide, circulate to make sure that they understand the challenges Washington faced early in his presidency. Provide assistance as needed.

 Explore More Video

Discovery School Video
This video explores the life of George Washington, the myths and his achievements as president.

Answer
Link Past and Present Many men attended the inauguration. The public watched from outside. A modern-day President's inauguration might be broadcast to the public on television or radio.

The Nation's First Economic Crisis

p. 284

Instruction
L2

- Have students read The Nation's First Economic Crisis. Remind students to look for details to answer the Section Focus Question.

- Ask: **What major challenge did President Washington face when he took office?** (*resolving the government's war debt*)

- Ask: **To whom did the government owe money?** (*The government owed money to individuals who had purchased bonds during the war and to the states.*)

- Discuss with students how purchasing bonds helped the war effort. (*By purchasing bonds, citizens loaned the government money to help fund the war.*)

- Ask: **Why might the government owe the states money?** (*The states probably spent a great deal of money to help fund the war.*)

Independent Practice

Have students continue filling in the study guide for this section.

📖 **Interactive Reading and Notetaking Study Guide,** Chapter 8, Section 1 (Adapted Version also available.)

Monitor Progress

As students fill in the Notetaking Study Guide, circulate and make sure individuals understand the nation's economic crisis. Provide assistance as needed.

Answers

✓**Checkpoint** the departments of Treasury, State, and War

✓**Checkpoint** The government had to borrow money to pay for the Revolutionary War.

Identifying Economic Costs $150,000

Establishing the Judiciary The Constitution also called for a judiciary, or court system. The Judiciary Act of 1789 provided for a Supreme Court of 6 justices. Under the Supreme Court were 3 circuit courts and 13 district courts. The main job of the federal courts was to hear appeals from the state courts. Washington appointed John Jay of New York as the first Chief Justice of the Supreme Court.

✓**Checkpoint** What were the new executive departments?

The Nation's First Economic Crisis

The American Revolution had left the nation deeply in debt. The federal government owed $52 million. That debt was mainly in the form of bonds. A **bond** is a certificate issued by a government for an amount of money that the government promises to pay back with interest. Both Americans and foreigners had <u>invested</u> in bonds to help the war effort. Would the government pay back this debt?

The issue was complicated because most people who had originally bought the bonds had sold them for less than they were worth. The buyers were **speculators**—people who invest in a risky venture in the hope of making a large profit. It seemed unfair to many Americans that speculators would make a profit after the original bondholders had lost money. Also in dispute was whether or not the federal government should pay back state debts.

The government was operating on a shoestring. It did not even have the money for George Washington's move to New York. Washington had to borrow $3,000 to pay his moving expenses.

✓**Checkpoint** Why was there such a large public debt?

Vocabulary Builder
invest (ihn VEHST) *v.* to purchase something with the hope that its value will grow

The Debt Problem
The U.S. government was collecting enough in taxes to pay its expenses, but hardly enough to pay back the debt. Hamilton's financial plan sought to find new sources of income to repay the debt. **Critical Thinking:** *Identifying Economic Costs* Without the amount of money owed, how much would the government have had left over after paying its costs?

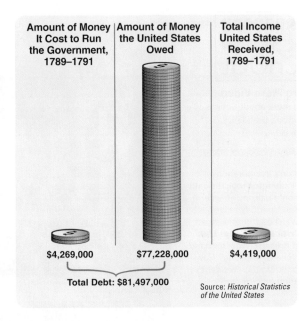

Amount of Money It Cost to Run the Government, 1789–1791	Amount of Money the United States Owed	Total Income United States Received, 1789–1791
$4,269,000	$77,228,000	$4,419,000

Total Debt: $81,497,000

Source: *Historical Statistics of the United States*

Differentiated Instruction

L1 Less Proficient Readers

Study Aid To help less proficient readers understand the impact of Washington's presidency, make a two-column chart on the board. In the first column, write down three of the challenges Washington faced at the beginning of his presidency: organizing the government, war debt, the Whiskey Rebellion. Use the Numbered Heads strategy (TE, p. T24) to call on students to fill in the second column of the chart with information from the text about the ways Washington responded to the challenges.

Hamilton's Financial Plan

The person responsible for developing a plan to solve the country's financial crisis was Alexander Hamilton, the secretary of the treasury.

Hamilton's program had three parts: (1) The U.S. government would fully assume, or agree to pay, all federal *and* state debts. (2) The U.S. government would charter a national bank for depositing government funds. (3) The government would <u>impose</u> a high tax on goods imported into the country.

Paying the Debt Hamilton knew that paying the debt would be a huge burden on the U.S. government. However, he wanted to prove to people here and abroad that the United States would honor its debts in full. Then, people would be willing to invest again in the future.

Many southerners opposed the plan to repay state debts. Several southern states had paid off their wartime debts on their own. Southerners thought other states should do the same.

Congress debated the plan for six months in 1790. Then, an agreement was reached. Southerners would support Hamilton's plan to have the federal government repay the wartime debt. In return, the government would build its new capital city in the South. The capital would rise along the banks of the Potomac River, between Virginia and Maryland.

A National Bank The second part of Hamilton's plan called for the creation of a privately owned bank of the United States. It would provide a safe place to deposit government funds. The bank would be able to issue paper money that would serve as a national currency.

The debate over the bank of the United States went beyond the bank itself and focused on the powers the government had under the Constitution. Opponents of the bank, such as Thomas Jefferson, insisted that the law establishing the bank was **unconstitutional**—contrary to what is permitted by the Constitution.

Jefferson argued that nowhere in the Constitution was there a provision allowing Congress to set up a national bank. Jefferson's view, that the Constitution permits only what it specifically says, is called a "strict" interpretation of the Constitution. Hamilton argued for a "loose" interpretation. He pointed out that Article 1, Section 8 of the Constitution gave Congress the power to make all laws "necessary and proper" for fulfilling its duties. This suggested that there were things not directly permitted by the Constitution that Congress could do.

Vocabulary Builder
<u>impose</u> (ihm POHZ) *v.* to place a burden on something or someone

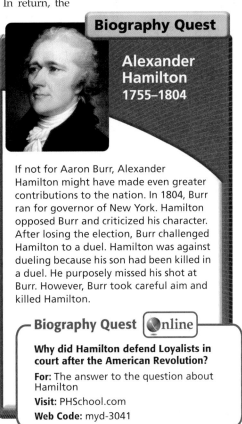

Biography Quest

Alexander Hamilton
1755–1804

If not for Aaron Burr, Alexander Hamilton might have made even greater contributions to the nation. In 1804, Burr ran for governor of New York. Hamilton opposed Burr and criticized his character. After losing the election, Burr challenged Hamilton to a duel. Hamilton was against dueling because his son had been killed in a duel. He purposely missed his shot at Burr. However, Burr took careful aim and killed Hamilton.

Biography Quest **Online**

Why did Hamilton defend Loyalists in court after the American Revolution?

For: The answer to the question about Hamilton
Visit: PHSchool.com
Web Code: myd-3041

Hamilton's Financial Plan

p. 285

Instruction L2

- To help students better understand the concept of loose and strict construction, which is important to the understanding of this section, use the Concept Lesson Loose and Strict Construction. Provide students with copies of the Concept Organizer.

  All in One Teaching Resources, Unit 3, Concept Lesson, p. 27, Concept Organizer, p. 7

- Read Hamilton's Financial Plan with students. Remind students to look for support of the main idea.

- Ask students to complete the worksheet Debating the National Bank. Have them discuss how Hamilton's financial plan led to debates about constitutional rights. (*Students should identify Hamilton's and Jefferson's opposing views regarding loose and strict interpretations of the Constitution and the establishment of the National Bank.*)

  All in One Teaching Resources, Unit 3, Debating the National Bank, p. 21

- Ask: **Why do you think it was important for Washington to support Hamilton's financial plan?** (*Possible answer: It was important for Washington to set a precedent for dealing with debt and interpreting the Constitution.*)

Independent Practice

Have students continue filling in the study guide for this section.

Interactive Reading and Notetaking Study Guide, Chapter 8, Section 1 (Adapted Version also available.)

Monitor Progress

As students fill in the Notetaking Study Guide, circulate and make sure that they understand Hamilton's financial plan. Provide assistance as needed.

Answer

Biography Quest He was born in the West Indies and under the Constitution, the president must be born in the United States.

History Background

Misconceptions about George Washington Students may have heard many stories about George Washington, but not all of them are true. A famous myth is the story that he cut down his father's cherry tree and later admitted his act with the famous line "I cannot tell a lie." This tale was invented by a parson named Mason Locke Weems in a biography of Washington. The story emphasized Washington's honesty and contributed greatly to his popularity.

Another myth: He threw a silver dollar across the Potomac River. The river is over a mile wide! This tale, illustrating his strength, enhanced his heroic image. Both stories contributed to our national culture.

The Whiskey Rebellion

p. 287

Instruction　L2

- Read The Whiskey Rebellion with students. Remind students to keep the Section Focus Question in mind.

- Ask: **How did George Washington react to the Whiskey Rebellion?** (*He led an army of 13,000 men to stop the rebellion.*) **Why do you think Washington used an armed force rather than negotiating with the farmers?** (*He wanted to establish the government's policy that rebellion would not be tolerated.*)

Independent Practice

Have students complete the study guide for this section.

Interactive Reading and Notetaking Study Guide, Chapter 8, Section 1 (Adapted Version also available.)

Monitor Progress

- As students fill in the Notetaking Study Guide, circulate to make sure that they understand the importance of the Whiskey Rebellion. Provide assistance as needed.

- Tell students to fill in the last column of the Reading Readiness Guide. Ask them to consider whether what they learned was what they had expected to learn.

All in One Teaching Resources, Unit 3, Reading Readiness Guide, p. 17

Answers

Detect Points of View Farmers thought taxing whiskey was unfair. George Washington thought the rebellion threatened the authority of the government and the rights of the people.

Checkpoint Congress debated the plan at first, but eventually passed all except the tariff on imports into law.

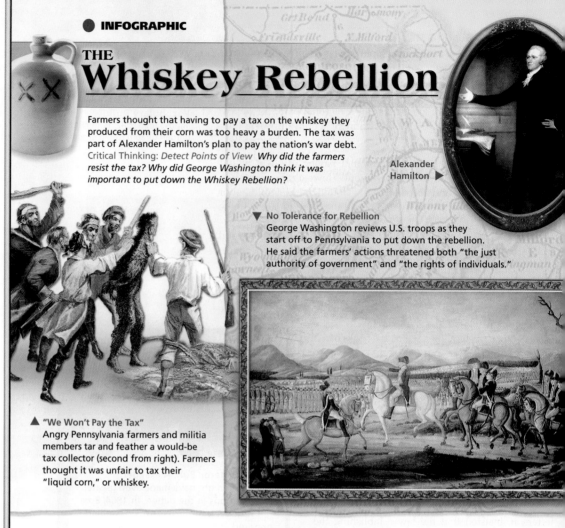

● **INFOGRAPHIC**

THE Whiskey Rebellion

Farmers thought that having to pay a tax on the whiskey they produced from their corn was too heavy a burden. The tax was part of Alexander Hamilton's plan to pay the nation's war debt.
Critical Thinking: *Detect Points of View* **Why did the farmers resist the tax? Why did George Washington think it was important to put down the Whiskey Rebellion?**

Alexander Hamilton ▶

▼ **No Tolerance for Rebellion**
George Washington reviews U.S. troops as they start off to Pennsylvania to put down the rebellion. He said the farmers' actions threatened both "the just authority of government" and "the rights of individuals."

▲ **"We Won't Pay the Tax"**
Angry Pennsylvania farmers and militia members tar and feather a would-be tax collector (second from right). Farmers thought it was unfair to tax their "liquid corn," or whiskey.

In 1791, Congress did pass a law establishing the bank, and the President signed it. However, to this day Americans disagree about whether the Constitution should be interpreted strictly or loosely.

A High Tariff The final part of Hamilton's plan called for a high tariff—a tax on imported goods. It would raise money for the federal government. It would also protect U.S. manufacturers from foreign competition by making imported goods more expensive.

The tariff was the only part of Hamilton's plan that Congress did not pass, and that was because southerners opposed it. They argued that a high tariff would help the North, where most industries were located, while making southerners pay more for the goods they bought.

Checkpoint How did Congress respond to Hamilton's plan?

Differentiated Instruction

L1 English Language Learners　　**L1** Special Needs

Reviewing Vocabulary Check students' understanding of the words *burden* and *would-be*. Have them rewrite the following sentences in their own words. When students have finished, ask them to share their sentences with the class.

- The farmers felt that paying the tax was a *burden*.

- The *would-be* tax collector did not succeed in collecting taxes.

　(*Students' sentences will vary. Possible sentences: The farmers felt oppressed by the tax; The farmers refused to pay any tax to the person who tried to collect.*)

The Whiskey Rebellion

In 1791, Congress imposed a tax on all whiskey made and sold in the United States. Hamilton hoped this tax would raise funds for the Treasury. Instead, it led to a revolt that tested the strength of the new government.

Many backcountry farmers made extra money by turning the corn they grew into whiskey. Therefore, they bitterly resented the new whiskey tax. Farmers compared it to the hated taxes that Britain had imposed on the colonies before the Revolution. Many farmers organized protests and refused to pay the tax.

In 1794, officials in western Pennsylvania tried to collect the tax. Farmers rebelled, burning down the home of a tax collector. Soon, a large, angry mob was marching through Pittsburgh like a gathering storm. The violent protest became known as the Whiskey Rebellion.

Washington responded quickly to this challenge to federal authority. He sent the militia to Pennsylvania. When the rebels heard that 13,000 troops were marching against them, they quickly scattered. Washington later pardoned the leaders of the rebellion.

The Whiskey Rebellion tested the will of the new government. Washington's forceful response showed Americans that armed rebellion was not acceptable in a republic.

Identify Similes Find the simile in this paragraph. What two things are being compared?

✓**Checkpoint** What was the cause of the Whiskey Rebellion?

⭐ **Looking Back and Ahead** George Washington set a firm course for the federal government, while Alexander Hamilton began to attack the debt problem. In the next section, you will read how the nation's first political parties developed.

Section 1 | Check Your Progress

Progress Monitoring Online
For: Self-test with instant help
Visit: PHSchool.com
Web Code: mya-3041

Comprehension and Critical Thinking

1. **(a) Describe** How did Washington's inauguration reflect the nation's deep respect for him?
(b) Organize Information Create a chart showing the top posts in the executive branch and judiciary at this time. Define each position and name the first person to occupy each post.

2. **(a) Recall** What was the nation's first economic crisis? How was it further complicated?
(b) Explain Problems What was Hamilton's plan to solve the crisis? Why was it controversial?

Reading Skill

3. **Identify Similes** Identify the simile in this sentence: The new President was as tough as nails. What two things does it compare?

Key Terms

4. Write two definitions for each key term: inauguration, precedent, bond, speculator, unconstitutional, tariff. First, write a formal definition for your teacher. Second, write a definition in everyday English for a classmate.

Writing

5. A newspaper account of George Washington's inauguration referred to him as "the savior of his country." That was a reference to Washington's service as commander in chief during the Revolutionary War. If you were to begin reading an essay about the life of George Washington, list five questions you would like it to answer.

Section 1 Check Your Progress

1. **(a)** Washington's inauguration drew huge crowds.
(b) Executive—Treasury, State, and War departments, headed by Hamilton, Jefferson, and Knox; Judiciary—Supreme Court with Chief Justice John Jay, 3 circuit courts, 13 district courts

2. **(a)** managing its war debt; people disagreed over who should be repaid
(b) a three-part plan including the repayment of federal and state debts,

the creation of a national bank, and the imposition of a national tariff; they opposed the national tariff and prevented its enactment

3. The President is compared to nails; both are "tough"—or strong.

4. Answers will vary. Students should demonstrate an understanding of the terms.

5. Students' answers should demonstrate the parts of Washington's life about which students are interested in learning.

Assess and Reteach

Assess Progress L2

Have students complete Check Your Progress. Administer the Section Quiz.

 All in One Teaching Resources, Section Quiz, p. 28

To further assess student understanding, use the Progress Monitoring Transparency.

Progress Monitoring Transparencies, Chapter 8, Section 1

Reteach L1

If students need more instruction, have them read this section in the Interactive Reading and Notetaking Study Guide.

📖 **Interactive Reading and Notetaking Study Guide,** Chapter 8, Section 1 (Adapted Version also available.)

Extend L3

Have students conduct research to find out more about Alexander Hamilton. Ask students to write a short biography of Hamilton. Tell students to focus on a particular period of his life, such as his early career, his Federalist leadership, or his conflicts with Burr. Have students present their biographies to the class.

Extend Online
For: Help with starting the Extend activity
Visit: PHSchool.com
Web Code: mye-0247

Progress Monitoring Online

Students may check their comprehension of this section by completing the Progress Monitoring Online graphic organizer and self-quiz.

Answers

 Reading Skill A mob is compared to a gathering storm.

✓**Checkpoint** A tax on whiskey was opposed by farmers—especially those in western Pennsylvania, who used corn to make whiskey.

The Arts of Early America
p. 288

Build Background Knowledge **L2**

Using the Idea Wave technique (TE, p. T24), have students brainstorm for different types of art, architecture, and music that they associate with the United States.

Instruction **L2**

- Read Life at the Time with students. Ask: **How did the architecture of the Federal Period reflect a departure from British influence?** (*The architecture of this period followed the Greek and Roman styles.*)

- Tell students that many types of folk art included items that were functional as well as decorative. Then, ask: **Why might people have wanted to create folk art?** (*Possible answer: Craftspeople may have wanted to decorate items with images that were important to them.*)

- Ask: **How does the song "Yankee Doodle" show the pride Americans had in their nation?** (*Words were added describing the importance of free elections, one of the important values on which the nation was founded.*)

- Show students the transparency Music of the 1800s to extend the lesson. Ask: **Why do you think Americans purposely avoided using British models for the arts?** (*It was another way to show their independence from Great Britain.*)

Color Transparencies, Music of the 1800s

Independent Practice

Ask students to visit the History Interactive online and to share their findings with the class.

> Extend Online
> **For:** Help with the History Interactive
> **Visit:** PHSchool.com
> **Web Code:** myp-3047

Monitor Progress

Ask students to complete the Analyze Life at the Time activity. Circulate to make sure students understand how early American art shows a sense of pride in the nation. Provide assistance as needed.

The Arts of Early America

After winning independence, Americans began to develop their own styles in the arts. Often, they deliberately turned away from the model of their former British rulers.

Architecture

American architects of the Federal Period (1790–1830) turned away from the influence of England. They looked instead to two ancient civilizations, Greece and Rome. Domes and pillars were common. Buildings were designed to create a sense of harmony and balance. This picture shows the White House as it looked in 1807.

> **History** *Interactive*
> **Explore Art and Music of the 1800s**
> **Visit:** PHSchool.com
> **Web Code:** myp-3047

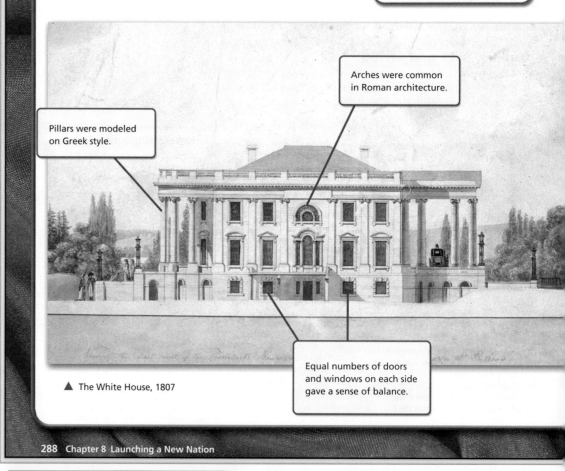

Pillars were modeled on Greek style.

Arches were common in Roman architecture.

Equal numbers of doors and windows on each side gave a sense of balance.

▲ The White House, 1807

Differentiated Instruction

L1 English Language Learners **L1** Less Proficient Readers **L1** Special Needs

Creating Artwork Have students create a piece of art that shows their own feelings about their country. Encourage students to use images that represent what is impor- tant to them. When students are finished, have them share their artwork with the class and describe what the different imag- es mean.

Folk Art

Folk art is art created by ordinary people rather than trained artists. Common types of American folk art included hand-stitched samplers, weather vanes, ships' figureheads, and tavern signs. Much of the folk art of this time included patriotic images that revealed pride in the new nation. This Pennsylvania Dutch watercolor shows George Washington and his wife, Martha.

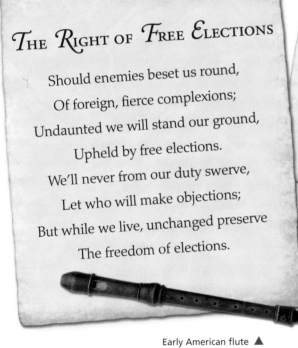

Pennsylvania Dutch watercolor ▶

Music

Many early American popular songs—including "Yankee Doodle"(below, right)—were adapted from old English melodies. In 1796, Americans put a new set of words to "Yankee Doodle" (below, left) to show pride in their democracy.

The Right of Free Elections

Should enemies beset us round,
Of foreign, fierce complexions;
Undaunted we will stand our ground,
Upheld by free elections.
We'll never from our duty swerve,
Let who will make objections;
But while we live, unchanged preserve
The freedom of elections.

Early American flute ▲

Yankee Doodle

There was Captain Washington
Upon a slapping stallion
A-giving orders to his men
I guess there was a million.
Yankee Doodle, keep it up
Yankee Doodle dandy
Mind the music and the step
And with the girls be handy.

Analyze LIFE AT THE TIME

Choose one of the examples of art, architecture, or music shown on these pages. Write a paragraph explaining how it shows a sense of pride in being an American.

Life at the Time 289

Writing Rubric

Score 1 Does not address assigned topic, is poorly organized.
Score 2 Details and organization are often unclear or incorrect.
Score 3 Has organization suited to topic, some appropriate details, some original ideas.
Score 4 Many appropriate details, original ideas, well-organized and developed.

History Background

Early American Portrait Artists Folk art was not the only early American art that reflected important American values. Portraits by artists such as Charles Willson Peale and Gilbert Stuart also showed the pride people had in the nation. Peale painted many Revolutionary heroes, including George Washington. Perhaps the most famous portrait of Washington was created by Stuart. The portrait was never finished, but in 1869 the image was adapted to appear on the one-dollar bill, where it remains today. In 1932, the same portrait was reproduced and millions of copies were distributed to schools for the bicentennial celebration of Washington's birth.

Answer

Analyze LIFE AT THE TIME Students' paragraphs will vary, but should describe how early American art, architecture, and music reflected a departure from British influence. Students should also recognize that early American art used visual symbols and descriptions that represented important American values.

The arguments over the proper course for the nation showed the divisions among the leaders. Students will now learn how these differences led to the creation of political parties.

Section Focus Question

How did two political parties emerge?

Before you begin the lesson for the day, write the Section Focus Question on the board. (*Lesson focus: People had different ideas about the role of government.*)

Prepare to Read

Build Background Knowledge **L2**

Ask students to preview the headings and visuals in this section and make predictions about how political parties first emerged in the United States. After they make predictions about what they will learn, address any misconceptions that students may have about the topic. Remind them to confirm or revise their predictions after they read the section. Use the Idea Wave technique (TE, p. T24) to generate a list.

Set a Purpose **L2**

■ Read each statement in the Reading Readiness Guide aloud. Ask students to mark the statements True or False.

All in One Teaching Resources, Unit 3, Reading Readiness Guide, p. 18

■ Have students discuss the statements in pairs or groups of four, then mark their worksheets again. Use the Numbered Heads strategy (TE, p. T24) to call on students to share their group's perspectives. The students will return to these worksheets later.

Violence Erupts in Congress

❝Directly before me stood Mr. Griswold laying on blows with all his might upon Mr. Lyon. . . . Lyon made an attempt to catch his cane, but failed—he pressed towards Griswold and endeavoured to close with him, but Griswold fell back and continued his blows on the head. . . .❞

—Federalist Representative George Thacher, describing a fight in Congress, 1798

◀ Fight between Federalist Representative Griswold and Republican Representative Lyon

The Birth of Political Parties

Objectives
- Explain how early political parties emerged.
- Compare the political views of the Republicans and the Federalists.
- Discuss the result of the election of 1796.

🔄 Reading Skill

Infer Meanings of Similes Similes compare things that may seem unrelated. The comparison helps you to see things in a new way. When you read a simile, think about how the items being compared are similar. Try to determine what point the writer is making.

Key Terms and People

faction   Alexander Hamilton
James Madison   John Adams
Thomas Jefferson

Why It Matters The arguments over Hamilton's financial plan reflected serious disagreements among the new nation's leaders. Americans also disagreed about the role of their nation's government.

❓ Section Focus Question: How did two political parties emerge?

Political Parties Emerge

The Framers of the Constitution did not expect political parties to develop in the United States. Rather, they thought that government leaders would rise above personal or local interests. The leaders, they believed, would work together for the sake of the country.

In those days, people spoke of *factions* rather than *political parties*. A **faction** was an organized political group, and the word was not complimentary. **James Madison** considered factions to be selfish groups, unconcerned with the well-being of the whole nation. Madison argued in the *Federalist Papers* that an effective national government would prevent the growth of factions. As he put it,

❝Among the numerous advantages promised by a well-constructed Union, none deserves to be more accurately developed than its tendency to break and control the violence of faction.❞

—James Madison, *The Federalist* No. 10, 1787

Thomas Jefferson and **Alexander Hamilton**, who were rarely in agreement, both disliked factions. Hamilton warned that the "spirit of faction" might work like a spark to bring mob rule and chaos.

290 Chapter 8 Launching a New Nation

Differentiated Instruction

L3 Advanced Readers   **L3 Gifted and Talented**

Creating a Poster or Pamphlet After reading the chapter, form students into two groups—Federalists and Republicans. Have each group create a poster or pam- phlet to persuade others to join its party. Ask the groups to present their posters or pamphlets to the class.

No one was more <u>hostile</u> to factions than George Washington. The President watched unhappily as Jefferson and Hamilton, the leading members of his Cabinet, grew apart. Washington tried to reduce the quarreling. In a letter to Henry Lee, he predicted that factions would destroy the "best fabric of human government and happiness."

Despite Washington's efforts, by the early 1790s two political parties were beginning to form. One group supported Thomas Jefferson and his close ally, James Madison. The other supported Alexander Hamilton and his ideas.

✓ **Checkpoint** Why did many of the nation's leaders dislike political parties?

Republicans Against Federalists

The two parties that took shape during the first half of the 1790s eventually got the names Republicans and Federalists.

The Republicans took their name from political clubs called Democratic-Republican Societies that had been organized in various parts of the country. They argued that the federal government was growing too strong under President Washington. They wanted to keep most power at the state or local level. They feared that a strong central government would act like a monarchy.

Vocabulary Builder
hostile (HAHS tihl) *adj.* unfriendly; adverse or opposed

Infer Meanings of Similes
To what is a strong central government compared to in the final sentence of this paragraph? What does the comparison mean?

Republicans Versus Federalists

Republicans	Federalists
1. Were led by Thomas Jefferson	1. Were led by Alexander Hamilton
2. Believed people should have political power	2. Believed wealthy and educated should lead
3. Favored strong state government	3. Favored strong central government
4. Emphasized agriculture	4. Emphasized manufacturing, shipping, and trade
5. Favored strict interpretation of Constitution	5. Favored loose interpretation of Constitution
6. Were pro-French	6. Were pro-British
7. Opposed national bank	7. Favored national bank
8. Opposed protective tariff	8. Favored protective tariff

Reading Charts
Skills Activity

The nation's first political parties were the Federalists and the Republicans. They took opposing stands on many political issues.

(a) **Read a Chart** How did the parties differ on federal power?

(b) **Apply Information** Why did the party that favored strong state governments insist on a strict interpretation of the Constitution?

Vocabulary Builder

Use the information below to teach students this section's high-use words.

High-Use Word	Definition and Sample Sentence
hostile, p. 291	*adj.* unfriendly; adverse or opposed Native Americans were often **hostile** to colonial settlements established on Native American lands.
fundamental, p. 293	*adj.* basic; most important; forming the foundation of an idea or action; essential A **fundamental** principle of democracy is that the people rule.

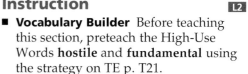

Teach

Political Parties Emerge
p. 290

Instruction   L2

■ **Vocabulary Builder** Before teaching this section, preteach the High-Use Words **hostile** and **fundamental** using the strategy on TE p. T21.

Key Terms Have students continue to fill in the See It–Remember It chart for the Key Terms in this chapter.

■ Have students read Political Parties Emerge, using the Paragraph Shrinking strategy (TE, p. T23).

■ Ask: **On what issue did most of the nation's founders agree?** (*They agreed that the U.S. should avoid the formation of factions, or political parties.*)

■ Discuss the reasons for the founders' views toward factions. (*They believed that factions were disruptive to the unity of a nation and could lead to violence and chaos.*)

■ Ask: **What do you think Washington meant by the "best fabric" of government?** (*the basic principles on which governments are based*)

Independent Practice

Have students begin filling in the study guide for this section.

📖 **Interactive Reading and Notetaking Study Guide,** Chapter 8, Section 2 (Adapted Version also available.)

Monitor Progress

As students fill in the Notetaking Study Guide, circulate to make sure individuals understand how factions came to be. Provide assistance as needed.

Answers

✓ **Checkpoint** They thought political parties threatened the country's unity.

🔵 **Reading Skill** It is compared to a monarchy. Some thought that a strong central government would be like being ruled by Britain again.

Reading Charts (a) The Federalists favored a strong central government; the Republicans favored strong state governments. **(b)** They believed that states should have the powers not explicitly granted to the central government in the Constitution because they feared that the federal government would become too powerful.

Republicans Against Federalists

p. 291

The Election of 1796

p. 293

Instruction [L2]

- Have students read Republicans Against Federalists and The Election of 1796. Remind them to look for details that answer the Section Focus Question.

- Ask: **What kind of government did Republicans support?** (*strong state governments and a limited federal government*) **What kind of government did Federalists support?** (*a strong federal government*)

- Discuss how the Vice President was elected in 1796. (*The people voted for candidates from different political parties. The person with the most votes became President, and the person with the second highest number of votes became Vice President.*)

- Ask: **How might the election process have affected the way the President and Vice President worked together?** (*Because the President and Vice President could be from opposing parties with different political views, it might have been difficult for them to agree on government policies and procedures.*)

Independent Practice

Have students continue filling in the study guide for this section.

📖 **Interactive Reading and Notetaking Study Guide,** Chapter 8, Section 2 (Adapted Version also available.)

Monitor Progress

- As students complete the Notetaking Study Guide, circulate to make sure individuals have an understanding of the election of 1796. Provide assistance as needed.

- Tell students to fill in the last column of the Reading Readiness Guide. Probe for what they learned that confirms or invalidates each statement.

All in One Teaching Resources, Unit 3, Reading Readiness Guide, p. 18

Links Across Time

Political Parties Then and Now

1790s Political differences between Thomas Jefferson and Alexander Hamilton led to the development of America's first political parties.

1850s By the 1850s, the parties we know today had taken shape. Today's Democratic Party actually traces its roots to Jefferson's Republican Party. The modern Republican Party, which was born during the 1850s over the issue of slavery, has no connection to Jefferson's Republicans.

Link to Today Online

Political Parties Today The two major parties play a leading role in the American political system. How do the parties stand on today's political issues?

For: Political parties in the news
Visit: PHSchool.com
Web Code: myc-3042

The donkey is the modern-day symbol associated with the Democractic Party.

The symbol for today's Republican Party is an elephant.

This early Republican Party drew its main strength from southern planters and northern farmers and artisans. Key leaders were James Madison and Thomas Jefferson. Unhappy with the federal government's policies, Jefferson resigned as secretary of state in 1793.

The Federalists took their name from the people who had supported the adoption of the Constitution after 1787. A prominent leader was Alexander Hamilton. As in the debates over the Constitution, Federalists said the United States needed a strong federal government to hold the country together and deal with its problems.

Federalists drew support mainly from merchants, other property owners, and ordinary workers whose jobs depended on manufacturing and trade. They were especially strong in the North.

Organizing and Arguing At the time that both parties were organizing, the Federalists had an advantage. President Washington usually supported Hamilton and his policies. One Hamilton supporter running for office proudly said, "I am a FEDERALIST, the friend of order, of government, and of the present administration."

A newspaper editor who supported the Republicans saw the situation very differently. In 1792, he printed a series of questions in the *National Gazette* implying that the Federalists wanted to betray the Constitution and bring back a king. "Are not some amongst us . . . advocates for monarchy and aristocracy?" he asked. "Are not the principles of all such [people] hostile to the principles of the constitution?"

Differentiated Instruction

L1 English Language Learners   **L1 Less Proficient Readers**   **L1 Special Needs**

Reading a Chart To give these students a better understanding of the election process, have them complete the worksheet Presidential Elections, 1789–1800. If they need help answering the questions, they may refer to this section in the Student Edition. Have students share the winner of each election and the party he belonged to with the class.

All in One Teaching Resources, Unit 3, Presidential Elections, 1789–1800, p. 22

Other Disagreements In addition to their <u>fundamental</u> disagreement about the power of the federal government, Federalists and Republicans disagreed about other issues. Federalists favored the national bank and a national tariff. The Republicans opposed both. Federalists favored close ties with England. Republicans were sympathetic to France, where a revolution overthrew the king in 1789. (You will read more about the French Revolution in Section 3.)

✓Checkpoint   How did Federalists and Republicans differ?

The Election of 1796

In 1796, George Washington said he would not seek a third term. This set an important precedent. Not until Franklin Roosevelt ran for and won a third term in 1940 would any President seek more than two terms. (In 1951, the Twenty-second Amendment legally limited the President to two terms.)

The Republican candidate for President in 1796 was Thomas Jefferson. The Federalists nominated John Adams, a New Englander, who had been Washington's Vice President.

In 1796, President and Vice President were not elected together as a ticket, as they are today. Instead, the candidate getting the most votes became President and the second-place candidate became Vice President.

Adams finished first and Jefferson second. The country thus gained a Federalist President and a Republican Vice President. Not surprisingly, this led to serious tensions during the next four years.

✓Checkpoint   Which party won the presidency in 1796?

⭐ **Looking Back and Ahead** The Republicans and Federalists had conflicting visions of what the federal government should do. In the next section, you will read how President Washington dealt with challenges at home and abroad.

Vocabulary Builder
<u>fundamental</u> (fuhn duh MEHN tahl)
adj. basic; most important; forming the foundation of an idea or action; essential

---

Section 2 | Check Your Progress

Progress Monitoring Online
For: Self-test with instant help
Visit: PHSchool.com
Web Code: mya-3042

Comprehension and Critical Thinking

1. **(a) Describe** How did the Framers of the Constitution feel about political parties?
   (b) Draw Conclusions Do you believe having political parties helps or hurts the nation? Explain.

2. **(a) Recall** What was the fundamental difference between the two political parties?

(b) Detect Points of View If you were a worker at a northern textile mill during Washington's presidency, would you have supported the Republicans or the Federalists? Explain.

🔁 **Reading Skill**

3. **Infer Meanings of Similes** Explain the simile in this sentence: Alexander Hamilton acted like a friend to government.

Key Terms

Complete this sentence so it clearly shows your understanding of the key term.

4. As a result of factions, _____.

Writing

5. Use Internet or library resources to find and read an article giving an overview of the life of George Washington. Then, create a timeline showing the most important events in Washington's life.

Assess and Reteach

Assess Progress   L2

Have students complete Check Your Progress. Administer the Section Quiz.

All in One Teaching Resources, Unit 3, Section Quiz, p. 29

To further assess student understanding, use the Progress Monitoring Transparency.

Progress Monitoring Transparencies, Chapter 8, Section 2

Reteach   L1

If students need more instruction, have them read this section in the Interactive Reading and Notetaking Study Guide.

📖 **Interactive Reading and Notetaking Study Guide,** Chapter 8, Section 2 (Adapted Version also available.)

Extend   L3

Form students into two groups, one representing the Federalists and the other representing the Republicans. Have each group compile a list of the major views of its assigned political party. Then, ask students to conduct a debate in which they respond to the question "How should the federal government interpret the Constitution to make laws?" Make sure students use facts to support their position.

Extend Online
For: Help with starting the Extend activity
Visit: PHSchool.com
Web Code: mye-0248

Progress Monitoring Online

Students may check their comprehension of this section by completing the Progress Monitoring Online graphic organizer and self-quiz.

Section 2 Check Your Progress

1. **(a)** They opposed political parties.
   (b) Responses will vary, but students should show an understanding of political parties and support their answers with details from the section.

2. **(a)** They had opposing views about the role and power of the federal government.
   (b) Students will probably answer that they would have supported the Federalists because they favored the national tariff to protect American industries.

3. "Like a friend to government" means Hamilton worked to help and protect government, the way a friend helps and protects another friend.

4. Possible answer: political parties developed, which caused tension in the government.

5. Responses will vary. Timelines should show significant events in Washington's life.

Answers

✓Checkpoint Federalists supported strong federal government; Republicans supported strong state governments

✓Checkpoint the Federalists

Review and Preview

The Federalists and the Republicans had conflicting views of the proper course for the United States. Students will now read how the country responded to a variety of challenges.

How did the actions of Britain and France affect the United States?

Before you begin the lesson for the day, write the Section Focus Question on the board. (*Lesson focus: Tension resulted when Americans disagreed on how to respond to the actions of Britain and France.*)

Prepare to Read

Build Background Knowledge **L2**

Tell students that in this section, they will learn about the impact of British and French actions on the United States. Ask students to scan the section and the Chapter Summary and make a short list of incidents that caused controversy in the United States. Use the Numbered Heads strategy (TE, p. T24) to make a list on the board.

Set a Purpose **L2**

■ Read each statement in the Reading Readiness Guide aloud. Ask students to mark the statements True or False.

All in One **Teaching Resources, Unit 3,** Reading Readiness Guide, p. 19

■ Have students discuss the statements in pairs or groups of four, then mark their worksheets again. Use the Numbered Heads strategy (TE, p. T24) to call on students to share their group's perspectives. The students will return to these worksheets later.

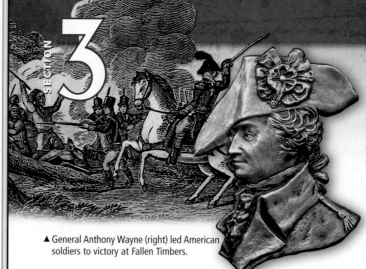

▲ General Anthony Wayne (right) led American soldiers to victory at Fallen Timbers.

Vital to Its Survival

❝Two hundred years ago the United States, a Confederation of Indian tribes and Great Britain all sought control of the land known as the Northwest Territory, a vast area north of the Ohio and east of the Mississippi rivers. For the young United States, the control of this area was vital to its survival.❞

—Dr. G. Michael Pratt, address at 1994 commemoration of Battle of Fallen Timbers

Troubles at Home and Abroad

Objectives

• Discuss the conflicts with Native Americans in the Northwest Territory.

• Describe how Americans reacted to the French Revolution.

• Identify the main points of Washington's Farewell Address.

• Summarize Washington's accomplishments as President.

🔄 Reading Skill

Infer Meanings of Metaphors As you read, notice metaphors that speak of one item as if it were another. For example, "he is the foundation of our success" means that his work supports our success, as a foundation supports a building. The word *like* is absent but is suggested by the comparison. As you read this section, look for metaphors.

Key Terms and People

Anthony Wayne   impressment
neutral   John Jay

Why It Matters Political parties emerged because Americans had differing viewpoints about the government and economy. Americans also disagreed on foreign policy issues.

❓ Section Focus Question: How did the actions of Britain and France affect the United States?

Conflicts in the Northwest Territory

As a result of the Treaty of Paris that ended the American Revolution, the United States won the vast territory north and west of the Ohio River to the Mississippi River. Although the British still had forts in the region, they promised to withdraw within a "reasonable" time. A decade later, the British soldiers were still there. Moreover, the British were supplying Native Americans with guns and ammunition. The British hoped that this would limit American settlement in the Northwest Territory.

A Struggle Over Lands Native Americans in the Northwest Territory wanted to keep their lands. During the 1780s, they attacked many American settlements. Several Native American groups joined together to oppose settlement.

Many American leaders believed that the country's future depended on settling its western lands. Therefore, the federal government tried to force Native Americans in the territories to sell their lands. By 1790, the United States had succeeded in buying Native American lands in most of Kentucky and in part of Tennessee. North of the Ohio River, Native Americans refused to sell. Even there, though, the flow of white settlement continued.

Differentiated Instruction

L1 English Language Learners   **L1** Less Proficient Readers   **L1** Special Needs

Using Symbols When Reading Give students a plastic page protector to put over the text. Have them reread the section "The French Revolution" and mark each sentence with a ? if they are uncertain or do not understand the sentence, a * if they understand the sentence, or a ! (Wow!) if they find the information interesting or new. Review any sentences they marked with a question mark. Pair students to compare their ! sentences, then have them write a sentence about the most interesting fact they found in the section.

A Series of Battles In 1790, Washington sent a small force to end the Native American attacks on settlers. Warriors led by Little Turtle of the Miami Nation and Blue Jacket of the Shawnees defeated the soldiers. The next year, Washington sent a larger force. This time, Little Turtle won an even bigger victory. More than 900 soldiers were killed or wounded. It was the worst defeat the army would ever suffer in a battle with Native Americans.

Washington then turned to a Revolutionary War hero, General Anthony Wayne, to lead the forces against the Native Americans. Native Americans gathered for battle at a place where fallen trees covered the ground. They thought the trees would cause trouble for Wayne and his soldiers. But in August 1794, Wayne won a major victory at the Battle of Fallen Timbers.

That battle broke the Native American hold on the Northwest. In the 1795 Treaty of Greenville, leaders of the defeated Native American nations gave up most of their lands from the Ohio River in the south to Lake Erie in the north. Today, that is most of the state of Ohio.

✓**Checkpoint** How were the conflicting claims of settlers and Native Americans resolved?

Treaty of Greenville

MAP•MASTER®
Skills Activity

In the Treaty of Greenville, Native Americans gave up, or ceded, territory to the United States. The cessions (lands ceded) are shown in color.

(a) Read a Map How many areas were ceded?

(b) Analyze Cause and Effect What event shown on the map led to the cessions?

KEY
Indian cessions
Miami Indian tribes

MapMaster Online

For: Interactive map
Visit: PHSchool.com
Web Code: myp-3043

The French Revolution

The French Revolution began in 1789. Most Americans at first supported the French revolutionaries. In their eyes, France was following the lead of the United States in fighting monarchy.

Soon, though, the French Revolution became controversial in the United States. One reason was that it became more violent. This process peaked in mid-1793 with a period called the Reign of Terror. The French revolutionaries executed about 17,000 people, including the king and queen. For the Federalists, the Revolution was a bloodthirsty monster. But Jefferson and his supporters argued that in a fight by oppressed people to win freedom, some injustices were to be expected.

Secondly, by early 1793, France and Britain were at war. In that war, said President Washington, the United States would remain neutral—not favoring either side in a dispute.

The United States wanted to trade with both sides. However, each European country feared such trade would benefit the other. Both countries began stopping American ships and seizing their cargoes.

Infer Meanings of Metaphors
Explain the metaphor in the second-to-last sentence of this paragraph.

Section 3 Troubles at Home and Abroad **295**

Vocabulary Builder

Use the information below to teach students this section's high-use words.

High-Use Word	Definition and Sample Sentence
cease, p. 296	*v.* to cause to come to an end; to stop After hours of battle, the soldiers on both sides **ceased** their firing.
emphasize, p. 297	*v.* to stress; to give more importance to The Declaration of Independence **emphasizes** equality and the natural rights of humankind.

Teach

Conflicts in the Northwest Territory
p. 294

The French Revolution
p. 295

Instruction L2

- **Vocabulary Builder** Before teaching this section, preteach the High-Use Words **cease** and **emphasize** using the strategy on TE p. T21.

  Key Terms Have students continue to fill in the See It–Remember It chart for the Key Terms.

- Read Conflicts in the Northwest Territory and The French Revolution aloud with students, using the Choral Reading strategy (TE, p. T22).

- Discuss the conflict between Native Americans and the settlers. Ask: **What was the impact of the Treaty of Greenville?** (*Defeated Native Americans lost their lands in the Northwest.*)

- Compare the French and American revolutions. Ask: **In what ways were the goals of the French Revolution similar to the ideals of the founders of the United States?** (*They both were fighting a monarchy and were inspired by the principles of liberty.*)

Independent Practice

Have students begin filling in the study guide for this section.

📖 **Interactive Reading and Notetaking Study Guide,** Chapter 8, Section 3 (Adapted Version also available.)

Monitor Progress

As students fill in the Notetaking Study Guide, circulate and make sure individuals understand the conflicts between the United States, France, and Britain. Provide assistance as needed.

Answers

MAP•MASTER Skills Activity **(a)** five **(b)** the Battle of Fallen Timbers

✓**Checkpoint** Washington sent troops to suppress the Native Americans.

🔵 **Reading Skill** The phrase "bloodthirsty monster" means the Revolution was very violent and cruel.

Washington Retires From Public Life

p. 297

Instruction L2

- Read Washington Retires From Public Life aloud with students. Remind students to look for details that answer the Section Focus Question.

- Ask: **What did Washington warn the American people about in his "Fare-well Address"?** (*to avoid political divisions at home and political involvement with foreign nations*)

- Discuss the list of accomplishments that ends the section. Ask: **What do you think were important factors in Washington's success?** (*Students may say that Washington's desire to serve his "fellow citizens," as well as the support of the people, helped him make decisions for the good of the nation.*)

- Display the transparency Portrait of President Washington. Follow the transparency lesson plan to lead students in a discussion about the public's attitudes toward President Washington.

Color Transparencies, Portrait of President Washington

Independent Practice

Have students continue filling in the study guide for this section.

Interactive Reading and Notetaking Study Guide, Chapter 8, Section 3 (Adapted Version also available.)

Monitor Progress

- As students fill in the Notetaking Study Guide, circulate and make sure individuals understand Washington's accomplishments. Provide assistance as needed.

- Tell students to fill in the last column of the Reading Readiness Guide. Probe for what they learned that confirms or invalidates each statement.

All in One Teaching Resources, Unit 3, Reading Readiness Guide, p. 19

Answers

Reading Primary Sources (a) it was cruel and inhumane **(b)** Students may say that attendees thought Louis XVI was a tyrant and supported his execution.

✓Checkpoint Republicans opposed Jay's Treaty but Federalists supported it.

American Reaction to the Reign of Terror

In this excerpt, a British observer describes the reactions of some Americans to the execution of Louis XVI.

"Never was the memory of any man so cruelly insulted as that of this mild and humane monarch [Louis XVI]. He was guillotined in effigy [using a dummy to represent a real person], in the capital of the Union [Philadelphia], twenty or thirty times every day, during one whole winter and part of the summer. Men, women, and children flocked to the tragical exhibition, and not a single paragraph appeared in the papers to shame them from it."

—William Cobbett, *History of the American Jacobins* (Philadelphia, 1796)

In this illustration, an executioner displays the severed head of Louis XVI.

Reading Primary Sources
Skills Activity

During the Reign of Terror, revolutionaries used the guillotine to behead the French king Louis XVI in January 1793. Queen Marie Antoinette was executed in October 1793.

(a) **Detect Points of View** How did the author view Louis XVI's execution?

(b) **Draw Conclusions** How do you think Philadelphians who attended the "tragical exhibition" felt about the king's execution? Explain.

Vocabulary Builder
cease (sees) *v.* to cause to come to an end; to stop

The British made matters worse by the **impressment** of sailors on American ships, which meant seizing the sailors and forcing them to serve in the British navy. Some of the sailors were British sailors who had fled the British navy, but many were Americans.

As tensions rose, Hamilton urged the President to stay friendly with Britain. He argued that American prosperity depended on trade with Britain. The British purchased 75 percent of American exports and supplied 90 percent of American imports.

Washington agreed and tried to repair relations with Britain. He sent John Jay to London to try to solve the most serious problems.

Jay returned with a treaty in 1795. In it, the United States agreed to pay debts long owed to British merchants. In return, Britain agreed to pay for the ships it had seized. It also agreed to withdraw its troops from the Northwest Territory and stop aiding Native Americans there. However, the British refused to recognize a U.S. right to trade with France. They also refused to cease impressment of U.S. sailors.

The Jay Treaty angered Republicans. They claimed the United States had given away too much and gotten too little. Federalists, in contrast, liked the treaty because it kept peace with Britain. Since Federalists controlled the Senate, the Jay Treaty won approval by a narrow margin.

✓Checkpoint How did Americans react to the Jay Treaty?

Differentiated Instruction

L3 Advanced Readers   **L3 Gifted and Talented**

Biography Assign the worksheet Martha Washington. After each student has answered the question, have him or her prepare a short oral report to share with the class detailing how Martha Washington set a precedent for First Ladies. Encourage them to include adjectives to

describe the characteristics they think a President's wife should have and how these might have changed since the time of Martha Washington.

All in One Teaching Resources, Unit 3, Martha Washington, p. 23

Washington Retires From Public Life

In 1796, Washington published a letter to fellow Americans that had lasting influence. Washington's Farewell Address made two major points. First, the President warned against political divisions at home. He feared that violent divisions might tear the nation apart.

Washington's second piece of advice concerned foreign policy. In a famous passage, Washington <u>emphasized</u> his belief that the United States must not get entangled in the affairs of Europe. He said:

> **❝** Europe has a set of primary interests which to us have none or a very remote relation. . . . Why . . . entangle our peace and prosperity in the toils [traps] of European ambition? . . . It is our true policy to steer clear of permanent alliances with any portion of the foreign world. **❞**
>
> —George Washington, Farewell Address, 1796

As he left office, Washington could take pride in his accomplishments: (1) The United States now had a functioning federal government. (2) The economy was improving. (3) Washington had avoided war. (4) The British had been forced to leave their forts in the Northwest Territory, an area that was now safe for settlement.

Still, political divisions were growing and challenges remained.

☑**Checkpoint** What were Washington's chief accomplishments?

⭐ **Looking Back and Ahead** As President, George Washington created conditions for a strong federal government. In the next section, you will read how his successor sought to deal with divisions at home and challenges abroad.

Vocabulary Builder
<u>emphasize</u> (EM fuh syz) **v.** to stress; to give more importance to

---

Section 3	**Check Your Progress**

Progress Monitoring ⦾nline
For: Self-test with instant help
Visit: PHSchool.com
Web Code: mya-3043

Comprehension and Critical Thinking

1. (a) Describe How did Washington deal with Britain's policy of impressment?
(b) Compare and Contrast How did Washington's policy on matters at home differ from his foreign policy?

2. (a) Recall What were the two main arguments Washington made in his Farewell Address?
(b) Distinguish Facts From Opinions Support the following opinion with facts from the chapter: George Washington was a great first President.

⦾ Reading Skill

3. Infer Meanings of Metaphors Identify and explain the metaphor in this sentence: In the heated political atmosphere, this warning had little impact.

Key Terms

Read each sentence that follows. If the sentence is true, write YES. If the sentence is not true, write NO and explain why.

4. As a neutral nation, the United States should trade only with Britain and not France.

5. The Jay Treaty did not end the impressment of American sailors by the British navy.

Writing

6. Based on what you have read about George Washington in this section, write a description of the personality traits he showed as President of the United States. Include at least two specific examples of actions that he took as President.

Section 3 Troubles at Home and Abroad **297**

Assess and Reteach

Assess Progress 🔲 L2

Have students complete Check Your Progress. Administer the Section Quiz.

AII in One Teaching Resources, Unit 3, Section Quiz, p. 30

To further assess student understanding, use the Progress Monitoring Transparency.

Progress Monitoring Transparencies, Chapter 8, Section 3

Reteach 🔲 L1

If students need more instruction, have them read this section in the Interactive Reading and Notetaking Study Guide.

📖 **Interactive Reading and Notetaking Study Guide,** Chapter 8, Section 3 (Adapted Version also available.)

Extend 🔲 L3

Assign students to groups to brainstorm for possible outcomes if Washington had: failed to get British troops out of the Northwest Territory; allied with France in its war with Britain; and ignored the Constitution when organizing the government. Then, ask: **In what condition would the nation—and its guarantee of liberty and justice—have been?** (*Possible answers: loss of independence, less individual freedom.*)

Progress Monitoring Online

Students may check their comprehension of this section by completing the Progress Monitoring Online graphic organizer and self-quiz.

Section 3 Check Your Progress

1. (a) He demonstrated that the nation's government could back up its intentions with military force.
(b) Washington was against involvement in foreign wars, but forceful in responding to rebellion at home.

2. (a) He warned against political divisions at home and involvement in foreign affairs.
(b) Students should choose apt details about Washington's accomplishments.

3. The mood of the country was like a heated atmosphere in which a thunderstorm is brewing.

4. No, Washington believed that as a neutral nation the United States should trade with both France and Britain.

5. Yes

6. Responses may vary, but may include honesty, leadership, diplomacy, and power.

Answer

☑**Checkpoint** Establishing a successful government, bringing the country out of debt, keeping the country out of war, forcing the British to leave the Northwest Territory.

Review and Preview

Students have read about the course set for the nation by President Washington. They will now read how foreign pressures affected President John Adams's administration.

Section Focus Question

How did problems with France intensify the split between the Federalists and Republicans?

Before you begin the lesson for the day, write the Section Focus Question on the board. (*Lesson focus: Political divisions grew bitter during the presidency of John Adams, as he struggled to keep peace with France.*)

Prepare to Read

Build Background Knowledge L2

Ask students to preview the headings and visuals in the section. Use the Give One, Get One strategy (TE, p. T25) to help students create a list of what they predict they will learn.

Set a Purpose

■ Read each statement in the Reading Readiness Guide aloud. Ask students to mark the statements True or False.

All in One Teaching Resources, Unit 3, Reading Readiness Guide, p. 20

■ Have students discuss the statements in pairs or groups of four, then mark their worksheets again. Use the Numbered Heads strategy (TE, p. T24) to call on students to share their group's perspectives. The students will return to these worksheets later.

Make Haste to Wage War

"We must make haste to *wage war*, or we shall be lost. . . . Something energetic and decisive must be done soon. Congress fiddles while our Rome is burning. America . . . can interdict [prohibit] France the ocean."

—Fisher Ames, urging war with France, 1798

◄ French ship attacking an American ship

The Presidency of John Adams

Objectives

• Discuss the reasons for tension between the United States and France.

• Describe the main provisions of the Alien and Sedition acts.

• Explain how controversy arose over states' rights.

⊙ Reading Skill

Identify Analogies In an analogy, two pairs of items are connected with the same sort of comparison. For example, both pairs might compare synonyms, or words with similar meanings. You must understand the comparison between the first pair in order to complete the comparison between the second pair. Some common types of analogies are cause-effect, antonyms, and synonyms.

Key Terms

alien
sedition

nullify
states' rights

Why It Matters John Adams succeeded Washington as President. He struggled to reduce the country's divisions and to steer a neutral course in foreign policy.

❓ Section Focus Question: How did problems with France intensify the split between the Federalists and Republicans?

Troubles With France

Adams immediately faced a crisis over relations with France. The French were angered by U.S. neutrality in the war between France and Britain. France had hoped for U.S. support. Had not French assistance been the key to success in the American Revolution? Why didn't Americans show their gratitude by helping the French now?

The Jay Treaty only increased tensions with France. As the French saw it, the treaty put the United States on Britain's side. France reacted late in 1796 by snubbing a U.S. diplomat. Moreover, the French continued to attack American merchant ships.

The XYZ Affair In 1797, Adams sent a new three-person mission to France. Agents of the French government demanded that the United States pay a bribe of $250,000. The agents also wanted the United States to lend France several million dollars.

The Americans said they would pay "not a sixpence [a coin worth six pennies]." Later, that statement led to the slogan, "Millions for defense, but not one sixpence for tribute [a forced payment]."

The bribe attempt was a sensation when it became public. Because the names of the French agents were kept secret, they were called X, Y, and Z. The incident became known as the XYZ Affair.

Differentiated Instruction

L3 Advanced Readers   **L3 Gifted and Talented**

Group Activity Form small groups to work together to create a media campaign to persuade people to support or oppose President Adams's handling of the XYZ Affair. Assign a position for each group. Have each group create a button, a print advertisement, and a one-minute announcement to communicate its view-

point. Students should consider the fears and concerns that arose as people learned the details of the affair. Campaigns should also take into account that although Adams was a Federalist, all Federalists did not support his decisions. Have students present their work to the class.

War Fever The XYZ Affair caused an outbreak of war fever in the United States. Many Federalists demanded that Adams ask Congress to declare war on France.

With war fever rising, Adams asked Congress to increase the size of the army and rebuild the navy. It did both, thus enhancing the power of the central government. Adams also convinced Congress to create a separate department of the navy. Between 1798 and 1800, the United States fought an undeclared naval war with France.

Nonetheless, the President and many other Americans opposed a full-scale war. To avoid war, Adams sent a new mission to France. Napoleon Bonaparte, France's dictator, was busy dealing with war in Europe. In 1800, he agreed to stop seizing American ships.

President Adams had avoided war. But the agreement angered leaders of his own Federalist Party, especially the pro-British Hamilton. This disapproval weakened Adams politically.

Still, Adams was satisfied. He told a friend that he wanted his tombstone to read: "Here lies John Adams, who took upon himself the responsibility of peace with France in the year 1800."

☑ **Checkpoint** How did Adams settle differences with France?

The Alien and Sedition Acts

The war fever deepened the split between Federalists and Republicans. Federalists' fear of revolutionary France spilled over into a mistrust of immigrants. Federalists suspected them of bringing in dangerous ideas and feared that they would back the Republicans.

Identify Analogies
The phrase *war fever* is an analogy. Think about what having a fever does to a person's body. How is that similar to what the desire for war might do to the country?

The Five-Headed Monster

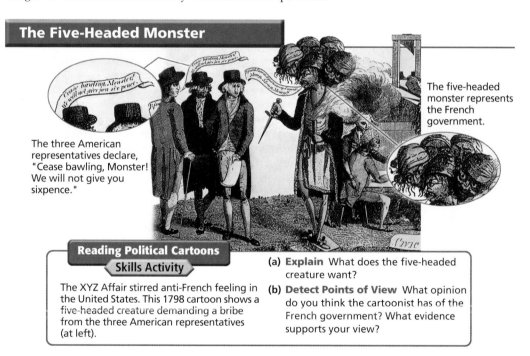

The three American representatives declare, "Cease bawling, Monster! We will not give you sixpence."

The five-headed monster represents the French government.

Reading Political Cartoons
Skills Activity

The XYZ Affair stirred anti-French feeling in the United States. This 1798 cartoon shows a five-headed creature demanding a bribe from the three American representatives (at left).

(a) Explain What does the five-headed creature want?

(b) Detect Points of View What opinion do you think the cartoonist has of the French government? What evidence supports your view?

Section 4 The Presidency of John Adams **299**

Vocabulary Builder

Use the information below to teach students this section's high-use words.

High-Use Word	Definition and Sample Sentence
duration, p. 300	*n.* length of time Civilians faced hardships for the **duration** of the war.
provoke, p. 301	*v.* to cause to anger; to excite; to cause an action When France seized U.S. ships, it must have known that its actions would **provoke** great anger among the American people.

Instruction

- **Vocabulary Builder** Before teaching this section, preteach the High-Use Words **duration** and **provoke** using the strategy on TE p. T21.

  Key Terms Have students complete the See It–Remember It chart for the Key Terms in this chapter.

- Read Troubles with France aloud with students, using the Structured Silent Reading strategy (TE, p. T22).

- Ask: **What issues caused increased tension in the United States between 1793 and 1797?** (*the failure of the United States to ally itself with France during the war between France and Britain; Jay's Treaty*)
  Ask: **Why did the XYZ Affair anger Americans so much?** (*The United States had approached France to negotiate, and Americans felt that France had responded unfairly.*)

- Ask: **Why do you think the Federalists were angry at Adams for avoiding war with France?** (*Students may suggest that France's attack on American merchant ships and the XYZ Affair angered Americans. Also, the Federalists tended to support Britain in that country's struggles with France.*)

Independent Practice

Have students begin filling in the study guide for this section.

📖 **Interactive Reading and Notetaking Study Guide,** Chapter 8, Section 4 (Adapted Version also available.)

Monitor Progress

As students fill in the Notetaking Study Guide, circulate and make sure individuals understand how Adams dealt with the tensions between the United States and France. Provide assistance as needed.

Answers

🔊 **Reading Skill** fevers spread throughout a person's body, as the desire for war spread throughout the country

☑**Checkpoint** He compromised to avoid war.

Reading Political Cartoons (a) money from the Americans **(b)** The cartoonist has a negative view of the French government; he drew the country as a monster.

The Alien and Sedition Acts

p. 299

States' Rights

p. 300

Instruction L2

- Read The Alien and Sedition Acts aloud with students.

- Have students complete the worksheet Debating the Alien Act. Ask them to compare and contrast how each party viewed the power of the federal government. (*Federalists—strong federal government; Republicans—limited power of federal government*)

  All in One Teaching Resources, Unit 3,
  Debating the Alien Act, p. 24

- Ask: **Why were the Virginia and Kentucky resolutions passed?** (*Because Republicans were not sure the Supreme Court could declare laws unconstitutional, they wanted the states to end the Alien and Sedition Acts.*) **What was the long-term impact of these resolutions?** (*They strengthened the arguments for states' rights, the claim that states could overrule federal laws.*)

Independent Practice

Have students continue filling in the study guide for this section.

Monitor Progress

- As students fill in the Notetaking Study Guide, circulate and make sure students understand the Alien and Sedition acts and their consequences. Provide assistance as needed.

- Tell students to fill in the last column of the Reading Readiness Guide. Probe for what they learned that confirms or invalidates each statement.

- Have students go back to their Word Knowledge Rating Form. Rerate their word knowledge and complete the last column with a definition or example.

  All in One Teaching Resources, Unit 3,
  Reading Readiness Guide, p. 20; Word Knowledge Rating Form, p. 16

Answers

Detect Points of View States could nullify laws if they disliked them.

☑**Checkpoint** They limited immigration and free speech.

300 Chapter 8

New Life for a Debate
Passage of the Alien and Sedition acts renewed the debate over federal versus state power. Jefferson and Madison wrote the Kentucky and Virginia resolutions in defense of states' rights. **Critical Thinking: *Detect Points of View*** *According to defenders of states' rights in 1798, what could states do if they disliked a federal law?*

Vocabulary Builder
duration (doo RAY shun) ***n.*** length of time

Arguments for States' Rights	Arguments for Federal Power
■ The federal government derives its power from rights given to it by the states.	■ The federal government derives its power from rights given to it by the American people.
■ Because the states created the United States, individual states have the power to nullify a federal law.	■ States have no power to nullify federal laws. ■ States cannot revoke federal powers set forth in the Constitution.

Trouble on the Horizon
Within 25 years of the Alien and Sedition acts, people in New England and South Carolina would threaten to leave the Union because they either disagreed with American foreign policy or opposed laws passed by Congress.

Federalist leaders decided that to restore order at home they must destroy their political opponents. Congress passed an act in 1798 aimed at immigrants. Another 1798 law targeted Republicans.

The act directed at immigrants was the Alien Act. An alien is an outsider or someone from another country. The Alien Act increased the duration from 5 to 14 years that a person had to live in the United States to become a citizen. The President gained the power to deport or imprison any alien he considered dangerous.

The act targeting Republicans was the Sedition Act. Sedition is activity designed to overthrow a government. The Sedition Act probably was the harshest law limiting free speech ever passed in the United States. It made it a crime for anyone to write or say anything insulting or anything false about the President, Congress, or the government in general. During 1798 and 1799, ten people were convicted under the act. Most were Republican editors and printers.

☑**Checkpoint** What did the Alien and Sedition acts do?

States' Rights

The Republicans denounced the Alien and Sedition acts. They charged that the Sedition Act violated the Constitution, especially the First Amendment, which guarantees freedom of speech.

However, the Republicans faced a problem opposing the law. At the time, it was not clearly established that the Supreme Court had the power to strike down a law as unconstitutional. Because of this, the Republicans expressed their opposition through the state legislatures.

Differentiated Instruction

L1 English Language Learners   **L1** Less Proficient Readers   **L1** Special Needs

Reading a Chart To help students understand the support for and opposition to the Alien Act, assign The Alien and Sedition Acts after the class has read the section. Form students into two groups. Have one group present the Federalist view of the Alien and Sedition acts to the class. Ask the other group to present the Republican view of the acts.

All in One Teaching Resources, Unit 3, The Alien and Sedition Acts, p. 25

Republicans James Madison and Thomas Jefferson, both Virginians, led the campaign. Madison wrote a resolution attacking the Alien and Sedition acts. It was passed by the Virginia legislature. Jefferson wrote a similar resolution that was passed by the Kentucky legislature. Together, the Virginia and Kentucky resolutions stated that the Alien and Sedition acts were unconstitutional. They declared that states had the right to declare laws passed by Congress to be unconstitutional.

No other states supported Virginia and Kentucky, so the two resolutions had little immediate impact. As for the Alien and Sedition acts, they were not in force for long. The law that gave the President the power to imprison or deport dangerous aliens expired after two years. The Sedition Act expired in 1801. The waiting period for immigrants to become citizens was restored to five years in 1802.

However, over the long term the Virginia and Kentucky resolutions were far more important than the laws that <u>provoked</u> them. The resolutions claimed that states could nullify—deprive of legal force—a law passed by Congress. The resolutions also boosted the idea of states' rights. This is the idea that the union binding "these United States" is an agreement between the states and that they therefore can overrule federal law. In decades to come, a number of states would refuse to obey certain federal laws. States' rights would become the rallying cry for southern defenders of slavery.

☑Checkpoint **Why did the issue of states' rights arise at this time?**

⭐ **Looking Back and Ahead** You have read how the United States got up and running under its first two Presidents. The next chapter deals with the next two Presidents, Thomas Jefferson and James Madison, and the challenges they faced.

James Madison

Vocabulary Builder
<u>provoke</u> (prah VOHK) **v.** to cause to anger; to excite; to cause an action

---

Section 4 | Check Your Progress

Progress Monitoring Online
For: Self-test with instant help
Visit: PHSchool.com
Web Code: mya-3044

Comprehension and Critical Thinking

1. **(a) Recall** What problem did President Adams face abroad?
(b) Explain Problems How did Adams resolve this problem?

2. **(a) Summarize** Why did the Federalist Congress pass the Alien and Sedition acts?
(b) Analyze Cause and Effect Explain the following statement: State reaction to the Alien and Sedition acts caused further tension between the political parties.

Reading Skill

3. **Identify Analogies** Explain the analogy in this sentence: As the call for war heated up, John Adams tried to be the nation's firefighter.

Key Terms

Answer the following questions in complete sentences that show your understanding of the key terms.
4. Why did Federalists mistrust aliens?
5. Why did newspaper editors accused of sedition tend to be Republicans?

6. Why did Republicans want to nullify the Alien and Sedition acts?
7. How can states' rights be used to oppose federal laws?

Writing

8. Use Internet or library resources to research the life of John Adams. List the principal events in his life. Then, describe the personality traits he displayed as President of the United States. Write a thesis statement that could be used to introduce a biographical essay about Adams.

Assess Progress L2

Have students complete Check Your Progress. Administer the Section Quiz.

All in One Teaching Resources, Unit 3, Section Quiz, p. 31

To further assess student understanding, use the Progress Monitoring Transparency.

Progress Monitoring Transparencies
Chapter 8, Section 4

Reteach L1

If students need more instruction, have them read this section in the Interactive Reading and Notetaking Study Guide.

📖 **Interactive Reading and Notetaking Study Guide,** Chapter 8, Section 4 (Adapted Version also available.)

Extend L3

Assign one half of the students to the Federalist Party and the other half to the Republican Party. Have each group create several newspaper articles that express the viewpoints of its party. Articles may be on the Alien Act, the Sedition Act, the XYZ Affair, and any other issue from the section.

Progress Monitoring Online

Students may check their comprehension of this section by completing the Progress Monitoring Online graphic organizer and self-quiz.

Section 4 Check Your Progress

1. **(a)** France thought the United States should support it in its war with Britain and responded to U.S. neutrality by attacking American ships and refusing to deal with American diplomats.
(b) Adams compromised with the French instead of going to war.

2. **(a)** to limit immigration and restrict free speech in response to a mistrust of immigrants during the French Revolution

(b) Republicans supported states' rights and opposed the Federalist-backed Alien and Sedition acts. This disagreement emphasized the differences between the parties.

3. Possible answer: As a firefighter tries to put out a fire, Adams tried to end the nation's desire for war.

4–7. Students' sentences should reflect an understanding of the key terms. Students' statements will vary.

8. Students' thesis statements should express a statement about John Adams's personality. Possible traits include firm, responsible, and diplomatic.

Answer

☑Checkpoint Republicans opposed the Alien and Sedition acts, but Republican-backed state legislatures could do nothing to overturn federal law.

Objective

Distinguishing facts from opinions can help students increase their awareness of historical points of view about events and developments. Considering ways to prove or confirm facts can also help students understand how historians use primary and secondary sources.

Distinguish Facts From Opinions

Instruction L2

1. Write the steps to distinguish facts from opinions on the board and ask the class to read the steps aloud.

2. Have students look at the diary entry. Ask them to explain whether they would expect a diary entry to express opinions. (*Possible answer: yes, because people often use their diaries to write down their personal thoughts and ideas*)

3. Practice the skill by following the steps on p. 302 as a class. Model each step to distinguish facts from opinions in the diary entry. (*1. (a) Possible answer: The publisher of the newspaper is John Fenno. The Bank, established by Congress in 1791, has the power to make loans to businesses. (b) Possible answer: You can look up the newspaper to find out who the publisher was, and you can look up the National Bank to see what its powers were. 2. (a) Possible answer: In my opinion, he is right to favor the Federalist leader. To me it is a more worthwhile policy than Mr. Jefferson's support of the farmers. (b) Possible answer: They use the phrases "In my opinion" and "to me." 3. (a) Possible answer: The federal bank is opposed by that friend of the states, Thomas Jefferson, who isn't thinking of our country's future. Fact: Thomas Jefferson opposed the bank. Opinion: Jefferson is not thinking of the country's future. (b) Possible answer: The writer has strong opinions and may see his opinions as fact, so he may not realize that he is mixing facts and opinions.*)

It is important to be able to tell the difference between facts and opinions when you read historical stories and narratives. A fact is something that can be proved to be true or can be observed. An opinion is a statement that reflects a person's feelings, judgments, or beliefs about a subject.

This diary entry, which is historical fiction, was written by a merchant living in colonial Philadelphia in the 1790s.

February 28

After dinner tonight I finished reading today's edition of the *Gazette of the United States.* The publisher of the newspaper is John Fenno. In my opinion, he is right to favor the Federalist leader, Alexander Hamilton. Of course, I am a merchant and I agree with Hamilton's support of trade and manufacturing. To me it is a more worthwhile policy than Mr. Jefferson's support of the farmers.

I believe that I have Hamilton alone to thank for the National Bank. This Bank, established by Congress in 1791, has the power to make loans to businesses, such as my dry goods store. Of course, the federal Bank is opposed by that friend of the states, Thomas Jefferson, who isn't thinking of our country's future. I only hope that Mr. Hamilton's party wins the next election.

—Isaac Smith

Learn the Skill
Use these steps to identify facts and opinions.

1. **Decide which statements are facts.** Facts are statements that are based on direct evidence and can be proved to be true. Facts tell what really happened. You can look up a statement in a research source to prove it is a fact.

2. **Decide which statements are opinions.** An opinion is a personal interpretation of an event, an idea, or a person. Words such as "I think," "I believe," or "I feel" are often used in a statement of opinion. Look for these words when you read.

3. **Recognize how writers or speakers mix facts and opinions.** Sometimes writers use facts to support their personal opinion. Or, writers use facts and opinions to persuade the reader to support their point of view.

Practice the Skill
Answer the following questions about the journal entry on this page.

1. **Decide which statements are facts.** (a) Find two facts in this journal entry. (b) How can you prove that each statement is a fact?

2. **Decide which statements are opinions.** (a) Find two statements of opinion in this journal entry. (b) How can you tell that each is an opinion?

3. **Recognize how writers or speakers mix facts and opinions.** (a) Find an example of a statement that mixes fact and opinion. What is the fact? What is the opinion? (b) Why do you think the writer mixed fact and opinion in this selection?

Apply the Skill
See the Review and Assessment at the end of this chapter.

302 Chapter 8 Launching a New Nation

Monitor Progress

Ask students to do the Apply the Skill activity. Then assign the Skills for Life worksheet. As students complete the worksheet, circulate to make sure individuals are applying the skill steps effectively. Provide assistance as needed.

All in One Teaching Resources, Unit 3, Skills for Life Worksheet, p. 26

Reteach L1

If students need more instruction, use the Social Studies Skills Tutor to reteach this skill.

Social Studies Skills Tutor CD-ROM, Distinguishing Fact and Opinion

How did Americans respond to internal and external challenges?

Section 1
Washington Takes Office

- George Washington was inaugurated as the first President in April of 1789.
- Washington and Congress organized the executive and judiciary branches.
- Alexander Hamilton developed a financial plan to repay the country's large war debt.
- Federal forces put down the Whiskey Rebellion in 1794.

Section 2
The Birth of Political Parties

- Deepening differences between factions led to the first political parties.
- Republicans wanted a limited national government, while Federalists favored a strong federal government.
- John Adams, a Federalist, won the presidency in 1796. Thomas Jefferson, a Republican, won the vice presidency.

Section 3
Troubles at Home and Abroad

- Washington responded forcefully to conflict in the Northwest Territory between settlers and Native Americans.
- The United States remained neutral when France and Britain went to war.
- In his Farewell Address, George Washington warned the nation against disunity and against becoming involved in foreign wars.

Section 4
The Presidency of John Adams

- John Adams was elected President of the United States in 1796.
- The United States and France avoided full-scale war under Adams but fought an undeclared naval war.
- The Federalist-sponsored Alien and Sedition acts provoked a strong reaction by Republicans in favor of states' rights.

Exploring the Essential Question

Use the online study guide to explore the essential question.

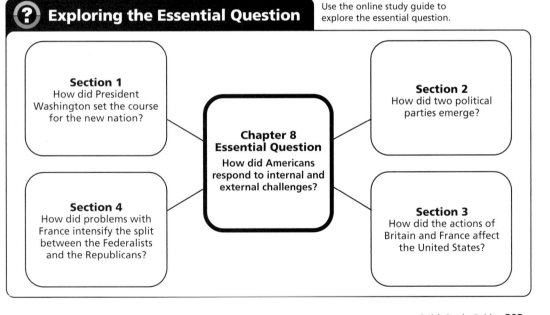

Section 1
How did President Washington set the course for the new nation?

Chapter 8 Essential Question
How did Americans respond to internal and external challenges?

Section 2
How did two political parties emerge?

Section 4
How did problems with France intensify the split between the Federalists and the Republicans?

Section 3
How did the actions of Britain and France affect the United States?

Quick Study Guide **303**

Essential Question

Remind students of the Chapter Focus Question: **How did Americans respond to internal and external challenges?** Have them review the bulleted statements and the Visual Preview at the beginning of the chapter to help them answer this question.

To bolster students' retention, at this time they should complete the study guide in print or online. Remind students that they should also continue notetaking for the Unit and Chapter Focus Questions.

Interactive Reading and Notetaking Study Guide, Chapter 8

 Study Guide *Online,* Chapter 8

Chapter Challenge

To wrap up this chapter, students should apply the knowledge they have gained to answer this question: **Did early Presidents respond successfully to the challenges faced by the country?** (*Answers will vary, but should demonstrate an understanding of the issues involved in successfully navigating the challenges facing the nation during this period.*)

Assessment at a Glance

Formal Assessment

    Chapter Tests A/B (L1/L2)

    AYP Monitoring Assessment

    Test Prep Workbook With Document-Based Assessment

    Test-Taking Strategies With Transparencies

Performance Assessment

    Group/Individual Activities, TE pp. 278g, 278h

    Teacher's Edition, pp. 287, 293, 297, 301

    Assessment Rubrics

Assessment Through Technology

    ExamView CD-ROM

    MindPoint CD-ROM

    Progress Monitoring Transparencies

    Progress Monitoring Online

Key Terms

1. precedent
2. unconstitutional
3. neutral
4. Sedition

Comprehension and Critical Thinking

5. **(a)** to advise Washington about government issues **(b)** Answers will vary, but should suggest that today's government is larger.

6. **(a)** the Whiskey Rebellion and the British-backed Native American resistance in the Northwest Territory; Washington sent troops in response to both situations. **(b)** Washington disagreed with the rebellion so strongly that he personally oversaw troop preparations to stop it.

7. **(a)** He did not want the United States to get entangled in the affairs of Europe. **(b)** He was afraid the country would be torn apart by divisions.

8. **(a)** They limited people's constitutional rights. **(b)** Responses will vary, but should be supported by reasoned arguments.

History Reading Skill

9. Possible answer: Washington was respected as the most important founder of the United States. Student answers may vary, but should use logic to support their view.

Writing

10. Paragraphs should include at least two events in their president's administration and a description of their president's personality.

11. Paragraphs should demonstrate an understanding of the causes of the rebellion or the soldier's feelings about stopping it.

For a more complete four-point rubric, see the Writing Rubrics in the Teaching Resources.

All in One Teaching Resources, Unit 3, p. 115

Key Terms
Fill in the blanks with the correct key terms.

1. Many of the customs that Washington started set a _____ for how other Presidents were to act in the future.

2. Jefferson said the national bank was _____ because it was not written in the Constitution that Congress had authority to establish one.

3. Neither France nor Britain agreed that the United States could be a _____ nation and trade with both sides during their war.

4. The _____ Act violated the First Amendment of the Constitution.

Comprehension and Critical Thinking

5. **(a) Recall** What was the purpose of George Washington's Cabinet?
   (b) Link Past and Present Why do you think current Presidents have more advisers than the number required in Washington's day?

6. **(a) Describe** What were two internal problems and their resolutions during Washington's second term as President?
   (b) Explain Problems What does the picture below indicate about Washington's view of the Whiskey Rebellion?

7. **(a) Recall** In Washington's Farewell Address, he talked about neutrality toward European nations. Why did Washington believe that the United States needed to be neutral in the war between France and Britain?
   (b) Draw Conclusions In Washington's Farewell Address, he also talked about national unity. Why was building unity an important goal for Washington?

---

8. **(a) Recall** Why were the Alien and Sedition acts unpopular with many people?
   (b) Apply Information Would you defend or oppose the government's right to silence people who criticize it? Explain.

History Reading Skill

9. **Analyze Comparisons** George Washington is often referred to as the Father of Our Country. What is the meaning of this metaphor? Do you think this is a valid comparison? Explain.

Writing

10. **Write a paragraph about either George Washington or John Adams.** Include major events and describe your subject's personality.
    Your paragraph should:
    • begin with a thesis statement;
    • expand on that main idea with facts, examples, and other information;
    • conclude by stating what you think was your subject's most important contribution to the new nation.

11. **Write a Narrative:** Study the pictures and text in Section 1 about the Whiskey Rebellion. Write a two-paragraph narrative describing the rebellion. Write from the point of view of either a farmer or a soldier.

Skills for Life
Distinguish Facts From Opinions
Use the fictional journal entry below to answer the questions that follow.

> "I am grateful that at least our Vice President, Thomas Jefferson, is a Republican. I believe that his policies are the only hope for farmers, such as myself and my neighbors. In my opinion, our political leaders don't have to be rich or well-educated. The people can lead as well as follow. Of course, the Federalist Mr. Hamilton, with his fine clothes, favors the wealthy merchants."

12. **(a)** Identify one fact in the journal entry.
    (b) How can you prove the statement is a fact?

13. **(a)** What is an example of an opinion?
    (b) How can you tell the statement is an opinion?

14. Find a statement that mixes fact and opinion. What is the fact? What is the opinion?

Skills for Life

12. **(a)** The Federalist Mr. Hamilton, with his fine clothes, favors the wealthy merchants. **(b)** You can look up Alexander Hamilton to find out what his policies were and if they favored wealthy merchants.

13. **(a)** Possible answer: I believe that his policies are the only hope for farmers. **(b)** Possible answer: The author uses the phrase "I believe."

14. **(a)** Possible answer: I am grateful that at least our Vice-President, Thomas Jefferson, is a Republican. **(b)** Possible answer: The fact is that Thomas Jefferson was a Republican. The opinion is that the author is grateful that Jefferson was elected Vice-President.

Chapter 8
Review and Assessment

Test Yourself

1. Which of the following led to tension between France and the United States during Adams's presidency?
   A Treaty of Greenville
   B Jay Treaty
   C Treaty of Paris
   D Declaration of Independence

Refer to the quotation below to answer Question 2.

> "It is in my judgment necessary under the circumstances of the case to take measures for calling forth the militia in order to . . . cause the laws to be duly executed."

2. What event is the subject of the quotation?
   A French Revolution
   B XYZ Affair
   C Battle of Fallen Timbers
   D Whiskey Rebellion

Refer to the chart below to answer Question 3.

The First Political Parties	
Federalists	Republicans
Favored strong central government	Favored state government
Emphasized manufacturing, shipping, and trade	Emphasized agriculture
Supported loose interpretation of the Constitution	Supported strict interpretation of the Constitution
Favored national bank	Opposed national bank

3. Which statement describes a fundamental difference between the two parties?
   A Federalists believed in a strong central government, and Republicans did not.
   B Federalists believed in a strict interpretation of the Constitution, and Republicans did not.
   C Republicans believed in a strong central government, and Federalists did not.
   D Republicans believed in a loose interpretation of the Constitution, and Federalists did not.

Document-Based Questions

Task: Look at Documents 1 and 2, and answer their accompanying questions. Then, use the documents and your knowledge of history to complete this writing assignment:

Write a newspaper editorial supporting or attacking President Adams's decision to avoid war with France.

Document 1: In 1797, France began seizing American ships. Enraged Americans called for war, but President John Adams urged a policy of peace. *What action does Adams say he will take toward France?*

> "It is my sincere desire . . . to preserve peace and friendship with all nations; and believing that neither the honor nor the interest of the United States absolutely forbid the repetition of advances for securing these desirable objects with France, I shall institute a fresh attempt at negotiation, and shall not fail to promote and accelerate an accommodation on terms compatible with the rights, duties, interests, and honor of the nation."

Document 2: After the XYZ Affair, newspapers published cartoons such as the one shown below. It depicts the United States as a young woman surrounded by members of the French government. *What is the cartoonist's view of the XYZ Affair?*

PROPERTY PROTECTED à la Françoise.

Test Yourself
1. B
2. D
3. A

Document-Based Questions
Answers

Document 1 Adams says he will negotiate with France.

Document 2 The XYZ Affair involved a French attempt to bribe U.S. negotiators.

Rubric: Write an Essay

Share the rubric with students before they begin writing.

Score 1 Ideas unclear, organization poor.

Score 2 Essay has few details in support of stand taken, fails to answer questions completely.

Score 3 Essay accurately answers questions, has clear organization and some supporting arguments. (*Pros for war: gain respect for United States, protect American ships; Cons to war: American military not strong enough, cost in money and lives lost*)

Score 4 Essay is comprehensive and detailed with clear organization and supporting arguments, shows creativity.

The Era of Thomas Jefferson (1800–1815)

History Background

The Significance of the Jefferson Era

Thomas Jefferson became President after a heated election in which he and his Republican Party ousted the Federalist Party incumbent, John Adams. Although Jefferson may have intended to reduce the power of the central government and increase the powers of the states, many of his actions had the opposite effect.

Jefferson cut federal involvement in foreign affairs, stripping embassies and military support drastically. Yet, he responded to a challenge by the Barbary States with military action.

Jefferson canceled the judicial appointments made in the last days of the previous administration. This led to a landmark Supreme Court case, *Marbury* v. *Madison*, in which the Court established its authority to review the constitutionality of laws. This decision strengthened the power of the judicial branch of government and the power of the federal government over the actions of the states.

The Louisiana Purchase was another example of Jefferson's taking actions that strengthened executive power. Jefferson's ambassadors to France accepted an offer to purchase all of the Louisiana Territory from cash-strapped France. Some critics said that Jefferson's administration was usurping the treaty-authorizing power of the Congress. Yet the purchase went through.

Threats from abroad continued during the presidency of Jefferson's successor, James Madison. Conflicts with Britain led to the War of 1812. The war ended with a strengthened United States poised to resume its territorial expansion across the continent.

As a result of these conflicts and the responses of Jefferson and Madison, the office of President became more important than either man would have initially found acceptable.

Essential Questions

Use this graphic organizer to see the relationship between key concepts and the Chapter Essential Question.

Focus Question/Section 1
How did Jefferson chart a new course for the government?
(p. 310)
Concepts: Limited Government, Judicial Review

Focus Question/Section 2
What was the importance of the purchase and exploration of the Louisiana Territory?
(p. 314)
Concept: Expansion

Chapter Essential Question
How did Jefferson and Madison deal with unresolved problems?

Focus Question/Section 4
What were the causes and effects of the War of 1812?
(p. 327)
Concept: Nationalism

Focus Question/Section 3
How did Jefferson respond to threats to the security of the nation?
(p. 322)
Concept: Conflict

Differentiated Instruction

Mapping Word Definitions

Research shows that mapping word definitions helps students develop the ability to investigate word meanings independently and provide elaborated definitions (as opposed to simple one- or two-word definitions).

Model mapping word definitions by developing a graphic organizer similar to the one shown on TE p. 309 for the high-use word *decline*.

- The definition in their own words—to lose strength or deteriorate

- A synonym or example—*fade, weaken*

- A sentence using the word—*When Jefferson cut the navy's budget, U.S. military strength declined.*

- A non-example—*strengthen*

Concepts Across Time

Have students develop an understanding of the enduring concepts of history by connecting these ideas.

Concept: Limited Government

Many of the freedoms enjoyed by citizens of the United States are possible because the nation has a limited government and because the process of judicial review ensures the constitutionality of laws. Have students recall what they read in the Citizenship Handbook about checks and balances in the Constitution. Ask: **How do checks and balances help to limit the power of our government?** (*They give each branch of government a way to block actions by other branches, thus preventing any one branch from becoming too powerful.*) Ask: **How can the judicial branch restrain the actions of other branches?** (*Through judicial review, it can block acts it deems to be unconstitutional.*) Use these questions when discussing judicial review in Section 1.

Concept: Expansion

Compare the expansion of the United States into the Louisiana Territory to the European expansion that led to the settlement of North and South America. Ask: **How were the periods of exploration similar?** (*In both cases, the governments were looking to increase wealth, find resources, and learn about the world.*) Ask: **How had the world changed by the time Lewis and Clark explored the Louisiana Territory?** (*The major continents had been reliably mapped, communication had improved, and scientists had a more sophisticated understanding of geography.*) Use this question when discussing the Lewis and Clark expedition in Section 2.

Concept: Revolution

Compare the War of 1812 to the Revolutionary War. Ask: **Why would some Americans call the War of 1812 the Second Revolution?** (*The United States reasserted its independence from Great Britain and, having proved itself again, gained the respect of European nations.*) Ask: **Why were the Americans in a better position to fight against Britain in 1812 than they had been during the Revolution?** (*Americans had a more established economy, there were more people to fight the war, and Britain had already lost a war to the Americans.*) Use these questions when discussing the War of 1812 in Section 4.

Section 1 **Jefferson Takes Office** *1.5 periods, .75 block*

Objectives

Students will

1. Describe the outcome of the election of 1800.
2. Explain Jefferson's policies as President.
3. Discuss the importance of *Marbury* v. *Madison*.

Differentiated Instruction Key

L1 Basic to Average
L2 All Students
L3 Average to Advanced

AR Advanced Readers
ELL English Language Learners
GT Gifted and Talented
LPR Less Proficient Readers
SN Special Needs

Prepare to Read

Build Background Knowledge
Preview the section and review Chapter 4 and have students brainstorm for changes that Jefferson might have made based on his political party.

Set a Purpose for Reading
Have students begin to fill out the Reading Readiness Guide.

Preview Key Terms
Preview the section's key terms.

Instructional Resources

All in One Teaching Resources, Unit 3
- **L2** Chapter Prereading Guide, p. 5
- **L2** History Reading Skill, p. 45
- **L2** Reading Readiness Guide, p. 47
- **L2** Word Knowledge Rating Form, p. 46

Discovery School Video
- **L2** The Era of Thomas Jefferson

Teacher's Edition
- **L2** Vocabulary Builder, pp. 309, 311

Differentiated Instruction

🔘 **Guided Reading Audio CD**
Spanish **ELL, LPR, SN**

Teach

Instruction
Republicans Take Charge
Describe Jefferson's inauguration.

Jefferson Charts a New Course
Explain Jefferson's new policies.

The Supreme Court and Judicial Review
Discuss *Marbury* v. *Madison*

Instructional Resources

📖 **Interactive Reading and Notetaking Study Guide**
- **L2** Chapter 9, Section 1

All in One Teaching Resources, Unit 3
- **L2** Jefferson's Inaugural Address, p. 51

Color Transparencies
- **L2** Mad Tom in a Rage

Differentiated Instruction

📖 **Interactive Reading and Notetaking Study Guide, Adapted Version (English/Spanish)**
- **L1** Chapter 9, Section 1

Teacher's Edition
- **L1** Visualizing the Word, p. 309 **ELL, LPR, SN**
- **L3** Research, p. 310 **AR, GT**
- **L1** Gaining Comprehension, p. 312 **ELL, LPR, SN**

Assess and Reteach

Assess Progress
Evaluate student comprehension with Check Your Progress and Section Quiz.

Reteach
Assign the Interactive Reading and Notetaking Study Guide to help struggling students.

Extend
Extend the lesson by having groups of students create a poster on the accomplishments of a key figure from this section.

Instructional Resources

📖 **Interactive Reading and Notetaking Study Guide**
- **L2** Chapter 9, Section 1

All in One Teaching Resources, Unit 3
- **L2** Reading Readiness Guide, p. 47
- **L2** Section Quiz, p. 60

Progress Monitoring Transparencies
- **L2** Chapter 9, Section 1

Differentiated Instruction

Teacher's Edition
- **L1** Checkpoints, TE, pp. 311, 312, 313

🔘 **SE on Audio CD**
- **L1** Chapter 9 **ELL, LPR, SN**

Internet Resources
PHSchool.com

1 period, .5 block

Objectives

Students will

1. Explain the importance of New Orleans and the crisis over its port.

2. Describe how the United States gained the Louisiana Purchase.

3. Discuss Lewis and Clark's expedition.

Differentiated Instruction Key

L1 Basic to Average
L2 All Students
L3 Average to Advanced

AR Advanced Readers
ELL English Language Learners
GT Gifted and Talented
LPR Less Proficient Readers
SN Special Needs

Prepare to Read

Build Background Knowledge
Preview the section and have students imagine the U.S. border ending at the Mississippi River.

Set a Purpose for Reading
Have students begin to fill out the Reading Readiness Guide.

Preview Key Terms
Preview the section's key terms.

Instructional Resources

All in One Teaching Resources, Unit 3
L2 Reading Readiness Guide, p. 48

Teacher's Edition
L2 Vocabulary Builder, p. 315

Differentiated Instruction

📀 **Guided Reading Audio CD**
Spanish ELL, LPR, SN

Teach

Instruction
The Nation Looks West
Explain the importance of New Orleans and the crisis over its port.

Buying Louisiana
Describe how the United States expanded west.

Lewis and Clark Explore the West
Discuss Lewis and Clark's expedition.

Instructional Resources

📖 **Interactive Reading and Notetaking Study Guide**
L2 Chapter 9, Section 2

All in One Teaching Resources, Unit 3
L2 Concept Lesson, p. 59
L2 Concept Organizer, p. 7
L2 Mandan Traders, p. 52

Color Transparencies
L2 Expansion of the United States

Discovery School Video
L2 Lewis and Clark

Differentiated Instruction

📖 **Interactive Reading and Notetaking Study Guide, Adapted Version (English/ Spanish)**
L1 Chapter 9, Section 2

Teacher's Edition
L3 Predicting, p. 314 AR, GT
L1 Describe, p. 316 ELL, LPR, SN
L3 Dramatizing Events, p. 318 AR, GT
L1 Create a Timeline, p. 320 LPR

All in One Teaching Resources, Unit 3
L3 On the Road with Lewis and Clark, p. 53

Assess and Reteach

Assess Progress
Evaluate student comprehension with Check Your Progress and Section Quiz.

Reteach
Assign the Interactive Reading and Notetaking Study Guide to help struggling students.

Extend
Extend the lesson by having students write journal entries of Lewis and Clark's adventures.

Instructional Resources

📖 **Interactive Reading and Notetaking Study Guide**
L2 Chapter 9, Section 2

All in One Teaching Resources, Unit 3
L2 Reading Readiness Guide, p. 48
L2 Section Quiz, p. 61

Progress Monitoring Transparencies
L2 Chapter 9, Section 2

Differentiated Instruction

Teacher's Edition
L1 Checkpoints, TE, pp. 315, 316, 319

📀 **SE on Audio CD**
L1 Chapter 9 ELL, LPR, SN

📀 **Exploring Primary Sources in U.S. History CD-ROM**
L3 Diary: The Journals of Lewis and Clark

Section 3 A Time of Conflict

 1 period, .5 block

Objectives

Students will

1. Discuss how the United States defeated the Barbary pirates.
2. Explain how war in Europe hurt American trade.
3. Discuss the causes and effects of the Embargo Act.
4. Identify the events leading up to the Battle of Tippecanoe.

Differentiated Instruction Key

L1 Basic to Average

L2 All Students

L3 Average to Advanced

AR Advanced Readers
ELL English Language Learners
GT Gifted and Talented
LPR Less Proficient Readers
SN Special Needs

Prepare to Read

Build Background Knowledge
Preview the section and discuss the benefits and risks of neutrality.

Set a Purpose for Reading
Have students begin to fill out the Reading Readiness Guide.

Preview Key Terms
Preview the section's key terms.

Instructional Resources

All in One Teaching Resources, Unit 3

L2 Reading Readiness Guide, p. 49

Teacher's Edition

L2 Vocabulary Builder, p. 323

Differentiated Instruction

🎧 **Guided Reading Audio CD**

Spanish ELL, LPR, SN

Teach

Instruction
Defeating the Barbary States
Discuss how the United States defeated the Barbary pirates.

American Neutrality Is Challenged
Discuss why Britain and France were interfering with U.S. shipping.

Jefferson Responds With an Embargo
Explain the Embargo Act.

Tecumseh and the Prophet
Identify the events leading up to the Battle of Tippecanoe.

Instructional Resources

📖 **Interactive Reading and Notetaking Study Guide**

L2 Chapter 9, Section 3

All in One Teaching Resources, Unit 3

L2 Jefferson Addresses Foreign Conflict, p. 55

Differentiated Instruction

📖 **Interactive Reading and Notetaking Study Guide, Adapted Version (English/Spanish)**

L1 Chapter 9, Section 3

Teacher's Edition

L3 Research, p. 322 AR, GT

L1 Gaining Comprehension, p. 324 ELL, LPR, SN

All in One Teaching Resources, Unit 3

L1 Jefferson's Conflicts Overseas, p. 56

Assess and Reteach

Assess Progress
Evaluate student comprehension with Check Your Progress and Section Quiz.

Reteach
Assign the Interactive Reading and Notetaking Study Guide to help struggling students.

Extend
Extend the lesson by having students debate one of Jefferson's policies.

Instructional Resources

📖 **Interactive Reading and Notetaking Study Guide**

L2 Chapter 9, Section 3

All in One Teaching Resources, Unit 3

L2 Reading Readiness Guide, p. 49

L2 Section Quiz, p. 62

Progress Monitoring Transparencies

L2 Chapter 9, Section 3

Differentiated Instruction

Teacher's Edition

L1 Checkpoints, TE pp. 323, 324, 325, 326

🎧 **SE on Audio CD**

L1 Chapter 9 ELL, LPR, SN

Section 4 The War of 1812 *1.5 periods, .75 block*

Objectives

Students will

1. Explain why the United States declared war on Britain.
2. Describe what happened in the early days of the war.
3. Discuss the American invasion of Canada and the fighting in the South.
4. Identify the events leading to the end of the War of 1812.

Differentiated Instruction Key

L1 Basic to Average
L2 All Students
L3 Average to Advanced

AR Advanced Readers
ELL English Language Learners
GT Gifted and Talented
LPR Less Proficient Readers
SN Special Needs

Prepare to Read

Build Background Knowledge
Preview the section and ask students to predict what they will learn.

Set a Purpose for Reading
Have students begin to fill out the Reading Readiness Guide.

Preview Key Terms
Preview the section's key terms.

Instructional Resources

All in One Teaching Resources, Unit 3
L2 Reading Readiness Guide, p. 50

Teacher's Edition
L2 Vocabulary Builder, p. 327

Differentiated Instruction

🔊 **Guided Reading Audio CD**
Spanish **ELL, LPR, SN**

Teach

Instruction
The Move Toward War
Explain why the United States declared war on Britain.

Early Days of the War
Describe what happened in the beginning of the war.

The War in the West and South
Discuss the American invasion of Canada and the effects the war had on Native Americans.

Final Battles
Identify the events leading to the end of the War of 1812.

Instructional Resources

📖 **Interactive Reading and Notetaking Study Guide**
L2 Chapter 9, Section 4

All in One Teaching Resources, Unit 3
L2 Dolley Madison, p. 57
L2 Skills for Life Worksheet, p. 58

Color Transparencies
L2 Old Ironsides and the War of 1812

Differentiated Instruction

📖 **Interactive Reading and Notetaking Study Guide, Adapted Version (English/Spanish)**
L1 Chapter 9, Section 4

Teacher's Edition
L1 Vocabulary Development, p. 328 **ELL, LPR, SN**
L3 Research and Reenact, p. 330 **AR, GT**

Assess and Reteach

Assess Progress
Evaluate student comprehension with Check Your Progress and Section Quiz.

Reteach
Assign the Study Guide to help students.

Extend
Extend the lesson by having students use the History Interactive to prepare a news report about the USS *Constitution*.

Instructional Resources

📖 **Interactive Reading and Notetaking Study Guide**
L2 Chapter 9, Section 4

All in One Teaching Resources, Unit 3
L2 Reading Readiness Guide, p. 50
L2 Word Knowledge Rating Form, p. 46
L2 Section Quiz, p. 63
L2 Chapter Test, p. 67

Progress Monitoring Transparencies
L2 Chapter 9, Section 4

Differentiated Instruction

Teacher's Edition
L1 Checkpoints, TE pp. 327, 328, 330, 331

All in One Teaching Resources, Unit 3
L1 Chapter Test, p. 64

🔊 **SE on Audio CD**
L1 Chapter 9 **ELL, LPR, SN**

🔊 **Skills Tutor CD-ROM**
Identifying Frame of Reference and Point of View

Internet Resources
PHSchool.com

Use the following research activities to help students deepen their understanding of the Chapter Essential Question: **How did Jefferson and Madison deal with unresolved problems?** Students should use library or Internet resources. The Web Codes provided offer access to Internet resources students can use to complete each activity. Use the appropriate four-point rubric in Assessment Rubrics to evaluate the activity.

📖 **Assessment Rubrics**

Create a Descriptive Report

Have students research the Lewis and Clark expedition and prepare a summary of the journey that might have been presented to President Jefferson upon their return. Summaries should be three to five paragraphs long explaining the successes of the trip. Remind students to use descriptive language since the President and other easterners had no idea what the explorers had seen. Ask volunteers to read their summaries for the class when studying Lewis and Clark Explore the West in Section 2.

🚶 **Individual research activity**　　L2

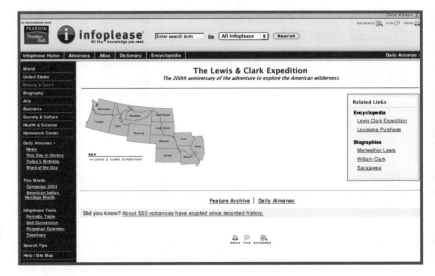

Go Online **Web Code:** mye-0231
PHSchool.com

Write a Speech

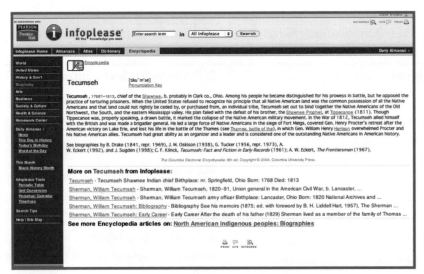

Have students research the life of Tecumseh. Using their understanding of the concept of nationalism, have them write a persuasive speech that Tecumseh might have delivered to encourage other Native Americans to organize against the expanding white settlers. Speeches should be no more than 5 minutes long. They should state a position clearly and should support the position with facts, examples, and details. Use this activity in Section 3 when reading Tecumseh and the Prophet.

🚶 **Individual research activity** AR, GT　　L3

Go Online **Web Code:** mye-0232
PHSchool.com

Create a Timeline

Have students work in small groups to create a timeline to understand the sequence of events in the War of 1812. Tell them to use information from the Internet as well as key events from Chapter 9 on the timeline. Timelines should have 12 to 15 events listed. Using their timelines, have students explain what they think were the positive outcomes of the war. Have students share their work. Use this activity when studying Section 4, The War of 1812.

 Group research activity ELL, LPR, SN **L1**

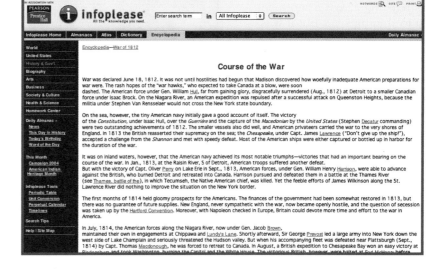

.Go Online **Web Code:** mye-0233
PHSchool.com

Write a Newspaper Article

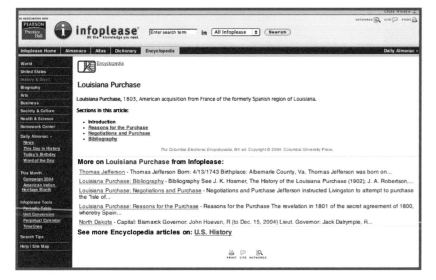

.Go Online **Web Code:** mye-0234
PHSchool.com

Have students research the Louisiana Purchase and write a newspaper article that could have appeared in an 1803 newspaper shortly after the event. Encourage students to create an attention-grabbing headline for their articles. Tell them to be sure they include important details about the event and the people and countries involved. Have students share their articles with a partner before sharing them with the class. Use this activity when studying The Louisiana Purchase in Section 2.

 Individual research activity **L2**

Why It Matters

We think of the United States as a republic stretching across a continent "from sea to shining sea." But it was only under Thomas Jefferson the U.S. territory first reached the Pacific. Lewis and Clark crossed an area of many different, unrelated nations. When Lewis spoke to the Tushepaw Indians in present-day Idaho, the speech had to be translated five times before the Tushepaw could understand it: from English to French, from French to Minataree, from Minataree to Shoshone, and from Shoshone to the Tushepaw language.

Although the United States expanded to span a continent, the challenge of uniting many diverse peoples and cultures into a unified country is not only significant to the history of the United States but also a continuing challenge for the nation's future.

Chapter Essential Question

How did Jefferson and Madison deal with unresolved problems?

Think Like a Historian

- To preview this chapter, have students review the content on these pages of the Student Edition. Ask: **What will you be learning about in this chapter?** (*Jefferson's time in office and the War of 1812*)

- Have students read the quotation. **What effect did the Louisiana Purchase have on the United States?** (*It doubled the territory of the United States.*)

- Have students study the image of the Lewis and Clark expedition meeting a group of Native Americans. Ask: **What do you think the reaction of each side might be?** (*Native American with head-dress seems confident, unafraid; those on the left side seem to be more uncertain, watchful.*) **Why do you think the Lewis and Clark group was made up of many diverse people?** (*Lewis and Clark were venturing into new territory and needed experienced wilderness guides and possibly translators to help them survive.*)

The Era of Thomas Jefferson

1800-1815

306

Bibliography

For the Teacher

Ellis, Joseph J. *American Sphinx: The Character of Thomas Jefferson.* New York: Vintage Books, 1998.

For the Student

L1 Klingel, Cynthia and Robert B. Noyed. *Dolley Madison: First Lady.* Minnesota: The Child's World, Inc., 2002.

L2 Collier, James Lincoln and Greg Copeland. *The Tecumseh You Never Knew (You Never Knew).* Connecticut: Children's Press, 2004.

L3 Tatlor, Lonn. *Star Spangled Banner: The Flag That Inspired the National Anthem.* New York: Harry N. Abrams, Inc., 2000.

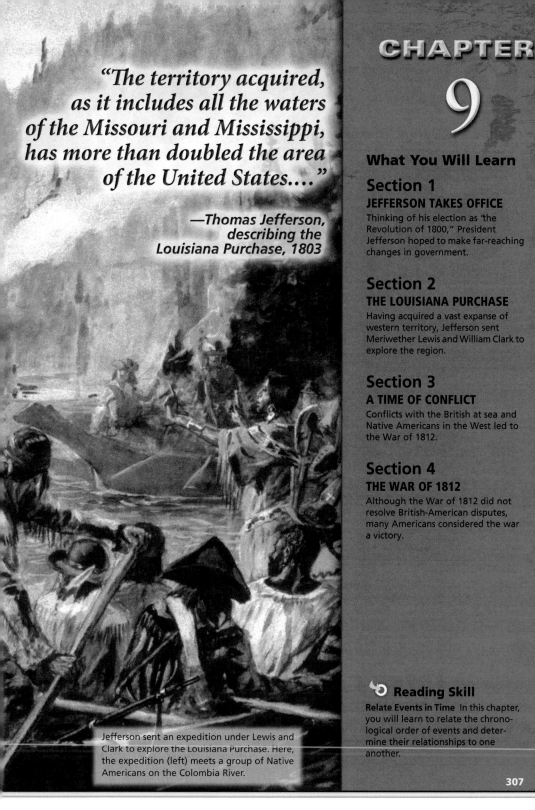

> "The territory acquired, as it includes all the waters of the Missouri and Mississippi, has more than doubled the area of the United States...."
>
> —Thomas Jefferson, describing the Louisiana Purchase, 1803

Jefferson sent an expedition under Lewis and Clark to explore the Louisiana Purchase. Here, the expedition (left) meets a group of Native Americans on the Colombia River.

CHAPTER 9

What You Will Learn

Section 1
JEFFERSON TAKES OFFICE
Thinking of his election as 'the Revolution of 1800," President Jefferson hoped to make far-reaching changes in government.

Section 2
THE LOUISIANA PURCHASE
Having acquired a vast expanse of western territory, Jefferson sent Meriwether Lewis and William Clark to explore the region.

Section 3
A TIME OF CONFLICT
Conflicts with the British at sea and Native Americans in the West led to the War of 1812.

Section 4
THE WAR OF 1812
Although the War of 1812 did not resolve British-American disputes, many Americans considered the war a victory.

Reading Skill
Relate Events in Time In this chapter, you will learn to relate the chronological order of events and determine their relationships to one another.

307

History Background

Destroying the USS *Philadelphia*
During the military conflict with the Barbary States, the USS *Philadelphia* was captured after it ran aground. Enemy pirates from the Barbary States boarded the ship and took its sailors hostage. The Americans worried that this ship could be used against them, so they carried out a secret mission to destroy it. Navy crew members disguised themselves as locals and approached the *Philadelphia* in the middle of the night. They quickly set fire to the ship and left before flames could reach their own small boat. The *Philadelphia* burned to the waterline and sank. The mission was a success.

Prepare to Read

Use the following for reading skill support.

All in One Teaching Resources, Unit 3, Chapter Prereading Guide, p. 5; History Reading Skill, p. 45

History Reading Skill *Online*
Web code: mve-3000

Differentiated Instruction

The following Teacher Edition strategies are suitable for students of varying abilities.

- **L3 Advanced Readers,** pp. 310, 314, 318, 322, 330 AR
- **L1 English Language Learners,** pp. 309, 312, 316, 324, 328 ELL
- **L3 Gifted and Talented,** pp. 310, 314, 318, 322, 330 GT
- **L1 Less Proficient Readers,** pp. 309, 312, 316, 320, 324, 328 LPR
- **L1 Special Needs,** pp. 309, 312, 316, 324, 328 SN

Chapter Resources

Teaching Resources, Unit 3
Chapter Prereading Guide, p. 5
Word Knowledge Rating Form, p. 46
History Reading Skill, p. 45
Skills for Life Worksheet, p. 58
Chapter Tests A/B (L1/L2), pp. 64, 67
Letter Home (English/Spanish), pp. 38, 39

Spanish Support
L1 Interactive Reading and Notetaking Study Guide, Spanish, Adapted Version
L1 Guided Reading Audio CD, Spanish

Media and Technology
L1 SE on Audio CD
L2 Social Studies Skills Tutor CD-ROM
ExamView Test Bank CD-ROM

DISCOVERY SCHOOL

Quick View Video
View the chapter video for a quick preview of the main ideas.

Visual Preview

How did Jefferson and Madison deal with unresolved problems?

Build Background Knowledge **L2**

In Chapter 8, students read about the problems the new country faced. Lead a structured discussion about the word "unresolved." Tell students that some problems often seem to be settled, but then may reoccur in a different time or form in their lives. (See TE p. T24 for more on structured discussion.) Ask students why they think some problems are difficult to completely resolve, or settle. Have them give examples from their lives about problems that keep resurfacing. (*issues of peer pressure, friction with parents or school figures*)

Instruction **L2**

- For background information on conducting a lesson for the Visual Preview, see TE p. T20.

- Write the Chapter Essential Question on the board. Use the Think-Write-Pair-Share strategy on TE p. T25 to have students recall some of the internal and external challenges they read about under Presidents Washington and Adams. Ask: **Of the problems the new country faced, which would likely reoccur?** (*land issues with Native Americans, the need for respect from France and Britain, states' rights*)

- Call students' attention to the color-coding of the map and the key to what the colors represent. Ask: **What can you tell about the beige part of the map?** (*It is Spanish territory.*) **How does the Louisiana Territory compare in size to the United States?** (*It is similar in size.*)

- Have students study the timeline on these pages. Ask: **When did the United States buy Louisiana?** (*1803*) **Who was it bought from?** (*France*) **What similarity do you notice about the events between 1811 and 1815?** (*They all involve fighting.*)

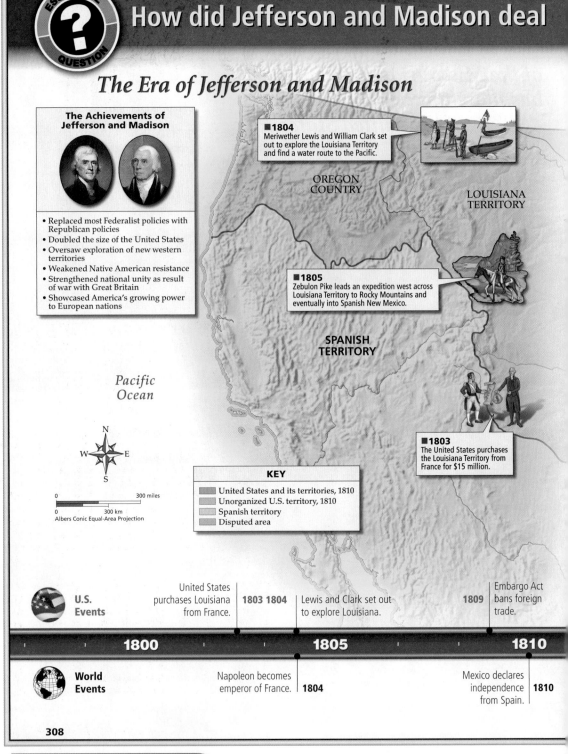

How did Jefferson and Madison deal

The Era of Jefferson and Madison

The Achievements of Jefferson and Madison

- Replaced most Federalist policies with Republican policies
- Doubled the size of the United States
- Oversaw exploration of new western territories
- Weakened Native American resistance
- Strengthened national unity as result of war with Great Britain
- Showcased America's growing power to European nations

■1804 Meriwether Lewis and William Clark set out to explore the Louisiana Territory and find a water route to the Pacific.

OREGON COUNTRY

LOUISIANA TERRITORY

■1805 Zebulon Pike leads an expedition west across Louisiana Territory to Rocky Mountains and eventually into Spanish New Mexico.

SPANISH TERRITORY

Pacific Ocean

■1803 The United States purchases the Louisiana Territory from France for $15 million.

KEY

- United States and its territories, 1810
- Unorganized U.S. territory, 1810
- Spanish territory
- Disputed area

0   300 miles
0   300 km
Albers Conic Equal-Area Projection

U.S. Events | United States purchases Louisiana from France. | **1803 1804** | Lewis and Clark set out to explore Louisiana. | **1809** Embargo Act bans foreign trade.

1800 | **1805** | **1810**

World Events | Napoleon becomes emperor of France. **1804** | Mexico declares independence from Spain. **1810**

308

History Background

Gaining Respect Gaining international recognition of American sovereignty was a challenge for the early presidents. Adams had negotiated the Jay Treaty in the hope of creating a relationship with Britain. However, the treaty did not stop the British from interfering with American maritime rights.

The United States faced formidable naval forces. The American navy consisted of 16 vessels, compared to 97 British ships on this side of the Atlantic. Knowing that the United States did not have the power to take on the British navy, Jefferson hoped to force Britain into recognizing American independence through the embargo. It failed, leaving the problem for Madison to resolve through warfare.

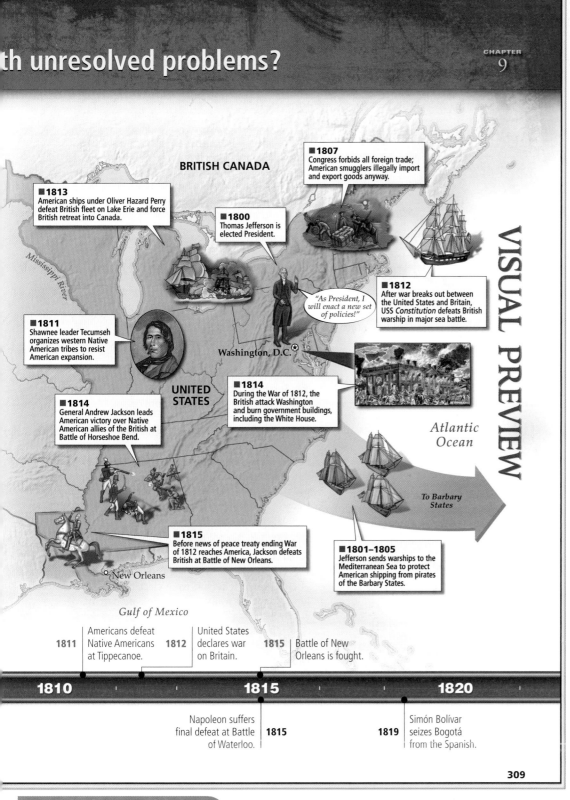

VISUAL PREVIEW

BRITISH CANADA

■1807
Congress forbids all foreign trade; American smugglers illegally import and export goods anyway.

■1813
American ships under Oliver Hazard Perry defeat British fleet on Lake Erie and force British retreat into Canada.

■1800
Thomas Jefferson is elected President.

Mississippi River

■1811
Shawnee leader Tecumseh organizes western Native American tribes to resist American expansion.

"As President, I will enact a new set of policies!"

■1812
After war breaks out between the United States and Britain, USS *Constitution* defeats British warship in major sea battle.

Washington, D.C. ⊛

UNITED STATES

■1814
General Andrew Jackson leads American victory over Native American allies of the British at Battle of Horseshoe Bend.

■1814
During the War of 1812, the British attack Washington and burn government buildings, including the White House.

Atlantic Ocean

■1815
Before news of peace treaty ending War of 1812 reaches America, Jackson defeats British at Battle of New Orleans.

○ New Orleans

■1801–1805
Jefferson sends warships to the Mediterranean Sea to protect American shipping from pirates of the Barbary States.

To Barbary States

Gulf of Mexico

| 1811 | Americans defeat Native Americans at Tippecanoe. | 1812 | United States declares war on Britain. | 1815 | Battle of New Orleans is fought. |

1810　　　　**1815**　　　　**1820**

| | Napoleon suffers final defeat at Battle of Waterloo. | 1815 | | 1819 | Simón Bolívar seizes Bogotá from the Spanish. |

309

Instruction (continued)

■ Have students review the graphics and captions on the map. Ask: **What happened in 1804?** (*Lewis and Clark began to explore the Louisiana Territory.*)

■ Organize the class into groups. Have each group select a graphic to analyze. Draw a timeline on the board and have students place their event in the proper order.

■ Divide the room in half, with one side labeled *internal issue* and the other side labeled *external issue.* Have each group decide which type of label the event represents and ask one member of the group to go to that side of the room. Discuss as a class why they think the event should be placed in that category.

■ Have students rewrite the Essential Question in simple terms in their notes. **How did Jefferson and Madison handle the nation's problems?** You may also post this question in a prominent place in the classroom and leave it there while discussing the chapter. Tell students to use the section focus questions as a guide to answering the Essential Question as they read the chapter.

■ Tell students that as they complete the Notetaking Study Guide for this chapter, they will be building the answer to the Chapter Essential Question.

📖 **Interactive Reading and Notetaking Study Guide,** Chapter 9 (Adapted Version also available.)

Review and Preview

Students have studied how the Federalists controlled the government. Now they will read about how the Republicans governed the nation.

Section Focus Question

How did Jefferson chart a new course for the government?

Before you begin the lesson for the day, write the Section Focus Question on the board. (*Lesson focus: Jefferson's goal to limit the power of the federal government*)

Prepare to Read

Build Background Knowledge L2

Ask students to recall from Chapter 8 the major disagreement between the Federalists and the Republicans. (*Federalists wanted a powerful central government, while Republicans felt it should have less power.*) Ask students to recall which political party Thomas Jefferson belonged to. (*Republican*) Ask students to begin to think about the types of governmental changes that Jefferson might have made based on his beliefs. Use the Idea Wave strategy (TE, p. T24) to elicit responses. Have students make a list of responses. Ask them to adjust the list as they read the section.

Set a Purpose L2

■ Read each statement in the Reading Readiness Guide aloud. Ask students to mark the statements as True or False.

All in One Teaching Resources, Unit 3, Reading Readiness Guide, p. 47

■ Have students discuss the statements in pairs or groups of four, and then mark their worksheets again. Use the Numbered Heads strategy (TE, p. T24) to call on students to share their group's perspectives. The students will return to these worksheets later.

Good Government

"A wise and frugal Government . . . shall restrain men from injuring one another, . . . shall leave them otherwise free to regulate their own pursuits . . . , and shall not take from the mouth of labor the bread it has earned. This is the sum of good government."

—Thomas Jefferson, First Inaugural Address, 1801

◄ Jefferson Memorial statue in Washington, D.C.

Jefferson Takes Office

Objectives
- Describe the outcome of the election of 1800.
- Explain Jefferson's policies as President.
- Discuss the importance of *Marbury* v. *Madison*.

🕤 Reading Skill

Understand Sequence of Events A historian must master the sequence of events that make up a historical episode. To understand the sequence, determine what happened first, next, or last. Look for clues such as dates and sequence signal words. Compare when events occurred. This will help you identify connections between events.

Key Terms and People

Thomas Jefferson	John Marshall
Aaron Burr	judicial review
laissez faire	

Why It Matters The Federalists had controlled the national government until the election of 1800. As a result of this election, the new Republican administration of Thomas Jefferson reversed some federalist policies. In fact, Jefferson referred to the election as the "Revolution of 1800."

❷ Section Focus Question: How did Jefferson chart a new course for the government?

Republicans Take Charge

Margaret Smith attended the inauguration of Thomas Jefferson as President of the United States in March 1801. After the inauguration, she wrote a letter explaining how proud she was of the United States. In other countries, the transfer of power usually involved "confusion . . . and bloodshed." However, "in our happy country" that transfer was peaceful and orderly.

A Bitter Campaign The presidential election of 1800 was viciously contested. The Federalists raised the prospect of civil war if Jefferson were elected. Republicans accused John Adams of wanting to create a monarchy.

By receiving 73 electoral votes, Jefferson defeated Adams. According to the Constitution, the person who received the next highest total of electoral votes would be Vice President. However, Aaron Burr, Jefferson's running mate, also received 73 votes. It was up to the House of Representatives to decide who would be President. For six days, the House was deadlocked. On the 36th vote, Jefferson won the election.

To avoid this situation in the future, the Twelfth Amendment to the Constitution changed how electors voted. Beginning in 1804, electors would vote separately for President and Vice President.

Differentiated Instruction

L3 Advanced Readers   **L3 Gifted and Talented**

Research Have students do research to learn about the current method of electing the President and Vice President of the United States. Have students also find out when the Twelfth Amendment was changed to reflect the current policy. Have students summarize their findings in a brief report.

Jefferson's Inauguration Thomas Jefferson was the first President to be inaugurated in Washington, D.C., the country's new capital. Jefferson believed the government should be less aristocratic. To make the point, he walked to his inauguration instead of riding in a fancy carriage. He also ended the custom of people bowing to the President. Instead, they just shook his hand.

Jefferson used his inaugural address to bring a divided country together. He told the American people:

> ❝Let us, then, fellow-citizens, unite with one heart and one mind. . . . Every difference of opinion is not a difference of principle. . . . We are all Republicans; we are all Federalists.❞
> —Thomas Jefferson, First Inaugural Address, March 4, 1801

☑ **Checkpoint** Why did the election of 1800 have to be decided in the House of Representatives?

Jefferson Charts a New Course

Jefferson thought of his election as the "Revolution of 1800." Jefferson's first goal as President was to limit the federal government's power over states and citizens. The new President thought that under Washington and Adams the federal government had become too involved in economic affairs. He believed in the idea known as laissez faire (LEHS ay fehr), from the French term for "let alone." **Laissez faire** means that the government should not interfere in the economy.

New Republican Policies Jefferson put his laissez faire ideas into practice when he reduced the number of people in government. He fired all tax collectors and cut the number of U.S. diplomats.

Vocabulary Builder
aristocratic (uh ris tuh KRAT ik)
adj. of an aristocracy or upper class

Thomas Jefferson's Home
Thomas Jefferson designed his home, Monticello. In the design, he included elements of Greek architecture, such as columns, and Roman architecture, such as domes. **Critical Thinking: Link Past and Present** What elements of Greek and Roman culture are still important to us today?

311

Vocabulary Builder

Use the information below to teach students this section's high-use words.

High-Use Word	Definition and Sample Sentence
aristocratic, p. 311	*adj.* of an aristocracy or an upper class Many settlers in colonial America disliked the appointed British governors because of their **aristocratic** customs.
revenue, p. 312	*n.* the income from taxes, licenses, etc. as of a city, state, or nation Great Britain relied on taxing the colonies for its **revenue**.

Teach

Republicans Take Charge

p. 310

Instruction ⬛ L2

- **Vocabulary Builder** Before teaching this section, preteach the High-Use Words **aristocratic** and **revenue** before reading, using the strategy on TE p. T21.

  Key Terms Following the instructions on p. 7, have students create a See It–Remember It chart for the Key Terms in this chapter.

- Read Republicans Take Charge with students, using the Structured Silent Reading strategy (TE, p. T22).

- Discuss the reason the Twelfth Amendment was enacted. (*Before this amendment, there could be a tie in the vote of the electoral college, causing delay and controversy in electing a President.*)

- Ask: **How did Jefferson's inauguration demonstrate his new approach to government?** (*Possible answer: He made it more informal and showed his desire to simplify government.*)

- Distribute Jefferson's Inaugural Address worksheet. Have students work with a partner to rewrite the speech in their own words and answer the questions.

  All in One Teaching Resources, Unit 3, Jefferson's Inaugural Address, p. 51

Independent Practice

Have students begin filling in the study guide for this section.

  📖 **Interactive Reading and Notetaking Study Guide,** Chapter 9, Section 1 (Adapted Version also available.)

Monitor Progress

As students fill in the Notetaking Study Guide, circulate to make sure individuals understand how Jefferson tried to end the bitterness of the presidential election. Provide assistance as needed.

Answers

☑ **Checkpoint** In the election of 1800, two candidates received the same number of votes, forcing the House to decide who would be President and who would be Vice President.

Link Past and Present architecture, law, philosophy, art, literature

Jefferson Charts a New Course

p. 311

The Supreme Court and Judicial Review

p. 312

Instruction L2

- Have students read Jefferson Charts a New Course and The Supreme Court and Judicial Review.

- Ask: **What were some of the policies that Jefferson changed when he took office?** (*He reduced the number of government officials, cut the army budget, replaced expensive warships with inexpensive gunboats, eliminated federal taxes, and freed those imprisoned under the Sedition Act.*)

- Display *Mad Tom in a Rage* transparency. Have students answer the questions at the bottom of the transparency.

Color Transparencies, Mad Tom in a Rage

- Ask: **Did the *Marbury* v. *Madison* ruling give Congress more or less power? Explain.** (*Less power; it stated that Congress did not have the right to give power to the Court and gave the Court more power over Congress.*) **What was the significance of this ruling?** (*It changed the relationship of the three branches of government, giving the courts a more equal role.*)

Independent Practice

Have students complete the study guide for this section.

Monitor Progress

- Check Notetaking Study Guide entries for student understanding of the importance of the *Marbury* v. *Madison* case.

- Tell students to fill in the last column of the Reading Readiness Guide. Probe for what they learned that confirms or invalidates each statement.

Answers

Reading Charts **(a)** reduce government expenses to reduce federal power; reconcile party differences **(b)** Questions will vary but should demonstrate an understanding of Jefferson's goals and policies and how they might differ from those of Washington and Adams.

Checkpoint He refused to renew the Sedition Act, refunded the fines that had been collected under the act, and released all those imprisoned under the act.

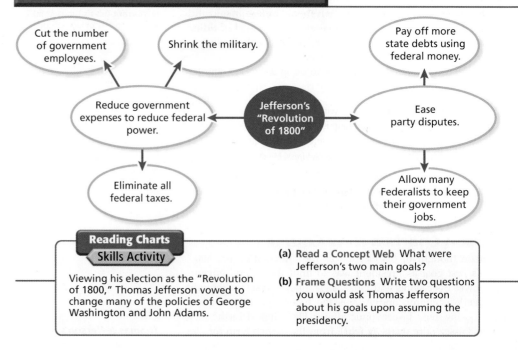

Goals and Policies of Thomas Jefferson

Reading Charts
Skills Activity

Viewing his election as the "Revolution of 1800," Thomas Jefferson vowed to change many of the policies of George Washington and John Adams.

(a) Read a Concept Web What were Jefferson's two main goals?

(b) Frame Questions Write two questions you would ask Thomas Jefferson about his goals upon assuming the presidency.

Vocabulary Builder
revenue (REV uh noo) **n.** the income from taxes, licenses, etc., as of a city, state, or nation

Larger cuts came from shrinking the military. Jefferson cut the army's budget in half, reducing the army's size from 4,000 to about 2,500 soldiers. At the same time, Jefferson eliminated all federal taxes inside the country. Now, most tax revenue came from the tariff on imported goods.

The Sedition Act was another of Jefferson's targets. As you have read, a number of people had been convicted and fined under the act. Jefferson ordered those fines refunded. Those imprisoned under the Sedition Act were released.

Federalist Policies Remain Jefferson could not reverse all Federalist policies. He believed that the United States had to keep repaying its national debt. He also did not fire most of the Federalist officeholders. He said they could keep their jobs if they did them well and were loyal citizens.

Checkpoint What action did Jefferson take as President to help those convicted under the Sedition Act?

The Supreme Court and Judicial Review

One Federalist who did not keep his job was Judge William Marbury. Adams had appointed Marbury and several other judges in the last hours before he left office. The Republicans argued that these appointments were aimed at maintaining Federalist power.

Differentiated Instruction

L1 English Language Learners   **L1** Less Proficient Readers   **L1** Special Needs

Gaining Comprehension Work with students to paraphrase the excerpt from Jefferson's inaugural address to help them understand its meaning. Begin by defining difficult words and phrases, such as *difference of opinion*, *principle*, *Republicans*, *Feder-*alists, and *unite*. Working one sentence at a time, read the sentence aloud and then lead a discussion on what it means. Finally, have students work in pairs to write down the meaning of the excerpt in their own words.

When Jefferson took office, he ordered James Madison, his secretary of state, to cease work on the appointments. Marbury then sued Madison, citing the Judiciary Act of 1789. This act gave the Supreme Court the power to review cases brought against a federal official.

The outcome of the case forever changed the relationship of the three branches of government. In his ruling, Chief Justice John Marshall spoke for a unanimous Court. He ruled that the Judiciary Act of 1789 was unconstitutional. Marshall stated that the Court's powers came from the Constitution, not from Congress. Therefore, Congress did not have the right to give power to the Supreme Court in the Judiciary Act. Only the Constitution could do that.

The Court's actual decision—that it could not help Marbury gain his commission—was not highly significant. However, the ruling did set an important precedent. Marshall used the case of *Marbury* v. *Madison* to establish the principle of judicial review—the authority of the Supreme Court to strike down unconstitutional laws. Today, judicial review remains one of the most important powers of the Supreme Court.

☑**Checkpoint** **What is judicial review?**

⭐ **Looking Back and Ahead** Thomas Jefferson had long argued that the federal government's powers were limited to what was set down in the Constitution. The Constitution did not specifically give the government the power to buy land from a foreign country. In the next section, you will read of Jefferson's dilemma when France offered to sell the United States the huge territory known as Louisiana.

Understand Sequence of Events What words in this paragraph are clues to sequence?

Section 1 | Check Your Progress

Progress Monitoring Online
For: Self-test with instant help
Visit: PHSchool.com
Web Code: mya-3051

Comprehension and Critical Thinking
1. (a) Recall How did Jefferson's inauguration demonstrate the changes he planned for the U.S. government?
(b) Apply Information How did Jefferson's policies change the American government?

2. (a) Identify What was Chief Justice Marshall's decision in the case of *Marbury* v. *Madison*?
(b) Make Predictions How did the outcome of *Marbury* v. *Madison* affect the relationship of the three branches of government?

Reading Skill
3. Understand Sequence of Events Read the first paragraph under the heading "Jefferson Charts a New Course." What was Jefferson's *first* priority as President?

Key Terms
Read each sentence below. If the sentence is true, write YES. If the sentence is not true, write NO and explain why.
4. Jefferson believed in laissez faire, the idea that the federal government should not interfere in economic affairs.

5. John Marshall cited judicial review as the reason why only the Senate had the right to decide whether acts of Congress are constitutional.

Writing
6. Based on what you have read in this section about Jefferson's early days in office, write a thesis statement about Jefferson's influence on American government. Then, list the kinds of supporting information that would back up your thesis statement.

Assess Progress L2
Have students complete Check Your Progress. Administer the Section Quiz.

All in One Teaching Resources, Section Quiz, Chapter 9, p. 60

To further assess student understanding, use the Progress Monitoring Transparency.

Progress Monitoring Transparencies, Chapter 9, Section 1

Reteach L1
If students need more instruction, have them read this section in the Interactive Reading and Notetaking Study Guide and complete the accompanying question.

📖 **Interactive Reading and Notetaking Study Guide,** Chapter 9, Section 1 (Adapted Version also available.)

Extend L3
Have students form groups of four. Give each group a large piece of poster board and assign one of the following key figures from the section: Thomas Jefferson, James Madison, or John Marshall. Ask students to use the information from the section, previous chapters, and the online biographies to create a poster highlighting the person's accomplishments and importance in history. Encourage students to include illustrations and other visuals. Provide students with the Web Code below.

Extend Online
For: Help in starting the Extend activity
Visit: PHSchool.com
Web Code: mye-0235

Progress Monitoring Online
Students may check their comprehension of this section by completing the Progress Monitoring Online graphic organizer and self-quiz.

Answers

🔄 **Reading Skill** when, then

☑**Checkpoint** the principle that the Supreme Court can decide if an act of Congress is constitutional or not

---

Section 1 Check Your Progress

1. (a) He wore simple clothing, shook hands, walked to the ceremony, and delivered a speech to reconcile differences.
(b) Jefferson's policies shrank the government and limited its power over states and citizens.

2. (a) Marshall ruled that the Judiciary Act of 1789 was unconstitutional.
(b) The case placed the Supreme Court in a more central position in the government; established judicial review

3. to limit the federal government's power over states and citizens

4. Yes.

5. No; Marshall stated that the Supreme Court, not the Senate, had the right to decide whether acts of Congress are constitutional.

6. Students should show understanding of the beginning of the "Jefferson Era," when the power of the government over the people and the states was limited.

Review and Preview

Students have learned about the early settlement of the United States. Now they will focus on the territorial expansion during Jefferson's presidency.

Section Focus Question

What was the importance of the purchase and exploration of the Louisiana Territory?

Before you begin the lesson for the day, write the Section Focus Question on the board. (*Lesson focus: It greatly increased the size of the nation.*)

Prepare to Read

Build Background Knowledge   L2

Have students turn to the political map of the United States on p. 316 of the Student Edition. Explain to students that the United States once only extended from the east coast to the Mississippi River. Have them trace their finger over the boundaries of this territory. Ask students to suggest ways that the country would be different today if it were still only made up of this territory. Use the Give One, Get One participation strategy (TE, p. T25) to elicit responses.

Set a Purpose   L2

■ Form students into pairs or groups of four. Distribute the Reading Readiness Guide. Ask students to fill in the first two columns of the chart.

> **All in One** **Teaching Resources, Unit 3,** Reading Readiness Guide, p. 48

■ Use the Numbered Heads strategy (TE, p. T24) to call on students to share one piece of information they already know and one piece of information they want to know. The students will return to these worksheets later.

SECTION 2

The Louisiana Territory

❝[The Missouri River] passes through a rich fertile and one of the most beautifully picturesque countries that I ever beheld.... Innumerable herds of living animals are seen.... Its lofty and open forests are the habitation of myriads of the feathered tribes.❞

—Meriwether Lewis, journal entry describing the Louisiana Territory, 1805

◀ Many Indian nations lived in the Louisiana Territory.

The Louisiana Purchase

Objectives
- Explain the importance of New Orleans and the crisis over its port.
- Describe how the United States gained the Louisiana Purchase.
- Discuss Lewis and Clark's expedition.

🔁 Reading Skill

Distinguish Events in Sequence As you read, it will help you to identify events that occur at about the same time in different locations. Ask yourself if these events share a common cause. Was there any advantage for people to make these events happen at the same time? Would faster communication have changed the sequence at all?

Key Terms and People

expedition	continental divide
Meriwether Lewis	Zebulon Pike
William Clark	

Why It Matters Jefferson focused on reducing the power and size of the federal government. But his foreign policy was more expansive. President Jefferson expanded the country's borders far to the west.

❓ **Section Focus Question: What was the importance of the purchase and exploration of the Louisiana Territory?**

The Nation Looks West

The tide of westward settlement speeded up in the years after the United States won independence. By 1800, more than one million settlers lived between the Appalachian Mountains and the Mississippi River.

Most western settlers were farmers. Because there were few roads in the West, they relied on the Mississippi River to ship their crops to the port at New Orleans. From there, the goods were loaded on ships and carried to markets in the East.

Spain, which controlled the Mississippi and New Orleans, had several times threatened to close the port to American ships. To prevent this from happening again, in 1795 the United States negotiated a treaty with Spain. The Pinckney Treaty guaranteed the Americans' right to ship their goods down the Mississippi to New Orleans. There, they could be stored until they were transferred to ocean-going ships for the journey east.

For a time, Americans shipped their goods through New Orleans peacefully. Then, in 1801, a crisis developed. Jefferson discovered that Spain had secretly given New Orleans and the rest of its Louisiana Territory to France.

Differentiated Instruction

L3 Advanced Readers   **L3** Gifted and Talented

Predicting Have students work in pairs. Have each select a major event from this section and assume either it had not occurred or that it had a different outcome. (For example, what if the revolution led by L'Ouverture in Haiti had not occurred?) Have each pair give a brief newscast in which they predict how subsequent events in American history might have been different.

Jefferson was alarmed by this development. The French ruler, Napoleon Bonaparte, had already set out to conquer Europe. Jefferson feared that he now intended to make France the <u>dominant</u> power in America as well. If Napoleon controlled Louisiana, the westward expansion of the United States would be blocked.

✓Checkpoint What important right did the United States gain with the Pinckney Treaty of 1795?

Buying Louisiana

Even before the actual transfer of Louisiana to France took place, America's position in Louisiana was threatened. In 1802, the Spanish governor of Louisiana withdrew the right of Americans to ship their goods through New Orleans. Westerners exploded in anger. They demanded that Jefferson go to war to win back their rights.

The situation was explosive. What would happen, Jefferson worried, when the French took over New Orleans?

A Surprise Offer The President decided the best approach was to try to buy the city of New Orleans from the French. He sent his friend James Monroe to France to make a deal. Monroe had the help of Robert Livingston, the American minister in Paris. Jefferson instructed the two men to buy New Orleans and a territory to the east called West Florida.

In Paris, the Americans discovered an <u>altered</u> situation. A revolution led by Toussaint L'Ouverture (too SAN loo vehr TYOOR) had driven the French from their Caribbean colony of Haiti. Without Haiti as a base, the French would have trouble defending Louisiana in the event of a war. At the same time, tensions between France and Britain were again on the rise. War was looming and Napoleon needed money to support the war effort. France offered to sell the United States not only New Orleans but the *entire* Louisiana Territory.

It would take months to get Jefferson's advice. So Livingston and Monroe agreed to buy the whole Louisiana Territory for $15 million— about 4 cents an acre. This included an enormous area stretching from the Gulf of Mexico to Canada and from the Mississippi River to the Rocky Mountains.

Vocabulary Builder
dominant (DAHM uh nunt)
adj. dominating; ruling; prevailing

Vocabulary Builder
alter (AWL ter) ***v.*** to change in some way; to make different

Haitian Independence
Toussaint L'Ouverture (right) helped lead the Haitian struggle to expel the French. **Critical Thinking: *Analyze Cause and Effect*** Why would France have trouble defending Louisiana if it did not control Haiti?

Vocabulary Builder

Use the information below to teach students this section's high-use words.

High-Use Word	Definition and Sample Sentence
dominant, p. 315	*adj.* dominating; ruling; prevailing Although people came to colonial America from many countries, the English language became **dominant**.
alter, p. 315	*v.* to change in some way; to make different Cornwallis's decision to camp on the Yorktown peninsula **altered** the course of the American Revolution.

Teach

The Nation Looks West
p. 314

Instruction [L2]

■ **Vocabulary Builder** Before teaching this section, preteach the High-Use Words **dominant** and **alter** before reading, using the strategy on TE p. T21.

  Key Terms Have students continue to fill in the See It–Remember It chart for the Key Terms in this chapter.

■ To help students better understand the concept of expansion, which is important to the understanding of this section, use the concept lesson on expansion.

  All in One Teaching Resources, Unit 3, Concept Lesson, p. 59; Concept Organizer, p. 7

■ Read The Nation Looks West with students, using the Partner Paragraph Shrinking reading strategy (TE, p. T23).

■ Ask: **How did most American farmers get their crops to market?** (*They shipped the goods to New Orleans down the Mississippi River.*)

■ Ask: **What effect do you think Spain's closing of the port of New Orleans had on the American economy?** (*Possible answer: The economy probably would have declined because farmers could not make as much money and therefore would have less money to buy other goods and services in the United States.*)

Independent Practice

Have students begin filling in the study guide for this section.

  Interactive Reading and Notetaking Study Guide, Chapter 9, Section 2 (Adapted Version also available.)

Monitor Progress

As students fill in the Notetaking Study Guide, circulate to make sure students realize the economic importance of New Orleans to farmers and to the nation.

Answers

✓Checkpoint the right to ship goods down the Mississippi River to New Orleans

Analyze Cause and Effect France would not have a place to station soldiers or an easy way to communicate with the leaders in Louisiana. It would be forced to ship people and goods across the Atlantic Ocean.

Buying Louisiana

p. 315

Instruction L2

- Have students refer to the map on this page as they read Buying Louisiana.

- Ask: **What did the American ambassadors intend to do in France?** (*They intended to negotiate the purchase of New Orleans.*)

- Ask students what they would have done had they been the ambassadors to France—would they have decided to purchase the entire Louisiana Territory? Have them explain why or why not. (*Students' answers will vary but should reflect an understanding that the price was very reasonable. Some may think that Jefferson should have been consulted first.*)

- Show the Expansion of the United States transparency and overlay. Have students work with a partner to answer the questions and then have them share their answers with the class.

Color Transparencies, Expansion of the United States

Independent Practice

Have students continue filling in the study guide for this section.

📖 **Interactive Reading and Notetaking Study Guide,** Chapter 9, Section 2 (Adapted Version also available.)

Monitor Progress

- As students fill in the Notetaking Study Guide, make sure individuals understand the complexity of the Louisiana Purchase. If students do not seem to have a good understanding of the material, have them reread the section.

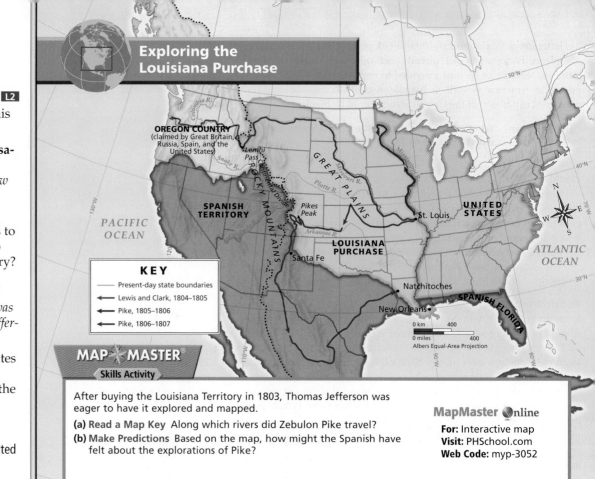

Exploring the Louisiana Purchase

KEY

— Present-day state boundaries
← Lewis and Clark, 1804–1805
← Pike, 1805–1806
← Pike, 1806–1807

MAP MASTER
Skills Activity

After buying the Louisiana Territory in 1803, Thomas Jefferson was eager to have it explored and mapped.

(a) Read a Map Key Along which rivers did Zebulon Pike travel?
(b) Make Predictions Based on the map, how might the Spanish have felt about the explorations of Pike?

MapMaster Online
For: Interactive map
Visit: PHSchool.com
Web Code: myp-3052

The Louisiana Purchase proved an amazing bargain for the United States. Its area almost doubled the size of the country. Although largely unexplored, the region clearly had millions of acres of fertile farmland and other natural resources. Ownership of Louisiana gave the United States control of the Mississippi River. As Livingston put it, "From this day, the United States take their place among the powers of the first rank."

Jefferson's Dilemma Jefferson was delighted with the deal. At the same time, he had a serious problem. The Constitution nowhere states that the President has the power to buy land from a foreign country. Adding the huge Louisiana Territory would dramatically change the character of the nation.

In the end, Jefferson decided that he did have authority to buy Louisiana. The Constitution, he reasoned, allowed the President to make treaties. The Senate approved the treaty and Congress quickly voted to pay for the land.

✓**Checkpoint** Why did President Jefferson hesitate to approve the purchase of the Louisiana Territory?

Differentiated Instruction

L1 English Language Learners   **L1** Less Proficient Readers   **L1** Special Needs

Describe Ask students to describe the map in their own words. Descriptions may be oral or written. Ask students to answer the following questions in their descriptions:

- What area does the map show?

- Who are the explorers identified on the map?

- How can you tell what route they took?

- What part of the United States did the explorers cover?

Answers

✓Checkpoint Jefferson knew that the Constitution did not specifically grant a President the right to buy land from foreign powers.

MAP MASTER
Skills Activity **(a)** Mississippi, Arkansas, Rio Grande **(b)** The Spanish might fear Pike was spying for America, since his route was so far into their territory.

Lewis and Clark Explore the West

In January 1803, even before the United States had bought Louisiana, Jefferson convinced Congress to spend $2,500 on a western expedition (eks puh DISH uhn). An **expedition** is a long and carefully organized journey.

Jefferson chose army captain Meriwether Lewis to lead the exploration. Lewis chose William Clark, also an army officer, as his coleader. The men were ordered to report back on the geography, plants, animals, and other natural features of the region.

The expedition also had other goals. Jefferson wanted Lewis and Clark to make contact with Native Americans who lived in the Louisiana Territory. The President also wanted Lewis and Clark to find out if a waterway existed between the Mississippi River and the Pacific Ocean.

Into the Unknown In the spring of 1804, Lewis and Clark left St. Louis and headed up the Missouri River. Their three boats carried tons of supplies and about 40 men. Most were Americans, although there were several French Canadians. The expedition also included an enslaved African American named York.

In mid-July, the party reached the mouth of the Platte River, a powerful tributary that flows into the Missouri. In early August, they met Native Americans for the first time. Three weeks later, the expedition reached the eastern edge of the Great Plains.

Links Across Time

1969 American astronauts Buzz Aldrin (shown here) and Neil Armstrong landed on the moon.

Exploration

1804–1806 Lewis and Clark explored the lands of the Louisiana Purchase. Their journals, maps, and drawings inspired the rapid settlement of the West.

1960s American explorers ventured into the "new frontier" of outer space. On July 20, 1969, the United States became the first nation to land a man on the moon. People around the world watched the landing on television.

Link to Today

Exploration Today The United States has sent additional missions to the moon and beyond. What kinds of exploration are going on today?

For: Recent activities of the U.S. space program
Visit: PHSchool.com
Web Code: mvc-3052

Section 2 The Louisiana Purchase **317**

Lewis and Clark Explore the West

p. 317

Instruction L2

■ Have students read Lewis and Clark Explore the West. Remind students to look for the sequence of events.

■ Ask: **What were the goals of the Lewis and Clark expedition?** (*Lewis and Clark were to report on the geography and natural resources, to establish an American claim to the land west of the Rocky Mountains, and to make contact with Native Americans of the region.*)

■ Review with students the number of men and boats that went on the long journey (*40 men and 3 boats*). Have students brainstorm for the types of supplies that might have been important to take on the journey (*examples: hunting weapons, fresh water, warm clothing*).

■ Assign Connections With Economics: Mandan Traders worksheet. Have students complete the activity and then discuss how Lewis and Clark benefited from staying with the Mandan people.

All in One Teaching Resources, Unit 3, Mandan Traders, p. 52

■ Ask: **Why did the Spanish fear Zebulon Pike's explorations?** (*They were afraid Pike was a spy, helping America to take over the region.*)

■ Ask students to think about what they know about the Southwest. Ask them to predict what may have interested Americans in the area. (*Possible answer: natural resources and the prospect of having more land available for expansion.*)

Economic Background

Problems for York When the Lewis and Clark expedition returned to the United States, each expedition member received double the payment of money and land he was promised at the start of the trip— except York. He received no payment at all since all his work was property of his master. Although York enjoyed much freedom and equal treatment on the journey, he was not granted his freedom until 10 years after the expedition ended.

Explore More Video

Discovery School Video

This video reveals the hardships experienced by Lewis and Clark and the other men of their expedition as they traveled thousands of miles from St. Louis to the Pacific Ocean and back. It mentions the two long winters during which the explorers had to camp and the difficult trip around the Great Falls of the Missouri River. It also presents the role of Sacagawea, the Native American woman who joined the expedition that first winter and helped guide the explorers.

Independent Practice

Have students complete the study guide for this section.

Interactive Reading and Notetaking Study Guide, Chapter 9, Section 2 (Adapted Version also available.)

Monitor Progress

- Check Notetaking Study Guide entries for student understanding of the difficulties and importance of the Lewis and Clark expedition.

- Tell students to fill in the last column of the Reading Readiness Guide. Ask them to consider whether what they learned was what they expected to learn.

All in One **Teaching Resources, Unit 3,** Reading Readiness Guide, p. 48

Answer

Apply Information Lewis and Clark faced extreme cold, rough waters, and difficult travel against strong currents.

Explore More Video
To learn more about Lewis and Clark's expedition, view the video.

Lewis and Clark: A Hard Journey At times during their travel up the Missouri River, members of the Lewis and Clark party had to carry their boats around rapids and falls. Here, Sacagawea, Clark, Lewis, and York examine the Great Falls in present-day Montana. *Critical Thinking: Apply Information* What other hazards did Lewis and Clark face on their river voyages?

In late October 1804, the expedition reached the territory of the Mandan people, in what is now North Dakota. Lewis and Clark decided to camp there for the winter. They were joined in camp by a French Canadian trader and his wife, a Native American named Sacagawea (sahk uh juh WEE uh). She was a Shoshone (shoh SHOH nee) who would travel with them and serve as translator.

Crossing the Rockies In April 1805, the party set out again. By summer they were in what is now Montana. They began to climb the Rockies. By August, they had reached the Continental Divide. A **continental divide** is the place on a continent that separates river systems flowing in opposite directions. The view to the west was beautiful but also deeply disappointing. Lewis had hoped to see a wide river that would take the group to the Pacific. Instead, all he saw were "immense ranges of mountains still to the west."

The next day, Lewis met a group of Shoshone warriors. When Sacagawea arrived to interpret, she was astonished to see that the Shoshone chief was her brother. She jumped up and threw her arms around him. Thanks to Sacagawea, the Shoshones agreed to sell the expedition horses that were needed to cross the mountains.

At the Pacific On the west side of the Rockies, Lewis and Clark reached the Columbia River. Here, they stopped to build canoes for the downriver voyage. At one point, they had to cross a 55-mile stretch of rapids and rough water. Finally, through a dense early November fog, they saw the Pacific Ocean.

Differentiated Instruction

L3 Advanced Readers

L3 Gifted and Talented

Dramatizing Events Have students work in a group to create a shadow puppet play dramatizing Lewis and Clark's expedition. After student groups have finished creating the puppets and writing a script, they should present their plays to the class.

All in One **Teaching Resources, Unit 3,** On the Road With Lewis and Clark, p. 53

The travelers spent the wet and gloomy winter of 1805–1806 near the point where the Columbia River flows into the Pacific. They began the return journey in March 1806. It took the party half a year to return to St. Louis. Their return, however, brought the American people a new awareness of a rich and beautiful part of the continent.

Pike's Expedition At the same time that Lewis and Clark were trekking back home, other Americans also hoped to learn more about the West. From 1806 to 1807, Zebulon Pike explored the southern part of the Louisiana Territory.

Pike led an expedition due west to the Rocky Mountains. There, he tried to climb a mountain that rose out of the Colorado plains. He made it about two thirds of the way to the top. Standing in snow up to his waist, he was forced to turn back. Today, this mountain is known as Pikes Peak.

Pike's return route took him into Spanish New Mexico. Early in 1807, Spanish troops arrested the members of the party as spies. The Spanish feared Pike was gathering information so that the Americans could take over the region. After several months of captivity, the men were released and escorted back to the United States. As the Spanish had feared, Pike's reports about the Spanish borderlands created great American interest in the region.

✓**Checkpoint** What goals did President Jefferson set for Lewis and Clark's expedition?

⭐ **Looking Back and Ahead** Lewis and Clark and Pike gave the United States detailed knowledge of the West. However, Americans had little time to digest this information. They soon found themselves caught up again in Europe's conflicts.

Distinguish Events in Sequence
What do the words "at the same time" tell you about the sequence of events? What was happening at the same time?

Section 2 | Check Your Progress

Progress Monitoring Online
For: Self-test with instant help
Visit: PHSchool.com
Web Code: mya-3052

Comprehension and Critical Thinking
1. **(a) Recall** Why was New Orleans important to the United States?
   (b) Identify Benefits What was the significance of the Louisiana Purchase?

2. **(a) Identify** Who was Sacagawea, and how was she important to the success of the Lewis and Clark expedition?
   (b) Compare and Contrast How was Pike's expedition similar to that of Lewis and Clark's? How was it different?

Reading Skill
3. **Distinguish Events in Sequence** Describe how the sequence of Lewis and Clark's expedition related to that of Zebulon Pike.

Key Terms
4. Draw a table with two rows and two columns. In the first column, list the key terms from this section: expedition, continental divide. In the next column, write the definition of each word.

Writing
5. Use this section and the following items to write a thesis statement about the life of Meriwether Lewis. **Items:** Born in 1774; Virginian; family friend of Jefferson; in 1792 asked by Jefferson to lead exploration of the Northwest; with Clark led expedition through Louisiana Territory; was appointed governor of Louisiana Territory in 1808; died mysteriously in 1809.

Section 2 Check Your Progress

1. **(a)** New Orleans was a major trading center for farmers.
   (b) The Louisiana Purchase expanded the nation and gave the United States control over New Orleans and all of the Mississippi River.

2. **(a)** Sacagawea was a Shoshone Native American who served as a guide and interpreter for the expedition.
   (b) Both explored the Louisiana Territory, but Pike explored the southern region while Lewis and Clark explored the northern region. Pike was not as successful as Lewis and Clark, having been captured and returned to the east by Spanish troops.

3. Answers should include details about the departure, success, and dangers of each expedition in the proper sequence.

4. Students' charts should include an accurate definition of the key terms.

5. Students should include the highlights from the life of Lewis in their thesis.

Assess and Reteach

Assess Progress L2
Have students complete Check Your Progress. Administer the Section Quiz.

All in One Teaching Resources, Section Quiz, Chapter 9, p. 61

To further assess student understanding, use the Progress Monitoring Transparency.

Progress Monitoring Transparencies, Chapter 9, Section 2

Reteach L1
If students need more instruction, have them read this section in the Interactive Reading and Notetaking Study Guide.

📖 **Interactive Reading and Notetaking Study Guide,** Chapter 9, Section 2 (Adapted Version also available.)

Extend L3
Have students read the excerpts from the journals of Lewis and Clark on the Primary Sources CD-ROM. Then ask students to rewrite the description of the team's expedition on pp. 317–319 in the form of journal entries.

💿 **Primary Sources CD-ROM,** Diary: The Journals of Lewis and Clark

Progress Monitoring Online
Students may check their comprehension of this section by completing the Progress Monitoring Online graphic organizer and self-quiz.

Answers

Reading Skill They tell you that two events were happening at the same time. Livingston and Monroe had made a deal with the French. At the same time, there was a revolution in Haiti that overthrew French colonialism.

✓**Checkpoint** Lewis and Clark were to report on the resources of the West, to make contact with Native Americans, and to establish claim to the land west of the Rockies.

Exploring the Louisiana Purchase

p. 320

Build Background Knowledge `L2`

Have students compare the map on these pages to the political map of the modern United States found in the Atlas of the Student Edition. Ask them to list the states through which Lewis and Clark traveled (*Missouri, Kansas, Nebraska, Iowa, South Dakota, North Dakota, Montana, Idaho, Oregon, Washington*) Explain that the information Lewis and Clark gathered about the West helped lead to settlement in these future states.

Instruction `L2`

- Read the introduction aloud with students. Then have students trace their fingers along the expedition route, pausing to read the captions as they reach each one.

- Direct students' attention again to the map. Ask: **In which direction did Lewis and Clark travel?** (*west*) Ask students to name the geographic features through which they traveled. (*Missouri, Jefferson, Snake, and Columbia rivers; Rocky Mountains*)

- Have students read Legacy of the Expedition. Ask students to predict how Manifest Destiny would affect Native Americans in the West. (*Answers will vary but students should recognize that many Native Americans would probably be forced from their lands and that their ways of life might change.*) Address any misconceptions that students may have about the topic. Remind them to confirm or revise their predictions after they read the next section.

Monitor Progress

Ask students to think about a time they traveled somewhere they had never been. Have them write 10 adjectives describing the experience. Ask them to consider which of these adjectives might be used to describe Lewis and Clark's journey and why.

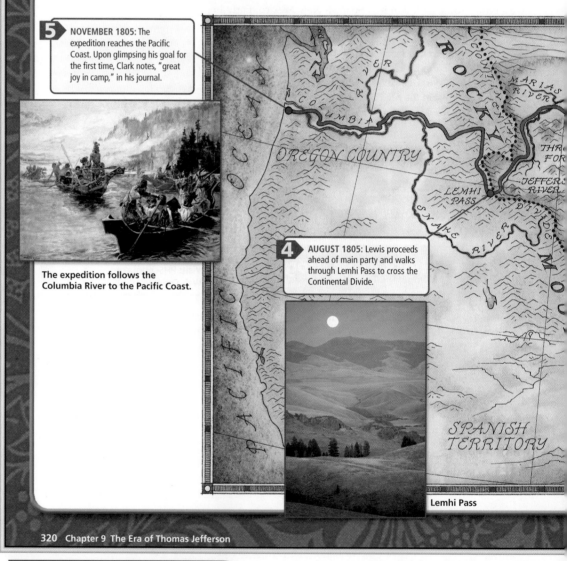

GEOGRAPHY AND HISTORY

Exploring the Louisiana Purchase

An atmosphere of eager anticipation filled the air as Meriwether Lewis and William Clark and their men set out to explore the vast lands that lay west of the Mississippi River. Use the map below to follow Lewis and Clark on their journey to the Pacific Ocean.

5 NOVEMBER 1805: The expedition reaches the Pacific Coast. Upon glimpsing his goal for the first time, Clark notes, "great joy in camp," in his journal.

The expedition follows the Columbia River to the Pacific Coast.

4 AUGUST 1805: Lewis proceeds ahead of main party and walks through Lemhi Pass to cross the Continental Divide.

Lemhi Pass

320 Chapter 9 The Era of Thomas Jefferson

Differentiated Instruction

`L1` **Less Proficient Readers**

Create a Timeline Give students a large piece of poster board and have students make a timeline of the events shown on the map to enhance their comprehension of Lewis and Clark's journey. Ask students to illustrate each event above or below the event's description on the timeline.

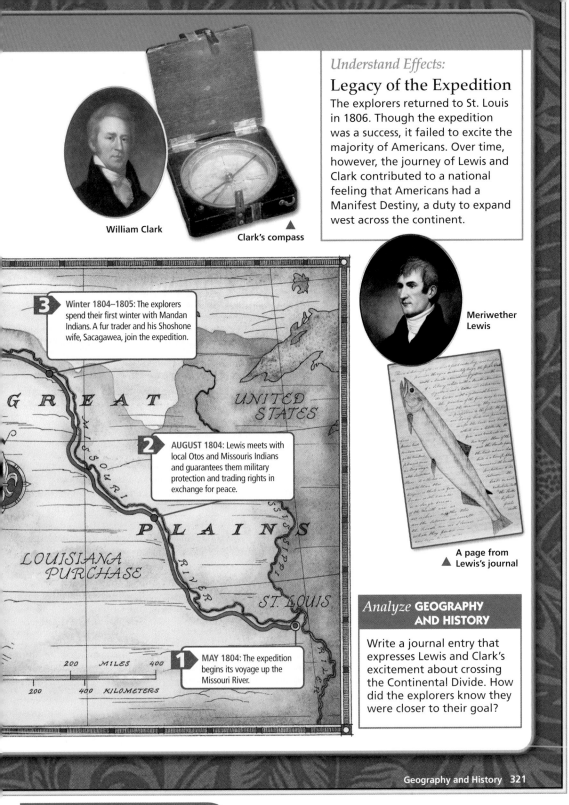

Understand Effects:

Legacy of the Expedition

The explorers returned to St. Louis in 1806. Though the expedition was a success, it failed to excite the majority of Americans. Over time, however, the journey of Lewis and Clark contributed to a national feeling that Americans had a Manifest Destiny, a duty to expand west across the continent.

William Clark

▲ **Clark's compass**

Meriwether Lewis

▲ **A page from Lewis's journal**

3 Winter 1804–1805: The explorers spend their first winter with Mandan Indians. A fur trader and his Shoshone wife, Sacagawea, join the expedition.

GREAT

UNITED STATES

2 AUGUST 1804: Lewis meets with local Otos and Missouris Indians and guarantees them military protection and trading rights in exchange for peace.

P L A I N S

LOUISIANA PURCHASE

RIVER

ST. LOUIS

| 200 MILES 400 |
| 200 400 KILOMETERS |

1 MAY 1804: The expedition begins its voyage up the Missouri River.

Analyze GEOGRAPHY AND HISTORY

Write a journal entry that expresses Lewis and Clark's excitement about crossing the Continental Divide. How did the explorers know they were closer to their goal?

History Background

Honoring Sacagawea There are many memorials in the United States dedicated to Sacagawea. Among them are Sacagawea State Park and Lake Sacagawea in Washington, and a bronze Sacagawea Monument in Salmon, Idaho, that marks what is thought to be her birthplace. Sacagawea is also pictured on the U.S. dollar coin.

Writing Rubric Share the rubric with students before they begin writing.

Score 1 Sentences are incomplete, unrelated to topic.

Score 2 Sentences address topic, but are unsupported.

Score 3 Sentences are thoughtful, supported by facts.

Score 4 Sentences are accurate, use good examples, creative.

Answer

Analyze GEOGRAPHY AND HISTORY

Students should write a short journal entry about each of the five events described on the map.

Review and Preview

Students have read about the disputes the United States had with Great Britain and France under Washington and Adams. Now students will learn how Jefferson responded to entanglements with foreign nations.

Section Focus Question

How did Jefferson respond to threats to the security of the nation?

Before you begin the lesson for the day, write the Section Focus Question on the board. (*Lesson focus: Jefferson responded with attacks and embargos.*)

Prepare to Read

Build Background Knowledge　L2

Ask a student volunteer to define the word *neutral*. Explain that the United States under Jefferson had a neutrality policy, which kept the U.S. out of conflicts between other nations. Have students brainstorm the possible benefits of neutrality (*no wars and the ability to trade with many nations*) and possible problems that could stem from it (*warring nations might attack, no strong allies*). Use the Give One, Get One participation strategy (TE, p. T25) to elicit responses.

Set a Purpose　L2

- Read each statement in the Reading Readiness Guide aloud. Ask students to mark the statements True or False.

   All in One Teaching Resources, Unit 3, Reading Readiness Guide, p. 49

- Have students discuss the statements in pairs or groups of four, then mark their worksheets again. Use the Numbered Heads participation strategy (TE, p. T24) to call on students to share their group's perspectives. The students will return to these worksheets later.

This Dreadful Fight

“The Indians are committing depredations [attacks] upon the white inhabitants located upon our Western frontier.... The British furnish them with arms, ammunition, and rations.... Many... are made widows and orphans by this dreadful fight.”

—Lydia B. Bacon, wife of U.S. army officer in Indiana Territory, 1811

◄ American troops and Indians clash at the Battle of Tippecanoe.

A Time of Conflict

Objectives
- Discuss how the United States defeated the Barbary pirates.
- Explain how war in Europe hurt American trade.
- Discuss the causes and effects of the Embargo Act.
- Identify the events leading up to the Battle of Tippecanoe.

Reading Skill

Explain How Events Are Related in Time Many events that occur in sequence have cause-and-effect relationships. Explaining how events are related in time will help you find these cause-and-effect links. As you read this section, look for events that have this relationship.

Key Terms and People

tribute
Stephen Decatur
embargo
smuggling

Tecumseh
William Henry
　Harrison

Why It Matters Under Washington and Adams, the United States had become entangled in the dispute between France and Britain. That problem did not go away. It rose again with added fury during the administration of Thomas Jefferson.

❓ **Section Focus Question: How did Jefferson respond to threats to the security of the nation?**

Defeating the Barbary States

Trade with Europe was critical to the U.S. economy. Americans sold crops and natural resources to customers in Europe. They purchased manufactured goods made in Europe.

After the American Revolution, pirates began attacking American ships in the Mediterranean Sea. The pirates came from four small countries on the North African coast—Morocco, Algiers, Tunisia, and Tripoli. Together, these countries were known as the Barbary States.

Barbary pirates raided European and American ships, taking property and enslaving sailors and holding them for ransom. European governments stopped such raids by paying the Barbary States **tribute**—money paid by one country to another in return for protection. In exchange, their rulers agreed to leave European ships alone.

For a time, the United States also paid tribute. But Jefferson stopped this practice and sent warships to the Mediterranean Sea to protect American merchant ships. At first, these military patrols went badly. The warship *Philadelphia* ran aground near the Tripoli coast and its crew was imprisoned. To keep the pirates from using the ship, American sailors led by **Stephen Decatur** raided Tripoli harbor in 1804 and burned the *Philadelphia* down to the waterline.

322　Chapter 9　The Era of Thomas Jefferson

Differentiated Instruction

L3 Advanced Readers　　**L3 Gifted and Talented**

Research Tell students that the policy of impressment was not new in the 1700s. Have students research impressment and identify other warring nations that prac-

ticed impressment. In a brief report, have them summarize one of the conflicts they read about and tell how the conflict was resolved.

The next year, a small force of American marines marched 600 miles across the Sahara and captured Tripoli. A line in the U.S. Marine Corps anthem—"To the shores of Tripoli"—recalls that victory. It inspired a wave of confidence in the ability of the United States to deal forcefully with foreign powers that threatened American security and prosperity.

✓**Checkpoint** How did European nations protect themselves against raids by the Barbary pirates?

American Neutrality Is Challenged

A more serious threat to American overseas trade came from two much more powerful countries, Britain and France. By 1803, the two nations once again were at war. The United States remained neutral.

Because it was neutral, the United States continued trading with both Britain and France. The war in Europe had created opportunities for Americans to sell their products there.

Meanwhile, Britain and France looked for ways to weaken each other. One method was to cut off the other country's foreign trade. British warships started seizing American ships trading with France. French warships did the same to American ships trading with Britain. Between 1803 and 1807, France seized 500 American ships and Britain seized more than 1,000.

Britain badly needed sailors for its war against France. So it turned again to impressment. As a result, thousands of American sailors were forced to serve in the British navy.

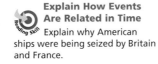
Explain How Events Are Related in Time Explain why American ships were being seized by Britain and France.

Impressment
A nineteenth-century woodprint shows unfortunate American sailors being impressed by British gangs. Conditions on board British warships were harsh.
Critical Thinking: *Draw Conclusions* *What impact do you think impressment had on the performance of the British navy?*

Section 3 A Time of Conflict **323**

Vocabulary Builder

Use the information below to teach students this section's high-use words.

High-Use Word	Definition and Sample Sentence
decline, p. 324	*v.* to gradually lose strength or power The strength of the Continental army **declined** after Valley Forge.
restore, p. 326	*v.* to bring back to a former condition The Loyalists hoped to **restore** British power in the colonies.

Jefferson Responds With an Embargo

p. 324

Instruction L2

- Read Jefferson Responds With an Embargo with students. Remind them to look for the sequence of events.

- Ask: **Why was the embargo ineffective for the United States?** (*Neither foreign country relied on the U.S. for shipping or goods so the embargo did not hurt them. The United States did rely on trade so it ended up hurting the country's economy.*)

- Assign the worksheet Jefferson Addresses Foreign Conflict and have students work in pairs to identify the risks and benefits associated with Jefferson's foreign policies. Then recreate the chart on the board and have student volunteers fill it in with their answers. At this time, you can also assign the worksheet Jefferson's Conflicts Overseas. (See Differentiated Instruction activity below.)

  All in One Teaching Resources, Unit 3, Jefferson Addresses Foreign Conflict, p. 55

Independent Practice

Have students continue filling in the study guide for this section.

Interactive Reading and Notetaking Study Guide, Chapter 9, Section 3

Monitor Progress

As students fill in the Notetaking Study Guide, circulate to make sure individuals understand the causes and effects of Jefferson's decision to impose an embargo. Provide assistance as needed.

Carving Up the World

George III   Napoleon

Reading Political Cartoons

Skills Activity

Britain's King George III and French leader Napoleon Bonaparte are shown dividing the world in this American cartoon. Their rivalry drew the United States into a conflict it did not want to enter.

(a) Identify Main Ideas What portion of the globe is Napoleon taking? What portion is King George taking?

(b) Detect Points of View What do you think the cartoonist's opinion is of the two European leaders?

Beginning in 1805, Britain and France increased their efforts to attack trade with their foes. No matter what American merchant ships did, they risked being seized by either Britain or France.

Checkpoint Why did Britain and France attack American merchant ships?

Jefferson Responds With an Embargo

The President looked for peaceful methods to force Britain and France to respect American neutrality. He decided to use an **embargo**—a government order that forbids foreign trade. In 1807, Congress passed the Embargo Act. It imposed a total embargo on American ships sailing to any foreign port. Jefferson predicted that both countries would soon cease attacking American ships.

Things did not turn out as Jefferson expected. Indeed, the big loser proved to be the United States. In just one year, American exports fell from $109 million to $25 million. Prices of American crops declined, hurting farmers and planters. Tens of thousands of Americans lost their jobs.

Many Americans were outraged by the embargo. Anger was greatest in New England, where merchants depended heavily on foreign trade. Thousands of Americans turned to **smuggling**—the act of illegally importing or exporting goods—in order to evade the embargo.

Vocabulary Builder
decline (dee KLĪN) **v.** to gradually lose strength or power

324 Chapter 9 The Era of Thomas Jefferson

Answers

Reading Political Cartoons (a) the portion containing Europe; much of the Western Hemisphere **(b)** The cartoonist thinks the leaders are greedy.

Checkpoint Impressment was the practice of kidnapping and forcing American sailors to serve in the British navy. It angered Americans because it demonstrated a lack of respect for the United States as a sovereign nation.

324 Chapter 9

Differentiated Instruction

L1 English Language Learners   **L1 Less Proficient Readers**   **L1 Special Needs**

Gaining Comprehension Assign the worksheet Jefferson's Conflicts Overseas to students who need extra help understanding the concepts of the section. Have students work together in pairs to identify the causes and effects. Provide assistance as needed.

All in One Teaching Resources, Unit 3, Jefferson's Conflicts Overseas, p. 56

Congress finally repealed the Embargo Act in 1809, just before Jefferson left office. Then, Congress passed a less severe law that reopened foreign trade with every country except Britain and France. The law stated that the United States would reopen trade with those countries when they started respecting America's trading rights as a neutral nation.

☑Checkpoint **Why did President Jefferson place an embargo on foreign goods in 1807?**

Tecumseh and the Prophet

In the years after the Battle of Fallen Timbers, tens of thousands of settlers moved westward. Ohio became a state in 1803. Americans continued to push into new areas. They settled in the territory of Indiana and other lands farther west.

The tide of settlement had a grave impact on Native Americans. Diseases such as measles, smallpox, and influenza killed thousands of Native Americans who had never been exposed to such diseases before. Settlers took over large parts of the Native American hunting grounds. Deer and other animals the Native Americans depended on were driven away as farmers cleared the forests for planting. The Native American population decreased, and the power of their traditional leaders declined.

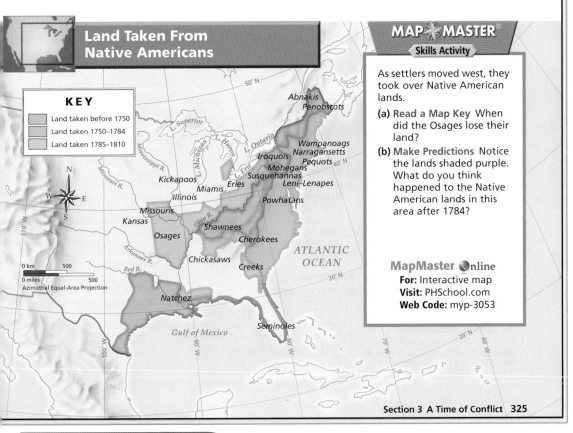

Land Taken From Native Americans

KEY
- Land taken before 1750
- Land taken 1750–1784
- Land taken 1785–1810

MAP MASTER®
Skills Activity

As settlers moved west, they took over Native American lands.

(a) Read a Map Key When did the Osages lose their land?

(b) Make Predictions Notice the lands shaded purple. What do you think happened to the Native American lands in this area after 1784?

MapMaster Online
For: Interactive map
Visit: PHSchool.com
Web Code: myp-3053

History Background

Tecumseh's Warning When Tecumseh saw the approach of the War of 1812, he joined forces with the British, who also wanted to stem the tide of white settlement in the West. Tecumseh's goal was to drive all settlers out of the Northwest Territory. He issued this warning to the white settlers:

"You are continually driving the red people [from their land] when at last you will drive them into the [ocean]. . . . You ought to know what you are doing with the Indians. . . . It is a very bad thing and we do not like it."

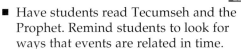

Tecumseh and the Prophet
p. 325

Instruction L2

- Have students read Tecumseh and the Prophet. Remind students to look for ways that events are related in time.

- Ask: **What impact did the white settlers have on the Native Americans?** (*White settlers brought diseases that killed thousands of Native Americans, took their land, and drove away much of the game Native Americans hunted for food, shrinking population even further.*)

- Ask students to explain why Tecumseh was a threat to the security of the United States. (*He was organizing the many different Native American tribes to fight together against the white settlers. He also received support from Britain.*)

Independent Practice

Have students complete the study guide for this section.

📖 **Interactive Reading and Notetaking Study Guide,** Chapter 9, Section 3 (Adapted Version also available.)

Monitor Progress

- Check Notetaking Study Guide entries for student understanding of the impact of Tecumseh's activities on the nation.

- Tell students to fill in the last column of the Reading Readiness Guide. Probe for what they learned that confirms or invalidates each statement.

All in One **Teaching Resources, Unit 3,** Reading Readiness Guide, p. 49

Answers

☑**Checkpoint** to try to force Britain and France to respect American neutrality

MAP MASTER Skills Activity **(a)** 1785–1810 **(b)** They were occupied by white settlers.

Assess and Reteach

Assess Progress L2

Have students complete Check Your Progress. Administer the Section Quiz.

All in One Teaching Resources, Section Quiz, Chapter 9, p. 62

To further assess student understanding, use the Progress Monitoring Transparency.

Progress Monitoring Transparencies, Chapter 9, Section 3

Reteach L1

If students need more instruction, have them read this section in the Interactive Reading and Notetaking Study Guide and complete the accompanying question.

Interactive Reading and Notetaking Study Guide, Chapter 9, Section 3 (Adapted Version also available.)

Extend L3

Many of the foreign policy decisions that Jefferson made were hotly contested in Congress. Have students, acting as members of Congress, hold a debate over one of the policies covered in the section. Divide students into two groups. Have one group of students criticize Jefferson's policy and another group defend it. Allow time for each group to prepare their arguments.

Progress Monitoring Online

Students may check their comprehension of this section by completing the Progress Monitoring Online graphic organizer and self-quiz.

Answer

☑**Checkpoint** to preserve traditional ways, resist further settlement, and stop quarreling with each other; Tecumseh organized the western tribes into a league.

New Leaders Take Charge The Shawnee people were hard hit by these developments. After 1805, two Shawnee brothers—Tenskwatawa (tehn SKWAH tuh wuh) and Tecumseh (tih KUHM suh)—began urging Native American resistance. Tecumseh and Tenskwatawa, who was also known as the Prophet, called on Native Americans to preserve traditional ways.

Tecumseh organized the western tribes into a league to <u>restore</u> Indian lands. He traveled widely spreading his message.

Harrison's Victory American officials were deeply concerned by Tecumseh's activities. In 1811, William Henry Harrison, governor of the Indiana Territory, decided to take action. While Tecumseh was traveling in search of allies, Harrison marched a thousand soldiers against Shawnee villages on the Tippecanoe River. In the Battle of Tippecanoe, Harrison defeated the Native Americans.

The Battle of Tippecanoe marked the high point of Native American opposition to settlement. Even though the alliance declined in power after the battle, Tecumseh and his warriors continued their struggle during the next several years.

☑**Checkpoint** What actions did Tecumseh and the Prophet urge on their followers?

⭐ **Looking Back and Ahead** Tensions remained high in the West even after Harrison's victory. Many Americans blamed the British, who continued to send arms to the Native Americans. There were widespread calls for war with Britain. Could the President and Congress resist them?

Section 3 | Check Your Progress

Progress Monitoring Online
For: Self-test with instant help
Visit: PHSchool.com
Web Code: mya-3053

Comprehension and Critical Thinking

1. (a) Identify Who were the Barbary pirates?
(b) Identify Costs What was the United States risking when it refused to pay tribute to the Barbary pirates? Why do you think Jefferson believed it was worth the risk?

2. (a) Describe How did settlement in the West affect the Native Americans who lived there?
(b) Clarify Problems Why were Native Americans of the West more likely to favor the British than the Americans?

Reading Skill

3. Explain How Events Are Related in Time What happened after Congress passed a law to undo the Embargo Act? Explain the connection between the Embargo Act and the new law.

Key Terms

4. Write two definitions for each key term: tribute, embargo, smuggling. First, write a formal definition for your teacher. Second, write a definition in everyday English for a classmate.

Writing

5. Read the following thesis statement: "Thomas Jefferson's presidency was clouded by international problems." Review the information in this section and choose four facts or details from the section that support this thesis statement. Then, based on the supporting items you chose, write several sentences developing the thesis statement.

Section 3 Check Your Progress

1. (a) They were seamen from the Barbary States in North Africa who attacked foreign ships, taking property and kidnapping sailors for ransom.
(b) It risked the lives of American sailors. It was important to prove American military strength.

2. (a) Native Americans caught diseases from settlers, had land taken from them, and their game fled from lands cleared by the settlers.

(b) The British also resisted the expansion of American settlement.

3. The United States began trading with countries other than Britain and France. The new law made this trade possible.

4. Students' definitions should accurately define each vocabulary word.

5. Students should include details about the Barbary pirates, British and French attacks on American ships, the Embargo Act, and Tecumseh's activities.

I Must Leave This House

"I am still here within sound of the cannon! . . . I have had [a wagon] filled with the . . . most valuable portable articles. . . . I insist on waiting until the large picture of Gen. Washington is secured. . . . And now, dear sister, I must leave this house."

—Dolley Madison, letter describing British attack on the White House, 1814

◄ British soldiers burn the White House.

The War of 1812

Objectives

- Explain why the United States declared war on Britain.
- Describe what happened in the early days of the war.
- Discuss the American invasion of Canada and the fighting in the South.
- Identify the events leading to the end of the War of 1812.

🔁 Reading Skill

Explain How Events Are Related in Time Events can be related in time in many ways. One event may directly cause another or events may unfold over time. As you read this section, try to relate the many events to one another in time. Use the skills you practiced in Sections 1–3 as tools. Also, use sequence verbs as a tool. These verbs describe how events progress over time.

Key Terms and People

nationalism
war hawk
blockade

Oliver Hazard
   Perry
Andrew Jackson
secede

Why It Matters Presidents Washington, Adams, and Jefferson had all worked hard to avoid war with Britain and France. But finally, in 1812, the United States declared war on Britain.

❓ **Section Focus Question: What were the causes and effects of the War of 1812?**

The Move Toward War

Tension with Britain was high when James Madison took office in 1809. Americans were angry at Britain for arming Native Americans in the Northwest. Americans also resented the continued impressment of American sailors by the British.

To most Americans, the country's honor was at stake. They felt a new sense of American nationalism—pride in one's country. In 1810, two strong nationalists, Henry Clay of Kentucky and John C. Calhoun of South Carolina, became leaders in the House of Representatives.

Clay, Calhoun, and their supporters were called war hawks—those who were eager for war with Britain. Opposition to war was strongest in New England. Many New Englanders believed war with Britain would harm American trade.

Relations with Britain worsened steadily in the early months of 1812. In the spring, the British told the United States they would continue impressing sailors. Meanwhile, Native Americans in the Northwest began new attacks on frontier settlements. In June, Congress declared war on Britain.

☑**Checkpoint** **In what regions of the United States was the support for war with Britain the strongest?**

Section 4 The War of 1812 **327**

Vocabulary Builder

Use the information below to teach students this section's high-use words.

High-Use Word	Definition and Sample Sentence
reinforce, p. 328	*v.* to strengthen with additional troops At Yorktown, American forces were **reinforced** by the French navy.
critic, p. 331	*n.* someone who makes judgments on the value of actions The Antifederalists were **critics** of the U.S. Constitution.

Chapter 9 Section 4 **327**

Teach

The Move Toward War
p. 327

Early Days of the War
p. 328

Instruction L2

- **Vocabulary Builder** Before teaching this section, preteach the High-Use Words **reinforce** and **critic** using the strategy on TE p. T21.

  Key Terms Have students complete the See It–Remember It chart.

- Read The Move Toward War and Early Days of the War with students using the Partner Paragraph Shrinking strategy (TE, p. T23).

- Ask students to name the Congressmen who were most eager for war. (*Henry Clay and John C. Calhoun*)

- Ask: **How do you think the early days of the war might have been different if Jefferson had not cut military spending?** (*Students might think that Americans would have been able to better defend themselves with more weapons, ships, and better trained officers.*)

- Show students the History Interactive transparency *Old Ironsides and the War of 1812.* Ask: **What made Old Ironsides so strong?** (*its thick hull*)

Color Transparencies, Old Ironsides and the War of 1812

Independent Practice

Have students begin filling in the study guide.

Monitor Progress

As students fill in the Notetaking Study Guide, circulate to make sure individuals understand why the War of 1812 began. Provide assistance as needed.

Answers

☑**Checkpoint** Its military was small and underfunded.

Identify Benefits They made it harder for the British to defeat the United States.

Early Days of the War

The war did not come at a good time for the British, who were still at war in Europe. However, Britain was not willing to meet American demands to avoid war. Providing Native Americans with support was one way of protecting Canada against an American invasion.

When the war began, Americans were confident that they would win. It soon became apparent that the United States was not prepared for war. Jefferson's spending cuts had weakened American military strength. The navy had only 16 warships ready for action. The army also was small, with fewer than 7,000 men.

In the first days of the war, the British set up a blockade of the American coast. A **blockade** is the action of shutting a port or road to prevent people or supplies from coming into an area or leaving it. By 1814, the British navy had 135 warships blockading American ports. After reinforcing their troops, the British were able to close off all American ports by war's end.

A major sea battle was fought at the beginning of the war. In August 1812, the USS *Constitution* defeated the British warship *Guerrière* (gai ree AIR) in a fierce battle. According to tradition, American sailors nicknamed the *Constitution* "Old Ironsides" because British artillery fire bounced off the ship's thick wooden hull. To the Americans, it seemed as if the *Constitution* were made of iron.

☑**Checkpoint** Why was the United States unprepared for war?

Vocabulary Builder
reinforce (ree ihn FORS) **v.** to strengthen with additional troops

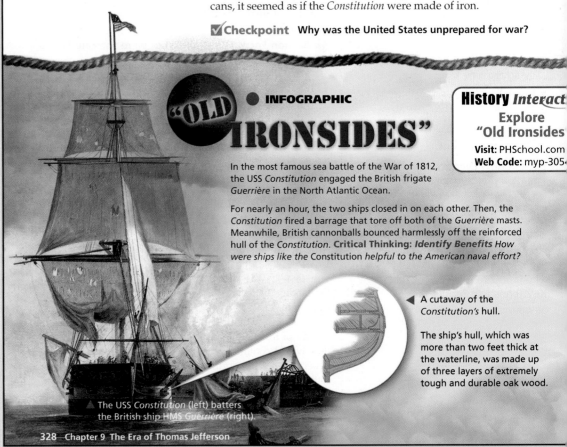

● **INFOGRAPHIC**

"OLD IRONSIDES"

History *Interact*
Explore
"Old Ironsides
Visit: PHSchool.com
Web Code: myp-305

In the most famous sea battle of the War of 1812, the USS *Constitution* engaged the British frigate *Guerrière* in the North Atlantic Ocean.

For nearly an hour, the two ships closed in on each other. Then, the *Constitution* fired a barrage that tore off both of the *Guerrière* masts. Meanwhile, British cannonballs bounced harmlessly off the reinforced hull of the *Constitution*. **Critical Thinking:** *Identify Benefits How were ships like the* Constitution *helpful to the American naval effort?*

◀ A cutaway of the *Constitution's* hull.

The ship's hull, which was more than two feet thick at the waterline, was made up of three layers of extremely tough and durable oak wood.

▲ The USS *Constitution* (left) batters the British ship HMS *Guerrière* (right).

328 Chapter 9 The Era of Thomas Jefferson

Differentiated Instruction

L1 **English Language Learners**   L1 **Less Proficient Readers**   L1 **Special Needs**

Vocabulary Development Have students make a list of the key terms and high-use words in this section. Then have them create flashcards with the word on one side and its definition on the other. Pair each student with a partner and have them quiz each other on the definitions of the words, using the flashcards. For English Language Learners, have students add pictures to the flashcards.

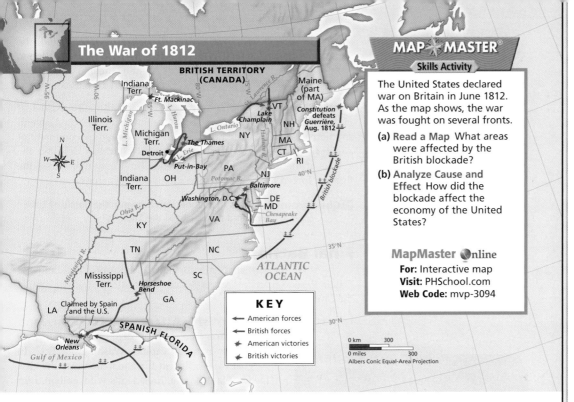

The War of 1812

BRITISH TERRITORY (CANADA)

MAP★MASTER®
Skills Activity

The United States declared war on Britain in June 1812. As the map shows, the war was fought on several fronts.

(a) Read a Map What areas were affected by the British blockade?

(b) Analyze Cause and Effect How did the blockade affect the economy of the United States?

MapMaster Online
For: Interactive map
Visit: PHSchool.com
Web Code: mvp-3094

KEY
← American forces
← British forces
✦ American victories
✦ British victories

0 km 300
0 miles 300
Albers Conic Equal-Area Projection

The War in the West and South

In the West, the Americans and British fought for control of the Great Lakes and the Mississippi River. Both sides had Native American allies.

Invasion of Canada Even before the war began, war hawks were demanding an invasion of Canada. They expected Canadians to welcome the chance to throw off British rule.

In July 1812, American troops under General William Hull invaded Canada from Detroit. Hull was unsure of himself. Fearing he did not have enough soldiers, he soon retreated.

The British commander, General Isaac Brock, took advantage of Hull's confusion. His army of British soldiers and Native American warriors quickly surrounded Hull's army and forced it to surrender. The British captured more than 2,000 American soldiers. It was a serious defeat for the United States.

American forces had better luck on Lake Erie. Both sides were aware of the importance of controlling the lake. A key three-hour battle took place at Put-In-Bay, in the western part of the lake, in 1813.

During the battle, the American flagship was badly damaged. The American commander, Oliver Hazard Perry, switched to another ship and continued the fight until it was won. Perry announced his victory with a dramatic message: "We have met the enemy and they are ours." With Americans in control of the lake, the British were forced to leave Detroit and retreat back into Canada.

History Background

Uncle Sam During the War of 1812, Samuel "Uncle Sam" Wilson of Troy, New York, supplied meat to the American army. The barrels containing meat were marked U.S., for United States, but many assumed that the initials stood for Uncle Sam. Soon "Uncle Sam" became the nickname for the government of the United States.

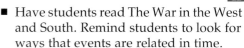

The War in the West and South

p. 329

Instruction [L2]

- Have students read The War in the West and South. Remind students to look for ways that events are related in time.

- Discuss the results of Hull's invasion of Canada. (*The British forced Hull's army to surrender and captured more than 2,000 American soldiers.*)

- Ask students to draw conclusions about why the Great Lakes were so important in the War of 1812. (*Control of the Great Lakes meant control over access to the center of the nation.*)

- Have students discuss the effects of the war on Native Americans. (*They suffered many defeats and had to give up a great deal of territory.*)

Independent Practice

Have students continue filling in the study guide for this section.

Interactive Reading and Notetaking Study Guide, Chapter 9, Section 4 (Adapted Version also available.)

Monitor Progress

As students fill in the Notetaking Study Guide, circulate to make sure individuals understand the military actions that took place in the West and in the South. Provide assistance as needed. If students do not seem to have a good understanding of the material, have them reread the section.

Answers

MAP★MASTER Skills Activity **(a)** the Atlantic coast, the Gulf of Mexico **(b)** It limited trade with other nations. As a result, American merchants lost profits. Also, Americans had limited access to the foreign goods that they wanted.

Final Battles

p. 330

Instruction `L2`

- Have students read Final Battles. Point out the reading Checkpoint question and tell students to look for details that support it as they read.

- Ask: **How did the war change after the British made peace with France?** (*The British had more resources to send to fight the war in America.*)

- Assign the Dolley Madison worksheet and discuss how Madison's actions would have inspired great pride among Americans. (*She showed courage, taking a risk to rescue a national treasure.*)

    All in One Teaching Resources, Dolley Madison, p. 57

- Ask: **What were some of the effects of the War of 1812?** (*Some people believed it forced Europe to treat the United States with more respect; New Englanders were critical of the war and the government and wanted to secede; Washington, D.C., was burned; "The Star-Spangled Banner" was written.*)

Independent Practice

Have students complete the study guide for this section.

Monitor Progress

- Check Notetaking Study Guide entries for student understanding of the final battles and the effects of the war.

- Tell students to fill in the last column of the Reading Readiness Guide.

- Have students go back to their Word Knowledge Rating Form. Rerate their word knowledge and complete the last column with a definition or example.

    All in One Teaching Resources, Unit 3, Reading Readiness Guide, p. 50; Word Knowledge Rating Form, p. 46

Answers

Reading Skill The Battle of the Thames took place after the Battle of Lake Erie.

Checkpoint Americans won control of Lake Erie and followed the British into Canada, defeating them in the Battle of the Thames.

Biography Quest Answer: The British were breaking their promise to help fight U.S. troops.

Explain How Events Are Related in Time Did the Battle of the Thames take place before or after the Battle of Lake Erie?

As the British and their Native American allies retreated, the Americans under General William Henry Harrison pursued them. They followed the British into Canada, defeating them in the Battle of the Thames. Tecumseh was among those killed in the battle.

Conflict in the South Native Americans also suffered defeat in the South. In the summer of 1813, Creek warriors attacked several southern American settlements. Andrew Jackson took command of American forces in Georgia. In March 1814, Jackson defeated the Creeks at the Battle of Horseshoe Bend. The treaty that ended the fighting forced the Creeks to give up millions of acres of land.

Checkpoint What is the connection between the Battle of Lake Erie and the Battle of the Thames?

Final Battles

In 1814, the British finally defeated Napoleon. This allowed Britain to send many more troops across the Atlantic to fight against the United States.

The British Attack Washington and Baltimore The new British strategy was to attack the nation's capital, Washington, D.C. In August 1814, a British force marched into the city. Dolley Madison, the President's wife, gathered up the President's important papers and fled the White House. The British set fire to several government buildings, including the White House. Americans were shocked to learn that their army could not defend Washington.

The British now moved on to Baltimore. Their first objective was Fort McHenry, which defended the city's harbor. British warships bombarded the fort throughout the night of September 13, 1814. Francis Scott Key, a young American, watched the attack. At dawn, Key saw the American flag still flying over the fort. The Americans had beaten off the attack.

On the back of an old envelope, Key wrote a poem that he called "The Star-Spangled Banner." It told the story of his night's watch. The poem became popular and was set to music. In 1931, Congress made it the national anthem of the United States.

The War Ends By 1814, Britain had tired of war. Peace talks began in Ghent (gehnt), Belgium. On Christmas Eve 1814, the two sides signed the Treaty of Ghent, which ended the war. The treaty returned things to the way they had been before the war.

Biography Quest

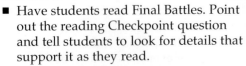

Tecumseh
1768–1813

The Shawnee war chief Tecumseh challenged the tide of white settlement. Tecumseh visited Native Americans from the Great Lakes to Florida, urging them to unite. He was away recruiting when General Harrison defeated the Shawnee at Tippecanoe. After the battle, Tecumseh allied his forces with the British, hoping that a British victory would mean the return of Native American lands. His death at the Battle of the Thames dealt a blow to Native American resistance.

Biography Quest Online

Why did Tecumseh issue an angry challenge to his allies, the British?

For: The answer to the question about Tecumseh

Visit: PHSchool.com

Web Code: myd-3054

Differentiated Instruction

L3 Advanced Readers   **L3 Gifted and Talented**

Research and Reenact Assign students to small groups. Have each group choose one of the battles of the War of 1812 to further research. Then have them create a play reenacting the events of the battle. Encourage students to create props appropriate to the time period. Have each group act out their play in front of the class.

News of the treaty took several weeks to reach the United States. In that time, the two sides fought one more battle. In January 1815, American forces under General Andrew Jackson won a stunning victory over the British at the Battle of New Orleans.

Protests and Peace From the start, there had been opposition to the War of 1812 within the United States. As the war dragged on, Federalist <u>critics</u> of President Madison spoke out more strongly, criticizing what they called "Mr. Madison's War." New Englanders in particular disliked the war, mainly because the blockade had badly damaged New England trade.

In December 1814, a group of Federalists met in Hartford, Connecticut. Some delegates to the Hartford Convention suggested that the New England states secede, or withdraw, from the United States. While the delegates debated, news of the peace treaty arrived. With the war over, the Hartford Convention quickly ended.

To some Americans, the War of 1812 was the "Second War of Independence." Once and for all, the United States secured its independence from Britain. European nations would now have to treat the young republic with respect. Pride at this achievement brought the confidence of Americans to a new height.

☑**Checkpoint** **What was the purpose of the Hartford Convention?**

⭐ **Looking Back and Ahead** After the War of 1812, Americans entered a new era of confidence. Tensions between regions, which had been high during the war, cooled with the coming of peace. In the postwar period, Americans enjoyed a period of calm and unity. As you will read in the next chapter, this era paved the way for a major expansion of American democracy.

Vocabulary Builder
critic (KRIHT ihk) **n.** someone who makes judgments on the value of actions

---

Section 4 | **Check Your Progress**

Progress Monitoring ⬤**nline**
For: Self-test with instant help
Visit: PHSchool.com
Web Code: mya-3054

Comprehension and Critical Thinking

1. (a) Identify Who were the war hawks? Why did they push for war with Britain?
(b) Draw Conclusions Were the war hawks overconfident? What did they overlook in their evaluation of British power?

2. (a) Recall How did the War of 1812 end?
(b) Analyze Cause and Effect What were some results of the war that were not expressly written in the treaty?

⬤ **Reading Skill**

3. Explain How Events Are Related in Time What battle was taking place at about the same time that William Hull was invading Canada?

Key Terms

Add a second sentence to each of the following sentences that clearly shows your understanding of the key term.
4. The War of 1812 increased U.S. nationalism. _____.
5. At the Hartford Convention, dissatisfied Federalists made plans

for the New England states to secede. _____.

Writing

6. Read the following notes about First Lady Dolley Madison and rearrange them in the best order for a biographical essay. **Notes:** Died in 1849; stylish woman; married James Madison in 1794; served as President Jefferson's official hostess; saved many valuables from White House when British invaded in 1814; turned Washington from a "dull swamp" into lively social city.

Assess Progress L2

Have students complete Check Your Progress. Administer the Section Quiz.

All in One Teaching Resources, Section Quiz, Chapter 9, p. 63

To further assess student understanding, use the Progress Monitoring Transparency.

Progress Monitoring Transparencies, Chapter 9, Section 4

Reteach L1

If students need more instruction, have them read this section in the Interactive Reading and Notetaking Study Guide and complete the accompanying question.

 Interactive Reading and Notetaking Study Guide, Chapter 9, Section 4 (Adapted Version also available.)

Extend L3

Have students use the History Interactive to explore the role of the USS *Constitution* in the War of 1812 online. Have students prepare a short news report of the event, giving the importance of the battle and the reaction of the people to the news. Have them present their work to the class. Provide students with the Web Code below.

Extend ⬤**nline**
For: Help in starting the Extend activity
Visit: PHSchool.com
Web Code: mye-3054

Progress Monitoring Online

Students may check their comprehension of this section by completing the Progress Monitoring Online graphic organizer and self-quiz.

Section 4 Check Your Progress

1. (a) Led by Clay and Calhoun, the war hawks were eager for war with Britain. Westerners wanted to end Native American resistance and seize Canada. Southerners wanted to seize Florida.
(b) The war hawks were probably overconfident. They overlooked the weakness of the American military and misjudged the power of the British military.

2. (a) It ended with the Treaty of Ghent. It returned things to the way they had been before the war.
(b) Many Americans felt great pride at having stood up to Britain; New Englanders were upset about the war and thought about seceding; Europe began to respect the United States more.

3. The Battle of Lake Erie

4. Possible answer: Americans felt an increased sense of pride in their nation.

5. Possible answer: They so opposed the war that they considered separating from the United States.

6. Notes should show how events are related.

Answer

☑**Checkpoint** to decide if New England should secede from the United States

Objective

People in the past, like people in the present, saw events through their own personal point of view. Finding and understanding these points of view will help students better understand historical issues and people. This analysis skill lesson will teach students how to detect historical points of view in primary sources.

Detect Historical Points of View

Instruction L2

1. Write the steps to detect historical points of view on the board and ask the class to read the steps aloud.

2. Ask students what kind of document this primary source is. (*a letter*) Have them suggest why a letter might be a good document to show historical point of view. (*Possible answer: A letter is written by an individual and expresses his or her opinions.*)

3. Practice the skill by following the steps on p. 332 as a class. Model each step to detect the point of view of the document. (*1. (a) to respond to the Danbury Baptist Association's question about national days of fasting and thanksgiving (b) The Bill of Rights banned a national church or religion. 2. Possible answer: that the government should not make laws about religious practices. 3. Possible answers: religion is a matter that is solely between a man and his god, no law respecting the establishment of religion, wall of separation between church and state 4. The writer feels that it would be wrong for him to establish national day of fasting and thanksgiving. 5. Possible answer: Jefferson was influenced by the passage of the Bill of Rights and the ideas in it about the separation of government and religion.*)

Monitor Progress

Ask students to do the Apply the Skill activity. Then assign the Skills for Life worksheet. As students complete the worksheet, circulate to make sure individuals are applying the skill steps effectively. Provide assistance as needed.

All in One Teaching Resources, Unit 3, Skills for Life Worksheet, p. 58

When reading a historical document, it is important to remember that the writer has a particular point of view, or way of looking at a subject. It is also important to consider how events of the time may have influenced the author's feelings.

The Danbury Baptist Association wrote to President Jefferson, asking why he would not establish national days of fasting and thanksgiving, as previous Presidents had done. Jefferson answered the letter in 1802. His carefully worded reply reflects his opinion about the separation of government and religion in the new nation.

Primary Source

"Believing with you that religion is a matter which lies solely between man & his god, that he owes account to none other for his faith or his worship, that the legitimate powers of government reach actions only, and not opinions, I contemplate with sovereign reverence that act of the whole American people which declared that their legislature should make no law respecting an establishment of religion, or prohibiting the free exercise thereof, thus building a wall of separation between church and state."

—Thomas Jefferson, Jan. 1, 1802

Learn the Skill

Use these steps to put historical points of view in context.

1. **Identify the context.** If you know the history of the period when a document was written, you can better understand the writer's point of view.

2. **Identify the main idea.** What main point does the writer make?

3. **Look for important words or phrases.** The writer may use key words or phrases that sum up the point of view being expressed.

4. **Identify point of view.** How does the writer or speaker feel about the subject?

5. **Relate point of view to context.** How was the point of view affected by historical context?

Practice the Skill

Answer the following questions about the primary source on this page.

1. **Identify the context.** (a) Why was this letter written? (b) How did the Bill of Rights address the issue of an American national church?

2. **Identify the main idea.** What is the main point of this letter?

3. **Look for important words or phrases.** What is an example of a key word or phrase that sums up the writer's point of view?

4. **Identify point of view.** How does the writer feel about the subject of the letter?

5. **Relate point of view to context.** How was Jefferson's point of view influenced by the events of the time?

Apply the Skill

See the Review and Assessment at the end of this chapter.

Reteach L1

If students need more instruction, use the Social Studies Skills Tutor to reteach this skill.

Social Studies Skills Tutor CD-ROM
Identifying Frame of Reference and Point of View

Quick Study Guide

How did Jefferson and Madison deal with unresolved problems?

Section 1
Jefferson Takes Office

- The Twelfth Amendment was added to the Constitution to prevent the deadlock in government that occurred when Jefferson and Burr received the same number of electoral votes in the election of 1800.
- In *Marbury* v. *Madison*, Chief Justice John Marshall and the Supreme Court established judicial review.

Section 2
The Louisiana Purchase

- In 1803, the United States purchased the Louisiana Territory from France.
- The Louisiana Purchase gave the United States control of the Mississippi River.
- Jefferson sent Lewis and Clark on an expedition to explore the new territory.

Section 3
A Time of Conflict

- In an attempt to punish Britain and France, Jefferson proposed the Embargo Act. The embargo hurt the U.S. economy.
- Native Americans were defeated when they opposed U.S. settlement in the Northwest Territory.

Section 4
The War of 1812

- The war hawks blamed Britain for trouble with the Native Americans and decreased trade.
- The War of 1812 ended without a clear victor, but the United States achieved a new sense of nationalism.

Exploring the Essential Question

Use the online study guide to explore the essential question.

Section 1
How did Jefferson chart a new course for the government?

Section 4
What were the causes and effects of the War of 1812?

Chapter 9 Essential Question
How did Jefferson and Madison deal with unresolved problems?

Section 2
What was the importance of the purchase and exploration of the Louisiana Territory?

Section 3
How did Jefferson respond to threats to the security of the nation?

Chapter 9

Essential Question

Remind students of the Chapter Essential Question: **How did Jefferson and Madison deal with unresolved problems?** Have them review the bulleted statements and the Visual Preview at the beginning of the chapter to help them answer this question.

To bolster students' retention, at this time they should complete the Study Guide in print or online. Remind students that they should also continue notetaking for the Unit and Chapter Essential Questions.

Interactive Reading and Notetaking Study Guide, Chapter 9 (Adapted Version also available.)

 Study Guide *Online,* Chapter 9

Chapter Challenge

To wrap up this chapter, students should apply the knowledge they have gained to answer this question. **How would the United States have been different if Britain had decisively defeated the United States in the War of 1812?** (*Answers may vary but students should recognize that the United States might not have become such a powerful nation and an economic leader.*)

Assessment at a Glance

Formal Assessment
- Chapter Tests A/B (L1/L2)
- AYP Monitoring Assessment
- Test Prep Workbook With Document-Based Assessment
- Test-Taking Strategies With Transparencies

Performance Assessment
- Group/Individual Activities, TE pp. 306g, 306h
- Teacher's Edition, pp. 313, 319, 326, 331
- Assessment Rubrics

Assessment Through Technology
- *ExamView* CD-ROM
- MindPoint CD-ROM
- Progress Monitoring Transparencies
- Progress Monitoring Online

Key Terms

1. judicial review
2. expedition
3. embargo
4. smuggling
5. continental divide

Comprehension and Critical Thinking

6. **(a)** Jefferson's view was that the federal government should have limited power. **(b)** Jefferson's purchase of Louisiana contradicted his view of limited powers. **(c)** Answers may vary, but students should recognize that many people today share Jefferson's philosophy that the government should have limited power over citizens and states.

7. **(a)** He felt that the last-minute appointments were a tactic by the Federalists to keep their power. **(b)** Marshall agreed with Marbury, but said the Judiciary Act was unconstitutional.

8. **(a)** dangerous rapids and strong currents in rivers, discouragingly long distances, cold winters, high mountains, and the danger of hostile Native Americans **(b)** The expeditions helped Americans learn more about the land, climate, and rivers of western lands. **(c)** Answers might include journeys to the ocean depths, to space, and to the Arctic regions.

9. **(a)** An act passed by Congress that prohibited foreign trade. **(b)** Congress reopened trade with all foreign countries except Britain and France.

10. **(a)** to protect their homeland, preserve their traditional ways, unite Native Americans, and resist further settlement of the West by white people **(b)** Settlers wanted to clear the forests for farmland. The Shawnee wanted to preserve the forests and continue living there.

11. **(a)** The British also wanted to stop the spread of American settlement to the West. **(b)** It helped Native Americans because they received guns from the British. It hurt them because the British were not as wholly committed to resisting American settlement as the Native Americans were.

Key Terms

Fill in the blanks with the correct key terms.

1. The principle of _____ gave the Supreme Court a central role in American government.

2. Lewis and Clark's _____ inspired many Americans to move west.

3. When Congress repealed Jefferson's _____ on trade, foreign trade was allowed again with every country except Britain and France.

4. During the Embargo Act, thousands of Americans turned to _____.

5. After crossing the _____ in the Rocky Mountains, Lewis and Clark began traveling on rivers that flowed to the Pacific Ocean.

Comprehension and Critical Thinking

6. **(a) Recall** What was Jefferson's view about the powers the federal government should have? **(b) Clarify Problems** How did he apply these views to the situation of buying Louisiana? **(c) Draw Conclusions** Use these situations and other information from the chapter to evaluate Jefferson's record as President.

7. **(a) Summarize** Why did Jefferson not want to keep William Marbury and other last-minute appointments of former President Adams on the federal payroll? **(b) Explain Problems** How did Chief Justice John Marshall deal with the problem created by James Madison's inaction?

8. **(a) Describe** What obstacles did Lewis and Clark's expedition encounter? **(b) Draw Conclusions** In what ways did Lewis and Clark's expedition help western settlers? **(c) Link Past and Present** What modern-day explorations compare to Lewis and Clark's and Pike's expeditions?

9. **(a) Recall** What was the Embargo Act of 1807? **(b) Identify Alternatives** What did Congress do to ease the economic effects of the embargo?

10. **(a) Summarize** What were the goals of Tecumseh and the Prophet? **(b) Detect Points of View** How did settler views differ from Shawnee views?

11. **(a) Recall** Why were many Native Americans allied with the British during the War of 1812? **(b) Identify Costs** Do you think siding with the British military helped or hurt the Native American cause? Explain.

History Reading Skill

12. **Relate Events in Time** Read the text under the heading "Lewis and Clark Explore the West." Which of these events happened first: Lewis and Clark headed up the Missouri River, or Lewis and Clark reached the mouth of the Platte River? What signal words offer clues to the sequence?

Writing

13. Write two paragraphs discussing Thomas Jefferson's experiences as President.
Your paragraphs should:
   - begin with a thesis statement that expresses your main impressions;
   - expand on that main idea with facts, examples, and other information;
   - conclude by stating Jefferson's most important contribution to the new nation.

14. **Write a Narrative:**
   What would it have been like to be an American sailor impressed by the British? Write a paragraph describing what the experience might have been like. Be sure to describe the conflicting emotions sailors may have felt.

Skills for Life

Detect Historical Points of View
Use the quotation below to answer the questions.

> "I consider the government of the United States as [prevented] by the Constitution from intermeddling religious institutions, their doctrines, discipline, or exercise. This results not only from the provision that no law shall be made respecting the establishment, or free exercise, of religion, but from that also which reserves to the states the powers not delegated to the U.S."
>
> —Thomas Jefferson, to Samuel Miller, Jan. 23, 1808

15. What is Jefferson's point of view?

16. How was Jefferson's point of view affected by historical events?

History Reading Skill

12. Lewis and Clark first headed up the Missouri River. The phrases that are clues to this sequence are "In the spring of 1804" and "In mid-July."

Writing

13. Paragraphs should include his views on government and the major events in Jefferson's administration, such as the *Marbury* v. *Madison* decision, the Louisiana Purchase, and his use of an embargo to keep Britain and France from interfering with American neutrality.

14. Paragraphs should show an understanding of being forced to serve in the British navy against one's will. The sailor needs to perform well to survive, but feels as if he is betraying his own country.

Progress Monitoring Online
For: Self-test with instant help
Visit: PHSchool.com
Web Code: mya-3056

Chapter 9
Review and Assessment

Test Yourself

1. Which of the following of Jefferson's policies negatively affected the American ability to fight the British in the War of 1812?

   A the increase of federal taxes

   B the Embargo Act of 1807

   C the purchase of the Louisiana Territory

   D the reduction of the military

2. Which present-day states were formed from the Louisiana Purchase?

   A Pennsylvania, New York, Massachusetts, and Maine

   B South Dakota, Nebraska, Kansas, and Oklahoma

   C Washington, Oregon, California, and Nevada

   D South Carolina, Virginia, Florida, and Georgia

Refer to the quotation below to answer Question 3.

> "Where are the Narragansett, the Mohican, the Pocanet, and other powerful tribes of our people? They have vanished before the avarice and oppression of the white man. . . . Will we let ourselves be destroyed in our turn?. . . Shall we, without a struggle, give up our homes . . .?"

3. Who was the likely speaker of this quotation?

   A President Thomas Jefferson

   B Chief Justice John Marshall

   C Native American leader Tecumseh

   D Secretary of State John Quincy Adams

Document-Based Questions

Task: Look at Documents 1 and 2, and answer their accompanying questions. Then, use the documents and your knowledge of history to complete this writing assignment:

Write a draft of a document explaining New England's opposition to the War of 1812 and expressing the region's views on the rights of states to challenge, or even separate from, the federal government.

Document 1: During the War of 1812, the British blockaded American ports. *Based on this map, how would the blockade affect merchants in New England?*

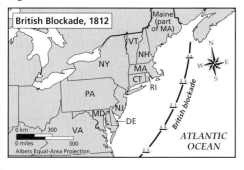

British Blockade, 1812

Maine (part of MA)
VT
NH
NY
MA
CT
RI
PA
NJ
MD
DE
VA
British blockade
ATLANTIC OCEAN
0 km 300
0 miles 300
Albers Equal-Area Projection

Document 2: In 1814, New Englanders meeting in the Hartford Convention called for increased states' rights and even considered secession from the Union. *In the portion of the document below, issued by the Hartford Convention, what causes are cited as reasons for separating from the Union?*

> "Events may prove that the causes of our calamities are deep and permanent. . . . They may be traced to implacable combinations of individuals, or of states, to monopolize power and office, and to trample without remorse upon the rights and interests of commercial sections of the Union.
> Whenever it shall appear that these causes are radical and permanent, a separation, by equitable arrangement, will be preferable to an alliance by constraint, among nominal friends. . . ."

Test Yourself

1. D
2. B
3. C

Document-Based Questions
Answers

Document 1 The blockade would drastically cut merchants' business.

Document 2 The document asserts that non-New Englanders control the Union and have acted against New England's interests.

Rubric: Write a Document

Share the rubric with students before they begin writing.

Score 1 Few facts, poorly organized, vague on reasons for New England's opposition.

Score 2 Meets some of requirements but misses others, lacks clarity in discussing how states might challenge federal government.

Score 3 Strong organization, includes details, but fails to link arguments effectively.

Score 4 Thorough and well organized, with varied sentence structure; makes a thoughtful analysis of New England's position and the issue of secession.

Chapter Review and Assessment **335**

For a more complete four-point rubric, see the Writing Rubrics in the Teaching Resources.

All in One Teaching Resources, Unit 3, p. 115

Skills for Life

15. Jefferson believed the Constitution forbade the federal government to make laws about religion.

16. Many of the early colonists came to America to have freedom of religion.

Professional Development

History Background

A Developing Sense of Nationalism and a Country's Place in the World

As the separate states developed a unified sense of goals and purpose, a sense of national pride and identity grew in the United States. This growing sense of nationalism accelerated when the new nation pulled together against the British in the War of 1812. The United States entered a period known as the Era of Good Feelings. Americans developed a strong feeling of unity and purpose.

This attitude affected the country's domestic and foreign policies for many years. Nationalism expressed itself in a belief that the United States was destined to expand to lands to its west. Actions by the Congress, the President, and the Supreme Court all increased federal authority to bind the country together.

By winning the War of 1812, the United States had ensured its own security against European intervention. With the Monroe Doctrine, it moved to stake out American leadership in the Western Hemisphere. It also presented a model for Europe's remaining colonies in the Americas. As they developed their own sense of nationalism, revolutions for independence became common.

Despite growing national pride and unity, there was an ongoing tension within the United States on two issues. First was the continuing argument about national versus state power. Second was the clash that was the result of varied regional economic interests.

These differences revealed themselves when the issue of tariffs arose in the early 1800s. The stringent tariffs proposed by representatives of Northeast merchants would help the industries that predominated in that area. Southern and Western farmers, on the other hand, believed tariffs would only hurt them. A debate also developed around several issues regarding slavery. Gradually, the nationalist tide gave way to rising sectionalism.

Essential Questions

Use this graphic organizer to see the relationship between key concepts and the Chapter Essential Question.

Focus Question/Section 1
How was the power of the federal government strengthened during the Era of Good Feelings?
(p. 340)

Concept: Compromise

Focus Question/Section 2
How did U.S. foreign affairs reflect new national confidence?
(p. 345)

Concept: Trade

Chapter Essential Question
How did the nation reflect a growing sense of national pride and identity?

Focus Question/Section 5
How did old issues take a new shape in the conflict over a national bank and tariffs?
(p. 362)

Concept: States' Rights

Focus Question /Section 4
Why did Jackson use force to remove Native Americans from the Southeast?
(p. 355)

Concept: Migration

Focus Question/Section 3
How did the people gain more power during the Age of Jackson?
(p. 349)

Concept: Power

Differentiated Instruction

Learning to Paraphrase

Analyze a Passage One active way of helping students learn how to paraphrase is to show them how to analyze a passage. Have students follow these steps.

1. Select a passage from the text that is 2–3 sentences long. Read and reread the passage.

2. Look up in a dictionary the meaning of any words that may be confusing.

3. Replace some of the words in the passage or combine several words into one idea.

4. Combine the sentences in a way that does not alter the main idea of the passage.

5. Ask yourself if the paraphrased sentence conveys the same meaning as the original.

6. List the words that you have left out of the original sentence. If any are important to the meaning of the passage, replace them in the paraphrased sentence.

Concepts Across Time

Have students develop an understanding of the enduring concepts of history by connecting these ideas.

Concept: Compromise

Students learning about how regional differences emerged during efforts to pass legislation affecting the national economy should recall what they learned about the Constitutional Convention. Ask: **What issues did delegates find it hard to agree on during the Convention?** (*slavery; national versus state power*) Discuss whether the compromises the delegates reached were likely to have permanently resolved the issues that had divided them. Explore this concept when discussing Building the National Economy in Section 1.

Concept: Trade

As students learn about trade expansion in the United States, have them recall the main trade issue between the colonies and Britain. Ask: **What was the trade theory that Britain wanted to follow but the colonies resisted?** (*The theory of mercantilism, under which the colonies were to supply raw materials for British factories to process into goods for sale to the colonies.*) Ask: **Why did Britain want to prevent the colonies from developing a strong manufacturing base?** (*to protect British manufacturers from competition*) Use these questions when discussing The Tariff of 1816 and Clay's American System in Section 1.

Concept: Migration

As students learn about the pressure of settlers to move to the frontier, have them recall what drove various groups to migrate to North America. Ask: **What peoples came to live in North America? What reasons did they have for leaving their old homes?** (*Native Americans had migrated to the continent long ago, looking for food and land. Europeans came seeking religious freedom and economic opportunities. Many Africans came against their will, having been captured and enslaved.*) Use these questions when discussing Indian Removal in Section 4.

Concept: States' Rights

As students read about the conflict over states' rights, have them recall why the Constitution replaced the Articles of Confederation as the governing document. Ask: **What problems did the United States have when the government operated under the Articles of Confederation?** (*The United States was very weak because Congress could not impose taxes, regulate trade, or collect money owed by the states.*) Discuss with students why many public officials today take an oath of office that includes a promise to "preserve, protect and defend the Constitution of the United States." Explore this concept when discussing Finance and States' Rights in Section 5.

Section 1 Building a National Identity

🕐 *1.5 periods, .75 block*

Objectives

Students will

1. Describe the feeling of national unity that followed the War of 1812.
2. Explain how Congress tried to strengthen the national economy.
3. Discuss how Supreme Court rulings supported federal power and economic growth.

Differentiated Instruction Key

L1 Basic to Average	**AR** Advanced Readers
L2 All Students	**ELL** English Language Learners
L3 Average to Advanced	**GT** Gifted and Talented
	LPR Less Proficient Readers
	SN Special Needs

Prepare to Read	Instructional Resources	Differentiated Instruction
Build Background Knowledge Preview the section and discuss students' impressions of tariffs. **Set a Purpose for Reading** Have students begin to fill out the Reading Readiness Guide. **Preview Key Terms** Preview the section's key terms.	**All in One** Teaching Resources, Unit 3 **L2** Chapter Prereading Guide, p. 5 **L2** History Reading Skill Worksheet, p. 78 **L2** Reading Readiness Guide, p. 80 **L2** Word Knowledge Rating Form, p. 79 **Teacher's Edition** **L2** Vocabulary Builder, p. 339, 341	💿 **Guided Reading Audio CD** **Spanish** ELL, LPR, SN

Teach	Instructional Resources	Differentiated Instruction
Instruction **The Era of Good Feelings** Describe the feeling of national unity that followed the War of 1812. **Building the National Economy** Discuss the second Bank of the United States and the Tariff of 1816. **Three Important Supreme Court Rulings** Explain the changes the Supreme Court had on American life.	📖 **Interactive Reading and Notetaking Study Guide** **L2** Chapter 10, Section 1 **All in One** Teaching Resources, Unit 3 **L2** Concept Lesson, p. 92 **L2** Concept Organizer, p. 7 **Color Transparencies** **L2** How Tariffs Work	📖 **Interactive Reading and Notetaking Study Guide, Adapted Version (English/Spanish)** **L1** Chapter 10, Section 1 ELL, LPR, SN **Teacher's Edition** **L1** Visualizing the Word, p. 339 ELL, LPR, SN **L1** Vocabulary Development, p. 340 ELL, LPR, SN **L3** Writing a Poem, p. 342 GT **L3** Research, p. 342 AR

Assess and Reteach	Instructional Resources	Differentiated Instruction
Assess Progress Evaluate student comprehension with Check Your Progress and Section Quiz. **Reteach** Assign the Interactive Reading and Notetaking Study Guide to help struggling students. **Extend** Extend the lesson by having students complete the History Interactive activity on tariffs online.	📖 **Interactive Reading and Notetaking Study Guide** **L2** Chapter 10, Section 1 **All in One** Teaching Resources, Unit 3 **L2** Reading Readiness Guide, p. 80 **L2** Section Quiz, p. 93 **Progress Monitoring Transparencies** **L2** Chapter 10, Section 1	**Teacher's Edition** **L1** Checkpoints, TE, pp. 340, 343, 344 💿 **SE on Audio CD** **L1** Chapter 10 ELL, LPR, SN **Internet Resources** PHSchool.com

Section 2 Dealing With Other Nations *1 period, .5 block*

Objectives

Students will

1. Explain why Spain ceded Florida to the United States.
2. Describe how Spanish territories in the Americas gained independence.
3. Explain why the Monroe Doctrine was issued.
4. Discuss how Canada became self-governing.

Differentiated Instruction Key

L1 Basic to Average	**AR** Advanced Readers
L2 All Students	**ELL** English Language Learners
L3 Average to Advanced	**GT** Gifted and Talented
	LPR Less Proficient Readers
	SN Special Needs

Prepare to Read	**Instructional Resources**	**Differentiated Instruction**
Build Background Knowledge Preview the section and ask students to make predictions about what they will learn. **Set a Purpose for Reading** Have students begin to fill out the Reading Readiness Guide. **Preview Key Terms** Preview the section's key terms.	**All in One** Teaching Resources, Unit 3 **L2** Reading Readiness Guide, p. 81 **Teacher's Edition** **L2** Vocabulary Builder, p. 345	🎧 **Guided Reading Audio CD** Spanish **ELL, LPR, SN**

Teach	**Instructional Resources**	**Differentiated Instruction**
Instruction **Relations With Spain** Discuss why Spain sold Florida to the United States. **Spanish Colonies Win Independence** Describe how the Spanish territories in America gained independence. **The Monroe Doctrine** Explain how the Monroe Doctrine came into being. **Relations With Canada** Discuss how Canada gained self-government.	📖 **Interactive Reading and Notetaking Study Guide** **L2** Chapter 10, Section 2 **All in One** Teaching Resources, Unit 3 **L2** Hail America, p. 85	📖 **Interactive Reading and Notetaking Study Guide, Adapted Version (English/ Spanish)** **L1** Chapter 10, Section 2 **ELL, LPR, SN** **Teacher's Edition** **L1** Gaining Comprehension, p. 346 **ELL, LPR, SN**

Assess and Reteach	**Instructional Resources**	**Differentiated Instruction**
Assess Progress Evaluate student comprehension with Check Your Progress and Section Quiz. **Reteach** Assign the Interactive Reading and Notetaking Study Guide to help struggling students. **Extend** Extend the lesson by having students create a timeline of important events in Canada's history.	📖 **Interactive Reading and Notetaking Study Guide** **L2** Chapter 10, Section 2 **All in One** Teaching Resources, Unit 3 **L2** Reading Readiness Guide, p. 81 **L2** Section Quiz, p. 94 **Progress Monitoring Transparencies** **L2** Chapter 10, Section 2	**Teacher's Edition** **L1** Checkpoints, TE, pp. 345, 347, 348 🎧 **SE on Audio CD** **L1** Chapter 10 **ELL, LPR, SN** **Internet Resources** PHSchool.com

Section 3 The Age of Jackson

 1 period, .5 block

Objectives

Students will

1. Discuss the conflict between Andrew Jackson and John Quincy Adams over the election of 1828.

2. Explain how the right to vote expanded in the United States.

3. Describe Andrew Jackson's victory in the election of 1828.

Differentiated Instruction Key

L1 Basic to Average
L2 All Students
L3 Average to Advanced

AR Advanced Readers
ELL English Language Learners
GT Gifted and Talented
LPR Less Proficient Readers
SN Special Needs

Prepare to Read	Instructional Resources	Differentiated Instruction
Build Background Knowledge Preview the section and ask students to make predictions about whether Jackson's actions benefited ordinary Americans. **Set a Purpose for Reading** Have students begin to fill out the Reading Readiness Guide. **Preview Key Terms** Preview the section's key terms.	**All in One** Teaching Resources, Unit 3 **L2** Reading Readiness Guide, p. 82 **Teacher's Edition** **L2** Vocabulary Builder, p. 349	● **Guided Reading Audio CD** **Spanish** ELL, LPR, SN

Teach	Instructional Resources	Differentiated Instruction
Instruction **Adams and Jackson In Conflict** Describe the election of 1824 and Adams's presidency. **A New Era in Politics** Discuss the increased suffrage in the United States. **Jackson Becomes President** Explain the election of 1828 and how Jackson saw himself as an average American.	📖 **Interactive Reading and Notetaking Study Guide** **L2** Chapter 10, Section 3 **All in One** Teaching Resources, Unit 3 **L2** Andrew Jackson and the Spoils System, p. 86 **Color Transparencies** **L2** The Election of 1824 **L2** The Election of 1828	📖 **Interactive Reading and Notetaking Study Guide, Adapted Version (English/ Spanish)** **L1** Chapter 10, Section 3 ELL, LPR, SN **Teacher's Edition** **L1** Gaining Comprehension, p. 350 ELL, SN **L3** Researching Political Parties, p. 352 AR, GT

Assess and Reteach	Instructional Resources	Differentiated Instruction
Assess Progress Evaluate student comprehension with Check Your Progress and Section Quiz. **Reteach** Assign the Interactive Reading and Notetaking Study Guide to help struggling students. **Extend** Extend the lesson by having students make a timeline of Andrew Jackson's life.	📖 **Interactive Reading and Notetaking Study Guide** **L2** Chapter 10, Section 3 **All in One** Teaching Resources, Unit 3 **L2** Reading Readiness Guide, p. 82 **L2** Section Quiz, p. 95 **Progress Monitoring Transparencies** **L2** Chapter 10, Section 3	**Teacher's Edition** **L1** Checkpoints, TE, pp. 351, 352, 354 ● **SE on Audio CD** **L1** Chapter 10 ELL, LPR, SN

Section 4 Indian Removal

 1 period, .5 block

Objectives

Students will

1. Describe the culture of Native Americans in the Southeast.
2. Describe the conflict over land occupied by Native Americans in the Southeast.
3. Discuss the forced removal of Native Americans.

Differentiated Instruction Key

L1 Basic to Average

L2 All Students

L3 Average to Advanced

AR Advanced Readers

ELL English Language Learners

GT Gifted and Talented

LPR Less Proficient Readers

SN Special Needs

Prepare to Read

Build Background Knowledge
Preview the section and discuss students' impressions of the President's powers.

Set a Purpose for Reading
Have students begin to fill out the Reading Readiness Guide.

Preview Key Terms
Preview the section's key terms.

Instructional Resources

All in One Teaching Resources, Unit 3

L2 Reading Readiness Guide, p. 83

Teacher's Edition

L2 Vocabulary Builder, p. 355

Differentiated Instruction

Guided Reading Audio CD

Spanish ELL, LPR, SN

Teach

Instruction
Native Americans of the Southeast
Describe the white customs many Native Americans adopted.

Conflict Over Land
Discuss why President Jackson ignored Supreme Court rulings to remove Cherokees.

On the Trail of Tears
Explain the Trail of Tears.

Instructional Resources

Interactive Reading and Notetaking Study Guide

L2 Chapter 10, Section 4

All in One Teaching Resources, Unit 3

L2 Tsali of the Cherokees, p. 87

Discovery School Video

L2 The Trail of Tears

Differentiated Instruction

Interactive Reading and Notetaking Study Guide, Adapted Version (English/Spanish)

L1 Chapter 10, Section 4 ELL, LPR, SN

All in One Teaching Resources, Unit 3

L1 John Burnett and the Trail of Tears, p. 89

Teacher's Edition

L3 Retracing the Trail of Tears, p. 356 GT

L1 Exploring the Main Idea, p. 358 ELL, LPR, SN

L1 Comparing Alphabets, p. 360 ELL

Assess and Reteach

Assess Progress
Evaluate student comprehension with Check Your Progress and Section Quiz.

Reteach
Assign the Interactive Reading and Notetaking Study Guide to help struggling students.

Extend
Extend the lesson by having students research the life of Cherokee leader John Ross.

Instructional Resources

Interactive Reading and Notetaking Study Guide

L2 Chapter 10, Section 4

All in One Teaching Resources, Unit 3

L2 Reading Readiness Guide, p. 83

L2 Section Quiz, p. 96

Progress Monitoring Transparencies

L2 Chapter 10, Section 4

Differentiated Instruction

Teacher's Edition

L1 Checkpoints, TE, pp. 355, 357, 359, 361

SE on Audio CD

L1 Chapter 10 ELL, LPR, SN

Section 5 States' Rights and the Economy ⏱ *3 periods, 1.5 blocks*

Objectives

Students will

1. Describe the disagreement over the Bank of the United States.
2. Discuss the differing viewpoints on the balance of federal and state powers.
3. Explain why South Carolina threatened to secede from the Union.
4. Describe the economic crisis that began in 1837.

Differentiated Instruction Key

L1 Basic to Average	**AR** Advanced Readers
L2 All Students	**ELL** English Language Learners
L3 Average to Advanced	**GT** Gifted and Talented
	LPR Less Proficient Readers
	SN Special Needs

Prepare to Read

Build Background Knowledge
Preview the section and ask students to predict what they will learn.

Set a Purpose for Reading
Have students begin to fill out the Reading Readiness Guide.

Preview Key Terms
Preview the section's key terms.

Instructional Resources

📘 **All in One** Teaching Resources, Unit 3
L2 Reading Readiness Guide, p. 84

Teacher's Edition
L2 Vocabulary Builder, p. 363

Differentiated Instruction

💿 **Guided Reading Audio CD**
Spanish ELL, LPR, SN

Teach

**Instruction
The Bank War**
Discuss why Jackson disliked the Bank.

The Question of States' Rights
Explain states' rights.

The Nullification Crisis
Discuss why South Carolina threatened to secede from the Union.

The End of the Jackson Era
Describe the Panic of 1837.

Instructional Resources

📖 **Interactive Reading and Notetaking Study Guide**
L2 Chapter 10, Section 5

📘 **All in One** Teaching Resources, Unit 3
L2 Daniel Webster, p. 90
L2 Skills for Life Worksheet, p. 91

Color Transparencies
L2 Andrew Jackson Battles the Bank of the United States

Differentiated Instruction

📖 **Interactive Reading and Notetaking Study Guide, Adapted Version (English/ Spanish)**
L1 Chapter 10, Section 5 ELL, LPR, SN

Teacher's Edition
L1 Definition, p. 362 ELL, LPR, SN
L3 Political Cartoons, p. 364 GT
L3 Speculating, p. 366 AR, GT

Assess and Reteach

Assess Progress
Assign Check Your Progress and Section Quiz.

Reteach
Assign the Study Guide to help students.

Extend
Have students interview community members about the effect of unpaid loans.

Think Like a Historian
Using information from primary sources and the chapters in this unit, revisit the unit essential question.

Instructional Resources

📖 **Interactive Reading and Notetaking Study Guide**
L2 Chapter 10, Section 5

📘 **All in One** Teaching Resources, Unit 3
L2 Reading Readiness Guide, p. 84
L2 Word Knowledge Rating Form, p. 79
L2 Section Quiz, p. 97
L2 Chapter Test, p. 101

Progress Monitoring Transparencies
L2 Chapter 10, Section 5

Color Transparencies
L2 Think Like a Historian, Unit 3

Differentiated Instruction

Teacher's Edition
L1 Checkpoints, TE, pp. 363, 364, 366, 367

📘 **All in One** Teaching Resources, Unit 3
L1 Chapter Test, p. 98

💿 **SE on Audio CD**
L1 Chapter 10 ELL, LPR, SN

💿 **Social Studies Skills Tutor CD-ROM**
Analyzing Graphic Data

Use the following research activities to help students deepen their understanding of the Chapter Essential Question: **How did the nation reflect a growing sense of national pride and identity?** Students should use library or Internet resources. The Web Codes provided offer access to Internet resources students can use to complete each activity. Use the appropriate four-point rubric in Assessment Rubrics to evaluate the activity.

 Assessment Rubrics

Make a Timeline of the Public Life of John Quincy Adams

Have students research the major events in the public life of John Quincy Adams to make a timeline of Adams's contributions to the United States, which began long before his presidency and continued until his collapse on the floor of the House of Representatives. Students should annotate the timeline by adding information on those events that had a significant impact on national issues. Then have students write a brief analysis of Adams's character as it revealed itself in his public roles. Use this activity after students have completed Section 2.

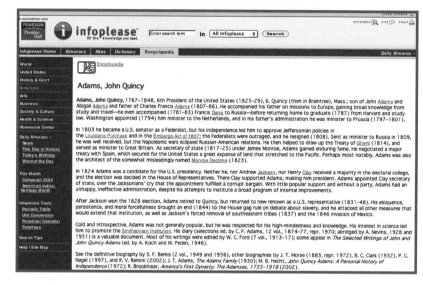

 Individual research activity AR

 Web Code: mye-0220

Compare the Major Players in the Battle Over the Second Bank

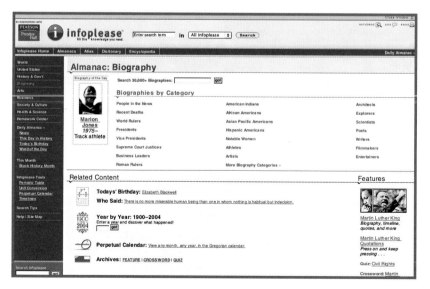

Have students use information they have gathered to make a graphic organizer, such as a chart, that compares the positions and actions of the three major participants in the battle over the charter of the second Bank of the United States: Nicholas Biddle, Senator Henry Clay, and President Andrew Jackson. The information should present as accurately as possible each man's motives, political and otherwise. Then, ask students to write their evaluation of how successfully each man pursued his position on the Bank. Use this activity after students have read about the Bank War in Section 5.

 Individual research activity AR, GT

 Web Code: mye-0221

Why It Matters

Learning more about how politics worked in past elections may help students make wise voting decisions in the future.

When election time draws near, politicians will flood the radio, television, newspapers, and other media with campaign sound bites. As students will read about the vigorous elections of the 1820s and 1830s, they can relate how some candidates today will either try to present issues in a way that is favorable to their campaigns or try to avoid discussing them at all.

Often the messages from opposing candidates sound equally appealing. For this reason, it is important for voters to learn as much as they can about the issues and about each candidate's proposals. Campaign issues such as education or budget priorities can affect students' lives and communities, so it is essential that they prepare to be informed voters.

Chapter Essential Question

How did the nation reflect a growing sense of national pride and identity?

Think Like a Historian

- To preview this chapter, have students review the content on these pages of the Student Edition. Ask: **What will you be learning about in this chapter?** *(how the United States gained new sense of confidence; issues faced by the early Republic)*

- Have students study the image on these pages. Ask: **How does this rally resemble an election rally today? How does it differ?** *(The rally is like today's in that many people attended and they were very interested in what the speaker was saying. It differs in that the setting is more intimate and informal than today and there are no women present.)*

- Ask: **What do you think de Tocqueville meant by saying that Jackson was a "slave" the majority?** *(De Tocqueville thought Jackson was not thinking for himself, but rather trying to please the majority.)*

A Changing Nation

1815–1840

Bibliography

For the Teacher
Jahoda, Gloria. *Trail of Tears.* Wings, 1995.

For the Student
L1 Whitelaw, Nancy. *Andrew Jackson: Frontier President.* Morgan Reynolds Publishing, 2000.

L2 Bruchac, Joseph. *The Journal of Jesse Smoke: A Cherokee Boy.* Scholastic, 2001.

L3 Alagna, Magdalena. *The Monroe Doctrine: An End to European Colonies in America.* Rosen Publishing, 2003.

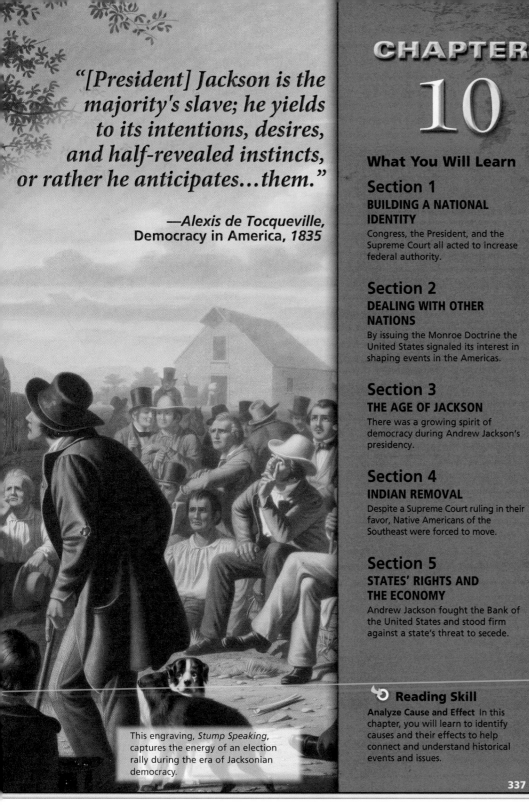

"[President] Jackson is the majority's slave; he yields to its intentions, desires, and half-revealed instincts, or rather he anticipates...them."

—*Alexis de Tocqueville,*
Democracy in America, 1835

This engraving, *Stump Speaking*, captures the energy of an election rally during the era of Jacksonian democracy.

CHAPTER 10

What You Will Learn

Section 1
BUILDING A NATIONAL IDENTITY
Congress, the President, and the Supreme Court all acted to increase federal authority.

Section 2
DEALING WITH OTHER NATIONS
By issuing the Monroe Doctrine the United States signaled its interest in shaping events in the Americas.

Section 3
THE AGE OF JACKSON
There was a growing spirit of democracy during Andrew Jackson's presidency.

Section 4
INDIAN REMOVAL
Despite a Supreme Court ruling in their favor, Native Americans of the Southeast were forced to move.

Section 5
STATES' RIGHTS AND THE ECONOMY
Andrew Jackson fought the Bank of the United States and stood firm against a state's threat to secede.

Reading Skill
Analyze Cause and Effect In this chapter, you will learn to identify causes and their effects to help connect and understand historical events and issues.

337

History Background

Jacksonian and Jeffersonian Democracy Although based in part on ideals expressed by Thomas Jefferson, Jacksonian Democracy marked a departure from previous political thought in the United States. Jefferson and the other Founding Fathers had envisioned a nation dominated by political elites, with educated citizens selecting leaders for the common good. Jacksonian Democracy, however, included a spirit of participatory egalitarianism—at least for white men. The expansion of the franchise was accompanied by the belief that all men, created equal, should have and exercise an equal political voice.

Prepare to Read

Use the following for reading skill support.

All in One Teaching Resources, Unit 3, Chapter Prereading Guide, p. 5; History Reading Skill, p. 78

History Reading Skill *Online*
Web code: mve-3000

Differentiated Instruction

The following Teacher Edition strategies are suitable for students of varying abilities.

- **L3 Advanced Readers,** pp. 342, 352, 366 AR
- **L1 English Language Learners,** pp. 339, 340, 346, 350, 358, 360, 362 ELL
- **L3 Gifted and Talented,** pp. 342, 352, 356, 364, 366 GT
- **L1 Less Proficient Readers,** pp. 339, 340, 346, 358, 362 LPR
- **L1 Special Needs,** pp. 339, 340, 346, 350, 358, 362 SN

Chapter Resources

Teaching Resources, Unit 3
Chapter Prereading Guide, p. 5
Word Knowledge Rating Form, p. 79
History Reading Skill, p. 78
Skills for Life Worksheet, p. 91
Chapter Tests A/B (L1/L2), pp. 98, 101
Letter Home (English/Spanish), pp. 70, 71

Spanish Support
- **L1 Interactive Reading and Notetaking Study Guide, Spanish,** Adapted Version
- **L1 Guided Reading Audio CD,** Spanish

Media and Technology
- **L1 SE** on Audio CD
- **L2 Social Studies Skills Tutor CD-ROM**
ExamView **Test Bank CD-ROM**

Discovery SCHOOL
Quick View Video
View the chapter video for a quick preview of the main ideas.

Visual Preview

How did the nation reflect a growing sense of national pride and identity?

Build Background Knowledge `L2`

Students have learned that after the War of 1812, the United States felt a new sense of pride and national unity. Lead a structured discussion of what "national unity" means. (See TE p. T24 for more on structured discussion.) Bring out the idea that unity inspires confidence and that teamwork often can accomplish more than individual efforts. Have students give examples of success they had when they were part of a team or group that had pride and confidence in its ability to achieve a goal. Ask students how they can show pride in America today. (*parades, fly the American flag, patriotic music*)

Instruction `L2`

- For background information on conducting a lesson for the Visual Preview, see TE p. T20.

- Write the Chapter Essential Question on the board. Ask: **What events have you learned about that contributed to a sense of national pride?** (*Americans won their independence; they felt they had defeated Britain for a second time in the War of 1812; Louisiana Purchase*)

- Have students examine the key for the large map. Ask: **What do the colored lines on the map show?** (*roads and canals*) **What does the arrow indicate?** (*Native Americans are moved westward.*)

- On the map showing Jackson's Landslide Victory, what area of the country did Adams win? (*northeast*)

- Direct attention to the timeline. **What years are covered by the timeline?** (*1810-1842*) **What happened in 1838-1839?** (*Cherokees were forced to move to Oklahoma.*)

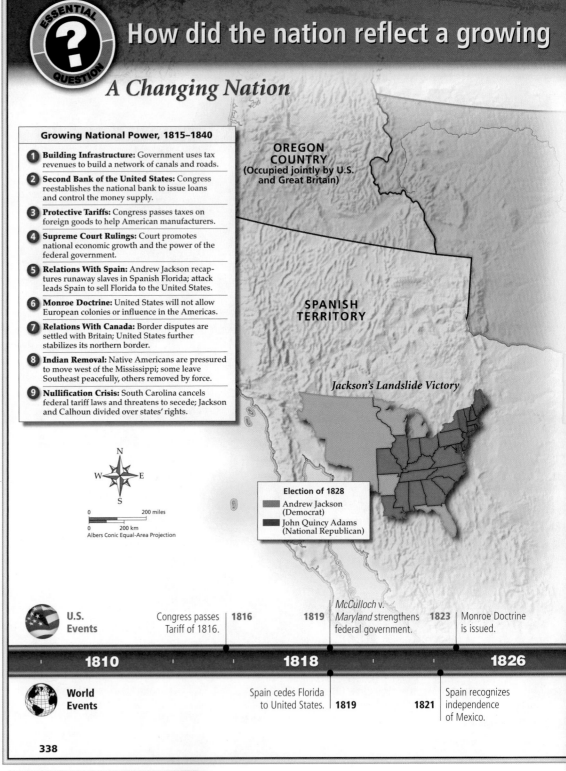

? How did the nation reflect a growing

A Changing Nation

Growing National Power, 1815–1840

1. **Building Infrastructure:** Government uses tax revenues to build a network of canals and roads.
2. **Second Bank of the United States:** Congress reestablishes the national bank to issue loans and control the money supply.
3. **Protective Tariffs:** Congress passes taxes on foreign goods to help American manufacturers.
4. **Supreme Court Rulings:** Court promotes national economic growth and the power of the federal government.
5. **Relations With Spain:** Andrew Jackson recaptures runaway slaves in Spanish Florida; attack leads Spain to sell Florida to the United States.
6. **Monroe Doctrine:** United States will not allow European colonies or influence in the Americas.
7. **Relations With Canada:** Border disputes are settled with Britain; United States further stabilizes its northern border.
8. **Indian Removal:** Native Americans are pressured to move west of the Mississippi; some leave Southeast peacefully, others removed by force.
9. **Nullification Crisis:** South Carolina cancels federal tariff laws and threatens to secede; Jackson and Calhoun divided over states' rights.

OREGON COUNTRY (Occupied jointly by U.S. and Great Britain)

SPANISH TERRITORY

Jackson's Landslide Victory

Election of 1828
- Andrew Jackson (Democrat)
- John Quincy Adams (National Republican)

0   200 miles
0   200 km
Albers Conic Equal-Area Projection

U.S. Events — Congress passes Tariff of 1816. | **1816** | **1819** | *McCulloch* v. *Maryland* strengthens federal government. | **1823** | Monroe Doctrine is issued.

1810 | **1818** | **1826**

World Events — Spain cedes Florida to United States. | **1819** | **1821** | Spain recognizes independence of Mexico.

338

History Background

Pressure for Land Wanting more land to plant cotton in the early 1800s, white settlers pressured the federal government to acquire Native American lands in the South. This was home to the Cherokee, Creek, Choctaw, Chickasaw, and Seminole nations. Between 1814 and 1824, the United States negotiated nine treaties with Native American tribes that traded their southern land for western land. In 1823, the Supreme Court handed down a decision that stated that Native Americans could occupy U.S. land, but not hold title to it because their "right of occupancy" was less important than the U.S.'s "right of discovery." However, Jackson's later Indian Removal Policy opened twenty-five million acres of land to white settlement and to slavery.

sense of national pride and identity?

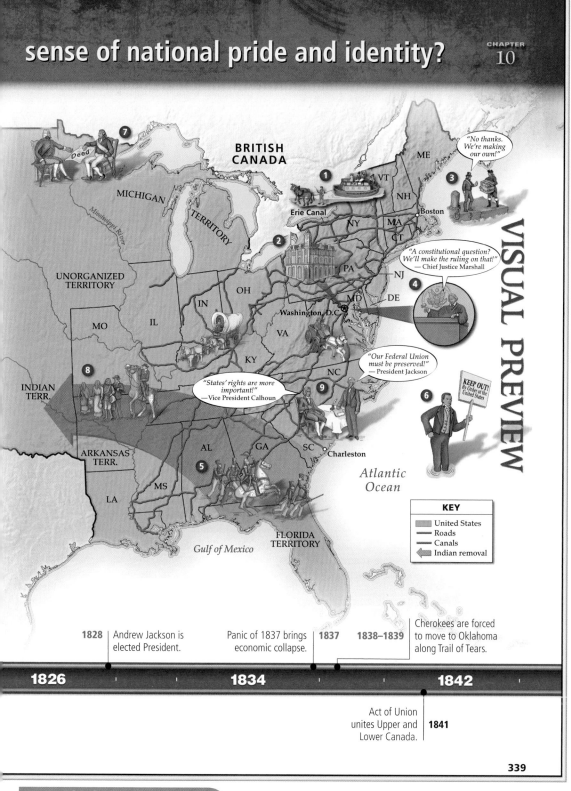

BRITISH CANADA

ME

VT

NH

"No thanks. We're making our own!"

Erie Canal

NY

MA

Boston

CT

MICHIGAN TERRITORY

Mississippi River

"A constitutional question? We'll make the ruling on that!" — Chief Justice Marshall

PA

NJ

UNORGANIZED TERRITORY

OH

IN

MD

DE

Washington, D.C.

VA

MO

IL

KY

"Our Federal Union must be preserved!" — President Jackson

NC

KEEP OUT! By Order of the United States

INDIAN TERR.

"States' rights are more important!" — Vice President Calhoun

ARKANSAS TERR.

AL

GA

SC

Charleston

Atlantic Ocean

MS

LA

KEY
United States
— Roads
— Canals
← Indian removal

FLORIDA TERRITORY

Gulf of Mexico

VISUAL PREVIEW

| 1828 | Andrew Jackson is elected President. | Panic of 1837 brings economic collapse. | 1837 | 1838–1839 | Cherokees are forced to move to Oklahoma along Trail of Tears. |

1826   **1834**   **1842**

Act of Union unites Upper and Lower Canada. | **1841**

Instruction *(continued)*

- Have a student read number 1 on the chart "Growing National Power." Define *infrastructure*. Tell students that *infrastructure* refers to the large-scale public systems and services that a country needs to function efficiently. Then ask students to name some examples of the nation's infrastructure. *(roads, water supplies, schools)* Discuss why this is important to a developing country. *(Possible answer: enables transportation of goods and services)*

- Using the Think-Write-Pair-Share strategy (TE, p. T25), have students read and analyze the remainder of the events on the chart. Have them explain why each would be helpful or harmful to the growth of national power.

- Have students rewrite the Essential Question in simple terms in their notes. **How did America's sense of pride and unity affect its policies?** You may also post this question in a prominent place in the classroom and leave it there while discussing the chapter. Tell students to use the section focus question as a guide to answering the Essential Question as they read the chapter.

- Tell students that as they complete the Notetaking Study Guide for this chapter, they will be building the answer to the Essential Question.

Interactive Reading and Notetaking Study Guide, Chapter 10 (Adapted Version also available.)

Vocabulary Builder

Preview the Vocabulary Have students preview the vocabulary in the chapter and rate how well they know each word on the Word Knowledge Rating Form. Collect the sheets and explain that they will have a chance to go over the forms later.

All in One Teaching Resources, Unit 3, Word Knowledge Rating Form, p. 79

Monitor Progress Pronounce each word and have students repeat it. Have a student read the definition. Then pair students and have them make flashcards, writing the vocabulary word on one side and the definition on the back. Have each student hold up a card and ask his or her partner for the definition of the word.

Section 1

Step-by-Step Instruction

Review and Preview

Students have read about the territorial expansion of the United States. Now they will focus on how the federal government faced economic issues.

Section Focus Question

How was the power of the federal government strengthened during the Era of Good Feelings?

Before you begin the lesson for the day, write the Section Focus Question on the board. (*Lesson focus: Congress, the President, and the Supreme Court all acted to increase the authority of the federal government.*)

Prepare to Read

Build Background Knowledge L2

Ask students to look at the chart on p. 342 and recall what they know about tariffs. (*They are a charge on imports.*) Ask students to predict who benefits from tariffs on imports. After they make their predictions, address any misconceptions they may have. Remind them to confirm or revise their predictions after they read Section 1. Use the Idea Wave strategy (TE, p. T24) to elicit responses.

Set a Purpose L2

■ Read each statement in the Reading Readiness Guide aloud. Ask students to mark the statements True or False.

> **All in One Teaching Resource, Unit 3,** Reading Readiness Guide, p. 80

■ Have students discuss the statements in pairs or groups of four, then mark their worksheets again. Use the Numbered Heads strategy (TE, p. T24) to call on students to share their group's perspectives. Students will return to these worksheets later.

Answer

✓**Checkpoint** It disappeared after President James Monroe's landslide election victory in 1816.

Drawing the Country Together

❝ There are existing powers in Congress to effectuate a comprehensive system of roads and canals, the effect of which would be to draw the different parts of the country more closely together. ❞

—Henry Clay, speech to House of Representatives, 1818

◀ Seaports like Charleston (left) were vital to America's growing economy.

Building a National Identity

Objectives
- Describe the feeling of national unity that followed the War of 1812.
- Explain how Congress tried to strengthen the national economy.
- Discuss how Supreme Court rulings supported federal power and economic growth.

🔄 Reading Skill

Analyze Cause and Effect Events in history are often linked by cause and effect. This means that one event makes another happen. However, you cannot assume that because events occur together or in sequence they have a cause-and-effect link. Ask yourself: Why did this event or result happen? What happened because of this event? The answers will show if a cause-and-effect relationship exists.

Key Terms and People

Henry Clay
John C. Calhoun
Daniel Webster
charter
dumping
contract
capitalism
interstate commerce

Why It Matters With peace restored after the War of 1812, the United States focused more on internal affairs. American leaders wanted to build national unity and improve the nation's economy.

❓ Section Focus Question: How was the power of the federal government strengthened during the Era of Good Feelings?

The Era of Good Feelings

With the end of the War of 1812, the Republicans took firm control of the government. The presidential election of 1816 resulted in a landslide victory for Republican candidate James Monroe of Virginia. He defeated Rufus King, the Federalist candidate, by 183 to 34 electoral votes. Stung by this defeat, the Federalist Party began to lose power. Within a few years, the party had disappeared.

President Monroe wanted to promote national unity. In the spring and summer of 1817, he made a goodwill circuit of the middle and northern sections of the country. He was warmly greeted in Connecticut and Massachusetts, the only states that had not voted for him in 1816. The old arguments over the War of 1812 seemed to have faded away.

While Monroe was in Boston, a local newspaper described the new sense of national unity as the "Era of Good Feelings." The name stuck and was used to describe Monroe's two terms in office. When he ran for reelection in 1820, no candidate opposed him.

✓**Checkpoint** What happened to the Federalist Party after the War of 1812?

340 Chapter 10 A Changing Nation

Differentiated Instruction

L1 English Language Learners **L1 Less Proficient Readers** **L1 Special Needs**

Vocabulary Development Give students added practice with key terms and high-use words. Have them make flashcards with the word on one side and its defini-

tion on the other. Pair students with a partner so that they can use the flashcards to quiz each other on the definitions.

Building the National Economy

After 1815, many Americans believed the federal government should take action to increase economic prosperity in all regions of the country. Even the Republicans began to see merit in certain federal programs. This was a change, because in previous years Republicans had been known for stressing states' rights. Support for federal measures to promote economic prosperity came from many regions.

These beliefs were expressed by a number of bright young members of Congress from different regions. Outstanding among those who favored federal action were Henry Clay of Kentucky, John C. Calhoun of South Carolina, and Daniel Webster of Massachusetts.

- Clay spoke for people in the West who thought the country needed better roads and canals to transport goods from one region to another.

- Calhoun spoke for the interests of the South. While first a defender of national unity, he later put more emphasis on the idea of states' rights.

- Webster became a spokesperson for the Northeast. At first, he opposed high tariffs, but he later came to support them as a way of protecting industry.

 Analyze Cause and Effect Explain what Americans believed was needed to make national unity grow. What would cause that growth to happen?

Vocabulary Builder
emphasis (EM fuh sis) *n.* special importance or significance

New Leaders Speak for Their Regions

During the Era of Good Feelings, three young members of Congress became spokespersons for their regions.

Daniel Webster - Massachusetts
He supported tariffs because they allowed New England's factories to compete against European manufacturers.

John C. Calhoun - South Carolina
He opposed tariffs because they raised the price of goods that southerners bought.

Henry Clay - Kentucky
He supported the construction of roads and canals because they would enable the three regions of the country to trade with one another.

Critical Thinking: *Apply Information* Which of the three leaders would you expect to be the strongest supporter of slavery? Explain.

341

The Era of Good Feelings

p. 340

Instruction L2

- **Vocabulary Builder** Before teaching this section, preteach the High-Use Words **emphasis** and **infrastructure,** using the strategy on TE p. T21.
Key Terms Following the instructions on p. 7, have students create a See It–Remember It chart for the key terms in this chapter.

- **Concept Lesson** To help students better comprehend the concept of economic growth, which is important to the understanding of this chapter, use the Concept Lesson about *Economic Growth.* Distribute the Concept Organizer.

  All in One Teaching Resources, Unit 3, Concept Lesson, p. 92; Concept Organizer, p. 7

- Read The Era of Good Feelings with students, using the Structured Silent Reading strategy (TE, p. T22).

- Ask: **Why do you think the outcome of the War of 1812 led to a sense of national unity?** (*Possible answer: People felt proud and patriotic because of how the country stood up to Britain.*)

Independent Practice

Have students begin filling in the study guide for this section.

Interactive Reading and Notetaking Study Guide, Chapter 10, Section 1 (Adapted Version also available.)

Monitor Progress

As students fill in the Notetaking Study Guide, circulate to make sure that they understand why this period became known as the "Era of Good Feelings."

Answers

Reading Skill A strong economy that helped all parts of the nation prosper and depend on one another would lead to increased national unity.

Apply Information Calhoun; He represented the South, where slavery was important to the economy.

Vocabulary Builder

Use the information below to teach students this section's high-use words.

High-Use Word	Definition and Sample Sentence
emphasis, p. 341	*n.* special importance or significance The Bill of Rights puts an **emphasis** on individual freedom.
infrastructure, p. 343	*n.* basic public works, like bridges and roads, needed for a society to function By building roads and bridges, the planners hoped to improve the country's **infrastructure**.

Building the National Economy

p. 341

Instruction L2

■ Have students read Building the National Economy with you. Remind them to look for cause-and-effect relationships between events.

■ Ask: **What did many Americans believe the federal government should do to improve national unity?** (*take measures to strengthen the country's economy so that all regions prospered and had strong economic ties with other parts*)

■ Ask: **What services did the second National Bank of the United States perform?** (*It restored order to the money supply and lent money to individuals.*)

■ Display the History Interactive transparency How Tariffs Work. With students, discuss the arguments for and against protective tariffs and write them on the board. (*For—wealth produced by tariffs would enable one region to purchase goods from another region; the federal government could use the money to improve the infrastructure in the South and West; factory owners were losing business to imported goods; Against—people in the South, where there were not as many factories, had to pay higher prices.*)

Color Transparencies, How Tariffs Work

■ Ask: **Why did Clay think his American System would appeal to all?** (*All sections would benefit financially. The profits gained in the North would enable northerners to buy products from the West and South.*)

Independent Practice

Have students continue filling in the study guide for this section.

📖 **Interactive Reading and Notetaking Study Guide,** Chapter 10, Section 1 (Adapted Version also available.)

Monitor Progress

As students fill in the Notetaking Study Guide, circulate to make sure that they understand how the national economy developed. Provide assistance as needed.

Answer

Identify Economic Costs The British could produce cloth more cheaply because they had well-established factories.

How Tariffs Work

By increasing the cost of imported goods, tariffs helped U.S. manufacturers to compete with foreign manufacturers. But the higher prices hurt consumers.
Critical Thinking: *Identify Economic Costs* Why was the cost of cloth higher in the United States than in Britain?

	United States	Great Britain
Cost of cloth	$6.00	$5.00
Cost to manufacture final product	$0.85	$0.50
Shipping costs	$0.20	$0.25
Tariff	—	$1.50
Total	$7.05	$7.25

The Second Bank of the United States As you have read, Congress passed a law in 1791 creating the first Bank of the United States. In 1811, the Bank ceased to exist. Its charter—a legal document giving certain rights to a person or company—had run out. Without the Bank, the economy suffered. State banks made too many loans and issued too much money. This caused an increase in spending and led to rising prices.

To cure these problems, Congress established the second Bank of the United States in 1816. Like the first Bank, the new Bank was privately owned and had a charter to operate for twenty years. It lent money to individuals and controlled the money supply. This gave a boost to American businesses.

The Tariff of 1816 Another problem the nation faced after the War of 1812 was foreign competition. Most British goods had been kept out of the United States by the Embargo Act and the War of 1812. This helped American industry grow rapidly. New American factories made textiles, smelted iron, and produced many other products.

After the War of 1812, British manufacturers looked to sell their goods in the United States. They could still produce goods more cheaply than the Americans because they had well-established factories and more customers. This gave the British an opportunity to drive their American competitors out of business by dumping their goods in the United States. Dumping is selling goods in another country below market prices.

Differentiated Instruction

L3 Gifted and Talented

Writing a Poem Have gifted writers compose a poem about the new sense of nationalism that developed in the 1800s. Have students summarize the main idea in a chorus that repeats throughout the poem. Have students read their poem to the class.

L3 Advanced Readers

Research A marker by Henry Clay's grave has a quotation from one of his speeches: "I know no North—no South—no East—no West." Suggest that students research Clay's career to learn what he meant and explore how well he practiced this philosophy. Invite students to share their conclusions with the class.

British dumping caused dozens of New England businesses to fail. As their investments collapsed, angry factory owners turned to Congress for help. They demanded protective tariffs to raise the price of foreign goods.

Congress responded with the Tariff of 1816, which put a tax on foreign textiles, iron, leather goods, paper, and other products. In 1818 and 1824, Congress passed even higher tariffs.

These tariffs were popular in the North, where most factories were located. However, the tariffs were deeply resented in the South, where they forced southerners to pay more for their goods. John C. Calhoun became a bitter foe of tariffs. He argued that they made northern manufacturers rich at the expense of the South.

Clay's American System As the debate over tariffs raged, Henry Clay came up with a plan that he believed would help the economy of each section of the country. He called his plan the American System. It proposed high tariffs and a federal program of public works.

Clay believed that high tariffs helped all regions of the country, not just the North. According to Clay, the wealth produced by tariffs would enable northerners to buy farm products from the West and the South. The tariff also would provide revenue for the federal government. The government could then use the money to build up the infrastructure—roads, bridges, and canals—in the South and West.

Clay's American System never fully became government policy. Presidents Madison and Monroe both refused to support some of Clay's projects. Also, southerners continued to oppose protective tariffs. They were not convinced by Clay's argument that high tariffs would aid the South in the long run.

☑**Checkpoint** **According to Henry Clay, how would his American System benefit the economy?**

Three Important Supreme Court Rulings

The Supreme Court also promoted national economic growth and the power of the federal government during this era. Led by Chief Justice John Marshall, a Federalist sympathizer, the Court issued a series of important rulings between 1819 and 1824.

In *McCulloch* v. *Maryland* (1819), the Court protected the second Bank of the United States. The case grew out of an attempt by the state of Maryland to put a tax on the branch of the Bank operating in that state. The Bank refused to pay the tax.

The Court's 1819 decision, written by Marshall, strengthened the power of the federal government. It ruled that states had no power to interfere with federal institutions. A tax, said the Court, was a dangerous interference because "the power to tax involves the power to destroy." Moreover, according to Marshall, a state cannot pass any law that violates a federal law. This reasoning would be used in future years to expand the power of the federal government.

British Leather Boots
The U.S. tariff on imports such as leather goods helped New England manufacturers to compete.

Vocabulary Builder
infrastructure (IHN frah struhk chahr) *n.* basic public works, like bridges and roads, needed for a society to function

Three Important Supreme Court Rulings
p. 343

Instruction L2

- Read Three Important Supreme Court Rulings together as a class. Remind students to look for details that answer the Section Focus Question.

- Ask: **How did the Supreme Court strengthen the power of the federal government?** (*by emphasizing the power of the federal government in cases in which states challenged it*)

- Ask: **How did the Supreme Court promote capitalism?** (*By protecting private contracts, it protected private businesses so they could compete in a free market.*)

Independent Practice

Have students complete the study guide for this section.

📖 **Interactive Reading and Notetaking Study Guide,** Chapter 10, Section 1 (Adapted Version also available.)

Monitor Progress

As students complete the Notetaking Study Guide, circulate to make sure that they understand the importance of these three Supreme Court rulings. Provide assistance as needed. Tell students to fill in the last column of the Reading Readiness Guide. Probe for what they learned that confirms or invalidates each statement.

All in One **Teaching Resources, Unit 3,** Reading Readiness Guide, p. 80

History Background

Dartmouth College Behind the Dartmouth College case lay an echo of British-American history. It was King George III who granted Dartmouth a charter as a private school. With independence, the states inherited the rights of such charters.

In opposing New Hampshire's actions, the school insisted that the royal charter was still valid. Arguing, and winning, the case was the well-known Dartmouth graduate, Daniel Webster.

Answer

☑**Checkpoint** It stressed high tariffs to protect northern manufacturers, which would act as an incentive for northerners to buy more agricultural products from the West and South. The tariff would also provide more revenue for the federal government, which could in turn be used to improve the infrastructure.

Assess and Reteach

Assess Progress   L2

Have students complete Check Your Progress. Administer the Section Quiz.

All in One Teaching Resources, Unit 3, Section Quiz, p. 93

To further assess student understanding, use the Progress Monitoring Transparency.

Progress Monitoring Transparencies, Chapter 10, Section 1

Reteach   L1

If students need more instruction, have them read this section in the Notetaking Study Guide and complete the accompanying question.

Interactive Reading and Notetaking Study Guide, Chapter 10, Section 1 (Adapted Version also available.)

Extend   L3

Have students complete the History Interactive activity online. Provide students with the Web Code below.

> **Extend Online**
> **For:** Help in starting the Extend activity
> **Visit:** PHSchool.com
> **Web Code:** myp-3061

Progress Monitoring Online

Students may check their comprehension of this section by completing the Progress Monitoring Online graphic organizer and self-quiz.

Answer

✔Checkpoint By protecting private contracts, the Court protected private businesses.

Interstate Commerce
No individual state could grant a monopoly to a steamboat company to use a river that divides two states, the Supreme Court ruled in *Gibbons* v. *Ogden*.

Two other decisions helped shape American life. In *Dartmouth College* v. *Woodward* (1819), the Court ruled that the charter of Dartmouth College in New Hampshire was a private contract. A **contract** is an agreement between two or more parties that can be enforced by law. Since the Constitution protected private contracts, New Hampshire could not change Dartmouth's charter. In protecting private contracts, the Court was protecting private businesses. In doing that, it helped promote **capitalism**—the economic system in which privately owned businesses compete in a free market.

In *Gibbons* v. *Ogden* (1824), the Court again supported federal power. It ruled that New York State could not give a steamboat company a monopoly to carry passengers on the Hudson River. The Court pointed out that travel on the Hudson River included stops in New Jersey as well as New York. Therefore, it was **interstate commerce**—trade between two or more states. Under the Constitution, only Congress can regulate interstate commerce. Again, the Court had strengthened the federal government at the expense of the states.

✔Checkpoint How did the Supreme Court ruling in *Dartmouth College* v. *Woodward* support economic growth?

⭐ **Looking Back and Ahead** Americans turned their attention to economic growth after the War of 1812. But while Americans were debating Henry Clay's American System, events in Latin America were drawing the concern of American leaders.

> **Progress Monitoring Online**
> **For:** Self-test with instant help
> **Visit:** PHSchool.com
> **Web Code:** mya-3061

Section 1 | Check Your Progress

Comprehension and Critical Thinking

1. **(a) Recall** Which groups supported and which opposed tariffs?
   (b) Draw Conclusions Do you think the American System offered a good solution to regional differences? Explain.

2. **(a) Recall** What did *McCulloch* v. *Maryland* decide?
   (b) Compare What did the Supreme Court decisions in *McCulloch* v. *Maryland* and *Gibbons* v. *Ogden* have in common?

Reading Skill

3. **Analyze Cause and Effect** Reread the text following the headings "The Tariff of 1816" and "Clay's American System." What did Clay believe would result from high tariffs?

Key Terms

Fill in the blanks with the correct key terms.

4. To set up the Bank of the United States, the government granted it a ____.
5. Private businesses compete in the American economic system called ____.

Writing

6. Decide which is the best closing sentence for an essay on James Monroe. Explain your choice.
   Sentences:
   (a) James Monroe, the fifth President of the United States, won two landslide victories.
   (b) Clearly, James Monroe deserved to have his presidency called the Era of Good Feelings.
   (c) James Monroe is, without a doubt, one of the greatest men ever elected President.

Section 1 Check Your Progress

1. **(a)** supported—the North; opposed—the South
   (b) Possible answers: Yes—all regions would have benefited. No—the benefits to the manufacturers might have been greater and happened sooner.

2. **(a)** States could not interfere with federal institutions or violate federal laws.
   (b) They both strengthened the power of the federal government by ruling that states had no power to interfere with federal institutions.

3. benefits to all regions; revenues for the federal government

4. charter

5. capitalism

6. Answer should support the choice.

SECTION 2

The Monroe Doctrine

"In the wars of the European powers in matters relating to themselves we have never taken any part. . . . We owe it, therefore, to candor and to the amicable relations existing between the United States and those powers to declare that we should consider any attempt on their part to extend their system to any portion of this hemisphere as dangerous to our peace and safety."

—President James Monroe,
address to Congress, 1823

◄ President James Monroe

Dealing With Other Nations

Objectives
- Explain why Spain ceded Florida to the United States.
- Describe how Spanish territories in the Americas gained independence.
- Explain why the Monroe Doctrine was issued.
- Discuss how Canada became self-governing.

Reading Skill

Identify Multiple Effects As you read about historical events, note that some events have multiple, or more than one, effects. Several effects may happen at the same time or one effect may lead to the next. As you read this section, look for multiple effects of each event.

Key Terms and People
cede
Miguel Hidalgo
Simón Bolívar
James Monroe
John Quincy Adams
self-government

Why It Matters After the War of 1812, the United States took a firm position against European influence in the Americas. President Monroe established a policy that would have a lasting impact on U.S. relations with Latin America.

② **Section Focus Question: How did U.S. foreign affairs reflect new national confidence?**

Relations With Spain

At the time of the War of 1812, the United States and Haiti were the only parts of the Americas not under European control. Spain controlled more territory in the Americas than any other European country. However, Spain's power had steadily weakened over several hundred years.

Spain's control was especially weak in Florida. Spain could not stop enslaved African Americans who escaped from plantations in Georgia and Alabama from crossing into Florida. Once in Florida, many of the escapees joined the Seminole Nation. The Seminoles often crossed into the United States to raid American settlements.

In 1817, the U.S. government sent Andrew Jackson to recapture those who had escaped slavery. Jackson attacked and destroyed Seminole villages. He then went far beyond his orders. He seized two important Spanish towns and forced the governor to flee Florida.

Jackson's attack on Florida showed that the United States could take over Florida whenever it wanted. Since Spain could not protect Florida, it decided to give up the territory. In the Adams-Onís Treaty of 1819, Spain ceded, or gave up, Florida to the United States.

✓Checkpoint What effect did Andrew Jackson's attack on Florida have on the government of Spain?

Section 2 Dealing With Other Nations 345

Vocabulary Builder

Use the information below to teach students this section's high-use words.

High-Use Word	Definition and Sample Sentence
province, p. 346	*n.* governmental division of a country, similar to a state Quebec is a **province** of Canada.
domestic, p. 348	*adj.* relating to one's country; internal President Washington was focused on dealing with **domestic** affairs.

Section 2
Step-by-Step Instruction

Review and Preview
Students have read about how the government dealt with economic concerns. Now they will focus on why the U.S. issued the Monroe Doctrine.

Section Focus Question
How did U.S. foreign affairs reflect new national confidence?
Before you begin the lesson for the day, write the Section Focus Question on the board. (*Lesson focus: The United States signaled that it was ready to take an active role in shaping events in the Western Hemisphere.*)

Prepare to Read

Build Background Knowledge **L2**
Preview the section and ask students to make predictions about what they will learn. Use the Idea Wave technique (TE, p. T24) to elicit responses.

Set a Purpose **L2**
- Read each statement in the Reading Readiness Guide aloud. Ask students to mark the statements True or False.

  All in One Teaching Resources, Unit 3, Reading Readiness Guide, p. 81

- Have students discuss the statements in pairs or groups of four, then mark their worksheets again. Use the Numbered Heads strategy (TE, p. T24) to call on students to share their group's perspectives. Students will return to these worksheets later.

Answer
✓Checkpoint Spain realized it could not protect Florida, so it sold the territory to the United States.

Teach

Relations With Spain
Spanish Colonies Win Independence

pp. 345–346

Instruction

L2

- **Vocabulary Builder** Before teaching this section, preteach the High-Use Words **province** and **domestic,** using the strategy on TE p. T21.

  Key Terms Have students continue to fill in the See It–Remember It chart for the key terms in this chapter.

- Read Relations with Spain and Spanish Colonies Win Independence, using the Choral Reading strategy (TE, p. T22).

- Ask: **How did Andrew Jackson's actions against the Seminoles demonstrate the power of the United States?** (*By seizing Spanish towns as well as destroying Seminole villages, he showed Spain that the United States could take Florida any time it wanted.*)

- Ask: **How do you think the struggles for independence in Mexico, South America, and Central America were similar?** (*Possible answers: They all had strong leaders to organize armies; most won their independence from Spain.*)

Independent Practice

Have students begin filling in the study guide for this section.

📖 **Interactive Reading and Notetaking Study Guide,** Chapter 10, Section 2 (Adapted Version also available.)

Monitor Progress

As students fill in the Notetaking Study Guide, circulate and make sure individuals understand the details about relations between the United States and Spain and the importance of the independence of Spain's former colonies.

Answers

 Reading Skill Mexico, Venezuela, Colombia, Ecuador, Panama, Nicaragua, Cost Rica, El Salvador, Honduras, Guatemala, Brazil

MAP MASTER Skills Activity **(a)** Cuba, Puerto Rico, British Honduras, British Guiana, Dutch Guiana, French Guiana **(b)** The United States acquired northern Mexico from just north of Baja California east to southern Texas.

Spanish Colonies Win Independence

By 1810, opposition to Spanish rule ran strong in Spain's American colonies. The American and French revolutions had inspired Latin Americans to want to control their own affairs. Revolutionary movements were growing in almost all of the Spanish colonies. Spain seemed unable to control the pressure for change in Latin America.

Mexico Breaks Away Mexico's struggle for independence began in 1810. In that year, Father Miguel Hidalgo (ee DAHL goh) organized an army of Native Americans that freed several Mexican provinces. However, in 1811, Hidalgo was captured and executed by troops loyal to Spain.

Another revolution broke out in Mexico in 1820. This time, Spain was unable to end the fighting. In 1821, Spain agreed to Mexico's independence.

At first, Mexico was ruled by an emperor. Then, in 1823, the monarchy was overthrown. A new constitution, patterned after the United States Constitution, made Mexico a federal republic of nineteen states and four territories.

Independence for South and Central America South America, too, was affected by revolutionary change. Here, the best-known leader of the struggle for independence from Spain was Simón Bolívar (see MOHN boh LEE vahr).

Vocabulary Builder
province (PRAHV ahns)
n. governmental division of a country, similar to a state

🔎 **Identify Multiple Effects**
Reading Skill What other nations were influenced by the American and French revolutions?

New Nations of Latin America

MAP MASTER®
Skills Activity

Wars of independence led to the creation of many new countries in Latin America in the first half of the 1800s.

(a) Read a Map What parts of Latin America remained colonies of European nations?

(b) Apply Information Use the world map in the Atlas in this textbook to identify how the border between the United States and Mexico has changed.

MapMaster ●nline

For: Interactive map
Visit: PHSchool.com
Web Code: myp-3062

KEY

▢ New nations
▢ European colonies

0 km 2,000
0 miles 2,000
Azimuthal Equal-Area Projection

PACIFIC OCEAN

ATLANTIC OCEAN

UNITED STATES · MEXICO · British Honduras · Cuba (Sp.) · HAITI · Puerto Rico (Sp.) · UNITED PROVINCES OF CENTRAL AMERICA · GRAN COLOMBIA · BRITISH GUIANA · DUTCH GUIANA · FRENCH GUIANA · PERU · BRAZIL · BOLIVIA · PARAGUAY · CHILE · ARGENTINA · URUGUAY

346

Differentiated Instruction

L1 English Language Learners   **L1** Less Proficient Readers   **L1** Special Needs

Gaining Comprehension Suggest to students that they use a ruler to help them keep their place as they read, line to line, down a page. Have students mark unfamiliar words or phrases with a sticky note, or jot down questions that occur as they are reading. Periodically provide assistance to the students to clarify these issues.

Bolívar is often called the Liberator for his role in leading independence movements in the northern part of South America. In August 1819, he led an army on a daring march from Venezuela over the ice-capped Andes Mountains and into Colombia. There, he defeated the Spanish and became president of the independent Republic of Great Colombia. It included today's nations of Venezuela, Colombia, Ecuador, and Panama.

Farther north, the people of Central America declared their independence from Spain in 1821. Two years later, they formed the United Provinces of Central America. It included today's nations of Nicaragua, Costa Rica, El Salvador, Honduras, and Guatemala.

In 1822, Brazil announced its independence from Portugal. Soon after, the United States recognized the independence of Mexico and six other former colonies in Central and South America. By 1825, most parts of Latin America had thrown off European rule.

☑Checkpoint **Why was Miguel Hidalgo important to the history of Mexico?**

The Monroe Doctrine

The future of these new countries was soon clouded. Several European powers, including France and Russia, indicated that they might help Spain regain its colonies.

This worried President James Monroe and Secretary of State John Quincy Adams. It also worried the British. Both nations wanted to protect trade with Latin America. In 1823, Britain suggested that the two countries issue a joint statement. The statement would announce their determination to protect the freedom of the new nations of Latin America.

Adams told President Monroe he thought the United States should take action alone. He believed a joint statement would make the United States look like Britain's junior partner. Monroe agreed.

In a message to Congress in December 1823, the President stated what is known as the Monroe Doctrine. The United States would not allow European nations to create American colonies or interfere with the free nations of Latin America. The United States would consider any attempt to do so "dangerous to our peace and safety."

At the time, the United States was not strong enough to block European action. Only the British navy could do that. As U.S. power grew, however, the Monroe Doctrine boosted the influence of the United States in the region.

☑Checkpoint **What was Adams's advice to Monroe?**

Links Across Time

Beyond the Monroe Doctrine

1823 The Monroe Doctrine warned European nations not to interfere in Latin America.

1900s U.S. Presidents cited the Monroe Doctrine to justify armed actions in Latin America. The actions often angered Latin Americans.

1930s President Franklin D. Roosevelt launched a Good Neighbor Policy. It stressed cooperation and trade to promote U.S. interests in the hemisphere.

Link to Today Online

Connection to Today What is the state of our relations with the countries of Latin America today?

For: U.S. relations with Latin America today
Visit: PHSchool.com
Web Code: myc-3062

Answers

☑Checkpoint He was a priest who led Mexico's struggle for independence from Spain. Though he was defeated, Spain eventually recognized that it could not maintain its rule over Mexico.

☑Checkpoint Adams said that cooperation between the two countries would make the U.S. seem to be Britain's junior partner.

The Monroe Doctrine
Relations With Canada
pp. 347–348

Instruction

- Have students read The Monroe Doctrine and Relations With Canada and look for details to answer the reading Checkpoint question.

- Ask: **How does John Quincy Adams's rejection of Britain's suggestion for a joint statement reflect the nation's new confidence?** (*Adams thought that it would detract from the nation's image as a strong, independent country.*)

- Ask: **Do you think there is a cause-and-effect link between the rebellions in Canada and the growing strength and independence of the United States? Explain.** (*Possible answer: Canadians were aware of how the United States won its independence and were probably inspired by it to seek self-government too.*)

- Contrast the British reactions to rebellions by Canadians and the American colonists. Ask: **Why did Britain react differently?** (*Britain learned a lesson from the American experience and realized it would have to grant Canadians some self-government to keep Canada loyal to Britain.*)

- After students have completed this discussion, distribute the "Hail America" worksheet.

  All in One Teaching Resources, Unit 3, "Hail America," p. 85

Independent Practice

Have students complete the study guide for this section.

  Interactive Reading and Notetaking Study Guide, Chapter 10, Section 2 (Adapted Version also available.)

Monitor Progress

- As students fill in the Notetaking Study Guide, make sure they understand the importance of the Monroe Doctrine and Canada's achievement of self-government.

- Tell students to fill in the last column of the Reading Readiness Guide. Probe for what they learned that confirms or invalidates each statement.

  All in One Teaching Resources, Unit 3, Reading Readiness Guide, p. 81

Assess and Reteach

Assess Progress `L2`

Have students complete Check Your Progress. Administer the Section Quiz.

All in One Teaching Resources, Section Quiz, p. 94

To further assess student understanding, use the Progress Monitoring Transparency.

Progress Monitoring Transparencies,
Chapter 10, Section 2

Reteach `L1`

If students need more instruction, have them read this section in the Interactive Reading and Notetaking Study Guide and complete the accompanying question.

Interactive Reading and Notetaking Study Guide, Chapter 10, Section 2 (Adapted Version also available.)

Extend `L3`

Have students do Internet research to prepare a timeline of important events in Canada, with special emphasis on connections with the United States. Provide students with the Web Code below.

> **Extend Online**
> **For:** Help in starting the Extend activity
> **Visit:** PHSchool.com
> **Web Code:** mye-0222

Progress Monitoring Online

Students may check their comprehension of this section by completing the Progress Monitoring Online graphic organizer and self-quiz.

Answer

Checkpoint Britain granted some self-government to Canada in order to stop rebellion and maintain Canada as a colony.

Section 2 Check Your Progress

1. (a) President Monroe's statement that the United States would not allow European nations to interfere with the independent nations of Latin America
(b) Possible answer: Yes, because it might seem to suggest that it would require Britain to enforce the doctrine.

Relations With Canada

Canada remained a British colony after the American Revolution. In 1791, the country was divided into two parts. Upper Canada was mainly English, and Lower Canada was mainly French. In 1837, there were rebellions against British rule in both parts of Canada.

Although the British put down the rebellions, they learned a lesson. They could no longer deny rights to Canadians. Britain would have to give Canadians more powers of self-government—the right of people to rule themselves independently. The Act of Union of 1841 was a major step in that direction. It merged Canada's two parts into a single unit governed by a Canadian legislature. Britain, however, still had ultimate control.

Canada and the United States had their own disagreements. Tensions were particularly high when the United States unsuccessfully tried to invade Canada during the War of 1812.

The situation slowly improved after the war. Between 1818 and 1846, the United States and Britain settled several border disputes regarding Canada. Eventually, the United States and Canada established excellent relations. Their relations remain strong to this day.

Checkpoint Why did Britain grant some self-government to Canada?

⭐ **Looking Back and Ahead** The Monroe Doctrine convinced Americans that their southern borders were safe from European expansion. Treaties with Britain lessened the tensions along the northern border with Canada. With a new sense of confidence, Americans prepared to make great strides on the domestic front. The 1820s and 1830s would see an upsurge in the democratic spirit.

Vocabulary Builder
domestic (doh MEHS tihk) *adj.*
relating to one's country; internal

> **Progress Monitoring Online**
> **For:** Self-test with instant help
> **Visit:** PHSchool.com
> **Web Code:** mya-3062

Section 2 | Check Your Progress

Comprehension and Critical Thinking
1. (a) Summarize What was the Monroe Doctrine?
(b) Clarify Problems Would the United States have looked weak if it had jointly issued a warning with Britain? Explain.

2. (a) List Name six of today's Latin American countries that were independent by 1825.
(b) Identify Economic Benefits How did Great Britain and the United States benefit from the independence of Spain's American colonies?

Reading Skill
3. Identify Multiple Effects European powers, such as France and Russia, considered helping Spain regain its South and Central American colonies. What were the effects of this situation? Reread the text under the heading "The Monroe Doctrine."

Key Terms
Answer the following questions in complete sentences that show your understanding of the key terms.
4. What did Spain cede to the United States in the Adams-Onís Treaty?

5. How did Canadians benefit when Britain granted them more self-government?

Writing
6. Revise the following sentences to make them flow better. **Sentences:** The Monroe Doctrine stated that the United States would not allow Spain to take back its former colonies. The doctrine helped the new Latin American states remain free. The doctrine supported the cause of democracy in the Western Hemisphere.

---

2. (a) Answers will vary but should include Mexico, Peru, Brazil, Bolivia, Paraguay, Chile, Argentina, Haiti, and Uruguay.
(b) With Spain no longer limiting the trade of its former colonies, they were now free to trade with Britain and the United States.

3. Accept any two or more of these: British and U.S. governments became concerned; Britain suggested alliance; Monroe issued the Monroe Doctrine rejecting alliance.

4. Florida

5. They could now govern themselves.

6. Sentences should demonstrate an understanding of events and use connecting words to flow smoothly.

Jackson Forever!
The Hero of Two Wars and of Orleans!
The Man of the People!
HE WHO COULD NOT BARTER NOR BARGAIN FOR THE
PRESIDENCY!

BECAUSE
It should be derived from the
PEOPLE!

KNOCK DOWN

OLD HICKORY
AND THE ELECTORAL LAW.

Election Fever
" The election fever which is constantly raging through the land . . . engrosses every conservation, it irritates every temper, it substitutes party spirit for personal esteem. . . . "

—Frances Trollope, comments on the election of 1832

◄ Supporters of Andrew Jackson were proud of his military exploits and elected him President.

The Age of Jackson

Objectives
- Discuss the conflict between Andrew Jackson and John Quincy Adams over the election of 1824.
- Explain how the right to vote expanded in the United States.
- Describe Andrew Jackson's victory in the election of 1828.

Reading Skill

Identify Short-Term Effects Some events have effects that take place shortly after the event. Other events create changes that last only a short time. Both of these types of effects are short-term effects. As you read Section 3, look for examples of the short-term effects of events.

Key Terms and People

Andrew Jackson   nominating
suffrage   convention
caucus   spoils system

Why It Matters The Constitution had established a system based on representative government. But not all citizens could fully participate in the early American republic. During the Age of Jackson, however, the democratic spirit grew and more Americans played an active role in government.

? **Section Focus Question: How did the people gain more power during the Age of Jackson?**

Adams and Jackson in Conflict

Andrew Jackson served two terms as President, from 1829 to 1837. His presidency marked the opening of a new and more democratic era in American political life. So great was his influence that the twenty-year period after he became President is often called the Age of Jackson.

Andrew Jackson was a wealthy man by the time he became President. However, he began life with very little. Born in a log cabin on the border of North and South Carolina, he was an orphan by the age of 14. Jackson was ambitious, brave, and tough. He survived smallpox as a child and severe gunshot wounds as an adult.

During a difficult march with his troops in 1812, one soldier described him as "tough as hickory." Hickory trees are extremely strong, and their wood is very hard. The description fit Jackson so well that it stuck as a nickname. Jackson became known as Old Hickory.

Jackson stood for the idea that ordinary people should participate in American political life. As a general and later as President, Andrew Jackson was deeply loved by millions of ordinary Americans. They loved him for his humble beginnings and his firm leadership.

Section 3 The Age of Jackson   **349**

Vocabulary Builder

Use the information below to teach students this section's high-use words.

High-Use Word	Definition and Sample Sentence
react, p. 350	*v.* to act in response to another action; to respond King George III **reacted** with anger when he heard of the colonists' demands.
participate, p. 351	*v.* to take part in The delegates to the Constitutional Convention **participated** in a historical debate over the nature of government.

Review and Preview

Students have studied how the early Republic dealt with domestic and foreign concerns. Now they will read about political changes in the 1820s and 1830s.

Section Focus Question

How did the people gain more power during the Age of Jackson?

Before you begin the lesson for the day, write the Section Focus Question on the board. (*Lesson focus: During Andrew Jackson's presidency, a growing spirit of democracy resulted in more people being allowed to vote.*)

Prepare to Read

Build Background Knowledge

Explain to students that in this section, they will read more about Andrew Jackson and learn how his presidency affected the lives of Americans. Ask students to preview the headings and Main Idea statements in this section to speculate on whether Jackson's actions benefited ordinary Americans. Use the Idea Wave technique (TE, p. T24) to elicit responses.

Set a Purpose

- Read each statement in the Reading Readiness Guide aloud. Ask students to mark the statements True or False.

  All in One Teaching Resources, Unit 3, Reading Readiness Guide, p. 82

- Have students discuss their statements in pairs or groups of four, then mark their worksheets again. Use the Numbered Heads strategy (TE, p. T24) to call on students to share their group's perspectives. The students will return to these worksheets later.

Teach

Adams and Jackson in Conflict

p. 349

Instruction

L2

- **Vocabulary Builder** Before teaching this section, preteach the High-Use Words **react** and **participate,** using the strategy on TE p. T21.
  Key Terms Have students continue to fill in the See It–Remember It chart for the key terms in this chapter.

- Read Adams and Jackson in Conflict with students, using the Choral Reading strategy (TE, p. T22).

- Ask: **What did Andrew Jackson want to see in American political life?** (*the participation of ordinary people*)

- Ask: **Why did the election of 1824 seem to be taken out of the hands of the people?** (*Because even though Jackson had more of the popular vote, he did not have a majority of the electoral votes. The House of Representatives had to decide the election.*)

- Display *The Election of 1824* transparency. Work through the map and key together with students. Call on students to answer the questions.

Color Transparencies, The Election of 1824

Independent Practice

Have students begin filling in the study guide for this section.

📖 **Interactive Reading and Notetaking Study Guide,** Chapter 10, Section 3 (Adapted Version also available.)

Monitor Progress

As students fill in the Notetaking Study Guide, circulate and make sure individuals understand the election process. Provide assistance as needed.

Answer

Draw Conclusions With their new right to vote, people would work on a political campaign so their candidate would win.

350 Chapter 10

The Election of 1824 Jackson first ran for President in 1824. His opponents were John Quincy Adams, Henry Clay, and William H. Crawford of Georgia. Jackson received the most electoral votes, but not a majority. According to the Constitution, the House of Representatives would have to decide the election.

The choice was between Jackson and Adams, the two who had received the most votes. As Speaker of the House, Clay had great influence. He told his supporters to vote for Adams. The House then elected Adams on the first ballot.

Jackson <u>reacted</u> with fury. He had won the most popular votes and the most electoral votes, but still had lost the election. When Adams appointed Clay secretary of state, Jackson's supporters claimed the two men had made a "corrupt bargain."

The Presidency of John Quincy Adams Adams was burdened by the charges of a secret deal. He accomplished little, even though he had ambitious plans for the nation. He supported Clay's American System and wanted the federal government to play a larger role in supporting the American economy.

Adams proposed a national program to build roads and canals and a high tariff to protect industry. He also planned to set up a national university and an observatory for astronomers in Washington, D.C. However, he lacked the political skill to push his programs through Congress. Adams never won the trust of the American people. As a result, he served only one term.

Vocabulary Builder
<u>react</u> (ree AKT) **v.** to act in response to another action

● **INFOGRAPHIC**

Democracy in Action

Voter Participation in Presidential Elections, 1824–1840

The Age of Jackson saw the first stirrings of democracy in action in the United States. More men could and did vote, and many more people joined political parties and participated in election campaigns.

It would be many years until women and African Americans also gained the right to vote. However, the kinds of political contests that are familiar to Americans today had their beginnings in the presidential elections of the 1820s and 1830s. **Critical Thinking:** *Draw Conclusions Why would people become more actively involved in political campaigns as the right to vote was extended to new groups?*

350

Differentiated Instruction

L1 English Language Learners   **L1** Special Needs

Gaining Comprehension Students may have difficulty understanding why a candidate who had the most votes did not win the election of 1824. Explain that in order to have a majority of votes (rather than only a plurality), a candidate must win more than half the total cast. Have students role-play voters by nominating three or more favorite foods or objects, then voting for the one they favor most. Only the one with a majority of votes—that is, more than half the total—wins. Explain that the difficulty of getting a majority increases when there are more than two candidates.

Despite his failures, Adams was an eloquent supporter of what he saw as America's special place in the world. He stated his ideas in a Fourth of July speech in 1821. He said the United States had no designs on the territory of other nations:

> "Wherever the standard of freedom and independence has been or shall be unfurled, there will her [America's] heart, . . . and her prayers be. But she goes not abroad in search of monsters to destroy. She is the well-wisher to the freedom and independence of all."
> —John Quincy Adams, Fourth of July 1821 Address

✓**Checkpoint** Why did Jackson's supporters claim there had been a "corrupt bargain" in the election of 1824?

A New Era in Politics

The election of 1824 disappointed Andrew Jackson and his followers. Still, that election began a new era in American politics.

Back in the 1790s, states had begun extending suffrage—the right to vote. Many states dropped the requirement that men had to own property to be able to <u>participate</u> in voting. Voting requirements varied slightly from state to state. However, almost all adult white males now could vote and hold office.

Vocabulary Builder
participate (pahr TIHS ah payt)
v. to take part in; to share in an activity

◄ *The County Election,* George Caleb Bingham

◄ Portrait of Andrew Jackson shown inside a souvenir box from an early presidential campaign.

351

Instruction L2

- Read A New Era of Politics with students. Remind them to look for answers to the Section Focus Question.

- Ask: **What is suffrage and who had it at that time?** (*Suffrage is the right to vote, and only white males had it.*) Discuss how extending suffrage was an example of expanding democracy in the Jackson era.

- Ask: **In what way did the formation of a second party make for a more representative democracy?** (*Previously, during the Era of Good Feelings, there was only one party. A second party could represent those people with differing views.*)

- Have students compare the caucus system to the nominating convention. Then ask: **How did ordinary people gain more political influence through this change?** (*The caucus system involved only a few members of a particular party. The convention system opened the nominating process to more people.*)

Independent Practice

Have students continue filling in the study guide for this section.

📖 **Interactive Reading and Notetaking Study Guide,** Chapter 10, Section 3 (Adapted Version also available.)

Monitor Progress

As students fill in the Notetaking Study Guide, circulate to be sure students understand suffrage. Provide assistance as needed.

History Background

Rights of Women In addition to the right to vote, other rights were denied to women in the early 1800s. They were not admitted to colleges, and married women could not make contracts, own property, or control their own earnings. As the 1800s progressed, coeducational colleges and colleges just for women opened, and women were allowed to control their own property after marriage. The Nineteenth Amendment granted suffrage at the national level in 1920.

Answer

✓**Checkpoint** Henry Clay threw his support to John Quincy Adams. Then, as President, Adams appointed Clay as his secretary of state.

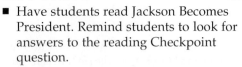

Jackson Becomes President

p. 353

Instruction L2

- Have students read Jackson Becomes President. Remind students to look for answers to the reading Checkpoint question.

- Discuss with students why Jackson's victory in 1828 was described as being a victory for the "common man." (*Jackson won support from ordinary Americans.*)

- Ask: **Why was Jackson able to explain his use of the "spoils system" as being a way to further democracy?** (*He was putting new people into government jobs.*)

- Display the transparency *The Election of 1828* and call on students to answer the questions. Then ask students to compare the elections of 1828 and 1824. (*Jackson won the later election decisively against only one candidate—President John Quincy Adams.*)

Color Transparencies, The Election of 1828

Answers

Biography Quest Possible answer: As a self-made success, he seemed to be one of the average people. He opposed special privilege for the wealthy and encouraged ordinary people to hold public office.

Reading Skill More people were involved in the nominating process.

Checkpoint all women, all enslaved African American men, most free African American men

---

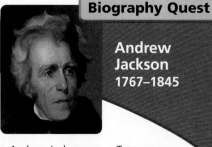

Biography Quest

Andrew Jackson
1767–1845

Andrew Jackson was a Tennessee landowner, lawyer, and judge. His military campaigns against the British in the War of 1812 and against Native Americans in Florida made him a war hero. Political opponents called him a country hick. But supporters admired him as a self-made man who spoke out for ordinary people. His election as President was a sign that the United States was becoming a more democratic nation.

Biography Quest nline

How did Jackson gain a reputation as a supporter of ordinary people?

For: The answer to the question about Jackson
Visit: PHSchool.com
Web Code: myd-3063

Identify Short-Term Effects
What was the immediate effect of using nominating conventions to choose presidential candidates?

States also were changing how they chose presidential electors. Previously, state legislatures chose them. Now, that right went to the voters. In 1824, voters chose the presidential electors in 18 out of 24 states.

Of course, suffrage was still restricted in the United States. Women could not participate in government. Nor could enslaved African Americans, male or female. In most states, even free African Americans could not vote.

Democracy in the Age of Jackson

Extending the right to vote was part of a larger spread of democratic ideas. Supporters of Andrew Jackson believed that ordinary people should vote in elections, hold public office, and do anything else they had the ability to do. Jackson's supporters strongly opposed special privileges for those of high social status.

Wealthy observers were sometimes dismayed by this spirit of equality. One visitor complained, "the rich and the poor, the educated and the ignorant, the polite and the vulgar, all . . . feed at the same table."

Jackson and his supporters did not trust government. They believed it often favored the rich and powerful. The Jacksonians also were suspicious of banks, which they believed favored the rich.

New Political Parties The Age of Jackson brought back the two-party system that had briefly ended during the Era of Good Feelings. During the 1824 election, the Republican Party split. Supporters of Adams called themselves National Republicans. Jackson's supporters used the name Democrats.

In 1831, the National Republicans nominated Henry Clay to run against Jackson. Jackson won easily, with strength in all parts of the country. However, by 1836, the anti-Jackson forces had formed a new party, the Whigs. From then until 1852, the Democrats and the Whigs were the country's two major political parties.

The new parties adopted a new way of choosing their presidential candidates. Previously, a party's members of Congress held a caucus—a meeting of members of a political party. These caucuses involved only a small group of people. Beginning in 1831, political parties started holding national nominating conventions—large meetings of party delegates to choose candidates for office. National conventions opened the nominating process to many more people and made it more democratic.

Checkpoint Which groups did not benefit from increased suffrage in the United States?

Differentiated Instruction

L3 Advanced Readers **L3 Gifted and Talented**

Researching Political Parties Have students research the political parties in the election of 1832, the Democrats and the National Republicans. Have groups of students develop a campaign to enlist members in each party, using text and graphics appropriate to the period. Have them share their work with the class.

Jackson Becomes President

Three times as many people voted in the election of 1828 as had voted in 1824. Most of these new voters supported Jackson, who easily defeated Adams.

The election revealed growing sectional and class divisions among American voters. Jackson did best in the West and the South, where planters and small farmers supported him. He also did well among small business people, artisans, and workers in cities and towns nationwide. Adams was most popular in his home region of New England.

Jackson's Inauguration Jackson's supporters called the election a victory for the "common man." His inauguration in March 1829 showed what they meant. Thousands of ordinary working people jammed into Washington for the event. After the inauguration at the Capitol, Jackson rode a horse to the White House. A journalist described the scene:

> **❝**As far as the eye could reach, the sidewalks of the Avenue were covered with people on foot . . . with . . . carriages and persons on horseback. . . . For a full half hour, I stood waiting for the stream to run by; but like a never failing fountain people continued pouring forth.**❞**
> —Amos Kendall in the *Argus of Western America,*
> March 29, 1829

Jackson's Inauguration
Joyful crowds welcomed Andrew Jackson to the White House upon his inauguration in 1829. The artist who created this picture made sly fun of the celebrants. **Critical Thinking: Apply Information** *Why were some people upset by what happened at Jackson's inauguration?*

Instruction (continued)

■ Have students complete the primary source worksheet Andrew Jackson and the Spoils System. Ask students if they think the spoils system was fair. (*Answers will vary but may include it was unfair because it removed people who had a background in the job, or it was fair because it gave new people the opportunity to try to change things for the better.*)

[All in One] **Teaching Resources, Unit 3,** Andrew Jackson and the Spoils System, p. 86

Independent Practice

Have students complete the study guide for this section.

Interactive Reading and Notetaking Study Guide, Chapter 10, Section 3 (Adapted Version also available.)

Monitor Progress

As students fill in the Notetaking Study Guide, circulate to make sure students understand the details of Jackson's inauguration and term. Provide assistance as needed.

Tell students to fill in the last column of the Reading Readiness Guide. Ask them to consider whether what they learned was what they had expected to learn.

[All in One] **Teaching Resources, Unit 3,** Reading Readiness Guide, p. 82

History Background

Jackson's Inauguration Margaret Bayard Smith was an author and socialite who wrote about Washington society. She attended Andrew Jackson's first inauguration at the White House to celebrate. In her book *The First Forty Years of Washington Society,* she wrote about the day. "The President, after having been literally nearly pressed to death and almost suffocated and torn to pieces by the people in their eagerness to shake hands with Old Hickory, had retreated . . . This wild scene had not been anticipated and therefore not provided against. Ladies and gentlemen only had been expected, not the people en masse. But it was the people's day, and the people's President would rule."

Answer
Apply Information They thought that mobs took over the White House.

Assess Progress L2

Have students complete Check Your Progress. Administer the Section Quiz.

All in One Teaching Resources, Unit 3, p. 95

To further assess student understanding, use the Progress Monitoring Transparency.

Progress Monitoring Transparencies, Chapter 10, Section 3

Reteach L1

If students need more instruction, have them read this section in the Interactive Reading and Notetaking Study Guide and complete the accompanying question.

Interactive Reading and Notetaking Study Guide, Chapter 10, Section 3 (Adapted Version also available.)

Extend L3

Have students research the life of Andrew Jackson on the Internet. Have them make a timeline of important events in his life.

Extend Online
For: Help in starting the Extend activity
Visit: PHSchool.com
Web Code: mye-0223

Progress Monitoring Online

Students may check their comprehension of this section by completing the Progress Monitoring Online graphic organizer and self-quiz.

Answer

✓**Checkpoint** He believed that putting new people into government jobs furthered democracy.

Twenty thousand people crowded in and around the White House for a reception in Jackson's honor. They did not all behave well. Some broke furniture, spilled drinks, trampled rugs, and broke several thousand dollars worth of glassware and dishes. Officials finally lured the unruly crowd outside by moving the punch bowl onto the White House lawn.

Jackson's opponents were shocked. One member of the Supreme Court complained about the "reign of King Mob." A Jackson supporter saw things more positively: "It was the People's day, and the People's President, and the People would rule."

The Spoils of Victory Jackson began his term by replacing some government officials with his supporters. Previous Presidents had done the same thing. In fact, during his two terms Jackson replaced only about 20 percent of federal officeholders.

The difference was that Jackson openly defended what he was doing. He claimed putting new people into government jobs furthered democracy. One of his supporters put it more selfishly when he compared the process to a conquering army after a war, saying "to the victors belong the spoils [loot]." People quickly applied the term spoils system to the practice of rewarding government jobs to loyal supporters of the party that wins an election.

✓**Checkpoint** How did Andrew Jackson justify the spoils system?

⭐ **Looking Back and Ahead** As President, Andrew Jackson supported the right of ordinary people to participate in government. Jackson's belief in equality, however, left out many, including Native Americans. In the next section, you will read how government policies denied basic rights to Native Americans.

Section 3 | **Check Your Progress**

Progress Monitoring Online
For: Self-test with instant help
Visit: PHSchool.com
Web Code: mya-3063

Comprehension and Critical Thinking

1. (a) Recall What was the "corrupt bargain"?
(b) Evaluate Information Who benefited from accusations of a "corrupt bargain"?

2. (a) Recall How did the United States become more democratic between the 1790s and the 1830s?
(b) Draw Conclusions How did these democratic changes contribute to Jackson's election in 1828?

 Reading Skill
3. Identify Short-Term Effects What was the immediate effect when Henry Clay told his supporters to vote for Adams?

Key Terms
Read each sentence below. If the sentence is true, write YES. If the sentence is not true, write NO and explain why.
4. By 1828, suffrage had been extended to white women and African Americans.
5. In 1824, a nominating convention chose John Quincy Adams to run for President.

6. Tens of thousands of ordinary citizens showed up for the caucus celebrating Jackson's victory.

Writing
7. Using vivid, specific words will make your writing livelier and more accurate. Rewrite these sentences using more specific, colorful words. **Sentences:** Many people liked Andrew Jackson, and he was very popular. People liked Jackson better than John Quincy Adams. They felt Jackson was a man of the people and Adams was not a man of the people.

Section 3 Check Your Progress

1. (a) It is what appeared to be a secret deal between John Quincy Adams and Henry Clay. Clay told his supporters to vote for Adams, who later made Clay his secretary of state.
(b) Andrew Jackson

2. (a) Suffrage was extended to more white males, and more voters could choose presidential electors.

(b) Many more people voted in 1828 than previously, and Jackson drew support from these newer voters.

3. Adams won the election.

4. No, voting rights had not been extended to women and African Americans.

5. No. Nominating conventions did not begin until 1831.

6. No. They came for the inauguration.

7. Students might use words and phrases such as *beloved, disliked, corrupt.*

Jackson's Viewpoint

❝It will incalculably strengthen the southwestern frontier and render the adjacent states strong enough to repel future invasions without remote aid . . . and enable those states to advance rapidly in population, wealth, and power.❞

—Andrew Jackson, explaining the benefits of Indian removal, 1830

◄ Seminole woman

Indian Removal

Objectives
- Describe the culture of Native Americans in the Southeast.
- Describe the conflict over land occupied by Native Americans in the Southeast.
- Discuss the forced removal of Native Americans.

🔵 Reading Skill

Identify Long-Term Effects Many historical events have long-term effects—lasting effects that build up over time. As you read Section 4, look for events that have long-term effects. Think about why these causes have had such a lasting effect.

Key Person
Sequoyah

Why It Matters As a general, Andrew Jackson won great popularity for his victories over Indians in Georgia and Florida. As President, he worked to remove Native Americans from their homelands. This forced migration still affects Native Americans today.

❓ **Section Focus Question: Why did Jackson use force to remove Indians from the Southeast?**

Native Americans of the Southeast

When Andrew Jackson became President, more than 100,000 Native Americans still lived east of the Mississippi River. Many were farmers or lived in towns.

The Choctaw, Chickasaw, Cherokee, and Creek nations lived in parts of Mississippi, Alabama, Georgia, North Carolina, and Tennessee. The Seminoles, who lived in Florida, had an unusual origin. They were a combination of Creeks who had moved into Florida, Florida Native Americans, and escaped African American slaves.

The Cherokees had adopted some white customs. Aside from farming, they ran successful businesses, such as grain and lumber mills. Some could speak and read English. Many had converted to Christianity.

The Cherokees even had a written alphabet for their language. It had been created by a learned leader named Sequoyah (sih KWOY uh). In 1827, the Cherokees established a government based on a written constitution. They claimed status as a separate nation. The next year, they started a newspaper in both English and Cherokee.

✅**Checkpoint** What were some of the customs and ways of life of the Cherokees?

Section 4 Indian Removal **355**

Vocabulary Builder

Use the information below to teach students this section's high-use words.

High-Use Word	Definition and Sample Sentence
voluntary, p. 357	*adj.* done willingly, of one's own free will Settlers began a huge **voluntary** movement westward.
quote, p. 357	*v.* to repeat the exact words spoken or written The newspaper **quoted** long excerpts from the President's speech.

Section 4
Step-by-Step Instruction

Review and Preview

Students have learned about the election of Andrew Jackson. Now they will study his policies toward Native Americans.

Section Focus Question

Why did Jackson use force to remove Native Americans from the Southeast?

Before you begin the lesson for the day, write the Section Focus Question on the board. (*Lesson focus: Whites wanted their land, and Native Americans would not move voluntarily. The government decided that Native Americans stood in the way of westward expansion.*)

Prepare to Read

Build Background Knowledge L2

Tell students that in this section, they will read how Andrew Jackson used his power as President. Ask students to speculate about whether a President of today could take actions contrary to a Supreme Court decision.

Set a Purpose L2

- Form students into pairs or groups of four. Distribute the Reading Readiness Guide. Ask students to fill in the first two columns of the chart.

  All in One **Teaching Resources, Unit 3,** Reading Readiness Guide, p. 83

- Use the Numbered Heads strategy (TE, p. T24) to call on students to share one piece of information they already know and one piece of information they want to know. The students will return to these worksheets later.

Answer
✅**Checkpoint** Many converted to Christianity, spoke English, and ran businesses.

Teach

Native Americans of the Southeast

p. 355   L2

Instruction

- **Vocabulary Builder** Before teaching this section, preteach the High-Use Words **voluntary** and **quote,** using the strategy on TE p. T21.
  Key Terms Have students continue to fill in the See It–Remember It chart for the key terms in this chapter.

- Read Native Americans of the Southeast, using the ReQuest strategy (TE, p. T23).

- Students may have misconceptions about the customs and lifestyle of Native Americans in the 1800s. Based on movies and novels, they may think Indians were only hunters and warriors. Address these impressions when discussing this section. (*Many Cherokees were farmers or businessmen. They had their own schools. Some could read and write English. Many had converted to Christianity.*)

- Discuss the status of the Cherokees in 1827. (*Although they had adapted many white customs, they had their own government with a constitution written in their own language. They claimed status as a separate nation living in the United States.*)

Independent Practice

Have students begin filling in the study guide for this section.

📖 **Interactive Reading and Notetaking Study Guide,** Chapter 10, Section 4 (Adapted Version also available.)

Monitor Progress

As students fill in the Notetaking Study Guide, circulate to make sure students understand how the Cherokees adapted to whites. Provide assistance as needed.

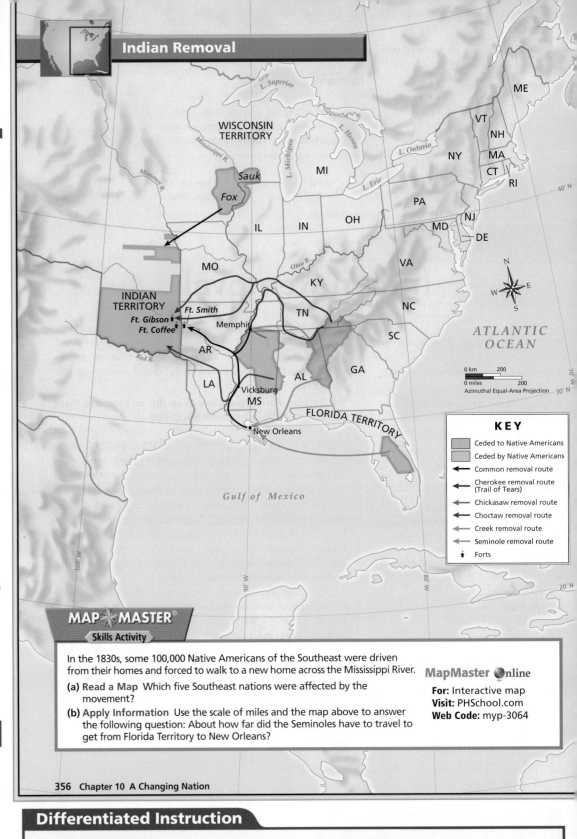

Indian Removal

KEY
- Ceded to Native Americans
- Ceded by Native Americans
- Common removal route
- Cherokee removal route (Trail of Tears)
- Chickasaw removal route
- Choctaw removal route
- Creek removal route
- Seminole removal route
- Forts

MAP★MASTER®

Skills Activity

In the 1830s, some 100,000 Native Americans of the Southeast were driven from their homes and forced to walk to a new home across the Mississippi River.

(a) Read a Map Which five Southeast nations were affected by the movement?

(b) Apply Information Use the scale of miles and the map above to answer the following question: About how far did the Seminoles have to travel to get from Florida Territory to New Orleans?

MapMaster Online

For: Interactive map
Visit: PHSchool.com
Web Code: myp-3064

356 Chapter 10 A Changing Nation

Differentiated Instruction

L3 Gifted and Talented

Retracing the Trail of Tears Have students work in pairs to plan a walking trip that retraces the Trail of Tears. Tell them to make lists of everything they would need to take in order to get from Georgia to the Indian Territory by foot. Suggest that one group plan to make the trip in the summer, while another plans for a winter trip. Have groups share their lists.

Answers

MAP★MASTER **(a)** Cherokee, Choctaw, Chickasaw, Creek, Seminole **(b)** 525 miles
Skills Activity

Conflict Over Land

To government leaders, the presence of Native Americans in the Southeast stood in the way of westward expansion of the United States. Furthermore, the Native Americans lived on fertile land. White farmers wanted that land for growing cotton.

Forced Movement Policies to move Native Americans from their lands dated from the presidency of Thomas Jefferson. Jefferson hoped the movement would be <u>voluntary</u>. He believed that moving west was the only way the Native Americans could preserve their cultures.

After the War of 1812, the federal government signed treaties with several Native American groups of the Old Northwest. Under those treaties, the groups gave up their lands and moved west of the Mississippi River.

However, the Native Americans of the Southeast would not move. In 1825, President James Monroe suggested a plan to move all Native Americans living east of the Mississippi to land west of the river. However, nothing came of the plan. Yet, year by year, the pressure on the Native Americans of the Southeast grew. By the 1820s, many white southerners were demanding that Native Americans be removed by force.

In 1825 and 1827, the state of Georgia passed a law forcing the Creeks to give up most of their land. In 1828, Georgia tried to get the Cherokees to do the same. The state said the Cherokees were not a separate nation and they had to move off their land.

Support for Native Americans Georgia's actions were challenged in two suits that reached the Supreme Court. The decision in the first suit went against the Cherokees. In *Cherokee Nation* v. *Georgia* (1831), the Court refused to stop Georgia from enforcing its law. But in *Worcester* v. *Georgia* (1832), the Court declared that Georgia's laws "can have no force" within Cherokee territory.

Chief Justice John Marshall wrote the Court's majority opinion in *Worcester* v. *Georgia*. He <u>quoted</u> treaties that the United States had signed, guaranteeing certain territory to Native Americans. Under the Constitution, treaties are the supreme law of the land. Therefore, Marshall said, Georgia had no say over Cherokee territory.

Like the state of Georgia, President Jackson wanted to remove the Native Americans from their land. He was furious when he heard of the ruling in *Worcester* v. *Georgia*. "John Marshall has made his decision," he is reported to have said. "Now let him enforce it!"

Jackson was already putting into effect a federal law called the Indian Removal Act of 1830. The law gave him authority to offer Native American nations land west of the Mississippi in exchange for their lands in the East. It also provided money so the law could be carried out.

☑ **Checkpoint** According to Marshall, why was Georgia barred from applying its laws to Cherokee territory?

Vocabulary Builder
<u>voluntary</u> (VAHL ahn tair ee)
adj. done willingly, of one's own free will

Vocabulary Builder
<u>quote</u> (kwoht) ***v.*** to repeat the exact words spoken or written

---

Conflict Over Land
p. 357

Instruction

- Have students read Conflict Over Land. Remind students to look for details to answer the Section Focus Question.

- Ask: **Why did Jackson want the Native American groups to move?** (*To government leaders, the Native Americans stood in the way of westward expansion.*)

- Discuss the Supreme Court cases involving the Cherokees. Ask: **Which case supported the Cherokees?** (*Worcester* v. *Georgia*)

- Ask: **In what way do you think Jackson's defiance of the Supreme Court's decision was typical of his history and character?** (*Possible answers: He was used to doing things on his own, as when he attacked Spanish settlements in Florida. He knew that whites would support his decision, and he was accustomed to meeting the general public's wishes.*) Ask: **Why did Jackson enforce the Indian Removal Act of 1830?** (*It was a way to bypass the Court's decision.*)

- Have students look at the map on the opposite page. Ask: **Which Americans had the most to gain with the Indian Removal Act?** (*southerners and westerners*)

Independent Practice
Have students continue filling in the study guide for this section.

📖 **Interactive Reading and Notetaking Study Guide,** Chapter 10, Section 4 (Adapted Version also available.)

Monitor Progress

As students fill in the Notetaking Study Guide, circulate to make sure students understand how the government leaders made the Native Americans move from their land. Provide assistance as needed.

History Background

Georgia's Gold Rush Cherokee country in northern Georgia was the site of one of the earliest gold rushes in U.S. history. In the early 1800s, gold had been discovered in Georgia near the Cherokee town of Sixes. People began rushing to Georgia in hopes of finding gold. However, the Cherokees inhabited most of the land in the region. Georgia tried to remove them from their land. The state held lotteries that gave both land and gold rights to whites. But Cherokees were not allowed to mine for gold. By 1830, more than 300 ounces of gold were being mined daily. This rush continued until 1849 when the California gold rush began and many of the miners left the area.

Answer

☑ **Checkpoint** Marshall said that the Cherokees had a right to their land because they were a Native American tribe that had treaties with the United States. The state of Georgia could not violate federal laws and treaties.

Explore More Video

Discovery School Video

This video examines the expulsion of the Cherokee people from their traditional lands in the south-central United States. Although the Cherokees adopted American customs, they were forced to move. Many died on the difficult march to present-day Oklahoma.

On the Trail of Tears

p. 358

Instruction L2

- Have students read On the Trail of Tears. Remind students to look for the sequence of events.

- Ask: **What step was taken before the actual removal of Native Americans?** (*Native Americans signed treaties giving up their lands and agreed to move to what is now Oklahoma.*)

- Distribute worksheet Tsali of the Cherokees. Have students read the excerpt and answer the questions.

  All in One Teaching Resources, Unit 3, Tsali of the Cherokees, p. 87

Independent Practice

Have students complete the study guide for this section.

Interactive Reading and Notetaking Study Guide, Chapter 10, Section 4 (Adapted Version also available.)

Monitor Progress

As students fill in the Notetaking Study Guide, circulate to make sure students understand the importance of the Trail of Tears. Provide assistance as needed.

Tell students to fill in the last column of the Reading Readiness Guide. Probe for what they learned that confirms or invalidates each statement.

All in One Teaching Resources, Reading Readiness Guide, p. 83

Answer

Interpret Art Possible answer: The owl represents the "flight" of the Native Americans.

Explore More Video To learn more about the Cherokees' journey, view the video.

A Tragic Journey This painting, *Shadow of the Owl*, by Cherokee artist John Guthrie portrays the Trail of Tears. More than 4,000 Cherokees died along the trail. The tombstone of one of them is shown below. *Critical Thinking: Interpret Art What do you think the owl in the main picture represents?*

WHITEPATH
CHEROKEE WARRIOR CHIEF
DIED 1838
TRAIL OF TEARS

On the Trail of Tears

Believing they had no choice, most Native American leaders signed new treaties giving up their lands. They agreed to move to what was called the Indian Territory. Today most of that area is in the state of Oklahoma.

Removal of the Choctaws The Choctaws signed the first treaty in 1830. The Treaty of Dancing Rabbit Creek stated that

> "the United States under a grant . . . shall cause to be conveyed to the Choctaw Nation a tract of country west of the Mississippi river . . ."
>
> —Article II, Treaty of Dancing Rabbit Creek, 1830

Closely guarded by American soldiers, the Choctaws moved west between 1831 and 1833.

The federal government did not provide enough tents, food, blankets, shoes, winter clothes, or other supplies. Heavy rain and snow caused enormous suffering. An army lieutenant wrote that one group "walked for 24 hours barefoot through the snow and ice" before reaching shelter.

Cherokee Removal The Cherokees held out a few years longer. They were still on their land in 1837 when Jackson left office.

Differentiated Instruction

L1 English Language Learners   **L1 Less Proficient Readers**   **L1 Special Needs**

Exploring the Main Idea Distribute worksheet John Burnett and the Trail of Tears to students. After they complete it, discuss how it might have felt to be either a Cherokee on the Trail of Tears or a soldier ordered to accompany Cherokees. Have students discuss their reading when reviewing Trail of Tears.

All in One Teaching Resources, Unit 3, John Burnett and the Trail of Tears, p. 89

Finally, in 1838, President Martin Van Buren forced the Cherokees to move. In the winter of 1838–39, they went to Indian Territory, guarded by 7,000 soldiers. The route is called the Trail of Tears. A soldier's description helps explain why:

“On the morning of November 17th, we encountered a terrific sleet and snow storm with freezing temperatures, and from that day until we reached the end of the fateful journey on March the 26th, 1839, the sufferings of the Cherokee were awful. The trail of the exiles was a trail of death.”

—Memoirs of Private John G. Burnett, December 1890

The Cherokees were forced to march hundreds of miles. They had little food or shelter. Many did not survive. Of 15,000 Cherokees who began the trip, 4,000 died along the way.

One group refused to move. The Seminoles fought three wars against removal. However, in the 1840s most Seminoles were forced to move. In their new homes in the Indian Territory, Native Americans struggled to rebuild their lives under very difficult conditions.

 Identify Long-Term Effects President Jackson sent federal agents to finalize treaties for Native American removal. Summarize the long-term effects of this policy. Explain how the policy affected the Native Americans in the region.

☑**Checkpoint** What mistakes in planning did the government make before removing Native Americans?

⭐ **Looking Back and Ahead** Andrew Jackson was determined to be a strong President. He defied the Supreme Court by enforcing the Indian Removal Act. In Section 5, you will learn about his stands against the nation's bankers and his dramatic actions to save the Union.

Section 4 | Check Your Progress

Progress Monitoring Online
For: Self-test with instant help
Visit: PHSchool.com
Web Code: mya-3064

Comprehension and Critical Thinking

1. **(a) Recall** How did the Supreme Court rule in the case of *Worcester* v. *Georgia*?
(b) Detect Bias Why do you suppose President Jackson objected to the Court's decision?

2. **(a) Compare and Contrast** Describe the removal of the Choctaws and the Cherokees.
(b) Identify Economic Benefits Why would the Cherokees be particularly opposed to removal from their land?

Reading Skill

3. **Identify Long-Term Effects** A long-term effect is an effect that lasts over a long period of time. White farmers wanted the lands belonging to Native Americans of the Southeast. Write three sentences summarizing the long-term effects of this desire for land.

Writing

4. A paragraph should focus on a single topic. Rewrite the following paragraph to get rid of any sentences that stray from the topic. **Paragraph:** By the 1830s, Native Americans had fought several legal battles over land. Many Native Americans wore traditional clothing. The states tried to make the Native Americans move. However, the Supreme Court decided that states could not force them from their homes.

Assess and Reteach

Assess Progress L2

Have students complete Check Your Progress. Administer the Section Quiz.

All in One Teaching Resources, Unit 3, p. 96

To further assess student understanding, use the Progress Monitoring Transparency.

Progress Monitoring Transparencies, Chapter 10, Section 4

Reteach L1

If students need more instruction, have them read this section in the Interactive Reading and Notetaking Study Guide and complete the accompanying question.

📖 **Interactive Reading and Notetaking Study Guide,** Chapter 10, Section 4 (Adapted Version also available.)

Extend L3

Ask students to research the life of Cherokee leader John Ross. Have students share what they have learned in a written or oral report.

Extend Online
For: Help in starting this activity
Visit: PHSchool.com
Web Code: mye-3064

Progress Monitoring Online

Students may check their comprehension of this section by completing the Progress Monitoring Online graphic organizer and self-quiz.

Section 4 Check Your Progress

1. **(a)** It ruled against Georgia. The Cherokees and the United States had signed treaties acknowledging that certain territories were theirs.
(b) He was determined that Native Americans be moved from land that white settlers wanted.

2. **(a)** Possible answer: The removals were not well prepared for, and the Choctaws and the Cherokees had to walk in winter conditions without enough tents, food, blankets, shoes, winter clothes, or other supplies. Many died from hunger, disease, and cold.
(b) Possible answer: They had adapted to many white customs and claimed status as a separate nation.

3. Possible answer: Native Americans were moved westward. Their lives were very difficult on the new land. Settlers took over their traditional homelands.

4. Paragraphs should focus on the main idea.

Answers

🔵 **Reading Skill** Five groups of Native Americans were forced to move west. The removals caused great hardship.

☑**Checkpoint** It did not provide enough tents, food, blankets, shoes, winter clothes, or other supplies.

Sequoyah and the Cherokee Alphabet

Build Background Knowledge `L2`

Biographies help to understand the role of people in history. Review what students know about the Cherokee Nation and Trail of Tears. Ask: **How did Cherokees adapt to white customs?** (*They farmed, ran businesses, and had schools. Many became Christian, and many could speak and read English.*) Ask if these adaptations benefited Cherokees. Use the Idea Wave strategy to elicit responses (TE, p. T24).

 Reading Skill

Remind students that characters usually have reasons for their actions and that understanding these motives can help us understand a character. As students read, ask them to look for the reasons or motives for Sequoyah's actions.

Vocabulary *Builder*
Teach Key Terms `L2`

Pronounce each word in the Vocabulary *Builder* list and have students repeat the word. Ask a student to read the definitions. Pair students and have them make flashcards, writing the vocabulary word on one side and the definition on the back. Then have students hold up a card and ask their partner for the definition of the word.

Instruction `L2`

- Using the Structured Silent Reading strategy (TE, p. T22), have students read *Sequoyah and the Cherokee Alphabet.*

- Ask: **How did Sequoyah try to show his friends that books were not only white people's magic?** (*Possible answer: Sequoyah showed them that the Cherokee language could be written.*) Ask: **Why weren't Sequoyah's friends convinced by his demonstration?** (*They thought making up symbols for every Cherokee word would take too long.*) Ask: **How do you think Sequoyah could convince them that the Cherokee language should be written?** (*Answers will vary but should show students' understanding of Sequoyah's strong desire to have a written Cherokee language.*)

Sequoyah and the Cherokee Alphabet *by Robert Cwiklik*

Prepare to Read

Introduction

The leader Sequoyah became convinced that the Cherokee needed a system to write in their own language. The following selection is from a biography of Sequoyah. In this excerpt, Sequoyah becomes interested in the "talking leaves" of an English book.

Reading Skill

Analyze Motivation A character's motives are the reason for his or her actions. As you read this excerpt, look for clues that tell why Sequoyah wanted the book.

Vocabulary *Builder*

As you read this literature selection, look for the following underlined words:

leaves (leevz) *n.* pages or sheets

wampum belt (WAHM pum) *n.* belt woven with images made with beads or shells, used to record historic events

pelts (pehltz) *n.* animal skins

bristled (BRIHS ahld) *v.* became angry

⭐ Background

The images on the wampum belt were a record of events in Cherokee history. Details like names of people and places were passed down from one medicine man to the next. The medicine men would tell the history of the tribe based on the images on the belt.

Sequoyah picked up the book to examine it. He saw that it was made of thin <u>leaves</u> of paper. Instead of the pictures on a <u>wampum belt</u>, there were marks of some kind on the paper, like the footprints of a crow. And the marks were in neat rows like the rows of corn planted in a garden. When the reader looked at those rows, the leaves of the book "talked" to him. The reader then told his friends what the leaves said. Sequoyah found these talking leaves fascinating.

Sequoyah mentally compared the markings on the talking leaves to the designs on a wampum belt. The colorful belt was much prettier, but the book was filled with many thin leaves, each covered with markings. It must surely "remember" more than the wampum belt. Wu The had told Sequoyah that books made the white people's medicine powerful. She had said that just one of their books of talking leaves could remember more than all the medicine men of Taskigi together. And the white men had many, many such books. This is why Wu The wanted Sequoyah to learn English—so he could learn the secret of the talking leaves, the secret of the white people's powerful medicine.

Sequoyah was so curious about the talking leaves that he bought the book from the hunter for two good deer <u>pelts</u>. The men laughed, thinking they had again cheated an Indian. Sequoyah knew his pelts were worth more in silver than this book. Still he wished to have it. He wanted to ponder the secret of its talking leaves.

Agi Li and Rabbit Eyes kidded Sequoyah as the three hiked home after the rain stopped, "You gave good pelts for a book you cannot even understand," they said, laughing.

Later the boys fell to talking about the talking leaves. "Surely," Rabbit Eyes said, "it was a magic power of the white man to be able to put his speeches into books."

360 Chapter 10 A Changing Nation

Differentiated Instruction

`L1` English Language Learners

Comparing Alphabets Tell students that many languages have different alphabets, such as Greek, Russian, Chinese, and Hebrew. If students are familiar with a non-English alphabet, have them share unique symbols of the language. Have them compare these symbols to the English letters for any similarities. Point out that Sequoyah developed the alphabet for Cherokees, which allowed them to write their constitution in their own language.

"Surely," Agi Li said, "one must learn the white man's language to gain the power of the talking leaves."

Sequoyah <u>bristled</u> at this. "Bah," he said. "These are mere scratchings, mere crow's prints. It is not magic. I could invent them for the Cherokee language, and we, too, could have our own talking leaves."

The other boys laughed at this. "How can you do such a thing?" asked Agi Li, chuckling.

Sequoyah picked up a flat stone and scratched out a picture of a deer on it with the blade of his knife. "There," he said, showing them the stone. "That means 'deer,' see?" Then Sequoyah drew an arrow through the deer. "And that means 'to hunt a deer,'" he said.

His friends laughed again. "At this rate, you will be scratching on stones until you are an old man, Sequoyah, to make pictures of every word there is in our language. It is impossible. The talking leaves belong to the white man. They are not meant for us."

Sequoyah stood his ground. "You are wrong," he said. "You think the white man has special medicine. That is why you wear his clothes," Sequoyah said, pointing to their trousers and shirts. "Well, our medicine can be just as strong, if we wish it."

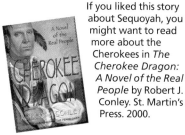

Analyze Motivation
At the beginning of the excerpt, Sequoyah's curiosity motivates him to buy the book. What is his motivation for wanting to write his language?

From *Sequoyah and the Cherokee Alphabet*, by Robert Cwiklik.
© 1989 Silver Burdett Press.

☑**Checkpoint** Why did Wu The want Sequoyah to learn English?

Sequoyah and his Cherokee alphabet

If you liked this story about Sequoyah, you might want to read more about the Cherokees in *The Cherokee Dragon: A Novel of the Real People* by Robert J. Conley. St. Martin's Press. 2000.

Analyze **LITERATURE**
Sequoyah went on to create an alphabet for the Cherokees. Imagine that you are Sequoyah. Write a paragraph explaining to the Cherokees why they should learn to write.

Literature **361**

History Background

The Cherokee Syllabary Sequoyah's first attempt to write the Cherokee language used a separate symbol for each word. When the number of symbols quickly became overwhelming, he tried a new idea. Sequoyah's second system used 85 phonetic symbols to represent syllables with sounds such as "no," "tsi," and "dla." Using this alphabet of syllables, Sequoyah easily taught his brother-in-law and his daughter to read and write. When he began sharing the alphabet more widely, Cherokee literacy expanded dramatically within weeks.

Instruction (continued)
■ Ask: **How do you think being able to write in their own language would benefit the Cherokee people?** (*Answers will vary but should show students' understanding of the value and power of literacy.*)

Monitor Progress

Discuss with students the development of Sequoyah's interest in literacy. Ask: **According to this passage, what first attracted Sequoyah to books?** (*Possible answer: Sequoyah saw that the leaves of a book "talked" to a reader and that a book could "remember" more information than a wampum belt.*) Ask: **How did Sequoyah pursue his interest in the "talking leaves"?** (*Possible answer: He bought the book to study it. Then he began to invent a written alphabet for the Cherokee language.*)

Writing Rubric Share this writing rubric with students.

Score 1 Does not address assigned topic and is poorly organized.
Score 2 Details, arguments, and organization are often unclear or incorrect.
Score 3 Has organization suited to topic, some appropriate details, some original ideas.
Score 4 Has clear organization suited to topic, many appropriate details, and original ideas.

Analyze **LITERATURE** Answers will vary, but students should offer 2–3 reasons why the Cherokees should learn to read.

Answers

🔵 **Reading Skill** He wanted to make his people's knowledge as strong as the white people's through reading and writing.

☑**Checkpoint** Wu wanted Sequoyah to learn English so he would know the secret of white people's medicine.

Review and Preview

Students have read about the popular support for Jackson. They will now learn how the issues of a national bank and tariffs showed the sectional divisions in the country.

Section Focus Question

How did old issues take a new shape in the conflict over a national bank and tariffs?

Before you begin the lesson for the day, write the Section Focus Question on the board. (*Lesson focus: The issue of national powers versus state rights resurfaced in the struggle between Andrew Jackson and the Bank of the United States and Jackson's refusal to allow states to nullify the tariff laws of the federal government.*)

Prepare to Read

Build Background Knowledge   **L2**

Invite students to preview this section by looking at the headings and visuals and making predictions about what they will learn. Provide examples to get students started. Use the Idea Wave technique (TE, p. T24) to generate a list.

Set a Purpose   **L2**

■ Read each statement in the Reading Readiness Guide aloud. Ask students to mark the statements True or False.

All in One Teaching Resources, Unit 3, Reading Readiness Guide, p. 84

■ Have students discuss the statements in pairs or groups of four, then mark their worksheets again. Use the Numbered Heads strategy (TE, p. T24) to call on students to share their group's perspectives. Students will return to these worksheets later.

An Interfering Government

"We must be blind to the lessons of reason and experience not to see that the more a government interferes with the labor and wealth of a community, the more it exacts from one portion and bestows on another. . . ."

—Vice President John C. Calhoun, protesting tariffs collected by U.S. Customs agents, 1832

▲ U.S. Custom House in Charleston, South Carolina

States' Rights and the Economy

Objectives

- Describe the disagreement over the Bank of the United States.
- Discuss the differing viewpoints on the balance of federal and state powers.
- Explain why South Carolina threatened to secede from the Union.
- Describe the economic crisis that began in 1837.

Reading Skill

Identify Multiple Causes Just as events can have multiple effects, so too can they have multiple causes. Major events in history often have many causes. As you read Section 5, look for events that have multiple causes.

Key Terms and People

nullification
Martin Van Buren

William Henry
Harrison

Why It Matters The issue of states' rights versus the power of the federal government had been debated since the founding of the United States. The debate became more urgent when Americans disagreed on important economic measures.

Section Focus Question: How did old issues take a new shape in the conflict over a national bank and tariffs?

The Bank War

Between 1816 and the early 1830s, the second Bank of the United States earned strong support from business people. They liked the fact that the Bank made loans to businesses. Moreover, the Bank was a safe place for the federal government to keep its money. The paper money it issued formed a stable currency. Its careful policies helped create confidence in banks all over the country.

On the other hand, many Americans disliked the Bank. They opposed the way the Bank restricted loans made by state banks. Fearing that state banks were making too many loans, Bank directors often limited the amount of money banks could lend. This angered farmers and merchants who wanted to borrow money to buy land. Many southerners and westerners blamed the Bank for the economic crisis that broke out in 1819. In that crisis, many people lost their farms.

The Bank's most powerful enemy was Andrew Jackson, who called the Bank "the Monster." According to Jackson, the Bank allowed a small group of the wealthy people to enrich themselves at the expense of ordinary people. Jackson believed that the wealthy stood for unfair privilege. Jackson especially disliked Nicholas Biddle, the Bank's president. Biddle, who came from a wealthy Philadelphia family, was skilled at doing favors for powerful politicians.

362   Chapter 10   A Changing Nation

Differentiated Instruction

L1 English Language Learners   **L1 Less Proficient Readers**   **L1 Special Needs**

Definition Students may need help in understanding what a crisis is. To help them, explain that the word comes from an ancient Greek word meaning "decision." Point out that in a time of crisis, making a decision is very important, because the

wrong decision can be dangerous. Invite students to give examples of a crisis in which someone has had to make a very important decision. You may wish to point out that the plural of *crisis* is *crises*.

Biddle got Congress to renew the Bank's charter in 1832, although the charter still had four years to go. The news reached Jackson when he was sick in bed. The President vowed, "The Bank . . . is trying to kill me, but I will kill it!"

Jackson immediately vetoed the bill. The fight over the Bank became a major issue in the 1832 presidential election. Henry Clay, who ran against Jackson, strongly supported the Bank. But most voters stood solidly behind Jackson's veto of the Bank bill. Jackson won reelection by a huge margin.

Jackson's victory over the Bank helped to increase the powers of the presidency. It showed that a determined President could stir up the voters and face down powerful opponents in Congress.

The second Bank ceased to exist when its charter ran out in 1836. Unfortunately for Jackson's successor, an economic crisis struck a few months after Jackson left office. Without a Bank of the United States, it was harder for the new President to end the crisis.

✓ **Checkpoint** What were the arguments for and against the second Bank of the United States?

The Question of States' Rights

Since the founding of the United States, Americans had debated what should be the balance between the powers of the states and the powers of the federal government.

King Andrew the First

A king's crown

Trampling on rights

Reading Political Cartoons

Skills Activity

The national press ridiculed Jackson for his quick temper and steely will.

(a) Detect Points of View Name two negative images in the cartoon. Why do you think Jackson is shown stepping on the bank document?

(b) Distinguish Relevant Information Would this cartoon have the same impact in Britain if, instead of Jackson, it showed a British leader? Explain your answer.

Vocabulary Builder

Use the information below to teach students this section's high-use words.

High-Use Word	Definition and Sample Sentence
resolve, p. 364	*v.* to decide; to solve Debates during the Constitutional Convention did not **resolve** the issue of slavery.
dissolve, p. 365	*v.* break up into smaller parts As Parliament passed unpopular laws and taxes for the colonies, the colonists' loyalty towards England **dissolved.**

Teach

The Bank War

The Question of States' Rights

pp. 362–363

Instruction   L2

■ **Vocabulary Builder** Before teaching this lesson, preteach the High-Use Words **resolve** and **dissolve,** using the strategy on TE p. T21.
  Key Terms Have students complete the See It–Remember It chart for the key terms in this chapter.

■ Read The Bank War and The Question of States' Rights, using the Choral Reading strategy (TE, p. T22).

■ Ask: **What reasons did people have to be against the Bank or be in support of the Bank?** (*support the Bank—it was a safe place to keep money; against the Bank—it limited the amount of money available for borrowing*)

■ Ask: **Why was there conflict over the powers available to state and federal governments?** (*The Constitution did not tell exactly where the federal government's power ended and the states' power began.*)

Independent Practice

Have students begin filling in the study guide for this section.

Monitor Progress

As students fill in the Notetaking Study Guide, circulate to make sure students understand the opposition to the Bank rights. Provide assistance as needed.

Answers

✓ **Checkpoint** For: It helped business; it kept federal money safe; it issued a stable currency; it created confidence in U.S. banks. Against: It hurt farmers and small merchants; it restricted state banks; it helped the wealthy; it caused the economic crisis of 1819.

Reading Political Cartoons (a) Jackson is dressed like a king and he is stepping on a legal document; because he vetoed the bank bill. **(b)** No. The British supported their monarchy. Yes. The king had to uphold the law.

The Nullification Crisis

p. 364

Instruction `L2`

- Have students read The Nullification Crisis. Remind students to look for causes and effects.

- Ask: **Why did South Carolina want to secede from the United States?** (*The state did not agree with the tariff laws. At a special convention, leaders said that the laws did not apply to South Carolina. If the federal government tried to forcibly impose the tariffs, South Carolina would secede.*)

- Ask: **How did John Calhoun and Daniel Webster symbolize the controversy?** (*Calhoun was from South Carolina, where anger over federal power was strongest, and he proposed that states had the right of nullification. Webster was from Massachusetts, and he argued that the United States had been formed not by states but by its people.*)

- Discuss how the crisis was resolved. Ask students to predict other issues that might cause similar crises (*slavery, opposition to war, civil rights*).

- Distribute worksheet on Daniel Webster and have students answer the questions.

All in One Teaching Resources, Unit 3, Daniel Webster, p. 90

- Display the transparency Andrew Jackson Battles the Bank of the United States. Discuss the key figures in the political cartoon.

Color Transparencies, Andrew Jackson Battles the Bank of the United States

- Have students review the timeline. Ask: **What is the cause of the states' rights debates?** (*The Constitution divided the power between the states and federal government. When there was a difference of opinion, both sides claimed final authority.*)

Answer

✓**Checkpoint** It states that any powers not specifically given to the federal government are reserved to the state government.

The Constitutional Convention of 1787 had created a government based on federalism, the division of power between the national government and the states. The Constitution gave the federal government many significant powers. At the same time, the Tenth Amendment set limits on federal power. It states that any powers not specifically given to the federal government are "reserved to the States respectively, or to the people."

Over the years, the issue of balancing federal and state power had come up repeatedly. The Alien and Sedition acts had raised the issue. So had the Virginia and Kentucky resolutions and the Hartford convention. The issue could never be fully <u>resolved</u>. During Andrew Jackson's presidency, arguments over federal power and states' rights caused a serious crisis.

Vocabulary Builder
<u>resolve</u> (ree SAHLV) **v.** to decide; to solve

✓**Checkpoint** How does the Tenth Amendment limit federal powers?

The Nullification Crisis

The crisis erupted when Congress passed a law in 1828 raising the tariff on iron, textiles, and other products. The tariff helped manufacturers in the North and some parts of the West. But it made southerners pay more for manufactured goods. It seemed to southerners that the federal government was forcing them to obey an unfair law.

Vice President John C. Calhoun of South Carolina argued that the states had the right of **nullification,** an action by a state that cancels a federal law to which the state objects. If accepted, Calhoun's ideas would seriously weaken the federal government.

Arguments for Nullification To many southerners, the tariff issue was part of a much larger problem. If the federal government could enforce what they considered an unjust law, could it also use its power to end slavery?

John C. Calhoun had based his theory of nullification on his view of how the Union was formed. He said the Union grew from an agreement between the various states. After the Union was formed, each state kept certain powers. One of them was the power to nullify federal laws the people of the state considered unfair.

Milestones in the States' Rights Debate

1787: The Constitution divides power between the states and federal government.

1798: Kentucky and Virginia claim that states can nullify laws deemed unconstitutional.

1814–1815: At the Hartford Convention, opponents of the War of 1812 insist that states have the right to secede.

1832: South Carolina claims the right to nullify tariffs, but it backs down when President Jackson threatens to use force against it.

1787 — 1802 — 1817 — 1832

364 Chapter 10 A Changing Nation

Differentiated Instruction

L3 Gifted and Talented

Political Cartoons Students should use the timeline on this page to review other cases of states declaring their right of nullification. Then have students create political cartoons supporting or opposing the right of a state to nullify a federal law. Students should display their cartoons and offer brief explanations of each cartoon's characters, symbols, and meaning.

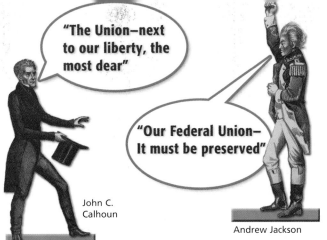

"The Union—next to our liberty, the most dear"

"Our Federal Union—It must be preserved"

John C. Calhoun

Andrew Jackson

Federal Power Versus States' Rights
President Andrew Jackson and Vice President John C. Calhoun took opposing views on states' rights and nullification. They had once been friends. However, by 1830, the two men were fierce enemies. **Critical Thinking:** *Detect Points of View How may Andrew Jackson's views about nullification have been affected by his responsibility as President of the United States?*

Arguments Against Nullification The clearest argument against nullification came from Massachusetts Senator Daniel Webster. He argued that the United States had not been formed by the states, but by the entire American people. In a dramatic speech on the floor of the Senate in January 1830, Webster defended his belief, saying "We are all agents of the same supreme power, the people."

A few months later, President Jackson dramatically defended the Union. At a banquet, Jackson stared directly at Vice President Calhoun and said, "Our Federal Union—It must be preserved." Ominously, Calhoun responded: "The Union—next to our liberty, the most dear." The challenge was clear. To Calhoun, states' rights was more important than saving the Union.

South Carolina Threatens to Secede In 1832, Congress passed another tariff law. Although it lowered some tariffs, it passed high tariffs on iron and textiles. South Carolina then called a state convention, which voted to nullify the tariffs. The tariffs of 1828 and 1832, it said, did not apply to South Carolina. The state also warned the federal government not to use force to impose the tariffs. If it did, South Carolina would secede from the Union.

A furious Jackson responded strongly. In December 1832, he put federal troops in South Carolina on alert. Then he issued a "Proclamation to the People of South Carolina." It said that the Union could not be <u>dissolved</u>. It also warned that "disunion by armed force is treason." With tensions running high, Calhoun resigned as Vice President.

Early in 1833, Jackson asked Congress to allow the federal government to collect its tariff in South Carolina by force if necessary. At the same time, he supported a compromise bill that would lower the tariffs. In March 1833, Congress passed both laws.

Unable to win support for its position from other states, South Carolina then repealed its tariff nullification. Many Americans breathed a sigh of relief. The crisis had been settled peacefully.

Vocabulary Builder
<u>dissolve</u> (dih ZAHLV) **v.** break up into smaller parts

Independent Practice
Have students continue filling in the study guide for this section.

Interactive Reading and Notetaking Study Guide, Chapter 10, Section 5 (Adapted Version also available.)

Monitor Progress

As students fill in the Notetaking Study Guide, circulate to make sure students understand the Nullification Crisis. Provide assistance as needed.

History Background

Proclamation to the People of South Carolina Andrew Jackson felt that John C. Calhoun's argument for nullification by South Carolina was a threat to the federal union and to national authority. He said, "I consider, then, the power to annul a law of the United States, assumed by one state, incompatible with the existence of the Union, contradicted explicitly by the letter of the Constitution, unauthorized by its spirit, inconsistent with every principle on which it was founded, and destructive of the great object for which it was formed." South Carolina retreated due to lack of support from other southern states and Jackson's threat to employ military force.

Answer
Detect Points of View As president, Jackson had to preserve the Union, so he could not support the right of states to nullify federal laws.

The End of the Jackson Era

p. 366

Instruction L2

- Have students read The End of the Jackson Era. Remind students to look for causes and effects.

- Ask: **What strategy did the Whigs use to try to upset Martin Van Buren, Jackson's handpicked candidate for President?** (*They ran three candidates, each of whom might appeal to a different region of the country.*)

- With the Panic of 1837, Van Buren quickly lost popular support. Have students discuss how an economic downturn in Britain affected the U.S.

Independent Practice

Have students complete the study guide for this section.

 Interactive Reading and Notetaking Study Guide, Chapter 10, Section 5 (Adapted Version also available.)

Monitor Progress

- As students fill in the Notetaking Study Guide, circulate to make sure students understand how the Jackson Era came to an end. Provide assistance as needed.

- Tell students to fill in the last column of the Reading Readiness Guide. Probe for what they learned that confirms or invalidates each statement.

- Have students go back to their Word Knowledge Rating Form. Rerate their word knowledge and complete the last column with a definition or example.

All in One Teaching Resources, Unit 3, Reading Readiness Guide, p. 84; Word Knowledge Rating Form, p. 79

Answers

Link Past and Present Similar: both try to appeal to patriotism and the majority of people. Different: Today we have television, radio, and the Internet for campaigning.

✓Checkpoint Calhoun believed that nullification was a right that individual states had.

The Election of 1840
Both the Whigs and the Democrats tried new methods in the presidential election of 1840. They broadened their appeal, hoping to win the vote of the "common man."
Critical Thinking: *Link Past and Present How are presidential campaigns today similar to the 1840 campaign? How are they different?*

Jackson had successfully defended federal power, while states' rights supporters had suffered a setback. However, the issue of states' rights would not go away. Americans would continue to debate the balance between states' rights and federal powers until the Civil War broke out in 1861.

✓Checkpoint What was the position of Vice President John C. Calhoun on nullification?

The End of the Jackson Era

A weary Andrew Jackson retired from office after two terms. Martin Van Buren was Andrew Jackson's choice to succeed him. Van Buren, the son of a New York tavern owner, had played a central role in organizing Jackson's first election victory in 1828. He had been secretary of state during Jackson's first term and Vice President during his second term. He had long been a close political adviser to Jackson.

In the election of 1836, the Whigs ran three candidates, each from a different region of the country. Their goal was to prevent any candidate from receiving a majority of electoral votes. This would throw the election into the House of Representatives. However, the strategy did not work. Van Buren received a majority of both the electoral and the popular vote.

Differentiated Instruction

L3 Advanced Readers   **L3 Gifted and Talented**

Speculating Have students work in pairs. Have each select a major event from this chapter and assume either it had not occurred or that it had had a different outcome. Have each group give a brief newscast in which they speculate how subsequent events in American history might have been different.

The Panic of 1837 Van Buren took office at a time when the American economy was beginning a severe slump. Because Britain was experiencing an economic slowdown, British manufacturers were buying less cotton. This caused cotton prices to fall sharply. American banks could not collect on the loans they had made to cotton growers. As a result, hundreds of banks went bankrupt.

The result was an economic collapse in the United States called the Panic of 1837. The economic hard times that followed lasted six years. The hardships of those years ruined Van Buren's presidency.

The Election of 1840 Van Buren ran for reelection in 1840 against the Whig candidate, William Henry Harrison. This time the Whigs ran a skillful campaign. They used parades, barbecues, and other forms of entertainment to reach ordinary voters. They portrayed Harrison as a "man of the people" who would feel right at home in a simple log cabin. Helped by his "log cabin" campaign, Harrison easily defeated Van Buren. The Whigs were in power and the Age of Jackson was over.

☑ **Checkpoint** What was the main cause of the Panic of 1837?

⭐ **Looking Back and Ahead** Throughout the administrations of John Quincy Adams, Andrew Jackson, and Martin Van Buren, Americans continued to push westward. By the 1830s, Americans had settled most of the land east of the Mississippi River. By the 1840s, they were crossing the Mississippi in large numbers. You will read about this movement in the next unit.

Identify Multiple Causes

In 1837, the United States experienced an economic collapse. What were two causes of this collapse?

Section 5 | Check Your Progress

Progress Monitoring Online
For: Self-test with instant help
Visit: PHSchool.com
Web Code: mya-3065

Comprehension and Critical Thinking

1. **(a) Recall** Why did states' rights become an issue in the 1820s?
(b) Distinguish Relevant Information Agree or disagree with the following statement and provide relevant facts to support your position: "The issue of states' rights had plagued the nation from the time of the Constitutional Convention."

2. **(a) Summarize** What were John C. Calhoun's and Daniel Webster's positions on nullification?
(b) Detect Points of View What did John C. Calhoun mean when he said, "The Union—next to our liberty, the most dear"?

Reading Skill

3. **Identify Multiple Causes** After the nullification crisis, South Carolina repealed its nullification of the federal tariffs. What were two causes of the state's action?

Key Terms

4. Write two definitions for the key term nullification. First, write a formal definition for your teacher. Second, write a definition in everyday English for a classmate.

Writing

5. Correct the errors in grammar, spelling, and punctuation in the following passage. **Passage:** The Nullification Crises represent a conflict between the South and the federal government. president Jackson at a banquet said that the Union must be preserved. John Calhoun answered "The Union—next to our liberty, the most dearest."

Assess Progress L2

Have students complete Check Your Progress. Administer the Section Quiz.

All in One **Teaching Resources, Unit 3,** Section Quiz, p. 97

To further assess student understanding, use the Progress Monitoring Transparency.

Progress Monitoring Transparencies, Chapter 10, Section 5

Reteach L1

If students need more instruction, have them read this section in the Interactive Reading and Notetaking Study Guide and complete the accompanying question.

📖 **Interactive Reading and Notetaking Study Guide,** Chapter 10, Section 5 (Adapted Version also available.)

Extend L3

Students can interview members of their family or community and ask them how their businesses and lives would be affected if they found themselves unable to get a bank loan, as happened to many people during the Panic of 1837. Invite them to share their findings with the class.

Progress Monitoring Online

Students may check their comprehension of this section by completing the Progress Monitoring Online graphic organizer and self-quiz.

Answers

Reading Skill Accept any two of these: Britain experienced an economic slowdown; British manufacturers bought less cotton; American banks could not collect on loans.

☑ **Checkpoint** The main cause was an economic crisis in Britain.

Section 5 Check Your Progress

1. **(a)** The federal government passed a new law raising tariffs on iron and textiles. A convention in South Carolina said that the tariffs did not apply to that state.
(b) Students who agree may cite the deep conflicts over the Alien and Sedition acts and the tariffs. Students who disagree may state that despite differences, the states had been able to find compromises.

2. **(a)** Webster opposed the idea that states had the right to nullify a federal law. John C. Calhoun argued that states did have this right.
(b) He meant that upholding states' rights was more important than holding the union together.

3. Jackson issued the "Proclamation to the People of South Carolina," warning them against secession; Calhoun resigned as Vice President; Congress passed laws authorizing force to collect federal tariffs in South Carolina and to lower the tariffs.

4. Possible answer: Nullification is the action of a state to cancel any federal law with which it does not agree. If states had the right of nullification, any state that did not like a federal law could ignore it.

5. Check to see that the grammar, spelling, and punctuation are correct.

Skills for Life

Objective

Recognizing bias means being aware of information and ideas that are one-sided or that present only a partial view of a subject. Knowing how to recognize bias helps students better understand historical events. The ability to spot bias will help students analyze information.

Identify Bias

Instruction   L2

1. Write the steps to identify bias on the board.

2. Have students look at the excerpt.

3. Practice the skill by following the steps on p. 368 as a class. Model each step to identify bias. (**1. (a)** *Andrew Jackson* **(b)** *December 7, 1835* **(c)** *Jackson had fought many battles against Native Americans and had proposed the Indian Removal Act.* **2.** *that the Native Americans should not be living near white settlements and should be moved to a territory west of Missouri and Arkansas* **3. (a)** *This account claims the government policy is generous; Native Americans, however, did not want to move and did not see it as a generous offer.* **(b)** *Possible answer: It seems now to be an established fact that they cannot live in contact with a civilized community and prosper.* **(c)** *Many white Americans wanted the land owned by the Native Americans.* **4.** *Jackson wants the audience to believe that Native Americans are uncivilized and cannot be improved, and so they should not live close to white Americans.*)

Monitor Progress

Ask students to do the Apply the Skill activity. Then assign the Skills for Life Worksheet. As students complete the worksheet, circulate to make sure individuals are applying the skill steps effectively. Provide assistance as needed.

All in One Teaching Resources, Unit 3, Skills for Life Worksheet, p. 91

Reteach   L1

If students need more instruction, use the Social Studies Skills Tutor to reteach this skill.

Social Studies Skills Tutor CD-ROM, Recognizing Bias

Skills for Life — Identify Bias

Bias is slanted writing that communicates a certain point of view about an idea or event. The writer either leaves out information or purposely changes the facts in order to create a certain impression. Bias is different from objective writing, which presents the facts in a balanced way.

> The following excerpt, from Andrew Jackson's seventh annual message to Congress, focuses on his Indian removal policy.
>
> **Primary Source**
>
> "... The plan of removing the [native] people to ... country west of the Mississippi River approaches its [conclusion]. ... All preceding experiments for the improvement of the Indians have failed. It seems now to be an established fact that they can not live in contact with a civilized community and prosper. ...
>
> The plan for their removal ... is founded upon the knowledge we have gained of their character and habits, and has been dictated by a spirit of [generosity]. A territory exceeding in extent that [given up] has been granted to each tribe. Of its climate, fertility, and capacity to support an Indian population the representations are highly favorable. ...
>
> ... A country west of Missouri and Arkansas has been assigned to them, into which the white settlements are not to be pushed. ... A barrier has thus been raised for their protection ... guarding the Indians as far as possible from those evils which have brought them to their present condition."
>
> —Andrew Jackson, December 7, 1835

Learn the Skill
Use these steps to identify bias.

1. **Identify the source.** Knowing the speaker or writer and the audience helps you understand why the point of view might be biased.

2. **Find the main idea.** Summarize the main point in the primary source.

3. **Compare the primary source with objective writing.** Look for differences between the biased writing and an objective account of the same subject. Does the biased writer leave out information or alter facts? Does the biased writer use broad generalizations that support a particular point of view? Does the biased writer use emotionally charged words?

4. **Draw conclusions.** What does the writer or speaker hope to accomplish?

Practice the Skill
Answer the following questions about the primary source on this page.

1. **Identify the source.** (a) Who is the author? (b) Why might the author's position be biased?

2. **Find the main idea.** What is the main point of the speech?

3. **Compare the primary source with objective writing.** Read the information about the government's Indian removal policy in Section 4. (a) What is one way that this account differs from the account in Section 4? (b) What is an example of a broad generalization that creates a biased view? (c) What information about the real reason for Indian removal is not included?

4. **Draw conclusions.** What message does the author want to present to the audience?

Apply the Skill
See the Review and Assessment at the end of this chapter.

Quick Study Guide

? **How did the nation reflect a growing sense of national pride and identity?**

Section 1
Building a National Identity

- James Monroe's time as President was called the Era of Good Feelings.
- Tariffs protected northern factories but forced the South to pay more for goods.
- Key Supreme Court decisions strengthened the power of the federal government.

Section 2
Dealing With Other Nations

- The United States acquired Florida in 1819.
- Spanish territories in the Americas revolted and gained their independence.
- Britain granted Canadians more rights.

Section 3
The Age of Jackson

- John Quincy Adams served only one term.
- Democratic reforms allowed more white men to vote.

Section 4
Indian Removal

- The government forced Native Americans to move west of the Mississippi River.
- Thousands of Native Americans died resisting removal or along the journey west.

Section 5
States' Rights and the Economy

- Jackson vetoed a bill to renew the charter of the second Bank.
- South Carolina said that states had the right to nullify federal laws.
- Jackson insisted that states could not nullify federal laws.
- Eventually, South Carolina backed down on nullification.

? Exploring the Essential Question

Use the online study guide to explore the essential question.

Section 1
How was the power of the federal government strengthened during the Era of Good Feelings?

Section 5
How did old issues take a new shape in the conflict over a national bank and tariffs?

Chapter 10 Essential Question
How did the nation reflect a growing sense of national pride and identity?

Section 2
How did U.S. foreign affairs reflect new national confidence?

Section 3
How did the people gain more power during the Age of Jackson?

Section 4
Why did Jackson use force to remove Native Americans from the Southeast?

Quick Study Guide **369**

Think Like A Historian

Enrich Learning To enrich this unit, have students revisit the Unit Essential Question. Using information from the chapters in the unit and the primary sources on pp. 372–375, have students demonstrate their understanding of this period by holding a Congressional hearing on the issues of the time.

Think Like a Historian, pp. 372–375

Pressed for Time? If you do not have time to complete the activity, return to the essential question on the unit opener. Post the flip chart pages and ask students to review and revise the list. As a summary, display the Unit 3 Think Like a Historian transparencies.

Color Transparencies, Think Like a Historian, Unit 3

Essential Question

Remind students of the Chapter Essential Question: **How did the nation reflect a growing sense of national pride and identity?** Have them review the bulleted statements and the Visual Preview at the beginning of the chapter to help them answer this question.

To bolster students' retention, at this time they should complete the Study Guide in print or online. Remind students that they should also continue filling in the Interactive Reading and Notetaking Study Guide for the Unit and Chapter Essential Questions.

📖 **Interactive Reading and Notetaking Study Guide,** Chapter 10 (Adapted Version also available.)

Interactive Textbook **Study Guide** *Online,* Chapter 10

Chapter Challenge

To wrap up this chapter, students should apply the knowledge they have gained to answer this question: **How did the expansion of voting rights affect the pride Americans felt in their country during the Age of Jackson?** (*Answers should demonstrate understanding of Jackson's popularity with the "common people," who supported him in great numbers and were assuming a larger role in shaping the nation's destiny.*)

Assessment at a Glance

Formal Assessment
Chapter Tests A/B (L1/L2)

AYP Monitoring Assessment

Test Prep Workbook With Document-Based Assessment

Test-Taking Strategies With Transparencies

Performance Assessment
Group/Individual Activities, TE p. 336h

Teacher's Edition, pp. 344, 348, 354, 359, 367

Assessment Rubrics

Assessment Through Technology
ExamView CD-ROM

MindPoint CD-ROM

Progress Monitoring Transparencies

Progress Monitoring Online

Key Terms

1. It hurt American business because the British manufacturers sold goods for prices lower than American manufacturers could charge, thus putting Americans out of business.

2. Suffrage means that those who have it are eligible to vote and participate in the democratic process.

3. A political party might hold a caucus.

4. Calhoun believed that each state had the right to nullify a federal law.

Comprehension and Critical Thinking

5. **(a)** He believed that all regions plus the federal government would benefit: the North because manufacturers would be protected by tariffs; the South and West because they would sell more goods to the North; the federal government because it would have more money to spend on infrastructure, which in turn would help the nation. **(b)** It is likely that the North would have benefited the most because their industries would be protected, but there were no guarantees that the rest of the plan would work as Clay predicted.

6. **(a)** Russia and France were threatening to help Spain regain its newly liberated colonies. **(b)** It warned away any European interference with those countries' independence. **(c)** They may have been grateful for the U.S. coming to their defense, but they may have also feared possible U.S. interference.

7. **(a)** Andrew Jackson had more electoral votes, although not a majority. The House of Representatives decided the election in Adams's favor when Henry Clay's supporters voted for Adams. **(b)** Suffrage was extended, so more Jackson supporters could vote. Adams was not popular with the public after the "corrupt bargain" scandal.

8. **(a)** the route the Cherokees were forced to take to Indian Territory from Georgia **(b)** Indian Territory eventually became part of the state of Oklahoma.

9. **(a)** Elected officials reward their supporters with positions in government. **(b)** It might get more support from people who thought they would benefit

---

Key Terms

Answer the following questions in complete sentences that show your understanding of the key terms.

1. How would British dumping hurt American business?

2. What are the advantages of suffrage?

3. Which group of people might hold a caucus?

4. Who did John C. Calhoun believe had the right of nullification?

Comprehension and Critical Thinking

5. **(a) List** How did Henry Clay believe the United States would benefit from his American System?
   (b) Analyze Cause and Effect Which regions of the country were likely to benefit most from the plan? Why?

6. **(a) Explain** Why did President Monroe issue the Monroe Doctrine?
   (b) Apply Information How might the Monroe Doctrine aid Latin American nations?
   (c) Draw Conclusions How do you think Latin American leaders felt about the Monroe Doctrine?

7. **(a) Describe** Why did Andrew Jackson lose the presidential election in 1824?
   (b) Analyze Cause and Effect What changes occurred between 1824 and 1828 that resulted in Jackson winning the 1828 election?

8. **(a) Identify** What was the Trail of Tears?
   (b) Link Past and Present Why does the state of Oklahoma today have a large Native American population?

9. **(a) Describe** How did the spoils system work?
   (b) Draw Conclusions How would it affect a political party?
   (c) Detect Points of View Why did Jackson say the spoils system furthered democracy?

10. **(a) Identify** What was the Panic of 1837?
   (b) Draw Inferences How might the panic have contributed to the election of William Henry Harrison in 1840?

History Reading Skill

11. **Analyze Cause and Effect** Reread the text in Section 1 under the heading "Three Important Supreme Court Rulings." What was the cause of the Supreme Court's decision in *McCulloch* v. *Maryland*? What were the results of the decision? Which results were short-term? Which were long-term?

Writing

12. **Revise the following paragraph to correct the errors in grammar, spelling, and punctuation:** In 1832, congress pass a new law, which lowered some tariffs but continued the high tarriffs on iron and textiles. Generally the South opposed tarifs. South Caroline actually voted to oppose the tariff legislation. Because President Jackson regard this act as a challenge to his authority. He issued a "Proclamation to the People of South Carolina." Which said that leaving the Union would be an act of treeson.

13. **Write a Narrative:** Imagine you are a Cherokee in 1838–1839. Write a narrative describing your journey to the Indian Territory.

Skills for Life
Identify Bias

Use the excerpt below to answer the questions.

> "More than eight millions of the stock of this bank are held by foreigners. By this act the American Republic proposes virtually to make them a present of some millions of dollars. . . . If we must have a bank with private stockholders, every consideration of sound policy and every impulse of American feeling admonishes that it should be *purely American*. . . ."
>
> —Andrew Jackson, "Bank Veto Message," July 10, 1832

14. **(a)** Who is the author? **(b)** Why would the author's position be biased?

15. What is the main point of the message?

16. Give an example of emotionally charged words used to support the writer's point of view.

17. What message does the writer want to convey to the audience?

---

from it later. **(c)** It brought new people to government service.

10. **(a)** an economic crisis similar to a depression **(b)** Many people felt it was the result of economic decisions made during Jackson's time, and Van Buren was Jackson's ally.

History Reading Skill

11. The cause was the attempt by the state of Maryland to tax the second Bank of

the United States. The results were that Maryland was not allowed to tax the Bank, and the federal government got stronger. The first was a short-term result, while the second was a long-term result.

Writing

12. In 1832, Congress passed a new law that lowered some tariffs, but continued the high tariffs on iron and textiles.

Test Yourself

1. **What was the principal reason Andrew Jackson opposed the second Bank of the United States?**

   A Its policies hurt revenue Jackson expected to get from tariffs.

   B The second Bank refused to loan money to state banks.

   C Jackson believed it gave power to a small group of wealthy people.

   D The second Bank backed John C. Calhoun on the issue of nullification.

2. **Which issue was Andrew Jackson referring to when he said, "John Marshall has made his decision. Now let him enforce it"?**

   A a case about the importance of private contracts

   B a state attempt to apply its laws to Cherokee territory

   C interstate commerce

   D the dumping of goods by Britain in the United States

Refer to the map below to answer Question 3.

3. **Based on the map above, what was the major reason Jackson won the election of 1828?**

   A Jackson won only the states with large electoral vote totals.

   B New states that joined the Union between 1824 and 1828 voted for Jackson.

   C Many states that had voted for Adams in 1824 switched to Jackson.

   D Jackson swept the electoral votes of states in the South and West.

Document-Based Questions

Task: Look at Documents 1 and 2, and answer their accompanying questions. Then, use the documents and your knowledge of history to complete this writing assignment:

Write a short essay describing how changing political practices reflected new views of democracy that began to take hold during the Age of Jackson.

Document 1: William Henry Harrison's 1840 presidential campaign was filled with advertising, slogans, organized rallies, and campaign songs like this one. *What image of Harrison was this song trying to create?*

"Come swell the throng and join the song,
Make the circle wider
Join the round for Harrison, Log Cabin and Hard Cider.
With Harrison our country's won,
No treachery can divide her.
Thy will be done
With Harrison, Log Cabin and Hard Cider."

Document 2: This campaign poster combines images of a humble log cabin with slogans about Harrison's exploits as a general. *What image of Harrison does this poster create? How does this image compare to Andrew Jackson's image?*

Test Yourself
1. **C**
2. **B**
3. **D**

Document-Based Questions
Answers

Document 1 the image of a "common man" and a patriot

Document 2 Harrison's campaign techniques were technically more primitive than those used today but just as prone to exaggeration and oversimplification.

Rubric: Write an Essay

Share the rubric with students before they begin writing.

Score 1 Has weak organization, few facts or details about expansion of suffrage.

Score 2 Gives more information but does so randomly, without tying related ideas together.

Score 3 Provides facts and supporting details that are usually on target, shows clear organization. (*New views of democracy may include the following: many states dropped the property ownership requirement for voting; belief that ordinary people should hold public office; opposition to special privileges for those of high social status; idealized image of the "common man."*)

Score 4 Clear and logical presentation, no spelling or grammatical errors, includes details to support all assertions.

Generally, the South opposed tariffs. South Carolina actually voted to oppose the tariff legislation. President Jackson regarded this act as a challenge to his authority. He issued a "Proclamation to the People of South Carolina." It said that leaving the Union would be an act of treason.

13. Narratives should show an understanding of the difficulty of the Cherokee journey.

For a more complete four-point rubric, see the writing rubrics in the Teaching Resources.

All in One Teaching Resources, Unit 3, p. 115

Skills for Life
14. **(a)** Andrew Jackson **(b)** He was strongly against the Bank of the United States; he believed it favored the wealthy at the expense of ordinary people.

15. that foreigners would have control of the Bank

16. virtually make them a present, purely American

17. that the Bank is not good for America and should be vetoed

Unit 3

Think Like a Historian

? What problems might a new nation face?

Build Background Knowledge **L2**

Discuss the problems associated with making the new country work. Lead a structured discussion about how the Constitution created a framework for government and how that framework had to be filled in. (See TE p. T24 for more on structured discussion.) Give students the example of forming a club in school. Have students identify all the things that have to be done to get a club, or any organization of people, up and running. Discuss electing club officers, collecting dues, and making rules. Have students keep this analogy in mind as they consider how the new nation began to function.

Instruction **L2**

- Write the Unit Essential Question on the chalkboard. Have students put this in their own words. *(Possible answer: What problems did the new nation have?)* Have students preview the documents on these pages to list some of the problems facing the new nation.

- Have students review the essential questions for chapters 8–10. Draw a web diagram on the chalkboard, showing how the chapter questions feed into the unit question. (See **Teaching Resources, Unit 3,** p. 4.) Discuss how each chapter question helps answer the unit question.

- Tell students that after they study the documents they will participate in a Congressional meeting to discuss problems faced by the new nation.

Answers

Document 1: The government owed investors millions of dollars but was unable to collect enough money to repay those debts.

Document 2: Because many people had opposed paying taxes to the British and did not want to pay them to the new government.

Unit 3 — ESSENTIAL QUESTION — THINK LIKE A HISTORIAN

What problems might a new nation face?

DIRECTIONS: Analyze the following documents from the period of the new American republic. Answer the questions that accompany each document or series of documents. You will use your answers to build an answer to the unit question: What problems might a new nation face?

HISTORIAN'S CHECKLIST

WHO produced the document?
WHERE was it made?
WHEN was it produced?
WHY was it made and for what audience?
WHAT is its viewpoint?
HOW does it connect to what I've learned?
WHY is the document important?

document 1 — Economic Problems

PROBLEM	HAMILTON'S SOLUTION
• States owe money on loans made during American Revolution	Federal government repays state debts to restore lenders' confidence
• Government needs income to pay off debts	Government places tariff on imports
• Government needs a safe place to deposit its funds	Government creates national bank

Why did the new government have a debt problem?

document 2 — Whiskey Rebellion

"I, George Washington, President of the United States, do hereby command all persons, being insurgents, ... to disperse and retire peaceably to their respective abodes."

—*George Washington, 1794*

Why did Washington's new government have trouble collecting taxes?

372

Differentiated Instruction

L3 Advanced Readers   **L3** Gifted and Talented

Solving Problems Encourage students to use this activity to better understand the impact of solutions to historical problems. Have them consider why people in the past decided on a certain solution to a problem. For example, students can make a chart listing the problems facing the new republic, the chosen solutions, and the results. Then have them evaluate whether what seemed like the best solution at the time proved successful in the long term. Tell them to consider this as they prepare for their role in the Congressional debate.

3 Party Politics

document

" Let us, then, fellow-citizens, unite with one heart and one mind. Let us restore to social intercourse that harmony and affection without which liberty and even life itself are but dreary things.... Every difference of opinion is not a difference of principle. We have called by different names brethren of the same principle. We are all Republicans, we are all Federalists. "

—*Thomas Jefferson,
First Inaugural Address, 1801*

According to Jefferson, what was causing disharmony?

4 The Supreme Court

document

" It is emphatically the province and duty of the judicial department to say what the law is. Those who apply the rule to particular cases, must of necessity expound and interpret that rule. If two laws conflict with each other, the courts must decide on the operation of each. "

—*John Marshall,
Marbury v. Madison, 1803*

How did Marshall address the problem of some laws being unconstitutional?

5 The Louisiana Purchase

document

How did the Louisiana Purchase increase the likelihood of wars in the West?

☞ Go On

373

Instruction (continued)

■ If your students have already examined these documents as enrichment to the chapters, have them answer the Historian's Checklist questions as a review.

■ If you have not used these documents yet, students will need more time to work with these sources. For documents that present challenging reading, use these steps:

1. As the students study the documents, remind them to use the question associated with each document as the focus question.

2. Have students review the topics of the documents by going back into the chapters in which they read about them. Help students use the section summaries at the beginning of the chapters to locate the topics of the documents.

3. Ask students to apply the Paragraph Shrinking strategy to Document 3. (See TE p. T23.) Have students summarize in 10–15 words what Jefferson is saying here. (*Although Republicans and Federalists have different opinions, everyone has the good of the republic at heart.*)

4. Have students go through the documents and list unfamiliar words to look up in a dictionary. For example, for Document 4 knowing the meanings of words such as *emphatically*, *judicial*, and *expound* will enable students to understand the document and answer the question.

5. Have one student read a document aloud, breaking it into short segments. Then, as a class, work to paraphrase the document. For example, the beginning of the first sentence in Document 4 could be summarized as "It is the business of the courts…"

6. Have students review their Reading and Note Taking Study Guide to understand what else was happening at the time of the Louisiana Purchase to understand Document 5.

History Background

Interpreting the Constitution John Marshall served as Chief Justice of the United States for 34 years (1801-1835). This is the longest tenure of any Chief Justice in history. Marshall is credited with both establishing the Supreme Court as the final authority on interpreting the Constitution and with solving the problem of integrating laws into the new constitutional government. A strong nationalist with a forceful personality, Marshall sought to uphold the supremacy of the federal government over the states. In its effort to encourage economic growth, the Marshall Court worked to protect property and contracts by limiting state interference.

Answers

Document 3: The philosophical differences between the two parties.

Document 4: He used the *Marbury* v. *Madison* case to establish the Court's authority to strike down unconstitutional laws.

Document 5: The Louisiana Territory was home to many Native American tribes, some of whom resisted American expansion.

Instruction (continued)

- Preview the documents and assign selections according to student abilities. You may organize students into groups to review documents.

- Assign Document 6 to students with less proficient reading skills. Ask: **What sight is Key writing about in "The Star-Spangled Banner"?** *(the sight of the American flag still waving after a night of British bombardment)* Ask students how they would feel in this situation if they were Francis Scott Key and how they would express their feelings of relief and pride. *(Answers will vary, but students might say they would cheer or shout with joy.)*

- Assign Document 8 to advanced readers. Ask: **What did the Cherokees request? What did they base their request on?** *(to stay on their own land; treaties they had with the United States)* **Did the prediction of the Cherokee come true?** *(yes)* **How do you know this?** *(Under the Indian Removal Act, they were forced to move westward.)*

- Assign gifted students Document 9. Ask: **Which words and phrases can be considered propaganda? What effect do they have on the reader?** *(Possible answers: "Hero of Two Wars," "Man of the People"; the effect is to elicit a power positive reaction to Jackson.)* Have students sketch a drawing on the board to illustrate this poster and explain the symbols they use to the class.

Answers

Document 6: Key's words inspired American soldiers to rally against the British invasion and fight harder to win the war.

Document 7: They disagreed over the issue of federal power versus states' rights.

---

continued

6 The War of 1812

document

"Oh, say, can you see, by the dawn's early light,
What so proudly we hail'd at the twilight's last gleaming? Whose broad stripes and bright stars, thro' the perilous fight, O'er the ramparts we watch'd, were so gallantly streaming? And the rockets' red glare, the bombs bursting in air,
Gave proof thro' the night that our flag was still there.
O say, does that star-spangled banner yet wave
O'er the land of the free and the home of the brave?"

—*Francis Scott Key, "The Star-Spangled Banner," 1814*

How do you think Key's words affected American soldiers fighting against the British?

7 Differing Views

document

"Our federal Union—it must be preserved!"
—*President Andrew Jackson, April 13, 1830*

"To the Union. Next to our liberty, most dear."
—*Vice President John C. Calhoun, April 13, 1830*

What were Jackson and Calhoun disagreeing about?

Andrew ▶ Jackson

◀ John C. Calhoun

374

Differentiated Instruction

L1 English Language Learners   **L1** Less Proficient Readers   **L1** Special Needs

Emphasize Vocabulary Have students make a list of the key terms and unfamiliar words in Documents 6–9. Then have them create flashcards with the word on one side and its definition on the other. Pair each student with a partner and have them quiz each other on the definitions of the words, using the flashcards. For English language learners, have students add pictures to the flashcards where appropriate. To prepare for their role in the Congressional hearing activity, have them write one sentence for each document using one of these key terms or words.

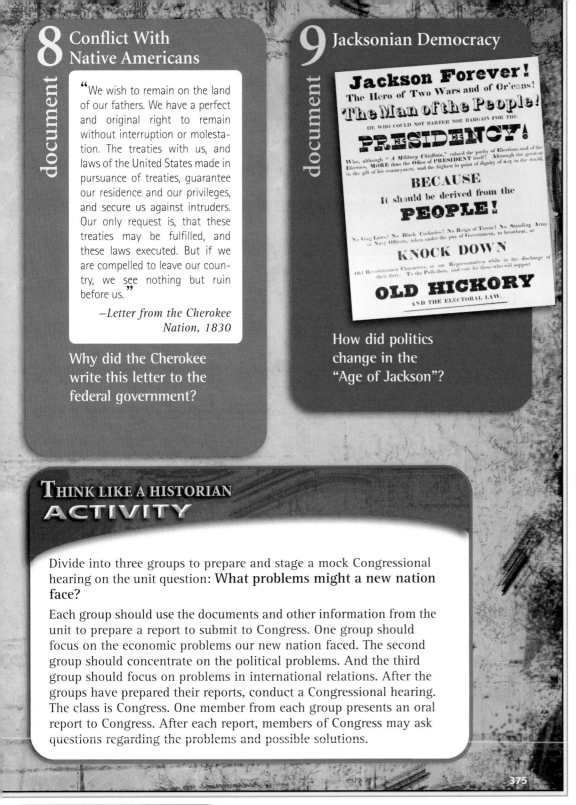

8 Conflict With Native Americans

document

"We wish to remain on the land of our fathers. We have a perfect and original right to remain without interruption or molestation. The treaties with us, and laws of the United States made in pursuance of treaties, guarantee our residence and our privileges, and secure us against intruders. Our only request is, that these treaties may be fulfilled, and these laws executed. But if we are compelled to leave our country, we see nothing but ruin before us."

—Letter from the Cherokee Nation, 1830

Why did the Cherokee write this letter to the federal government?

9 Jacksonian Democracy

document

Jackson Forever!
The Hero of Two Wars and of Orleans!
The Man of the People!
HE WHO COULD NOT BARTER NOR BARGAIN FOR THE
PRESIDENCY!

Who, although "A Military Chieftain," valued the purity of Elections and of the Electors, MORE than the Office of PRESIDENT itself! Although the greatest in the gift of his countrymen, and the highest in point of dignity of any in the world,

BECAUSE
It should be derived from the
PEOPLE!

No Gag Laws! No Black Cockades! No Reign of Terror! No Standing Army or Navy Officers, when under the pay of Government, to browbeat, or

KNOCK DOWN

Old Revolutionary Characters, or our Representatives while in the discharge of their duty. To the Polls then, and vote for those who will support

OLD HICKORY
AND THE ELECTORAL LAW.

How did politics change in the "Age of Jackson"?

THINK LIKE A HISTORIAN
ACTIVITY

Divide into three groups to prepare and stage a mock Congressional hearing on the unit question: **What problems might a new nation face?**

Each group should use the documents and other information from the unit to prepare a report to submit to Congress. One group should focus on the economic problems our new nation faced. The second group should concentrate on the political problems. And the third group should focus on problems in international relations. After the groups have prepared their reports, conduct a Congressional hearing. The class is Congress. One member from each group presents an oral report to Congress. After each report, members of Congress may ask questions regarding the problems and possible solutions.

375

Unit 4

Why It Matters

As the 1800s progressed, the North built up industry while the rural South developed its system of slavery. New issues arose that remain relevant today.

- The Industrial Revolution set in motion a cascade of changes. Today, manufacturing is moving overseas. The U.S. economy depends more on services, such as banking and information technology. The technology revolution has much in common with the industrial revolution, forcing many workers to learn new skills and changing the nature of business.

- Education remains a burning issue, with increased federal involvement in recent years. The No Child Left Behind Act of 2001 sought to improve school performance and assure all children a good education.

Unit Essential Question

What forces unite and divide a nation?

Think Like a Historian

- To preview this unit, have students review the content on these pages of the Student Edition. Ask them: **What will you be learning about in this unit?** (*growth and changes in different parts of the United States in the first half of the 1800s*) Tell students that some of these changes led to regional differences that began to divide the nation.

- Write the Unit Focus Question on the board. Using the Idea Wave strategy (TE, p. T24), have students brainstorm answers to the question. In considering the Unit Focus Question, ask students: **What were some similarities and differences between the thirteen original states? How did they resolve some of their differences?** (*similarities: self-government; differences: economies, slavery. They resolved their differences through compromises.*)

- Record students' answers on a flip chart. Keep a copy of them. Once students have completed their responses, tell

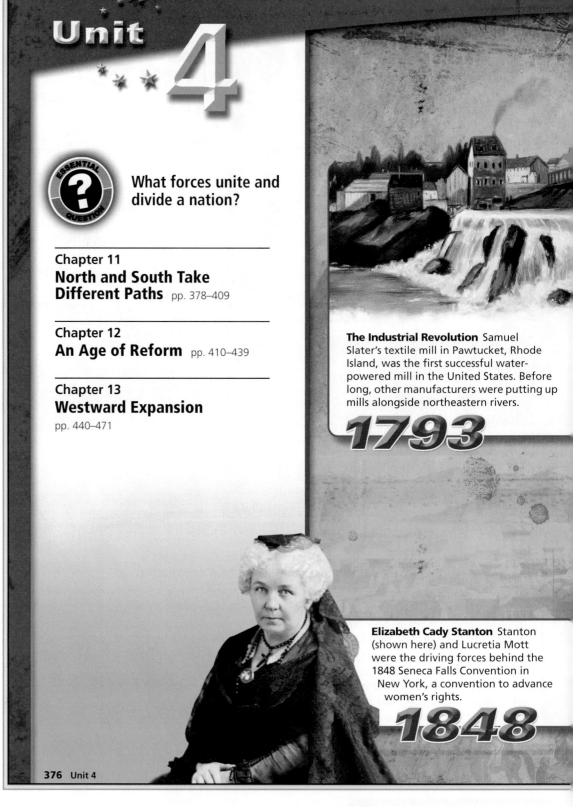

Unit 4

What forces unite and divide a nation?

The Industrial Revolution Samuel Slater's textile mill in Pawtucket, Rhode Island, was the first successful water-powered mill in the United States. Before long, other manufacturers were putting up mills alongside northeastern rivers.

1793

Elizabeth Cady Stanton Stanton (shown here) and Lucretia Mott were the driving forces behind the 1848 Seneca Falls Convention in New York, a convention to advance women's rights.

1848

376 Unit 4

them that they will be learning about increasing differences between the North and South and about United States expansion into the West. Let them know that you will return to this same question at the end of the unit and review their responses for possible additions or changes. (*See Think Like a Historian, p. 469.*)

- Preview the primary sources in Think Like a Historian on pp. 472–475. You may wish to introduce and discuss these documents to enrich chapter content.

The Nation Expands and Changes

"Am I Not a Man and a Brother?" An emblem of a man in chains became the symbol of the struggle against slavery. In 1827, Samuel Cornish and John Russwurm set up an abolitionist newspaper called *Freedom's Journal.*

1827

Battle of Buena Vista Outnumbered two to one, an American force under General Zachary Taylor (on his white horse) forced General Santa Anna's Mexican army to retreat under cover of night back into central Mexico.

1847

San Francisco Boom Within a few years of the California gold rush, San Francisco had become a thriving town with rows of houses looking out at a busy waterfront.

1850s

377

Unit Skills

■ Skills for Life

Evaluate Internet Sources
Chapter 11, p. 406

Evaluate Summaries
Chapter 12, p. 436

Evaluate Written Sources
Chapter 13, p. 468

■ Reading Skills

Identify and Explain Central Issues
Chapter 11, p. 379

Draw Conclusions from Sources
Chapter 12, p. 411

Frame Research Questions
Chapter 13, p. 441

■ Writing Workshop *Online*

Expository Essay: Multiple Causes or Effects
Web Code: mve-4000

■ Think Like a Historian

Students complete an activity in which they use pirmary sources to explore the Essential Question. pp. 472–475.

┌ Home Involvement ─

Students will be studying about the divergent paths of the American people in the early nineteenth century. A summary of the content and suggested activities adults at home can do with their student are available in a reproducible outline in the Teaching Resources.

All in One **Teaching Resources, Unit 4,** Letter Home, Chapters 11, 12, 13

 eTeach

Read the essay on eTeach for further ideas on Reading in the Content Area.
Visit: PHSchool.com
Web Code: myf-0301

DK World Desk Reference

Use the resources on the DK World Desk Reference for further information about Mexico today.
Visit: PHSchool.com
Web Code: mye-0302

History Background

Wedgwood's Abolitionist Symbol In the late 1700s, the British Wedgwood company—famous for making fine china and ceramics—produced a small ornament expressing opposition to slavery. Many of the original pieces were given to British and American abolitionists, including Benjamin Franklin. Some abolitionists wore them in jewelry, such as bracelets and tie pins. A medallion based on the piece is pictured on p. 377. The picture of a man in chains soon became a widely recognized symbol of slavery and oppression, which was used by the American abolitionist movement and remains powerful today.

North and South Take Different Paths (1800–1845)

History Background

The Effects of the Industrial Revolution

The first half of the nineteenth century was a period of revolutionary developments in transportation and industrial technology, which brought with them the beginnings of sweeping social change. The Industrial Revolution brought steam power and the factory system from England to the United States. Soon, canals, railroads, and steamships were efficiently transporting goods and people over increasing distances. Although these developments affected the entire country, they did so in different ways, often intensifying existing differences between North and South.

The Industrial Revolution affected the North directly. The region's farming, fishing, and trading economy became one characterized by mills and factories, manufacturing, and a large number of people working outside the home. Mass production brought a flood of unskilled laborers—such as young women, children, and new immigrants—into the workforce. Cities grew around factories.

The Industrial Revolution also transformed the South. Increased industrial capacity in the North and better transportation led to a dramatic increase in the demand for cotton, which could be processed more quickly using the cotton gin. Despite the fact that a minority of southern whites owned slaves—and only a very few were large planters—the ascendance of cotton both increased the dependence of the southern economy on slave labor and established the plantation lifestyle as the southern ideal.

Slavery in the South functioned both as a labor system and as a means of social control. Slave owners feared uprisings and passed harsh laws to discourage revolt. Slave codes extended to free African Americans, who faced legal restrictions, prejudice, and discrimination. They often faced similar obstacles in the North.

These economic divisions between North and South grew more pronounced by the mid-1800s. The divisions had far-reaching consequences. By the time the Civil War broke out in 1861, the Industrial Revolution had given the North a major advantage in factories and munitions.

Essential Questions

Use this graphic organizer to see the relationship between key concepts and the Chapter Essential Question.

Focus Question/Section 1
How did the new technology of the Industrial Revolution change the way Americans lived?
(p. 382)

Concept: Mass Production

Focus Question/Section 2
How did urbanization, technology, and social change affect the North?
(p. 390)

Concept: Technology

Chapter Essential Question
Why did Americans take different paths in the early 1800s?

Focus Question/Section 4
How did Americans move west, and how did this intensify the debate over slavery?
(p. 401)

Concept: Power

Focus Question/Section 3
How did cotton affect the social and economic life of the South?
(p. 396)

Concept: Slavery

Professional Development

Differentiated Instruction

Taking an Active Part by Sharing Ideas

Give One, Get One Strategy In this chapter, students will use the Give One, Get One strategy to participate in class discussion. This strategy has three stages: independent reflection, peer interaction, and class discussion. The independent reflection stage requires students to generate and evaluate their own ideas. The peer interaction and class discussion stages have them exchange ideas and then present each other's ideas.

Tips on Using This Strategy Encourage students to consider their own ideas carefully to determine which are strongest and best to share with others. Remind students that accurately copying a partner's idea and then identifying it with the partner's name is an important step in the idea exchange that not only records the source of the idea but makes sure that the idea is presented correctly in the class discussion. Suggest that students use a simple chart to record their own and others' ideas.

Concepts Across Time

Have students develop an understanding of the enduring concepts of history by connecting these ideas.

Concept: Mass Production

Students learning about the use of mass production in factories should contrast nineteenth-century techniques and work habits with how goods were made by early Native Americans. Ask: **Why were Native American techniques poorly suited to mass production?** (*Possible answer: Native Americans lacked the wheel, which Europeans and others used to harness the energy of animals or flowing water for mass production.*) Use this question when discussing The Industrial Revolution in Section 1.

Concept: Technology

Remind students how hard it was for colonial Americans to transport goods, or merely to travel long distances. Explain that early settlements in Virginia were located along the Atlantic coast or at nearby river ports that were readily accessible by boat. Remind students that technology enables people to perform tasks and make products more efficiently. It changes how people live and work and has often been key to the development of civilizations. Ask: **How is the Erie Canal an example of an advance in technology?** (*Building the canal required organizational skills and the application of new techniques such as the building of locks to help boats pass over uneven terrain. The canal became a tool for improving people's lives.*) Ask: **Why were waterways like the Erie Canal a great help in economic growth?** (*They permitted cheap transport of grain and other bulky goods at a time when roads were poorly built and often impassable.*) Use these questions when discussing improvements in transportation in Sections 2 and 4.

Concept: Slavery

As they study slavery in the southern states, students should recall how American slavery differed from slavery in places such as Africa and ancient Greece. Tell students that in those places slaves were often treated as servants rather than as property, and enslaved people were often of the same race as their masters. In some places, enslaved people or their children might rise to prominent positions in society. Ask: **Why was American slavery considered to be an especially cruel form of slavery?** (*Whole families were enslaved from generation to generation, and families might be broken apart when children were sold to separate owners. Also, in the United States, enslaved people were overwhelmingly of African descent, while owners were mainly of European descent, leading to enduring racial stereotypes and prejudices.*) Use this question when discussing Section 3.

Section 1 The Industrial Revolution *1.5 periods, .75 block*

Objectives

Students will

1. Explain the changes that the Industrial Revolution brought to American life.
2. Discuss the importance of Samuel Slater's cotton mill.
3. Describe the growth of industry in the United States after 1812.
4. Identify important developments in factories and the problems that factory life produced.

Differentiated Instruction Key

L1 Basic to Average
L2 All Students
L3 Average to Advanced

AR Advanced Readers
ELL English Language Learners
GT Gifted and Talented
LPR Less Proficient Readers
SN Special Needs

Prepare to Read	**Instructional Resources**	**Differentiated Instruction**
Build Background Knowledge Preview the section and discuss life without machines. **Set a Purpose for Reading** Have students begin to fill out the Reading Readiness Guide. **Preview Key Terms** Preview the section's Key Terms.	**All in One** Teaching Resources, Unit 4 **L2** Chapter Prereading Guide, p. 4 **L2** History Reading Skill Worksheet, p. 14 **L2** Word Knowledge Rating Form, p. 15 **L2** Reading Readiness Guide, p. 16 **Teacher's Edition** **L2** Vocabulary Builder, pp. 381, 383 **Discovery School Video** **L2** North and South Take Different Paths	🎧 **Guided Reading Audio CD** **Spanish** ELL, LPR, SN

Teach	**Instructional Resources**	**Differentiated Instruction**
Instruction **A Revolution in Technology** **The American Industrial Revolution** Analyze the effect the Industrial Revolution had on work in the United States. **American Industry Grows** Explain Francis Lowell's factory system. **The Revolution Takes Hold** Analyze the changes caused by mass production.	📖 **Interactive Reading and Notetaking Study Guide** **L2** Chapter 11, Section 1 **Color Transparencies** **L2** Spinning Mill **L2** James Watt's Steam Engine	📖 **Interactive Reading and Notetaking Study Guide, Adapted Version (English/ Spanish)** **L1** Chapter 11, Section 1 ELL, LPR, SN **Teacher's Edition** **L1** Visualizing the Word, p. 381 ELL, LPR, SN **L3** Spinning Mill, p. 382 GT **L3** Factory Conditions, p. 384 AR **L1** Unfamiliar Words, p. 386 ELL, LPR, SN **All in One** Teaching Resources, Unit 4 **L3** A Factory Report in 1846, p. 20

Assess and Reteach	**Instructional Resources**	**Differentiated Instruction**
Assess Progress Evaluate student comprehension with Check Your Progress and Section Quiz. **Reteach** Assign the Interactive Reading and Notetaking Study Guide to help struggling students. **Extend** Extend the lesson by having students complete James Watt's Steam Engine online.	📖 **Interactive Reading and Notetaking Study Guide** **L2** Chapter 11, Section 1 **All in One** Teaching Resources, Unit 4 **L2** Reading Readiness Guide, p. 16 **L2** Section Quiz, p. 27 **Progress Monitoring Transparencies** **L2** Chapter 11, Section 1	**Teacher's Edition** **L1** Checkpoints, TE pp. 383, 384, 385, 387 💿 **SE on Audio CD** **L1** Chapter 11 ELL, LPR, SN **Internet Resources** PHSchool.com

Section 2 The North Transformed *1 period, .5 block*

Objectives

Students will

1. Explain why American cities grew in the 1800s.
2. List the new inventions and advances in agriculture and manufacturing.
3. Describe the improvements in transportation during the early 1800s.
4. Discuss the wave of immigration to the United States in the 1840s and 1850s.
5. Describe the problems African Americans faced in the North.

Differentiated Instruction Key

- **L1** Basic to Average
- **L2** All Students
- **L3** Average to Advanced
- **AR** Advanced Readers
- **ELL** English Language Learners
- **GT** Gifted and Talented
- **LPR** Less Proficient Readers
- **SN** Special Needs

Prepare to Read

Build Background Knowledge
Preview the section and ask students about the North's characteristics during the 1800s.

Set a Purpose for Reading
Have students begin to fill out the Reading Readiness Guide.

Preview Key Terms
Preview the section's Key Terms.

Instructional Resources

All in One Teaching Resources, Unit 4
L2 Reading Readiness Guide, p. 17

Teacher's Edition
L2 Vocabulary Builder, p. 391

Differentiated Instruction

Guided Reading Audio CD
Spanish ELL, LPR, SN

Teach

Instruction
Northern Cities
The Growth of Northern Industry
A Transportation Revolution
Explain how new inventions and improvements in transportation helped industry and cities grow.

A New Wave of Immigrants
Explain how Irish and German immigrants settled in the United States.

African Americans in the North
Discuss discrimination against African Americans.

Instructional Resources

Interactive Reading and Notetaking Study Guide
L2 Chapter 11, Section 2

Color Transparencies
L2 Telegraph

Differentiated Instruction

Interactive Reading and Notetaking Study Guide, Adapted Version (English/Spanish)
L1 Chapter 11, Section 2 ELL, LPR, SN

Teacher's Edition
L1 Understanding Sentences, p. 388 ELL, LPR
L3 City Growth, p. 390 AR
L1 Comprehension Reinforcement, p. 392 LPR, SN
L1 Word Definitions, p. 394 ELL

Assess and Reteach

Assess Progress
Evaluate student comprehension with Check Your Progress and Section Quiz.

Reteach
Assign the Study Guide to help students.

Extend
Have students research African American abolitionists.

Instructional Resources

Interactive Reading and Notetaking Study Guide
L2 Chapter 11, Section 2

All in One Teaching Resources, Unit 4
L2 Reading Readiness Guide, p. 17
L2 Section Quiz, p. 28

Progress Monitoring Transparencies
L2 Chapter 11, Section 2

Differentiated Instruction

Teacher's Edition
L1 Checkpoints, TE pp. 391, 392, 393, 394, 395

SE on Audio CD
L2 Chapter 11 ELL, LPR, SN

Internet Resources
PHSchool.com

Section 3 The Plantation South *1 period, .5 block*

Objectives

Students will

1. Explain the significance of cotton and the cotton gin to the South.

2. Describe what life was like for free and enslaved African Americans in the South.

Differentiated Instruction Key

L1	Basic to Average	AR	Advanced Readers
L2	All Students	ELL	English Language Learners
L3	Average to Advanced	GT	Gifted and Talented
		LPR	Less Proficient Readers
		SN	Special Needs

Prepare to Read

Build Background Knowledge
Preview the section and discuss how northern industry will affect the South.

Set a Purpose for Reading
Have students begin to fill out the Reading Readiness Guide.

Preview Key Terms
Preview the section's Key Terms.

Instructional Resources

All in One Teaching Resources, Unit 4
L2 Reading Readiness Guide, p. 18

Teacher's Edition
L2 Vocabulary Builder, p. 397

Differentiated Instruction

🔘 **Guided Reading Audio CD**
Spanish ELL, LPR, SN

Teach

Instruction
The Cotton Kingdom
Analyze the relationship between cotton production and slavery.

African Americans in the South
Compare the lives of free and enslaved African Americans.

Instructional Resources

📖 **Interactive Reading and Notetaking Study Guide**
L2 Chapter 11, Section 3

Discovery School Video
L2 Plantation Life

Differentiated Instruction

📖 **Interactive Reading and Notetaking Study Guide, Adapted Version (English/Spanish)**
L1 Chapter 11, Section 3 ELL, LPR, SN

Teacher's Edition
L1 Word Meanings, p. 396 ELL
L3 Oral History, p. 398 AR, GT

Assess and Reteach

Assess Progress
Evaluate student comprehension with Check Your Progress and Section Quiz.

Reteach
Assign the Interactive Reading and Notetaking Study Guide to help struggling students.

Extend
Extend the lesson by having students review the journal of Fanny Kemble.

Instructional Resources

📖 **Interactive Reading and Notetaking Study Guide**
L2 Chapter 11, Section 3

All in One Teaching Resources, Unit 4
L2 Reading Readiness Guide, p. 18
L2 Section Quiz, p. 29

Progress Monitoring Transparencies
L2 Chapter 11, Section 3

Differentiated Instruction

Teacher's Edition
L1 Checkpoints, TE pp. 398, 400

🔘 **SE on Audio CD**
L2 Chapter 11 ELL, LPR, SN

Internet Resources
PHSchool.com

Section 4 The Challenges of Growth

 1.5 periods, .75 block

Objectives

Students will

1. Identify the problems Americans moving westward faced.
2. Describe the impact of the building of the Erie Canal.
3. Discuss the debate over slavery and the Missouri Compromise.

Differentiated Instruction Key

L1 Basic to Average
L2 All Students
L3 Average to Advanced

AR Advanced Readers
ELL English Language Learners
GT Gifted and Talented
LPR Less Proficient Readers
SN Special Needs

Prepare to Read

Build Background Knowledge
Preview the section and discuss what settlers needed in order to move west.

Set a Purpose for Reading
Have students begin to fill out the Reading Readiness Guide.

Preview Key Terms
Preview the section's Key Terms.

Instructional Resources

All in One Teaching Resources, Unit 4
L2 Reading Readiness Guide, p. 19

Teacher's Edition
L2 Vocabulary Builder, p. 401

Differentiated Instruction

🔘 **Guided Reading Audio CD**
Spanish ELL, LPR, SN

Teach

Instruction
Moving West
Roads and Turnpikes
Discuss the western frontier and how settlers reached it.

Canals
Analyze the impact of the Erie Canal.

The Extension of Slavery
Discuss the debate over slavery and the Missouri Compromise.

Instructional Resources

📖 **Interactive Reading and Notetaking Study Guide**
L2 Chapter 11, Section 4

All in One Teaching Resources, Unit 4
L2 Population and Territory, p. 22
L2 The Erie Canal, p. 24
L2 Concept Lesson, p. 26
L2 Concept Organizer, p. 6
L2 Skills for Life Worksheet, p. 25

Differentiated Instruction

📖 **Interactive Reading and Notetaking Study Guide, Adapted Version (English/Spanish)**
L1 Chapter 11, Section 4 ELL, LPR, SN

Teacher's Edition
L1 Along the Erie Canal, p. 402 ELL, LPR, SN
L3 Present Graphic Data, p. 404 GT

All in One Teaching Resources, Unit 4
L1 Along the Erie Canal, p. 23

Assess and Reteach

Assess Progress
Assign Check Your Progress and Section Quiz.

Reteach
Assign the Study Guide to help students.

Extend
Have students research Henry Clay online.

Instructional Resources

📖 **Interactive Reading and Notetaking Study Guide**
L2 Chapter 11, Section 4

All in One Teaching Resources, Unit 4
L2 Word Knowledge Rating Form, p. 15
L2 Reading Readiness Guide, p. 19
L2 Section Quiz, p. 30
L2 Chapter Test, p. 34

Progress Monitoring Transparencies
L2 Chapter 11, Section 4

Differentiated Instruction

Teacher's Edition
L1 Checkpoints, TE pp. 402, 403, 404, 405

All in One Teaching Resources, Unit 4
L1 Chapter Test, p. 31

🔘 **SE on Audio CD**
L2 Chapter 11 ELL, LPR, SN

Internet Resources
PHSchool.com

Use the following research activities to help students deepen their understanding of the Chapter Essential Question: **Why did Americans take different paths in the early 1800s?** Students should use library or Internet resources. The Web Codes provided offer access to Internet resources students can use to complete each activity. Use the appropriate four-point rubric in Assessment Rubrics to evaluate the activity.

 Assessment Rubrics

Write a Report About Factories in Lowell, Massachusetts

Have groups of three or four students use the Web site to learn more about factories in Lowell. Have each member write a paragraph on one aspect of the Lowell factories for a report to someone who is starting a factory in the early 1800s. Ask the group to make a recommendation on whether the Lowell system is a good model. Have groups make a brief presentation to the class. Use this activity when studying American Industry Grows in Section 1.

 Group research activity AR, GT   L3

Go Online **Web Code:** mye-0255
PHSchool.com

Send and Receive Messages in Morse Code

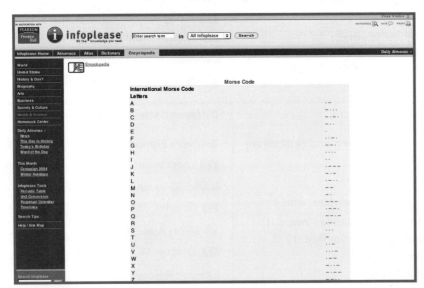

Have students use the Web site to look up the key to international Morse Code. Ask them to write brief sentences about new inventions in the 1800s in Morse Code. Then have them exchange papers and decode each other's sentences. Use this activity when studying The Growth of Northern Industry in Section 2.

 Individual research activity   L2

Go Online **Web Code:** mye-0256
PHSchool.com

Write an Essay Comparing and Contrasting Leaders of Slave Revolts

Have students research the leaders of famous slave revolts, such as Nat Turner, Denmark Vesey, and Gabriel Prosser. Have students choose two of these men and write a three-paragraph essay comparing and contrasting their lives and goals, as well as the results of their revolts. Ask students to present their findings to the class. Use this activity when studying African Americans in the South in Section 3.

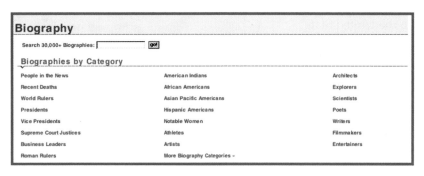

 Individual research activity AR   **L3**

Go Online **Web Code:** mye-0257
PHSchool.com

Make a Timeline of the Construction of the National Road

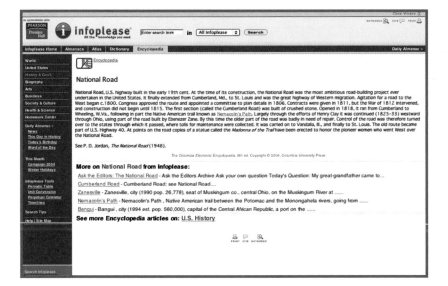

Go Online **Web Code:** mye-0258
PHSchool.com

Have students make a timeline of the construction of the National Road, including when different parts were begun and completed. Remind them to include information on Nemacolin's Path, over which part of the National Road was built. On the timeline, have them add historical events that affected the construction of the path and road, with a sentence explaining the impact of each event. Have students share their timelines with the class. Ask the class to use the information from the timelines to make generalizations about government construction projects and about the need for roads. Use this activity when studying Roads and Turnpikes in Section 4.

 Individual research activity   **L2**

Why It Matters

Inventions in the mid-1800s brought on many changes in the United States. New machines improved farming, industry, and communication. Railroads and telegraph lines stretched across the nation. Economic interdependence grew as cotton from the South was shipped to factories in the North, while crops from the West were sent to the East coast cities. These changes worked to unify the country.

Yet regional differences were also a result of these same changes. In the North, people flocked to the factories, causing a rapid growth of large cities. In the South, cotton production grew more and more dependent on slave labor. The flood of people moving west intensified these differences, as people debated whether to allow slavery in these new territories. The bitter controversy eventually split the country in half and led to the worst fighting on United States' soil that Americans would ever know.

Chapter Essential Question

Why did Americans take different paths in the early 1800s?

Think Like a Historian

- To preview this chapter, have students review the content of these pages of the Student Edition. Ask: **What will you be learning about in this chapter?** *(possible answer: the Industrial Revolution, differences between the North and South, the slavery issue, the challenges associated with increased western settlement)*

- Have students read the quote at the top of page 381. Work with students to rephrase the quote so that it is easier for them to understand. Ask: **Why do you think President Jackson was concerned about the "efforts" to pull the North and South apart?** *(accept any answer that describes Jackson's concern for the country, the importance of keeping the country united, avoiding conflict)*

- Have students look at the images on the student pages. Ask: **What is the mood of the crowd on viewing this new steam locomotive? How were you able to come to this conclusion?** *(The crowd is excited and curious; they are cheering and staring)*

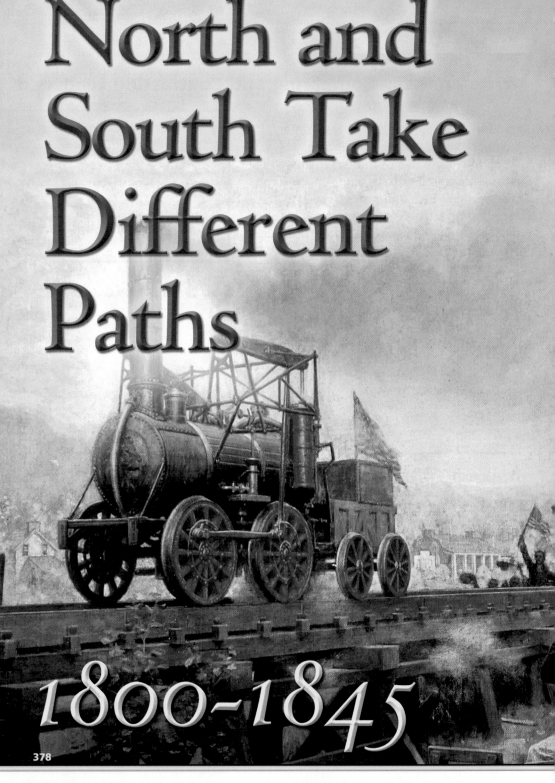

North and South Take Different Paths

1800–1845

378

Bibliography

For the Teacher

Jewett, Clayton E., and John O. Allen. *Slavery in the South: A State-by-State History.* Greenwood Press, 2004.

Moran, William. *The Belles of New England: The Women of the Textile Mills and the Families Whose Wealth They Wove.* Thomas Dunne Books, 2002.

For the Student

L1 McCormick, Anita Louise. *The Industrial Revolution in American History.* Enslow Publishers, 1998.

L2 Patterson, Katherine. *Lyddie.* Thorndike Press, 1993.

L3 Dudley, William. *American Slavery.* Greenhaven Press, 2000.

> *"We behold systematic efforts ...to excite the South against the North and the North against the South...."*
>
> —President Andrew Jackson,
> *Farewell Address, 1837*

Although scenes like this one spurred American nationalism, sectional differences grew during the first half of the nineteenth century.

CHAPTER 11

What You Will Learn

Section 1
THE INDUSTRIAL REVOLUTION
New inventions brought new ways of making basic products.

Section 2
THE NORTH TRANSFORMED
Differences between the North and the South increased with the growth of industry.

Section 3
THE PLANTATION SOUTH
The invention of the cotton gin increased the South's dependence on the labor of enslaved people.

Section 4
THE CHALLENGES OF GROWTH
As settlement spread westward, debates over slavery increased tensions between North and South.

Reading Skill

Identify and Explain Central Issues In this chapter, you will learn to identify central issues and describe them in the context of the times and places in which they occurred.

379

History Background

Steam Locomotives The first trains were imported to the United States from England. In the early 1800s, the English inventor Richard Trevithick created a steam engine on a carriage that could roll along a track, which became the first successful locomotive. The first public freight railroad began operating in England in 1825, followed, in 1830, by the first passenger railroad with a regular schedule. The Delaware and Hudson Canal Company of Pennsylvania ran the English-built Stourbridge Lion on wooden tracks in 1829, making it the first full-sized locomotive to travel on North American tracks.

Prepare to Read

Use the following for reading skill support.

All in One Teaching Resources, Unit 4, Chapter Prereading Guide, p. 4; History Reading Skill, p. 14

History Reading Skill, *Online*
Web code: mve-3000

Differentiated Instruction

The following Teacher's Edition strategies are suitable for students of varying abilities.

L3 Advanced Readers, pp. 384, 390, 398 AR

L1 English Language Learners, pp. 381, 386, 388, 394, 396, 402 ELL

L3 Gifted and Talented, pp. 382, 398, 404 GT

L1 Less Proficient Readers, pp. 381, 386, 388, 392, 402 LPR

L1 Special Needs, pp. 381, 386, 392, 402 SN

Chapter Resources

Teaching Resources, Unit 4
Chapter Prereading Guide, p. 4
Word Knowledge Rating Form, p. 15
History Reading Skill, p. 14
Skills for Life Worksheet, p. 25
Chapter Tests A/B (L1/L2), pp. 31, 34
Letter Home (English/Spanish), pp. 7, 8

Spanish Support
L1 Interactive Reading and Notetaking Study Guide, Spanish, Adapted Version
L1 Guided Reading Audio CD, Spanish

Media and Technology
L1 SE on Audio CD
L2 Social Studies Skills Tutor CD-ROM
ExamView Test Bank CD-ROM

Quick View Video
View the chapter video for a quick preview of the main ideas.

Visual Preview

? **Why did Americans take different paths in the early 1800's?**

Build Background Knowledge **L2**

Have students review the map and map key. Point out the different economies in the North and South and the existence of slave and free states. Discuss how these different paths led to sectional differences. Emphasize that for a nation of united states, differences among members was a serious situation. Sectional differences threatened to pull the nation apart. Lead a structured review connecting what students have learned with the Essential Question. (For information on structured discussion, see TE p. T24.) **L2**

Instruction

■ For background information on conducting a lesson for the Visual Preview, see TE p. T20.

■ Write the Chapter Essential Question on the board. Explain to students that the maps and the graph on pp. 380–381 represent economic differences between the North and the South. Ask: **How did the economies of the North and the South differ?** *(Possible answer: The South was mainly agricultural. The North was mainly industrial.)*

■ Using the key, have students explain the differences between those states that are marked blue and those that are marked red. Explain that the issue of slavery caused tension between the North and the South. Point out that the reference to territories in the Key is important because the controversy of whether or not a territory would allow slavery threatened the balance of power between North and South in the nation's Congress. Then have students look at the map on these pages. Ask: **What city had the largest population in 1840?** *(New York City)*

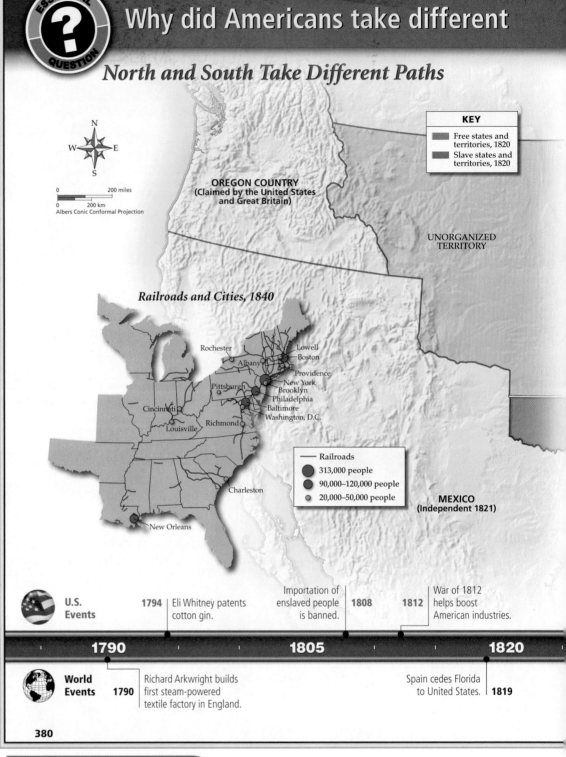

? **ESSENTIAL QUESTION** **Why did Americans take different**

North and South Take Different Paths

Railroads and Cities, 1840

KEY
- Free states and territories, 1820
- Slave states and territories, 1820

OREGON COUNTRY
(Claimed by the United States and Great Britain)

UNORGANIZED TERRITORY

0 — 200 miles
0 — 200 km
Albers Conic Conformal Projection

Rochester
Lowell
Boston
Albany
Providence
New York
Pittsburgh
Brooklyn
Philadelphia
Cincinnati
Baltimore
Washington, D.C.
Louisville
Richmond
Charleston
New Orleans

— Railroads
● 313,000 people
● 90,000–120,000 people
● 20,000–50,000 people

MEXICO
(Independent 1821)

U.S. Events
1794 | Eli Whitney patents cotton gin.
Importation of enslaved people is banned. | 1808
1812 | War of 1812 helps boost American industries.

1790 — **1805** — **1820**

World Events
1790 | Richard Arkwright builds first steam-powered textile factory in England.
Spain cedes Florida to United States. | 1819

380

History Background

Moving West After the War of 1812, there was a huge surge of westward migration. In 1790, 95 percent of the population lived in states bordering the Atlantic Ocean; by 1800, 25 percent of the people lived west of the Appalachian Mountains.

There were only a few roads traveling west. Northerners tended to travel along northern routes, while southerners used their regional southern roads. Although expansion brought a sense of national unity, the settlers from different regions did not intermingle. They brought their own regional identities into the new territory. As a result, the West did not form a third, distinct political region.

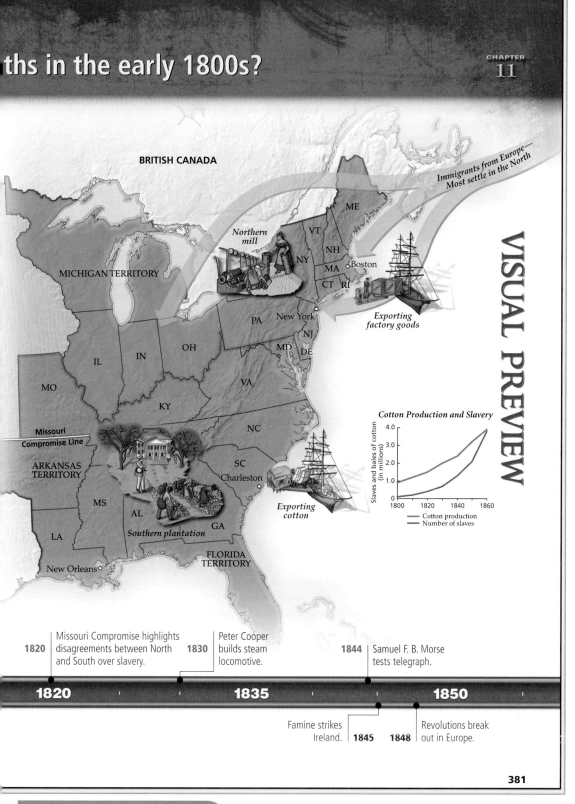

BRITISH CANADA

MICHIGAN TERRITORY

Immigrants from Europe—Most settle in the North

ME

Northern mill

VT

NH

NY

MA Boston

CT RI

PA New York

NJ

MD DE

Exporting factory goods

IL

IN

OH

VA

MO

KY

Missouri Compromise Line

NC

ARKANSAS TERRITORY

SC

Charleston

MS

AL

GA

Southern plantation

LA

New Orleans

FLORIDA TERRITORY

Exporting cotton

VISUAL PREVIEW

Cotton Production and Slavery

Slaves and bales of cotton (in millions)

4.0
3.0
2.0
1.0
0

1800 1820 1840 1860

— Cotton production
— Number of slaves

| 1820 | Missouri Compromise highlights disagreements between North and South over slavery. | 1830 | Peter Cooper builds steam locomotive. | 1844 | Samuel F. B. Morse tests telegraph. |

1820 | **1835** | **1850**

Famine strikes Ireland. | **1845** | **1848** | Revolutions break out in Europe.

381

Instruction (continued)

- Have students look at the timeline. Ask: **What span of American history is covered on the timeline?** *(1790–1850)* **What new inventions were created in this era?** *(cotton gin, steam locomotive, telegraph)*

- Have students look at the line graph. Trace the green line for students and explain that it shows a steep increase in cotton production. Have students repeat the process with the red line. Then ask: **Why did the number of enslaved people increase between 1800 and 1860?** *(Possible answer: The number of enslaved people increased in proportion to the increase in cotton production.)*

- Have students review the map. Ask: **How would you describe the populations of the North and the South in 1840?** *(Possible answer: The North had many large cities. The South had few large cities.)*

- Have students rewrite the Essential Question in simple terms in their notes: **Why did Americans have different goals in the early 1800s?** You may also post this question in a prominent place in the classroom and leave it there while discussing the chapter. Tell students to use the section focus questions as a guide to answering the Essential Question as they read the chapter.

- Tell students that as they complete the Notetaking Study Guide for this chapter, they will be building the answer to the Essential Question.

Interactive Reading and Notetaking Study Guide, Chapter 11, (Adapted Version also available.)

Vocabulary Builder

Preview the Vocabulary Have students preview the vocabulary in the chapter and rate how well they know each word on the Word Knowledge Rating Form. Collect the sheets and explain that they will have a chance to go over the forms later.

All in One Teaching Resources, Unit 4, Word Knowledge Rating Form, p. 15

Monitor Progress Have students substitute the correct vocabulary term for the underlined word in the following sentences in order to demonstrate their understanding.

- The machines in the mill are <u>effective</u> for producing cloth. *(efficient)*

- France sold the Louisiana Territory to the United States during the <u>rule</u> of Napoleon. *(reign)*

Review and Preview

The early 1800s saw the new nation growing larger and developing a sense of pride. Students will now focus on the impact of the new technology of the Industrial Revolution.

Section Focus Question

How did the new technology of the Industrial Revolution change the way Americans lived?

Before you begin the lesson for the day, write the Section Focus Question on the board. (*Lesson focus: Many people went from working on farms to working in factories in the North, while industrial needs and new inventions encouraged planters to raise more cotton in the South, increasing the need for slaves.*)

Prepare to Read

Build Background Knowledge L2

In this section students will read about the Industrial Revolution and how it affected life in the United States. Ask students to think about how life would be without machines. Use the Idea Wave strategy (TE, p. T24) to encourage responses. Then discuss how technology can change the way people live.

Set a Purpose L2

■ Read each statement in the Reading Readiness Guide aloud. Ask students to mark the statements True or False.

All in One Teaching Resources, Unit 4, Reading Readiness Guide, p. 16

■ Have students discuss the statements in pairs or groups of four, then mark their worksheets again. Use the Numbered Heads strategy (TE, p. T24) to call on students to share their group's perspectives. The students will return to these worksheets later.

You Will Be Astounded

❝ There are more than 5,000 females employed in Lowell; and when you come to see the amount of labor performed by them, in superintending the different machinery, you will be astonished.... Everything moves on like clockwork....❞

—Congressman Davy Crockett of Tennessee, after visiting mills in Lowell, Massachusetts, 1834

▲ New England mill town, early 1800s

The Industrial Revolution

Objectives

- Explain the changes that the Industrial Revolution brought to American life.
- Discuss the importance of Samuel Slater's cotton mill.
- Describe the growth of industry in the United States after 1812.
- Identify important developments in factories and the problems that factory life produced.

↻ Reading Skill

Identify Central Issues From the Past
To effectively study history, you can identify important—or central—issues and then seek to make generalizations from them. To make a generalization, identify main points or ideas in a text. Then, devise a general principle or broad statement that applies to all of them and to other situations.

Key Terms and People

Industrial Revolution
factory system
capitalist

Francis Cabot Lowell
mass production
interchangeable parts

Why It Matters In early America, most people worked as farmers. Men worked in the fields to produce food for their families. Women helped in the fields and made simple goods, like candles and soap, at home. The Industrial Revolution changed all this.

❓ **Section Focus Question: How did the new technology of the Industrial Revolution change the way Americans lived?**

A Revolution in Technology

In the 1700s, a great change began that we now call the **Industrial Revolution.** Gradually, machines took the place of many hand tools. Much of the power once provided by people and horses began to be replaced, first by flowing water and then by steam engines.

The Industrial Revolution began in Britain, in the textile, or cloth-making, industry. For centuries, workers had spun thread in their homes on spinning wheels. The thread was then woven into cloth on hand looms. Making thread was time-consuming. It took one person, spinning one strand at a time, almost two weeks to produce a pound of cotton thread.

Machines and Factories In the 1760s, the spinning jenny speeded up the thread-making process. The jenny allowed a person to spin many strands at once. However, thread still had to be made by hand.

Then, in 1764, Richard Arkwright invented the water frame, a spinning machine powered by running water rather than human energy. Other inventions speeded up the weaving process. To house the large machines, manufacturers built textile mills on the banks of rivers.

382 Chapter 11 North and South Take Different Paths

Differentiated Instruction

L3 Gifted and Talented

Spinning Mill Ask students to suppose that they work in a spinning mill, such as the one shown in the transparency Spinning Mill (see p. 383). Have students write several diary entries describing the mill, the machines in it, and their particular job.

Encourage students to include details and references to the positive and negative aspects of work in a mill. Ask students to share highlights of their diary entries with the class.

The new mills created a new way of working, known as the factory system. The **factory system** brings workers and machinery together in one place. Instead of spinning at home, textile workers had to go to the factories and begin and end work at specific hours. Workers now had to keep up with the machines instead of working at their own pace.

British mill owners soon recognized the potential of the new water frames and the factory system. However, the system required huge amounts of money to be <u>invested</u> in buildings and machines. Thus, the mill owners turned to **capitalists,** people who invest capital, or money, in a business to earn a profit. Factories proved to be a good investment for the capitalists and mill owners. By 1784, British workers were producing 24 times as much thread as they had in 1765.

Steam Power Building factories on riverbanks had some disadvantages. In a dry season, the machines had no power. Also, most factories were far from cities, and labor was hard to find in rural areas.

In 1790, Arkwright built the first steam-powered textile plant. The steam engine was a reliable source of power. Factories no longer had to be built on riverbanks. They could be built in cities, where young women and children provided cheap labor.

Britain tried to guard the secrets of its industrial success. It forbade anyone to take information about textile machinery out of Britain. Skilled workers were forbidden to leave the country.

✓**Checkpoint** How did the Industrial Revolution change the way work was performed?

Vocabulary Builder

invest (ihn VEHST) **v.** to supply money for a project in order to make a profit

A Steam Engine

1 Cylinder Steam from boiling water rises into the cylinder.

3 Flywheel The other end of the beam goes down, moving gears to turn the flywheel.

2 Piston rod Pressure from the rising steam pushes the piston rod up and raises one end of the beam.

History *Interactive*

Study a Steam Engine in Action

Visit: PHSchool.com
Web Code: myp-4071

Steam Engine

Steam engines use the energy created by boiling water to push rods and wheels. **Critical Thinking: *Identify Economic Benefits*** *What advantage would the steam engine have given to a manufacturer over competitors who depended on water power to operate their machinery?*

Vocabulary Builder

Use the information below to teach students this section's high-use words.

High-Use Word	Definition and Sample Sentence
invest, p. 383	*v.* to supply money for a project in order to make a profit Shipowners **invested** in voyages to distant lands.
efficient, p. 386	*adj.* acting effectively, without wasted cost or effort New inventions often led to more **efficient** ways of doing business.

Teach

A Revolution in Technology

The American Industrial Revolution

pp. 382–384

Instruction   L2

- **Vocabulary Builder** Before teaching this lesson, preteach the High-Use Words **invest** and **efficient,** using the strategy on TE p. T21.

  Key Terms Following the instructions on p. 7, have students create a See It–Remember It chart for the Key Terms in this chapter.

- Read A Revolution in Technology and The American Industrial Revolution with students, using the Oral Cloze strategy (TE, p. T22).

- Ask: **How did the factory system work?** (*It brought together workers and machinery in one place.*)

- To help students understand early factories, show the transparency Spinning Mill and discuss the questions.

- Show the History Interactive transparency James Watt's Steam Engine. Have students discuss the questions.

Color Transparencies, Spinning Mill; James Watt's Steam Engine

Independent Practice

Have students begin filling in the study guide for this section.

Interactive Reading and Notetaking Study Guide, Chapter 11, Section 1 (Adapted Version also available.)

Monitor Progress

As students fill in the study guide, circulate to make sure they understand the importance of the Industrial Revolution.

Answers

✓**Checkpoint** Possible answer: Machines took the place of hand tools.

Identify Economic Benefits A manufacturer who used a steam engine would not be limited to building a factory on a riverbank, but could choose a location closer to cheap labor.

American Industry Grows

p. 384

Instruction

- Have students read American Industry Grows. Remind students to look for cause and effect.

- Ask: **What sparked the growth of industry in the United States?** (*During the War of 1812, the British blockade forced Americans to supply their own goods.*)

- Ask: **Why did Lowell's mill town have boardinghouses, a library, and a hospital for its workers?** (*Lowell wanted better lives for his workers.*)

- Ask: **Why do you think Charles Dickens was amazed when he saw Lowell?** (*He was probably surprised that conditions in Lowell were so good compared to those in England.*)

Independent Practice

Have students continue filling in the study guide for this section.

   Interactive Reading and Notetaking Study Guide, Chapter 11, Section 1 (Adapted Version also available.)

Monitor Progress

As students fill in the study guide, circulate and make sure students understand how the growth of American industry affected workers. Provide assistance as needed.

Signs of Progress
The Industrial Revolution put people to work in large factories like the one shown here. **Critical Thinking: *Distinguish Relevant Information*** *From the evidence in this picture, how might the presence of a factory affect the surrounding communities?*

The American Industrial Revolution

In 1789, a young apprentice in one of Arkwright's factories decided to immigrate to the United States. Samuel Slater knew that his knowledge of Arkwright's machines could be worth a fortune. He studied hard and memorized the plans of Arkwright's machines. Then, he boarded a ship for New York.

In the United States, Slater joined forces with a wealthy merchant, Moses Brown. Brown had rented a textile mill in Pawtucket, Rhode Island. Relying entirely on his memory, Slater constructed a spinning machine based on Arkwright's. Slater's factory began producing cotton thread at a rate never before seen in the United States.

✓Checkpoint **Why did Samuel Slater have to build his machines from memory?**

American Industry Grows

The success of Slater's mill marked the beginning of American industrialization. Industrialization began in the Northeast. The region was home to a class of merchants who had capital to build factories and to buy raw materials.

Still, U.S. industry did not grow significantly until the War of 1812. As the British navy blockaded U.S. ports, Americans had to depend on their own industries to supply goods.

The Lowell Mills Francis Cabot Lowell found a way. Before the war, he had visited England and seen the latest weaving machines. When he returned to the United States, Lowell and an associate built an improved version of the English machines.

Differentiated Instruction

L3 Advanced Readers

Factory Conditions Assign students the worksheet A Factory Report in 1846. Have them answer the questions and define the underlined words in the text. Then have students read the document aloud to the class, explaining the underlined words as they read. Discuss with the class why working conditions deteriorated.

   All in One Teaching Resources, Unit 4, A Factory Report in 1846, p. 20

Answers

Distinguish Relevant Information Possible answer: Smoke from the factories might fill the air; there might be more traffic on roads; there would be a place for people to work.

✓Checkpoint It was against British law to take technology out of England, so he had to memorize the plans for machines.

With several other capitalists, Lowell opened a mill in Waltham, Massachusetts. The mill was organized in a new way. Instead of obtaining thread from separate spinning mills, Lowell's factory brought together spinning and weaving in one building.

After Lowell died in 1817, his partners expanded the business. Wanting better lives for their workers, the partners built a new town, with boardinghouses, a library, and a hospital. They named their mill town Lowell after their late partner.

Lowell Girls The new factories were staffed with young women from nearby farms. "Lowell girls" lived in boardinghouses under strict supervision. After work, they might attend lectures or visit libraries. As a result, many women gained an education they probably would not have received on their family farms. The British novelist Charles Dickens was amazed when he saw Lowell:

Identify Central Issues From the Past
What generalization can you make about the link between war, trade, and inventiveness?

> ❝Firstly, there is a . . . piano in a great many of the boardinghouses. Secondly, nearly all these young ladies subscribe to circulating libraries. Thirdly, they have [created] a periodical called 'The Lowell Offering.' . . .❞
> —Charles Dickens, *American Notes,* 1842

✓**Checkpoint** How was the Lowell factory system different from the European factory system?

Links Across Time

2000s Office workers and researchers use computers for much of what they do.

Technology and Work

1820s The Industrial Revolution opened the way for new developments in technology, which changed the way people worked.

1981–2000s Since the invention of the personal computer, changes in technology have affected not only *how* people work but also *where* they work. With speedy laptops and hand-held devices, workers are able to work successfully at home or at the office.

Link to Today ⬤nline

Technology's Impact Technology continues to advance. How are technological innovations changing people's lives today?

For: Technology in the workplace
Visit: PHSchool.com
Web Code: myc-4071

Section 1 The Industrial Revolution **385**

Instruction   L2

- Have students read The Revolution Takes Hold. Remind them to look for details to answer the Section Focus Question.

- Discuss mass production. Ask: **What were some advantages of interchangeable parts?** (*They allowed parts to be replaced easily, they could be assembled quickly by unskilled workers, they made manufacturing more efficient, and they made goods cheaper.*)

- Discuss the disadvantages of mass production. Ask: **What do you think craftspeople thought of mass production?** (*Possible answer: They were not happy about it, because unskilled workers could make the same products more quickly.*)

- Discuss working conditions in factories in the 1800s. Ask: **What problems did workers in factories face?** (*Conditions were not safe, and injured workers lost their income. Days were long, pay was low, and there was little light or fresh air in factories. Child workers could not play or get an education.*)

- Ask: **Why do you think people were willing to work in such poor conditions?** (*Possible answer: People needed jobs to earn wages. Many uneducated and unskilled factory workers couldn't get work elsewhere.*)

History Background

Women's Wages In the early 1800s, women factory workers who were married were expected to turn their wages over to their husbands, who could spend the money as they wished. This injustice was one of many that women fought against through the women's rights movement later in the century.

Answers

🔵 **Reading Skill** Possible answer: War may sometimes result in the halting of trade, causing people to come up with new ways to fill the need to supply goods.

✓**Checkpoint** Instead of obtaining thread from separate spinning mills, Lowell's factory brought together spinning and weaving in one building.

Independent Practice

Have students continue filling in the study guide for this section.

📖 **Interactive Reading and Notetaking Study Guide,** Chapter 11, Section 1 (Adapted Version also available.)

Monitor Progress

- As students fill in the study guide, circulate to make sure individuals understand the problems with factory life. Provide assistance as needed.

- Tell students to fill in the last column of the Reading Readiness Guide. Probe for what they learned that confirms or invalidates each statement.

All in One Teaching Resources, Unit 4, Reading Readiness Guide, p. 16

Assess and Reteach

Assess Progress　　　L2

Have students complete Check Your Progress. Administer the Section Quiz.

All in One Teaching Resources, Unit 4, Section Quiz, p. 27

To further assess student understanding, use the Progress Monitoring Transparency.

Progress Monitoring Transparencies, Chapter 11, Section 1

Factory Workers
This picture shows young girls at work in a textile factory about 1834.
Critical Thinking: *Draw Conclusions* *What were some disadvantages for children who worked in early American factories?*

The Revolution Takes Hold

The Lowell system was an example of a unique American outlook. Without a long tradition of doing things a certain way, Americans experimented with new methods. One of the most important developments was **mass production,** or the rapid manufacture of large numbers of identical objects.

Before the 1800s, skilled craftsworkers manufactured clocks, guns, and other mechanical products. Each part of the gun or clock was handcrafted. When a part broke, a craftsworker had to create a unique piece to fit the product. In the 1790s, American inventor Eli Whitney devised a system of **interchangeable parts,** identical pieces that could be assembled quickly by unskilled workers.

Interchangeable parts soon came to be used in the manufacture of other products. Manufacturing became more <u>efficient</u>. The price of many goods dropped. As people bought more goods, U.S. industry expanded to satisfy their needs.

Factory Life As you have read, the Lowell mills treated factory workers in a new and kinder way. However, this was not the general rule. Samuel Slater employed children in his textile mill, as had been done for decades in British factories. As time went on, working conditions for children and adults became harsher.

Vocabulary Builder
<u>efficient</u> (ee FISH ehnt) *adj.* acting effectively, without wasted cost or effort

Differentiated Instruction

　L1 **English Language Learners**　　L1 **Less Proficient Readers**　　L1 **Special Needs**

Unfamiliar Words Suggest to students that they use a ruler to help them keep their place as they read, line to line, down a page. Have students mark unfamiliar words or phrases (such as *handcrafted* on this page) with a sticky note. Review with them from time to time what they have marked.

Answer

Draw Conclusions Possible answers: They could be injured, didn't get to play outdoors, worked long hours for little pay, had no time for school, and had big responsibilities.

Child Labor Children routinely worked on family farms in the 1800s. Their labor was often needed to help feed their families. Working on a home farm was different from working in a factory, however. American textile mills, coal mines, and steel foundries employed children as young as 7 or 8. These children had no opportunities for education. They often worked in unsafe conditions. By 1880, more than a million children between the ages of 10 and 15 worked for pay.

Factory Conditions Working conditions were appalling. Factories were poorly lighted. There was little fresh air. Machines were designed to perform a task, not to protect the worker. As a result, many workers were injured on the job. A worker who lost a hand or a foot received no help. He or she needed to depend on family for support. Business owners provided no payments for disabled workers, as they do by law today.

To keep machines running as long as possible, workdays lasted 12 or 14 hours. By 1844, workers were demanding shorter days. "Eight hours for work, eight hours for sleep, and eight hours for God and the brethren" was an early slogan. Conditions gradually improved, but the 8-hour workday was far in the future.

✓**Checkpoint** How did Eli Whitney's system of interchangeable parts speed up the manufacturing process?

⭐ **Looking Back and Ahead** Although the new factories were hard on workers, industrialization led to vastly increased production and lower prices. In the next section, you will read how the growth of northern industry helped to widen the gap between the North and the South.

Section 1 | Check Your Progress

Progress Monitoring Online
For: Self-test with instant help
Visit: PHSchool.com
Web Code: mya-4071

Comprehension and Critical Thinking

1. (a) **Describe** How did the War of 1812 affect U.S. industry?
   (b) **Draw Conclusions** Why did advances in industry occur mainly in the North?

2. (a) **Recall** What are interchangeable parts?
   (b) **Draw Conclusions** How did the system of interchangeable parts affect employment in the United States?

🔄 **Reading Skill**

3. **Identify Central Issues From the Past** Based on this section, what generalization can you make about the impact of inventiveness during the early Industrial Revolution?

Key Terms

4. Write two definitions for each key term: factory system, capitalist, interchangeable parts. First, write a formal definition for your teacher. Second, write a definition in everyday English for a classmate.

Writing

5. Rewrite the following lists of causes and effects, so that causes are correctly paired up with their effects.

Causes: Francis Lowell; Arkwright's textile plant; Samuel Slater's emigration; Eli Whitney

Effects: efficiency in mass production; libraries for factory workers; factories built in cities; increased American production of cotton thread

---

Reteach L1

If students need more instruction, have them read this section in the Interactive Reading and Notetaking Study Guide.

📖 **Interactive Reading and Notetaking Study Guide,** Chapter 11, Section 1 (Adapted Version also available.)

Extend L3

To help students expand their understanding of new technology, have them complete the History Interactive online activity on James Watt's Steam Engine.

Extend ⦾nline
For: History Interactive activity
Visit: PHSchool.com
Web Code: myp-4071

Progress Monitoring Online

Students may check their comprehension of this section by completing the Progress Monitoring Online graphic organizer and self-quiz.

Answer

✓**Checkpoint** Through mass production, American factories made identical pieces that could be assembled by unskilled workers; skilled workers were not needed.

Section 1 Check Your Progress

1. (a) Possible answer: It made shipping and importing goods difficult; Americans had to develop their own industries.
   (b) The Northeast was home to merchants with capital to build factories and buy materials.

2. (a) identical pieces that can be assembled by unskilled workers
   (b) Factories could hire unskilled laborers at lower wages.

3. Possible answer: Inventiveness changed the way that people worked and lived.

4. Possible formal definitions include: factory system—a system that brings workers and machinery together in one place; capitalist—person who invests capital, or money, in a business to earn a profit; interchangeable parts—identical pieces that can be assembled quickly by unskilled workers. Possible informal definitions include: factory system—people working together with

machines; capitalist—person who invests money; interchangeable parts—pieces of a thing that are exactly the same

5. Francis Lowell caused libraries for factory workers. Arkwright's textile plant caused factories built in cities. Samuel Slater's emigration caused increased American production of cotton thread. Eli Whitney's system of interchangeable parts caused efficiency in mass production.

Mill Workers

Build Background Knowledge **L2**

Reading a memoir helps students identify with individuals from the past. Review with students what they know about factory life in America. Ask: **How do you think a woman working in a mill would feel about her job?** Use the Idea Wave strategy to elicit responses (TE, p. T24).

Reading Skill

Remind students that the time and place are important parts of the setting. As students read, ask them to look for details about the setting and how it affects Lucy's mood and tone.

Vocabulary *Builder*
Teach Key Terms **L2**

Pronounce each word in the Vocabulary *Builder* list, and have students repeat the word. Ask a student to read the definitions. Have students give a sentence for each term.

Instruction **L2**

- Using the Reciprocal Questioning reading strategy (TE, p. T23), read the first three paragraphs of the memoir. Ask students to identify two ways that Lucy interacts with the setting. (*Possible answers: She changes bobbins on the spinning-frames; she explores the carding-room, dressing-room, and weaving-room; she plays among the spinning-frames; she doesn't like the noise of the machines; she is amazed by the waterwheel.*)

- Have students read the remaining paragraphs. Ask: **How does Lucy's view of the mill setting compare in these paragraphs to the previous paragraphs?** (*Possible answer: Previously, she was enthusiastic about the mill. In the later paragraphs, Lucy still felt that the mill setting was agreeable, but she was less enthusiastic about it. She saw that she could become a drudge by staying there, felt confined, and sometimes yearned to leave.*)

Mill Workers
by Lucy Larcom

Prepare to Read

Introduction

Lucy Larcom was born in Massachusetts in 1824. After her father died when she was 11, Lucy went to work in the Lowell textile mills. Years later, she wrote about her experiences. The following selection is an excerpt from her memoirs.

Reading Skill

Analyze Setting In literature, a character's actions and attitudes often are affected by his or her surroundings. In the memoir below, we learn how the physical conditions in a textile mill affect Lucy Larcom's outlook on work. As you read, pay attention to her descriptions of the mill.

Vocabulary *Builder*

As you read this literature selection, look for the following underlined words:

bobbin (BAHB ihn) *n.* spool for thread or yarn, used in spinning, weaving, or in a sewing machine

board (bord) *n.* meals provided regularly for pay

drudge (druhj) *n.* person who does hard, menial, or tedious work

⭐ **Background**
Women and girls who worked in northern mills were educated. Some mills published collections of workers' essays and poetry.

I went to my first day's work in the mill with a light heart. The novelty of it made it seem easy, and it really was not hard just to change the <u>bobbins</u> on the spinning-frames every three-quarters of an hour or so, with half a dozen other little girls who were doing the same thing. When I came back at night, the family began to pity me for my long, tiresome day's work, but I laughed and said, "Why, it is nothing but fun. It is just like play."

And for a while it was only a new amusement. . . . We were not occupied more than half the time. The intervals were spent frolicking around the spinning-frames, teasing and talking to the older girls, or entertaining ourselves with games and stories in the corner, or exploring, with the overseer's permission, the mysteries of the carding-room, the dressing-room, and the weaving-room.

I never cared much for machinery. The buzzing and hissing of pulleys and rollers and spindles and flyers around me often grew tiresome. I could not see into their complications, or feel interested in them. But in a room below us we were sometimes allowed to peer in through a sort of blind door at the great waterwheel that carried the works of the whole mill. It was so huge that we could only watch a few of its spokes at a time, and part of its dripping rim, moving with a slow, measured strength through the darkness that shut it in. It impressed me with something of the awe which comes to us in thinking of the great Power which keeps the mechanism of the universe in motion. . . .

When I took my next three months at the grammar school, everything there was changed, and I too was changed. . . . It was a great delight to me to study, and at the end of the three months the master told me that I was prepared for the high school.

388 Chapter 11 North and South Take Different Paths

Differentiated Instruction

L1 English Language Learners   **L1** Less Proficient Readers

Understanding Sentences Provide a page protector to place over the text. Have students read the literature selection. Ask students to mark each sentence with a **?** if they don't understand the sentence, a ***** if they understand the sentence, and a **!** (for "wow") if they find the information new or interesting. Review any sentences students have with a question mark. Pair students to compare their "wow" sentences.

Lowell girls weaving in a Massachusetts textile mill in the 1850s

But alas! I could not go. The little money I could earn—one dollar a week, besides the price of my <u>board</u>—was needed in the family, and I must return to the mill. . . .

At this time I had learned to do a spinner's work, and I obtained permission to tend some frames that stood directly in front of the windows, with only them and the wall behind me, extending half the length of the mill. . . .

The last window in the row behind me was filled with flourishing houseplants—fragrant-leaved geraniums, the overseer's pets. . . . T[he] perfume and freshness tempted me there often. . . . On the whole, it was far from being a disagreeable place to stay in. The girls were bright looking and neat, and everything was kept clean and shining. The effect of the whole was rather attractive to strangers. . . .

Still, we did not call ourselves ladies. We did not forget that we were working girls, wearing coarse aprons suitable to our work, and that there was some danger to our becoming <u>drudges</u>. I know that sometimes the confinement of the mill became very wearisome to me. In the sweet June weather I would lean far out of the window, and try not to hear the unceasing clash of the sound inside. Looking away to the hills, my whole stifled being would cry out, "Oh that I had wings!"

From *A New England Girlhood,* by Lucy Larcom. Peter Smith, 1973. First published in 1887 by Macmillan.

☑ **Checkpoint** Why did Larcom return to the mill after finishing three months at grammar school?

Analyze LITERATURE

Lucy Larcom's words describe a mill in New England during the 1800s. Consider the sights and sounds around her, and how working in the mill made her feel. Write a paragraph in which you describe what it is like to work in a mill.

⭐ **Background**

The wages paid for millwork offered new opportunities to many women and girls, but workers lived apart from their families and often felt lonely.

🎯 **Analyze Setting**

Lucy's attitude toward the mill changes somewhat over the course of this excerpt. How does setting contribute to this change?

If you liked this passage from *A New England Girlhood,* you might want to read more first-person accounts in *Ordinary Americans: U.S. History Through the Eyes of Everyday People,* edited by Linda R. Monk. Close Up Foundation. 2003.

Literature **389**

Monitor Progress

Discuss with students how Lucy's life changed when she went to work at the mill. Ask: **If Lucy had not gone to work at the mill, what do you think her life would have been like?** (*Answers will vary but should show an understanding that her life would have been hard.*)

Answers

🎯 **Reading Skill** She began to feel confined indoors and longed to be outside.

☑ **Checkpoint** Her family needed the money she earned at the mill.

Writing Rubrics Share this writing rubric with students.

Score 1 Paragraph does not contain any details and is poorly organized.
Score 2 Paragraph contains few details or impressions.
Score 3 Paragraph presents many details.
Score 4 Paragraph presents a vivid picture of a factory.

History Background

Child Labor In 1836, Massachusetts became the first state to pass a child labor law. The law prohibited children under age 15 from being employed unless they had attended school for at least three months in the last year. The first federal child labor law was passed in 1916, but it was overturned by the Supreme Court. It was not until the Fair Labor Standards Act of 1938 that basic child labor reforms were instituted nationally.

Analyze **LITERATURE** Students should describe the details of the daily life in a mill. When would they report for work? How long was the workday? Did they get breaks? They should also describe the physical layout of the factory and their impressions of the workplace. The more details they can provide in their account, the better.

Review and Preview

Geography affected how colonies developed economically. Students will now analyze the impact of the Industrial Revolution on the North.

Section Focus Question

How did urbanization, technology, and social change affect the North?

Before you begin the lesson for the day, write the Section Focus Question on the board. (*Lesson focus: With the arrival of new waves of immigrants and the growth of industry, northern cities grew, as did the differences between the North and South.*)

Prepare to Read

Build Background Knowledge L2

In this section, students will learn about life in the North in the early 1800s. Ask students to preview the headings in Section 2. Then ask: **What qualities characterized the North in the early 1800s?** (*Possible answers: urban growth and problems, growing industry, new transportation, new immigrants*) Use the Numbered Heads strategy (TE, p. T24) to encourage discussion.

Set a Purpose L2

■ Form students into pairs or groups of four. Distribute the Reading Readiness Guide. Ask students to fill in the first two columns of the chart.

> **All in One Teaching Resources, Unit 4,** Reading Readiness Guide, p. 17

■ Use the Numbered Heads strategy (TE, p. T24) to call on students to share one piece of information they already know and one piece of information they want to know. The students will return to these worksheets later.

▲ New York harbor, 1840

Plenty of Work to Be Had

❝Now I will tell you something about . . . New York. Provisions are very cheap; plenty of work to be had; clothes are dear, but men paid well for their work; house rent is very dear in New York, it is a very healthy place. . . .❞

—English immigrant boy's letter to his mother, 1850

The North Transformed

Objectives

- Explain why American cities grew in the 1800s.
- List the new inventions and advances in agriculture and manufacturing.
- Describe the improvements in transportation during the early 1800s.
- Discuss the wave of immigration to the United States in the 1840s and 1850s.
- Describe the problems African Americans faced in the North.

🄳 Reading Skill

Explain Central Issues From the Past As you read about the events of the past, you'll discover that people struggled with issues, much as they do today. Explain those issues to yourself—try to identify what people's concerns were, how they felt about issues, what the issues were about. This will make issues more real and understandable for you.

Key Terms and People

urbanization	famine
telegraph	nativist
Samuel F.B. Morse	discrimination

Why It Matters From colonial times, the North and South developed as distinct regions. At first these differences were small. But during the Industrial Revolution, the differences between the North and South widened dramatically.

❓ Section Focus Question: How did urbanization, technology, and social change affect the North?

Northern Cities

American cities had long been the centers of commerce and culture. By today's standards, these early cities were small. New York, the largest, had a population of slightly more than 33,000 in 1790. Compared to the major cities of Europe, or even the ancient Aztec capital of Tenochtitlán, New York was hardly more than a town.

Growth of Cities In the 1800s, however, U.S. cities grew larger. The Industrial Revolution spurred urbanization, or the growth of cities due to movement of people from rural areas to cities. As capitalists built more factories, agricultural workers were attracted to the new types of work available in the cities.

As cities along the eastern coast became crowded, newly arrived immigrants headed west. Pittsburgh, Pennsylvania, had about 23,000 people in 1840. Ten years later, the city had more than doubled in population. Farther west, the Kentucky city of Louisville was also growing. German and Irish immigrants increased the city's population to more than 43,000 by 1850, making Louisville larger than Washington, D.C.

390 Chapter 11 North and South Take Different Paths

Differentiated Instruction

L3 Advanced Readers

City Growth Ask students to research the growth of northern cities in the early 1800s. Have students make concept webs showing both the hazards and the attractions that these cities offered. Then have students write a paragraph comparing the hazards and attractions of cities today with those of the 1800s. Ask students to share their ideas with the class.

Urban Problems Growing cities faced many problems. Filthy streets, the absence of good sewage systems, and a lack of clean drinking water encouraged the spread of disease.

> "One finds in the streets [of New York] dead cats and dogs, which make the air very bad; dust and ashes are thrown out into the streets, which are swept perhaps once every [two weeks]."
>
> —Baron Axel Klinckowstrom of Sweden

Citywide fires were another common problem. Most structures were made of wood. Volunteer firefighters were often poorly trained and equipped. Insurance companies paid firefighters for saving an insured building. Racing to fire scenes to earn the insurance money, rival fire companies sometimes ended up fighting one another instead of the fire.

☑**Checkpoint** What problems did cities face in the early 1800s?

The Growth of Northern Industry

New inventions revolutionized communications. The most important was the telegraph, a device that used electrical signals to send messages quickly over long distances.

The Telegraph Samuel F.B. Morse's invention worked by sending electrical signals over a wire. A code devised by Morse used shorter and longer bursts of electricity. In his system, known as the Morse code, each letter of the alphabet is represented by its own mix of short signals ("dots") and long signals ("dashes").

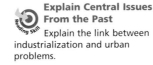 **Explain Central Issues From the Past** Explain the link between industrialization and urban problems.

Growing Cities
American cities became bustling centers of enterprise during the 1800s. This is a view along State Street in Boston. **Critical Thinking: *Explain Problems*** What problems did the rapid growth of cities pose for city dwellers?

391

Teach

Northern Cities
The Growth of Northern Industry
pp. 390–391

Instruction   L2

- **Vocabulary Builder** Before teaching this section, preteach the High-Use Words **reign** and **inferior**, using the strategy on TE p. T21.

  Key Terms Have students continue to fill in the See It–Remember It chart for the Key Terms in this chapter.

- Read Northern Cities and The Growth of Northern Industry with students, using the Structured Silent Reading strategy (TE, p. T22).

- Display the Telegraph transparency, and discuss the impact of faster communication. Ask: **How did businesses communicate with customers and suppliers before the invention of the telegraph?** (*Possible answer: by mail for long distances and by messenger for short distances*)

Color Transparencies, Telegraph

Independent Practice
Have students begin filling in the study guide for this section.

📖 **Interactive Reading and Notetaking Study Guide,** Chapter 11, Section 2 (Adapted Version also available.)

Monitor Progress

As students fill in the study guide, make sure they understand how the Industrial Revolution helped urbanize the North.

Answers

🔁 **Reading Skill** Possible answer: Industrialization required large numbers of workers in cities. This created urban problems, such as crowding, disease, and fire danger.

☑**Checkpoint** They were unclean and had poor drinking water, which spread disease; the air was poor; fires were common, and firefighters were often ill-equipped.

Explain Problems People lived crowded together, leading to poor sanitation and fire hazards.

Vocabulary Builder

Use the information below to teach students this section's high-use words.

High-Use Word	Definition and Sample Sentence
reign, p. 393	*n.* period of dominance or rule The American Revolution took place during the **reign** of King George III.
inferior, p. 395	*adj.* less worth; less valuable; of lower rank Old factories are **inferior** to newer, more modern ones.

A Transportation Revolution

p. 392

Instruction L2

- Have students read A Transportation Revolution. Remind students to look for the sequence of events.

- Ask students to name forms of transportation that helped American industry grow in the 1800s. (*steamboats, clipper ships, railroads*)

- Ask: **How do you think these new forms of transportation affected industry in the North?** (*Possible answer: They made it easier and faster both to obtain raw materials and to get goods to markets.*)

Independent Practice

Have students continue filling in the study guide for this section.

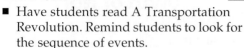 **Interactive Reading and Notetaking Study Guide,** Chapter 11, Section 2 (Adapted Version also available.)

Monitor Progress

As students fill in the study guide, circulate and make sure individuals understand how improvements in transportation helped industry grow. Provide assistance as needed.

Answers

Biography Quest He overheard a conversation about a new discovery: the electromagnet.

☑**Checkpoint** the telegraph, mechanical reaper, improvements in threshers, the combine, and sewing machine

---

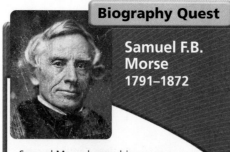

Biography Quest

Samuel F.B. Morse
1791–1872

Samuel Morse began his career as a painter. By 1835, however, he was working on the invention that would make him famous. For years, he struggled to find funding. In 1843, he convinced Congress to back his efforts.

The following year, he arranged to link the nation's capital and the city of Baltimore with telegraph lines. The historic first message was sent from the Capitol building in Washington, D.C.

Biography Quest Online

What chance event led Morse to attempt to develop the telegraph?

For: The answer to the question about Morse
Visit: PHSchool.com
Web Code: myd-4072

In 1844, Morse tested his system. He wired a message from Washington, D.C., to his assistant in Baltimore: "What hath God wrought?" A few minutes later, a response came back from Baltimore.

The telegraph soon became part of American life. Thousands of miles of wires were strung across the nation. Factories in the East could communicate with their markets in the West in a matter of hours rather than weeks.

Advances in Agriculture The mechanical reaper, invented by Cyrus McCormick, made it easier for farmers to settle the prairies of the Midwest. The reaper cut stalks of wheat many times faster than a human worker could. This enabled farmers to cultivate more land and harvest their crops with fewer workers.

Improvements in threshers also speeded up the harvesting of grain. Threshers separate the grains of wheat from their stalks. The wheat grains are then ground into flour. Eventually, the mechanical reaper and the thresher were put together into one machine called a combine.

These advances in agriculture also affected industry. Farm laborers who had been replaced by machines went to cities to work in shops and factories. Cities like Cincinnati grew as both agricultural and industrial centers.

Advances in Manufacturing Other inventions revolutionized the way goods were made. In 1846, Elias Howe patented a machine that could sew seams in fabric. A few years later, Isaac Singer improved on Howe's design. The sewing machine made it much more efficient to produce clothing in quantity. As clothes became less expensive, people of modest means began to dress almost as well as wealthier Americans.

By 1860, factories in New England and the Middle Atlantic states were producing most of the nation's manufactured goods. That year, Americans had over $1 billion invested in businesses. Of that total, more than 90 percent was invested in businesses in the North.

☑**Checkpoint** What new inventions helped northern industry to grow?

A Transportation Revolution

Improvements in transportation spurred the growth of American industry. As transportation became faster and easier, factories could make use of raw materials from farther away. Improved transportation also allowed factory owners to ship their goods to distant markets.

Differentiated Instruction

L1 Less Proficient Readers **L1** Special Needs

Comprehension Reinforcement Have students read the text of The Growth of Northern Industry as they listen to the Student Edition on Audio CD. Pause the CD after each subsection, and ask students if they have any questions. If needed, provide students with a copy of the CD to work independently at home or in the School Resource Center.

🔊 **SE on Audio CD,** Chapter 11, Section 2

Steamboats and Clipper Ships In 1807, Robert Fulton, an American inventor, used a steam engine to power a boat. Fulton's *Clermont* was the first practical steamboat. It was 133 feet long and had wooden side paddles that pulled it through the water.

Although side-paddle steamboats were ideal for traveling on rivers, they were not suited to ocean travel. In 1850, a new type of American-built ship appeared, the clipper ship. Long and slender, with tall masts, the clipper ships were magnificent, swift vessels. The Yankee clippers, as they were called, were the world's fastest ships. Their reign was brief, however. By the 1850s, Great Britain was producing oceangoing steamships. These ironclad steamships were faster and could carry more cargo.

Vocabulary Builder
reign (rayn) *n.* period of dominance or rule

Railroads Of all forms of transportation, railroads did the most to tie together raw materials, manufacturers, and markets. Steamboats had to follow the paths of rivers, which sometimes froze in winter. Railroads, however, could be built almost anywhere.

America's first railroad, the Baltimore and Ohio, was begun in 1828. As with most European railroads, its cars were drawn along the track by horses. Then, in 1830, Peter Cooper built the first American-made steam locomotive. By 1840, about 3,000 miles of railway track had been built in the United States.

☑ **Checkpoint** Why were railroads a better means of transportation than steamboats?

A New Wave of Immigrants

The American population grew rapidly in the 1840s. Millions of immigrants entered the United States, mostly from western Europe. Some came because they had heard of opportunities to buy cheap land. Others believed their skills would serve them well in the United States. Still others had little choice, because they could not survive at home.

Fulton's Steamboat
Robert Fulton's steamboat, the *Clermont*, carried passengers between New York and Albany on the Hudson River. **Critical Thinking:** *Interpret Pictures Why would the* Clermont *not be suitable for ocean travel?*

Section 2 The North Transformed 393

History Background

McCormick's Competition Cyrus McCormick, whose invention of the reaper made cultivation of the prairie possible, faced competition in manufacturing his machinery. One competitor of McCormick was represented by a young lawyer named Abraham Lincoln. In a patent dispute against McCormick, Lincoln's client won, and Lincoln earned $1,000. This money later helped him underwrite his famous debates with Stephen Douglas.

A New Wave of Immigrants
p. 393

Instruction
L2

- Have students read A New Wave of Immigrants. Remind them to look for causes and effects.

- Discuss the waves of immigrants to the United States in the 1840s. Ask: **From where did most immigrants come?** (*western Europe*) Ask: **Why did large numbers of immigrants come from Ireland and Germany?** (*They were escaping the potato famine in Ireland; many Germans had taken part in failed revolutions against harsh rulers and needed to escape punishment.*)

- Ask: **How might newcomers from different cultural backgrounds affect a region?** (*Possible answers: People would bring new languages, skills, ideas, foods, and customs to existing communities.*)

- Discuss the response of the nativists to the new immigrants. (*Nativists wanted the United States to be preserved for white, American-born Protestants.*)

Independent Practice
Have students continue filling in the study guide for this section.

📖 **Interactive Reading and Notetaking Study Guide,** Chapter 11, Section 2 (Adapted Version also available.)

Monitor Progress

As students fill in the study guide, circulate to make sure individuals understand how immigration affected the United States in the mid-1800s. Provide assistance as needed.

Answers

☑ **Checkpoint** Unlike steamboats, railroads could be built almost anywhere and travel in any season.

Interpret Pictures It was too narrow and low and had paddle wheels. Ocean waves and currents would be too strong and make the boat uncontrollable.

Chapter 11 Section 2 393

African Americans in the North

p. 395

Instruction

- Have students read African Americans in the North. Remind students to look for details to answer the reading Checkpoint question.

- Ask: **Did the abolition of slavery in the North erase all problems for free African Americans? Why or why not?** (*Possible answer: No, they still faced discrimination.*)

- Ask: **How did African Americans respond to discrimination?** (*They started their own churches and publications.*)

Independent Practice

Have students complete the study guide for this section.

 Interactive Reading and Notetaking Study Guide, Chapter 11, Section 2 (Adapted Version also available.)

Monitor Progress

- As students fill in the study guide, circulate to make sure individuals understand that African Americans faced discrimination in the North. Provide assistance as needed.

- Tell students to fill in the last column of the Reading Readiness Guide. Ask them to evaluate if what they learned was what they had expected to learn.

All in One Teaching Resources, Unit 4, Reading Readiness Guide, p. 17

Answers

Draw Inferences Possible answers: Many Irish thought next year would be better; they were overwhelmed and did not want to leave their homes and family and friends.

✓Checkpoint The Irish were fleeing from a famine, and the Germans were fleeing from failed revolutions.

Irish Immigration, 1845–1853

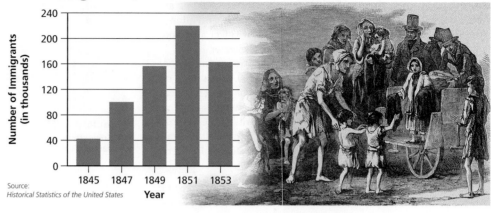

Source: *Historical Statistics of the United States*

Fleeing the Famine
A famine in the 1840s drove many Irish to the United States. They contributed to a sharp rise in immigration. **Critical Thinking: Draw Inferences** *Why do you suppose the peak did not come immediately after the famine started in 1845?*

The Great Hunger Ireland had long been under British rule. While the best farmland was owned by British landlords, the potato was the staple, or basic, food for most of the population. Then, in 1845, a fungus destroyed the potato crop, leading to famine, or widespread starvation. The years that followed are often called the Great Hunger. More than a million people starved to death. About a million more left Ireland.

Most of the Irish immigrants who came to the United States during this period had been farm laborers at home. The men found work doing the lowliest jobs in construction or laying railroad track in the East and Midwest. Young Irish women were often employed as household workers.

German Newcomers Germans came to America during this period as well. Many had taken part in revolutions against harsh rulers. When the revolutions failed, the Germans fled to the United States.

Unlike the Irish, German immigrants came from many different levels of society. After arriving in the United States, most Germans moved west. Many settled in the Ohio Valley and the Great Lakes region.

Reaction Against Immigrants Some Americans worried about the growing foreign population. These were nativists, or people who wanted to preserve the country for white, American-born Protestants. Nativists especially opposed Irish immigration because most of the Irish were Roman Catholics.

One group of nativists in New York formed a secret group. When asked about their secret order, members replied, "I know nothing." In time, the Know-Nothings became a political party. In 1856, the Know-Nothing candidate for President won 21 percent of the vote. Soon after, the party split over the issue of slavery and dissolved.

✓Checkpoint Why did Irish and German immigration to the United States increase in the 1840s?

Differentiated Instruction

L1 English Language Learners

Word Definitions Have students make a list of the Key Terms and High-Use Words for this chapter. Then have them create flashcards with the word on one side and its definition on the other. Pair students with a partner, and have them quiz each other on the definitions of the words using the flashcards.

African Americans in the North

Even more than immigrants, African Americans in the North faced discrimination. Discrimination is the denial of equal rights or equal treatment to certain groups of people.

Slavery had largely ended in the North by the early 1800s. Free African Americans there were joined by new arrivals from the South. Freedom, however, did not grant equal treatment. African Americans were often denied the right to vote. They were not allowed to work in factories or in skilled trades. Even when they sought the least desirable jobs, they were at a disadvantage. Many employers preferred to hire white immigrants rather than African Americans.

Prejudice against African Americans led to the racial segregation of schools and public facilities. Turned away by white congregations, African Americans formed their own churches. For example, people who had been freed from slavery started the African Methodist Episcopal Church in Philadelphia in 1816.

White newspapers often portrayed African Americans as inferior. African Americans responded by starting their own publications. The first newspaper owned and run by African Americans was *Freedom's Journal,* which was established in 1827 in New York. Its editor, John B. Russwurm, had been one of the first African Americans to graduate from an American college.

Vocabulary Builder
inferior (ihn FIR ee uhr) *adj.* less worthy; less valuable; of lower rank

☑**Checkpoint** What obstacles did African Americans face in the North?

⭐ **Looking Back and Ahead** Northern cities grew with the arrival of immigrants from abroad and African Americans from rural areas. Meanwhile, as you will read in the next section, the South depended more and more on cotton and slavery.

Section 2 | Check Your Progress

Progress Monitoring Online
For: Self-test with instant help
Visit: PHSchool.com
Web Code: mya-4072

Comprehension and Critical Thinking
1. **(a) Recall** What factors led to the growth of cities?
(b) Evaluate Information How did the rapid growth of cities affect urban living conditions?
2. **(a) Recall** How did the telegraph improve communication?
(b) Identify Economic Benefits How might improved communication help the growing economy?

Reading Skill
3. **Explain Central Issues From the Past** Reread the text following the heading "Advances in Agriculture." Explain how changes in agriculture affected workers in the nineteenth century.

Key Terms
Read each sentence below. If the sentence is true, write YES. If the sentence is not true, write NO and explain why.
4. Urbanization is the movement of people from urban areas to farms.

5. More than a million people died in a famine during "the Great Hunger" that started in Ireland in 1845.
6. Even though many African Americans living in the North were legally free, they still suffered from discrimination.

Writing
7. Based on what you have read in this section, list as many causes as you can for the growth of industry in the North. Put stars next to the causes that you think are most important.

Section 2 Check Your Progress

1. **(a)** new inventions that aided the growth of industry; more immigration
(b) It caused overcrowding, uncleanliness, and the risk of fire in cities.

2. **(a)** It let people communicate across long distances quickly.
(b) Since factories in the East could communicate with their markets in the West quickly, this could help the economy to grow because orders could be taken and filled more quickly.

3. **Possible answer:** Many new machines were invented to speed up agricultural work. They replaced many farm workers, who went to cities to work in factories and shops.

4. No, it is the movement of people from rural areas to cities.

5. Yes

6. Yes

7. List should demonstrate an understanding of the growth of industry in the North. Possible causes: urbanization, advances in technology and transportation, influx of immigrants and African Americans into the cities.

Answer

☑**Checkpoint** They faced discrimination in terms of the right to vote, getting jobs, and segregation in schools and other public places.

Assess and Reteach

Assess Progress L2

Have students complete Check Your Progress. Administer the Section Quiz.

All in One **Teaching Resources, Unit 4,** Section Quiz, p. 28

To further assess student understanding, use the Progress Monitoring Transparency.

Progress Monitoring Transparencies, Chapter 11, Section 2

Reteach L1

If students need more instruction, have them read this section in the Interactive Reading and Notetaking Study Guide.

Interactive Reading and Notetaking Study Guide, Chapter 11, Section 2 (Adapted Version also available.)

Extend L3

Have students do an Internet search on African American abolitionists in the North. Possible leaders they might research are James Forten, Robert Purvis, Charles Remond, Sarah Parker Remond, Frederick Douglass, and Sojourner Truth.

Extend Online
For: Help starting the Extend activity
Visit: PHSchool.com
Web Code: mye-0259

Progress Monitoring Online

Students may check their comprehension of this section by completing the Progress Monitoring Online graphic organizer and self-quiz.

Review and Preview

The Industrial Revolution led the North to develop factories and cities. Students will now learn how the South became more dependent on cotton and slavery.

Section Focus Question

How did cotton affect the social and economic life of the South?

Before you begin the lesson for the day, write the Section Focus Question on the board. (*Lesson focus: The invention of the cotton gin made growing cotton more profitable, resulting in a need for more workers and increasing the South's dependence on slavery.*)

Prepare to Read

Build Background Knowledge   L2

In this section, students will read about the development of an agrarian economy in the South. Remind students that they read in Section 2 about new technology and industrial developments in the North. Ask: **How do you think these developments will affect the rest of the country?** (*Answers will vary but may refer to more effective transportation and communication, as well as the increased availability of goods.*) Use the Give One, Get One strategy (TE, p. T25) to encourage discussion.

Set a Purpose   L2

- Read each statement in the Reading Readiness Guide aloud. Ask students to mark the statements True or False.

    All in One **Teaching Resources, Unit 4,** Reading Readiness Guide, p. 18

- Have students discuss the statements in pairs or groups of four, then mark their worksheets again. Use the Numbered Heads strategy (TE, p. T24) to call on students to share their group's perspectives. The students will return to these worksheets later.

The Slaves' Quarters

❝As to beds to sleep on, they were known to none of the field hands; nothing but a coarse blanket . . . was given them, and this only to the men and women. The children stuck themselves in holes and corners, about the quarters; often in the corner of the huge chimneys, with their feet in the ashes to keep them warm.❞

—Frederick Douglass, *My Bondage and My Freedom*, describing his early life as a slave

▲ The plantation owner's house was very different from the slaves' quarters.

The Plantation South

Objectives

- Explain the significance of cotton and the cotton gin to the South.
- Describe what life was like for free and enslaved African Americans in the South.

Reading Skill

Explain Problems From the Past Why did problems occur in the past? Try to answer this question as you read. It will help you connect events and understand people's beliefs and actions. Put yourself in the shoes of the people about whom you read. What problems would you have with these same issues? Explain these problems to clarify them.

Key Terms and People

cotton gin
slave code

spiritual
Nat Turner

Why It Matters The Industrial Revolution brought change to both the North and South. In the North, industry, immigration, and cities all grew. But in the South, the economy became more dependent on cotton and slave labor.

❷ **Section Focus Question: How did cotton affect the social and economic life of the South?**

The Cotton Kingdom

As the North became more urban and industrialized, the South remained largely rural. Two events changed life in the South. First, a boom in textiles caused by the Industrial Revolution created a huge demand for cotton. Second, a new invention allowed the South to satisfy that demand.

The Cotton Gin In 1793, Eli Whitney devised a simple machine that speeded the processing of cotton. His cotton gin used a spiked cylinder to remove seeds from cotton fibers.

Before the introduction of the cotton gin, the seeds had to be picked out of the cotton fibers by hand. This was a slow process. Working by hand, a laborer could clean only a pound of cotton a day.

The cotton gin was revolutionary technology. A worker could process fifty times more cotton fiber with the gin than by hand. Cotton growing became far more profitable.

Slave Labor To grow more cotton, planters used more slave labor. In 1790, there were about 698,000 enslaved African Americans in the United States. By 1860, the census recorded nearly 4 million. During that time, the price of a slave increased ten or twenty times.

396 Chapter 11 North and South Take Different Paths

Differentiated Instruction

L1 **English Language Learners**

Word Meanings English language learners may have difficulty understanding the term *cotton kingdom*. Looking up *kingdom* in the dictionary will tell students that it is "a government, country, state, or popula-

tion ruled by a king or queen." Explain that in the term *cotton kingdom*, the South is the kingdom and cotton is the king. Ask students to explain why cotton "ruled" the South.

Cotton became the greatest source of wealth for the United States. It enriched planters in the South, as well as bankers and shipowners in the North. Cotton production rose at an astonishing rate. Planters grew one and a half millon pounds of cotton in 1790. In 1820, they grew ten times as much.

Southern states were not all alike. States like Alabama and Mississippi, which depended on cotton, had large populations of enslaved people. Other states, such as Kentucky, <u>devoted</u> less attention to cotton. Fewer enslaved people lived there.

In the southern "Cotton Kingdom," society was dominated by owners of large plantations. This small but wealthy class lived in luxury and sent their children to the finest schools. But more than half of all southern farmers did not have slaves. They grew corn and raised hogs and chickens.

Defending Slavery Most southern whites accepted the system of slavery. Many feared that any weakening of controls over African Americans might encourage violent uprisings. By the 1830s, some people in the North were urging that slavery be banned. (You will read about the movement to end slavery in the next chapter.) In response, southern whites hardened their support for slavery.

Supporters of slavery said it was more humane than the free labor system of the North. Unlike northern factory workers, they argued, enslaved African Americans did not worry about unemployment.

Vocabulary Builder
devote (dee VOHT) **v.** to commit; to apply (time and energy, for example)

Explain Problems From the Past Explain the disagreements between supporters and critics of slavery.

Cotton Production and Slavery

Cotton Production

Bales of Cotton (in millions) vs. Year (1800–1860)

Source: *Historical Statistics of the United States*

Growth of Slavery

Number of Slaves (in millions) vs. Year (1800–1860)

Source: *Historical Statistics of the United States*

Reading Charts
Skills Activity

The rise in cotton production in the South was paralleled by a rise in the number of enslaved African Americans.

(a) **Read Graphs** How much did cotton production increase between 1800 and 1850? In what 10-year period did slavery grow the fastest?

(b) **Make Predictions** If cotton production had decreased, would the number of slaves have declined? Explain your reasoning.

Vocabulary Builder

Use the information below to teach students this section's high-use words.

High-Use Word	Definition and Sample Sentence
devote, p. 397	*v.* to commit; to apply (time and energy, for example) To become a judge, one must **devote** many years to the study of law.
revolt, p. 400	*n.* uprising; rebellion Slaveholders feared times when enslaved African Americans would rise up in **revolt** and fight for freedom.

Teach

The Cotton Kingdom
p. 396

Instruction

- **Vocabulary Builder** Before teaching this section, preteach the High-Use Words **devote** and **revolt**, using the strategy on TE p. T21.

  Key Terms Have students continue to fill in the See It–Remember It chart for the Key Terms in this chapter.

- Read The Cotton Kingdom with students, using the Paragraph Shrinking strategy (TE, p. T23). Remind students to look for support of the main idea.

- Tell students that southerners grew tobacco, rice, sugar cane, and cotton. Ask: **Why was there an increased demand for cotton?** (*The Industrial Revolution led to a growth in textiles, which in turn demanded more cotton.*) **How did the cotton gin make growing cotton more profitable?** (*Workers could process fifty times more cotton with the gin than by hand.*)

- Discuss the impact of the cotton boom. (*increased wealth for planters, bankers, shipowners; plantation owners dominated southern society; spread of slavery*)

- Point out that the graphs show the parallel growth of cotton production and slave labor. Discuss the use of slave labor on cotton plantations. Ask: **Why did cotton production and the number of slaves in the United States both increase at the same time?** (*Having more slaves allowed southern plantation owners to produce more cotton.*)

Answers

Reading Skill Supporters of slavery claimed that it was humane and that slaves did not have to worry about unemployment. Critics of slavery pointed out that slaves did not have the basic right to leave their work if conditions became too harsh, that slaves were often mistreated, and that all people should be free.

Reading Charts (a) by about two million bales; 1840–1850 **(b)** Possible answer: Yes, because fewer workers would be needed.

Instruction (continued)

- Students may have the misconception that most white southerners lived on large plantations and owned many slaves. Ask: **Why did most southern white people support slavery even though many of them did not own slaves?** (*Possible answers: Many feared slave uprisings and violence, felt superior to enslaved people, resented the interference of the North, or believed that enslaved workers were better off than northern factory workers.*)

Independent Practice

Have students continue filling in the study guide for this section.

Interactive Reading and Notetaking Study Guide, Chapter 11, Section 3 (Adapted Version also available.)

Monitor Progress

As students fill in the study guide, circulate to make sure that individuals understand the importance of cotton in the southern economy. Provide assistance as needed.

Explore More Video

Discovery School Video

Have students view Plantation Life to help with their understanding of slavery in the United States. The video points out the harsh lives that enslaved people lived and the ways they tried to maintain their spirits. It also examines how enslaved African Americans tried to resist and rebel against slavery.

Answers

☑Checkpoint Fewer than half of white southerners owned slaves.

Compare and Contrast Possible answer: The pictures show that owners were free to enjoy the comforts of life. Slaves, on the other hand, were not free, and they spent their days doing backbreaking labor.

Critics of slavery, however, challenged this reasoning. They argued that northern workers were free to quit a job and take another if conditions became too harsh. Also, the critics said, people held in slavery often suffered physical or other abuse from white owners. There was no satisfactory substitute for freedom.

☑Checkpoint **How widespread was slave ownership?**

African Americans in the South

Not all of the 4 million African Americans in the South were enslaved. About 253,000 (or 6 percent) were free. Many had purchased their freedom. A few did well, especially in cities like New Orleans. But most did not share in the prosperity around them.

Restrictions on Free African Americans Laws denied basic rights even to African Americans who were free. By law, they were excluded from all but the most menial jobs. Their children were denied the right to attend public schools. African Americans could not vote, serve on juries, or testify against white defendants in court.

Free African Americans were discouraged from traveling. In a petition, some described the conditions they faced:

Explore More Video
To learn more about southern plantations, view the video.

❝[When] we have occasion to . . . Travel . . . [b]y Steem boat or Stage, we have been exceedingly anoyd And put to very considerable inconvenience and eaven compeled to Leave the boat and thereby entirely defeated from accomplishing our just and lawful business because we have not [had] a certificate from some White person.❞

—Petition to Delaware legislature, 1850s

⬤ **INFOGRAPHIC**

Plantation Life
Life on a southern plantation showed vast contrasts. The families of large plantation owners enjoyed many luxuries. Families bound to slavery experienced hard work and many cruelties.
Critical Thinking: *Compare and Contrast How do these pictures support the view that plantation owners and enslaved African Americans lived very different lives?*

Keeping Cool
Refreshing breezes from fans like this kept wealthy women cool. ▼

▼ **A Family on the Patio**
A wealthy southern family relaxes on their patio as they survey their estate.

398

Differentiated Instruction

L3 Advanced Readers

L3 Gifted and Talented

Oral History Tell students that one major source of information about the life of enslaved African Americans is a series of interviews conducted in the late 1800s. Tell students that at this time, people interviewed former slaves to record their recollections of life under slavery. In pairs, have students research some of these accounts. Then have them role-play, with one person as the interviewer and the other as the subject interviewed. Have them write a script and present a brief interview for the class.

The freedom of African Americans in the South was never secure. Slave catchers prowled the streets looking for escapees. They often kidnapped free African Americans and sold them into slavery.

In spite of all the restrictions placed upon them, many free African Americans made valuable contributions to southern life. Norbert Rillieux revolutionized the sugar industry. His method of refining sugar made the process faster, safer, and less costly. Another African American inventor, Henry Blair, developed a seed-planting device that reduced the time a farmer spent sowing a crop.

Life Under Slavery For all the problems faced by free African Americans, those who were enslaved faced much greater trials. They had no rights at all. Laws known as **slave codes** controlled every aspect of their lives. As a Kentucky court ruled in 1828, "... a slave by our code is not treated as a person but as a ... thing...."

Many enslaved African Americans became skilled workers. Their skills kept the plantations operating efficiently. Others worked in the owners' homes as housekeepers, butlers, or nannies and became trusted house servants.

The vast majority did heavy farm labor. Most slaveholders stopped short of working a laborer to death. Some came close, however. On the large plantations, white overseers administered punishment—often a whipping—for many offenses.

Enslaved African Americans had only one real protection against mistreatment: Owners looked on them as valuable property that they needed to keep healthy and productive.

Families of enslaved African Americans were often broken apart when slave owners sold one or more of their family members. Many children had only the slightest memory of their parents.

▼ **A Family in the Fields**
Children worked in the fields with their enslaved parents. This Georgia family was picking cotton.

▲ **Farming Tools**
Slaves used tools like the hedge clippers and pitchfork shown above.

◀ **Bonds of Slavery**
Shackles such as these were used to restrain slaves who tried to escape or who otherwise displeased a master.

399

History Background

Nat Turner Nat Turner, leader of the 1831 slave revolt in Virginia, saw himself acting as a divine agent to free his people. He believed that an eclipse of the sun was a sign that the time for his revolt had arrived. In response to his revolt, slave laws became more severe in the South. More than 50 whites were killed before Turner and his followers were stopped. News of the revolt spread, encouraging more slave rebellions. In South Carolina, two slaves were executed for plotting a revolt. In response, most southern states enacted tougher laws regarding emancipation, freedom of movement, and all aspects of slave behavior.

African Americans in the South

p. 398

Instruction

- Have students read African Americans in the South. Remind students to look for causes and effects.

- Ask: **What was one way for an enslaved person to gain freedom?** (*purchase it*)

- Ask students who have completed the History Reading Skill Worksheet to share what they learned about spirituals and the central issues those spirituals addressed.

- Discuss with students the life of free and enslaved African Americans in the South. Ask: **Why do you think slave codes make it illegal to teach enslaved workers?** (*Owners felt they had more control if slaves were illiterate.*)

- Ask: **Why do you think there were so many restrictions on free blacks in the South?** (*Possible answer: White southerners did not want free African Americans to have equal rights because white people wanted to stay in power.*)

- Ask: **How did life for free blacks in the South compare with life for free blacks in the North?** (*Possible answer: Some free blacks in the North could vote, and some went to school. No free blacks in the South could vote or go to school. But free blacks in the North, like free blacks in the South, faced discrimination in employment.*)

Independent Practice

Have students complete the study guide for this section.

Interactive Reading and Notetaking Study Guide, Chapter 11, Section 3 (Adapted Version also available.)

Monitor Progress

- As students fill in the study guide, circulate and make sure individuals understand the challenges that enslaved and free African Americans faced in the South. Provide assistance as needed.

- Tell students to fill in the last column of the Reading Readiness Guide. Probe for what they learned that confirms or invalidates each statement.

All in One Teaching Resources, Unit 4, Reading Readiness Guide, p. 18

Assess and Reteach

Assess Progress `L2`

Have students complete Check Your Progress. Administer the Section Quiz.

All in One **Teaching Resources, Unit 4,** Section Quiz, p. 29

To further assess student understanding, use the Progress Monitoring Transparency.

Progress Monitoring Transparencies, Chapter 11, Section 3

Reteach `L1`

If students need more instruction, have them read this section in the Interactive Reading and Notetaking Study Guide.

Interactive Reading and Notetaking Study Guide, Chapter 11, Section 3 (Adapted Version also available.)

Extend `L3`

Fanny Kemble was an English actress and abolitionist married to an American who later inherited a plantation and hundreds of slaves. To better understand plantation life from the perspective of an "outsider," have students research and summarize Fanny Kemble's *Journal of a Residence on a Georgian Plantation.*

Progress Monitoring Online

Students may check their comprehension of this section by completing the Progress Monitoring Online graphic organizer and self-quiz.

Answer

☑**Checkpoint** Many adapted to slavery by finding support in the Bible, African customs, and music. Some worked slowly or badly on purpose, some turned to violence, and some escaped.

1. (a) Possible answer: Northern mills needed cotton; southern plantations supplied this cotton; the cotton gin
(b) Northern textile factories need cotton; Whitney invents cotton gin; need for slaves increases; population of cotton-

---

Nat Turner captured

Vocabulary Builder
revolt (ree VOHLT) **n.** uprising; rebellion

After 1808, it was illegal to import enslaved Africans to the United States. As a result, African Americans had little direct contact with Africa. Nevertheless, African customs, music, and dance survived in their daily lives from one generation to another.

Many African Americans found a message of hope in the Bible. African Americans composed spirituals, religious folk songs that blended biblical themes with the realities of slavery.

Resistance to Slavery Many African Americans did what they could to resist the slaveholders. Some worked slowly or pretended not to understand what they were told to do. Others deliberately broke farm equipment. The most daring fled north to freedom.

Sometimes, resistance became rebellion. Nat Turner led the most famous slave <u>revolt</u> in 1831. Turner said he had a vision that told him to kill whites. He and others killed about 60 whites. In reprisal, many innocent African Americans were executed.

☑**Checkpoint** How did enslaved African Americans adapt to slavery and resist it?

⭐ **Looking Back and Ahead** The more cotton they grew, the more southern planters depended on the labor of enslaved African Americans. At the same time, African Americans in the South struggled to endure or resist slavery. In the next section, you will read how the settling of western areas caused new tensions between North and South.

Section 3 | **Check Your Progress**

Progress Monitoring Online
For: Self-test with instant help
Visit: PHSchool.com
Web Code: mya-4073

Comprehension and Critical Thinking

1. (a) Summarize How were northern textile mills and southern cotton plantations linked? What key invention deepened this connection?
(b) Understand Sequence Place the following events in the order in which they happened: population of cotton-producing states triples; Whitney invents the cotton gin; Nat Turner leads slave revolt; the need for slaves increases; northern textile factories have need for cotton; support for slavery hardens among southern whites.

2. (a) Describe What might a typical workday be like for an enslaved African American on a southern cotton plantation?
(b) Draw Conclusions Why do you think enslaved people rebelled, even though the risk was so great and the likelihood of success so small?

Reading Skill
3. Explain Problems From the Past Connect the problems facing southern planters and southern African Americans.

Key Terms
Answer the following questions in complete sentences that show your understanding of the key terms.

4. How does the cotton gin work?
5. How did slave codes control every aspect of the lives of enslaved African Americans?
6. What would be a common theme of an African American spiritual?

Writing
7. Based on what you have read in this section, list as many effects as you can that resulted from the invention of the cotton gin by Eli Whitney. List the effects in the order in which they happened. If one effect led to another effect, draw an arrow between those two developments.

---

producing states triples; support for slavery hardens among southern whites; Nat Turner's slave revolt.

2. (a) Possible answer: up before dawn, work in fields until dark, work after dark
(b) Possible answer: They may have felt that freedom was worth any risk.

3. Possible answer: Southern planters needed cotton to survive and large labor forces to grow it. Slaves provided that

labor force but suffered terrible conditions and inhumane treatment.

4. The cotton gin uses a cylinder with spikes to remove seeds from cotton fibers.

5. Slave codes were laws that controlled what enslaved people could and could not do.

6. the Bible and the realities of slavery

7. Answers will vary but should be in sequence.

The Wagons Were So Numerous

❝ The wagons were so numerous that the leaders of one team had their noses in the trough at the end of the next wagon ahead. . . . Besides the coaches and wagons, there were gentlemen travelling singly in the saddle, with all their luggage stuffed into their saddlebags. There were enormous droves of sheep and herds of cattle, which raised the dust like a cloud along their path. ❞

—A traveler's recollection of traffic on the National Road, early 1800s

▲ Settlers heading West.

The Challenges of Growth

Objectives

- Identify the problems Americans moving westward faced.
- Describe the impact of the building of the Erie Canal.
- Discuss the debate over slavery and the Missouri Compromise.

🔍 Reading Skill

Place Events in a Matrix of Time and Place Each event in history takes place in the context of a specific time and place. As you read this textbook or other history textbooks, try to remember additional events from the same time or place. Then, look for possible connections among the events discussed in the different parts of a chapter or unit.

Key Terms and People

Daniel Boone
turnpike
corduroy road
canal
Henry Clay

Why It Matters Americans kept moving westward. As northerners and southerners migrated and settled in new lands, they brought their differing ways of life with them.

❓ **Section Focus Question: How did Americans move west, and how did this intensify the debate over slavery?**

Moving West

During colonial times, Americans looked on the back-country between the Atlantic Coast and the Appalachian Mountains as the western frontier. By the 1750s, the Scotch-Irish and the Germans of Pennsylvania had begun to settle the backcountry.

The most famous early pioneer was Daniel Boone. In 1775, Boone and a party of 30 men cleared a new route to the West—the Wilderness Road. It crossed the Appalachian Mountains through the Cumberland Gap into Kentucky. The Wilderness Road became the main route across the Appalachians. In time, pioneers created many other routes for westward travel. (See the map on the next page.)

A Growing Population By the early 1800s, the flow of immigrants to the West had become a flood. As western populations grew, many areas applied to become states. From 1792 to 1819, eight states joined the Union: Kentucky (1792), Tennessee (1796), Ohio (1803), Louisiana (1812), Indiana (1816), Mississippi (1817), Illinois (1818), and Alabama (1819).

Section 4 The Challenges of Growth **401**

Section 4
Step-by-Step Instruction

Review and Preview

The South depended heavily on slave labor. Students will now explore how the division over slavery became more evident as Americans settled in the western territories.

Section Focus Question

How did Americans move west, and how did this intensify the debate over slavery?

Before you begin the lesson for the day, write the Section Focus Question on the board. (*Lesson focus: Settlers who arrived in western territories via roads, turnpikes, and canals debated over whether slavery should be allowed in those areas.*)

Prepare to Read

Build Background Knowledge L2

In this section, students will learn how the push westward led to new transportation routes and increased the conflict over slavery between the North and the South. Remind students that they learned about Lewis and Clark's exploration of the West in Chapter 9. Ask students what changes will be necessary for settlers to begin to move to these territories. Use the Think-Write-Pair-Share strategy (TE, p. T25) to encourage participation.

Set a Purpose L2

- Read each statement in the Reading Readiness Guide aloud. Ask students to mark the statements True or False.

  All in One **Teaching Resources, Unit 4,** Reading Readiness Guide, p. 19

- Have students discuss the statements in pairs or groups of four, then mark their worksheets again. Use the Numbered Heads strategy (TE, p. T24) to call on students to share their group's perspectives. The students will return to these worksheets later.

Vocabulary Builder

Use the information below to teach students this section's high-use words.

High-Use Word	Definition and Sample Sentence
pursue, p. 402	*v.* to chase after; to try to capture Latin American leaders vowed to **pursue** liberty in their fight for freedom from European control.
isolated, p. 403	*v.* set apart Lord Cornwallis was trapped on the **isolated** Yorktown peninsula.

Teach

Moving West
Roads and Turnpikes

pp. 401–402

Instruction   L2

- **Vocabulary Builder** Before teaching this section, preteach the High-Use Words **pursue** and **isolated**, using the strategy on TE p. T21.

  Key Terms Have students complete the See It–Remember It chart for the Key Terms in this chapter.

- Read Moving West and Roads and Turnpikes with students, using the Choral Reading strategy (TE, p. T22).

- Ask: **Where was the western frontier in the early 1800s?** (*west of the Appalachian Mountains, for example in Kentucky*)

- Discuss the development of the national road network. Ask: **What is the difference between a turnpike and other roads on which Americans traveled west?** (*Possible answer: A turnpike was a private toll road; people had to pay money to travel on it, unlike many other roads.*)

- To help students understand the connections between the growth of the United States in territory and population, assign the worksheet Population and Territory.

  All in One Teaching Resources, Unit 4, Population and Territory, p. 22

Independent Practice

Have students begin filling in the study guide for this section.

📖 **Interactive Reading and Notetaking Study Guide,** Chapter 11, Section 4 (Adapted Version also available.)

Monitor Progress

As students fill in the study guide, circulate and make sure individuals understand how roads and turnpikes helped the country expand westward.

Answers

MAP MASTER Skills Activity **(a)** Pennsylvania Road, Pennsylvania Canal **(b)** Possible answer: obstacles such as mountains and forests

✓**Checkpoint** on backcountry paths and trails

◔ **Reading Skill** the Louisiana Purchase and the War of 1812

402 Chapter 11

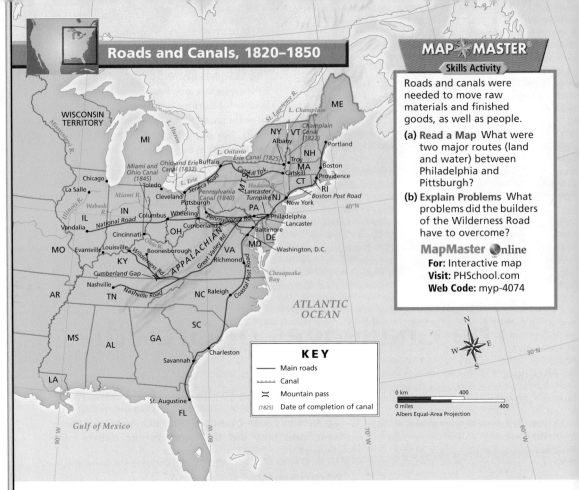

Roads and Canals, 1820–1850

MAP MASTER
Skills Activity

Roads and canals were needed to move raw materials and finished goods, as well as people.

(a) Read a Map What were two major routes (land and water) between Philadelphia and Pittsburgh?

(b) Explain Problems What problems did the builders of the Wilderness Road have to overcome?

MapMaster Online
For: Interactive map
Visit: PHSchool.com
Web Code: myp-4074

KEY
— Main roads
⊢⊢⊢ Canal
⋈ Mountain pass
(1825) Date of completion of canal

0 km 400
0 miles 400
Albers Equal-Area Projection

Vocabulary Builder
pursue (per SYOO) **v.** to chase after; to try to capture

Traveling west was not easy. Many early roads began as paths for deer or bison. Indians used these well-worn paths to pursue game. Then, white settlers began to drive their wagons over these paths. Not surprisingly, the roads were terrible. They were unpaved, dotted with tree stumps, and easily washed out by rain.

✓**Checkpoint** How did American settlers heading west reach their new homes?

◔ **Place Events in a Matrix of Time and Place** Name two important events from the early nineteenth century that contributed to America's growth as a nation. Consider the topics covered in this chapter and in previous chapters.

Roads and Turnpikes

Clearly the nation needed better roads. Farmers and merchants had to have a way to move their goods to market quickly and cheaply. Some capitalists decided to provide that way.

Private companies began to build turnpikes, or toll roads. At certain points, a bar on a hinge swung out across the road. The bar resembled a spear, or pike. Travelers would have to stop and pay a toll in order to pass.

402 Chapter 11 North and South Take Different Paths

Differentiated Instruction

L1 English Language Learners   **L1 Less Proficient Readers**   **L1 Special Needs**

Along the Erie Canal Pair students with more able readers to complete the worksheet Along the Erie Canal. If possible, obtain a recording of the song, and let students listen to it. Tell students that there are many versions of this song. Suggest that they write a verse of their own based on information they have learned about the canal. Have students share their verses with the class.

All in One Teaching Resources, Unit 4, Along the Erie Canal, p. 23

In 1795, a private company in Pennsylvania built a turnpike between Lancaster and Philadelphia. The Lancaster Turnpike was the first long-distance stone road in the United States. The road provided cheap, reliable transportation to <u>isolated</u> agricultural areas.

In marshy areas, wagons traveled on **corduroy roads**, roads made of sawed-off logs, laid side by side. This meant a bumpy ride as wagons bounced over each log. Corduroy roads were a hazard to horses, because they could break their legs if they slipped through the logs.

The National Road was the first federally funded road. Begun in 1811 in Cumberland, Maryland, it stretched to Wheeling, in western Virginia, by 1818 and reached Vandalia, Illinois, in 1850. The road crossed hundreds of miles of varying terrain. Bridges carried it over many rivers and streams.

☑ **Checkpoint** **What was the National Road?**

Canals

Slow road travel isolated western farmers from eastern markets. The fastest, cheapest way to ship goods was by water. However, the major rivers ran north and south. The solution was to build canals from east to west. A **canal** is a channel that is dug across land and filled with water. Canals allow boats to reach more places.

In 1816, New York Governor DeWitt Clinton proposed a canal from the Hudson River to Lake Erie. Critics scoffed at the idea. Still, work began on "Clinton's Ditch" in 1817.

Building the canal was a challenge for canal engineers—and for workers, who were mostly Irish immigrants. The land in upstate New York is not level. Locks had to be built to raise or lower boats in the canal. Locks are chambers just big enough to hold a boat. When a boat enters a lock, gates close at both ends of the chamber. If the boat is to be raised, water flows into the lock. If the boat must be lowered, water drains out.

At Lockport, five double locks raised the canal 50 feet. One canal traveler wrote:

❝As one passes along this deep cavern and sees . . . the rough perpendicular walls pierced in every part with drill-holes used for blasting the rock, he is astonished at the perseverance, labor, and expense which it cost.❞
—from the *Diary of Jonathan Pearson*, 1833

Within two years of its opening in 1825, the canal had paid for itself. Produce from the Midwest came across Lake Erie, passed through the Erie Canal, and was carried down the Hudson River to New York City. Because of its location at the end of the river, New York soon became the richest city in the nation.

Vocabulary Builder
<u>isolated</u> (ī sah lay tehd) **adj.** set apart

Crazy Over Canals
American popular culture celebrated the new canals with songs, stories, and even jokes.

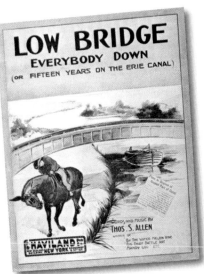

LOW BRIDGE
EVERYBODY DOWN
(OR FIFTEEN YEARS ON THE ERIE CANAL)

WORDS AND MUSIC BY
THOS. S. ALLEN

HAVILAND
NEW YORK

Section 4 The Challenges of Growth **403**

Canals

p. 403

Instruction

- Have students read Canals. Remind students to look for causes and effects.

- Ask: **What canal extended from the Hudson River to Lake Erie?** (*the Erie Canal*)

- Ask students to look at the map that shows roads and canals on p. 402. Ask: **Why were most canals built east to west?** (*Most major rivers flow north and south, and canals allowed people and goods to move west.*)

- Ask: **How did the Erie Canal benefit New York City?** (*Produce from the Midwest could be sent by water all the way to New York, and manufactured goods could be sent to the Midwest, making New York City the richest city in the nation.*)

- Have students learn more about the Erie Canal by assigning the worksheet The Erie Canal. Ask them to complete the questions on the worksheet.

All in One Teaching Resources, Unit 4, The Erie Canal, p. 24

Independent Practice

Have students continue filling in the study guide for this section.

📖 **Interactive Reading and Notetaking Study Guide,** Chapter 11, Section 4 (Adapted Version also available.)

Monitor Progress

As students fill in the study guide, circulate to make sure individuals understand the importance of canals. Provide assistance as needed.

History Background

The Early West and American Culture Many of the "trappings" of American culture are epitomized by the early West. Log cabins, moccasins, fringed leather jackets and pants reflect Native American influence on our earliest pioneers. Folklore and folk songs about "The Erie Canal," "Johnny Appleseed," "Paul Bunyan," "John Henry," and "Davy Crockett" all come from this period of westward expansion.

Americans sought to expand their frontiers by looking beyond their borders, seeking to conquer natural barriers, and express their individualism. American mores developed based on these earliest experiences.

Answer

☑Checkpoint The National Road was the first federally funded road. It went from Maryland through Virginia, Ohio, and Indiana to Illinois.

The Extension of Slavery

p. 404

Instruction ▪️L2

- Have students read The Extension of Slavery. Remind students to look for the sequence of events.

- Ask: **What was the most serious problem caused by westward expansion?** (*the extension of slavery*)

- To help students better understand the concept of *compromise*, which is important to the understanding of this section, use the Concept Lesson about Compromise. Provide students with copies of the Concept Organizer.

  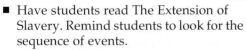 **Teaching Resources, Unit 4,** Concept Lesson, p. 26; Concept Organizer, p. 6

- Discuss Jefferson's quote. Explain to students that a knell can be a mournful funeral bell. Ask: **What did Jefferson fear when he referred to "the knell of the Union"?** (*Possible answer: that the nation will be split by slavery*)

Independent Practice

Have students complete the study guide for this section.

📖 **Interactive Reading and Notetaking Study Guide,** Chapter 11, Section 4 (Adapted Version also available.)

Monitor Progress

- As students fill in the study guide, circulate to make sure individuals understand the problems caused by the expansion of slavery. Provide assistance as needed.

- Tell students to fill in the last column of the Reading Readiness Guide. Probe for what they learned that confirms or invalidates each statement.

- Have students go back to their Word Knowledge Rating Form. Rerate their word knowledge, and complete the last column with a definition or example.

  All in One Teaching Resources, Unit 4, Reading Readiness Guide, p. 19; Word Knowledge Rating Form, p. 15

Answers

☑️**Checkpoint** The Erie Canal enabled them to get their produce to eastern markets more easily.

Reading Charts (a) Ohio (b) to maintain the balance of free and slave states in the Senate

---

The success of the Erie Canal sparked a surge of canal building. In 1829, a canal was built through Delaware. Canals were soon underway in Virginia, Pennsylvania, Ohio, Indiana, and Illinois.

☑️**Checkpoint** How did the building of the Erie Canal help farmers in the interior of the country?

The Extension of Slavery

Westward expansion strengthened the nation. It also caused problems. The most serious problem was the extension of slavery.

Slave and Free States In 1819, the nation consisted of 11 "slave states," which permitted slavery, and 11 "free states," which prohibited slavery. However, Missouri had been seeking admission as a slave state since 1817.

Northerners had reacted strongly. Adding another slave state would upset the balance in the Senate, where each state had two votes. Adding two more senators from a slave state would make the South more powerful than the North.

In 1819, Representative James Tallmadge of New York proposed that Missouri be admitted as a slave state. However, once it was admitted, no more slaves could be brought into the state.

The bill passed the House of Representatives, but it failed in the Senate. Southern senators feared that slavery itself—and thus the South's economic well-being—was being threatened.

The Missouri Compromise In the next session of Congress, Maine applied for admission to the Union. Unlike Missouri, Maine prohibited slavery. The admission of both a free state and a slave state would maintain the balance in the Senate.

In 1820, Senator Henry Clay persuaded Congress to adopt the Missouri Compromise. It permitted Maine to be admitted to the Union as a free state and Missouri to be admitted as a slave state. In addition, the compromise provided that the Louisiana Territory north of the southern border of Missouri would be free of slavery. The compromise had one other important feature. It gave southern slave owners a clear right to pursue escaped fugitives into "free" regions and return them to slavery.

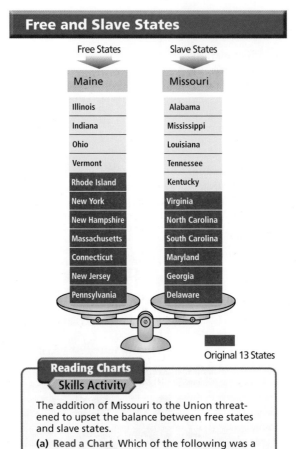

Free and Slave States

Free States	Slave States
Maine	Missouri
Illinois	Alabama
Indiana	Mississippi
Ohio	Louisiana
Vermont	Tennessee
Rhode Island	Kentucky
New York	Virginia
New Hampshire	North Carolina
Massachusetts	South Carolina
Connecticut	Maryland
New Jersey	Georgia
Pennsylvania	Delaware

Original 13 States

Reading Charts

Skills Activity

The addition of Missouri to the Union threatened to upset the balance between free states and slave states.

(a) Read a Chart Which of the following was a free state: Kentucky, Tennessee, or Ohio?

(b) Explain Problems Why did northern states wish to have Missouri and Maine enter the Union at the same time?

Differentiated Instruction

▪️L3 Gifted and Talented

Present Graphic Data Have students research states by order of entry into the Union. Ask students to make a chart of the states that entered the Union between the time of the Missouri Compromise and 1850, noting which were slave states and which were free states. Have students present their charts to the class.

A Continuing Problem The Missouri Compromise revealed how much sectional rivalries divided the states of the Union. The compromise seemed to balance the interests of the North and the South. However, white southerners were not happy that Congress had given itself the power to make laws regarding slavery. Many northerners, in turn, were angry that Congress had allowed slavery to expand into another state.

Thomas Jefferson was alarmed by the fierce debate over the Missouri Compromise. The former President, much older now, saw that the issues raised by the compromise could tear the nation apart. He wrote to a friend:

> **❝**This momentous question, like a firebell in the night, awakened and filled me with terror. I considered it at once as the knell of the Union. . . . [W]e have the wolf by the ears, and we can neither hold him, nor safely let him go.**❞**
>
> —Thomas Jefferson, letter of April 22, 1820

As Jefferson observed, the bitterness of feelings about slavery posed a serious threat to national unity. In time, the issue of slavery would indeed split the nation in two.

☑Checkpoint Why was Jefferson alarmed at the bitterness of the debate over the extension of slavery?

⭐ **Looking Back and Ahead** In this chapter, you learned about increasing differences between North and South. In the next chapter, you will read about the movement to end slavery and other efforts to bring social change.

Section 4 | Check Your Progress

Progress Monitoring 🌐nline
For: Self-test with instant help
Visit: PHSchool.com
Web Code: mya-4074

Comprehension and Critical Thinking

1. (a) Recall How did building better roads and canals transform the United States?
(b) Identify Economic Benefits How did improved transportation lead to economic growth?

2. (a) List What were the main points of the Missouri Compromise?
(b) Make Predictions Why would the issues addressed by the Missouri Compromise continue to tear the nation apart?

🔁 Reading Skill

3. Place Events in a Matrix of Time and Place What event in the early nineteenth century led to the creation of the Missouri Territory and later to the state of Missouri? Describe this event.

Key Terms

4. Draw a table with three rows and three columns. In the first column, list the key terms from this section: turnpike, corduroy road, canal. In the next column, write the definition of each term. In the last column, make a small illustration that shows the meaning of the term.

Writing

5. Based on what you have read in this section, write a thesis statement about the most important change caused by the development of new routes to the West.

Assess Progress **L2**

Have students complete Check Your Progress. Administer the Section Quiz.

All in One Teaching Resources, Unit 4, Section Quiz, p. 30

To further assess student understanding, use the Progress Monitoring Transparency.

Progress Monitoring Transparencies, Chapter 11, Section 4

Reteach **L1**

If students need more instruction, have them read this section in the Interactive Reading and Notetaking Study Guide.

📖 **Interactive Reading and Notetaking Study Guide,** Chapter 11, Section 4 (Adapted Version also available.)

Extend **L3**

Have students use the Internet to research Henry Clay of Kentucky. Ask students to find out why Clay was nicknamed the "Great Compromiser" and to explain the compromises in which he was involved to the class.

Extend 🌐nline
For: Help starting the Extend activity
Visit: PHSchool.com
Web Code: mye-0260

Progress Monitoring Online

Students may check their comprehension of this section by completing the Progress Monitoring Online graphic organizer and self-quiz.

Section 4 Check Your Progress

1. (a) Traveling to the West became easier, as did moving goods to markets.
(b) Farmers and factory owners could ship their produce and goods to far-away markets more easily and cheaply.

2. (a) Missouri enters Union as slave state, Maine as free state, maintaining the balance in the Senate. The Louisiana Territory north of the southern border of Missouri would be free of slavery. Southern slave owners could pursue fugitives into free regions.
(b) Each new state would raise the issue of maintaining the balance of power in Congress. It required northerners to support slavery by turning in fugitive slaves.

3. Possible answer: The Louisiana Purchase transferred ownership of land from France to the United States. The Missouri Territory was part of this land.

4. Students should construct an illustrated table with definitions as follows: turnpike—a toll road; corduroy road—road made of sawed off logs, laid side by side; canal—channel dug across land and filled with water. Illustrations will vary.

5. Thesis statements will vary but should address broad issues, such as the expansion of slavery.

Answer

☑Checkpoint Jefferson was alarmed. He saw that slavery could cause the nation to split apart.

Objective

The Internet connects millions of Web sites sponsored by businesses, governments, educational groups, and individuals all over the world. With so many sites available, it is important to evaluate a site to determine if the information is unbiased and legitimate.

Evaluate Internet Sources

Instruction L2

1. Write the steps to evaluate Internet sources on the board, and ask the class to read the steps aloud.

2. Ask students to read the Web image. Using the Idea Wave strategy, have students suggest what keywords might have been used to find this page. (*Samuel Morse, telegraph, inventors, 19th century America, communication*)

3. Practice the skill by following the steps on p. 406 as a class. Model each step to evaluate Internet sources. (*1. It presents information about Samuel F. B. Morse. 2. (a) topic, source of information, what types of information on Morse can be found on this site, time period of documents available (b) It includes correspondence, letterbooks, diaries, scrapbooks, printed matter, maps, and drawings from 1793–1919; it links to the Library of Congress homepage and to the Manuscript Division of the Library of Congress; keyword search 3. It documents Morse's invention of the telegraph and its importance to the United States. 4. (a) Library of Congress (b) Yes; it is sponsored by a U.S. government agency.*)

Monitor Progress

Ask students to do the Apply the Skill activity. Then assign the Skills for Life Worksheet. As students complete the worksheet, circulate to make sure individuals are applying the skill steps effectively. Provide assistance as needed.

All in One Teaching Resources, Unit 4,
Skills for Life Worksheet, p. 25

When you are doing research on the Internet, it is important to evaluate the Web sites to determine if the information is valid and objective. The page below is from a Web site about Samuel F.B. Morse.

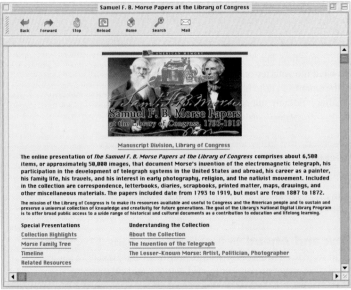

Source: The Library of Congress

Learn the Skill
Use these steps to learn how to evaluate Internet sources.

1 **Determine the Web site's purpose.** Does the Web site provide information? Is it trying to sell something or to promote a particular point of view?

2 **Examine the information.** Does the site include visuals? Does it include first-person accounts and other primary source materials?

3 **Compare the information to what you already know.** Does the information agree with what you have read in a textbook or in another reliable print source? What other information is provided?

4 **Evaluate the source.** Is the source an established organization? Can you tell who provided the information?

Practice the Skill
Use the information above to answer the following questions.

1 **Determine the Web site's purpose.** What is the purpose of this Web site?

2 **Examine the information.** (a) What kinds of information can you find on this page? (b) What other features does it include?

3 **Compare the information to what you already know.** What additional information does this Web site give that supplements the information in this chapter?

4 **Evaluate the source.** (a) Who is the provider for this site? (b) If you were writing a paper about Samuel F.B. Morse, do you think you could use the information on this Web site? Why or why not?

Apply the Skill
See the Review and Assessment at the end of this chapter.

406 Chapter 11 North and South Take Different Paths

Quick Study Guide

 Why did Americans take different paths in the early 1800s?

Section 1
The Industrial Revolution

- By the end of the 1700s, advances in technology allowed goods to be produced cheaply and quickly by machines.
- In the United States, the Industrial Revolution centered in the Northeast, which had an ample supply of labor and raw materials.
- Factory conditions became increasingly dangerous, and laborers fought for better working conditions.

Section 2
The North Transformed

- Cities grew rapidly during the 1800s, and crowding, disease, and fast-spreading fires were common problems.
- Northern industries grew due to advances in technology.

Section 3
The Plantation South

- Eli Whitney's cotton gin made possible a huge increase in cotton production.
- As cotton production grew, the number and value of enslaved African Americans increased dramatically.
- In the face of cruel conditions, many enslaved African Americans resisted slavery.

Section 4
The Challenges of Growth

- By the early 1800s, a flood of settlers westward helped many territories qualify for statehood.
- Better roads and canals further increased the rate of western settlement.
- Tension arose over slavery in the territories, but the Missouri Compromise settled the issue temporarily.

? Exploring the Essential Question

Use the online study guide to explore the essential question.

Section 1
How did the new technology of the Industrial Revolution change the way Americans lived?

Chapter 11 Essential Question
Why did Americans take different paths in the early 1800s?

Section 2
How did urbanization, technology, and social change affect the North?

Section 4
How did Americans move west, and how did this intensify the debate over slavery?

Section 3
How did cotton affect the social and economic life of the South?

Chapter 11

Essential Question
Remind students of the Chapter Essential Question: **Why did Americans take different paths in the early 1800s?** Have students review the bulleted statements and the Visual Preview at the beginning of the chapter to help them answer this question.

To bolster students' retention, at this time they should complete the study guide in print or online. Remind students that they should also continue notetaking for the Unit and Chapter Essential Questions.

 **Interactive Reading and Notetaking Study Guide,** Chapter 11 (Adapted Version also available.)

Interactive Textbook **Study Guide** *Online,* Chapter 11

Chapter Challenge
To wrap up this chapter, students should apply the knowledge they have gained to answer this question: **How does geography affect history?** (*Answers will vary, but students should recognize that the rivers and viability of building canals in the North allowed for industrialization and for concentrated populations in cities, whereas the South's climate led to the development of a cotton-growing economy dependent on enslaved labor.*)

Assessment at a Glance

Formal Assessment
  Chapter Tests A/B (L1/L2)
  AYP Monitoring Assessment
  Test Prep Workbook With Document-Based Assessment
  Test-Taking Strategies With Transparencies

Performance Assessment
  Group/Individual Activities, TE pp. 378g, 378h
  Teacher's Edition, pp. 386, 395, 400, 405
  Assessment Rubrics

Assessment Through Technology
  ExamView CD-ROM
  MindPoint CD-ROM
  Progress Monitoring Transparencies
  Progress Monitoring Online

Key Terms

1. Industrial Revolution

2. nativists

3. spirituals

4. turnpikes

Comprehension and Critical Thinking

5. **(a)** They were factory workers at mills owned by Lowell and his associate. **(b)** Possible answer: It was more efficient to bring weaving and spinning into one building.

6. **(a)** He devised the system of inter-changeable parts. **(b)** It made manufac-turing more efficient and lowered the price of goods.

7. **(a)** Steamboats had to follow the paths of rivers, while railroads could be built in most places. **(b)** Both helped trans-port raw materials and products between manufacturers and markets.

8. **(a)** The cotton gin enabled southern planters to process cotton fiber more quickly and to profit more from grow-ing cotton. Northern manufacturers could in turn make more cotton cloth. **(b)** Because the cotton gin made grow-ing cotton more profitable, planters grew more cotton and so needed more slave labor to work in the fields.

9. **(a)** Southerners argued that enslaved people were better off than factory workers because they didn't have to worry about unemployment, food, shelter, or medical care. Northerners said that workers were free to quit a job and take another and didn't suffer abuse from owners. **(b)** Enslaved Afri-can Americans resisted by working slowly, pretending not to understand, breaking farm equipment, trying to escape, and revolting.

10. **(a)** The roads were terrible—unpaved, easily washed out with rain, dotted with tree stumps. **(b)** Improved trans-portation made it easier for people to travel west and settle in the backcoun-try and for farmers and merchants to move their goods to market quickly and cheaply. **(c)** Possible answers: As immigrants arrived and headed west, they needed ways to travel and routes to travel over; Irish immigrants helped to build canals.

Key Terms
Fill in the blanks with the correct key terms.

1. The _____ was the change in the way people made goods beginning in the late 1700s.

2. People who wanted to keep immigrants out of the country were called _____.

3. African Americans sang _____ to keep hope during their difficult lives.

4. Travelers had to pay tolls on _____ in order to pass.

Comprehension and Critical Thinking

5. **(a) Describe** Who were the Lowell girls?
(b) Apply Information How do you think the Lowell system affected production?

6. **(a) Identify** What contribution did Eli Whitney make to manufacturing?
(b) Identify Economic Benefits How did this contribution benefit consumers?

7. **(a) Summarize** How did the physical limita-tions of steamboats differ from those of rail-roads?
(b) Draw Conclusions Why were both means of transportation important to the growth of industry?

8. **(a) Summarize** How did the cotton gin benefit southern planters? How did it benefit northern textile manufacturers?
(b) Analyze Cause and Effect How did the cotton gin change life for enslaved people?

9. **(a) Contrast** What arguments did some south-erners use to defend slavery? What were some points raised by northern critics of slavery to challenge those arguments?
(b) Apply Information What were some tac-tics that enslaved African Americans employed in order to endure or resist slavery?

10. **(a) Describe** What were some of the difficul-ties Americans faced as they traveled west?
(b) Analyze Cause and Effect How did improved transportation affect western settle-ment? How did it affect industry?
(c) Draw Conclusions How were immigrants important to the transportation revolution?

11. **(a) Recall** How was slavery an issue in the debate over Missouri's statehood?
(b) Detect Points of View Why did northern-ers believe that it would be damaging to the North if the South became more powerful in the Senate?

History Reading Skill

12. **Identify and Explain Central Issues** Write a paragraph that explains the issues central to the Missouri Compromise. Orient the issues in the context of the times and places in which they occurred.

Writing

13. **Write a paragraph explaining *either* the causes *or* the effects of one of the following developments:**
   - Industrialization of the North
   - The cotton empire of the South

   Your paragraph should:
   - begin with a sentence that expresses your main idea;
   - indicate whether you will focus on the sub-ject's causes or its effects;
   - expand on your main idea with facts, exam-ples, and other information.

14. **Write a Narrative:**
Choose one of the inventions developed during the first half of the nineteenth century. Write a narrative that describes how people were affected by the invention.

Skills for Life
Evaluate Internet Sources
Visit this Web site: www.eriecanalmuseum.org. Then, use the information to answer the following questions.

15. What seems to be the purpose of this Web site?

16. **(a)** What kinds of information can you find on this page? **(b)** What other features and links does it include?

17. What additional information does this Web site give to supplement the information in your textbook?

18. **(a)** Who is the provider for this site? **(b)** If you were writing a paper about the Erie Canal, do you think you could use the information on this Web site? Why or why not?

---

11. **(a)** Missouri allowed slavery, and it would upset the balance in Congress to add a slave state. **(b)** Possible answer: They feared that southerners might expand slavery.

History Reading Skills
12. Possible answer: The Missouri Compro-mise arose because northerners wanted to limit the spread of slavery, with which they largely disagreed and which was not important to their most-ly industrial economy, and southerners wanted to expand slavery because their rural agricultural economy depended on it. The admission of a free state and slave state maintained the balance in the Senate.

Writing
13. Paragraphs should demonstrate an understanding of the importance of these developments. Both had a pro-found effect on the economic and social life of the country.

Test Yourself

1. **Which of the following inventions did the most to advance the connection between goods, raw materials, and markets?**

   A interchangeable parts

   B steamboats

   C telegraphs

   D railroads

2. **In the mid-1800s, many immigrants came to the United States from Ireland to escape**

   A revolutions.

   B famine.

   C political unrest.

   D religious persecution.

Refer to the quotation below to answer Question 3.

> "This momentous question, like a firebell in the night, awakened and filled me with terror. I considered it at once as the knell of the Union. . . ."

3. **To which issue does this quotation refer?**

   A transportation

   B slavery

   C immigration

   D mass production

Document-Based Questions

Task: Look at Documents 1 and 2, and answer their accompanying questions. Then, use the documents and your knowledge of history to complete this writing assignment:

Write an essay describing what life was like for enslaved African Americans in the South. Use information from the graph to explain why slaveholders felt restrictive measures were necessary.

Document 1: This graph gives information about the population of some slave-holding states in 1840. *Use the graph to make a generalization about the South's slave population.*

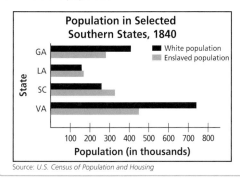

Population in Selected Southern States, 1840

■ White population
▨ Enslaved population

State: GA, LA, SC, VA

Population (in thousands): 100 200 300 400 500 600 700 800

Source: *U.S. Census of Population and Housing*

Document 2: The excerpt below is from a 1930s interview with Fountain Hughes, born a slave in 1848 near Charlottesville, Virginia. *How does Fountain Hughes describe what it meant to be a slave?*

"Well, I belonged to B., when I was a slave. My mother belonged to B. But we was all slave children. . . .
   Now I couldn' go from here across the street . . . [with]out I have a note, or something from my master. . . . Whoever he sent me to, they'd give me another pass an' I'd bring that back so as to show how long I'd been gone. . . . An' when I come back, why I carry it to my master an' give that to him, that'd be all right. But I couldn' jus' walk away like the people does now. . . .
   We belonged to people. They'd sell us like they sell horses an' cows an' hogs an' all like that. Have a auction bench, an' they'd put you on, up on the bench an' bid on you jus' same as you bidding on cattle."

Test Yourself

1. D

2. B

3. B

Document-Based Questions
Answers

Document 1 Possible answer: In some states, the enslaved population was larger than the white population.

Document 2 Hughes describes being a slave as having to report to and answer to someone whenever he did anything or went anywhere. He also describes how ownership of an enslaved person could change at any time, as with an animal.

Rubric: Write a Letter to the Editor

Share the rubric with students before they begin writing.

Score 1 Is poorly organized, lacks defense of the treatment of slaves.

Score 2 Has few details, meaning unclear.

Score 3 Is reasonably well written, shows understanding of planter's point of view. (*Possible details include: feelings of enslaved people toward restriction and justifications for restitution by slaveholders.*)

Score 4 Has clear organization and is well developed and creative, shows understanding of a southern planter's point of view, gives detailed defense of treatment of slaves.

---

14. Possible topics include the spinning jenny, steam engine, interchangeable parts, telegraph, mechanical reaper, threshers, sewing machine, and steamboats. Answer should indicate how the invention changed the lives of people.

For a more complete four-point rubric, see the Writing Rubrics in the Teaching Resources.

All⬛in⬛One Teaching Resources, Unit 4, p. 111

Skills for Life

15. to give information about the Erie Canal Museum

16. **(a)** history, exhibits, programs, membership, volunteer information, museum shops, special features, how to contact the museum, visiting hours **(b)** 1850 Weighlock Building, museum tours, school programs, Syracuse Heritage Area Visitor Center

17. It provides the history of the Erie Canal and information about the canal boats.

18. **(a)** The Erie Canal Museum **(b)** Yes, because it is sponsored by a nonprofit agency and has educational programs. It is associated with the city of Syracuse.

An Age of Reform (1820–1860)

History Background

The Importance of Early Reform Movements

The study of mid–nineteenth-century reform and cultural movements provides an excellent opportunity to understand the roots of American society and culture. In the mid-1800s, religious revivals inspired many Americans to improve both themselves and their society. The expansion of democracy under President Andrew Jackson also helped spark efforts to improve American society.

Inspired by political or religious ideals, reformers tackled social problems, from alcohol abuse to prison reform, care of the mentally ill, and inadequate education. But one issue stood out: abolishing slavery. In the North, the movement to end slavery grew. Abolitionists, including former slaves, publicly denounced the horrors of slavery. They also began to help slaves escape to freedom using the Underground Railroad. Not all northerners opposed slavery, however, and most southerners strongly favored it. In the South, slavery was spreading along with the cotton boom, and southerners began to use new techniques to defend their way of life.

One unexpected result of the abolitionist movement was the movement for women's rights. When abolitionist women were excluded from participating in an antislavery convention, they began to realize the inequalities women faced. At a convention in Seneca Falls, New York, the goals of the American women's rights movement were formally articulated, and the struggle for women's suffrage, education, and overall equality began.

Reformers' determination to improve individuals and society was shared by a new generation of American writers, painters, and composers. Transcendentalists emphasized individualism and the emotional ties between humans and nature. Shunning European themes, writers and painters celebrated American life and themes in their works. African American spirituals, as well as popular songs by composers such as Stephen Foster, formed a new American style of music. Even as a new American culture began to take form, however, increasing disagreements over the issue of slavery continued to divide the country.

Essential Questions

Use this graphic organizer to see the relationship between key concepts and the Chapter Essential Question.

Focus Question/Section 1
How did key people bring about reform in education and society?
(p. 414)
Concept: Reform

Focus Question/Section 2
How did abolitionists try to end slavery?
(p. 422)
Concepts: Slavery, Abolition

Chapter Essential Question
How did reformers and writers inspire change and spark controversy?

Focus Question/Section 4
How did American literature and art have an impact on American life?
(p. 431)
Concept: Nationalism

Focus Question/Section 3
How did the women's suffrage movement begin?
(p. 427)
Concept: Democracy

Professional Development

Differentiated Instruction

Simplified Outlining

Organizing Ideas When taking notes, utilizing the Power Notes strategy may help students differentiate between main ideas and details from their reading. Remind students that a Power Notes outline differs from a traditional outline in that it labels and organizes relationships among ideas in the reading. Level 1 should reflect the main idea or the level it follows. Write the sample Power Notes outline on the board for the first section of the chapter.

Level 1: Improving Society

    Level 2: The Reforming Spirit

        Level 3: Jacksonian Democracy

        Level 3: The Second Great Awakening

        Level 3: Utopian Communities

    Level 2: Social Reformers at Work

Developing an Outline Explain to students what the levels mean and how to create a Power Notes outline. Have students develop their own Power Notes outline for the other sections in the chapter. Remind students that the outlines are good reference tools for answering section assessment questions or studying for quizzes and tests.

Concepts Across Time

Have students develop an understanding of the enduring concepts of history by connecting these ideas.

Concept: Reform

Remind students that "reform" is an enduring theme in history. Ask: **What was the goal of the Great Awakening in colonial America in the 1700s?** (*To bring sinful colonists back to God and revive religious devotion*) Ask: **Why was a Second Great Awakening deemed to be necessary in the 1800s?** (*Many people believed that Americans had again lost interest in religion and slipped back into sinful ways.*) Use these questions when discussing reform movements in Section 1.

Concepts: Slavery, Abolition

Students should recall the beginnings of slavery in the Americas. Ask: **How did early Spanish settlers in the Americas deal with labor shortages?** (*They made Native Americans work for them under the* encomienda *system.*) Ask: **Why did the Spanish later bring enslaved Africans to do their labor?** (*Many Native Americans died from unfamiliar diseases and brutal working conditions.*) Remind students that some Spanish settlers, like the priest Bartolomé de las Casas, tried to end the oppression of Native Americans. Use these questions when discussing the fight against slavery in Section 2.

Concept: Democracy

Students learning about the struggle for women's suffrage should recall that some males have also had to struggle to receive voting rights. Ask: **When did U.S. suffrage expand to include all adult white males?** (*By Andrew Jackson's election as President in 1828, white male suffrage was widespread.*) Use these questions when discussing women's rights in Section 3.

Concept: Nationalism

Students should consider the many ways in which people develop a sense of national uniqueness. Remind students that the struggle for political freedom from Great Britain helped colonists develop a loyalty to the new United States of America. Ask: **How did American independence encourage the development of distinctly American forms of literature and art?** (*Possible answer: Independence weakened old cultural ties to Europe and led creative Americans to focus on a range of American themes.*) Use this question when discussing American literature and arts in Section 4.

Section 1 Improving Society

 1.5 periods, .75 block

Objectives

Students will

1. Discuss what led many Americans to try to improve society in the 1800s.
2. Identify the social problems that reformers tried to solve.
3. Summarize the improvements in public education in the 1800s.

Differentiated Instruction Key

- **L1** Basic to Average
- **L2** All Students
- **L3** Average to Advanced
- **AR** Advanced Readers
- **ELL** English Language Learners
- **GT** Gifted and Talented
- **LPR** Less Proficient Readers
- **SN** Special Needs

Prepare to Read

Build Background Knowledge
Discuss how reformers address issues of today and addressed those of the nineteenth century.

Set a Purpose for Reading
Have students begin to fill out the Reading Readiness Guide.

Preview Key Terms
Preview the section's Key Terms.

Instructional Resources

All in One Teaching Resources, Unit 4
- **L2** Chapter Prereading Guide, p. 4
- **L2** History Reading Skill Worksheet, p. 44
- **L2** Word Knowledge Rating Form, p. 45
- **L2** Reading Readiness Guide, p. 46

Teacher's Edition
- **L2** Vocabulary Builder, pp. 413, 415

Discovery School Video
- **L2** An Age of Reform

Differentiated Instruction

🔊 **Guided Reading Audio CD**
Spanish ELL, LPR, SN

Teach

Instruction
The Reforming Spirit
Describe the Second Great Awakening and how it spurred reform movements.

Social Reformers at Work
Explain the problems reformers worked to solve.

Education Reform
Discuss Horace Mann and the improvement of public education.

Instructional Resources

📖 **Interactive Reading and Notetaking Study Guide**
- **L2** Chapter 12, Section 1

All in One Teaching Resources, Unit 4
- **L2** Horace Mann, p. 50

Differentiated Instruction

📖 **Interactive Reading and Notetaking Study Guide, Adapted Version (English/ Spanish)**
- **L1** Chapter 12, Section 1 ELL, LPR, SN

Teacher's Edition
- **L1** Visualizing the Word, p. 413 ELL, LPR, SN
- **L1** Gaining Comprehension, p. 414 LPR, SN
- **L3** American Utopias, p. 416 AR
- **L1** Vocabulary Development, p. 418 ELL, LPR, SN

Assess and Reteach

Assess Progress
Evaluate student comprehension with Check Your Progress and Section Quiz.

Reteach
Assign the Interactive Reading and Notetaking Study Guide to help struggling students.

Extend
Extend the lesson by having students research and make a chart of nineteenth-century reformers.

Instructional Resources

📖 **Interactive Reading and Notetaking Study Guide**
- **L2** Chapter 12, Section 1

All in One Teaching Resources, Unit 4
- **L2** Reading Readiness Guide, p. 46
- **L2** Section Quiz, p. 58

Progress Monitoring Transparencies
- **L2** Chapter 12, Section 1

Differentiated Instruction

Teacher's Edition
- **L1** Checkpoints, TE pp. 416, 417, 419

🔊 **SE on Audio CD**
- **L1** Chapter 12 ELL, LPR, SN

Internet Resources
PHSchool.com

Section 2 The Fight Against Slavery

 *1 period, .5 block*

Objectives

Students will

1. Describe efforts in the North to end slavery.
2. Discuss the contributions of William Lloyd Garrison, Frederick Douglass, and other abolitionists.
3. Describe the purpose and risks of the Underground Railroad.
4. Explain why many people in the North and South defended slavery.

Differentiated Instruction Key

L1 Basic to Average
L2 All Students
L3 Average to Advanced

AR Advanced Readers
ELL English Language Learners
GT Gifted and Talented
LPR Less Proficient Readers
SN Special Needs

Prepare to Read

Build Background Knowledge
Preview the section and discuss why slavery was a target of reform.

Set a Purpose for Reading
Have students begin to fill out the Reading Readiness Guide.

Preview Key Terms
Preview the section's Key Terms.

Instructional Resources

All in One Teaching Resources, Unit 4
L2 Reading Readiness Guide, p. 47

Teacher's Edition
L2 Vocabulary Builder, p. 423

Differentiated Instruction

Guided Reading Audio CD
Spanish ELL, LPR, SN

Teach

Instruction
Roots of the Antislavery Movement
Describe how slavery ended in the North.

Growing Opposition to Slavery
Explain the abolitionist movement's efforts to end slavery.

The Underground Railroad
Discuss the Underground Railroad and Harriet Tubman.

Opposing Abolition
Discuss why some northerners and southerners defended slavery.

Instructional Resources

Interactive Reading and Notetaking Study Guide
L2 Chapter 12, Section 2

All in One Teaching Resources, Unit 4
L2 The Grimké Sisters, p. 52
L2 Concept Lesson, p. 57
L2 Concept Organizer, p. 6

Discovery School Video
L2 The Underground Railroad

Differentiated Instruction

Interactive Reading and Notetaking Study Guide, Adapted Version (English/Spanish)

L1 Chapter 12, Section 2 ELL, LPR, SN

Teacher's Edition
L1 Comprehension Aid, p. 422 LPR, SN
L1 The Underground Railroad, p. 424 SN, ELL
L3 Harriet Tubman, p. 425 AR, GT

All in One Teaching Resources, Unit 4
L1 The Underground Railroad, p. 54

Assess and Reteach

Assess Progress
Evaluate student comprehension with Check Your Progress and Section Quiz.

Reteach
Assign the Interactive Reading and Notetaking Study Guide to help struggling students.

Extend
Extend the lesson by having students create posters based on the antislavery movement.

Instructional Resources

Interactive Reading and Notetaking Study Guide
L2 Chapter 12, Section 2

All in One Teaching Resources, Unit 4
L2 Reading Readiness Guide, p. 47
L2 Section Quiz, p. 59

Progress Monitoring Transparencies
L2 Chapter 12, Section 2

Differentiated Instruction

Teacher's Edition
L1 Checkpoints, TE pp. 422, 424, 426

SE on Audio CD
L1 Chapter 12 ELL, LPR, SN

Internet Resources
PHSchool.com

Section 3 A Call for Women's Rights

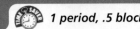 *1 period, .5 block*

Objectives

Students will

1. Explain how the women's suffrage movement began.
2. Describe the goals of the Seneca Falls Convention in 1848.
3. Identify the new opportunities that women gained in the mid-1800s.

Differentiated Instruction Key

L1 Basic to Average
L2 All Students
L3 Average to Advanced

AR Advanced Readers
ELL English Language Learners
GT Gifted and Talented
LPR Less Proficient Readers
SN Special Needs

Prepare to Read	Instructional Resources	Differentiated Instruction
Build Background Knowledge Preview the section and discuss the connection between women's activity in reform movements and the struggle for women's rights. **Set a Purpose for Reading** Have students begin to fill out the Reading Readiness Guide. **Preview Key Terms** Preview the section's Key Terms.	**All in One** Teaching Resources, Unit 4 **L2** Reading Readiness Guide, p. 48 **Teacher's Edition** **L2** Vocabulary Builder, p. 427	🎧 **Guided Reading Audio CD** Spanish ELL, LPR, SN

Teach	Instructional Resources	Differentiated Instruction
Instruction **The Struggle Begins** Discuss the rights of women in 1820 and why they needed more rights. **Seneca Falls Convention** Explain the Seneca Falls Convention and the Declaration of Sentiments. **New Opportunities for Women** Describe the advances in education for women.	📖 **Interactive Reading and Notetaking Study Guide** **L2** Chapter 12, Section 3 **All in One** Teaching Resources, Unit 4 **L2** Declaration of Sentiments, p. 55 **Color Transparencies** **L2** Are Not the Women Half the Nation?	📖 **Interactive Reading and Notetaking Study Guide, Adapted Version (English/ Spanish)** **L1** Chapter 12, Section 3 ELL, LPR, SN **Teacher's Edition** **L1** Gaining Comprehension, p. 428 ELL, LPR, SN **L3** Writing an Editorial, p. 429 AR, GT

Assess and Reteach	Instructional Resources	Differentiated Instruction
Assess Progress Evaluate student comprehension with Check Your Progress and Section Quiz. **Reteach** Assign the Interactive Reading and Notetaking Study Guide to help struggling students. **Extend** Extend the lesson by having students create a concept web about one woman mentioned in this section.	📖 **Interactive Reading and Notetaking Study Guide** **L2** Chapter 12, Section 3 **All in One** Teaching Resources, Unit 4 **L2** Reading Readiness Guide, p. 48 **L2** Section Quiz, p. 60 **Progress Monitoring Transparencies** **L2** Chapter 12, Section 3	**Teacher's Edition** **L1** Checkpoints, TE pp. 427, 428, 430 🎧 **SE on Audio CD** **L1** Chapter 12 ELL, LPR, SN **Internet Resources** PHSchool.com

Section 4 American Literature and Arts *1.5 periods, .75 block*

Objectives
Students will

1. Identify the common themes in American literature and art in the mid-1800s.
2. Describe the flowering of American literature in the mid-1800s.
3. Discuss the development of unique American styles in art and music.

Differentiated Instruction Key

L1 Basic to Average
L2 All Students
L3 Average to Advanced

AR Advanced Readers
ELL English Language Learners
GT Gifted and Talented
LPR Less Proficient Readers
SN Special Needs

Prepare to Read

Build Background Knowledge
Preview the section and discuss reform-related themes in nineteenth-century American art and literature.

Set a Purpose for Reading
Have students begin to fill out the Reading Readiness Guide.

Preview Key Terms
Preview the section's Key Terms.

Instructional Resources

All in One Teaching Resources, Unit 4
L2 Reading Readiness Guide, p. 49

Teacher's Edition
L2 Vocabulary Builder, p. 431

Differentiated Instruction

🔘 Guided Reading Audio CD
Spanish **ELL, LPR, SN**

Teach

Instruction
An American Culture Develops
Discuss transcendentalism and how writers and artists explored American themes.

Flowering of American Literature
Identify the poets and authors of the mid-1800s.

Art and Music
Explain the themes of American painting and music.

Instructional Resources

📖 Interactive Reading and Notetaking Study Guide
L2 Chapter 12, Section 4
All in One Teaching Resources, Unit 4
L2 Analysis Skill Worksheet, p. 56

Color Transparencies
L2 Kindred Spirits

Differentiated Instruction

📖 Interactive Reading and Notetaking Study Guide, Adapted Version (English/ Spanish)
L1 Chapter 12, Section 4 **ELL, LPR, SN**

Teacher's Edition
L1 Study Aid, p. 432 **ELL, LPR, SN**
L3 Creating an Art Exhibit Pamphlet, p. 434 **AR, GT**

Assess and Reteach

Assess Progress
Evaluate student comprehension with Check Your Progress and Section Quiz.

Reteach
Assign the Interactive Reading and Notetaking Study Guide to help struggling students.

Extend
Extend the lesson by having students create a poem expressing ideas about transcendentalism and individualism.

Instructional Resources

📖 Interactive Reading and Notetaking Study Guide
L2 Chapter 12, Section 4
All in One Teaching Resources, Unit 4
L2 Reading Readiness Guide, p. 49
L2 Word Knowledge Rating Form, p. 45
L2 Section Quiz, p. 61
L2 Chapter Test, p. 65

Progress Monitoring Transparencies
L2 Chapter 12, Section 4

Differentiated Instruction

Teacher's Edition
L1 Checkpoints, TE pp. 433, 434, 435
All in One Teaching Resources, Unit 4
L1 Chapter Test, p. 62

🔘 SE on Audio CD
L1 Chapter 12 **ELL, LPR, SN**

Extend the Lesson Through Technology Research

Use the following research activities to help students deepen their understanding of the Chapter Essential Question: **How did reformers and writers inspire change and spark controversy?** Students should use library or Internet resources. The Web Codes provided offer access to Internet resources students can use to complete each activity. Use the appropriate four-point rubric in Assessment Rubrics to evaluate the activity.

 Assessment Rubrics

Write an Essay About Changes in Teacher Training

Have students use the Web site to learn more about the ways teachers have been trained in the United States since the time of Horace Mann. Have each student write a two- or three-paragraph essay about the changes in teacher training from the mid-1800s to the present. Have students present their findings to the class. Use this activity when studying Education Reform in Section 1.

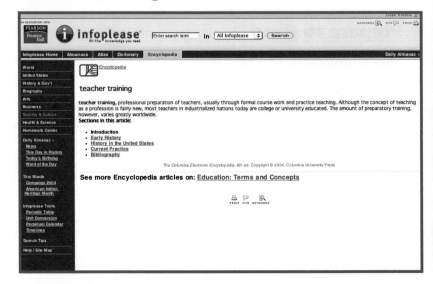

 Individual research activity AR **L3**

 Go Online PHSchool.com **Web Code:** mye-0207

Write a Letter to Frederick Douglass

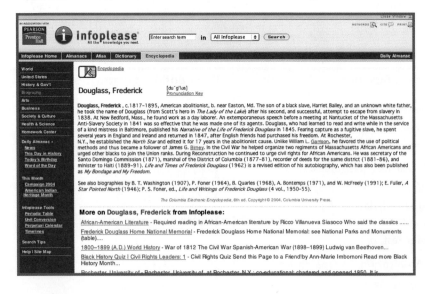

Have students use the information on the Web site to learn more about the life of Frederick Douglass. Then have them write a letter to Douglass at any point in his adult life. Remind them to refer to or ask questions about Douglass's experiences and ideas. Ask students to share their letters with the class when studying Section 2, Growing Opposition to Slavery.

 Individual research activity **L2**

 Go Online PHSchool.com **Web Code:** mye-0208

Create a Timeline About Women's Suffrage

Have students use the information on the Web site to make a timeline, beginning with the Seneca Falls Convention and ending with the passage of the Nineteenth Amendment, about key events leading up to women gaining the right to vote. The timeline should have between 8 and 10 events. Have students share with the class the ways Elizabeth Cady Stanton and Susan B. Anthony continued to contribute to the movement after the Seneca Falls Convention. Use this activity when studying the Seneca Falls Convention in Section 3.

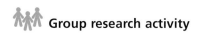 **Group research activity** `L2`

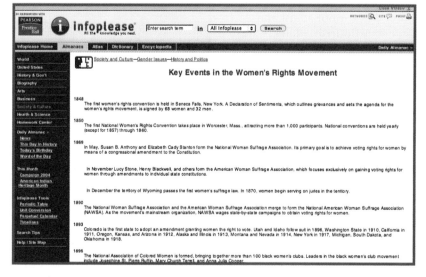

Go Online **Web Code:** mye-0209
PHSchool.com

Review a Stephen Foster Song or Concert

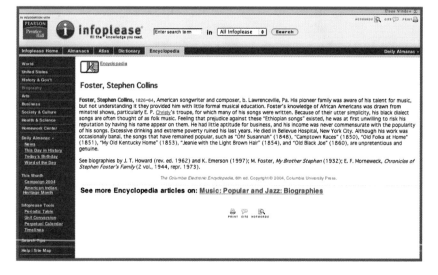

Have students working in pairs use the information on the Web site to learn more about Stephen Foster songs. Tell students to suppose that they have attended a concert of Stephen Foster songs. With their partners, have students give a review of either an individual song or the entire concert experience. Remind them to include what nineteenth-century audiences would have found appealing about the music and lyrics. Ask them to share their reviews with the class. Use this activity when studying Art and Music in Section 4.

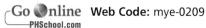 **Group research activity** GT `L3`

Go Online **Web Code:** mye-0210
PHSchool.com

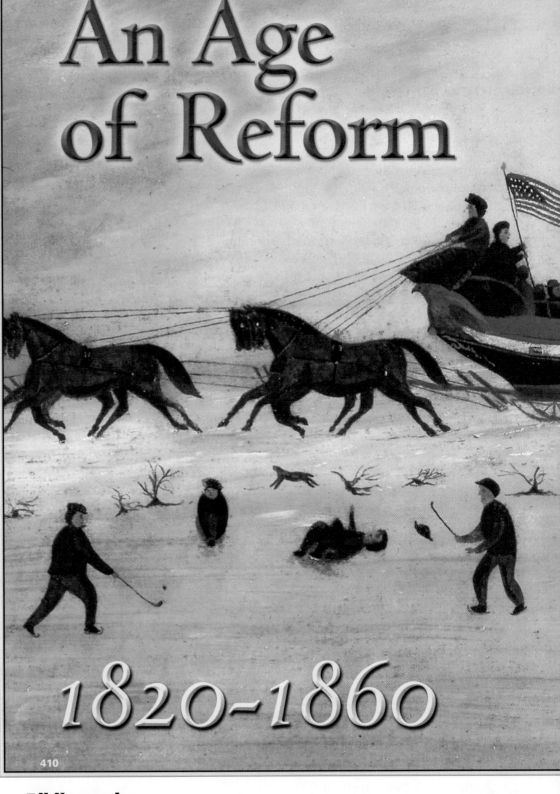

Chapter 12

An Age of Reform

1820–1860

Why It Matters

A plant that does not grow and change dies; a nation that cannot adapt and change can never flourish. Many of the things we take for granted today—women's right to vote, medical help for the mentally ill, free public schools, and freedom from slavery—are goals that reformers fought for during this period.

At the same time that reformers worked for social change, American writers and artists initiated a creative revolution leaving behind the old European influences to shape a uniquely American expression. Painters, poets, novelists, and essayists developed original styles based on the American landscape and society. Their work expressed themes—such as the desire for liberty or the love of nature—that appeals to audiences even today.

Chapter Essential Question

How did reformers and writers inspire change and spark controversy?

Think Like a Historian

- To preview this chapter, have students review the content of these pages of the Student Edition. Ask: **What will you be learning about in this chapter?** (*Possible answer: reforms in education and other areas, the fight against slavery, the effort to gain equality for women, and the distinctive style developed by American artists, writers, and musicians*)

- Have students read the quote at the top of page 411. Ask: **What "privileges" do you think women and African Americans did not have?** (*Possible answers: students should mention right to vote, right to live a free life*)

- Have students study the image and caption on these pages. Ask: **What kind of citizens do you think the women riding the sleigh are? What helped you make that conclusion?** (*Possible answers: proud, responsible, determined; they are organized and holding a flag.*)

Bibliography

For the Teacher

Walters, Ronald G. *American Reformers, 1815–1860.* Rev. ed. New York: Hill & Wang Publishers, 1997.

For the Student

L1 Hawthorne, Nathaniel. *Tanglewood Tales.* Tor Books, 1999.

L2 Fradin, Dennis Brindell. *Bound for the North Star: True Stories of Fugitive Slaves.* Houghton Mifflin Company, 2000.

L3 Ward, Geoffrey, and Ken C. Burns. *Not for Ourselves Alone: The Story of Elizabeth Cady Stanton and Susan B. Anthony.* Knopf Publishing Group, 2001.

"For while the man is born to do whatever he can, to the woman and the negro there is no such privilege."

—Elizabeth Cady Stanton,
*speech to the
American Anti-Slavery Society, 1860*

In this painting, the women riding in the sleigh were campaigning to win the right to vote.

CHAPTER 12

What You Will Learn

Section 1
IMPROVING SOCIETY
By the mid-1800s, people were seeking reform in many areas of American life, including education.

Section 2
THE FIGHT AGAINST SLAVERY
Abolitionists sought an end to slavery in the United States.

Section 3
A CALL FOR WOMEN'S RIGHTS
Some reformers sought to win political and economic equality for women.

Section 4
AMERICAN LITERATURE AND ARTS
In the early 1800s, American artists, writers, and musicians began to develop a distinct style.

🔄 **Reading Skill**

Draw Conclusions From Sources In this chapter, you will learn how to use details from primary and secondary sources to draw conclusions.

411

History Background

Women and the Constitution
"Women" were never mentioned in the Constitution. It stated that "the people" and "citizens" elected representatives to Congress, without defining what these terms meant. Most Americans assumed they referred to white males.

Most Americans also believed that when men voted, they represented everyone in their family. Even as late as 1848, at the Seneca Falls Women's Rights Convention, the resolution for women's suffrage was considered too radical by many attendees, and passed by only a few votes.

It took several more generations for the idea of women's suffrage to be accepted by the majority of American women and men.

Prepare to Read

Use the following for reading skill support.

All in One Teaching Resources, Unit 4, Chapter Prereading Guide, p. 4; History Reading Skill, p. 44

History Reading Skill *Online*
Web code: mve-3000

Differentiated Instruction

The following Teacher's Edition strategies are suitable for students of varying abilities.

L3 Advanced Readers, pp. 416, 425, 429, 434 AR

L1 English Language Learners, pp. 413, 418, 420, 424, 428, 432 ELL

L3 Gifted and Talented, pp. 425, 429, 434 GT

L1 Less Proficient Readers, pp. 413, 414, 418, 422, 428, 432 LPR

L1 Special Needs, pp. 413, 414, 418, 420, 422, 424, 428, 432 SN

Chapter Resources

Teaching Resources, Unit 4
Chapter Prereading Guide, p. 4
Word Knowledge Rating Form, p. 45
History Reading Skill, p. 44
Skills for Life Worksheet, p. 56
Chapter Test A/B (L1/L2), pp. 62, 65
Letter Home (English/Spanish), pp. 37, 38

Spanish Support
L1 Interactive Reading and Notetaking Study Guide, Spanish, Adapted Version
L1 Guided Reading Audio CD, Spanish

Media and Technology
L1 SE on Audio CD
L2 Social Studies Skills Tutor CD-ROM
ExamView **Test Bank CD-ROM**

DISCOVERY SCHOOL

Quick View Video
View the chapter video for a quick preview of the main ideas.

Visual Preview

? **How did reformers and writers inspire change and spark controversy?**

Build Background Knowledge L2

Discuss with students the definition of the word *reform*. Explain that reform during the mid-1800s refers to the changes demanded and made to improve American education and society. Point out to students that reform movements still exist. Use the example of the efforts to protect and improve the environment. Ask students how they are contributing to this worldwide reform movement.

Instruction L2

- For background information on conducting a lesson for the Visual Preview, see TE p. T20.

- Write the Essential Question on the board. Establish an understanding of the word *controversy*. Explain that this refers to a debate or quarrel of opposing opinions and that at times people purposely stir up controversy as a way to get people's attention. Ask students to identify some current controversies.

- Have students look at the timeline. Ask: **What American works of literature were published in the 1850s?** (*The Scarlet Letter, Moby Dick, Walden, and Leaves of Grass*) **Who was Charles Finney?** (*He helped start a religious revival.*)

- Have students review the map and read the captions. Ask: **What do the arrows show?** (*Underground Railroad routes*) **Where do the arrows begin?** (*in slave states*) **What were the destinations of some Underground Railroad routes?** (*Mexico, Canada, West Indies*)

- Ask: **What event in this chapter do you think will be considered an important step toward gaining voting rights for women?** (*the women's rights convention in Seneca Falls, New York*)

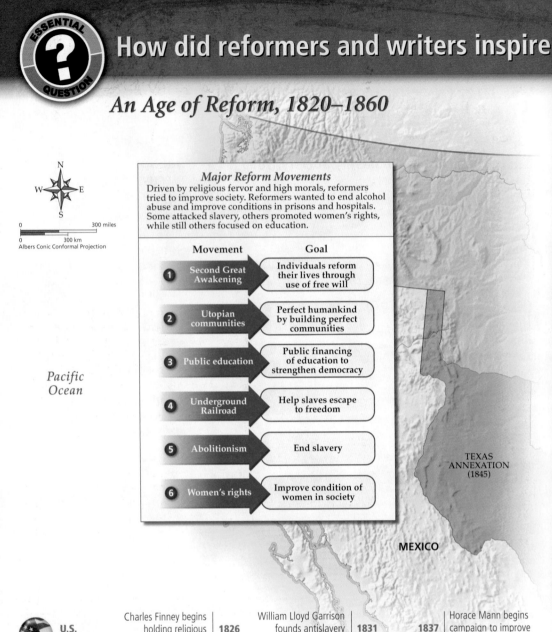

? ESSENTIAL QUESTION

How did reformers and writers inspire

An Age of Reform, 1820–1860

Pacific Ocean

0 — 300 miles
0 — 300 km
Albers Conic Conformal Projection

Major Reform Movements
Driven by religious fervor and high morals, reformers tried to improve society. Reformers wanted to end alcohol abuse and improve conditions in prisons and hospitals. Some attacked slavery, others promoted women's rights, while still others focused on education.

Movement	Goal
1 Second Great Awakening	Individuals reform their lives through use of free will
2 Utopian communities	Perfect humankind by building perfect communities
3 Public education	Public financing of education to strengthen democracy
4 Underground Railroad	Help slaves escape to freedom
5 Abolitionism	End slavery
6 Women's rights	Improve condition of women in society

TEXAS ANNEXATION (1845)

MEXICO

U.S. Events

Charles Finney begins holding religious revival meetings. **1826**

William Lloyd Garrison founds antislavery newspaper. **1831**

1837 Horace Mann begins campaign to improve public schools.

1820   **1830**   **1840**

World Events

1822 Colony of Liberia is founded in West Africa.

1833 Slavery is banned in all British colonies.

History Background

Educational Equality The struggle for equal educational opportunities dates back to 1848. In Boston, Benjamin Roberts, a black abolitionist and printer, wanted to enroll his five-year-old daughter in an all-white school. When his daughter was turned away, he took his case to court. In 1849, the Massachusetts Supreme Court ruled that "separate but equal schools" for black and white students were constitutional. (This decision formed the basis of the *Plessy v Ferguson* ruling almost 50 years later.)

However, public opinion carried the issue forward. In 1855, the Massachusetts legislature outlawed segregated schools.

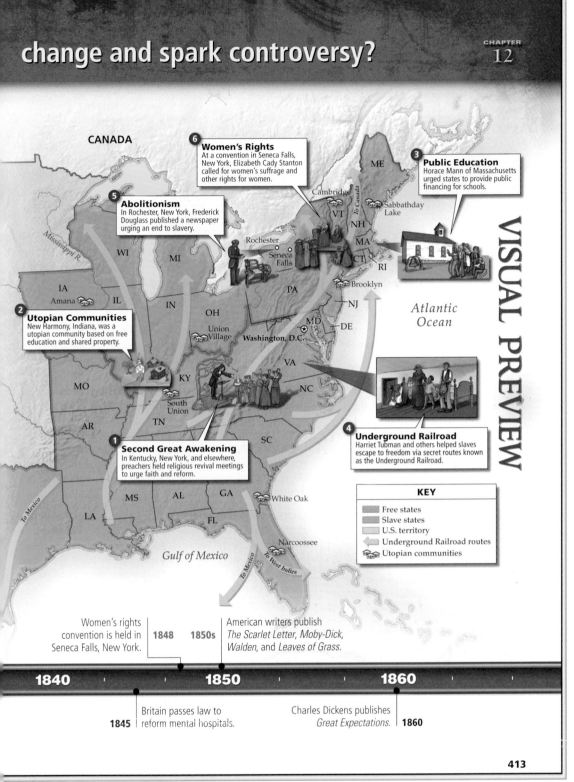

CANADA

6 **Women's Rights**
At a convention in Seneca Falls, New York, Elizabeth Cady Stanton called for women's suffrage and other rights for women.

3 **Public Education**
Horace Mann of Massachusetts urged states to provide public financing for schools.

5 **Abolitionism**
In Rochester, New York, Frederick Douglass published a newspaper urging an end to slavery.

2 **Utopian Communities**
New Harmony, Indiana, was a utopian community based on free education and shared property.

1 **Second Great Awakening**
In Kentucky, New York, and elsewhere, preachers held religious revival meetings to urge faith and reform.

4 **Underground Railroad**
Harriet Tubman and others helped slaves escape to freedom via secret routes known as the Underground Railroad.

ME, VT, NH, MA, CT, RI, Cambridge, Sabbathday Lake, Rochester, Seneca Falls, Brooklyn, Atlantic Ocean, PA, NJ, OH, MD, DE, Union Village, Washington, D.C., VA, NC, KY, South Union, TN, AR, SC, MS, AL, GA, White Oak, LA, FL, Narcoossee, Gulf of Mexico, Amana, IA, IL, IN, WI, MI, MO

Mississippi R., To Canada, To Mexico, To West Indies

VISUAL PREVIEW

KEY
- Free states
- Slave states
- U.S. territory
- ← Underground Railroad routes
- Utopian communities

Women's rights convention is held in Seneca Falls, New York. | **1848** **1850s** | American writers publish *The Scarlet Letter*, *Moby-Dick*, *Walden*, and *Leaves of Grass*.

1840 **1850** **1860**

1845 Britain passes law to reform mental hospitals.

Charles Dickens publishes *Great Expectations*. **1860**

413

Instruction (continued)

- Have students review the map and chart. Explain that the chart lists the major reform movements. Further details of the efforts are shown on the map. Ask: **Why did reformers push for public education?** *(to provide citizens with the opportunity to gain basic knowledge and skills that would strengthen democracy)*

- Ask: **Which movement's members probably helped slaves escape to freedom on routes known as the Underground Railroad?** *(abolitionist movement)* **What important issues were discussed at the Seneca Falls Convention?** *(women met to demand women's suffrage and rights)*

- Use the Idea Wave Strategy (TE p. T24) to lead a structured review of earlier reform efforts. For example, students can review the Great Awakening, the religious revival of the mid-1700s. Alternatively, they can discuss the Puritan experiment of a "City Upon a Hill" as an earlier attempt to create a utopian society.

- Have students rewrite the Essential Question in simple terms in their notes: **What changes did reformers bring about?** You may also post this question in a prominent place in the classroom and leave it there while discussing the chapter. Tell students to use the section focus questions as a guide to answering the Essential Question as they read the chapter.

- Tell students that as they complete the Notetaking Study Guide for this chapter, they will be building the answer to the Essential Question.

Interactive Reading and Notetaking Study Guide, Chapter 11 (Adapted Version also available.)

Vocabulary Builder

Preview the Vocabulary Have students preview the vocabulary in the chapter and rate how well they know each word on the Word Knowledge Rating Form. Collect the sheets and explain that they will have a chance to go over the forms later.

All in One Teaching Resources, Unit 4, Word Knowledge Rating Form, p. 45

Monitor Progress Have students demonstrate their understanding of the vocabulary words by completing these activities:

- Ask students to tell about a time they did something on *impulse*.
- Have students describe the *emotion* they feel during a thunderstorm.
- Ask students to *reproduce* a favorite picture.

Review and Preview

Students have read about the political reforms made under President Jackson. Now they will focus on the efforts by reformers to solve social problems.

◀ Charles Finney

Their Hearts Will Be Changed

"When the churches are thus awakened and reformed, the reformation and salvation of sinners will follow, going through the same stages of conviction, repentance, and reformation. Their hearts will be broken down and changed."

—Charles Finney, a religious revival preacher, 1834

Section Focus Question

How did key people bring about reform in education and society?

Before you begin the lesson for the day, write the Section Focus Question on the board. (*Lesson focus: They were inspired by religious ideas and Jacksonian democracy to push for reforms in lifestyle, human rights, and education.*)

Prepare to Read

Build Background Knowledge L2

Tell students that in this section they will learn about a spirit of reform that grew in the early nineteenth century. Have students use the Think-Write-Pair-Share strategy (TE, p. T25) to list things that people want to reform or improve today. Ask students to think about how these reforms address today's issues, and tell them that nineteenth-century reforms addressed issues of that time.

Set a Purpose L2

■ Form students into pairs or groups of four. Distribute the Reading Readiness Guide. Ask students to fill in the first two columns of the chart.

All in One Teaching Resources, Unit 4, Reading Readiness Guide, p. 46

■ Use the Numbered Heads strategy (TE, p. T24) to call on students to share one piece of information they already know and one piece of information they want to know. The students will return to these worksheets later.

Improving Society

Objectives

- Discuss what led many Americans to try to improve society in the 1800s.
- Identify the social problems that reformers tried to solve.
- Summarize the improvements in public education in the 1800s.

Reading Skill

Assess Evidence for a Conclusion In reading history, you will encounter many descriptive details that help you draw conclusions about historical events. Evaluate the details carefully with questions such as these: Are they accurate and from reliable sources? Do the sources have firsthand knowledge of the situations? What conclusions do the details point to?

Key Terms and People

social reform	prohibition
predestination	Dorothea Dix
Charles Finney	public school
revival	Horace Mann
temperance movement	

Why It Matters The Age of Jackson was a time of expanding democracy in the United States. This democratic spirit, combined with religious ideas, inspired people to improve American society.

Section Focus Question: How did key people bring about reform in education and society?

The Reforming Spirit

In the 1830s, many Americans became interested in social reform, or organized attempts to improve conditions of life. The effort to create a better society had both political and religious roots.

Jacksonian Democracy The expansion of democracy in the Age of Jackson encouraged reform. Most states dropped property requirements for voting. As a result, more white American men were able to vote than ever before. Political parties also developed a more open way of choosing candidates for President.

In the spirit of Jacksonian democracy, some people worked to make the political system even fairer. A number of reformers believed that all men should vote and be able to hold office. Others supported greater legal rights for women. Increasingly, reformers also spoke out strongly against slavery. They argued that no society that allowed one human being to own another could call itself democratic.

414 Chapter 12 An Age of Reform

Differentiated Instruction

L1 Less Proficient Readers   **L1 Special Needs**

Gaining Comprehension Suggest to students that they use a ruler to help them keep their place as they read, line by line, down a page. Have students mark unfamiliar words or phrases (such as *conditions of life* on this page) with a sticky note, or jot down questions that occur as they are reading. Periodically provide assistance to the students to clarify these issues.

The Second Great Awakening Religious feelings and ideas also sparked the reforming <u>impulse</u>. Beginning in the early 1800s, a new generation of ministers challenged some traditional views. This movement became known as the Second Great Awakening.

Changing religious ideas sparked the Second Great Awakening. In colonial days, many American Protestants believed in predestination, the idea that God decided the fate of a person's soul even before birth. But leaders of the Second Great Awakening preached that people's own actions determined their salvation. This "doctrine of free will" blended easily with political ideas about democracy and independence.

The most important of this new generation of preachers was Charles Finney. Finney held the first of many religious revivals in 1826. A revival is a huge outdoor religious meeting. Before long, Finney and other preachers were conducting revivals across the nation. A single revival might go on for several days or even a week. Ministers of different faiths preached day and night, trying to <u>convert</u> sinners and urging people to reform their lives.

Finney believed that the emotion of a revival could touch even the most hopeless sinner. "All sorts of abandoned characters are awakened and converted," he wrote. "The worst part of human society is softened and reclaimed, and made to appear as a lovely specimen of the beauty of holiness."

Vocabulary Builder
<u>impulse</u> (IHM puhls) *n.* sudden push or driving force

Vocabulary Builder
<u>convert</u> (kahn VERT) *v.* to change from one political party, religion, or way of life to another

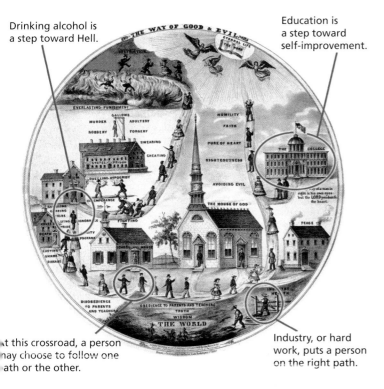

Drinking alcohol is a step toward Hell.

Education is a step toward self-improvement.

At this crossroad, a person may choose to follow one path or the other.

Industry, or hard work, puts a person on the right path.

The Way to Salvation
This symbolic painting, *The Way of Good and Evil*, shows two paths a person can take. One path leads to Hell and the other leads to Heaven. **Critical Thinking: Apply Information** How does this painting reflect the doctrine of free will that was part of the Second Great Awakening?

The Reforming Spirit
p. 414

Instruction L2

- **Vocabulary Builder** Before teaching this section, preteach the High-Use Words **impulse** and **convert** using the strategy on p. T21.
  Key Terms Following the instructions on p. 7, have students create a See It–Remember It chart for the Key Terms in this chapter.

- Read The Reforming Spirit with students using the Structured Silent Reading strategy (TE, p. T22).

- Ask: **What was the Second Great Awakening, and who was Charles Finney?** (*a widespread religious movement based on the idea that people had free will and could improve themselves; it sparked change and reform. He was its most important leader.*)

- Ask students how the Second Great Awakening fostered the spirit of reform in this period. (*It inspired people to improve themselves and their society. It led to the creation of utopian communities.*)

Independent Practice
Have students begin filling in the study guide for this section.

Interactive Reading and Notetaking Study Guide, Chapter 12, Section 1 (Adapted Version also available.)

Monitor Progress

As students fill in the Notetaking Study Guide, circulate to make sure that individuals understand the roots of the reform movement in this period. Provide assistance as needed.

Vocabulary Builder

Use the information below to teach students this section's high-use words.

High-Use Word	Definition and Sample Sentence
impulse, p. 415	*n.* sudden push or driving force Reformers had an **impulse** to try to improve society.
convert, p. 415	*v.* to change from one political party, religion, or way of life to another The preacher's goal was to **convert** his listeners from a life of sin to a life of good works.

Answer
Apply Information It shows that a person has free will to choose between drinking and going to Hell or temperance and going to Heaven.

Social Reformers at Work

p. 416

Instruction [L2]

- Have students read Social Reformers at Work. Remind them to look for details that answer the Section Focus Question.

- Ask: **What was the temperance movement and what problems did it hope to solve?** (*an organized effort to end alcohol abuse and the problems it created, such as mistreatment of women and children by husbands and fathers who drank too much*)

- Discuss with students the goals and successes of Dorothea Dix. Ask: **What did Dorothea Dix try to reform, and what did she achieve?** (*She worked to improve conditions for prisoners and the mentally ill and helped create many mental hospitals.*)

Independent Practice

Have students continue filling in the study guide for this section.

📖 **Interactive Reading and Notetaking Study Guide,** Chapter 12, Section 1 (Adapted Version also available.)

Monitor Progress

As students fill in the Notetaking Study Guide, circulate to make sure individuals understand the goals of the reform movements. Provide assistance as needed.

Preaching at a revival meeting

Thus, the religious revivals of the Second Great Awakening encouraged reform. People came to believe that, if they had the power to improve themselves, they could improve society as well.

Utopian Communities The desire to create a more perfect society spurred some reformers to found utopian communities. (*Utopia* was a book about a fictional ideal society.) Utopian reformers hoped their communities would become models for others to follow.

Robert Owen founded a utopian community in Indiana in 1825. He called this colony New Harmony. New Harmony was based on common ownership of property. Residents were to raise their own food and manufacture their own goods. However, New Harmony turned out to be anything but harmonious. Members argued among themselves about goals and actions. The colony dissolved after about two years. Indeed, most utopian communities did not last very long.

✓**Checkpoint** What was the goal of the Second Great Awakening?

Social Reformers at Work

Utopian reformers tried to create perfect, separate communities. However, most reform-minded Americans chose to work within the existing society. The reforming impulse took many forms.

The Temperance Movement Many reformers supported the temperance movement, an organized effort to end alcohol abuse and the problems created by it. Alcohol was widely used in the United States. Whiskey was cheaper than milk or beer. Often, it was safer to drink than water, which was frequently contaminated. As a result, alcohol abuse reached epidemic proportions.

Many women were drawn to the temperance movement. They pointed out how many women and children suffered at the hands of husbands and fathers who drank too much. Such organizations as the American Temperance Society published pamphlets denouncing "strong drink."

Most reformers favored temperance, or moderation in drinking. But others called for prohibition, a total ban on the sale and consumption of alcohol. During the 1850s, supporters of prohibition got nine states to pass laws banning the sale of alcohol. The movement was interrupted by the Civil War but reemerged later.

Prison Reform Other reformers sought to improve the nation's prison system. Prisons had traditionally been harsh places, designed to make people want to stay out of them. Poorly heated buildings, inadequate food, and cramped conditions were typical. Many people in prison were not criminals at all but were people who owed money they could not pay back. Because debtors could seldom earn money while in jail, they often remained locked up for years.

Differentiated Instruction

L3 Advanced Readers

American Utopias Have students research more information about one of the utopian communities of this era, such as New Harmony or the Oneida Community, and write a paragraph about that community. Be sure that students include information about who founded the community, what its goals and principles were, any special rules it had, how long it lasted, and why it dissolved. Ask students to share their findings with the class.

Answer

✓**Checkpoint** to encourage people to reform their lives

Chains and cages used on prisoners

Reforming Prison Conditions
The two drawings shown at left are from an 1858 magazine article about prison conditions. Such sights led Dorothea Dix (right) and other reformers to call for more humane treatment of prisoners.
Critical Thinking: Frame Questions *Based on these drawings, write two questions that you would ask Dorothea Dix to answer.*

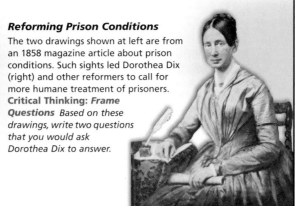

Dorothea Dix

Social reformers began investigating conditions in jails. Dorothea Dix, a Massachusetts schoolteacher, was one of those who took up the cause of prison reform. Over the years, she worked to convince state legislatures to build new, more sanitary, and more humane prisons. In addition, debtors were no longer sent to jail.

Reforms for the Mentally Ill Dix was outraged to find that prisons were also used to house individuals with mental illnesses. After a careful investigation, she reported to the Massachusetts legislature on the horrifying conditions she had witnessed: "A woman in a cage . . . [One man] losing the use of his limbs from want of exercise . . . One man and one woman chained."

Dix's shocking report helped persuade the Massachusetts legislature to fund a new mental hospital. She then continued her efforts in other states. She urged city and state governments around the country to create separate institutions, called asylums, for those with mental illnesses. The new asylums provided treatment, rather than punishment.

☑**Checkpoint** How did Dorothea Dix contribute to social reform?

Education Reform

Education was another area of concern to reformers. The first American schools were set up for religious purposes. The Puritans of Massachusetts believed that all people needed to be able to read and understand the Bible. In 1642, they passed a law requiring all large towns to hire teachers and build schools. In this way, Massachusetts set up the first public schools, or free schools supported by taxes.

Need for Better Education By the early 1800s, Massachusetts was still the only state to require public schools. In other states, children from wealthy families were educated privately, whereas poor children generally received no education outside the home. Under these circumstances, many Americans could not read or write.

History Background

Improvements in Mental Health Care Dorothea Dix was nearly 40 when she began teaching at a Boston-area jail. She found that many inmates were mentally ill, not criminals. Inspired to improve conditions for mentally ill people, she gave a report based on her survey of every prison in Massachusetts to the state legislature in 1843. It led to an expansion of the state mental hospital. In the next three years, Dix traveled 30,000 miles around the country inspecting prisons and reporting her findings. When she began, there were 13 hospitals for the mentally ill in the country. By 1880, there were 123, 32 of which Dix helped found.

Instruction (continued)

- In order to understand Horace Mann's achievements, have students complete the worksheet Horace Mann. Then have them discuss Mann's legacy.

  All in One Teaching Resources, Unit 4, Horace Mann, p. 50

- Discuss with students the status of education for African Americans at this time. (*Education was unavailable to many African Americans. Southern states prohibited teaching enslaved people to read. In the North, African American children were usually denied entry to the same schools white children attended, but African Americans were admitted to public schools in Massachusetts and attended some private colleges.*)

Independent Practice

Have students complete the study guide for this section.

Interactive Reading and Notetaking Study Guide, Chapter 12, Section 1 (Adapted Version also available.)

Monitor Progress

- As students complete the Notetaking Study Guide, circulate and make sure individuals understand the changes in American education.

- Tell students to fill in the last column of the Reading Readiness Guide. Ask them to evaluate whether what they learned was what they expected to learn.

  All in One Teaching Resources, Unit 4, Reading Readiness Guide, p. 46

- To further assess student understanding, use the Progress Monitoring Transparencies.

Progress Monitoring Transparencies, Chapter 12, Section 1

Answer

🔵 **Reading Skill** The source is credible, as Mann was the foremost education reformer of the time. He wanted children to be good citizens, develop their talents, and be educated.

Links Across Time

Public Education

1852 Massachusetts became the first state to pass a law that required all children to attend school up to a certain age. This was known as compulsory education.

1918 By this date, compulsory education laws had been passed in every state in the Union. As a result, for the first time, every state required children to attend school at least up to the tenth grade.

Link to Today 🔵 Online

Education Today Today, billions of dollars in federal, state, and local taxes go to support public education. But not everybody agrees on the best way to spend that money and to educate American children.

For: Education in the news
Visit: PHSchool.com
Web Code: myc-4081

Public school classroom, around 1920

The reforms of the Jacksonian Era increased the number of eligible voters. Reformers grew concerned that the education system was not keeping up with the political system. They argued that education was necessary to ensure that voters were intelligently informed. With immigration on the rise, reformers also pointed out that better schools would help immigrants assimilate, or become part of, American culture.

Mann and Public Education Horace Mann of Massachusetts took the lead in education reform. To Mann, public financing of education was essential for democracy to work. He said:

Assess Evidence for a Conclusion Read the quotation by Horace Mann. Assess the credibility of this source in supporting the following conclusion: Mann believed that strong character, moral behavior, and wide knowledge were equally important qualities. List three examples from the quotation that support this conclusion.

> ❝If we do not prepare children to become good citizens; if we do not develop their capacities, if we do not enrich their minds with knowledge . . . then our republic must go down to destruction as others have gone before it.❞
>
> —Horace Mann, quoted in *A Century of Childhood* (Heininger)

After becoming head of the state board of education in 1837, Mann convinced Massachusetts to improve its public school system. It created colleges to train teachers, raised the salaries of teachers, and lengthened the school year. (To learn more about public education in the 1800s, see the Life at the Time feature.)

Differentiated Instruction

L1 English Language Learners   **L1 Less Proficient Readers**   **L1 Special Needs**

Vocabulary Development Have students make a list of the key terms and high-use words. Then have them create flashcards with the word on one side and its definition on the other. Pair students and have them quiz each other on the definitions of the words using the flashcards. For English Language Learners, have students add pictures to go with the flashcards. Check their understanding as they continue to read the section.

Other states soon followed Massachusetts's example. By the 1850s, public schools had gained much acceptance in the Northeast. Southern and western states lagged behind, however. They would not create their own public school systems until many decades later.

Education for African Americans The improvements in public education did little for African Americans. Southern states prohibited teaching enslaved persons to read. In the North, free black children were seldom admitted to the same schools as white children.

Reformers who tried to improve educational opportunities for African Americans often met with resistance. Prudence Crandall, a Quaker teacher, opened a school for African American girls in Connecticut. Hostile neighbors attacked and destroyed the school.

Still, some opportunities did open up. In major northern cities, free African American educators opened their own schools. In 1855, Massachusetts became the first state to admit African American students to public schools. Some African Americans attended private colleges such as Harvard and Oberlin. In 1854, Pennsylvania chartered Ashmun Institute (later called Lincoln University), the nation's first college for African American men.

☑ **Checkpoint** How did public education improve in the mid-1800s?

⭐ **Looking Back and Ahead** Inspired by political or religious ideals, reformers tackled many social problems. But one issue towered above all others in the minds of reformers. In the next section, you will read about the growing efforts to end slavery.

Section 1 | Check Your Progress

Progress Monitoring Online
For: Self-test with instant help
Visit: PHSchool.com
Web Code: mya-4081

Comprehension and Critical Thinking
1. (a) **Identify** What were the ideas of predestination and the doctrine of free will?
(b) **Draw Conclusions** How might the doctrine of free will promote democracy?

2. (a) **Recall** Which reforms did Horace Mann convince the state of Massachusetts to make?
(b) **Detect Points of View** According to Mann, why is it important for a democracy to have educated citizens?

Reading Skill
3. **Assess Evidence for a Conclusion** Assess the quotation that follows by Dorothea Dix. Is the evidence reliable? Does it support the conclusion that the mentally ill were poorly treated?
Quotation: "[T]wo females . . . lie in wooden bunks filled with straw; always shut up. . . . The use of cages [is] all but universal."

Key Terms
Answer the following questions in complete sentences that show your understanding of the key terms.
4. What did the temperance movement seek?

5. What was the goal of social reform in the 1830s?
6. What is a religious revival?

Writing
7. A topic sentence sets the focus for a single paragraph. A thesis statement expresses a broader idea to be developed in an entire essay. Write three topic sentences for paragraphs that would support and develop the following thesis statement: A powerful reforming spirit swept through this country in the 1830s.

Section 1 Improving Society 419

Assess and Reteach

Assess Progress   L2
Have students complete Check Your Progress. Administer the Section Quiz.

All in One **Teaching Resources, Unit 4,** Section Quiz, p. 58

To further assess student understanding, use the Progress Monitoring Transparency.

Progress Monitoring Transparencies, Chapter 12, Section 1

Reteach   L1
If students need more instruction, have them read this section in the Interactive Reading and Notetaking Study Guide and complete the accompanying question.

📖 **Interactive Reading and Notetaking Study Guide,** Chapter 12, Section 1 (Adapted Version also available.)

Extend   L3
To extend the lesson, have students use the Internet to look up additional nineteenth-century reformers such as Mary Lyon, Samuel Gridley Howe, Bronson Alcott, and Lucy Stone and make a chart listing them, the cause(s) in which each was active, and their achievements. Have students share their work with the class. Provide students with the Web code below.

Extend Online
For: Help with this activity
Visit: PHSchool.com
Web Code: mye-0211

Progress Monitoring Online
Students may check their comprehension of this section by completing the Progress Monitoring Online graphic organizer and self-quiz.

Section 1 Check Your Progress

1. (a) predestination: belief that God decides the fate of a person's soul even before birth; doctrine of free will: people's actions determined their salvation
(b) Possible answer: If people believe that salvation comes from their own acts, they might pay more attention to their duties to others.

2. (a) create teacher colleges, increase teacher salaries, lengthen the school year

(b) Educated citizens participate in government and keep democracy alive.

3. Dorothea Dix inspected places where the mentally ill were kept, so what she says is reliable. The details she gives do support the conclusion.

4. The temperance movement tried to stop alcohol abuse.

5. The goal of social reform in the 1830s was to improve society.

6. A revival is a large religious meeting.

7. Possible topic sentences: Religious feelings and ideas sparked the reform spirit. The temperance movement wanted to improve society by ending alcohol abuse. Better education was another area of concern to the reformers.

Answer

☑ **Checkpoint** Public school systems and teacher colleges were established; African Americans were admitted to some schools and colleges.

Going to School

p. 420

Build Background Knowledge   L2

Have students recall the education reforms of Horace Mann. Ask: **Why were reformers such as Mann interested in expanding public education?** (*They believed it would make Americans better citizens.*) Then, ask: **What do you think early public schools were like?** (*Possible answer: Children of all grades went to school in the same classroom.*)

Instruction   L2

■ Read Life at the Time with students. Ask students to describe a one-room schoolhouse. (*Children of all ages were taught together. Most schools only went up to eighth grade. Students studied from McGuffey's Eclectic Readers, wrote on chalk slates, and recited lessons when their teacher called on them.*)

■ Ask: **What was discipline like in early classrooms?** (*Discipline was strict. Students were often punished or rewarded based on how well they learned their lessons.*) Ask: **How is this different from modern schools?** (*Possible answers: Students today do not have to wear dunce caps. Students who misbehave today might get detention or be sent to the principal's office. Today, students' work is graded.*)

■ Encourage students to draw inferences about the moral lessons in *McGuffey's Eclectic Readers*. Remind students of Horace Mann's reasons for promoting education. Ask: **Why do you think textbooks in the 1800s taught moral lessons as well as the "three Rs"?** Elicit that learning about character and values, as well as to read and write, was seen as an important part of becoming a good citizen.

Going to School

Following the lead of Massachusetts, other states in the North began to fund public schools. Not all children were able to attend school, and most of those who did only got as far as the eighth grade. What were these early American classrooms like?

The Classroom

Schools in the early 1800s were not like the large public buildings we know today. In rural areas especially, many children went to one-room schoolhouses, where children of all ages were taught together. Students wrote on chalk slates and were expected to recite their lessons when called upon by the teacher.

History *Interactive*
Explore an Early American Classroom
Visit: PHSchool.com
Web Code: myp-4081

Differentiated Instruction

L1 English Language Learners   **L1** Special Needs

Picturing a One-Room Schoolhouse
Have students work in groups to list unique items that might be found in a one-room schoolhouse, such as a dunce cap or a *McGuffey's Eclectic Reader*. Then have them make a poster showing a class in a one-room schoolhouse. Have them label the objects from their lists. Display the finished posters in the classroom.

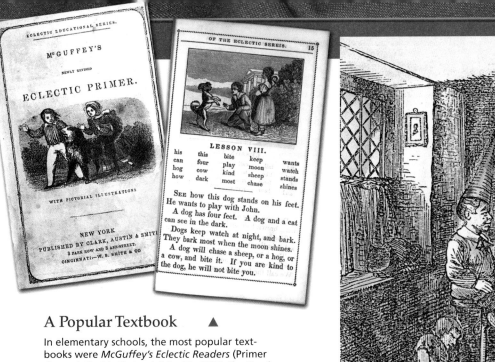

A Popular Textbook ▲

In elementary schools, the most popular text-books were *McGuffey's Eclectic Readers* (Primer through Sixth). First published in 1836, the Readers offered moral lessons along with the "three Rs"—reading, 'riting, and 'rithmetic. The lesson shown above was used to teach children how to read and how to treat pets.

Rewards and Punishments ▶

Discipline was strict in early classrooms. Students who failed to learn their lessons might have to sit in a corner wearing a "dunce cap" (right). But there were also rewards. Students might get certificates for learning their lesson well, for good behavior, or just for coming to school on time (below).

▼

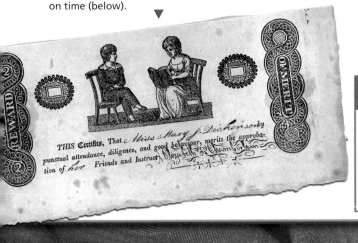

Analyze LIFE AT THE TIME

Look at the pages from *McGuffey's Eclectic Primer* shown at the top of this page. Then, write a lesson for the Primer about the importance of going to school. Use simple language that can be understood by elementary school students.

Independent Practice
Have students complete the History Interactive activity online.

Extend ● Online
For: Help in starting the History Interactive
Visit: PHSchool.com
Web Code: myp-4081

Monitor Progress

Ask students to complete the Analyze Life at the Time activity. Circulate to make sure individuals understand nineteenth-century education.

Writing Rubric

Score 1 Lesson is inappropriate or unrelated to the task.
Score 2 Lesson is sparse or confusing.
Score 3 Lesson is logical, shows understanding of task.
Score 4 Lesson is logical, creative, and well thought out.

History Background

A Modern One-Room Schoolhouse Most one-room schoolhouses were replaced by larger schools by the mid-twentieth century, but Granville Village School in Vermont remains in use today. Since its founding in 1857, however, the school has undergone a number of changes. Today, it goes only through the fourth grade and has expanded to two classes: one for first- and second-graders and one for third- and fourth-graders. As in most modern schools, there are computers in the classroom, and specialists teach subjects such as art. Despite these modernizations, the Granville Village School is proud to continue its one-room heritage.

Answer

Analyze **LIFE AT THE TIME** Lessons will vary but should be written in simple language and should show a clear understanding of the increasing value placed on education in the mid-1800s.

Review and Preview

Students have studied how reformers worked to end many problems in society. Now they will read how this reform effort focused on ending slavery.

Section Focus Question

How did abolitionists try to end slavery?

Before you begin the lesson for the day, write the Section Focus Question on the board. (*Lesson focus: Abolitionists used many different methods, including publishing books, newspapers, and pamphlets; holding rallies; and helping enslaved people escape. Former slaves shared their experiences, and a colony for free African Americans was started in Liberia. Politicians spoke against slavery in Congress.*)

Prepare to Read

Build Background Knowledge   L2

In this section, students will learn about the struggles to end slavery in the mid-1800s. Discuss with students why slavery was a target of reform in this period. Use the Idea Wave strategy (TE, p. T24) to elicit student ideas.

Set a Purpose   L2

■ Read each statement in the Reading Readiness Guide aloud. Ask students to mark the statements True or False.

   All in One Teaching Resources, Unit 4, Reading Readiness Guide, p. 47

■ Have students discuss the statements in pairs or groups of four, then mark their worksheets again. Use the Numbered Heads strategy (TE, p. T24) to call on students to share their group's perspectives. The students will return to these worksheets later.

Answer

✓Checkpoint Northern states began to make it illegal after the Revolution. By the end of 1804, every northern state had ended or pledged to end slavery.

An Abolitionist's Plea
❝Cease to oppress. . . . Bind him no longer by the cords of slavery, but with those of kindness and brotherly love.❞

—John Greenleaf Whittier, 1833 pamphlet opposing slavery

◀ Rioters destroy an abolitionist's press.

The Fight Against Slavery

Objectives
- Describe efforts in the North to end slavery.
- Discuss the contributions of William Lloyd Garrison, Frederick Douglass, and other abolitionists.
- Describe the purpose and risks of the Underground Railroad.
- Explain why many people in the North and South defended slavery.

🔄 Reading Skill

Form an Opinion Based on Evidence You can use details and evidence in primary and secondary sources to help you form opinions about history. Remember that primary sources come from people who saw or experienced events, whereas secondary sources (such as this textbook) build on many sources to recount historical information.

Key Terms and People

abolitionist
William Lloyd Garrison

Frederick Douglass
Harriet Tubman

Why It Matters Since colonial times, some Americans had opposed the enslavement of people. They condemned slavery on religious and moral grounds. In the mid-1800s, the reforming spirit spurred a vigorous new effort to end slavery.

❓ **Section Focus Question: How did abolitionists try to end slavery?**

Roots of the Antislavery Movement

A number of prominent leaders of the early republic, such as Alexander Hamilton and Benjamin Franklin, opposed slavery. They believed that slavery violated the most basic principle of the Declaration of Independence, "that all men are created equal."

Slavery Ends in the North In 1780, Pennsylvania became the first state to pass a law that gradually eliminated slavery. By 1804, every northern state had ended or pledged to end slavery. Congress also outlawed slavery in the Northwest Territory. As a result, when Ohio entered the Union in 1803, it became the first state to ban slavery in its state constitution.

The Colonization Movement The American Colonization Society, established in 1817, was an early antislavery organization. This society proposed that slaves be freed gradually and transported to Liberia, a colony founded in 1822 on the west coast of Africa.

The colonization movement did not work. Most enslaved people had grown up in the United States and did not desire to leave. By 1830 only about 1,400 African Americans had migrated to Liberia.

✓Checkpoint **How did slavery end in the North?**

Differentiated Instruction

L1 Less Proficient Readers   **L1 Special Needs**

Comprehension Aid Before reading the section, have students go through it and write down each heading to create an outline. As they read, have them jot down important words, concepts, or people they want to remember or questions they may have about the content under each heading. Check with students to see what questions they have. Encourage them to try to answer them on their own before asking for help from you.

Growing Opposition to Slavery

The Second Great Awakening inspired further opposition to slavery. Many people were influenced by the preaching of Charles Finney, who condemned slavery. By the mid-1800s, a small but growing number of people were abolitionists, reformers who wanted to abolish, or end, slavery. Rejecting gradual emancipation, abolitionists called for a complete and immediate end to slavery.

Garrison One of the most forceful voices for abolition was William Lloyd Garrison. A Quaker, he strongly opposed the use of violence to end slavery. Still, Garrison was more <u>radical</u> than many others, because he favored full political rights for all African Americans.

In 1831, Garrison launched an abolitionist newspaper, the *Liberator*. It became the nation's leading antislavery publication for 34 years, ending only when slavery itself ended.

Garrison cofounded the New England Anti-Slavery Society, which later became the American Anti-Slavery Society. Leaders of this group included Theodore Weld, a minister who had been a pupil of Charles Finney. Weld brought the zeal of a religious revival to antislavery rallies. Other members included Sarah and Angelina Grimke, daughters of a South Carolina slaveholder.

African American Abolitionists Prominent African Americans in the North took a leading role in the abolitionist movement. In 1829, David Walker published his *Appeal: to the Coloured Citizens of the World*. This strongly worded pamphlet urged enslaved people to rebel, if necessary, to gain their freedom.

Vocabulary Builder
radical (RAD ih kul) *adj.* favoring extreme change

The Liberator

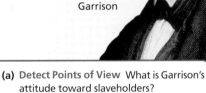

"Let Southern oppressors tremble—let all the enemies of the persecuted blacks tremble. . . . On this subject, I do not wish to think, or to speak, or write, with moderation. No! No! Tell a man whose house is on fire to give a moderate alarm . . . but urge me not to use moderation in a cause like the present. I am in earnest—I will not equivocate—I will not excuse—I will not retreat a single inch—AND I WILL BE HEARD."

—William Lloyd Garrison, *Liberator*, January 1831

William Lloyd Garrison

Reading Primary Sources
Skills Activity

In the above excerpt from the first issue of the *Liberator*, William Lloyd Garrison vows to take a firm stand against slavery.

(a) Detect Points of View What is Garrison's attitude toward slaveholders?

(b) Draw Conclusions What does Garrison mean when he writes, "Tell a man whose house is on fire to give a moderate alarm"?

Vocabulary Builder

Use the information below to teach students this section's high-use words.

High-Use Word	Definition and Sample Sentence
radical, p. 423	*adj.* favoring extreme change The signing of the Declaration of Independence was seen as a **radical** act by the English Parliament.
via, p. 424	*prep.* by way of Settlers went west **via** the Great Wagon Road.

The Underground Railroad

Opposing Abolition

pp. 425–426

Instruction

- With students, read The Underground Railroad and Opposing Abolition. Remind students to look for details that answer the reading Checkpoint question.

- Ask students how the Underground Railroad worked. (*Leaders called "conductors" led enslaved people trying to escape from one "station" to the next.*)

- Discuss Harriet Tubman's role in the Underground Railroad. Ask: **Why was Harriet Tubman nicknamed the "Black Moses"?** (*Possible answer: Like Moses in the Bible, Harriet Tubman helped lead her people out of slavery.*)

- Ask: **How did supporters of slavery fight abolition?** (*with violence, by claiming that slaves were better off than northern factory workers, and by passing a "gag rule" in Congress that prevented discussion of antislavery petitions*)

- Discuss with students how reliance on cotton in the North and South helped keep slavery alive. (*Possible answer: The free labor from slavery helped both regions make money from cotton.*)

Answers

 Reading Skill Answers will vary, but should be supported by details from the quote.

☑ **Checkpoint** He made public speeches describing his experiences as a slave and published the abolitionist newspaper *The North Star.*

 Form an Opinion Based on Evidence
What is your opinion of Frederick Douglass's speech? Do you think it was an effective statement against slavery? Use evidence to support your opinion.

Antislavery medallion

Vocabulary Builder
via (VEE ah) *prep.* by way of

Perhaps the most powerful speaker for abolitionism was Frederick Douglass. Born into slavery, Douglass had broken the law by learning to read. He later escaped to freedom in the North. Garrison and other abolitionists encouraged Douglass to describe his experiences at antislavery rallies. Douglass told one crowd:

> ❝I appear this evening as a thief and a robber. I stole this head, these limbs, this body from my master, and ran off with them.❞
>
> —Frederick Douglass, speech, 1842

By appearing in public, Douglass risked being sent back into slavery. Yet, he continued to speak before larger and larger audiences. He also published his own antislavery newspaper, the *North Star.*

A Former President Takes a Stand Abolitionists won the support of a few powerful people. Former President John Quincy Adams, now a member of Congress, read antislavery petitions from the floor of the House of Representatives. In 1839, Adams proposed a constitutional amendment that would ban slavery in any new state joining the Union. However, the amendment was not passed.

Two years later, Adams made a dramatic stand against slavery. Captive Africans aboard the slave ship *Amistad* had rebelled, killing the captain and ordering the crew to sail back to Africa. Instead, the crew sailed the ship to America. The 73-year-old Adams spoke to the Supreme Court for nine hours and helped the captives regain their freedom.

☑ **Checkpoint** What role did Frederick Douglass play in the abolitionist movement?

The Underground Railroad

Some courageous abolitionists dedicated themselves to helping people escape from slavery. They established a system known as the Underground Railroad. Despite its name, it was neither underground nor a railroad. It was a network of people—black and white, northerners and southerners—who secretly helped slaves reach freedom.

Working for the Underground Railroad was illegal and dangerous. "Conductors" led fugitive slaves from one "station" to the next. Stations were usually the homes of abolitionists, but might be churches or caves. Supporters helped by donating clothing, food, and money to pay for passage on trains and boats. Many people risked their lives to help runaway slaves. Levi Coffin, an Indiana Quaker, assisted more than 3,000 fugitives.

Harriet Tubman, who had herself escaped from slavery, escorted more than 300 people to freedom via the Underground Railroad. Tubman was nicknamed the Black Moses after the biblical leader who led the Israelites out of slavery in Egypt. She proudly told Frederick Douglass that, in 19 trips to the South, she "never lost a single passenger." Slave owners promised a $40,000 reward for her capture.

Differentiated Instruction

English Language Learners   **Special Needs**

The Underground Railroad To help students understand the extent and activities of the Underground Railroad, assign the worksheet The Underground Railroad after the class has read the section but before you begin the class discussion. Make sure students understand that the routes went from south to north. Have students add arrows pointing north to the routes on the map to clarify. Ask students to describe some of the routes in the Underground Railroad for the class.

All in One Teaching Resources, The Underground Railroad, p. 54

● INFOGRAPHIC
The UNDERGROUND RAILROAD

As many as 50,000 African Americans escaped from slavery in the South to freedom in the North or in Canada via the Underground Railroad.
Critical Thinking: *Identify Costs and Benefits* What were the risks of helping fugitive slaves escape? Why do you think conductors on the Underground Railroad chose to take those risks?

Discovery SCHOOL

Explore More Video
To learn more about how African Americans escaped slavery, view the video.

This song contained ▶ directions for escaping slaves. The "drinking gourd" is the Big Dipper.

"The riverbank makes a very good road.
The dead trees will show you the way.
Left foot, peg foot, traveling on,
If you follow the drinking gourd."

KEY
→ RAILROAD ROUTES
▢ FREE STATES
▢ SLAVE STATES
▢ TERRITORIES

Harriet Tubman, the ▶ most famous conductor on the Underground Railroad

---

🌐 Explore More Video

Discovery School Video
The Underground Railroad This video looks at the network of people who helped enslaved African Americans escape to the North—and freedom—in the years before the Civil War. It explains the coded words used by participants in the Underground Railroad to hide their actions and highlights the activities of abolitionists Thomas Garrett and Harriet Tubman, who had herself escaped from slavery.

Independent Practice
Have students complete the study guide for this section.

📖 **Interactive Reading and Notetaking Study Guide,** Chapter 12, Section 2 (Adapted Version also available.)

Monitor Progress

■ As students complete their work on the Notetaking Study Guide, circulate to make sure individuals understand the Underground Railroad and the forces abolitionists had to fight.

■ Tell students to fill in the last column of the Reading Readiness Guide. Probe for what they learned that confirms or invalidates each statement.

All in One Teaching Resources, Unit 4, Reading Readiness Guide, p. 47

History Background

L3 Advanced Readers   **L3 Gifted and Talented**

Harriet Tubman Have students visit the library to locate a copy of the biography *Harriet Tubman: Guide to Freedom,* by Ann Petry. After reading, have students use what they learned to make a timeline of important events in Tubman's life. Ask them to share how she was influenced by some of these key events.

Answer
Identify Costs and Benefits People helping slaves escape risked being arrested or killed. They believed it was the right thing to do.

Assess and Reteach

Assess Progress　L2

Have students complete Check Your Progress. Administer the Section Quiz.

All in One Teaching Resources, Unit 4, Section Quiz, p. 59

To further assess student understanding, use the Progress Monitoring Transparency.

Progress Monitoring Transparencies, Chapter 12, Section 2

Reteach　L1

If students need more instruction, have them read this section in the Interactive Reading and Notetaking Study Guide and complete the accompanying question.

Interactive Reading and Notetaking Study Guide, Chapter 12, Section 2 (Adapted Version also available.)

Extend　L3

To extend the lesson, have students use the Internet to research the antislavery movement. Then have students create antislavery posters based on the ideas and techniques of abolitionists. Provide students with the Web code below.

Extend Online
For: Help in starting the activity
Visit: PHSchool.com
Web Code: mye-0212

Progress Monitoring Online

Students may check their comprehension of this section by completing the Progress Monitoring Online graphic organizer and self-quiz.

Answers

☑**Checkpoint** "Conductors" led escaped people to "stations" along the way to freedom.

☑**Checkpoint** They depended on cotton produced by slave labor.

Each year, hundreds of slaves moved along the Underground Railroad to freedom in the North or in Canada. In total, perhaps as many as 50,000 gained their freedom in this way.

☑**Checkpoint** How did the Underground Railroad work?

Opposing Abolition

Abolitionists faced powerful obstacles in the North as well as in the South. Many northerners profited from the existence of slavery. Northern textile mill owners and merchants relied on the cotton produced by southern slave labor. Northern workers feared that freed slaves might come north and take their jobs.

Such fears sometimes prompted violence against abolitionists. Mobs attacked antislavery meetings. In 1835, William Lloyd Garrison was dragged through the streets of Boston with a rope around his neck.

As you have read, southerners had long defended slavery as a positive force. Now, as support for abolition grew louder, they went on the offensive. The state of Georgia offered a $5,000 reward for the arrest and conviction for libel of William Lloyd Garrison. Southerners in Congress won passage of a "gag rule" that blocked discussion of antislavery petitions. John Quincy Adams unsuccessfully fought for repeal of the gag rule.

☑**Checkpoint** Why did some northerners oppose abolition?

⭐ **Looking Back and Ahead** By the 1840s, the North and the South were increasingly divided by the issue of slavery. Abolitionists succeeded in making converts in the North. Slavery was spreading along with the cotton boom in the South.

Progress Monitoring Online
For: Self-test with instant help
Visit: PHSchool.com
Web Code: mya-4082

Section 2 | Check Your Progress

Comprehension and Critical Thinking

1. (a) List What solutions did the American Colonization Society propose to end slavery?
(b) Explain Problems Why did most African Americans reject the society's goals?

2. (a) Identify Which groups in the North were opposed to abolition? Why?
(b) Identify Alternatives How might the concerns of these groups have been calmed?

Reading Skill

3. Form an Opinion Based on Evidence Henry Brown mailed himself to freedom in a crate. What do you think was important to him? Use evidence quoted from his own narrative to form your opinion: "I was . . . placed on my head. . . . In this dreadful position, I remained the space of an hour and a half . . . my eyes were almost swollen out of their sockets, and the veins on my temples seemed ready to burst. I made no noise, however, determining to obtain 'victory or death.'"

Key Terms

4. Write two definitions for the key term abolitionist. First, write a formal definition for your teacher. Second, write a definition in everyday English for a classmate.

Writing

5. Choose three details from Section 2 that support the topic sentence that follows. Then, write a paragraph developing the topic based on these details. **Topic sentence:** Abolitionists used a variety of tactics to oppose slavery.

Section 2 Check Your Progress

1. (a) that enslaved people be gradually freed and transported to Liberia
(b) Most of them were born in the United States and did not want to leave.

2. (a) mill owners who depended on cotton produced with slave labor; workers who feared that formerly enslaved people would compete for their jobs
(b) if the price of cotton stayed low, the supply stayed high, and freed African Americans did not compete for northern workers' jobs

3. It was vital to him that he get to a place where he could be free.

4. formal: a reformer who wanted to abolish, or end, slavery; informal: someone who worked to end slavery

5. Answers will vary but should discuss specific abolitionist actions.

The Improvement of Women

❝As a general rule, men do not desire the improvement of women. . . . As *they* have determined that Jehovah has placed woman on a lower platform than man, they of course wish to keep her there; and hence the noble faculties of our minds are crushed, and our reasoning powers are almost wholly uncultivated. . . . ❞

—Sarah Grimke, protesting against poor educational opportunities, 1838

◀ Statue of women's rights leaders (from left) Lucretia Mott, Susan B. Anthony, and Elizabeth Cady Stanton

A Call for Women's Rights

Objectives
- Explain how the women's suffrage movement began.
- Describe the goals of the Seneca Falls Convention in 1848.
- Identify the new opportunities that women gained in the mid-1800s.

🔲 Reading Skill

State the Meaning of Evidence One way to draw conclusions from source material is to make a statement about the meaning of the evidence. This statement will be a conclusion drawn from the details of the evidence. Your statement should use your own words, fit with all the details, and make sense to you.

Key Terms and People

Sojourner Truth
Lucretia Mott
Elizabeth Cady Stanton

women's suffrage
women's rights movement
Susan B. Anthony

Why It Matters Women participated in abolitionism and other reform efforts. Some women activists also began to focus on equal rights for themselves. They hoped to win the right to vote as well as other advances.

❓ **Section Focus Question: How did the women's suffrage movement begin?**

The Struggle Begins

In 1820, the rights of American women were limited. They could not vote, serve on juries, attend college, or enter such professions as medicine or law. Married women could not own property or keep their own wages. Most Americans—both men and women—believed that a woman's place was in the private world of the home.

Women who were active in abolition or other social reform movements believed that they had important contributions to make to American society. They began to demand rights as equal citizens. Among these women was Sojourner Truth. Born into slavery in New York State, she was illiterate, but her words inspired the crowds that heard her. Truth became a powerful voice on behalf of both enslaved African Americans and women.

Lucretia Mott, a Quaker, had spent years working in the antislavery movement. Quakers allowed women to take public roles that other religions prohibited. Mott thus had organizing skills and public speaking experience that most women of her day did not.

☑**Checkpoint** Why did some reformers turn to the issue of women's rights?

Section 3 A Call for Women's Rights **427**

Vocabulary Builder

Use the information below to teach students this section's high-use words.

High-Use Word	Definition and Sample Sentence
exclude, p. 428	*v.* to keep out or expel; to reject Most colleges at that time **excluded** women and African Americans.
ally, p. 429	*n.* a person joined with another for a common purpose France became America's **ally** during the Revolution.

Review and Preview

Students have discussed how the abolitionist movement began. Now they will read about the beginnings of the women's suffrage movement.

Section Focus Question

How did the women's suffrage movement begin?

Before you begin the lesson for the day, write the Section Focus Question on the board. (*Lesson focus: When women became involved in reform movements, limits on their participation led some women to feel that they needed to work for equal rights for themselves, including the right to vote.*)

Prepare to Read

Build Background Knowledge L2

Tell students that in this section they will learn how the struggle for women's rights began. Remind students about the reform movements they studied in Sections 1 and 2. Ask: **How could the work of women reformers cause them to desire more rights?** (*Possible answer: Women working for rights for others began to consider their own lack of rights.*) Use the Idea Wave strategy (TE, p. T24) to elicit student responses.

Set a Purpose L2

- Read each statement in the Reading Readiness Guide aloud. Ask students to mark the statements True or False.

  All in One Teaching Resources, Unit 4, Reading Readiness Guide, p. 48

- Have students discuss the statements in pairs or groups of four, then mark their worksheets again. Use the Numbered Heads strategy (TE, p. T24) to call on students to share their group's perspectives. The students will return to these worksheets later.

Answer

☑**Checkpoint** Women were excluded from active participation in other reform movements and saw their own need for equal rights.

Chapter 12 Section 3 **427**

Teach

The Struggle Begins
Seneca Falls Convention

pp. 427–428

Instruction `L2`

- **Vocabulary Builder** Before teaching this section, preteach the High-Use Word **exclude** and **ally** using the strategy on p. T21.

  Key Terms Have students continue to fill in the See It–Remember It chart for the Key Terms in this chapter.

- Read The Struggle Begins and Seneca Falls Convention using the Paragraph Shrinking method (TE, p. T23).

- Ask: **What two women began to organize the women's rights movement after not being allowed to participate in a conference on abolition?** (*Elizabeth Cady Stanton and Lucretia Mott*)

- Have students complete the worksheet The Declaration of Sentiments. Have students discuss changes in women's rights since 1848.

  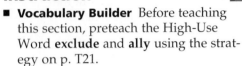 **Teaching Resources,** The Declaration of Sentiments, p. 55

- Display the transparency Are Not the Women Half the Nation? Use the questions to guide the discussion.

  Color Transparencies, Are Not the Women Half the Nation?

Independent Practice

Have students begin filling in the study guide for this section.

Monitor Progress

As students fill in the Notetaking Study Guide, circulate to make sure individuals understand the beginning of the women's rights movement.

Answers

Biography Quest Elizabeth Cady Stanton's wedding ceremony was unusual for its day because she did not promise to "obey" her husband in her vows.

☑**Checkpoint** to list the rights that the Seneca Falls Convention was demanding for women

---

Seneca Falls Convention

In 1840, Mott traveled to London to attend an international anti-slavery convention. There, she met another abolitionist, Elizabeth Cady Stanton. Stanton was honeymooning in London with her husband, a delegate to the conference. But when Mott and Stanton tried to attend a meeting, they were told that women were not permitted to take an active role in the proceedings.

Mott and Stanton were infuriated at being excluded. Sitting outside the convention hall, they agreed on the need for a convention to advance women's rights. They followed through on that idea in the summer of 1848. Their convention met in Seneca Falls, New York, "to discuss the social, civil, and religious rights of women." The Seneca Falls Convention attracted over 300 men and women.

Declaration of Sentiments Stanton wrote a Declaration of Sentiments, modeled on the Declaration of Independence. It began, "We hold these truths to be self-evident: that all men and women are created equal. . . ." The declaration then listed injustices women suffered, including being shut out from educational opportunities and good jobs. The Declaration of Sentiments demanded full equality for women in every area of life.

Like the colonial Patriots, Stanton opposed "taxation without representation." In a speech just before the convention, she declared:

> ❝[W]e are assembled to protest against a form of government existing without the consent of the governed—to declare our right to be free as man is free, to be represented in the government which we are taxed to support.❞
>
> —Elizabeth Cady Stanton, speech, July 19, 1848

Call for Suffrage Stanton's argument was the beginning of the long battle for women's suffrage, or the right of women to vote. However, not all of the delegates agreed when Stanton included a call for women's suffrage in the Declaration of Sentiments. Some, such as Frederick Douglass, strongly supported it. Others, including Lucretia Mott, feared that the call for women's suffrage would be so controversial that it would harm their other causes. Still, the convention narrowly voted to support the demand for women's suffrage.

☑**Checkpoint** What was the purpose of the Declaration of Sentiments?

Vocabulary Builder
exclude (ehks KLYOOD) **v.** to keep out or expel; to reject

Biography Quest

Elizabeth Cady Stanton
1815–1902

With seven children to care for, Elizabeth Cady Stanton still found time to try to change the world. She began her long political partnership with Susan B. Anthony in 1851. For much of the next 50 years, the two women pooled their talents to try to win women the right to vote. "[I am] a fine writer," Stanton noted. "Miss Anthony is a thorough manager." Sadly, Stanton died 18 years before women finally won the vote.

Biography Quest **Online**

Why was Stanton's wedding ceremony unusual for its day?

For: The answer to the question about Stanton

Visit: PHSchool.com

Web Code: myd-4083

Differentiated Instruction

L1 English Language Learners **L1 Less Proficient Readers** **L1 Special Needs**

Gaining Comprehension Have students read the text of Seneca Falls Convention as they listen to the Student Edition on Audio CD. Create exit cards for the students to complete at the end of the tape. The cards will read "What I learned about _____" or "It made me feel _____." Review their responses. Students can be provided a copy of the CD to work independently at home or in the school Resource Center.

🔊 **Student Edition on Audio CD,** Chapter 12, Section 3

New Opportunities for Women

The Seneca Falls Convention launched the women's rights movement in the United States. The women's rights movement was an organized effort to improve the political, legal, and economic status of women in American society.

Political Victories In the years after the Seneca Falls Convention, Susan B. Anthony became a close ally of Stanton. The two made a dynamic team. As an unmarried woman, Anthony was free to travel and devote herself to reform work. Stanton, the mother of a growing family, more often wrote speeches from her home. Together, they founded the National Woman Suffrage Association in 1869.

The fight for women's suffrage made little progress at first. Yet the women's rights movement won some victories. In 1860, Stanton and Anthony convinced New York to pass a law protecting women's property rights. Many other states followed. Some states revised their laws to allow married women to keep their wages.

Education for Women The women's rights movement focused much attention on education. American schools emphasized education for boys, who would grow up to be voters, citizens, and professionals. Girls seldom studied advanced subjects like math and science.

Even before the Seneca Falls Convention, reformers worked to give girls a chance for a better education. In 1821, Emma Willard started an academy in Troy, New York, that soon became the model for girls' schools everywhere. The Troy Female Seminary attracted the daughters of lawyers and doctors. The first year, 90 students enrolled. By 1831, the seminary had more than 300 students. Many female reformers of this era attended Willard's school.

Mary Lyon began an even bolder experiment when she opened Mount Holyoke Female Seminary in Massachusetts, in 1837. Lyon did not call her school a college. However, Mount Holyoke was, in fact, the first college for women in the United States. The school showed that women could indeed learn subjects like Latin, geometry, and chemistry.

Vocabulary Builder
ally (AL ī) **n.** a person joined with another for a common purpose

Cause and Effect

CAUSES
- Women could not vote, serve on juries, own property, or divorce abusive husbands.
- Many abolitionists believed that women also deserved equal rights.
- Women were denied equal educational opportunities.
- Seneca Falls Convention launched the women's rights movement.

THE WOMEN'S RIGHTS MOVEMENT

EFFECTS
- Suffragist movement demanded that women get the right to vote.
- States passed laws that protected women's property rights.
- Private schools for women opened, and some colleges accepted women as students.
- Women entered careers once closed to them.

Reading Charts
Skills Activity

The Seneca Falls Convention marked the start of an organized women's rights movement in the United States.

(a) Read a Chart Identify two effects of the women's rights movement.

(b) Analyze Cause and Effect Why is the abolition movement shown as a cause of the women's rights movement?

New Opportunities for Women
p. 429

Instruction

- With students, read New Opportunities for Women. Remind students to look for causes and effects.

- Ask: **What did the leaders in women's education accomplish?** (*Emma Willard opened a girls' school; Mary Lyon started the first college for women.*)

- Ask: **How could education be a key to improving women's rights?** (*Possible answer: An educated woman could use her knowledge to argue for her rights. An education could lead to career opportunities.*)

Independent Practice

Have students complete the study guide for this section.

Monitor Progress

- As students complete the Notetaking Study Guide, circulate to make sure they understand the vital role of women's education.

- Tell students to fill in the last column of the Reading Readiness Guide. Ask them to evaluate whether what they learned was what they had expected to learn.

- **All in One Teaching Resources, Unit 4,** Reading Readiness Guide, p. 48

- To further assess student understanding, use the Progress Monitoring Transparencies.

Progress Monitoring Transparencies, Chapter 12, Section 3

Differentiated Instruction

L3 Advanced Readers   **L3 Gifted and Talented**

Writing an Editorial Students may have the misconception that the vast majority of women supported the suffrage movement. In reality, the feminist activists did not attract broad support. Many women claimed winning suffrage would destroy the family. Have students research the arguments of the antisuffrage movement in the 1800s. Have them write letters to the editor giving this point of view. Remind them to use the arguments nineteenth-century readers would find convincing. Have several students read their letters to the class.

Answers

Reading Charts **(a)** Accept any two of the following: The suffragist movement demanded that women get the right to vote; states passed laws that protected women's property rights; private schools for women opened, and some colleges began to accept women students; and women entered careers once closed to them. **(b)** because many abolitionists advocated equal rights for women

Assess and Reteach

Assess Progress [L2]

Have students complete Check Your Progress. Administer the Section Quiz.

All in One **Teaching Resources, Unit 4,** Section Quiz, p. 60

To further assess student understanding, use the Progress Monitoring Transparency.

Progress Monitoring Transparencies, Chapter 12, Section 3

Reteach [L1]

If students need more instruction, have them read this section in the Interactive Reading and Notetaking Study Guide and complete the accompanying question.

Interactive Reading and Notetaking Study Guide, Chapter 12, Section 3 (Adapted Version also available.)

Extend [L3]

To extend the lesson, have students use the Internet to find out more about one of the women mentioned in Section 3. Using what they have learned, have them create a large concept web to profile the beliefs and achievements of the person. Have students use their concept webs to share a few facts about the person with the class. Provide students with the Web code below.

> Extend Online
> **For:** Help in starting the Extend activity
> **Visit:** PHSchool.com
> **Web Code:** mye-0213

Progress Monitoring Online

Students may check their comprehension of this section by completing the Progress Monitoring Online graphic organizer and self-quiz.

Answers

Reading Skill Possible answer: There was a great demand for the new women's schools.

Checkpoint Possible answers: The first college for women, Mount Holyoke, was established in 1837; women began to become teachers, journalists, and scientists.

Reading Skill **State the Meaning of Evidence** Make a general statement that is supported by the evidence in these three paragraphs.

Maria Mitchell (left) at her telescope

New Careers Gradually, American society came to accept that girls could be educated and that women could be teachers. More and more schools began hiring women teachers who had been trained at one of the new academies or colleges for women. Some women began trying to enter other professions as well.

Margaret Fuller made a career as a journalist, scholar, and literary critic. She spoke in public for pay at a time when it was illegal for women to do so. In 1845, Fuller published an influential book, *Women in the Nineteenth Century.* "We would have every . . . barrier thrown down. We would have every path laid open to Woman as freely as to Man," she wrote.

Other women excelled in science. Elizabeth Blackwell was admitted to Geneva Medical College in New York. Blackwell graduated first in her class in January 1849, becoming the first woman to graduate from an American medical school. The astronomer Maria Mitchell was the first professor hired at Vassar College. She was also the first woman elected to the American Academy of Arts and Sciences in 1848. A crater on the moon was later named in her honor.

✓Checkpoint Give two examples of advances in education for women.

⭐ **Looking Back and Ahead** The delegates at the Seneca Falls Convention hesitated to demand women's suffrage. As it turned out, getting the vote was a long struggle. Not until 1920 did a constitutional amendment guarantee women's right to vote. You will read more about the women's suffrage movement in a later chapter.

> **Progress Monitoring** Online
> **For:** Self-test with instant help
> **Visit:** PHSchool.com
> **Web Code:** mya-4083

Section 3 | Check Your Progress

Comprehension and Critical Thinking

1. (a) Summarize What were the goals of the women's rights movement?
(b) Compare and Contrast How were the goals of the women's rights movement similar to and different from those of the abolitionist movement?

2. (a) Recall Why was it considered more important for boys to get a good education than girls in the early 1800s?
(b) Explain Problems How did the lack of equal educational opportunities hurt women?

Reading Skill

3. State the Meaning of Evidence Make a statement about public views regarding women in politics, and then support it with the evidence in this paragraph: "Hers is the domestic altar; there she ministers and commands . . .; let her not seek madly to descend from this eminence to mix with the strife and ambition of the cares of government; the field of politics is not her appropriate arena."

Key Terms

Read each sentence below. If the sentence is true, write YES and explain why. If the sentence is not true, write NO and explain why not.
4. Supporters of women's suffrage opposed the right to vote.
5. The Seneca Falls Convention marked the start of the women's rights movement.

Writing

6. Imagine that you are a reporter in 1848 writing an article about the Seneca Falls Convention. Write a few sentences explaining why the convention met. Then, predict what might be the long-term effects of the convention.

Section 3 Check Your Progress

1. (a) to achieve equal rights for women
(b) The first goal of the abolitionist movement was to end slavery. Both the women's rights movement and abolitionists also wanted to expand the rights to vote, own property, and take part in society.

2. (a) Men were educated to earn a living and vote.
(b) Women could not hold professional jobs or gain respect in a society controlled by men.

3. Possible answer: Some men believed it was not "ladylike" for women to participate in politics.

4. No; suffragists supported the right to vote.

5. Yes. It was a formal gathering that endorsed social and political change.

6. Answers will vary, but should describe the goals of the convention and express and support an opinion of those goals.

A National Hero

"Until [James Fenimore] Cooper, most American writers borrowed their subject matter and literary styles from Europe.... Cooper proved that such imitation was not necessary.... He gave the American public what it desperately wanted—a national hero whose history was theirs."

—Frank Magill, editor and literary critic

◀ Natty Bumppo is the hero of Cooper's novel *The Last of the Mohicans*.

American Literature and Arts

Objectives

- Identify the common themes in American literature and art in the mid-1800s.
- Describe the flowering of American literature in the mid-1800s.
- Discuss the development of unique American styles in art and music.

🔵 Reading Skill

Draw Logical Conclusions As you review the details and evidence in text, make sure that the conclusions you draw are logical. In other words, they should make sense with all the details and with what you know about the events and about the world. Use your own experience to test, for example, whether particular attitudes make sense in a given situation. Do they fit the historical context?

Key Terms and People

transcendentalism
Ralph Waldo
  Emerson
individualism
Henry David
  Thoreau
civil disobedience
Herman Melville
Nathaniel
  Hawthorne
Louisa May Alcott

Why It Matters While sectionalism and slavery divided the nation, other ideas united the nation. Many Americans shared a belief in optimism and nationalism. They believed that individuals could improve themselves and society. They had pride in the United States of America.

❓ **Section Focus Question: How did American literature and art have an impact on American life?**

An American Culture Develops

Before 1800, American writers and artists modeled their work on European styles. Poets used complex, formal language and filled their poems with references to Greek and Roman myths. Most artists trained in Europe and learned European approaches to painting.

American Themes By the mid-1800s, American writers and artists had begun to develop styles that reflected American optimism and energy. Their work explored subjects that were uniquely American. Two early writers, Washington Irving and James Fenimore Cooper, reflected this interest in American themes.

Irving drew upon the Dutch history of New York in his stories "The Legend of Sleepy Hollow" and "Rip Van Winkle." Rip Van Winkle was a lazy farmer who slept through the American Revolution.

Cooper created the popular character Natty Bumppo, a frontiersman who kept moving westward. Uncomfortable with life in cities and towns, Bumppo criticized the destruction of nature. Cooper's novels about Bumppo, such as *The Deerslayer* and *The Last of the Mohicans,* helped American literature gain popularity in Europe.

Section 4 American Literature and Arts 431

Vocabulary Builder

Use the information below to teach students this section's high-use words.

High-Use Word	Definition and Sample Sentence
emotion, p. 432	*n.* strong feeling such as sadness, anger, or love His speech about the evils of slavery stirred the **emotions** of the audience.
reproduce, p. 435	*v.* to make a copy of In her paintings, she tried to **reproduce** the beauty of the natural world.

Section 4
Step-by-Step Instruction

Review and Preview

Students have learned how the reform impulse worked to improve society. American literature and art reflected the optimistic sense that individuals can perfect themselves and others.

Section Focus Question

How did American literature and art have an impact on American life?

Before you begin the lesson for the day, write the Section Focus Question on the board. (*Lesson focus: American artists and writers began to celebrate and express American places and ideas. This encouraged pride in the new nation.*)

Prepare to Read

Build Background Knowledge   L2

Tell students that in this section they will learn about the development of a new American style in literature and art. Have students think about the reforms and changes they learned about in Sections 1 through 3. Then have students predict ideas and themes that might appear in art and literature at this time. After they make predictions, address any misconceptions that students may have about the topic. Remind them to confirm or revise their predictions after they read the section. Use the Think-Pair-Share strategy (TE, p. T25) to elicit responses.

Set a Purpose   L2

- Read each statement in the Reading Readiness Guide aloud. Ask students to mark the statements True or False.

  All in One Teaching Resources, Unit 4, Reading Readiness Guide, p. 49

- Have students discuss the statements in pairs or groups of four, then mark their worksheets again. Use the Numbered Heads strategy (TE, p. T24) to call on students to share their groups' perspectives. The students will return to these worksheets later.

Teach

An American Culture Develops

p. 431

Instruction

L2

- **Vocabulary Builder** Before teaching this section, preteach the High-Use Words **emotion** and **reproduce** using the strategy on p. T21.

  Key Terms Have students complete the See It–Remember It chart for the Key Terms in this chapter.

- Read An American Culture Develops using the Choral Reading strategy (TE, p. T22).

- Discuss with students the beginning of an American culture. Ask: **What did Washington Irving and James Fenimore Cooper have in common?** (*They both wrote stories that reflected their interest in American themes.*)

- Ask: **How did Emerson and Thoreau encourage individualism?** (*Emerson wanted people to be guided by their "inner light." Thoreau believed individuals should judge right and wrong for themselves.*)

- Ask: **How are transcendentalism and individualism related?** (*Possible answer: Transcendentalism is based on emotions, which are experienced by individual humans, so the experiences, thoughts, and feelings of the individual are very important.*)

- Discuss with students how transcendentalism might have led people to work for reforms. (*Possible answer: It celebrated the value of each soul as a part of nature and highlighted the fact that people have a common humanity and responsibility for one another.*)

Independent Practice

Have students begin filling in the study guide for this section.

Monitor Progress

As students fill in the Notetaking Study Guide, circulate to make sure individuals understand the development of early American art.

Answer

Apply Information The speaker is very emotional and talks of pain and death.

Transcendentalism By the early 1800s, a new artistic movement took shape in Europe, called Romanticism. Unlike thinkers of the Enlightenment, who emphasized reason, Romantics placed greater value on nature, <u>emotions</u>, and imagination.

A small but influential group of writers and thinkers in New England developed an American form of Romanticism, called transcendentalism (trahnz ehn DEHNT uhl ihzm). **Transcendentalism** was a movement that sought to explore the relationship between humans and nature through emotions rather than through reason. It got its name because its goal was to transcend, or go beyond, human reason.

Transcendentalists believed in a close link between humans and nature. They urged people to live simply and to seek beauty, goodness, and truth within their own souls.

Emerson and Thoreau Ralph Waldo Emerson was the leading transcendentalist. In his popular speeches and essays, Emerson asked Americans to question the value of material goods. Civilization might provide wealth, he said, but nature reflected higher values that came from God. Emerson also stressed individualism, the unique importance of each individual. "Trust thyself," he taught. He challenged people to use their "inner light" to guide their lives and improve society.

Henry David Thoreau (thuh ROW) took up Emerson's challenge. He spent two years living in the woods at Walden Pond, meditating on nature. In his 1854 book *Walden,* Thoreau urged people to live

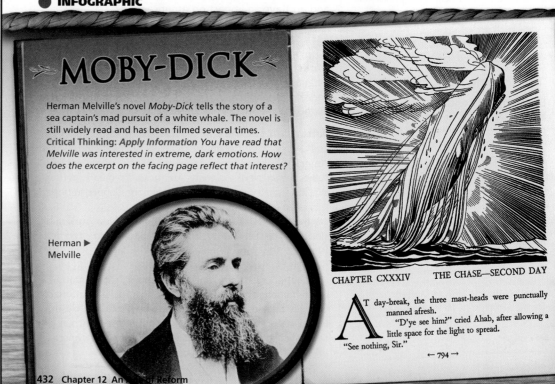

● **INFOGRAPHIC**

MOBY-DICK

Herman Melville's novel *Moby-Dick* tells the story of a sea captain's mad pursuit of a white whale. The novel is still widely read and has been filmed several times. **Critical Thinking:** *Apply Information* You have read that Melville was interested in extreme, dark emotions. How does the excerpt on the facing page reflect that interest?

Herman ▶ Melville

CHAPTER CXXXIV   THE CHASE—SECOND DAY

At day-break, the three mast-heads were punctually manned afresh.
   "D'ye see him?" cried Ahab, after allowing a little space for the light to spread.
"See nothing, Sir."

← 794 →

432 Chapter 12 An Age of Reform

Differentiated Instruction

L1 English Language Learners   **L1** Less Proficient Readers   **L1** Special Needs

Study Aid To help students remember the writers and artists in this section, have them make a two-column chart. In the first column, have them write the person's name. In the second column, have them list works and other important or interesting information about each person.

simply. "Most of the luxuries, and many of the so-called comforts of life, are not only not indispensable, but positive hindrances to the elevation of mankind," he wrote.

Like Emerson, Thoreau believed that individuals must judge right and wrong for themselves. He encouraged civil disobedience, the idea that people should peacefully disobey unjust laws if their consciences demand it. Thoreau spent a night in jail for refusing to pay a tax that he felt supported slavery. Thoreau's ideas about civil disobedience and nonviolent protest influenced later leaders like Martin Luther King, Jr.

☑Checkpoint   **What was the goal of transcendentalism?**

Flowering of American Literature

Irving and Cooper set a high standard for American writers. Two later novelists, Herman Melville and Nathaniel Hawthorne, began to change the tone of American literature.

Melville and Hawthorne Both Hawthorne and Melville were fascinated by psychology and extreme emotions. Melville's novel *Moby-Dick* (1851) told the story of a sea captain who is obsessed with pursuing a white whale. In the end, Captain Ahab's mad pursuit destroys himself, his ship, and his crew. *Moby-Dick* was largely ignored when it was first published. Today, however, it is considered one of the greatest American novels.

Draw Logical Conclusions

Draw a logical conclusion about Thoreau's values from the information and quotation in this paragraph.

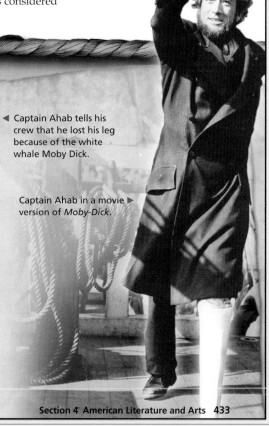

"Aye, my hearties all round; it was Moby Dick that dismasted me; Moby Dick that brought me to this dead stump I stand on now. Aye aye,' he shouted with a terrific, loud, animal sob, like that of a heart-stricken moose; 'Aye, aye! it was that accursed white whale that razeed me; made a poor pegging lubber for me for ever and a day!' Then, tossing both arms, with measureless imprecations he shouted out, 'Aye, aye! and I'll chase him round Good Hope, and round the Horn, and round the Norway Maelstrom, and round perdition's flames before I give him up. And this is what ye have shipped for, men! To chase that white whale on both sides of land, and over all sides of the earth. . . . "

◄ Captain Ahab tells his crew that he lost his leg because of the white whale Moby Dick.

Captain Ahab in a movie ► version of *Moby-Dick*.

Section 4 American Literature and Arts   **433**

History Background

An African American Writer William Wells Brown was the son of an enslaved woman and a slaveholder. In the first chapter of his novel *Clotel*, a slave once owned by Thomas Jefferson and the two daughters she bore to him are sold at auction. The book was published in London in 1853. In the version published in the United States in 1864, the character of Jefferson was replaced by a Southern senator. The original version of *Clotel* was not published in the United States until 1969.

Flowering of American Literature
p. 433

Instruction   L2

- With students, read Flowering of American Literature. Remind students to look for answers to the Section Focus Question.

- Ask: **How was the new literature uniquely American?** (*It expressed American ideas and values and celebrated what was important to Americans.*)

- Ask: **How did the new literature celebrate American culture and society?** (*Possible answer: Authors and poets of this period set their works in the American past or dealt with American issues. They also celebrated the American people and showed what their lives were like.*)

Independent Practice

Have students continue filling in the study guide for this section.

📖 **Interactive Reading and Notetaking Study Guide,** Chapter 12, Section 4 (Adapted Version also available.)

Monitor Progress

As students fill in the Notetaking Study Guide, circulate to make sure individuals understand the early development of American literature. Provide assistance as needed.

Answers

☑Checkpoint to explore the relationship between humans and nature through emotion rather than reason

🔄 **Reading Skill** Possible answer: He was concerned not with material things but with making humanity better.

Art and Music

p. 435

Instruction L2

- Read Art and Music with students. Remind them to look for answers to the reading Checkpoint question.

- Ask: **How did painters' work express an American style?** (*Painters focused on American landscapes, people, and everyday life.*)

- Display the transparency Kindred Spirits to help students better understand the Hudson River School of painting. Use the questions to guide a discussion.

Color Transparencies, Kindred Spirits

- Ask: **What do the many American work songs show about the period?** (*Possible answer: Most people were workers.*)

Independent Practice

Have students complete the study guide for this section.

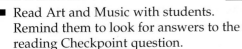 **Interactive Reading and Notetaking Study Guide,** Chapter 12, Section 4 (Adapted Version also available.)

Monitor Progress

- As students complete the Notetaking Study Guide, circulate to make sure individuals understand the themes of American music and art. Provide assistance as needed.

- Tell students to fill in the last column of the Reading Readiness Guide. Probe for what they learned that confirms or invalidates each statement.

- Ask students to go back to their Word Knowledge Rating Form. Rerate their word knowledge and complete the last column with a definition or example.

All in One Teaching Resources, Unit 4, Reading Readiness Guide, p. 49; Word Knowledge Rating Form, p. 45

- To further assess student understanding, use the Progress Monitoring Transparency.

Progress Monitoring Transparencies, Chapter 12, Section 4

Answers

Evaluate Information The people are a small part of nature.

☑**Checkpoint** by using historical themes and settings

The Hudson River School
This landscape painting by Thomas Cole shows Americans building a home in the middle of the wilderness. Like other paintings of the Hudson River school, it reflects a sense of the beauty and power of nature. **Critical Thinking:** *Evaluate Information* What is the relationship between people and nature in this painting?

Hawthorne was descended from the Puritans of Massachusetts. He often used historical themes to explore the dark side of the mind. In his 1850 novel *The Scarlet Letter*, a young minister is destroyed by secret guilt. The novel paints a grim picture of Puritan life.

Alcott Louisa May Alcott presented a gentler view of New England life. In 1868, Alcott published *Little Women*, a novel based on her own experiences growing up with three sisters. The main character, Jo March, was one of the first young American heroines to be presented as a believable, imperfect person rather than as a shining ideal.

Poets of Democracy Poets helped create a new national voice. Henry Wadsworth Longfellow based poems on American history, such as "Paul Revere's Ride." His long poem *The Song of Hiawatha* was one of the first works to honor Native Americans.

Walt Whitman published *Leaves of Grass* in 1855. This book of poems shocked many readers because it rejected formal rules. But today, Whitman is seen as the poet who best expresses the democratic American spirit. His poetry celebrated common people:

> ❝[T]he policeman travels his beat—the gate-keeper marks who pass; . . .
>
> The clean-hair'd Yankee girl works with her sewing-machine, or in the factory or mill.❞
>
> —Walt Whitman, "Song of Myself"

Some poets used their pens to support social reform. John Greenleaf Whittier, a Massachusetts Quaker, and Frances Watkins Harper, an African American woman from Maryland, wrote poems that described and condemned the evils of slavery.

☑**Checkpoint** How did writers explore the American past?

Differentiated Instruction

L3 Advanced Readers   **L3 Gifted and Talented**

Creating an Art Exhibit Pamphlet Have students research a painter from the Hudson River School and create an informational pamphlet that would accompany an exhibit of the artist's works. The pamphlet should include general background about the School and the artist, as well as a list of at least three works the students would include in an exhibit, with a note for each giving the title, date painted, and subject. Ask students to share their favorite work and tell what characteristics of the Hudson River School it shows.

Art and Music

After 1820, artists also began to create a unique American style. Turning away from European themes, they focused on the landscapes around them or on the daily lives of common Americans.

Painting America A group of artists painted scenes of the Hudson River valley. This group became known as the Hudson River school. Thomas Cole and the other painters of this school reflected the values of Romanticism. They sought to stir emotions by reproducing the beauty and power of nature.

Other American painters were inspired by everyday life. George Caleb Bingham created a timeless picture of life on the great rivers. George Catlin captured the ways and dignity of Native Americans.

Popular Songs Most early American songs, such as "Yankee Doodle," had roots in English, Irish, or Scottish tunes. Over time, a wide variety of new American songs emerged. Many were work songs, chanted by men as they sailed on whaling ships, laid railroad tracks, or hauled barges along canals. The spiritual was a special type of song developed by enslaved African Americans.

The most popular American songwriter of the 1800s was Stephen Foster. Many of his tunes, such as "Camptown Races" and "Old Folks at Home," are still familiar today.

☑Checkpoint   **Identify two themes of American painting.**

⭐ **Looking Back and Ahead** American culture of the 1800s had an influence that is still felt today. People still read *Moby-Dick* and *Little Women*. Concepts like individualism and civil disobedience continue to affect people's ideas and actions.

Vocabulary Builder
reproduce (ree prah DYOOS) **v.** to make a copy of

Section 4 | Check Your Progress

Progress Monitoring Online
For: Self-test with instant help
Visit: PHSchool.com
Web Code: mya-4084

Comprehension and Critical Thinking

1. **(a) Recall** Before 1800, what models influenced American writers and painters?
   (b) Draw Conclusions How did later works like *The Scarlet Letter* and the paintings of the Hudson River school reflect a change in American art and literature?

2. **(a) Recall** What did Henry David Thoreau mean by "civil disobedience"?
   (b) Link Past and Present How did Thoreau's ideas influence Martin Luther King, Jr.?

🔄 Reading Skill

3. **Draw Logical Conclusions** In a novel by James Fenimore Cooper, Natty Bumppo watches as settlers shoot hundreds of pigeons. Based on the following quotation, what conclusion can you draw about Natty's feelings for nature? Explain why your conclusion is logical. **Quotation:** "It's much better to kill only such as you want, without wasting your powder and lead, than to be firing into God's creatures in this wicked manner. . . . Wasn't the woods made for the beasts and birds to harbor in?"

Key Terms

4. Write two definitions for the key term transcendentalism. First, write a formal definition for your teacher. Second, write a definition in everyday English for a classmate.

Writing

5. What is the relationship between artists and society? Using examples from this section, write a paragraph explaining how writers, painters, and musicians reflect the society in which they lived and how they help to influence it.

Assess Progress   L2

Have students complete Check Your Progress. Administer the Section Quiz.

All in One Teaching Resources, Unit 4, Section Quiz, p. 61

To further assess student understanding, use the Progress Monitoring Transparency.

Progress Monitoring Transparencies, Chapter 12, Section 4

Reteach   L1

If students need more instruction, have them read this section in the Interactive Reading and Notetaking Study Guide and complete the accompanying question.

📖 **Interactive Reading and Notetaking Study Guide,** Chapter 12, Section 4 (Adapted Version also available.)

Extend   L3

Have students find an example of a painting by a member of the Hudson River School. Ask students to record the name of the painting and the artist and use the painting as an inspiration for writing a poem. Poems should not only relate to the painting but also express ideas about transcendentalism and individualism. Ask volunteers to read their poems to the class. If possible, have students display a copy of their inspiration painting while they read.

Progress Monitoring Online

Students may check their comprehension of this section by completing the Progress Monitoring Online graphic organizer and self-quiz.

Section 4 Check Your Progress

1. **(a)** European ones
   (b) They were focused on American subjects and history.

2. **(a)** the idea that people should protest or peacefully refuse to obey laws that they believe are wrong
   (b) He practiced civil disobedience as Thoreau did to fight against unjust laws.

3. Possible answer: Bumppo respected and cared about nature; the answer is logical because, in the quotation, Cooper writes that it is wicked to kill more of God's creatures than you need.

4. Possible answer: formal: a movement that sought to explore the relationship between humans and nature; informal: the idea that people should enjoy nature and live simpler lives

5. Answers will vary but should use specific examples of artists, their work, and their connections to the outside world.

Answer

☑Checkpoint Possible answers: American landscapes and everyday life

Objective

Evaluating summaries can aid student comprehension of the main ideas of reading passages. The skill will help students focus on the most important parts of what they read and help teach students the elements necessary to develop their own summaries.

Evaluate Summaries

Instruction L2

1. Write the steps to evaluate summaries on the board and ask the class to read the steps aloud.

2. Have students look at who wrote the passage, and for what occasion it was written. Using the Idea Wave strategy (TE, p. T24), have them suggest what they think the speech will be about.

3. Practice the skill by following the steps on p. 436 as a class. Model each step to explain the passage. (**1.** *Answers will vary, but should mention the contrast between slavery and independence.* **2.** *Possible answer: Enslaved Americans do not have independence.* **3.** *Answers will vary, but should support the main idea.* **4.** *Summary C; reasons will vary but should relate to the main idea.*)

Monitor Progress

Ask students to do the Apply the Skill activity. Then assign the Skills for Life worksheet. As students complete the worksheet, circulate to make sure individuals are applying the skill steps effectively. Provide assistance as needed.

All in One Teaching Resources, Unit 4, Skills for Life Worksheet, p. 56

Skills for Life — Evaluate Summaries

A summary briefly retells the main ideas of a selection, using different words. It also includes the most important details about the main ideas. Summaries should not include personal opinions about the selection. Read the primary source below, then read summaries A–C.

> **Primary Source**
>
> In 1852, Frederick Douglass, African American abolitionist, was invited to speak at a July 4th gathering in Rochester, New York.
>
> Fellow citizens, pardon me, allow me to ask, why am I called upon to speak here today? What have I, or those I represent, to do with your national independence? Are the great principles of political freedom and of natural justice, embodied in that Declaration of Independence, extended to us? . . . This Fourth of July is yours, not mine. You may rejoice. I must mourn. . . . Do you mean, citizens, to mock me by asking me to speak today? . . . My subject then, fellow citizens, is American slavery. I shall see this day and its popular characteristics from the slave's point of view.
>
> —Frederick Douglass, Independence Day speech, Rochester, 1852

Summary A: Douglass believes that all Americans should celebrate the Fourth of July. The freedoms established in the Declaration of Independence are meant for all.

Summary B: Douglass does not feel he is able to speak. He is a poor man who does not enjoy the wealth and good fortune shared by many members of the audience.

Summary C: Douglass reminds his audience that African Americans did not enjoy the freedoms and independence guaranteed in the Declaration of Independence.

Learn the Skill

Use these steps to determine which summary accurately captures the main idea of the speech.

1. **Identify the subject of the selection.** What is the selection about?

2. **Find the main idea of the selection.** Determine the writer or speaker's most important point about the subject.

3. **Find important details.** What details provide key information about the main idea?

4. **Evaluate the summary.** Does it accurately restate the main idea of the original in different words? Does it include important details? Does it communicate the basic meaning of the original text?

Practice the Skill

Answer the following questions about the summaries on this page.

1. **Identify the subject of the selection.** What is the selection about?

2. **Find the main idea of the selection.** What main point does Frederick Douglass make?

3. **Find important details.** What is one detail that provides information about the main idea?

4. **Evaluate the summary.** Which is the best summary of Douglass's speech? Give three reasons for your answer.

Apply the Skill

See the Review and Assessment at the end of this chapter.

How did reformers and writers inspire change and spark controversy?

Section 1
Improving Society

- Jacksonian democracy encouraged reform by focusing on ideals of liberty and equality.
- In the Second Great Awakening, ministers preached that people had free will and could reform their own lives.
- Reformers tackled a variety of causes, including temperance, prison reform, improved conditions for those with mental illnesses, and public education.

Section 2
The Fight Against Slavery

- Abolitionists such as William Lloyd Garrison and Frederick Douglass called for an end to slavery.
- Conductors on the Underground Railroad helped people escape from slavery to freedom.
- Abolitionists faced strong opposition in both the North and the South.

Section 3
A Call for Women's Rights

- People active in social reform began to demand equal rights for women.
- The Declaration of Sentiments at the Seneca Falls Convention called for women's equality in many areas of public life.
- The women's rights movement focused much of its attention on gaining better education for women.

Section 4
American Literature and Arts

- American writers and artists began to explore American themes in their work.
- Transcendentalists emphasized emotions, nature, and individualism.
- Melville and Hawthorne explored dark areas of psychology, while Whitman wrote poems celebrating democracy.

? **Exploring the Essential Question**

Use the online study guide to explore the essential question.

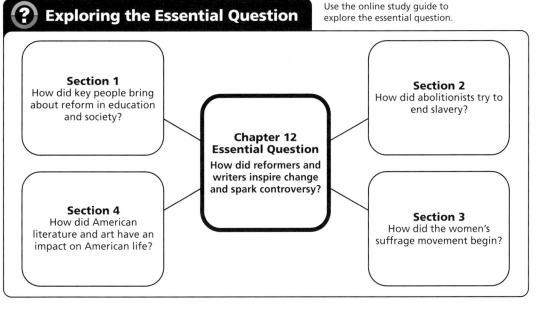

Section 1
How did key people bring about reform in education and society?

Chapter 12 Essential Question
How did reformers and writers inspire change and spark controversy?

Section 4
How did American literature and art have an impact on American life?

Section 2
How did abolitionists try to end slavery?

Section 3
How did the women's suffrage movement begin?

Chapter 12

Essential Question
Remind students of the Chapter Essential Question: **How did reformers and writers inspire change and spark controversy?** Have them review the bulleted statements and the Visual Preview at the beginning of the chapter to help them answer this question.

To bolster students' retention, at this time they should complete the study guide in print or online. Remind students that they should also continue notetaking for the Unit and Chapter Essential Questions.

Interactive Reading and Notetaking Study Guide, Chapter 12 (Adapted Version also available.)

 Study Guide *Online,* Chapter 12

Chapter Challenge
To wrap up this chapter, have students write a paragraph to answer this question: **How might the United States be different today if the educational reforms begun by Horace Mann had not taken place?** (*Answers will vary, but should demonstrate an understanding of the importance of education, especially publicly funded education, and how it enriches people's lives and contributes to democracy.*)

Assessment at a Glance

Formal Assessment

Chapter Tests A/B (L1/L2)

Test Prep Workbook With Document-Based Assessment

Test-Taking Strategies With Transparencies

Performance Assessment

Group/Individual Activites, TE pp. 410g, 410h

Teacher's Edition, pp. 419, 426, 430, 435

Assessment Rubrics

Assessment Through Technology

ExamView **CD-ROM**

MindPoint CD-ROM

Progress Monitoring Transparencies

Progress Monitoring Online

Key Terms

1. God determines the fate of a person's soul before birth.

2. abolish slavery

3. vote

Comprehension and Critical Thinking

4. **(a)** abuses of prisoners and of the mentally ill **(b)** She traveled around the country and spoke to state legislatures to call for reforms and improvements. **(c)** Possible answer: Today the mentally ill are treated, not imprisoned.

5. **(a)** Possible answers: The Declaration of Independence stated that all men are equal; religious beliefs that owning other people is immoral **(b)** Northern abolitionists believed that slavery was wrong for any reason; southern slaveholders depended on it for their economy and therefore rationalized its existence.

6. **(a)** the rights to vote, own property, and speak in public meetings **(b)** Women gained more educational opportunities and began to be admitted to some careers.

History Reading Skill

7. The writer values education. He says those with good education do a higher level of work and earn more money.

Writing

8. Students should relate the role of abolitionists in the reform movement to the sentiments in the poem.

9. Students' essays should include the goals and motives of the particular reformers they have heard at the meeting.

For a more complete four-point rubric, see the writing rubrics in the Teaching Resources.

All in One Teaching Resources, Unit 4, p. 111

Key Terms

Complete each of the following sentences so that the second part further explains the first part and clearly shows your understanding of the key term.

1. The doctrine of free will was almost the exact opposite of predestination, the belief that _____.

2. People in the United States who wanted to end slavery were called abolitionists because they wanted to _____.

3. Women who wanted to _____ supported women's suffrage.

Comprehension and Critical Thinking

4. **(a) Describe** Describe two problems Dorothea Dix uncovered.
   (b) Apply Information What did she do to correct them?
   (c) Link Past and Present How do you think Dix's work benefits people today?

5. **(a) List** Give two reasons why Americans opposed slavery.
   (b) Compare and Contrast Compare how northern abolitionists and southern slaveholders viewed slavery.

6. **(a) Recall** Which rights were denied women in the early 1800s?
   (b) Draw Conclusions What rights did women gain as a result of the victories won in the struggle for equal rights in the 1800s?

History Reading Skill

7. **Draw Conclusions From Sources** Based on the following quotation, what conclusion can you draw about the writer's view regarding education? Explain how you reached this conclusion.

> "Those who have been blessed with a good common-school education rise to a higher and higher point in the kinds of labor performed and also in the rate of wages paid, while the ignorant sink like dregs and are always found at the bottom."
>
> —Annual Reports of the Secretary of the Board of Education of Massachusetts, 1839–1844

Writing

8. **Read the following poem by Frances Watkins Harper. Then, write a paragraph explaining how this poem is related to the spirit of change that swept the United States in the mid-1800s:**

> "I ask no monument, proud and high,
> To arrest the gaze of passers-by;
> All that my yearning spirit craves,
> Is bury me not in a land of slaves."
>
> —Frances Watkins Harper, "Bury Me in a Free Land"

9. **Write a Narrative:**
   You are a student in the 1850s. Your parents have taken you to a public meeting about temperance, abolition, or women's rights. Write a letter to a friend describing what you saw and heard at the meeting and how it made you feel. Use information from this chapter to create your description.

Skills for Life
Evaluate Summaries

Review Section 3, "A Call for Women's Rights." Then, look at the three summaries below and answer the questions that follow.

> **Summary A:** The Seneca Falls Convention was a failure. American women failed to make any political or economic gains.
>
> **Summary B:** The Seneca Falls Convention did not change American society overnight. Still, the convention marked the start of a long struggle for women's rights that eventually succeeded.
>
> **Summary C:** The Seneca Falls Convention was a great success. Before long, many states gave women property rights and passed laws giving women suffrage.

10. What is the main idea of the section?

11. Which is the best summary of the section? Give three reasons for your answer.

Skills for Life

10. Possible answer: In the mid-1800s, women in the United States began to work for equal rights, achieving slow progress.

11. Summary B. Possible reasons: It is factual; it includes the fact that it took a long time for women to gain equal rights; it mentions that "American society" did not change overnight, which is important because equal rights for women was a huge, societal change at that time.

Chapter 12
Review and Assessment

Test Yourself

1. The idea that God decides the fate of each person is called

   A prohibition.

   B transcendentalism.

   C romanticism.

   D predestination.

2. Frederick Douglass and William Lloyd Garrison were

   A founders of the American Colonization Society.

   B leaders of the antislavery movement.

   C conductors on the Underground Railroad.

   D delegates to the Seneca Falls Convention.

Refer to the quotation below to answer Question 3.

> "Most of the luxuries, and many of the so-called comforts of life, are not only not indispensable, but positive hindrances to the elevation of mankind."

3. The quotation above describes the core ideas of which American author?

   A Herman Melville

   B Louisa May Alcott

   C Henry David Thoreau

   D James Fenimore Cooper

Document-Based Questions

Task: Look at Documents 1 and 2, and answer their accompanying questions. Then, use the documents and your knowledge of history to complete this writing assignment:

> Write a short essay about the Second Great Awakening. Include details about the emotional and moral impact of the movement.

Document 1: Charles Grandison Finney, a leading figure of the Second Great Awakening, conducted spellbinding revival meetings in many eastern cities. This excerpt is from Finney's Revival Lectures. *According to Finney, what role do revivals play in religion?*

> "Almost all the religion in the world has been produced by revivals. God has found it necessary to take advantage of the excitability there is in mankind, to produce powerful excitements among them, before he can lead them to obey. Men are so spiritually sluggish, there are so many things to lead their minds off from religion, and to oppose the influence of the Gospel, that it is necessary to raise an excitement among them, till the tide rises so high as to sweep away the opposing obstacles. They must be so excited that they will break over these counteracting influences, before they will obey God."

Document 2: Millions of American flocked to revival meetings, sometimes camping at the sites for several days. *Why were so many Americans attracted to the revival movement?*

Test Yourself

1. D

2. B

3. C

Document-Based Questions
Answers

Document 1 Revivals arouse people from their natural spiritual sluggishness and lead them to obey God.

Document 2 Possible answers: the excitement of a special event to break the humdrum of daily life, a desire for religious guidance, a wish to become a better person, a chance to hear interesting speakers and expand one's knowledge

Rubric

Share the rubric with students before they begin writing.

Score 1 Is off the point, poorly organized, lacks substance.

Score 2 Has few details of the revival experience, is sketchy on moral impact.

Score 3 Shows understanding of the revival experience, gives thoughtful but limited reflections on moral impact. (*Answers may include ideas about salvation, self-improvement, effect of mass appeal.*)

Score 4 Well written, shows imagination in describing a revival, gives personal reflections on how the experience might affect an attender.

Westward Expansion

History Background

The Lure of the West

The study of westward expansion provides an excellent opportunity to understand the ideals and determination of Americans, as well as the difficulties involved in pursuing these ideals. Many Americans overcame physical and political obstacles in order to build a better life in the West. Yet, the expansion of the nation into the new territory exacerbated some issues, such as the treatment of Native Americans and the expansion of slavery, which would continue to affect the course of American history.

The American West was settled by diverse people, including Native Americans, Spanish colonists, French trappers, Americans of all walks of life, and immigrants. The West was settled largely because it offered many

Americans the chance for a better life. The idea of Manifest Destiny—that it was God's will that the United States reach from ocean to ocean and control the continent—gave some settlers a spiritual as well as a practical goal.

American settlers in the West faced two major challenges. First, they faced immense physical hardships on their overland journey. The Oregon Trail, stretching from Independence, Missouri, to the Oregon Territory, was about 2,000 miles long. Many settlers traveled the entire distance on foot, walking alongside wagons that held all their possessions.

Second, the settlers faced armed Native Americans who fought to protect their land and way of life. Also, much of the territory—Texas, Califor-

nia, and the present-day Southwest—was part of Mexico, which had become independent in 1821. It was after the Texas War for Independence and the Mexican-American War that this territory became part of the United States.

Essential Questions

Use this graphic organizer to see the relationship between key concepts and the Chapter Essential Question.

Focus Question/Section 1
What cultures and ideas influenced the development of the West?
(p. 444)

Concept: Nationalism

Focus Question/Section 2
Why did people go west and what challenges did they face?
(p. 448)

Concept: Migration

Chapter Essential Question
How did westward expansion change the geography of the nation and demonstrate the determination of its people?

Focus Question/Section 4
How did Mormon settlement and the gold rush lead to changes in the West?
(p. 462)

Concept: Diversity

Focus Question/Section 3
What were the causes and effects of the Texas War for Independence and the Mexican-American War?
(p. 454)

Concept: Conflict

Differentiated Instruction

Structuring Paragraphs

Using a standard framework for writing paragraphs can help students write assignments that are effective and to the point. Ask students to write a paragraph using the following guidelines:

1. Begin with a topic sentence.

2. Add three to five examples with transition words.

3. Include a summary sentence.

Remind students to vary sentence length and structure. Model the assignment by providing students with a topic sentence, three examples, transition words, and a summary.

Topic Sentence: As the population increased, settlers in the early 1800s began to move west toward the Pacific Ocean.

Examples: Traders explored new trails searching for furs and markets where they could sell goods. Later, thousands of men and women made the journey west looking for fertile farmland and greater freedom. Freedom of religion also played a role in the desire to move west. Mormons, for example, chose to move west in their quest for religious freedom.

Summary Sentence: Settlers moved west to find wealth, adventure, and freedom.

Concepts Across Time

Have students develop an understanding of the enduring concepts of history by connecting these ideas.

Concept: Nationalism

Students learning about Manifest Destiny should consider the origins of American identity. Ask: **How did the loyalty of colonists change in the late 1700s?** (*Colonists transferred their loyalty from Great Britain to the American colony they lived in and then to the new United States.*) Ask: **Why would Americans want their country to spread across the continent?** (*Possible answer: Americans took pride in their new country and truly believed it was America's destiny to stretch from sea to sea.*) Use these questions when discussing Manifest Destiny in Section 1.

Concept: Migration

Remind students that the Americas were first settled by people from Asia walking across a land bridge connecting Asia and North America. Ask: **Why did those first people move to the Americas?** (*Possible answers: They were following game; they were fleeing overcrowding or enemies; they were adventurous.*) Ask: **Where were Native Americans living in North America when Europeans first came to settle?** (*Throughout the continent, from the*

Pacific to the Atlantic.) Use these questions when discussing the expansion of Western settlement in Sections 2 and 4.

Concept: Conflict

The struggle for territory has been an age-old conflict. Remind students that Native Americans fought wars over territory long before Europeans began to settle North America. Ask students to compare the causes and effects of the Mexican-American War with earlier North American wars fought for the control of territory. (*Possible answers: The efforts of Europeans to expand early settlements often led to wars against Native Americans. Sometimes tribes sided with the Europeans in order to get help against their own Native American enemies. Native Americans were involved on both sides in the French and Indian War of 1754–1763. Territory, as well as independence, was again at stake in the American Revolution and in the War of 1812. As in the Mexican War, the outcomes of these earlier wars determined who was to rule over a territory.*) Use this question when discussing the Mexican-American War in Section 3.

Section 1 The West *1.5 periods, .75 block*

Objectives

Students will

1. Identify the destinations of settlers heading west in the early 1800s.
2. Describe the unique culture of the Southwest.
3. Explain the meaning of Manifest Destiny.

Differentiated Instruction Key

L1 Basic to Average

L2 All Students

L3 Average to Advanced

AR Advanced Readers
ELL English Language Learners
GT Gifted and Talented
LPR Less Proficient Readers
SN Special Needs

Prepare to Read	Instructional Resources	Differentiated Instruction
Build Background Knowledge Preview the section and discuss with students the move west. **Set a Purpose for Reading** Have students begin to fill out the Reading Readiness Guide. **Preview Key Terms** Preview the section's Key Terms.	**All in One Teaching Resources, Unit 4** **L2** Chapter Prereading Guide, p. 4 **L2** History Reading Skill, p. 75 **L2** Word Knowledge Rating Form, p. 76 **L2** Reading Readiness Guide, p. 77 **Teacher's Edition** **L2** Vocabulary Builder, pp. 443, 445 **Discovery School Video** **L2** Westward Expansion	🔘 Guided Reading Audio CD Spanish ELL, LPR, SN

Teach	Instructional Resources	Differentiated Instruction
Instruction **What Was "The West"?** Discuss the sources of information that scholars use to learn about the past. **Mexican Settlements** Describe the culture of the Southwest. **Manifest Destiny** Discuss the idea of Manifest Destiny and the expansion of the United States.	📖 **Interactive Reading and Notetaking Study Guide** **L2** Chapter 13, Section 1 **All in One Teaching Resources, Unit 4** **L2** Concept Lesson, p. 89 **L2** Concept Organizer, p. 6 **L2** Manifest Destiny, p. 81	📖 **Interactive Reading and Notetaking Study Guide, Adapted Version (English/ Spanish)** **L1** Chapter 13, Section 1 ELL, LPR, SN **Teacher's Edition** **L1** Visualizing the Word, p. 443 ELL, LPR **L1** Learning with Flashcards, p. 444 ELL, LPR, SN **L3** Using Literature, p. 446 AR, GT

Assess and Reteach	Instructional Resources	Differentiated Instruction
Assess Progress Evaluate student comprehension with Check Your Progress and Section Quiz. **Reteach** Assign the Interactive Reading and Notetaking Study Guide to help struggling students. **Extend** Extend the lesson by having students compare the entrances of California and North Dakota to the Union.	📖 **Interactive Reading and Notetaking Study Guide** **L2** Chapter 13, Section 1 **All in One Teaching Resources, Unit 4** **L2** Reading Readiness Guide, p. 77 **L2** Section Quiz, p. 90 **Progress Monitoring Transparencies** **L2** Chapter 13, Section 1	**Teacher's Edition** **L1** Checkpoints, TE pp. 445, 446, 447 🔘 SE on Audio CD **L1** Chapter 13 ELL, LPR, SN

Section 2 Trails to the West *1 period, .5 block*

Objectives

Students will

1. Explain how traders and fur trappers helped open the West.

2. List the reasons pioneers traveled along the Oregon Trail and describe the hardships they faced.

3. Discuss the issues for women, Native Americans, and new settlers in the West.

Differentiated Instruction Key

L1 Basic to Average	**AR** Advanced Readers
L2 All Students	**ELL** English Language Learners
L3 Average to Advanced	**GT** Gifted and Talented
	LPR Less Proficient Readers
	SN Special Needs

Prepare to Read

Build Background Knowledge
Preview the section and remind students what they have learned about early American travelers.

Set a Purpose for Reading
Have students begin to fill out the Reading Readiness Guide.

Preview Key Terms
Preview the section's Key Terms.

Instructional Resources

All in One Teaching Resources, Unit 4

L2 Reading Readiness Guide, p. 78

Teacher's Edition

L2 Vocabulary Builder, p. 449

Differentiated Instruction

🎧 Guided Reading Audio CD

Spanish **ELL, LPR, SN**

Teach

Instruction
Traders Lead the Way
Discuss how traders and fur trappers helped open the West.

The Oregon Trail
Explain the rewards and hardships of settling the West.

Life in the West
Describe the status of women in the West and the conflicts that settlers had with Native Americans.

Instructional Resources

📖 Interactive Reading and Notetaking Study Guide

L2 Chapter 13, Section 2

All in One Teaching Resources, Unit 4

L2 Narcissa Whitman's Letter to Her Sister, p. 82

Color Transparencies

L2 Fur Traders Descending the Missouri

Differentiated Instruction

📖 Interactive Reading and Notetaking Study Guide, Adapted Version (English/Spanish)

L1 Chapter 13, Section 2 **ELL, LPR, SN**

Teacher's Edition

L3 Mountain Men, p. 448 **AR**

L1 Listening to the Text, p. 450 **ELL, SN**

L3 Westward Expansion, p. 452 **AR, GT**

All in One Teaching Resources, Unit 4

L3 Westward Ho!, p. 86

Assess and Reteach

Assess Progress
Evaluate student comprehension with Check Your Progress and Section Quiz.

Reteach
Assign the Interactive Reading and Notetaking Study Guide to help struggling students

Extend
Extend the lesson by having students write letters from mountain men.

Instructional Resources

📖 Interactive Reading and Notetaking Study Guide

L2 Chapter 13, Section 2

All in One Teaching Resources, Unit 4

L2 Reading Readiness Guide, p. 78

L2 Section Quiz, p. 91

Progress Monitoring Transparencies

L2 Chapter 13, Section 2

Differentiated Instruction

Teacher's Edition

L1 Checkpoints, TE pp. 449, 451, 453

🎧 SE on Audio CD

L1 Chapter 13 **ELL, LPR, SN**

Internet Resources
PHSchool.com

Section 3 Conflict With Mexico

1 period, .5 block

Objectives

Students will

1. Explain how Texas became independent from Mexico.
2. Discuss the issues involved in annexing Texas and Oregon.
3. Summarize the main events in the Mexican-American War.
4. Explain how the United States achieved Manifest Destiny.

Differentiated Instruction Key

L1 Basic to Average
L2 All Students
L3 Average to Advanced

AR Advanced Readers
ELL English Language Learners
GT Gifted and Talented
LPR Less Proficient Readers
SN Special Needs

Prepare to Read	Instructional Resources	Differentiated Instruction
Build Background Knowledge Preview the section and discuss whether or not American settlers and Mexicans would be likely to get along. **Set a Purpose for Reading** Have students begin to fill out the Reading Readiness Guide. **Preview Key Terms** Preview the section's Key Terms.	**All in One Teaching Resources, Unit 4** **L2** Reading Readiness Guide, p. 79 **Teacher's Edition** **L2** Vocabulary Builder, p. 455	**Guided Reading Audio CD** Spanish **ELL, LPR, SN**

Teach	Instructional Resources	Differentiated Instruction
Instruction **Texas Wins Independence** Explain how Texas became independent from Mexico. **Annexing Texas and Oregon** Identify the issues raised by adding new states to the Union. **The Mexican-American War** Discuss the Mexican-American War and the controversy it caused. **Achieving Manifest Destiny** Describe how the United States gained territory to achieve Manifest Destiny.	**Interactive Reading and Notetaking Study Guide** **L2** Chapter 13, Section 3 **All in One Teaching Resources, Unit 4** **L2** Texas War for Independence, p. 83 **Color Transparencies** **L2** Growth of the United States to 1853 **Discovery School Video** **L2** The Alamo	**Interactive Reading and Notetaking Study Guide, Adapted Version (English/Spanish)** **L1** Chapter 13, Section 3 **ELL, LPR, SN** **Teacher's Edition** **L1** Peer Assistance, p. 454 **ELL, LPR, SN** **L1** Sam Houston, p. 455 **ELL, LPR, SN** **L3** Defenders of the Alamo, p. 456 **AR, GT** **L1** The Mexican Point of View, p. 460 **ELL** **All in One Teaching Resources, Unit 4** **L1** Sam Houston, p. 84

Assess and Reteach	Instructional Resources	Differentiated Instruction
Assess Progress Evaluate student comprehension with Check Your Progress and Section Quiz. **Reteach** Assign the Interactive Reading and Notetaking Study Guide to help struggling students. **Extend** Extend the lesson by having students write a newspaper editorial on the Mexican-American War.	**Interactive Reading and Notetaking Study Guide** **L2** Chapter 13, Section 3 **All in One Teaching Resources, Unit 4** **L2** Reading Readiness Guide, p. 79 **L2** Section Quiz, p. 92 **Progress Monitoring Transparencies** **L2** Chapter 13, Section 3	**Teacher's Edition** **L1** Checkpoints, TE pp. 456, 457, 459 **SE on Audio CD** **L1** Chapter 13 **ELL, LPR, SN**

Section 4 A Rush to the West

 1.5 periods, .75 block

Objectives

Students will

1. Explain why the Mormons settled in Utah and the issues that divided Mormons and the federal government.

2. Discuss the effects of the 1849 California gold rush.

3. Describe how California's population had changed by 1850.

Differentiated Instruction Key

L1 Basic to Average	**AR** Advanced Readers
L2 All Students	**ELL** English Language Learners
L3 Average to Advanced	**GT** Gifted and Talented
	LPR Less Proficient Readers
	SN Special Needs

Prepare to Read

Build Background Knowledge
Preview the section and discuss how growth in population causes changes.

Set a Purpose for Reading
Have students begin to fill out the Reading Readiness Guide.

Preview Key Terms
Preview the section's Key Terms.

Instructional Resources

All in One Teaching Resources, Unit 4

L2 Reading Readiness Guide, p. 80

Teacher's Edition

L2 Vocabulary Builder, p. 463

Differentiated Instruction

🔊 **Guided Reading Audio CD**
Spanish **ELL, LPR, SN**

Teach

Instruction
Mormons Settle Utah
Discuss why the Mormons moved west.

The California Gold Rush
Identify the changes caused by the gold rush and the influx of forty-niners.

California's Changing Population
Discuss how the Gold Rush led to diversity and democracy in settling California.

Instructional Resources

📖 **Interactive Reading and Notetaking Study Guide**

L2 Chapter 13, Section 4

All in One Teaching Resources, Unit 4

L2 Skills for Life Worksheet, p. 88

Differentiated Instruction

Teacher's Edition

L3 Poly = many, p. 462 **GT**

L1 Word Derivation, p. 464 **ELL**

L3 Mariano Vallejo, p. 466 **AR, GT**

All in One Teaching Resources, Unit 4

L3 General Mariano Vallejo, p. 85

Assess and Reteach

Assess Progress
Assign Check Your Progress and Section Quiz.

Reteach
Assign the Study Guide to help students.

Extend
Have students write a diary entry as forty-niners.

Think Like a Historian
Using information from primary sources and the chapters in this unit, revisit the Unit Essential Question.

Instructional Resources

📖 **Interactive Reading and Notetaking Study Guide**

L2 Chapter 13, Section 4

All in One Teaching Resources, Unit 4

L2 Word Knowledge Rating Form, p. 76

L2 Reading Readiness Guide, p. 80

L2 Section Quiz, p. 93

L2 Chapter Test, p. 97

Progress Monitoring Transparencies

L2 Chapter 13, Section 4

Differentiated Instruction

Teacher's Edition

L1 Checkpoints, TE pp. 463, 465, 467

All in One Teaching Resources, Unit 4

L1 Chapter Test, p. 94

🔊 **SE on Audio CD**

L1 Chapter 13 **ELL, LPR, SN**

Internet Resources
PHSchool.com

🔊 **Social Studies Skills Tutor CD-ROM**

Analyzing Primary and Secondary Sources

Use the following research activities to help students deepen their understanding of the Chapter Essential Question: **How did westward expansion change the geography of the nation and demonstrate the determination of its people?** Students should use library or Internet resources. The Web Codes provided offer access to Internet resources students can use to complete each activity. Use the appropriate four-point rubric in Assessment Rubrics to evaluate the activity.

 Assessment Rubrics

Define Manifest Destiny

In pairs, have students look up *Manifest Destiny*. Using the information on the Web site, have students make posters giving Americans reasons why they should settle the West. Ask students to share their posters with the class. Use this activity when studying Manifest Destiny in Section 1.

 Group Research Activity GT **L3**

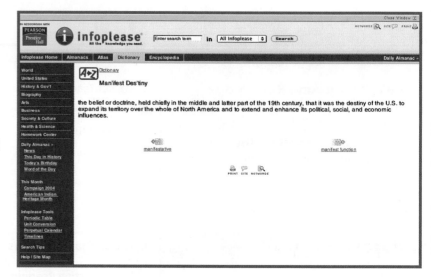

 Go Online PHSchool.com **Web Code:** mye-0261

Write a Diary Entry and Draw a Picture of Life on the Oregon Trail

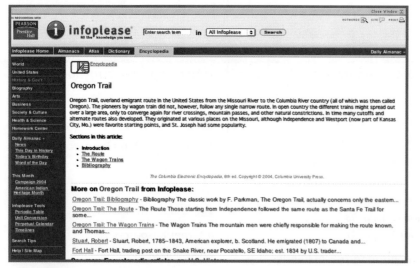

Have students work in pairs. Ask them to use the Web site to learn more about traveling on the Oregon Trail. Have each student write a two-paragraph diary entry that shows familiarity with the ways Oregon Trail travelers crossed different kinds of terrain. Then have them make a drawing that shows how wagon trains passed through one of the geographical features on the Oregon Trail. Have students present their diaries and drawings to the class. Use this activity when studying the Oregon Trail in Section 2.

 Group Research Activity AR, GT **L3**

 Go Online PHSchool.com **Web Code:** mye-0262

Create a Biography of Sam Houston

Have students use the information on the Web site to write a one-page biographical sketch of Sam Houston. Tell students to include information about Houston's role in the Texas Revolution, his role as a political leader of Texas as both an independent republic and a state, and his dedication to the Union. Use this activity when studying Texas Wins Independence in Section 3.

 Individual Research Activity   L2

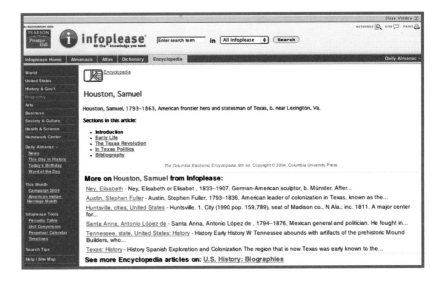

 **Web Code:** mye-0263

Write a Newspaper Article about John Sutter

Have students use information from the Web site to write a newspaper article about John Sutter and his role in the California gold rush. Have students read their articles aloud to the class. Tell the class to identify statements in each article that can be verified and explain how they would check the statements. Use this activity in studying the California Gold Rush in Section 4.

Individual Research Activity   L2

 **Web Code:** mye-0264

Why It Matters

E pluribus unum: from out of many, one. This is the motto on the seal of the United States. American society today is made out of many different regions, ethnic groups, and cultural heritages. The United States becomes a continental republic in the 1840s. It includes lands that create a much broader mix of peoples and cultures than were seen in the 13 colonies. Most importantly, the largely Hispanic peoples of California and the Southwest are now part of the United States. The first arrival of large numbers of Asians, beginning with Chinese immigrants during the Gold Rush, are included in our cultural mix as well.

The expansion achieved by the Mexican-American War made the United States the undeniably dominant power in North America. Expansion, once a force for unity, soon divided the nation into northerners and southerners who could not agree on the community they shared.

Chapter Essential Question

How did westward expansion change the geography of the nation and demonstrate the determination of its people?

Think Like a Historian

- To preview this chapter, have students review the content of these pages of the Student Edition. Ask: **What will you be learning about in this chapter?** *(about Americans moving west and a conflict with Mexico)*

- Have students read the quote at the top of page 441. Ask: **What difficulties did Lewis and his group face while traveling West?** *(Possible answer: mountainous terrain, food shortages)*

- Have students study the illustration. Ask: **What does this illustration tell you about the role cooperation played during the long journey west?** *(Possible answer: It played a very important role. Everyone, including the children, had jobs to do.)*

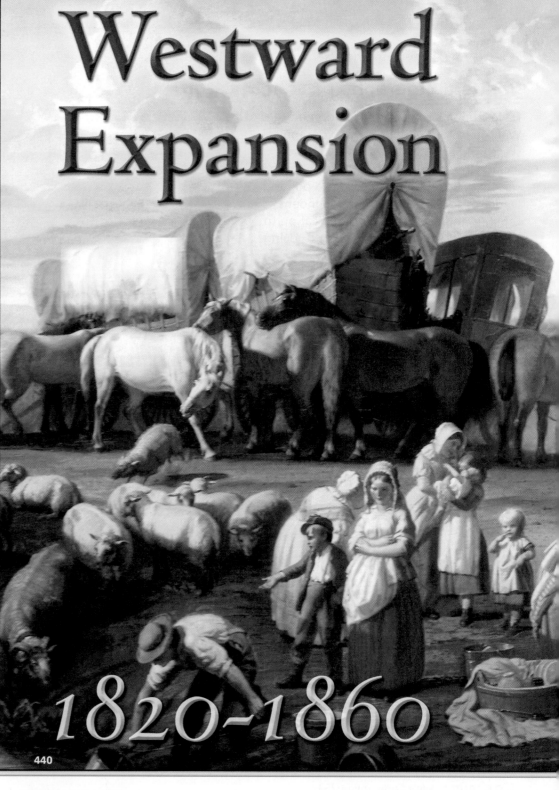

Westward Expansion

1820–1860

440

Bibliography

For the Teacher

Eisenhower, John S. D. *So Far from God: The U.S. War With Mexico, 1846–1848.* University of Oklahoma Press, 2000.

For the Student

L1 Garland, Sherry. *A Line in the Sand: The Alamo Diary of Lucinda Lawrence,*

Gonzales, Texas, 1836 (Dear America). Scholastic, 1998.

L2 Green, Carl R. *The Mission Trails in American History (In American History)* Enslow Publishers, 2001.

L3 Nardo, Don. *The Mexican-American War.* Greenhaven Press, 1999.

> *"Come through a poor mountainous country... it is difficult to get food for our horses our provisions is getting scarce and have a great trouble to get more here...."*
>
> —*Jane Voorhees Lewis,*
> **A Journey by Covered Wagon, 1847**

In this painting, settlers traveling to the West by wagon train pause on their long journey.

CHAPTER 13

What You Will Learn

Section 1
THE WEST
By the mid-1800s, many Americans wanted the nation to extend westward to the Pacific Ocean.

Section 2
TRAILS TO THE WEST
To journey westward, traders and settlers had to travel along difficult and dangerous trails.

Section 3
CONFLICT WITH MEXICO
The Texas War for Independence led to conflict and war between the United States and Mexico.

Section 4
A RUSH TO THE WEST
While the Mormons migrated to Utah, other settlers flocked to California in search of gold.

Reading Skill

Frame Research Questions In this chapter, you will learn how to ask questions that can be answered through research.

441

History Background

Teenager on the Trail The wagon train journey was long and difficult. Martha Ann Morrison was 13 years old when she traveled west with her family in 1844. Commenting on the rigors of the journey, she noted in her memoirs: "Some of the women I saw on the road went through a great deal of suffering and trial. I remember distinctly one girl my own age that died and was buried on the road. Her mother had a great deal of trouble and suffering. It strikes me as I think of it now that Mothers on the road had to undergo more trial and suffering than anybody else."

Prepare to Read

Use the following for reading skill support.

All in One Teaching Resources, Unit 4, Chapter Prereading Guide, p. 4; History Reading Skill, p. 75

History Reading Skill *Online*
Web code: mve-3000

Differentiated Instruction

The following Teacher's Edition strategies are suitable for students of varying abilities.

L3 Advanced Readers, pp. 446, 448, 452, 456, 466 AR

L1 English Language Learners, pp. 443, 444, 450, 454, 455, 460, 464 ELL

L3 Gifted and Talented, pp. 446, 452, 456, 462, 466 GT

L1 Less Proficient Readers, pp. 443, 444, 454, 455 LPR

L1 Special Needs, pp. 444, 450, 454, 455 SN

Chapter Resources

Teaching Resources, Unit 4
Chapter Prereading Guide, p. 4
Word Knowledge Rating Form, p. 76
History Reading Skill, p. 75
Skills for Life Worksheet, p. 88
Chapter Tests A/B (L1/L2), pp. 94, 97
Letter Home (English/Spanish), pp. 68, 69

Spanish Support
L1 **Interactive Reading and Notetaking Study Guide, Spanish,** Adapted Version
L1 **Guided Reading Audio CD,** Spanish

Media and Technology
L1 SE on Audio CD
L2 Social Studies Skills Tutor CD-ROM
ExamView Test Bank CD-ROM

DISCOVERY SCHOOL

Quick View Video
View the chapter video for a quick preview of the main ideas.

Chapter 13

Visual Preview

? **How did westward expansion change the geography of the nation and demonstrate the determination of its people?**

Build Background Knowledge L2

Discuss the idea of westward expansion. Have students look at the map. Point out that in 1800, the term *the West* referred to the area between the Appalachian Mountains and the Mississippi River. By 1860, the United States became a continental nation, stretching from the Atlantic Ocean to the Pacific Ocean. Ask: **In what different ways did the United States acquire land?** *(Possible answer: through exploration, purchase, war, and treaties; students may name specific instances.)*

Instruction L2

■ For background information on conducting a lesson for the Visual Preview, see TE page T20.

■ Write the Essential Question on the board. Discuss the phrase "demonstrate the determination of its people." Ask: **What does it mean to be determined?** *(having a fixed or firm purpose)* **How do people demonstrate determination?** *(they do not give up, keep trying to overcome challenges or difficulties)* Have students discuss the challenges western travelers faced.

■ Have students review the timeline. Ask: **When did the Mexican-American War begin?** *(1846)* **When did the California gold rush begin?** *(1849)*

■ Have students look at the key. Help students define the terms *annexed* and *ceded* as used in the key.

■ Have students look at the map. Point out that as people began to move West, trails were established to help ease travel—although there were still great difficulties. Have students note the major trails. Ask: **Why do you think most trails began in major cities?** *(Possible answer: easier to buy supplies, join wagon trains)*

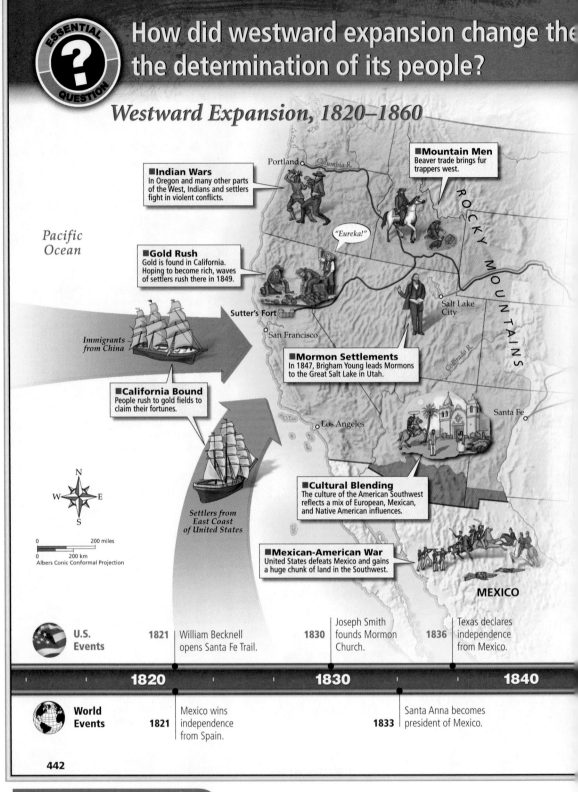

How did westward expansion change the the determination of its people?

Westward Expansion, 1820–1860

Indian Wars In Oregon and many other parts of the West, Indians and settlers fight in violent conflicts.

Mountain Men Beaver trade brings fur trappers west.

Gold Rush Gold is found in California. Hoping to become rich, waves of settlers rush there in 1849.

"Eureka!"

Pacific Ocean

Sutter's Fort

San Francisco

Salt Lake City

Immigrants from China

Mormon Settlements In 1847, Brigham Young leads Mormons to the Great Salt Lake in Utah.

California Bound People rush to gold fields to claim their fortunes.

Los Angeles

Santa Fe

Cultural Blending The culture of the American Southwest reflects a mix of European, Mexican, and Native American influences.

Settlers from East Coast of United States

Mexican-American War United States defeats Mexico and gains a huge chunk of land in the Southwest.

MEXICO

0   200 miles
0   200 km
Albers Conic Conformal Projection

U.S. Events	**1821** William Becknell opens Santa Fe Trail.	**1830** Joseph Smith founds Mormon Church.	**1836** Texas declares independence from Mexico.

1820   **1830**   **1840**

World Events	**1821** Mexico wins independence from Spain.	**1833** Santa Anna becomes president of Mexico.

442

History Background

Moving West Pioneers who wanted to move west had to carefully plan their journey. Pioneers began their trek west in the spring, to be sure that there was enough grass for the animals to graze on—leaving too early might prove deadly. The settlers also had to take with them all the food they would need for their trip. A family of four would need more than 1,000 pounds of food. Among the foodstuffs that pioneers packed into their wagons were flour, bacon, coffee, tea, lard, sugar, rice, and dried fruit. Settlers also carried guns and rifles, as well as tents, bedding, candles, soap, and cooking utensils. The cost of a trip was probably between $800 and $1,200.

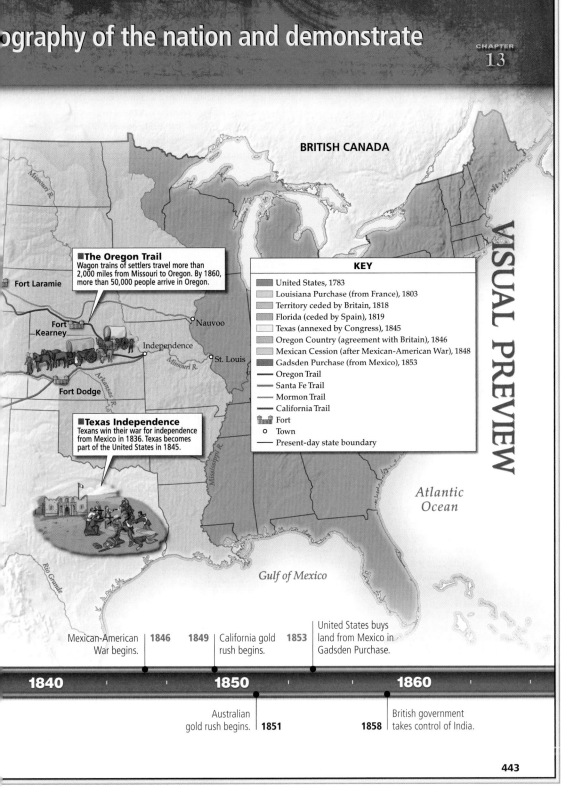

BRITISH CANADA

The Oregon Trail
Wagon trains of settlers travel more than 2,000 miles from Missouri to Oregon. By 1860, more than 50,000 people arrive in Oregon.

Fort Laramie

Fort Kearney

Nauvoo

Independence

St. Louis

Missouri R.

Fort Dodge

Arkansas R.

KEY

▪	United States, 1783
▪	Louisiana Purchase (from France), 1803
▪	Territory ceded by Britain, 1818
▪	Florida (ceded by Spain), 1819
▪	Texas (annexed by Congress), 1845
▪	Oregon Country (agreement with Britain), 1846
▪	Mexican Cession (after Mexican-American War), 1848
▪	Gadsden Purchase (from Mexico), 1853
—	Oregon Trail
—	Santa Fe Trail
—	Mormon Trail
—	California Trail
🏛	Fort
○	Town
—	Present-day state boundary

VISUAL PREVIEW

Texas Independence
Texans win their war for independence from Mexico in 1836. Texas becomes part of the United States in 1845.

Mississippi R.

Rio Grande

Atlantic Ocean

Gulf of Mexico

Mexican-American War begins. | 1846 | 1849 | California gold rush begins. | 1853 | United States buys land from Mexico in Gadsden Purchase.

1840 | **1850** | **1860**

Australian gold rush begins. | **1851**

British government takes control of India. | **1858**

443

Instruction (continued)

- Have students look at the arrow showing settlers heading to California. Explain that these settlers traveled by boat around South America to the West Coast.

- Have students review the map. Ask: **If you were a Mormon living in Nauvoo, Illinois, what route would you have taken to reach Salt Lake City, Utah?** *(the Oregon Trail)*

- Direct students' attention to the graphics on the map. Read the caption for Texas Independence. Ask: **When did Texas join the United States?** *(1845)* Pair students and have them select 2 graphics to analyze, using the Think-Write-Pair-Share strategy (TE p. T25.) Have students share their work with the class.

- Have students rewrite the Essential Question into two simple questions in their notes: **How did the move west change the country's geography? What actions showed that Americans were determined?** You may also post these questions in a prominent place in the classroom and leave them there while discussing the chapter. Tell students to use the section focus questions as a guide to answering the Essential Question as they read the chapter.

- Tell students that as they complete the Notetaking Study Guide for this chapter, they will be building the answer to the Essential Question.

📖 **Interactive Reading and Notetaking Study Guide,** Chapter 13 (Adapted Version also available.)

Vocabulary Builder

Vocabulary Preview Have students preview the vocabulary in the chapter and rate how well they know each word on the Word Knowledge Rating Form. Collect the sheets and explain that they will have a chance to go over the forms later.

All in One **Teaching Resources, Unit 4,** Word Knowledge Rating Form, p. 76

Monitor Progress Have students demonstrate their understanding of the vocabulary words by completing these activities.

- Ask students for an example of a *hostile* action.

- Have students describe a *policy* that they follow at school.

- Ask students to name types of music that have *distinct* qualities.

Review and Preview

Students have learned how settlers moved from the colonies on the Atlantic coast to the Appalachian Mountains. Now students will explore the continued westward movement.

Section Focus Question

What cultures and ideas influenced the development of the West?

Before you begin the lesson for the day, write the Section Focus Question on the board. (*Lesson focus: Native Americans, Spanish, Chinese, Americans from the East*)

Prepare to Read

Build Background Knowledge L2

The section deals with the idea of the West as the frontier. Remind students that they have read in Chapters 9 and 10 about earlier generations of Americans crossing mountains to settle new lands. Ask students to discuss what these Americans were looking for and what would motivate them to travel thousands of miles by wagon train to find it. Use the Idea Wave strategy (TE, p. T24) to elicit responses.

Set a Purpose L2

- Group students into pairs or groups of four. Distribute the Reading Readiness Guide. Ask students to fill in the first two columns of the chart.

  All in One Teaching Resources, Unit 4, Reading Readiness Guide, p. 77

- Use the Numbered Heads strategy (TE, p. T24) to call on students to share one piece of information they already know and one piece of information they want to know. The students will return to these worksheets later.

▲ Spanish mission in California

Mission San Luis Rey

"At this time (1829) its population was about three thousand Indians. . . . Some were engaged in agriculture, while others attended to the management of over sixty thousand head of cattle. Many were carpenters, masons, coopers, saddlers, shoemakers, weavers . . . while the females were employed in spinning and preparing wool for their looms. . . . "

—Alfred Robinson, *Life in California*, 1846

The West

Objectives

- Identify the destinations of settlers heading west in the early 1800s.
- Describe the unique culture of the Southwest.
- Explain the meaning of Manifest Destiny.

🔊 Reading Skill

Ask Analytical Questions Reading about historical events will often lead you to ask questions. When these questions are analytical—or require you to solve puzzles in the text to answer them—they can yield interesting research. Think about the *why* and *how* of history to help you ask questions about the text and then to frame possible research questions.

Key Terms

frontier   ranchero
land grant   expansion

Why It Matters Since colonial times, settlers had been moving westward over the Appalachian Mountains and beyond. As these settlers moved further westward, they encountered Native Americans and Mexicans. The mixing of these cultures affected the development of the West and the entire nation.

❓ Section Focus Question: What cultures and ideas influenced the development of the West?

What Was "The West"?

As the nation grew, Americans' idea of "the West" changed. Early Americans thought of the area between the Appalachians and the Mississippi River as the western frontier. A **frontier** is the land that forms the farthest extent of a nation's settled regions. By the 1820s, however, much of the land in this area had been settled. As the population soared, Americans began to look beyond the Mississippi River.

The Great Plains Stretching for seemingly endless miles to the west, the Great Plains lie between the Mississippi River and the Rocky Mountains. The Plains were easy to reach from eastern and southern states. However, settlers in the early 1800s were not attracted to this vast region. Farmers did not consider the land suitable for agriculture. The Plains were covered by grass that was anchored to the ground by deep root systems. Breaking up the dense sod would be hard manual labor.

For many settlers in the early 1800s, the Great Plains were simply a route to the Far West. Some were attracted to the area known as Oregon Country in the Northwest. Others were interested in the Mexican lands of the Southwest.

444 Chapter 13 Westward Expansion

Differentiated Instruction

L1 English Language Learners   **L1 Less Proficient Readers**   **L1 Special Needs**

Learning with Flashcards Have students make a list of the Key Terms and High-Use Words. Then, have them create flashcards with the word on one side and its definition on the other. Pair students with a partner and have them quiz each other on the definitions of the words using the flashcards. Check their understanding as they continue to read the section.

The Northwest In the Northwest, settlers were attracted to the fertile land stretching from beyond the Rocky Mountains to the Pacific Ocean. This region is now occupied by the states of Oregon and Washington as well as by most of British Columbia in Canada. In the early 1800s, the United States, Great Britain, Russia, and Spain all claimed this land as their own.

The Southwest The Mexican settlements in the Southwest were another major destination for settlers heading west. This area, known as the Spanish Borderlands, was part of New Spain. Together with Mexico, these lands had been claimed for Spain in the 1500s.

The lands of the Southwest included present-day California, Utah, Nevada, Arizona, New Mexico, Texas, and about half of Colorado. Ruled first by Spain, then by Mexico, these lands had a culture and history very different from that of the eastern United States.

☑**Checkpoint** **What did "the West" mean to Americans in the 1800s?**

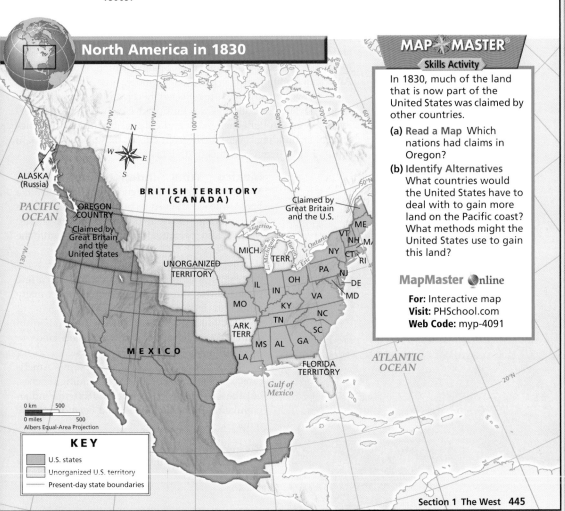

North America in 1830

MAP MASTER®
Skills Activity

In 1830, much of the land that is now part of the United States was claimed by other countries.
(a) Read a Map Which nations had claims in Oregon?
(b) Identify Alternatives What countries would the United States have to deal with to gain more land on the Pacific coast? What methods might the United States use to gain this land?

MapMaster ⬤nline

For: Interactive map
Visit: PHSchool.com
Web Code: myp-4091

KEY
- U.S. states
- Unorganized U.S. territory
- Present-day state boundaries

Section 1 The West **445**

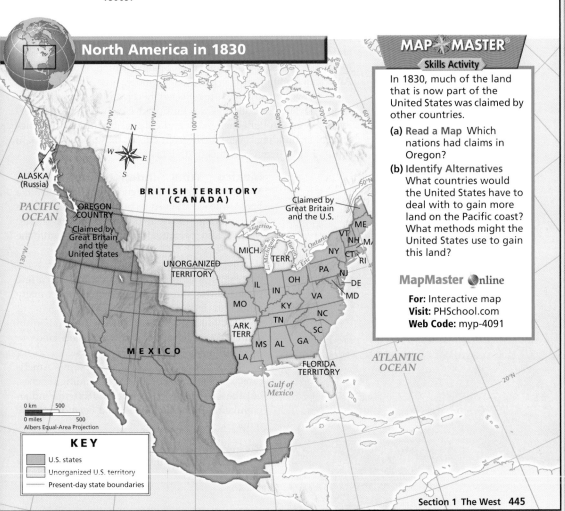

Vocabulary Builder

Use the information below to teach students this section's high-use words.

High-Use Word	Definition and Sample Sentence
policy, p. 446	*n.* plan or course of action, as pursued by a government The Missouri Compromise became **policy** in 1820.
distinct, p. 446	*adj.* clear or definite; different in its quality The Southwest had a **distinct** culture different from that of other parts of the country.

Ask Analytical Questions
What do you think were the land and climate features that attracted people to the Northwest? Suggest a possible research question to build on this topic.

Teach

What Was "The West"?

p. 444

Instruction L2

- **Vocabulary Builder** Before teaching this section, preteach the High-Use Words **policy** and **distinct** using the strategy on TE p. T21.

  Key Terms Following the instructions on p. 7, have students create a See It–Remember It chart for the Key Terms in this chapter.

- To help the students better understand the concept of the *frontier*, which is important to the understanding of this chapter, use the Concept Lesson Frontier. Distribute the Concept Organizer.

  All in One Teaching Resources, Unit 4, Concept Lesson, p. 89; Concept Organizer, p. 6

- Read What Was "The West"? with students using the Structured Silent Reading strategy (TE, p. T22).

- Ask students why most Americans moving west did not settle on the Great Plains. (*grasses made farming hard*)

- Ask students to consider who lived in the Northwest and Southwest. (*Native Americans lived in both; the Spanish only in the Southwest.*)

Independent Practice

Have students begin filling in the study guide for this section.

Monitor Progress

As students fill in the Notetaking Study Guide, circulate to make sure that they understand the idea of the West.

Answers

⬤ **Reading Skill** Possible answer: It had fertile soil, access to water, and a moderate climate. A research question: What factors explain settlement patterns during the westward expansion of the nineteenth century?

☑**Checkpoint** The West was the land west of the Mississippi River.

MAP MASTER Skills Activity **(a)** Great Britain and the United States **(b)** Mexico and Great Britain; diplomacy, war

Mexican Settlements
Manifest Destiny

pp. 446–447

Instruction **L2**

- Have students read Mexican Settlements and Manifest Destiny.

- Ask: **What were the groups in Spanish settlements?** (*peninsulares, creoles, mestizos*)

- Ask students who have completed the History Reading Skill Worksheet to share their research questions.

- Have students use the worksheet Manifest Destiny to explore debates on Manifest Destiny. Have students discuss how Channing's viewpoint is different from O'Sullivan's viewpoint.

All in One Teaching Resources, Unit 4, Manifest Destiny, p. 81; History Reading Skill Worksheet, p. 75

Independent Practice

Have students complete the study guide for this section.

Interactive Reading and Notetaking Study Guide, Chapter 13, Section 1 (Adapted Version also available.)

Monitor Progress

- As students fill in the Notetaking Study Guide, circulate to make sure students understand that the idea of Manifest Destiny gave Americans a claim to new land. Provide assistance as needed.

- Tell students to fill in the last column of the Reading Readiness Guide. Ask them to consider whether what they learned was what they expected to learn.

All in One Teaching Resources, Unit 4, Reading Readiness Guide, p. 77

Answers

Apply Information Native Americans and the Spanish, living together, shared their cultures.

Checkpoint The Spanish, Native Americans, and Africans shaped this culture.

Mission in the Southwest
Old Spanish missions, like this one in California, still dot the Southwest. Native Americans were forced to live and work on the mission grounds, where Spanish priests taught them about Christianity. **Critical Thinking: Apply Information** *How were missions like these an example of cultural blending?*

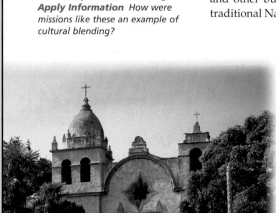

446

Mexican Settlements

Like England and France, Spain followed a <u>policy</u> of mercantilism toward its colonies. It was illegal for settlers in New Spain to trade with other countries. Raw materials were sent to Spain. Manufactured goods were shipped to the Spanish colonies for sale.

Over the years, many Spanish settlers, or peninsulares, had children. These American-born children were called creoles. Spanish settlers, Native Americans, and Africans also intermarried. The result was another group, the mestizos. By the 1800s, this combination of ethnic groups had created a <u>distinct</u> Southwestern culture.

Native Americans Spanish missionaries, such as Junípero Serro (ho NEE peh roh SEHR rah) in California, were determined to convert Native Americans to Catholicism. Many Indians in the borderlands were forced to live and work at missions. There, they herded sheep and cattle and raised crops. They also learned about the Catholic religion. In the end, the mission system took a terrible toll on Native Americans. Thousands died from overwork or disease.

Spanish settlers and Native Americans exchanged language, foods, and customs. The Spanish brought their language, religion, and laws to the region. The Indians introduced the Spanish to such foods as beans, squash, and potatoes. Spanish settlers adopted Native American clothing, such as ponchos and moccasins.

Southwestern architecture reflected this blending of cultures. The general style of the buildings was European. However, Native American laborers brought their skills and cultural traditions. Churches and other buildings were made from adobe, or sun-dried brick, a traditional Native American building material.

Mexico Wins Independence In 1821, Mexico won its independence from Spain. Unlike Spain, Mexico allowed its people to trade with the many foreign ships that landed on its shores. Mexico also permitted overland trade with the United States.

Under Spanish rule, land grants, or government gifts of land, had been given only to a few peninsulares. Mexico, however, made many grants to individual rancheros, or owners of ranches. Mexico also removed the missions from church control and distributed mission lands to rancheros and a few American settlers.

Much of this land belonged to Native Americans. Indians often responded by raiding ranches, but they were soon crushed. By 1850, the Indian population in the Southwest had been drastically reduced.

✓Checkpoint **What groups shaped the culture of the Southwest?**

Differentiated Instruction

L3 Advanced Readers

L3 Gifted and Talented

Using Literature Have a student with dramatic ability prepare to read "The Other Pioneers" by Roberto Félix Salazar aloud to the class. This poem is readily available in literature collections and anthologies. After reading, ask: **What did all pioneers have in common?** (*They plowed the land and built towns, houses, and churches.*)

Manifest Destiny

From the beginning, Americans had been interested in westward **expansion**, or extending the nation beyond its existing borders. Thomas Jefferson was one of many who believed that the nation must increase in size to make room for its growing population. As you have read, under Jefferson, the Louisiana Purchase doubled the territory of the nation.

By the 1840s, many Americans strongly favored westward expansion. Newspaper editor John L. O'Sullivan wrote in 1845:

> ❝The American claim is by the right of our manifest [obvious] destiny to overspread and possess the whole of the continent which Providence has given us for the development of the great experiment of liberty and . . . self-government entrusted to us.❞
>
> —John L. O'Sullivan, *United States Magazine and Democratic Review*

The phrase Manifest Destiny quickly became popular. It described the belief that the United States was destined, or meant, to extend from the Atlantic to the Pacific—"from sea to shining sea."

✓**Checkpoint** What did Americans mean by Manifest Destiny?

⭐ **Looking Back and Ahead** The drive to achieve Manifest Destiny would become one of the most powerful forces shaping American history. In the next sections, you will see how Americans pursued the goal of Manifest Destiny.

Section 1 | Check Your Progress

Progress Monitoring Online
For: Self-test with instant help
Visit: PHSchool.com
Web Code: mya-4091

Comprehension and Critical Thinking

1. (a) Recall Why did American farmers prefer to settle in the Northwest rather than the Great Plains?
(b) Evaluate Information How did the geography of the Great Plains affect U.S. settlement of that region in the early 1800s?

2. (a) Explain What is Manifest Destiny?
(b) Detect Points of View How do you think the Mexican government felt about the idea of Manifest Destiny?

🔁 **Reading Skill**
3. Ask Analytical Questions Suggest a possible research question related to this topic: The effect of Native American labor on slavery in Mexican settlements.

Key Terms
Fill in the blanks with the correct key terms.
4. Each time Americans settled farther west, the _____ moved.
5. Under Spanish rule, only peninsulares received _____, but under Mexican rule, rancheros received them as well.

Writing
6. Decide which is the best closing sentence for an essay discussing why Americans were drawn to the lands west of the Mississippi River. Explain your choice.
Sentences:
(a) So for many Americans, the West was a promise—of wealth, adventure, and freedom.
(b) The fertile lands of the Northwest drew many people who wanted to own farms.
(c) Therefore, the southwestern lands ruled by Mexico had developed a culture very different from that of easterners.

Assess Progress L2

Have students complete Check Your Progress. Administer the Section Quiz.

All in One **Teaching Resources, Unit 4,** Section Quiz, p. 90

To further assess student understanding, use the Progress Monitoring Transparency.

Progress Monitoring Transparencies, Chapter 13, Section 1

Reteach L1

If students need more instruction, have them read this section in the Interactive Reading and Notetaking Study Guide.

📖 **Interactive Reading and Notetaking Study Guide,** Chapter 13, Section 1 (Adapted Version also available.)

Extend L3

The dates when states joined the union tell a story about how the West was settled. Use the appendix in this book to compare California's date with the Great Plains state of North Dakota. Why did California become a state so much earlier? What earlier event may have helped California become a state? (*California: 1850, North Dakota: 1889; Settlers came to California earlier, whereas few settlers at that time moved to the hard-to-farm Great Plains; the 1849 gold rush*)

Progress Monitoring Online

Students may check their comprehension of this section by completing the Progress Monitoring Online graphic organizer and self-quiz.

Section 1 Check Your Progress

1. (a) The land was easier to farm.
(b) The pioneers bypassed most of the Great Plains in the early 1800s because they thought it was unsuitable for farming.

2. (a) the belief that the United States should expand to the Pacific Ocean
(b) Possible answer: threatened and angry

3. Possible question: How did the use of forced Native American labor in Mexican settlements compare to the forced labor system used by their Spanish predecessors?

4. frontier

5. land grants

6. Answers should be supported.

Answer

✓**Checkpoint** The United States should extend west across the continent to the Pacific Ocean.

Review and Preview

Students have learned about the merchants and Christian missionaries who were among the earliest settlers in the colonies. Now they will read about the role traders and missionaries had in the westward expansion.

Why did people go west and what challenges did they face?

Before you begin the lesson for the day, write the Section Focus Question on the board. (*Lesson focus: They wanted better lives; they faced a dangerous journey.*)

Prepare to Read

Build Background Knowledge L2

In this section, students will read about people who risked everything for a new life in the West. Remind students that they have read about earlier Americans who crossed the Appalachians for land and a new start in life. Ask students to consider the courage this decision took and how it has shaped how Americans see themselves. Use the Idea Wave strategy (TE, p. T24) to elicit responses.

Set a Purpose L2

- Read each statement in the Reading Readiness Guide aloud. Ask students to mark the statements True or False.

  All in One **Teaching Resources, Unit 4,** Reading Readiness Guide, p. 78

- Have students discuss the statements in pairs or groups of four, then mark their worksheets again. Use the Numbered Heads strategy (TE, p. T24) to call on students to share their group's perspectives. The students will return to these worksheets later.

◄ A mountain man

Thirty Thousand Beaver Skins

❝The annual quantity of these furs could not be exactly ascertained, but Mr. Smith was informed indirectly that they amounted to about thirty thousand beaver skins, besides otter skins and small furs. The beaver skins alone, at the New York prices, would be worth above two hundred and fifty thousand dollars. ❞

—Report of trappers Jedediah Smith, David Jackson, and W.L. Sublette, 1830

Trails to the West

Objectives

- Explain how traders and fur trappers helped open the West.

- List the reasons pioneers traveled along the Oregon Trail and describe the hardships they faced.

- Discuss the issues for women, Native Americans, and new settlers in the West.

🔁 Reading Skill

Ask Inferential Questions You can also ask inferential questions to explore a text and generate research ideas. Inferential questions require you to read between the lines. In other words, you have to use clues in the text and your own knowledge to make reasonable guesses about history. You can then conduct research to confirm or disprove your guesses.

Key Terms and People

William Becknell
John Jacob Astor
mountain man
rendezvous

Marcus and
Narcissa
Whitman

Why It Matters Like the settlers who traveled across the Atlantic to build the thirteen colonies, settlers who moved westward were drawn by a variety of factors and had to face difficult challenges.

❓ **Section Focus Question: Why did people go west and what challenges did they face?**

Traders Lead the Way

The first Americans to move into the Far West were traders. They were looking for new markets in which to sell their goods. In the process, they blazed important trails for the people who followed.

The Santa Fe Trail As you have read, when Mexico won independence, it began to allow overland trade with the United States. In 1821, Captain William Becknell led a wagon train filled with merchandise from Independence, Missouri, to Santa Fe, New Mexico. The route stretched for about 800 miles.

Becknell crossed treacherous rivers with bottoms of quicksand. He and the traders traveling with him barely survived the desert. Then, he had to find a way through nearly impassable mountains. In spite of these obstacles, Becknell's group reached Santa Fe with their wagons. Other Americans followed Becknell's route. It became known as the Santa Fe Trail. The Santa Fe Trail soon became a busy international trading route.

The Oregon Fur Trade Farther north, fur traders were making huge fortunes. John Jacob Astor, a German immigrant, sent the first American fur-trading expedition to Oregon. Astor established the American Fur Company in 1808 at Fort Astor, now Astoria, Oregon.

448 Chapter 13 Westward Expansion

Differentiated Instruction

L3 Advanced Readers

Mountain Men Have students research the lives of mountain men. Ask them to find facts about the life and accomplishments of one of these mountain men: Jedediah Smith, James Beckwourth, or Jim Bridger. Have students use what they learn to write a short biography of the person they chose, including why he went west and the challenges he faced. Have students contribute information to the class discussion of the life of the traders.

Astor's expedition consisted of two groups. The first group sailed around South America and up the Pacific coast. The second group traveled across the continent, using information that had been recorded by Lewis and Clark. On the way, they found the South Pass through the Rocky Mountains. This important route helped to open the Northwest for the missionaries and settlers who followed.

Mountain Men The fur trade made Astor the richest man in the country. The trappers who supplied him with furs were also eager to become rich. These mountain men, or fur trappers of the Northwest, would become legendary.

For most of the year, trappers led isolated lives in a dangerous environment. They endured bitter cold, intense heat, and attacks from wild animals. Jedediah Smith was once scalped by a grizzly bear. He persuaded a companion to sew his scalp back onto his head and to piece together his severed ear. Several weeks later, Smith returned to his work.

Once a year, trappers would bring their furs to a rendezvous (RAHN day voo), a meeting where the trappers would trade furs for supplies. Here, the mountain men would celebrate their time together—singing, laughing, and competing in contests. Then, they got down to serious bargaining. Beaver fur was in great demand in the East, so trappers were able to command high prices for their furs.

By the 1830s, the supply of beavers was nearly exhausted. Most trappers moved back east to become farmers, merchants, or even bankers. Others stayed as guides for the wagon trains that brought thousands of settlers west in the 1840s. One mountain man, an African American named James Beckwourth, discovered a pass through the Sierras that later became a major route to California.

☑**Checkpoint** Why did the mountain men travel to Oregon?

The Oregon Trail

The first white easterners to build permanent homes in Oregon were missionaries. In the 1830s, they began to travel west for the purpose of bringing their religious beliefs to the Indians.

Missionaries One couple, Marcus and Narcissa Whitman, set up a mission in Oregon to serve the Cayuse Indians. The Whitmans had trouble from the start. The Cayuses mistrusted them, partly because the Whitmans made little effort to understand Cayuse ways.

As more settlers arrived and took over Indian lands, the Cayuses grew increasingly hostile. Then, in 1847, an epidemic of measles killed many Cayuse adults and nearly all their children. Blaming the Whitmans, the Indians killed them along with 12 other settlers.

Still, missionaries like the Whitmans greatly spurred settlement of the West. Their glowing reports of Oregon led more easterners to make the journey west. Farmers sought the free and fertile land, the mild climate, and the plentiful rainfall of the river valleys. Settlers from all over the country were in the grip of "Oregon Fever."

Vocabulary Builder
environment (en VY ruhn mehnt)
n. surroundings

Vocabulary Builder
hostile (HAHS tihl) *adj.* unfriendly; intending to do harm

Vocabulary Builder

Use the information below to teach students this section's high-use words.

High-Use Word	Definition and Sample Sentence
environment, p. 449	*n.* surroundings Lewis and Clark's report included information on the **environment** of the Louisiana Territory.
hostile, p. 449	*adj.* unfriendly, intending to do harm White settlers encountered **hostile** groups of Native Americans as they moved westward.

Teach

Traders Lead the Way
p. 448

Instruction L2

- **Vocabulary Builder** Before teaching this section, preteach the High-Use Words **environment** and **hostile** using the strategy on TE p. T21.

  Key Terms Have students continue filling in the See It–Remember It chart for the Key Terms in this chapter.

- Have students read Traders Lead the Way using the Paragraph Shrinking strategy (TE, p. T23).

- Ask students how fur traders went to Oregon. (*Some came by boat around South America and up the Pacific coast. Others came by land, crossing the Rocky Mountains.*)

- Discuss with students challenges faced by traders in the West. Ask: **Why do you think people took on these hardships?** (*Students should infer that they made money by bringing goods west and bringing furs out of the Northwest.*)

- Use the Fur Traders Descending the Missouri transparency to engage students on the lives of fur trappers.

Color Transparencies, Fur Traders Descending the Missouri

Independent Practice

Have students begin to fill in the study guide for this section.

Interactive Reading and Notetaking Study Guide, Chapter 13, Section 2 (Adapted Version also available.)

Monitor Progress

As students fill in the Notetaking Study Guide, circulate and make sure that they understand why fur traders went to the West. Provide assistance as needed.

Answer

☑**Checkpoint** to get rich

The Oregon Trail

p. 449

Instruction
L2

- Have students read The Oregon Trail. Remind students to look for the sequence of events.

- Ask students why the Whitmans went to Oregon. (*to set up a mission to serve the Cayuse*)

- Have students read the worksheet Narcissa Whitman's Letter to Her Sister to learn more about what life was like on the Oregon Trail. Ask them to answer the questions that follow. Have students discuss why Narcissa Whitman calls this part of the country "buffalo country."

All in One Teaching Resources, Narcissa Whitman's Letter to Her Sister, p. 82

Independent Practice

Have students continue filling in the study guide for this section.

Interactive Reading and Notetaking Study Guide, Chapter 13, Section 2 (Adapted Version also available.)

Monitor Progress

As students fill in the Notetaking Study Guide, circulate and make sure that they understand the difficulties of travel on the Oregon Trail. Provide assistance as needed.

Answers

Reading Skill Possible answer: Some wanted adventure, while others had a religious calling. They must have believed that they were heading to a better life. Possible research question: What motivated Americans to explore and settle the West?

Identify Costs and Benefits Answers may vary, but should mention the risks of travel as well as the potential for greater freedom and riches.

Checkpoint to band together for protection

On the Oregon Trail Most settlers followed the Oregon Trail, a route that stretched more than 2,000 miles from Missouri to Oregon. They set out in spring and had to be in Oregon within five months. Travelers caught by winter in the Rockies risked a slow death. The trip itself was hazardous. Disease and accidents killed about one traveler out of every ten on the Oregon Trail.

Pioneers on the Oregon Trail banded together for protection. Most traveled in long trains of covered wagons. The wagons carried supplies, while the people walked. As the miles went by, the horses and oxen tired more easily. People began to discard personal items to lighten their wagons. The trail was scattered with "leeverites," short for "leave 'er right here."

Dust got into everything. Some people wore masks to keep it out of their faces and lungs. Clean, safe water was hard to find. Francis Parkman, a famous historian, observed the following incident:

> **"** I saw a tall slouching fellow . . . contemplating the contents of his tin cup, which he had just filled with water. 'Look here, you,' said he; 'it's chock full of animals!' The cup . . . exhibited in fact an extraordinary variety and profusion of animal life. **"**
> —Francis Parkman, *The Oregon Trail*

Despite such hardships, more than 50,000 people reached Oregon between 1840 and 1860.

Checkpoint Why did settlers travel by wagon train?

Ask Inferential Questions
Why do you think so many Americans were willing to face the hardships of westward settlement? Suggest a possible research topic to answer this question.

● INFOGRAPHIC

To many easterners, Oregon held out the promise of fertile, available farmland and greater freedom. But first, they had to pack their belongings and set off on the long, difficult Oregon Trail. **Critical Thinking** *Identify Costs and Benefits* **Do you think the benefits of moving to Oregon outweighed the risk? Why or why not?**

450 Chapter 13 Westward Expansion

Differentiated Instruction

L1 English Language Learners   **L1 Special Needs**

Listening to the Text Have students read the text of Trails to the West as they listen to the SE on Audio CD. Monitor student answers to Checkpoint questions to make sure they understand the material. Students can be provided with a copy of the CD to work independently at home or in the School Resource Center.

SE on Audio CD, Chapter 13, Section 2

Life in the West

Pioneer life was filled with hardships. Settlers arrived with few possessions. Working only with hand tools, they had to clear the land, plant crops, and build shelters. Disease, accidents, and natural disasters like storms and floods were an ever-present threat.

A. H. Garrison was 15 years old when his family went west in 1846. They traveled along the Oregon Trail with 74 other wagons. Along the way, his father became so ill he was unable to walk. Garrison later recalled the hardships of their first winter in Oregon.

> **"**On Christmas day, it began to snow, and it continued until the ground was covered to a depth of twenty inches. . . . At the beginning of the storm, father had thirteen head of oxen, and twelve head of cows, and one fine American mare. There was no feed to be had, and the grass was so covered that the cattle could get nothing to eat. . . . When spring came, we had four oxen and three cows left.**"**
>
> —*Reminiscences of A. H. Garrison*

Some settlers gave up and returned to the East. Others, like John Bidwell of California, met the challenges and went on to live extraordinary lives. Bidwell and his wife Annie each became civic leaders. John became a United States Congressman and even ran for President, while Annie fought for temperance and the right of women to vote.

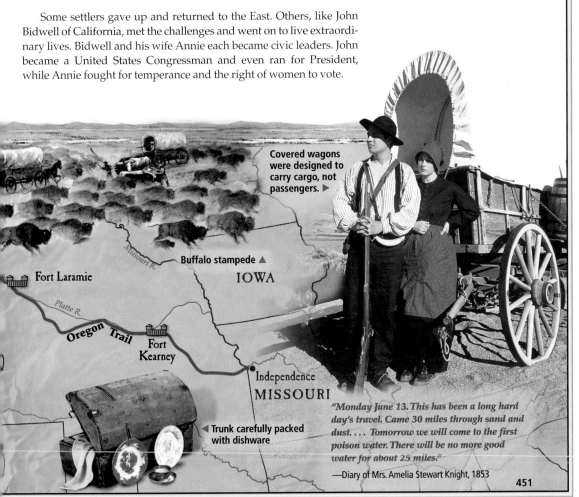

Covered wagons were designed to carry cargo, not passengers. ▶

Buffalo stampede ▲

IOWA

Fort Laramie

Missouri R.

Platte R.

Oregon Trail

Fort Kearney

Independence
MISSOURI

◀ Trunk carefully packed with dishware

"Monday June 13. This has been a long hard day's travel. Came 30 miles through sand and dust. . . . Tomorrow we will come to the first poison water. There will be no more good water for about 25 miles."
—Diary of Mrs. Amelia Stewart Knight, 1853

451

Seeing the Main Idea

On the Oregon Trail On the prairies of the Middle West and on the Great Plains, wagons could be used without the necessity of making roads, and there the covered wagon, or prairie schooner, predominated. The name *schooner* was an allusion to the white-topped schooners of the sea. The schooner was much lighter than the earlier Conestoga wagon, and rarely needed more than four horses, and sometimes only two, even on virgin prairie trails. Oxen were frequently used instead of horses.

Travel was slow, dangerous, and exhausting. Have students read the passage from the diary of Mrs. Knight. Using the Idea Wave, ask students to brainstorm for the next entries in the journal.

History Background

South Pass The key to the Oregon Trail was South Pass, which was first discovered in 1812 by several of Astor's men and rediscovered by the mountain man Jedediah Smith in 1824. South Pass is not a narrow pass through the mountains but rather a broad valley, about 20 miles wide, at an elevation of 8,000 feet, through which the Continental Divide passes. At South Pass, Oregon Trail travelers were only halfway and still had 1,000 miles left to travel.

Life in the West

p. 451

Instruction

L2

- Have students read Life in the West. Remind students to look for causes and effects.

- Ask: **What were some of the hardships pioneers faced in their move westward?** (*hard work to clear the land and build shelters, disease, accidents, natural disasters*) **What qualities do you think these pioneers had?** (*determined, realistic, self-reliant, hardy*)

- Have students discuss the role of women in the West. Ask: **How were women in the West rewarded for their contributions?** (*They received the right to vote.*)

- Have students brainstorm for images of the West they have gained through literature and movies. Ask: **What impact do you think the experience of these pioneers had on our national self-image?** (*Possible answer: We see ourselves as brave, determined, strong, and resourceful.*)

Independent Practice

Have students continue filling in the study guide for this section.

Monitor Progress

- As students fill in the Notetaking Study Guide, circulate and make sure that they understand the challenges of living in the West. Provide assistance as needed.

- Tell students to fill in the last column of the Reading Readiness Guide. Probe for what they learned that confirms or invalidates each statement.

All in One Teaching Resources, Unit 4, Reading Readiness Guide, p. 78

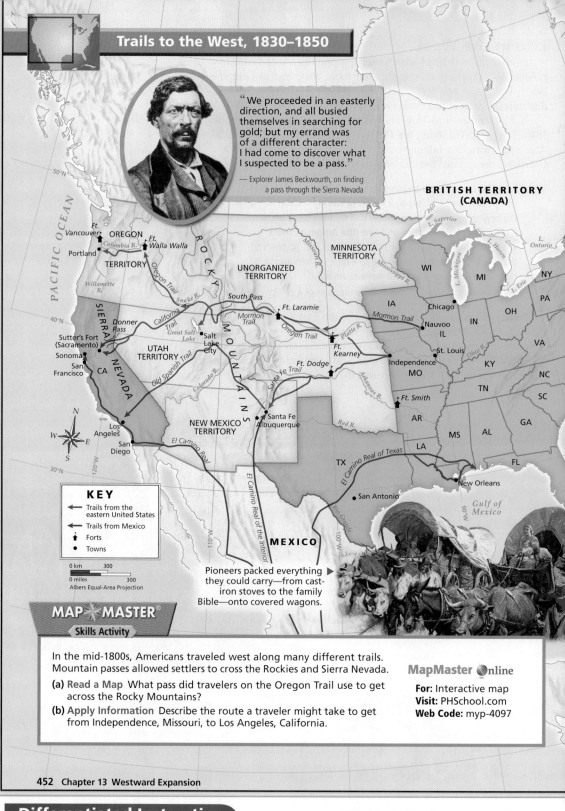

Trails to the West, 1830–1850

"We proceeded in an easterly direction, and all busied themselves in searching for gold; but my errand was of a different character: I had come to discover what I suspected to be a pass."

— Explorer James Beckwourth, on finding a pass through the Sierra Nevada

KEY

← Trails from the eastern United States

← Trails from Mexico

⚑ Forts

• Towns

0 km 300
0 miles 300
Albers Equal-Area Projection

Pioneers packed everything they could carry—from cast-iron stoves to the family Bible—onto covered wagons.

MAP MASTER
Skills Activity

In the mid-1800s, Americans traveled west along many different trails. Mountain passes allowed settlers to cross the Rockies and Sierra Nevada.

(a) Read a Map What pass did travelers on the Oregon Trail use to get across the Rocky Mountains?

(b) Apply Information Describe the route a traveler might take to get from Independence, Missouri, to Los Angeles, California.

MapMaster Online

For: Interactive map
Visit: PHSchool.com
Web Code: myp-4097

452 Chapter 13 Westward Expansion

Differentiated Instruction

L3 Advanced Readers   **L3 Gifted and Talented**

Westward Expansion Have students work in a group to plan a board game about westward expansion. Have them use the two-page Westward Ho! worksheet to plan and play the game. Students should bring in their finished product and

explain or play the game in class. If appropriate, students of varying levels may play the game.

All in One Teaching Resources, Westward Ho!, p. 86

Answers

 (a) South Pass **(b)** The Santa Fe Trail to Gila River and Overland Mail trails; or the Santa Fe Trail to the Old Spanish Trail

452 Chapter 13

Women in the West Women in the West worked alongside men to make a success of their family farms. The fact that their labor was necessary for a family's survival raised the status of western women.

Meanwhile, as you have read, women in the East had begun to campaign for greater political and legal rights. Chief among these was the right to vote. On a national level, women's struggle for the vote would take many years. But the West was quicker to reward the hard work of its women. In 1869, the Wyoming Territory became the first area of the United States to grant women the vote.

Native Americans and Settlers Native Americans in Oregon lived in an uneasy peace with the white settlers. Indians in the southern part of Oregon usually got along with whites. In northern Oregon, however, Native Americans were angered by the presence of strangers on their lands.

The discovery of gold in northern Oregon in the 1850s brought large numbers of white and Chinese miners into the area. War broke out there in 1855. The miners killed several dozen Native American men. Three months later, miners massacred an equal number of Indian women, children, and old men.

The Indians fought back, killing white and Chinese alike. The brief war ended when the U.S. government intervened. The Native Americans were forced to accept peace treaties.

Woman harvesting hay on a western farm

☑**Checkpoint** Why did women enjoy greater equality in the West than in the East?

⭐ **Looking Back and Ahead** The Oregon and Santa Fe trails created close links between east and west. In the next section, you will see how western lands became part of the United States.

Section 2 | **Check Your Progress**

Progress Monitoring ◉nline
For: Self-test with instant help
Visit: PHSchool.com
Web Code: mya-4092

Comprehension and Critical Thinking

1. (a) Recall Why did Americans go to Oregon in the early 1800s?
(b) Analyze Cause and Effect What factors might have discouraged Americans from traveling to Oregon?

2. (a) Explain Why did conflict arise between Native Americans and settlers in Oregon?
(b) Make Predictions Do you think such conflicts would be likely to continue later in the 1800s? Explain.

◉ Reading Skill

3. Ask Inferential Questions Reread the text following the heading "The Oregon Fur Trade." What qualities were needed to be successful as a fur trapper in Oregon? Suggest a possible research question to take this topic further.

Key Terms
Read each sentence below. If the sentence is true, write YES and explain why. If the sentence is not true, write NO and explain why not.
4. Mountain men made their living by farming the Great Plains.

5. A trapper would often trade his furs for supplies at a rendezvous.

Writing

6. For each of these transitions (connecting words), write a sentence that expresses a cause-effect relationship about the topic in parentheses. **Transitions:**
(a) because (Astor and the Oregon Trail)
(b) as a result (the decline in the fur trade)
(c) therefore (hardships on the Oregon Trail)

Assess Progress L2

Have students complete Check Your Progress. Administer the Section Quiz.

All in One Teaching Resources, Unit 4, Section Quiz, p. 91

To further assess student understanding, use the Progress Monitoring Transparency.

Progress Monitoring Transparencies, Chapter 13, Section 2

Reteach L1

If students need more instruction, have them read this section in the Interactive Reading and Notetaking Study Guide and complete the accompanying question.

📖 **Interactive Reading and Notetaking Study Guide,** Chapter 13, Section 2 (Adapted Version also available.)

Extend L3

Have students research on the Internet for information about mountain men. Ask students to write a brief letter "back home" from the point of view of a mountain man. The letter should mention the hardships they faced and why they undertook the journey. Provide students with the Web Code below.

Extend ◉nline
For: Help in starting the Extend activity
Visit: PHSchool.com
Web Code: mye-0265

Progress Monitoring Online

Students may check their comprehension of this section by completing the Progress Monitoring Online graphic organizer and self-quiz.

Section 2 Check Your Progress

1. (a) for the free and fertile land, mild climate, and rainfall in the river valleys
(b) The journey was long and hard. Native Americans sometimes attacked travelers and settlers because they were angered by the presence of strangers on their lands. There was danger of not making it across the Rockies before winter set in.

2. (a) Conflict between miners and Native Americans occurred in northern Oregon over land, and miners killed many Native Americans, causing war to break out.
(b) Yes. As more settlers arrived, they would take land and fishing areas away from Native Americans.

3. Possible answer: To be a successful fur trapper, one had to be adventurous, willing to take risks, and have capital to invest in a new business. Possible research question: Why was John Jacob Astor successful?

4. no; mountain men were fur traders.

5. yes, this is where trappers would trade their furs.

6. Sentences should show understanding of cause-and-effect relationships.

Answer

☑Checkpoint Women enjoyed greater equality because their labor was needed and valued.

Section 3
Step-by-Step Instruction

Review and Preview

Students have learned about traders moving west. Now they will find out how the increased tensions between the United States and Mexico led to war.

Section Focus Question

What were the causes and effects of the Texas War for Independence and the Mexican-American War?

Write the Section Focus Question on the board. (*Lesson focus: American settlement, the United States expanding*)

Prepare to Read

Build Background Knowledge L2

In this section, students will read about the years of conflict with Mexico that resulted in the independence of Texas and in the Mexican Cession. Remind students that they have read about settlers moving to Texas. Ask students to consider the cultural and religious differences between the American settlers and the Mexicans. Would they consider these people likely to live in harmony or not? Why? Use the Think-Write-Pair-Share strategy (TE, p. T25) to elicit responses.

Set a Purpose L2

■ Read each statement in the Reading Readiness Guide aloud. Ask students to mark the statements True or False.

> **All in One Teaching Resources, Unit 4,** Reading Readiness Guide, p. 79

■ Have students discuss the statements in pairs or groups of four, then mark their worksheets again. Use the Numbered Heads strategy (TE, p. T24) to call on students to share their group's perspectives. The students will return to these worksheets later.

SECTION **3**

I Wish to See Texas Free

❝I wish to see Texas free from . . . religious intolerance and other anti-republican restrictions, and independent at once; and as an individual have always been ready to risk my all to obtain it: . . . I now think the time has come for Texas to assert her natural rights; and were I in the convention I would urge an immediate declaration of independence.❞

—Stephen Austin, letter to Sam Houston, 1835

◀ Stephen Austin

Conflict With Mexico

Objectives
- Explain how Texas became independent from Mexico.
- Discuss the issues involved in annexing Texas and Oregon.
- Summarize the main events in the Mexican-American War.
- Explain how the United States achieved Manifest Destiny.

 **Reading Skill**

Ask Questions to Synthesize Information As you read history, recall what you already know about the topic. Consider as well what you know about related topics or experiences—even from modern times. Pull these many pieces of information together to ask and answer questions about the text. Then, use your questions to build research topics.

Key Terms and People

Stephen Austin	annex
dictatorship	James K. Polk
siege	cede
Sam Houston	John C. Frémont

Why It Matters Mexico became independent in 1821. That same year, American traders were traveling to the Southwest along the Santa Fe Trail. Meanwhile, American settlers arrived in the Mexican province of Texas. Growing tensions between Mexicans and Americans led to fighting.

❓ Section Focus Question: What were the causes and effects of the Texas War for Independence and the Mexican-American War?

Texas Wins Independence

In 1820, the Spanish governor of Texas gave Moses Austin a land grant to establish a small colony in Texas. After Moses died, his son, Stephen Austin, led a group of some 300 Americans into Texas.

Soon after, Mexico won independence from Spain. The Mexican government agreed to honor Austin's claim to the land. In return, Austin and his colonists agreed to become Mexican citizens and to worship in the Roman Catholic Church.

Growing Conflict Thousands of Americans flooded into Texas. They soon came into conflict with the Mexican government. The new settlers were Protestant, not Catholic. Also, many of the settlers were slaveholders from the American South who wanted to grow cotton in Texas. However, Mexico had abolished slavery.

For a while, Mexico tolerated these violations of its laws. Then, in 1830, Mexico banned further American settlement. Still, Americans kept arriving in Texas. Tensions increased as Mexico tried to enforce its laws banning slavery and requiring settlers to worship in the Catholic Church. Mexico also began to levy heavy taxes on American imports.

Differentiated Instruction

L1 English Language Learners **L1 Less Proficient Readers** **L1 Special Needs**

Peer Assistance The High-Use Words and Key Terms include several words that might be not only unfamiliar to students, but also difficult to pronounce. Words such as *levy, provoke, siege, annex,* and *cede* all present challenges. Once you have intro-duced the words to the entire class, pair English Language Learners, Less Proficient Readers, and Special Needs Students. Have each pair write a sentence for each of these words. Check that sentences demonstrate student understanding of the words.

Declaring Independence American settlers wanted more representation in the Mexican legislature. Some Tejanos (teh HAH nos), Texans of Mexican descent, also hoped for a democratic government that gave less power to the central government.

These hopes were dashed in 1833 when General Antonio López de Santa Anna became president of Mexico. Santa Anna wanted a strong central government, with himself at the head. Soon after, Santa Anna overturned Mexico's democratic constitution and started a **dictatorship**, or one-person rule.

Austin urged Texans to revolt against the Mexican government. In 1836, Texans declared independence from Mexico and created the Republic of Texas.

Texans at War Santa Anna responded with force. His troops laid siege to the Alamo, a mission in San Antonio where about 185 Anglo-Americans and Tejanos were gathered. A **siege** is an attack in which one force surrounds a city or fort. The defenders of the Alamo held out for 12 days under heavy cannon fire. At last, Mexican forces overran the Alamo. All of the defenders were killed in battle or executed afterward. Inspired by the bravery of the Alamo defenders, many American volunteers joined the Texan army.

The following April, the commander of the Texan forces, **Sam Houston**, led a small army in a surprise attack against Santa Anna's army at San Jacinto. Texans shouted "Remember the Alamo!" Within 18 minutes, the Texans had captured Santa Anna. They forced him to sign a treaty recognizing Texan independence.

Discovery SCHOOL

Explore More Video
To learn more about the Texas War for Independence, view the video.

Siege at the Alamo For 12 days, a small group of Texans held off Mexican troops at the Alamo. This print from the 1800s is not an eyewitness portrayal, but it gives an idea of the odds against the defenders of the Alamo. *Critical Thinking: Detect Points of View Based on this print (right), why do you think many Americans admired the defenders of the Alamo?*

The Alamo today

Vocabulary Builder

Use the information below to teach students this section's high-use words.

High-Use Word	Definition and Sample Sentence
decade, p. 456	*n.* a period of ten years The United States Census Bureau conducts a census of the population every **decade**.
provoke, p. 457	*v.* to cause to anger; to excite; to cause an action Laws that forced Native Americans off their land **provoked** an angry response.

Teach

Texas Wins Independence
p. 454

Instruction

■ **Vocabulary Builderds** Before teaching this section, preteach the High-Use Words **decade** and **provoke** using the strategy on TE p. T21.

Key Terms Have students continue to fill in the See It–Remember It chart.

■ Have students read Texas Wins Independence using the Choral Reading strategy (TE, p. T22).

■ Ask: **What were the conflicts between Mexicans and new settlers in Texas?** (*Mexico forbade slavery. Mexico was a Catholic country, whereas the American settlers were Protestant. Mexico also taxed American imports heavily.*)

■ Have students complete the worksheet Texas War for Independence. Have them refer to their timelines as you continue reading the section.

 **Teaching Resources, Unit 4,** Texas War for Independence, p. 83

Independent Practice
Have students begin filling in the study guide for this section.

Monitor Progress

As students fill in the Notetaking Study Guide, circulate and make sure that they understand the conflict between Texans and Mexican norms.

Explore More Video

Discovery School Video
The Alamo This video examines the fight at the Alamo between the Texan rebels and the Mexican army led by General Antonio López de Santa Anna.

Answer
Detect Points of View Possible answer: the defenders' bravery

Annexing Texas and Oregon

p. 456

Instruction `L2`

- Have students read Annexing Texas and Oregon. Remind them to look for the sequence of events.

- Ask: **How was the annexation of Texas linked to Oregon?** (*The balance of slave and free states was maintained.*)

- Help students see the link between national politics and foreign policy. Ask them to speculate why President Tyler presented Texas annexation to Congress before leaving office. (*Students should understand that Polk's election showed that voters supported annexation; Tyler believed he was fulfilling the will of the people.*)

Independent Practice

Have students continue filling in the study guide for this section.

Interactive Reading and Notetaking Study Guide, Chapter 13, Section 3 (Adapted Version also available.)

Monitor Progress

As students fill in the Notetaking Study Guide, circulate and make sure that they understand the overarching theme of expanding the United States. Provide assistance as needed.

Answers

 Reading Skill Possible answer: A state's status affected the balance of power between slave and free states. Possible research topic: What issues did Texas face seeking statehood?

Checkpoint Texans wanted freedom of religion and wanted to establish cotton plantations using slave labor.

MAP MASTER Skills Activity **(a)** Mexico **(b)** because there was a large disputed area

---

Why was it important whether a new state was a slave state or a free state? Suggest a possible research topic building on this question.

Vocabulary Builder
decade (DEK ayd) **n.** a period of ten years

Republic of Texas Sam Houston became president of the new Republic of Texas. He hoped that the United States would annex, or add on, Texas. But public opinion in the United States was divided. Southerners supported annexation of Texas as a slave state. Northerners opposed this, but still hoped for western expansion.

Presidents Andrew Jackson and Martin Van Buren refused to support annexation. Both feared that adding a slave state might spark a huge political fight that could split the Union.

Checkpoint Why did Texans want independence from Mexico?

Annexing Texas and Oregon

A <u>decade</u> after Texas won its independence, the annexation of Texas remained an unsettled question. It became a major issue in the presidential election of 1844.

Election of 1844 President John Tyler favored the annexation of Texas. But Tyler was not nominated for a second term. In 1844, the Whigs nominated Henry Clay instead.

Clay hoped to avoid the issue of annexation. But the Democratic candidate, James K. Polk, called for the annexation of both Texas and Oregon. At the time, Oregon was jointly held by Britain and the United States. Polk demanded that the British withdraw from all territory south of latitude 54°40'N. Polk, the candidate of expansion, won the election.

Annexation Shortly before Polk took office, Tyler asked Congress to annex Texas. Congress voted for admission of Texas as a state in 1845, three days before Tyler left office. A convention of Texan delegates quickly met and voted for annexation.

In keeping with his campaign promise, President Polk negotiated a treaty with Britain to divide Oregon. The United States got the lands south of latitude 49°N. Eventually, this territory became the states of Washington, Oregon, and part of Idaho.

Tensions With Mexico The annexation of Texas increased tensions with Mexico. Mexico had never formally recognized Texan independence. The treaty that Santa Anna had been forced to sign at San Jacinto set the southern boundary of Texas at the Rio Grande. The Mexican government claimed that the southern boundary of Texas was the Nueces River, farther to the north.

The Texas War for Independence

KEY
← Texan forces   ← Mexican forces
✦ Texan victories   ✦ Mexican victories

MAP MASTER
Skills Activity

After a brief but bloody war, the Republic of Texas won its independence from Mexico.

(a) Read a Map Key Who won the battle at Goliad?

(b) Make Predictions Based on this map, why might there be future conflict between Texas and Mexico?

MapMaster **Online**

For: Interactive map
Visit: PHSchool.com
Web Code: myp-4094

Differentiated Instruction

L3 Advanced Readers

Defenders of the Alamo Have students choose one of the three famous defenders of the Alamo—William Travis, Davy Crockett, or Jim Bowie—and research his life. Have students write a brief report

L3 Gifted and Talented

about the defender or work with other students to prepare a visual display about his life and contributions to the defense of the Alamo.

In fact, Texas had never controlled the area between the two rivers. But setting the Rio Grande as the border between Texas and Mexico would have given Texas much more land. President Polk put pressure on Mexico to accept this claim. Still, Mexico refused.

✓**Checkpoint** How did the annexation of Texas increase tensions with Mexico?

The Mexican-American War

Polk knew that the Mexican government needed cash. He offered money to settle the claim for the Rio Grande border. He also offered to purchase California and the rest of New Mexico. Outraged Mexicans refused the offer. They did not want to cede, or give up, more land to the United States.

Polk then changed his tactics. Hoping to provoke a Mexican attack on U.S. troops, he sent General Zachary Taylor south to the disputed land south of the Nueces. The Mexicans saw this as an act of war. After Mexican troops ambushed an American patrol on the disputed land, Polk asked Congress for a declaration of war. He claimed that Mexico had forced this war by shedding "American blood upon American soil."

Opposition to War Overall, the war with Mexico was very popular among Americans. Support for the war was strongest among southerners and westerners, who were willing to take up arms to gain more land.

Many northerners, however, argued that Polk had provoked the war. They scornfully referred to it as "Mr. Polk's war" and claimed that he was trying to extend slavery. Abraham Lincoln, a member of the House of Representatives from Illinois, pointed out that the land under dispute was not "American soil." He held that General Taylor's troops had invaded Mexico, not the other way around.

Rebellion in California Polk ordered troops under the command of Stephen Kearny to invade and capture Santa Fe, New Mexico. From there, Kearny was to lead his troops into California.

Even before Kearny's troops reached California, settlers near San Francisco had begun their own revolt against Mexico. Taking up arms, they raised a grizzly bear flag and declared California an independent republic. A bold young explorer, John C. Frémont, soon took command of the Bear Flag Rebellion. He moved to join forces with U.S. troops under the command of Kearny.

Vocabulary Builder
provoke (prah VOHK) **v.** to cause to anger; to excite; to cause an action

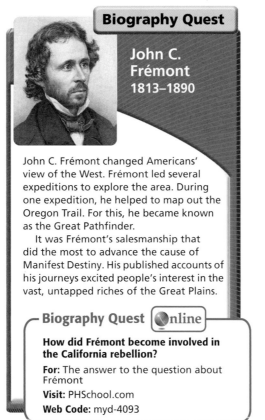

Biography Quest

John C. Frémont
1813–1890

John C. Frémont changed Americans' view of the West. Frémont led several expeditions to explore the area. During one expedition, he helped to map out the Oregon Trail. For this, he became known as the Great Pathfinder.

It was Frémont's salesmanship that did the most to advance the cause of Manifest Destiny. His published accounts of his journeys excited people's interest in the vast, untapped riches of the Great Plains.

Biography Quest 🌐 **Online**

How did Frémont become involved in the California rebellion?

For: The answer to the question about Frémont
Visit: PHSchool.com
Web Code: myd-4093

Section 3 Conflict With Mexico **457**

The Mexican-American War
p. 457

Instruction

- Have students read The Mexican-American War. Remind them to look for answers to the Section Focus Question.

- Ask: **How did the Mexican-American War start?** (*President Polk sent General Taylor to the disputed territory between the Nueces River and the Rio Grande. A Mexican force attacked Taylor's men. Polk asked for a declaration of war.*)

- Ask: **Do you agree or disagree with Lincoln's opinion that Taylor invaded Mexico, rather than that Mexico invaded the United States? Explain your view.** (*Students should see that Polk provoked the war by sending Taylor into the disputed territory.*)

- Ask students to compare and contrast the fights for California and Texas. (*Both became independent republics by fighting Mexican rule. Texans suffered defeats in a bloody fight. In California, there was less fighting.*)

Independent Practice

Have students continue filling in the study guide for this section.

📖 **Interactive Reading and Notetaking Study Guide,** Chapter 13, Section 3 (Adapted Version also available.)

Monitor Progress

As students fill in the Notetaking Study Guide, circulate and make sure that they understand the causes and results of the Mexican-American War. Provide assistance as needed.

History Background

Opposition to the Mexican-American War There was no shortage of prominent Americans who opposed the Mexican-American War. War opponents such as Lincoln were disturbed by the way the war started. Many were also bothered by the problems that new territory would present regarding slavery. Writer Henry David Thoreau was jailed overnight for his refusal to pay a poll tax that supported the war. As a result, he wrote the essay "Civil Disobedience," which later influenced Mohandas Gandhi in India and Dr. Martin Luther King, Jr.

Answers

✓**Checkpoint** Mexico had never accepted Texas's independence or the Rio Grande boundary.

Biography Quest Frémont was ordered to invade California at the outbreak of war in 1845. He and his troops arrived in time to aid the settlers in the revolt.

Achieving Manifest Destiny

p. 459

Instruction
L2

- Have students read Achieving Manifest Destiny. Remind students to look for causes and effects.

- Ask: **How did the Treaty of Guadalupe Hidalgo help the United States achieve Manifest Destiny?** (*The United States now stretched to both coasts.*)

- Discuss with students that the Treaty of Guadalupe Hidalgo was a blow to Mexico's national honor. The lost land had a long connection to Spanish and Mexican rule and culture.

- To help students visualize and understand how different parts of the West became part of the United States, use the Growth of the United States to 1853 transparency.

Color Transparencies, Growth of the United States to 1853

Independent Practice

Have students complete the study guide for this section.

📖 **Interactive Reading and Notetaking Study Guide,** Chapter 13, Section 3 (Adapted version also available.)

Monitor Progress

- As students complete the Notetaking Study Guide, circulate and make sure that they understand the geographic results of the Mexican-American War. Provide assistance as needed.

- Tell students to fill in the last column of the Reading Readiness Guide. Probe for what they learned that confirms or invalidates each statement.

All in One Teaching Resources, Unit 4, Reading Readiness Guide, p. 79

Growth of the United States to 1853

MAP MASTER
Skills Activity

By 1848, the United States stretched from the Atlantic Ocean to the Pacific Ocean.

(a) Read a Map What areas on the map did the United States own in 1853 that it did not own in 1830?

(b) Apply Information Look at a map of the present-day United States. When and how did your state become part of the United States?

MapMaster Online

For: Interactive map
Visit: PHSchool.com
Web Code: myp-4093

Mexico had very little military presence in California. Frémont's forces quickly captured Monterey and San Francisco. Meanwhile, General Kearny's troops captured Santa Fe and San Diego. There they united with naval units to occupy more of California. By early 1847, all of southern California was also under American control.

Invasion of Mexico Moving south from the Rio Grande, General Zachary Taylor captured the Mexican city of Monterrey. Santa Anna attacked Taylor at the Battle of Buena Vista. Though greatly outnumbered, Taylor's forces were better armed. Santa Anna retreated.

An American army under General Winfield Scott captured Veracruz, an important Mexican port. Scott then marched from Veracruz to Mexico City. Scott's army forced the Mexican army into the capital. Still, Santa Anna would not surrender.

Scott's campaign ended at Chapultepec, a stone palace above Mexico City. Like the Texans at the Alamo, the Mexicans fought bravely to defend Chapultepec. Most of them were killed. In Mexico, these young men are still honored for their bravery and patriotism.

458 Chapter 13 Westward Expansion

History Background

War Between Texas and Mexico The Texas War for Independence was short but noteworthy for its brutality, with atrocities on both sides. Santa Anna's position was that all rebellious Texans were traitors to Mexico. At the Alamo, the few survivors of the attack were executed. In what became known as the Goliad Massacre, James Fannin and about 338 men were executed after surrendering as prisoners of war. Houston's army at San Jacinto shouted "Remember Goliad" as well as "Remember the Alamo" as they charged the Mexican soldiers.

Answers

MAP MASTER
Skills Activity **(a)** Oregon country, Mexican Cession, Texas, Gadsden Purchase, Texas annexation **(b)** Answers will vary.

After Mexico's defeat at Chapultepec, Santa Anna left Mexico City. The Mexican capital was now in American hands. The United States had won the war. (To learn more about the key battles in the Mexican-American War, see the Geography and History feature.)

☑ **Checkpoint** How did Polk's actions lead to war with Mexico?

Achieving Manifest Destiny

Polk sent a representative, Nicholas Trist, to help General Scott negotiate a treaty with the Mexican government. Despite many difficulties, Trist negotiated the Treaty of Guadalupe Hidalgo, which was signed in 1848. It formally ended the Mexican-American War.

Under the treaty, Mexico recognized the annexation of Texas and ceded a vast territory to the United States. This territory, known as the Mexican Cession, included present-day California, Nevada, and Utah, as well as parts of Wyoming, Colorado, Arizona, and New Mexico. In return, the United States paid $18 million to Mexico.

In the Gadsden Purchase of 1853, the United States paid Mexico $10 million for a narrow strip of present-day Arizona and New Mexico. Manifest Destiny had been achieved.

☑ **Checkpoint** What was the Mexican Cession?

⭐ **Looking Back and Ahead** By 1853, the United States owned all the territory that would make up the first 48 states. Not until Alaska and Hawaii joined the Union in 1959 would any states outside this area be added.

Section 3 | **Check Your Progress**

> **Progress Monitoring Online**
> **For:** Self-test with instant help
> **Visit:** PHSchool.com
> **Web Code:** mya-4093

Comprehension and Critical Thinking

1. (a) Recall Why did the Republic of Texas hope the United States would annex Texas?
(b) Analyze Cause and Effect How would the addition of Texas as a slave state affect the Union? Explain.

2. (a) Recall What did the United States gain as a result of the Mexican-American War?
(b) Draw Conclusions How do you think the Mexican-American War affected the relationship between Mexico and the United States?

🔁 Reading Skill

3. Ask Questions to Synthesize Information Reread the text following the heading "Invasion of Mexico." Why might Santa Anna have been unwilling to surrender? Suggest a possible research topic to explore this question.

Key Terms

Complete each of the following sentences so that the second part clearly shows your understanding of the key term.
4. Many U.S. senators wanted to annex Texas, _____.
5. In Mexico, Santa Anna established a dictatorship, _____.

6. The Mexicans laid siege to the Alamo, _____.

Writing

7. Rewrite the following paragraph to eliminate sentence errors and improve sentence variety. **Paragraph:** Conflict between Mexicans and Anglo-Americans. There was a difference in religion. Mexicans were Catholics. Many Anglo-Americans Protestants. Mexico had outlawed slavery, but many Anglo-Americans owned slaves. This also created problems. Mexico began to tax American imports. Hostilities finally broke out. When Santa Anna attacked the Alamo.

Section 3 Conflict With Mexico **459**

Section 3 Check Your Progress

1. (a) Texans wanted the rights of American citizens.
(b) Texas would tip the balance in Congress in favor of slave states, thus allowing pro-slavery laws to be enacted.

2. (a) the land known as the Mexican Cession, including California, Nevada, and Utah and parts of Wyoming, Colorado, Arizona, and New Mexico

(b) Possible answer: It caused hostility and suspicion.

3. Possible answer: Perhaps he felt that surrender would be humiliating. Possible research topic: How does Mexican history view and present the time period of the Mexican-American War?

4. Possible answer: adding it onto the United States

5. Possible answer: since he was the only ruler

Assess and Reteach

Assess Progress [L2]

Have students complete Check Your Progress. Administer the Section Quiz.

> **All in One Teaching Resources, Unit 4,** Section Quiz, p. 92

To further assess student understanding, use the Progress Monitoring Transparency.

Progress Monitoring Transparencies, Chapter 13, Section 3

Reteach [L1]

If students need more instruction, have them read this section in the Interactive Reading and Notetaking Study Guide and complete the accompanying question.

> 📖 **Interactive Reading and Notetaking Study Guide,** Chapter 13, Section 3 (Adapted Version also available.)

Extend [L3]

Ask students to write a newspaper editorial on the Mexican-American War after the announcement of the Treaty of Guadalupe Hidalgo. They should express their opinions on how the war started, its ending, and its implications for the future of the United States. Ask several students to share their work with the class.

Progress Monitoring Online

Students may check their comprehension of this section by completing the Progress Monitoring Online graphic organizer and self-quiz.

Answers

☑ Checkpoint By ordering Taylor into disputed territory, Polk provoked a Mexican attack and got Congress to declare war on Mexico.

☑ Checkpoint land Mexico ceded to the United States, which is today California, Nevada, and Utah, and parts of Wyoming, Colorado, Arizona, and New Mexico

6. Possible answer: completely surrounding the fort

7. Check to see that students have a well-written paragraph.

The Mexican-American War

p. 460

Build Background Knowledge L2

Have students recall the Texas War for Independence. Ask students how Texan independence helped cause the Mexican-American War. (*Possible answer: Mexico did not accept the Texas border at the Rio Grande, and the United States saw that Manifest Destiny could be achieved.*) Have students locate the disputed border on the map.

Instruction L2

■ Have students read the introductory paragraph and discuss why hostilities broke out between Mexico and the United States. Ask students why Mexico was unhappy with the United States. (*The United States had annexed Texas.*) Then ask students why many people in the United States wanted to go to war. (*Americans felt that Mexico stood in the way of Manifest Destiny.*)

■ Show History Interactive transparency The Mexican-American War. Ask students to describe the United States' strategy on land and at sea. (*On land, American forces invaded Mexico in two directions. At sea, the United States Navy blockaded Mexico's east and west coasts.*) Ask: **What was similar about American land and sea strategies?** (*Both involved approaching Mexico from two directions.*)

Color Transparencies, The Mexican-American War

■ Ask students: **What led the Mexican government to move for peace?** (*The Mexicans had lost key battles, such as the Battle of Chapultepec, and U.S. forces had surrounded Mexico City. The Mexicans had also lost control of northern California and New Mexico to the United States.*)

GEOGRAPHY AND HISTORY

The Mexican-American War

By 1846, the United States and Mexico stood on the brink of war. Mexicans were furious at the American annexation of Texas the year before. Americans felt that Mexico stood in the way of Manifest Destiny. After a border dispute erupted in hostilities, U.S. troops attacked Mexico on two fronts in order to achieve quick victory.

History Interactive

Learn More About the Mexican-American War

Visit: PHSchool.com
Web Code: myp-4095

▶ U.S. soldier at the Battle of Buena Vista

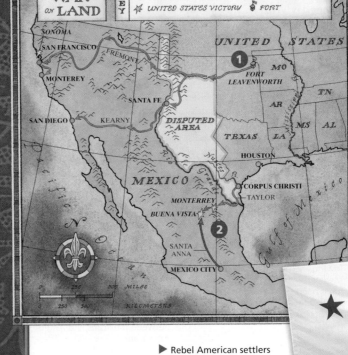

War on Land

American forces invaded Mexico in two directions. John C. Frémont and Stephen Kearny moved west from Fort Leavenworth ❶ to take control of California. They were aided by a revolt of American settlers near San Francisco. Zachary Taylor marched south across the Rio Grande and defeated a large Mexican force at Buena Vista ❷ .

▶ Rebel American settlers declared California a new nation—the Bear Flag Republic.

Differentiated Instruction

L1 English Language Learners

The Mexican Point of View Ask Spanish-speaking students to find a source that tells about the Mexican-American War from a Mexican point of view. Have students make a chart comparing the points of view of people in the two countries. Have students present or display their charts to the class.

War at Sea

The U.S. Navy blockaded Mexico's east and west coasts. American sailors helped secure California ❸ while another fleet in the Gulf of Mexico supported the assault at Veracruz ❹. Winfield Scott won a last battle against Mexican soldiers at the Battle of Chapultepec.

Understand Effects:

The War's Final Days

By the time of General Scott's victory outside Mexico City, U.S. forces had surrounded the Mexican capital. The northern territories of California and New Mexico were under Frémont's and Kearny's control, and Taylor had moved south to press for attack. With the loss of Mexico City, the Mexican government moved to make peace.

Independent Practice
To help students expand their understanding of the Mexican-American War, have them complete the History Interactive activity online.

Extend Online
For: Help with the History Interactive
Visit: PHSchool.com
Web Code: myp-4092

Monitor Progress

Ask students to complete the Analyze Geography and History activity. Circulate to make sure individuals understand the impact of the Mexican-American War.

WAR AT SEA

KEY
← UNITED STATES FORCES   ← MEXICAN FORCES
✦ UNITED STATES VICTORY

◄ The shako cap—topped with a tall plume of feathers—was part of the American uniform during the war.

▲ U.S. Navy ships guard the American landing at Veracruz.

Analyze **GEOGRAPHY AND HISTORY**

Select a key battle from the Mexican-American War, and write a journal entry about it from a U.S. soldier's point of view.

Writing Rubric Share the rubric with students.

Score 1 Journal entry is incomplete, vague, shows little effort.
Score 2 Ideas not developed well, opinions based on incorrect information.
Score 3 Has thoughtful entries, contains some details to develop ideas.
Score 4 Is well written and organized, opinions are supported with facts.

History Background

Zachary Taylor Despite a lack of political experience, Zachary Taylor's status as a hero of the Mexican-American War led to his election as President in 1848. His plain manners and sloppy clothing, which had earned him the nickname "Old Rough and Ready," helped him appeal to voters. Taylor was a southerner and a slave owner, but his successful army career also helped him appeal to northerners. Besides his role in the Mexican-American War, Taylor had served for many years on the frontier fighting Native Americans.

Answer

Analyze **GEOGRAPHY AND HISTORY**

The revolt in California helped the American war effort because it helped Frémont and Kearny take control of California. The geographic consequences of Frémont's and Kearny's victories were that the United States gained control of California and New Mexico. Journal entries will vary, but should show students' understanding of the United States and Mexican points of view about the war.

Review and Preview

Students have read how the United States gained territory after the war with Mexico. Now they will explore how Mormon settlement and the discovery of gold transformed the West.

Section Focus Question

How did Mormon settlement and the gold rush lead to changes in the West?

Before you begin the lesson for the day, write the Section Focus Question on the board. (*Lesson focus: People seeking religious freedom and gold greatly increased the area's population.*)

Prepare to Read

Build Background Knowledge `L2`

In the previous section, students read about how Californians rose up against Mexican rule and formed the Bear Flag Republic. Tell students that after the Mexican-American War a discovery took place that brought people from all around the world flooding into California. Use the Idea Wave strategy (TE, p. T24) to have students discuss how they think a very rapid growth in population might change a place.

Set a Purpose `L2`

■ Read each statement in the Reading Readiness Guide aloud. Ask students to mark the statements True or False.

All in One Teaching Resources, Unit 4, Reading Readiness Guide, p. 80

■ Have students discuss the statements in pairs or groups of four, then mark their worksheets again. Use the Numbered Heads strategy (TE, p. T24) to call on students to share their group's perspectives. The students will return to these worksheets later.

Chinese Immigrants

❝Every immigrant group has its own newspaper except for the Chinese. As a result, although the Chinese merchants are many in number, they have no influence. Because they are uninformed, they have no way to exercise their freedom of choice. . . . Since I feel strongly about this situation, I have founded a newspaper called *Golden Hills News* to record in Chinese the commercial news and government affairs happening every day.❞

—William D. M. Howard, announcing a Chinese-language newspaper in San Francisco, 1854

◄ Western miners, including a Chinese immigrant (right)

A Rush to the West

Objectives
- Explain why the Mormons settled in Utah and the issues that divided Mormons and the federal government.
- Discuss the effects of the 1849 California gold rush.
- Describe how California's population had changed by 1850.

🔵 Reading Skill

Ask Questions That Go Beyond the Text Research questions should build on the information you learn in your textbook. Use the many strategies you practiced in Sections 1–3 to build questions that link the text topic to larger issues. For example, you might look at how history fits with modern situations or why the people of history made the decisions they made.

Key Terms and People

Joseph Smith   forty-niner
polygamy   water rights
Brigham Young   vigilante

Why It Matters As a result of the war with Mexico, the United States gained the lands known as the Mexican Cession. Large numbers of Americans began to settle in this vast region.

❓ **Section Focus Question: How did Mormon settlement and the gold rush lead to changes in the West?**

Mormons Settle Utah

Even before the end of the war, a group of Americans had begun moving into the part of the Mexican Cession that is today Utah. These were the Mormons, members of the Church of Jesus Christ of Latter-day Saints. The church was founded in 1830 by Joseph Smith, a New York farmer. Smith said that heavenly visions had revealed to him the text of a holy book called the *Book of Mormon*.

Seeking Refuge The Mormon Church grew quickly, but some of its teachings often placed its followers in conflict with their neighbors. For example, Mormons at first believed that property should be held in common. Smith also favored **polygamy,** the practice of having more than one wife at a time.

Hostile communities forced the Mormons to move from New York to Ohio and then to Missouri. By 1844, the Mormons had settled in Nauvoo, Illinois. There, Joseph Smith was murdered by an angry mob.

462 Chapter 13 Westward Expansion

Differentiated Instruction

`L3` Gifted and Talented

Poly = many The vocabulary word *polygamy* introduces students to the prefix *poly-*, which means "many." Have them find at least five other words that begin with *poly*. As a contest, you could have students work in teams and see who can

write the funniest paragraph using as many "poly" words as possible. The key rule for the paragraphs is that students must define the words in the paragraph as well as use them.

Brigham Young, the new Mormon leader, realized that Nauvoo was no longer safe. He had heard about a great valley in the Utah desert, which at the time was still owned by Mexico. In 1847, he led a party of Mormons on a long, hazardous journey to the valley of the Great Salt Lake. Over the next few years, some 15,000 Mormon men, women, and children made the trek to Utah.

Although Utah was a safe refuge, the land was not hospitable. Farming was difficult in the dry desert. Then, in the summer of 1849, enormous swarms of crickets nearly destroyed the Mormons' first harvest. But a flock of seagulls flew in from the Pacific and devoured the crickets. The Mormons then set out to make the desert bloom. Under strict church supervision, they enclosed and distributed farmland and set up an efficient system of irrigation.

Conflict With the Government In 1848, as a result of the Mexican Cession, Utah became part of the United States. Congress then created the Utah Territory. Mormon leaders immediately came into conflict with officials appointed to govern the territory.

Three issues divided the Mormons and the federal government. First, the Mormon Church controlled the election process in the Utah Territory. Non-Mormons had no say. Second, the church supported businesses that were owned by Mormons. "Outsiders" had difficulty doing business. The third issue was polygamy, which was illegal in the rest of the country.

These issues were not resolved for more than 40 years. In time, Congress passed a law that took control of elections away from the Mormon Church. Church leaders agreed to ban polygamy and to stop favoring Mormon-owned businesses. Finally, in 1896, Utah became a state.

☑**Checkpoint** Why did the Mormons leave Illinois?

Vocabulary Builder
efficient (ee FISH ehnt) *adj.* done in a way that increases production with the least amount of waste

Mormons Come to Utah
Brigham Young (below) led the first wave of Mormons to migrate to Utah. In later years, settlers continued to arrive. Some, like those shown in the painting, were so poor they had to haul their belongings along the Mormon Trail by hand. **Critical Thinking: Identify Benefits** *Identify two benefits these Mormons might look forward to from settling in Utah.*

463

Mormons Settle Utah
p. 462

Instruction [L2]

- **Vocabulary Builder** Before teaching this section, preteach the High-Use Words **efficient** and **prospect** using the strategy on TE p. T21.

  Key Terms Have students complete the See It–Remember It chart for the Key Terms in this chapter.

- Read Mormons Settle Utah with students, using the Oral Cloze reading strategy (TE, p. T22).

- Ask: **Why did the Mormons have to move so many times before finding a home?** (*People where they lived disagreed with their beliefs.*)

- Discuss with students why people felt threatened by the Mormons. Extend the discussion to explore the conflict between the Mormons' pursuit of religious freedom and their denial of rights to non-Mormons.

Independent Practice
Have students continue filling in the study guide for this section.

📖 **Interactive Reading and Notetaking Study Guide,** Chapter 13, Section 4 (Adapted Version also available.)

Monitor Progress

As students complete the Notetaking Study Guide, circulate and make sure that they understand the Mormons' search for a home. Provide assistance as needed.

Vocabulary Builder

Use the information below to teach students this section's high-use words.

High-Use Word	Definition and Sample Sentence
efficient, p. 463	*adj.* done in a way that increases production with the least amount of waste The cotton gin provided a more **efficient** way of processing cotton.
prospect, p. 464	*n.* promise; something looked forward to The **prospect** of owning good farmland attracted many settlers to the West.

Answers
Identify Benefits Possible answers: freedom of religion; no outside interference in family life; could hold land in common

☑**Checkpoint** Joseph Smith was murdered and they feared for their safety.

The California Gold Rush

p. 464

Instruction [L2]

- Have students read The California Gold Rush. Remind students to look for causes and effects.

- Ask: **How did California's population change in 1849?** (*More than 80,000 miners came to California.*)

- Ask: **Why was lawlessness a problem in California mining towns?** (*There was no official law enforcement.*)

- Discuss with students the social dislocation caused by the gold rush. Ask students to suppose that the class is starting its own town 100 miles away. Have them list what they will need, problems they might face, and help they might have. Write the ideas on the board. Then compare them to the conditions of the gold rush.

Independent Practice

Have students continue filling in the study guide for this section.

📖 **Interactive Reading and Notetaking Study Guide,** Chapter 13, Section 4 (Adapted Version also available.)

Monitor Progress

As students fill in the Notetaking Study Guide, circulate and make sure that individuals understand the immediate impact of the gold rush. Provide assistance as needed.

Vocabulary Builder
<u>prospect</u> (PRAHS pehkt) *n.* promise; something looked forward to

Panning for Gold
Forty-niners, like the man in this picture, spent many back-breaking hours sifting through sand at the edge of the river. If they were lucky, their reward was a glimmer of gold in their pan.
Critical Thinking: *Apply Information Based on your reading, what method of gold mining did this prospector use?*

The California Gold Rush

When California was ceded to the United States in 1848, about 10,000 Californios, or Mexican Californians, were living in the territory. A handful of wealthy families owned most of the land. They lived an elegant, aristocratic life. Their ranches were worked by poorer Californios or by Native Americans.

After the Mexican Cession, easterners began to migrate to California. The wealthy Californios looked down on the newcomers from the East, and the newcomers felt contempt for the Californios. The two groups rarely mixed or intermarried.

Gold Is Discovered An event in January 1848 would bring a flood of other settlers to California. James Marshall was building a sawmill on John Sutter's land near Sacramento. One morning, he found a small gold nugget in a ditch. Sutter tried to keep his discovery a secret. But the news spread like wildfire throughout the country and abroad. By 1849, the California gold rush had begun.

The <u>prospect</u> of finding gold attracted about 80,000 fortune seekers. The nickname "forty-niners" was given to these people who came to California in search of gold. In just two years, the population of California zoomed from 14,000 to 100,000.

Sutter's Mill was just the beginning. Prospectors, or gold seekers, searched throughout the Sacramento Valley for gold. They dug into the land using picks and shovels. They also looked in streams. This process, called placer mining, did not take much labor, money, or skill. Miners washed dirt from a stream in a pan, leaving grains of gold in the bottom. Finding gold was called "hitting pay dirt."

Gold above ground was quickly found. But there was more gold in underground deposits, or lodes. Gold in lodes was difficult and expensive to mine. It required heavy and expensive machinery. As a result, large companies took over the mining of underground lodes.

Water Rights In the gold fields, disputes over water rights were common. Water rights are the legal rights to use the water in a river, stream, or other body. California has an abundance of land, but much of it is desert. Settlers needed water for irrigation and mining.

California had kept older Mexican laws regarding water rights. Landowners had the right to use the water that flowed through their land. At the same time, it was illegal to cut off water to one's neighbors. In most gold rush territories, though, the law was ignored. The first people to reach a stream used as much water as they wanted—sometimes even the whole stream! Disputes over water rights often erupted into violence.

Life in Mining Towns Mining towns were not very permanent places. Most sprang up overnight and emptied just as quickly when miners heard news of a gold strike in another place.

Mining towns attracted both miners and people hoping to make money from miners. Miners were often willing to pay high prices for food and supplies. They also needed entertainment. A typical mining town was made up of a row of businesses with a saloon at its center.

Differentiated Instruction

[L1] English Language Learners

Word Derivation Spanish-speaking students should recognize the word *vigilante* because it comes from Spanish, but in English it has a very different meaning. Work with students so that they see that in Spanish, *vigilante* means "watchman," or one who is vigilant, whereas in English it means someone who takes the law into his or her own hands. Have students use the English word in a sentence and then share the origin of the word with the class.

Answer
Apply Information panning for gold

California was not yet a state, so federal law did not apply within the mining towns. To impose some order, miners banded together and created their own rules. Punishment for crimes was often quick and brutal. **Vigilantes,** or self-appointed law enforcers, punished people for crimes, though they had no legal right to do so.

Role of Women Gold rushes were not like other migrations in American history. Most migrations included men and women, young and old. Most forty-niners, however, were young men. By 1850, the ratio of men to women in California was twelve to one!

Still, some women did come to California in search of fortune, work, or adventure. Unlike other areas of the country, California offered women profitable work. Some women mined, but many more stayed in town. They worked in or ran boardinghouses, hotels, restaurants, laundries, and stores.

Drifting and Settling Few forty-niners struck it rich. After the gold rush ended, many people continued to search for gold throughout the West. There were gold or silver strikes in British Columbia, Idaho, Montana, Colorado, Arizona, and Nevada. Other miners gave up the drifting life and settled in the West for good.

☑**Checkpoint** Why were water rights an important issue?

Links Across Time

Water Rights in the West

1849 During the gold rush, California law generally gave water rights to the first person to make use of a body of water.

1905 Los Angeles, still a small city, won rights to the Owens River, 200 miles away. Engineers later built aqueducts and dams to carry the water to the city. This water helped Los Angeles grow rapidly. But ranchers and farmers in the Owens Valley protested the loss of their water rights.

Link to Today nline

Connection to Today Water rights remain an issue in many areas of the nation today. Farms and communities still compete to win access to clean, available water.

For: Water rights in the news
Visit: PHSchool.com
Web Code: myc-4094

1913 Workers opened the gates of the newly completed Los Angeles aqueduct.

History Background

Levi Strauss The most famous success story of the gold rush was Levi Strauss, a German-Jewish immigrant who arrived in San Francisco with canvas fabric to make tents. Strauss quickly saw that there were plenty of tent suppliers. What miners really needed was sturdy pants that could stand up to the rigors of mining. So Strauss hired a tailor to use his canvas, later denim fabric, to make sturdy pants. He not only sold a lot of pants but also started a business that has become an American institution. His pants later became known as blue jeans.

Answer

☑Checkpoint Much of California is desert. Water rights were important for irrigation and mining.

California's Changing Population

p. 466

Instruction L2

- Have students read California's Changing Population. Remind them to look for the sequence of events.

- Ask: **Why did groups such as Irish, Jewish, and Italian workers often have an easier time in California?** (*Mining towns were more egalitarian than American society in general, so they often faced less prejudice.*)

- Ask: **Which groups did face prejudice in mining communities?** (*Chinese, African Americans, Native Americans*)

- Ask students how everyone being new to the area and having to work hard to find gold affected mining communities. (*Mining towns were more democratic because people in the gold fields had to depend on one another.*)

Independent Practice

Have students continue filling in the study guide for this section.

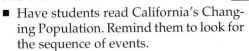 **Interactive Reading and Notetaking Study Guide,** Chapter 13, Section 4 (Adapted Version also available.)

Monitor Progress

- As students fill in the Notetaking Study Guide, circulate and make sure that they understand the impact of the gold rush on California's population. Provide assistance as needed.

- Tell students to fill in the last column of the Reading Readiness Guide. Probe for what they learned that confirms or invalidates each statement.

- Have students go back to their Word Knowledge Rating Form. Rerate their word knowledge and complete the last column with a definition or example.

All in One Teaching Resources, Reading Readiness Guide, p. 80; Word Knowledge Rating Form, p. 76

Answer

Distinguish Relevant Information People in the street are wearing clothes from different cultures and ways of life.

San Francisco During the Gold Rush

This painting shows San Francisco in the 1850s. "Where there was a vacant piece of ground one day," wrote one witness, "the next saw it covered with half a dozen tents or shanties." **Critical Thinking: Distinguish Relevant Information** *What information in this picture supports the conclusion that San Francisco had a diverse population?*

California's Changing Population

Many gold rush towns were temporary, but some grew and prospered. San Francisco had only 200 inhabitants in 1848. During the gold rush, immigrants who sailed to California passed through San Francisco's harbor. Its merchants provided miners with goods and services. Many newcomers remained in the city. Others returned to settle there after working in the mines. By 1870, San Francisco had a population of more than 100,000.

An Unusual Mix of People The gold rush brought enormous ethnic diversity to California. People came from Europe, Asia, Australia, and South America. By 1860, the population of California was almost 40 percent foreign-born.

European immigrants often enjoyed more freedom in California than in Europe. They also faced less prejudice than in the East. In some ways, mining societies were more democratic, as men in the gold fields had to rely on one another. One immigrant wrote home:

> **"**We live a free life, and the best thing . . . is that no human being here sets himself up as your lord and master. It is true that we do not have many of the luxuries of life, but I do not miss them.**"**
>
> —quoted in *Land of Their Choice* (Blegen)

Chinese Immigrants China's economy was in trouble in the 1840s. After news reached China of a "mountain of gold," about 45,000 Chinese men went to California. Most hoped to return home to China with enough money to take care of their families.

Chinese laborers faced prejudice. They generally were not given higher-paying jobs in the mines. Instead, they were hired to do menial labor. Some cooked or did laundry. Despite many difficulties, the Chinese worked hard. They helped build railroads and worked on farms. Their labor also helped cities like San Francisco to prosper.

Differentiated Instruction

L3 Advanced Readers   **L3 Gifted and Talented**

Mariano Vallejo Have students use the General Mariano Vallejo worksheet to read and answer questions about the life of a prominent Californio. Have them summarize their findings for the class.

All in One Teaching Resources, General Mariano Vallejo, p. 85

African Americans Several thousand free African Americans lived in California by 1850. They had their own churches and newspapers. Many ran their own businesses. However, they did not have equal rights. They could not vote or serve on juries.

Slavery did not take root in California. Some southerners did bring their slaves with them during the gold rush. However, the other miners objected. They believed that anyone who profited from mining should participate in the hard labor of finding gold.

Native Americans For Native Americans, the gold rush brought even more tragedy. Miners swarmed onto Indian lands to search for gold. Vigilante gangs killed Indians and stole their land. About 100,000 Indians, nearly two thirds of the Native American population of California, died during the gold rush.

Impact on Californios By 1850, only 15 percent of Californians were Mexican. The old ruling families did not have a strong say in the new territorial government. When a constitutional convention was held, only 8 of the 48 delegates were Californios.

Californio politicians could not stop the passage of laws that discriminated against their people. The legislature levied a high tax on ranches and required rancheros to prove that they owned their land. This was often difficult, because most had received their land grants from Spain or Mexico. By the time many Californios could prove ownership, they had had to sell their land to pay legal bills.

Ask Questions That Go Beyond the Text
Ask a question that explores beyond the text and requires research to answer. You might focus on the ways that the lives of Mexicans in California changed after the gold rush.

☑**Checkpoint** What effects did the gold rush have on Californios?

⭐ **Looking Back and Ahead** California had enough people by 1850 to apply for admission to the Union as a free state. As you will read in the next chapter, California's request for statehood would cause a national crisis.

Section 4 | **Check Your Progress**

Progress Monitoring Online
For: Self-test with instant help
Visit: PHSchool.com
Web Code: mya-4094

Comprehension and Critical Thinking

1. **(a) Recall** Why did the Mormons decide to move to Utah?
   (b) Identify Alternatives What other options might the Mormons have considered?

2. **(a) List** Which groups migrated to California after 1848?
   (b) Make Inferences Which groups benefited most from the discovery of gold? Which groups suffered most? Explain.

Reading Skill

3. **Ask Questions That Go Beyond the Text** Recall what you just read about California during the gold rush. Ask a question that goes beyond the text and requires research to answer.

Key Terms

4. Write two definitions of the term water rights. First, write a formal definition for your teacher. Second, write a definition in everyday English for a classmate.

Writing

5. Write a short paragraph explaining what happened as a result of the California gold rush in 1849. Then, exchange paragraphs with another student. Check your partner's work for errors. Work together to take the best elements from each paragraph and to create a new version.

Assess Progress L2

Have students complete Check Your Progress. Administer the Section Quiz.

All in One **Teaching Resources, Unit 4,** Section Quiz, p. 93

To further assess student understanding, use the Progress Monitoring Transparency.

Progress Monitoring Transparencies, Chapter 13, Section 4

Reteach L1

If students need more instruction, have them read this section in the Interactive Reading and Notetaking Study Guide and complete the accompanying question.

📖 **Interactive Reading and Notetaking Study Guide,** Chapter 13, Section 4 (Adapted Version also available.)

Extend L3

Have students suppose they are forty-niners recently arrived in California. Have them research life in the time. Ask them to write a diary entry about what they have found in the gold fields. Provide students with the Web Code below.

Extend Online
For: Help in starting the Extend activity
Visit: PHSchool.com
Web Code: mye-0266

Progress Monitoring Online

Students may check their comprehension of this section by completing the Progress Monitoring Online graphic organizer and self-quiz.

Section 4 Check Your Progress

1. **(a)** They feared violent attacks by non-Mormons.
   (b) giving up their religious beliefs

2. **(a)** Easterners, African Americans, Chinese, and other people from Asia, South America, and Australia
   (b) Eastern miners who struck it rich benefited. Chinese laborers and Native Americans suffered. The Chinese faced prejudice and Native Americans had their lands stolen by miners.

3. Possible question: What influenced the responses of existing California inhabitants to newcomers?

4. Formal: legal rights to use the water in a river, stream, or other body of water; informal: who gets to use the water and who doesn't

5. Paragraphs will vary, but should include the impact on life in mining towns and on California's population.

Answers

🔵 **Reading Skill** Possible question: In what ways did Californios face discrimination after 1849?

☑**Checkpoint** Californios lost political power and faced discrimination.

Skills for Life

Objective

It is important to evaluate the validity of a written source when performing research. Some sources are more accurate and reliable than others. In some instances, the evidence is presented as fact when it is simply the writer's opinion. It is critical for students to evaluate the source when they gather information on the topic.

Evaluate Written Sources

Instruction `L2`

1. Write the steps to evaluate a written source on the board. Ask the class to read the steps aloud.

2. Using the Numbered Heads strategy (TE, p. T24), have students share what they know about which clues can help them identify whether the information in a source is reliable. (*Possible answers: the author, the context in which it was written, the format in which it was published, the tone, and the purpose*) Ask students why they think it is important to evaluate the validity of sources when reading history. (*Possible answer: to determine how reliable the information is*)

3. Practice the skill by following the steps on p. 468 as a class. Model each step to evaluate a written source. (*1. Elizabeth Wood 2. July and September of 1851; their purpose was to describe the land and landforms that the writer sees on her journey west. 3. Possible answers: (a) She seems interested in the area and curious about seeing new things. (b) She describes the Red Buttes in great detail, Devil's Gate being "high enough to make one's head swim," and the beauty and grandeur of Mount St. Elias in the distance. 4. Possible answer: Yes, because the writer is describing what she sees, and would not otherwise know what these landforms look like.*)

Skills for Life — Evaluate Written Sources

Historical evidence comes from many sources. Evaluating the validity of written sources is important in putting together a picture of the past.

The following journal entries, written by Elizabeth Wood, describe portions of her two-and-a-half-month journey from Fort Laramie, Wyoming, to eastern Oregon in 1851.

Primary Source

"July 25. Since last date we camped at the ford where emigrants cross from the south to the north side of the Platte. . . . We stopped near the Red Buttes, where the hills are of a red color, nearly square and have the appearance of houses with flat roofs. . . . We also passed Independence Rock and the Devil's Gate, which is high enough to make one's head swim, and the posts reach an altitude of some 4 or 500 feet."

"Monday, September 15th. . . . Mount St. Elias is in the distance, and is covered with snow, so you can imagine somewhat the beauty and grandeur of the scene. We are now among the tribe of Wallawalla Indians."

—Journal of a Trip to Oregon, Elizabeth Wood

Learn the Skill
Use these steps to evaluate written sources.

1. **Identify the source.** Knowing who the writer is helps you to evaluate that person's account of events.

2. **Note the context.** When was the account written? In what form did it appear? What was the purpose of the account?

3. **Analyze the point of view.** What is the writer trying to say? How does the writer feel about the subject?

4. **Evaluate the validity of the material.** How true is this account? Why do you think so?

Practice the Skill
Answer the following questions to evaluate the source on this page.

1. **Identify the source.** Who wrote these journal entries?

2. **Note the context.** (a) When were these entries written? (b) What was their purpose?

3. **Analyze the point of view.** (a) How does the writer feel about the journey? (b) What words or phrases express the writer's feelings?

4. **Evaluate the validity of the material.** Do you think this journal entry accurately describes the journey west? Why or why not?

Apply the Skill
See the Review and Assessment at the end of this chapter.

468 Chapter 13 Westward Expansion

Monitor Progress

Ask students to do the Apply the Skill activity. Then assign the Skills for Life Worksheet. As students complete the worksheet, circulate to make sure individuals are applying the skill steps effectively. Provide assistance as needed.

All in One Teaching Resources, Unit 4, Skills for Life Worksheet, p. 88

Reteach `L1`

If students need more instruction, use the Social Studies Skills Tutor to reteach this skill.

Social Studies Skills Tutor CD-ROM, Using Reliable Information

How did westward expansion change the geography of the nation and demonstrate the determination of its people?

Section 1
The West

- By the 1820s, land-hungry Americans often had to look west of the Mississippi River for territory to settle.
- Some Americans moved to the Mexican-controlled lands of the Southwest.
- Manifest Destiny was the idea that the United States had the right to "spread and possess the whole of the continent."

Section 2
Trails to the West

- Traders and trappers helped open the West for settlement.
- Free land and the mild climate attracted settlers from all parts of the United States to Oregon.

Section 3
Conflict With Mexico

- American settlers in Texas rebelled against Mexico and created the independent Republic of Texas.
- American forces defeated Mexican troops in what became known as the Mexican-American War.
- The United States gained vast new territories as a result of the Treaty of Guadalupe-Hidalgo.

Section 4
A Rush to the West

- The Mormons moved west to Utah for religious freedom.
- Gold fever brought thousands of immigrants to California.

? Exploring the Essential Question

Use the online study guide to explore the essential question.

Section 1
What cultures and ideas influenced the development of the West?

Chapter 13 Essential Question
How did westward expansion change the geography of the nation and demonstrate the determination of its people?

Section 2
Why did people go west and what challenges did they face?

Section 4
How did Mormon settlement and the gold rush lead to changes in the West?

Section 3
What were the causes and effects of the Texas War for Independence and the Mexican-American War?

Think Like A Historian

Enrich Learning To enrich this unit, have students revisit the Unit Essential Question. Using information from the chapters in the unit and the primary sources on pp. 472–475, have students discuss unifying and dividing forces during this era and create a poster illustrating the answers.

Think Like a Historian, pp. 472–475

Pressed for Time? If you do not have time to complete the activity, return to the essential question on the unit opener. Post the flip chart pages and ask students to review and revise the list. As a summary, display the Unit 4 Think Like a Historian transparencies.

Color Transparencies, Think Like a Historian, Unit 4

Chapter 13

Essential Question

Remind students of the Chapter Essential Question: **How did westward expansion change the geography of the nation and demonstrate the determination of its people?** Have students review the bulleted statements and the Visual Preview at the beginning of the chapter to help them answer this question.

To bolster students' retention, at this time they should complete the study guide in print or online. Remind students that they should also continue notetaking for the Unit and Chapter Essential Questions.

Interactive Reading and Notetaking Study Guide, Chapter 13 (Adapted Version also available.)

 Study Guide *Online,* Chapter 13

Chapter Challenge

To wrap up this chapter, students should apply the knowledge they have gained to this activity. Have students generate a list of personal characteristics that a western settler might need for success. Have students rate the most important five and explain their choices. (*Answers will vary, but might include patriotism, determination, strong work ethic, courage, and a sense of adventure.*)

Assessment at a Glance

Formal Assessment
- Chapter Tests A/B (L1/L2)
- Test Prep Workbook With Document-Based Assessment
- Test-Taking Strategies With Transparencies

Performance Assessment
- Group/Individual Activities, TE pp. 440g, 440h
- Teacher's Edition, pp. 447, 453, 459, 467
- Assessment Rubrics

Assessment Through Technology
- *ExamView* CD-ROM
- MindPoint CD-ROM
- Progress Monitoring Transparencies
- Progress Monitoring Online

Key Terms

1. Disputes occurred because water was scarce.

2. They owned ranches.

3. They made money from acquiring free land.

4. Santa Anna laid siege to the Alamo.

Comprehension and Critical Thinking

5. **(a)** Peninsulares were Spaniards born in Spain but living in New Spain. Creoles were people of Spanish descent born in New Spain. Mestizos were people of mixed Spanish, African, and Native American descent. **(b)** Mestizos were most likely to support independence because they had fewer rights and privileges under Spanish rule.

6. **(a)** Manifest Destiny was the belief that the United States was destined to spread from the Atlantic to the Pacific oceans. **(b)** By achieving Manifest Destiny, the United States gained land and resources for a growing population.

7. **(a)** The mountain men were fur trappers. They lived in the woods and trapped furs, explored, and blazed trails in the West. **(b)** They helped open the West to settlement. Jedediah Smith found South Pass, the way over the Rocky Mountains for the Oregon Trail.

8. **(a)** Polk favored the annexation of Texas. His election made that happen. As President, Polk provoked a Mexican attack, resulting in the Mexican-American War and the Mexican Cession. **(b)** Great Britain claimed the Northwest. Britain's claim could have blocked the United States from stretching across the entire continent.

9. **(a)** The Mormons immigrated to Utah to find a safe place to live and to practice their religion. **(b)** the Puritans, the Jews, the Catholics, and the Quakers

10. **(a)** The forty-niners were people who came to California in 1849 to look for gold. **(b)** The huge surge in population represented by the forty-niners qualified California for statehood.

History Reading Skill

11. Possible questions: What were the pros and cons to the idea of Manifest Destiny? What challenges did travelers face on the Santa Fe Trail?

Key Terms

Answer the following questions in complete sentences that show your understanding of the key terms.

1. Why did settlers in California argue over water rights?

2. What did rancheros own?

3. How did wealthy families benefit from land grants?

4. To what did General Santa Anna lay siege in San Antonio during the war for Texas independence?

Comprehension and Critical Thinking

5. **(a) Identify** Who were the peninsulares, the creoles, and the mestizos?
   (b) Draw Inferences Which of these groups were most likely to support Mexican independence from Spain? Why?

6. **(a) Recall** What was Manifest Destiny?
   (b) Identify Economic Benefits What economic benefits could the United States get from following the ideals of Manifest Destiny?

7. **(a) Describe** Describe the life of a mountain man like the one pictured at right.
   (b) Draw Inferences How did these men contribute to the goal of Manifest Destiny?

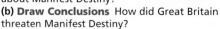
Mountain man

8. **(a) Explain** What did President James Polk do to bring about Manifest Destiny?
   (b) Draw Conclusions How did Great Britain threaten Manifest Destiny?

9. **(a) Recall** Why did the Mormons immigrate to Utah?
   (b) Compare What other groups in earlier American history came to North America for similar reasons?

10. **(a) Identify** Who were the forty-niners?
    (b) Analyze Cause and Effect How did the forty-niners contribute to California becoming a state?

⊙ History Reading Skill

11. **Frame Research Questions** Frame a research question about any aspect of this chapter. Start by reviewing headings and choosing one that interests you. Remember to frame questions that go beyond the text and require research to answer.

Writing

12. **Write two paragraphs discussing the results of the Mexican-American War.** Then, exchange papers with another student.
    As you look at your partner's paragraphs, you should:
    - correct every error you can find;
    - look for places to add transitions to make the sentences flow better and to connect the two paragraphs;
    - find opportunities to mix short and long sentences.

13. **Write a Narrative:**
    You are an easterner in the 1840s trying to decide whether to go to Oregon, Utah, or California. Write a diary entry in which you weigh the possible costs and benefits of such a trip and reach a final decision.

Skills for Life
Evaluate Written Sources
Use the diary entry below to answer the questions.

> "Tuesday May 20th. Travelled 20 miles and camped . . . saw several antelope, and an animal called prairie dogs, which resemble a puppy. There are acres of them . . . they plough the ground up and form little knolls all over the ground. . . ."
>
> —Journal of Travels to Oregon, Amelia Hadley, 1851

14. Who wrote this journal entry?

15. When was it written?

16. How does the writer feel about the journey?

17. Do you think this journal entry accurately describes prairie wildlife? Why or why not?

Writing

12. Paragraphs should include the following results: the United States annexed Texas; Mexico ceded vast territory in the West, known as the Mexican Cession, to the United States; the United States paid $18 million to Mexico; the United States achieved its goal of Manifest Destiny.

13. Narrative should give likely reasons why the writer would go to a specific location (Oregon—as missionaries or fur traders; Utah—for religious freedom; California—for mining) and the hardships and benefits each presented.

For a more complete four-point rubric, see the Writing Rubrics in the Teaching Resources.

All in One Teaching Resources, Unit 4, p. 111

Chapter 13
Review and Assessment

Test Yourself

1. Which of the following most directly led to achieving Manifest Destiny?

   A Women vote in the West.

   B Mormons move to Nauvoo, Illinois.

   C Santa Anna establishes dictatorship in Mexico.

   D President Polk negotiates a treaty with Great Britain to divide Oregon.

Refer to the quotation below to answer Question 2.

> "I am determined to sustain myself as long as possible and die like a soldier, who never forgets what is due to his honor and that of his country. Victory or Death!"

2. The person who made this statement was mostly likely

   A at the Alamo.

   B at a rendezvous.

   C at John Sutter's sawmill.

   D on the Oregon Trail.

Refer to the map below to answer Question 3.

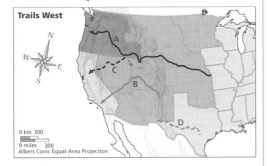

Trails West

0 km 300
0 miles 300
Albers Conic Equal-Area Projection

3. Which of the trails marked on the map led the forty-niners to their final destination?

   A trail A

   B trail B

   C trail C

   D trail D

Document-Based Questions

Task: Look at Documents 1 and 2, and answer their accompanying questions. Then, use the documents and your knowledge of history to complete this writing assignment:

List the reasons for and against the Mexican-American War. Then, write a short essay analyzing the arguments of each side. Draw a conclusion about the validity of each argument.

Document 1: In 1846, President Polk asked Congress to declare war against Mexico. *What does Polk accuse Mexico of doing?*

> "The grievous wrongs perpetrated by Mexico upon our citizens throughout a long period of years remains unredressed.... We have tried every effort of reconciliation.... But now ... Mexico has passed the boundary of the United States, has invaded our territory and shed American blood upon the American soil....
>
> ... I involve the prompt action of Congress to recognize the existence of the war, and to place at the disposition of the Executive the means of prosecuting the war with vigor, and thus hastening the restoration of peace."

Document 2: Abraham Lincoln, then a member of Congress, spoke out against the Mexican-American War. *How does Lincoln challenge Polk's reasons for war with Mexico?*

> "I carefully examined the President's messages.... The result of this examination was to make the impression that ... he falls far short of proving his justification [for the war].... The President ... declares that the soil was ours on which hostilities were commenced by Mexico....
>
> Let [the President] remember he sits where Washington sat, and so remembering, let him answer as Washington would answer.... And if, so answering, he can show that the soil was ours, where the first blood of the war was shed, ... then I am with him.... But if he can not do this ... then I shall be fully convinced ... that he is deeply conscious of being in the wrong."

Test Yourself

1. D

2. A

3. C

Document-Based Questions
Answers

Document 1 Polk accuses Mexico of invading U.S. territory and shedding U.S. blood on U.S. soil.

Document 2 Lincoln says Polk failed to justify his claim that Mexicans invaded the United States.

Arguments About the Mexican War. *For: America has a Manifest Destiny to expand; Mexico had refused a U.S. offer to buy territory; Mexican soldiers invaded U.S. territory and killed American soldiers. Against: Polk purposely provoked the war by invading Mexican territory; the United States has no moral right to take another nation's land; the war may lead to an extension of American slavery.*

Rubric: Write an Essay

Share the rubric with students before they begin writing.

Score 1 Contains many errors, shows lack of understanding of topic.

Score 2 Is poorly written, leaves out some key arguments for or against the war.

Score 3 Covers most of arguments and gives conclusions as to validity, fairly well written.

Score 4 Is well written with good sentence structure, full coverage of arguments, with a clear assessment of their validity.

Skills for Life

14. Amelia Hadley, a woman who traveled west to Oregon.

15. It was written in 1851.

16. The writer seems interested in the trip she is taking and curious about the wildlife that she sees along the way.

17. Possible answers: Yes, she is describing the animals and what they do from first-hand experience in their natural environment. No, she seems to have only a basic knowledge of wildlife; for example, she compares prairie dogs to puppies.

Unit 4

Think Like a Historian

? **What forces unite and divide a nation?**

Build Background Knowledge `L2`

Talk about some of the things that unite students, such as a football game against a local rival, and some of the things that divide students, such as student cliques. Then help students recall the circumstances that led the colonists to declare independence from Britain. Ask: **What were some of the factors that united the colonists? What were some of the factors that divided them?** (*Possible answer: Colonists were united by a desire for freedom; colonists were divided over their loyalty to the crown.*)

Instruction `L2`

- Write the Unit Essential Question on the chalkboard. Have students put the question in their own words. (*Possible answer: What are some of the things that pull citizens together or pull them apart?*) Ask students to recall the definitions for nationalism (*pride in one's own nation*) and sectionalism (*concern for interests of a particular region*). Tell them to apply these concepts as they read these documents.

- Have students review the Essential Question for chapters 11–13. Draw a web diagram on the chalkboard, showing how the chapter questions feed into the unit question. (See **Teaching Resources, Unit 4**, p. 3). Discuss how each chapter question helps answer the unit question.

- Tell students that after they study they will create a poster that will help them answer the unit question.

Answers

Document 1: Effects included the creation of factories and factory jobs, increased urban populations, and pollution.
Document 2: The South's economy relied on the production of cotton and the use of slave labor. The North's economy relied on the production of factory goods and the use of paid laborers.

What forces unite and divide a nation?

DIRECTIONS: Analyze the following documents regarding forces that united and divided the United States in the early 1800s. Answer the questions that accompany each document or set of documents. You will use your answers to build an answer to the unit question: *What forces unite and divide a nation?*

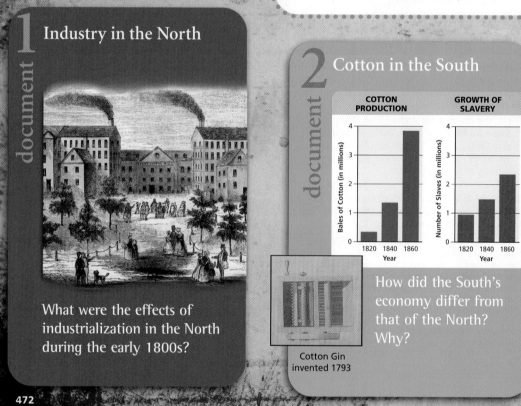

HISTORIAN'S CHECKLIST

WHO produced the document?
WHERE was it made?
WHEN was it produced?
WHY was it made and for what audience?
WHAT is its viewpoint?
HOW does it connect to what I've learned?
WHY is the document important?

document 1 Industry in the North

What were the effects of industrialization in the North during the early 1800s?

472

document 2 Cotton in the South

COTTON PRODUCTION

Bales of Cotton (in millions) — 1820, 1840, 1860 (Year)

GROWTH OF SLAVERY

Number of Slaves (in millions) — 1820, 1840, 1860 (Year)

Cotton Gin invented 1793

How did the South's economy differ from that of the North? Why?

Differentiated Instruction

`L1` English Language Learners

Understand Concepts Review the definition of the noun *force*. Tell students that a *force* is a powerful cause or factor that brings about a result or change. These forces can bring together, or unite, a nation. Or they can separate, or divide, a nation. When assigning a document, have students work in pairs to determine what forces are at work and what changes they bring about. Then have them put the forces and changes in simple cause-and-effect diagrams. Have students use their diagrams when completing the activity on p. 475.

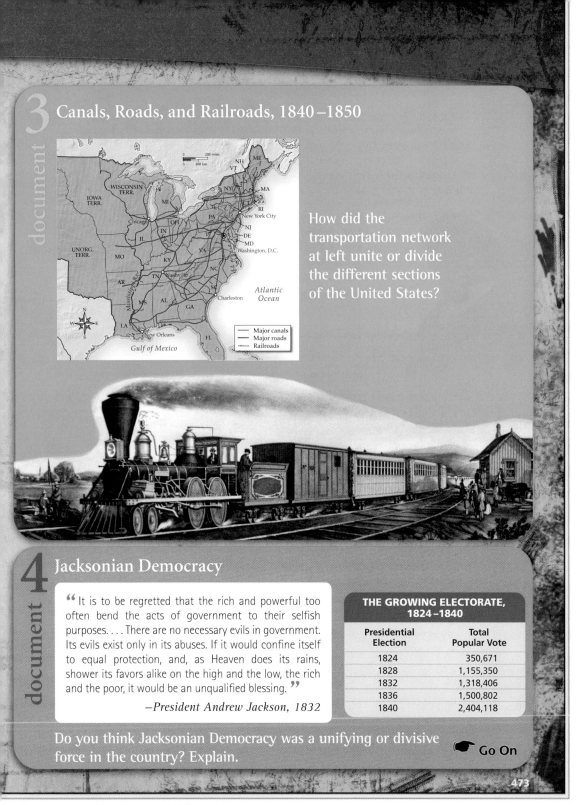

3 Canals, Roads, and Railroads, 1840–1850

How did the transportation network at left unite or divide the different sections of the United States?

Map legend:
— Major canals
— Major roads
---- Railroads

4 Jacksonian Democracy

" It is to be regretted that the rich and powerful too often bend the acts of government to their selfish purposes. . . . There are no necessary evils in government. Its evils exist only in its abuses. If it would confine itself to equal protection, and, as Heaven does its rains, shower its favors alike on the high and the low, the rich and the poor, it would be an unqualified blessing. "

—President Andrew Jackson, 1832

THE GROWING ELECTORATE, 1824–1840	
Presidential Election	Total Popular Vote
1824	350,671
1828	1,155,350
1832	1,318,406
1836	1,500,802
1840	2,404,118

Do you think Jacksonian Democracy was a unifying or divisive force in the country? Explain.

☞ Go On

473

History Background

Manifest Destiny A philosophy can sometimes unite a nation. During the 1800s, many Americans subscribed to Manifest Destiny. The concept became the dominant issue in national politics. Coined by John O'Sullivan, editor and Democratic politician, the phrase that soon became "the rallying cry throughout America" suggested expansion was good for the country and bound to happen. A strong feeling of national pride and the superiority of American democracy contributed to the belief in the inevitability of this expansion. This philosophy easily justified ignoring the Native Americans and Mexicans populating the desired lands.

Instruction (continued)

■ If students have examined these documents as enrichment to the chapters, have them answer the Historian's Checklist as review. Then, have them identify how each document helps answer the essential question. Ask them whether each document describes a force that "unites" or "divides."

If you have not used these documents yet, students will need more time to work with these sources. For documents that present challenging reading, use the following steps:

1. Remind students to use the questions associated with the documents as they read. Tell students that these questions will help them focus on each document.

2. Have pairs of students read the document aloud, stopping after each sentence or main idea. Then, have the pairs work together to paraphrase each of the sentences or main ideas. For example, for Document 4, the first part could be summarized as, "It is too bad that the rich and powerful use the law to help themselves."

3. Provide students with dictionaries. As they read the documents, have them jot down the meanings of unfamiliar words. Help less proficient readers who are having trouble determining the correct definition of multiple-meaning words.

4. Pose one of the Historian's Checklist questions. Using the Idea Wave strategy on TE p. T24, have students answer the question.

Answers

Document 3: The canals, roads, and railroads united the nation east of the Mississippi River by allowing the efficient exchange of goods between the different sections.

Document 4: Jacksonian Democracy was a unifying force because more people voted and average citizens became more politically active. However, it was also a divisive force because Jackson's policies triggered a crisis over states' rights versus national authority and sparked conflict between rich banking interests and the common people.

Instruction (continued)

- Preview the documents and assign selections according to student abilities. You may organize students into groups to review documents. For example, assign Document 1 to students with special needs or English language learners. Ask: **What does the picture tell you about the North in the early 1800s?** *(Possible answers: the North was industrialized; it had pollution; there were parks.)*

- Assign Document 5 to advanced readers. Ask the students why Douglass does not feel the July 4th celebration is a time for African Americans to rejoice. *(It does not celebrate the freedom of African Americans; it is a reminder of their bondage.)* Ask them which phrases in the document support this. *(the day reveals to him…the gross injustice…to which he is…victim; celebration is a sham; sounds of rejoicing are empty and heartless)*

- Assign Document 6 to less proficient readers. Review words and phrases such as *repeated injuries, usurpations, candid,* and *tyranny.* Organize students into groups and have each group paraphrase a key sentence of the document. Ask: **What is this document about?** *(women's rights)* Ask students to identify the rights women were denied. *(the right to vote and to participate in the formation of laws; property rights; control over her wages.)*

- Assign Document 7 to advanced readers. Point out the ellipses in the document and tell students this indicates that some text is missing from the original document. Ask: **How does the senator feel about the President's proposal?** *(The senator is against a war with Mexico.)* Study the poster and the map. **What argument would someone give supporting the war?** *(Gold was found in California and Americans wanted to get there without going through territory owned by Mexico.)*

Answers

Document 5: Abolitionists agreed with Douglass because they wanted slavery outlawed throughout the entire nation. Slave owners disagreed with Douglass because his ideas threatened their livelihood.

Document 6: They supported the extension of voting rights to ordinary Americans but were angry that women were not included in the political process.

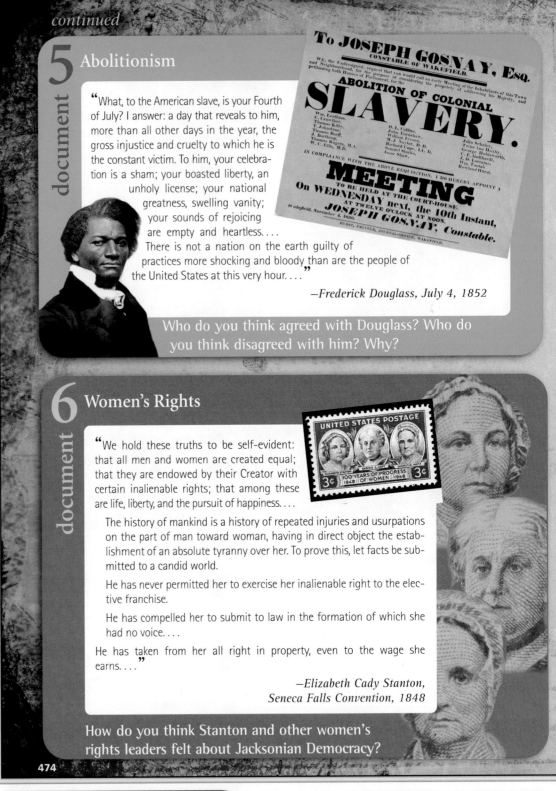

continued

5 Abolitionism

"What, to the American slave, is your Fourth of July? I answer: a day that reveals to him, more than all other days in the year, the gross injustice and cruelty to which he is the constant victim. To him, your celebration is a sham; your boasted liberty, an unholy license; your national greatness, swelling vanity; your sounds of rejoicing are empty and heartless.... There is not a nation on the earth guilty of practices more shocking and bloody than are the people of the United States at this very hour...."

—Frederick Douglass, July 4, 1852

Who do you think agreed with Douglass? Who do you think disagreed with him? Why?

6 Women's Rights

"We hold these truths to be self-evident: that all men and women are created equal; that they are endowed by their Creator with certain inalienable rights; that among these are life, liberty, and the pursuit of happiness....

The history of mankind is a history of repeated injuries and usurpations on the part of man toward woman, having in direct object the establishment of an absolute tyranny over her. To prove this, let facts be submitted to a candid world.

He has never permitted her to exercise her inalienable right to the elective franchise.

He has compelled her to submit to law in the formation of which she had no voice....

He has taken from her all right in property, even to the wage she earns...."

—Elizabeth Cady Stanton,
Seneca Falls Convention, 1848

How do you think Stanton and other women's rights leaders felt about Jacksonian Democracy?

Differentiated Instruction

L3 Advanced Readers

Emphasize Relevance Have students review the connections between uniting and divisive forces during the 1800s. As they discuss and prepare their posters, have them consider how life might have been different without the influence of one or more of the forces discussed in the unit.

L3 Gifted and Talented

What would life be like if it were not based on the idea that all people have the right to vote? How would life be different had the nation not embraced Manifest Destiny? Have students consider the answers to these questions as they create posters that answer the unit question.

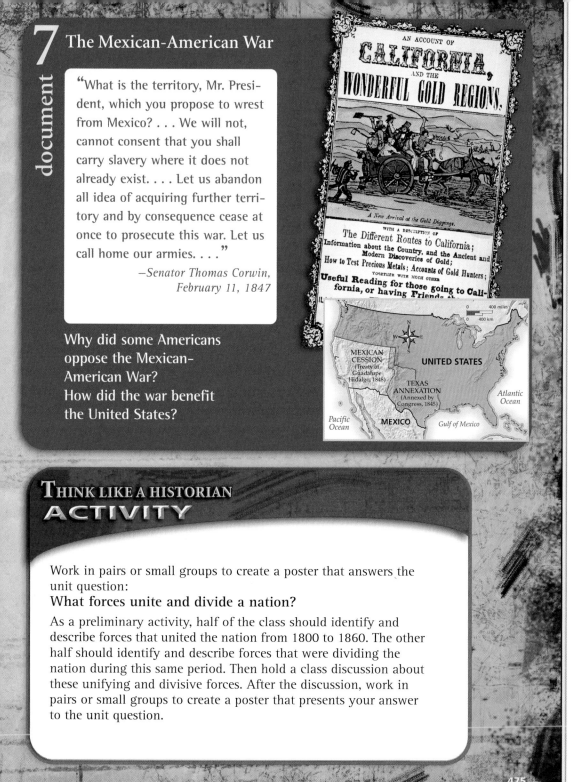

7 The Mexican-American War

document

"What is the territory, Mr. President, which you propose to wrest from Mexico? . . . We will not, cannot consent that you shall carry slavery where it does not already exist. . . . Let us abandon all idea of acquiring further territory and by consequence cease at once to prosecute this war. Let us call home our armies. . . ."

—Senator Thomas Corwin, February 11, 1847

Why did some Americans oppose the Mexican-American War? How did the war benefit the United States?

THINK LIKE A HISTORIAN
ACTIVITY

Work in pairs or small groups to create a poster that answers the unit question:

What forces unite and divide a nation?

As a preliminary activity, half of the class should identify and describe forces that united the nation from 1800 to 1860. The other half should identify and describe forces that were dividing the nation during this same period. Then hold a class discussion about these unifying and divisive forces. After the discussion, work in pairs or small groups to create a poster that presents your answer to the unit question.

475

Monitor Progress

Review the Unit Question and remind students about the brainstorming they did when they first began the unit. Bring out the flip charts you did with the students at the beginning of the unit. Have students review these answers and revise the list as appropriate.

Activity

Divide the class in half to complete the first part of the activity. Then organize the class into small groups or pairs to create their posters. Review these guidelines with students before they begin their work.

- Use a graphic organizer to show the forces that unite and divide a nation. Organize your notes into two columns, one labeled "uniting forces" and one labeled "divisive forces." Use information from the unit and the documents to help you decide which entries to put on the graphic organizer.

- Decide which of the forces you will use in your poster. Discuss your choice and decide on the best two or three forces from each category to use in your poster.

- Appoint one person in your group to draw a pencil sketch of the poster. Have another student or students work on headings and captions. Discuss the sketch and the headings before proceeding with the final poster.

Circulate to be sure students understand their assignment and that work is collaborative. Allow for class discussion and evaluation of the projects. Use the appropriate four-point rubric in the Assessment Rubrics to evaluate this activity.

 Assessment Rubrics

History Background

Connecting to Today The United States has gone to war many times throughout its history. While the reasons for engaging in war varied, so did the opinions of Americans. At times loyalties were divided, such as in the War of 1812. At other times, such as World War II, national opinion fully supported the reasons for the conflict. In recent years, the United States fought wars in Afghanistan and Iraq as part of the war on terror. Initially, Americans were united in support of the wars. Yet with time, public opinion changed and many Americans took a strong stand against the war.

Discuss this issue with the class. Ask: **When should a country go to war?**

Answers

Document 7: Some Americans opposed the war because they wanted to prevent the expansion of slavery to new territories. The American victory gave the United States a large swath of land from the Southwest to the Pacific coast.

Unit 5

Why It Matters

As compromises regarding slavery failed, violence consumed the nation. The Civil War tore the nation in two and its legacy remains with us today.

■ The Civil War is a terrible example of what can happen when people and nations fail to resolve differences peacefully. Recent examples can be seen in former Yugoslavia, Congo, Chechnya, and the Middle East.

■ Discrimination and hate crimes have not been limited to African Americans in the South in the 1800s. Recent hate crimes have targeted African Americans, Jews, Muslims, and immigrants, among others.

■ Among the "firsts" developed for the Civil War, and still used today, were aerial reconnaissance, the bugle call "Taps," the U.S. Secret Service, and a press corps that covered the war from the battle areas.

Unit Essential Question

How was the Civil War a political, economic, and social turning point?

Think Like a Historian

• To preview this unit, have students review the content on these pages of the Student Edition. Ask: **What will you be learning about in this unit?** (*the causes of the Civil War, the war itself, and the Reconstruction period that followed*) Tell students that the Civil War led to changes in both the North and the South.

• Write the Unit Focus Question on the board. Using the Idea Wave strategy (TE, p. T24), have students brainstorm for answers to the question. In considering the Unit Focus Question, ask students to recall the changes that followed the American Revolution.

• Record students' answers on a flip chart. Keep a copy of them. Once students have completed their responses, tell them that they will be learning about the causes and effects of the Civil War. Let them know that you will return to this same question at the end of the unit and

Unit 5

How was the Civil War a political, economic, and social turning point?

Chapter 14
The Nation Divided pp. 478–507

Chapter 15
The Civil War pp. 508–541

Chapter 16
Reconstruction and the New South pp. 542–567

Underground Railroad By the middle of the 1830s, opposition to slavery was rising among reformers. Abolitionists aided enslaved people who sought to escape via the Underground Railroad to the North or to Canada.

1830s

Lincoln's Gettysburg Address Lincoln's firm leadership inspired the Union side. In the Gettysburg Address, he vowed that "these dead shall not have died in vain . . . and that government of the people, by the people, for the people, shall not perish from the earth."

1863

review their responses for possible additions or changes. (*See Think Like a Historian, p. 565.*)

• Preview the primary sources in Think Like a Historian on pp. 568–571. You may wish to introduce and discuss these documents to enrich chapter content.

Civil War and Reunion

Decision at Gettysburg All attempts at compromise having failed, the United States endured a bloody four-year civil war. After the Battle of Gettysburg, the war turned in favor of the Union army.

1863

A New Voice in Government Before the Civil War, African Americans had no voice in southern government. During Reconstruction, they became a powerful voting force in southern elections. African Americans were elected to public office as sheriffs, mayors, state legislators, and members of Congress.

1868

477

Think Like a Historian

Students complete an activity in which they use primary sources to explore the Essential Question.
pp. 568–571

Home Involvement

A summary of the Civil War content students will be studying and suggested activities adults at home can do with their child are available in the Teaching Resources.

 **Teaching Resources, Unit 5,** Letter Home, Chapters 14, 15, 16

eTeach

Read the essay on eTeach for further ideas on Using the Internet in the Classroom.
Visit: PHSchool.com
Web Code: myf-0301

DK World Desk Reference

Use the resources on the DK World Desk Reference for further information about the United States.
Visit: PHSchool.com
Web Code: mye-0302

History Background

Lincoln's Changing Views The Gettysburg Address both honors the dead and shows Lincoln's changing view of the Civil War. In earlier speeches, Lincoln had focused on restoring the Union. In the Gettysburg Address, Lincoln expressed new ideas about the larger goals and principles behind the war: establishing freedom and equality under the law for all. These ideas, following the success of the Emancipation Proclamation, helped renew Union commitment to the war.

The Nation Divided (1846–1861)

History Background

The Importance of the 1850s

The 1850s began hopefully, but a series of unsatisfactory compromises, new legislation, and legal decisions increased tensions between North and South over the issue of slavery.

The admission of new states to the Union first fueled renewed debate. After much negotiation and compromise, Texas—as a slave state—and California—as a free state—joined the Union peacefully. In 1854, however, the Kansas-Nebraska Act allowed popular sovereignty to decide the issue of slavery in the Kansas and Nebraska Territories. This led pro- and antislavery forces into violent confrontation and the territories into political chaos.

Additional polarizing events soon followed. In 1857, the Supreme Court ruled in the Dred Scott case that slaves were property protected by the Fifth Amendment. Therefore Congress could not make any laws regulating slavery. This left the entire country open to the spread of slavery. In 1859, John Brown raided Harpers Ferry in an unsuccessful but bloody attempt to capture arms and lead a slave revolt. Both the raid and subsequent northern support for Brown frightened southerners, who began to realize how strong the antislavery movement had become in the North.

The Whig Party, unable to agree on a strong stance on the crucial issue of slavery, disappeared from the national scene by 1860. It was replaced by the Republican Party. Most Republicans opposed the spread of slavery to the territories. In 1860, Abraham Lincoln, running as a Republican, won a majority of the electoral vote. His election prompted several southern states to secede, and the Civil War soon followed.

Essential Questions

Use this graphic organizer to see the relationship between key concepts and the Chapter Essential Question.

Focus Question/Section 1
How did the question of admission of new states to the Union fuel the debate over slavery and states' rights?
(p. 482)

Concept: Constitution

Focus Question/Section 2
What was the Compromise of 1850, and why did it fail?
(p. 486)

Concept: Compromise

Chapter Essential Question
How did the nation try but fail to deal with growing sectional differences?

Focus Question/Section 4
Why did the election of Abraham Lincoln spark the secession of southern states?
(p. 499)

Concept: Sucession

Focus Question/Section 3
Why did the Lincoln-Douglas debates and John Brown's raid increase tensions between the North and South?
(p. 494)

Concept: Region

Differentiated Instruction

Discussion Ideas

Students will be more willing and interested in engaging in discussion if they are discussing a topic of high interest that is well-suited to the discussion format.

Choose a Topic As students read the chapter, ask them to write down one idea that could be used to conduct an interesting discussion. Ideas could relate to something they do not understand, something that seems interesting, or something that relates to something else they know, but should provoke interest and more ideas. Model the process by giving students both rich and poor ideas for a discussion.

Rich idea: Why was the Fugitive Slave Act of 1850 controversial?

Poor idea: What was the Compromise of 1850?

Choose a Format Also ask students to suggest a discussion format for their ideas. If their discussion idea suits a quick whip around the class, they should suggest an Idea Wave (TE, p. T24) type of format. If the discussion idea prompts a longer, more thoughtful discussion, they may suggest a Give One, Get One (TE, p. T25) or Think-Write-Pair-Share (TE, p. T25) type of discussion. Have students take turns discussing their ideas.

Concepts Across Time

Have students develop an understanding of the enduring concepts of history by connecting these ideas.

Concept: Compromise

Students should recall how American policy about slavery was shaped by a number of compromises over the years. Ask: **What compromise did the Constitutional Convention make regarding slavery?** (*the Three-fifths Compromise; three-fifths of the slaves would be included in the population count for representation and taxation*) Ask: **What did the Missouri Compromise of 1820 do?** (*It kept an equal balance between free states and slave states, barred slavery in part of the Louisiana Territory, and allowed slave owners to reclaim fugitive slaves from northern states.*) Ask: **Why were some northerners willing to compromise on issues of slavery?** (*Northern mill owners and merchants often profited from trade in slave-grown cotton, and many northern laborers feared increased competition for jobs if slavery ended.*) Use these questions when discussing the tensions over slavery and the Compromise of 1850 in Sections 1 and 2.

Concept: Region

Students learning about the debate over slavery should understand the South's economy. Ask:

How did the climate and environment of the southern colonies result in a unique economic system? (*The long growing season and fertile soil favored the development of plantation agriculture and slavery.*) Use this question when discussing the debate over slavery in Sections 1 and 2.

Concept: Constitution

Constitutional issues played a large part in the debate over slavery. Students learning about the background of the Civil War should recall the roots of the conflict. Ask: **Why did southern states argue at the Constitutional Convention that slaves should be counted as part of the population when determining how many seats in Congress each state would get?** (*They were afraid of being outvoted on issues important to the South, especially slavery.*) Ask: **How are states represented in the Senate?** (*Each state is represented by two senators.*) Ask: **Why would it matter if there were more slave states or free states?** (*It would affect voting in the Senate and the Electoral College.*) Use these questions when discussing the debate over slavery in Sections 1 and 2.

Section 1 Growing Tensions Over Slavery *1.5 periods, .75 block*

Objectives

Students will

1. Explain why conflict arose over the issue of slavery in the territories after the Mexican-American War.

2. Identify the goal of the Free-Soil Party.

3. Describe the compromise Henry Clay proposed to settle the issues that divided the North and the South.

Differentiated Instruction Key

L1 Basic to Average	**AR** Advanced Readers
L2 All Students	**ELL** English Language Learners
L3 Average to Advanced	**GT** Gifted and Talented
	LPR Less Proficient Readers
	SN Special Needs

Prepare to Read	Instructional Resources	Differentiated Instruction
Build Background Knowledge Preview the section and remind students how the issue of slavery was reopened. **Set a Purpose for Reading** Have students begin to fill out the Reading Readiness Guide. **Preview Key Terms** Preview the section's key terms.	**All in One** Teaching Resources, Unit 5 **L2** Chapter Prereading Guide, p. 4 **L2** History Reading Skill, p. 14 **L2** Word Knowledge Rating Form, p. 15 **L2** Reading Readiness Guide, p. 16 **Teacher's Edition** **L2** Vocabulary Builder, pp. 481, 483	🎧 **Guided Reading Audio CD** **Spanish** ELL, LPR, SN

Teach	Instructional Resources	Differentiated Instruction
Instruction **Slavery and the Mexican-American War** Describe the problem of adding new territory to the Union. **A Bitter Debate** Discuss debate over the Compromise of 1850.	📖 **Interactive Reading and Notetaking Study Guide** **L2** Chapter 14, Section 1 **All in One** Teaching Resources, Unit 5 **L2** Speech to the Senate, p. 22	📖 **Interactive Reading and Notetaking Study Guide, Adapted Version (English/ Spanish)** **L1** Chapter 14, Section 1 ELL, LPR, SN **Teacher's Edition** **L1** Visualizing the Word, p. 481 ELL, LPR, SN **L1** Decoding, p. 482 ELL, LPR, SN **L3** Civil War Debate, p. 484 AR, GT **All in One** Teaching Resources, Unit 5 **L3** A Civil War Debate, p. 20

Assess and Reteach	Instructional Resources	Differentiated Instruction
Assess Progress Evaluate student comprehension with Check Your Progress and Section Quiz. **Reteach** Assign the Interactive Reading and Notetaking Study Guide to help struggling students. **Extend** Extend the lesson by having students research the Compromise of 1850.	📖 **Interactive Reading and Notetaking Study Guide** **L2** Chapter 14, Section 1 **All in One** Teaching Resources, Unit 5 **L2** Reading Readiness Guide, p. 16 **L2** Section Quiz, p. 27 **Progress Monitoring Transparencies** **L2** Chapter 14, Section 1	**Teacher's Edition** **L1** Checkpoints, TE pp. 483, 485 🎧 **SE on Audio CD** **L1** Chapter 14 ELL, LPR, SN **Internet Resources** PHSchool.com

Objectives

Students will

1. Summarize the main points of the Compromise of 1850.
2. Describe the impact of the novel *Uncle Tom's Cabin.*
3. Explain how the Kansas-Nebraska Act reopened the issue of slavery in the territories.
4. Describe the effect of the Kansas-Nebraska Act.

Differentiated Instruction Key

L1 Basic to Average
L2 All Students
L3 Average to Advanced

AR Advanced Readers
ELL English Language Learners
GT Gifted and Talented
LPR Less Proficient Readers
SN Special Needs

Prepare to Read

Build Background Knowledge
Preview the section and remind students about the controversy over slavery caused by the Mexican Cession.

Set a Purpose for Reading
Have students begin to fill out the Reading Readiness Guide.

Preview Key Terms
Preview the section's key terms.

Instructional Resources

All in One Teaching Resources, Unit 5
L2 Reading Readiness Guide, p. 17

Teacher's Edition
L2 Vocabulary Builder, p. 487

Differentiated Instruction

Guided Reading Audio CD
Spanish ELL, LPR, SN

Teach

Instruction
The Compromise of 1850
Discuss the provisions of the Compromise of 1850.

Uncle Tom's Cabin
Describe the impact of *Uncle Tom's Cabin.*

The Kansas-Nebraska Act
Discuss the idea of popular sovereignty and its application in the Kansas-Nebraska territory.

Bleeding Kansas
Describe the effect of the Kansas-Nebraska Act on Kansas.

Instructional Resources

Interactive Reading and Notetaking Study Guide
L2 Chapter 14, Section 2

Color Transparencies
L2 Anthony Burns

Discovery School Video
L2 *Uncle Tom's Cabin*

Differentiated Instruction

Interactive Reading and Notetaking Study Guide, Adapted Version (English/Spanish)
L1 Chapter 14, Section 2 ELL, LPR, SN

Teacher's Edition
L1 Slavery, p. 486 ELL, LPR, SN
L3 Harriet Beecher Stowe, p. 488 AR, GT
L1 Marked Reading, p. 490 LPR
L1 Understanding Vernacular, p. 492 ELL, LPR

Assess and Reteach

Assess Progress
Evaluate student comprehension with Check Your Progress and Section Quiz.

Reteach
Assign the Interactive Reading and Notetaking Study Guide to help struggling students.

Extend
Extend the lesson by having students research Harriet Beecher Stowe.

Instructional Resources

Interactive Reading and Notetaking Study Guide
L2 Chapter 14, Section 2

All in One Teaching Resources, Unit 5
L2 Reading Readiness Guide, p. 17
L2 Section Quiz, p. 28

Progress Monitoring Transparencies
L2 Chapter 14, Section 2

Differentiated Instruction

Teacher's Edition
L1 Checkpoints, TE pp. 487, 488, 490, 491

SE on Audio CD
L1 Chapter 14 ELL, LPR, SN

Internet Resources
PHSchool.com

Historian's Apprentice Activity Pack

Section 3 The Crisis Deepens *1 period, .5 block*

Objectives

Students will

1. Explain why the Republican Party came into being in the 1850s.
2. Summarize the issues involved in the Dred Scott decision.
3. Identify Abraham Lincoln's and Stephen Douglas's views on slavery.
4. Describe the differing reactions in the North and the South to John Brown's raid.

Differentiated Instruction Key

- **L1** Basic to Average
- **L2** All Students
- **L3** Average to Advanced

- **AR** Advanced Readers
- **ELL** English Language Learners
- **GT** Gifted and Talented
- **LPR** Less Proficient Readers
- **SN** Special Needs

Prepare to Read

Build Background Knowledge
Preview the section and discuss the repeal of the Missouri Compromise.

Set a Purpose for Reading
Have students begin to fill out the Reading Readiness Guide.

Preview Key Terms
Preview the section's key terms.

Instructional Resources

All in One Teaching Resources, Unit 5
- **L2** Reading Readiness Guide, p. 18

Teacher's Edition
- **L2** Vocabulary Builder, p. 495

Differentiated Instruction

🔊 **Guided Reading Audio CD**
Spanish ELL, LPR, SN

Teach

Instruction
A New Antislavery Party
Discuss the success of the Republican Party.

The Dred Scott Decision
Explain the Dred Scott decision and its results.

The Lincoln-Douglas Debates
Explain the highlights and significance of the Lincoln-Douglas debates.

John Brown's Raid
Describe northerners' and southerners' reactions to John Brown's raid.

Instructional Resources

📖 **Interactive Reading and Notetaking Study Guide**
- **L2** Chapter 14, Section 3

Color Transparencies
- **L2** Lincoln-Douglas Debate

Differentiated Instruction

📖 **Interactive Reading and Notetaking Study Guide, Adapted Version (English/Spanish)**
- **L1** Chapter 14, Section 3 ELL, LPR, SN

Teacher's Edition
- **L1** Listening, p. 494 ELL, LPR, SN
- **L3** The Lincoln-Douglas Debates, p. 496 AR, GT

Assess and Reteach

Assess Progress
Evaluate student comprehension with Check Your Progress and Section Quiz.

Reteach
Assign the Interactive Reading and Notetaking Study Guide to help struggling students.

Extend
Extend the lesson by having students write a letter about John Brown's trial and sentence.

Instructional Resources

📖 **Interactive Reading and Notetaking Study Guide**
- **L2** Chapter 14, Section 3

All in One Teaching Resources, Unit 5
- **L2** Reading Readiness Guide, p. 18
- **L2** Section Quiz, p. 29

Progress Monitoring Transparencies
- **L2** Chapter 14, Section 3

Differentiated Instruction

Teacher's Edition
- **L1** Checkpoints, TE pp. 494, 495, 497, 498

🔊 **SE on Audio CD**
- **L1** Chapter 14 ELL, LPR, SN

Section 4 The Coming of the Civil War *1.5 periods, .75 block*

Objectives

Students will

1. Describe the results of the election of 1860.
2. Explain why the southern states seceded from the Union.
3. Summarize the events that led to the outbreak of the Civil War.

Differentiated Instruction Key

L1 Basic to Average

L2 All Students

L3 Average to Advanced

AR Advanced Readers

ELL English Language Learners

GT Gifted and Talented

LPR Less Proficient Readers

SN Special Needs

Prepare to Read

Build Background Knowledge
Preview the section and discuss whether the nation could have held together in the face of existing divisions.

Set a Purpose for Reading
Have students begin to fill out the Reading Readiness Guide.

Preview Key Terms
Preview the section's key terms.

Instructional Resources

All in One Teaching Resources, Unit 5

L2 Reading Readiness Guide, p. 19

Teacher's Edition

L2 Vocabulary Builder, p. 499

Differentiated Instruction

Guided Reading Audio CD

Spanish **ELL, LPR, SN**

Teach

Instruction
The Nation Divides
Discuss the regional political parties and their candidates and the secession of the southern states.

The Civil War Begins
Discuss the events at Fort Sumter.

Instructional Resources

Interactive Reading and Notetaking Study Guide

L2 Chapter 14, Section 4

All in One Teaching Resources, Unit 5

L2 1860 Electoral Votes, p. 23

L2 Concept Lesson, p. 26

L2 Concept Organizer, p. 6

L2 Skills for Life Worksheet, p. 25

Differentiated Instruction

Interactive Reading and Notetaking Study Guide, Adapted Version (English/Spanish)

L1 Chapter 14, Section 4 **ELL, LPR, SN**

Teacher's Edition

L1 The Election of 1860, p. 500 **ELL, LPR, SN**

L3 Secession Dialogue, p. 502 **AR, GT**

All in One Teaching Resources, Unit 5

L1 The Election of 1860, p. 24

Assess and Reteach

Assess Progress
Evaluate student comprehension with Check Your Progress and Section Quiz.

Reteach
Assign the Interactive Reading and Notetaking Study Guide to help struggling students.

Extend
Extend the lesson by having students complete the History Interactive activity on Fort Sumter online.

Instructional Resources

Interactive Reading and Notetaking Study Guide

L2 Chapter 14, Section 4

All in One Teaching Resources, Unit 5

L2 Word Knowledge Rating Form, p. 15

L2 Reading Readiness Guide, p. 19

L2 Section Quiz, p. 30

L2 Chapter Test, p. 34

Progress Monitoring Transparencies

L2 Chapter 14, Section 4

Differentiated Instruction

Teacher's Edition

L1 Checkpoints, TE pp. 501, 503

SE on Audio CD

L1 Chapter 14 **ELL, LPR, SN**

All in One Teaching Resources, Unit 5

L1 Chapter Test, p. 31

Extend the Lesson Through Technology Research

Use the following research activities to help students deepen their understanding of the Chapter Essential Question: **How did the nation try but fail to deal with growing sectional differences?** Students should use library or Internet resources. The Web Codes provided offer access to Internet resources students can use to complete each activity. Use the appropriate four-point rubric in Assessment Rubrics to evaluate the activity.

 Assessment Rubrics

Write a Newspaper Editorial Opposing the Fugitive Slave Law

Have students research the Fugitive Slave Law of 1850 and write a 3–4 paragraph editorial opposing the law. Tell students that the purpose of the editorial is to persuade others that the law is wrong. Remind them to use specific evidence to support their argument. Use this activity when studying A Bitter Debate in Section 1.

 Individual research activity   L2

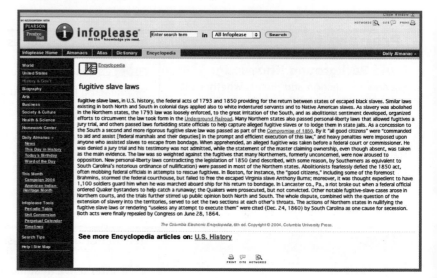

Go Online **Web Code:** mye-0225
PHSchool.com

Create a Timeline of the Battle Over Slavery

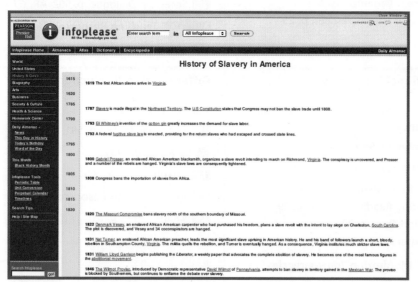

Have students look at a timeline on the Web site and then create their own timeline of events in the battle over slavery that preceded the Civil War. Ask students to place 6–8 major events on their timeline, with a sentence about the significance of each. Have students compare their timelines to check their work. Use the timeline when studying Compromises Fail in Section 2.

 Individual research activity   L2

Go Online **Web Code:** mye-0226
PHSchool.com

Write an Obituary About John Brown

Have students research John Brown on the Web site. Tell them to suppose that they are writing an obituary about him after he has been hanged in 1859. Ask them to consider the scope of Brown's life, his activities in Kansas and Harpers Ferry, and the strong tensions over the issue of slavery in 1859 in writing their obituary. Use this activity when studying John Brown's Raid in Section 3.

 Individual research activity AR, GT

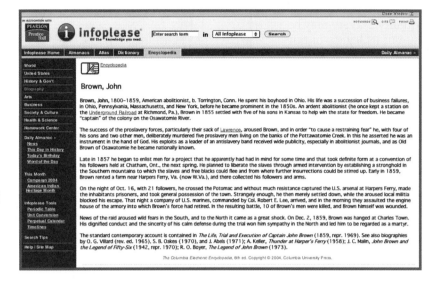

 Web Code: mye-0227

Create an Editorial Cartoon for a Candidate in the Election of 1860

Have students work in small groups to use the Web site to research one of the four candidates for president in the election of 1860: Abraham Lincoln, Stephen Douglas, John Bell, or John Breckinridge. Ask them to use what they have learned to create a political cartoon that gives voters a reason to vote for their candidate. Students should display their cartoons and offer brief explanations of the cartoon's symbols and meanings. Use this activity when studying Election of 1860 in Section 4.

 Group research activity AR, GT

Web Code: mye-0228

Why It Matters

The United States is still torn over the issue of racial equality. Slavery may be a thing of the past, but its legacy of poverty, inequality, and ignorance still troubles society.

For example, at the beginning of the 2000s, about 23 percent of African American families lived below the poverty level compared to about 8 percent of white families. About 26 percent of white Americans had completed four or more years of college while about 17 percent of African Americans had done so. But even more telling, the average annual earnings of white college graduates were almost $10,000 higher than those of African American college graduates.

Studying the origins of the Civil War will help students understand the problems of today and how they came about.

Chapter Essential Question

How did the nation try but fail to deal with growing sectional differences?

Think Like a Historian

- To preview this chapter, have students review the content of these pages of the Student Edition. Ask: **What will you be learning about in this chapter?** (about sectional differences on slavery)

- Have students study the image on these pages and read the quote. Ask: **How do you think enslaved people felt about escaping to freedom?** (desperate, fearful)

- Have students read the section summaries and recall what they learned in Chapter 11 about the economic differences between the North and the South. Ask: **Why do you think slavery continued to be a divisive subject between the North and the South?** (Many northerners opposed slavery because they did not depend on slave labor the way plantation owners in the South did.)

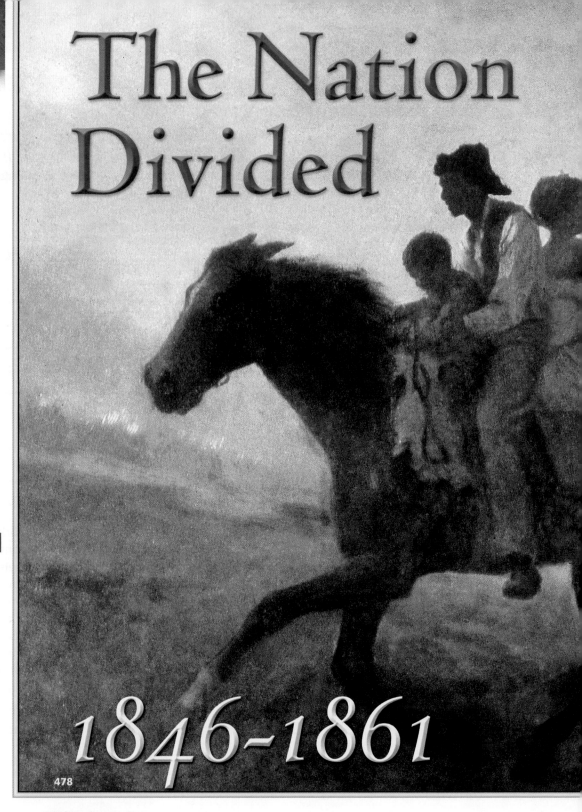

The Nation Divided

1846-1861

478

Bibliography

For the Teacher

Donald, David Herbert. *Lincoln.* New York: Simon & Schuster, 1996.

For the Student

L1 January, Brendan. *The Dred Scott Decision (Cornerstones of Freedom).* Connecticut: Children's Press, 1998.

L2 Lester, Julius and Tom Feelings. *To Be a Slave.* New York: Puffin Books, 2000.

L3 Devillers, David. *The John Brown Slavery Revolt Trial: A Headline Court Case (Headline Court Cases).* Enslow Publishers, 2000.

"I then whispered to my wife, 'Come, my dear, let us make a desperate leap for liberty!'"

—*William Craft,*
Running a Thousand
Miles for Freedom, 1860

This painting, *A Ride for Liberty—The Fugitive Slaves*, depicts a black family fleeing toward freedom.

CHAPTER 14

What You Will Learn

Section 1
GROWING TENSIONS OVER SLAVERY
With the addition of new western land, debate over the spread of slavery increased.

Section 2
COMPROMISES FAIL
After all efforts at compromise failed, violent fighting broke out in the Kansas Territory.

Section 3
THE CRISIS DEEPENS
As tensions increased, a new antislavery political party emerged.

Section 4
THE COMING OF THE CIVIL WAR
Abraham Lincoln's election led seven southern states to leave the Union.

⟲ Reading Skill

Analyze Cause and Effect In this chapter, you will learn to identify causes and their effects to help connect and understand historical events and issues.

479

History Background

The Underground Railroad The Fugitive Slave Law came about partly as a result of the success of the Underground Railroad. Escape for slaves was extremely difficult. They did not have maps, and they had difficulty finding food and shelter. Any unknown person of color was an immediate object of suspicion. The Underground Railroad helped more than 50,000 people escape from slavery. The increased number of successful escapes posed a crisis for slave owners. Given the investment slave owners made in their slaves, recapturing escapees was a matter of vital importance to many southerners.

Prepare to Read

Use the following for reading skill support.

All in One Teaching Resources, Unit 5, Chapter Prereading Guide, p. 4; History Reading Skill, p. 14

History Reading Skill *Online*
Web code: mve-3000

Differentiated Instruction

The following Teacher's Edition strategies are suitable for students of varying abilities.

- **L3** **Advanced Readers,** pp. 484, 488, 496, 502 AR
- **L1** **English Language Learners,** pp. 481, 482, 486, 492, 494, 500 ELL
- **L3** **Gifted and Talented,** pp. 484, 488, 496, 502 GT
- **L1** **Less Proficient Readers,** pp. 481, 482, 486, 490, 492, 494, 500 LPR
- **L1** **Special Needs,** pp. 481, 482, 486, 494, 500 SN

Chapter Resources

Teaching Resources, Unit 5
Chapter Prereading Guide, p. 4
History Reading Skill, p. 14
Word Knowledge Rating Form, p. 15
Skills for Life Worksheet, p. 25
Chapter Tests A/B (L1/L2), pp. 31, 34
Letter Home (English/Spanish), pp. 7, 8

Spanish Support
- **L1** **Interactive Reading and Notetaking Study Guide, Spanish,** Adapted Version
- **L1** **Guided Reading Audio CD,** Spanish

Media and Technology
- **L1** SE on Audio CD
- *ExamView* **Test Bank CD-ROM**

DISCOVERY SCHOOL

Quick View Video
View the chapter video for a quick preview of the main ideas.

Visual Preview

? **How did the nation try but fail to deal with growing sectional differences?**

Build Background Knowledge   L2

Discuss with students the definition of the word *compromise*. Bring out the concept that compromise is a settlement of differences in which each side agrees to give up some of what it wants. Lead a structured review connecting what the students have learned with the Essential Question. (See TE p. T24) Give students a relevant example of a compromise, such as the following: Students want no weekend homework, but teachers feel it is necessary. A compromise solution is that no major papers or projects will be assigned, but reading and short assignments are allowed. Have students give examples of compromises they have made in their own lives.

Instruction   L2

■ For background information on conducting a lesson for the Visual Preview, see TE p. T20.

■ Write the Essential Question on the board and explain the term "sectional differences." Establish the connection between the idea of sectional differences and the need for compromise. Use the Idea Wave strategy (TE p. T24) to lead a structured review of critical differences between the North and the South. Ask: **What were the major differences between North and South?** (*slavery, economies*)

■ Using the key, have students explain what the blue and red colors indicate. (*blue shows free states; red shows slave states*) Have them name a state that is red. (*Texas, Louisiana, Arkansas, Missouri, Mississippi, Tennessee, Kentucky, Alabama, Florida, Georgia, South Carolina, North Carolina, Virginia, Maryland, Delaware*) Have students identify the three primary sections of the nation. (*free states, slave states, territories*)

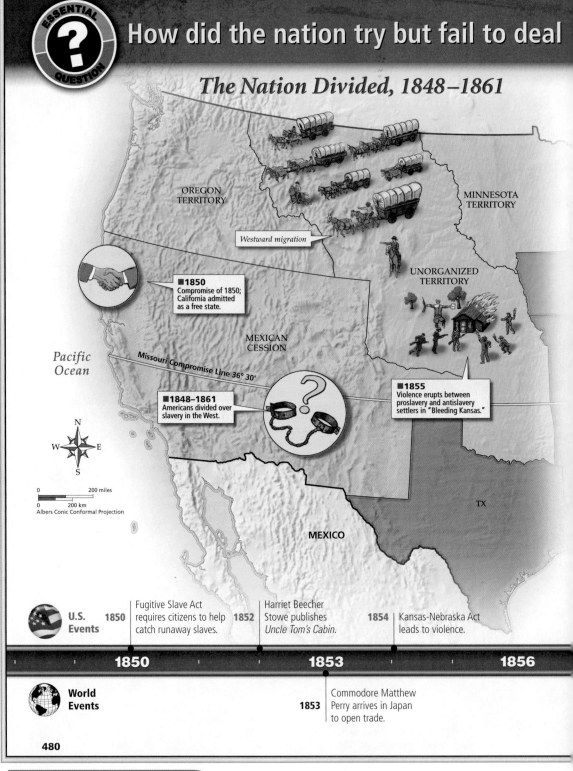

? **How did the nation try but fail to deal**

The Nation Divided, 1848–1861

OREGON TERRITORY

MINNESOTA TERRITORY

Westward migration

UNORGANIZED TERRITORY

■**1850**
Compromise of 1850; California admitted as a free state.

MEXICAN CESSION

Pacific Ocean

Missouri Compromise Line 36° 30'

■**1848–1861**
Americans divided over slavery in the West.

■**1855**
Violence erupts between proslavery and antislavery settlers in "Bleeding Kansas."

0   200 miles
0   200 km
Albers Conic Conformal Projection

TX

MEXICO

| | | U.S. Events | 1850 | Fugitive Slave Act requires citizens to help catch runaway slaves. | 1852 | Harriet Beecher Stowe publishes *Uncle Tom's Cabin*. | 1854 | Kansas-Nebraska Act leads to violence. |

1850   **1853**   **1856**

| | | World Events | | | 1853 | Commodore Matthew Perry arrives in Japan to open trade. |

480

History Background

Tipping the Balance The appeal of Manifest Destiny was offset by the controversy over the spread of slavery. Antislavery activists opposed anything that would add slaveholding states to the Union and upset the balance between free and slave states. Proslavery southerners, on the other hand, saw westward expansion as an opportunity to gain power by expanding slavery into the Western territories. The land gained during the Mexican-American War (1846–1848) was the focus of the dispute.

The main debate between the North and the South over slavery was not primarily a moral one. The question of slavery divided the North and the South over issues of power and control.

with growing sectional differences?

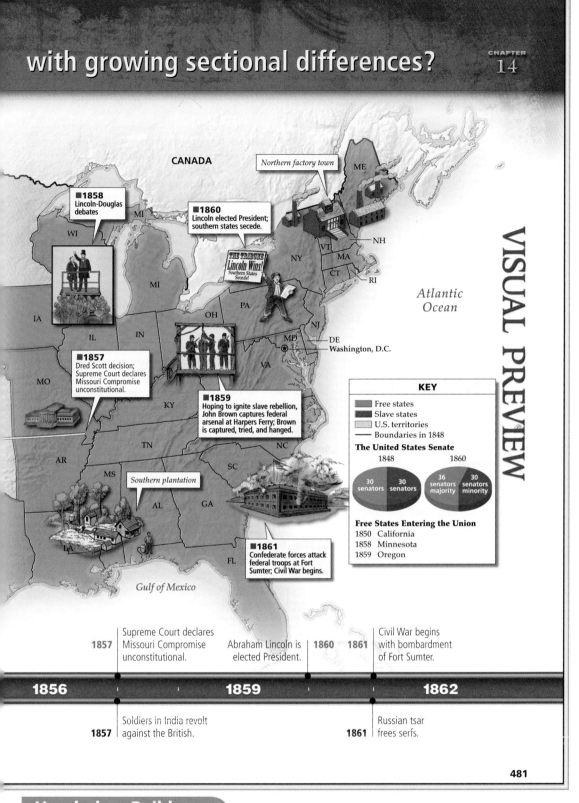

CANADA

Northern factory town

■1858
Lincoln-Douglas debates

■1860
Lincoln elected President; southern states secede.

THE TRIBUNE
Lincoln Wins!
Southern States Secede!

■1857
Dred Scott decision; Supreme Court declares Missouri Compromise unconstitutional.

■1859
Hoping to ignite slave rebellion, John Brown captures federal arsenal at Harpers Ferry; Brown is captured, tried, and hanged.

Southern plantation

■1861
Confederate forces attack federal troops at Fort Sumter; Civil War begins.

Atlantic Ocean

Washington, D.C.

Gulf of Mexico

ME, NH, VT, MA, CT, RI, NY, PA, NJ, DE, MD, VA, OH, IN, IL, MI, WI, IA, MO, KY, TN, NC, SC, GA, AL, MS, AR, LA, FL

VISUAL PREVIEW

KEY
- ▮ Free states
- ▮ Slave states
- ▯ U.S. territories
- — Boundaries in 1848

The United States Senate

1848	1860
30 senators / 30 senators	36 senators majority / 30 senators minority

Free States Entering the Union
1850 California
1858 Minnesota
1859 Oregon

1857	Supreme Court declares Missouri Compromise unconstitutional.		Abraham Lincoln is elected President.	1860	1861	Civil War begins with bombardment of Fort Sumter.

1856			**1859**			**1862**

| 1857 | Soldiers in India revolt against the British. | | | | 1861 | Russian tsar frees serfs. |

481

Instruction (continued)

- Have students look at the timeline. Ask: **What is the time period covered on the timeline?** *(1850–1862)* **What event directly preceded the Civil War?** *(Lincoln was elected President.)* **What event started the war?** *(bombardment of Fort Sumter)*

- Look at the graphics and captions on the map. In the middle of the map, there is an image of a house on fire. Read the caption. Ask: **What two groups are fighting?** *(proslavery and antislavery settlers)* **In what state does the violence occur?** *(Kansas)*

- Pair students and have them select two graphics to analyze. Using the Think-Write-Pair-Share strategy (TE p. T25), have them interpret their selections. Then, discuss the graphics with the entire class.

- Have students rewrite the Essential Question in simple terms in their notes. **Why didn't the North and the South find a way to settle their differences?** You may also post this question in a prominent place in the classroom and leave it there while discussing the chapter. Tell students to use the section focus questions as a guide to answering the Essential Question as they read the chapter.

- Tell students that as they complete the Notetaking Study Guide for this chapter, they will be building the answer to the Essential Question.

Interactive Reading and Notetaking Study Guide, Chapter 14 (Adapted Version also available)

Vocabulary Builder

Preview the Vocabulary Have students preview the vocabulary in the chapter and rate how well they know each word on the Word Knowledge Rating Form. Collect the sheets and explain that they will have a chance to go over the forms later.

All in One Teaching Resources, Unit 5, Word Knowledge Rating Form, p. 15

Monitor Progress Have students demonstrate their understanding of the vocabulary terms by completing these activities.

- Ask students how they can *clarify* their understanding of history.

- Ask students whether a week without any TV would pose a *crisis* situation for them.

Review and Preview

Students have read about the attempts to settle the issue of slavery. Now they will focus on how territorial expansion after the Mexican-American War renewed the debates about the spread of slavery.

Section Focus Question

How did the question of admission of new states to the Union fuel the debate over slavery and states' rights?

Before you begin the lesson for the day, write the Section Focus Question on the board. (*Lesson focus: It threatened to upset the balance between free states and slave states.*)

Prepare to Read

Build Background Knowledge L2

Remind students about the Missouri Compromise of 1820. Both northerners and southerners hoped that it had settled the issue of slavery. Ask students to name the events they read about in Chapter 13 that reopened the slavery issue. Use the Idea Wave strategy (TE, p. T24) to elicit responses.

Set a Purpose L2

■ Read each statement in the Reading Readiness Guide aloud. Ask students to mark the statements True or False.

 All in One Teaching Resources, Unit 5, Reading Readiness Guide, p. 16

■ Have students discuss the statements in pairs or groups of four, then mark their worksheets again. Use the Numbered Heads strategy (TE, p. T24) to call on students to share their group's perspectives. The students will return to these worksheets later.

SECTION 1

The Free-Soil Party

❝ Two years ago there existed in this State a party calling itself the "Free Soil" party. . . . opposed, not only to the extension, but to the existence of slavery, and carried out their principles by resolves and mutual political action. One principal item in their creed was, that no member of that party should vote for a slaveholder or a pro-slavery man. ❞

—From a letter to the editor, "The Semi-Weekly Eagle," Brattleboro, Vermont, 1850

◀ Free-Soil Party presidential campaign poster, 1848

Growing Tensions Over Slavery

Objectives
- Explain why conflict arose over the issue of slavery in the territories after the Mexican-American War.
- Identify the goal of the Free-Soil Party.
- Describe the compromise Henry Clay proposed to settle the issues that divided the North and the South.

🎯 Reading Skill

Analyze Causes Causes are the reasons that events happen. As the United States struggled over the issue of slavery, events such as new laws or important speeches had dramatic effects on the struggle. Understanding how these events made such an impact will help you make sense of this turbulent time in American history.

Key Terms and People

popular sovereignty	Henry Clay
secede	John C. Calhoun
fugitive	Daniel Webster

Why It Matters The Missouri Compromise of 1820 seemed to have quieted the differences between North and South. But the American victory in the Mexican-American War added new territory to the United States. As a result, the states renewed their struggle over slavery and states' rights.

❓ **Section Focus Question: How did the question of admission of new states to the Union fuel the debate over slavery and states' rights?**

Slavery and the Mexican-American War

Between 1820 and 1848, four new slaveholding states and four new free states were admitted to the Union. This maintained the balance between free and slaveholding states, with 15 of each. However, territory gained by the Mexican-American War threatened to destroy the balance.

The Wilmot Proviso The Missouri Compromise did not apply to the huge territory gained from Mexico in 1848. Would this territory be organized as states that allowed slavery? The issue was vital to northerners who wanted to stop slavery from spreading.

Fearing that the South would gain too much power, in 1846 Representative David Wilmot of Pennsylvania proposed that Congress ban slavery in all territory that might become part of the United States as a result of the Mexican-American War.

This proposal was called the Wilmot Proviso. The provision was passed in the House of Representatives, but it failed in the Senate. Although the Wilmot Proviso never became law, it aroused great concern in the South. Many supporters of slavery viewed it as an attack on slavery by the North.

482 Chapter 14 The Nation Divided

Differentiated Instruction

 L1 English Language Learners **L1 Less Proficient Readers** **L1 Special Needs**

Decoding The key terms *popular sovereignty, secede,* and *fugitive* all present decoding challenges to readers. Pronounce each word slowly, and point to the sounds so students understand that the *g* in *sovereignty* is silent, the *c* in *secede* is the same sound as the initial *s*, and the *g* in *fugitive* is soft instead of hard.

An Antislavery Party The <u>controversy</u> over the Wilmot Proviso also led to the rise of a new political party. Neither the Democrats nor the Whigs took a firm stand on slavery. Each hoped to win support in both North and South in the election of 1848.

The Democratic candidate for President in 1848, Senator Lewis Cass of Michigan, proposed a solution that he hoped would appeal to everyone. Cass suggested letting the people in each new territory or state decide for themselves whether to allow slavery. This process, called **popular sovereignty**, meant that people in the territory or state would vote directly on issues, rather than having their elected representatives decide.

Many Whigs and Democrats wanted to take a stronger stand against the spread of slavery. In August 1848, antislavery Whigs and Democrats joined forces to form a new party, which they called the Free-Soil Party. It called for the territory gained in the Mexican-American War to be "free soil," a place where slavery was banned.

The party chose former Democratic President Martin Van Buren as its candidate. Van Buren did poorly in the election. However, he won enough votes from the Democrats to keep Cass from winning. General Zachary Taylor, a Whig and a hero of the Mexican-American War, was elected instead.

☑**Checkpoint** Why was the Free-Soil Party founded?

Vocabulary Builder
<u>controversy</u> (KAHN truh vur see)
n. argument or dispute

The Election of 1848

That's you Dad! more
"FREE SOIL."
We'll rat'em out yet.
Long life to
Davy Wilmot.

Lewis Cass

Martin
Van Buren
and his son

Reading Political Cartoons
Skills Activity

This 1848 cartoon reflects a view that members of the Free-Soil Party were "barnburners," ready to burn down the barn (the Democratic Party) to get rid of proslavery "rats."

(a) Identify Main Ideas How does the cartoon relate to the Election of 1848?

(b) Apply Information In the cartoon bubble (top right), what are the meanings of "FREE SOIL" and "Davy Wilmot"?

Vocabulary Builder

Use the information below to teach students this section's high-use words.

High-Use Word	Definition and Sample Sentence
controversy, p. 483	*n.* argument or dispute The annexation of Texas by the United States caused **controversy**.
crisis, p. 484	*n.* turning point or deciding event in history During the winter at Valley Forge, General Washington faced a **crisis** in keeping his forces together.

Teach

Slavery and the Mexican-American War
p. 482

Instruction   L2

- **Vocabulary Builder** Before teaching this section, preteach the High-Use Words **controversy** and **crisis** using the strategy on TE p. T21.

  Key Terms Following the instructions on p. 7, have students create a See It–Remember It chart for the key terms in this chapter.

- Read Slavery and the Mexican-American War using the Choral Reading strategy (TE, p. T22).

- Ask: **What was the goal of the Free-Soil Party?** (*to prevent the spread of slavery to territory gained in the Mexican-American War*)

- Remind students that the North controlled the House of Representatives, but each state had two seats in the Senate. Ask: **Why was the South alarmed by the Wilmot Proviso?** (*Banning new slave states would give free states a majority in both houses of Congress.*)

Independent Practice

Have students begin filling in the study guide for this section.

📖 **Interactive Reading and Notetaking Study Guide,** Chapter 14, Section 1 (Adapted Version also available.)

Monitor Progress

As students fill in the Notetaking Study Guide, circulate and make sure individuals understand which events led to the renewed debate on slavery.

Answers

☑**Checkpoint** The Free-Soil Party formed to prevent slavery in new lands gained in the Mexican-American War.

Reading Political Cartoons (a) Cass and Van Buren were both presidential candidates; Van Buren is shown "burning" Cass out of the party. **(b)** "Free-Soil" refers to territory where slavery was banned; Davy Wilmot proposed banning slavery in all territory gained in the Mexican-American War.

A Bitter Debate

p. 484

Instruction L2

- Have students read A Bitter Debate. Remind students to look for the answer to the Section Focus Question.

- Ask: **Why was Calhoun opposed to California's admission to the Union?** (*It would tip the balance in the Senate against slave states.*)

- Have students use the worksheet Speech to the Senate to explore the debate on the Compromise of 1850. Have students discuss whether they think Webster's speech is persuasive.

  All in One Teaching Resources, Unit 5, Speech to the Senate, p. 22

Independent Practice

Have students complete the study guide for this section.

Interactive Reading and Notetaking Study Guide, Chapter 14, Section 1 (Adapted Version also available.)

Monitor Progress

- As students complete the Notetaking Study Guide, circulate and make sure individuals understand the debate on expanding slavery.

- Tell students to fill in the last column of the Reading Readiness Guide. Probe for what they learned that confirms or invalidates each statement.

  All in One Teaching Resources, Unit 5, Reading Readiness Guide, p. 16

Calhoun Versus Webster

❝[If] something is not done to arrest it, the South will be forced to choose between abolition and secession. . . . If you are unwilling we should part in peace, tell us so; and we shall know what to do when you reduce the question to submission or resistance.❞

—John C. Calhoun, March 4, 1850

John C. Calhoun

❝I wish to speak today, not as a Massachusetts man, nor as a Northern man, but as an American. . . . I speak today for the preservation of the Union. . . . I speak today . . . for the restoration to the country of that quiet and that harmony which make the blessings of this Union so rich, and so dear to us all.❞

—Daniel Webster, March 7, 1850

Daniel Webster

Reading Primary Sources
Skills Activity

During the Senate debate on Clay's Compromise of 1850, John C. Calhoun and Daniel Webster wrote dramatic speeches evaluating the compromise.

(a) Detect Points of View For what region does Daniel Webster claim to be speaking?

(b) Apply Information Calhoun says "[If] something is not done to arrest it, the South will be forced to choose between abolition and secession." To what does "it" refer?

A Bitter Debate

After the discovery of gold in California, thousands of people rushed west. California soon had enough people to become a state. Both sides realized that California's admission to the Union as a free state would upset the balance between free and slave states in the Senate.

Northerners argued that California should be a free state because most of the territory lay north of the Missouri Compromise line. But southerners feared that if free states gained a majority in the Senate, the South would not be able to block antislavery attacks like the Wilmot Proviso. Southern leaders began to threaten to secede, or withdraw, from the nation if California was admitted to the Union as a free state.

Analyze Causes What event did both southerners and northerners worry would destroy the balance of power between them?

There were other issues dividing the North and South. Northerners wanted the slave trade abolished in Washington, D.C. Southerners wanted northerners to catch people who had escaped from slavery. Southerners called for a law that would force the return of fugitives, or runaway enslaved people.

Vocabulary Builder crisis (KRĪ sihs) *n.* turning point or deciding event in history

For months it looked as if there was no solution. Then, in January 1850, Senator Henry Clay of Kentucky stepped forward with a plan to calm the crisis. Clay had won the nickname the Great Compromiser for working out the Missouri Compromise. Now, Clay made another series of proposals that he hoped would forever resolve the issues that bitterly divided northerners and southerners.

Differentiated Instruction

L3 Advanced Readers   **L3 Gifted and Talented**

Civil War Debate Have students research life in the United States in the first half of the 1800s, comparing and contrasting the major differences between the North and the South. They should then review the events leading to the conflict. To present their findings, have students debate whether the Civil War could have been avoided.

All in One Teaching Resources, Unit 5, A Civil War Debate, p. 20

Answers

Reading Primary Sources (a) for the entire country **(b)** attacks on slavery

Reading Skill California's admission to the Union

The Senate's discussion of Clay's proposals produced one of the greatest debates in American political history. South Carolina Senator John C. Calhoun was against compromise. Calhoun was gravely ill and just four weeks from death. He was too weak to give his speech, but he struggled to sit upright while his final speech was read to the Senate.

The admission of California as a free state, Calhoun wrote, would expose the South to continued attacks on slavery. There were only two ways to preserve the South's way of life. One was a constitutional amendment to protect states' rights. The other was secession.

Three days later, Massachusetts Senator Daniel Webster rose to support Clay's proposals and called for an end to the bitter sectionalism that was dividing the nation. Webster argued for Clay's compromise in order to preserve the Union.

Which view would prevail? The very existence of the United States depended on the answer.

✓ **Checkpoint** How did California's proposed admission to the Union affect the debate between the North and the South over slavery?

⭐ **Looking Back and Ahead** With the territories acquired by the Mexican-American War, the nation could no longer overlook the slavery issue. Statehood for each of these territories would upset the balance between free states and slaveholding states. For a short while, it seemed to many that Henry Clay's proposed compromise gave concessions to both sides. But, as you will read in the next section, the compromise soon fell apart. When it did, the nation once again plunged down the road to all-out war between the regions.

Section 1 | Check Your Progress

Progress Monitoring Online
For: Self-test with instant help
Visit: PHSchool.com
Web Code: mya-5101

Comprehension and Critical Thinking

1. (a) Recall What was the Wilmot Proviso?
(b) Analyze Cause and Effect Did the Wilmot Proviso successfully address the nation's divisions over slavery? What effect *did* it have on the nation?

2. (a) List What were the main issues that led to Henry Clay's proposed compromise?
(b) Detect Points of View Write a sentence describing how you would feel about the need to compromise if you were a member of Congress from the North.

🔄 **Reading Skill**

3. Analyze Causes What did southerners want Congress to do about enslaved people who had fled to the North?

Key Terms

Complete these sentences so they clearly show your understanding of the key terms.
4. The status of new western territories would be decided by popular sovereignty, which is _____.
5. If southern states seceded from the Union, then _____.

6. Many northerners would not report fugitives, who were _____.

Writing

7. Consider the broad topic "Conflicts Between Slave States and Free States Before the Civil War." Divide it into four or five narrower topics. Each of these narrower topics should be covered in a research paper of a few pages.

Assess Progress L2

Have students complete Check Your Progress. Administer the Section Quiz.

📋 **Teaching Resources, Unit 5,** Section Quiz, p. 27

To further assess student understanding, use the Progress Monitoring Transparency.

Progress Monitoring Transparencies, Chapter 14, Section 1

Reteach L1

If students need more instruction, have them read this section in the Interactive Reading and Notetaking Study Guide and complete the accompanying question.

📖 **Interactive Reading and Notetaking Study Guide,** Chapter 14, Section 1 (Adapted Version also available.)

Extend L3

Have students do Internet research on the Compromise of 1850 and write a paragraph presenting the new information they learn.

Extend Online
For: Help in starting the Extend activity
Visit: PHSchool.com
Web Code: mye-0229

Progress Monitoring Online

Students may check their comprehension of this section by completing the Progress Monitoring Online graphic organizer and self-quiz.

Section 1 Check Your Progress

1. (a) a proposed law that would have banned slavery from lands gained as a result of the Mexican-American War
(b) No; it angered and frightened the South.

2. (a) California applying to be a state, northern desire to ban the slave trade in the District of Columbia, and the South wanting a fugitive slave law

(b) Possible answers: Slavery is wrong, but I will compromise to keep the Union together; slavery is wrong, and no compromise is possible, not even to save the Union.

3. pass a law that would force the return of fugitives

4. when people vote directly on issues

5. the Union would be split in two

6. runaway slaves

7. Papers should focus on one major cause of conflict.

Answer

✓ **Checkpoint** It led to renewed controversy.

Review and Preview

Students have read how the acquisition of new territory after the Mexican-American War fueled the debates about the spread of slavery. Now they will focus on the Compromise of 1850, its provisions, and its failure to lead to a peaceful resolution.

Section Focus Question

What was the Compromise of 1850, and why did it fail?

Before you begin the lesson for the day, write the Section Focus Question on the board. (*Lesson focus: It was a compromise that allowed California into the Union as a free state and included a fugitive slave law; it angered both the North and the South.*)

Prepare to Read

Build Background Knowledge **L2**

In this section, students will read about the provisions of the Compromise of 1850 and the growing division over slavery. Have students recall the problems caused by the Mexican Cession. Ask them how California's desire to become a state added to these problems. (*It threatened the balance between free and slave states.*)

Set a Purpose **L2**

■ Read each statement in the Reading Readiness Guide aloud. Ask students to mark the statements True or False.

> **All in One Teaching Resources, Unit 5,** Reading Readiness Guide, p. 17

■ Have students discuss the statements in pairs or groups of four, then mark their worksheets again. Use the Numbered Heads strategy (TE, p. T24) to call on students to share their group's perspectives. The students will return to these worksheets later.

A Harsh Accusation

❝ Sir, the Nebraska Bill was in every respect a swindle. It was a swindle by the South of the North. . . . All efforts were now given to the dismal work of forcing slavery on free soil. ❞

—Senator Charles Sumner of Massachusetts, before being assaulted on the Senate floor, 1856

◀ Newspapers reported Sumner's caning by a southern congressman.

Compromises Fail

Objectives

- Summarize the main points of the Compromise of 1850.
- Describe the impact of the novel *Uncle Tom's Cabin*.
- Explain how the Kansas-Nebraska Act reopened the issue of slavery in the territories.
- Describe the effect of the Kansas-Nebraska Act.

🔁 Reading Skill

Analyze Effects The important events of the 1850s had far-reaching effects around the nation. As you read Section 2, try to identify and understand these effects. Remember that two events do not necessarily have a cause-and-effect link just because they occur in sequence. Use signal words such as *result* to help you identify effects.

Key Terms and People

Harriet Beecher Stowe
propaganda
Stephen Douglas
John Brown

Why It Matters Many Americans hoped that Henry Clay's proposed compromise would quiet the controversy over slavery. However, after 1850, the growing divide only worsened.

❓ **Section Focus Question: What was the Compromise of 1850, and why did it fail?**

The Compromise of 1850

In September 1850, Congress finally passed five bills based on Clay's proposals. This series of laws became known as the Compromise of 1850. President Zachary Taylor had opposed the Compromise. However, Taylor died in 1850. The new President, Millard Fillmore, supported the Compromise and signed it into law.

To Please the North The Compromise of 1850 was designed to end the crisis by giving both supporters and opponents of slavery part of what they wanted. To please the North, California was admitted to the Union as a free state. In addition, the Compromise banned the slave trade in the nation's capital. (However, Congress declared that it had no power to regulate the slave trade between slave states.)

To Please the South Under the terms of the Compromise, popular sovereignty would be used to decide the question of slavery in the rest of the Mexican Cession. People in the states created from that territory would vote whether to be a free state or a slave state when they requested admission to the Union. Also, in return for agreeing to outlaw the slave trade in Washington, D.C., southerners got a tough new fugitive slave law.

486 Chapter 14 The Nation Divided

Differentiated Instruction

L1 English Language Learners   **L1 Less Proficient Readers**   **L1 Special Needs**

Slavery Help students understand the legal status of enslaved people in the United States. See that they understand that enslaved people were regarded as property, not as people with any rights.

Under the law, a runaway slave was still the slave owner's property, so anyone who helped the slave escape was considered to be depriving the slave owner of his property.

The Fugitive Slave Act of 1850 allowed special government officials to arrest any person accused of being a runaway slave. Suspects had no right to a trial to prove that they had been falsely accused. All that was required to <u>deprive</u> them of their freedom was for a slaveholder or any white witness to swear that the suspect was the slaveholder's property. In addition, the law required northern citizens to help capture accused runaways if authorities requested assistance.

Outrage in the North The Fugitive Slave Act became the most controversial part of the Compromise of 1850. Many northerners swore that they would resist the hated new law.

Northerners were outraged to see people accused of being fugitive slaves deprived of their freedom. An Indiana man was torn from his wife and children and given to an owner who claimed the man had escaped 19 years earlier. A wealthy African American tailor was carried back to South Carolina after living in New York for years. His friends quickly raised enough money to buy his freedom. But most who were shipped south remained there. Thousands of northern African Americans fled to the safety of Canada, including many who had never been enslaved.

In city after city, residents banded together to resist the Fugitive Slave Law. When two white Georgians arrived in Boston to seize fugitives, Bostonians threatened the slave catchers with harm if they did not leave the city right away. Another group rescued an accused runaway and sent him to safety in Canada. When the mob leaders were arrested, local juries refused to convict them.

John C. Calhoun had hoped that the Fugitive Slave Law would force northerners to admit that slaveholders had rights to their property. Instead, every time the law was enforced, it convinced more northerners that slavery was evil.

☑**Checkpoint** How did the Compromise of 1850 deal with the admission of California to the Union?

Vocabulary Builder
deprive (dee PRĪV) **v.** to keep from happening; to take away by force or intent

Returned to Slavery
Guarded by federal troops, fugitives Anthony Burns and Thomas Sims are captured in Boston and returned to enslavement in South Carolina. Below is a poster distributed by a southern slaveholder. **Critical Thinking: Draw Conclusions** What details show the attitude of Bostonians to the return of Burns and Sims?

Vocabulary Builder

Use the information below to teach students this section's high-use words.

High-Use Word	Definition and Sample Sentence
deprive, p. 487	*v.* to keep from happening; to take away by force or intent During the administration of Andrew Jackson, many Native Americans were **deprived** of their homelands.
impose, p. 490	*v.* to place a burden on someone or something After the Boston Tea Party, the British **imposed** a harsh rule on Massachusetts.

The Compromise of 1850

p. 486

Instruction   L2

- **Vocabulary Builder** Before teaching this section, preteach the High-Use Words **deprive** and **impose** using the strategy on TE p. T21.

  Key Terms Following the instructions on p. 7, have students create a See It–Remember It chart for the key terms in this chapter.

- Read The Compromise of 1850 using the Paragraph Shrinking strategy (TE, p. T23).

- Ask: **What did the Compromise of 1850 do about slavery in the District of Columbia?** (*It outlawed the buying and selling of slaves there.*)

- To follow up, ask: **Why was slavery in the District of Columbia such an important issue?** (*As the nation's capital, the District of Columbia had special significance for northerners and southerners alike.*)

- Ask: **How did northerners react to enforcement of the Fugitive Slave Law?** (*They resisted it.*)

- Discuss how the Fugitive Slave Law inflamed northerners both because they opposed slavery and because the law denied them local control. Ask students how they might have felt about this law if they lived in a northern city during the 1850s.

- Use the transparency Anthony Burns to help students understand northerners' anger at the Fugitive Slave Law.

Color Transparencies, Anthony Burns

Independent Practice
Have students begin filling in the study guide for this section.

Monitor Progress

As students fill in the Notetaking Study Guide, make sure individuals understand the terms of the Compromise of 1850 and the Fugitive Slave Law in the North.

Answers

☑**Checkpoint** California was admitted to the Union as a free state.

Draw Conclusions girl crying, men protesting

Uncle Tom's Cabin

p. 488

Instruction

- Have students read *Uncle Tom's Cabin.* Remind them to look for details that answer the reading Checkpoint question.

- Ask: **Why did Harriet Beecher Stowe write Uncle Tom's Cabin?** (*She wanted to make people see slavery as evil.*)

- Discuss the effect of the novel on the nation. Ask: **How did southerners criticize the story?** (*They said it was propaganda and that it did not give a true picture of their lives.*)

Independent Practice

Have students continue filling in the study guide for this section.

Interactive Reading and Notetaking Study Guide, Chapter 14, Section 2 (Adapted Version also available.)

Monitor Progress

As students fill in the Notetaking Study Guide, circulate and make sure individuals understand the impact of *Uncle Tom's Cabin* on the nation. Provide assistance as needed.

 Explore More Video

Discovery School Video

This video looks at Harriet Beecher Stowe, the author of *Uncle Tom's Cabin,* a powerful novel against slavery written in the 1850s. The video examines the growing controversy over slavery between North and South and how Stowe came to experience slavery. It describes what led her to write her book and the impact that it had on both northern and southern attitudes.

Answers

Reading Skill Readers began to see slavery as a moral issue, not just political. The word *result* highlights the link.

☑**Checkpoint** Stowe's book made white southerners feel angry and threatened because it turned the North more strongly against slavery.

Identify Costs Possible answers: Cost: could be arrested for breaking the law; Benefit: will help enslaved person gain freedom

---

Uncle Tom's Cabin

One northerner deeply affected by the Fugitive Slave Act was Harriet Beecher Stowe. The daughter of an abolitionist minister, Stowe met many people who had escaped from slavery. She decided to write "something that will make this whole nation feel what an accursed thing slavery is."

In 1852, Stowe published *Uncle Tom's Cabin,* a novel about kindly Uncle Tom, an enslaved man who is abused by the cruel Simon Legree. In this passage, Tom dies after a severe beating:

> **❝**Tom opened his eyes, and looked upon his master. . . .
> 'There an't no more ye can do! I forgive ye with all my soul!'
> and he fainted entirely away.
>
> 'I b'lieve, my soul, he's done for, finally,' said Legree, stepping forward, to look at him. 'Yes, he is! Well, his mouth's shut up, at last,—that's one comfort!'**❞**
>
> —Harriet Beecher Stowe, *Uncle Tom's Cabin,* Chapter 38

Stowe's book was a bestseller in the North. It shocked thousands of people who previously had been unconcerned about slavery. As a result, readers began to view slavery as more than just a political conflict. It was a human, moral problem facing every American.

Many white southerners were outraged by Stowe's book. They criticized it as propaganda, false or misleading information that is spread to further a cause. They claimed the novel did not give a fair or accurate picture of the lives of enslaved African Americans.

☑**Checkpoint** What impact did *Uncle Tom's Cabin* have?

Analyze Effects
What was one effect of Harriet Beecher Stowe's horror over slavery? What word in this paragraph highlights the cause-effect link?

DISCOVERY SCHOOL

Explore More Video
To learn more about Harriet Beecher Stowe's book, view the video.

Uncle Tom's Cabin The novel *Uncle Tom's Cabin* had an impact that lasted long after slavery ended. An original illustration from the book and a scene on a decorative plate are shown here. *Critical Thinking: Identify Costs* You are a northerner during the 1850s. A fugitive comes to your door seeking help. Will you help her? List the costs and benefits of helping the person.

Differentiated Instruction

L3 **Advanced Readers**

L3 **Gifted and Talented**

Harriet Beecher Stowe Have students read a biography of Harriet Beecher Stowe, such as *Harriet Beecher Stowe and the Beecher Preachers* by Jean Fritz. Then have them give a short presentation to the class on how the author's life influenced her strong antislavery views.

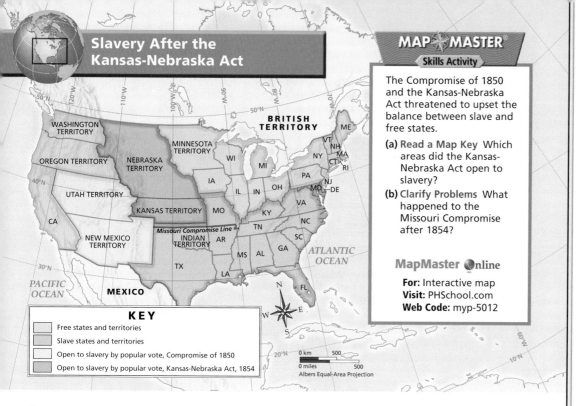

Slavery After the Kansas-Nebraska Act

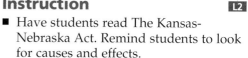

Skills Activity

The Compromise of 1850 and the Kansas-Nebraska Act threatened to upset the balance between slave and free states.

(a) Read a Map Key Which areas did the Kansas-Nebraska Act open to slavery?

(b) Clarify Problems What happened to the Missouri Compromise after 1854?

MapMaster Online

For: Interactive map
Visit: PHSchool.com
Web Code: myp-5012

KEY

- Free states and territories
- Slave states and territories
- Open to slavery by popular vote, Compromise of 1850
- Open to slavery by popular vote, Kansas-Nebraska Act, 1854

The Kansas-Nebraska Act

The nation moved closer to war after Congress passed the Kansas-Nebraska Act in 1854. The act was pushed through by Senator Stephen Douglas. Douglas was eager to develop the lands west of his home state of Illinois. He wanted to see a railroad built from Illinois through the Nebraska Territory to the Pacific Coast.

In 1853, Douglas suggested forming two new territories—the Kansas Territory and the Nebraska Territory. Southerners at once objected. Both territories lay in an area closed to slavery by the Missouri Compromise. This meant that the states eventually created from these territories would enter the Union as free states.

To win southern support, Douglas proposed that slavery in the new territories be decided by popular sovereignty. Thus, in effect, the Kansas-Nebraska Act undid the Missouri Compromise.

As Douglas hoped, southerners supported the Kansas-Nebraska Act. They were sure that slave owners from Missouri would move across the border into Kansas. In time, they hoped that Kansas would enter the union as a slave state.

Northerners, however, were outraged by the Kansas-Nebraska Act. They believed that Douglas had betrayed them by reopening the issue of slavery in the territories. "The more I look at it the more enraged I become," said one northern senator of Douglas's bill. "It needs but little to make me an out-and-out abolitionist."

History Background

Slavery and Cuba The expansion of slavery into new areas once threatened to push the United States into a war with Spain. In late 1854, several U.S. diplomats prepared a document at the behest of President Pierce, which recommended a U.S. takeover of Cuba if Spain refused to sell the island. Known as the Ostend Manifesto, the secret document surfaced in 1855, when it was published in several U.S. newspapers. Southerners supported the manifesto's proposal because they saw Cuba as another potential slave state, but northerners loudly protested. With tensions still high in the wake of the Kansas-Nebraska Act, Pierce backed away from the recommendation.

The Kansas-Nebraska Act

p. 489

Instruction

L2

- Have students read The Kansas-Nebraska Act. Remind students to look for causes and effects.

- Ask: **How did the Kansas-Nebraska Act affect the Missouri Compromise?** (*The Act repealed it, as it had outlawed slavery in that area.*)

- Ask them to determine the reason for the nickname "Bleeding Kansas." (*the violence in Kansas between pro- and antislavery fighters*)

- Discuss the reaction of both southerners and northerners to the Kansas-Nebraska Act. Ask: **Why did southerners support it?** (*The popular sovereignty clause meant the territories might allow slavery and enter the Union as slave states.*) **Why were northerners angry with it?** (*Under the Missouri Compromise, slavery had not been allowed in the territories; now that ban could be lifted.*)

Independent Practice

Have students continue filling in the study guide for this section.

Interactive Reading and Notetaking Study Guide, Chapter 14, Section 2 (Adapted Version also available.)

Monitor Progress

As students fill in the Notetaking Study Guide, circulate and make sure individuals understand how the Kansas-Nebraska Act led to increased controversy. Provide assistance as needed.

Answers

MAP MASTER Skills Activity **(a)** the Nebraska and Kansas territories **(b)** It was repealed.

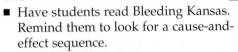

Bleeding Kansas

p. 490

Instruction

L2

- Have students read Bleeding Kansas. Remind them to look for a cause-and-effect sequence.

- Ask: **How did the Kansas-Nebraska Act affect the population of the territories?** (*The population increased as settlers flooded into the territory.*)

- Discuss with students the difficulty of putting popular sovereignty into practice in Kansas. Ask students if they think popular sovereignty was a fair way to decide whether to allow slavery. (*Answers will vary, but students should recognize the problems and violence it created.*)

Independent Practice

Have students complete the study guide for this section.

📖 **Interactive Reading and Notetaking Study Guide,** Chapter 14, Section 2 (Adapted Version also available.)

Monitor Progress

- As students fill in the Notetaking Study Guide, circulate and make sure individuals understand how the Kansas-Nebraska Act led to violence in Kansas. Provide assistance as needed.

- Tell students to fill in the last column of the Reading Readiness Guide. Ask them to consider whether what they learned was what they expected to learn.

All in One Teaching Resources, Unit 5 Reading Readiness Guide, p. 17

Answers

Interpret Maps Proslavery settlers came from the South.

✓Checkpoint By allowing the territories to use popular sovereignty to decide the slavery issue, the Missouri Compromise ban was ended.

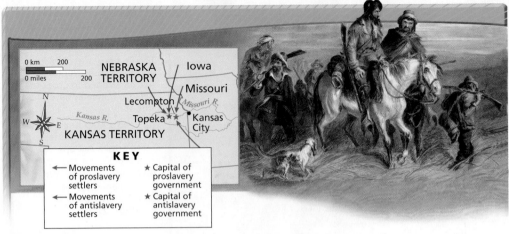

Bleeding Kansas

The migration of proslavery and antislavery settlers into Kansas led to the outbreak of violence known as Bleeding Kansas. **Critical Thinking: Interpret Maps** Why did some proslavery settlers take a more southerly route than did antislavery settlers?

After months of debate, southern support enabled the Kansas-Nebraska Act to pass in both houses of Congress. President Franklin Pierce, a Democrat elected in 1852, then signed the bill into law. Douglas predicted that, as a result of the Kansas-Nebraska Act, the slavery question would be "forever banished from the halls of Congress." But events would soon prove how wrong he was.

✓Checkpoint **How did Stephen Douglas's plan undo the Missouri Compromise?**

Bleeding Kansas

The Kansas-Nebraska Act left it to the white citizens of the territory to decide whether Kansas would be free or slave territory. Both proslavery and antislavery settlers flooded into Kansas within weeks after Douglas's bill became law. Each side was determined to hold the majority in the territory when it came time for the vote.

Thousands of Missourians entered Kansas in March 1855 to illegally vote in the election to select a territorial legislature. Although Kansas had only 3,000 voters, nearly 8,000 votes were cast on election day! Of 39 legislators elected, all but 3 supported slavery. The antislavery settlers refused to accept these results and held a second election.

Vocabulary Builder
impose (ihm POHZ) **v.** to place a burden on someone or something

Growing Violence Kansas now had two governments, each claiming the right to <u>impose</u> their government on the territory. Not surprisingly, violence soon broke out. In April, a proslavery sheriff was shot when he tried to arrest some antislavery settlers in the town of Lawrence. The next month, he returned with 800 men and attacked the town.

Differentiated Instruction

L1 Less Proficient Readers

Marked Reading Suggest to students that they use a ruler to help them keep their place as they read, line by line down a page. Have students mark unfamiliar words or phrases (such as *territorial legislature* on this page) with a sticky note, and periodically help them understand what they have marked.

Three days later, John Brown, an antislavery settler from Connecticut, led seven men to a proslavery settlement near Pottawatomie (paht uh wah TOH mee) Creek. There, they murdered five proslavery men and boys.

These incidents set off widespread fighting in Kansas. Bands of proslavery and antislavery fighters roamed the countryside, terrorizing those who did not support their views. The violence was so bad that it earned Kansas the name Bleeding Kansas.

Bloodshed in the Senate Even before Brown's raid at Pottawatomie Creek, the violence in Kansas spilled over into the United States Senate. Charles Sumner of Massachusetts was the leading abolitionist senator. In a fiery speech, Sumner denounced the proslavery legislature in Kansas. He then attacked his southern foes, singling out Andrew Butler, an elderly senator from South Carolina.

Butler was not present the day Sumner made his speech. A few days later, however, Butler's nephew, Congressman Preston Brooks, marched into the Senate chamber. Using a heavy cane, Brooks beat Sumner until he fell to the floor, bloody and unconscious. Sumner never completely recovered from his injuries.

Many southerners felt that Sumner got what he deserved. Hundreds of people sent canes to Brooks to show their support. To northerners, however, Brooks's violent act was just more evidence that slavery was brutal and inhuman.

✓**Checkpoint** What was the outcome of the election to select a legislature in the Kansas Territory?

⭐ **Looking Back and Ahead** By 1856, all attempts at compromise had failed. The bitterness between the North and the South was about to alter the political landscape of the United States.

Analyze Effects Describe the effect of the Kansas-Nebraska Act on Kansas.

HISTORIAN'S APPRENTICE ACTIVITY PACK

To further explore the topics in this chapter, complete the activity in the Historian's Apprentice Activity Pack to answer this essential question:

How can a nation be united and divided at the same time?

Section 2 | Check Your Progress

Progress Monitoring Online
For: Self-test with instant help
Visit: PHSchool.com
Web Code: mya-5102

Comprehension and Critical Thinking
1. **(a) Recall** What parts of the Compromise of 1850 were included to please the North?
(b) Draw Conclusions Why do you think northerners were still not satisfied?

2. **(a) Recall** What was the Kansas-Nebraska Act?
(b) Evaluate Information How did the Kansas-Nebraska Act contribute to tension between the North and the South?

Reading Skill
3. **Analyze Effects** What was one effect of Harriet Beecher Stowe's book *Uncle Tom's Cabin*?

Key Terms
Complete the following sentence so that the second part further explains the first part and clearly shows your understanding of the key term.
4. Many white southerners considered *Uncle Tom's Cabin* propaganda; _____ an unfair picture of slavery.

Writing
5. Imagine that you are researching the effects of Harriet Beecher Stowe's book *Uncle Tom's Cabin*. Write down five questions that would help you focus your research on this topic. The questions should point you to areas where you need to find more information about the influence of Stowe's book.

Section 2 Compromises Fail **491**

Assess and Reteach

Assess Progress [L2]

Have students complete Check Your Progress. Administer the Section Quiz.

All in One Teaching Resources, Unit 5, Section Quiz, p. 28

To further assess student understanding, use the Progress Monitoring Transparency.

Progress Monitoring Transparencies, Chapter 14, Section 2

Reteach [L1]

If students need more instruction, have them read this section in the Interactive Reading and Notetaking Study Guide and complete the accompanying question.

Interactive Reading and Notetaking Study Guide, Chapter 14, Section 2 (Adapted Version also available.)

Extend [L3]

Have students use the Internet to learn more about Harriet Beecher Stowe. Have them write a paragraph about her other literary works or her involvement with the abolitionists.

Extend Online
For: Help in starting the Extend activity
Visit: PHSchool.com
Web Code: mye-0230

Progress Monitoring Online

Students may check their comprehension of this section by completing the Progress Monitoring Online graphic organizer and self-quiz.

Section 2 Check Your Progress

1. **(a)** It admitted California as a free state.
(b) Possible answer: It reopened the question of the expansion of slavery in an area where it had previously been outlawed by the Missouri Compromise.

2. **(a)** It created two territories from the Nebraska territory. The slavery issue was to be decided by popular sovereignty.
(b) Southerners hoped slavery would be allowed, since the issue was to be decided by popular sovereignty. Northerners were angry that the ban of slavery under the Missouri Compromise was ended.

3. Possible answers: both northerners and southerners became more angry with each other; many began to see slavery as a moral issue.

4. it was false or misleading information which gave

5. Questions should focus on the impact of the novel.

Answers

Reading Skill Violence broke out as pro- and antislavery supporters fought for control.

✓**Checkpoint** The first election resulted in a legislature that favored slavery. Foes of slavery did not accept it and elected their own legislature.

Excerpt from *Uncle Tom's Cabin*

p. 492

Build Background Knowledge **L2**

Reading a novel can help students connect with universal and timeless human feelings experienced throughout history by relating to the characters' experiences and by analyzing the imagery. Review with students what they know about the arguments for and against slavery. (*Proponents of slavery argued that enslaved people were property and not people, therefore they did not deserve equal treatment. Proponents also thought that slavery was necessary to maintain the agricultural economy of the South. Critics argued that all enslaved people were human beings and that they deserved fair treatment. They believed that enslaving people was wrong for both moral and legal reasons.*) Ask students to recall what they know about the lives of people who were enslaved. (*They had no freedom—everything they did was determined by the people who claimed ownership of them.*)

Vocabulary *Builder*

Pronounce the words in the Vocabulary *Builder* list. Ask students to read the definitions. Then have them write sentences that use the vocabulary words correctly.

Instruction **L2**

- Using the Choral Reading strategy (TE, p. T22), read "Uncle Tom's Cabin." Ask students to identify the lead characters and to describe them. (*Possible answer: The lead characters are Shelby and Haley. Both men own slaves. Shelby seems to respect his slaves to a certain extent, regarding them with some kindness and thoughtfulness. Haley treats slaves as nothing other than property.*)

- Remind students to pay attention to how the author presents the characters. Ask: **What does Stowe really think of the slavetrader?** (*Possible answer: She paints a rough picture of Haley, so apparently she does not like him or approve of his attitude.*) Ask: **How can you tell?** (*Possible answer: Stowe has Haley speak as though enslaved people are not people.*)

Uncle Tom's Cabin
by Harriet Beecher Stowe

Prepare to Read

Introduction

Harriet Beecher Stowe rocked the nation in 1851 when she published *Uncle Tom's Cabin*. The novel won many converts to the antislavery cause. The excerpt below is from the opening chapter. Shelby, a Kentucky slave owner, must sell some of his enslaved servants to Mr. Haley, a slave trader. Haley is especially interested in buying a young woman named Eliza.

Reading Skill

Judging Characters In a work of fiction, characters may say things that the author thinks are wrong. We have to read carefully in order to understand how the author wants us to judge the characters. In the selection below, look for clues as to what Stowe really thinks of Mr. Haley, the slave trader.

Vocabulary *Builder*

As you read this literature selection, look for the following underlined words:

calculation (kal kyoo LAY shuhn) *n.* ability to figure out exactly what something is worth

humane (hyoo MAYN) *adj.* kind; considerate; merciful

candid (KAN dihd) *adj.* frank; honest

virtuous (VIR choo uhs) *adj.* highly moral

Background

Much of *Uncle Tom's Cabin* is written in dialect that reproduces how different types of characters speak. For example, to show the way Haley speaks, Stowe uses "ha'nt" for "haven't," "this yer" for "this here," "uns" for "ones," and "onpleasant" for "unpleasant."

"Come, how will you trade about the gal?—what shall I say for her—what'll you take?"

"Mr. Haley, she is not to be sold," said Shelby. "My wife would not part with her for her weight in gold."

"Ay, ay! women always say such things, cause they ha'nt no sort of <u>calculation</u>. Just show 'em how many watches, feathers, and trinkets, one's weight in gold would buy, and that alters the case, I reckon."

"I tell you, Haley, this must not be spoken of; I say no, and I mean no," said Shelby, decidedly.

"Well, you'll let me have the boy, though," said the trader; "you must own I've come down pretty handsomely for him."

"What on earth can you want with the child?" said Shelby.

"Why, I've got a friend that's going into this yer branch of the business—wants to buy up handsome boys to raise for the market. Fancy articles entirely—sell for waiters, and so on, to rich 'uns, that can pay for handsome 'uns. It sets off one of yer great places—a real handsome boy to open door, wait, and tend. They fetch a good sum; and this little devil is such a comical, musical concern, he's just the article!"

"I would rather not sell him," said Mr. Shelby, thoughtfully; "the fact is, sir, I'm a <u>humane</u> man, and I hate to take the boy from his mother, sir."

"O, you do?—La! yes—something of that ar natur. I understand, perfectly. It is mighty onpleasant getting on with women, sometimes, I al'ays hates these yer screechin', screamin' times. They are *mighty* onpleasant; but, as I manages business, I generally avoids

---

Differentiated Instruction

L1 English Language Learners   **L1** Less Proficient Readers   **L1** Special Needs

Understanding Vernacular Some students may have difficulty decoding the unfamiliar spelling used by Stowe to convey the dialect of the characters. Before reading the section with students, have them work in pairs to identify words written in dialect. Explain to students that

Stowe has written the words the way that the characters pronounce them. Encourage students to take advantage of this phonetic spelling by sounding out these words with their partners. Then, when choral reading with the class, enunciate these words and call on volunteers to decode their meaning.

Slave auction

'em, sir. Now, what if you get the girl off for a day, or a week, or so; then the thing's done quietly,—all over before she comes home. Your wife might get her some ear-rings, or a new gown, or some such truck, to make up with her."

"I'm afraid not."

"Lor bless ye, yes! These critters ain't like white folks, you know; they gets over things, only manage right. Now, they say," said Haley, assuming a <u>candid</u> and confidential air, "that this kind o' trade is hardening to the feelings; but I never found it so. Fact is, I never could do things up the way some fellers manage the business. I've seen 'em as would pull a woman's child out of her arms, and set him up to sell, and she screechin' like mad all the time;—very bad policy—damages the article—makes 'em quite unfit for service sometimes. I knew a real handsome gal once, in Orleans, as was entirely ruined by this sort o' handling. The fellow that was trading for her didn't want her baby; and she was one of your real high sort, when her blood was up. I tell you, she squeezed up her child in her arms, and talked, and went on real awful. It kinder makes my blood run cold to think on 't; and when they carried off the child, and locked her up, she jest went ravin' mad, and died in a week. Clear waste, sir, of a thousand dollars, just for want of management,—there's where 't is. It's always best to do the humane thing, sir; that's been my experience." And the trader leaned back in his chair, and folded his arm, with an air of <u>virtuous</u> decision, apparently considering himself a second Wilberforce.

From *Uncle Tom's Cabin*, by Harriet Beecher Stowe

Analyze LITERATURE

Imagine that you are a northerner in 1851 reading *Uncle Tom's Cabin* for the first time. Write a letter to a friend explaining how this excerpt made you feel about the slave trade.

Judging Characters
Stowe has Haley refer to enslaved Africans as "critters," showing he does not think of them as human beings. Yet, he also claims that slave-trading has not hardened his feelings. What does this indicate about Stowe's view of Haley?

Background
William Wilberforce was a famous English clergyman who campaigned to end slavery.

If you liked this selection, you might want to read more about the antislavery movement in *Escape From Slavery: Five Journeys to Freedom* by Doreen Rappaport, illustrated by Charles Lilly. Harper Collins Publishers. 1991.

Literature 493

History Background

Harriet Beecher Stowe Harriet Beecher Stowe was born in Connecticut in 1811. A minister's daughter, she had an opportunity to become educated when many women of her time were denied. Stowe became a teacher after she graduated from her sister's school at the age of 16. In 1832, she moved to Ohio where she continued teaching and began a prolific writing career. She published her first book, *The Mayflower*, nine years later. Although Ohio was a free state, Stowe had the opportunity to meet and learn from many people who had escaped slavery during the 18 years that she lived there. Stowe's experiences inspired her best-known and most influential work, *Uncle Tom's Cabin*.

Review and Preview

Now students will read about Lincoln's strong stand against the spread of slavery and the effect on the nation of John Brown's raid.

Section Focus Question

Why did the Lincoln-Douglas debates and John Brown's raid increase tensions between the North and South?

Before you begin the lesson for the day, write the Section Focus Question on the board. (*Lesson focus: Both events highlighted divisions on slavery.*)

Prepare to Read

Build Background Knowledge **L2**

Ask students to recall how the Missouri Compromise was repealed by later events. Use the Idea Wave strategy (TE, p. T24) to have students predict possible results from these events. (*Possible answer: increased division and tension*)

Set a Purpose **L2**

■ Group students into pairs or groups of four. Distribute the Reading Readiness Guide. Ask students to fill in the first two columns of the chart.

　All in One Teaching Resources, Unit 5, Reading Readiness Guide, p. 18

■ Use the Numbered Heads strategy (TE, p. T24) to call on students to share one piece of information they already know and one piece of information they want to know. The students will return to these worksheets later.

Answer

✓Checkpoint James Buchanan was elected President.

▲ Slaves laboring on a southern plantation

Gross Injustice and Cruelty

❝This rich inheritance of justice, liberty, prosperity, and independence bequeathed by your fathers is shared by you, not by me. . . . What, to the American slave is your Fourth of July? I answer: a day that reveals to him, more than all other days in the year, the gross injustice and cruelty to which he is the constant victim.❞

—Frederick Douglass, Independence Day speech delivered at Rochester, New York, 1852

The Crisis Deepens

Objectives
- Explain why the Republican Party came into being in the 1850s.
- Summarize the issues involved in the Dred Scott decision.
- Identify Abraham Lincoln's and Stephen Douglas's views on slavery.
- Describe the differing reactions in the North and the South to John Brown's raid.

🔄 Reading Skill

Analyze Causes and Effects
Historians often disagree over exactly what caused the Civil War. As you read Section 3, watch carefully for cause-and-effect links. Analyzing these links will help you answer this difficult question for yourself. Remember that sometimes the link is not directly stated. Identify an event, then ask yourself: What caused this event to happen? What were the effects of this event?

Key People

Dred Scott　　　　Abraham Lincoln
Roger B. Taney

Why It Matters Bitterness between northerners and southerners weakened the nation's two major political parties. As a result of the growing struggle over slavery, a new party and new leaders emerged.

❓ Section Focus Question: Why did the Lincoln-Douglas debates and John Brown's raid increase tensions between the North and South?

A New Antislavery Party

As the Whig Party split apart in 1854, many northern Whigs joined a new political party. It was called the Republican Party, and its main goal was to stop the spread of slavery into the western territories. The Republicans' antislavery stand also attracted northern Democrats and Free-Soil Party members.

The Republicans quickly became a powerful force in politics. The congressional elections of 1854 were held only months after the party was founded. Of the 245 candidates elected to the U.S. House of Representatives, 105 were Republicans. Republican victories in state races also cost the Democrats control of all but two northern state legislatures.

Two years later, in 1856, the Republican Party ran its first candidate for President. It chose John C. Frémont, the army officer who had helped California win independence during the Mexican-American War. The Republicans waged a strong antislavery campaign. Although the Democrat James Buchanan was elected, Frémont won in 11 of the nation's 16 free states.

✓Checkpoint What was the result of the election of 1856?

494 Chapter 14 The Nation Divided

Differentiated Instruction

L1 English Language Learners　　**L1 Less Proficient Readers**　　**L1 Special Needs**

Listening Have students read the text of A New Antislavery Party as they listen to the SE on Audio CD. Monitor student answers to Checkpoint questions to make sure they understand. Students can be pro-vided with a copy of the CD to work independently at home or in the School Resource Center.

　🔊 **SE on Audio CD** Chapter 14, Section 3

The Dred Scott Decision

In March 1857—only three days after Buchanan took office—the U.S. Supreme Court delivered a shattering blow to antislavery forces. It decided the case of *Dred Scott* v. *Sandford*.

Dred Scott was an enslaved person who had once been owned by a U.S. Army doctor. The doctor, and Scott, lived for a time in Illinois and in the Wisconsin Territory. Slavery was illegal in both places. After leaving the army, the doctor settled with Scott in Missouri.

With the help of antislavery lawyers, Scott sued for his freedom. He argued that he was free because he had lived where slavery was illegal. In time, the case reached the Supreme Court. Neither northerners nor southerners were prepared for what the Court decided.

The Court Decides Chief Justice Roger B. Taney wrote the decision for the Court. Scott was not a free man, he said, for two reasons. First, according to Taney, Scott had no right to sue in federal court because African Americans were not citizens. Second, Taney said, merely living in free territory did not make an enslaved person free. Slaves were property, Taney declared, and property rights were protected by the U.S. Constitution.

But the ruling went even further. Taney wrote that Congress did not have the power to prohibit slavery in any territory. Thus, the Missouri Compromise was unconstitutional.

Reaction Supporters of slavery rejoiced at the Dred Scott decision. The decision meant that slavery was legal in all territories—just as white southern leaders had been demanding all along.

Northerners, however, were stunned. African American leaders such as Frederick Douglass condemned the ruling. Still, Douglass declared, "my hopes were never brighter than now." He believed that outrage against the decision would bring more whites to the abolitionist cause.

Indeed, white northerners were also shocked by the ruling. Many had hoped that slavery would eventually die out if it were restricted to the South. Now, however, slavery could spread throughout the West.

One northerner who spoke out against the Dred Scott decision was an Illinois lawyer named Abraham Lincoln. The idea that African Americans could not be citizens, he said, was based on a false view of American history. In a very short time, Lincoln would become a central figure in the fight against the spread of slavery.

✓**Checkpoint** Why did Dred Scott claim he was no longer enslaved?

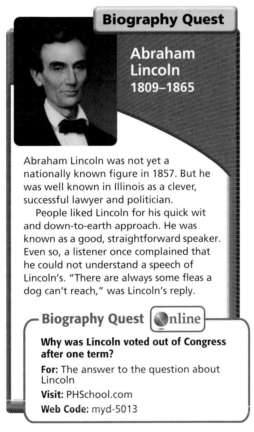

Biography Quest

Abraham Lincoln
1809–1865

Abraham Lincoln was not yet a nationally known figure in 1857. But he was well known in Illinois as a clever, successful lawyer and politician.

People liked Lincoln for his quick wit and down-to-earth approach. He was known as a good, straightforward speaker. Even so, a listener once complained that he could not understand a speech of Lincoln's. "There are always some fleas a dog can't reach," was Lincoln's reply.

Biography Quest ●nline

Why was Lincoln voted out of Congress after one term?

For: The answer to the question about Lincoln

Visit: PHSchool.com

Web Code: myd-5013

Section 3 The Crisis Deepens **495**

Vocabulary Builder

Use the information below to teach students this section's high-use words.

High-Use Word	Definition and Sample Sentence
embrace, p. 496	*v.* to hold tight; to readily accept With the battles of Lexington and Concord, many Americans **embraced** the idea of independence from Britain.
clarify, p. 497	*v.* to make the meaning of something clear The Virginia and Tennessee resolutions **clarified** the reasons for opposing the Alien and Sedition acts.

Instruction

- **Vocabulary Builder** Before teaching this section, preteach the High-Use Words **embrace** and **clarify** using the strategy on TE p. T21.

  Key Terms Have students continue to fill in the See It–Remember It chart for the key terms in this chapter.

- Have students read A New Antislavery Party and The Dred Scott Decision using the Oral Cloze reading strategy (TE, p. T22).

- Ask: **What was the main goal of the Republican Party?** (*to stop expansion of slavery in the territories*)

- Ask students why the Republican Party had such sudden success. Encourage them to consider the events of the 1850s they have read about in this chapter. (*The success of the Republican Party resulted from growing opposition in the North to the spread of slavery.*)

- Discuss Taney's chain of reasoning in the Dred Scott decision. Ask: **What were Taney's three conclusions?** (*First, Taney said that African Americans were not citizens, so they could not sue. Second, if Scott were allowed to sue, he would lose, as he was his owner's property. Third, all slaves were property protected by the Constitution, so Congress could not make any laws banning slavery in the territories.*)

Independent Practice

Have students begin filling in the study guide for this section.

Monitor Progress

As students fill in the Notetaking Study Guide, make sure individuals understand why the Republican Party became so popular and the effect of the Dred Scott decision.

Answers

✓**Checkpoint** He had lived in places where slavery was illegal.

Biography Quest He questioned the motives of the Mexican-American War, which seemed unpatriotic to his constituents.

The Lincoln-Douglas Debates

p. 496

Instruction L2

- Have students read The Lincoln-Douglas Debates. Remind them to look for answers to the Section Focus Question.

- Ask: **What brought Abraham Lincoln back into politics?** (*his opposition to the Kansas-Nebraska Act*)

- Discuss with students Lincoln's quote about a "house divided." Ask: **What did Lincoln mean by this?** (*The nation would have to make up its mind about slavery and allow it either everywhere or nowhere.*)

- Frame the significance of the Lincoln-Douglas debates. Ask: **Why do you think that debates between two candidates for Illinois senator were important to the whole country?** (*Answers will vary, but students should recognize that the slavery debate was taking place all over the country. They should also remember that Douglas was famous for writing the Kansas-Nebraska Act.*) Tell students that Douglas was starting to campaign for President in 1860 and that the debates also helped make Lincoln a national figure.

- Use the transparency Lincoln-Douglas Debate to help students understand the impact of the Lincoln-Douglas debates.

Color Transparencies, Lincoln-Douglas Debate

Independent Practice

Have students continue filling in the study guide for this section.

Interactive Reading and Notetaking Study Guide, Chapter 14, Section 3 (Adapted Version also available.)

Monitor Progress

As students fill in the Notetaking Study Guide, circulate and make sure individuals understand the significance of the Lincoln-Douglas debates. Provide assistance as needed.

Links Across Time

Elections and the Media

1858 Americans followed the Lincoln-Douglas debates as telegraph reports circulated around the country.

1960 Americans were for the first time able to watch presidential candidates debate live on television. Richard Nixon and John F. Kennedy debated before an enormous television audience. Many experts believe that the debates played a major role in Kennedy's victory.

Link to Today   Online

Elections and the Media Today The digital revolution is again changing American political campaigns. What media do candidates use today?

For: Voting and the media
Visit: PHSchool.com
Web Code: myc-5103

Vocabulary Builder
embrace (ehm BRAYS) *v.* to hold tight; to readily accept

The Lincoln-Douglas Debates

Lincoln had had only a brief career in politics. After serving in the Illinois state legislature, he was elected to Congress as a Whig. There, he voted for the Wilmot Proviso. After a single term, he returned to Illinois to practice law.

Lincoln's opposition to the Kansas-Nebraska Act brought him back into politics, this time embracing the Republican cause. He had long been a rival of Illinois Senator Stephen Douglas, the author of the Kansas-Nebraska Act. Their rivalry was personal as well as political. Both men had courted Mary Todd, who married Lincoln.

A House Divided In 1858, Illinois Republicans chose Lincoln to run for the Senate against Douglas. Accepting the nomination, Lincoln made a stirring speech in favor of the Union:

> **"** A house divided against itself cannot stand. I do not believe this government can endure, permanently, half slave and half free. I do not expect the Union to be dissolved—I do not expect the house to fall—but I do expect it will cease to be divided. It will become all one thing or all the other. **"**
>
> —Abraham Lincoln, Springfield, Illinois, June 16, 1858

Lincoln did not state that he wanted to ban slavery. Still, many southerners became convinced that Lincoln was an abolitionist.

Differentiated Instruction

L3 Advanced Readers   **L3 Gifted and Talented**

The Lincoln-Douglas Debates Have students work together to research more about the Lincoln-Douglas debates. Then have them write a newspaper article describing one of the debates and share it with the class.

Debating Slavery Lincoln then challenged Douglas to a series of public debates. Thousands of people gathered to hear them speak. Newspapers throughout the nation reported what each man said.

Douglas strongly defended popular sovereignty. "Each state of this Union has a right to do as it pleases on the subject of slavery," he said. "In Illinois we have exercised that sovereign right by prohibiting slavery. . . . It is none of our business whether slavery exists in Missouri." Douglas also painted Lincoln as a dangerous abolitionist who wanted equality for African Americans.

Lincoln took a stand against the spread of slavery. He declared, "If slavery is not wrong, nothing is wrong." Lincoln predicted that slavery would die on its own. In the meantime, he said, it was the obligation of Americans to keep it out of the western territories.

In reply to Douglas, Lincoln stated: "I am not, nor ever have been in favor of bringing about in any way the social and political equality of the white and black races." But he did <u>clarify</u> this view. He insisted that "there is no reason in the world why the Negro is not entitled to all the rights enumerated in the Declaration of Independence, the right to life, liberty and the pursuit of happiness."

In the end, Douglas won the Senate election. However, the debates had made Lincoln known throughout the country. Two years later, the men would be rivals again—this time for the presidency.

☑**Checkpoint** **What position did Douglas take on slavery?**

John Brown's Raid

The nation's attention soon was captured by the actions of John Brown. Driven out of Kansas after the Pottawatomie Massacre, Brown had returned to New England. There he hatched a plot to raise an army and free people in the South who were enslaved.

In 1859, Brown and a small band of supporters attacked the town of Harpers Ferry in Virginia. His goal was to seize guns the U.S. Army had stored there. He thought that enslaved African Americans would support him. He would then give them weapons and lead them in a revolt.

Brown quickly gained control of the arms. But troops commanded by Colonel Robert E. Lee surrounded Brown's force before it could escape. Ten of Brown's followers were killed. Brown was wounded and captured.

Vocabulary Builder
clarify (KLAIR ih fi) **v.** to make the meaning of something clear

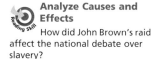

Analyze Causes and Effects
How did John Brown's raid affect the national debate over slavery?

John Brown in Kansas
John Steuart Curry began painting this 10-foot-high mural in 1937. It shows John Brown as a fiery abolitionist with a rifle in one hand and a Bible in the other. **Critical Thinking: *Detect Points of View*** *Based on this painting, do you think Curry admired John Brown?*

Instruction
L2
- Have students read John Brown's Raid. Remind them to look for the sequence of events.
- Ask students how southerners felt about the raid. (*threatened, angry*)
- Ask: **What was the effect of John Brown's raid?** (*It further increased the tension between the North and the South.*)

Independent Practice
Have students complete the study guide for this section.

📖 **Interactive Reading and Notetaking Study Guide,** Chapter 14, Section 3 (Adapted Version also available.)

Monitor Progress

- As students fill in the Notetaking Study Guide, circulate and make sure individuals understand the effects of John Brown's raid. Provide assistance as needed.
- Tell students to fill in the last column of the Reading Readiness Guide. Ask them to consider whether what they learned was what they expected to learn.

All in One **Teaching Resources, Unit 5,** Reading Readiness Guide, p. 18

Answers

☑**Checkpoint** voters should decide

🔄 **Reading Skill** Brown's raid made the debate more heated. Southerners were shocked and angered at northern support of Brown.

Detect Points of View Answers will vary. Some may feel Curry admired Brown, showing him as a dynamic figure, leading the fight against slavery. Others might say Curry was criticizing Brown as a violent, angry man.

History Background

Lincoln and Abolitionists Lincoln was not an abolitionist in 1858, and many historians argue that he never was. At the time, many abolitionists were ardent social reformers who sometimes also advanced such causes as women's suffrage, public education, and prison reform. The Free-Soil Party and its successor, the Republican Party, never called for the abolition of slavery. Their platforms only opposed the expansion of slavery into the territories.

Assess and Reteach

Assess Progress L2

Have students complete Check Your Progress. Administer the Section Quiz.

All in One Teaching Resources, Unit 5, Section Quiz, p. 29

To further assess student understanding, use the Progress Monitoring Transparencies.

Progress Monitoring Transparencies, Chapter 14, Section 3

Reteach L1

If students need more instruction, have them read this section in the Interactive Reading and Notetaking Study Guide and complete the accompanying question.

Interactive Reading and Notetaking Study Guide, Chapter 14, Section 3 (Adapted Version also available.)

Extend L3

Have students write a letter to the court that convicted John Brown expressing their opinions about the verdict. Ask them to tell the court whether or not they think John Brown deserved a lighter sentence and why.

Progress Monitoring Online

Students may check their comprehension of this section by completing the Progress Monitoring Online graphic organizer and self-quiz.

Answers

Contrast Curry's painting stirs up strong emotions and anger, Hovenden's creates feelings of sympathy or sadness.

Checkpoint His goal was to capture arms and start a slave rebellion.

Section 3 Check Your Progress

1. (a) northern Democrats and Free-Soil Party members
(b) Possible Answer: Their success encouraged Republicans.

2. (a) He had lived in territories where slavery was illegal.
(b) The South was happy, but the North was angry because the ruling meant slavery could spread west.

Death of John Brown
Thomas Hovenden painted this portrait of a saintly John Brown. On his way to his death, Brown stops to kiss a child. Hovenden did not personally witness the events he showed here. **Critical Thinking: Contrast** *Compare this painting to the one on the previous page. How do these two paintings try to stir different emotions?*

At his trial, Brown sat quietly as the court found him guilty of murder and treason. Before hearing his sentence, he gave a moving defense of his actions. The Bible, he said, instructed him to care for the poor and enslaved. "If it is deemed necessary that I should forfeit my life for the furtherance of the ends of justice . . . I say, let it be done." He showed no emotion as he was sentenced to death.

When the state of Virginia hanged Brown for treason on December 2, 1859, church bells across the North tolled to mourn the man who many considered a hero. But southerners were shocked. People in the North were praising a man who had tried to lead a slave revolt! More than ever, many southerners were convinced that the North was out to destroy their way of life.

✓Checkpoint What was John Brown's goal in launching the raid on Harpers Ferry?

⭐ **Looking Back and Ahead** The nation had suffered one dispute after another over the expansion of slavery since the end of the Mexican-American War in 1846. By the election of 1860, talk of the breakup of the United States was everywhere. In the next section, you will read how that breakup came about.

Section 3 | Check Your Progress

Progress Monitoring Online
For: Self-test with instant help
Visit: PHSchool.com
Web Code: mya-5103

Comprehension and Critical Thinking

1. (a) Summarize Which groups supported the newly formed Republican Party?
(b) Draw Conclusions How did the outcomes of the elections of 1854 and 1856 affect the Republican Party?

2. (a) Identify On what grounds did Dred Scott sue for his freedom in court?
(b) Draw Conclusions How did Taney's ruling further divide the North and the South?

3. (a) Recall What were the Lincoln-Douglas debates?
(b) Apply Information Why do you think the Lincoln-Douglas debates received national attention?

Reading Skill
4. Analyze Causes and Effects Identify one cause and one effect of John Brown's raid. Why did Brown and his followers attack Harpers Ferry? What happened as a result?

Writing
5. Reread the paragraphs in this section that describe the Lincoln-Douglas debates. When you have finished, paraphrase the excerpt from Lincoln's Springfield speech. Remember, when you paraphrase, you restate something said by someone else, using only your own words.

---

3. (a) The South became convinced that the North was out to destroy its way of life; John Brown was hanged.
(b) Enslaved African Americans did not join him; he was outnumbered by troops.

4. Brown's goal was to seize U.S. Army guns to supply enslaved African Americans with weapons so they could join the fight for their freedom. As a result of the raid, Brown was executed and southerners, shocked by the support Brown received in the North, were convinced that northerners wanted to destroy the southern way of life.

5. Paraphrasing should follow the content and sequence of Lincoln's speech.

◀ Confederate seal

The Confederate States

❝ In the exercise of a right so ancient, so well-established, and so necessary for self-preservation, the people of the Confederate states . . . passed [laws] resuming all their rights as sovereign and independent States and dissolved their connection with the other States of the Union. ❞

—President Jefferson Davis, message to the Confederate Congress, April 29, 1861

◀ Newspaper announcing secession of southern states

The Coming of the Civil War

Objectives

- Describe the results of the election of 1860.
- Explain why southern states seceded from the Union.
- Summarize the events that led to the outbreak of the Civil War.

🎯 Reading Skill

Analyze Multiple Causes or Effects
Many events in history have more than one cause, as the Civil War certainly did. Other events lead to more than one effect, which is also certainly true of the Civil War. As you read about this turning point in American history, look for causes with multiple effects and effects with multiple causes.

Key Term

civil war

Why It Matters John Brown's raid increased tensions between North and South. So did the growing power of the Republican Party. The nation was on the verge of a civil war.

❓ **Section Focus Question: Why did the election of Abraham Lincoln spark the secession of southern states?**

The Nation Divides

As the election of 1860 drew near, Americans everywhere felt a sense of crisis. The long and bitter debate over slavery had left the nation seriously divided.

Election of 1860 The Republicans chose Abraham Lincoln as their presidential candidate. His criticisms of slavery during his debates with Douglas had made him popular in the North.

Southern Democrats wanted the party to support slavery in the territories. But northerners refused to do so. In the end, the party split in two. Northern Democrats chose Stephen Douglas as their candidate. Southern Democrats picked Vice President John Breckinridge of Kentucky.

Some southerners still hoped to heal the split between North and South. They formed the Constitutional Union Party and nominated John Bell of Tennessee. Bell promised to protect slavery *and* keep the nation together.

Stephen Douglas was sure that Lincoln would win the election. However, he believed that Democrats "must try to save the Union." He pleaded with southern voters to stay with the Union, no matter who was elected. However, when Douglas campaigned in the South, hostile southerners often pelted him with eggs and rotten fruit.

Section 4 The Coming of the Civil War   499

Vocabulary Builder

Use the information below to teach students this section's high-use words.

High-Use Word	Definition and Sample Sentence
accommodation, p. 501	*n.* adjustment; adaptation With the Treaty of Ghent, Britain and the United States reached an **accommodation** to end the War of 1812.
isolate, p. 503	*v.* to set apart; to separate With the French fleet in place, Cornwallis was **isolated** on the Yorktown peninsula.

Teach

The Nation Divides

p. 499

Instruction L2

- **Vocabulary Builder** Before teaching this section, preteach the High-Use Words **accommodation** and **isolate** using the strategy on TE p. T21.

  Key Terms Have students complete the See It–Remember It chart for the key terms in this chapter.

- Have students read The Nation Divides using the Structured Silent Reading strategy (TE, p. T22).

- Ask: **Which party split along regional lines? Who were the candidates from each region?** (*the Democratic Party; North: Stephen Douglas, South: John Breckinridge*)

- Ask: **Why did the South and North choose separate candidates?** (*Neither felt it could trust a candidate from the other region.*)

- Have students use the 1860 Electoral Vote worksheet to analyze the results of the election of 1860. Discuss the implications of these results for the unity of the country.

  All in One Teaching Resources, Unit 5, 1860 Electoral Votes, p. 23

- At this time, you may also assign the worksheet The Election of 1860. (See Differentiated Instruction activity below.)

- Ask: **Why did southern states secede after Lincoln's election?** (*They believed that Lincoln was opposed to slavery.*)

- Discuss with students how Lincoln's election led to secession. Ask: **Why did many southerners feel that they had no choice?** (*The election of a President hostile to their interests, which is how they saw Lincoln and the Republicans, persuaded them to take the ultimate step of secession.*)

Answers

MAP MASTER Skills Activity **(a)** four political parties: green-Republican; purple-Northern Democrat; yellow-Constitutional Union; orange-Southern Democrat; Republicans won the northern states, Southern Democrats won the southern states **(b)** sections of the country voted as united blocks

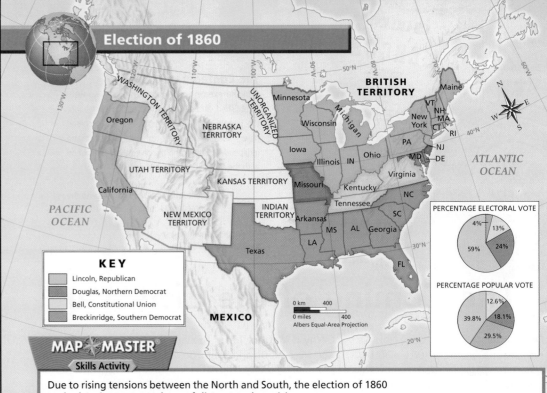

Election of 1860

KEY
- Lincoln, Republican
- Douglas, Northern Democrat
- Bell, Constitutional Union
- Breckinridge, Southern Democrat

MEXICO

0 km 400
0 miles 400
Albers Equal-Area Projection

PERCENTAGE ELECTORAL VOTE
4% / 13% / 24% / 59%

PERCENTAGE POPULAR VOTE
12.6% / 18.1% / 29.5% / 39.8%

MAP MASTER Skills Activity

Due to rising tensions between the North and South, the election of 1860 took place in an atmosphere of distrust and suspicion.

(a) Read a Map Key What do the four colors on the map stand for? Which party won nearly all the northern states? Which party won nearly all the southern states?

(b) Draw Conclusions How does the map show that sectionalism was important in the election?

MapMaster Online

For: Interactive map
Visit: PHSchool.com
Web Code: myp-5104

The election showed just how fragmented the nation had become. Lincoln won in every free state and Breckinridge in all the slave-holding states except four. Bell won Kentucky, Tennessee, and Virginia—all in the upper South. Douglas carried only Missouri. Although Lincoln got only 40 percent of the popular votes, he received enough electoral votes to win the election.

Southern States Secede Lincoln's election sent shock waves through the South. To many southerners, it seemed that the South no longer had a voice in the national government. They believed that the President and Congress were now set against their interests—especially slavery.

One Virginia newspaper expressed the feelings of many southerners. "A party founded on the single sentiment . . . of hatred of African slavery, is now the controlling power," it observed. "The honor, safety, and independence of the Southern people are to be found only in a Southern Confederacy."

South Carolina was the first southern state to secede from the Union. When news of Lincoln's election reached the state, the

Differentiated Instruction

L1 English Language Learners **L1 Less Proficient Readers** **L1 Special Needs**

The Election of 1860 Have students use the worksheet The Election of 1860 to analyze the results of the election of 1860. Discuss the implications of these results for the unity of the country.

All in One Teaching Resources, Unit 5, The Election of 1860, p. 24

legislature called for a special convention. On December 20, 1860, the convention passed a declaration that "the union now subsisting between South Carolina and the other states, under the name of the 'United States of America' is hereby dissolved."

The Confederate States of America With the hope of accommodation all but gone, six more states followed South Carolina out of the Union. However, not all southerners favored secession. Tennessee Senator Andrew Johnson and Texas Governor Sam Houston were among those who opposed it. Yet, the voices of the moderates were overwhelmed. "People are wild," said one opponent of secession. "You might as well attempt to control a tornado as attempt to stop them."

In early February, leaders from the seven seceding states met in Montgomery, Alabama, to form a new nation that they called the Confederate States of America. By the time Lincoln took office in March, they had written a constitution and named former Mississippi Senator Jefferson Davis as their president.

☑Checkpoint **Why did southern states secede from the Union?**

Vocabulary Builder
accommodation (ak kom moh DAY shuhn) **n.** adjustment; adaptation

The Civil War Begins

On March 4, 1861, Abraham Lincoln became President of a nation facing the greatest crisis in its history. In his inaugural address, he assured the seceded states that he meant them no harm. "I have no purpose, directly or indirectly, to interfere with the institution of slavery where it exists," he promised. But he also warned them about continuing on the course they had chosen:

> ❝In your hands, my dissatisfied fellow countrymen, and not in mine, is the momentous issue of . . . war. The government will not assail [attack] you. . . . We are not enemies, but friends. We must not be enemies. Though passion may have strained, it must not break our bonds of affection. ❞
> —Abraham Lincoln, Inaugural Address, March 4, 1861

Lincoln's assurance of friendship was rejected. The seceding states took over post offices, forts, and other federal property within their borders. The new President had to decide how to respond.

Fort Sumter Lincoln's most urgent problem was Fort Sumter, located on an island in the harbor of Charleston, South Carolina. The fort's commander would not surrender it. South Carolina authorities decided to starve the fort's 100 troops into surrender. They had been cut off from supplies since late December and could not hold out much longer.

Abraham Lincoln speaks at his first inauguration

501

Instruction (continued)
- To help the students better understand the concept of *secession*, which is important to the understanding of this chapter, use the Concept Lesson Secession. Provide students with copies of the Concept Organizer.

[All in One] **Teaching Resources, Unit 5,** Concept Lesson, p. 26; Concept Organizer, p. 6

Independent Practice
Have students continue filling in the study guide for this section.

📖 **Interactive Reading and Notetaking Study Guide,** Chapter 14, Section 4 (Adapted Version also available.)

Monitor Progress

As students fill in the Notetaking Study Guide, circulate and make sure individuals understand the political consequences of the slavery debate and why the South decided to secede. Provide assistance as needed.

The Civil War Begins
p. 501

Instruction   [L2]
- Have students read The Civil War Begins. Remind students to look for the sequence of events.
- Ask: **Why did the South decide to open fire on Fort Sumter?** (*Confederate leaders decided to capture the fort while it was isolated.*)

History Background

Jefferson Davis Although he believed in states' legal right to secede, Jefferson Davis opposed secession and spoke publicly in both the North and the South in the 1850s about the need for national harmony. Davis continued to hope for a peaceful resolution to the crisis even after secession.

When his own state of Mississippi seceded, Davis made a farewell speech to the Senate urging peace. His first act as president of the Confederacy in 1861 was to send a delegation to Washington, D.C., to prevent war—a delegation Lincoln refused to see.

Answer

☑Checkpoint Many southerners felt that with Lincoln's election, the South no longer had a voice in the national government.

Instruction (continued)

- Have students discuss whether Lincoln could have prevented war by surrendering Fort Sumter. Ask: **Could Lincoln allow the fort to be surrendered and not reply militarily?** (*Answers will vary, but students should understand the pressure for war from both sides.*)

- Show History Interactive transparency Attack on Fort Sumter. Ask: **Why did the attack on Fort Sumter begin the war?** (*It was the first time the Confederates fired on a Union fort.*)

Color Transparencies, Attack on Fort Sumter

Independent Practice

Have students complete the study guide for this section.

📖 **Interactive Reading and Notetaking Study Guide,** Chapter 14, Section 4 (Adapted Version also available.)

Monitor Progress

- As students fill in the Notetaking Study Guide, circulate and make sure individuals understand how the Civil War began. Provide assistance as needed.

- Tell students to fill in the last column of the Reading Readiness Guide. Probe for what they learned that confirms or invalidates each statement.

- Have students go back to their Word Knowledge Rating Form. Rerate their word knowledge and complete the last column with a definition or example.

All in One **Teaching Resources, Unit 5,** Reading Readiness Guide, p. 19; Word Knowledge Rating Form, p. 15

Answer

Analyze Cause and Effect Cause: The Union fort was in Confederate territory and its commander refused to surrender. Effect: The fort surrendered and the Civil War began.

● **INFOGRAPHIC**

ATTACK ON FORT SUMTER

America's most tragic conflict began early on the morning of April 12, 1861, at Fort Sumter. The dark night was suddenly lit up by Confederate shells fired from the mainland. Within a few hours, the fort's wooden barracks had caught fire and portions of the fort had crumbled. At midday, a Confederate shell knocked over the fort's flagpole. The firing went on throughout the day and evening. By the next day, the Union garrison was exhausted and every wooden structure in the fort was ablaze. "The men lay . . . on the ground, with wet handkerchiefs over their mouths and eyes, gasping for breath." **Critical Thinking:** *Analyze Cause and Effect* *What was the cause of the Confederate attack on Fort Sumter? What were the effects?*

History *Interactive*
Inside Fort Sumter
Visit: PHSchool.com
Web Code: myp-5107

American flag from Fort Sumter ▼

▼ **Confederate Troops Fire on the Fort**
Confederate artillery pounded Fort Sumter for 34 hours. Fires raged out of control and threatened to ignite the fort's magazine, where many barrels of gunpowder were stored. Facing shortages of food and ammunition, the Union commander surrendered. The bloodiest of all American wars had begun.

Major Robert ▶ Anderson, Union commander of Fort Sumter

502 Chapter 14 The Nation Divided

Differentiated Instruction

L3 Advanced Readers   **L3** Gifted and Talented

Secession Dialogue Have students work in pairs to write a dialogue between a moderate, pro-Union southerner and one who favors secession. Ask students to consider what they have read in this chapter and the likelihood of war if states secede. Ask students to perform their dialogues for the class.

Lincoln did not want to give up the fort. But he feared that sending troops might cause other states to secede. Therefore, he announced that he would send food to the fort, but that the supply ships would carry no troops or guns.

Confederate leaders decided to capture the fort while it was isolated. On April 12, Confederate artillery opened fire on the fort. After 34 hours, with the fort on fire, the U.S. troops surrendered.

Was War Avoidable? The Confederate attack on Fort Sumter marked the beginning of a long civil war. A civil war is a war between opposing groups of citizens of the same country.

The Civil War probably attracts more public interest today than any other event in American history. Americans continue to debate why the war took place and whether it could have been avoided.

In 1850, southerners might have been satisfied if they had been left alone. But by 1861, many Americans in both the North and the South had come to accept the idea that war could not be avoided. At stake was the nation's future. Four years later, a weary Lincoln looked back to the beginning of the conflict. He noted:

> **"** Both parties [condemned] war, but one of them would *make* war rather than let the nation survive, and the other would *accept* war rather than let it perish, and the war came.**"**
>
> —Abraham Lincoln, Second Inaugural Address, March 4, 1865

✓**Checkpoint** Why was Lincoln reluctant to give up Fort Sumter?

⭐ **Looking Back and Ahead** Confederate cannons had nearly destroyed Fort Sumter. To many, it seemed like a huge fireworks display. No one knew that the fireworks marked the beginning of a terrible war that would last four years.

Vocabulary Builder
isolate (ī sah layt) **v.** to set apart; to separate

Analyze Multiple Causes or Effects According to this section, what were two causes of the Civil War?

Section 4 | Check Your Progress

Progress Monitoring Online
For: Self-test with instant help
Visit: PHSchool.com
Web Code: mya-5104

Comprehension and Critical Thinking

1. **(a) Recall** How did divisions among the Democrats help lead to the election of Republican Abraham Lincoln in 1860?
(b) Explain Problems What was the South's reaction to Lincoln's election? How did Lincoln try to reassure the South?

2. **(a) Identify** What event marked the start of war between the North and the South?

(b) Evaluate Information Explain what Abraham Lincoln meant by the following remark: "Both parties [condemned] war, but one of them would *make* war rather than let the nation survive. . . ."

🌐 **Reading Skill**
3. **Analyze Multiple Causes or Effects** What were three effects of Lincoln's warning to the South?

Key Terms
4. Write two definitions for the key term civil war. First, write a formal definition for your teacher. Second, write a definition in everyday English for a classmate.

Writing
5. Based on what you have read in this section, write a thesis statement for an essay explaining why the election of Abraham Lincoln caused the South to secede.

Section 4 Check Your Progress

1. **(a)** Northern and southern Democratic candidates split the Democratic vote, which allowed Lincoln to win with a minority of the popular vote.
(b) Seven southern states seceded. Lincoln tried to assure the South of his good intentions.

2. **(a)** the Confederate attack on Fort Sumter
(b) The South would make war to secede, while the Union would fight only to keep the country together.

3. Accept any three of these: The seceding states took over U.S. property; South Carolina cut off food supplies to Fort Sumter; Lincoln sent food to the fort; Confederate artillery fired on the fort.

4. Formal: A civil war is a war between opposing groups in the same country. Informal: A civil war is when two groups in the same country fight.

5. Thesis should be clear and supported by details.

Assess and Reteach

Assess Progress L2
Have students complete Check Your Progress. Administer the Section Quiz.

All in One Teaching Resources, Unit 5, Section Quiz, p. 30

To further assess student understanding, use the Progress Monitoring Transparency.

Progress Monitoring Transparencies, Chapter 14, Section 4

Reteach L1
If students need more instruction, have them read this section in the Interactive Reading and Notetaking Study Guide and complete the accompanying question.

📖 **Interactive Reading and Notetaking Study Guide,** Chapter 14, Section 4 (Adapted Version also available.)

Extend L3
Have students complete the History Interactive activity online. Provide students with the Web Code below.

Extend Online
For: Help in starting the History Interactive activity
Visit: PHSchool.com
Web Code: myp-5107

Progress Monitoring Online
Students may check their comprehension of this section by completing the Progress Monitoring Online graphic organizer and self-quiz.

Answers

🌐 **Reading Skill** Lincoln's election; the Confederates firing on Ft. Sumter

✓**Checkpoint** Possible answer: Lincoln feared giving it up would show weakness and encourage further secession.

Objective

Many historical sources contain information on a variety of subjects. This analysis skill lesson will teach students how to focus on one central topic and decide which information is relevant to that topic.

Determine Relevance

Instruction   L2

1. Write the steps to determine relevance on the board and ask the class to read the steps aloud.

2. Have students suggest a title for the letter based on its subject.

3. Practice the skill by following the steps on p. 504 as a class. Model each step to determine relevance. (*1. William does not agree with his brother Joseph about the Kansas-Nebraska Act. 2. I am reading this letter for a personal point of view on the Kansas-Nebraska Act. 3. (a) Answers will vary, but students should cite parts of the letter about the Kansas-Nebraska Act or slavery. (b) Answers will vary but should explain the choices in part (a). 4. (a) Students should cite statements from the first paragraph, such as the statement about Joseph's store. (b) Answers will vary but should show students' understanding that this is not about the main idea.*)

Monitor Progress

Ask students to do the Apply the Skill activity. Then assign the Skills for Life worksheet. As students complete the worksheet, circulate to make sure individuals are applying the skill steps effectively. Provide assistance as needed.

All in One Teaching Resources, Unit 5,
Skills for Life Worksheet, p. 25

Not everything a writer includes in a selection is equally important. Some information is relevant because it is directly related to the subject of the text. Other information is less relevant because it does not directly relate to the subject. When you read, you must focus your attention on the main topic and the most relevant information. Read the fictional letter below to determine relevance.

> The letter below is historical fiction. That means that it is based on history, but is not a primary source. In the letter, William, a farmer who had moved to Kansas Territory, writes to his brother Joseph in Vermont.
>
> November 20, 1854
> Dear Joseph,
>   I was pleased to receive your last letter. The success of your store is a great achievement. Our new farm continues to prosper and little Sarah has recovered from the fever that had sickened her for a month. Of course, the issue of the Kansas-Nebraska Act continues to trouble me. I do not agree with your support of Senator Stephen Douglas of Illinois; however, I enjoy reading his speeches. Those who oppose slavery, as I do, do not want that cruel system in place in a territory where it had been banned. Under the terms of the Kansas-Nebraska Act, it is up to the people to decide the issue peacefully by voting their hearts. Yet, settlers who are for and against slavery in the territory seem intent on using force, instead of the ballot box. The elections next year will settle the issue once and for all.
>
>   Your loving brother,
>   William

Learn the Skill

Use these steps to determine which information is relevant and which is irrelevant.

1 **Identify the subject or topic.** What is the main topic of the selection?

2 **Identify your purpose for reading the selection.** Ask yourself: What am I trying to find out?

3 **Identify the information that is relevant to the topic.** What information is directly related to the subject? Why is it relevant?

4 **Identify the information that is irrelevant to the topic.** What information is not directly related to the subject? Why is it irrelevant?

Practice the Skill

Answer the following questions about the letter on the page.

1 **Identify the subject or topic.** What is the main topic of the letter?

2 **Identify the purpose for reading the selection.** Why am I reading this letter?

3 **Identify the information that is relevant to the subject.** (a) What are two statements that are directly related to the topic of the letter? (b) Why is each statement relevant?

4 **Identify the information that is irrelevant to the topic.** (a) What are two statements that are not directly related to the subject? (b) Why is each statement irrelevant?

Apply the Skill

See the Review and Assessment at the end of this chapter.

504 Chapter 14 The Nation Divided

Quick Study Guide

How did the nation try but fail to deal with growing sectional differences?

Section 1
Growing Tensions Over Slavery

- The acquisition of new territories in the West reopened the issue of slavery.
- Lawmakers debated how to keep a balance of power between free and slave-holding states.

Section 2
Compromises Fail

- The Compromise of 1850 attempted to settle the slavery question, but northerners refused to accept the Fugitive Slave Act.
- *Uncle Tom's Cabin* increased northern hatred of slavery and antagonized southern slaveholders.
- Popular sovereignty established by the Kansas-Nebraska Act triggered bloody fighting in Kansas.

Section 3
The Crisis Deepens

- The Republican Party was formed to oppose the spread of slavery.
- In the Dred Scott decision, the Supreme Court ruled that Congress could not ban slavery in any territory.
- Abraham Lincoln became a central political figure when he and Stephen Douglas debated slavery.
- John Brown, an abolitionist, and his followers attacked the federal arsenal at Harpers Ferry, Virginia, to protest slavery.

Section 4
The Coming of the Civil War

- After Lincoln won the presidential election of 1860, some southern states seceded from the Union.
- The Civil War began when Confederate troops fired on Fort Sumter.

? Exploring the Essential Question

Use the online study guide to explore the essential question.

Section 1
How did the question of admission of new states to the Union fuel the debate over slavery and states' rights?

Chapter 14 Essential Question
How did the nation try but fail to deal with growing sectional differences?

Section 2
What was the Compromise of 1850, and why did it fail?

Section 4
Why did the election of Abraham Lincoln spark the secession of southern states?

Section 3
Why did the Lincoln-Douglas debates and John Brown's raid increase tensions between the North and South?

Essential Question

Remind students of the Chapter Essential Question: **How did the nation try but fail to deal with growing sectional differences?** Have them review the bulleted statements and the Visual Preview at the beginning of the chapter to help them answer this question.

To bolster students' retention, at this time they should complete the Notetaking Study Guide in print or online. Remind students that they should also continue notetaking for the Unit and Chapter Essential Questions.

📖 **Interactive Reading and Notetaking Study Guide,** Unit 4, Chapter 14 (Adapted Version also available.)

 Study Guide *Online,* Chapter 14

Chapter Challenge

To wrap up this chapter, students should apply the knowledge they have gained to answer this question. Ask: **How might history have been different if Stephen Douglas had won the election of 1860?** (*Answers will vary but may suggest that war would have been postponed, but not avoided completely.*)

Assessment at a Glance

Formal Assessment

  Chapter Tests A/B (L1/L2)

  AYP Monitoring Assessment

  Test Prep Workbook With Document-Based Assessment

  Test-Taking Strategies With Transparencies

Performance Assessment

  Group/Individual Activities, TE pp. 478g, 478h

  Teacher's Edition, pp. 485, 491, 498, 503

  Assessment Rubrics

Assessment Through Technology

  ExamView CD-ROM

  MindPoint CD-ROM

  Progress Monitoring Transparencies

  Progress Monitoring Online

Key Terms

1. secede
2. propaganda
3. civil war

Comprehension and Critical Thinking

4. **(a)** Douglas wanted a railroad built from Illinois through the Nebraska territory to the west coast. He also wanted to create two states out of the Nebraska territory. **(b)** Proslavery forces elected a government, and antislavery forces elected a different legislature favoring their views. Kansas then erupted in chaos and violence. Divisions on slavery were too great to heal by compromise.

5. **(a)** Dred Scott was not a free man. Dred Scott could not sue, as he was not a citizen; he was the property of his owner. Slaves were property, so Congress could make no laws restricting slavery in the territories. **(b)** Possible answer: Stowe was probably furious.

6. **(a)** The Republican Party's main goal was to prevent the spread of slavery to the territories. **(b)** He took a strong stand against the spread of slavery into the territories.

7. **(a)** John Brown **(b)** Answers will vary but should show an understanding of John Brown's actions.

8. **(a)** Confederates wanted to take control of the fort and attacked it. **(b)** Answers will vary but should show students' understanding both of southern fears about Lincoln's views on slavery and of Lincoln's efforts to keep the Union together.

History Reading Skill

9. The election split the nation.

Key Terms

Fill in the blanks with the correct key terms.

1. Many southern states threatened to _____ from the Union if California was admitted as a free state.

2. Southerners claimed that *Uncle Tom's Cabin* was _____ because it did not give a fair picture of the lives of enslaved African Americans.

3. Slavery was the main issue that split the nation apart and led to a violent _____.

Comprehension and Critical Thinking

4. **(a) Recall** Why did Senator Stephen Douglas introduce the Kansas-Nebraska Act?
   (b) Understand Sequence How did the events in Kansas demonstrate the unrest that would eventually take shape throughout the nation?

5. **(a) Summarize** What was the Supreme Court's verdict in the Dred Scott case?
   (b) Detect Points of View How do you think Harriet Beecher Stowe reacted to the verdict?

6. **(a) Identify** What was the main goal of the Republican Party in the election of 1854?
   (b) Distinguish Relevant Information How did Abraham Lincoln represent Republican principles during the Lincoln-Douglas debates?

7. **(a) Identify** What is the subject of the painting below?
   (b) Draw Conclusions Do you agree with the artist's view of this person? Why or why not?

---

8. **(a) Describe** What happened at Fort Sumter?
   (b) Draw Conclusions Do you think southerners were justified in seceding despite Lincoln's assurances? Explain.

History Reading Skill

9. **Analyze Cause and Effect** Reread the text in Section 4 under the heading "The Nation Divides." How did the election of 1860 affect the unity of the United States?

Writing

10. **Choose one of the following topics for a research report:**
   • the Kansas-Nebraska Act
   • the Dred Scott decision
   • the early career of Abraham Lincoln

   List five questions you would want to pursue if you were going to research that topic. Write a thesis statement for the topic and find supporting evidence for that thesis from the chapter.

11. **Write a Narrative:**
   Imagine you are from a northern farm family and have just heard of the attack on Fort Sumter. Write a narrative describing your hopes and fears about the future.

Skills for Life

Determine Relevance

Use the fictional letter below to answer the questions that follow.

> October 18, 1856
>
> Dear Margaret,
>
> When the Republican Party was formed two years ago, we had no idea it would grow so quickly. I am so pleased with the party's choice of John Frémont as the Republican candidate for President. I know Mother would have agreed with me. I only hope you and I will be able to cast our votes in a presidential election soon.
>
> Your loving sister, Ellen

12. What is the letter about?

13. What is one statement directly related to the subject of the letter? Why is it relevant?

14. What is one statement that is irrelevant to the subject of the letter? Why is it irrelevant?

Writing

10. Check to be sure questions stay on topic and are focused on specific issues. Thesis should be clear and well-supported.

11. Narrative should explain whether or not the writer thinks fighting will continue, or if it can be avoided. The viewpoint should be clear and well-supported.

For a more complete four-point rubric, see the Writing Rubrics in the Teaching Resources.

 **Teaching Resources, Unit 5,** p. 108

Chapter 14
Review and Assessment

Test Yourself

1. All of the following were causes of the Civil War EXCEPT
   A John Brown's raid on Harpers Ferry.
   B the Dred Scott decision.
   C the use of child labor in northern factories.
   D the publication of Stowe's *Uncle Tom's Cabin.*

Refer to the quotation below to answer Question 2.

> "A house divided against itself cannot stand. . . .
> I do not expect the Union to be dissolved—I do
> not expect the house to fall—but I do expect it
> will cease to be divided. It will become all one
> thing or all the other."

2. What division does this quotation describe?
   A church and state
   B free states and slaveholding states
   C the House of Representatives and the Senate
   D Republicans and Democrats

Refer to the pie chart below to answer Question 3.

Percentage of Popular Vote, 1860

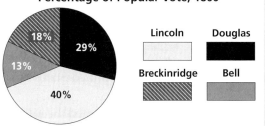

Lincoln   Douglas

Breckinridge   Bell

18%   29%   13%   40%

3. What conclusion can you draw from this pie chart?
   A Southerners voted for Douglas.
   B Lincoln won most of the popular vote.
   C Bell had little support in the North.
   D The two Democrats combined won more votes than Lincoln.

Document-Based Questions

Task: Look at Documents 1 and 2, and answer their accompanying questions. Then, use the documents and your knowledge of history to complete this writing assignment:

Write a two-paragraph essay comparing the goals of the Fugitive Slave Law with its actual effects.

Document 1: In this speech, Senator John Calhoun of South Carolina explained the need for the Fugitive Slave Law. *According to Calhoun, what would happen if Congress did not pass the law?*

> "How can the Union be saved? . . . There is but one way . . . , and that is by adopting such measures as will satisfy . . . the southern section that they can remain in the Union consistently with their honor and their safety. . . .
>   But can this be done? Yes, easily. . . . The North has only . . . to conced[e] to the South an equal right in [newly] acquired territory, and to caus[e] the stipulations relative to fugitive slaves to be faithfully fulfilled—to cease the agitation of the slave question. . . ."

Document 2: This poster reveals Bostonians' commitment to protect runaways or kidnapped African Americans. *Why were posters like this illegal?*

Test Yourself
1. C
2. B
3. D

Document-Based Questions
Answers

Document 1 The South might be forced to choose between accepting abolition and seceding from the Union.

Document 2 They urged people to openly disobey a national law.

Goals and Effects of Fugitive Slave Law of 1850. Goals: Stop agitation against slavery; retrieve fugitive slaves. Effects: Aroused greater opposition to slavery; retrieved some fugitive slaves.

Rubric: Write an Essay
Share the rubric with students before they begin writing.

Score 1 Is poorly organized, misses key points.

Score 2 Has unclear writing, few specifics.

Score 3 Contains competent discussion of law's goals and effects.

Score 4 Includes full examination of goals and effects, providing both context and details, clearly written and organized.

Skills for Life
12. Her support of the Republican Party.

13. Possible answer: I am so pleased with the party's choice of John Frémont, who opposes the spread of slavery, as the Republican candidate for President of the United States. It is relevant because it indicates why she supports the Republican Party.

14. . . . we had no idea it would grow so quickly. It is irrelevant because it does not give a reason for her support of the party.

The Civil War (1861–1865)

History Background

The Civil War

The Civil War began as a struggle to restore the Union after a complex series of events led to the secession of southern states. By the time of the surrender of Fort Sumter, numerous compromises over the spread of slavery had been attempted and had failed.

Both the North and the South were confident of victory at first. The South had superior military leadership and the advantage of fighting a defensive war on its own territory, while the North had a larger population, a strong industrial base, and more

resources. Nevertheless, the Civil War was destined to last four violent years, tearing apart families and causing the death of more Americans than any other war the United States has fought.

At first Lincoln handled the issue of slavery carefully, keeping in mind that four border states with slaves remained in the Union. However, by 1862, Lincoln recognized that he needed to broaden the goals of the war. To announce a plan to free slaves, Lincoln waited for a Union victory, which he got at Antietam. Then on January

1, 1863, he issued the Emancipation Proclamation. Although it did not immediately free slaves, it changed the war into a struggle to end slavery and paved the way for the Thirteenth Amendment (1865), which banned slavery in all the states of the unified nation. Ironically, although the Civil War was the bloodiest conflict the United States has ever fought, it served to reunite the nation instead of tearing it further apart.

Essential Questions

Use this graphic organizer to see the relationship between key concepts and the Chapter Essential Question.

Focus Question/Section 1
Why did each side in the Civil War think the war would be won easily?
(p. 512)

Concept: Sectionalism

Focus Question/Section 2
How did each side in the war try to gain an advantage over the other?
(p. 518)

Concept: Technology

Chapter Essential Question
How did people, places, and things affect the outcome of the Civil War?

Focus Question/Section 5
How did Lincoln and his generals turn the tide of the war?
(p. 533)

Concept: Civil War

Focus Question/Section 4
How did the war affect people and politics in the North and the South?
(p. 528)

Concept: Change

Focus Question/Section 3
What were the causes and effects of the Emancipation Proclamation?
(p. 524)

Concept: Emancipation

Differentiated Instruction

Pre-Teaching Vocabulary

Research literature on academic vocabulary instruction indicates that effective strategies require students to go beyond simply looking up dictionary definitions or examining the context. Vocabulary learning must be based on the learner's dynamic engagement in construction understanding.

Active Learning If students are not retaining the meaning of the Key Terms or High-Use Words, use this extended vocabulary sequence to engage them in learning new words.

1. Present the word in writing and point out the part of speech.

2. Pronounce the word and have students pronounce the word.

3. Provide a range of familiar synonyms (or "it's like" words) before offering definitions.

4. Provide an accessible definition and concrete examples, or "showing sentences."

5. Rephrase the definition or example sentence, asking students to complete the statement by substituting the word aloud.

6. Check for understanding by providing an application task/question requiring critical thinking.

Sample Instructional Sequence:

1. *Resource* is a noun, a word that names a person, place, or thing.

2. Say the word *resource* after me. (Students repeat.)

3. *Resource* means available assests or supplies. With more *resources*, the North was able to field, feed, and equip larger armies.

4. The _____ of the North included a large labor supply, good farmland, factories, and railroads. (Students substitute missing word.)

5. Is water an example of a *resource*? Yes-No-Why? (Students answer the question.)

Concepts Across Time

Have students develop an understanding of the enduring concepts of history by connecting these ideas.

Concept: Sectionalism

Sectionalism played a large role in the events that led up to the Civil War. Remind students that sectionalism also existed in colonial times, when there was no unifying American government and people were loyal to their colony. Ask: **What kept the colonies from fighting among themselves?** (*They were united by a common cause—the desire to win independence from Britain. Also, they faced a common danger—if Britain won, their leaders would be treated as rebels and traitors.*) Use the question when discussing the opening weeks of the war in Section 1.

Concept: Emancipation

Remind students that slavery had a long history in many different societies. Remind students that in the United States before the Civil War, emancipation was a personal action by a slave owner to free particular individuals. Ask: **What reasons might an owner have had to free a slave?** (*Possible answers: a belief that slavery was morally wrong, a desire to reward an enslaved individual for loyalty or long service, a desire to avoid the expense of maintaining an elderly slave*) Ask: **Why did many white southerners oppose even the individual emanci-**

pation of slaves? (*They thought that an increase in the South's free black population would undermine the slave system.*) Use these questions when discussing the Emancipation Proclamation in Section 3.

Concept: Technology

Remind students studying the battles of the Civil War that the technology of warfare has evolved gradually over the centuries. Explain that the introduction of cannons in the Middle Ages gave an advantage to large armies and helped kings to consolidate their power over lesser lords. Ask: **How do you think cannons would give an advantage to kings?** (*Cannons were expensive and required large armies, and kings had access to more resources and soldiers than did lesser lords.*) Have students recall some of the technology that was developed between the time of the American Revolution and the Civil War. Ask: **What new technology would be useful to the fighting forces in the Civil War?** (*Possible answers: Railroads to transport troops and supplies, the telegraph to transmit information, improved guns such as revolvers and rifles.*) Use these questions when discussing war developments in Sections 2 and 5.

Section 1 The Call to Arms *1.5 periods, .75 block*

Objectives

Students will

1. Identify the states that supported the Union, the states that seceded, and the states whose loyalties were divided.

2. Describe the advantages each side had in the war.

3. Compare the different strategies used by the North and the South.

4. Summarize the results of the First Battle of Bull Run.

5. Describe the conditions soldiers in camp faced.

Differentiated Instruction Key

L1 Basic to Average
L2 All Students
L3 Average to Advanced

AR Advanced Readers
ELL English Language Learners
GT Gifted and Talented
LPR Less Proficient Readers
SN Special Needs

Prepare to Read

Build Background Knowledge
Ask students to predict what they will learn.

Set a Purpose for Reading
Begin to fill out the Reading Guide.

Preview Key Terms
Preview the section's Key Terms.

Instructional Resources

All in One Teaching Resources, Unit 5
L2 Chapter Prereading Guide, p. 4
L2 History Reading Skill Worksheet, p. 45
L2 Word Knowledge Rating Form, p. 46
L2 Reading Readiness Guide, p. 47

Teacher's Edition
L2 Vocabulary Builder, pp. 511, 513

Differentiated Instruction

Guided Reading Audio CD
Spanish ELL, LPR, SN

Teach

Instruction
Taking Sides in the War
Identify the side each state took in the war.

North Against South
Explain the advantages of each side.

The Two Sides Plan Strategies
Examine each side's strategy to win the war.

Americans Against Americans
Discuss how the strategy on each side differed.

First Battle of Bull Run
Explain how the Union army failed to end the war quickly.

A Soldier's Life
Discuss the battle of Bull Run. Explain the conditions soldiers faced.

Instructional Resources

Interactive Reading and Notetaking Study Guide
L2 Chapter 15, Section 1

Color Transparencies
L2 Bull Run

Differentiated Instruction

Interactive Reading and Notetaking Study Guide, Adapted Version (English/Spanish)
L1 Chapter 15, Section 1 ELL, LPR, SN

Teacher's Edition
L1 Visualizing the Word, p. 511 ELL, LPR, SN
L3 Comparing Points of View, p. 512 AR
L1 Gaining Comprehension, p. 514 LPR, SN
L1 Define, p. 516 ELL, LPR

All in One Teaching Resources, Unit 5
L3 Fort Sumter: Two Views, p. 52

Assess and Reteach

Assess Progress
Assign Check Your Progress and Section Quiz.

Reteach
Assign the Study Guide to help students.

Extend
Extend the lesson by having students complete the online History Interactive activity.

Instructional Resources

Interactive Reading and Notetaking Study Guide
L2 Chapter 15, Section 1

All in One Teaching Resources, Unit 5
L2 Reading Readiness Guide, p. 47
L2 Section Quiz, p. 60

Progress Monitoring Transparencies
L2 Chapter 15, Section 1

Differentiated Instruction

Teacher's Edition
L1 Checkpoints, TE pp. 513, 514, 515, 516, 517

SE on Audio CD
L1 Chapter 15 ELL, LPR, SN

Internet Resources
PHSchool.com

Section 2 Early Years of the War

 1 period, .5 block

Objectives

Students will

1. Explain how new weapons made fighting the war more dangerous.
2. Describe the course of the war in the East in 1862.
3. Describe the early days of the war in the West and at sea.

Differentiated Instruction Key

L1 Basic to Average
L2 All Students
L3 Average to Advanced

AR Advanced Readers
ELL English Language Learners
GT Gifted and Talented
LPR Less Proficient Readers
SN Special Needs

Prepare to Read

Build Background Knowledge
Preview the section and discuss student's understanding of strategy.

Set a Purpose for Reading
Have students begin to fill out the Reading Readiness Guide.

Preview Key Terms
Preview the section's Key Terms.

Instructional Resources

All in One Teaching Resources, Unit 5
L2 Reading Readiness Guide, p. 48

Teacher's Edition
L2 Vocabulary Builder, p. 519

Differentiated Instruction

🔘 **Guided Reading Audio CD**
Spanish ELL, LPR, SN

Teach

Instruction
New Technology in the War
Examine how changing technology affected the way that the Civil War was fought.

The War in the East
Identify the new technology used in the Civil War. Analyze McClellan's caution in using the Union army.

The War in the West
Discuss the Battle of Shiloh.

Instructional Resources

📖 **Interactive Reading and Notetaking Study Guide**
L2 Chapter 15, Section 2

All in One Teaching Resources, Unit 5
L2 General Robert E. Lee, p. 53

Discovery School Video
L2 The *Monitor* and the *Merrimack*

Differentiated Instruction

📖 **Interactive Reading and Notetaking Study Guide, Adapted Version (English/Spanish)**
L1 Chapter 15, Section 2 ELL, LPR, SN

Teacher's Edition
L1 Gaining Comprehension, p. 518 ELL, LPR, SN
L3 Research, p. 520 GT
L3 Writing a Journal Entry, p. 522 AR, GT

Assess and Reteach

Assess Progress
Evaluate student comprehension with Check Your Progress and Section Quiz.

Reteach
Assign the Interactive Reading and Notetaking Study Guide to help struggling students.

Extend
Extend the lesson by having students create an illustrative biography of Ulysses S. Grant.

Instructional Resources

📖 **Interactive Reading and Notetaking Study Guide**
L2 Chapter 15, Section 2

All in One Teaching Resources, Unit 5
L2 Reading Readiness Guide, p. 48
L2 Section Quiz, p. 61

Progress Monitoring Transparencies
L2 Chapter 15, Section 2

Differentiated Instruction

Teacher's Edition
L1 Checkpoints, TE pp. 518, 520, 521

🔘 **SE on Audio CD**
L1 Chapter 15 ELL, LPR, SN

Internet Resources
PHSchool.com

Section 3 The Emancipation Proclamation ⏱ *1 period, .5 block*

Objectives

Students will

1. Explain why Lincoln issued the Emancipation Proclamation.
2. Identify the effects of the proclamation.
3. Describe the contributions of African Americans to the Union.

Differentiated Instruction Key

L1 Basic to Average
L2 All Students
L3 Average to Advanced

AR Advanced Readers
ELL English Language Learners
GT Gifted and Talented
LPR Less Proficient Readers
SN Special Needs

Prepare to Read	Instructional Resources	Differentiated Instruction
Build Background Knowledge Preview the section and review what students have already learned about slavery. **Set a Purpose for Reading** Have students begin to fill out the Reading Readiness Guide. **Preview Key Terms** Preview the section's Key Terms.	**All in One Teaching Resources, Unit 5** **L2** Reading Readiness Guide, p. 49 **Teacher's Edition** **L2** Vocabulary Builder, p. 525	🎧 **Guided Reading Audio CD** **Spanish** ELL, LPR, SN
Teach	**Instructional Resources**	**Differentiated Instruction**
Instruction **Emancipating the Enslaved** Discuss the Emancipation Proclamation and its effects. **African Americans Help the Union** Explain how African Americans helped the Union army.	📖 **Interactive Reading and Notetaking Study Guide** **L2** Chapter 15, Section 3 **All in One Teaching Resources, Unit 5** **L2** Concept Lesson, p. 59 **L2** Concept Organizer, p. 6 **Color Transparencies** **L2** African Americans Join the War	📖 **Interactive Reading and Notetaking Study Guide, Adapted Version (English/ Spanish)** **L1** Chapter 15, Section 3 ELL, LPR, SN **Teacher's Edition** **L3** Predicting, p. 524 AR, GT **L1** Comparing, p. 526 ELL, LPR, SN
Assess and Reteach	**Instructional Resources**	**Differentiated Instruction**
Assess Progress Assign Check Your Progress and Section Quiz. **Reteach** Assign the Interactive Reading and Notetaking Study Guide to help struggling students. **Extend** Extend the lesson by having students create a timeline of the major events of the section.	📖 **Interactive Reading and Notetaking Study Guide** **L2** Chapter 15, Section 3 **All in One Teaching Resources, Unit 5** **L2** Reading Readiness Guide, p. 49 **L2** Section Quiz, p. 62 **Progress Monitoring Transparencies** **L2** Chapter 15, Section 3	**Teacher's Edition** **L1** Checkpoints, TE pp. 526, 527 🎧 **SE on Audio CD** **L1** Chapter 15 ELL, LPR, SN

Section 4 The Civil War and American Life *1 period, .5 block*

Objectives

Students will

1. Explain how opposition to the war caused problems for both sides.
2. Identify the reasons that both sides passed draft laws.
3. Describe the economic hardships the war caused in the North and the South.
4. Describe the contributions of women to the war efforts.

Differentiated Instruction Key

L1 Basic to Average
L2 All Students
L3 Average to Advanced

AR Advanced Readers
ELL English Language Learners
GT Gifted and Talented
LPR Less Proficient Readers
SN Special Needs

Prepare to Read

Build Background Knowledge
Discuss students' impressions of the draft.

Set a Purpose for Reading
Have students begin to fill out the Reading Readiness Guide.

Preview Key Terms
Preview the section's Key Terms.

Instructional Resources

All in One Teaching Resources, Unit 5
L2 Reading Readiness Guide, p. 50

Teacher's Edition
L2 Vocabulary Builder, p. 529

Differentiated Instruction

🎧 **Guided Reading Audio CD**
Spanish ELL, LPR, SN

Teach

Instruction

Divisions Over the War
Discuss how the war divided the country.

The Draft Laws
Explain the draft laws.

The War and Economic Strains
Examine how the cost of goods was affected by the war.

Women in the Civil War
Identify the ways the war affected northern and southern economies. Discuss the ways women contributed to the war effort.

Instructional Resources

📖 **Interactive Reading and Notetaking Study Guide**
L2 Chapter 15, Section 4

Differentiated Instruction

📖 **Interactive Reading and Notetaking Study Guide, Adapted Version (English/Spanish)**
L1 Chapter 15, Section 4 ELL, LPR, SN

Teacher's Edition
L1 Define, p. 528 ELL, LPR, SN
L3 Using Literature, p. 530 AR, GT

All in One Teaching Resources, Unit 5
L3 "Beat! Beat! Drums!", p. 54

Assess and Reteach

Assess Progress
Assign Check Your Progress and Section Quiz.

Reteach
Assign the Interactive Reading and Notetaking Study Guide to help struggling students.

Extend
Extend the lesson by having students write a letter as a woman who played a role in the Civil War.

Instructional Resources

📖 **Interactive Reading and Notetaking Study Guide**
L2 Chapter 15, Section 4

All in One Teaching Resources, Unit 5
L2 Reading Readiness Guide, p. 50
L2 Section Quiz, p. 63

Progress Monitoring Transparencies
L2 Chapter 15, Section 4

Differentiated Instruction

Teacher's Edition
L1 Checkpoints, TE pp. 529, 530, 531, 532

🎧 **SE on Audio CD**
L1 Chapter 15 ELL, LPR, SN

Section 5 Decisive Battles

 1.5 periods, .75 block

Objectives

Students will

1. Describe the significance of the battles at Vicksburg and Gettysburg.
2. Explain how Union generals used a new type of war to defeat the Confederacy.
3. Explain how the war ended.

Differentiated Instruction Key

L1 Basic to Average
L2 All Students
L3 Average to Advanced

AR Advanced Readers
ELL English Language Learners
GT Gifted and Talented
LPR Less Proficient Readers
SN Special Needs

Prepare to Read

Build Background Knowledge
Discuss students' impressions of "turning point."

Set a Purpose for Reading
Have students begin the Reading Guide.

Preview Key Terms
Preview the section's Key Terms.

Instructional Resources

All in One Teaching Resources, Unit 5
L2 Reading Readiness Guide, p. 51

Teacher's Edition
L2 Vocabulary Builder, p. 533

Differentiated Instruction

🔊 **Guided Reading Audio CD**
Spanish ELL, LPR, SN

Teach

Instruction
The Tide Turns
Identify the events that marked a turning point in the war.

Closing In on the Confederacy
Explain how the Union began to defeat the South in the war's final battles.

Peace at Last
Discuss why General Lee surrendered.

Instructional Resources

📖 **Interactive Reading and Notetaking Study Guide**
L2 Chapter 15, Section 5

All in One Teaching Resources, Unit 5
L2 Photographing the War, p. 56
L2 Skills for Life Worksheet, p. 58

Color Transparencies
L2 The Final Battles

Differentiated Instruction

📖 **Interactive Reading and Notetaking Study Guide, Adapted Version (English/ Spanish)**
L1 Chapter 15, Section 5 ELL, LPR, SN

Teacher's Edition
L1 Analyze Photographs, p. 534 ELL, LPR, SN
L3 Using Literature, p. 536 AR, GT

📖 **Readings in Social Studies, America in Progress**
L3 *The Red Badge of Courage*, pp. 165–166

All in One Teaching Resources, Unit 5
L1 Civil War Powder Monkey, p. 55

Assess and Reteach

Assess Progress
Assign Check Your Progress and Section Quiz.

Reteach
Assign the Study Guide to help students.

Extend
Have students write a speech about Memorial Day.

Instructional Resources

📖 **Interactive Reading and Notetaking Study Guide**
L2 Chapter 15, Section 5

All in One Teaching Resources, Unit 5
L2 Reading Readiness Guide, p. 51
L2 Section Quiz, p. 64
L2 Chapter Test, p. 68

Progress Monitoring Transparencies
L2 Chapter 15, Section 5

Differentiated Instruction

Teacher's Edition
L1 Checkpoints, TE pp. 535, 536, 537

All in One Teaching Resources, Unit 5
L1 Chapter Test, p. 65

🔊 **SE on Audio CD**
L1 Chapter 15 ELL, LPR, SN

Use the following research activities to help students deepen their understanding of the Chapter Essential Question: **How did people, places, and things affect the outcome of the Civil War?** Students should use library or Internet resources. The Web Codes provided offer access to Internet resources students can use to complete each activity. Use the appropriate four-point rubric in Assessment Rubrics to evaluate the activity.

 Assessment Rubrics

Present a Biography

Ask students to choose a military leader during the Civil War and research information about his life and background. Students might write about one of the following leaders or someone of their own choosing: Ulysses S. Grant, George McClellan, William Tecumseh Sherman, Ambrose Burnside, David Farragut, Joseph Hooker, Irwin McDowell, Robert E. Lee, Albert Johnston, Joseph Johnston, Thomas Jackson, or George E. Pickett. Remind students to focus on the role the leader played, his motivations, and how he affected the outcome of the war. Have students present their biographies to the class.

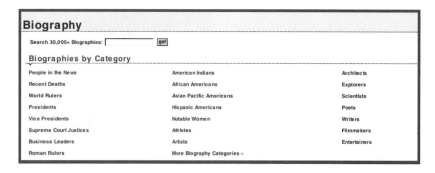

 **Web Code:** mye-0267

 Individual research activity AR   **L3**

Deliver a Newscast About a Civil War Battle

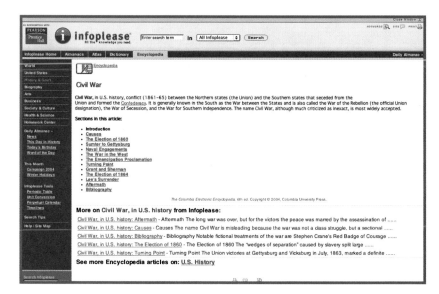

Have students work in groups to prepare a newscast and analysis about a major Civil War battle. One student might be the anchor; others might be guest analysts; still others might assume responsibility for showing maps and photographs. Groups can present their newscasts after the class has read the relevant section of the chapter.

 Group research activity   **L2**

 **Web Code:** mye-0268

Why It Matters

One definition of a democracy might be "a system in which people have a say in how they are governed." If that is the case, the American Civil War is one example of the system breaking down. The slave states refused to accept the results of the democratic presidential election of 1860 and chose to secede. One major cause of the conflict, slavery and the future of African Americans, reflected an issue which challenged the nation for many years after the war.

Many historians consider the Civil War to be a major turning point in U.S. history. The most dramatic result of the Civil War was the abolition of slavery. Other effects were also important. One was the development of a strong federal government. Another legacy was the supremacy of the nation-state. Until 1860, it was common to refer to *these* United States, as a union of states. Since the Civil War, Americans refer to *the* United States, a nation.

Chapter Essential Question

How did people, places, and things affect the outcome of the Civil War?

Think Like a Historian

- To preview this chapter, have students review the content of these pages of the Student Edition. Ask: **What will you be learning about in this chapter?** *(the Civil War)*

- Remind students of books they may have read and films they may have seen based on the Civil War. Have students look at the painting and read the quote from a soldier in the field of battle. Ask: **How does the soldier describe his battlefield experience?** *(in terms of the horrible sounds of battle)*

The Civil War

1861–1865

Bibliography

For the Teacher

McPherson, James M. *Battle Cry of Freedom: The Civil War Era.* Oxford, England: Oxford University Press, 2003.

For the Student

L1 Stanchak, John E. *Civil War.* New York: DK Publishing, 2000.

L2 Murphy, Jim. *Journal of James Edmond Pease: A Civil War Union Soldier: Virginia, 1863.* Scholastic, 1998.

L3 Reit, Seymour V. *Behind Rebel Lines: The Incredible Story of Emma Edmonds, Civil War Spy.* Harcourt, 2001.

> *"The wild cries of charging lines, the rattle of musketry, the booming of artillery and the shrieks of wounded were ...like very hell itself...."*
>
> —Lt. Porter Farley,
> 140th New York Infantry Regiment

In a painting by Don Troiani, a Union soldier and a Confederate soldier fight during the Battle of Gettysburg.

CHAPTER 15

What You Will Learn

Section 1
THE CALL TO ARMS
As the war began and states took sides, the North and the South drew up plans and hoped for an early victory.

Section 2
EARLY YEARS OF THE WAR
The early years of the war were indecisive, as neither side seemed able to defeat the other.

Section 3
THE EMANCIPATION PROCLAMATION
President Lincoln's decision to issue the Emancipation Proclamation opened the way for African Americans to join the Union army.

Section 4
THE CIVIL WAR AND AMERICAN LIFE
The war caused divisions in both North and South while changing the lives of civilians and soldiers alike.

Section 5
DECISIVE BATTLES
Union victories at Gettysburg and Vicksburg in 1863 forced the South's surrender in April 1865.

⤴ Reading Skill
Understand Sequence In this chapter, you will learn to relate the chronological order of events and determine their relationships to one another.

509

History Background

Battle Hymn of the Republic The United States did not have an official national anthem until 1931, when Congress proclaimed "The Star-Spangled Banner" the national song. Before that time, a rousing hymn with lyrics by Julia Ward Howe was often sung at state events.

Howe was a New York writer who published an abolitionist newspaper with her husband. After visiting Union soldiers in a hospital, she decided to write new lyrics to the popular melody "John Brown's Body." The editor of the *Atlantic Monthly*, James Field, gave the lyrics the title "Battle Hymn of the Republic" and printed them in the February 1862 issue of the magazine. The song soon became the Union's battle cry.

Prepare to Read

Use the following for reading skill support.

All in One Teaching Resources, Unit 5, Chapter Prereading Guide, p. 4; History Reading Skill, p. 45

History Reading Skill *Online*
Web code: mve-3000

Differentiated Instruction

The following Teacher Edition strategies are suitable for students of varying abilities.

L3 Advanced Readers, pp. 512, 522, 524, 530, 536 AR

L1 English Language Learners, pp. 511, 516, 518, 526, 528, 534 ELL

L3 Gifted and Talented, pp. 520, 522, 524, 530, 536 GT

L1 Less Proficient Readers, pp. 511, 514, 516, 518, 526, 528, 534 LPR

L1 Special Needs, pp. 511, 514, 518, 526, 528, 534 SN

Chapter Resources

Teaching Resources, Unit 5
Chapter Prereading Guide, p. 4
Word Knowledge Rating Form, p. 46
History Reading Skill, p. 45
Skills for Life Worksheet, p. 58
Chapter Tests A/B (L1/L2), pp. 65, 68
Letter Home (English/Spanish), pp. 37, 38

Spanish Support
L1 Interactive Reading and Notetaking Study Guide, Spanish, Adapted Version
L1 Guided Reading Audio CD, Spanish

Media and Technology
L1 SE on Audio CD
L2 Social Studies Skill Tutor CD-ROM
ExamView Test Bank CD-ROM

Discovery SCHOOL

Quick View Video
View the chapter video for a quick preview of the main ideas.

Visual Preview

? **How did people, places, and things affect the outcome of the Civil War?**

Build Background Knowledge **L2**

Have students discuss the kinds of issues that would cause people to go to war. Lead a structured review of the causes of the American Revolution (see TE p.T24). Students can also review, from chapter 14, the events that eventually divided the nation before the Civil War. Ask: **Are these issues that would start a conflict? Why?** *(Yes, because these issues were key to how the North and South defined themselves and caused deep rifts that compromise could no longer disguise.)*

Instruction **L2**

- For background information on conducting a lesson for the Visual Preview, see TE, p. T20.

- Write the Chapter Essential Question on the board. Discuss the ways in which an individual can impact a situation. Ask if the students have ever met a person who changed their lives in some way. Then, have students choose a person they have read about—George Washington, for example. What effect did his leadership have on the new republic?

- Have students review the timeline. In 1862, Lincoln announced a plan of emancipation. Ask: **What does "emancipation" mean?** *(setting free)* **Who do you think it applied to?** *(enslaved African Americans)* **From the time of the secession of eleven southern states to Lee's surrender, how long did the war last?** *(four years)*

- Have students study the map key. Discuss what each symbol represents. On the map, have students note the section of the country where much of the fighting occurred. Ask: **Why is the place where combat occurs important?** *(because combat devastates a wide area)*

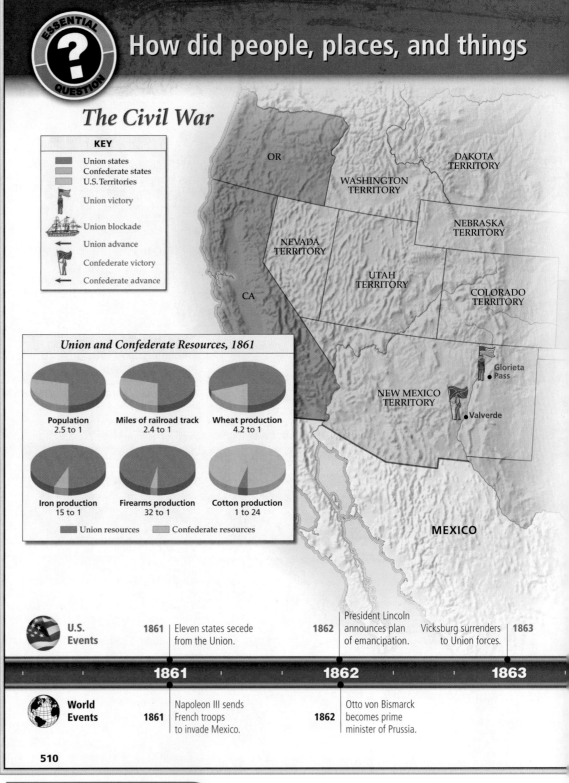

? **How did people, places, and things**

The Civil War

KEY

- Union states
- Confederate states
- U.S. Territories
- Union victory
- Union blockade
- Union advance
- Confederate victory
- Confederate advance

Union and Confederate Resources, 1861

Population 2.5 to 1

Miles of railroad track 2.4 to 1

Wheat production 4.2 to 1

Iron production 15 to 1

Firearms production 32 to 1

Cotton production 1 to 24

■ Union resources ■ Confederate resources

OR · WASHINGTON TERRITORY · DAKOTA TERRITORY · NEBRASKA TERRITORY · NEVADA TERRITORY · UTAH TERRITORY · COLORADO TERRITORY · CA · NEW MEXICO TERRITORY · Glorieta Pass · Valverde · MEXICO

U.S. Events 1861 | Eleven states secede from the Union.   1862 | President Lincoln announces plan of emancipation.   Vicksburg surrenders to Union forces. | 1863

1861   **1862**   **1863**

World Events 1861 | Napoleon III sends French troops to invade Mexico.   1862 | Otto von Bismarck becomes prime minister of Prussia.

510

History Background

Impact of Economics The Civil War was the violent end to decades of economic differences between the North and the South. The North had smaller farms, more natural resources, and many more large cities than the South. Slavery had been replaced by immigrant labor from Europe. Overland transportation was easier because two-thirds of the railroad tracks were in the North.

The South, on the other hand, had large plantations worked by slave labor. Because growing tobacco and cotton had always been profitable, Southerners saw no reason to industrialize. There were few large cities, and overland transportation was difficult.

In 1860, the South's economy was beginning to stall while the North's economy was booming.

affect the outcome of the Civil War?

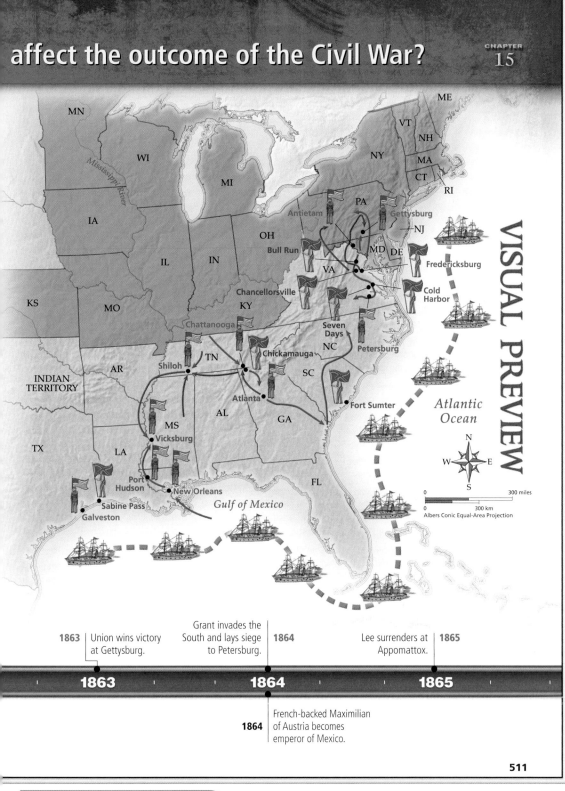

VISUAL PREVIEW

| 1863 | Union wins victory at Gettysburg. | Grant invades the South and lays siege to Petersburg. | 1864 | Lee surrenders at Appomattox. | 1865 |

1863   **1864**   **1865**

1864 | French-backed Maximilian of Austria becomes emperor of Mexico.

511

Instruction (continued)

- Review the resources inset. Instruct students to list the resources of both the Union and the Confederacy. Ask: **Why do you think railroad track was an important resource? Explain.** *(because tracks carried materials and supplies that supported both civilians and the army)* Using the Think-Write-Pair-Share strategy on TE p. T25, have students choose one resource and discuss how that resource was an advantage or disadvantage for either the Union or the Confederacy.

- Have students rewrite the Essential Question in simple terms in their notes. **What led to the North's victory in the Civil War?** You may also post this question in a prominent place in the classroom and leave it there while discussing the chapter. Tell students to use the section focus questions as a guide to answering the Essential Question as they read.

- Tell students that as they complete the Notetaking Study Guide for this chapter, they will be building the answer to the Essential Question.

Interactive Reading and Notetaking Study Guide, Chapter 15, (Adapted Version also available.)

Vocabulary Builder

Preview the Vocabulary Have students preview the vocabulary in the chapter and rate how well they know each word on the Word Knowledge Rating Form. Collect the sheets and explain that they will have a chance to go over the forms later.

All in One Teaching Resources, Unit 5, Word Knowledge Rating Form, p. 46

Monitor Progress Have students substitute the correct vocabulary term for the underlined word in the following sentences in order to demonstrate their understanding.

- The spy stayed out of sight so she wouldn't <u>meet</u> any enemy troops. *(encounter)*

- The addition of 500 soldiers <u>strengthened</u> the army. *(reinforced)*

Review and Preview

Students have learned how sectional differences led to the Civil War. They will now read how hopes for a quick war were dashed.

Miserable Conditions

❝Miserable as our condition was, that of the enlisted men was far worse. . . . There was no shelter for them. There was not enough food. They were thinly clad; many had no shoes, few had overcoats, and hundreds had only ragged trousers and shirt to cover their nakedness.❞

—Maj. Abner B. Small, Sixteenth Maine Volunteers, *Memoirs of a Prisoner of War*

◀ Union troops

Section Focus Question

Why did each side in the Civil War think the war would be won easily?

Before you begin the lesson for the day, write the Section Focus Question on the board. (*Lesson Focus: Both sides had distinct advantages and both had strategies for winning.*)

Prepare to Read

Build Background Knowledge L2

Make two columns on the board and title them "North" and "South." Then ask students to preview the section by reading the headings and looking at the images. Ask students to predict what they will learn about the North and the South. Write their answers in the appropriate column on the board. Use the Numbered Heads participation strategy (TE, p. T24) to elicit responses.

Set a Purpose L2

■ Read each statement in the Reading Readiness Guide aloud. Ask students to mark the statements True or False.

   All in One Teaching Resources, Unit 5, Reading Readiness Guide, p. 47

■ Have students discuss the statements in pairs or groups of four, then mark their worksheets again. Use the Numbered Heads strategy (TE, p. T24) to call on students to share their groups' perspectives. The students will return to these worksheets later.

The Call to Arms

Objectives

• Identify the states that supported the Union, the states that seceded, and the states whose loyalties were divided.

• Describe the advantages each side had in the war.

• Compare the different strategies used by the North and the South.

• Summarize the results of the First Battle of Bull Run.

• Describe the conditions soldiers in camp faced.

🔟 Reading Skill

Understand Sequence of Events The Civil War began as a result of a complex sequence of events. As that war proceeded in its early days, events continued at a furious pace. To form a full understanding of this phase of the war, pause regularly to summarize the sequence of events. Use your own words to recount the important events in the correct order.

Key Terms

| border state | martial law |
| neutral | blockade |

512 Chapter 15 The Civil War

Why It Matters As two American nations prepared for war, many Northerners and Southerners were confident that their side would win a quick victory. They were wrong. The Civil War would be a long, bloody, and costly conflict.

❓ Section Focus Question: Why did each side in the Civil War think the war would be won easily?

Taking Sides in the War

Two days after Fort Sumter's surrender, President Lincoln declared that a rebellion existed in the South. To put it down, he asked the nation's governors to raise 75,000 troops. Across the North, young men eagerly volunteered. Support was so widespread that the governors of Ohio, Indiana, and several other states begged to send more troops than the President had requested.

More States Secede Not all states were so enthusiastic, however. In Tennessee, the governor said that his state "will not furnish a single man" to fight against "our southern brothers." The governors of Kentucky and Missouri made similar replies to Lincoln's request. Maryland and Delaware did not respond at all.

The President's call for troops led more southern states to secede. On April 17, Virginia left the Union. In May, Arkansas, Tennessee, and North Carolina also joined the Confederacy. However, the western counties of Virginia, where there was little support for slavery, refused to secede. In 1863, these 50 counties were admitted to the Union as the state of West Virginia.

Differentiated Instruction

L3 Advanced Readers

Comparing Points of View Have students read the two accounts of events at Fort Sumter on the worksheet Fort Sumter: Two Views and answer the questions. Ask students to work with a partner to discuss which writer seems to be more aware of the future consequences of the battle. Sug-

gest that students ask themselves: Which writer is concerned mainly with the present and which is looking to the future?

All in One Teaching Resources, Unit 5, Fort Sumter: Two Views, p. 52

The Border States Loyalties remained divided in the border states—slave states that did not secede. Delaware had few enslaved people, and its support of the Union was strong. However, many people in Kentucky, Missouri, and Maryland favored the South. Kentucky and Missouri were important to controlling the Ohio and Mississippi rivers. And unless the Union could hold Maryland, Washington would be surrounded by the Confederacy.

At first, Kentucky declared itself neutral, or not favoring either side. Union generals wanted to occupy Kentucky, but Lincoln refused. He feared that such a move would push the state to secede. His strategy was wise. When Confederate forces invaded it in September 1861, Kentucky decided to support the North.

By contrast, the President acted forcefully to hold Missouri and Maryland. When Missouri's government sided with the South, Union supporters set up their own state government. Fighting broke out within the state. Finally, Lincoln sent troops, and the state stayed in the Union throughout the war.

In Maryland, southern sympathizers destroyed railroad and telegraph lines. So Lincoln placed eastern Maryland under martial law. This is a type of rule in which the military is in charge and citizens' rights are suspended. Maryland officials and others suspected of disloyalty were jailed without trials.

Understand Sequence of Events
Summarize the events as North and South geared up for full-scale conflict. Make sure to recount events in the correct sequence.

☑ **Checkpoint** How did the border states line up in the war?

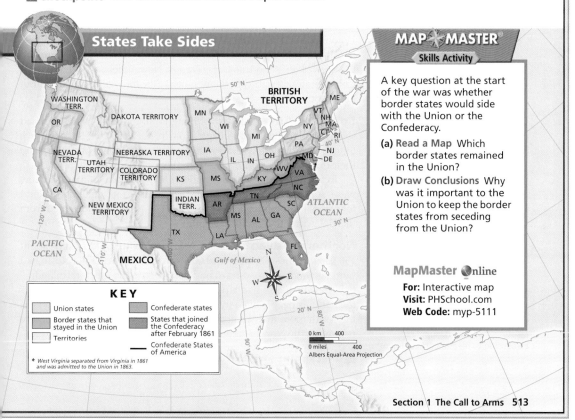

States Take Sides

MAP ✦ MASTER®
Skills Activity

A key question at the start of the war was whether border states would side with the Union or the Confederacy.

(a) Read a Map Which border states remained in the Union?

(b) Draw Conclusions Why was it important to the Union to keep the border states from seceding from the Union?

MapMaster ●nline
For: Interactive map
Visit: PHSchool.com
Web Code: myp-5111

KEY
- Union states
- Border states that stayed in the Union
- Territories
- Confederate states
- States that joined the Confederacy after February 1861
- Confederate States of America

* West Virginia separated from Virginia in 1861 and was admitted to the Union in 1863.

0 km 400
0 miles 400
Albers Equal-Area Projection

Section 1 The Call to Arms **513**

Vocabulary Builder

Use the information below to teach students this section's high-use words.

High-Use Word	Definition and Sample Sentence
distinct, p. 514	*adj.* clear or definite; different in quality Each Civil War general had his own **distinct** methods of fighting.
resource, p. 514	*n.* supply of something to meet a particular need As the war dragged on, the South's war effort suffered from a lack of **resources.**

Teach

Taking Sides in the War
p. 512

Instruction L2

■ **Vocabulary Builder** Before teaching this section, preteach the High-Use Words **distinct** and **resource,** using the strategy on TE p. T21.

Key Terms Following the instructions on p. 7, have students create a See It–Remember It chart for the Key Terms in this chapter.

■ Read Taking Sides in the War with students, using the Choral Reading technique (TE, p. T22). Ask: **What was the immediate result of the surrender of Fort Sumter?** (*Lincoln asked the states to raise 75,000 troops to put down the rebellion in the South.*)

Independent Practice
Have students begin filling in the study guide for this section.

📖 **Interactive Reading and Notetaking Study Guide,** Chapter 15, Section 1 (Adapted Version also available.)

Monitor Progress

As students fill in the Notetaking Study Guide, circulate to make sure they understand how the states took sides. Provide assistance as needed.

Answers

🔵 **Reading Skill** Possible answer: The Confederates took Fort Sumter, Lincoln declared them in rebellion and ordered an army raised. Several states debated whether to support the Union or the Confederacy. Confederate forces invaded Kentucky, which then rallied to the Union. Lincoln used force to keep Missouri and Maryland in the Union.

☑ **Checkpoint** They were all on the Union side.

MAP ✦ MASTER Skills Activity **(a)** Delaware, Maryland, West Virginia, Missouri, and Kentucky **(b)** Their geographical locations were important to the Union.

Chapter 15 **513**

North Against South

p. 514

Instruction `L2`

- Have students read North Against South. Remind students to look for the sequence of events.

- Have students create a table listing the southern military advantages and the North's advantages. (*Southern advantages: fighting on their own territory; could count on local people for help; had the most experienced military officers. Northern advantages: more factories, railroad track, and farmland; larger population; more resources.*)

- Ask: **Why would the greater number of factories and factory workers be an advantage to the North?** (*Possible answer: More goods and war materials could be produced.*) Ask: **What disadvantages might the North have had in invading the South?** (*Possible answer: The North had to move troops, materials, and other supplies over long distances and unfamiliar geography.*)

Independent Practice

Have students continue filling in the study guide for this section.

> **Interactive Reading and Notetaking Study Guide,** Chapter 15, Section 1 (Adapted Version also available.)

Monitor Progress

As students fill in the Notetaking Study Guide, circulate to make sure that they understand the advantages of each side. If students do not seem to have a good understanding, have them reread the section. Provide assistance as needed.

Answers

Reading Charts (a) Factory production **(b)** The North was able to field, feed, and equip larger armies because it had a larger population, more factories, and more railroads to move troops and supplies. **(c)** the North—because of its ability to equip a larger army and provide railroad transportation

✓Checkpoint The South had more experienced military officers and would be fighting on its own land among its own people. The North had more factories, farmland, railroad tracks, and a larger population, so it could better feed and equip its army.

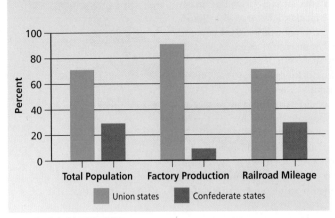

Comparing Resources, 1861

Percent (y-axis: 0, 20, 40, 60, 80, 100)

Total Population | Factory Production | Railroad Mileage

■ Union states ■ Confederate states

Source: *The Times Atlas of World History*

Reading Charts
Skills Activity

The Union had an advantage over the Confederacy in a number of resources.

(a) Read a Bar Graph In which of the three comparisons is the Union's advantage the greatest?

(b) Draw Conclusions For each of these three resources, how would you expect the Union to benefit from its advantage?

(c) Make Predictions Based on the information in these graphs, which side would you expect to win the war? Explain.

North Against South

As the armies prepared, people on both sides were confident. A Union soldier declared that he was "willing . . . to lay down all my joys in this life to help maintain this government." Southerners compared themselves to Americans of 1776. A New Orleans poet wrote of Confederates: "Yes, call them rebels! 'tis the name/Their patriot fathers bore."

Vocabulary Builder
distinct (dihs TIHNKT) *adj.* clear or definite; different in quality

Southern Advantages Although outnumbered, the South had some <u>distinct</u> military advantages. To win, northern armies would have to invade and conquer the South. Confederates would be fighting on their own territory, with help from the local people.

In addition, most of the nation's experienced military officers were southerners. The Confederacy's three top generals—Albert Johnston, Joseph Johnston, and Robert E. Lee—all had resigned from the U.S. Army to fight for the South.

Northern Advantages In 1861, the United States had about 130,000 factories. Of those, 110,000 were in the North. The North had twice as much railroad track and almost twice as much farmland.

Vocabulary Builder
resource (REE sors) *n.* supply of something to meet a particular need

The North also had a population advantage. Some two thirds of the nation's people lived in states that remained in the Union, and in the South more than a third of the people were enslaved. With more <u>resources</u>, the North was able to field, feed, and equip larger armies.

✓Checkpoint What were each side's advantages?

Differentiated Instruction

L1 Less Proficient Readers   **L1 Special Needs**

Gaining Comprehension Suggest to students that they use a ruler to help them keep their place as they read, line by line, down a page. Have students mark unfamiliar words or phrases (such as *resigned* on this page) with a sticky note, or jot down questions that occur as they read. Periodically provide assistance to the students to clarify these issues.

The Two Sides Plan Strategies

Union leaders hoped to win a quick victory. To isolate the Confederacy, Lincoln had the navy blockade southern seaports. A **blockade** is a military action to prevent traffic from coming into an area or leaving it. Lincoln hoped to cut off the South's supply of manufactured goods and block overseas sales of cotton.

An important part of northern strategy was to gain control of the Mississippi River, the South's major transportation link. This would split the South in two. The Union also planned to invade Virginia and seize Richmond, the Confederate capital. It was just 100 miles from Washington, D.C.

The South's strategy was simpler. The Confederates did not need to invade the North. They had only to defend their land until northerners got tired of fighting. The Confederates sought aid from Britain and other European nations. They hoped that Britain's need of cotton for its textile mills would force the British to support the South.

✓ **Checkpoint** How did strategies on the two sides differ?

Americans Against Americans

On both sides, men rushed to be part of the fight. "I had never dreamed that New England ... could be fired with so warlike a spirit," wrote Mary Ashton Livermore in Boston. In South Carolina, Mary Chesnut said that men rushed to enlist in the army for "fear the war will be over before they get a sight of the fun."

This war between Americans broke families apart, setting brother against brother, father against son. Kentucky Senator John Crittenden had two sons in the war fighting on different sides. Four brothers of Mary Lincoln, the President's wife, fought for the Confederacy.

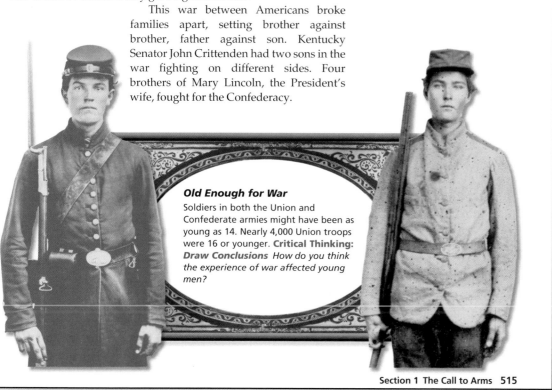

Old Enough for War
Soldiers in both the Union and Confederate armies might have been as young as 14. Nearly 4,000 Union troops were 16 or younger. **Critical Thinking: Draw Conclusions** How do you think the experience of war affected young men?

History Background

A Moment's Hesitation Uniforms were a cause of much confusion during the Battle of Bull Run. For two hours, the Union soldiers had steadily pushed the Confederates back toward and up the slopes of Henry House Hill (named for the home of Judith Henry, a bedridden widow). Two Union artillery batteries were blasting gaps in the Confederate lines when a blue-clad regiment emerged from the woods. Thinking the regiment was the infantry support it had requested, Union soldiers stopped firing. The regiment, which turned out to be Confederate, leveled muskets, fired, and wiped out the Union guns. From that point on in the battle, the tide shifted to the Confederates.

The Two Sides Plan Strategies

Americans Against Americans

p. 515

Instruction
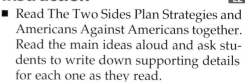

- Read The Two Sides Plan Strategies and Americans Against Americans together. Read the main ideas aloud and ask students to write down supporting details for each one as they read.

- Discuss the strategy plan of each side. Ask: **Why was it important to the North to take Richmond?** (*It was the Confederate capital so taking it could cripple the South's government. It was also very close to Washington, D.C., the nation's capital.*)

- Review the term "civil war." Explain that the word *civil* refers to citizens and their relations to one another and a state or government. Ask: **Why was this war called a civil war?** (*It was a war in which citizens fought against one another.*)

Independent Practice

Have students continue filling in the study guide for this section.

📖 **Interactive Reading and Notetaking Study Guide,** Chapter 15, Section 1 (Adapted Version also available.)

Monitor Progress

As students fill in the Notetaking Study Guide, circulate to make sure individuals understand the strategies of each side and how the war divided the nation's citizens. Provide assistance as needed.

Answers

✓**Checkpoint** The North hoped to blockade southern seaports, to gain control of the Mississippi River to control transportation and cut the South in two, and to capture Richmond. The South's plan was simpler—southerners planned to defend their territory until the northerners tired of fighting.

Draw Conclusions Possible answer: Some may have grown up quickly and acquired new skills; many may have become scared, tired, and disillusioned.

First Battle of Bull Run
A Soldier's Life

pp. 516–517

Instruction ▪ L2

- Read First Battle of Bull Run and A Soldier's Life with students. Remind them to look for sequence of events.

- Ask: **Why did citizens ride out to see the armies meet at Manassas?** (*They expected a quick Union victory.*) **How did the inexperience of both armies show during the battle?** (*The northerners lost their initial advantage and had to flee; the southerners couldn't follow up and chase them because they were too tired.*)

- Show students the History Interactive transparency Bull Run and discuss the effect this battle had on both sides.

Color Transparencies, Bull Run

- Discuss the conditions of camps and prisons. Ask: **Why were the poor conditions in prisons and camps a disadvantage to both sides?** (*Soldiers were too weak with illness and hunger to fight; morale would suffer.*)

Independent Practice

Have students complete the study guide for this section.

📖 **Interactive Reading and Notetaking Study Guide,** Chapter 15, Section 1 (Adapted Version also available.)

Monitor Progress

- As students complete the Notetaking Study Guide, circulate to make sure they understand the importance of Bull Run and the harsh conditions soldiers faced. Provide assistance as needed.

- Tell students to fill in the last column of the Reading Readiness Guide. Probe for what they learned that confirms or invalidates each statement.

All in One **Teaching Resources, Unit 5,** Reading Readiness Guide, p. 47

Answers

Draw Conclusions Both sides were aware of their advantages and felt their cause was right. Neither side appreciated the advantages of the other sufficiently, nor did they accurately estimate their own weaknesses.

Before the First Battle of Bull Run, both sides expected an easy victory. But they were wrong. Here, Union soldiers have panicked and are fleeing the Bull Run battlefield. Bull Run was an early sign that the war would be long and costly. **Critical Thinking: Draw Conclusions** *What reasons did each side have to think it would win an early victory? Why were both sides' expectations unreasonable?*

History *Interactive*
Explore the Lessons of a Battle
Visit: PHSchool.com
Web Code: myp-5177

The soldiers came from many backgrounds. Nearly half of the North's troops were farmers. One fourth were immigrants.

Three fourths of the South's 1 million white males between ages 18 and 45 served in the army. Two thirds of the 3.5 million northern males of the same age fought for the Union. Some soldiers were as young as 14.

✓ **Checkpoint** Who were the soldiers in this war?

First Battle of Bull Run

Union General Irvin McDowell wanted time to turn his soldiers into an effective fighting force. But by July 1861, northern newspapers were demanding the capture of Richmond and a quick end to the war.

McDowell's 30,000 men left Washington and marched southwest into Virginia. About the same number of Confederates waited at Manassas, a railroad center about 25 miles away. Hundreds of people rode out from Washington to see the battle, expecting an easy Union victory.

The armies clashed along Bull Run, a river just north of Manassas, on July 21. At first, the Union army pushed forward. But a southern commander rallied his men to hold firm. "Look, there is Jackson with his Virginians, standing like a stone wall," he shouted. From then on, the general, Thomas Jackson, was known as "Stonewall" Jackson.

Slowly the battle turned in favor of the Confederates. The poorly trained Union troops began to panic. Soldiers and sightseers fled back to Washington. The Confederates were too exhausted to pursue them.

✓ **Checkpoint** What was the result of the First Battle of Bull Run?

✓**Checkpoint** They were ordinary men from many backgrounds; many were farmers and immigrants.

✓**Checkpoint** The battle was inconclusive and the war continued.

Differentiated Instruction

L1 English Language Learners

L1 Less Proficient Readers

Define Have students make a list of Key Terms and High-Use Words. Then have students create flashcards with a word on one side and its definition on the other. Pair students with partners to use the flashcards to study the words.

A Soldier's Life

Most soldiers spent three fourths of their time in camp, not fighting. Training took up to 10 hours a day. When not training, soldiers stood guard, wrote home, and gathered firewood. A meal might be simply a dry, cracker-like product called hardtack.

Harsh Conditions Camp conditions were often miserable, especially when wet weather created muddy roads and fields. The lack of clean water was a major health threat. Outbreaks of smallpox, typhoid fever, and other diseases swept through the ranks. It was not unusual for half the men in a regiment to be too sick to fight.

Prisoners of War Both sides built prison camps for captured soldiers. Overcrowded prison camps became deathtraps. Nearly 10 percent of soldiers who died in the war perished in prison camps.

The camps at Elmira, New York, and Andersonville, Georgia, were the worst. Elmira camp, built to hold 5,000 Confederate prisoners, held 10,000. The camp cut rations to bread and water, forcing prisoners to eat rats to survive. Thousands died. At Andersonville, nearly 35,000 Union soldiers lived in a fenced, open field intended to hold 10,000 men. As many as 100 prisoners died each day, usually from starvation or exposure.

✓ **Checkpoint** What conditions did soldiers have to endure?

⭐ **Looking Back and Ahead** The North's hopes for an early victory had been dashed. The war would be long and brutal. In the next section, you will read more about the early years of the war.

Hardtack

Section 1 | Check Your Progress

> **Progress Monitoring Online**
> **For:** Self-test with instant help
> **Visit:** PHSchool.com
> **Web Code:** mya-5111

Comprehension and Critical Thinking

1. **(a) Recall** How did President Lincoln respond to the surrender of Fort Sumter?
(b) Apply Information What caused three border states to remain in the Union?

2. **(a) List** What were three advantages held by the South? What were three advantages held by the North?
(b) Analyze Cause and Effect How did the First Battle of Bull Run shatter the belief that the Civil War would be a quick Union victory?

Reading Skill

3. **Understand Sequence of Events** Choose a state that wavered about supporting the North or the South. Summarize the sequence of events that led this state to a final decision.

Key Terms

Complete each of the following sentences so that the second part explains the first and shows your understanding of the key term.

4. Union leaders planned a blockade; _____.

5. Lincoln placed Maryland under martial law; _____.

Writing

6. Create an outline that covers the information presented in this section, copying the form below. A few entries have been filled in.

I. Taking sides in the war (first important topic)
  A. More states secede (first issue for that topic)
    1. A number of border states refused to send troops to support the Union (first point)
    2. _____ (second point)
  B.
    1.
    2.
II.

Assess and Reteach

Assess Progress   L2

Have students complete Check Your Progress. Administer the Section Quiz.

All in One Teaching Resources, Unit 5, Section Quiz, p. 60

To further assess student understanding, use the Progress Monitoring Transparency.

Progress Monitoring Transparencies, Chapter 15, Section 1

Reteach   L1

If students need more instruction, have them read this section in the Interactive Reading and Notetaking Study Guide.

📖 **Interactive Reading and Notetaking Study Guide,** Chapter 15, Section 1 (Adapted Version also available.)

Extend   L3

To help students expand their understanding of the significance of the Battle of Bull Run, have them complete the online History Interactive activity. Provide students with the Web Code below.

> **Extend Online**
> **For:** Help with the History Interactive activity
> **Visit:** PHSchool.com
> **Web Code:** myp-5117

Progress Monitoring Online

Students may check their comprehension of this section by completing the Progress Monitoring Online graphic organizer and self-quiz.

Section 1 Check Your Progress

1. **(a)** He ordered 75,000 troops to put down the rebellion.
(b) Kentucky joined when it was invaded by Confederate troops; troops were sent to Missouri to maintain order; Maryland was put under martial law.

2. **(a)** The South was defending its own territory; it could count on help from local people; it had experienced military leaders. The North had more factories, railroad tracks, farmland, and people.
(b) The battle was not as easy as expected, and both sides showed inexperience.

3. Possible answer: Kentucky was neutral and would not take sides. After Confederate forces invaded Kentucky, it decided to support the North.

4. Possible answer: They would use military force to keep traffic from coming into or leaving southern seaports.

5. Possible answer: The military ran it and citizens' rights were suspended.

6. Outlines may vary, but students should generally use the headings as guides for the main topics and details.

Answer

✓ **Checkpoint** Camps lacked clean water, and disease was widespread. Prisons were overcrowded, and there was not enough food for prisoners.

Review and Preview

Students have learned that the Battle of Bull Run showed both sides that the war would not be easy to win. Now students will read how each side tried to rethink its strategy in order to defeat its enemy.

Section Focus Question

How did each side in the war try to gain an advantage over the other?

Before you begin the lesson for the day, write the Section Focus Question on the board. (*Lesson focus: McClellan tried to make his army bigger and stronger; Lee tried to invade the North to win support abroad and change northerners' public opinion about the war; Grant pushed to gain control over Confederate territory.*)

Prepare to Read

Build Background Knowledge **L2**

Have students write a description of the differences between an offensive and defensive strategy. Suggest that they think about strategies in sports such as football, basketball, or tennis. Use the Think-Write-Pair-Share (TE, p. T25) strategy to structure this activity.

Set a Purpose **L2**

- Form students into pairs or groups of four. Distribute the Reading Readiness Guide. Ask students to fill in the first two columns of the chart.

  All in One Teaching Resources, Unit 5, Reading Readiness Guide, p. 48

- Use the Numbered Heads strategy (TE, p. T24) to call on students to share one piece of information they want to know. The students will return to these worksheets later.

Answer

☑Checkpoint new rifles and cannons that were more accurate and had greater range than earlier ones; ironclad ships

◀ Confederate troops

Battlefield Report

"Our men were vomiting with excessive fatigue, over-exhaustion, and sunstroke; our tongues were parched and cracked for water, and our faces blackened with powder and smoke, and our dead and wounded were piled indiscriminately in the trenches."

—Confederate soldier, describing a battle in Georgia

Early Years of the War

Objectives

- Explain how new weapons made fighting the war more dangerous.
- Describe the course of the war in the East in 1862.
- Describe the early days of the war in the West and at sea.

🔁 Reading Skill

Distinguish Events in Sequence As you read this section, it is important to keep events in sequence. Ask yourself: Which event happened first? Next? Last? You might number events to help you organize their sequence. This will help you to understand the unfolding drama of the Civil War.

Key Terms and People

ironclad casualty
George McClellan Ulysses S. Grant

Why It Matters The Union's crushing defeat at Bull Run made northerners realize that a long and difficult struggle lay ahead. Both the North and South tried to find the strategies and the leaders that would ensure victory and preserve their way of life.

❓ Section Focus Question: How did each side in the war try to gain an advantage over the other?

New Technology in the War

New weapons made the Civil War more deadly than any previous war. Traditionally, generals had relied on an all-out charge of troops to overwhelm the enemy. But new rifles and cannons were far more accurate and had a greater range than the old muskets and artillery. They could also be loaded much faster. As a result, the attacking army could be bombarded long before it arrived at the defenders' position.

Unfortunately, Civil War generals were slow to recognize the problem and change tactics. Thousands of soldiers on both sides were slaughtered by following orders to cross open fields against these deadly new weapons.

Both sides also made use of ironclads. These were warships covered with protective iron plates. Cannon fire bounced harmlessly off this armor. The most famous naval battle of the war occurred when two ironclads, the Union's *Monitor* and the Confederacy's *Merrimack*, fought to a draw in March 1862. The use of ironclads marked the end of thousands of years of wooden warships. The Confederates used ironclads against the Union's naval blockade. Ironclad Union gunboats played an important role in the North's efforts to gain control of the Mississippi River.

☑Checkpoint What new technologies were used in the Civil War?

518 Chapter 15 The Civil War

Differentiated Instruction

L1 English Language Learners **L1 Less Proficient Readers** **L1 Special Needs**

Gaining Comprehension Have students read the text of Early Years of the War as they listen to the Student Edition on audio CD. Monitor student answers to the Checkpoint question to make sure they understand. Students can be provided with a copy of the CD to work independently at home or in the school Resource Center.

🔘 **SE on Audio CD,** Chapter 15, Section 2

The War in the East

After the Union's defeat at Bull Run, Lincoln removed McDowell and put General George McClellan in command. The general was a good organizer, but he was very cautious. For seven months, he trained his army but did not attack. "If General McClellan does not want to use the army," a frustrated Lincoln complained, "I would like to borrow it for a time."

In March 1862, McClellan was finally ready. He moved some 100,000 soldiers by boat along Chesapeake Bay to a peninsula southeast of Richmond. As McClellan advanced toward the Confederate capital, he discovered that his force was far <u>superior</u> to the 15,000 enemy soldiers blocking the way. However, McClellan still did not have as many soldiers as he wanted because Lincoln had ordered 37,000 soldiers to stay behind to guard Washington, D.C. The general stopped his advance and asked for more troops.

McClellan waited nearly a month before moving again. This delay gave the Confederates time to <u>reinforce</u> their small army of defenders. On May 31, 1862, the Confederates stopped McClellan's advance near Richmond. In late June, McClellan had to retreat.

With Richmond no longer threatened, Lee decided to invade the North. He hoped that a victory on Union soil would help win support for the South in Europe and turn northern public opinion against the war. In early September, he slipped his army into western Maryland.

Now McClellan had a stroke of luck. A Union officer found a paper showing Lee's battle plan. McClellan thus learned that the Confederate army had divided into two parts.

Vocabulary Builder
superior (sah PIR ee ahr) *adj.* of greater importance or value; above average

Vocabulary Builder
reinforce (ree ihn FORS) *v.* to make stronger; to make more effective

DISCOVERY SCHOOL

Explore More Video
To learn more about this historic battle, view the video.

● INFOGRAPHIC
Battle of Two Ironclads

The Civil War introduced ironclad warships. Here, an artist shows the battle between the Confederacy's *Merrimack* (left) and the Union's *Monitor* (right) off Hampton Roads, Virginia, in 1862. **Critical Thinking: Draw Conclusions** *How would you expect an ironclad ship to fare in a battle against an older warship that lacked armor? Explain.*

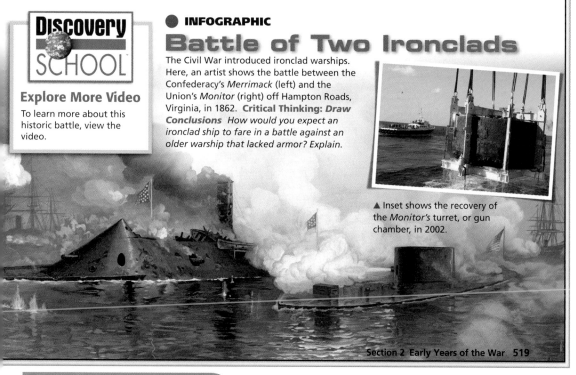

▲ Inset shows the recovery of the *Monitor's* turret, or gun chamber, in 2002.

Vocabulary Builder

Use the information below to teach students this section's high-use words.

High-Use Word	Definition and Sample Sentence
superior, p. 519	*adj.* of greater importance or value; above average In some battles, a smaller force proved **superior** to a larger one.
reinforce, p. 519	*v.* to make stronger; to make more effective Expecting an enemy attack, soldiers tried to **reinforce** their defenses.

Teach

New Technology in the War

The War in the East

pp. 518–519

Instruction L2

■ **Vocabulary Builder** Before teaching this lesson, preteach the High-Use Words **superior** and **reinforce,** using the strategy on TE p. T21.

Key Terms Have students continue to fill in the See It–Remember It chart for the Key Terms in this chapter.

■ Read New Technology in the War and The War in the East with students, using the Oral Cloze technique (TE, p. T22).

■ Discuss the new technology and its effect on strategy. Ask: **How did the new rifles and cannons force military leaders to change their tactics?** (*They could no longer order soldiers to charge against these weapons because the results were deadly.*)

■ Ask: **Why did Lee want to invade the North?** (*After McClellan failed to take Richmond, Lee thought a victory on Union soil would gain European support for the South and turn northern public opinion against the war.*) Have students complete the biography worksheet General Robert E. Lee and ask them to explain why President Lincoln had hoped that Lee would lead the federal army.

All in One Teaching Resources, Unit 5, General Robert E. Lee, p. 53

Independent Practice
Have students begin filling in the study guide for this section.

Monitor Progress

As students fill in the Notetaking Study Guide, circulate to make sure they understand the results of the battles.

🌐 Explore More Video

Discovery School Video
The *Monitor* and the *Merrimack* Show the video to help students understand this battle of the ironclads.

Answer
Draw Conclusions It would be able to do a lot of damage to the older ship without being badly damaged itself.

The War in the West

p. 520

Instruction

L2

- Ask students to read The War in the West. Remind them to look for the sequence of events.

- Ask: **How did Grant change the direction of the Union army?** (*His military campaigns in the West were successful and enabled the North to gain important advantages.*) **Why was Grant more effective than McClellan?** (*He was willing to take chances.*)

- Discuss the Battle of Shiloh and its consequences. Ask: **Why was control of the railroad junction at Corinth and the eventual control of the Mississippi River important to the Union army?** (*These were major transportation routes for moving troops and supplies.*)

Independent Practice

Have students complete the study guide for this section.

Interactive Reading and Notetaking Study Guide, Chapter 15, Section 2 (Adapted Version also available.)

Monitor Progress

- As students complete the Notetaking Study Guide, circulate to make sure they understand the events of the early years of the war. Provide assistance as needed.

- Tell students to fill in the last column of the Reading Readiness Guide. Ask them to evaluate whether what they learned was what they had expected to learn.

All in One Teaching Resources, Unit 5, Reading Readiness Guide, p. 48

Assess and Reteach

Assess Progress

L2

Have students complete Check Your Progress. Administer the Section Quiz.

All in One Teaching Resources, Unit 5, Section Quiz, p. 61

To further assess student understanding, use the Progress Monitoring Transparency.

Progress Monitoring Transparencies, Chapter 15, Section 2

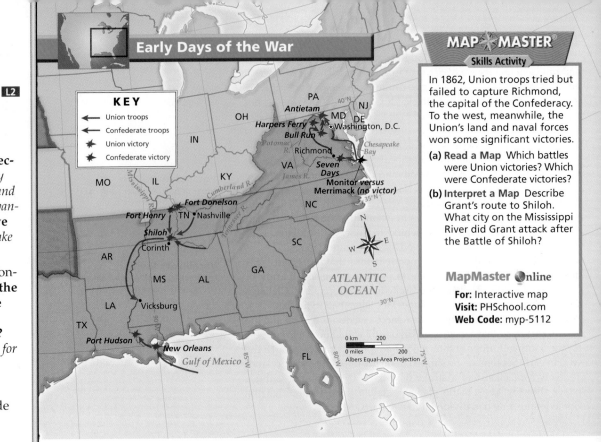

MAP MASTER
Skills Activity

Early Days of the War

KEY
- Union troops
- Confederate troops
- ★ Union victory
- ★ Confederate victory

In 1862, Union troops tried but failed to capture Richmond, the capital of the Confederacy. To the west, meanwhile, the Union's land and naval forces won some significant victories.

(a) Read a Map Which battles were Union victories? Which were Confederate victories?

(b) Interpret a Map Describe Grant's route to Shiloh. What city on the Mississippi River did Grant attack after the Battle of Shiloh?

MapMaster Online

For: Interactive map
Visit: PHSchool.com
Web Code: myp-5112

McClellan's troops attacked the larger part of Lee's army at Antietam Creek, near Sharpsburg, Maryland, on September 17, 1862. This was the bloodiest day of the Civil War. The Union army attacked again and again. It suffered about 12,000 casualties—the military term for persons killed, wounded, or missing in action. Lee lost nearly 14,000 men—almost one third of his army. He was forced to pull his battered army back into Virginia. To Lincoln's dismay, McClellan did not press his advantage by pursuing Lee.

Neither side won a clear victory at the Battle of Antietam. But because Lee had ordered a retreat, the North claimed victory.

✓Checkpoint How did McClellan's caution hurt the Union?

The War in the West

As McClellan moved cautiously, Union armies in the West went on the attack. General Ulysses S. Grant led the most successful of these armies. McClellan and Grant were very different. McClellan wore carefully fitted uniforms. Grant, once a poor store clerk, wore rumpled clothes. McClellan was cautious. Grant took chances.

Answers

MAP MASTER Skills Activity **(a)** Check to see that students find these places correctly. **(b)** Grant traveled from Fort Henry to Fort Donelson and then to Shiloh; Vicksburg

✓Checkpoint It gave the Confederates time to reinforce their troops at Richmond and force the Union army to retreat. It prevented the Union army from further hurting Lee's troops at Sharpsburg.

Differentiated Instruction

L3 Gifted and Talented

Research Have students research the kinds of equipment that Union and Confederate soldiers typically carried. Then, have students either draw a picture of a representative from each side and label the items they carried or write a description.

Union forces made major advances in western land and naval battles in 1862, seizing control of most of the Mississippi River. In February 1862, Grant moved his army south from Kentucky. First, he captured Fort Henry on the Tennessee River. Then, he captured Fort Donelson on the Cumberland River.

Two water routes into the western Confederacy were now wide open. Grant's army continued south along the Tennessee River toward Corinth, Mississippi, an important railroad center.

Before Grant could advance on Corinth, Confederate General Albert Sidney Johnston attacked. On April 6, 1862, he surprised Grant's troops at the Battle of Shiloh. (For more on this battle, see the Geography and History feature in this chapter.)

The Battle of Shiloh was costly yet important for both sides. The South suffered nearly 11,000 casualties and the North more than 13,000. However, the Union forced the Confederate army to withdraw from the railroad center. Union forces also gained control of western Tennessee and part of the Mississippi River.

Two weeks after the Battle of Shiloh, a Union fleet commanded by David Farragut entered the Mississippi River from the Gulf of Mexico. On April 26, Farragut captured New Orleans, Louisiana. By summer, nearly the entire river was in Union hands.

Distinguish Events in Sequence
What was the sequence of battles in the West? When did these occur?

✓**Checkpoint** What was the result of the Battle of Shiloh?

⭐ **Looking Back and Ahead** Northern and southern generals both tried to carry the war into enemy territory. At first, neither side gained a decisive advantage. In the next section, you will read how the Emancipation Proclamation changed the nature of the war.

Section 2 | Check Your Progress

Progress Monitoring Online
For: Self-test with instant help
Visit: PHSchool.com
Web Code: mya-5112

Comprehension and Critical Thinking

1. (a) Describe Explain how new weapons made the Civil War more deadly than previous American wars.
(b) Evaluate Information How did harsh conditions and new technology result in a high number of casualties?

2. (a) Summarize Why was General McClellan considered to be an ineffective leader?
(b) Organize Information Make a chart that shows the place, casualties, leaders, outcome, and importance of the battles at Shiloh and Antietam Creek.

Reading Skill

3. Distinguish Events in Sequence During the Battle of Shiloh, which came first: Grant captured Fort Henry, Johnston attacked, Grant won a stunning victory? Identify the signal clues that you used.

Key Terms

Read each sentence. If the sentence is true, write YES. If the sentence is not true, write NO and explain why.
4. Both the Union and the Confederacy suffered many casualties.
5. Ironclads were of little importance in the war at sea.

Writing

6. Use library or Internet resources to find more information about one of the topics covered in this section. Suggestions for topics include the ironclad warships, the Battle of Shiloh, or the Battle of Antietam. Then, write a short introduction to a research paper that would present information about the topic.

If students need more instruction, have them read this section in the Interactive Reading and Notetaking Study Guide.

📖 **Interactive Reading and Notetaking Study Guide,** Chapter 15, Section 2 (Adapted Version also available.)

Extend L3

Have students do further Internet research on Ulysses S. Grant. Then ask them to create an illustrative biography using what they learned about his life. For example, the biography could be in the form of a timeline with illustrations or a picture book. Then have students share their work with the class. Provide students with the Web Code to help start the activity.

Extend Online
For: Help with the History Interactive activity
Visit: PHSchool.com
Web Code: mye-0269

Progress Monitoring Online

Students may check their comprehension of this section by completing the Progress Monitoring Online graphic organizer and self-quiz.

Answers

Reading Skill In February 1862, Grant captured Fort Henry and then Fort Donelson. In April 1862, troops met at the Battle of Shiloh. Late in April, Union forces captured New Orleans.

✓**Checkpoint** The South lost control of western Tennessee, a railroad junction, and part of the Mississippi River.

Section 2 Check Your Progress

1. (a) harsh, boring, miserable
(b) New guns killed more soldiers, and malnutrition and exposure killed many prisoners.

2. (a) He was overly cautious and failed to take advantage of opportunities.
(b) Chart should include the following information: Shiloh—Corinth, Tennessee; 11,000 Confederates killed; 13,000 Union soldiers killed; Grant led Union and Johnston led Confederates; Confederates had to withdraw; the Union gained control of western Tennessee, a railroad junction, and part of the Mississippi River. Antietam Creek—Sharpsburg, Maryland; 14,000 Confederates killed; 12,000 Union soldiers killed; McClellan led the Union troops and Lee led the Confederates; Lee was forced to retreat but McClellan did not pursue the Confederates, squandering an opportunity for a more decisive Union victory.

3. Grant captured Fort Henry. Signal clues include the word *first*.

4. Yes

5. No, they were important to the North to control the Mississippi River.

6. Paragraphs should include 2 or 3 major facts about the topic.

The Battle of Shiloh
p. 522

Build Background Knowledge `L2`

Have students recall what they learned about the Battle of Shiloh in Section 2. Ask: **Which side lost more troops?** (*the North*) **What did the North gain from the battle?** (*It won control over Corinth's railroad junction, western Tennessee, and part of the Mississippi River.*)

Instruction `L2`

- Have student volunteers read the introduction and captions aloud.

- Ask: **Why did Confederates call the Union's position the "Hornet's Nest"?** (*The Union soldiers fired intensely at the Confederates from their position along a sunken road.*)

- Ask: **Why were Confederate troops at a disadvantage as they approached the Union positions?** (*Union soldiers were crouched behind mounds of earth along a sunken road; the Confederates had no such protection as they marched against Union positions.*)

Monitor Progress

Have students share their answers to the Analyze Geography and History question on the Student Edition page. Correct any misunderstandings.

The Battle of Shiloh

In April 1862, the Confederacy seized an opportunity to attack Union forces in the West. Two Union armies were attempting to join each other in southwestern Tennessee. Confederate troops were camped close by in Corinth, Mississippi. The Confederates attacked near Pittsburgh Landing, Tennessee, on April 6, hoping to crush one Union force before the other could arrive.

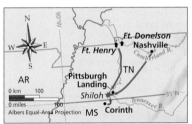

KEY
← Union troops
← Confederate troops

Confederate troops attacked Union forces at the Battle of Shiloh.

1 A Sunken Road

The initial Confederate attack caught Union troops by surprise. They retreated a mile before establishing a defensive position along a sunken road. Troops crouched behind the road bank and fought off a dozen Confederate charges.

522 Chapter 15 The Civil War

Differentiated Instruction

`L3` **Advanced Readers**	`L3` **Gifted and Talented**
Writing a Journal Entry Have students write a journal entry as if they were General Johnston during the Battle of Shiloh. Tell them to include information about the bat-	tle and how the general may have felt about it. Have students share their entries with the class. Ask: **What impact would this journal entry have on his troops?**

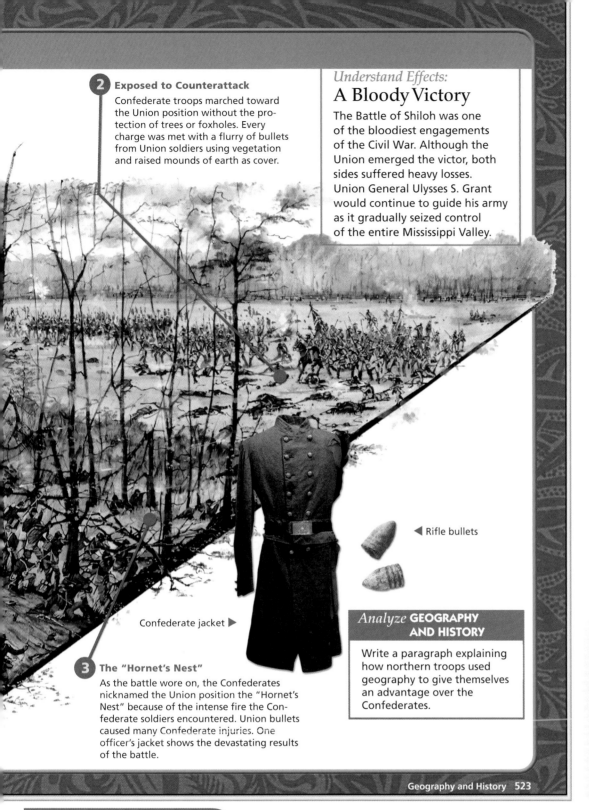

2 Exposed to Counterattack
Confederate troops marched toward the Union position without the protection of trees or foxholes. Every charge was met with a flurry of bullets from Union soldiers using vegetation and raised mounds of earth as cover.

Understand Effects:
A Bloody Victory
The Battle of Shiloh was one of the bloodiest engagements of the Civil War. Although the Union emerged the victor, both sides suffered heavy losses. Union General Ulysses S. Grant would continue to guide his army as it gradually seized control of the entire Mississippi Valley.

◀ Rifle bullets

Confederate jacket ▶

3 The "Hornet's Nest"
As the battle wore on, the Confederates nicknamed the Union position the "Hornet's Nest" because of the intense fire the Confederate soldiers encountered. Union bullets caused many Confederate injuries. One officer's jacket shows the devastating results of the battle.

Analyze **GEOGRAPHY AND HISTORY**

Write a paragraph explaining how northern troops used geography to give themselves an advantage over the Confederates.

History Background

Success and Failure General Don Carlos Buell's troops helped the Union defeat the Confederates at the Battle of Shiloh in the spring of 1862, but a fall campaign in Kentucky by Buell's troops was not as successful. At the Battle of Perryville, Buell failed to quickly pursue the Confederates as they retreated. His failure to decisively win the battle and his objection to strategic plans given to him by the Union government led to Buell's removal from command.

Writing Rubric Share the rubric with students before they begin.

Score 1 Essay is unorganized and missing facts.

Score 2 Essay has simple sentences and few facts.

Score 3 Essay has good organization and some details.

Score 4 Essay is clear, has many details, shows careful thought.

Answer

Analyze **GEOGRAPHY AND HISTORY**

They positioned themselves along a sunken road to fight off the Confederates. Answers will vary, but should highlight the natural cover used by the northern troops against Confederate rifle and cannon fire.

Section 3

Step-by-Step Instruction

Review and Preview

Students have read about the early fighting and heavy casualties in the Civil War. They will now read how President Lincoln's Emancipation Proclamation expanded the goals of the war to include the ending of slavery.

Section Focus Question

What were the causes and effects of the Emancipation Proclamation?

Before you begin the lesson for the day, write the Section Focus Question on the board. (*Lesson focus: Causes: Lincoln understood that slavery was important to the South's success in the war; abolitionists were calling for emancipation. Effects: It changed the war into a war for freedom, kept Britain from supporting the South's independence, united African Americans in support of the war.*)

Prepare to Read

Build Background Knowledge L2

Ask students to recall what they learned about slavery in Chapter 14. Draw a concept web on the board and write "Slavery" in the center circle. Use the Give One, Get One (TE, p. T25) participation strategy to expand the web. Suggest that students include the names of important politicians and their views, and the views of the North and the South in the web. Then have students preview the headings in the section and predict whether slavery would end under Lincoln.

Set a Purpose L2

■ Read each statement in the Reading Readiness Guide aloud. Ask students to mark the statements True or False.

  All in One Teaching Resources, Unit 5, Reading Readiness Guide, p. 49

■ Have students discuss the statements in pairs or groups of four, then mark their worksheets again. Use the Numbered Heads strategy (TE, p. T24) to call on students to share their group's perspectives. The students will return to these worksheets later.

SECTION **3**

Justice Has Awakened
❝After two hundred years of bondage and suffering a returning sense of justice has awakened the great body of American people to make amends for the unprovoked wrongs committed against us for over two hundred years.❞

—African American Tennesseans,
letter to the Federal Government, 1865

◀ Artist's representation of Lincoln greeting freed slaves.

The Emancipation Proclamation

Objectives
- Explain why Lincoln issued the Emancipation Proclamation.
- Identify the effects of the proclamation.
- Describe the contributions of African Americans to the Union.

Reading Skill

Explain How Events Are Related in Time President Lincoln and others made many choices in fighting the war. They made these choices in the context of the events at the time. When reading about history, it is important to see how events in a period are related in time. Do events influence the attitudes and decisions of people going forward in time? Do they change people's actions and freedoms?

Key Terms and People
emancipate
Horace Greeley

Why It Matters President Lincoln had been reluctant to abolish slavery. But he changed his mind. His Emancipation Proclamation would dramatically alter the nature of the war, the lives of African Americans, and the future of the United States.

❓ **Section Focus Question: What were the causes and effects of the Emancipation Proclamation?**

Emancipating the Enslaved

Many abolitionists rejoiced when the war began. They urged Lincoln to end slavery and thus punish the South for starting the war.

Lincoln Changes His Mind At first, the President resisted. He knew most northerners did not want to end slavery. "You . . . overestimate the number in the country who hold such views," he told one abolitionist. He feared that any action to emancipate, or free, enslaved African Americans might make the border states secede.

Lincoln said his goal was to restore the Union, even if that meant letting slavery continue. He stated this very clearly in a letter to abolitionist newspaper publisher Horace Greeley.

❝If I could save the Union without freeing *any* slave, I would do it, and if I could save it by freeing *all* the slaves, I would do it. . . . What I do about slavery . . . I do because I believe it helps to save the Union.❞

524 Chapter 15 The Civil War

Differentiated Instruction

L3 Advanced Readers   **L3 Gifted and Talented**

Predicting Have students work in pairs. Have each select a major event from this chapter and assume either that it had not occurred or that it had a different outcome. (For example, what if Lincoln had not issued the Emancipation Proclamation?) Have each pair give a brief newscast in which they speculate how subsequent events in American history might have been different.

Gradually, Lincoln began to change his mind. He realized how important slavery was to the South's war effort. He told his Cabinet that he intended to issue an Emancipation Proclamation. But Cabinet members advised him to wait until after a success on the battlefield.

A Famous Proclamation On September 22, 1862, a few days after Lee's retreat from Antietam, Lincoln met again with his Cabinet and issued a <u>preliminary</u> proclamation.

On January 1, 1863, Lincoln issued the final Emancipation Proclamation. This document had little immediate effect, however, because it freed enslaved people only in areas that were fighting the Union. Those were places where the Union had no power. The proclamation did not apply to parts of the South already under Union control. Nor did it free anyone in the border states.

The proclamation was both criticized and praised. Some abolitionists said it should be applied throughout the country. White southerners accused Lincoln of trying to cause a slave revolt. But many Union soldiers were enthusiastic. They welcomed anything that weakened the South. "This army will <u>sustain</u> the Emancipation Proclamation and enforce it with the bayonet," an Indiana soldier said.

Effects of the Proclamation Even though the proclamation freed few slaves at first, it had other important effects. Above all, it changed the Civil War into a struggle for freedom. This was no longer just a fight to save the nation. It was now also a fight to end slavery.

> **Vocabulary Builder**
> **preliminary** (pree LIM uh nehr ee) **adj.** leading up to the main action

> **Vocabulary Builder**
> **sustain** (suh STAYN) **v.** to keep going; to endure; to supply with food; to support as just

The Emancipation Proclamation

❝That on the first day of January, in the year of our Lord [1863], all persons held as slaves within any State or designated part of a State, the people whereof shall then be in rebellion against the United States, shall be then, thenceforward, and forever free. . . .❞

—Emancipation Proclamation, January 1, 1863

A Union general posted the announcement at right, declaring the freedom of enslaved African Americans in the part of Virginia occupied by his troops.

FREEDOM TO SLAVES!

Whereas, the President of the United States did, on the first day of the present month, issue his *Proclamation* declaring "that **all persons held as Slaves** in certain designated *States, and parts of States, are, and henceforward shall be free,*" and that the Executive Government of the United States, including the Military and Naval authorities thereof, would recognize and maintain the freedom of said persons. *And Whereas,* the county of Frederick, in which the *Slaves should become free,* I therefore hereby notify the citizens of the city of Winchester, and of said County, of said Proclamation, and of my intention to maintain and enforce the same.

I expect all citizens to yield a ready compliance with the Proclamation of the Chief Executive, and I admonish all persons disposed to resist its peaceful enforcement, that upon manifesting such disposition by acts, they will be regarded as rebels in arms against the lawful authority of the Federal Government and dealt with accordingly.

All persons liberated by said Proclamation are admonished to abstain from all violence, and immediately betake themselves to useful occupations.

The officers of this command are admonished and ordered to act in accordance with said proclamation and to yield their ready co-operation in its enforcement.

Winchester Va
Jan. 5th, 1863.

R. H. Milroy,
Brig. Gen'l Commanding.

Reading Primary Sources
Skills Activity

President Lincoln's proclamation specified that it applied only to certain parts of the United States.

(a) Understand Sequence In what order were these two declarations issued?

(b) Compare In what way is the declaration on the right more specific than the one by President Lincoln?

Vocabulary Builder

Use the information below to teach students this section's high-use words.

High-Use Word	Definition and Sample Sentence
preliminary, p. 525	*adj.* leading up to the main action Expanding trade in Europe and the East was a **preliminary** step to the Age of Exploration.
sustain, p. 525	*v.* to keep going; to endure; to supply with food; to support as just Using horse carts to haul food and ammunition, the army was able to **sustain** its troops through a long campaign

Emancipating the Enslaved

p. 524

Instruction

- **Vocabulary Builder** Before teaching this lesson, preteach the High-Use Words **preliminary** and **sustain,** using the strategy on TE p. T21.

  Key Terms Have students continue to fill in the See It–Remember It chart for the Key Terms in this chapter.

- Have students read Emancipating the Enslaved using the Paragraph Shrinking technique (TE, p. T23).

- To help students better understand the concept of emancipation, use the Concept Lesson *Emancipation*.

  All in One Teaching Resources, Unit 5, Concept Lesson, p. 59; Concept Organizer, p. 6

- Point out how Lincoln's point of view about slavery changed. Ask: **How did Lincoln think ending slavery would weaken the South?** (*Slaves were a vital labor source in the South's war effort; ending slavery would lessen the South's fighting capabilities.*)

- Ask: **How did the focus of the war change?** (*It became a struggle for freedom.*) **How did the proclamation affect Britain's view?** (*Although Britain might have favored an independent South, it would not support a government fighting to keep people enslaved.*)

Independent Practice

Have students begin filling in the study guide for this section.

Monitor Progress

As students fill in the Notetaking Study Guide, circulate to make sure they understand the effect of the Emancipation Proclamation. Provide assistance as needed.

Answers

Reading Primary Sources (a) Emancipation Proclamation, then the general's announcement; **(b)** The President's declaration applies in areas still fighting the Union. The general's applies in the City of Winchester in the county of Frederick.

African Americans Help the Union

p. 526

Instruction

L2

- Have students read African Americans Help the Union. Remind students to look for how events are related in time.

- Ask: **Why was a war about freedom more appealing to African Americans than a war to hold the country together?** (*African Americans wanted freedom; without it, the state of the nation probably made little difference to them.*)

- Display the African Americans Join the War transparency and have students answer the questions on it.

Color Transparencies, Africans Americans Join the War

- Ask: **In what other ways did African Americans help weaken the South's war effort?** (*They provided information useful to Union armies, many refused to work on plantations while their owners were away.*)

Independent Practice

Have students complete the study guide for this section.

Monitor Progress

- As students fill in the Notetaking Study Guide, circulate to make sure individuals understand how African Americans contributed to the Union war effort.

- Tell students to complete the Reading Readiness Guide. Probe for what they learned that confirms or invalidates each statement.

All in One Teaching Resources, Unit 5, Reading Readiness Guide, p. 49

Answers

Apply Information Possible answer: African American soldiers received less pay, faced extra risks if captured, and served in segregated units under white officers.

✓Checkpoint It changed the Civil War into a struggle for freedom, dashed any hopes that Britain would recognize the South's independence, and united African Americans in the North in support of the war.

Reading Skill Many African Americans were not allowed to serve in the army until after the Emancipation Proclamation was issued.

African American Soldiers
These are guards of the 107th Colored Infantry at Fort Corcoran in Washington, D.C.
Critical Thinking: Apply Information How did conditions for African American soldiers differ from those for white soldiers?

Explain How Events Are Related in Time Explain why these two events are related in time: African American soldiers fought for the Union; President Lincoln issued the Emancipation Proclamation.

Also, the Emancipation Proclamation dashed any hopes that Britain would recognize the South's independence. Britain would not help a government that was fighting to keep people enslaved.

In both the North and the South, Lincoln's proclamation united African Americans in support of the war. "We shout for joy that we live to record this righteous decree," wrote Frederick Douglass.

✓Checkpoint How did the proclamation affect the war?

African Americans Help the Union

When the Civil War began, African American volunteers were not permitted to join the Union army. Northern African Americans appealed for the chance to help fight for the nation. However, not until after the Emancipation Proclamation were many allowed to serve.

Volunteering for Service The Emancipation Proclamation encouraged African Americans to enlist. Ultimately, 189,000 African Americans served in the Union army or navy. More than half were former slaves who had escaped or been freed by the fighting. All faced extra risks. If captured, they were not treated as prisoners of war. Most were returned to slavery and some were killed.

Black and white sailors served together on warships. In the army, however, African American soldiers served in all-black regiments under white officers. They earned less pay than white soldiers.

Despite these disadvantages, African American regiments fought with pride and courage. "They make better soldiers in every respect than any troops I have ever had under my command," a Union general said of an African American regiment from Kansas.

Differentiated Instruction

L1 English Language Learners   **L1 Less Proficient Readers**   **L1 Special Needs**

Comparing Give students a page protector to put over the text. Have students reread the section Emancipating the Enslaved and mark each sentence with a **?** if they are uncertain or don't understand the sentence, a ***** if they understand the sentence, or a **!** (wow) if they find the information interesting or new. Review any sentences students have marked with a question mark. Pair students to compare the "wow" sentences. Then, have them write one sentence about the importance of the Emancipation Proclamation.

African American troops took part in about 40 major battles and hundreds of minor ones. The most famous was the attack on Fort Wagner in South Carolina by the 54th Massachusetts Infantry on July 18, 1863. The unit volunteered to lead the assault. As the soldiers charged, Confederate cannon fire rained down. Yet the 54th reached the top of the fort's walls before being turned back in fierce hand-to-hand fighting. The regiment suffered terrible losses. Nearly half of its soldiers were casualties.

Thousands of African Americans supported the Union in noncombat roles. Free northern and emancipated southern African Americans often worked for Union armies as cooks, wagon drivers, and hospital aides.

Resisting Slavery In the South, many enslaved African Americans did what they could to hurt the Confederate war effort. Some provided military and other kinds of information to Union armies. Enslaved people had always quietly resisted slavery by deliberately working slowly or damaging equipment. But with many slaveholders off fighting the war, large numbers of slaves refused to work.

☑Checkpoint **How did African Americans help the Union cause?**

⭐ **Looking Back and Ahead** The Emancipation Proclamation made the Civil War a fight to end slavery. After the war, the Thirteenth Amendment banned slavery throughout the nation. The next section tells how the war affected civilians on both sides.

Section 3 | **Check Your Progress**

> **Progress Monitoring** ⬤**nline**
> **For:** Self-test with instant help
> **Visit:** PHSchool.com
> **Web Code:** mya-5113

Comprehension and Critical Thinking

1. **(a) Identify** Why did Lincoln at first resist identifying slavery as an issue of the Civil War?
(b) Analyze Cause and Effect What effect did the Emancipation Proclamation have on slavery?

2. **(a) Recall** In what ways did African Americans participate in the Civil War?
(b) Explain Problems What were three problems faced by African American soldiers?

⟳ Reading Skill

3. **Explain How Events Are Related in Time** Identify events that happened after the Emancipation Proclamation. Explain how these events are connected.

Key Terms

4. Write two definitions for emancipate. First, write a formal definition for your teacher. Second, write a definition in everyday English for a classmate.

Writing

5. Use library or Internet resources to find information about the African American 54th Massachusetts Infantry. Then, list the subtopics to be included in a research paper about the regiment. Write a paragraph about one of those subtopics. Identify some photographs and other nontext items that you would include in a research report on the 54th.

Section 3 Check Your Progress

1. **(a)** He feared losing the border states.
(b) It had little immediate effect.

2. **(a)** They fought in the Union army, worked in noncombat roles, passed on information, and resisted slavery.
(b) If captured, they were returned to slavery; they served in all-black regiments with white commanders; they earned less pay.

3. Possible answer: As a result of the Emancipation Proclamation, the war became a fight to end slavery and African Americans united to support the war and to volunteer service.

4. formal: to free; informal definitions will vary but should reflect an understanding of the meaning of the word.

5. Possible list of subtopics: battles fought; leaders; training of troops

---

Assess and Reteach

Assess Progress ⬛L2

Have students complete Check Your Progress. Administer the Section Quiz.

All in One **Teaching Resources, Unit 5,** Section Quiz, p. 62

To further assess student understanding, use the Progress Monitoring Transparency.

Progress Monitoring Transparencies, Chapter 15, Section 3

Reteach ⬛L1

If students need more instruction, have them read this section in the Interactive Reading and Notetaking Study Guide.

📖 **Interactive Reading and Notetaking Study Guide,** Chapter 15, Section 3 (Adapted Version also available.)

Extend ⬛L3

Have students create a timeline that includes the major events described in the section. Tell students to be sure to label the dates and provide a brief description of each event. Then have students choose two dates on the timeline and write a few sentences explaining how the events are related in time.

Progress Monitoring Online

Students may check their comprehension of this section by completing the Progress Monitoring Online graphic organizer and self-quiz.

Answer

☑Checkpoint They fought as soldiers, worked in noncombat roles, passed on military information, and refused to work on southern plantations.

Review and Preview

Students have read about the impact of the Emancipation Proclamation on the war. They will now learn how the demands of the war affected civilians on both sides, causing much hardship and bitterness.

Section Focus Question

How did the war affect people and politics in the North and the South?

Before you begin the lesson for the day, write the Section Focus Question on the board. (*Lesson focus: The war caused political divisions in both the North and the South while changing the lives of civilians and soldiers alike.*)

Prepare to Read

Build Background Knowledge **L2**

In this section, students will learn how the military draft affected Americans during the Civil War. Write the word "draft" on the board and discuss what students know about its meaning. Ask students to think about why a draft might be necessary during a war, and why some people might oppose a draft. Use Think-Write-Pair-Share (TE, p. T25) to engage students.

Set a Purpose **L2**

■ Read each statement in the Reading Readiness Guide aloud. Ask students to mark the statements True or False.

All in One **Teaching Resources, Unit 5,** Reading Readiness Guide, p. 50

■ Have students discuss the statements in pairs or groups of four, then mark their worksheets again. Use the Numbered Heads strategy (TE, p. T24) to call on students to share their groups' perspectives. The students will return to these worksheets later.

▲ A nurse cares for an injured soldier.

A Nurse's Day

❝[Today] I have covered crutches, ripped up arm slings, washed and made them over, gone to commissary with order from doctor for material for pads for wounded or amputated limbs. . . . ❞

—Elvira Powers,
a nurse at a Northern hospital, 1863

The Civil War and American Life

Objectives

- Explain how opposition to the war caused problems for both sides.
- Identify the reasons that both sides passed draft laws.
- Describe the economic hardships the war caused in the North and the South.
- Describe the contributions of women to the war efforts.

🎧 Reading Skill

Explain How Events Are Related in Time As soldiers were fighting the Civil War on the battlefield, Americans in both the North and the South were facing other wartime challenges. You will have a better understanding of the Civil War Era if you can relate events on the battlefield to events in civilian life.

Key Terms

habeas corpus	income tax
draft	inflation

Why It Matters The Civil War was not just about the winning and losing of battles and the freeing of slaves. The conflict affected men and women from all walks of life. In both the North and the South, civilians had to cope with the pains of war.

❓ Section Focus Question: How did the war affect people and politics in the North and the South?

Divisions Over the War

The Civil War not only divided the nation. It also caused divisions *within* the North and the South. Not all northerners supported a war to end slavery or even to restore the Union. Not all white southerners supported a war to defend slavery or secession.

Division in the South In the South, opposition to the war was strongest in Georgia and North Carolina. Barely half of Georgians supported secession. There were nearly 100 peace protests in North Carolina in 1863 alone. Yet only Virginia provided more troops to Confederate armies than did North Carolina. Generally, regions with large slaveholding plantations supported the war more strongly than poor back-country regions, where there were fewer enslaved people.

Strong support for states' rights created other divisions. For example, South Carolina's governor objected to officers from other states leading South Carolina troops. And the governors of Georgia and North Carolina did not want the Confederate government to force men from their states to do military service.

528 Chapter 15 The Civil War

Differentiated Instruction

L1 English Language Learners **L1** Less Proficient Readers **L1** Special Needs

Define As they read, students may come across words or phrases that are unfamiliar or difficult for them to understand. Encourage students to keep a list of these words as they read. Check with them periodically to clarify the meaning of each

word. When students have finished reading the section, ask them to create their own glossaries by writing a sentence or drawing a picture that helps to explain each new term. Have students share their glossaries with the class.

Division in the North Northerners were also divided over the war. Many opposed the Emancipation Proclamation. Others believed that the South had a right to secede. Some northern Democrats blamed Lincoln and the Republicans for forcing the South into a war. Northern Democrats who opposed the war were called Copperheads, after the poisonous snake. Copperheads were strongest in Ohio, Indiana, and Illinois. They criticized the war and called for peace with the Confederacy.

Dealing With Disruptions Some people on both sides tried to disrupt the war effort. A common tactic was to encourage soldiers to desert. Some northerners helped Confederate prisoners of war to escape. In the South, peace groups tried to end the war by working against the Confederacy. They tried to prevent men from volunteering for military service and urged Confederate soldiers to desert.

To deal with such problems, both Lincoln and Confederate President Jefferson Davis suspended the right of habeas corpus in some places during the war. Habeas corpus is a constitutional protection against unlawful imprisonment. It empowers judges to order that imprisoned persons be brought into court to determine if they are being legally held. In the North, more than 13,000 people were arrested and jailed without trials.

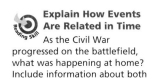
Explain How Events Are Related in Time
As the Civil War progressed on the battlefield, what was happening at home? Include information about both North and South in your answer.

✔**Checkpoint** How did the Civil War divide both North and South?

Copperheads

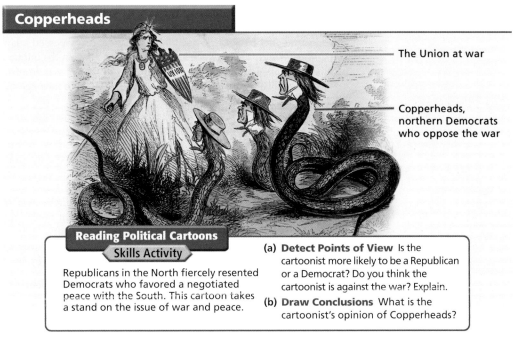

The Union at war

Copperheads, northern Democrats who oppose the war

Reading Political Cartoons
Skills Activity

Republicans in the North fiercely resented Democrats who favored a negotiated peace with the South. This cartoon takes a stand on the issue of war and peace.

(a) Detect Points of View Is the cartoonist more likely to be a Republican or a Democrat? Do you think the cartoonist is against the war? Explain.

(b) Draw Conclusions What is the cartoonist's opinion of Copperheads?

Vocabulary Builder

Use the information below to teach students this section's high-use words.

High-Use Word	Definition and Sample Sentence
levy, p. 531	*v.* to impose by law It is common for governments to **levy** a tax on imports.
currency, p. 531	*n.* money used to make purchases The government prints paper **currency** that people can use for their purchases.

Divisions Over the War
p. 528

Instruction [L2]

- **Vocabulary Builder** Before teaching this lesson, preteach the High-Use Words **levy** and **currency** using the strategy on TE p. T21.

  Key Terms Have students continue to fill in the See It–Remember It chart.

- Read Divisions Over the War with students, using the Oral Cloze technique (TE, p. T22).

- Ask: **What caused supporters of states' rights to oppose the war?** (*They objected to officers from other states commanding their troops; they also felt drafting men from their states violated states' rights.*)

- Ask: **Why did both Davis and Lincoln feel they had to suspend the right of habeas corpus?** (*Possible answer: Neither wanted dissenters to interfere with their war efforts.*)

Independent Practice

Have students begin filling in the study guide for this section.

📖 **Interactive Reading and Notetaking Study Guide,** Chapter 15, Section 4 (Adapted Version also available.)

Monitor Progress

As students fill in the Notetaking Study Guide, circulate to make sure they understand the divisions that existed in the North and the South. Provide assistance as needed.

Answers

🔁 **Reading Skill** Students' answers should include information about disruptive efforts, calls for peace, and suspension of habeas corpus.

✔**Checkpoint** Not all northerners supported a war to preserve the Union or end slavery, and not all southerners favored a war to defend secession or support slavery.

Reading Political Cartoons (a) Probably Republican; he probably is not against the war, because he shows the Copperheads threatening the Union, which is at war. **(b)** Possible answer: They are dangerous and poisonous to the Union.

The Draft Laws

p. 530

Instruction

L2

- Have students read The Draft Laws. As they read, remind them to look for answers to the Section Focus Question.

- Ask: **Why did many men desert on a temporary basis?** (*They were farmers who went home, tended their fields, and then returned.*)

- Have students define the draft. (*system of required military service*) Ask: **Why might factory workers and laborers riot?** (*Possible answers: They didn't want to leave their jobs; they were angry that those who could afford to could avoid the draft.*)

Independent Practice

Have students continue filling in the study guide for this section.

Interactive Reading and Notetaking Study Guide, Chapter 15, Section 4 (Adapted Version also available.)

Monitor Progress

As students fill in the Notetaking Study Guide, circulate to make sure they understand why the draft was established and why it caused problems. Provide assistance as needed.

Join or Be Drafted
Volunteers rushed to enlist at first, but antiwar feeling soon grew. During the New York draft riots of 1863, a mob set fire to a home for African American orphans.
Critical Thinking: Detect Points of View What motivated the people who rioted against the draft?

The Draft Laws

Desertion was a problem for both sides. Between 300,000 and 550,000 Union and Confederate soldiers left their units and went home. About half returned after their crops were planted or harvested. However, at times, from one third to one half of an army's soldiers were away from their units without permission.

To meet the need for troops, each side established a draft, a system of required military service. The South, with its smaller population, was first to act. In April 1862, the Confederacy passed a law requiring white men between ages 18 and 35 to serve in the military for three years. Later, the age range expanded to cover men from 17 to 50. The North adopted a similar draft law in 1863, for men ages 20 to 45.

Exceptions existed, however. Wealthy people had many ways of escaping fighting. In the South, a man who held at least 20 enslaved people did not have to serve. Both sides allowed draftees to hire substitutes to serve in their place. Northerners could avoid the draft by paying the government $300. For many workers, however, this was about a year's pay.

People on both sides complained that the draft made the war "a poor man's fight." Anger against the draft led to violent riots in the North in July 1863. The worst took place in New York City. Mobs of factory workers and laborers rioted for several days, destroying property and attacking African Americans and wealthy white men.

☑ **Checkpoint** Why was the Civil War sometimes called a poor man's fight?

Differentiated Instruction

L3 Advanced Readers

L3 Gifted and Talented

Using Literature Have students read and complete the worksheet *"Beat! Beat! Drums!"* Then ask them to prepare a dramatic choral reading of the poem. Some students might explain the meaning of the

underlined words before reading the poem aloud.

All in One Teaching Resources, Unit 5, "Beat! Beat! Drums!" p. 54

Answers

Detect Points of View Possible answer: They resented having to serve in the war. Because the war was centered around the issue of slavery, they saw African Americans as the cause of the war.

☑ **Checkpoint** Wealthy men could pay to avoid the draft while poor men could not afford to do so.

The War and Economic Strains

Northern industries boomed as they turned out goods the Union needed in the war. Plenty of jobs were available. But the draft drained away workers so there was a constant shortage.

To pay the costs of fighting the war, Congress <u>levied</u> the first income tax in American history in August 1861. An income tax is a tax on the money people receive. The Union also printed $400 million of paper money to help pay its expenses. This was the first federal paper money, or <u>currency</u>. Putting this additional money into circulation led to inflation, or a general rise in prices. In the North, the prices of goods increased an average of 80 percent during the war.

The South was less able than the North to sustain a war. The Union blockade prevented the South from raising money by selling cotton overseas. Shortages made goods more expensive. This led to much greater inflation than in the North. A pair of shoes that had cost $18 dollars in 1862 cost up to $800 in the South in 1864. The price of a pound of beef soared from 12 cents in 1862 to $8 in 1865.

Southern food production fell as invading Union armies destroyed farmland and crops. Shortages of food led to riots in some southern cities. In Richmond, more than 1,000 women looted shops for food, cloth, and shoes in 1863. A woman in North Carolina complained:

> **❝**A crowd of we poor women went to Greensboro yesterday for something to eat as we do not have a mouthful of bread nor meat. . . . I have 6 little children and my husband in the army and what am I to do?**❞**
>
> —farm woman in North Carolina, April 1863

Enslaved people also suffered from wartime shortages. What little they did have was often seized by Confederate soldiers.

☑ Checkpoint What strains did the war put on people?

Women in the Civil War

Women in both the North and the South contributed to the war in many ways. At least 400 women disguised themselves as men and joined the Union or Confederate armies. Others became spies behind enemy lines. Many women took over businesses, farms, and plantations while their fathers, brothers, and husbands served on the battlefields.

In both North and South, women ran farms and plantations. Some southern women worked in the fields to help meet the needs of the Confederacy. They continued to work despite fighting that destroyed their crops and killed their livestock.

Women also ran many northern farms. "I saw more women driving teams [of horses] on the road and saw more at work in the fields than men," a traveler in Iowa reported in 1862.

Vocabulary Builder
levy (LEHV ee) **v.** to impose by law

Vocabulary Builder
currency (KER rehn see) **n.** money used to make purchases

History Background

Anesthetics on the Battlefield In 1860, anesthetics such as chloroform and ether, which work by putting a patient to sleep, were a recent development. A laboratory in Brooklyn run by Dr. Edward Robinson Squibb supplied much of the anesthetics used during the war. Thousands of amputations were performed during the Civil War because musketballs battered limbs in such a way that they had to be removed within 24 hours or the patient would die. However, the success rate of using chloroform was high; many soldiers survived the shock of surgery and lived. Helping the wounded were women nurses. They volunteered even though they faced the resentment of many male physicians.

The War and Economic Strains
Women in the Civil War

p. 531

Instruction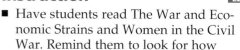

- Have students read The War and Economic Strains and Women in the Civil War. Remind them to look for how events are related in time.

- Discuss the economic issues that the war caused for both sides. Ask: **How did the shortages of goods cause people to behave?** (*They stole, looted, and pleaded for help.*)

- Ask: **What effect did the war have on women?** (*They contributed in numerous ways, including fighting in the armies, acting as spies, taking over businesses, and running farms and plantations. Many women, such as Clara Barton, worked as nurses.*)

Independent Practice

Have students complete the study guide for this section.

📖 **Interactive Reading and Notetaking Study Guide,** Chapter 15, Section 4 (Adapted Version also available.)

Monitor Progress

- As students complete the Notetaking Study Guide, circulate to make sure individuals understand how the Civil War affected women and the economy. Provide assistance as needed.

- Tell students to fill in the last column of the Reading Readiness Guide. Probe for what they learned that confirms or invalidates each statement.

All in One Teaching Resources, Unit 5, Reading Readiness Guide, p. 50

Answer

☑ Checkpoint It caused financial hardships, as well as shortages of food and other necessities.

Assess and Reteach

Assess Progress   L2

Have students complete Check Your Progress. Administer the Section Quiz.

 All in One Teaching Resources, Unit 5, Section Quiz, p. 63

To further assess student understanding, use the Progress Monitoring Transparency.

Progress Monitoring Transparencies, Chapter 15, Section 4

Reteach   L1

If students need more instruction, have them read this section in the Interactive Reading and Notetaking Study Guide.

 Interactive Reading and Notetaking Study Guide, Chapter 15, Section 4 (Adapted Version also available.)

Extend   L3

Ask students to think about the different roles filled by women during the Civil War, such as soldier, spy, and head of a business. Have students choose one role and compose a letter that a woman in that role might have written to a friend or loved one during the Civil War. Ask students to share their letters with the class.

Progress Monitoring Online

Students may check their comprehension of this section by completing the Progress Monitoring Online graphic organizer and self-quiz.

Answers

☑Checkpoint They took on many roles that would not have been possible during peacetime.

Biography Quest While in Switzerland she learned about the International Red Cross. Under its sponsorship, she went to France to help organize relief during the Franco-Prussian War.

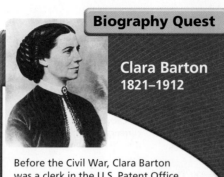

Biography Quest

Clara Barton
1821–1912

Before the Civil War, Clara Barton was a clerk in the U.S. Patent Office. When hostilities began, she became a nurse. Her work under dangerous conditions earned her the nickname Angel of the Battlefield from her Union and Confederate patients.

After the war, Barton worked for a time with the International Red Cross. Returning to the United States, Barton helped set up an American branch of the Red Cross.

Biography Quest **Online**

How did Barton become involved in a European war?

For: The answer to the question about Barton

Visit: PHSchool.com

Web Code: myd-5114

Women on both sides did factory work. Some performed dangerous jobs, such as making ammunition. Others took government jobs. For example, the Confederate government employed dozens of women to sign and number Confederate currency.

The war created many new opportunities for women. Some women became teachers. About 10,000 northern women became nurses. Men had dominated these professions before the war.

Barriers to women especially fell in the field of nursing. Elizabeth Blackwell, America's first female physician, trained nurses for the Union army. Social reformer Dorothea Dix became the head of Union army nurses. Harriet Tubman, who continued to lead enslaved people to freedom during the war, also served as a Union nurse. Clara Barton cared for wounded soldiers on the battlefield. Although nursing was not considered a "proper" job for respectable southern women, some volunteered anyway.

☑Checkpoint How did the war affect women?

⭐ **Looking Back and Ahead** Both sides suffered political and economic hardships during the war. Draft laws affected every family, while new jobs opened up for women. In the next section, you will read how the war finally ended in the defeat of the Confederacy.

Section 4 | Check Your Progress

Progress Monitoring Online
For: Self-test with instant help
Visit: PHSchool.com
Web Code: mya-5114

Comprehension and Critical Thinking

1. (a) Identify What were two reasons some northerners opposed the war? What were two reasons some southerners opposed the war?
(b) Explain Problems Why did the military draft lead some people to describe the war as a poor man's fight?

2. (a) Describe Explain the changing role for women during the Civil War.
(b) Identify Costs What effects did the Civil War have on the economies of the North and of the South?

Reading Skill

3. Explain How Events Are Related in Time What was happening to the American economy as the Civil War raged on?

Key Terms

4. Draw a table with four rows and three columns. In the first column, list the key terms from this section: habeas corpus, draft, income tax, inflation. In the next column, write the definition of each term. In the last column, make a small illustration that shows the meaning of the term.

Writing

5. Reread the text under the heading "Women in the Civil War." Then, write a short paragraph about the role that women played in the Civil War. Include material directly quoted from this section. Be sure to copy the quotation exactly, to punctuate it correctly, and to identify the source.

532 Chapter 15 The Civil War

Section 4 Check Your Progress

1. (a) Some opposed the Emancipation Proclamation; some believed the South had a right to secede. Some southerners did not support secession; some felt the war intruded on states' rights.
(b) Those who could, paid to avoid the draft; poor men could not and were forced to fight.

2. (a) Women began to have more opportunities, because they took on many roles that had previously been performed by men.
(b) Northern industries profited by producing goods necessary for the war. However, both the Union and Confederate governments began printing more paper money, leading to inflation.

3. Possible answer: The economies of both the North and South were declining.

4. Students' definitions should be based on those given in the text.

5. Paragraphs should describe several roles.

A Valiant Foe

❝I felt . . . sad and depressed at the downfall of a foe who had fought so long and valiantly, and had suffered so much for a cause, though that cause was, I believe, one of the worst for which a people ever fought.❞

—General Grant, expressing his feelings about General Lee

◀ General Grant (left) accepts General Lee's surrender.

Decisive Battles

Objectives
- Describe the significance of the battles at Vicksburg and Gettysburg.
- Explain how Union generals used a new type of war to defeat the Confederacy.
- Explain how the war ended.

🔵 Reading Skill

Relate Events in a Sequence Events in sequence are often connected by a cause-and-effect link. One event causes an event that occurs next. This event in turn can cause another to occur. As you read Section 5, look for sequential events, and then determine if they have a cause-and-effect relationship. Remember, however, that not all events in sequence have this link.

Key Terms and People

siege   total war
William Tecumseh
   Sherman

Why It Matters By 1863, the Civil War had produced hundreds of thousands of dead and wounded. As the fighting raged on, there seemed to be no end in sight. But decisive battles at Gettysburg and Vicksburg would change the war's course and enable the Union to win the Civil War.

❓ **Section Focus Question: How did Lincoln and his generals turn the tide of the war?**

The Tide Turns

After the Union victory at the 1862 Battle of Antietam, the war again began to go badly for the North. As before, the problem was poor leadership. When McClellan failed to pursue Lee's beaten army, Lincoln replaced him with General Ambrose Burnside.

Confederate Victories Burnside knew McClellan had been fired for being too cautious. So Burnside decided on a bold stroke. In December 1862, he marched his army of 120,000 men directly toward Richmond. Lee massed 75,000 men at Fredericksburg, Virginia, to block their path. Using traditional tactics, Burnside ordered charge after charge. The Union suffered nearly 13,000 casualties in the Battle of Fredericksburg and the Confederates nearly 5,000.

Lincoln next turned to General Joseph Hooker, nicknamed "Fighting Joe." "May God have mercy on General Lee, for I will have none," Hooker boasted as he marched the Union army toward Richmond. In May 1863, Hooker's army was smashed at the Battle of Chancellorsville by a force that was half its size. But the victory was a costly one for the South. During the battle, Stonewall Jackson was shot and wounded. A few days later, Jackson died.

Section 5 Decisive Battles   **533**

Vocabulary Builder

Use the information below to teach students this section's high-use words.

High-Use Word	Definition and Sample Sentence
encounter, p. 534	*v.* to meet in an unexpected way; to experience Soldiers who entered the enemy territory did not know what dangers they might **encounter**.
exceed, p. 535	*v.* to go beyond what is expected; to be greater than what was planned The general had expected to win, but his victory **exceeded** his greatest hopes.

Section 5
Step-by-Step Instruction

Review and Preview

Students have read about the suffering, death, and destruction of the Civil War. Students will now learn how the war finally ended.

Section Focus Question

How did Lincoln and his generals turn the tide of the war?

Before you begin the lesson for the day, write the Section Focus Question on the board. (*Lesson focus: The Union gained the upper hand with victories at Gettysburg and Vicksburg. Lincoln appointed Grant commander of the Union forces, which also helped turn the tide.*)

Prepare to Read

Build Background Knowledge   L2

In this section, students will learn about the major turning points in the Civil War. Ask students to think about what the phrase "turning point" means. Suggest that they think of times in their own lives when they reached a turning point. Use the Give One, Get One strategy (TE, p. T25) to foster discussion of this concept.

Set a Purpose   L2

■ Read each statement in the Reading Readiness Guide aloud. Ask students to mark the statements True or False.

All in One Teaching Resources, Unit 5, Reading Readiness Guide, p. 51

■ Have students discuss the statements in pairs or groups of four, then mark their worksheets again. Use the Numbered Heads strategy (TE, p. T24) to call on students to share their groups' perspectives. The students will return to these worksheets later.

Teach

The Tide Turns

p. 533

Instruction

L2

- **Vocabulary Builder** Before teaching this lesson, preteach the High-Use Words **encounter** and **exceed,** using the strategy on TE p. T21.

  Key Terms Have students complete the See It–Remember It chart.

- Have students read The Tide Turns using the Paragraph Shrinking technique (TE, p. T23).

- Discuss the problems of leadership in the Union army. Ask: **How did these problems lead Lee to initiate an attack on Union soil?** (*The Union army suffered badly at several battles under different generals, giving Lee confidence that he could win a major victory on Union soil.*)

- Ask: **How did Grant overcome Vicksburg?** (*He led a siege until the Confederates gave up.*)

- Ask: **How did Lincoln take advantage of the Gettysburg victory?** (*He gave a speech there to honor soldiers and to suggest the healing that should follow when the war ended.*)

Independent Practice

Have students begin filling in the study guide for this section.

Interactive Reading and Notetaking Study Guide, Chapter 15, Section 5 (Adapted Version also available.)

Monitor Progress

As students fill in the Notetaking Study Guide, circulate to make sure individuals understand why the battles at Gettysburg and Vicksburg were turning points in the war. Provide assistance as needed.

Answers

MAP MASTER Skills Activity **(a)** Chancellorsville, Fredericksburg, Appomattox Court House, Atlanta, Chattanooga, Corinth, Jackson, Vicksburg; Gettysburg **(b)** The South suffered more damage than the North because most of the battles took place in the South.

Vocabulary Builder
encounter (ehn KOWN ter) **v.** to meet in an unexpected way; to experience

The Battle of Gettysburg These Confederate victories made Lee bolder. He was convinced that a major victory on Union soil would force northerners to end the war. In June 1863, Lee's troops crossed Maryland and marched into Pennsylvania. The Union army, which was now commanded by General George Meade, pursued them.

On July 1, some Confederate soldiers approached the quiet town of Gettysburg. They were looking for shoes, which were in short supply in the South because of the Union blockade. Instead of shoes, the Confederates encountered part of Meade's army. Shots were exchanged. More troops joined the fight on both sides. By evening, the southerners had pushed the Union forces back through Gettysburg.

The next day, more than 85,000 Union soldiers faced some 75,000 Confederates. The center of the Union army was on a hill called Cemetery Ridge. The center of the Confederate position was nearly a mile away, on Seminary Ridge. The fighting raged into the next day as Confederate troops attacked each end of the Union line.

On the afternoon of July 3, Lee ordered an all-out attack on the center of the Union line. General George E. Pickett led about 15,000 Confederates across nearly a mile of open field toward Cemetery Ridge. As they advanced, Union artillery shells and rifle fire rained down on them. Only a few hundred men reached the Union lines, and they were quickly driven back. About 7,500 Confederates were killed or wounded in what is known as Pickett's Charge.

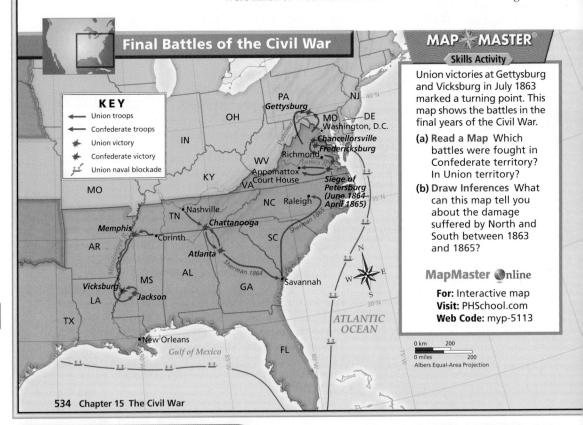

Final Battles of the Civil War

KEY
- Union troops
- Confederate troops
- Union victory
- Confederate victory
- Union naval blockade

MAP MASTER®

Skills Activity

Union victories at Gettysburg and Vicksburg in July 1863 marked a turning point. This map shows the battles in the final years of the Civil War.

(a) Read a Map Which battles were fought in Confederate territory? In Union territory?

(b) Draw Inferences What can this map tell you about the damage suffered by North and South between 1863 and 1865?

MapMaster Online

For: Interactive map
Visit: PHSchool.com
Web Code: myp-5113

Differentiated Instruction

L1 English Language Learners   **L1 Less Proficient Readers**   **L1 Special Needs**

Analyze Photographs Ask students to complete the worksheet Civil War Powder Monkey and answer the questions. Have students share what they learned, as well as their impressions of the photograph on the worksheet, with the rest of the class.

All in One Teaching Resources, Unit 5, Civil War Powder Monkey, p. 55

In all, the Confederacy suffered more than 28,000 casualties during the three-day Battle of Gettysburg. Union losses exceeded 23,000. For a second time, Lee had lost nearly a third of his troops. "It's all my fault," he said as he rode among his surviving soldiers. "It is I who have lost this fight."

The Fall of Vicksburg On July 4, 1863, as Lee's shattered army began its retreat from Gettysburg, the South suffered another major blow far to the south and west. Vicksburg surrendered to General Grant. It had been one of the last cities on the Mississippi River to remain in Confederate hands. Unable to take Vicksburg by force, Grant had begun a siege of the city in May 1863. A **siege** is an attempt to capture a place by surrounding it with military forces and cutting it off until the people inside surrender.

Day after day, Union guns bombarded Vicksburg. Residents took shelter in cellars and in caves they dug in hillsides. They ate mules and rats to keep from starving. After six weeks, the 30,000 Confederate troops at Vicksburg finally gave up. A few days later, the last Confederate stronghold on the Mississippi River, Port Hudson, Louisiana, also gave up. The entire river was now under Union control.

These events, coupled with Lee's defeat at Gettysburg, make July 1863 the major turning point of the Civil War. Now the Union had the upper hand.

The Gettysburg Address In November 1863, about 15,000 people gathered on the battlefield at Gettysburg to honor the soldiers who had died there. In what is now known as the Gettysburg Address, Lincoln looked ahead to a final Union victory. He said:

> ❝We here highly resolve that these dead shall not have died in vain—that this nation, under God, shall have a new birth of freedom—and that government of the people, by the people, for the people, shall not perish from the earth.❞
> —Abraham Lincoln, Gettysburg Address, November 19, 1863

☑**Checkpoint** Identify two events that marked turning points in the Civil War.

Closing In on the Confederacy

In Ulysses S. Grant, President Lincoln found the kind of commander he had long sought. In 1864, the President gave him command of all Union forces. Grant decided that he must attack Richmond, no matter how large the Union losses.

Grant Versus Lee Grant's huge army hammered at the Confederates in a series of battles in northern Virginia in the spring of 1864. Grant was unable to break through Lee's troops. But Grant did not retreat. Instead, he continued the attack.

Vocabulary Builder
exceed (ehks SEED) **v.** to go beyond what is expected; to be greater than what was planned

Union General Ulysses S. Grant

History Background

Cotton and the Red River Campaign
While Sherman was pursuing his campaign to capture Atlanta, Union General Nathaniel P. Banks was leading the Red River Campaign in Louisiana. The goal was to gain control of Louisiana, Texas, and Arkansas, and prevent southern forces from getting supplies. Union officials also hoped to take cotton, which was abundant in the region, to provide to northern mills. Confederate general Richard Taylor was aware of the Union's desire to secure cotton, and limited the sale of it to northern buyers. When that proved a failure, Taylor ordered that all baled and seeded cotton be burned.

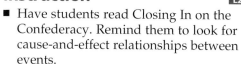

Closing In on the Confederacy

p. 535

Instruction

L2

- Have students read Closing In on the Confederacy. Remind them to look for cause-and-effect relationships between events.

- Ask: **What advantage did Grant have over Lee?** (*He had a steady stream of men and supplies while Lee was running out of both.*)

- Ask: **Why was Sherman's capture of Atlanta a boost for Lincoln?** (*Northerners had grown tired of the war and the victory gave them hope.*)

- Have students complete the worksheet Photographing the War. Discuss how visual images might have affected the public's attitudes toward the war.

  All in One Teaching Resources, Unit 5, Photographing the War, p. 56

- Discuss with students the policy of total warfare. Explain that this strategy was new in American military history and was the model for modern warfare. Ask students whether they think it was an effective strategy. (*Students' answers will vary, but should recognize the devastation it caused to the civilian society as well as the ability of the military to fight.*)

Independent Practice

Have students continue filling in the study guide for this section.

📖 **Interactive Reading and Notetaking Study Guide,** Chapter 15, Section 5 (Adapted Version also available.)

Monitor Progress

As students fill in the Notetaking Study Guide, circulate to make sure individuals understand how Sherman closed in on the Confederacy. Provide assistance as needed.

Answer

☑**Checkpoint** the Union's victories at Gettysburg and Vicksburg

Peace at Last

p. 536

Instruction L2

- Ask students to read Peace at Last together with you. Remind students to look for details that answer the Section Focus Question.

- Discuss the behavior of Lee and Grant at Appomattox. Ask: **How can you tell that both men were aware of the toll of the war?** (*Lee surrendered rather than subject his remaining troops to another defeat. Grant offered generous terms and reminded his men that the rebels were once again fellow countrymen.*)

- Display the transparency The Final Battles and have students answer the questions.

Color Transparencies, The Final Battles

Independent Practice

Have students complete the study guide for this section.

📖 **Interactive Reading and Notetaking Study Guide,** Chapter 15, Section 5 (Adapted Version also available.)

Monitor Progress

- As students complete the Notetaking Study Guide, circulate to make sure they understand how peace was achieved. Provide assistance as needed.

- Tell students to fill in the last column of the Reading Readiness Guide. Probe for what they learned that confirms or invalidates each statement.

All in One **Teaching Resources, Unit 5,** Reading Readiness Guide, p. 51; Word Knowledge Rating Form, p. 46

Answers

Reading Charts (a) because it would disrupt the balance of political power, giving slave states more votes in Congress **(b)** Total war destroyed the South's economy and left hundreds of thousands of southerners killed; Hundreds of thousands of northerners killed

🔵 **Reading Skill** Victory in Atlanta happened first. It helped Lincoln get reelected.

☑Checkpoint He burned Atlanta and left a path of destruction 60 miles wide from Atlanta to the Atlantic Ocean.

Cause and Effect

CAUSES
- Issue of slavery in the territories divides the North and South.
- Abolitionists want slavery to end.
- Southern states secede after Lincoln's election.

⬇ **THE CIVIL WAR** ⬇

EFFECTS
- Lincoln issues the Emancipation Proclamation.
- Total war destroys the South's economy.
- Hundreds of thousands of Americans killed.

Reading Charts
Skills Activity

The Civil War had multiple causes—and multiple effects.

(a) Analyze Cause and Effect Why did the North fear the extension of slavery to the West?

(b) Draw Conclusions Which effects were felt mainly in the South? Which effects were felt mainly in the North?

🔵 **Relate Events in a Sequence**
What happened first, the Union's victory in Atlanta or President Lincoln's reelection? Explain how these events are related in sequence.

After seven weeks of fighting, Grant had lost about 55,000 men; the Confederates had lost 35,000. Grant realized that his army could count on a steady stream of men and supplies. Lee, on the other hand, was running out of both.

The two armies clashed at Petersburg, an important railroad center south of Richmond. There, in June 1864, Grant began a siege, the tactic he had used at Vicksburg.

While Grant besieged Lee, another Union army under General William Tecumseh Sherman advanced toward Atlanta. Like Grant, Sherman was a tough soldier. He believed in total war—all-out attacks aimed at destroying an enemy's army, its resources, and its people's will to fight. Sherman later said:

> ❝We are not only fighting hostile armies, but a hostile people, and must make young and old, rich and poor, feel the hard hand of war.❞
>
> —William T. Sherman,
> *Memoirs,* 1886

March to the Sea The Confederates could not stop Sherman's advance. The Union army marched into Atlanta on September 2, 1864. Atlanta's capture gave President Lincoln's reelection campaign a boost. In the months before the capture of Atlanta, many northerners had grown tired of the war. Support for Lincoln had been lagging. But after Atlanta's fall, Lincoln won a huge election victory over General George McClellan, the Democrats' candidate.

In November, Sherman ordered Atlanta burned. He then marched east toward the Atlantic Ocean. Along the way, Union troops set fire to buildings, seized crops and livestock, and pulled up railroad tracks. They left a path of destruction up to 60 miles wide. In February 1865, the army headed north across the Carolinas.

☑Checkpoint How did Sherman show "the hard hand of war"?

Peace at Last

In March 1865, Grant's army still waited outside Petersburg. For months, Grant had been extending his battle lines east and west of Petersburg. Lee knew it was only a matter of time before Grant would capture the city.

Differentiated Instruction

L3 Advanced Readers   **L3 Gifted and Talented**

Using Literature *The Red Badge of Courage* is a story about a young soldier's response to the Civil War. Have students read the literature selection in Readings in Social Studies, America in Progress. Suggest that students share the selection with the class by preparing a dramatic reading of it. After students are done, discuss the significance of the last paragraph. (*The interaction Henry has with an enemy makes him realize that the war is being fought between men just like himself.*)

All in One **Readings in Social Studies, America in Progress,** *The Red Badge of Courage*, pp. 165–166

Lincoln, too, saw that the end of the war was near. In his Second Inaugural Address in March 1865, he asked Americans to forgive and forget. "With malice toward none; with charity for all; . . . let us strive together . . . to bind up the nation's wounds," said Lincoln.

Surrender at Appomattox On April 2, Grant's troops finally broke through Confederate lines. By evening, Richmond was in Union hands. Lee's army retreated to the town of Appomattox Court House. There, on April 9, 1865, his escape cut off, Lee surrendered.

Grant offered Lee generous surrender terms. The Confederates had only to give up their weapons and leave in peace. As Lee rode off, some Union troops started to celebrate the surrender. But Grant silenced them. "The war is over," he said. "The rebels are our countrymen again."

The War's Terrible Toll The Civil War was the bloodiest conflict the United States has ever fought. About 260,000 Confederate soldiers gave their lives in the war. The number of Union dead exceeded 360,000, including 37,000 African Americans. Nearly a half million men were wounded. Many returned home disfigured for life.

The war had two key results: It reunited the nation and put an end to slavery. However, a century would pass before African Americans would begin to experience the full meaning of freedom.

☑Checkpoint **Why did Lee finally decide to surrender?**

⭐ **Looking Back and Ahead** With Lee's surrender, the long and bitter war came to an end. In the next chapter, you will read how U.S. leaders tried to patch the Union together again.

Section 5 | Check Your Progress

> **Progress Monitoring ◉nline**
> **For:** Self-test with instant help
> **Visit:** PHSchool.com
> **Web Code:** mya-5115

Comprehension and Critical Thinking

1. (a) Identify Why are the battles at Gettysburg and Vicksburg considered a turning point?
(b) Understand Sequence How did the advantages of the North at the start of the war continue to be advantages?

2. (a) Classify Classify each of the following people as either a Union general or a Confederate general: Ambrose Burnside, Robert E. Lee, Ulysses S. Grant, William Tecumseh Sherman.
(b) Distinguish Facts From Opinions Write three facts and three opinions Grant might have stated about the Civil War.

⟳ Reading Skill

3. Relate Events in a Sequence What events led to the turning point of the Civil War in July 1863? How did those events change the war?

Key Terms

Complete each of the following sentences so that the second part further explains the first part and clearly shows your understanding of the key term.
4. Grant placed Vicksburg under a siege; _____.
5. Sherman pursued a total war; _____.

Writing

6. This section says that the Civil War took more than 620,000 American lives. Research and record the number of American deaths in World War I, World War II, Korea, and Vietnam. Compare the total number of American lives lost in these wars to the number lost in the Civil War. Then, write a paragraph to make a point about your findings. Also, credit the sources of published information you used.

Section 5 Decisive Battles 537

Assess Progress L2

Have students complete Check Your Progress. Administer the Section Quiz.

All in One Teaching Resources, Unit 5, Section Quiz, p. 64

To further assess student understanding, use the Progress Monitoring Transparency.

Progress Monitoring Transparencies, Chapter 15, Section 5

Reteach L1

If students need more instruction, have them read this section in the Interactive Reading and Notetaking Study Guide.

📖 **Interactive Reading and Notetaking Study Guide,** Chapter 15, Section 5 (Adapted Version also available.)

Extend L3

Explain that in the late 1860s, Memorial Day emerged as a day to honor soldiers who had died in the Civil War. Today, the holiday honors those whose lives were sacrificed in all American wars. Ask students to write a Memorial Day speech explaining why it is important to honor those who have given their lives in American wars. Students should read their speeches aloud to the class.

Progress Monitoring Online

Students may check their comprehension of this section by completing the Progress Monitoring Online graphic organizer and self-quiz.

Answer

☑Checkpoint He was surrounded with no escape; he had lost too many men in a long, bloody conflict and had little hope of reinforcements.

Section 5 Check Your Progress

1. (a) The victories gave the Union the upper hand.
(b) The Union was able to replenish troops and supplies because of its larger population and industries.

2. (a) Burnside was Union, Lee Confederate, and both Grant and Sherman were Union.
(b) Students' answers will vary, but should include appropriate facts. When writing the opinions, students should keep in mind that Grant did not retreat when challenged, and believed in the importance of unity after the war.

3. Possible answer: The Union won the Battle of Antietam, but was defeated at a number of battles afterward. In 1863, the Union won at the battles of Gettysburg and Vicksburg, which gave its leaders confidence that they could win the war.

4. He cut it off from food and supplies until the city surrendered.

5. His aim was to destroy the Confederate army, its resources, and the will of the South to fight.

6. Students' paragraphs will vary, but should make accurate comparisons between the loss of American lives in the Civil War and in the other wars.

Chapter 15 Section 5 **537**

Skills for Life

Objective

Analyzing speeches can help students increase their awareness of historical points of view and events. Finding the main idea and analyzing the speaker's point of view will help students better understand historical issues and people. This skill lesson will teach students how to analyze a speech.

Analyze a Speech

Instruction   L2

1. Write the steps to analyze a speech on the board. Ask the class to read the steps aloud.

2. Using the Numbered Heads strategy (TE, p. T24), have students share what they know about finding the main idea of a passage. (*Students should note that the main idea is the most important idea of a passage.*) Remind students that sometimes the main idea is plainly stated, but other times it is implied.

3. Practice the skill by following the steps on p. 538 as a class. Model each step to analyze a speech. (*1. (a) Abraham Lincoln wrote the speech. (b) It was given on November 19, 1863. (c) It was given in honor of soldiers who died during the Battle of Gettysburg. 2. The main idea is that the Union must win the war, so the nation can be free and reunited. 3. (a) The Civil War is a noble cause for the Union, a test whether it can be preserved as a free nation. (b) "they who have fought here thus far so nobly" and "this nation . . . shall have a new birth of freedom—and . . . shall not perish . . ." (c) Possible answers: He wants freedom for everyone; By winning, he believes the war will have been worth fighting.*)

Monitor Progress

Ask students to do the Apply the Skill activity. Then assign the Skills for Life Worksheet. As students complete the worksheet, circulate to make sure individuals are applying the skill steps effectively. Provide assistance as needed.

All in One **Teaching Resources, Unit 5,** Skills for Life Worksheet, p. 58

A primary source is information about people or events presented by someone who lived through what is being described. Speeches are primary sources that can give important information about historical figures and events.

> **Primary Source**
>
> President Lincoln gave this speech at the dedication of the battlefield cemetery at Gettysburg.
>
> "Fourscore and seven years ago our fathers brought forth on this continent a new nation, conceived in Liberty, and dedicated to the proposition that all men are created equal.
>
> Now we are engaged in a great civil war, testing whether that nation, or any nation so conceived and so dedicated, can long endure. We are met on a great battlefield of that war. We have come to dedicate a portion of that field as a final resting place for those who here gave their lives that the nation might live. It is altogether fitting and proper that we should do this.
>
> But in a larger sense, we cannot dedicate, we cannot consecrate, we cannot hallow, this ground. The brave men, living and dead, who struggled here have consecrated it, far above our poor power to add or detract. The world will little note, nor long remember, what we say here, but it can never forget what they did here. It is for us the living, rather, to be dedicated here to the unfinished work which they who fought here have thus far so nobly advanced. It is rather for us to be here dedicated to the great task remaining before us—that from these honored dead we take increased devotion to that cause for which they gave the last full measure of devotion—that we here highly resolve that these dead shall not have died in vain—that this nation, under God, shall have a new birth of freedom—and that government of the people, by the people, for the people, shall not perish from the earth."
>
> —Abraham Lincoln, November 19, 1863

Learn the Skill
Use these steps to analyze a speech.

1. **Identify the source.** Find out who gave the speech, when it was given, and why it was given.

2. **Identify the main idea.** Read carefully to discover what the main idea of the speech is. What do you think the speaker wanted to tell his or her audience?

3. **Identify the point of view.** Often a speechmaker wants to persuade listeners to share his or her feelings. Read carefully to determine the point of view of the speechmaker. Look for language that expresses strong feelings.

Practice the Skill
Answer the questions about the speech above.

1. **Identify the source.** (a) Who wrote the speech? (b) When was the speech given? (c) Why was it given?

2. **Identify the main idea.** What is the most important idea in the speech?

3. **Identify the point of view.** (a) What is the speaker's opinion of the Civil War? (b) What words or phrases express his feelings? (c) Why do you think he feels this way?

Apply the Skill
See the Review and Assessment at the end of this chapter.

Quick Study Guide

 How did people, places, and things affect the outcome of the Civil War?

Section 1
The Call to Arms

- The Civil War was a war of Americans against Americans.
- Both the North and the South used their advantages in planning military strategy.

Section 2
Early Years of the War

- New weapons made fighting the war more dangerous.
- Despite many battles early in the war, neither side gained a clear advantage.

Section 3
The Emancipation Proclamation

- The Emancipation Proclamation freed enslaved people in areas of rebellion.
- The Emancipation Proclamation changed the Civil War into a fight to end slavery.
- Approximately 189,000 African Americans served in the Union army and navy.

Section 4
The Civil War and American Life

- The Civil War caused divisions in both the North and the South.
- Draft laws that seemed to favor the wealthy led to protests and riots.
- The Civil War caused economic hardships and also led to changes in women's roles.

Section 5
Decisive Battles

- Major Confederate losses at Gettysburg and Vicksburg marked a turning point.
- Lee surrendered to Grant on April 9, 1865, at Appomattox Court House.
- Some 620,000 soldiers died in the Civil War.

? Exploring the Essential Question

Use the online study guide to explore the essential question.

Section 1
Why did each side in the Civil War think the war would be won easily?

Chapter 15 Essential Question
How did people, places, and things affect the outcome of the Civil War?

Section 2
How did each side in the war try to gain an advantage over the other?

Section 5
How did Lincoln and his generals turn the tide of the war?

Section 3
What were the causes and effects of the Emancipation Proclamation?

Section 4
How did the war affect people and politics in the North and the South?

Chapter 15

Essential Question

Remind students of the Chapter Essential Question: **How did people, places, and things affect the outcome of the Civil War?** Have them review the bulleted statements and the Visual Preview at the beginning of the chapter to help them answer this question. After they've answered the Chapter Focus Question about the people, places, and events that affected the outcome of the Civil War, address any misconceptions that students may still have about the topic.

To bolster students' retention, at this time they should complete the study guide in print or online. Remind students that they should also continue notetaking for the Unit and Chapter Essential Questions.

Interactive Reading and Notetaking Study Guide, Chapter 15 (Adapted Version also available.)

Study Guide *Online,* Chapter 15

Chapter Challenge

To wrap up this chapter, students should apply the knowledge they have gained to answer this question: **Why might the problems and suffering of the Civil War have continued even after the fighting stopped?** (*Answers will vary, but students should recognize the divisions between the North and the South and that the war may not have solved the issues over which people disagreed.*)

Assessment at a Glance

Formal Assessment

Chapter Tests A/B (L1/L2)

AYP Monitoring Assessment

Test Prep Workbook With Document-Based Assessment

Test-Taking Strategies With Transparencies

Performance Assessment

Group/Individual Activities, TE p. 508h

Teacher's Edition, pp. 517, 520–521, 527, 532, 537

Assessment Rubrics

Assessment Through Technology

ExamView CD-ROM

MindPoint CD-ROM

Progress Monitoring Transparencies

Progress Monitoring Online

Key Terms

1. The Union army had the greatest number of casualties.

2. When Confederate forces invaded Kentucky, it decided to support the North.

3. They wanted to stop rioting and dissension that would hurt their war effort.

4. After six weeks, residents and soldiers were starving because they had no supplies of food.

Comprehension and Critical Thinking

5. **(a)** If it seceded, Washington, D.C., would be surrounded by the Confederacy. **(b)** Maryland stayed in the Union.

6. **(a)** The South needed the slaves' labor for the war effort, so freeing them would weaken the South. **(b)** Any two of the following: it did not apply to parts of the South already under Union control; it did not free anyone in the border states; the federal government had no power to enforce the proclamation in states that were still fighting the Union.

7. **(a)** They served as spies; took over businesses while the men were away; ran farms and plantations; worked in the fields, factories, and government; and formed groups to send supplies to troops. **(b)** Because the men were away at war, women were able to work in jobs that were dominated by men before the war. **(c)** Possible answers: military service, nursing, teaching, farming

8. **(a)**

Bull Run	neither side
Antietam Creek	Union
Shiloh	Union
Fredericksburg	Confederate
Vicksburg	Union
Gettysburg	Union
Petersburg	Union

(b) Possible answer: It probably was more comforting to northerners because they were fighting for freedom.

9. **(a)** Students' sentences may include information about the battles at Gettysburg and Vicksburg, Grant's siege at Petersburg, Sherman's capture of Atlanta, and Lee's surrender at Appomattox. **(b)** Possible answer: It

---

Key Terms
Answer the following questions in complete sentences that show your understanding of the key terms.

1. Which army, the Union or the Confederate, sustained more casualties?

2. Why did Kentucky cease being neutral?

3. What was both Lincoln's and Davis's purpose in suspending habeas corpus?

4. How did Grant's siege of Vicksburg lead to the surrender of Confederate troops?

Comprehension and Critical Thinking

5. **(a) Recall** Why was it critical to keep Maryland in the Union?
(b) Analyze Cause and Effect What was the effect of Lincoln's declaring martial law in Maryland?

6. **(a) Identify** Why did President Lincoln issue the Emancipation Proclamation?
(b) Explain Problems What were two limitations of the Emancipation Proclamation?

7. **(a) Describe** What roles did women play in the Civil War?
(b) Identify Economic Benefits In what way did the hardships of the Civil War provide new opportunities for women?
(c) Link Past and Present Make a list of three opportunities that are open to women today that once were limited to men.

8. **(a) Classify** Create a chart of the battles fought at these places: Bull Run, Antietam Creek, Shiloh, Fredericksburg, Vicksburg, Gettysburg, Petersburg. Classify each battle as either a Union victory or a Confederate victory.
(b) Detect Bias Reread the excerpt from Lincoln's Gettysburg Address found in Section 5. Do you think the address gave more comfort to northerners or to southerners? Why?

9. **(a) Summarize** Write three sentences that explain how the Civil War ended.
(b) Make Predictions Do you think the surrender of the Confederate army at Appomattox Court House brought an end to the conflict between the northern and southern states? Explain.

History Reading Skill
10. **Understand Sequence** In a paragraph, summarize the events in the Civil War on the battlefield and on the home front. Use signal words to clarify the sequence. Where appropriate, show cause-effect links between events in sequence.

Writing
11. **Write on the following topic:**
Find more information about a Civil War general. Write four paragraphs about him, using the guidelines below.
- The first paragraph should introduce the general and present a thesis.
- The second and third paragraphs should support this thesis by giving some background about the general's life, actions, and character.
- The fourth paragraph should draw a conclusion about the general.

12. **Write a Narrative:**
Choose one of the following roles: soldier, civilian, or nurse. Write two paragraphs of descriptive narrative telling about your experience in the Civil War.

Skills for Life
Analyze a Speech
Use the quotation below to answer the questions.

> ". . . the people of the Confederate States, in their conventions, determined that the wrongs which they had suffered and the evils with which they were menaced required that they should revoke the delegation of powers to the Federal Government which they had ratified in their several conventions. They consequently passed ordinances [laws] resuming all their rights as sovereign and independent States. . . ."
>
> —Jefferson Davis, April 29, 1861

13. **(a)** Who is the writer?
(b) When was this written?

14. What is the main idea?

15. **(a)** What words or phrases show the writer's feelings?
(b) Why do you think he feels this way?

---

probably did not end conflict because disagreements over slavery and the Union may have continued.

History Reading Skill
10. Students' paragraphs should accurately summarize the events described in the chapter. Paragraphs must include signal words and show cause-and-effect links between events in sequence.

Writing
11. Paragraphs should include the impact of the general on the war effort for his side, his successes or failures.

12. Narrative should clearly define the role being taken and have reasonable descriptions of events.

For a more complete four-point rubric, see the Writing Rubrics in the Teaching Resources.

Progress Monitoring Online

For: Self-test with instant help
Visit: PHSchool.com
Web Code: mya-5116

Chapter 15
Review and Assessment

Test Yourself

Refer to the quotation below to answer Question 1.

> "I now hold in contemplation of universal law and of the Constitution [that] the Union of these States is perpetual. . . . It follows from these views that no State upon its own mere motion can lawfully get out of the Union. . . ."
>
> —Abraham Lincoln, March 4, 1861

1. This quotation shows that Lincoln wanted to

A allow southern states to secede.

B amend the Constitution.

C abolish slavery.

D preserve the Union.

2. Which of the following granted freedom to all African Americans in areas of rebellion against the Union in 1863?

A Gettysburg Address

B Thirteenth Amendment

C Emancipation Proclamation

D surrender at Appomattox Court House

3. Which of the following was the North's most important advantage in the Civil War?

A Britain and other European nations sent economic aid.

B The nation's most experienced military leaders were northerners.

C The North had a larger population and more resources than the South.

D Northerners were united in their support for the war.

Document-Based Questions

Task: Look at Documents 1 and 2, and answer their accompanying questions. Then, use the documents and your knowledge of history to complete this writing assignment:

Write an essay describing the disagreement between the Copperheads and northern supporters of the Civil War. Include specific details about each side's position.

Document 1: Clement L. Vallandigham, an Ohio congressman, gave this speech in New York City in March 1863. *What does Vallandigham propose? How does that represent the Copperhead position?*

> "When I see that the experiment of blood has failed, . . . I am not one of those who proclaim . . . that we shall have separation and disunion. I am for going back to the instrumentality through which this Union was first made, and by which alone it can be restored.
>
> I am for peace, because it is the first step toward conciliation and compromise. You cannot move until you have first taken that indispensable preliminary—a cessation of hostilities. . . .
>
> Let men of intelligence judge: let history attest it hereafter. My theory . . . then, is this—stop this war."

Document 2: Copperheads were probably the most outspoken critics of the war in the North. *What opinion of Copperheads does this cartoon present?*

Skills for Life

13. (a) Jefferson Davis wrote this; **(b)** April 29, 1861

14. The Confederate States want to withdraw from the Union and become independent states.

15. (a) "the wrongs which they had suffered and the evils with which they were menaced;" **(b)** Possible answer: He feels this way because he is a southerner and believes the Confederacy has a right to exist because the southern states have not been treated well.

Test Yourself
1. D
2. C
3. C

Document-Based Questions
Answers

Document 1 Vallandigham favors a cease-fire as a first step to reaching a compromise settlement between North and South.

Document 2 that Copperheads are dangerous snakes

Rubric: Write an Essay

Share the rubric with students before they begin writing.

Score 1 Is poorly written, does not address topic.

Score 2 Gives weak description of one or both positions, little supporting evidence.

Score 3 Gives accurate statement of opposing positions, with evidence in support.

Score 4 Is clearly organized, shows careful thought, with full treatment of war positions and supporting details.

Reconstruction and the New South (1863–1896)

History Background

The Significance of Reconstruction

Beyond the physical rebuilding of the South, two major issues faced the nation after the Civil War: under what conditions would the 11 states that had seceded be returned to the Union, and what would be the economic, political, and social future of 4 million freed African Americans, most of whom lived in the South? The Republicans wanted to secure the protection of freedmen and obtain an oath of loyalty from seceded states before they would be allowed back into the Union. Freed African Americans sought the right to vote, in addition to educational and economic opportunities. Southern whites wanted to turn back the clock as much as possible and keep African Americans in subservient positions.

Before Lincoln was assassinated, he presented a lenient plan for reunion. Only 10 percent of male voters in a southern state had to swear loyalty to the Union before a new state government could be organized. If the state government agreed to ban slavery, the state could rejoin the Union.

Lincoln's successor, Andrew Johnson, also offered a lenient plan. However, former Confederate leaders were soon gaining control of their state governments and thwarting efforts of freedmen to gain political and economic power. In response, Republicans in Congress passed the Civil Rights Act of 1866 and overrode Johnson's veto of the Fourteenth Amendment.

Radical Reconstruction, fashioned by congressional Republicans, brought changes to the South that advanced the rights of African Americans. But this would not last. Increasingly, African American efforts to gain and maintain their rights were met with violent opposition from southern whites. Any vestige of federal help ended with the contested election of 1876, when Rutherford B. Hayes agreed to withdraw federal troops from the South in exchange for support in the House of Representatives for his election.

By 1876, the southern states were back in the Union and free to establish their own laws limiting the opportunities of African Americans. These laws remained unchallenged by the federal government until well into the twentieth century.

Essential Questions

Use this graphic organizer to see the relationship between key concepts and the Chapter Essential Question.

Focus Question/Section 1
How did the government try to solve key problems facing the nation after the Civil War?
(p. 546)

Concept: Reconstruction

Focus Question/Section 2
How did disagreements over Reconstruction lead to conflict in government and in the South?
(p. 552)

Concept: Impeachment

Chapter Essential Question
What were the short-term and long-term effects of the Civil War?

Focus Question/Section 3
What were the effects of Reconstruction?
(p. 558)

Concept: Segregation

Differentiated Instruction

Summarizing

The ability to summarize effectively can help improve students' abilities to comprehend and recall text. Good summarizers make notes on the text and reread as they write. Poor summarizers read the text once and begin writing. Share this information with your students, and then use the following steps to model how to create a useful summary.

1. Review structural aids, such as headings, Key Terms, Checkpoints, and visual information in the text.

2. Predict what you think you will learn from the selection.

3. Read the selection and sort through the main ideas and details. Reread and take notes on key words from topic sentences that express the main idea of each paragraph.

4. Organize the ideas in your notes. Cluster ideas that go together.

5. Write your summary. As you write, be sure to cross out any information that does not seem important.

Have students write a summary of Section 1 of this chapter, using the steps outlined here.

Concepts Across Time

Have students develop an understanding of the enduring concepts of history by connecting these ideas.

Concept: Reconstruction

Students learning about Reconstruction should understand that reconstructing a region after a war not only includes rebuilding homes and shops, but also rebuilding social and political systems. Have students recall that after the American Revolution, Americans needed to work together to set up state and national governments. Ask: **What group was formed to develop a plan for national government for the United States?** (*the Constitutional Convention*) Discuss how the Convention drew up the Constitution and the process needed for approval. Use this concept when discussing all three sections.

Concept: Impeachment

Have students recall that the Constitution provides for impeachment as a means of removing a United States official, including the President and Vice President. Ask: **According to the Constitution, on what grounds can an official be impeached?** ("*treason, bribery, or other high crimes and misdemeanors [lesser crimes]*") Have students

recall that impeachment is the formal bringing of charges by the House, followed by a trial before the Senate. Review these provisions in the Constitution when discussing the impeachment of President Johnson in Section 2.

Concept: Checks and Balances

Have students recall the debates over ratification of the Constitution. Ask: **What method does the Constitution provide to keep any of the three branches of government from dominating the others?** (*checks and balances*) Review with students the checks and balances in the Constitution. As students study this chapter, ask them to identify examples of checks and balances in action. (*Lincoln vetoing the Wade-Davis bill, Congress overriding Johnson's veto of the Civil Rights Act of 1866, Congress passing the Fourteenth Amendment to prevent the Supreme Court from overruling the Civil Rights Act of 1866, the House impeaching President Johnson*) Use this concept when discussing all three sections.

Section 1 Lesson Plan

Objectives

Students will

1. Describe the postwar challenges that faced the nation.
2. Compare and contrast President Lincoln's plan for Reconstruction with the plan proposed by Congress.
3. Identify the goals of the Freedmen's Bureau.
4. Describe the immediate impact of Lincoln's assassination.

Differentiated Instruction Key

- **L1** Basic to Average
- **L2** All Students
- **L3** Average to Advanced
- **AR** Advanced Readers
- **ELL** English Language Learners
- **GT** Gifted and Talented
- **LPR** Less Proficient Readers
- **SN** Special Needs

Prepare to Read

Build Background Knowledge
Have students preview the section and predict what they will learn about early Reconstruction plans.

Set a Purpose for Reading
Have students begin to fill out the Reading Readiness Guide.

Preview Key Terms
Preview the section's key terms.

Instructional Resources

All in One Teaching Resources, Unit 5
- **L2** Chapter Prereading Guide, p. 4
- **L2** History Reading Skill, p. 77
- **L2** Reading Readiness Guide, p. 79
- **L2** Word Knowledge Rating Form, p. 78

Teacher's Edition
- **L2** Vocabulary Builder, pp. 545, 547

Differentiated Instruction

Guided Reading Audio CD
Spanish **ELL, LPR, SN**

Teach

Instruction
Preparing for Reunion
Describe Lincoln's Ten Percent Plan and Congress's Wade-Davis Bill.

The Freedmen's Bureau
Explain the tasks of the Freedmen's Bureau.

Lincoln Is Murdered
Discuss Lincoln's assassination and its effect on Reconstruction.

Instructional Resources

Interactive Reading and Notetaking Study Guide
- **L2** Chapter 16, Section 1

Discovery School Video
- **L2** Abraham Lincoln

Differentiated Instruction

Interactive Reading and Notetaking Study Guide, Adapted Version (English/Spanish)
- **L1** Chapter 16, Section 1 **ELL, LPR, SN**

Teacher's Edition
- **L1** Visualizing the Word, p. 545 **ELL, LPR, SN**
- **L1** Comparing and Contrasting, p. 546 **ELL, LPR, SN**
- **L1** Analyzing Historical Poems, p. 548 **LPR**
- **L3** Analyzing Historical Poems, p. 548 **GT**
- **L3** Drawing a Poster, p. 550 **GT**

All in One Teaching Resources, Unit 5
- **L3** *O Captain! My Captain!*, p. 82

Assess and Reteach

Assess Progress
Evaluate student comprehension with Check Your Progress and Section Quiz.

Reteach
Assign the Interactive Reading and Notetaking Study Guide to help struggling students.

Extend
Extend the lesson by having students read Lincoln's Second Inaugural Address and rewrite one of its paragraphs in their own words.

Instructional Resources

Interactive Reading and Notetaking Study Guide
- **L2** Chapter 16, Section 1

All in One Teaching Resources, Unit 5
- **L2** Reading Readiness Guide, p. 79
- **L2** Section Quiz, p. 87

Progress Monitoring Transparencies
- **L2** Chapter 16, Section 1

Differentiated Instruction

Teacher's Edition
- **L1** Checkpoints, TE pp. 547, 548, 549

SE on Audio CD
- **L1** Chapter 16 **ELL, LPR, SN**

Exploring Primary Sources in U.S. History CD-ROM
- **L3** Lincoln's Second Inaugural Address

Section 2 The Battle Over Reconstruction

 1 period, .5 block

Objectives

Students will

1. Explain why conflicts developed over plans for Reconstruction.
2. Describe the changes in the South brought about by Radical Reconstruction.
3. Explain how Congress tried to remove President Johnson from office.
4. Describe how the Ku Klux Klan and other secret societies tried to prevent African Americans from exercising their rights.

Differentiated Instruction Key

L1 Basic to Average	**AR** Advanced Readers
L2 All Students	**ELL** English Language Learners
L3 Average to Advanced	**GT** Gifted and Talented
	LPR Less Proficient Readers
	SN Special Needs

Prepare to Read

Build Background Knowledge
Preview the section and review with students the amendments they have learned about in the past and how these amendments changed the nation.

Set a Purpose for Reading
Have students begin to fill out the Reading Readiness Guide.

Preview Key Terms
Preview the section's key terms.

Instructional Resources

All in One Teaching Resources, Unit 5
L2 Reading Readiness Guide, p. 80

Teacher's Edition
L2 Vocabulary Builder, p. 553

Differentiated Instruction

🔊 **Guided Reading Audio CD**
Spanish **ELL, LPR, SN**

Teach

Instruction
A Growing Conflict
Describe the Thirteenth Amendment and President Johnson's Reconstruction plan.

The Fourteenth Amendment
Explain the purpose of the Fourteenth Amendment.

Radical Reconstruction
Discuss the changes that were made to the South and the advancement of African Americans under the Reconstruction Act of 1867.

Instructional Resources

📖 **Interactive Reading and Notetaking Study Guide**
L2 Chapter 16, Section 2

All in One Teaching Resources, Unit 5
L2 Readmitting the Confederacy, p. 83

Color Transparencies
L2 Ku Klux Klan

Differentiated Instruction

📖 **Interactive Reading and Notetaking Study Guide, Adapted Version (English/Spanish)**
L1 Chapter 16, Section 2 **ELL, LPR, SN**

Teacher's Edition
L1 Gaining Comprehension, p. 552 **ELL, LPR, SN**
L3 Debating, p. 554 **AR, GT**
L1 Geography and History, p. 556 **LPR, SN**

All in One Teaching Resources, Unit 5
L1 Rejoining the Union, p. 84

Assess and Reteach

Assess Progress
Evaluate student comprehension with Check Your Progress and Section Quiz.

Reteach
Assign the Interactive Reading and Notetaking Study Guide to help struggling students.

Extend
Extend the lesson by having students write a news report on racial terrorism in the South during Reconstruction.

Instructional Resources

📖 **Interactive Reading and Notetaking Study Guide**
L2 Chapter 16, Section 2

All in One Teaching Resources, Unit 5
L2 Reading Readiness Guide, p. 80
L2 Section Quiz, p. 88

Progress Monitoring Transparencies
L2 Chapter 16, Section 2

Differentiated Instruction

Teacher's Edition
L1 Checkpoints, TE pp. 553, 554, 557

🔊 **SE on Audio CD**
L1 Chapter 16 **ELL, LPR, SN**

Section 3 The End of Reconstruction

 3 periods, 1.5 blocks

Objectives

Students will

1. Explain why support for Reconstruction declined.
2. Describe how African Americans in the South lost many newly gained rights.
3. Describe the sharecropping system and how it trapped many in a cycle of poverty.
4. Identify the signs that the South began to develop a stronger economy by the 1880s.

Section 3 Lesson Plan

Differentiated Instruction Key

L1 Basic to Average
L2 All Students
L3 Average to Advanced

AR Advanced Readers
ELL English Language Learners
GT Gifted and Talented
LPR Less Proficient Readers
SN Special Needs

Prepare to Read

Build Background Knowledge
Preview the section and recall with students how the South changed during Reconstruction.

Set a Purpose for Reading
Have students begin to fill out the Reading Readiness Guide.

Preview Key Terms
Preview the section's key terms.

Instructional Resources

All in One Teaching Resources, Unit 5
L2 Reading Readiness Guide, p. 81

Teacher's Edition
L2 Vocabulary Builder, p. 559

Differentiated Instruction

Guided Reading Audio CD
Spanish ELL, LPR, SN

Teach

Instruction
Reconstruction's Conclusion
Discuss the events that led to the end of Reconstruction.

African Americans Lose Rights
Explain how southern states took away the rights of African Americans.

A Cycle of Poverty
Describe the poverty of sharecroppers.

Industrial Growth
Discuss the South's efforts to boost its economy by developing manufacturing.

Instructional Resources

Interactive Reading and Notetaking Study Guide
L2 Chapter 16, Section 3

All in One Teaching Resources, Unit 5
L2 Concept Lesson, p. 86
L2 Concept Organizer, p. 6
L2 Skills for Life Worksheet, p. 85

Color Transparencies
L2 Voting Patterns During Reconstruction
L2 History Interactive: Explore the Sharecropping Cycle

Differentiated Instruction

Interactive Reading and Notetaking Study Guide, Adapted Version (English/Spanish)
L1 Chapter 16, Section 3

Teacher's Edition
L1 Gaining Comprehension, p. 558 ELL, LPR, SN
L3 Comparing, p. 560 AR, GT
L3 Predicting, p. 562 AR, GT

Assess and Reteach

Assess Progress
Assign Check Your Progress and Section Quiz.

Reteach
Assign the Study Guide to help students.

Extend
Extend the lesson by having students complete the History Interactive activity.

Think Like a Historian
Using information from primary sources and the chapters in the unit, revisit the Unit Essential Question.

Instructional Resources

Interactive Reading and Notetaking Study Guide
L2 Chapter 16, Section 3

All in One Teaching Resources, Unit 5
L2 Reading Readiness Guide, p. 81
L2 Section Quiz, p. 89
L2 Chapter Test, p. 93

Color Transparencies
L2 Think Like a Historian, Unit 5

Progress Monitoring Transparencies
L2 Chapter 16, Section 3

Differentiated Instruction

Teacher's Edition
L1 Checkpoints, TE pp. 559, 561, 562, 563
All in One Teaching Resources, Unit 5
L1 Chapter Test, p. 90

SE on Audio CD
L1 Chapter 16 ELL, LPR, SN

Social Studies Skill Tutor CD-ROM
Analyze a Migration Map

Internet Resources
PHSchool.com

Historian's Apprentice Activity Pack

Use the following research activities to help students deepen their understanding of the Chapter Essential Question: **What were the short-term and long-term effects of the Civil War?** Students should use library or Internet resources. The Web Codes provided offer access to Internet resources students can use to complete each activity. Use the appropriate four-point rubric in Assessment Rubrics to evaluate the activity.

 Assessment Rubrics

Create a Timeline

Have students work in small groups to create a timeline to understand the sequence of events that led to African Americans gaining full civil rights in the United States, which began during Reconstruction. Tell students to use information from the Internet as well as key events from Chapter 16 on the timeline. Timelines should have 12–15 events listed. Encourage students to illustrate the events. Have students share their timelines with the class.

 Group research activity L2

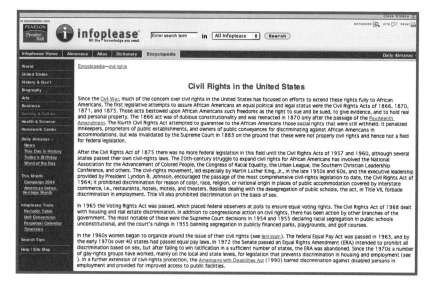

Go Online PHSchool.com **Web Code:** mye-0205

Debate the Proposals

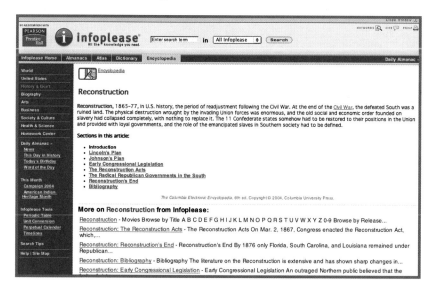

Have students research one of the Reconstruction plans they learned about in the chapter—Lincoln's Ten Percent Plan, the Wade-Davis Bill, Johnson's plan, or the Radical Reconstruction plan. Then have students prepare a speech explaining why the plan they researched should be adopted and used for Reconstruction. Have students debate the various positions for the class.

 Individual research activity AR, GT L3

 **Web Code:** mye-0206

Why It Matters

While many people believe a single vote cannot possibly affect the outcome of a presidential election, there have been some very close calls. In the presidential elections of 1876 and 2000, the Democratic candidates, Samuel Tilden and Al Gore, respectively, won the popular votes but lost the elections. Because the Gore-Bush race hinged on a few hundred votes in Florida, the outcome of the election was ultimately decided by the U.S. Supreme Court. In the Hayes-Tilden presidential race of 1876, 20 disputed votes ultimately forced the contest to be decided by an electoral commission. That race had a profound effect: The election of Rutherford B. Hayes marked the end of Reconstruction.

The end of Reconstruction meant a slow erosion of hard-won rights for African Americans. It would be another century, and another hard fought political battle, before these rights were fully restored.

Chapter Essential Question

What were the short-term and long-term effects of the Civil War?

Think Like a Historian

- To preview this chapter, have students review the content of these pages of the Student Edition. Ask: **What will you be learning about in this chapter?** *(the reuniting of the North and the South after the Civil War)*

- Have students read the quote from Felix Haywood and the section headings. Ask: **Why do you think Felix Haywood felt that "getting rich" was part of being free?** *(Students responses will vary, but students should recognize that formerly enslaved people might have assumed that they needed only freedom to become successful.)*

- Have students study the photo. There are African Americans of all ages in this photo. Ask: **Why do you think they wanted an education?** *(African Americans wanted to avoid being taken advantage of and to get ahead.)*

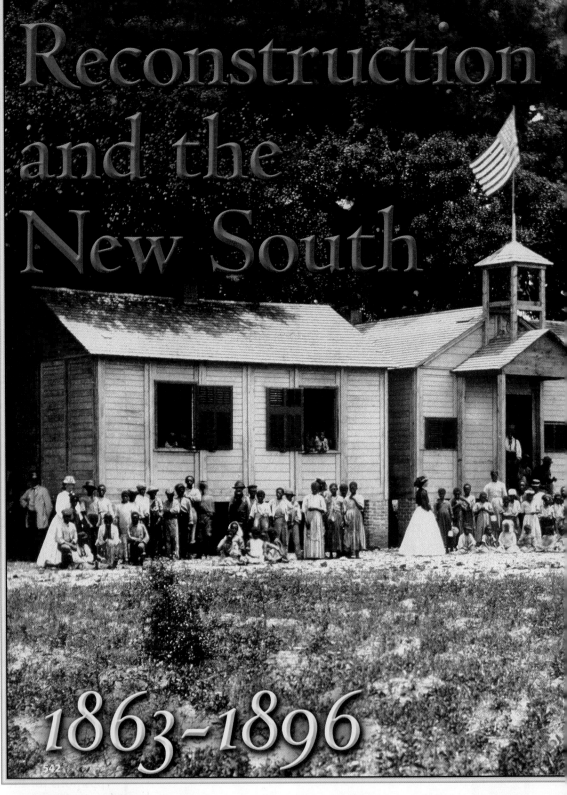

Reconstruction and the New South

1863–1896

Bibliography

For the Teacher

Donald, David Herbert. *Lincoln.* New York: Simon and Schuster, 1996.

Wade, Wyn Craig. *The Fiery Cross.* Oxford University Press, 1998.

For the Student

L1 McKissack, Patricia, et al. *Days of Jubilee.* Connecticut: Scholastic, 2003.

L2 Otfinoski, Peter. *Abraham Lincoln.* Connecticut: Children's Press, 2004.

L3 Schlesinger, Arthur Meir (ed), et al. *The Election of 1876 and the Administration of Rutherford B. Hayes.* Pennsylvania: Mason Crest Publishers, 2002.

*"We knowed freedom was on us....
We thought we was going
to get rich like the white folks....
But it didn't turn out that way."*

—Felix Haywood,
former slave, on Reconstruction

Students and teachers pose
outside the Freedmen's Bureau
school in Beaufort, South Carolina.

CHAPTER 16

What You Will Learn

Section 1
REBUILDING THE NATION
As the Civil War ended, Americans faced the problem of how to reunite the nation.

Section 2
THE BATTLE OVER RECONSTRUCTION
Disagreements over Reconstruction led to conflict in the government and in the South.

Section 3
THE END OF RECONSTRUCTION
With the end of Reconstruction, African Americans in the South lost many of the rights they had gained.

↺ **Reading Skill**

Analyze and Evaluate Proposals In this chapter, you will learn to identify central issues and frame good research questions in order to analyze and evaluate proposals.

543

Chapter 16

Visual Preview

? **What were the short-term and long-term effects of the Civil War?**

Build Background Knowledge L2

Discuss the definitions of "short-term" and "long-term." Have students look at the image of Richmond, Virginia, after the Civil War, on page 547. Explain that the rebuilding of homes and communities was one of the long-term effects of the war. It would take many years to repair the economic and social destruction found throughout the South. Short-term, or immediate effects, while devastating, could be addressed fairly rapidly. For example, restoring food supplies or offering temporary shelter to citizens might be accomplished more quickly than re-establishing railroad lines. Use the Idea Wave strategy (TE, p. T24) to lead a structured review of what the terms mean. Ask: **What were the long- and short-term effects of Hurricane Katrina?** *(Possible answers: the loss of lives and property; the role of the government in giving assistance; displacement of people)*

Instruction L2

■ For background information on conducting a lesson for the Visual Preview, see TE p. T20.

■ Write the Essential Question on the board. Discuss the concept of reconstruction. Explain to students that because of the war, many things changed, and that the people and the country had to rebuild their lives. Ask them which region of the country would probably face the most change and to give reasons for their answer.

■ Have students connect effects and reconstruction by reviewing the Cause and Effect chart on SE p. 536. Ask: **What effects do you think the end of slavery would have upon the nation?** *(Possible answer: The nation would have to absorb a formerly enslaved population and the South would have to change its economy because it lost its slave labor.)*

Reconstruction and the New South

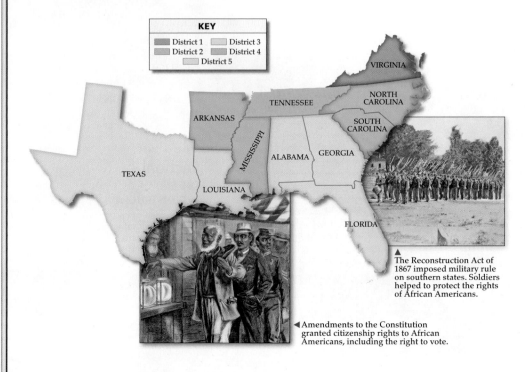

Military Districts, 1867

KEY
- District 1
- District 2
- District 3
- District 4
- District 5

VIRGINIA
NORTH CAROLINA
TENNESSEE
ARKANSAS
SOUTH CAROLINA
MISSISSIPPI
ALABAMA GEORGIA
TEXAS
LOUISIANA
FLORIDA

▲ The Reconstruction Act of 1867 imposed military rule on southern states. Soldiers helped to protect the rights of African Americans.

◀ Amendments to the Constitution granted citizenship rights to African Americans, including the right to vote.

U.S. Events

President Lincoln proposes mild Reconstruction plan. | **1863** | **1865** | Lincoln is assassinated five days after war ends. | **1867** | Radical Reconstruction begins.

1860 | **1865** | **1870**

World Events

1867 | Dominion of Canada is formed.

544

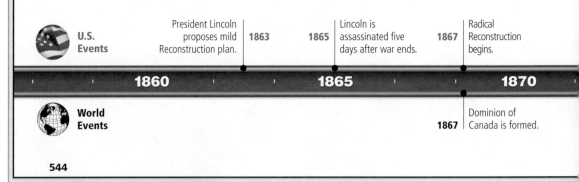

History Background

Losing Status In the years following Reconstruction, African Americans watched their constitutional rights erode as a result of several Supreme Court decisions that promoted racial segregation. In addition to *Plessy v. Ferguson* of 1896, *Cumming v. County Board of Education* in 1899 ruled that separate schools for the races were valid. In 1905, Georgia passed a law requiring separate public parks. In 1909, Mobile, Alabama, set a 10 p.m. curfew for African Americans.

Social segregation had an impact on other aspects of African American life. Economic segregation followed, causing black men to be excluded from newer trades and to lose their position of dominance in traditional trades such as carpentry. Lower incomes lead to poorer housing as well.

Self-Rule Returns to the South

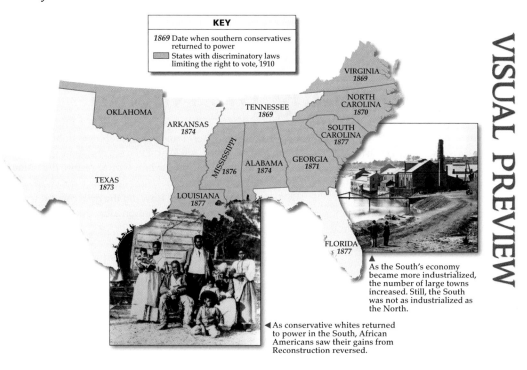

KEY

1869 Date when southern conservatives returned to power

States with discriminatory laws limiting the right to vote, 1910

OKLAHOMA

VIRGINIA
1869

TENNESSEE
1869

NORTH
CAROLINA
1870

ARKANSAS
1874

MISSISSIPPI

SOUTH
CAROLINA
1877

ALABAMA
1874

GEORGIA
1871

TEXAS
1873

MISSISSIPPI
1876

LOUISIANA
1877

FLORIDA
1877

As the South's economy became more industrialized, the number of large towns increased. Still, the South was not as industrialized as the North.

◄ As conservative whites returned to power in the South, African Americans saw their gains from Reconstruction reversed.

VISUAL PREVIEW

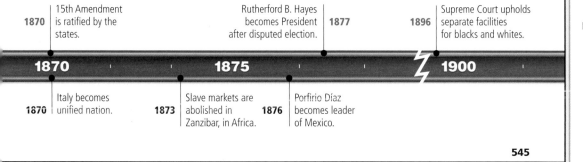

1870	**15th Amendment** is ratified by the states.	Rutherford B. Hayes becomes President after disputed election.	**1877**

1870   1875   1900

1896 Supreme Court upholds separate facilities for blacks and whites.

1870 Italy becomes unified nation.

1873 Slave markets are abolished in Zanzibar, in Africa.

1876 Porfirio Díaz becomes leader of Mexico.

545

Instruction (continued)

- Have students look at the timeline. Ask: **When did Lincoln propose a mild Reconstruction Plan?** *(1863)* **When did Radical Reconstruction begin?** *(1867)* **What do you think the difference might be between "mild" and "radical"?** *(mild meant kind and forgiving; radical meant strict or drastic)*

- Have students look at the maps and captions. As they review the *Military Districts, 1867* map, ask: **How many districts were created after the Civil War?** *(5)* **Which state was not affected?** *(Tennessee)* **Identify one short-term effect of the Civil War.** *(African Americans were granted citizenship and voting rights.)*

- Looking at the *Self-Rule Returns to the South* map, ask: **How did the economy in the South change?** *(It became less agricultural and began to move toward industry*

- Using the Think-Write-Pair-Share strategy (TE, p. T25), have students analyze the maps and images. Discuss with them some of the long-term effects of Reconstruction. *(Possible answers: the South became more industrialized; the number of large towns increased)*

- Have students rewrite the Essential Question in simple terms in their notes. **What were the immediate results of the Civil War and what happened later?** You may also post this question in a prominent place in the classroom and leave it there while discussing the chapter. Tell students to use the section focus questions as a guide to answering the Essential Question as they read.

- Tell students that as they complete the Notetaking Study Guide for this chapter, they will be building the answer to the Essential Question.

📖 **Interactive Reading and Notetaking Study Guide,** Chapter 16, (Adapted Version also available.)

Vocabulary Builder

Preview the Vocabulary Have students preview the vocabulary in the chapter and rate how well they know each word on the Word Knowledge Rating Form. Collect the sheets and explain that they will have a chance to go over the forms later.

All in One Teaching Resources, Unit 5, Word Knowledge Rating Form, p. 78

Monitor Progress Organize students into groups of three or four. Each group will complete a word map for two or three terms. Have them write the new term in the center of the page. Then, in each corner of the paper, have them write these labels: definition, sentence/picture, example, and nonexample. Review the completed word maps with the students.

Review and Preview

Students have learned about the causes and devastation of the Civil War. Now they will focus on the problems of reuniting the nation.

Section Focus Question

How did the government try to solve key problems facing the nation after the Civil War?

Before you begin the lesson for the day, write the Section Focus Question on the board. (*Lesson focus: The government developed a plan for Reconstruction and set up the Freedmen's Bureau to try to solve postwar problems.*)

Prepare to Read

Build Background Knowledge   **L2**

Ask students to preview the section by reading the headings and looking at the images. Then have students predict what they will be learning about in this section. Use the Numbered Heads strategy (TE, p. T24) to elicit responses.

Set a Purpose   **L2**

■ Read each statement in the Reading Readiness Guide aloud. Ask students to mark the statements True or False.

All in One Teaching Resources, Unit 5, Reading Readiness Guide, p. 79

■ Have students discuss the statements in pairs or groups of four, then mark their worksheets again. Use the Numbered Heads strategy (TE, p. T24) to call on students to share their group's perspectives. The students will return to these worksheets later.

Bind Up the Nation's Wounds

❝With malice toward none, with charity for all, with firmness in the right as God gives us to see the right, let us strive on to finish the work we are in, to bind up the nation's wounds, to care for him who shall have borne the battle and for his widow and his orphan—to do all which may achieve and cherish a just and lasting peace . . . .❞

—Abraham Lincoln,
Second Inaugural Address, 1865

◄ As Civil War soldiers returned home, President Lincoln hoped to swiftly heal the nation.

Rebuilding the Nation

Objectives

- Describe the postwar challenges that faced the nation.
- Compare and contrast President Lincoln's plan for Reconstruction with the plan proposed by Congress.
- Identify the goals of the Freedmen's Bureau.
- Describe the immediate impact of Lincoln's assassination.

Reading Skill

Identify Proposals In turbulent times, such as after the Civil War, people may have many different ideas about how to move forward. They identify goals to achieve and propose solutions to problems. For example, each proposal made by a government leader was intended to achieve a specific goal. As you read Section 1, identify these proposals and goals.

Key Terms and People

Abraham Lincoln   freedman
amnesty   John Wilkes Booth

Why It Matters After four years of bitter fighting, the Union had won the Civil War. Even so, problems remained as Americans tried to find the best way to restore the union and rebuild the nation.

❷ **Section Focus Question: How did the government try to solve key problems facing the nation after the Civil War?**

Preparing for Reunion

As the Civil War ended, enormous problems faced the nation, especially the South. Vast stretches of the South lay in ruins. What provisions would be made for people who had been freed from slavery? Homeless refugees—both African American and white—needed food, shelter, and work. (For more on conditions in the South after the Civil War, see the Life at the Time feature at the end of this section.)

Somehow, though, Americans had to master their hard feelings and bring the North and the South together again. This process, known as Reconstruction, would occupy the nation for years to come.

Lincoln's Ten Percent Plan Abraham Lincoln wanted to make it easy for the southern states to rejoin the Union. His goal was to bind up the wounds of war as quickly as possible.

In December 1863, Lincoln introduced what was called the Ten Percent Plan. As soon as ten percent of a state's voters swore an oath of loyalty to the United States, the voters could organize a new state government. That government would have to declare an end to slavery. Then, the state could send members to Congress and take part in the national government again.

546 Chapter 16 Reconstruction and the New South

Differentiated Instruction

L1 English Language Learners   **L1 Less Proficient Readers**   **L1 Special Needs**

Comparing and Contrasting Have students create a two-column chart comparing and contrasting Lincoln's Ten Percent Plan and the Wade-Davis Bill. Have them list the similarities in one column and the differences in the other column. Then create a chart on the board and have all students fill in their answers. Students should then add any answers to their charts that they may have missed.

Lincoln's plan included amnesty for former Confederates who took the loyalty oath. An amnesty is a group pardon. The offer of amnesty did not apply to Confederate government leaders and top military officers.

The Wade-Davis Bill Six months later, Congress passed a much stricter plan for Reconstruction called the Wade-Davis Bill. Under that bill, 50 percent of voters would have to sign a loyalty oath before a state could return to the Union. Moreover, anyone who had <u>voluntarily</u> fought for the Confederacy would be barred from voting for delegates to a convention to write a new state constitution. The bill did not give them a right to vote. Lincoln would not sign the Wade-Davis Bill, so it never became law.

Lincoln and his fellow Republicans hoped to see a strong Republican Party in the new South. Lincoln thought that his "soft," or lenient, Reconstruction policy would win support from influential southerners. Supporters of a strict policy toward the South, known as Radical Republicans, disagreed. They argued that only a strict plan would keep the people who had led the South into secession from regaining power and weakening the control of the Radical Republicans.

☑️**Checkpoint** How did Lincoln's plan for Reconstruction differ from that of the Radical Republicans in Congress?

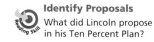

Identify Proposals What did Lincoln propose in his Ten Percent Plan?

Vocabulary Builder
voluntary (VAHL ahn tair ee) *adj.* not forced; done of one's own free will

Destruction in the South
Parts of Richmond, capital of the Confederacy, lay in ruins at war's end. **Critical Thinking: *Interpret Photographs*** *What do you think would be the most urgent need of the people of Richmond?*

547

The Freedmen's Bureau
Lincoln Is Murdered

pp. 548–549

Instruction
 L2

- Have students read The Freedmen's Bureau and Lincoln Is Murdered. Remind them to look for answers to the Section Focus Question.

- Ask: **How do you know that education was very important to newly freed slaves?** (*They traveled long distances to attend school.*)

- Assign the worksheet *O Captain! My Captain!* Then lead a class discussion on what the poet's feelings were about Lincoln.

  All in One Teaching Resources, Unit 5, *O Captain! My Captain!*, p. 82

- Remind students that Andrew Johnson became President under difficult circumstances. Ask: **Do you think Radical Republicans would support President Johnson?** (*Yes, because they thought he would take a hard line on Reconstruction.*)

Independent Practice
Have students complete the study guide for this section.

Monitor Progress

- Check Notetaking Study Guide entries for student understanding of the function of the Freedmen's Bureau and the effects of Lincoln's assassination.

- Tell students to fill in the last column of the Reading Readiness Guide. Probe for what they learned that confirms or invalidates each statement.

Explore More Video

Discovery School Video
This video summarizes the life and presidency of Abraham Lincoln.

Answers

✓Checkpoint It was a government agency to provide emergency relief and to establish schools, particularly for freedmen.

Make Predictions Possible answer: It may have delayed the start of Reconstruction and dashed hopes for a lenient Reconstruction plan.

The Freedmen's Bureau

It was urgent to deal with the needs of freedmen, enslaved people who had been freed by the war, as well as other war refugees. Congress created the Freedmen's Bureau in March 1865. The bureau's first duty was to provide emergency relief to people displaced by the war.

Education The Freedmen's Bureau set up schools to teach freedmen to read and write. So great was the hunger for education that many African American communities started schools on their own. To pay a teacher, people pooled their pennies and dollars.

Many teachers were northern white women, but a large number were northern African American women. Edmonia Highgate, the daughter of freed slaves, taught at a Freedmen's Bureau school in Louisiana. "The majority of my pupils come from plantations, three, four and even eight miles distant," she wrote. "So anxious are they to learn that they walk these distances so early in the morning."

Most southern states had lacked systems of public education before the war. Now, public schools began to educate both blacks and whites. The Freedmen's Bureau helped to start schools at which African Americans could extend their education. These schools gave rise to such present-day institutions as Fisk University in Tennessee and Hampton University in Virginia.

Defending Freedmen The Freedmen's Bureau helped freedmen find jobs and <u>resolved</u> disputes between whites and blacks. Some people tried to cheat the freedmen. The Freedmen's Bureau set up its own courts to deal with such disputes.

✓Checkpoint What was the Freedmen's Bureau?

Vocabulary Builder
<u>resolve</u> (ree SAHLV) **v.** to decide; to solve

Explore More Video
To learn more about Lincoln's life and presidency, view the video.

Assassinated! Lincoln's assassination set off an intense hunt for the killer, John Wilkes Booth. ***Critical Thinking: Make Predictions*** *What effect do you think the assassination of Lincoln would have on the nation?*

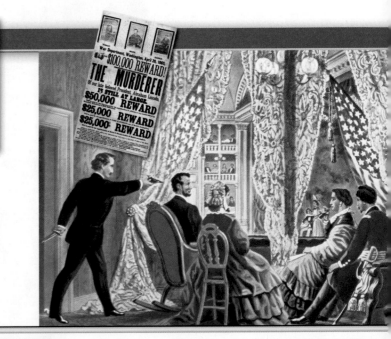

548

Differentiated Instruction

L3 Gifted and Talented

Analyzing Historical Poems Before you assign the worksheet *O Captain! My Captain!*, assign a student with dramatic talent to prepare in advance to read the poem with appropriate delivery. The reading of

L1 Less Proficient Readers

this poem with proper emphasis and pauses will help less able readers and auditory learners to comprehend its meaning more clearly.

Lincoln Is Murdered

As the war drew to a close, President Lincoln hoped for a peaceful Reconstruction. But Lincoln had no chance to put his plans into practice. He was shot dead on April 14, 1865, five days after Lee's surrender.

A Confederate sympathizer, John Wilkes Booth, slipped up behind Lincoln while he and his wife were attending a play at the Ford's Theatre in Washington. Booth fired a single pistol shot into the President's head. Lincoln died a few hours later.

Booth was shot dead two weeks later after pursuers trapped him in a barn and set it on fire. Eight people were convicted and four were hanged for their parts in the plot to kill Lincoln.

News of Lincoln's death shocked the nation. A special funeral train carried Lincoln's body back to Illinois for burial. In town after town, vast crowds paid their last respects.

Lincoln's successor was Vice President Andrew Johnson of Tennessee. Johnson was a southern Democrat who had remained loyal to the Union. Because Johnson had expressed bitterness toward the Confederates, many expected him to take a strict approach to Reconstruction.

✔ **Checkpoint**   Why did many people expect Johnson to take a hard line on Reconstruction?

⭐ **Looking Back and Ahead**   Many people feared the effect of Lincoln's assassination on the process of Reconstruction. In the next section, you will learn how Reconstruction was affected by tensions between Lincoln's successor and members of Congress.

Section 1 | Check Your Progress

Progress Monitoring Online
For: Self-test with instant help
Visit: PHSchool.com
Web Code: mya-5121

Comprehension and Critical Thinking

1. **(a) Recall** What problems faced the South at the end of the Civil War?
   (b) Contrast Why did the South have greater difficulty than the North in recovering from the Civil War?

2. **(a) Recall** How did Lincoln's plan for Reconstruction differ from the Wade-Davis Bill?
   (b) Explain Problems What problems do you see for reuniting the nation in each plan?

Reading Skill

3. **Identify Proposals** Reread the paragraphs under the heading "The Freedmen's Bureau." What did the bureau propose to do to help the freedmen?

Key Terms

Answer the following questions in complete sentences that show your understanding of the key terms.
4. What did former Confederates have to do to get amnesty under Lincoln's plan to rebuild the Union?
5. Who were the freedmen?

Writing

6. Choose the best sentence to end a research paper about Abraham Lincoln. Explain your choice.
   Sentences:
   (a) Abraham Lincoln was humbly born on February 12, 1809, but he went on to be one of our greatest Presidents.
   (b) Because Abraham Lincoln did not win a majority of the votes cast, his presidency turned out to be the nation's most turbulent period.
   (c) His trials as President changed Lincoln into the steady leader who saved the Union in its darkest hour.

Assess Progress   L2

Have students complete Check Your Progress. Administer the Section Quiz.

All in One **Teaching Resources,** Section Quiz, Chapter 16, p. 87

To further assess student understanding, use the Progress Monitoring Transparency.

Progress Monitoring Transparencies, Chapter 16, Section 1

Reteach   L1

If students need more instruction, have them read this section in the Interactive Reading and Notetaking Study Guide and complete the accompanying question.

📖 **Interactive Reading and Notetaking Study Guide,** Chapter 16, Section 1 (Adapted Version also available.)

Extend   L3

Have students read President Lincoln's Second Inaugural Address. Have them write a paragraph explaining whether they think Lincoln's plan for Reconstruction was in keeping with the ideas in his Second Inaugural Address. Have students present their work to the class.

🌐 **Exploring Primary Sources in U.S. History CD-ROM,** *Lincoln's Second Inaugural Address*

Progress Monitoring Online

Students may check their comprehension of this section by completing the Progress Monitoring Online graphic organizer and self-quiz.

Section 1 Check Your Progress

1. **(a)** The South was in ruins and refugees needed food, shelter, and work.
   (b) Because of the vast destruction, the South had fewer resources to work with.

2. **(a)** Lincoln's plan was more lenient. It required that only 10 percent of voters swear an oath of loyalty to the United States and offered amnesty to Confederate fighters and supporters, except for leaders. The Wade-Davis Bill required 50 percent of a state's voters to swear loyalty to the Union and denied political rights to anyone who volunteered to fight for the Confederacy.
   (b) Lincoln's plan might make it easier for former Confederates to regain control of the state governments; Congress's plan might cause resentment.

3. It tried to find them jobs.

4. Possible answer: In order to get amnesty under Lincoln's plan, they had to take the loyalty oath to the U.S.

5. Possible answer: The freedmen were enslaved people who had been freed as a result of the Civil War.

6. Answers will vary, but should be well supported. Students should indicate that the answer would depend on the focus of the research paper.

Answer

✔ **Checkpoint** Johnson expressed bitterness toward the Confederates.

The South After the Civil War

p. 550

Build Background Knowledge L2

Ask students to recall what they learned in Chapter 15 about the Civil War battles. Ask: **Where did most of the battles take place?** (*in the South*) Using the Idea Wave strategy (TE, p. T24), have students list possible problems this might have caused in the South.

Instruction L2

■ Read the introduction aloud with students. Have students study the pictures and have volunteers read the captions aloud.

■ Ask: **According to these pictures and the picture on p. 547, what challenges faced the South after the Civil War?** (*Both whites and blacks had to find a way to earn a living; schools had to be provided; buildings and railroads had to be rebuilt.*) **How do you think this level of devastation affected the region?** (*Possible answer: It made economic recovery very slow.*)

■ Ask: **What problems would the collapse of the banking system cause?** (*Possible answer: It would be hard for people to get loans to start businesses that would provide employment.*)

Monitor Progress

Ask students to work with a partner to study the pictures on these pages and to use what they have learned to write a new caption for each picture. Monitor what students have written.

The South After the Civil War

The Civil War had a devastating impact on the South. All southerners—rich and poor, black and white—faced a long struggle to rebuild their lives and their land.

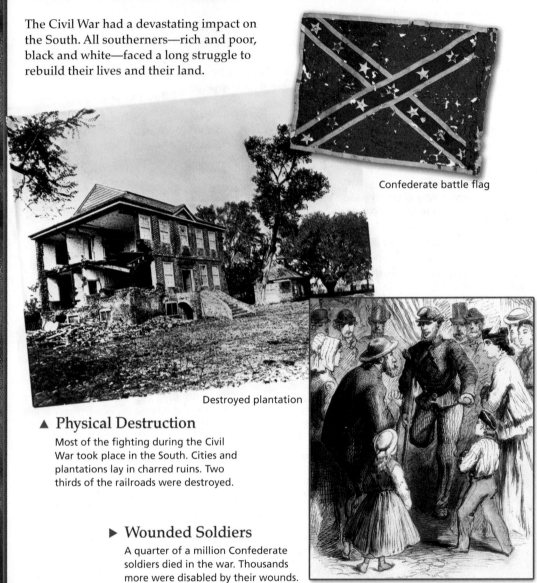

Confederate battle flag

Destroyed plantation

▲ **Physical Destruction**

Most of the fighting during the Civil War took place in the South. Cities and plantations lay in charred ruins. Two thirds of the railroads were destroyed.

▶ **Wounded Soldiers**

A quarter of a million Confederate soldiers died in the war. Thousands more were disabled by their wounds.

Returning Confederate veteran

550 Chapter 16 Reconstruction and the New South

Differentiated Instruction

L3 **Gifted and Talented**

Drawing a Poster Remind students that the Freedmen's Bureau helped freedmen learn to read by setting up schools across the South. Have students create a poster advertising one of these new schools and encouraging freedmen to attend. Tell students that the poster should include several visuals and little, if any, text because most of the former slaves could not read.

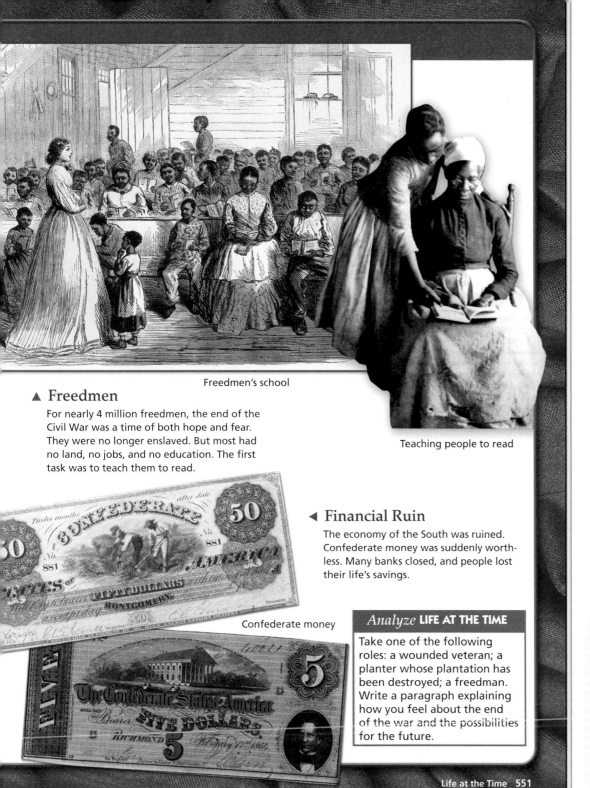

Freedmen's school

Teaching people to read

▲ Freedmen

For nearly 4 million freedmen, the end of the Civil War was a time of both hope and fear. They were no longer enslaved. But most had no land, no jobs, and no education. The first task was to teach them to read.

Confederate money

◀ Financial Ruin

The economy of the South was ruined. Confederate money was suddenly worthless. Many banks closed, and people lost their life's savings.

Analyze **LIFE AT THE TIME**

Take one of the following roles: a wounded veteran; a planter whose plantation has been destroyed; a freedman. Write a paragraph explaining how you feel about the end of the war and the possibilities for the future.

History Background

A Helping Hand Freed slaves and whites who were left starving, injured, or homeless after the Civil War received help from the Freedmen's Bureau. From 1865 to 1869, the Bureau distributed about 15 million food rations to blacks and 5 million to whites. By 1867, it had set up 45 hospitals.

It also helped some freedmen settle on abandoned lands. Once President Johnson granted amnesty to former Confederates, however, freedmen lost access to this land and most were reduced to laboring for others.

Writing Rubric Share the rubric with the students.

Score 1 Response has unsupported opinions, does not address topic.
Score 2 Response addresses some of the issues, little support given.
Score 3 Response is thoughtful, support given for opinions.
Score 4 Response is thorough, well-written, well-supported.

Answer

Analyze **LIFE AT THE TIME** Students' paragraphs should reflect what they have learned from the chapter and this feature, and display an understanding of what the person's perspective would probably be based on how the person has been affected by the war.

Review and Preview

Students have learned that President Lincoln and Congress disagreed on a plan for reuniting the nation. Now they will focus on how the Radical Republicans controlled Reconstruction.

Section Focus Question

How did disagreements over Reconstruction lead to conflict in government and in the South?

Before you begin the lesson for the day, write the Section Focus Question on the board. (*Lesson focus: President Johnson and Radical Republicans had different ideas for Reconstruction, which led Republicans to attempt to remove Johnson from office. Some white southerners who did not agree with Reconstruction used violence to keep African Americans out of power.*)

Prepare to Read

Build Background Knowledge   L2

Tell students that they will learn about three constitutional amendments in this section. Using the Idea Wave strategy (TE, p. T24), have students brainstorm for what they know about constitutional amendments—what they are and how they come about.

Set a Purpose   L2

■ Read each statement in the Reading Readiness Guide aloud. Ask students to mark the statements True or False.

  All in One Teaching Resources, Unit 5, Reading Readiness Guide, p. 80

■ Have students discuss the statements in pairs or groups of four, then mark their worksheets again. Use the Numbered Heads strategy (TE, p. T24) to call on students to share their group's perspectives. The students will return to these worksheets later.

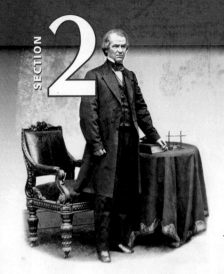

◀ President Andrew Johnson

Who Shall Rule the South?

❝ Rebels found themselves in places of trust, while the truehearted Unionists, who had watched for the coming of our flag and ought to have to have enjoyed its protecting power, were driven into hiding places. ❞

—Senator Charles Sumner, criticizing President Johnson's Reconstruction actions in the South, 1868

The Battle Over Reconstruction

Objectives

• Explain why conflicts developed over plans for Reconstruction.

• Describe the changes in the South brought about by Radical Reconstruction.

• Explain how Congress tried to remove President Johnson from office.

• Describe how the Ku Klux Klan and other secret societies tried to prevent African Americans from exercising their rights.

🔄 Reading Skill

Analyze Proposals Proposals must be carried out in order to be effective. The proposal must include details on how to put the proposal into action. As you read Section 2, look at the suggested ideas for carrying out proposals.

Key Terms and People

Andrew Johnson
black codes
Hiram Revels
Blanche Bruce
scalawag
carpetbagger
impeachment

Why It Matters The Radical Republicans in Congress wanted a strict form of Reconstruction. However, President Johnson had a more lenient plan. The stage was set for a battle between Congress and the Presidency.

❓ **Section Focus Question: How did disagreements over Reconstruction lead to conflict in government and in the South?**

A Growing Conflict

Like President Lincoln, Andrew Johnson proposed a relatively lenient plan of Reconstruction. He followed Lincoln's example in putting his plan into effect himself, without consulting legislators.

The Thirteenth Amendment In January 1865, Congress approved a constitutional amendment to abolish slavery throughout the nation. When ratified later that year, the Thirteenth Amendment banned both slavery and forced labor. It gave Congress the power to make laws to enforce its terms.

Johnson's Plan Like Lincoln, Johnson issued a broad amnesty to most former Confederates. Johnson allowed southern states to organize new governments and elect representatives to Congress. Each state, though, was required to abolish slavery and ratify the Thirteenth Amendment. By late fall, most of the states had met Johnson's requirements. When Congress met in December 1865, the representatives and senators elected by white southerners included many former Confederate leaders.

552   Chapter 16 Reconstruction and the New South

Differentiated Instruction

L1 English Language Learners   **L1 Less Proficient Readers**   **L1 Special Needs**

Gaining Comprehension English language learners may have difficulty understanding the term *black codes*. Looking up each of the words in the dictionary will be of little help. Explain that *codes* can be defined as a set of rules for how to act. Ask students to use that definition of *codes* to explain the meaning of the term *black codes*.

Violence Against Freedmen

Popular magazines carried pictures of violence against freedmen, including the burning of a school (above) and the riots in Memphis (left). **Critical Thinking: *Make Predictions*** *How do you think northerners might have reacted to these pictures?*

Congress quickly rejected Johnson's approach. First, it refused to seat the southern senators and representatives. Next, the two houses appointed a committee to form a new plan for the South.

In a series of public hearings, the committee heard testimony about black codes—new laws used by southern states to control African Americans. Critics claimed that the codes replaced the system of slavery with near-slavery. In Mississippi, for example, African Americans could not vote or serve on juries. If unable to pay a fine as ordered by a court, they might be hired out by the sheriff to any white person who paid the fine.

Anger at these developments led Congress to adopt an increasingly hard line. The hardest line was taken by the Radical Republicans. The Radicals had two key goals. One was to prevent former Confederates from regaining control over southern politics. The other was to protect the freedmen and guarantee them a right to vote.

☑Checkpoint **How did Congress respond to Johnson's plan for Reconstruction?**

The Fourteenth Amendment

The struggle over Reconstruction led to direct clashes between the President and Congress during 1866. At issue were two laws and a constitutional amendment.

Voicing alarm at the treatment of African Americans in the South, Congress passed the Civil Rights Act of 1866. It granted citizenship rights to African Americans and guaranteed the civil rights of all people except Native Americans.

President Johnson vetoed the bill and another one extending the life of the Freedmen's Bureau. Congress voted to overturn both vetoes. Under the Constitution, a vetoed bill becomes law if it wins the votes of two thirds of each house. Both bills received enough votes to become law.

Vocabulary Builder
critic (KRIHT ihk) ***n.*** someone who makes judgments on the value of objects or actions

A Growing Conflict
The Fourteenth Amendment

pp. 552–553

Instruction 　　L2

- **Vocabulary Builder** Before teaching this lesson, preteach the High-Use Words **critic** and **register,** using the strategy on TE p. T21.

  Key Terms Have students continue to fill in the See It–Remember It chart.

- Read A Growing Conflict and The Fourteenth Amendment with students using the Oral Cloze strategy (TE, p. T22)

- Ask: **What was the purpose of the Thirteenth Amendment?** (*to ban slavery throughout the United States*) **Why was it necessary?** (*Even after the Civil War, slavery was legal in some parts of the country.*)

- Have students describe the two key goals of Radical Republicans. (*to prevent southern planters from regaining control of the government and to protect freedmen and guarantee them the right to vote*) Ask: **Why do you think the struggle over Reconstruction was getting more bitter?** (*Possible answer: Radical Republicans saw signs that the southern states were trying to turn back the clock.*)

- Ask students to describe in their own words the details of the Fourteenth Amendment. (*Answers will vary, but students should mention due process, equal protection of the laws, definition of a citizen, and reduction of a state's representation in Congress if any male citizen over age 21 was denied the right to vote.*)

Vocabulary Builder

Use the information below to teach students this section's high-use words.

High-Use Word	Definition and Sample Sentence
critic, p. 553	***n.*** someone who makes judgments on the value of objects or actions The war hawks were **critics** of Madison's lenient policy with the British.
register, p. 555	***v.*** enroll or record officially American citizens who are over 18 can **register** to vote.

Answers

Make Predictions Possible answer: Northerners probably reacted with horror and outrage.

☑Checkpoint Congress rejected his approach and appointed a committee to form a new plan.

Instruction (continued)

■ **Ask: Why do you think the Fourteenth Amendment failed to win approval until Radical Republicans took control of Reconstruction?** (*Possible answer: Former Confederate leaders did not want to give the vote to African Americans.*)

Independent Practice

Have students continue filling in the study guide for this section.

📖 **Interactive Reading and Notetaking Study Guide,** Chapter 16, Section 2 (Adapted Version also available.)

Monitor Progress

As students fill in the Notetaking Study Guide, circulate to make sure individuals understand the purpose of the Thirteenth and Fourteenth amendments and the nature of the conflict between President Johnson and Congress over Reconstruction. Provide assistance as needed. If students do not seem to have a good understanding of the material, have them reread the section.

Answers

Reading Charts (a) Radical Republican plan **(b)** Johnson's plan allowed former Confederate officials political rights and did not do enough to protect African Americans.

🕐 **Reading Skill** It says that everyone born or naturalized in the U.S. is a citizen with the rights guaranteed to citizens; states cannot pass laws that take away these rights; and states cannot pass laws that deprive citizens of equal protection from laws. These laws helped protect the rights of freedmen.

✔**Checkpoint** It gave freedmen the same rights as people of other races and forbade states from passing laws that took away their rights.

554 Chapter 16

Opposing Plans for Reconstruction

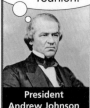

I want a quick reunion.

President Andrew Johnson

President Andrew Johnson (1865)	Radical Republicans (1867)
• Majority of white men must swear oath of loyalty	• Must disband state government
• Must ratify 13th Amendment	• Must write new constitution
• Former Confederate officials may vote and hold office	• Must ratify 13th and 14th Amendments
	• Must allow African American men to vote

We want real change.

Congressman Thaddeus Stevens

Reading Charts
Skills Activity

President Andrew Johnson and Republican members of Congress, led by Thaddeus Stevens, disagreed about the process of Reconstruction.

(a) Read a Chart Which plan required states to write new constitutions?

(b) Detect Points of View Why did Radical Republicans think Johnson's plan was not strict enough?

Congress also drew up the Fourteenth Amendment to the Constitution, seeking to make sure that the Supreme Court did not strike down the Civil Rights Act. Republicans remembered the Court's Dred Scott decision. In that ruling, the Court declared that no one descended from an enslaved person could be a United States citizen.

The amendment failed at first to win the approval of three fourths of the states. It finally was approved in 1868, after Radicals took control of Reconstruction.

The Fourteenth Amendment says that all people born or naturalized in the United States are citizens. The amendment also declares that states may not pass laws that take away a citizen's rights. Nor can a state "deprive any person of life, liberty, or property, without due process of law; nor deny to any person . . . the equal protection of the laws."

Another provision declares that any state that denies the vote to any male citizen over the age of 21 will have its representation in Congress reduced. That provision was not enforced until the 1970s.

🕐 **Analyze Proposals**
Congress proposed the Fourteenth Amendment to give freedmen a way to defend their rights. How would the amendment put that goal into action?

The Fourteenth Amendment became a powerful tool for enforcing civil rights. However, almost a century passed before it was used for that purpose.

✔**Checkpoint** How did the Fourteenth Amendment seek to protect the freedmen?

Radical Reconstruction

Tempers rose as the elections of 1866 approached. White rioters and police attacked and killed many African Americans in two southern cities, Memphis and New Orleans. Outrage at this violence led Congress to push a stricter form of Reconstruction.

Differentiated Instruction

L3 Advanced Readers   **L3 Gifted and Talented**

Debating Tell students to suppose it is 1867 and Congress is debating whether the Reconstruction Act is necessary. Divide students into two groups—one group should argue for the passing of the act and the other should argue against it. Have groups develop evidence using library or Internet sources for their position on the issue and then hold the debate in class.

Radicals in Charge By early 1867, the Radical Republicans had won enough support from moderates to begin a "hard" Reconstruction. This period is known as Radical Reconstruction.

The Reconstruction Act of 1867 removed the governments of all southern states that had refused to ratify the Fourteenth Amendment. It then imposed military rule on these states, dividing them into five military districts. Before returning to the Union, each state had to write a new constitution and ratify the Fourteenth Amendment. Each state also had to let African Americans vote.

Under military rule, the South took on a new look. Soldiers helped <u>register</u> southern blacks to vote. In five states, African American voters outnumbered white voters. In the election of 1868, Republicans won all southern states. The states wrote new constitutions and, in June 1868, Congress seated representatives from seven "reconstructed" states.

Time of Hope and Advancement For the first time, African Americans in the South played an active role in politics. Prominent among them were free-born African Americans—carpenters, barbers, preachers—and former Union soldiers.

African Americans were elected as sheriffs, mayors, judges, and legislators. Sixteen African Americans served in the U.S. House of Representatives between 1872 and 1901. Two others, Hiram Revels and Blanche Bruce, served in the Senate.

Historians once took a critical view of Radical Reconstruction, focusing on the widespread corruption and excessive spending during this period. More recently, however, historians have written about important accomplishments of Reconstruction. They noted that during Reconstruction, southern states opened public schools for the first time. Legislators spread taxes more evenly and made fairer voting rules. They gave property rights to women. In addition, states rebuilt bridges, roads, and buildings destroyed by the war.

Radical Reconstruction brought other sweeping changes to the South. Old leaders lost much of their power. The Republican Party built a strong following based on three key groups. One group, called scalawags by their opponents, were southern whites who had opposed secession. Freedmen voters made up a second group.

The third group were carpetbaggers, a name given by southerners to northern whites who went south to start businesses or pursue political office. Critics claimed that these northerners were in such a rush to head south that they just tossed their clothes into cheap satchels called carpetbags.

Vocabulary Builder
register (REJ is tur) *v.* enroll or record officially

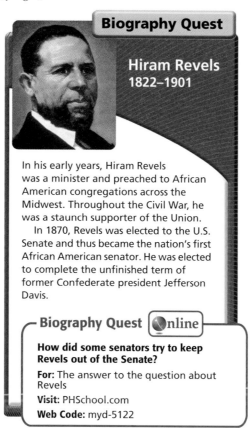

Biography Quest

Hiram Revels
1822–1901

In his early years, Hiram Revels was a minister and preached to African American congregations across the Midwest. Throughout the Civil War, he was a staunch supporter of the Union.

In 1870, Revels was elected to the U.S. Senate and thus became the nation's first African American senator. He was elected to complete the unfinished term of former Confederate president Jefferson Davis.

Biography Quest **Online**

How did some senators try to keep Revels out of the Senate?

For: The answer to the question about Revels

Visit: PHSchool.com

Web Code: myd-5122

History Background

African Americans in Government In 1966, Republican Edward W. Brooke of Massachusetts became the first African American to be elected to the Senate since Reconstruction. In 1992, Democrat Carol Moseley Braun of Illinois became the first African American woman to be elected senator. In 1995, there was a record number of African Americans in Congress—40.

Instruction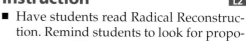

- Have students read Radical Reconstruction. Remind students to look for propositions and their support.

- Discuss the details of the Reconstruction Act of 1867. (*It threw out any southern state government that had refused to ratify the Fourteenth Amendment and divided the South into five military districts that were governed by army commanders.*) Ask: **Under the Radical Republican plan, what did southern states have to do to rejoin the Union?** (*write new constitutions, ratify the Fourteenth Amendment, and allow African Americans to vote*)

- Ask students to list the important accomplishments of Reconstruction. (*African Americans played an active role in politics for the first time; southern states opened public schools for the first time; legislators spread taxes more evenly, made fairer voting rights, and gave property rights to women; states rebuilt bridges, roads, and buildings destroyed by the war.*)

- Ask: **Why do you think Radical Republicans wanted President Johnson removed from office?** (*Possible answers: Johnson and the Radicals disagreed on many aspects of Reconstruction, so the Radicals may have believed it would be easier to carry out Reconstruction their way if Johnson was removed from office.*)

- Distribute the Readmitting the Confederacy worksheet. After students have completed the activity individually, have them share their answers with the class. Use their answers to guide a class discussion on why they think southern states resisted approving the Fourteenth Amendment. (*African American voters often outnumbered white voters, and whites did not want to lose control of the government.*)

All in One Teaching Resources, Unit 5, Readmitting the Confederacy, p. 83

Answer

Biography Quest Some senators tried to keep Revels out of the Senate by arguing that he had not been a citizen for the nine required years, as they believed African Americans had only become citizens with the passage of the 1866 Civil Rights Act.

Instruction (continued)

- Ask students to explain the purpose of the Fifteenth Amendment. (*to bar states from denying the right to vote on account of race, color, or previous status as a slave*)
  Ask: **How were some southern states still able to prevent African Americans from voting?** (*by requiring that voters own property or pay a tax, which African Americans often could not afford*)

- Display the Ku Klux Klan transparency and have students answer the questions.

Color Transparencies, Ku Klux Klan

Independent Practice

Have students complete the study guide for this section.

Interactive Reading and Notetaking Study Guide, Chapter 16, Section 2 (Adapted Version also available.)

Monitor Progress

- Check Notetaking Study Guide entries for student understanding of the accomplishments of Radical Reconstruction and the strides and setbacks associated with the African American right to vote.

- Tell students to fill in the last column of the Reading Readiness Guide. Probe for what they learned that confirms or invalidates each statement.

All in One Teaching Resources, Unit 5, Reading Readiness Guide, p. 80

Assess and Reteach

Assess Progress   L2

Have students complete Check Your Progress. Administer the Section Quiz.

All in One Teaching Resources, Section Quiz, p. 88

To further assess student understanding, use the Progress Monitoring Transparency.

Progress Monitoring Transparencies, Chapter 16, Section 2

Answers

Reading Political Cartoons (a) Two of the following: the skull and crossbones, the weapons, the burning school, the KKK member, the White League member, the hanging person, the frightened couple; Possible answers: frightened, sad, distressed, devastated, worried **(b)** Nast thinks the Klan is evil and violent.

The Impact of Violence

The terror— "WORSE THAN SLAVERY"

Burning school-house

The Ku Klux Klan used terror and violence to keep African Americans from voting. Northern cartoonist Thomas Nast shows his point of view about the Klan and other secret societies in this cartoon.

(a) Distinguish Relevant Information Point out two negative images in the cartoon. Give one word to describe the family.

(b) Detect Points of View What do you think is Nast's opinion of the Ku Klux Klan?

Targeting President Johnson Meanwhile, the Radicals mounted a major challenge against President Johnson. The Radicals tried to remove Johnson from office by impeachment. Impeachment is the bringing of formal charges against a public official. The Constitution says the House may impeach a President for "treason, bribery, or other high crimes and misdemeanors." After impeachment, there is a trial in the Senate. If convicted, the President is removed from office.

Johnson escaped removal—but barely. The House voted to impeach him in February 1868. The Senate trial took place from March to May. In the end, the votes went 35 for and 19 against Johnson. This was one vote short of the required two-thirds majority.

The Election of 1868 General Ulysses S. Grant, a war hero, won the presidential election for the Republicans in the fall of 1868. With southern states back in the Union under military rule, some 500,000 African Americans voted, mainly for Republicans. Grant won the electoral votes of 26 of the 34 states.

Grant was a moderate who had support from many northern business leaders. With his election, the Radicals began losing their grip on the Republican Party.

Fifteenth Amendment Over opposition from Democrats, Congress approved the Fifteenth Amendment in 1869. It barred all states from denying African American males the right to vote "on account of race, color, or previous condition of servitude."

Differentiated Instruction

L1 Less Proficient Readers   **L1 Special Needs**

Geography and History If students are having trouble understanding how southern states were readmitted to the Union, distribute the Rejoining the Union worksheet. Have students work with a partner to read the passage and answer the questions. Remind students that the underlined portions of the text and highlighted portions of the map will help them answer the questions. Circulate as pairs complete the worksheet, and provide assistance as needed.

All in One Teaching Resources, Unit 5, Rejoining the Union, p. 84

Some African Americans said the amendment was too weak. It did not prevent states from requiring voters to own property or pay a voting tax. The amendment took effect in 1870, after three fourths of the states gave their approval.

The Ku Klux Klan Angry at being shut out of power, some whites resorted to violence. They created secret societies to terrorize African Americans and their white allies.

The best-known secret society was the Ku Klux Klan. Its members donned white robes with hoods that hid their faces. Klansmen rode by night to the homes of African American voters, shouting threats and burning wooden crosses. If threats failed, the Klan would whip, torture, shoot, or hang African Americans and white Republicans. Klan violence took hundreds of lives during the election of 1868.

The terror went on even after Congress responded with new laws. The Ku Klux Klan Acts of 1870 and 1871 barred the use of force against voters. Although the original Klan dissolved, new groups took its place. In the face of the terrorism, voting by African Americans declined. The stage was set for the end of Reconstruction.

☑ **Checkpoint** What were the key elements of Radical Reconstruction?

⭐ **Looking Back and Ahead** Although Reconstruction guaranteed rights to more Americans, huge challenges remained. In the next section, you will learn more about the process of rebuilding the South. You will also learn that as time went on, Americans became less interested in Reconstruction. This set the scene for a return of power to former Confederates.

Terror and Violence
To spread terror, Ku Klux Klan members wore hoods like the one above when they attacked their victims. They also left miniature coffins as warnings. **Critical Thinking: Draw Conclusions** Why do you think the hoods helped spread terror?

Section 2 | Check Your Progress

Progress Monitoring Online
For: Self-test with instant help
Visit: PHSchool.com
Web Code: mya-5122

Comprehension and Critical Thinking

1. **(a) Recall** Which amendment guaranteed African Americans the right to vote: the Thirteenth, Fourteenth, or Fifteenth?
(b) Apply Information How did each of these three amendments help to expand democracy?

2. **(a) Recall** What was the Ku Klux Klan?
(b) Evaluate Information Why do you think the Klan was not formed before the Civil War?

🔘 **Reading Skill**

3. **Analyze Proposals** In 1867, the Radical Republicans in Congress proposed the Reconstruction Act. What actions did this proposal involve?

Key Terms

Complete each of the following sentences so that the second part clearly shows your understanding of the key term.

4. Radical Republicans in the House of Representatives tried to remove the President by impeachment, which is _____.

5. Former Confederates wanted to control the lives of freedmen through black codes, which were _____.

Writing

6. Rewrite the following passage to correct the grammar, spelling, and punctuation errors that you find. **Passage:** President Johnson wanting to show mercy to the defeated confederacy. Many of the republicans in Congress, however, opposed him. Because they wanted to protect the freedman. This conflict led congress to held impeechment hearings.

Section 2 The Battle Over Reconstruction **557**

Section 2 Check Your Progress

1. **(a)** Fifteenth Amendment
(b) Thirteenth: By banning slavery, it served as a first step toward granting more rights to African Americans. Fourteenth: It gave citizenship to all people born or naturalized in the United States, except most Native Americans, and gave everyone equal protection of the laws. Fifteenth: It gave African American males the right to vote by forbidding states to deny anyone the right to vote based on race, color, or previous condition of servitude.

2. **(a)** a secret society that terrorized African Americans and their white allies
(b) Possible answer: African Americans in the South were enslaved before the war and had few rights, so they posed no threat to the white southern way of life.

3. Actions included replacing southern governments that would not ratify the Fourteenth Amendment, imposing military rule on those states, requiring states to ratify the amendment and then write a new constitution, requiring states to let African Americans vote, and helping with voter registration.

4. Possible answer: the bringing of formal charges against a public official

5. laws used by southern states to restrict the rights of African Americans

6. Check for good writing skills.

Reteach ▮L1

If students need more instruction, have them read this section in the Interactive Reading and Notetaking Study Guide and complete the accompanying question.

📖 **Interactive Reading and Notetaking Study Guide,** Chapter 16, Section 2 (Adapted Version also available.)

Extend ▮L3

Have students work in pairs to write a news report on racial terrorism in the South during Reconstruction. Have several students share their work with the class.

Progress Monitoring Online

Students may check their comprehension of this section by completing the Progress Monitoring Online graphic organizer and self-quiz.

Answers

☑ **Checkpoint** to have southern states write new constitutions and ratify the Fourteenth Amendment before rejoining the Union; to give African Americans the right to vote

Draw Conclusions Possible answer: Hoods hid the identities of Klansmen. It was more frightening to the victims if they did not know who the attacker was.

Review and Preview

Radical Republicans succeeded in passing three amendments in an effort to secure rights of freedmen. Students will now focus on the demise of Reconstruction efforts and the resulting hardships for African Americans in the South.

Section Focus Question

What were the effects of Reconstruction?

Before you begin the lesson for the day, write the Section Focus Question on the board. (*Lesson focus: military rule in the South; Democrats regaining power in southern states; African Americans losing rights they had gained during Reconstruction; many freedmen left poor and landless; the South's economy beginning to recover*)

Prepare to Read

Build Background Knowledge `L2`

Have students recall the changes that took place in the South during Reconstruction. Use the Idea Wave strategy (TE, p. T24) to elicit responses and list them on the board. Tell students that they will learn that the South changed again after Reconstruction ended.

Set a Purpose `L2`

- Form students into pairs or groups of four. Distribute the Reading Readiness Guide. Ask students to fill in the first two columns of the chart.

  All in One Teaching Resources, Unit 5, Reading Readiness Guide, p. 81

- Use the Numbered Heads strategy (TE, p. T24) to call on students to share one piece of information they already know and one piece of information they want to know. The students will return to these worksheets later.

SECTION 3

A Southern Viewpoint

❝It would be best for the peace, harmony, and prosperity of the whole country that there should be an immediate restoration, an immediate bringing back of the states into their original practical relations.❞

— Alexander H. Stephens, urging an end to federal control of southern states, 1866

◄ Cartoon criticizing northern carpetbaggers in the South

The End of Reconstruction

Objectives
- Explain why support for Reconstruction declined.
- Describe how African Americans in the South lost many newly gained rights.
- Describe the sharecropping system and how it trapped many in a cycle of poverty.
- Identify the signs that the South began to develop a stronger economy by the 1880s.

Reading Skill

Evaluate Proposals When you read a proposal, ask yourself: Is the proposal likely to work as a way of advancing its goal?

Key Terms and People

poll tax · segregation
literacy test · Homer Plessy
grandfather clause · sharecropper

Why It Matters The South experienced reforms during the Reconstruction era. However, many of the changes were quite temporary. When Reconstruction ended, African Americans were subjected to new hardships and injustices. It would take more than a century to overcome these injustices.

❓ **Section Focus Question: What were the effects of Reconstruction?**

Reconstruction's Conclusion

Support for Radical Republicans declined as Americans began to forget the Civil War and focus on bettering their own lives. Scandals within President Grant's administration played an important role. Grant made poor appointments to public offices, often appointing personal friends. Many of the appointees proved to be corrupt. Although Grant himself had no part in the corruption that took place, his reputation suffered. Grant won reelection in 1872, but many northerners lost faith in the Republicans and their policies.

Self-rule for the South Meanwhile, many people in both North and South were calling for the withdrawal of federal troops and full amnesty for former Confederates. Starting with Virginia in 1869, opponents of Republicans began to take back the South, state by state. Slowly, they chipped away at the rights of African Americans.

In some states, campaigns of terror by secret societies were a major factor in restoring their power. By 1874, Republicans had lost control of all but three southern states. By 1877, Democrats controlled those, too.

The Election of 1876 The end of Reconstruction was a direct result of the presidential election of 1876. Because of disputes over election returns, the choice of the President was

---

Differentiated Instruction

L1 English Language Learners **L1 Less Proficient Readers** **L1 Special Needs**

Gaining Comprehension Have students read the text of The End of Reconstruction as they listen to the Student Edition on Audio CD. Create exit cards for the students to complete at the end of the CD. The cards will read "What I learned about _____" or "It made me feel _____." Review their responses. Students can be given a copy of the CD to work independently at home or in the school Resource Center.

💿 **SE on Audio CD,** Chapter 16

decided by Congress. There, a deal between the Republicans and Democrats settled the election—and sealed the fate of Reconstruction.

The candidates in 1876 were Rutherford B. Hayes of Ohio for the Republicans and Samuel J. Tilden of New York for the Democrats. The Republicans said they would continue Reconstruction, and the Democrats said they would end it.

Tilden won the popular vote by 250,000 votes. However, 20 electoral votes were in dispute. Without them, Tilden fell one vote short of the 185 needed to win in the electoral college.

To resolve the issue, Congress appointed a special commission of 15 members. Most of them were Republicans. The commission gave all 20 electoral votes to Hayes. Rather than fight the decision in Congress, Democrats agreed to accept it. Hayes had privately told them that he would end Reconstruction. Once in office, Hayes removed all federal troops from the South.

Evaluate Proposals
What proposal did Hayes make to the Democrats in order to end their opposition? How did this proposal meet the goals of both the Democrats and Republicans?

✓**Checkpoint** What factors contributed to the end of Reconstruction?

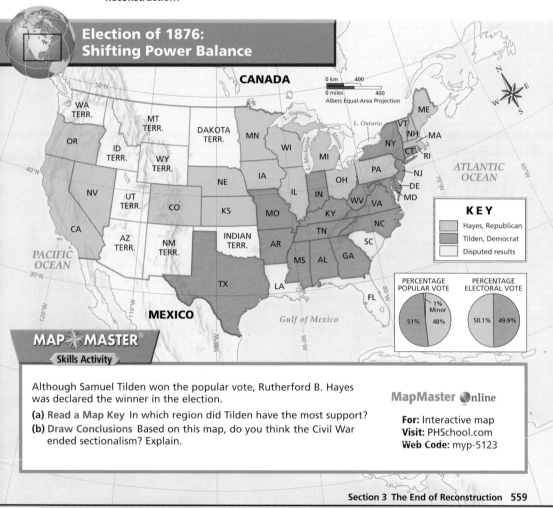

Election of 1876: Shifting Power Balance

KEY
- Hayes, Republican
- Tilden, Democrat
- Disputed results

| PERCENTAGE POPULAR VOTE | PERCENTAGE ELECTORAL VOTE |

51% 48% 1% Minor   50.1% 49.9%

MAP MASTER®
Skills Activity

Although Samuel Tilden won the popular vote, Rutherford B. Hayes was declared the winner in the election.
(a) Read a Map Key In which region did Tilden have the most support?
(b) Draw Conclusions Based on this map, do you think the Civil War ended sectionalism? Explain.

MapMaster Online
For: Interactive map
Visit: PHSchool.com
Web Code: myp-5123

Section 3 The End of Reconstruction **559**

Vocabulary Builder

Use the information below to teach students this section's high-use words.

High-Use Word	Definition and Sample Sentence
require, p. 560	*v.* to order or command President Martin Van Buren **required** the Cherokees to leave their land in Georgia.
inferior, p. 561	*adj.* of lower rank or status, or of poorer quality At first, American manufacturers were **inferior** in quality to British goods.

Teach

Reconstruction's Conclusion

p. 558

Instruction L2

■ **Vocabulary Builder** Before teaching this lesson, preteach the High-Use Words **require** and **inferior,** using the strategy on TE p. T21.

Key Terms Have students complete the See It–Remember It chart.

■ Read Reconstruction's Conclusion with students using the Choral Reading technique (TE, p. T22).

■ Ask students to explain how Republicans began to lose power. (*Scandals during Republican President Grant's term led northerners to lose faith in Republicans. People began calling for the end of military rule, which led to Democrats taking back control of southern states.*)

■ Ask: **What event marked the end of Reconstruction?** (*the election of 1876*) **What do you think might have happened if Reconstruction continued for many more years?** (*Answers will vary, but should reflect prior knowledge of the changes made during Reconstruction.*)

■ Display the Voting Patterns During Reconstruction transparency. Discuss the changes that might have come when representation in Congress switched from mostly Republican in 1872 to mostly Democrat in 1876. (*Possible answers: end of Reconstruction; fewer rights for African Americans; end to military rule in the South.*)

Color Transparencies, Voting Patterns During Reconstruction

Answers

⟳ **Reading Skill** Hayes proposed to end Reconstruction. The Democrats wanted to end Reconstruction and the Republicans wanted to win the presidency.

✓**Checkpoint** northerners' losing faith in Republicans because of government corruption; Democratic candidates taking back the South; the election of 1876

MAP MASTER Skills Activity **(a)** the South **(b)** No; the map shows that people in the South primarily voted one way—Democratic—and people in the North and West primarily voted a different way—Republican.

Chapter 16 **559**

Have students begin filling in the study guide for this section.

Monitor Progress

As students fill in the Notetaking Study Guide, circulate to make sure individuals understand how and why Reconstruction ended. Provide assistance as needed.

African Americans Lose Rights

p. 560

Instruction L2

- Read African Americans Lose Rights with students. Have students look for evidence that southern whites achieved their goal—keeping African Americans from voting.

- Ask: **What was the grandfather clause?** (*a provision that allowed a voter to skip a literacy test if his father or grandfather had been eligible to vote on January 1, 1867*) **Why was it passed?** (*to ensure that only white men could vote*)

- Lead a discussion on how the lives of African Americans and whites in the South might have differed when segregation was law. (*Answers will vary, but students should point out that whites probably had access to better education, jobs, and facilities.*)

- To help students better understand the concept of segregation, which is important to the understanding of this section, use the Concept Lesson Segregation. Distribute copies of the concept organizer.

  All in One Teaching Resources, Unit 5, Concept Lesson, p. 86; Concept Organizer, p. 6

Independent Practice

Have students continue filling in the study guide for this section.

Monitor Progress

As students fill in the Notetaking Study Guide, circulate to make sure individuals understand how African Americans lost rights they had gained during Reconstruction. Provide assistance as needed.

Answer

Draw Conclusions They could not make enough money to pay back their debt to landowners and buy their own land.

African Americans Lose Rights

With the end of Reconstruction, African Americans began to lose their remaining political and civil rights in the South. Southern whites used a variety of techniques to stop African Americans from voting. They passed laws that applied to whites and African Americans but were enforced mainly against African Americans.

One such law imposed a **poll tax**—a personal tax to be paid before voting. This kept a few poor whites and many poor freedmen from voting. Another law required voters to pass a **literacy test,** or a test to see if a person can read and write. In this case, voters were <u>required</u> to read a section of the Constitution and explain it.

However, a grandfather clause allowed illiterate white males to vote. The **grandfather clause** was a provision that allowed a voter to avoid a literacy test if his father or grandfather had been eligible to vote on January 1, 1867. Because no African American in the South could vote before 1868, nearly all were denied the right to vote.

Southern states created a network of laws requiring **segregation,** or enforced separation of races. These so-called Jim Crow laws barred the mixing of races in almost every aspect of life. Blacks and whites were born in separate hospitals and buried in separate cemeteries. The laws decreed separate playgrounds, restaurants, and schools. They required African Americans to take back seats or separate cars on railroads and streetcars. When African Americans challenged the restrictions in court, they lost. State and local courts consistently ruled that Jim Crow laws were legal.

Vocabulary Builder
require (rih KWYR) **v.** to order or command

● INFOGRAPHIC

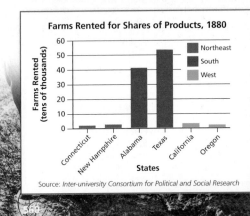

SHARECROPPING
CYCLE OF POVERTY

Farming land they did not own, sharecroppers were locked into a cycle of debt, as shown by the illustration.
Critical Thinking: *Draw Conclusions* Why was it hard for sharecroppers to escape the debt cycle?

1. Planting the Crop
Landowners give the sharecropper land, seed, and tools in exchange for a share in the crop. Sharecroppers buy goods and supplies from the landowner on credit.

Farms Rented for Shares of Products, 1880

Y-axis: Farms Rented (tens of thousands), 0–60
Legend: Northeast, South, West
States (x-axis): Connecticut, New Hampshire, Alabama, Texas, California, Oregon

Source: *Inter-university Consortium for Political and Social Research*

Differentiated Instruction

L3 Advanced Readers

Comparing Explain that like the election for President in 1876, the election of 2000 resulted in the winner of the popular vote losing the election. Have students research this election, in which George W. Bush

L3 Gifted and Talented

defeated Al Gore. Point out that third-party candidate Ralph Nader also played a role in the results. Then ask students to identify the similarities and differences between the two elections.

In 1896, the U.S. Supreme Court upheld segregation laws. Homer Plessy had been arrested for sitting in a coach marked "for whites only." In the case of *Plessy* v. *Ferguson,* the Court ruled in favor of a Louisiana law requiring segregated railroad cars. The Court said a law could require "separate" facilities, so long as they were "equal."

This "separate but equal" rule was in effect until the 1950s. In fact, facilities for African Americans were rarely equal. For example, public schools for African Americans were almost always <u>inferior</u> to schools for whites.

✓Checkpoint What methods did southern states use to deprive African Americans of their rights?

Vocabulary Builder
inferior (ihn FIR ee uhr) **adj.** of lower rank or status, or of poorer quality

A Cycle of Poverty

At emancipation, many freedmen owned little more than the clothes they wore. Poverty forced many African Americans, as well as poor whites, to become sharecroppers. A **sharecropper** is a laborer who works the land for the farmer who owns it, in exchange for a share of the value of the crop.

The landlord supplied living quarters, tools, seed, and food on credit. At harvest time, the landlord sold the crop and tallied up how much went to the sharecroppers. Often, especially in years of low crop prices or bad harvests, the sharecroppers' share was not enough to cover what they owed the landlord for rent and supplies. As a result, most sharecroppers became locked into a cycle of debt.

2. Harvesting the Crop and Settling Accounts
The sharecropper gives the landowner his crop. Landowner sells it and gives the tenant his share, minus the amount owed at the company store.

History *Interactive*
Explore the Sharecropping Cycle
Visit: PHSchool.com
Web Code: myp-5127

3. Cycle of Debt
After a year of hard work, the sharecroppers often owed more than they had earned and had no choice but to offer the landlord a greater percentage of next year's crop.

History Background

Harlan's Predictions Supreme Court Justice John Harlan was the only voice of dissent in the *Plessy* v. *Ferguson* case. He showed incredible foresight in his opinion when he wrote: "Our Constitution is color-blind, and neither knows nor tolerates classes among citizens. In respect of civil rights, all citizens are equal before the law . . . In my opinion, the judgment this day rendered will, in time, prove to be quite as pernicious as the decision made by this tribunal in the *Dred Scott* case . . . The present decision, . . . , will not only stimulate aggressions, . . . , upon the admitted rights of colored citizens, but will encourage the belief that it is possible, by means of state [laws], to defeat the [good] purposes which the people of the United States had in view when they adopted the recent amendments of the Constitution."

A Cycle of Poverty
p. 561

Instruction

- Read A Cycle of Poverty with students. Have students look for causes and effects.

- Have students look at the Sharecropping Cycle of Poverty feature and ask them to describe the cycle in their own words. (*Students' answers will vary, but should reflect an understanding of how sharecroppers got trapped in a cycle of debt.*) Ask: **Were African Americans in towns and cities struggling with poverty as well? Explain.** (*Yes, opportunities for skilled workers dwindled and many African Americans had to take any job they could find.*)

- Display the History Interactive transparency Sharecropping Cycle of Poverty. Ask students if they think there is a point where the cycle might be broken.

Color Transparencies, Explore the Sharecropping Cycle

Independent Practice

Have students continue filling in the study guide for this section.

Interactive Reading and Notetaking Study Guide, Chapter 16, Section 3 (Adapted Version also available.)

Monitor Progress

As students fill in the Notetaking Study Guide, circulate to make sure individuals understand why many African Americans struggled with poverty. Provide assistance as needed.

Answer

✓Checkpoint They used poll taxes and literacy tests to prevent African Americans from voting, and passed Jim Crow laws that prevented African Americans from using facilities that whites used.

Industrial Growth

p. 562

Instruction
L2

- Read Industrial Growth with students. As students read, circulate and make sure individuals can answer the Checkpoint question.

- Ask: **What part of the South's economy began to recover first during Reconstruction?** (*agriculture*)

- Ask: **How did the South use its resources to develop manufacturing? Give an example.** (*It built mills and factories to develop its resources. For example, furniture factories were built to turn the South's lumber into furniture; textile factories used the region's cotton; factories used the South's iron and oil.*)

Independent Practice

Have students complete the study guide for this section.

Interactive Reading and Notetaking Study Guide, Chapter 16, Section 3 (Adapted Version also available.)

Monitor Progress

- Check Notetaking Study Guide entries for student understanding of how the South developed its industries during and after Reconstruction.

- Tell students to fill in the last column of the Reading Readiness Guide. Ask them to consider whether what they learned was what they had expected to learn.

- Have students go back to their Word Knowledge Rating Form. Rerate their word knowledge and complete the last column with a definition or example.

All in One Teaching Resources, Unit 5, Reading Readiness Guide, p. 81; Word Knowledge Rating Form, p. 78

Answer

☑**Checkpoint** Sharecroppers bought farming supplies from landowners on credit and shared the profits from crops. They often did not make enough money to pay back the debt, so they had to keep working for the landowners to repay them.

Links Across Time

1963 Dr. Martin Luther King, Jr., speaks to Americans in Washington, D.C.

Fighting for Civil Rights

1896 In *Plessy* v. *Ferguson*, the Supreme Court upheld segregation laws in the South. These restrictions continued for more than 50 years.

1950s–1960s Some Americans launched a campaign to bring equal rights to African Americans. This civil rights movement used marches, petitions, and other public actions to end discrimination in education, use of public facilities, and voting.

Link to Today | Online

Civil Rights Today Did the civil rights movement win equal rights for all Americans? Not everyone agrees. Go online to find out more about recent developments in civil rights.

For: Civil rights in the news
Visit: PHSchool.com
Web Code: myc-5123

Opportunities dwindled for African Americans in southern towns and cities, too. African American artisans who had been able to find skilled jobs during Reconstruction increasingly found such jobs closed to them. Those with some education could become schoolteachers, lawyers, or preachers in the African American community. But most urban African Americans had to take whatever menial job they could find.

☑**Checkpoint** **How did many freedmen and whites become locked in a cycle of poverty?**

Industrial Growth

It would be a long process, but during Reconstruction the South's economy began to recover. By the 1880s, new industries appeared. Southerners hailed a "New South," based on industrial growth.

The first element of the South's economy to begin recovery was agriculture. Cotton production, which had lagged during the war, quickly revived. By 1875, it was setting new records. Planters put more land into tobacco production, and output grew.

Southern investors started or expanded industries to turn raw materials into finished products. The textile industry came to play an important role in the southern economy.

Differentiated Instruction

L3 Advanced Readers   **L3 Gifted and Talented**

Predicting Have students work in pairs. Have each select a major event from this chapter and assume that either it had not occurred or that it had a different outcome. (For example, what if Samuel Tilden had been elected President rather than Rutherford B. Hayes?) Have each pair give a brief oral presentation in which they speculate how subsequent events in American history might have been different.

The South had natural resources in abundance, but it had done little to develop them in the past. Atlanta newspaper editor Henry Grady described the funeral of a man from Georgia as follows:

❝They buried him in the heart of a pine forest, and yet the pine coffin was imported from Cincinnati. They buried him within touch of an iron mine, and yet the nails in his coffin and the iron in the shovel that dug his grave were imported from Pittsburgh.❞

—Henry Grady to the Bay State Club of Boston, 1889

The South began to develop its own resources. New mills and factories grew up to use the South's iron, timber, and oil. Lumber mills and furniture factories processed yellow pine and hardwoods from southern forests.

Southern leaders took great pride in the region's progress. They spoke of a "New South" that was no longer dependent on "King Cotton." An industrial age was underway, although the North was still far more industrialized.

☑Checkpoint What was the "New South" that was emerging by 1900?

⭐ **Looking Back and Ahead** When Reconstruction ended in 1877, its record showed many successes and some failures. Most importantly, all African Americans were finally citizens. Laws passed during Reconstruction, such as the Fourteenth Amendment, became the basis of the civil rights movement that took place almost 100 years later.

HISTORIAN'S APPRENTICE ACTIVITY PACK

To further explore the topics in this chapter, complete the activity in the Historian's Apprentice Activity Pack to answer this essential question:

Was Reconstruction a success or a failure?

Factory in the "New South"

Progress Monitoring ⬤nline
For: Self-test with instant help
Visit: PHSchool.com
Web Code: mya-5123

Section 3 | **Check Your Progress**

Comprehension and Critical Thinking
1. **(a) Identify** Who were share-croppers? How did they differ from landowners?
(b) Draw Conclusions Why did so many sharecroppers live in poverty?

2. **(a) Recall** What is segregation?
(b) Analyze Cause and Effect How did *Plessy* v. *Ferguson* make the fight against segregation more difficult?

🔄 **Reading Skill**
3. **Evaluate Proposals** In *Plessy* v. *Ferguson*, the Supreme Court proposed the idea of "separate but equal" facilities. Do you think this idea meets the goal of ensuring equal rights?

Key Terms
Complete each of the following sentences so that the second part clearly shows your understanding of the key term.
4. African Americans and whites had to pay a poll tax before _____.

5. Because of laws in the South requiring segregation, African Americans and whites _____.

Writing
6. Rewrite the following passage to correct the errors. **Passage:** The 1876 presidential election decided by a special commission. Samuel J. Tilden a democrat won the Popular vote over republican Rutherford B. Hayes. However, their were 20 disputed electorial votes. A special commission made an agreement with the democrats.

Assess Progress L2

Have students complete Check Your Progress. Administer the Section Quiz.

All in One Teaching Resources, Section Quiz, p. 89

To further assess student understanding, use the Progress Monitoring Transparency.

Progress Monitoring Transparencies, Chapter 16, Section 3

Reteach L1

If students need more instruction, have them read this section in the Interactive Reading and Notetaking Study Guide and complete the accompanying question.

📖 **Interactive Reading and Notetaking Study Guide,** Chapter 16, Section 3 (Adapted Version also available.)

Extend L3

Have students complete the History Interactive activity online. Provide students with the Web Code below.

Extend ⬤nline
For: Help in starting the History Interactive activity
Visit: PHSchool.com
Web Code: myp-5127

Progress Monitoring Online

Students may check their comprehension of this section by completing the Progress Monitoring Online graphic organizer and self-quiz.

Section 3 Check Your Progress

1. **(a)** Sharecroppers were farmers who rented land and paid a share of each year's crop as rent; they did not own the land they worked.
(b) Sharecroppers often owed landlords more than they made at the end of a year.

2. **(a)** enforced separation of races
(b) It ruled in favor of segregation as long as facilities were equal.

3. The Court reasoned that laws calling for separate facilities for whites and blacks were acceptable as long as facilities were equal. Students will probably disagree with the Court's proposition because the facilities for blacks were never equal to those for whites.

4. they could vote.

5. had to use separate facilities such as restaurants and playgrounds.

6. Check for grammar and organization of content.

Answer

☑Checkpoint The New South began to develop its own resources, setting up mills and factories to turn its resources into useful goods.

Objective

Complex information can often be presented in a visual way in maps. Thematic maps can help show important historical patterns. This analysis skill lesson will teach students how to better understand historical information by analyzing a migration map.

Analyze a Migration Map

Instruction   L2

1. Write the steps to analyze migration maps on the board and ask the class to read the steps aloud.

2. Ask students what historical pattern they think this map will help them understand. (*African Americans migrating during Reconstruction.*) Ask how the map will help them understand this pattern. (*Possible answer: The map shows where African Americans came from and where they went during the years 1866–1877.*)

3. Practice the skill by following the steps on this page as a class. Model each step to analyze the migration map. (*1. African American Migration, 1866–1877 2. areas to which African Americans migrated 3. north and east 4. Possible answer: African Americans migrated to the North and West during Reconstruction.*)

Monitor Progress

Ask students to do the Apply the Skill activity. Then assign the Skills for Life worksheet. As students complete the worksheet, circulate to make sure individuals are applying the skill steps effectively. Provide assistance as needed.

All in One Teaching Resources, Unit 5, Skills for Life Worksheet, p. 85

Reteach   L1

If students need more instruction, use the Social Studies Skills Tutor to reteach this skill.

Social Studies Skills Tutor CD-ROM, Analyzing and Interpreting Special Purpose Maps

---

Skills for Life — Analyze a Migration Map

Thematic maps focus on special topics, such as food products, physical features, or political boundaries. Information presented in a visual way is easier to understand and absorb. One type of thematic map shows the migration or movement of people within a particular area.

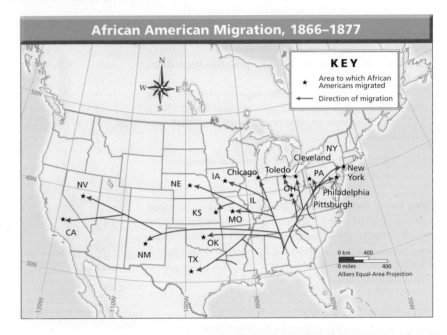

African American Migration, 1866–1877

KEY
★ Area to which African Americans migrated
← Direction of migration

Learn the Skill
Use these steps to learn how to trace migrations on maps.

1. **Identify the subject of the map.** Read the title of the map. Look for dates that identify the time period.

2. **Look at the map key.** The map key explains special symbols and colors used on the map.

3. **Determine direction.** To trace the route of a migration, use the direction arrows on the compass rose to identify north, south, east, and west. Then, identify the direction or directions of the route.

4. **Make a generalization.** Use the information on the map to make a general statement about the historic migration.

Practice the Skill
Answer the following questions about the map on this page.

1. **Identify the subject of the map.** What is the title of the map?

2. **Look at the map key.** What does the star symbol show?

3. **Determine direction.** In which direction did African Americans travel to migrate to New York?

4. **Make a generalization.** In general, to which areas of the country did African Americans migrate during Reconstruction?

Apply the Skill
See the Review and Assessment at the end of this chapter.

What were the short-term and long-term effects of the Civil War?

Section 1
Rebuilding the Nation

- The South faced major economic and social challenges at the end of the Civil War.
- Reconstruction plans and programs like the Freedmen's Bureau were designed to rebuild the South.
- The death of Abraham Lincoln threatened lenient plans for Reconstruction.

Section 2
The Battle Over Reconstruction

- President Andrew Johnson and the Radical Republicans clashed over Reconstruction plans.
- Conflict over Reconstruction led to Andrew Johnson's impeachment.
- During Reconstruction, African American males gained the right to vote. Republicans came to power in each southern state.

Section 3
The End of Reconstruction

- With the end of Reconstruction, African Americans in the South lost many rights they had gained after the Civil War.
- Many African Americans and poor whites were forced to become sharecroppers.
- The South's agriculture revived, and its industries expanded.

⑦ Exploring the Essential Question

Use the online study guide to explore the essential question.

Section 1
How did the government try to solve key problems facing the nation after the Civil War?

Chapter 16 Essential Question
What were the short-term and long-term effects of the Civil War?

Section 2
How did disagreements over Reconstruction lead to conflict in government and in the South?

Section 3
What were the effects of Reconstruction?

Quick Study Guide **565**

Enrich Learning To enrich this unit, have students revisit the Unit Essential Question. Using information from the chapters in the unit and the primary sources on pp. 568–571, have students demonstrate their understanding of the Civil War by preparing a documentary news program to present the issues.

Think Like a Historian, pp. 568–571.

Pressed for Time? If you do not have time to complete the activity, return to the essential question on the unit opener. Post the flip chart pages and ask students to review and revise the list. As a summary, display the Unit 5 Think Like a Historian transparencies.

Color Transparencies, Think Like a Historian, Unit 5

Chapter 16

Essential Question
Remind students of the Chapter Essential Question: **What were the short-term and long-term effects of the Civil War?** Have them review the bulleted statements and the Visual Preview at the beginning of the chapter to help them answer this question.

To bolster students' retention, at this time they should complete the study guide in print or online. Remind students that they should also continue notetaking for the Unit and Chapter Essential Questions.

📖 **Interactive Reading and Notetaking Study Guide,** Chapter 16 (Adapted Version also available.)

 Study Guide *Online,* Chapter 16

Chapter Challenge
To wrap up this chapter, students should apply the knowledge they have gained to answer this question: **Was Reconstruction successful?** (*Possible answer: Reconstruction was successful in helping rebuild the South's economy, readmitting states to the Union, and helping freed African Americans gain rights and begin new lives in society. But African Americans lost their rights shortly after Reconstruction and the views of people in the North and South remained different, as evidenced by how they voted in presidential elections.*)

Assessment at a Glance

Formal Assessment
  Chapter Tests A/B (L1/L2)
  AYP Monitoring Assessment
  Test Prep Workbook With Document-Based Assessment
  Test-Taking Strategies With Transparencies

Performance Assessment
  Group/Individual Activities, TE p. 542f
  Teacher's Edition, pp. 549, 556–557, 563
  Assessment Rubrics

Assessment Through Technology
  ExamView CD-ROM
  MindPoint CD-ROM
  Progress Monitoring Transparencies
  Progress Monitoring Online

Chapter 16
Review and Assessment

Key Terms

1. freedmen
2. carpetbaggers
3. literacy tests
4. sharecropper

Comprehension and Critical Thinking

5. (a) The Wade-Davis Bill made it more difficult for southern states to rejoin the Union than Lincoln's plan. It required 50 percent of a state's white men to swear loyalty to the United States and denied the right to vote or hold office to anyone who volunteered to fight for the Confederacy. Lincoln's plan required that only 10 percent of voters swear an oath of loyalty and offered amnesty to Confederate fighters and supporters, except for leaders. **(b)** Southerners probably would have reacted more favorably to Lincoln's plan.

6. (a) Johnson's Reconstruction plan was not as strict as the Radicals had hoped it would be. Johnson later vetoed many Reconstruction acts passed by Congress, which was controlled by the Radicals. **(b)** Students should suggest that he was less effective because Republicans still did not support him and most had voted to impeach and remove him from office.

7. (a) the right to vote **(b)** It shows an African American man voting.

8. (a) It set up schools to educate freedmen, helped them find jobs, and resolved disputes between freedmen and whites. **(b)** Possible answer: Education—Many of the schools set up by the Freedmen's Bureau still provide education today.

9. (a) Democrats did not fight against Hayes receiving all the votes he needed to win because he had secretly agreed to end Reconstruction. **(b)** When Reconstruction ended, they lost many of their rights.

History Reading Skill

10. Possible answer: Johnson proposed a broad amnesty to most former Confederates. He allowed southern states to organize new governments and elect representatives to Congress. Each state was required to abolish slavery and ratify the Thirteenth Amendment. Congress proposed extending

---

Key Terms
Fill in the blanks with the correct key terms.

1. _____ were people who had been enslaved before emancipation.

2. Northerners who moved south after the Civil War were sometimes called _____.

3. Southern states gave _____, which required voters to read and explain part of the Constitution.

4. A _____ farmed land in return for a portion of the value of the crop.

Comprehension and Critical Thinking

5. (a) Recall How did the Wade-Davis Bill differ from Lincoln's plan for reuniting the country? **(b) Make Predictions** How do you think southerners would have reacted to Reconstruction if Lincoln's plan had been followed?

6. (a) Recall How did Johnson and the Radicals come into conflict? **(b) Analyze Cause and Effect** How effective do you think Johnson was after the failure of the impeachment process?

7. (a) Recall What right is guaranteed by the Fifteenth Amendment? **(b) Interpret Art** How does the painting *His First Vote* (below) reflect how the Fifteenth Amendment affected African Americans?

8. (a) Recall How did the Freedman's Bureau help African Americans after the Civil War? **(b) Make Predictions** Which of the actions of the Freedmen's Bureau has probably had the longest lasting impact on African Americans? How?

9. (a) Recall What were the terms of the compromise that gave Rutherford B. Hayes the presidency in 1876? **(b) Draw Conclusions** How were African Americans in the South affected by this compromise?

History Reading Skill

10. Analyze and Evaluate Proposals Review what you have read about the conflict between Johnson and Radical Republicans. What did each side propose? Which proposal makes the most sense to you? Explain.

Writing

11. Write an essay on the following topic: Explain how events and developments during Reconstruction highlighted differences between North and South, even as the two tried to reunite.

Your essay should:
- state a thesis or purpose for writing;
- explain the subject you are writing about;
- offer evidence, examples, or details to support your explanation;
- conclude with a short summary of your main points.

12. Write a Narrative: Imagine you are Hiram Revels. Write a narrative describing your first days in the Senate.

Skills for Life
Analyze a Migration Map
Use the map in the Skills for Life feature to answer the questions that follow.

13. What time period is covered in this map?

14. What does the arrow symbol show?

15. In which direction did African Americans travel to migrate to Oklahoma and New Mexico?

16. Based on the information in the map, what decision did many African Americans make during Reconstruction?

---

the Freedmen's Bureau, granting citizenship rights to African Americans, and guaranteeing civil rights for all except Native Americans. Students may answer that the proposals of Congress did more to protect the rights of freedmen.

Writing

11. Student essays should consider the reasons and reactions to the programs and amendments established during Reconstruction

12. Narratives should consider Revels' point of view as the first African American senator and the reaction of others to his position.

For a more complete four-point rubric, see the Writing Rubrics in the Teaching Resources.

 **Teaching Resources, Unit 5,** p. 108

Test Yourself

Refer to the quotation below to answer Question 1.

> "A system of oppression so rank that nothing could make it seem small except the fact that [African Americans] had already been ground under it for a century and a half."

1. Which system does this quotation refer to?

A amnesty

B Reconstruction

C sharecropping

D segregation

2. How did African Americans benefit from the passage of the Fourteenth Amendment?

A Their right to vote was protected.

B They became citizens.

C They were given land.

D They no longer had to pass literacy tests.

3. A chief goal of the Freedmen's Bureau was to promote

A abolition.

B industrial growth.

C education.

D segregation.

Document-Based Questions

Task: Look at Documents 1 and 2, and answer their accompanying questions. Then, use the documents and your knowledge of history to complete the following writing assignment:

Write a two-paragraph essay about the goals and methods of the Ku Klux Klan. Using specific details, draw a conclusion about whether Document 1 or Document 2 gives a more accurate description of the Klan.

Document 1: The "Organization and Principles" of the Ku Klux Klan, stated below, was written in 1868. It describes the goals of the Klan. *What does the Klan say is its attitude toward violence?*

> "This is an institution of chivalry, humanity, mercy, and patriotism; embodying in its genius and its principles all that is chivalric in conduct, noble in sentiment, generous in manhood, and patriotic in purpose; its peculiar objects being:
>
> First, to protect the weak, the innocent, and the defenseless from the [insults], wrongs, and outrages of the lawless, the violent, and the brutal; to relieve the injured and oppressed. . . .
>
> *Questions to be asked each [Klan] candidate:*
> • Are you in favor of a white man's government in this country? . . ."

Document 2: This political cartoon was published in a northern magazine in 1874. *Describe what has happened to the African American family.*

Test Yourself

1. D

2. B

3. C

Document-Based Questions
Answers

Document 1 The document says the Klan aims to protect "the weak, the innocent, and the defenseless" from violence.

Document 2 The family has been terrorized by the Klan and its apparent partner, the White League.

Rubric: Write an Essay

Share the rubric with students before they begin writing.

Score 1 Is poorly organized, strays from assigned topic.

Score 2 Has unclear writing, is weak in interpreting Klan document or cartoon.

Score 3 Has logical presentation, includes appropriate commentary and detail, recognizes weakness of Klan's self-justification.

Score 4 Is well written, clearly organized, with interesting choice of language and detail.

Skills for Life

13. 1866–1877

14. The arrow symbol shows direction of migration.

15. West

16. Based on the information in the map, many African Americans moved to the North and West during Reconstruction.

Think Like a Historian

? **How was the Civil War a political, economic, and social turning point?**

Build Background Knowledge L2

Discuss the concept of "turning point." Tell students that this is a particular time or event that marks the beginning of a completely new stage of life. Going to college or getting married are usually turning points in life. Using the Idea Wave strategy (TE p. T24), have students give other examples of turning points.

Instruction L2

■ Write the Unit Essential Question on the chalkboard. Have students put this in their own words. (*Possible answer: How did the Civil War change life in the North and in the South?*) Have students identify some of the changes that occurred as a result of the war. Ask: **Why would the Civil War have been a turning point regardless of which side won?** (*because it would have resulted in widespread moral, economic, and political change either way*)

■ Have students review the essential questions for Chapters 14–16. Draw a web diagram on the chalkboard, showing how the chapter questions feed into the unit question. (See **Teaching Resources, Unit 5**, p. 3.) Discuss how each chapter question helps answer the unit question.

■ Tell students that after they study the documents they will create a documentary news program using them to help answer this question.

Answers

Document 1: This poster is antislavery because it is a warning to enslaved people on the run to avoid those who might capture them and return them to slavery.

Document 2: Hostility continued because of southern bitterness over the end of slavery and the devastation brought by Union armies in the South.

How was the Civil War a political, economic, and social turning point?

DIRECTIONS: Analyze the following documents from the years before, during, and after the Civil War. Answer the questions that accompany each document or set of documents. You will use your answers to build an answer to the unit question: How was the Civil War a political, economic, and social turning point?

HISTORIAN'S CHECKLIST

WHO produced the document?
WHERE was it made?
WHEN was it produced?
WHY was it made and for what audience?
WHAT is its viewpoint?
HOW does it connect to what I've learned?
WHY is the document important?

1 document — **Handbill, Boston, 1851**

CAUTION!! COLORED PEOPLE OF BOSTON, ONE & ALL, You are hereby respectfully CAUTIONED and advised, to avoid conversing with the Watchmen and Police Officers of Boston, For since the recent ORDER OF THE MAYOR & ALDERMEN, they are empowered to act as KIDNAPPERS AND Slave Catchers, And they have already been actually employed in KIDNAPPING, CATCHING, AND KEEPING SLAVES. Therefore, if you value your LIBERTY, and the Welfare of the Fugitives among you, Shun them in every possible manner, as so many HOUNDS on the track of the most unfortunate of your race. Keep a Sharp Look Out for KIDNAPPERS, and have TOP EYE open. APRIL 24, 1851.

Was this poster antislavery or proslavery? Explain.

2 document — **Battle of Antietam, 1862**

Why did hostility between the North and the South continue even after the Civil War was over?

568

Differentiated Instruction

L1 English Language Learners   **L1** Less Proficient Readers

Understanding Propaganda Review the definition of *propaganda*. Tell students that *propaganda* is any material that tries to get people to think a certain way about something. When assigning Document 4, have students work in pairs to identify the propaganda points in the article. Have students construct a web diagram. In the center circle, have them state the writer's main point. In the outer circles, have students identify the supporting details the writer uses to support or prove his main idea. Have students brainstorm how to incorporate this document in the news program activity.

3 The Emancipation Proclamation

"Coming generations will celebrate the first of January as the day which brought liberty and manhood to American slaves.... That paper Proclamation must now be made iron, lead and fire, by the prompt employment of the negro's arm in this contest."

—*Frederick Douglass, 1863*

What were the effects of the Emancipation Proclamation?

4 Northern Newspaper's Viewpoint

"There is one, and only one, sure and safe policy for the immediate future: namely: the North must remain the absolute Dictator of the Republic until the spirit of the North shall become the spirit of the whole country....

The South is still unpurged of her treason. Prostrate in the dust she is no less a traitor at this hour than when her head was erect.... They cannot be trusted with authority over their former slaves.... The only hope for the South is to give the ballot to the Negro and in denying it to the rebels."

—The Independent, *May 5, 1865*

Do you think this editorial helped the nation heal after the Civil War? Why or why not?

5 The South's Postwar Economy

"Our losses have been frightful, and we have, now, scarcely a support. My Father had five plantations on the coast, and all the buildings were burnt, and the negroes ... are roaming in a starved condition. Our farm near Charleston was abandoned.... All is now lost, and the negroes, left to themselves ... seek a little food, about the city. Our residence in the city, was sacked ... and the house well riddled by shell & shot. Our handsome Residence in the country was burnt. The Enemy passed over all our property on the coast in their march from Savannah to Charleston, the whole country, down there, is now a howling wilderness.... [I]t will be many years, before this once productive country will be able to support itself."

—*Edward Barnwell Heyward, South Carolina planter, 1866*

How did the Civil War affect the South's economy?

 Go On

569

Instruction (continued)

- If your students have examined these documents as enrichment to the chapters, have them answer the Historian's Checklist questions as a review.

- If you have not used these documents yet, students will need more time to work with these sources. For documents that present challenging reading, use the following steps:

1. As the students study the documents, remind them to use the question associated with each document as the focus question.

2. Have one student read a document aloud, breaking it into short segments. Then, have the class summarize the main ideas. For example, for Document 5, ask students to list each hardship that Heyward describes. Ask: **How did the war directly affect southern planters and their slaves?** *(The planters were ruined, and the devastated plantations left the freed slaves with nowhere to go and no way to support themselves.)*

3. Organize the class into groups. Using the Idea Wave strategy (TE p. T 24), have each group answer the Historian's Checklist Questions for one of the documents. If they need more information about a document, tell them to go back to the chapter to find out relevant information. Remind them to use the section summaries at the beginning of the chapters to find which chapter covers the material. They may also use their Interactive Reading and Note Taking Study Guide to review.

4. Review the answers to the Historian's Checklist. Have students identify how each doument helps answer the essential question. Ask students whether the document addresses political, economic, or social issues.

Answers

Document 3: It freed enslaved people in areas that were fighting the Union. Because it changed the war into a fight to end slavery, the proclamation dashed southern hopes that Britain would help the South.

Document 4: It probably did not help heal the nation because it called for the North to dominate the South after the war.

Document 5: The war ruined the South's economy by the destruction of both cities and plantations and by the freeing of the slaves.

History Background

Turning Point According to historian James McPherson, the Civil War led to a radical change in the development of America. The balance between the economies—northern industrial and southern agrarian—tipped decisively towards industrialization. The northern version of capitalism was based on competitive, free labor. This was a fairly new concept, not only for the South, but also for much of the world, which was still mainly agricultural and labor intensive.

The Union military victory defined the economic direction the nation would take. The South, however, continued to struggle to maintain its way of life and values. This difference of view would persist and lead to social conflict that continued long past the Reconstruction era.

Instruction (continued)

- Preview the documents and assign selections according to student abilities. You may organize students into groups to review documents. For example, assign Document 3 to advanced readers. Ask: **What does Douglass mean when he says "That paper...must be made iron, lead, and fire"?** *(The Union must use military force to implement the document.)* **How would this be achieved?** *(African Americans should join the northern army to help win the war.)* **What is the tone of this document?** *(positive, confident)*

- Assign Document 6 to less proficient readers. Have them work in pairs to define *downtrodden, animosities,* and *elevate.* Have students paraphrase this speech in their own words. Ask: **What does Senator Revels say former enslaved people want?** *(to enjoy liberty and equality with white citizens)*

- Assign Document 7 to special needs students. Have students note all the horrifying details of this political cartoon of the time. *(Students should pick up on the hanging man, burning schoolhouse, dead or injured child, the slogans both on and over the shield, the heavily armed Ku Klux Klansman, and so on.)* Ask: **What does the slogan "Worse than slavery" mean?** *(that the condition of former slaves is now even more perilous than it was during slavery)* **What feeling is the slogan meant to convey?** *(fear)*

- Assign Document 8 to English language learners. Ask: **What do you learn from the map key?** *(that much land was devoted to sharecropping)* Direct students to study the picture and explain what is happening. *(Answers will vary, but students might note that the African American sharecroppers are working the field, dependent on a white man, much as they did when they were enslaved.)*

Answers

Document 6: Revels' goals of black and white equality could not be achieved in the South because of the failure of Reconstruction and other aftereffects of the Civil War.

Document 7: Radical white southerners formed terrorist groups like the Ku Klux Klan to intimidate African Americans, keep them from voting, and scare them into accepting fewer rights and privileges than white people.

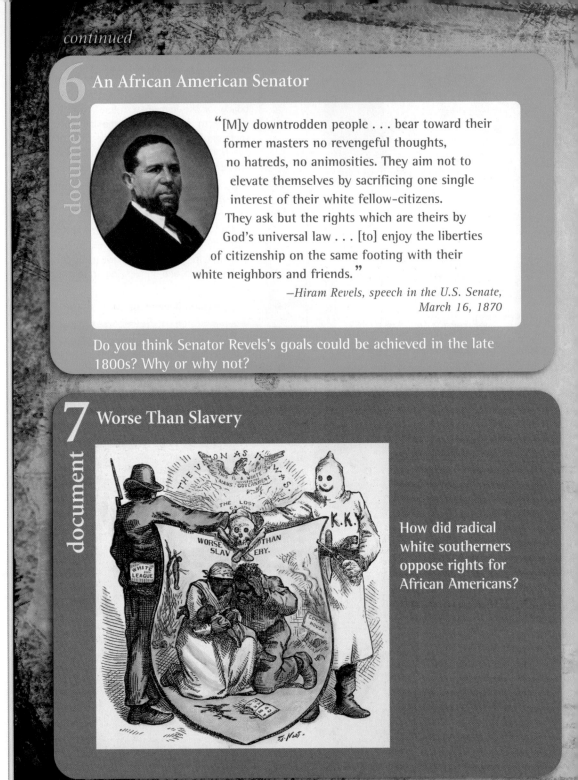

continued

6 An African American Senator

"[M]y downtrodden people . . . bear toward their former masters no revengeful thoughts, no hatreds, no animosities. They aim not to elevate themselves by sacrificing one single interest of their white fellow-citizens. They ask but the rights which are theirs by God's universal law . . . [to] enjoy the liberties of citizenship on the same footing with their white neighbors and friends."

—Hiram Revels, speech in the U.S. Senate, March 16, 1870

Do you think Senator Revels's goals could be achieved in the late 1800s? Why or why not?

7 Worse Than Slavery

How did radical white southerners oppose rights for African Americans?

Differentiated Instruction

L3 Advanced Readers   **L3** Gifted and Talented

Emphasize Relevance Have students consider the relationship between political, economic, social issues represented by these documents. Tell them to brainstorm how these issues affect each other. For example, the political issue of freeing enslaved people directly affected their economic status. Former slaves now had to find work and the system of sharecropping was one result of this political change. Have students make a cause-and-effect diagram showing how one document had a connection to another. Have students use this organizer when preparing their documentary to help explain or demonstrate links among and between issues.

8 Sharecropping

document

Why did many African American farmers remain trapped in poverty?

Percentage of
sharecropped
farms (by county)
- 0%–20%
- 21%–34%
- 35%–80%

Conic Projection
0   100   200 mi
0   100 200 km

VIRGINIA
TENNESSEE
NORTH CAROLINA
ARKANSAS
SOUTH CAROLINA
MISS. ALABAMA GEORGIA
TEXAS
LOUISIANA
FLORIDA
Atlantic Ocean
Gulf of Mexico
95°W   85°W

THINK LIKE A HISTORIAN
ACTIVITY

Divide into three groups to prepare a documentary news program on the unit question: **How was the Civil War a political, economic, and social turning point?**

One group should use the Think Like a Historian documents to describe the Civil War's political effects. Another group should use the documents to describe the economic effects of the war. The last group should cover the war's social effects. After each group has had time to prepare a presentation, it should report its findings to the rest of the class in the format of a documentary news program.

571

Monitor Progress

To monitor progress, have students recall the brainstorming they did when they first began the unit. Teachers should bring out the flip charts they did with the students at the beginning of the unit. Have students review these answers and revise the list as appropriate.

Activity

Organize the class into groups to work on the activity. Review these guidelines with students before they begin their work.

- Use a web diagram to summarize the points you want to make. In the center circle, write either *Political Effects, Economic Effects*, or *Social Effects*. Then the smaller circles coming from the center circle can contain summarized facts to support the points you want to make.

- Work towards your topic. Be sure the supporting circles in your graphic organizer relate just to the category with which you are dealing.

- Use as many of the documents as you can to support your position and make your presentation interesting to the class.

- Edit your information so that you are speaking to the point and not including extraneous information.

- Incorporate any useful information from the chapters in Unit 5 that supports your presentation.

- Determine in what order the participants in each group will present their piece of the overall presentation. Practice the presentation as a group so that the transition from one person to the next is seamless.

- Each group should be prepared to answer questions from the class.

Circulate to be sure students understand their assignment and that work is collaborative. Allow for class discussion and evaluation of the projects. Use the appropriate four-point rubric in the Assessment Rubrics to evaluate this activity.

 Assessment Rubrics

Answer

Document 8: African American farmers remained poor because they could not afford to buy land and had to sharecrop. Sharecroppers gave their crops to a landowner to sell, but low crop values meant most sharecroppers owed more money than they earned.

Pearson Prentice Hall
Professional Development

Epilogue (1865–Present)

History Background

The Rise of a Superpower

After the Civil War, the United States turned its focus to domestic growth. Transcontinental railroads lured settlers and businesses to the West, and millions of immigrants settled in eastern cities. Big businesses welcomed the inexpensive labor, and innovations such as electricity furthered the growth and expansion of cities. As American trade expanded, so did American interest in the world.

Around the beginning of the twentieth century, the United States began to take an active role in world affairs. The Spanish-American War had left the United States with territories in Latin America and the Pacific, increasing the nation's power on a global scale. Although the United States was committed to isolationism, this new position of power soon drew the nation into World War I. Following victory, the nation retreated to enjoy a brief period of prosperity before the economy crashed.

While Americans struggled through the Great Depression, dictatorships took hold in Germany, Italy, and Japan. These countries took aggressive actions on distant continents, yet the United States once again chose neutrality. These aggressive events soon grew into World War II and threatened the security of the United States. Now, continued neutrality was impossible. With U.S. forces joining the Allies, victory came slowly but surely. However, this second "war to end all wars" gave rise to new tensions between democracy and communism.

A new type of war, the Cold War, began as the United States and the Soviet Union built up arms and gathered allies across the globe. These two superpowers fought each other through their alliances in places such as Korea, Cuba, and Vietnam. As the Vietnam War came to an end, the Cold War began to thaw. Years of investment in the arms race had drained the Soviet economy. In 1989, the Soviet Union collapsed and new nations rose from its ashes.

Today, tensions and conflicts persist around the world. Current struggles in the Middle East now occupy the attention of the United States. Our nation continues to face many challenges. As in the past, Americans will embrace these challenges with courage and determination.

Essential Questions

Use this graphic organizer to see the relationship between key concepts and the Chapter Essential Question.

Focus Question/Section 1
How did rapid industrialization affect the American economy and society?
(p. 576)

Concept: Industrialization

Focus Question/Section 2
How did a more powerful United States expand its role in the world?
(p. 584)

Concept: Power

Chapter Essential Question
How has the American nation met challenges at home and abroad?

Focus Question/Section 4
What changes and challenges are shaping the United States today?
(p. 596)

Concept: Immigration

Focus Question/Section 3
How has the United States tried to increase democracy at home and abroad?
(p. 590)

Concept: Democracy

Differentiated Instruction

Emphasize Important Points

Strategies Students with special needs may have difficulty determining what is important within the content of their textbook. Use these strategies to emphasize important points.

- Circle, underline, or highlight important information on handouts, test instructions, and overhead transparencies.

- Provide verbal cues during discussions, such as, "This is important."

- Provide the number of things included in listed information prior to giving the list. For example, "There are *three* key events that led to this event."

- Require students to demonstrate that they are listening and following along (e.g., taking notes, running a finger along the text).

- Utilize realia and visuals (e.g., photographs, objects, color transparencies) to make important concepts less abstract.

- Lead a quick text prereading, or "text tour," focusing student attention on important topics, illustrations, titles and subtopics, and boldfaced words.

Concepts Across Time

Have students develop an understanding of the enduring concepts of history by connecting these ideas.

Concept: Power

Students may recall that as colonists, Americans believed that they should have the right to form a government and make decisions for themselves. Point out that today, the United States exercises its influence to assist smaller, less developed nations which also seek the right to form a government and make decisions for themselves. Ask: **What are some examples of American influence on today's world?** (*Answers will vary, but students may note that the United States has helped create democratic governments in Afghanistan and Iraq. Students may also note the proliferation of American culture, such as movies, music, and fashion.*) Emphasize the impact of the United States on other nations throughout its history. Use this question when discussing Section 2.

Concept: Democracy

Explain to students that during World War I and World War II, the United States took a leading role in world politics in support of its democratic ideals. This role continued through the Vietnam War, but with less successful consequences. The mission to shape the global political stage increased further after the Cold War ended. Ask: **Do you think that the governments of large, powerful countries should have influence in shaping the policies of smaller countries?** (*Possible answers: No, because each nation knows what is best for itself. If a nation needs assistance, it will ask for it. Yes, larger countries can play a key role because they are uniquely suited to aid smaller countries, and should do so.*) Point out that domestic interests and international goals may sometimes conflict. Use this question when discussing Section 3.

Concept: Immigration

Remind students that many early immigrants came to the United States during times of economic hardship and political upheaval. Have students recall other periods of immigration that they have studied. Ask: **What are some of the reasons people might migrate to the United States today?** (*Although the details of peoples' reasons may differ, the same basic reasons are common today. People come to the United States seeking economic opportunity and political refuge.*) Discuss the pressures faced by immigrants. Use this question when discussing Section 4.

Section 1 The Nation Grows *1.5 periods, .75 block*

Objectives

Students will

1. Describe the impact of western settlement on Native Americans.

2. Explain the connection between the expansion of industry and the growing labor union movement.

3. Understand how an expanding economy and a surge of immigration led to an explosive growth of American cities.

4. Identify the leading reforms of the Progressive Era.

Differentiated Instruction Key

L1 Basic to Average	**AR**	Advanced Readers
L2 All Students	**ELL**	English Language Learners
L3 Average to Advanced	**GT**	Gifted and Talented
	LPR	Less Proficient Readers
	SN	Special Needs

Prepare to Read	Instructional Resources	Differentiated Instruction
Build Background Knowledge Preview the section and have students predict what they will learn about westward expansion.	**All in One** Teaching Resources, Unit 5 **L2** Chapter Prereading Guide, p. 4 **Teacher's Edition** **L2** Vocabulary Builder, pp. 575, 577	🎧 **Guided Reading Audio CD** **Spanish** ELL, LPR, SN

Teach	Instructional Resources	Differentiated Instruction
Instruction **The Western Frontier** Analyze the impact of westward expansion on settlers, Native Americans, and industry. **Business and Labor** Describe the issues between business and labor at the turn of the twentieth century. **Immigration and the Growth of Cities** Identify the causes and effects of immigration and urban life in the United States. **The Progressive Era** Examine the goals and accomplishments of the Progressives.	💿 Constitution CD-ROM **Color Transparencies** **L2** Immigration, 1960–2000	**Teacher's Edition** **L1** Interpreting History, p. 576 ELL, LPR, SN **L3** Write a Biography, p. 578 AR, GT **L3** The Right Decision, p. 580 AR, GT

Assess and Reteach	Instructional Resources	Differentiated Instruction
Assess Progress Evaluate student comprehension with Check Your Progress.		**Teacher's Edition** **L1** Checkpoints, TE pp. 577, 579, 581 💿 SE on Audio CD **L1** Epilogue, Section 1

Section 2 A New Role for the Nation *1 period, .5 block*

Objectives

Students will

1. Describe how the United States gained an empire after the Spanish-American War.

2. Identify the causes of World War I.

3. Explain the social changes that occurred in the United States during the 1920s.

4. Describe how hard times affected American families during the 1930s.

Differentiated Instruction Key

L1 Basic to Average	**AR** Advanced Readers
L2 All Students	**ELL** English Language Learners
L3 Average to Advanced	**GT** Gifted and Talented
	LPR Less Proficient Readers
	SN Special Needs

Prepare to Read	Instructional Resources	Differentiated Instruction
Build Background Knowledge Preview the section and have students predict what they will learn about U.S. involvement in international conflicts.	**Teacher's Edition** **L2** Vocabulary Builder, p. 585	💿 **Guided Reading Audio CD** **Spanish** ELL, LPR, SN

Teach	Instructional Resources	Differentiated Instruction
Instruction **Becoming a World Power** Identify the impact of the Spanish-American War on the United States. **World War I and the Postwar Decade** Explain the United States' policy of isolationism, and describe life in the United States in the decade after World War I. **The Great Depression** Examine the causes and effects of the Great Depression.	**Color Transparencies** **L2** Employment Agency **L2** Social Security	**Teacher's Edition** **L1** Outline and Summarize, p. 584 ELL, LPR, SN **L3** Make a Flow Chart, p. 586 AR, GT **L1** Write an Essay, p. 588 ELL, LPR, SN

Assess and Reteach	Instructional Resources	Differentiated Instruction
Assess Progress Evaluate student comprehension with Check Your Progress.		**Teacher's Edition** **L1** Checkpoints, TE pp. 585, 587, 589 💿 **SE on Audio CD** **L1** Epilogue, Section 2

Section 3 Toward the Modern Age *1 period, .5 block*

Objectives

Students will

1. Describe the causes and results of World War II.
2. Explain the major events of the Cold War.
3. Tell how the civil rights movement changed American society.
4. Examine U.S. involvement in the Vietnam War.

Differentiated Instruction Key

L1 Basic to Average	**AR** Advanced Readers
L2 All Students	**ELL** English Language Learners
L3 Average to Advanced	**GT** Gifted and Talented
	LPR Less Proficient Readers
	SN Special Needs

Prepare to Read	Instructional Resources	Differentiated Instruction
Build Background Knowledge Preview the section and have students predict what they will learn about the reasons the United States was pulled back into international conflict.	**Teacher's Edition** **L2** Vocabulary Builder, p. 591	**Guided Reading Audio CD** Spanish **ELL, LPR, SN**

Teach	Instructional Resources	Differentiated Instruction
Instruction **World War II** Identify the causes and effects of U.S. involvement in World War II. **The Cold War Begins** Describe the impact of the Cold War on decades of U.S. foreign policy. **The Civil Rights Movement** Examine various groups' struggles for civil rights. **The Vietnam War** Explain the controversy surrounding U.S. participation in the Vietnam War.	**Exploring Primary Sources in History CD-ROM** **L3** A Nurse Reflects **Color Transparencies** **L2** Suburban Life **L2** Cities and Suburbs in Contrast **L2** A Civil Rights Sit-In **L2** *Sonny's Quilt* **L2** *Working Woman* **L2** *Ghosts of the Barrio*	**Teacher's Edition** **L1** Make a Chart, p. 590 **ELL, LPR, SN** **L3** Write a Descriptive Paragraph, p. 592 **AR, GT** **L1** Summarize Events, p. 594 **ELL**

Assess and Reteach	Instructional Resources	Differentiated Instruction
Assess Progress Evaluate student comprehension with Check Your Progress.		**Teacher's Edition** **L1** Checkpoints, TE pp. 592, 593, 594, 595 **SE on Audio CD** **L1** Epilogue, Section 3 **HAAP** Historian's Apprentice Activity Pack

Objectives

Students will

1. List the goals of the conservative Presidents such as Ronald Reagan and George H. W. Bush.
2. Tell how different foreign policy challenges arose after the end of the Cold War.
3. Examine U.S. foreign policy in the Middle East after the September 11 attacks.
4. Discuss environmental and technological challenges that face Americans today.

Differentiated Instruction Key

L1 Basic to Average	**AR**	Advanced Readers
L2 All Students	**ELL**	English Language Learners
L3 Average to Advanced	**GT**	Gifted and Talented
	LPR	Less Proficient Readers
	SN	Special Needs

Prepare to Read

Build Background Knowledge
Preview the section and have students predict what they will learn about the challenges facing the nation in the twenty-first century.

Instructional Resources

Teacher's Edition
L2 Vocabulary Builder, p. 597

Differentiated Instruction

🎧 **Guided Reading Audio CD**
Spanish ELL, LPR, SN

Teach

Instruction

Rise of the Conservative Movement
Explain the growth of the conservative movement in the 1980s.

New Conflicts in the World
Discuss the effects of the fall of Communism on the Soviet Union and Eastern Europe.

New Directions in Foreign Policy
Explain U.S. foreign policy in world hot spots such as the Middle East and the Balkans.

Changes and Challenges
Examine energy and environmental issues facing the nation.

Instructional Resources

Color Transparencies
L2 Selected Results: California Recall Election, 2003

Discovery School Video
L2 Heroes of Ground Zero

Differentiated Instruction

Teacher's Edition
L1 Write a Fact Sheet, p. 596 ELL, LPR, SN
L3 Make an Illustrated Timeline, p. 598 AR, GT
L3 Write Parallel Accounts, p. 600 AR, GT

Assess and Reteach

Assess Progress
Evaluate student comprehension with Check Your Progress.

Instructional Resources

Differentiated Instruction

Teacher's Edition
L1 Checkpoints, TE pp. 597, 598, 600, 601

🎧 **SE on Audio CD**

L1 Epilogue, Section 4

🏛 **HAAP** **Historian's Apprentice Activity Pack**

Use the following research activities to help students deepen their understanding of the Chapter Essential Question: **How has the American nation met challenges at home and abroad?** Students should use library or Internet resources. The Web Codes provided offer access to Internet resources students can use to complete each activity. Use the appropriate four-point rubric in Assessment Rubrics to evaluate the activity.

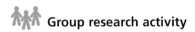 **Assessment Rubrics**

Present an Inventor or Industrial Leader

In groups of four, have students research the accomplishments of a major inventor or industrial leader, such as Thomas Edison, Alexander Graham Bell, Andrew Carnegie, or John D. Rockefeller. Have each group prepare an oral report to share with the class on its person and the person's achievements. Ask the class to evaluate how each of the people contributed to the nation. Use this activity when studying Section 1.

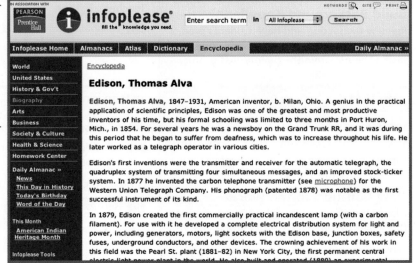

 Group research activity   L2

 Go Online PHSchool.com **Web Code:** mve-0206

Create a Timeline of Overseas Expansion

Have students conduct research to learn more about U.S. territories. Have them relate what they learn by creating a timeline that lists the year each territory came under U.S. control, why the United States took control of the territory, and, if applicable, the year its people became U.S. citizens. Use this activity when learning about U.S. expansion in Section 2.

Individual research activity   L2

 Go Online PHSchool.com **Web Code:** mve-0207

Write a Cause-and-Effect Chain

Have students research the causes and effects of the Cold War. From their research, have them create a graphic organizer that shows the causes of the Cold War and the effects that it had on U.S. foreign policy. Encourage students to illustrate their organizers with illustrations and cartoons they find in their research. Have them display their work in the classroom and compare their findings. Use this activity after students have completed Section 3.

 Individual research activity AR, GT   L3

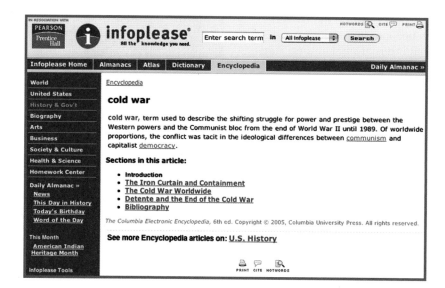

 **Web Code:** mve-0208

Prepare a Public Service Announcement

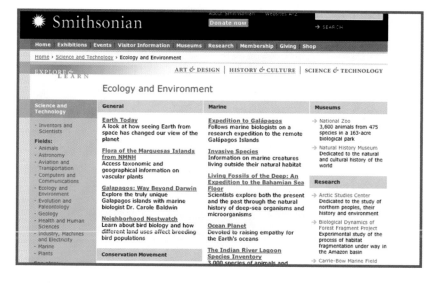

Assign students to work in four groups, then assign each group one of following issues: reducing fuel consumption, reducing waste, raising awareness of alternative fuel sources, and reducing trade deficits. Instruct each group to prepare a radio public service announcement to raise awareness about their assigned issue. If possible, have each group tape-record their announcement and play it for the other groups. Use this activity when students have completed Section 4.

 Group research activity AR, GT   L3

 Web Code: mve-0209

Epilogue

Why It Matters

During the past century, the United States has become increasingly involved in international affairs. Starting with its involvement in the Spanish-American War, the United States has exercised its power by annexing territories, supporting democracy, and fostering its economic interests in the process.

Today, Americans are still wondering what should be done with the territories they obtained at the turn of the twentieth century. Although the Philippines was granted independence and Hawaii became a state, Guam and Puerto Rico remain territorial possessions.

Although Americans acknowledge their responsibility to support nations in converting to democratic rule, some controversy exists over the best way to accomplish it.

Chapter Essential Question

How has the American nation met challenges at home and abroad?

Think Like a Historian

- To preview this chapter, have students review the content of these pages of the Student Edition. Ask: **What will you be learning about in this chapter?** (*national and international issues that the United States faced in the twentieth and twenty-first centuries*)

- Have the students read the quote from Al Gore. Discuss the definition of the word *technology*. Explain that technology is the application of the latest scientific developments resulting in devices that make life easier or more exciting. Have students give examples of the impact of technology on their lives.

- Help students define the terms *superpower* and *industrial giant* as used in the caption.

Epilogue

1865–Present

572

Bibliography

For the Teacher

Brown, David E. *Inventing Modern America: From the Microwave to the Mouse.* MIT Press, 2003.

For the Student

L1 Freedman, Russell. *Immigrant Kids.* Puffin Reprint, 1995.

L2 Collier, Christopher. *Progressivism, Depression, New Deal: 1901–1941.* Benchmark Books, 2000.

L3 Stolley, Richard B. *LIFE: Our Century in Pictures for Young People.* Little, Brown, 2000.

"There are all kinds of exciting new technologies that can create millions of new good jobs, put the U.S. back in a position of leadership in the world economy, and solve lots of problems at the same time."

—Al Gore,
economic policy speech, 2002

Since 1865, the United States has become an industrial giant and a global superpower. But in the 21st century, America faces new challenges to its prosperity.

EPILOGUE

What You Will Learn

Section 1
THE NATION GROWS

An expanding economy and a surge of immigration led to an explosive growth in American cities.

Section 2
A NEW ROLE FOR THE NATION

Around 1900, the United States reversed a century of isolation and began taking an active role in world events.

Section 3
TOWARD THE MODERN AGE

After World War II, the United States entered a long period of heightened tensions with the Soviet Union, known as the Cold War.

Section 4
INTO THE FUTURE

Challenges to Americans today include the threat of terrorism, technological change, and preservation of the environment.

🔖 Reading Skill

Frame Research Questions In this chapter, you will learn how to ask questions that can be answered through research.

573

History Background

New Technologies As the millennium approached, the push toward faster communication encouraged, as Al Gore said, "new technologies." The use of cell phones, beepers, fax machines, and shrinking computers that could hold more information, greatly increased.

However, with the great rush of information, Americans now faced the modern dilemma of too much information. That dilemma introduced new problems, such as: How much of one's personal information is safe? The national obsession to give information may have led Americans to reveal more private information to others than they would like. Furthermore, because there is as much bad information relayed as good, it becomes necessary to find ways to sift the doubtful from the reliable information. New challenges have arrived with the new technologies.

Prepare to Read

Use the following for reading skill support.

All in One Teaching Resources,
Chapter Prereading Guide, p. 4

History Reading Skill *Online*
Web code: mve-3000

Differentiated Instruction

The following Teacher Edition strategies are suitable for students of varying abilities.

L3 Advanced Readers, pp. 578, 580, 586, 592, 598, 600 AR

L1 English Language Learners, pp. 575, 576, 582, 584, 588, 590, 594, 596 ELL

L3 Gifted and Talented, pp. 578, 580, 586, 592, 598, 600 GT

L1 Less Proficient Readers, pp. 575, 576, 582, 584, 588, 590, 596 LPR

L1 Special Needs, pp. 575, 576, 582, 584, 588, 590, 596 SN

Chapter Resources

Teaching Resources, Unit 5
Chapter Prereading Guide, p. 4

Spanish Support
L1 Guided Reading Audio CD, Spanish

Media and Technology
L1 SE on Audio CD
L2 Social Studies Skills Tutor CD-ROM
ExamView Test Bank CD-ROM

Discovery SCHOOL

Quick View Video
View the chapter video for a quick preview of the main ideas.

Epilogue

Visual Preview

❓ How has the American nation met challenges at home and abroad?

Build Background Knowledge `L2`

Discuss with students the qualities they think a strong leader should have. A good leader may be found in many different situations, such as sports, school, or among their own friends. Have them give examples of people they think qualify as strong leaders. Ask them to give reasons to support their choices.

Instruction `L2`

■ For background information on conducting a lesson for the Visual Preview, see TE p. T20.

■ Write the Essential Question on the board. As a superpower, America is a world leader. Connect the idea of leaderships as an individual to leadership as a nation. Then ask: **What kinds of problems would challenge the leader of a large and powerful nation, such as the United States?** *(Possible answers: making important decisions for many people; dealing with economic, health, and political issues; making sure the country is safe; dealing with the challenges presented by other countries)*

■ Using the key, have students explain what the blue indicates. *(states entering the Union between 1867 and 1912)* Have students name a state that entered the Union in 1959. *(Alaska, Hawaii)* Ask: **What do the green-colored states show?** *(the original 13 colonies)*

■ Explain that the map shows the geographic growth of the United States from thirteen colonies to a large and powerful nation. Have students recall the difficulties of the early republic during the Articles of Confederation. Compare the young republic to the present-day republic. Ask: **How has the sense of American leadership changed?** *(Possible answers: weakness under the Articles of Confederation, growing confidence with War of 1812, Spanish-American War, World Wars I and II, superpower today)*

How has the American nation met

The Growing Nation, 1865–Present

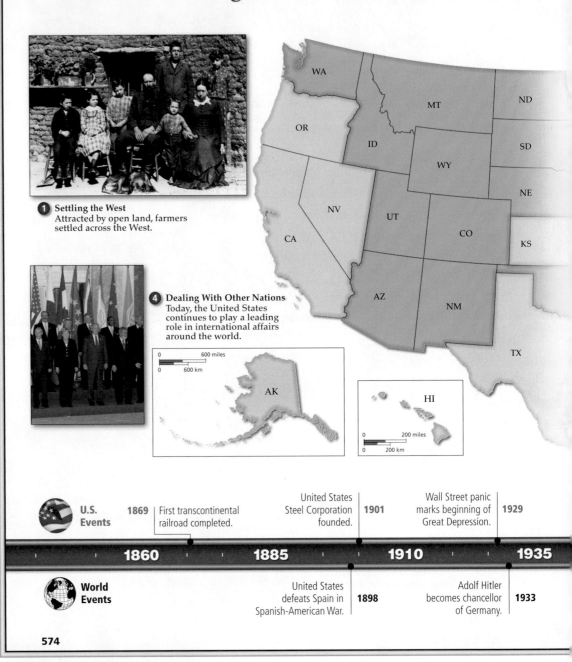

① Settling the West
Attracted by open land, farmers settled across the West.

④ Dealing With Other Nations
Today, the United States continues to play a leading role in international affairs around the world.

	U.S. Events		
1869 First transcontinental railroad completed.	United States Steel Corporation founded. **1901**	Wall Street panic marks beginning of Great Depression. **1929**	

1860	1885	1910	1935

World Events
United States defeats Spain in Spanish-American War. **1898**

Adolf Hitler becomes chancellor of Germany. **1933**

574

History Background

Your World One of the greatest challenges that all countries now face is the threat of terrorism. Following 9/11, the federal government authorized a $40 billion emergency spending package for homeland security and defense. Intelligence gathering authority was strengthened. Six weeks after the 9/11 attack, President Bush signed the Patriot Act, which called for federal authorities to use more foreign intelligence information, gave authorities broader wiretapping authority, and expanded penalties for terrorist acts. Although some see the Patriot Act as a threat to civil liberties, many people support the government's attempts to stop an attack before it happens.

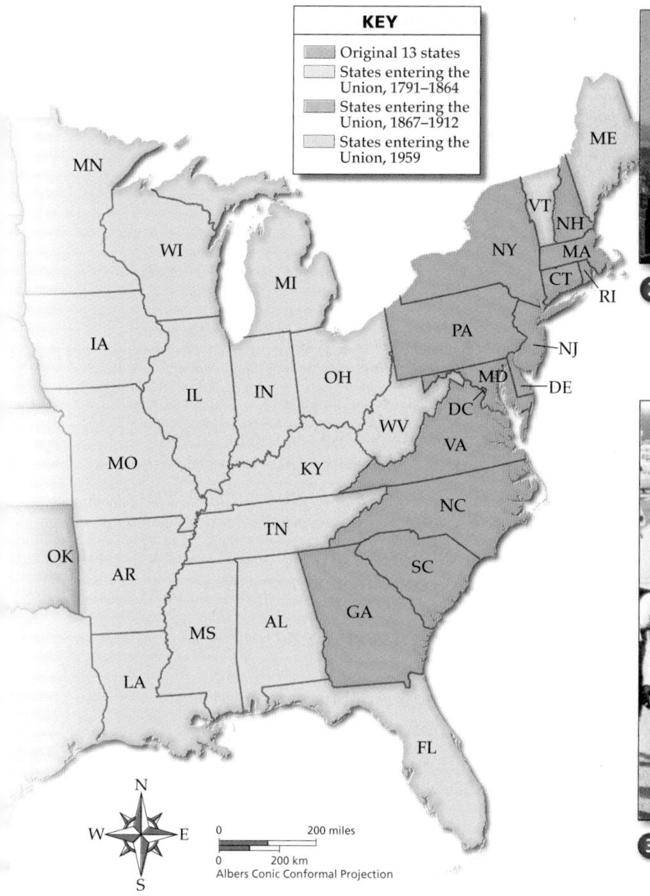

challenges at home and abroad? EPILOGUE

KEY

- Original 13 states
- States entering the Union, 1791–1864
- States entering the Union, 1867–1912
- States entering the Union, 1959

ME
MN
VT
NH
WI
NY
MA
MI
CT
RI
PA
NJ
IA
OH
MD
DE
IL
IN
DC
WV
MO
VA
KY
NC
TN
OK
SC
AR
GA
MS
AL
LA
FL

N
W E
S
0   200 miles
0   200 km
Albers Conic Conformal Projection

VISUAL PREVIEW

2 Building America's Cities
Industrialization and immigration led to the rapid growth of cities.

3 Striving for Social Equality
Martin Luther King, Jr., and other activists struggled to win equality for all citizens.

| 1935 | Social Security system signed into law. | 1954 | Supreme Court outlaws school segregation in *Brown v. Board of Education*. | | 2001 | United States attacked by Middle Eastern terrorists. |

1935 — **1960** — **1985** — **2010**

| 1941 | Japanese attack on Pearl Harbor forces United States into World War II. | | U.S.-led coalition ousts Iraqi dictator Saddam Hussein. | 2003 |

575

Review and Preview

Students have read about Reconstruction following the Civil War. Now they will learn about the movement West and industrialization.

How did rapid industrialization affect the American economy and society?

Before you begin the lesson for the day, write the Section Focus Question on the board. (*Lesson focus: Rapid industrialization was good for the economy, but caused problems in society.*)

Prepare to Read

Build Background Knowledge L2

Tell students that in this section they will read about people who took significant risks for a new life in the West. Remind students that they have read about earlier Americans who crossed the Appalachians for land and new opportunities. Ask students to consider the courage that this decision took and how it has shaped the way Americans see themselves today. Use the Idea Wave strategy (TE, p. T24) to elicit responses.

Teach

The Western Frontier

p. 576

Instruction L2

- **Vocabulary Builder** Before teaching this section, preteach the High-Use Words **dominate** and **minimize** using the strategy on TE p. T21.

  Key Terms Following the instructions on p. 7, have students create a See It-Remember It chart for the Key Terms in this chapter.

- Read The Western Frontier with students using the Oral Cloze strategy (TE, p. T22).

▲ A farm family on the Great Plains

The Pioneer Spirit

❝There were many tearful occasions for the tearful type. There were days and months without human fellowship, there were frightful blizzards . . . and many pitiful deprivations, but there were also compensations for the brave, joyous, determined pioneer.❞

—Lulu Fuhr, reflecting on life as a Kansas pioneer, 1916

The Nation Grows

Objectives
- Describe the impact of western settlement on Native Americans.
- Explain the connection between the expansion of industry and the growing labor union movement.
- Understand how an expanding economy and a surge of immigration led to an explosive growth of American cities.
- Identify the leading reforms of the Progressive Era.

🔄 Reading Skill

Ask Extension Questions In discussing one central event, history books will often mention a related event. You may find yourself interested in the related event. Why did it happen? What made it important? How did it affect those involved? Framing questions in specific language will help you research to find the answers.

Key Terms and People

reservation
corporation
monopoly

Theodore Roosevelt
suffrage

Why It Matters With the Civil War over, the nation turned its attention to westward settlement and economic expansion. This growth made the United States a leading economic power and transformed American society.

❓ **Section Focus Question: How did rapid industrialization affect the American economy and society?**

The Western Frontier

After the Civil War, the United States grew and changed. Americans looked westward, hoping to find new opportunities in the wide, empty prairies. The West, however, was already home to many groups of Native Americans who would, in time, lose their lands.

Moving West A rush to the West began in the 1840s, drawing miners, ranchers, farmers, and other pioneers. Gold and silver strikes attracted miners to many parts of the West, including California and Alaska. Some mining boomtowns grew into permanent settlements.

Cattle ranching became a boom industry in the 1870s. Ranchers shipped meat to a growing population in the East. The Homestead Act (1862) gave prairie land to anyone who would farm it for five years. Eager for land, families from the East endured hardships and harsh weather. African Americans also moved West, looking for freedom they did not have in the South. To protect their interests, farmers joined with members of labor unions and formed the Populist Party.

Differentiated Instruction

L1 English Language Learners   **L1** Less Proficient Readers   **L1** Special Needs

Interpreting History Remind students that westward expansion in the 1800s affected both American settlers and Plains Indians. Help students review the material in the first part of this section to gain a deeper understanding of the effects of westward expansion on these two groups. Then ask each student to share his or her ideas about the struggles faced by one of these two groups. Students can brainstorm about ways that these groups tried to overcome their struggles.

Technology helped sustain western settlement. With the new steel plow, farmers could cut the tough prairie soil. To encourage railroad building, the government granted the railroad 10 square miles of land for every mile of track. In 1869, the Union Pacific Railroad, building west, met the Central Pacific, building east, at Promontory, Utah. This first transcontinental railroad helped unite the country.

Plains Indians Lose Their Lands Settlement of the West meant the near destruction of Native American cultures. Plains Indians were buffalo hunters. The buffalo supplied meat for food and skins for clothing, warm rugs, and tepees.

In spite of treaties protecting Indian lands, miners and settlers claimed ownership. Soldiers and hunters wiped out the huge buffalo herds. Leaders such as Sitting Bull, Crazy Horse, Chief Joseph, and Geronimo led their people in wars with government troops. The contest was hopeless. Gradually, the federal government forced Native Americans onto reservations, land set aside for Native Americans to live on.

✓**Checkpoint** What impact did the destruction of the buffalo herds have on Native Americans of the Great Plains?

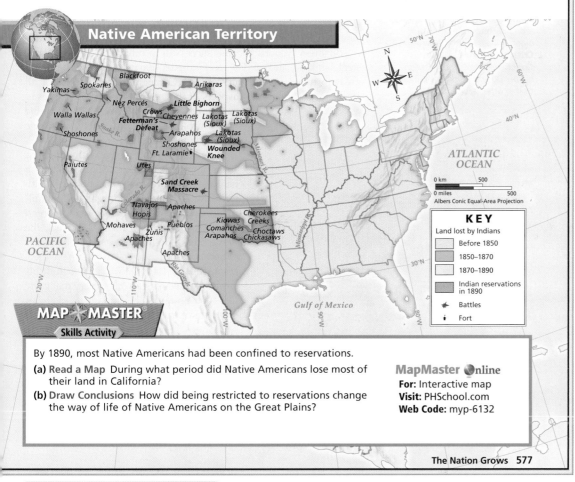

Native American Territory

MAP MASTER
Skills Activity

By 1890, most Native Americans had been confined to reservations.

(a) Read a Map During what period did Native Americans lose most of their land in California?

(b) Draw Conclusions How did being restricted to reservations change the way of life of Native Americans on the Great Plains?

MapMaster Online
For: Interactive map
Visit: PHSchool.com
Web Code: myp-6132

KEY

Land lost by Indians

- Before 1850
- 1850–1870
- 1870–1890
- Indian reservations in 1890
- ✦ Battles
- ⚑ Fort

0 km 500
0 miles 500
Albers Conic Equal-Area Projection

The Nation Grows **577**

- Discuss with students the difficulty of settling in a new area. Have students suggest ways that settlers were assisted by the government. (*The government provided settlers with land through the Homestead Act.*) Ask: **Why do you think the government wanted to support settlers?** (*Possible answers: to expand the nation, to reduce the population in the East*)

- Discuss how Native Americans in the West lived after the Civil War. (*Some farmed, but many depended on buffalo for their way of life.*)

- Ask: **How did life change for Plains Indians when miners, settlers, and railroads moved west?** (*Miners and railroad companies ignored treaties protecting Native American lands. Soldiers and hunters wiped out the buffalo. Native Americans resisted, but were forced onto reservations by the government.*)

Monitor Progress

Circulate to make sure students understand the effects of westward expansion on American settlers and Native Americans. Provide assistance as needed.

Vocabulary Builder

Use the information below to teach students this section's high-use words.

High-Use Word	Definition and Sample Sentence
dominate, p. 578	*v.* to rule or control Great Britain **dominated** the original thirteen colonies.
minimize, p. 580	*v.* to reduce; to make smaller; to make of less importance At first, northerners **minimized** the fighting capacity of the Confederates.

Answers

✓**Checkpoint** The destruction of the buffalo herds left the Native Americans without food and skins used for clothing and housing.

MAP MASTER Skills Activity **(a)** 1850–1870 **(b)** Native Americans lost their traditional lifestyles. They were expected to settle down, stop following the buffalo, and become farmers.

Business and Labor

p. 578

Instruction L2

- Have students read Business and Labor. Remind students to look for the sequence of events.

- Ask: **What innovations shaped the 1800s?** (*the railroad, refrigeration, the telephone, the light bulb, electricity, the phonograph, and moving pictures*)

- Ask students to name several business tycoons and their contributions. (*Vanderbilt built railroad empires, Carnegie controlled all aspects of steel production and gave to charity, J.P. Morgan invested in railroads and steel, and John D. Rockefeller made a fortune in oil.*)

- Ask: **Are all corporations monopolies?** (*No. A corporation is a type of business organization. A corporation becomes a monopoly if it buys up most or all of its competitors or otherwise severely limits competition.*)

- Ask: **What was the effect of industrial growth on workers?** (*More jobs were created, but often working conditions were dangerous and the pay was low.*)

Monitor Progress

Circulate to make sure students understand the inventions that appeared and the businesses that boomed during the late 1800s. Provide assistance as needed.

Answer

Draw Conclusions Possible answers: Edison meant that hard work is required for success. Yes, his opinions are true. People have to work hard to be successful in other areas of life such as sports and school.

578 Chapter Epilogue

Business and Labor

American business and industry boomed after the Civil War. A network of rail lines crossed the country. Railroads carried materials to factories and cattle to meatpacking plants. Inventions such as refrigeration, the telephone, and the electric street car changed both business and daily life. Thomas Edison and his workers invented products that shaped today's world—not only the first practical light bulb but also the electric power plant, the phonograph, and motion pictures. Late in the 1800s, inventors in America and Europe built the first automobiles.

Vocabulary Builder
<u>dominate</u> (DAHM uh nayt) **v.** to rule or control

Inventive Genius
Thomas Edison once said, "Genius is one percent inspiration and ninety-nine percent perspiration." **Critical Thinking: *Draw Conclusions*** *What did Edison mean? Do you think his opinion is true in other areas of life?*

Growth of Big Business The railroad industry <u>dominated</u> the American economy. "Railroad barons" bought up smaller lines and built great railroad empires. The most powerful was Cornelius Vanderbilt, owner of the New York Central Railroad. Railroad owners sometimes abused their power by fixing prices and bribing public officials. At the same time, though, the railroads created jobs and spurred the growth of industry.

To expand, businesses organized as corporations. A corporation sells shares of stock to investors in exchange for money, or capital. If the business prospers, investors get dividends, and the value of their stock grows. The corporate structure protects individual owners if a company fails because they could not lose more than they invested.

Business tycoons became successful in other areas, particularly steel, banking, and oil. The steel industry expanded quickly, creating great fortunes. Steelmaker Andrew Carnegie gained control of all aspects of the business, from iron mines to steel mills to shipping lines. Believing the wealthy had a duty to society, Carnegie gave millions to charity.

Big banks grew along with industry. They invested in corporations, allowing bankers to control company policies. With his fortune, banker J. P. Morgan bought railroads and steel companies. He merged several companies to form U.S. Steel, the first billion-dollar American business. Other fortunes were based on a new resource—oil. John D. Rockefeller built his family fortune with an oil refinery that grew into the Standard Oil Company. Rockefeller organized a trust to control the stock of rival companies. That made Standard Oil a monopoly—a company that dominates an industry.

Critics charged that these business practices reduced competition, hurting smaller companies and consumers. Others defended giant corporations, saying they brought lower prices and improved people's lives.

578

Differentiated Instruction

L3 Advanced Readers   **L3 Gifted and Talented**

Write a Biography Ask students to further research the life of one of the people discussed in this section. Have students find out how this person's early life contributed to and influenced his success. Students should compile their research and observations into a biographical essay to share with the class. Have the class rank the importance of these people based on the impact of their businesses and inventions on American society.

Rise of Organized Labor The growth of American industry created thousands of new jobs. Working conditions, however, were often harsh and dangerous. Many workers were immigrants, women, and children, who labored for long hours and low pay in crowded sweatshops.

Workers began to organize for better conditions. The Knights of Labor wanted shorter hours and an end to child labor. In 1886, the American Federation of Labor (AFL) brought together trade unions, which represented workers who were skilled in particular crafts. Some unions used strikes to gain better pay. In the 1886 Haymarket Riot in Chicago, police clashed violently with protesting workers. Public officials and the courts generally sided with factory owners.

✔Checkpoint How did economic conditions affect the labor union movement?

Immigration and the Growth of Cities

In the late 1800s, millions of immigrants streamed into the United States. Fleeing poverty, they hoped for factory jobs or to acquire farmland. The immigrants swelled city populations. Housing was scarce, and city services were lacking. At the same time, city life offered a rich mix of cultures and amusements.

The New Immigrants Before the Civil War, most immigrants were from northern and western Europe. In the late 1800s, this pattern changed. More people came from southern or eastern Europe—Italy, Poland, Russia, and other countries. A growing number of Asians, mainly Chinese, arrived on the West Coast.

Language, religion, and culture set newcomers apart from their neighbors. Usually the older immigrants kept traditional ways, and their children hurried to learn English and become citizens.

Many Americans opposed the flood of immigrants, saying that newcomers would never fit into American culture. On the West Coast, anti-Chinese feelings were especially strong. An 1882 federal law barred most Chinese immigrants. Other laws set limits on immigration.

American Cities Grow and Change The United States was once mainly a rural, farming nation. That changed as people flocked to cities. One large group of migrants was African Americans from the South. They formed thriving new communities in northern cities such as Chicago and Detroit.

City life was very different for the rich and the poor. The poor often lived in small, dark, crowded tenement apartments. In these unhealthy conditions, diseases like tuberculosis spread easily. Fires were frequent and crime common. Middle-class families, on the other hand, lived in comfortable houses. The very wealthy built mansions far from the crowds.

✔Checkpoint How did industrialization and immigration change life in American cities?

Child coal miners

Instruction   L2

- Have students read Immigration and the Growth of Cities. Remind students to look for causes and effects.

- Ask: **How were immigrants that came to the United States in the late 1800s different from pre-Civil War immigrants?** (*Before the Civil War, most immigrants were from northern and western Europe. In the late 1800s, they came from southern or eastern Europe and were eager to learn English and become citizens.*)

- Discuss the impact of the immigration movement of the late 1800s on the United States. (*growth of cities, nativist reaction, laws limiting immigration*)

- Ask: **What group of migrants came to cities from the South?** (*African Americans*) Discuss with students the reasons that African Americans migrated from the South. (*Possible answers: There were job opportunities in the cities; there was less discrimination.*)

- Use the transparency Immigration: 1960–2000 to extend knowledge of immigration at the turn of the twentieth century.

Color Transparencies, Immigration, 1960–2000

Monitor Progress

Circulate to make sure students understand the changes caused by industrialization and immigration in American cities. If students do not seem to have a good understanding, have them reread the section. Provide assistance as needed.

History Background

Long Days, Low Wages Some of the conditions that workers had to endure at the beginning of the twentieth century are almost impossible to imagine. For example, in 1900 the average factory worker earned less than 22 cents per hour. The average workweek was 59 hours, which meant about 10 hours per day except Sunday. Steelworkers spent even more time at their grueling jobs. They worked 12 hours a day, 7 days a week.

Answers

✔Checkpoint Workers organized to gain better working conditions, including better pay and fewer hours.

✔Checkpoint Possible answers: New communities were formed in cities; skyscrapers and public parks were built.

The Progressive Era

p. 580

Instruction L2

- Have students read The Progressive Era. Remind students to look for the sequence of events.

- Discuss with students the downside of the business boom that occurred at the turn of the century. Have students consider why corruption occurs in business and politics. (*Students may suggest that people want more money and power, and they use their leadership positions to obtain them.*) Ask students if they think the government has a role to play in ending corruption. (*Possible answers: Yes, the government should make sure that business and politics operate for the public good. No, businesses should be trusted to regulate themselves; government should not interfere.*)

- Ask: **What were the goals of the Progressives?** (*to reduce the power of business, improve social conditions, and clean up political corruption*)

- Ask: **How did Progressive politics affect the presidency?** (*Theodore Roosevelt brought Progressive policies to the presidency. He used his administration to influence the quality of life in America.*)

Suffragettes march for the right to vote in the early 1900s

Vocabulary Builder

<u>minimize</u> (MIHN ah mīz) **v.** to reduce; to make smaller; to make of less importance

Ask Extension Questions
The conflict between Theodore Roosevelt and William Howard Taft is an interesting aspect of American history. Suggest a possible research question building on the election of 1912.

The Progressive Era

Though prosperity created the Gilded Age in the late 1800s, American society had many problems. In the Progressive Era, reformers worked to reduce the power of big business, improve social conditions, and clean up political corruption.

Progressive Reformers Though they had different targets, Progressives were united in wanting to improve society. Some reformers were journalists, known as muckrakers. They reported on slum conditions and unsafe meatpacking plants. Other Progressives backed political reforms such as primary elections.

Progressives also attacked corruption in government. Powerful "bosses," such as Boss Tweed in New York City, controlled business and politics. One early reform set up the Civil Service Commission. It awarded federal jobs on the basis of exam scores rather than political influence. Reformers also tried to <u>minimize</u> the power of big business. In 1887, Congress passed the Interstate Commerce Act to regulate railroads. The Sherman Antitrust Act (1890) limited business tactics that hurt competition.

Progressive Presidents By 1900, reform ideas reached presidential politics. Theodore Roosevelt became President in 1901, after William McKinley's assassination. Roosevelt believed the presidency could influence the quality of American life. He attacked unfair business practices and supported labor. His conservation policy set aside land for national parks and forests. New laws made food products and medicines safer. Roosevelt's successor, William Howard Taft, continued reforms.

In 1912, Woodrow Wilson, also a Progressive, was elected President. He backed laws to encourage business competition. Congress also began to regulate the banking system.

The Women's Suffrage Movement Even though many leading reformers were women, American women had few political rights. Reformers such as Elizabeth Cady Stanton had long fought

Differentiated Instruction

L3 Advanced Readers **L3 Gifted and Talented**

The Right Decision Progressives believed that people would make the right decisions if given the chance. They fought for reforms that gave more power to voters because of this belief. Have students meet

in groups of four to discuss this idea. Then ask students to defend or disagree with the Progressives' position in a letter to the editor. Tell students to include examples to support their position.

Answer

Reading Skill Possible research question: Why did Wilson win support of the Progressives during election, even though Taft continued Progressive reform?

for **suffrage**—the right to vote. American women first gained the vote in some western states. In 1920, the Nineteenth Amendment to the Constitution protected women's right to vote.

Women sought equality in other areas, too, such as the chance to study law and medicine. They tried to end social problems such as child labor. Women also led the fight to ban alcoholic beverages. In 1919, the Eighteenth Amendment established Prohibition, a ban on the sale of alcohol in the United States.

Seeking Equality The reforms of the early 1900s did not achieve much for nonwhites. Since Reconstruction's end, African Americans had lost many rights. They faced prejudice and segregation in schools, housing, and jobs. Two leaders offered different answers. Booker T. Washington advised people to concentrate on education and gradual progress. W.E.B. Du Bois believed that African Americans should work actively against discrimination. Du Bois joined with white reformers to found the National Association for the Advancement of Colored People (NAACP).

Other minority groups also faced discrimination. The Mexican American population in the Southwest grew quickly after 1910. Immigration to the United States from China was barred, but Asians from Japan and the Philippines immigrated to the West Coast. Discrimination against the Asians was widespread. An agreement with Japan kept out more workers.

✓**Checkpoint** List some accomplishments of the Progressive Presidents Roosevelt, Taft, and Wilson.

⭐ **Looking Back and Ahead** By the beginning of the twentieth century, Americans were settled across the continent. American industry was thriving, and immigration had swelled the nation's cities. In the next section, you will see how this new status thrust the United States into a leading role on the world scene.

Booker T. Washington

W.E.B. Du Bois

HISTORIAN'S APPRENTICE ACTIVITY PACK

To further explore the topics in this chapter, complete the activity in the Historian's Apprentice Activity Pack to answer this essential question:

How did industrialization affect the United States?

- Have students consider the patience it took for women to win the right to vote. Ask: **How do you think the Progressive movement affected women's desire to vote?** (*Possible answer: After working so hard for others' rights, women were inspired to gain more rights for themselves. Women thought they could choose uncorrupted leaders if they had the right to vote.*)

- Have students view the Constitution CD-ROM to learn more about the passing of the Nineteenth Amendment.

  💿 **Constitution CD-ROM**

- Discuss with students the struggles that African Americans faced after Reconstruction ended. Ask: **How did Booker T. Washington's approach to reform for African Americans differ from that of W.E.B. Du Bois?** (*Washington advised people to concentrate on education and gradual progress, while Du Bois believed that African Americans should work actively against discrimination.*)

Monitor Progress

Circulate to make sure students understand the struggles various groups faced when seeking equal rights. Provide assistance as needed.

Answer

✓**Checkpoint** Possible answers: Roosevelt set aside land for conservation, and regulated food products and medicines. Taft continued Roosevelt's policies. Wilson backed laws that encouraged business competition and regulated the banking system.

Section 1 | **Check Your Progress**

Comprehension and Critical Thinking

1. (a) Identify Who was Chief Joseph?
(b) Detect Points of View In 1879, Chief Joseph appeared before Congress. He said, "Treat all men alike. Give them all the same law. Give them all an even chance to live and grow. All men were made by the same Great Spirit Chief." What was Chief Joseph trying to tell Congress? How do you think members of Congress responded to his words?

2. (a) Describe Why did cities grow rapidly after the Civil War?
(b) Apply Information How did the growth of cities lead to problems for many residents?

🔲 **Reading Skill**

3. Ask Extension Questions The displacement of Native Americans of the Great Plains and Southwest is a controversial part of American history. Suggest a possible research question building on this topic.

Key Terms

4. Draw a table with four rows and two columns. In the first column, list the key terms from this section: reservation, corporation, monopoly, suffrage. In the next column, write the definition of each term.

Writing

5. "Life in a city is more rewarding than life outside a city." List two or three arguments in favor of that opinion, and list two or three arguments opposing that opinion.

Section 1 Check Your Progress

1. (a) Chief Joseph was a Plains Indian who led his people in wars against government troops to preserve Native American lands and ways of life.
(b) Chief Joseph was asking Congress to treat his people fairly. Congress probably took very little notice of his words.

2. (a) New inventions, industrialization, and immigration caused cities to grow rapidly after the Civil War.

(b) Possible answers: Many poor residents had to live in overcrowded conditions, which made disease, the threat of fire, and crime widespread.

3. Possible questions: Was it necessary for Americans to displace the Native Americans? How democratic was the displacement of Native Americans?

4. reservation: land set aside for Native Americans to live on; corporation: type of business organization that sells shares of stock to investors in exchange for

capital; monopoly: a company that dominates an industry; suffrage: the right to vote

5. Students' arguments should be reasonable and based on information presented in the text.

An Immigrant's Journey

Build Background Knowledge L2

Ask students to recall what they know about life for immigrants at the turn of the twentieth century. (*Most worked long, hard hours for little pay, and lived in unhealthy and unsafe conditions.*) Have students consider the factors that made life easier for immigrants and the factors that made life harder. Use the Idea Wave strategy (TE, p. T24) to elicit responses. (*Immigrants tended to live together in ethnic neighborhoods. New immigrants learned English and sought citizenship.*) Tell students that in this feature, they will learn what it was like for immigrants to travel to, arrive in, and begin a new life in the United States.

Instruction L2

- Have students read An Immigrant's Journey. Remind students to relate the information in the pictures to the information in the captions.

- Discuss with students the reasons why people came to the United States, even though the journey was long and difficult. Ask: **What were some of the hopes, fears, and challenges newcomers shared when they arrived in the United States?** (*hope for a new life; fear of being deported; the challenge of learning new customs and a new language*)

- Ask: **According to the passage from the Irish immigrant, how were some people treated when they arrived?** (*Some people were treated with disrespect.*) Ask students why they think this happened. (*Possible answers: Immigration officials met with thousands of people every day and had to move quickly.*)

An Immigrant's Journey

From all over the world, immigrants poured into the United States. Wherever they came from, these newcomers shared many of the same hopes, fears, and challenges.

1 Passage

Immigrants faced a long, difficult ocean crossing crowded into ship holds that were designed to carry cargo or cattle.

"Day after day the weather was bad and the sea stormy. The hatch was tightly closed and there was no circulation of air, so we were all tortured by the bad odor."

–Japanese immigrant
describes the voyage

European immigrants arrive in New York

2 Arrival

New York's Ellis Island was the point of entry for many European immigrants. Asians were detained on Angel Island outside San Francisco.

"Immigration officials slammed a tag on you with your name, address, country of origin, etc. . . . Then they pushed you and they'd point, because they didn't know whether you spoke English or not."

–Irish immigrant
describes arrival at Ellis Island

Differentiated Instruction

L1 English Language Learners   **L1 Less Proficient Readers**   **L1 Special Needs**

Identify Alternatives Explain to students that 4 out of every 10 Americans today have ancestors who passed through Ellis Island between 1892 and 1954. Have students name at least four other ways in which the ancestors of present-day Americans might have arrived in the United States. Share students' ideas with the class. (*Possible answers: They were already here, as Native Americans; they were forced to come here as slaves; they migrated prior to the establishment of Ellis Island; they came through San Francisco; they migrated across the Mexican-American border; they flew here.*)

3 Ethnic Neighborhoods

Crowded into ethnic neighborhoods, immigrants preserved familiar ways as they adjusted to their new culture.

"When we first arrived we still wore our wooden shoes. . . . We conquered the English language beautifully. My father spoke well. But in the home we spoke Frisian."

–Dutch immigrant describes life in America

History *Interactive*
Learn More About Immigration
Visit: PHSchool.com
Web Code: mvl-9294

A street in a Jewish neighborhood in New York

4 Citizenship

For many immigrants, becoming a citizen was the proudest moment of their lives.

A new citizen is sworn in

"I am the youngest of America's children, and into my hands is given all her priceless heritage. . . . Mine is the whole majestic past, and mine is the shining future."

–Russian immigrant expresses pride in becoming U.S. citizen

Analyze LIFE AT THE TIME

Suppose that you are an immigrant in 1900. For each stage of the journey from passage to citizenship, write a sentence describing your hopes or your fears.

History Background

Ellis Island The immigration facilities at Ellis Island opened in January of 1892 and were not permanently closed until 1954. It is estimated that around 12 million immigrants passed through Ellis Island. The use of an island as the checkpoint for new immigrants was hardly coincidental. Its geography supported the legislative and social concerns of the times. By containing new arrivals on an island, they could be sequestered from the general population as needed for health or legal reasons. In 1965, Ellis Island was opened as a museum of immigration history. It remains open for that purpose today.

Instruction (continued)

■ Encourage students to draw inferences about the swearing-in of a new citizen. Point out the passage from the Russian immigrant to help elicit responses.

■ Ask: **What factors could make the swearing-in the proudest moment of an immigrant's life?** (*Possible answers: The immigrant might have had to face many difficult challenges to achieve citizenship.*)

Monitor Progress

Circulate to make sure individuals understand the challenges immigrants overcame to make a life in the United States. Provide assistance as needed.

Writing Rubric Share this writing rubric with the students.

Score 1 Sentences do not relate to the topic.
Score 2 Sentences partially relate to the topic. Some information is incorrect.
Score 3 Response is thoughtful and uses information correctly.
Score 4 Response is thoughtful, accurate, thorough, and well written.

Answer

Analyze **LIFE AT THE TIME** Sentences will vary, but should demonstrate a clear understanding of the experiences of immigrants, their hopes for the future, and their fears of new experiences.

Section 2
Step-by-Step Instruction

Review and Preview

Students have read about the United States' domestic expansion. Now they will learn about the nation's international expansion.

Section Focus Question

How did a more powerful United States expand its role in the world?

Before you begin the lesson for the day, write the Section Focus Question on the board. (*Lesson focus: The United States acquired new territories and allied with other powerful nations against common enemies.*)

Prepare to Read

Build Background Knowledge   L2

This section discusses the territory that the United States acquired in the 1800s. Ask students to list the states and territories that are currently part of the United States, but not adjacent to the other states. Use the Idea Wave strategy (TE, p. T24) to elicit responses. (*States include Alaska and Hawaii. Territories include Puerto Rico, American Samoa, Federated States of Micronesia, Guam, and the Midway Islands.*) After students respond, address any misconceptions they may have regarding geography or territories owned by the United States.

Teach

Becoming a World Power

p. 584

Instruction   L2

- **Vocabulary Builder** Before teaching this section, preteach the High-Use Words **invest** and **restore** using the strategy on TE p. T21.

  Key Terms Have students continue to fill in the See It-Remember It chart for the Key Terms in this chapter.

Americans Mean Business

66 The chief business of the American people is business. They are profoundly concerned with producing, buying, selling, investing, and prospering in the world. . . . We want peace and honor, and that charity which is so strong an element of all civilization. The chief ideal of the American people is idealism. 99

—President Calvin Coolidge, 1925

◄ Automobile production strengthened U.S. trade around the world.

A New Role for the Nation

Objectives

- Describe how the United States gained an empire after the Spanish-American War.
- Identify the causes of World War I.
- Explain the social changes that occurred in the United States during the 1920s.
- Describe how hard times affected American families during the 1930s.

🔄 Reading Skill

Ask Analytical Questions Reading about history may sometimes leave you puzzled. Ask questions that focus on these puzzles, and then research to find answers. Start by looking at what does not make sense to you, such as why people acted in a particular way. Use the question starters *who, what, when, why,* and *how.* Then, think about how events changed over time and what caused the changes.

Key Terms and People

Woodrow Wilson   Franklin Delano
isolationism   Roosevelt
on margin

Why It Matters Following George Washington's early advice to avoid the political affairs of other nations, later Presidents pursued policies that limited U.S. involvement in world affairs. Yet, as American trade expanded, the United States abandoned isolationism and emerged as a new power on the global stage.

❓ **Section Focus Question: How did a more powerful United States expand its role in the world?**

Becoming a World Power

Once Americans reached the Pacific Coast, they looked toward winning even more trade and territory. In the 1850s, visits by the U.S. Navy opened ports in Japan to trade with the West. In 1867, the United States purchased the resource-rich Alaska Territory from Russia.

U.S. expansion in the Pacific rested on naval power. The country acquired the islands of Midway and Samoa, where ships bound for Asia could refuel. The next large acquisition was the island chain of Hawaii, ruled by its royal family. Starting in the mid-1800s, Americans had set up large sugar plantations in Hawaii. In 1893, with the help of the U.S. Marines, American sugar planters overthrew the last Hawaiian queen, Liliuokalani. The United States soon annexed the islands. In mainland Asia, the United States competed with European nations for influence in China. The Open Door Policy guaranteed access to Chinese ports and trade.

Differentiated Instruction

L1 English Language Learners   **L1** Less Proficient Readers   **L1** Special Needs

Outline and Summarize To give students practice with writing skills, have them outline this section and summarize its main points. Students can use the main ideas in the section as the main heads in the outline. Subheads can be the supporting details. Have students use their outlines to write a short summary of the section.

The United States and Latin America Backers of expansion next looked closer to home. In nearby Cuba, people were rebelling against rule by Spain. Sensational newspaper stories made many Americans want to help the rebels. In 1898, the American battleship *Maine* blew up in Havana harbor. Newspaper headlines blamed Spain. Soon the country was at war with Spain, not only in Cuba but also in the Philippine Islands. A quick victory gave the United States control of Cuba, Puerto Rico, Guam, and the Philippines. Cubans were given self-rule, though under American control.

Theodore Roosevelt believed in using power to promote American expansion. He actively followed a "big stick" policy in challenging European expansion in Latin America. One of his goals was a canal across the narrow Isthmus of Panama. It would let ships sail between the Atlantic and the Pacific oceans rather than going around South America. Taking advantage of a local rebellion, Roosevelt obtained land for the canal. Despite tropical diseases and engineering challenges, the Panama Canal was completed by 1914. Roosevelt took another step in establishing an American role in Latin America. The Roosevelt Corollary stated the right of the United States to intervene in Latin American affairs in order to prevent European nations from trying to establish control. U.S. troops protected American investments in Haiti and the Dominican Republic. From 1914 through 1916, U.S. troops intervened in the Mexican Revolution.

☑Checkpoint **What lands did the United States gain control of as a result of the Spanish-American War?**

The Big Stick in the Caribbean Sea

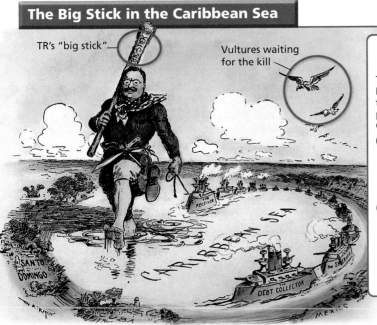

TR's "big stick"

Vultures waiting for the kill

Reading Political Cartoons

Skills Activity

This 1904 cartoon shows President Roosevelt using the U.S. Navy to block European interference in the Caribbean Sea.

(a) Detect Relevant Information What is the meaning of the object in Roosevelt's right hand?

(b) Detect Points of View Do you think the cartoonist approved of Roosevelt's Latin American policies?

Vocabulary Builder

Use the information below to teach students this section's high-use words.

High-Use Word	Definition and Sample Sentence
invest, p. 587	*v.* to purchase something with money with the hope that its value will grow; to give power or authority Cornelius Vanderbilt **invested** wisely in the infant railroad industry.
restore, p. 589	*v.* to bring back to a normal state; to put back; to reestablish Quick action by President Washington **restored** peace to the uneasy western frontier.

Instruction (continued)

■ Read Becoming a World Power with students using the Choral Reading strategy (TE, p. T24).

■ Ask: **How did the United States practice isolationism prior to the late 1800s?** (*It took little part in foreign affairs.*)

■ Ask: **How did U.S. expansion help its industries?** (*It opened new markets, such as Japan and China, and took over useful resources, such as plantations in Hawaii.*)

■ Discuss with students the event that led the United States into war against Spain. Ask: **What role did newspapers play in the war?** (*They sparked it by blaming Spain for the explosion of the* Maine.*)

■ Have students discuss Roosevelt's "big stick" policy. Ask: **What territories were acquired using this approach?** (*Puerto Rico, Guam, and the Philippines*)

■ Remind students that Americans sympathized with Cubans rebelling against Spanish rule, which contributed to U.S. involvement in the war. Ask: **How did American sympathies prior to the war contradict U.S. actions after it?** (*At first the United States helped Cuba rebel against Spanish rule. Afterwards, the United States restricted Cuba's independence.*)

Monitor Progress

Circulate to make sure students understand the causes and effects of U.S. expansion into the Pacific and Latin America. Provide assistance as needed.

Answers

☑Checkpoint Puerto Rico, Guam, and the Philippines; Cuba ruled itself, but under American control.

Reading Political Cartoons **(a)** Possible answer: The stick represents the power of the United States. **(b)** Possible answer: Probably not. The cartoonist may have thought that Roosevelt's policies were heavy-handed.

World War I and the Postwar Decade

p. 586

Instruction L2

- Have students read World War I and the Postwar Decade. Remind students to look for causes and effects.

- Discuss with students the reasons for the war. Point out that the United States remained neutral during the beginning of the war. Ask: **Why did the United States enter the war?** (*German submarines began attacking American ships.*)

- Ask: **Why did Congress seek a return to isolationism after World War I?** (*Possible answers: The war was costly in resources and human lives. Americans did not want to remain involved in world affairs.*) **What step did the Senate take to ensure this isolationism?** (*It rejected U.S. membership in the League of Nations.*)

- Ask: **In what ways did American society change during the 1920s?** (*Possible answers: Women gained many rights; people enjoyed a new type of music called jazz; alcoholic beverages were banned.*)

Monitor Progress

Circulate to make sure students understand the causes and effects of World War I. Provide assistance as needed.

Answer

🔁 **Reading Skill** The United States entered the war because German submarines began attacking American ships. Possible research questions: Why did German submarines attack American ships? Did the United States have alternatives other than entering the war?

2005 An honor guard keeps 24-hour watch at the Tomb of the Unknowns.

Links Across Time

Honoring Veterans

1921 The day World War I ended has been remembered ever since. On November 11, 1921, the body of an unidentified American soldier was laid to rest in the Tomb of the Unknowns at Arlington National Cemetery.

1938 November 11 was made a national holiday, Armistice Day. The name of Armistice Day was later changed to Veterans Day.

Link to Today 🌐 Online

Veterans Day Today Each year, on November 11, we continue to honor those who have served in our nation's armed forces.

For: Veterans Day in the news
Visit: PHSchool.com
Web Code: mvc-7213

World War I and the Postwar Decade

In 1914, long-standing tensions in Europe erupted into war. Imperialism was one cause—major nations were competing for territory. To maintain power, nations made alliances with one another, promising support if their allies were attacked.

In June 1914, in Sarajevo, Bosnia, a Serbian nationalist killed the heir to the Austro-Hungarian throne. The alliance system soon drew one nation after another into war. The war pitted the Central powers—Germany, Austria-Hungary, and the Ottoman, or Turkish, Empire—against the Allied powers of France, Britain, and Russia. In time, more than 20 countries were involved.

Ask Analytical Questions
Reread the text following the subheading "Entering the War." Why did the United States finally enter the war in 1917? Suggest a possible research question on this topic.

Entering the War President Woodrow Wilson tried to keep the United States neutral. However, American opinion soon became anti-German because of German submarine attacks on American ships. The United States entered the war in April 1917.

Results of World War I When the United States joined the war, things looked bad for the Allies—Britain, France, and Russia. Then, Russia withdrew from the war after a revolution overthrew the tsar's government. However, by June 1918, the Germans were in retreat. The war ended in November. Its costs were staggering. More than 8 million people were dead. Much of Europe was in ruins.

Differentiated Instruction

L3 Advanced Readers   **L3** Gifted and Talented

Make a Flow Chart Help students keep track of the sequence of events surrounding World War I by making a flow chart. In their charts, students should outline the progression of events prior to, during, and following the war. Have students increase the complexity of their charts by adding a sentence or two to each entry that analyzes the motivations for, and the consequences of, each event. Have students share their charts with the class.

President Wilson tried to shape the peace settlement. His Fourteen Points plan outlined a League of Nations, an organization that would settle international disputes. However, the final peace treaty left out many of Wilson's ideas. Instead, the Treaty of Versailles imposed extremely harsh terms on Germany. Congress sought a return to isolationism, avoiding becoming involved in world affairs. It rejected U.S. membership in the League of Nations.

The Prosperous Twenties The 1920s began as a hopeful, prosperous time. The postwar economy grew quickly.

The auto industry was important in the booming economy. Factories turned out new consumer goods such as radios, vacuum cleaners, and refrigerators. Many people also <u>invested</u> in the stock market for the first time. Stock prices rose steadily.

American society changed during the 1920s. Women could now vote. More women joined the workforce. Some young women, known as flappers, shocked older Americans with their short skirts and unconventional behavior. Having more leisure time, people enjoyed sports, radio programs, and movies, along with a new kind of music—jazz. African American culture flourished during the Harlem Renaissance.

Reformers had tried to change society by banning alcoholic beverages. Prohibition had disastrous side effects, however. Many people broke the law. Organized crime thrived by supplying liquor to illegal speakeasies. Prohibition was repealed in 1933.

The Crash Some of the prosperity of the 1920s was not real. People bought things they could not afford, paying in installments. They bought stocks on margin, paying only a fraction of the cost.

Then, the economy began to slow. Though factories still made goods, people could not afford them. Factories laid off workers or closed. Some investors began to sell their stocks. Stock prices fell. Brokers demanded full payment for stocks bought on margin. Many investors had to sell. In October 1929, panic struck the stock market.

✓Checkpoint What were the results of World War I?

The Great Depression

The economy now plunged into the worst economic slump in American history. The Great Depression deepened throughout the 1930s. Banks closed, wiping out people's savings. Unemployment soared. Hungry people lined up at soup kitchens. A severe drought in the Great Plains made things worse. High winds and dust storms blew away the topsoil, turning farmland into a region named the Dust Bowl.

President Herbert Hoover tried to fight the Great Depression with some public works programs. Still, people blamed him for the hard times. They wanted a leader who would act more forcefully. In 1932, they elected Franklin Delano Roosevelt, also known as FDR. The new President made people feel more confident.

Vocabulary Builder

<u>invest</u> (ihn VEHST) **v.** to purchase something with money with the hope that its value will grow; to give power or authority

Flappers balance on the ledge of a building.

The Great Depression
p. 587

Instruction
L2

- Have students read The Great Depression. Remind students to look for the sequence of events.

- Discuss with students the state of the economy prior to the stock market crash.

- Ask: **What was the Great Depression?** (*A period from the late 1920s through the 1930s in which the economy suffered. Banks and businesses closed and unemployment soared.*)

- Ask: **How do you think the economy is affected when millions of people are unemployed?** (*Possible answer: When people are unemployed and have little money, they cannot afford to buy things. Declining demand means more factories and stores will close, leading to further unemployment. Also, banks will not be repaid loans made to companies and to people, so they will close as well.*)

- Have students explain how President Hoover tried to fight the Great Depression. Ask: **Was he successful?** (*Hoover started some public works programs, but his programs did not work.*) Ask: **How did President Roosevelt fight the Great Depression?** (*Roosevelt instituted a public works program called the New Deal, which gave relief to the unemployed, made plans for economic recovery, and instituted reforms to prevent another depression.*)

- Use the transparency Employment Agency to extend understanding of the effects of unemployment during the Great Depression.

Color Transparencies, Employment Agency

History Background

Life Goes On Despite hard times, there were some major accomplishments during the Great Depression.

- Inventors at the Massachusetts Institute of Technology introduced an early computer in 1930.

- Also in 1930, American astronomer Clyde Tombaugh discovered Pluto, the ninth planet from the sun.

- New York's Empire State Building, the world's tallest building at the time, opened in 1931.

Answer

✓Checkpoint The Allies won World War I and the United States retreated behind isolationist policies. The Treaty of Versailles imposed harsh terms on Germany.

Instruction (continued)

- Discuss the New Deal with students. Ask them to describe the New Deal program that they feel was the most effective. Have them explain their opinions. (*Answers will vary, but should demonstrate an awareness of the types of New Deal programs and their effects.*)

- Ask: **How did the New Deal change the role of the government?** (*It gave the government a bigger role in the economy. The government became responsible for controlling the economy and preventing another downturn like the Great Depression from happening again.*) Have students work in small groups to discuss whether they think the government should be involved in managing the economy. Use the Give-One-Get-One strategy (TE, p. T25) to elicit responses.

- Use the transparency Social Security to extend understanding of New Deal responses to economic suffering.

Color Transparencies, Social Security

Monitor Progress

Circulate to make sure students understand how and why life changed during the Great Depression. Provide assistance as needed.

Answer

Link Past and Present Answers will vary, but students may say that they would be afraid of losing everything, or that they would want to help their parents and friends.

● **INFOGRAPHIC**

THE GREAT DEPRESSION: Misery in the Cities

The misery of the Great Depression touched all America Much of the most visible suffering took place in the nation's cities. **Critical Thinking: *Link Past and Presen*** *How do you think you would react if another depression like this one struck the United States?*

Desperate for food, the jobless lined up at soup kitchens operated by churches and private charities. ▼

◀ Apple sellers were a common sight on street corners.

Unemployment, 1927–1933

Source: *Historical Statistics of the United States*

Unemployment reached its highest levels in American history during the 1930s.

The homeless gathered in miserable shantytowns, nicknamed Hoovervilles.

588 Epilogue

Differentiated Instruction

L1 English Language Learners   **L1** Less Proficient Readers   **L1** Special Needs

Write an Essay Have students reread the content discussing the Great Depression on pp. 587–589. Ask students to write a short essay describing life during the Great Depression from the point of view of someone their age. For help in starting this activity, have students suggest questions that may help them when rereading the text and organizing their essays. (*Possible questions: What was daily life like during the Great Depression? How had life been beforehand? How might a young person's life change if one or both parents become unemployed?*) As they write, encourage students to keep in mind the goals of the New Deal and how Roosevelt's reforms made life better.

FDR's Program FDR promised the American people a New Deal. His programs had three main goals: relief for the unemployed, plans for recovery, and reforms to prevent another severe depression. The Works Progress Administration (WPA), for example, built schools and public buildings and gave work to artists and writers. The Tennessee Valley Authority (TVA) built dams to supply electric power and control floods in parts of the South. The Federal Deposit Insurance Corporation (FDIC) protected bank accounts. The Social Security system provided benefits for retired or disabled people.

Impact of the New Deal Some critics thought the New Deal went too far. They wanted less government interference in business.

Other critics said that it did not go far enough to assist the poor. The New Deal did not <u>restore</u> the prosperity of the 1920s. However, it changed people's relationship with the federal government. Government grew bigger, with more influence on everyday life. Government spending increased greatly, building up a deficit. On the other hand, New Deal programs helped millions of people. Many thought that social programs helped people keep their faith in democracy during the crisis.

Vocabulary Builder
<u>restore</u> (ree STOR) **v.** to bring back to a normal state; to put back; to reestablish

☑Checkpoint **What were the three goals of the New Deal?**

⭐ **Looking Back and Ahead** By the late 1930s, the New Deal had restored hope, though it had not ended the Depression. While Americans fought the Depression, ominous events were occurring in other parts of the world. Dictatorships in Germany, Italy, the Soviet Union, and Japan took aggressive actions that once again threatened the security of the United States.

Section 2 | Check Your Progress

Comprehension and Critical Thinking

1. (a) Identify What role did the press play in rallying American support for a war in Cuba?
(b) Analyze Cause and Effect By the end of the war, how had the United States replaced Spain as a colonial power?

2. (a) Recall Why did the United States enter World War I?
(b) Draw Conclusions Do you think the United States should have stayed out of World War I?

3. (a) List Name three ways American society changed during the 1920s.

(b) Detect Points of View In 1925, President Calvin Coolidge commented, "The business of America is business." What did Coolidge mean by this? How did his words reflect the confidence of Americans in the strength of their economy?

Reading Skill
4. Ask Analytical Questions Reread the text following the subheading "The United States and Latin America." What were the reasons why Theodore Roosevelt wanted a canal built across the Isthmus of Panama? Suggest a possible research question on this topic.

Key Terms
Read each sentence below. If the sentence is true, write YES. If the sentence is not true, write NO and explain why.

5. Isolationism was based on the desire of Americans to take a leading role in world affairs.

6. Investors who bought on margin always paid in full for the stocks they were purchasing.

Writing
7. What evidence in this section suggests the reasons why poor Americans were so drawn to the wealthy FDR? Write a paragraph explaining your opinion.

Answer

☑Checkpoint The three goals of the New Deal were relief for the unemployed, plans for recovery, and reforms to prevent another severe depression.

Section 2 Check Your Progress

1. (a) The press published articles that encouraged Americans to sympathize with the rebels and implicated Spain in the Havana harbor bombing.
(b) The United States took over territories in Latin America and in the Pacific.

2. (a) German submarines were sinking American ships.
(b) Possible answers: Yes, because the lives and resources lost were not worth it. No, because without help from the United States, the Allies probably would have lost the war.

3. (a) Unemployment rose, factories and stores closed, and banks closed.
(b) Possible answer: Coolidge meant that business was essential to America and its economy. His words reflected the confidence of Americans in their economy by suggesting that if the economy was strong, then America was strong.

4. Roosevelt wanted a canal to allow ships to sail from the Atlantic to the Pacific without having to go around South America. Possible questions: How would a canal benefit Americans?

5. No. Isolationism was based on the American desire to remove itself from foreign affairs.

6. No. They only paid a fraction of the cost.

7. Students' paragraphs should explain their opinions and give supporting evidence based on information from the text. Possible supporting evidence: Roosevelt's relief programs were aimed at helping the poor.

Review and Preview

Students have read about the expanded role of the United States in the world during the early 1900s. Now they will learn how that role evolved during the middle of the twentieth century.

How has the United States tried to increase democracy at home and abroad?

Before you begin the lesson for the day, write the Section Focus Question on the board. (*Lesson focus: through diplomacy, economic aid, and military intervention*)

Prepare to Read

Build Background Knowledge   **L2**

Have students suppose that they live in a country that was once a world power. Now its government is weak and its economy is in crisis. Ask: **How might you respond to a politician who promises to restore your nation to its former glory?** (*Possible answer: I would support him or her because I want my nation to return to its former glory.*) Explain to students that nations such as Italy and Germany struggled economically after World War I, and that their people put their faith in dictators.

Teach

World War II
p. 590

Instruction   **L2**

- **Vocabulary Builder** Before teaching this section, preteach the High-Use Words **convert** and **satellite** using the strategy on TE p. T21.

  Key Terms Have students continue filling in the See It–Remember It chart for the Key Terms in this chapter.

- Read World War II with students using the ReQuest strategy on TE p. T23.

SECTION 3

Our National Policy

❝Our national policy in foreign affairs has been based on a decent respect for the rights and dignity of all nations, large and small. And the justice of morality must and will win in the end. . . . In fulfillment of this purpose we will not be intimidated by the threats of dictators.❞

—President Franklin D. Roosevelt,
Four Freedoms Speech, 1941

◀ A soldier returns home after
World War II.

Toward the Modern Age

Objectives
- Describe the causes and results of World War II.
- Explain the major events of the Cold War.
- Tell how the civil rights movement changed American society.
- Examine U.S. involvement in the Vietnam War.

🔄 Reading Skill

Focus Research Topics Research topics must be specific. Formulate questions for which information to answer them is likely to be available. Frame questions to a particular time and place. Avoid questions that would require *yes* or *no* answers. Connect questions to the context of your history reading. Work toward asking questions that can be answered with evidence from available and reliable research sources.

Key Terms and People

totalitarian state	Cold War
appeasement	Martin Luther
Harry S Truman	King, Jr.

Why It Matters After World War I, Americans were threatened by yet another war as dictators in Europe and Asia threatened democracy. The United States would defeat this threat by winning World War II. After defending democracy abroad, Americans looked inward to expand civil liberties and freedoms at home.

? Section Focus Question: How has the United States tried to increase democracy at home and abroad?

World War II

World War I was supposed to make the world "safe for democracy." In the 1930s, however, democracy disappeared in many places. Fascist dictators took power in Germany, Italy, and Spain. In the Soviet Union, Joseph Stalin established a totalitarian Communist state. In a totalitarian state, a single party controls the government and every aspect of people's lives. In East Asia, Japan built an empire.

Fascism was fostered by the troubles many countries had with their economies. In Italy, Benito Mussolini and the Fascist Party played on extreme nationalist feelings. In Germany, there was much resentment of the harsh peace treaties that ended World War I. Adolf Hitler blamed Germany's losses in the war on Jews and others. His National Socialist—or Nazi—Party was brutal and militaristic. During the war years, Hitler and his officers carried out his systematic plan to destroy European Jews. In what is now called the Holocaust, Nazi troops rounded up Jews in every occupied country. More than 6 million died or were killed in concentration camps. Millions of other "enemies" of the Nazis were also brutally murdered.

590 Epilogue

Differentiated Instruction

L1 English Language Learners   **L1** Less Proficient Readers   **L1** Special Needs

Make a Chart To help students build a solid idea of World War II alliances, use this activity to help students understand the Axis leaders. Create a chart on the board as you reread World War II with students. Call on volunteers to fill in the table with each leader's name, country, and the type of government that he formed. Have students make a copy of the completed table to use as a study aid for the section and chapter assessments.

Hitler secretly began to rebuild the German army and break peace treaty terms. Then, his armies invaded neighboring countries. At first, Britain and France followed a policy of appeasement, a policy of giving in to aggression in order to avoid war. However, when Hitler invaded Poland in 1939, they declared war. Soon, Italy, Japan, and other nations joined Germany to form the Axis powers. The Allies included Britain, France, China, the Soviet Union, and many others.

At first, the United States tried to remain neutral, though it sent aid to the Allies. On December 7, 1941, Japan launched a surprise attack on American military bases in Hawaii. The United States went to war alongside the Allies.

The Home Front America mobilized for war quickly. Factories converted to war production. To conserve supplies for the military, the government rationed the amounts of meat, gasoline, sugar, clothing, and other goods that civilians could buy. Millions of women went to work in defense jobs.

During the war, prejudice against Americans of Japanese ancestry caused a great injustice. Fearing that they might be disloyal, the U.S. government moved about 110,000 Japanese Americans into "relocation camps." They lost homes and businesses.

The Allied Victory In 1942, the Allies faced losses on most fronts. Then, several Allied victories marked turning points in the war: The U.S. Navy defeated the Japanese at Midway Island. Russians held back the German siege of Stalingrad, and the British drove back the Germans in North Africa. In 1943, the Allies invaded Italy. The major invasion of western Europe came on D-Day, June 6, 1944. Allied troops landed on the coast of Normandy, France, and pressed eastward toward Germany.

Vocabulary Builder
convert (kuhn VERT) *v.* to change from one purpose or function to another; to change from one political party or religion to another

Fighting Front and Home Front
Winning World War II depended on the bravery of soldiers and the strength of the economy. At left, GIs storm onto the Normandy beachhead. At right, women respond to the urgent need to produce the goods of war.
Critical Thinking: *Make Inferences How did the growth of the American economy make the United States a more formidable fighting force?*

- Ask: **In which countries did Fascist dictators take power?** (*Germany, Italy, and Spain*)

- Ask: **What was the connection between Italian and German aggression and the Versailles Treaty?** (*As a result of the Versailles Treaty, both Germany and Italy felt powerless and overburdened by debt. This led to the rise of nationalism and dictatorships.*)

- Have students identify the sequence of events leading to World War II. (*Hitler broke the Treaty of Versailles by secretly building up an army. Then he invaded nearby countries, and broke an appeasement agreement by invading Poland. That was when the Allies declared war.*)

- Ask: **Why do you think the United States fought as part of the Allies?** (*Possible answers: The Allies were the countries that the United States had helped in World War I. They shared common beliefs and values with the United States. The United States could not support the dictatorial leadership of the Axis Powers.*)

- Have students consider the role of civilians during World War II. Ask: **Was home front support important to the war effort?** (*Yes, people on the home front provided needed supplies by working in factories and by making sacrifices for the soldiers.*) Ask: **What happened on the home front that caused great injustice to Americans of Japanese ancestry?** (*The U.S. government showed prejudice by forcing Americans of Japanese ancestry into "relocation camps" on the grounds that they might be disloyal.*)

Monitor Progress

Circulate to make sure students understand the causes and effects of World War II. Provide assistance as needed.

Vocabulary Builder

Use the information below to teach students this section's high-use words.

High-Use Word	Definition and Sample Sentence
convert, p. 591	*v.* to change from one purpose or function to another During World War I, flower gardens were **converted** into vegetable gardens.
satellite, p. 592	*n.* a small state that is economically or politically dependent on a larger, more powerful state Poland became a **satellite** state of the Soviet Union after World War II.

Answer
Make Inferences Possible answer: With a growing economy, the United States was able to produce more tools and weapons for the war effort.

The Cold War Begins

p. 592

Instruction

L2

- Have students read The Cold War Begins. Remind students to look for causes and effects.

- Ask: **What effect might the U.S. bombings in Japan have had on Cold War tensions?** (*Possible answer: After seeing the destructive force of America's nuclear weapons, the Soviet Union wanted nuclear weapons. This caused tension between the United States and the Soviet Union.*) Ask students to consider why Cold War tensions resulted in an arms race between superpowers. (*Each nation feared that the other nation would build more or better weapons, so each nation raced to keep up with the other.*)

- Ask: **How did the two sides "fight" each other in the Cold War?** (*While there was no direct armed conflict between the superpowers, they engaged in conflicts with each other by assisting allies with weapons and troops in places such as Berlin and Korea.*)

- Ask: **How did the goal of containing Communism abroad impact American society?** (*Attempts were made to contain, or stop, any Communist efforts within the United States, such as loyalty checks on government workers and the rise of McCarthyism.*)

Monitor Progress

Circulate to make sure students understand the significance of the Cold War. If students do not seem to have a good understanding, have them reread the section. Provide assistance as needed.

Answers

MAP MASTER Skills Activity **(a)** Norway, West Germany, Greece, and Turkey bordered Warsaw Pact nations. **(b)** Possible answer: Yes, because it is so close geographically to both NATO nations and to Warsaw Pact nations.

✓Checkpoint Midway Island, Stalingrad, North Africa, the invasion of Italy, and the invasion of western Europe on D-Day

---

The Cold War in Europe

MAP MASTER®
Skills Activity

By 1955, the Cold War divided Europe into two camps: those nations belonging to NATO and those nations belonging to the Warsaw Pact.

(a) Read a Map Which NATO nations bordered Warsaw Pact nations?

(b) Apply Information Do you think it would be difficult for Yugoslavia to remain neutral? Explain.

MapMaster Online
For: Interactive map
Visit: PHSchool.com
Web Code: mvp-8251

0 km 400
0 miles 400
Albers Conic Equal-Area Projection

NORWAY, SWEDEN, FINLAND, IRELAND, DENMARK, GREAT BRITAIN, NETH., BELG., EAST GERMANY, POLAND, SOVIET UNION, LUX., WEST GERMANY, CZECHOSLOVAKIA, FRANCE, SWITZ., AUSTRIA, HUNGARY, ROMANIA, PORTUGAL, SPAIN, ITALY, YUGOSLAVIA, BULGARIA, ALBANIA, GREECE, TURKEY

North Sea, Baltic Sea, ATLANTIC OCEAN, Black Sea, Mediterranean Sea

KEY
- NATO nations, 1955
- Warsaw Pact, 1955
- Neutral nations
- Areas added to the Soviet Union after World War II

President Roosevelt died in April 1945 and was succeeded by Harry S Truman. However, the Allies' march to victory continued. In May, Germany surrendered. Use of a new weapon—the atomic bomb—brought Japan's surrender. People everywhere hoped that a new world body, the United Nations (UN), would prevent future wars.

✓Checkpoint What victories for the Allies marked turning points in World War II?

The Cold War Begins

At the end of the war, the Allies divided Germany into occupation zones. Although the other Allies objected, Soviet troops set up Communist <u>satellites</u> in Eastern Europe.

President Truman resolved to contain Soviet expansion. Hostility developed into a Cold War, a state of tension. An arms race began, and both superpowers spent billions on defense and weapons.

Postwar Crises The war had left Europe in ruins. Secretary of State George C. Marshall proposed to rebuild the continent. With $12 billion of Marshall Plan help, Western Europe began to recover.

The East-West split led to serious clashes. In 1948, the Soviets blockaded supplies coming into West Berlin. Truman's answer was the Berlin Airlift. For nearly a year, American planes dropped tons of food and supplies to West Berliners. In May 1949, Stalin lifted the blockade. Berlin remained a trouble spot. In 1961, the East German government built a wall dividing East and West Berlin.

Vocabulary Builder
satellite (SAT uh lyt) **n.** a small state that is economically or politically dependent on a larger, more powerful state

---

Differentiated Instruction

L3 Advanced Readers

Write a Descriptive Paragraph Using the text and map on pp. 592–593, have students write a paragraph describing the causes and effects of significant events during the Cold War era. Students may organize their paragraphs chronologically or categorically by country or event.

L3 Gifted and Talented

Encourage students to add a paragraph that relates Cold War tensions and competition between superpowers in the 1950s and 1960s with the contemporary nuclear arms situation between nations such as India and Pakistan.

The Korean War After World War II, communism gained a foothold in Asia. On the Korean Peninsula, a Communist government ruled the north and a non-Communist government ruled the south.

In June 1950, North Korean troops invaded the South. UN troops organized to stop them. As the UN troops fought their way northward, Chinese soldiers joined the North Koreans. Douglas MacArthur, the American commander, wanted to invade China. Truman, however, wanted to limit the war. He fired MacArthur. In 1953, a truce was negotiated, but Korea remained divided.

Cold War Fears Communist advances in Asia and Europe frightened many Americans. They worried that Communists were working inside the United States. In 1950, Wisconsin Senator Joseph McCarthy made dramatic charges about Communists in government, in schools, and even in the army. McCarthy attracted attention but had little real evidence.

Global Conflicts In 1959, communism came closer to home. Fidel Castro led a Communist revolution in Cuba. Thousands of Cubans fled to the United States.

In October 1962, the Soviets attempted to ship weapons to Castro. President John F. Kennedy then announced that American ships would stop any Soviet ships taking missiles to Cuba. After a few tense days, the Soviet ships turned back.

☑**Checkpoint** How did the Korean War end?

The Civil Rights Movement

All Americans had worked together to win the war. Many people, though, still faced discrimination in jobs, education, and housing.

The Movement Begins In many southern states, laws supported "separate but equal" facilities in schools and other public places. In *Brown* v. *Board of Education of Topeka* (1954), the Supreme Court ruled that segregated schools could not provide children with an equal education. It ordered schools everywhere to integrate black students and white students.

In 1955, African Americans in Montgomery, Alabama, organized a boycott of the city's segregated bus system. It followed the arrest of Rosa Parks, who had refused to give up her seat to a white man, as the law required.

There were many black activists, but Dr. Martin Luther King, Jr., soon emerged as a fearless and compelling national leader. King urged the use of nonviolent protests against unjust laws.

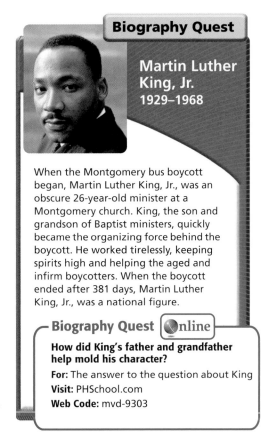

Biography Quest

Martin Luther King, Jr.
1929–1968

When the Montgomery bus boycott began, Martin Luther King, Jr., was an obscure 26-year-old minister at a Montgomery church. King, the son and grandson of Baptist ministers, quickly became the organizing force behind the boycott. He worked tirelessly, keeping spirits high and helping the aged and infirm boycotters. When the boycott ended after 381 days, Martin Luther King, Jr., was a national figure.

Biography Quest 🌐**nline**

How did King's father and grandfather help mold his character?

For: The answer to the question about King
Visit: PHSchool.com
Web Code: mvd-9303

Instruction   L2

- Have students read The Civil Rights Movement. Remind students to look for answers to the Section Focus Question.

- Ask: **What was decided in the case of Brown v. Board of Education?** (*The court decided that segregated schools were unconstitutional.*)

- Discuss the early activities of the civil rights movement with students. Ask: **Why do you think many civil rights protests took place in the South?** (*Possible answers: Civil rights workers may have thought that change was needed more in the South, or because racial discrimination and segregation were more prevalent there than in the North.*)

- Use the transparencies *Sonny's Quilt* and A Civil Rights Sit-In to extend understanding of the civil rights movement.

Color Transparencies, A Civil Rights Sit-In; *Sonny's Quilt*

- Use the transparencies Suburban Life and Cities and Suburbs in Contrast to explore the changes in American social and economic life after World War II.

Color Transparencies, Suburban Life; Cities and Suburbs in Contrast

---

History Background

Blacklisting The House Un-American Activities Committee (HUAC) was dedicated, in theory, to finding American Communists in government, show business, and other occupations. The committee hearings in 1947 resulted in many people being blacklisted, or denied work, based solely on suspicions. One group of producers, directors, screenwriters, and actors—known as the Hollywood Ten—refused to testify before the committee. First they were sentenced to jail for their silence. Once released, they found themselves blacklisted. As a result, many of them never worked in Hollywood again.

Answers

☑**Checkpoint** Korea remained divided after a truce in 1953 that ended the war.

Biography Quest Possible answer: His father and grandfather, both ministers, might have influenced King's feelings toward nonviolence and equality.

Instruction (continued)

- Have students consider how it was possible to make such changes by using simple protest techniques. Use the Idea Wave strategy (TE, p. T24) to elicit responses. Ask: **Why do you think Lyndon Johnson carried on Kennedy's civil rights policies?** (*Possible answer: Johnson also believed in civil rights.*)

- Ask: **Why do you think groups other than African Americans also fought for their civil rights?** (*Possible answers: Other groups wanted fair treatment as well. They were inspired by the successes of African Americans to take on their own struggles. They wanted to show that everyone in America deserves equal treatment.*)

- Use the transparencies *Working Woman* and *Ghosts of the Barrio* to extend understanding of the civil rights struggles of groups other than African Americans.

Color Transparencies, *Working Woman*; *Ghosts of the Barrio*

🔘 **Exploring Primary Sources in History CD-ROM,** A Nurse Reflects

Monitor Progress

Circulate to make sure students understand why and how African Americans fought for civil rights and how groups also struggled for equal rights. If students do not seem to have a good understanding, have them reread the section. Provide assistance as needed.

A Nurse Reflects

"Those of us who went to Vietnam practiced a lifetime of nursing in one year—our tour of duty there. We were the young, caring for the young. The average age of the wounded soldier in Vietnam was 19.4 years. The average age of the nurse was 23. We quickly learned that the primary reason we were in Vietnam was to get each other home."

—Diane Carlson Evans, speech in Washington, D.C., 1998

Nurses care for wounded soldiers about to be shipped home.

Reading Primary Sources
Skills Activity

As many as 10,000 women served in uniform with U.S. military forces in the Vietnam War, most as nurses.

(a) Rank What three characteristics do you think were most important for a nurse serving in Vietnam?

(b) Draw Conclusions What does the speaker mean when she says the main goal was "to get each other home"?

The 1960s The 1960s brought great social change. Civil rights became a national issue. In August 1963, more than 200,000 people gathered on the Mall in Washington, D.C., where King made his famous "I have a dream" speech.

In 1963, John F. Kennedy was assassinated. His successor, Lyndon Johnson, was skilled in getting laws passed. Under his leadership, Congress passed strong Civil Rights and Voting Rights acts.

The 1960s brought other protests. Despite new civil rights laws, many thought that change was coming too slowly. In the hot summers, riots broke out in several cities.

The Movement Widens The struggle for civil rights inspired other groups to demand greater equality. Latinos had several goals. For example, many Mexican Americans were migrant farm workers, working for low pay in dangerous conditions. In the 1960s, César Chávez organized the United Farm Workers. With a national boycott of grapes, the union won better working conditions. Native American and Asian American groups also gained political influence.

Women were not a minority, but they faced many barriers. Working women earned less than men—about 63 cents for every dollar—for doing the same kind of work. It was hard for women to enter professions. The National Organization for Women (NOW) worked for equality in those areas.

✔**Checkpoint** What did the Supreme Court rule in *Brown* v. *Board of Education of Topeka*?

HISTORIAN'S APPRENTICE ACTIVITY PACK

To further explore the topics in this chapter, complete the activity in the Historian's Apprentice Activity Pack to answer this essential question:

What major influences have helped shape American society and culture?

Differentiated Instruction

L1 English Language Learners

Summarize Events Pair students who are learning English with students who are fluent in English. Ask students to work together to prepare a summary of The Vietnam War. Then, match pairs and have them share summaries with each other. Students may use their summaries as a study aid for the section and chapter assessments.

Answers

Reading Primary Sources (a) Possible answers: good nursing skills, good health, an understanding and caring demeanor; **(b)** to do what had to be done in order to end the war as soon as possible

✔**Checkpoint** The court ruled that segregation in public schools is unconstitutional.

The Vietnam War

After World War II, a civil war broke out in Vietnam. That war divided Vietnam into a Communist North and a non-Communist South. Over several years, the United States built up its forces in Vietnam. Fighting in Vietnam was jungle warfare against guerrilla fighters. There were few clear-cut victories.

Americans were bitterly divided over the war. Some, often referred to as "hawks," wanted to escalate the war for a victory over the Communist North. Others, referred to as "doves," however, believed that the United States should not be in Vietnam at all. Antiwar protests were widespread.

President Johnson did not run again in 1968. The new President, Richard Nixon, promised to end the war. Peace talks led to a cease-fire agreement in 1973. In 1975, the last American soldiers left, and all of Vietnam fell under Communist rule.

 Checkpoint What was the outcome of the Vietnam War?

⭐ **Looking Back and Ahead** The Vietnam War was a painful episode in American history. Besides its huge cost, the war deeply divided the nation. But, as the war wound down, the Cold War showed signs of a thaw. In the next section, you will see how the nation turned its attention to new issues in the 1980s.

Focus Research Topics
Reread the text under the heading "The Vietnam War." Suggest a more focused research topic that is based on the divisions between "hawks" and "doves" during the Vietnam era.

Section 3 | Check Your Progress

Comprehension and Critical Thinking

1. **(a) Recall** How did Americans feel about world involvement during the 1930s?
   (b) Link Past and Present Do you think it is possible for the United States to be isolationist today? Explain your answer.

2. **(a) Recall** Describe two results of the Vietnam War.
   (b) Contrast Contrast the Korean War and the Vietnam War in terms of causes and results.

3. **(a) Recall** Who was Senator Joseph McCarthy?
   (b) Link Past and Present Television played a key role in the downfall of Senator McCarthy.

Give at least three examples of how television influences public opinion today.

Reading Skill

4. **Focus Research Topics** Reread the text under the heading "World War II." Suggest a more-focused research question that is based on the following: Why do democracies sometimes try to appease dictators?

Key Terms

5. Write two definitions for the following key terms: totalitarian state, appeasement, Cold War. First, write a formal definition for your teacher. Second, write a definition in everyday English for a classmate.

Writing

6. Choose two details from within this section that support the topic sentence that follows. Then, write a paragraph developing the topic based on these details. **Topic sentence:** The 1960s were a time of conflict for Americans both home and abroad.

Section 3 Check Your Progress

1. **(a)** Americans favored isolationism.
   (b) Possible answers: Yes, the United States is powerful enough to do anything it wants to do. No, the United States is intricately linked to the economies and politics of nations worldwide.

2. **(a)** Possible answer: President Johnson did not seek re-election and Vietnam fell under Communist rule.
   (b) Both wars resulted from a struggle between Communist and non-Commu-

nist interests. People in the United States supported the Korean War. They were divided over the Vietnam War. Korea remained divided into two countries: one Communist and one non-Communist. Vietnam became entirely Communist.

3. **(a)** Joseph McCarthy was a senator from Wisconsin who accused people in the government, in schools, and in the army of being Communists.
   (b) Answers may vary, but students' responses should explain how television influenced public opinion.

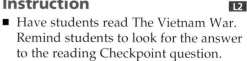

The Vietnam War
p. 595

Instruction L2

- Have students read The Vietnam War. Remind students to look for the answer to the reading Checkpoint question.

- Discuss the Vietnam War with students. Have them compare and contrast the Korean War and the Vietnam War. (*Both nations were split into Communist and non-Communist nations. Superpowers gave supplies and troops to help their side win in both wars. Fighting in Korea was the conventional battle of soldiers; fighting in Vietnam was jungle warfare against guerrilla fighters. The Vietnam War severely divided the American public. The Korean War did not.*)

- Ask: **How did Americans become divided over the Vietnam War?** (*Possible answer: "Hawks" wanted to keep fighting to defeat the Communists. "Doves" wanted the United States to pull out of the war.*)

- Discuss the results of the Vietnam War. (*President Johnson did not run for re-election; Vietnam reunited under Communist rule.*)

Monitor Progress

Circulate to make sure students understand the divisiveness of the Vietnam War. Provide assistance as needed.

Answers

Reading Skill Possible research topic: American opinions about Communism during the Vietnam War

 Checkpoint Peace talks led to a cease-fire in 1973. In 1975, the last American troops left and the entire nation fell under Communist rule.

4. Possible research question: What can happen if dictators begin to gain too much influence globally?

5. totalitarian state: a nation in which one party controls everything; appeasement: a policy of giving in to aggression to avoid war; cold war: a tense and unfriendly relationship between two nations

6. Paragraphs should contain the chosen topic sentence and two supporting details from the section, such as the civil rights movement, boycotts, and the Vietnam War.

Review and Preview

Students have read about changes in the United States during the twentieth century. Now they will learn about challenges facing the United States during the twenty-first century.

Section Focus Question

What changes and challenges are shaping the United States today?

Before you begin the lesson for the day, write the Section Focus Question on the board. (*Lesson focus: Challenges and changes include conflicts in the Middle East, terrorism, and environmental issues.*)

Prepare to Read

Build Background Knowledge   **L2**

Ask students to consider the role that the federal government plays in the lives of ordinary citizens. Tell students that some people believe that the government has too large a role, while others believe that it doesn't go far enough to help its citizens.

Teach

Rise of the Conservative Movement

p. 596

Instruction   **L2**

■ **Vocabulary Builder** Before teaching this section, preteach the High-Use Words **radical** and **consume**, using the strategy on TE p. T21.

Key Terms Have students complete the See It–Remember It chart for the Key Terms in this chapter.

■ Read Rise of the Conservative Movement with students using the Structured Silent Reading strategy on TE p. T22.

SECTION 4

A Renewal of Spirit

❝ I want my candidacy to unify our country, to renew the American spirit and sense of purpose. I want to carry our message to every American, regardless of party affiliation. ❞

—Ronald Reagan, addressing the Republican National Convention, 1980

◀ Ronald Reagan ushered in a new conservative era in 1980.

Into the Future

Objectives

- List the goals of the conservative Presidents such as Ronald Reagan and George H.W. Bush.
- Tell how different foreign policy challenges arose after the end of the Cold War.
- Examine U.S. foreign policy in the Middle East after the September 11 attacks.
- Discuss environmental and technological challenges that face Americans today.

🎯 Reading Skill

Ask Questions That Connect to the Present Does history repeat itself? Investigate by asking questions that connect history to the present. Compare or contrast a historical situation with a current situation. Or look at ways that historical situations have led to current situations. Ask questions that require research to answer.

Key Terms and People

Ronald Reagan	détente
deregulation	terrorism
George H.W. Bush	al Qaeda
George W. Bush	

Why It Matters Just like generations before them, Americans of today face challenges at home and abroad. American leaders continue to search for the best way to secure democracy and prosperity at home. At the same time, they must confront how best to deal with foreign threats.

❓ Section Focus Question: What changes and challenges are shaping the United States today?

Rise of the Conservative Movement

The unpopular Vietnam War helped bring Richard Nixon, a Republican, to office. In response to an economic crisis—rising prices, slow growth, and high unemployment—Nixon cut back spending. Then, political scandal rocked his administration.

The Watergate affair began during Nixon's 1972 reelection campaign, with a break-in at the Democratic headquarters. A Senate investigation showed that Nixon and his advisers had lied in trying to cover up the incident. By midsummer 1974, the House of Representatives seemed ready to impeach Nixon and the Senate ready to convict him. Instead, he resigned—the first President to do so.

Vice President Gerald Ford succeeded Nixon. Wanting to end the scandal, he pardoned the former President, though many people objected. Ford was also beset by economic problems, and in 1976, he lost the election to Jimmy Carter, a Democrat. Carter had trouble working with Congress. Inflation remained a problem, made worse by an energy crisis. In 1980, voters preferred the upbeat message of the Republican candidate, Ronald Reagan.

596 Epilogue

Differentiated Instruction

L1 English Language Learners   **L1** Less Proficient Readers   **L1** Special Needs

Write a Fact Sheet Students will learn about several presidents in this section. Help students keep track of the information by having them compile a brief fact sheet about each president. Fact sheets can contain several important pieces of information for each president. You can assist students as you read the first part of the section together by using verbal cues, such as "This is an important fact," and repeating the fact. When students have completed their fact sheets, pair them to compare notes and to check for accuracy.

The New Conservative Movement Conservative voters backed Reagan for different reasons. Some wanted a smaller federal government and deregulation, or reduction of restrictions on business. Others focused on morality and a return to traditional family values. Many belonged to evangelical Christian churches, which emphasized a personal experience with God.

As President, Reagan put conservative ideas into action. His economic plan cut taxes and dropped many regulations. Spending for social programs fell, and military spending soared. After Reagan's two terms, his Vice President, George H.W. Bush, was elected in 1988. He continued many of Reagan's policies.

Presidents Clinton and Bush Conservatives remained strong in Congress in the 1990s. Now, however, there was a Democrat in the White House—Bill Clinton, a former Arkansas governor. President Clinton was often at odds with Congress. However, Congress and the President managed to agree on major changes in the welfare system and on balancing the federal budget.

Clinton's personal popularity was high. The economy was growing so fast that there was a budget surplus. However, an investigation turned up evidence of his improper relationship with a White House intern, which he at first denied under oath. In late 1998, the House of Representatives voted to impeach Clinton. In a historic trial in February 1999, the Senate acquitted him.

The impeachment trial was only the second in history, but the 2000 election was unique. Clinton's Vice President, Al Gore, ran against Texas Governor George W. Bush, a son of the former President. Gore won the popular vote by a narrow margin. The electoral college tally, however, was in doubt while votes were recounted in Florida. In December 2000, the Supreme Court ruled the Florida recount illegal, making Bush the President. In his first term, Bush won major victories by fulfilling campaign pledges to lower taxes and to raise standards for public schools. Reelected by a comfortable margin in 2004, Bush pledged to make reform of the nation's social security system the centerpiece of his second term. However, controversy over American policy in the Middle East overshadowed Bush's second term.

✓**Checkpoint** List two main goals of Presidents Reagan and George W. Bush.

Clinton Signs a Bill
Children of minimum-wage earners cluster around President Clinton as he signs a bill to raise the minimum wage. **Critical Thinking: Contrast** *Contrast the records of Ronald Reagan and Bill Clinton.*

Instruction (continued)

- Discuss with students the events that occurred during President Nixon's 1972 re-election campaign that came to be known as the Watergate affair. Ask students whether they believe that Nixon would have been impeached had he not resigned. (*Students should base their answers on the facts of the case.*)

- Discuss Reagan's presidency with the class. Ask: **What conservative ideas did Reagan put into action?** (*Reagan cut taxes, reduced spending for social programs, increased military spending, and reduced business regulation.*) Ask students why they think George H.W. Bush continued Reagan's policies. (*Possible answer: Bush was also a conservative.*)

- Have students summarize the 2000 election. (*Gore won the popular vote, but there was doubt over the electoral college tally in Florida. The Florida recount was deemed illegal by the Supreme Court, and George W. Bush became president.*)

- Use the transparency Selected Results: California Recall Election, 2003 to extend knowledge of the rise of the conservative movement.

Color Transparencies, Selected Results: California Recall Election, 2003

Monitor Progress

Circulate to make sure students understand the goals and values of conservative leaders during the past 20 years. If students do not seem to have a good understanding, have them reread the section. Provide assistance as needed.

Answers

✓**Checkpoint** Their goals included cutting taxes and reducing business regulations.

Contrast Possible answers: President Clinton was often at odds with Congress, but President Reagan was not. During the Clinton administration, the economy grew and there was a budget surplus. President Reagan's economic plan cut taxes and dropped many regulations; spending for social programs fell, and military spending soared.

Vocabulary Builder

Use the information below to teach students this section's high-use words.

High-Use Word	Definition and Sample Sentence
radical, p. 599	*adj.* favoring fundamental or extreme change John Brown was tried and convicted for his **radical** actions in Virginia.
consume, p. 600	*v.* to use up; to eat or drink The French and Indian War **consumed** vast amounts of British resources.

New Conflicts in the World

p. 598

Instruction [L2]

- Have students read New Conflicts in the World. Remind students to look for details to answer the Section Focus Question.

- Review with students how Nixon dealt with Communist nations. (*Nixon's policy of détente improved relations with Communist nations.*) Have students suggest reasons why Ford and Carter continued this policy. (*Possible answer: Both Ford and Carter wanted less tension between the United States and Communist nations.*)

- Ask: **What effect did the arms race ultimately have on the Soviet Union?** (*The arms race put great pressure on the Soviet economy. When the Soviet government tried to save communism by relaxing control, Communist governments in Eastern Europe collapsed.*)

- Ask: **Did the Cold War's end result in world peace?** (*No. Conflicts continued worldwide. Civil wars broke out in nations in Africa and Central America. War erupted in the Balkans. Hostility and conflict also continued in the Middle East.*)

- Ask: **Why is foreign oil important in U.S. international affairs?** (*Possible answers: Arab countries cut off oil shipments to the United States in 1973, causing high prices and shortages. Oil was one of the causes of the brief Persian Gulf War in 1991.*)

Monitor Progress

Circulate to make sure students understand what conflicts arose after the Cold War ended. If students do not seem to have a good understanding, have them reread the section. Provide assistance as needed.

Answers

Reading Skill Possible question: What social or economic problems do Russia and the other former Soviet republics face today that they would not have had to face under communism?

Checkpoint Soviet republics began to declare their independence.

New Conflicts in the World

From the late 1940s on, the Cold War dominated foreign policy. Then, Communist rule began to crumble all over Europe. By the mid-1990s, communism was no longer a major threat. New kinds of conflicts erupted in trouble spots all over the world.

The Cold War Ends The Cold War began to thaw during the Nixon administration. Although a strong anti-Communist, Nixon established ties with Communist China. He visited China and the Soviet Union in 1972. The policy of détente—a relaxing of tensions—continued during the Ford and Carter administrations.

All this time, however, the arms race was putting great pressure on the failing Soviet economy. A new Soviet leader, Mikhail Gorbachev, attempted to save communism by relaxing controls on speech and political opposition. However, the Soviet system was too corrupt to survive. Beginning in 1989, every Communist government in Eastern Europe eventually collapsed. The Berlin Wall was torn down. East and West Germany were soon reunited under a democratic government.

Change overtook the Soviet Union itself. In August 1991, hardline Communists tried to reverse the reforms, but thousands of Russian people opposed them. One by one, the Soviet republics declared their independence. By the end of 1991, the Soviet Union was gone. The United States began to help Russia and the other republics build democracy and a free-market economy.

An Age of Regional Conflicts The end of the Cold War did not mean world peace. Civil wars tore apart countries in Africa and Central America. When the Communist government of Yugoslavia fell, old ethnic and religious hatreds flared up in the Balkans. In 1991, the republics of Croatia and Bosnia split off from Yugoslavia. Millions of people were displaced as Serbs, Croats, and Bosnians fought one another. A second Balkan war erupted in 1998 between Serbs and Albanians in Kosovo. NATO forces intervened, and American soldiers joined European troops as peacekeepers.

The Middle East was another hot spot. A major source of trouble was hostility between the Jewish state of Israel and its Arab neighbors. Another was ongoing violence between Palestinians and Israelis. Ever since the founding of Israel in 1948, each U.S. President tried to bring peace, but terrorism and reprisals continued.

American support for Israel angered some Arab countries. In 1973, oil-producing Arab countries cut off oil shipments, causing shortages and high prices. The supply of Mideastern oil also caused the brief Persian Gulf War in 1991. Saddam Hussein, the dictator of Iraq, invaded neighboring oil-rich Kuwait. A UN coalition of the United States and its allies launched an air attack. After six weeks, Iraq left Kuwait, although Hussein remained in power.

Ask Questions That Connect to the Present The end of the Cold War changed the relationship of the United States with Russia and the former Soviet republics. Ask a question that connects the collapse of communism in the Soviet Union with events in the region today. Your question should require research to answer.

Breaking down the Berlin Wall

Checkpoint What was the immediate result of the collapse of the Soviet Union?

Differentiated Instruction

[L3] Advanced Readers

Make an Illustrated Timeline Have students make a timeline that tracks the sequence of global events before, during, and after the end of the Cold War. Students should annotate their entries with a few

[L3] Gifted and Talented

sentences about the causes and effects of each event. They should also illustrate key events. Provide students with space on the bulletin board to display their timelines.

New Directions in Foreign Policy

After the 1960s, terrorist bombings, kidnappings, and hijackings became more common in Europe, the Middle East, and elsewhere. Terrorism is the deliberate use of random acts of violence, often against civilians, in order to achieve a political goal.

The Challenge of Terrorism In the Middle East, a number of radical Muslim groups sponsored terrorism. These extremists were outraged by U.S. support for Israel, as well as by the Persian Gulf War. As a result, Americans overseas sometimes became targets of terrorism.

Terrorism also became a threat within the United States itself. In 1993, a bomb rocked the World Trade Center in New York City. Six Arab men were later convicted of the crime. In 1995, two Americans who resented the government exploded a bomb that destroyed a federal office building in Oklahoma City, killing 168 people.

The United States Is Attacked On September 11, 2001, terrorists seized control of four American passenger airplanes. The hijackers crashed two of the planes into the Twin Towers of the World Trade Center in New York City. As onlookers watched in horror, the two skyscrapers collapsed. A third hijacked airliner crashed into the Pentagon near Washington, D.C. The fourth airplane crashed in Pennsylvania after courageous passengers attacked the hijackers. More than 3,000 people were killed in the terrorist attacks of September 11.

Vocabulary Builder
radical (rad ih kul) *adj.* favoring fundamental or extreme change

HISTORIAN'S APPRENTICE ACTIVITY PACK

To further explore the topics in this chapter, complete the activity in the Historian's Apprentice Activity Pack to answer this essential question:

How has the United States tried to remain safe and to defend democracy?

Explore More Video
To learn more about the attacks of September 11, 2001, view the video.

Attack on America After the September 11 attack on the World Trade Center, President George W. Bush went to New York City to give encouragement to rescue workers. The events of September 11 produced dramatic changes in American foreign policy. *Critical Thinking: Analyze Cause and Effect* Do you think the attacks had the impact on the American people that the attackers expected?

Into the Future **599**

History Background

Responses to Disaster After the terrorist attacks of September 11, 2001, students across the nation did their part to help out. Students in Manchester Township, New Jersey, created posters, signs, and banners expressing their sorrow for the victims and support for their country. They also collected money for victims and supplies for rescuers. In Lexington, South Carolina, 1,300 students contributed to a fund for a new fire truck for the Red Hook community in Brooklyn, New York. An Internet bulletin board in South Carolina gave students in grades 8–12 a chance to correspond with students in areas affected by the attacks. And at a middle school in Attleboro, Massachusetts, students quickly collected $25,000 for the victims of terrorism.

New Directions in Foreign Policy

p. 599

Instruction [L2]

- Have students read New Directions in Foreign Policy. Remind students to look for causes and effects.

- Discuss with students the definition of terrorism. Have students suggest why terrorism is considered different than war. (*Possible answer: Terrorist acts are not waged by legitimate governments, but wars are.*)

- Ask: **Did terrorist attacks on the United States begin on September 11, 2001?** (*No. There were several attacks on the United States before September 11, 2001.*)

- Ask students to summarize the events that took place on September 11, 2001. (*On the morning of September 11, terrorists crashed two planes into the World Trade Center and one plane into the Pentagon. A fourth plane crashed in Pennsylvania when passengers attacked the terrorists.*)

- Ask: **How did Americans respond to the attacks?** (*They donated blood, money, and supplies to help the victims and their families.*)

 Explore More Video

Discovery School Video

This video discuses the attacks of September 11, 2001.

Answer

Analyze Cause and Effect Possible answers: No, because the terrorists did not think that the United States would invade Afghanistan. Yes, because the terrorists wanted to start a war.

Instruction (continued)

- Ask: **Why did the United States invade Afghanistan?** (*Osama bin Laden, whose group was considered responsible for the September 11 attacks, was hiding in Afghanistan under the protection of the Taliban government.*) Ask: **Were U.S. troops successful?** (*Possible answers: Yes, they toppled the Taliban. No, they did not capture Osama bin Laden.*)

- Ask: **Why did the United States invade Iraq?** (*President Bush believed that Iraqi leader Saddam Hussein had ties to Osama bin Laden, and that Hussein was developing weapons of mass destruction.*) Ask students why this war was controversial in the United States. (*Possible answers: Some Americans felt that Iraq had not been a threat. Other Americans supported the war because they believed Hussein had been a brutal dictator.*)

Monitor Progress

Circulate to make sure students understand the government's reaction to the September 11 attacks. Provide assistance as needed.

Hurricane Katrina
On August 29, 2005, Hurricane Katrina swirled out of the Gulf of Mexico and on to land. Winds of up to 175 miles per hour caused death, injury, and destruction. Here, a helicopter rescues people trapped on the roof of their house. **Critical Thinking: Analyze Effects** How does the environment affect people? How do people affect the environment?

Vocabulary Builder
consume (kahn SYOOM) *v.* to use up; to eat or drink

Americans Respond American citizens were quick to respond to the tragedy. Millions lined up to give blood, aided in rescue efforts, or donated money and supplies to help the victims and rescuers.

It soon became clear that the attack was the work of al Qaeda (ahl KY duh) (also spelled *al-Qaida*). **Al Qaeda** is a terrorist network led by a wealthy Saudi, Osama bin Laden. Bin Laden was living in Afghanistan, protected by a brutal dictatorship, the Taliban. In November 2001, an American-led force attacked military sites and terrorist training camps in Afghanistan. The Taliban were soon toppled. However, Osama bin Laden escaped, and the search for him continued.

War in Iraq President Bush next targeted Iraq as a threat. Bush accused Iraqi dictator Saddam Hussein of having ties with Bin Laden. He also claimed that Hussein was developing weapons of mass destruction (WMD), such as nuclear and chemical weapons.

In March 2003, the United States and Britain led a coalition of about 30 nations in an attack on Iraq. Using advanced weapons, coalition forces smashed Iraq's defenses in six weeks. As the fighting subsided, coalition advisers set up the Coalition Provisional Authority to supervise the establishment of a new democratic government for Iraq. In 2005, Iraqis voted in the nation's first free election in 50 years.

Despite these efforts at reconstruction, militants began a terror campaign to kill American troops and Iraqis. Attacks continued even after Hussein was brought to justice. Captured in 2003, the dictator was tried and executed in 2006. Meanwhile, Shiite and Sunni Muslims took up arms against each other across Iraq.

Americans Divided Many Americans supported the Iraq War. Bush's strong actions, they said, toppled a brutal dictator and promoted democracy. Others criticized Bush's actions. They felt Iraq had not posed an immediate threat. Other critics charged that the war consumed valuable money, supplies, and troops.

☑ Checkpoint What reasons did President Bush give for toppling the government of Saddam Hussein?

Changes and Challenges

The United States faced crucial new challenges in the twenty-first century. Trade and technology made the world smaller and more interdependent.

Answers

Analyze Effects Answers will vary, but should reflect the fact that the environment can destroy people and, conversely, that people can destroy the environment.

☑ Checkpoint Bush asserted that Hussein had ties with all Qaeda, and that he was developing weapons of mass destructions.

New Technologies The Internet and other new technologies have brought nations closer together. The possibilities of these technologies seem endless. However, our dependence on technology makes businesses and individuals more vulnerable to attack.

The Environment Natural disasters cause great destruction. In 2005, Hurricane Katrina resulted in hundreds of deaths and billions of dollars in damage. Global warming is a growing problem. Many scientists warn that the burning of fossil fuels causes global warming by emitting carbon dioxide into the atmosphere.

School Violence Too often, students bully or hurt other students. In 1999, two students at Columbine High School in Colorado killed 12 classmates and a teacher. In 2007, a Virginia Tech student murdered nearly 50 students and teachers. In response, schools have heightened security and taught students how to resolve disputes peacefully.

New Immigration Patterns America's face also has changed. After the fall of the Soviet Union, many former Soviet citizens moved to the United States. Today, most new immigrants come from Latin America, the Caribbean, and Asia. These patterns mean that Latinos are now the largest ethnic minority in the United States.

✓**Checkpoint** What are two challenges facing Americans today?

⭐ **Looking Back and Ahead** Today, the United States faces complex issues. Yet, Americans have met such challenges before. In 1776, the problems were so great that many believed the new nation would not survive. Instead, the United States grew into a superpower and a model for nations everywhere.

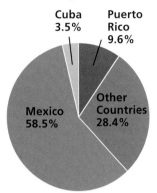

Latinos by Region of Origin, 2000

Cuba 3.5%
Puerto Rico 9.6%
Other Countries 28.4%
Mexico 58.5%

Source: *Statistical Abstract of the United States*

A Diverse Population
The pie graph above shows the varied origins of the nation's growing Latino population.

Section 4 | Check Your Progress

Comprehension and Critical Thinking

1. (a) Summarize Why did the Soviet Union collapse in the late 1980s?
(b) Explain Problems Describe two ways in which the United States could help former Communist nations make the shift to democracy.

2. (a) Recall Describe two environmental problems the United States faces.
(b) Explain Problems Why are these problems also global in impact?

Reading Skill

3. Ask Questions That Connect to the Present Ask a question that connects the Cold War to the present and requires research to answer. You might focus on the relationships of the nations of Eastern Europe to the United States.

Key Terms

4. Draw a table with three rows and two columns. In the first column, list these key terms: deregulation, détente, terrorism. In the next column, write the definition of each word.

Writing

5. Imagine that you will be writing an editorial meant to influence readers of your school newspaper about environmental issues in your community. Create an outline for the editorial that organizes your thoughts. Create two main topic headings for the editorial: I. Environmental problems in our community; II. What can be done about them.

Changes and Challenges
p. 600

Instruction
L2

- Have students read Changes and Challenges. Remind students to look for causes and effects.

- Ask: **How does the use of fossil fuels affect the environment?** (*Burning fossil fuels sends carbon dioxide into the atmosphere, which scientists believe causes global warming.*)

- Have students identify how immigration to the United States has changed. (*Many new immigrants are from the former Soviet Union, Latin America, the Caribbean, and Asia.*) Ask: **How does greater diversity improve American culture?** (*Possible answer: American culture becomes enriched with languages, religions, and customs.*)

Monitor Progress

Circulate to make sure students understand challenges to the environment and changes in the population. Provide assistance as needed.

Answer

✓**Checkpoint** Global warming could cause disasters, such as floods or droughts.

Section 4 Check Your Progress

1. (a) The Soviet Union collapsed due to overspending on arms production.
(b) The United States could provide economic assistance, and it could teach the nations how to establish and run a democratic government.

2. (a) The United States faces the effects of global warming and a lack of alternatives to its dependence on oil.

(b) The geographic and economic nature of these problems makes them global in their impact.

3. Possible questions: Is the world better off now that the Cold War has ended? How does the Cold War continue to overshadow international events?

4. deregulation: reduction of restrictions on business; détente: a relaxing of tensions; terrorism: the deliberate use of random acts of violence, often against civilians, to achieve a political goal

5. Outlines should be organized, have a clear point of view, and contain the two topic headings.

Skills for Life

Objective

Making predictions will help students more easily understand what they are reading. Using prior knowledge, students can compare similar experiences to a present situation and make a prediction of that situation's outcome.

Make Predictions

Instruction L2

1. Write the steps to making predictions on the board. Ask the class to read the steps aloud.

2. Using the Numbered Heads strategy (TE, p. T24), have students share what they know about circle graphs. (*Possible answers: Circle graphs present information by showing the breakdown of parts to the whole.*) Remind students that the entire pie chart represents 100% of the information being shown. In this case, each pie chart represents 100% of the population in the United States for the stated year.

3. Help students learn the skill by following the steps on p. 602 as a class. Model each step to make predictions. (*1.(a) Percent of Total U.S. Population by Age Group, 1960–2050 (b) 1960, 2000, and 2050 (c) U.S. Bureau of the Census, Projections of the Population of the U.S., by Age, Sex, and Race: 1995 to 2050 (2002) 2.(a) 35.7 percent (b) 45 & Over (c) 0–17 3.(a) Possible answer: Fewer schools will be built since there will be fewer children. Perhaps more houses and apartments will be built since there will be more older adults to buy them. (b) Possible advice: The increase in the number of older people may require additional facilities as well as increased specialization in the areas of aging and care for those with geriatric diseases.*)

Monitor Progress

Ask students to do the Apply the Skill activity. As students complete the activity, circulate to make sure individuals are applying the skill steps effectively. Provide assistance as needed.

Skills for Life Make Predictions

To predict consequences, or results, you must analyze what has happened in the past and compare it to the present situation. The data below show demographic, or population, trends. Demographic data help social scientists, as well as town and city planners, form a more complete picture of a certain population and establish trends over a period of time.

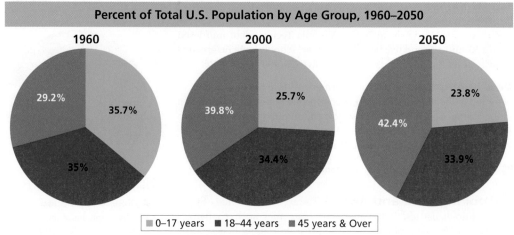

Percent of Total U.S. Population by Age Group, 1960–2050

1960: 35.7%, 35%, 29.2%
2000: 25.7%, 34.4%, 39.8%
2050: 23.8%, 33.9%, 42.4%

■ 0–17 years ■ 18–44 years ■ 45 years & Over

Source: U.S. Bureau of the Census, *Projections of the Population of the U.S., by Age, Sex, and Race: 1995 to 2050* (2002)

Learn the Skill
Use these steps to make predictions.

❶ **Identify the subject of the data.** Read the graph or chart title to understand what is being measured. Always look for the source of the data.

❷ **Analyze the data.** Study the data to see trends or patterns. Remember, information can be presented in different ways: tables, graphs, charts, or as text. Data may appear as percentages or in thousands or millions.

❸ **Predict possible future developments.** Draw conclusions or make generalizations based on the data on the chart.

Practice the Skill
Answer the following questions about the data on this page.

❶ **Identify the subject of the data.** (a) What is the title of the pie graphs? (b) What years are shown on the graphs? (c) What is the source of the data?

❷ **Analyze the data.** (a) What percentage of the population was between 0 and 17 years of age in 1960? (b) Which age group shows the most growth between 1960 and 2050? (c) Which group decreases the most?

❸ **Predict possible future developments.** (a) How do you think changes in the population will affect the construction of schools and houses built between 2000 and 2050? (b) What advice would you offer to hospitals and health care facilities based on this data?

Apply the Skill
See the Review and Assessment at the end of this chapter.

Quick Study Guide

How has the American nation met challenges at home and abroad?

Section 1
The Nation Grows

- Settlement of the western frontier led to the near destruction of the Plains Native American way of life.
- A booming economy led to the rise of wealthy business tycoons and a growing labor union movement.
- A surge in immigration swelled city populations and helped change the United States from a rural to an urban nation.

Section 2
A New Role for the Nation

- After the Civil War, the United States extended its control over parts of the Pacific region and Latin America.
- After its victory in World War I, the United States enjoyed a period of prosperity.
- The 1929 stock market crash marked the beginning of the Great Depression.

Section 3
Toward the Modern Age

- After early defeats on all fronts, the Allies rallied to win victory in World War II.
- Cold War tensions led to a number of dangerous confrontations.
- After World War II, African Americans began to demand their full civil rights.
- The Vietnam War was a costly conflict that deeply divided Americans.

Section 4
Into the Future

- The conservative movement sought to reduce the role of the federal government.
- U.S. foreign policy focused on the Middle East and the Balkans.
- After the 9/11 attacks, the U.S. invaded Afghanistan and Iraq.
- Environmental issues increasingly have global and economic effects.

(?) Exploring the Essential Question

Use the online study guide to explore the essential question.

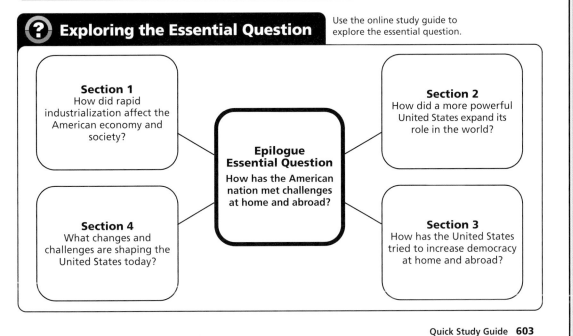

Section 1
How did rapid industrialization affect the American economy and society?

Epilogue Essential Question
How has the American nation met challenges at home and abroad?

Section 2
How did a more powerful United States expand its role in the world?

Section 4
What changes and challenges are shaping the United States today?

Section 3
How has the United States tried to increase democracy at home and abroad?

Quick Study Guide **603**

Epilogue

Essential Question

Remind students of the Chapter Essential Question: **How has the American nation met challenges at home and abroad?** Have them review the bulleted statements and the Visual Preview at the beginning of the chapter to help them answer this question.

Chapter Challenge

To wrap up this chapter, students should apply the knowledge they have gained to answer this question: **How have American values and goals affected lives worldwide?** *(Possible answer: As a superpower, the United States has a strong impact on other nations in terms of its policies and values. A recent example would be the war in Iraq and the replacement of its dictatorship with a democracy.)*

Assessment at a Glance

Performance Assessment

Group/Individual Activities, TE pp. 572g, 572h

Teacher's Edition, pp. 581, 589, 595, 601

Assessment Rubrics

Key Terms

1. They wanted to live freely on land of their choice.

2. The Nineteenth Amendment guaranteed women the right to vote.

3. The United States withdrew from foreign affairs, so it did not join the League of Nations after World War I.

4. Possible answer: They wanted to avoid becoming involved in a military conflict.

5. Nixon visited China and the Soviet Union in 1972.

Comprehension and Critical Thinking

6. **(a)** It meant the near destruction of their way of life. **(b)** They lost and were forced off their land and on to reservations.

7. **(a)** They were forced to work long hours for little pay. **(b)** Workers wanted to improve their working conditions. Labor unions sought shorter hours, better pay, and an end to child labor.

8. **(a)** Edison invented the light bulb, the phonograph, and the electric power plant. **(b)** Possible answer: Electricity became widely available and the mass entertainment industry began to grow.

9. **(a)** There was a mass migration to cities. **(b)** The growth of industry encouraged mass migration to cities, which resulted in overpopulation and unhealthy living conditions.

10. **(a)** The United States entered World War II. **(b)** Americans rallied together against a common enemy and the government lashed out with military force.

History Reading Skill

11. Questions should be focused, insightful, and useful for guiding research. Possible questions: Section 1: What factors contributed to the rise in U. S. population in the beginning of the twentieth century? Section 2: What are some effects of Roosevelt's New Deal that are still in evidence today? Section 3: What national and international issues deeply divided Americans in the mid-to-late twentieth century? Section 4: What role can history play in helping Americans face the complex issues of today?

Key Terms
Answer the following questions in complete sentences that show your understanding of the key terms.

1. Why did many Native Americans of the Plains move onto reservations?

2. Which amendment of the Constitution guaranteed American women the right of suffrage?

3. How did isolationism in the United States affect the peace settlement after World War I?

4. Why did the European democracies resort to appeasement of Adolf Hitler?

5. What action by President Richard Nixon established the policy of détente during the Cold War?

Comprehension and Critical Thinking

6. **(a) Describe** How did the westward migration of Americans change the lives of Plains Indians? **(b) Analyze Cause and Effect** How did wars with government troops affect Native American life?

7. **(a) Recall** How did changes in the economy affect workers in the late 1800s? **(b) Draw Conclusions** Why was there an effort to organize workers into labor unions?

8. **(a) Identify** Identify two devices invented by Thomas Edison. **(b) Draw Conclusions** How did Edison's inventions improve daily life in American cities?

9. **(a) Summarize** The newspaper editor Horace Greeley said, "We cannot all live in cities, yet nearly all seem determined to do so." What did he mean? **(b) Evaluate Information** How did the growth of industry affect the way people lived in the cities?

10. **(a) Describe** What were the results of the Japanese attack on Pearl Harbor? **(b) Link Past and Present** How was the reaction of Americans to the attack on Pearl Harbor similar to the reaction of Americans to the terrorist attacks of September 11, 2001?

🕐 History Reading Skill

11. **Frame Research Questions** Review Sections 1 through 4 of the Epilogue, and frame one research question for each section. For every research question, choose a general topic. Then, narrow your question to make it more specific. Remember to frame questions that go beyond the text and require research to answer.

Writing

12. **Write a Persuasive Paragraph:** Choose one headline from the list below, and write a persuasive paragraph that gives your opinion on the issue. Remember to support your opinion with facts, examples, and reasons.
    • Settlement of the West: Triumph or Tragedy?
    • Rockefeller and Carnegie: Heroes or Tyrants?
    • The Vietnam War: Justified or Unjustified?

13. **Write a Narrative:** Imagine that you are an immigrant arriving in New York City around 1900. Write a narrative describing your experiences at Ellis Island.

Skills for Life
Make Predictions
Use the graph below to answer the questions.

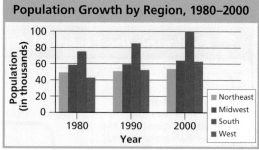

Population Growth by Region, 1980–2000

Source: U.S. Bureau of the Census, *The Statistical History of the U.S.* (1976) and 2000 Census of the U.S. www.census.gov

14. What is being measured by the data?

15. **(a)** In 1980, how many people lived in the Northeast? **(b)** What happened to the population of the South from 1980 to 2000?

16. Make a prediction about how this graph might look in 2020.

Writing

12. Paragraphs should present a strong, well-defined position with appropriate reasons and supporting facts.

13. Narratives should show careful thought and original ideas, and should be creatively executed.

Skills for Life

14. Population Growth by Region, 1980–2000

15. **(a)** About 50 million people lived in the Northeast. **(b)** It increased from about 75 million to more than 100 million.

16. Possible answer: Based on the previous 30 years, a graph in 2020 would also show an increase in the number of people living in the South.

Epilogue
Review and Assessment

Test Yourself

1. Which of the following most benefited big business?

   A rise of the American Federation of Labor

   B strikes called by unions

   C dangerous working conditions in sweatshops

   D development of the corporation

Refer to the quotation below to answer questions 2 and 3.

> "My fellow Americans, our long national nightmare is over. Our Constitution works; ours is a Government of laws and not of men. . . . [L]et us restore the golden rule to our political process, and let brotherly love purge our hearts of suspicion and hate."
>
> —President Gerald Ford, August 9, 1974, hours after the resignation of Richard Nixon

2. Of what is President Ford speaking when he refers to a "long national nightmare"?

   A Vietnam

   B Watergate

   C the rule of law

   D inflation

3. Which phrase suggests that President Ford is thinking of pardoning Nixon?

   A "Our Constitution works"

   B "ours is a government of laws"

   C "restore the golden rule"

   D "purge our hearts of . . . hate"

Document-Based Questions

Task: Look at Documents 1 and 2, and answer their accompanying questions. Then, use the documents and your knowledge of history to complete the following writing assignment:

> Write a three-paragraph essay about the role of government in American life today. Using specific details, indicate whether you think that President Roosevelt's views or President Reagan's views are more appropriate to the role of government in our society today.

Document 1: FDR's first inaugural address was given at a time when the economy was in shambles and Americans were desperate for action. *How does Roosevelt propose to attack the Depression?*

> "This Nation asks for action, and action now. Our greatest primary task is to put people to work. This is no unsolvable problem if we face it wisely and courageously. It can be accomplished in part by direct recruiting by the Government itself, treating the task as we would treat the emergency of a war, but at the same time, through this employment, accomplishing greatly needed projects to stimulate and reorganize the use of our natural resources."
>
> —Franklin Delano Roosevelt, First Inaugural Address, 1933

Document 2: Forty-eight years later, Ronald Reagan's first inaugural address was given at a time when many Americans were concerned by the growing size of federal government programs. *What does Reagan suggest is the core of the problem?*

> "In this present crisis, government is not the solution to our problem; government is the problem. From time to time we've been tempted to believe that society has become too complex to be managed by self-rule, that government by an elite group is superior to government for, by, and of the people. But if no one among us is capable of governing himself, then who among us has the capacity to govern someone else?"
>
> —Ronald Reagan, First Inaugural Address, 1981

Test Yourself

1. D

2. B

3. C

Document-Based Questions

Document 1 Roosevelt plans to attack the Depression by putting people to work through government hiring.

Document 2 Reagan suggests that government is too large and complex, and has become the problem.

Rubric: Write a Paragraph

Share the rubric with students before they begin writing.

Score 1 Ideas are unclear, organization is poor.

Score 2 Essay has few details, fails to explain whether or not people's views have changed.

Score 3 Essay accurately explains whether people's views have changed, has clear organization and some details.

Score 4 Essay is comprehensive and detailed with clear organization and supporting details, shows creativity.

Reference Section

Table of Contents

Primary Source Readings in American History

The Creation of Cherokee Country

Build Background Knowledge

Discuss Native American civilization in North America. Ask: **How long before European exploration did Native Americans live in North America?** (*thousands of years*) Ask: **What do you know about how the Cherokee lived?** (*Possible answers: The Cherokee hunted deer and other animals for food and hides, and they farmed corn, beans, and squash primarily. The Cherokee lived in large towns in log houses.*)

Vocabulary *Builder*

Teach Key Terms

Pronounce each word in the Vocabulary *Builder* list, and have students repeat the word. Ask a student to read the definitions. Have students use each word in a sentence.

Instruction

• Read The Creation of Cherokee Country with the students using the Oral Cloze Reading strategy (TE, p. T22).

• Ask: **What is the role of the Great Buzzard in this creation story?** (*The animals send out the Great Buzzard to find dry land. The Great Buzzard grew tired over Cherokee country, and his wings began to beat the ground. His wings formed the mountains and valleys of Cherokee country.*)

Monitor Progress

To monitor progress, have students answer the questions. Possible answers:

1. They wanted more space because it was very crowded where they lived before, but they needed dry earth on which to land and live.

2. The Appalachian Mountains were formed by the beating of the Great Buzzard's wings. When the buzzard's wings struck the earth, they formed valleys, and when they lifted again, they formed the mountains.

3. **Apply Information** Answers will vary but may discuss the significance of animals in the lives of early peoples. Many early civilizations lived closely with the animals in their environment, dependent upon them for food, shelter, and labor.

Background

The Cherokees were one of the dominant Native American groups of the Southeast culture region. They originally lived in the area that is now North Carolina, South Carolina, and Georgia. Other major groups in the Southeast included the Natchez and Creeks.

Like other Native Americans, the Cherokees had a strong tradition of oral literature. History, folk tales, and religious beliefs were memorized and recited, passing from one generation to the next. Creation stories were an important part of this oral tradition. The following story tells how the Cherokee lands in Georgia and the surrounding area were created. The mountains described are the Appalachians.

Vocabulary *Builder*

suspend (suh SPEND) *v.* to hang from

cardinal (KAHRD uh nuhl) *adj.* main; most important

vault (vawlt) *n.* arched roof or ceiling

dart (dahrt) *v.* to move suddenly or rapidly

alight (uh LĪT) *v.* to come to rest from the air

buzzard (BUHZ uhrd) *n.* any of various breeds of vultures

The earth is a great island floating in a sea of water, and <u>suspended</u> at each of the four <u>cardinal</u> points by a cord hanging down from the sky <u>vault</u>, which is of solid rock. When the world grows old and worn out, the people will die and the cords will break and let the earth sink down into the ocean, and all will be water again. The Indians are afraid of this.

When all was water, the animals were above . . . beyond the arch, but it was very much crowded, and they were wanting more room. They wondered what was below the water and at last . . . the little Water-beetle, offered to go and see if it could learn. It <u>darted</u> in every direction over the surface of the water, but could find no firm place to rest. Then it dived to the bottom and came up with some soft mud, which began to grow and spread on every side until it became the island which we call the earth. It was afterward fastened to the sky with four cords, but no one remembers who did this.

At first the earth was flat and very soft and wet. The animals were anxious to get down, and sent out different birds to see if it was yet dry, but they found no place to <u>alight</u> and came back again to [the world above]. At last it seemed to be time, and they sent out the Great <u>Buzzard</u>, the father of all the buzzards we see now. He flew all over the earth, low down near the ground, and it was still soft. When he reached the Cherokee country, he was very tired, and his wings began to flap and strike the ground, and wherever they struck the earth there was a valley, and where they turned up again there was a mountain. When the animals above saw this, they were afraid that the whole world would be mountains, so they called him back, but the Cherokee country remains full of mountains to this day.

Nineteenth Annual Report of the Bureau of American Ethnology, 1897–1898

Comprehension and Critical Thinking

1. Why did the animals want dry land?

2. According to this creation story, how were the Appalachian Mountains formed?

3. **Critical Thinking:** *Apply Information* Why do you think animal figures play an important role in this and other creation stories?

History Background

The Cherokee The Cherokee people first lived in the Great Lakes region. They migrated south to the Appalachian Mountains in present-day Tennessee and North and South Carolina following defeats by the Delaware and Iroquois peoples. The Cherokee believed that the universe comprised three worlds: the upper world, the lower world, and this world, or earth. This world was an island suspended between an upper world of perfect order and goodness and a lower world of disorder and chaos. The Cherokee believed that human beings must find some kind of balance between the upper and lower worlds while living on earth.

Chapter 1

Pericles, *Funeral Oration*

Background

Ancient Greece was divided into many small city-states, among them Athens and Sparta. Today, we consider Athens the birthplace of democracy.

In the fifth century B.C., a great conflict called the Peloponnesian War broke out between Athens and an alliance of city-states under the leadership of Sparta. At the time, the most respected leader in Athens was Pericles.

While the war was going on, Pericles was asked to deliver a speech honoring the city's war dead. He chose the occasion to also praise Athens, its government, its military, and its way of life. In the following selection from the speech, Pericles explains why he thinks the government of Athens is superior to those of other city-states.

Vocabulary *Builder*

capacity (kuh PAS ih tee) *n.* ability; skill

obscurity (ahb SKYOOR uh tee) *n.* state of being unclear or unknown

surveillance (suhr VAIL uhns) *n.* careful watching

injurious (ihn JYOOR ee uhs) *adj.* harmful

magistrate (MAJ uh strayt) *n.* official who enforces the law

statute (STACH oot) *n.* formal written law

Our constitution does not copy the laws of neighboring states; we are rather a pattern to others than imitators ourselves. Its administration favors the many instead of the few; this is why it is called a democracy. If we look to the laws, they afford equal justice to all in their private differences; if to social standing, advancement in public life falls to reputation for <u>capacity</u>, class considerations not being allowed to interfere with merit; nor again does poverty bar the way, if a man is able to serve the state, he is not hindered by the <u>obscurity</u> of his condition.

The freedom which we enjoy in our government extends also to our

Bust of Pericles

ordinary life. There, far from exercising a jealous <u>surveillance</u> over each other, we do not feel called upon to be angry with our neighbor for doing what he likes, or even to indulge in those <u>injurious</u> looks which cannot fail to be offensive, although they inflict no positive penalty. But all this ease in our private relations does not make us lawless as citizens. Against this fear is our chief safeguard, teaching us to obey the <u>magistrates</u> and the laws, particularly such as regard the protection of the injured, whether they are actually on the <u>statute</u> book, or belong to that code which, although unwritten yet cannot be broken without acknowledged disgrace.

Thucydides, History of the Peloponnesian War

Comprehension and Critical Thinking

1. According to Pericles, what makes Athens a democracy?

2. What freedoms do Athenians enjoy in their private lives?

3. Critical Thinking: *Compare* Based on this description, in what ways was the government of Athens similar to the government of the United States today?

Differentiated Instruction

L2 All Students

Identifying Information Write the following statements on the board. Have students identify the parts of the passage that contain these ideas:

• Our system is unique and is a model for other nations.

• A person's occupation or background

does not prevent him or her from pursuing higher goals.

• People do not need to spy on and persecute each other.

• The rule of law protects our people from disintegration and chaos.

Funeral Oration

Build Background Knowledge

Discuss government in the United States. Ask: **What type of government does the United States have?** (*Possible answers: federal republic, representative democracy*) Ask: **What document is the basis of the U.S. government?** (*the U.S. Constitution*) Ask: **What purpose does the Bill of Rights serve?** (*It guarantees and protects certain civil liberties.*)

Vocabulary *Builder*

Teach Key Terms

Pronounce each word in the Vocabulary *Builder* list, and have students repeat the word. Ask a student to read the definitions. Have students suggest a synonym for each word. For example, what is a synonym for *surveillance*? (*Possible answer: observation*)

Instruction

• Have students read Funeral Oration using the Choral Reading strategy (TE, p. T22).

• Ask: **What do Athens' laws provide?** (*equal justice to all*)

• Ask: **What determines a person's ability to advance socially?** (*merit*)

• Ask: **What should not prevent a person from advancing socially?** (*class, poverty, obscurity*)

Monitor Progress

To monitor progress, have students answer the questions. Possible answers:

1. According to Pericles, Athens' government is a democracy because it favors the many instead of the few.

2. Athenians enjoy the freedom to pursue their individual lives with equal liberties and opportunities and without fear of surveillance.

3. **Compare** Answers will vary but should discuss the United States' form of representative democracy and its constitutional guarantees of individual liberties and equal opportunities.

The Destruction of the Indies

Build Background Knowledge

Discuss the early interactions of European explorers and Native Americans. Ask: **What was the Columbian Exchange?** (*The process by which animals, plants, and ideas passed back and forth between the Western Hemisphere and the Eastern Hemisphere.*) Ask: **What negative effects did European explorers and colonists have on Native Americans?** (*Possible answers: Europeans brought new diseases to the Western Hemisphere that killed many Native Americans. Europeans enslaved Native Americans.*)

Vocabulary *Builder*

Teach Key Terms

Pronounce each word in the Vocabulary *Builder* list, and have students repeat the word. Ask a student to read the definitions. Have students write a sentence for each vocabulary word.

Instruction

- Have students read The Destruction of the Indies using the Structured Silent Reading strategy (TE, p. T22).

- Ask: **According to Las Casas, in what two ways have Europeans destroyed Native American peoples?** (*by waging war against them and by killing anyone who resists*)

- Ask: **How does Las Casas say the Spaniards have treated the Native Americans?** (*Las Casas says the Spaniards have treated Native Americans worse than they treat their animals.*)

Monitor Progress

To monitor progress, have students answer the questions. Possible answers:

1. Las Casas indicates that the Spanish treated the Native Americans badly out of greed for gold.

2. The Native Americans thought the Europeans were gods or spirits from heaven.

3. **Detect Points of View** Answers will vary but should discuss that the conquistadores did not behave as Christians should but instead attacked and killed many Native Americans and treated them brutally.

Primary Sources

Bartolomé de Las Casas, *The Destruction of the Indies*

Background

Bartolomé de Las Casas was a Roman Catholic priest born in Seville, Spain, in 1484. In his youth, he met Christopher Columbus and traveled to the West Indies. There, he observed the conquest of the Americas and was horrified by the treatment of Native Americans by the conquistadors.

Las Casas dedicated his long life to protecting Native Americans from Spanish abuse.

On several occasions, he returned to Spain to plead their case before the Spanish throne. His writings and discussions shocked Spanish leaders who attempted to pass laws to protect the Indians. The conquistadors' friends at court, however, often had the policies reversed. Below is an excerpt from a 1542 work detailing the abusive policies of the Spanish.

Vocabulary *Builder*

tyrannical (tih RAN ih kuhl) *adj.* harsh; using power unjustly

instrumental (ihn struh MEHN tuhl) *adj.* serving as an important tool; very helpful

annihilation (uh nī uh LAY shuhn) *n.* complete destruction

Sacrament (SAK ruh mehnt) *n.* sacred rite of the Christian church

indigenous (ihn DIHJ uh nehs) *adj.* native to a region or counry

tribulation (trihb yoo LAY shuhn) *n.* great sorrow or trouble

There are two main ways in which those who have traveled to this part of the world pretending to be Christians have uprooted these pitiful peoples and wiped them from the face of the earth. First, they have waged war on them: unjust, cruel, bloody and <u>tyrannical</u> war. Second, they have murdered anyone and everyone who has shown the slightest sign of resistance. . . . This latter policy has been <u>instrumental</u> in suppressing the native leaders, and, indeed, given that the Spaniards normally spare only women and children, it has led to the <u>annihilation</u> of all adult males. . . .

The reason the [Spanish] have murdered on such a vast scale and killed anyone and everyone in their way is purely and simply greed. They have set out to line their pockets with gold. . . . The Spaniards have shown not the slightest consideration for these people, treating them (and I speak from first-hand experience, having been there from the outset) not as brute animals—indeed, I would to God they had done and had shown them the consideration they afford their animals—so much as piles of dung in the middle of the road. They have had as little concern for their souls as for their bodies, all the millions that have perished having gone to their deaths with no knowledge of God and without the benefit of the <u>Sacraments</u>. . . .

The <u>indigenous</u> peoples never did the Europeans any harm whatever; on the contrary, they believed them to have descended from the heavens, at least until they or their fellow-citizens had tasted, at the hands of these oppressors, a diet of robbery, murder, violence, and all other manner of trials and <u>tribulations</u>.

Bartolomé de Las Casas, The Destruction of the Indies

Comprehension and Critical Thinking

1. According to Las Casas, why did the Spanish treat Native Americans the way they did?

2. Who did the Native people think the Europeans were at first?

3. **Critical Thinking:** *Detect Points of View* Why does Las Casas accuse the conquistadors of "pretending to be Christians"? What evidence does he offer for this accusation?

History Background

Before the Europeans Scholars estimate that about 75 million native peoples inhabited the Americas prior to European contact in 1492, although there is great debate about the figure and some scholars put the number as low as 15 million. Scholars do agree that European diseases dramatically decreased Native American populations between 1500 and 1900. Native American ancestors migrated to the Americas before the evolution of many modern "old world" diseases. Their population reproduced and increased for thousands of years without the influence of such diseases so their bodies were not prepared to fight the viruses and bacteria brought by Europeans. Influenza, smallpox, measles, and other diseases reduced Native American populations by as much as 90 percent.

Chapter 2

Jacques Marquette, *Reaching the Mississippi*

Background

Jacques Marquette was born in northern France in 1637. He joined the Jesuits at the age of 17 and worked as a priest in France for more than a decade. In his late twenties, Marquette was sent to Quebec, in the heart of France's North American empire. Marquette served as a missionary to the native people of the continent. There, he heard rumors of a great river southwest of Quebec, which the French hoped would be a "Northwest Passage" to the Pacific Ocean. In 1673, Marquette joined Canadian-born explorer Louis Joliet and five other adventurers to find the river. Here, he describes reaching the Mississippi River.

Vocabulary *Builder*

dissuade (dihs WAYD) *v.* to advise against; discourage

salvation (sal VAY shuhn) *n.* saving of a person's soul, especially referring to life after death

depute (dee PYOOT) *v.* to select someone for a task or mission

---

On the 17th day of May, 1673, we started from the mission of St. Ignatius. . . . [T]he first nation that we came to was that of the Folle Avoine [Menominee]. . . . I told these people . . . of my design to go and discover those remote nations, in order to teach them the mysteries of our holy religion. They . . . did their best to <u>dissuade</u> me. They represented to me that I would meet nations who never show mercy to strangers. . . .

I thanked them for their advice . . . but told them that I could not follow it, because the <u>salvation</u> of souls was at stake. . . .

We left the waters flowing to Quebec . . . to float on those that would thenceforward take us through strange lands.

. . . [W]e arrived at . . . the Mississippi on the 17th of June, with a joy that I cannot express.

Finally on the 25th of June we perceived on the water's edge some tracks of men, and a narrow . . . beaten path. . . . [A]fter walking about two leagues, we discovered a village. . . . We . . . decided to reveal ourselves. . . . by shouting with all our energy, and stopped without advancing any farther. On hearing the shout, the savages [the Illinois] . . . having probably recognized us as Frenchmen, especially when they saw a black gown—or, at least, having not cause for distrust, as we were only two men, and had given them notice of our arrival—they <u>deputed</u> four old men to come and speak to us. . . . They afterward invited us to enter their village.

Jacques Marquette, *The Jesuit Relations*, Vol. LIX

Comprehension and Critical Thinking

1. What warning did the Menominee give Marquette and Joliet?

2. How long was the journey from St. Ignatius to the Mississippi?

3. Critical Thinking: *Predict* What dangers do you think Marquette and Joliet will face as they continue on their journey?

Marquette and Joliet on the Mississippi

Primary Sources **611**

Reaching the Mississippi

Build Background Knowledge

Discuss the exploration and settlement of North America. Ask: **What was the first permanent settlement in North America?** (*the Spanish settlement at St. Augustine in present-day Florida*) Ask: **What nations explored and set up colonies in North America?** (*Spain, England, France, the Netherlands*)

Vocabulary *Builder*

Teach Key Terms

Pronounce each word in the Vocabulary *Builder* list, and have students repeat the word. Ask a student to read the definitions. Pair students and have them make flashcards, writing the vocabulary word on one side and the definition on the back. Then have students hold up a card and ask their partner for the definition of the word.

Instruction

- Have students read Reaching the Mississippi using the Choral Reading strategy (TE, p. T22).

- Ask: **Why did Marquette want to explore North America and encounter new peoples?** (*to spread Christianity*)

- Ask: **About how much time passed between Marquette's departure from St. Ignatius and his meeting with the Illinois?** (*about five weeks*)

Monitor Progress

To monitor progress, have students answer the questions. Possible answers:

1. that if they continued on their journey they would meet dangerous groups of people

2. The trip took Marquette and Joliet exactly one month.

3. **Predict** Answers will vary but should discuss that Marquette and Joliet were unfamiliar with both the land and the peoples who lay ahead.

Differentiated Instruction

L2 All Students

Paraphrasing Pair students to read the excerpt from *Reaching the Mississippi* and to rewrite each paragraph in their own words. Have several students share their work orally with the class. Have students discuss whether they agree that the interpretation matches the meaning of the document.

Primary Sources

History of Plimoth Plantation

Build Background Knowledge

Discuss the Pilgrims who established the Plymouth colony. Ask: **Why did the Pilgrims leave England?** (*The Pilgrims left England to practice religious freedom. They were English Protestants who wanted to separate from the official Church of England.*) Ask: **What was the Mayflower Compact?** (*The Mayflower Compact was a written set of rules that the male Pilgrims agreed to. The compact provided for a system of elected government.*)

Vocabulary *Builder*

Teach Key Terms

Pronounce each word in the Vocabulary *Builder* list, and have students repeat the word. Ask a student to read the definitions. Have students use each vocabulary word in a sentence.

Instruction

• Have students read History of Plimoth Plantation using the Structured Silent Reading strategy (TE, p. T22).

• Ask: **What did the Pilgrims find when they made landfall?** (*The Pilgrims found undeveloped wilderness, with wild animals and Native Americans.*)

• Ask: **What season was it when the Pilgrims landed, and how does Bradford describe it?** (*It was winter. Bradford describes the winter as sharp, violent, cruel, and dangerous with fierce storms.*)

Monitor Progress

To monitor progress, have students answer the questions. Possible answers:

1. Bradford means the land. The Pilgrims had been at sea but their "proper element" was the land.

2. The Pilgrims face undeveloped wilderness, including wild animals and unfamiliar people they consider savage. They also face a harsh winter season. Bradford says their one source of hope is "the spirit of God and his grace."

3. **Detect Bias** Answers will vary but should note that Bradford refers to the Native Americans as "savage barbarians" and "wild men." Answers should also note how strange the Pilgrims, with their different clothes, tools, and ships, must have appeared to the Native Americans.

612

Primary Sources

William Bradford, *History of Plimoth Plantation*

Background
On September 6, 1620, the Pilgrims departed from Plymouth, England, on board the *Mayflower*. The journey across the Atlantic Ocean took 66 days. Their intended destination was the mouth of the Hudson River, site of present-day New York City. During the second half of the trip, they encountered rough weather. The threat of shipwreck if they continued on to the Hudson led them to halt, explore Cape Cod, and settle in Massachusetts.

Among the passengers was William Bradford. He later served as governor of the Plymouth Colony for more than 25 years. Bradford also wrote *History of Plimoth Plantation*, a valuable source of information about the colony. In this excerpt, Bradford describes the arrival of the Pilgrims at Cape Cod.

Vocabulary *Builder*
succor (SUHK uhr) *n.* help or aid
barbarian (bahr BEHR ee uhn) *n.* uncivilized person
desolate (DEHS uh liht) *adj.* empty; lacking in life or comfort
sustain (SUH stayn) *v.* support; keep alive

Being thus arrived in a good harbor and brought safe to land, they fell upon their knees and blessed the God of Heaven who had brought them over the vast and furious ocean and delivered them from all the perils and miseries thereof, again to set their feet on the firm and stable, their proper element.

But here I cannot but stay and make a pause and stand half amazed at this poor people's present condition; and so I think will the reader too, when he well considers the same. Being thus past the vast ocean and a sea of troubles before in their preparation . . . they had now no friends to welcome them, nor inns to entertain or refresh their weather-beaten bodies, no houses or much less towns to repair to, to seek for

Pilgrims of Plymouth Colony

succor. . . . These savage <u>barbarians</u>, when they met with them (as after will appear) were readier to fill their sides of arrows than otherwise. And for the season, it was winter, and they that know the winters of that country know them to be sharp and violent and subject to cruel and fierce storms, dangerous to travel to known places, much more to search an unknown coast. Besides, what could they see but a hideous and <u>desolate</u> wilderness full of wild beasts and wild men? And what multitudes there might be of them they knew not. . . . What could now <u>sustain</u> them but the spirit of God and his grace?

William Bradford, *History of Plimoth Plantation*

Comprehension and Critical Thinking

1. What does Bradford mean when he speaks of the Pilgrims' "proper element"?

2. What fears do the Pilgrims face? According to Bradford, what is their one source of hope?

3. **Critical Thinking:** *Detect Bias* What is Bradford's view of Native Americans? How do you think Native Americans viewed the Pilgrims?

612 Reference Section

History Background

Pilgrims and Puritans The Pilgrims who landed on Plymouth Rock in 1620 were religious separatists fleeing persecution under the Church of England. In 1691, the Plymouth colony of the Pilgrims became part of the larger Massachusetts Bay Colony. The settlers of Massachusetts Bay were Puritans. Like the Pilgrims, the Puritans left England primarily to practice their religion freely, but unlike the Pilgrims, the Puritans were not Separatists. The Puritans remained a part of the Church of England and hoped to reform it from within. The Puritans believed the Church of England was corrupt and ritualistic, and wanted people to develop a more personal and committed relationship with their God through preaching, scripture, prayer, and work.

Chapter 3

Maryland Act of Toleration

Background

Lord Baltimore was the founder of the Maryland Colony and served as Lord Proprietary, or head of the government. He had hoped to make Maryland a Catholic colony. However, the majority of colonists turned out to be Protestants. Nevertheless, Catholic settlers got the large grants and held the positions of power in the colony. Protestant settlers were unhappy with those conditions.

In 1649, Lord Baltimore encouraged the Maryland legislature to pass an act of toleration. The law gave the colony a measure of religious freedom. The act was designed to protect Protestants but, in fact, protected the Catholic minority as well. The following excerpt from the Act of Toleration identifies some of the people and actions that would and would not be tolerated in the colony.

Vocabulary *Builder*

blaspheme (blas FEEM) *v.* to speak against God or holy matters

confiscation (kahn fihs KAY shuhn) *n.* seizure of property by a government

forfeiture (FOR fuh chuhr) *n.* act of giving up something as a penalty

amity (AM ih tee) *n.* peaceful relations

discountenance (dihs KOWNT uhn ehns) *v.* make to feel shame

Forasmuch as, in a well-governed and Christian commonwealth, matters concerning religion and the honor of God ought in the first place to be taken into serious consideration, . . . be it therefore ordered and enacted by the Right Honorable Cecilius Lord Baron of Baltimore, absolute Lord and Proprietary of this Province with the advise and consent of this General Assembly:

That whatsoever person or persons within the Province thereunto belonging shall from henceforth blaspheme God, that is, curse Him; or deny our Savior Jesus Christ to be the son of God, or shall deny the Holy Trinity, the Father, Son, and Holy Ghost . . . shall be punished with death and confiscation or forfeiture of all his or her lands and goods to the Lord Proprietary and his heirs.

And be it also enacted . . . that whatsoever person or persons shall from henceforth use or utter any reproachful words or speeches concerning the Blessed Virgin Mary, the Mother of our Savior, or the Holy Apostles . . . shall in such case for the first offense forfeit to the said Lord Proprietary and his heirs . . . the sum of five pounds sterling. . . . And that every person or persons before mentioned offending herein the third time, shall for such third Offence forfeit all

his lands and Goods and be for ever banished and expelled out of this Province. . . .

And for the more quiet and peaceable government of this Province, and the better to preserve mutual love and amity amongst the Inhabitants thereof, be it therefore [enacted] that no person or persons whatsoever within this Province . . . professing to believe in Jesus Christ, shall from henceforth be any ways troubled, molested or discountenanced for or in respect of his or her religion nor in the free exercise thereof within this Province or the Islands thereunto belonging nor any way compelled to the belief or exercise of any other Religion against his or her consent.

An Act Concerning Religion, April 24, 1649

Comprehension and Critical Thinking

1. What actions were punishable by death under the Maryland Act of Toleration?

2. What people were given religious freedom in Maryland? Why?

3. Critical Thinking: *Contrast* Based on your reading, how did colonial Maryland differ from Puritan New England in terms of religious toleration?

Primary Sources **613**

Differentiated Instruction

L2 All Students

Paraphrasing Pair students to read the excerpt from Maryland Act of Toleration and rewrite each paragraph in their own words. Have several students share their work orally with the class. Have students discuss whether they agree that the interpretation matches the meaning of the document.

Maryland Act of Toleration

Build Background Knowledge

Remind students that, during the 1600s, most of the colonies had little toleration for religious differences. Tell students that there was a civil war in England at this time concerning the issue of religion. Point out that there were some beliefs that still would not be tolerated under the provisions of the 1649 act. Ask: **Why did Lord Baltimore need to issue an act of religious toleration in Maryland?** (*Catholicism was persecuted in Britain and in the Puritan colonies of New England. Maryland was established as a Catholic colony. The act was written to address complaints of discrimination against Protestants.*)

Vocabulary *Builder*

Teach Key Terms

Pronounce each word in the Vocabulary *Builder* list and have students repeat the word. Ask a student to read the definitions. Have students use each word in a sentence. Ask students to suggest synonyms for these vocabulary words. For example, ask a student to provide a synonym for for "amity." (*friendliness, civility*)

Instruction

- Read Maryland Act of Toleration with students using the Oral Cloze Strategy (TE, p. T22)

- Ask: **By what authority does Lord Baltimore issue this act of toleration?** (*He is the proprietary head of the colony.*)

- Ask: **What evidence is in this excerpt that Lord Baltimore hoped to achieve practical political goals with the toleration act?** (*He refers to the "more quiet and peaceable government of this Province" as a goal.*)

Monitor Progress

To monitor progress have students answer the Comprehension and Critical thinking questions. Possible answers:

1. Death penalty could result from blaspheming or cursing God, denying Jesus, or denying the Holy Trinity.

2. People who professed Christian faith were allowed religious freedom. Possible answer: to preserve peaceful relations among the colonists.

3. **Contrast** In Puritan colonies, deviation from accepted beliefs was severely punished. In Maryland, a much wider range of Christian beliefs was tolerated.

613

Primary Sources

The Magna Carta

Build Background Knowledge

Remind students that the Magna Carta is a medieval document that gave English nobles certain rights and restricted the powers of the king. Have students recall why the Magna Carta is important in American history. Ask: **Where did American colonists get many of their ideas about government and justice?** (*American colonists got many of their ideas about government and justice from English law and government, including the Magna Carta.*) Ask: **How did the Magna Carta influence the Declaration of Independence?** (*The colonists declared their independence because King George was denying them rights guaranteed to Englishmen by the Magna Carta.*)

Vocabulary *Builder*

Teach Key Terms

Pronounce each word in the Vocabulary *Builder* list and have students repeat the word. Ask a student to read the definitions. Have students use each word in a sentence.

Instruction

- Using the Choral Reading strategy (TE, p. T22), read sections 12, 30, and 31 with students. Stop after each section and have students describe in their own words what each section means. Then ask: **What problems are these sections trying to fix?** (*Possible answers: unfair taxation, tax collectors taking people's property*)

- Have students finish reading the document. Ask: **Why do you think King John had to be forced to sign the Magna Carta?** (*Possible answer: It took away some of his power to act as he wished.*)

- Ask students to tell which section of the document they think is the most important and why.

Monitor Progress

To monitor progress, have students answer the questions. Possible answers:

1. Sections 30 and 31

2. Section 12 promises not to impose taxes (except for specific purposes) without the consent of the kingdom.

3. **Link Past and Present** In the United States today, people have the right to a fair trial by a jury of their peers.

614

Primary Sources

The Magna Carta

Background

King John ruled England from 1199 to 1216. During his troubled reign, he found himself in conflict with England's feudal barons. The nobles especially resented John's attempts to tax them heavily.

In 1215, the barons forced John to sign the Magna Carta, or Great Charter. Most of this document was intended to protect the rights of the barons.

However, over time, the document came to guarantee some basic rights of English citizens. When English colonists came to North America, they brought these ideas with them. Eight of the 63 clauses of the Magna Carta are printed here.

Vocabulary *Builder*

<u>counsel</u> (KOWN suhl) *n.* advice; consent

<u>bailiff</u> (BAY lihf) *n.* tax collector in medieval England

<u>credible</u> (KREHD uh buhl) *adj.* believable

<u>peer</u> (peer) *n.* person of equal rank

<u>realm</u> (rehlm) *n.* kingdom

<u>enjoin</u> (ehn JOIN) *v.* to order; to enforce

12. No [tax] nor aid shall be imposed on our kingdom, unless by common <u>counsel</u> of our kingdom, except for ransoming our person, for making our eldest son a knight, and for once marrying our eldest daughter; and for these there shall not be levied more than a reasonable aid. . . .

30. No sheriff or <u>bailiff</u> of ours, or other person, shall take the horses or carts of any freeman for transport duty, against the will of the said freeman.

31. Neither we nor our bailiffs shall take, for our castles or for any other work of ours, wood which is not ours, against the will of the owner of that wood. . . .

38. No bailiff for the future shall, upon his own unsupported complaint, put any one to his "law," without <u>credible</u> witnesses brought for this purpose.

39. No freeman shall be taken or imprisoned . . . or exiled or in any way destroyed, nor will we go upon him nor send upon him, except by the lawful judgment of his <u>peers</u> or by the law of the land.

40. To no one will we sell, to no one will we refuse or delay, right or justice. . . .

45. We will appoint as justices, constables, sheriffs, or bailiffs only such as know the law of the <u>realm</u> and mean to observe it well. . . .

63. Wherefore it is our will, and we firmly <u>enjoin</u>, that the English Church be free, and that the men in our kingdom have and hold all the aforesaid liberties, rights, and concessions, well and peaceably, freely and quietly, fully and wholly, for themselves and their heirs, of us and our heirs, in all respects and in all places for ever, as is aforesaid.

The Magna Carta, in *Source Problems in English History,* ed. White and Notestein

Comprehension and Critical Thinking

1. Which clauses of the Magna Carta listed here protect the right of people to their own private property?

2. What promise is made in clause 12?

3. **Critical Thinking:** *Link Past and Present* How do the principles expressed in clauses 38–40 apply to the United States today?

614 Reference Section

History Background

The Impact of the Magna Carta The Magna Carta was a revolutionary document in the development of constitutional government. In England, the Magna Carta's demand for "common counsel" to pass taxes was later used as a justification for having a Parliament. Although many of the Magna Carta's provisions focus on the feudal rights of nobles, the document's aims of limiting royal power and protecting all freemen inspired the creators of later constitutional governments. The Magna Carta provided inspiration for both the Declaration of Independence and the French Revolution's Declaration of the Rights of Man and of the Citizen.

Chapter 4

Jonathan Mayhew, *On Unlimited Submission to Rulers*

Background

During the Great Awakening, American preachers spoke out on both political and religious issues. One of these preachers was Jonathan Mayhew, the Congregationalist minister at Boston's West Church. In a 1750 sermon, Mayhew argued against the idea that people owed complete submission, or obedience, to their rulers. Mayhew based

his argument on the teachings of an early Christian leader, the apostle Paul.

Mayhew's lengthy sermon was printed and widely read in the colonies. In this excerpt, he explains his view of the purpose of government.

Vocabulary *Builder*

welfare (WEHL fair) *n.* well-being

parity (PAR ih tee) *n.* similarity

allegiance (uh LEE jehntz) *n.* loyalty

implicit (ihm PLIH siht) *adj.* by suggestion; not stated directly

---

The [goal of government] is the good of civil society. . . .

If it be our duty, for example, to obey our king merely for this reason, that he rules for the public <u>welfare</u> (which is the only argument the apostle makes use of), it follows, by a <u>parity</u> of reason, that when he turns tyrant and makes his subjects his prey to devour and to destroy instead of his charge to defend and cherish, we are bound to throw off our <u>allegiance</u> to him and to resist. . . . Not to discontinue our allegiance, in this case, would be to join with the sovereign

Jonathan Mayhew

JONATHAN MAYHEW, D-D-PASTOR OF THE WEST CHVRCH IN BOSTON, IN NEW ENGLAND, AN ASSERTOR OF THE CIVIL AND RELIGIOVS LIBERTIES OF HIS COVNTRY AND MANKIND.

in promoting the slavery and misery of that society, the welfare of which we ourselves, as well as our sovereign, are indispensably obliged to secure and promote as far as in us lies.

It is true the apostle puts no such case of such a tyrannical prince; but, by his grounding his argument for submission wholly upon the good of civil society, it is plain he <u>implicitly</u> authorizes and even requires us to make resistance whenever this shall be necessary to the public safety and us to make happiness.

Jonathan Mayhew, A Discourse Concerning Unlimited Submission and Non-Resistance to the Higher Powers

Comprehension and Critical Thinking

1. According to Mayhew, what is the chief goal of a government?

2. What does Mayhew think people should do if a ruler becomes tyrannical?

3. Critical Thinking: *Make Predictions* How do you think ideas like Mayhew's might contribute to a spirit of resistance and revolution in the colonies?

Primary Sources   615

History Background

The Great Awakening and Universities Besides bringing people together to express their religious and political ideas, the Great Awakening led to the establishment of educational institutions. Princeton University in New Jersey was founded by evangelical Presbyterians in 1746, Brown University in Rhode Island

was founded by the Baptists in 1764, and the university now known as Rutgers, in New Jersey, was founded by the Dutch Reformed Church in 1766.

On Unlimited Submission to Rulers

Build Background Knowledge

Remind students that many of the 13 English colonies were founded by people seeking religious freedom. Have them discuss the impact of the Great Awakening in the colonies. Use the Idea Wave strategy (TE, p. T24) to have students predict how the Great Awakening might have influenced colonists who believed British rule had become unfair. (*Possible answer: The colonists probably thought that they had the right to govern themselves.*)

Vocabulary *Builder*

Teach Key Terms

Pronounce each word in the Vocabulary *Builder* list and have students repeat the word. Ask a student to read the definitions. Have students use each word in a sentence.

Instruction

- Read On Unlimited Submission to Rulers with students, using the Oral Cloze strategy (TE, p. T22).

- Ask: **When does Mayhew believe people should turn against their government?** (*when it becomes tyrannical*) Then ask: **What aspects of society are threatened by a tyrannical ruler?** (*public safety and happiness*)

- Ask: **What did Mayhew believe would be the result if a society continued to support a tyrannical ruler?** (*The welfare of the society would be at risk because the people would be promoting the slavery and misery of that society.*)

Monitor Progress

To monitor progress, have students answer the questions. Possible answers:

1. According to Mayhew, the chief goal of a government is to ensure the welfare of civil society.

2. They should offer resistance against the ruler.

3. **Make Predictions** The idea that a society should resist tyrannical rule might have led the American colonists to consider rebellion against British rule and seek independence.

The Fifty States

State	Date of Entry to Union (Order of Entry)	Land Area in Square Miles	Population (In Thousands)	Number of Representatives in House*	Capital	Largest City
Alabama	1819 (22)	50,750	4,447	7	Montgomery	Birmingham
Alaska	1959 (49)	570,374	627	1	Juneau	Anchorage
Arizona	1912 (48)	113,642	5,131	8	Phoenix	Phoenix
Arkansas	1836 (25)	52,075	2,673	4	Little Rock	Little Rock
California	1850 (31)	155,973	33,872	53	Sacramento	Los Angeles
Colorado	1876 (38)	103,730	4,301	7	Denver	Denver
Connecticut	1788 (5)	4,845	3,406	5	Hartford	Bridgeport
Delaware	1787 (1)	1,955	784	1	Dover	Wilmington
Florida	1845 (27)	53,997	15,982	25	Tallahassee	Jacksonville
Georgia	1788 (4)	57,919	8,186	13	Atlanta	Atlanta
Hawaii	1959 (50)	6,423	1,212	2	Honolulu	Honolulu
Idaho	1890 (43)	82,751	1,294	2	Boise	Boise
Illinois	1818 (21)	55,593	12,419	19	Springfield	Chicago
Indiana	1816 (19)	35,870	6,080	9	Indianapolis	Indianapolis
Iowa	1846 (29)	55,875	2,926	5	Des Moines	Des Moines
Kansas	1861 (34)	81,823	2,688	4	Topeka	Wichita
Kentucky	1792 (15)	39,732	4,042	6	Frankfort	Louisville
Louisiana	1812 (18)	43,566	4,469	7	Baton Rouge	New Orleans
Maine	1820 (23)	30,865	1,275	2	Augusta	Portland
Maryland	1788 (7)	9,775	5,296	8	Annapolis	Baltimore
Massachusetts	1788 (6)	7,838	6,349	10	Boston	Boston
Michigan	1837 (26)	56,809	9,938	15	Lansing	Detroit
Minnesota	1858 (32)	79,617	4,919	8	St. Paul	Minneapolis
Mississippi	1817 (20)	46,914	2,845	4	Jackson	Jackson
Missouri	1821 (24)	68,898	5,595	9	Jefferson City	Kansas City
Montana	1889 (41)	145,556	902	1	Helena	Billings
Nebraska	1867 (37)	76,878	1,711	3	Lincoln	Omaha
Nevada	1864 (36)	109,806	1,998	3	Carson City	Las Vegas
New Hampshire	1788 (9)	8,969	1,236	2	Concord	Manchester
New Jersey	1787 (3)	7,419	8,414	13	Trenton	Newark
New Mexico	1912 (47)	121,365	1,819	3	Santa Fe	Albuquerque
New York	1788 (11)	47,224	18,976	29	Albany	New York
North Carolina	1789 (12)	48,718	8,049	13	Raleigh	Charlotte
North Dakota	1889 (39)	68,994	642	1	Bismarck	Fargo
Ohio	1803 (17)	40,953	11,353	18	Columbus	Columbus
Oklahoma	1907 (46)	68,679	3,451	5	Oklahoma City	Oklahoma City
Oregon	1859 (33)	96,003	3,421	5	Salem	Portland
Pennsylvania	1787 (2)	44,820	12,281	19	Harrisburg	Philadelphia
Rhode Island	1790 (13)	1,045	1,048	2	Providence	Providence
South Carolina	1788 (8)	30,111	4,012	6	Columbia	Columbia
South Dakota	1889 (40)	75,898	755	1	Pierre	Sioux Falls
Tennessee	1796 (16)	41,220	5,689	9	Nashville	Memphis
Texas	1845 (28)	261,914	20,852	32	Austin	Houston
Utah	1896 (45)	82,168	2,233	3	Salt Lake City	Salt Lake City
Vermont	1791 (14)	9,249	609	1	Montpelier	Burlington
Virginia	1788 (10)	39,598	7,079	11	Richmond	Virginia Beach
Washington	1889 (42)	66,582	5,894	9	Olympia	Seattle
West Virginia	1863 (35)	24,087	1,808	3	Charleston	Charleston
Wisconsin	1848 (30)	54,314	5,364	8	Madison	Milwaukee
Wyoming	1890 (44)	97,105	494	1	Cheyenne	Cheyenne
District of Columbia		61	572	1 (nonvoting)		

Self-Governing Areas, Possessions, and Dependencies	Land Area in Square Miles	Population (In Thousands)	Capital
Puerto Rico	3,515	809	San Juan
Guam	209	155	Agana
U.S. Virgin Islands	132	121	Charlotte Amalie
American Samoa	77	65	Pago Pago

Sources: Department of Commerce, Bureau of the Census   *As of 108th Congress.

 Alabama

 Alaska

 Arizona

 Arkansas

 California

 Colorado

 Connecticut

 Delaware

 Florida

 Georgia

 Hawaii

 Idaho

 Illinois

 Indiana

 Iowa

 Kansas

 Kentucky

 Louisiana

 Maine

 Maryland

 Massachusetts

 Michigan

 Minnesota

 Mississippi

 Missouri

 Montana

 Nebraska

 Nevada

 New Hampshire

 New Jersey

 New Mexico

 New York

 North Carolina

 North Dakota

 Ohio

 Oklahoma

 Oregon

 Pennsylvania

 Rhode Island

 South Carolina

 South Dakota

 Tennessee

 Texas

 Utah

 Vermont

 Virginia

 Washington

 West Virginia

 Wisconsin

Wyoming

Contents

The Economics Handbook will provide you with key economic concepts and terms, so you may understand economic issues and decision making throughout history.

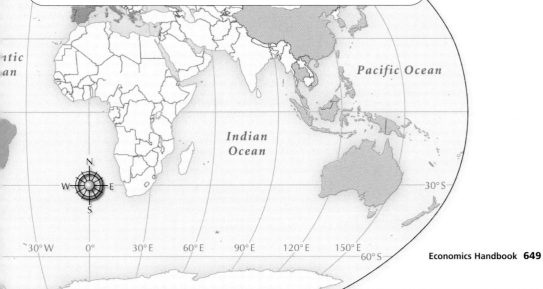

Objectives

- Be able to define economics, and the role needs and wants play in economic systems.
- Understand what trade-offs and opportunity costs are.

Building Background Knowledge

Students may have difficulty developing a working definition of economics, as it applies to their lives. Begin a discussion which helps define the study of economics, and ask students to come up with examples of buying, selling, or trading to meet their needs and wants. Explain how economists wish to understand people's motives in buying, selling, or trading.

Instruction

Ask students to find examples of buying, selling, or trading in a daily newspaper or periodical. Ask students to demonstrate the similarities and differences between their examples of buying, selling or trading, and the examples they found in a newspaper or periodical.

Review Questions

1. Economics is the study of how people make choices when they face a limited supply of resources.

2. Trade-offs are the items or opportunities people give up when they choose one course of action over the other. The opportunity cost is the item or opportunity lost when a person decides on one course of action. Further examples can help clarify this idea for students.

What is Economics?

Making Choices About Resources

Which sweater to buy? How many hours to study? Which restaurant to go to? If you are like most people, you constantly face decisions because you don't have enough time and money to do everything. Economics is the study of how people make choices when they face a limited supply of resources.

The study of economics begins with the idea that people cannot have everything they need and want. A need is something like air, food, or shelter. A want is an item that we would like to have but that is not necessary for survival. Because people cannot have everything they need or want, they must consider their choices and decide how best to fill their needs.

As an individual, you have to decide what to do with your time and money. Businesses have to decide how many people to employ and how much to produce. A city government may have to decide whether to spend its budget to build a park or a library.

Trade-offs and Opportunity Costs

When people make decisions, they face trade-offs because they choose one course of action over another. A person who chooses one item gives up other opportunities. The thing a person gives up is called the opportunity cost. Suppose you have to choose between sleeping late or getting up early to study for a test. The opportunity cost of extra study time is less sleep.

Review Questions

1. What is economics?
2. Define trade-off and opportunity cost.

Scarcity

Why Must People Make Choices?

People have to make choices because of scarcity. Scarcity is the term used to explain that there are not enough resources to meet everyone's wants or needs. One person may be able to buy hundreds of bicycles or guitars, but no one can have an unlimited supply of everything. At some point, a limit is reached. Scarcity always exists because our needs and wants are always greater than our resource supply.

Meeting Basic Needs
Agriculture allowed early Native Americans to grow and store food for survival.

Meeting Needs and Wants

Until modern times, people mostly focused on resources related to agriculture to meet their needs and wants. They farmed the land to produce food, mainly for their own use. This traditional way of meeting basic needs still exists in some countries today. However, modern societies have also developed other economic systems to deal with increased trade and industry. An economic system is the method used by a society to produce and distribute goods and services.

Review Questions

1. What is scarcity?

2. How does scarcity cause people to make choices?

Objectives

- Understand scarcity, in terms of using resources to meet demand for needs and wants.
- Learn what an economic system is.

Building Background Knowledge

Ask students to list several needs and wants. Write student answers on the board, and divide answers into two columns, according what is a need, and what is a want. Discuss how economic systems attempt to meet these needs and wants.

Instruction

Have students review a time period of excessive scarcity, such as the Jamestown and Plymouth Colonies, or the Great Depression. Ask: **How did individuals or governments address the lack of resources during these times?** Ask: **Did these individuals succeed in meeting people's needs and wants?**

Review Questions

1. Scarcity is the term used to describe the limited amount, or lack of resources that must meet people's needs or wants.

2. Scarcity forces people to choose which want or need they should fulfill due to a lack of resources. If there were unlimited resources, meeting wants and needs would be easier.

Objectives

- Learn what the three key economic questions are.
- Understand the difference between producers and consumers.

Building Background Knowledge

Ask students to think about how people meet their needs. Ask: **Where do the food, clothes, and shelter we need to survive come from?** Ask: **Who produces the things we need?**

Instruction

Have students review the three key economic questions, as well as the follow up questions provided in the chart. Ask students how they think their community or country should answer the three key economic questions. Discuss student answers. (*Possible answer: We should spend more money for education*).

Review Questions

1. Goods include any item that can be bought or sold, including clothes and food. Services are activities people do for others, including teaching, firefighting, or working in government.

2. Student answers may vary, though understanding key values of the U.S. economy would include understanding the importance of efficiency and economic freedom.

Basic Economic Questions

Through its economic system, society answers three key questions. 1) What goods and services should be produced? 2) How should goods and services be produced? 3) Who consumes the goods and services? Goods are objects, such as cars and clothes. Services are actions that people do for others, such as teaching. Producers make and sell goods and services. Consumers buy and use goods and services.

How a society answers these three questions shows what economic goals it values and shapes its economic system.

Three Key Economic Questions		
What goods and services should be produced?	How should goods and services be produced?	Who consumes the goods and services?
How much of our resources should we devote to national defense, education, public health, or consumer goods? Which consumer goods should we produce?	Should we produce food on large corporate farms or on small family farms? Should we produce electricity with oil, nuclear power, coal, or solar power?	How do goods and services get distributed? The question of who gets to consume which goods and services lies at the very heart of the differences between economic systems. Each society answers the question of distribution based on its combination of social values and goals.

Economic Goals	
Economic efficiency	Making the most of resources
Economic freedom	Freedom from government intervention in the production and distribution of goods and services
Economic security and predictability	Assurance that goods and services will be available, payments will be made on time, and a safety net will protect individuals in times of economic disaster
Economic equity	Fair distribution of wealth
Economic growth and innovation	Innovation leads to economic growth, and economic growth leads to a higher standard of living.
Other goals	Societies pursue additional goals, such as environmental protection.

Review Questions

1. List examples of both goods and services.

2. Which economic goals are most valued in the U.S.?

Modern Economic Systems

As you read on page 651, an economic system is the method a society uses to produce and distribute goods and services. Four different economic systems have developed as societies attempt to answer the three economic questions according to their goals. This table provides information about the main economic systems in the world today.

Modern Economic Systems

	Description	Origin	Location Today
Traditional	People make economic decisions based on custom or habit. They produce what they have always produced and just as much as they need, using long-established methods.	Accompanied the rise of agriculture and home crafts	Mainly in rural areas within developing nations
Market (Capitalist, Free-Enterprise)	Economic decisions are made in the marketplace through interactions between buyers and sellers according to the laws of supply and demand. Individuals own the means of production. Government regulates some economic activities and provides such "public goods" as education.	Capitalism has existed since the earliest buying and selling of goods in a market. The market economic system developed in response to Adam Smith's ideas and the shift from agriculture to industry in the 1800s.	Australia, Canada, Japan, United States, and a handful of other nations
Centrally Planned (Command, Socialist, Communist)	Central government planners make most economic decisions for the people. In theory, the workers own the means of production. In practice, the government does. Some private businesses, but government is in control.	In the 1800s, criticism of capitalism by Karl Marx and others led to calls for distributing wealth according to need. After the 1917 Russian Revolution, the Soviet Union developed the first command economy.	Communist countries, including Cuba, North Korea, Venezuela and Vietnam
Mixed (Social Democratic, Liberal Socialist)	A system with markets in which the government plays an important role in making economic decisions.	The Great Depression of the 1930s ended laissez-faire capitalism in most countries. People insisted that government take a stronger role in fixing economic problems. The fall of communism in Eastern Europe in the 1990s ended central planning in most countries. People insisted on freer markets.	Most nations, including Brazil, France, India, Italy, Poland, Russia, and Sweden

Objectives

- Learn about the four modern economic systems and where these systems exist.
- Learn how each system attempts to answer the three key economic questions.

Building Background Knowledge

Students may not understand the relationship between a country's government and how that country answers the three key economic questions. Review major countries on a world map with students and identify the types of government of each country, and give examples —through historic or current events—to compare the differences between two or more countries.

Instruction

Ask each student to read the description, origin and location of one modern economic system. Ask students to describe how their assigned economy, whether traditional, centrally planned, market, or mixed, answers the three key economic questions. Locate countries with these economies on a world map and identify how these differences affect the daily lives of citizens in each country.

Objectives

■ Learn what a market is and its basic function.

■ Understand the relationship between producers and consumers in a market economy.

Building Background Knowledge

Ask students to give examples of when they have bought or sold goods. Discuss how when buying or selling, students are part of a market, an arrangement where goods—needs and wants—can be exchanged. Discuss the similarities between a student's personal example of a market and larger, more complex examples, such as the stock market (the buying and selling of investments in companies), or the employment market.

Instruction

Refer students to "The Debt Problem," and "Hamilton's Financial Plan," found on pages 284 and 285, or the graph, "Unemployment, 1933-1941," found on page 797. Discuss how government activity can affect the market of the United States. Ask: **What effect can government decisions have on markets?** Ask: **How can events which seem to have no relationship to the economy affect markets?**

Review Questions

1. Markets exist in order to provide needs and wants people would, or could not provide for themselves. Markets exchange the goods and services produced.

2. In a free market, consumers and producers determine the kind of goods and services are created, sold and bought.

The Market Economy

Individuals Buy and Sell

What do a crafts fair, a music store, and the New York Stock Exchange all have in common? All are examples of markets. A market is an arrangement that allows buyers and sellers to exchange things.

Markets exist because none of us can make, or produce, all we require to satisfy our needs and wants. You probably didn't grow the wheat used to make the cereal you had for breakfast. Instead, you purchased your cereal at a store, which is an example of a market. Markets allow us to exchange the things we have for the things we want.

In a market system, people and businesses have the freedom to make, to sell, and to buy what they want. Producers choose what to make and sell. Consumers decide what goods and services to buy. In other words, individuals answer the three key economic questions that you learned about on page 652. It is an efficient system because producers make only what buyers want, when they want it, and generally at prices they are willing to pay.

New York Stock Exchange

Review Questions

1. Why do markets exist?

2. In a free market, who decides what to make, to sell, and to buy?

Centrally Planned Economies

The Government Decides

In a centrally planned economy, the central government alone answers the key economic questions. Centrally planned economies are sometimes called command economies because a central authority is in command of the economy. It owns all resources and decides what is produced and at what price things will be sold.

The government in centrally planned economies tries to encourage faster economic growth and more equal distribution of goods and services. Economic growth means there is an increase in production and people are spending more money.

Often, the government has a hard time making a plan that will meet these goals. There is no competition among sellers and producers do not keep the profit if they make better products. As a result, producers do not try to improve their products, and consumers must accept poorly made merchandise.

Centrally planned economies mostly exist in countries with a communist form of government, such as North Korea and the former Soviet Union. In communist countries, the government controls both economic and political decisions. Individual freedoms are limited.

Decision Making in a Centrally Planned Economy

Limited amount of cotton
↓
Government decides producers should make more uniforms than sweaters
↓
Less cotton goes to sweater factories | More cotton goes to uniform factories
↓ | ↓
Fewer sweaters for consumers | More uniforms for soldiers

Review Questions

1. In a centrally planned economy who makes the important economic decisions?

2. **Diagram Skills** How does the government's decision affect consumers and soldiers?

Objectives

- Learn what a centrally planned, or command economy is.
- Understand how centrally planned economies try to encourage economic growth, as well as the drawbacks of a centrally planned economy.

Building Background Knowledge

Discuss the origins and goals of the command, or centrally planned economy, as well as the appeal of distributing wealth according to need. Give examples of modern countries that operate under a command economy. Ask: **Why would the idea of distributing wealth according to need appeal to so many?**

Instruction

Write the following quotation on the board from John Adams, second president of the United States, speaking against the Stamp Act in 1765:

"We have called this a burdensome tax, because the duties are so numerous and so high, and the embarrassments to business…so great, that it would be totally impossible for the people to subsist under it."

Have students discuss the ideological differences between this statement and the goals of centrally planned economies, which determine how wealth should be distributed.

Review Questions

1. In a centrally planned economy, the central government determines how key economic questions will be answered.

2. By deciding how a limited resource will be used, the government determines the availability of sweaters for consumers. In this example, the government places more value on military uniforms than in providing goods for consumers.

Economics Handbook

Objectives

- Learn what mixed economies are.
- Understand the relationship between the market and the government in a mixed economy.

Building Background Knowledge

Ask students to think about the services the U.S. government provides to its citizens. Ask: **Were these services always available to U.S. citizens?** Ask: **Has the level of government involvement changed over time?**

Instruction

Discuss Franklin Roosevelt's New Deal program as an example of increased government participation in the economy.

Ask: **What parts of the New Deal legislation are still in effect today?** Ask: **How do services of the U.S. government provides compare to other countries?** *(Possible answer: Canada provides some form of health insurance to its citizens, while the U.S. allows competition between private companies in providing health insurance.)*

Review Questions

1. A mixed economy involves both a market economy and some government involvement. In a mixed economy, the government may provide funding or services for defense, education and public roads.

2. Student answers will vary, depending on their research. Students should explain the government's reasoning behind the government recall.

Mixed Economies

Government Helps the Economy

No country has an economy that is strictly a free market or a command economy. Most economies are actually market economies, with some level of government involvement. This is called a mixed economy. While most areas of the economy may be free, the government may step in to provide certain goods and services. In a mixed economy, the government generally provides defense, education, and public roads.

Review Questions

1. Describe a mixed economy.

2. In a mixed economy, the government enforces safety standards. If a product is found to be unsafe, the government requires that the product be recalled, or removed from stores. Do research on the Internet to identify two products that have been recalled in the last year. Explain the reasons for the recalls.

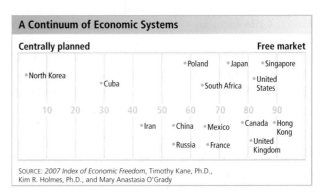

A Continuum of Economic Systems

SOURCE: *2007 Index of Economic Freedom,* Timothy Kane, Ph.D., Kim R. Holmes, Ph.D., and Mary Anastasia O'Grady

How Involved Is the Government?

As you read on page 653, the economic systems of the nations around the world vary greatly. The chart above shows the continuum or range of economic systems in the world. The countries on the left side of the diagram have a large amount of government involvement in the economy. The countries on the right have less government involvement in the economy. Compared to most other countries, the United States has an economy with little government involvement and a great deal of economic freedom. Its system is called a free enterprise system.

Economics at Work

Factors of Production

Now that you are familiar with the different economic systems that exist, it is important to understand how producers make decisions about resources and how the marketplace works.

All the resources that are used to make all goods and services are called factors of production. As the diagram below shows, there are three types: land, labor, and capital. Because resources are scarce, societies try to make the most of the resources they have to work with. When societies use resources efficiently, the economy grows. Efficiency means an economy is using resources in such a way as to maximize the production of goods and services.

The Marketplace

In a local market, goods and services are exchanged among people who live within a smaller community such as a town or city. Over the years, however, technology and improved transportation systems have allowed producers to exchange goods with people who live across the world. As you will read on the next page, the relationship between sellers and buyers help decide how much to produce and at what price.

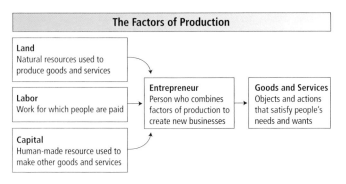

The Factors of Production

Land Natural resources used to produce goods and services

Labor Work for which people are paid

Capital Human-made resource used to make other goods and services

Entrepreneur Person who combines factors of production to create new businesses

Goods and Services Objects and actions that satisfy people's needs and wants

Entrepreneurs are individuals who take risks to develop new ideas and start businesses. Their efforts help the economy grow.

Review Questions

1. **Diagram Skills** What are the three types of resources used to make goods and services?

2. Why is it important to use resources efficiently?

3. How has technology and transportation changed the marketplace?

Objectives

- Learn about the factors of production and the importance of efficiency.
- Understand the relationship between factors of production, entrepreneurs, and the distribution of goods and services in the marketplace.

Building Background Knowledge

Ask students to think about how the goods they buy were made. Ask: **What materials were used to make the clothes they wear?** Ask: **Where were the clothes they wear made?**

Instruction

Have students read a recent article from a newspaper or periodical on the economic growth of China or India. Ask: **What factors of production are most important in enabling these countries to produce a large number of goods?** Ask students to compare the United States to China or India in terms of the goods each country produces, and the factors of production available to each country.

Review Questions

1. The three types of resources used to create goods and services are land, labor and capital.

2. Using resources efficiently allows for the maximum production of goods and services. Because resources are limited, it is in the interest of producers and consumers to use resources in a way that is not wasteful.

3. Technology allows goods and services to be exchanged over greater distances. People who have access to technology are less limited by geography, in terms of what they can buy or sell.

Objectives

■ Understand the relationship between the price of a good and demand for that good.

■ Learn about the relationship between consumers and demand for goods.

Building Background Knowledge

Discuss why people buy more of a good when a company offers that item or service at a discount. Provide examples to begin discussion.

Instruction

Ask students to think of something that they would like to purchase. List student examples on the board. List the approximate costs of each student example and discuss whether students would be willing to pay the approximate cost. Discuss how the price they, as consumers, are willing to pay influences the final price of a good or service.

Review Questions

1. The relationship between price and consumer demand is such that as price increases, demand for an item will go down. As the price for an item decreases, the demand for that item will increase.

2. At $ .50 per slice of pizza, there will be demand for 250 slices per day.

Consumer Demands

Producers make decisions about how to use resources, but consumers decide which goods to buy and use. Economists use the term **demand** to describe the ability and desire of consumers to buy a good.

In a market system, buyers demand goods and sellers supply those goods. Both buyers and sellers help to set prices through their interactions. For example, more people will buy a slice of pizza if it costs $1 than if it costs $10. As the price of an item increases, people will buy less of it. As the price goes down, people will buy more of the same item. Buying more when prices are low, and buying less when prices are high is called the **law of demand**.

When fewer people buy pizza because the price is too high, economists say that the quantity demanded of pizza has dropped. When prices drop and people buy more, they say the quantity demanded of pizza has increased.

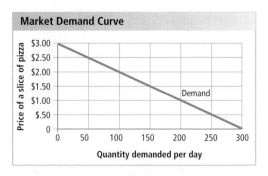

Market Demand Curve

Economists use a line graph to show how price and the demand for a good relate to each other. Because quantity demanded increases as prices decrease, the line on the graph above slopes down to the right.

Review Questions

1. What is the relationship between price and consumer demand?

2. According to the graph, at $.50 per slice, what is the demand for pizza per day?

The Supply of Goods and Services

When demand for a good increases, the price rises. In order to make more money, companies will supply more of the good or service as prices increase. Supply is the amount of goods available in the marketplace. When prices rise, other companies might begin producing the good because they also want to make money. As a result, there is a greater supply of the good available to consumers. If the price of a good decreases, companies will produce less and some companies may stop selling the good completely. The law of supply states that producers will offer more of a good if prices rise, and less of a good if prices fall.

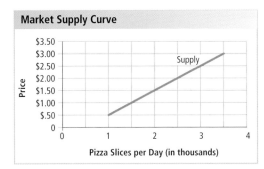

Market Supply Curve

The line on a supply graph will always rise from left to right. The line shows that higher prices lead to higher production. If the price of a slice of pizza is $2.00, all the pizzerias in a city will produce 2,500 slices.

Review Questions

1. According to the law of supply, what happens to the quantity of goods produced if prices fall?

2. Graph Skills According to the graph, how many slices of pizza will be produced if the cost per slice is $1.00?

Objectives

■ Learn about the law of supply.
■ Understand the relationship between the quantity of a good and the price of that product or service.

Building Background Knowledge

Discuss the limited supply of a new, popular video game, or video game system. Ask: **How much does new technology cost in comparison to older technology?** Ask: **Why do companies produce a limited number of video games, or video game systems?**

Instruction

Relate the law of supply to the previous discussion of demand for goods or services. Ask: **How are supply and demand related?** Ask: **How do companies adjust the quantity of goods produced to maximize profit?**

Review Questions

1. According to the law of supply, if prices fall, the quantity of goods produced will also decline.

2. If the cost per slice of pizza is $1.00, there will be 1,500 slices produced per day.

Objectives

- Learn about the efficient distribution of resources between countries.
- Understand the incentive to specialize in production of a good or service.

Building Background Knowledge

Ask students to identify goods (food, clothes, etc.) manufactured or harvested in your area. Ask: **Why is your region well suited to produce these goods?**

Instruction

Refer students to "Geography of New England," Chapter 3, Section 2, or to "Why Industry Boomed," in Chapter 18, Section 1. Discuss how geography and the availability of resources create markets specific to certain regions. Ask: **Why do some regions specialize in providing certain goods?**

Why Nations Trade

Making the Best Use of Resources

As you have read, markets exist because people cannot produce all we require to satisfy our needs and wants. This is true of nations, as well.

Countries produce different goods and services because they have different resources. They focus on certain products that they can make easily and cheaply. For example, coffee can be grown easily in warm areas like Central America, so it is inexpensive to produce there. If Canadians wanted to produce coffee, however, they would have to grow it in greenhouses, which would be more difficult and costly. Because countries cannot efficiently produce everything their citizens need and want, they engage in trade. By specializing or focusing on the production of certain goods and services, nations make the best use of their resources.

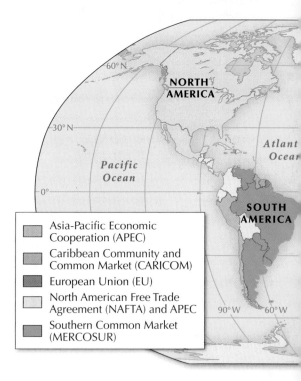

Asia-Pacific Economic Cooperation (APEC)

Caribbean Community and Common Market (CARICOM)

European Union (EU)

North American Free Trade Agreement (NAFTA) and APEC

Southern Common Market (MERCOSUR)

Nations Work Together

Trading among nations is an exchange of goods and services in an international market. It has played an important role in the U.S. economy. Free-trade zones help encourage trade among nations. A free-trade zone is a region where a group of countries agree to reduce or eliminate tariffs, or taxes on imported goods. These agreements make trading less expensive.

The North American Free Trade Agreement (NAFTA) was developed to eliminate all fees and other trade barriers between Canada, Mexico, and the United States. Supporters of NAFTA say the agreement increases trade between the countries. Approximately 100 trading organizations like NAFTA operate throughout the world today.

Major Trade Organization Members

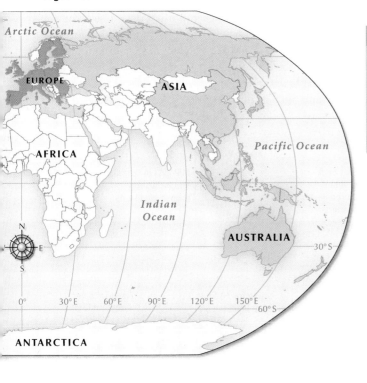

Review Questions

1. How does trade help societies meet their needs and wants?

2. How do countries join together to encourage economic growth for all?

Objectives

- Learn about the elimination of tariffs as a means to encourage trade between economies.

- Learn about the North American Free Trade Agreement as one trade organization, established to encourage trade between Canada, the United States, and Mexico.

Building Background Knowledge

On the board, list the three countries (Canada, Mexico, United States) included in the North American Free Trade Agreement (NAFTA). Have students list goods they think might be produced in each country (Mexico exports: fruits, vegetables, coffee, cotton; Canada exports: crude petroleum, fertilizers, forest products, natural gas, and aluminum; United States exports: soybeans, fruit, corn, motor vehicle parts, computers) and discuss how each country's exports benefit the countries that are a part of NAFTA.

Instruction

Discuss the pros and cons of trade. Refer students to "Hamilton's Financial Plan," Chapter 8, Section 1, or to "A World Linked by Trade," Chapter 29, Section 2. Ask: **Why do countries impose tariffs?** Ask: **Are there circumstances when it is better to reduce or eliminate tariffs?**

Review Questions

1. Trade helps a society meet its needs and wants by providing a way to acquire goods and services efficiently and cheaply.

2. Countries work together to encourage economic growth by creating free trade zones through the elimination of tariffs, which increases trade between countries.

Objectives
- Learn about free enterprise in the American economy..
- Learn about the government's involvement in the U.S. economy through its fiscal policy.

Building Background Knowledge

Have students think of people they know, or figures in history who have pursued economic opportunity through opening a business, moving to a new country, or moving to a different area within the same country. Discuss the meaning of free enterprise and how student examples reflect the exercise of free enterprise.

Instruction

Refer students to Chapter 18, Section 2, "Big Business and Organized Labor" or "The American Industrial Revolution," in Chapter 11, Section 1. Ask: **What are the drawbacks to free enterprise?** Ask: **How did the drawbacks of free enterprise change the government's role in the economy?**

The American Economy

A Tradition of Free Enterprise

The United States economy encourages free enterprise, which means people are allowed to try out their business ideas and compete in the free market. Its vast land, resources, and many people who are willing to work have all contributed to economic growth in the United States.

The free market has helped the economy in the United States, but the government set up the foundation for economic success. Government laws, such as those protecting the right to private property and enforcing contracts, help Americans profit from free enterprise. The Constitution also specifies limits on how government can tax, and it prohibits government from interfering in business contracts. Federal and state agencies regulate industries whose goods and services affect the well-being of the public.

The Government's Role in the Economy

The federal government also makes important decisions about the economy by setting fiscal policy. Fiscal policy means that the government decides how to both collect money and spend money in the best interest of the economy. Government officials debate about raising or cutting taxes and about how much should be spent on specific programs such as defense, education, and welfare.

Key Events in American Economic History

| 1791 First Bank of the United States chartered | 1834 Mill girls in Lowell, Massachusetts, protest wage cuts | 1867 Knights of Labor formed |

1750　　　　　1800　　　　　1850

| 1835 Strike for 10-hour workday in Philadelphia | 1869 Financial panic sweeps nation |

662 Reference Section

Americans often argue about the proper balance of government involvement in the economy. Some people want more government services, while others say that the government already intervenes too much in the economy.

Sometimes government fiscal policy decisions bring gradual shifts or changes to an established system. For example, in the United States during the Great Depression many new federal programs changed the role of the government in the American economy. With the New Deal, the federal government moved away from *laissez faire*, or leaving the economy alone. Instead, the federal government took specific actions to improve the economy.

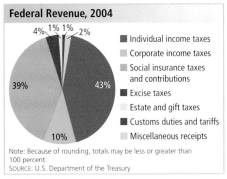

Federal Revenue, 2004

- 4%
- 1% 1%
- 2%
- 43%
- 39%
- 10%

- ■ Individual income taxes
- ■ Corporate income taxes
- ■ Social insurance taxes and contributions
- ■ Excise taxes
- ■ Estate and gift taxes
- ■ Customs duties and tariffs
- ■ Miscellaneous receipts

Note: Because of rounding, totals may be less or greater than 100 percent.
SOURCE: U.S. Department of the Treasury

This graph shows the revenue sources or sources of money in the governments budget.

Review Questions

1. Describe the economic system of the United States.

2. **Graph Skills** What are the largest sources of the U.S. Government's income?

3. What are two ways the government encourages economic growth in the U.S. economy?

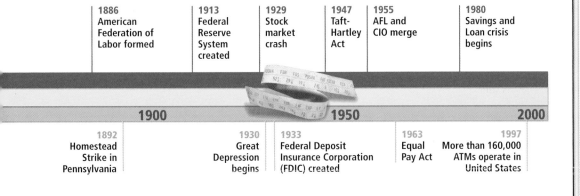

| 1886 American Federation of Labor formed | 1913 Federal Reserve System created | 1929 Stock market crash | 1947 Taft-Hartley Act | 1955 AFL and CIO merge | 1980 Savings and Loan crisis begins |

1900 **1950** **2000**

| 1892 Homestead Strike in Pennsylvania | 1930 Great Depression begins | 1933 Federal Deposit Insurance Corporation (FDIC) created | 1963 Equal Pay Act | 1997 More than 160,000 ATMs operate in United States |

Economics Handbook **663**

Objectives

- Continue to learn about the role of government in the U.S. economy, particularly in contrast to laissez faire.

Building Background Knowledge

Discuss the beginnings of laissez faire in the United States, starting with the Jefferson Administration (Chapter 9, Section 1, under "Jefferson Charts a New Course"), and how the policy of laissez faire changed as a result of the Great Depression. Ask: **How did people come to see the government's role in the economy?**

Instruction

Have students list the items, services or programs the government spends money on. Write these on the board and ask students to reach a consensus on how government money should be spent. Compare this to actual government spending figures, which can be found on the U.S. Office of Management and Budget website.

Review Questions

1. The economic system in the United States includes both government involvement, as well as the practice of free enterprise. The government serves as a check on free enterprise, enforcing laws to protect consumers, as well as setting limits on government involvement. The government, through tax collection and spending, has a great influence on the overall economy.

2. The U.S. Government derives most of its income from individual income taxes and social insurance contributions.

3. The government can take an active part in promoting job growth, as with the New Deal, and it encourages free enterprise, allowing businesses to compete in the open marketplace.

Objectives

- Learn about tools economists use to measure the American economy.
- Understand the role of the Federal Reserve, including its analysis of the Gross Domestic Product and the rate of inflation.

Building Background Knowledge

Students may not understand the purpose of monetary policy. Review the "Causes and Effects" of the Great Depression in Chapter 23, Section 4. By drawing relationships between the causes and effects in this chart, explain to students why the government has an interest in managing the economy. Ask: **How might a widening gap between rich and poor Americans hurt the economy?**

Instruction

Have students collect information from a newspaper or periodical that discusses the Federal Reserve, interest rates, inflation, or monetary policy in the United States. Ask: **How does the U.S. government regulate the economy?** Ask: **How does raising or lowering interest rates, for example, affect regular people? What does raising or lowering interest rates do to the overall economy?**

Review Questions

1. Monetary policy is the collection of decisions intended to manage economic growth.

2. Economists study the Gross Domestic Product—the total dollar value of goods produced in a country—as well as the rate of inflation which is the general increase in prices.

Economics Handbook

Measuring the Economy

The Federal Reserve or Fed is the central banking system of the United States. It functions as a bank for other banks and for the federal government. The Fed is responsible for monetary policy, which means it makes decisions that help to manage the growth of the economy. The Fed attempts to encourage economic growth by controlling the money supply, availability of credit, and interest rates.

Monetary policy is based on careful study of economic indicators including the rate of inflation and the Gross Domestic Product (GDP). These factors help economists predict changes in the economy.

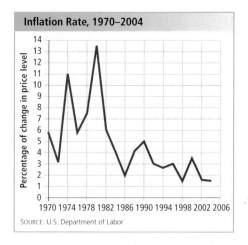

Inflation Rate, 1970–2004

SOURCE: U.S. Department of Labor

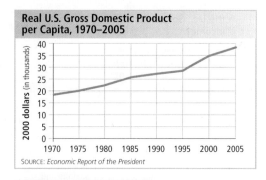

Real U.S. Gross Domestic Product per Capita, 1970–2005

SOURCE: *Economic Report of the President*

Review Questions

1. What is monetary policy?

2. What factors do economists study to measure the economy?

Inflation is a general increase in prices. In a period of inflation, as prices rise, the same amount of money buys less. As a result, people cannot afford to buy as many goods and services.

The GDP is the total dollar value of goods produced in a country. The GDP grows when more goods and services are being produced. If consumers spend less, fewer goods and services will be produced and the GDP decreases.

The strength of the economy can also be measured by how much people are saving and investing. When you save money, it doesn't just stay in the bank. Banks use your saved money to make loans to businesses. This investment helps the economy grow.

English and Spanish Glossary

The glossary defines all high-use words and many key historical words and terms. The high-use words appear underlined the first time that they are used in the text. The key words and terms appear in blue type the first time that they are used. Each word in the glossary is defined in both English and Spanish. The page number(s) after the English definition refers to the page(s) on which the word or phrase is defined in the text. For other references, see the index.

Pronunciation Key

When difficult names or terms first appear in the text, they are respelled to help you with pronunciation. A syllable printed in small capital letters receives the greatest stress. The pronunciation key below lists the letters and symbols that will help you pronounce the word. It also includes examples of words using each of the sounds and shows how each word would be pronounced.

Symbol	Example	Respelling
a	hat	(hat)
ay	pay, late	(pay), (layt)
ah	star, hot	(stahr), (haht)
ai	air, dare	(air), (dair)
aw	law, all	(law), (awl)
eh	met	(meht)
ee	bee, eat	(bee), (eet)
er	learn, sir, fur	(lern), (ser), (fer)
ih	fit	(fiht)
ī	mile	(mīl)
ir	ear	(ir)
oh	no	(noh)
oi	soil, boy	(soil), (boi)
oo	root, rule	(root), (rool)
or	born, door	(born), (dor)
ow	plow, out	(plow), (owt)

Symbol	Example	Respelling
u	put, book	(put), (buk)
uh	fun	(fuhn)
yoo	few, use	(fyoo), (yooz)
ch	chill, reach	(chihl), (reech)
g	go, dig	(goh), (dihg)
j	jet, gently bridge	(jeht), (JEHNT lee), (brihj)
k	kite, cup	(kīt), (kuhp)
ks	mix	(mihks)
kw	quick	(kwihk)
ng	bring	(brihng)
s	say, cent	(say), (sehnt)
sh	she, crash	(shee), (krash)
th	three	(three)
y	yet, onion	(yeht), (UHN yuhn)
z	zip, always	(zihp), (AWL wayz)
zh	treasure	(TREH zher)

A

abolitionist (a boh LIH shuhn ihst) person who wanted to end slavery (p. 423)
abolicionista persona que quería abolir la esclavitud

accommodation (ak kom moh DAY shuhn) adjustment; adaptation (p. 501)
acomodo ajuste; adaptación

accumulate (uh KYOOM yoo layt) to collect slowly; to increase in amount over time (p. 81)
acumular reunir lentamente; aumentar una cantidad con el tiempo

adobe (uh DOH bee) sun-dried, unburned brick made of clay and straw (p. 12)
adobe seco al sol, ladrillo no quemado hecho de arcilla y paja

alien (AY lee ihn) outsider; someone from another country (p. 300)
extranjero persona que no pertenence a un grupo; persona de otro país

alliance (ah LĪ ans) agreement between nations or groups to aid and support one another (pp. 57, 141, 183)
alianza convenio entre países por el que se comprometen a ayudarse y apoyarse mutuamente

ally (AL eye) a person joined with another for a common purpose (p. 429)
aliado una persona ensambló con otra para un propósito común

alter (AWL ter) to change; to make different (p. 315)
alterar cambiar; hacer algo diferente

alternative (awl TUR nuh tiv) providing a choice between two or among more than two things (p. 19)
alternativa opción de escoger entre dos o más cosas

amend (ah MEHND) to change or revise (p. 264)
enmendar cambiar o revisar

amendment (ah MEHND mehnt) revision or addition to a bill, law, or constitution (p. 221)
enmienda revisión o adición a un proyecto de ley, ley o constitución

amnesty (AM nehs tee) government pardon (p. 547)
amnistía indulto que otorga el gobierno

annex (an NEHKS) to add on or take over (p. 456)
anexar agregar o apoderarse de algo

appeal (ah PEEL) to ask that a court decision be reviewed by a higher court (p. 262)
apelar pedir que una decisión de un tribunal sea revisada por un tribunal superior

appeasement (uh PEEZ mehnt) policy of giving into aggression in order to avoid war (p. 591)
apaciguamiento política de consentir la agresión para evitar la guerra

apprentice (uh PREHN tihs) person who learns a trade or craft from a master (p. 110)
aprendiz persona que aprende un oficio o destreza de un maestro

aristocratic (uh ris tuh KRAT ik) of an aristocracy or upper class (p. 311)
aristocrático de la aristocracia o clase alta

B

backcountry (bak KUHN tree) frontier region located along the eastern slope of the Appalachian Mountains (p. 81)
backcountry región fronteriza ubicada a lo largo de la ladera oriental de los montes Apalaches

bill (bihl) proposed law (p. 259)
proyecto de ley ley propuesta

bill of rights (bihl uhv rīts) written list of freedoms that a government promises to protect (p. 103)

declaración de derechos lista escrita de las libertades que un gobierno se compromete a proteger

black codes (blak kohds) southern laws that severely limited the rights of African Americans after the Civil War (p. 553)
códigos negros leyes sureñas que limitaron severamente los derechos de los afroamericanos después de la Guerra Civil

blockade (BLAHK ayd) shutting a port or roadway to prevent people or supplies from coming into or leaving an area (pp. 161, 328, 515)
bloqueo cierre de un puerto o camino para impedir que entren o salgan personas o provisiones en cierta zona

bond (bahnd) certificate issued by a government for a certain amount of money that the government promises to pay back with interest (p. 284)
bono certificado emitido por un gobierno por cierta cantidad de dinero que el gobierno promete devolver con intereses

border state (BOR der stayt) slave state that remained in the Union during the Civil War (p. 513)
estado fronterizo estado esclavista que permaneció en la Unión durante la Guerra Civil

borderland (BOR der land) land along a frontier (p. 91)
tierra limítrofe tierra a lo largo de una frontera

boycott (BOI kaht) organized campaign to refuse to buy or use certain goods and services (p. 147)
boicot campaña organizada para rehusar comprar o usar ciertos bienes y servicios

C

canal (kah NAHL) artificial waterway dug across land to improve transportation (p. 403)
canal vía navegable artificial excavada a lo largo de un terreno para mejorar el transporte

capitalism (KA piht ahl ihz uhm) economic system in which people put money, or capital, into a business or project in order to make a profit later on; economic system in which privately owned businesses compete in a free market (p. 344)

capitalismo sistema económico en el que las personas invierten dinero (capital) en un negocio o proyecto para obtener ganancias más adelante; sistema económico en el que los negocios de propiedad privada compiten en un mercado libre

capitalist (KA piht ahl ihst) person who invests capital, or money, in a business to earn a profit (p. 383)
capitalista persona que invierte capital (dinero) en un negocio para obtener ganancias

carpetbagger (KAHR peht BAG er) uncomplimentary nickname for a northern white who went to the South after the Civil War to start a business or pursue a political career (p. 555)
carpetbagger sobrenombre despreciativo dado a los norteños blancos que se mudaron al Sur después de la Guerra Civil para emprender un negocio o seguir una carrera política

casualty (KA su ahl tee) military term for a person killed, wounded, or missing in action (p. 520)
baja término militar que describe a una persona muerta, herida o desaparecida en combate

caucus (KAW kuhs) private meeting of members of a political party (p. 352)
reunión de comité encuentro privado de los integrantes de un partido político

cavalry (KAV uhl ree) units of troops on horseback (p. 183)
caballería unidades de tropas a caballo

cease (sees) to stop; to come to an end (p. 296)
cesar detenerse; llegar a su fin

cede (seed) to give up (pp. 144, 345, 457)
ceder entregar

censorship (SEHN sor shihp) the power to review, change, or prevent the publication of news (p. 267)
censura poder de revisar, cambiar o evitar la publicación de noticias

charter (CHAHR ter) official document that gives certain rights to an individual or a group (pp. 67, 342)
carta de privilegio documento oficial que confiere ciertos derechos a un individuo o grupo

checks and balances (chehks and BAL an sez) a principle of the U.S. Constitution that gives each branch of government the power to check, or limit, the actions of the other branches (p. 257)
control y equilibrio principio de la Constitución de Estados Unidos que otorga a cada rama del gobierno el poder de controlar o limitar las acciones de las otras ramas

circumnavigate (ser kuhm NAV ih gayt) to travel all the way around Earth (p. 40)
circunnavegar hacer un recorrido completo alrededor de la Tierra

citizen (SIHT ih zehn) person who owes loyalty to a particular nation and is entitled to all its rights and protections (p. 270)
ciudadano persona que debe lealtad a una determinada nación y que tiene derecho a recibir todos sus derechos y protecciones

civil disobedience (SIHV ihl dih soh BEE dee ehns) idea based on nonviolence that people have a right to disobey a law they consider unjust, if their consciences demand it (p. 433)
desobediencia civil idea de que las personas tienen derecho, sin usar la violencia, a desobedecer una ley que consideren injusta, si su conciencia así lo exige

civil war (SIHV ihl wor) war between people of the same country (p. 503)
guerra civil guerra entre habitantes de un mismo país

civilian (suh VIHL yuhn) person not in the military (p. 187)
civil persona que no pertenece a las fuerzas armadas

civilization (sihv uh luh ZAY shuhn) advanced culture in which people have developed cities, science, and industries (p. 8)
civilización cultura avanzada en la cual la gente ha desarrollado ciudades, la ciencia y la industria

clan (klan) group of families that are related to one another (p. 15)
clan grupo de familias que están relacionadas entre sí

clarify (KLAIR ih fī) to make the meaning of something clear (p. 497)
aclarar explicar el significado de algo

Cold War   **culture**

Cold War (kohld wor) after World War II, long period of intense rivalry between the Soviet Union and the United States (p. 592)
guerra fría después de la Segunda Guerra Mundial, largo período de intensa rivalidad entre la Union Soviética y Estados Unidos

compromise (KAHM proh mīz) agreement in which each side gives up part of what it wants to end a disagreement (p. 214)
acuerdo compromiso por el que cada una de las partes renuncia a una parte de lo que desea con el fin de acabar con una desavenencia

confine (kuhn FĪN) to keep within certain limits; to shut or imprison (p. 188)
confinar mantener dentro de ciertos límites; encerrar o encarcelar

conquistador (kahn KWIHS tuh dor) conqueror, especially one of the sixteenth-century Spanish soldiers who defeated the Indian civilizations of Mexico, Central America, or Peru (p. 44)
conquistador persona que conquista, especial- mente uno de los soldados españoles del siglo XVI que derrotaron a las civilizaciones indígenas de México y América Central o Perú

constitution (kahn stih TYOO shuhn) document in which the laws, principles, organization, and pro- cesses of a government are established (p. 204)
constitución documento que establece las leyes, principios, organización y procedimientos de un gobierno

consume (kuhn SYOOM) to use up (p. 600)
consumir usar

continental (kahn tihn EHN tuhl) paper money printed during the American Revolution (p. 188)
continental forma de papel moneda impreso durante la Guerra de la Independencia

continental divide (kahn tihn EHN tuhl dih VĪD) mountain ridge that separates river systems flowing toward opposite sides of a continent (p. 318)
divisoria continental cadena montañosa que separa sistemas fluviales que corren hacia lados opuestos de un continente

contract (KAHN trakt) agreement between two or more parties that can be enforced by law (p. 344)

contrato convenio entre dos o más partes que se puede hacer valer por ley

contrast (KAHN trast) difference shown between things when compared (pp. 89, 214)
contraste diferencia que se manifiesta entre dos cosas cuando son comparadas

controversy (KAHN truh vur see) argument or dispute (p. 483)
controversia discusión o disputa

convert (kuhn VERT) to change from one purpose or function to another; to change from one political party or religion to another (pp. 91, 415, 591)
convertir cambiar de un propósito o función a otro; cambiar de un partido político o de una religión a otra

corduroy road (KOR der oi rohd) road made of sawed-off logs, laid side by side (p. 403)
camino de troncos camino hecho de troncos aserrados y colocados uno al lado de otro

corporation (kor por AY shuhn) business owned by many investors (p. 578)
compañía empresa que es propiedad de muchos inversionistas

cotton gin (KAHT tuhn jihn) machine that removed seeds from cotton fibers (p. 396)
despepitadora de algodón máquina que servía para quitar las semillas a las fibras de algodón por medio de un cilindro de madera con púas

coureur de bois (koo REHR duh BWAH) French term for "runner of the wood" (p. 54)
coureur de bois término francés para "corre- dor del bosque" o contrabandista de pieles

crisis (KRĪ sihs) turning point or deciding event; situation involving great risk (p. 484)
crisis momento crucial o acontecimiento decisivo; una situación que implica un gran riesgo

critic (KRIHT ihk) someone who makes judgments about objects or actions (pp. 331, 553)
crítico persona que hace juicios sobre objetos o acciones

culture (KUHL cher) way of life (p. 10)
cultura forma de vida

culture area (KUHL cher AIR ee uh) region in which groups of people have a similar way of life (p. 11)
área cultural región en la cual grupos de personas tienen una forma de vida similar

currency (KER rehn see) money used to make purchases (pp. 11, 531)
moneda dinero que se usa para realizar compras

D

dame school (daym skool) school run by a woman, usually in her own home (p. 119)
escuela de señoritas escuela administrada por una mujer, generalmente en su propia casa

debtor (DEH tor) person who cannot pay his or her debts (p. 87)
deudor persona que no puede pagar sus deudas

decade (DEK ayd) a period of ten years (p. 456)
década un período de diez años

decline (dee KLĪN) to lose strength or power over a period of time (pp. 54, 324)
decaer perder fuerza o poder a lo largo de cierto tiempo

deprive (dee PRĪV) to keep from happening; to take away something needed by force or intent (pp. 7, 487)
privar impedir que suceda; tomar por la fuerza o con intención algo que se necesita

deregulation (dee rehg yuh LAY shuhn) reduction of federal or state restrictions on businesses (p. 597)
desregulación reducción de las restricciones federales o estatales sobre los negocios

détente (day TAHNT) policy to reduce tension between two countries (p. 598)
détente política de reducir las tensiones entre las superpotencias

devise (dee VĪZ) to carefully think out; to invent (p. 206)
idear hacer planes cuidadosamente; inventar

devote (dee VOHT) to commit; to apply time and energy (p. 397)
dedicar comprometer; destinar tiempo y energía

dictatorship (dihk TAY tor shihp) government in which one person or a small group holds complete authority (pp. 252, 455)
dictadura gobierno en el que una persona o un grupo pequeño ejerce una autoridad total

direct democracy (dir EHKT deh MAH kra see) system of government in which ordinary citizens have the power to govern (p. 24)
democracia directa sistema de gobierno en el que los ciudadanos comunes tienen poder para gobernar

discrimination (dihs krihm ihn AY shuhn) denial of equal rights or equal treatment to certain groups of people (p. 395)
discriminación negación de igualdad de derechos o de un tratamiento igualitario a ciertos grupos de personas

dissent (dihs SEHNT) disagreement (p. 267)
disensión desacuerdo

dissolve (dih ZAHLV) to break up into smaller parts (p. 365)
disolver separar en partes más pequeñas

distinct (dihs TIHNKT) clear or definite; clearly different in its quality (pp. 12, 446, 514)
distinto claro o definido; que difiere claramente en cuanto a su calidad

divine right (dih VĪN rīt) belief that a ruler's authority comes directly from God (p. 122)
derecho divino creencia en que la autoridad de un gobernante proviene directamente de Dios

domestic (doh MEHS tihk) having to do with the home or household; pertaining to a country's internal affairs (pp. 108, 348)
doméstico relacionado con la casa o el hogar; relativo a los asuntos internos de un país

dominant (DAHM uh nunt) dominating; ruling; prevailing (p. 315)
dominante que domina, rige, o prevalece

dominate (DAHM uh nayt) to rule or control (p. 578)
dominar regir o controlar

draft (draft) system of required military service (p. 530)
leva sistema del servicio militar obligatorio

dumping (DUHMP ing) selling goods in another country at very low prices (p. 342)

inundación de mercado venta de productos en otro país a precios muy bajos

duration (doo RAY shun) length of time (p. 300)
duración un tiempo determinado

duty (DOOT ee) import tax (p. 146)
aranceles impuestos a las importaciones

E

economic depression (eh koh NAH mihk dee PREH shuhn) period when business activity slows, prices and wages drop, and unemployment rises (p. 208)
depresión económica período en el que la actividad comercial disminuye, los precios y los salarios bajan y el desempleo aumenta

efficient (ee FISH ehnt) acting effectively, without wasted cost or effort (pp. 386, 463)
eficiente que actúa con eficacia, sin desperdiciar costos ni esfuerzos

emancipate (ee MAN sih payt) to set free (p. 524)
emancipar liberar

embargo (ehm BAHR goh) government order that forbids foreign trade (p. 324)
embargo orden gubernamental que prohíbe el comercio exterior

embrace (ehm BRAYS) to accept; to hold tight to; to readily accept (p. 496)
abrazar aceptar; aferrarse a; aceptar sin dificultad

emotion (ee MOH shuhn) strong feeling such as sadness, anger, or love (pp. 214, 432)
emoción sentimiento intenso; por ejemplo, tristeza, ira o amor

emotional (ee MOH shuh nuhl) appealing to the emotions, or feelings, of people (p. 147)
emocional relativo a las emociones o sentimientos de la gente

emphasis (EM fuh sis) special importance or significance (p. 341)
énfasis importancia o significado importante

emphasize (EM fuh syz) to stress; to make more important (p. 297)
recalcar destacar; dar más importancia

encomienda (ehn koh mih EHN dah) land granted to Spanish settlers that included the right to demand labor or taxes from Native Americans (p. 147)
encomienda terreno otorgado a los colonos españoles, que incluía el derecho a exigir trabajo o impuestos de los indígenas americanos

encounter (ehn KOWN ter) to meet in an unexpected way; to experience (p. 534)
tropezar con encontrar de modo inesperado; experimentar

enlist (ehn LIHST) to sign up for military duty (p. 187)
enlistarse inscribirse para el servicio militar

environment (en VY run munt) surroundings (p. 449)
entorno lo que rodea

establish (uh STAB lish) to set up, found (p. 67)
establecer instituir, fundar

exceed (ehks SEED) to go beyond what is expected or planned (p. 535)
exceder ir más allá de lo esperado; superar lo proyectado

exclude (ehks KLOOD) to keep out or expel; to reject or not be considered (p. 428)
excluir mantener fuera o expulsar; rechazar o no considerar

executive (ehks ZEHK yoo tihv) in government, person who runs the government and sees that the laws are carried out (p. 205)
ejecutivo en un gobierno, persona que dirige el gobierno y hace cumplir las leyes

expansion (ehks PAN shuhn) extending of a nation beyond its existing borders (p. 447)
expansión acto de extender un país más allá de sus fronteras existentes

expedition (ehks peh DIH shuhn) journey undertaken by a group of people with an objective (p. 317)

expedición viaje que emprende un grupo de personas con un objetivo concreto

extended family (ehks TEHN dehd FAM ih lee) close-knit family group that includes parents, children, grandparents, aunts, uncles, and cousins (p. 107)
familia extensa grupo familiar unido que incluye a los padres, hijos, abuelos, tías, tíos y primos

F

faction (FAK shuhn) organized political group (p. 290)
facción grupo político organizado

factor (FAK tor) condition or quality that causes something else to happen (p. 45)
factor condición o cualidad que provoca que ocurra algo distinto

factory system (FAK tor ee SIHS tehm) methods of production that bring workers and machinery together in one place (p. 383)
sistema de fábricas métodos de producción que reúnen trabajadores y maquinaria en un mismo lugar

famine (FAM ihn) widespread starvation (p. 394)
hambruna escasez generalizada de alimentos

fateful (FAYT ful) having important consequences; decisive (p. 192)
fatídico de graves consecuencias; decisivo

federalism (FEHD er uhl ihz uhm) principle of the U.S. Constitution that establishes the division of power between the federal government and the states (p. 257)
federalismo principio de la Constitución de Estados Unidos que establece la división de poderes entre el gobierno federal y los estados

feudalism (FYOOD uhl ihz uhm) system in which a ruler grants parts of his land to lords in exchange for military service and financial assistance (p. 25)
feudalismo sistema en el cual el gobernante otorga parte de su tierra a los señores a cambio de servicio militar y ayuda financiera

finance (FĪ nans) to pay for; to supply with money (p. 120)
financiar pagar por algo; proveer dinero

flexible (FLEHKS ah bahl) capable of change (p. 221)
flexible capaz de cambiar

forty-niner (FOR tee NĪ ner) person who came to California in search of gold (p. 464)
los del cuarenta y nueve personas que vinieron a California en busca de oro

fragment (FRAG mehnt) broken part or piece; small section of something (p. 501)
fragmento parte rota o pieza de algo; sección pequeña de algo

freedmen (FREED mehn) men and women who were legally freed from slavery after the Civil War (p. 548)
libertos hombres y mujeres liberados jurídicamente de la esclavitud después de la Guerra Civil

freedom of the press (FREE duhm uhv thuh prehs) right of newspapers and other public media to publish articles believed to be accurate (p. 105)
libertad de prensa derecho de los diarios y otros medios públicos de comunicación a publicar artículos cuyo contenido consideran como cierto

frontier (fruhn TIR) land that forms the furthest extent of a nation's settled regions (p. 444)
frontera territorio que constituye la extensión más lejana de las regiones establecidas de un país

fugitive (FYOO jih tihv) runaway (p. 484)
fugitivo persona que huye

function (FUHNK shuhn) purpose; proper use; official duty (p. 91)
función propósito; uso adecuado; responsabilidades que conlleva un cargo

fundamental (fuhn duh MEHN tahl) most important part; foundation of an idea or action; the essential quality (pp. 78, 293)
fundamental lo más importante; la base de una idea o acción; la cualidad esencial

G

gentry (JEHN tree) upper class of colonial society (p. 110)
alta burguesía clase alta de la sociedad colonial

glacier (GLAY sher) thick sheet of ice (p. 6)
glaciar gruesa capa de hielo

grandfather clause (GRAND fah ther klawz) law that excused a voter from a literacy test if his father or grandfather had been eligible to vote on January 1, 1867 (p. 560)
cláusula del abuelo ley que eximía a un votante de la prueba de alfabetización si su padre o abuelo había tenido derecho a votar el 1 de enero de 1867

grievance (GREE vans) formal complaint (p. 172)
querella queja formal

guerrilla (guh RIHL uh) fighter who works as part of a small band to make hit-and-run attacks (p. 191)
guerrillero combatiente dentro de un pequeño grupo que realiza ataques relámpago

H

habeas corpus (HAY bee ihs KOR puhs) the right not to be held in prison without first being charged with a specific crime; constitutional protection against unlawful imprisonment (pp. 104, 252, 529)
habeas corpus derecho a no ser encarcelado sin antes haber sido acusado de un delito específico; protección constitucional contra el encarcelamiento ilegal

hostile (HAHS tihl) unfriendly; intending to do harm (pp. 291, 449)
hostil poco amistoso; que se propone hacer daño

I

impeachment (ihm PEECH mehnt) process of bringing formal charges against a public official (p. 556)
juicio político proceso que consiste en presentar una acusación formal contra un funcionario público

impose (ihm POHZ) to place a burden on something or someone (pp. 285, 490)
imponer colocar una carga sobre algo o alguien

impressment (ihm PREHS mehnt) practice of seizing sailors on American ships and forcing them to serve in the British navy (pp. 296, 388)
leva práctica de obligar a una persona a prestar servicio militar; captura de marineros de navíos estadounidenses para obligarlos a servir en la armada británica

impulse (IHM puhls) sudden push or driving force; sudden action; driving force behind an action (p. 415)
impulso empujón repentino o fuerza motriz; acción repentina; la fuerza motriz detrás de una acción

inauguration (ihn awg er AY shuhn) ceremony in which the President officially takes the oath of office (p. 283)
toma de mando ceremonia en la que el presidente hace el juramento propio de su cargo

incident (IN suh dunt) happening; occurrence (p. 151)
incidente acontecimiento; suceso

income tax (IHN kuhm taks) tax on the money people earn or receive (p. 531)
impuesto a los ingresos impuesto sobre el dinero que la gente gana

indentured servant (ihn DEHN cherd SER vehnt) person who signs a contract to work for a set number of years in exchange for ocean passage to the colonies (p. 111)
sirviente contratado persona que firma un contrato para trabajar durante un número determinado de años a cambio de un pasaje oceánico a las colonias

individual (in duh VIJ oo ul) of, for, or by a single person or thing (p. 205)
individual de, para o por una sola persona o cosa

individualism (ihn dih VIHD yoo uhl ihz uhm) concept that stresses the importance of each individual (p. 432)
individualismo concepto que hace hincapié en la importancia de cada individuo

Industrial Revolution (ihn DUHS tree uhl rehv oh LYOO shuhn) gradual replacement of many hand tools by machines (p. 382)
Revolución Industrial sustitución gradual de muchas herramientas manuales por máquinas

inferior (ihn FIR ee uhr) less worthy; less valuable; of lower rank; of poorer quality (pp. 395, 561)
inferior menos digno; menos valioso; de categoría más baja; de menor calidado

inflation (ihn FLAY shuhn) general rise in prices (p. 531)
inflación aumento generalizado de los precios

infrastructure (IHN frah struhk cher) basic public works needed for a society to function, including the systems of roads, bridges, and tunnels (p. 343)
infraestructura obras públicas básicas necesarias para el funcionamiento de una sociedad, como los sistemas de carreteras, puentes y túneles

interchangeable parts (ihn ter CHAYNJ ah buhl pahrts) identical pieces that can be assembled quickly by unskilled workers (p. 386)
partes intercambiables piezas idénticas que pueden ser ensambladas con rapidez por trabajadores no calificados

interest group (IHN trehst groop) organization that represents the concerns of a particular group (p. 271)
grupo de intereses organización que representa los asuntos que conciernen a un grupo en particular

interstate commerce (IHN ter stayt KAHM mers) trade between two or more states (p. 344)
comercio interestatal intercambio comercial entre dos o más estados

invest (ihn VEHST) to purchase something with money with the hope that its value will grow; to supply money for a project in order to make a profit (pp. 284, 383, 587)
invertir adquirir algo a cambio de dinero con la esperanza de que su valor aumente; facilitar dinero para un proyecto para que dé ganacias

ironclad (Ī ern klad) warship covered with protective iron plates (p. 518)
acorazado barco de guerra cubierto con placas protectoras de hierro

irrigate (IR uh gayt) to water crops by channeling water from rivers or streams (p. 7)
irrigar regar los cultivos canalizando el agua de los ríos o arroyos

isolate (Ī soh layt) to set apart; to separate (p. 503)
aislar apartar; separar

isolated (Ī soh lay tehd) set apart; separated (p. 403)
aislado apartado; separado

isolationism (Ī soh LAY shuhn ihz uhm) avoiding involvement in other countries' affairs (p. 587)
aislacionismo práctica de evitar la participación en los asuntos de otros países

J

judicial branch (jyoo DIH shuhl branch) system of courts to settle disputes involving national issues (p. 213)
poder judicial sistema de tribunales para dirimir pleitos referentes a cuestiones nacionales

judicial review (jyoo DIH shuhl ree VYOO) principle that the Supreme Court has the right to decide whether acts of Congress are constitutional or not (p. 313)
revisión judicial principio según el cual la Corte Suprema tiene derecho a decidir si los actos del Congreso son constitucionales

jurisdiction (jer ihs DIHK shuhn) power of a court to hear and decide cases (p. 262)
jurisdicción potestad de un tribunal para conocer y resolver sobre casos

K

kayak (KĪ ak) boat consisting of a light wooden frame covered with watertight skins and propelled by a double-bladed paddle (p. 12)

kayac bote que consta de una ligera estructura de madera cubierta de pieles impermeables a excepción de una única o doble abertura en el centro, y que se impulsa por medio de un remo de dos paletas

L

laissez faire (LAY seh fair) idea that government should not interfere in the economy (p. 311)
laissez faire idea de que el gobierno no debe entrometerse en la economía

land grant (land grant) government gift of land (p. 446)
concesión de tierras donación de tierras por parte del gobierno

legislature (LEHJ ihs lay cher) part of a government that makes laws (p. 103)
legislatura parte de un gobierno que se encarga de elaborar leyes

levy (LEHV ee) to impose a tax by law; to force to be paid (pp. 104, 531)
gravar imponer una contribución por ley; obligar a que se pague

libel (LĪ behl) publishing of false statements that unjustly damage a person's reputation (pp. 105, 267)
libelo publicación de afirmaciones falsas que dañan injustamente la reputación de una persona

limited government (LIHM ih tehd GUHV ern mehnt) the principle that the government has only the powers that the Constitution gives it (p. 256)
gobierno limitado el principio de que el gobierno tiene únicamente los poderes que la Constitución le otorga

literacy test (LIH ter ah see tehst) examination to see if a person can read and write; used in the past to restrict voting rights (p. 560)
prueba de alfabetización examen para establecer si una persona sabe leer y escribir, se usaba en el pasado para restringir el derecho al voto

logic (LAH jihk) reason; good sense; careful thought (p. 171)
lógica razón; buen juicio; reflexión cuidadosa

M

martial law (MAHR shuhl law) type of rule in which the military is in charge and citizens' rights are suspended (p. 513)
ley marcial tipo de gobierno en el que los militares están al mando y se suspenden los derechos de los ciudadanos

mass production (mas proh DUHK shuhn) manufacturing of large numbers of identical products quickly and cheaply (p. 386)
producción en masa manufactura rápida y a bajo costo de un gran número de productos idénticos

mercantilism (MER kan tihl ihz uhm) economic policy that held that a nation prospered by exporting more goods to foreign nations than it imported from them (p. 50)
mercantilismo principio económico según el cual una nación prospera exportando más bienes a países extranjeros que los que importa de ellos

mercenary (MER sehn air ee) soldier who fights merely for pay, often for a foreign country (pp. 161, 181)
mercenario soldado que combate tan sólo por una paga, casi siempre en favor de un país extranjero

middle class (MIHD uhl klas) a portion of the colonial population that included small planters, independent farmers, and skilled craftsworkers (p. 111)
clase media en las 13 colonias, parte de la población colonial que incluía a los pequeños cultivadores, a los granjeros independientes y a los artesanos

militia (mih LIH shah) organized body of armed volunteers (p. 140)
milicia cuerpo organizado de voluntarios armados

minimize (MIHN ah mīz) to reduce to the lowest possible amount (p. 580)
reducir al mínimo disminuir a la cantidad más pequeña posible

minimum (MIHN ah muhm) smallest amount possible or allowed (p. 146)
mínimo cantidad más pequeña posible o permitida

minuteman (MIHN uht man) colonial militia volunteer who was prepared to fight at a minute's notice (p. 152)
miliciano de la Guerra de Independencia voluntario de la milicia colonial que estaba siempre preparado para luchar

mission (MIHSH uhn) religious settlement run by Catholic priests and friars; settlement that aims to spread a religion into a new area (p. 47)
misión colonia religiosa administrada por sacerdotes católicos y frailes; asentamiento cuya finalidad es diseminar la religión en una nueva zona

monopoly (muhn AH poh lee) company that controls all or nearly all business in a particular industry (pp. 151, 578)
monopolio compañía que controla toda o casi toda la actividad de una industria en particular

monotheism (MAHN oh thee ihz uhm) belief that there is only one god (p. 22)
monoteísmo creencia de que solamente hay un dios

motive (MOH tihv) thought or feeling behind an action (p. 55)
motivo pensamiento o sentimiento detrás de una acción

mountain man (MOWN tehn man) fur trapper of the Northwest (p. 449)
hombre de montraña cazador de pieles del Noroeste

myth (mihth) story or legend; imaginary object; invented story (p. 37)
mito cuento o leyenda; objeto imaginario; relato inventado

N

nationalism (NA shuhn uhl ihz uhm) devotion to the interests of one's own country; pride in one's own nation or ethnic group (p. 327)
nacionalismo lealtad a los intereses del propio país; orgullo respecto a la propia nación o grupo étnico

nativist (NAY tihv ihst) person who was opposed to immigration (p. 394)
nativista persona que buscaba reservar Estados Unidos para los protestantes blancos nacidos en el país, y que se oponía a la inmigración

natural rights (NA cher uhl rīts) rights that belong to every human being from birth (p. 122)
derechos naturales derechos de los que goza todo ser humano desde el momento de su nacimiento

naturalization (na cher uhl ih ZAY shuhn) legal process guaranteeing citizenship (p. 270)
naturalización procedimiento jurídico que garantiza la ciudadanía

navigation (nav uh GAY shuhn) science of locating the position and plotting the course of ships (p. 19)
navegación ciencia de ubicar la posición y de trazar el trayecto de los barcos

negative (NEHG ah tihv) in opposition to an idea; not positive (p. 41)
negativo opuesto a una idea; no positivo

neutral (NEW truhl) not favoring either side in a dispute (pp. 295, 513)
neutral que no favorece a ninguna de las partes en un pleito

nominating convention (NAHM ih nay ting kuhn VEHN shuhn) large meeting of party delegates to choose candidates for office (p. 352)
convención de postulación gran encuentro de delegados de un partido para elegir candidatos a un cargo

northwest passage (NORTH wehst PAS saj) water route through or around North America (p. 51)
paso del noroeste ruta navegable a través o alrededor de América del Norte

nullification (nuhl ih fih KAY shuhn) idea that a state has the right to nullify, or cancel, a federal law that the state leaders consider to be unconstitutional (p. 364)
anulación idea de que un estado tiene derecho a anular o cancelar una ley federal que los dirigentes del estado consideran inconstitucional

nullify (NUHL ih fī) to cancel a federal law; to deprive of legal force (p. 301)
anular cancelar una ley federal; privar de fuerza jurídica

O

occupy (AHK yoo py) take possession of (p. 158)
ocupar tomar posesión o apoderarse de algo

on margin (ohn MAHR jehn) practice that allows people to buy stock with a down payment of a portion of the full value (p. 587)
con margen práctica que permite a las personas comprar acciones abonando una entrada del diez por ciento del valor total

option (AHP shuhn) choice; possible course of action (p. 192)
opción elección; posible manera de actuación

override (OH ver rīd) set aside; disregard; overrule; replace (p. 259)
invalidar dejar de lado; no tener en cuenta; no admitir; sustituir

P

participate (pahr TIHS ah payt) to take part in; to share in an activity (pp. 24, 351)
participar tomar parte en algo; compartir una actividad

peninsular (peh nihn suh LAR) Spanish colonist who was born in Spain (p. 48)
peninsular colono español nacido en España

petition (peh TIH shuhn) formal written request to someone in authority that is signed by a group of people (p. 147)
petición solicitud formal por escrito, firmada por un grupo de personas y dirigida a una autoridad

phase (fayz) stage of development (p. 143)
fase etapa de desarrollo

pilgrim (PIHL gruhm) person who takes a religious journey (p. 69)
peregrino persona que emprende un viaje religioso

plantation (plan TAY shuhn) large estate farmed by many workers (pp. 47, 87)
plantación finca grande cultivada por muchos trabajadores

policy (PAHL uh see) plan or course of action, as pursued by a government (p. 446)
política plan o normas a seguir por un gobierno

poll tax (pohl taks) personal tax to be paid before voting (p. 560)
impuesto al voto impuesto personal que debía pagarse para poder votar

polygamy (poh LIHG ah mee) practice of having more than one wife at a time (p. 462)
poligamia práctica de tener más de una esposa al mismo tiempo

popular sovereignty (PAH pyoo lahr SAH ver ehn tee) principle that asserts that people are the primary source of the government's authority; right of people to vote directly on issues (pp. 256, 483)
soberanía popular derecho de los habitantes de un territorio o estado a votar directamente sobre ciertas cuestiones en vez de que sus representantes electos decidan

potlatch (PAHT lach) ceremony held by some Native American groups at which the hosts showered their guests with gifts such as woven cloth, baskets, canoes, and furs (p. 12)
potlach ceremonia realizada por algunos grupos de indígenas americanos en la cual los anfitriones agasajaban a sus huéspedes con regalos como tejidos, cestas, canoas y pieles

preamble (PREE am buhl) introduction to a declaration, constitution, or other official document (p. 172)
preámbulo introducción a una declaración, constitución u otro documento oficial

precedent (PREH seh dehnt) example to be followed by others in the future (p. 283)
precedente ejemplo a seguir por otros en el futuro

precise (pree SĪS) exact; accurate (p. 27)
preciso exacto; acertado, certero

predestination (pree dehs tihn AY shuhn) idea
that God decides the fate of a person's soul
even before birth (p. 415)
predestinación idea de que Dios decide el
destino del alma de una persona incluso antes
de su nacimiento

preliminary (pree LIM uh nehr ee) leading up to
the main action (p. 525)
preliminar preámbulo a la acción principal

presidio (prih SIHD ee oh) military post where
soldiers lived in the Spanish colonies (p. 92)
presidio puesto militar donde vivían los soldados en las colonias españolas

private property (PRĪ veht PRAH per tee) property owned by an individual (p. 252)
propiedad privada propiedad que pertenece a
una persona

privateer (prī vuh TEER) armed civilian ship that
had the government's permission to attack
enemy ships and keep goods seized (p. 190)
corsario barco civil armado con el permiso del
gobierno para atacar a los barcos enemigos y
quedarse con los bienes capturados

prohibition (proh ih BIH shuhn) total ban on the
sale and consumption of alcohol (p. 416)
ley seca prohibición total de la venta y
consumo de alcohol

propaganda (prah peh GAN dah) false or misleading information that is spread to further a
cause; information used to sway public opinion
(p. 488)
propaganda información falsa o engañosa que
se difunde para apoyar una causa; información
usada para influir en la opinión pública

proprietary colony (proh PRĪ eh tair ee KAHL uhn
ee) English colony in which the king gave land
to one or more proprietors, or owners, in
exchange for a yearly payment (p. 78)
colonia de propietarios colonia inglesa donde
el rey concedía tierras a uno o más propietarios
o dueños a cambio de un pago anual

proprietor (proh PRĪ ah tor) owner of a business
or colony (p. 86)
propietario dueño de una empresa o colonia

prospect (PRAHS pehkt) expectation; something to
look forward to happening (pp. 110, 464)

prospecto expectativa; algo que se desea
que ocurra

province (PRAHV ahns) governmental division
of a country, similar to a state (pp. 51, 346)
provincia división gubernamental de un país,
semejante a un estado

provoke (prah VOHK) to cause to anger; to excite;
to cause an action (pp. 301, 457)
provocar incitar al enojo; excitar; dar lugar
a una acción

public school (PUHB lihk skool) school supported
by taxes (pp. 118, 417)
escuela pública escuela financiada con
impuestos

pueblo (PWEHB loh) town in the Spanish colonies;
Anasazi village (p. 93)
pueblo asentamiento en las colonias españolas;
aldea anasazi

pursue (per SYOO) to chase after; to try to capture
(p. 402)
perseguir ir tras de algo; tratar de capturar

Q

quote (kwoht) to repeat the exact words spoken
or written (p. 357)
citar repetir las palabras exactas habladas o
escritas

R

racism (RAY sihz uhm) belief that one race is
superior or inferior to another (p. 116)
racismo creencia de que una raza es superior o
inferior a otra

radical (RAD ih kul) favoring fundamental or
extreme change (pp. 423, 599)
radical que favora cambio fundamental o
extreme

ranchero (ran CHAIR oh) owner of a ranch (p. 446)
ranchero dueño de un rancho

ratify (RAT ih fī) to approve (pp. 218, 264)
ratificar aprobar

react (ree AKT) to act in response to an action;
to respond (pp. 152, 350)

reaccionar actuar en respuesta a una acción; responder

register (REJ is tur) enroll or record officially (p. 555)
registrar inscribir o anotar oficialmente

reign (rayn) period of dominance or rule (p. 393)
reinado período de dominación o gobierno

reinforce (ree ihn FORS) to strengthen; to make more effective (pp. 122, 328, 519)
reforzar fortalecer; hacer más eficaz

rendezvous (RAHN day voo) yearly meeting where trappers would trade furs for supplies (p. 449)
rendezvous encuentro anual en el que los tramperos intercambiaban pieles por provisiones

repeal (ree PEEL) to cancel (pp. 152, 255)
revocar cancelar

representative government (reh pree SEHN tah tihv GUHV ern mehnt) political system in which voters elect others to make laws (p. 69)
gobierno representativo sistema político en el que los votantes eligen a otras personas para que elaboren las leyes

reproduce (ree prah DOOS) to make a copy (p. 435)
reproducir hacer una copia

republic (ree PUHB lihk) system of government in which the people choose representatives to govern them (pp. 25, 252)
república sistema de gobierno en el que la gente elige representantes que los gobernarán

require (rih KWYR) to order or command (p. 560)
requerir ordenar o mandar

reservation (reh zer VAY shuhn) area set aside by the government for Native Americans to live on (p. 577)
reservación territorio que el gobierno destina a ser habitado por indígenas americanos

reside (ree ZĪD) to live in; to dwell for a while; to exist in (p. 8)
residir vivir en algún lugar; habitar por un tiempo; existir

resolution (rehz uh LOO shuhn) formal statement of opinion or policy (p. 171)
resolución declaración formal de una opinión o política

resolve (ree SAHLV) strong determination; *also* to decide; to solve (pp. 143, 364, 548)

resolver decidir; dar solución

resource (REE sors) supply of something to meet a particular need (pp. 188, 514)
recurso abasto de algo que satisface una necesidad en particular

restore (ree STOR) to bring back to a normal state; to put back; to reestablish (pp. 50, 158, 326, 589)
restaurar devolver a una condición normal; reponer; restablecer

restrict (ree STRIHKT) to confine; to keep within a certain boundary or limit; to place limitations on something or somebody (p. 75)
restringir confinar; mantener dentro de ciertas fronteras o límites; poner limitaciones a algo o alguien

retain (rih TAYN) to keep (p. 103)
retener mantener

revenue (REV uh noo) the income from taxes, licenses, etc., as of a city, state, or nation (p. 312)
ingreso utilidad de impuestos, licencias, etc., de la ciudad, estado o la nación

revival (ree VĪ vuhl) huge outdoor religious meeting (p. 415)
reunión evangelista encuentro religioso de grandes proporciones al aire libre

revolt (ree VOHLT) uprising; rebellion; to rebel (pp. 116, 400)
revuelta sublevación; rebelión

rigid (RIH jihd) strict; not easily bent or changed (p. 48)
rígido estricto; que no se dobla o cambia con facilidad

royal colony (ROI uhl KAHL uh nee) colony under direct control of the English crown (p. 78)
colonia real colonia bajo control directo de la corona inglesa

S

sachem (SAY chuhm) member of the tribal chief council in the League of the Iroquois (p. 15)
sachem (representante en tiempo de paz) miembro del consejo del jefe tribal de la Liga de los iroqueses

salvation (sal VAY shuhn) in Christianity, the means for saving one from evil; everlasting afterlife (p. 23)
salvación en la cristiandad, la manera para librarse del mal; la vida eterna

satellite (SAT uh lyt) a small state that is economically or politically dependent on a larger, more powerful state (p. 592)
satélite un estado pequeño dependiente económicamente y políticamente de un estado más grande y poderoso

scalawag (SKAL eh wag) southern white who had opposed secession (p. 555)
scalawag blanco sureño que se oponía a la secesión

secede (seh SEED) to withdraw from membership in a group (pp. 331, 484)
separarse retirarse como miembro de un grupo

sedition (seh DIH shuhn) stirring up of rebellion against a government (p. 300)
sedición acto de fomentar la rebelión contra un gobierno

segregation (sehg reh GAY shuhn) enforced separation of races (p. 560)
segregación separación obligada de dos razas

self-government (sehlf GUHV ern mehnt) right of people to rule themselves independently (p. 348)
autogobierno derecho de las personas a gobernarse a sí mismas de forma independiente

separation of powers (seh pahr AY shuhn uhv POW ers) principle by which the powers of government are divided among separate branches (pp. 123, 253)
separación de poderes principio por el cual los poderes del gobierno se dividen entre sus distintas ramas

sharecropper (SHAIR krah per) person who rents a plot of land and farms it in exchange for a share of the crop (p. 561)
aparcero persona que alquila un terreno y lo cultiva a cambio de una parte de la cosecha

siege (seej) military blockade or bombardment of an enemy town or position in order to force it to surrender (pp. 455, 535)

sitio cerco militar o bombardeo de una población o posición enemiga a fin de obligarla a rendirse

slave code (slayv kohd) laws that controlled enslaved African Americans' lives and denied them basic rights (pp. 116, 399)
código de la esclavitud una de un grupo de leyes que regulaban la vida de los esclavos afroamericanos y les negaban los derechos fundamentales

smuggling (SMUH glihng) act of illegally importing or exporting goods (p. 324)
contrabando importación o exportación ilegal de mercancías

social reform (SOH shuhl ree FORM) organized attempts to improve conditions of life (p. 414)
reforma social intentos organizados de mejorar las condiciones de vida

specify (SPEHS uh fī) to describe or to point out in detail (p. 73)
especificar describir o señalar en detalle

speculator (SPEHK yoo lay tor) person who invests in a risky venture in the hope of making a large profit (p. 284)
especulador persona que invierte en una empresa arriesgada con la esperanza de tener grandes ganancias

sphere (sfeer) rounded shape; area of interest or influence (p. 17)
esfera figura redondeada; zona de interés o influencia

spirituals (SPIR ih chyoolz) religious folk songs that blended biblical themes with the realities of slavery (p. 400)
canto espiritual canto religioso tradicional que combinaba temas bíblicos con las realidades de la esclavitud

spoils system (spoilz SIHS tehm) act of replacing government officials with supporters of a newly elected President (p. 354)
sistema de sinecuras sustitución de funcionarios gubernamentales por partidarios del presidente recién electo

states' rights (stayts rīts) the right of states to limit the power of the federal government (p. 301)

derechos de los estados derecho de los estados a limitar el poder del gobierno federal

strait (strayt) narrow passage that connects two large bodies of water (p. 40)
estrecho travesía estrecha que conecta dos grandes masas de agua

suffrage (SUH frihj) right to vote (pp. 351, 581)
sufragio derecho al voto

superior (suh PIR ee er) of greater importance or value; above average in quality; higher in position or rank (p. 519)
superior de mayor importancia o valor; por encima del promedio en cuanto a calidad; que ocupa una posición o categoría más alta

surplus (SER pluhs) excess; quantity that is left over (p. 7)
superávit excedente; cantidad sobrante

sustain (suh STAYN) to keep going; to support as just (pp. 68, 525)
sostener mantener en marcha; apoyar como justo

T

tariff (TAIR ihf) tax placed on goods entering a country from another country (p. 286)
arancel impuesto con que se gravan las mercancías que entran en un país provenientes de otro

telegraph (TEHL eh graf) invention that allows messages to be sent quickly by sending electrical signals along a wire (p. 391)
telégrafo invento que permite enviar mensajes rápidamente a grandes distancias por medio de señales eléctricas que viajan por un cable

temperance movement (TEHM per ehns MOOV mehnt) organized effort to end alcohol consumption (p. 416)
movimiento por la temperancia esfuerzo organizado en contra del consumo de alcohol

temporary (TEM puh rehr ee) not permanent (p. 115)
temporal que no es permanente

terrorism (TEHR er ihz uhm) deliberate use of violence, often against civilian targets, to achieve political or social goals (p. 599)

terrorismo uso deliberado de la violencia, a menudo en contra de objetivos civiles, con el fin de alcanzar objetivos políticos o sociales

toleration (tahl er AY shuhn) recognition that other people have the right to different opinions (p. 73)
tolerancia reconocimiento de que otras personas tienen el derecho de mantener opiniones distintas

total war (TOH tuhl wor) all-out attacks aimed at destroying not only an enemy's army but also its resources and its people's will to fight (p. 536)
guerra total ataques masivos encaminados a destruir no sólo al ejército enemigo, sino también sus recursos y la voluntad de luchar de la población

totalitarian state (toh tal uh TER ee uhn stayt) nation in which a single party controls the government and every aspect of people's lives (p. 590)
estado totalitario país en el que un sólo partido político controla el gobierno y todos los aspectos de la vida de las personas

town meeting (town MEET ing) meeting in colonial New England during which settlers discussed and voted on issues; form of direct democracy in which residents meet to make decisions for the community (p. 75)
cabildo abierto reunión en la Nueva Inglaterra colonial donde los colonos discutían y votaban sobre sus asuntos; forma de democracia directa en la que los residentes se reúnen para tomar decisiones que conciernen a la comunidad

traitor (TRAY ter) person who betrays his or her country or cause and helps the other side (p. 192)
traidor persona que traiciona a su país

transcendentalism (trans sehn DEHN tuhl ihz uhm) movement that sought to explore the relationship between humans and nature through emotions rather than through reason (p. 432)
trascendentalismo movimiento que se proponía explorar la relación entre los seres humanos y la naturaleza mediante las emociones en vez de la razón

transform (trans FORM) to change in appearance or form; to change the condition of something (p. 183)
transformar cambiar la apariencia o la forma; cambiar la condición de algo

triangular trade (trī ANG yuh ler trayd) three-way colonial trade route between the colonies, the islands of the Caribbean, and Africa (p. 115)
comercio triangular ruta de comercio colonial a tres bandas entre las colonias, las islas del Caribe y África

tribute (TRIH byoot) money paid by one country to another in return for protection (p. 322)
tributo dinero que un país paga a otro a cambio de protección

turnpike (TERN pīk) road built by a private company that charges a toll to use it (p. 402)
camino de peaje camino construido por una compañía privada que cobra una cuota por su uso

U

unconstitutional (uhn kahn stih TOO shuhn uhl) contrary to what is permitted by the U.S. Constitution (pp. 263, 285)
inconstitucional contrario a lo que permite la Constitución de Estados Unidos

urbanization (er ban ihz AY shuhn) movement of large numbers of people from rural areas to cities; rapid growth of city populations (p. 390)
urbanización desplazamiento de un gran número de personas de las zonas rurales a las ciudades; crecimiento rápido de la población de las ciudades

V

veto (VEE toh) to reject, as when the President rejects a law passed by Congress (p. 259)
vetar rechazar, como cuando el Presidente rechaza una ley aprobada por el Congreso

via (VEE ah) by way of (p. 424)
vía paso por algún lugar

vigilante (vihj ihl AN tee) self-appointed law enforcer (p. 465)
vigilante persona que se designa a sí misma para hacer cumplir la ley

violate (VY uh layt) fail to keep or observe; infringe on (p. 172)
violar que no logra adherirse o observar; que infringe

vital (VĪ tuhl) necessary for life; of great importance; spirited; lively (p. 183)
vital necesario para la vida; de gran importancia; lleno de vida; animado

voluntary (VAHL ahn tair ee) not forced; done of one's free will (pp. 357, 547)
voluntario no forzado; hecho por voluntad propia

W

war hawk (wor hawk) one of the members of Congress who called for war with Britain prior to the War of 1812 (p. 327)
halcón de guerra uno de los miembros del Congreso de representantes del Sur y del Oeste que instaban a la guerra con Gran Bretaña antes de la guerra de 1812

water rights (WAW ter rīts) legal right to use water from a body of water (p. 464)
derecho de aguas derecho jurídico a utilizar el agua de un río, arroyo u otra masa de agua con un fin determinado

women's rights movement (WOO mehns rīts MOOV mehnt) organized campaign to win property, education, and other rights for women (p. 429)
movimiento por los derechos femeninos campaña organizada para obtener el derecho a la propiedad, a la educación y otros derechos para la mujer

women's suffrage (WOO mehns SUH frihj) right of women to vote (p. 428)
sufragio femenino derecho de las mujeres a votar

writ of assistance (riht uhv uh SIHS tehns) court order that allowed officials to make undefined searches (p. 148)
auto de asistencia orden judicial que permitía a determinados funcionarios a realizar registros sin tener que revelar lo que andaban buscando

Acknowledgments

Staff Credits

The people who made up the *America: History of Our Nation* team—representing design services, editorial, editorial services, education technology, manufacturing and inventory planning, market research, marketing services, planning and budgeting, product planning, production services, publishing processes, and rights and permissions—are listed below. Boldface type denotes the core team members.

Rosalyn Arcilla, **Nancy Barker,** Harold DelMonte, **Jim Doris, Allen Gold, Shelby Gragg,** Michael Hornbostel, John Kingston, **Doreen Kruk, Marian Manners, Anne McLaughlin,** Michael McLaughlin, Xavier Niz, **Maureen Raymond, Ryan Richards,** Melissa Shustyk, **Rose Sievers, Marc Wezdecki**

Additional Credits

Jennifer Ciccone, Dalia Misevicius, Debi Taffet, Humberto Ugarte, Kristen VanEtten

Map and Art Credits

Maps: Mapping Specialist Limited, except where noted with additional type set by Justin Contursi **Visual Preview Maps** XNR Productions **4-5, 34-35, 64-65, 100-101, 138-139, 168-169, 202-203, 280-281, 308-309, 338-339, 380-381, 412-413, 442-443, 450-451, 480-481, 510-511, 544-545, 574-575 and TLAH Maps 131, 373, 472, 475, 571** Anthony Morse **20, 82, 210, 320-321, 425, 460-461** with additional type set by Artur Mkrtchyan **Illustrated Maps** Anthony Morse **20, 82, 210, 320-321, 425** Kevin Jones Associates **13**

Art: Keithley and Associates, all charts/graphs/instructional art and photo composites except where noted **Illustrations** XNR Productions **4-5, 13, 34-35, 64-65, 100-101, 138-139, 168-169, 202-203, 280-281, 308-309, 338-339, 380-381, 412-413, 442-443, 450-451, 480-481, 510-511, 544-545, 574-575 Timelines** Humberto Ugarte **Instructional Art/Photo Composites** One Visual Mind **13, 38-39, 72-73, 109, 160, 194, 216, 286, 328, 350-351** Kerry Cashman **398-399, 425, 432-433, 450-451, 502, 560-561** Humberto Ugarte **74, 80, 450-451, 452, 588** Justin Contursi **Atlas design and Skills Activity photo treatments** GDPS **All Skills for Life art** Brainworx **210-211, 288-289, 320-321, 341, 420-421, 460-461, 522-523, 550-551**

Every effort has been made to credit all vendors. Any omissions brought to our attention will be corrected in subsequent printings.

Photo Credits

Cover and Title page Getty Images **A-1** Getty Images, Inc.; **A-2 T** Esbin/Anderson/Omni-Photo Communications, Inc.; **A-3 B** Dallas and John Heaton/CORBIS; **A-3 T** AP/Wide World Photos; **A-4 T** Tom & Susan Bean; **A-5 T** Julie Habel/CORBIS; **A-5 B** Marvin Newman; **A-6 T** Grant Heilman Photograph; **A-7 T** Giancarlo de Bellis/Omni-Photo Communications, Inc.; **A-7 B** Bill Ross/CORBIS; **A-10** Larry Downing/Reuters/CORBIS; **A-11** © CORBIS; **A-12 TL** Connie Ricca/CORBIS; **A-12 TR** Smithsonian American Art Museum, Washington, DC/Art Resource, NY; **A-12 B** Bettmann/CORBIS; **A-13 T** Bettmann/CORBIS; **A-13 B** Jay Dorin/Omni-Photo Communications, Inc.; **A-15 T** Anaheim Public Library; **A-15 B** D. Boone/CORBIS; **A-16 TL** © Royalty-Free/Corbis; **A-16 B** © CORBIS; **ii** Jamestown-Yorktown Educational Trust, VA, USA/The Bridgeman Art Library, London/New York; **v** John Guthrie, Guthrie Studios; **vii** The Granger Collection, New York; **viii** Courtesy National Archives; **ix** O.C. Seltzer, Lewis and Clark with Sacagawea, at the Great Falls of the Missouri River, #0137.871. From the Collection of Gilcrease Museum, Tulsa; **x** Collection of The New-York Historical Society, negative no. 26280ON; **xi** AP/Wide World Photos; **xii** © Royalty-Free/Corbis; **HT 01** Omni-Photo Communications, Inc.; **HT 02 L** Courtesy National Archives; **Ht 02 R** Omni-Photo Communications, Inc.; **HT 03** Lawrence Migdale/Pix; **HT 04** © CORBIS/Bettmann; **HT 05** © David Young-Wolff/PhotoEdit inc.; **HT 08 L** David Stoecklein/CORBIS; **HT 08 R** Sime s.a.s./eStock/PictureQuest; **HT 10** Silver Burdett Ginn; **HT 14** Copyright © North Wind/North Wind Picture Archives—All rights reserved; **HT 15** CC Lockwood/Animals Animals; **HT 16** Mary Evans Picture Library; **HT 17** The Granger Collection, New York; **HT 21** KAL/The Baltimore Sun/CartoonArts International/CWS; **HT 23** Brand X Pictures/PictureQuest; **HT 24** © Jeff Greenberg/PhotoEdit Inc.; **0 B** Copyright © North Wind/North Wind Picture Archives—All rights reserved.; **0 T** The Art Archive/Museo de la Torre del Oro Seville/Dagli Orti/The Picture Desk; **01 TR** Jamestown-Yorktown Educational Trust, VA, USA/The Bridgeman Art Library, London/New York; **01 TL** Hair Comb (Seneca Iroquois) late 17th century, carved moose antler, 4 1/2" H (11.4 cm.). From the collections of the Rochester Museum & Science Center, Rochester, New York (RM 2932); **01 B** © CORBIS/Bettmann; **02-03** Tom Bean/CORBIS; **04 B** Jorge Ianiszewski/Art Resource, NY; **04 M** Stock Montage, Inc.; **05 T** The Granger Collection, New York; **05 R** Figure of Shou Lao (jade), Chinese School, (17th century)/Fitzwilliam Museum, University of Cambridge, UK/Bridgeman Art Library; **06** Erich Lessing/Art Resource, NY; **08** Charles & Josette Lenars/CORBIS; **08 Inset** The Granger Collection, New York; **09** Jorge Ianiszewski/Art Resource, NY; **10** Richard Nowitz Photography; **11 R** The Granger Collection, New York; **11 L** Michel Zabe/© Dorling Kindersley; **11 M** Michel Zabe/© Dorling Kindersley; **14** Hair Comb (Seneca Iroquois) late 17th century, carved moose antler, 4 1/2" H (11.4 cm.). From the collections of the Rochester Museum & Science Center, Rochester, New York (RM 2932); **15** The Art Archive/Cherokee Indian Museum North Carolina/Mireille Vautier; **16** Courtesy, Dept. of Library Services, American Museum of Natural History; **17 L** Courtesy of the Freer Gallery of Art, Smithsonian Institution, Washington, D.C.: Purchase, F1946.12, f. 38b; **17 TR** Peter Chadwick/© Dorling Kindersley; **17 BR** Roger Phillips/© Dorling Kindersley; **17 MR** Philip Dowell © Dorling Kindersley; **18** Giraudon/Art Resource, NY; **19** Figure of Shou Lao (jade), Chinese School, (17th century)†/Fitzwilliam Museum, University of Cambridge, UK/Bridgeman Art Library; **20 L** photolibrary.com; **20 R** © Tom Stoddart/Woodfin Camp & Associates; **21 M** The Granger Collection, New York; **21 T** © Markus Matzel/Peter Arnold, Inc.; **21 B** Philip Dowell © Dorling Kindersley; **22** The Granger Collection, New York; **23** Tissot, James Jacques Joseph (1836-1902) Moses and the 10 Commandments c. 1896-1902. Gouache on board. 10 11/16 × 5 5/8". Gift of the Heirs of Jacob Schiff, x1952-190. Photo by John Parnell. The Jewish Museum, New York, NY, U.S.A./Art Resource, NY; **24** Bildarchiv Preussischer Kulturbesitz/Art Resource, NY; **25** AP/Wide World Photos; **26** The Granger Collection, New York; **29** Bildarchiv Preussischer Kulturbesitz/Art Resource, NY; **30** Figure of Shou Lao (jade), Chinese School, (17th century)†/Fitzwilliam Museum, University of Cambridge, UK/Bridgeman Art Library; **31** © Royalty-Free/CORBIS; **32-33** Amos Zemer/Omni-Photo Communications, Inc.; **36** © Bettmann/CORBIS; **37** Ridolfo Ghirlandaio (1483-1561) "Christopher Columbus". Museo Navale di Pegli, Genoa, Italy. Scala/Art Resource, NY.; **38 B** Astrolabe, copper, by Ahmad Ibn Khalaf an Iraqi Arab, 9th century, O_DATA†/†Bibliotheque Nationale de Cartes et Plans, Paris, France/Bridgeman Art Library; **39 R** The Art Archive/Museo de la Torre del Oro Seville/Dagli Orti/The Picture Desk; **39 L** The Art Archive/Marine Museum Lisbon/Dagli Orti; **40 (5)** Corel Professional Photos CD-ROM™; **40 MR** Roger Phillips/© Dorling Kindersley; **42 M** National Gallery Collection; by kind permission of the Trustess of the National Gallery, London/CORBIS; **42 TL** Copyright © North Wind/North Wind Picture Archives—All rights reserved; **43 BL** James Stevenson/© National Maritime Musuem, London, © Dorling Kindersley; **43 M** Mary Evans Picture Library; **43 TR** The Granger Collection, New York; **44** © Bettmann/CORBIS; **45** The Granger Collection, New York; **47** The Granger Collection, New York; **49** © HIP/Art Resource; **50 R** Peter M. Fisher/Corbis; **50 TL** © Dorling Kindersley; **50 B** Bettmann/CORBIS; **51** Queen Elizabeth I playing the lute (miniature) (see also 3912), Hilliard, Nicholas (1547-1619), Berkeley Castle, Gloucestershire, UK/Bridgeman Art Library; **52** Tate Gallery, London/Art Resource, NY; **53** The Granger Collection, New York; **55** The Granger Collection, New York; **56** © Monica Graff/The Image Works; **57** The Granger Collection, New York; **60** Copyright © North Wind/North Wind Picture Archives—All rights reserved; **62-63** © CORBIS/Bettmann; **66** © Jamestown Yorktown Foundation, Williamsburg, VA; **68** State Capitol, Commonwealth of Virginia. Courtesy The Library of Virginia; **69** Courtesy of the Library of Congress. Art © Romare Bearden Foundation/Licensed by VAGA, New York, NY; **70** Head of Squanto (d.1622), an American Indian of the Pawtuxet tribe who became a good friend to the Pilgrims (wood), American School, (17th century)/Private Collection/Bridgeman Art Library; **71** North Wind Picture Archives; **72 B** Courtesy of The Salem Witch Museum, Salem, Massachusetts; **72 TL** Getty Images; **72 TR** Getty Images Inc.–Hulton Archive Photos; **72-73 Bkgrnd** Getty Images/Richard Dobson; **73 R** Courtesy, American Antiquarian Society; **73 L** © CORBIS; **74 TR** North Wind Picture Archives; **74 B** Portrait of Anne

Hutchinson (1591-1643), American School, (20th century)/Schlesinger Library, Radcliffe Institute, Harvard University,/The Bridgeman Art Library; **74 TL** © H. Stanley Johnson/SuperStock; **74 MR** SuperStock, Inc.; **76** Mary Evans Picture Library; **77** The Picture Collection of the New York Public Library; **78** © Private Collection/© Philip Mould Ltd, London/The Bridgeman Art Library; **79** The Granger Collection, New York; **80 MR** The Granger Collection, New York; **80 TL** Library of Congress; **80 B** The New York Public Library/Art Resource, NY; **83 T** Roy Rainford/Robert Harding World Imagery; **83 M** © Charles E. Rotkin/CORBIS; **83 B** © Philip Gould/CORBIS; **84 Bkgrnd** SuperStock Inc.; **84** The Granger Collection, New York; **85** The Granger Collection, New York; **87** Portrait of General James Edward Oglethorpe (1696-1785) founder of the State of Georgia, copy of original portrait in Atlanta, c.1932 (oil on canvas), Ravenet, Simon Francois (1706/21-74) (after)/Corpus Christi College, Oxford, UK/Bridgeman Art Library; **89** Hulton Archive/Getty Images Inc.; **90** © Jon Arnold/SuperStock; **92 L** Tumacacori Mission, 1855 (oil on canvas), Pratt, Henry Cheever (1803-80)/© Phoenix Art Museum, Arizona, Francis Hover Stanley and Carolanne Smurthwaite/Bridgeman Art Library; **92 R** Jack Dykinga/Getty Images; **96** The Granger Collection, New York; **98-99** Embroidered by: Eunice Bourne, Massachusetts (Barnstable), 1732- before 1781. Overmantel (detail). American, Colonial, mid-18th century. Plain weave linen embroidered with wool, silk and metallic yarns, glass beads, and wood frame with glass. 63 × 129 cm (24 13/16 × 50 13/16 in) (Including frame). Museum of Fine Arts, Boston. Seth K. Sweetser Fund, 21.2233. Photograph © 2006 Museum of Fine Arts, Boston; **100 M** The Granger Collection, New York; **100 TR** Copyright © North Wind/North Wind Picture Archives—All rights reserved; **100 BL** Slaves preparing tobacco, Virginia, America, c.1790, from 'Le Costume Ancien et Moderne', Volume II, plate 50, by Jules Ferrario, engraved by Angelo Biasioli (1790-1830), published c.1820s-30s (colour litho), Bramati, G. (19th century) (after)/Private Collection, The Stapleton Collection/Bridgeman Art Library; **101 B** North Wind Picture Archives; **102** Private Collection, © John Noott Galleries, Broadway, Worcestershire, UK/The Bridgeman Art Library; **103** The Granger Collection, New York; **105 R** The New York Public Library, Rare Book Division/Art Resource; **105 L** Copyright © North Wind/North Wind Picture Archives—All rights reserved; **106** Courtesy of the Library of Congress; **107** The Granger Collection, New York; **109 BR** © CORBIS/Bettmann; **109 BL** © Richard T. Nowitz/CORBIS; **109 TL** The Granger Collection, New York; **109 R** Wilberforce House, Hull Museums, Hull City Council, UK. DK; **110 R** Victoria & Albert Museum, London/Art Resource, NY; **110 L** Wenham Museum; **111** The Granger Collection, New York; **112** The Granger Collection, New York; **113** SuperStock, Inc.; **115** The Granger Collection, New York; **116** Slaves preparing tobacco, Virginia, America, c.1790, from 'Le Costume Ancien et Moderne', Volume II, plate 50, by Jules Ferrario, engraved by Angelo Biasioli (1790-1830), published c.1820s-30s (colour litho), Bramati, G. (19th century) (after)†/Private Collection, The Stapleton Collection/Bridgeman Art Library; **117** © CORBIS; **118** The Granger Collection, New York; **119 B** © CORBIS; **119 M** The Granger Collection, New York; **119 R** The Granger Collection, New York; **120** Schomburg Center/Art Resource, NY; **121** Copyright © North Wind/North Wind Picture Archives—All rights reserved; **123** Archivo Icongrafico, S.A/CORBIS; **125 T** Collection of The New-York Historical Society; **125 B** Pearson Education/PH School Division; **128** The Granger Collection, New York; **129** The Granger Collection, New York; **130** Maryland Province of the Society of Jesus. Photo by Don Doll, SJ; **131** The Granger Collection, New York; **132 T** Library of Congress; **132 B** North Wind Picture Archives; **133** The Granger Collection, New York; **134-135 BL** Courtesy National Archives; **134 T** Tony Freeman/PhotoEdit; **135 BR** Copyright © North Wind/North Wind Picture Archives—All rights reserved; **135 TL** The Granger Collection, New York; **136-137** © Bettmann/CORBIS; **140** The Granger Collection, New York; **141** The Granger Collection, New York; **143** Robert Griffing/Paramount Press, Inc.; **144** Mary Evans Picture Library; **145 L** Colonial Williamsburg Foundation; **145 R** Corbis/Bettmann; **147** Copyright © North Wind/North Wind Picture Archives—All rights reserved; **148** The Granger Collection, New York; **149** The Granger Collection, New York; **150** © North Wind Picture Archive; **151 T** The Granger Collection, New York; **151 B** Boston Tea Party tea leaves in a glass bottle, collected by T.M. Harris, Dorchester Neck, December 1773, American School, (18th century)/© Massachusetts Historical Society, Boston, MA, USA/Bridgeman Art Library; **151 BL** Courtesy, American Antiquarian Society; **153** Jim Conaty/Omni-Photo Communications, Inc.; **154 T** Courtesy of the Library of Congress; **154 B** John Singleton Copley (American, 1738-1815), "Mrs. James Warren (Mercy Otis)," ca.1763. Oil on canvas. 9 5/8 × 39 1/2 in. (126 × 100.3 cm). Bequest of Winslow Warren. Courtesy, Museum of Fine Arts, Boston. Reproduced with permission. (c)2000 Museum of Fine Arts, Boston. All Rights Reserved. Photograph © 2006 Museum of Fine Arts, Boston.; **154 BR** Jim Barber/StockRep, Inc.; **154 M** The Granger Collection, New York; **155** The Granger Collection, New York; **156** © Art Resource, NY; **157** The Granger Collection, New York; **158** Fort Ticonderoga Museum; **159** Fort Ticonderoga Museum; **160 M** Copyright © North Wind/North Wind Picture Archives—All rights reserved.; **160 BL** American 18th Century, Attack on Bunker's Hill, with the Burning of Charles Town, oil on canvas, .533 × .708 (21 × 27 7/8); framed: .603 × .774 × .038 (23 3/4 × 30 1/2 × 1 1/2). Gift of Edgar Williams and Bernice Chrysler Garbisch, Photograph (c) 2000 Board of Trustees, National Gallery of Art, Washington, 1783 or after, oil on canvas.; **160 TR** The Granger Collection; **160 BR** The Granger Collection; **160 T** © CORBIS; **166-167** Paintings by Don Troiani; historicalartprints.com; **170** The Granger Collection, New York; **171** Bettmann/CORBIS; **172** The Granger Collection, New York; **173** Maryland Historical Society, Baltimore; **174** Courtesy National Archives and Records Administration, College Park, Maryland, photo no. (USH001TF 011 004); **175** Index Stock Imagery, Inc.; **179** The Granger Collection, New York; **181** The Granger Collection, New York; **182 BL** Uniforms of the American Revolution: 1777 Private Field Dress from the 1st Georgia Continental Infantry (gouache & w/c on paper), Lefferts, Charles MacKubin (1873-1923)/© New-York Historical Society, New York, USA/Bridgeman Art Library; **182 TR** Colonial Williamsburg Foundation; **182 BR** Courtesy National Park Service, Museum Management Program and Valley Forge National Historical Park. Rifle, 1760-1770, Pennsylvania "Mountain" flintlock rifle. Steel, iron, wood. L 137.8 Barrel L 99.7 cm. The George C. Neumann Collection, Valley Forge Historical Park, VAFO 172. http://www.cr.nps.gov/museum/exhibits/revwar/image_gal/vafoimg/vafo172.html; **182 BM** The Connecticut Historical Society Museum, Hartford, Connecticut; **183** The Granger Collection, New York; **184** PhotoDisc, Inc./Getty Images; **185** Pearson Education/PH School Division; **186** The Granger Collection, New York; **187** © CORBIS/Bettman; **188** The Granger Collection, New York; **190** The Granger Collection, New York; **191** SuperStock, Inc.; **192** Copyright © North Wind/North Wind Picture Archives—All rights reserved.; **194 TL** The Granger Collection, New York; **194 M** The Granger Collection, New York; **194 TR** The Granger Collection, New York; **194 BL** The Granger Collection, New York; **194 BR** Fort Ticonderoga Museum; **194 Bkgrnd** The Granger Collection, New York; **197** PhotoDisc, Inc./Getty Images; **198** Corel Professional Photos CD-ROM; **200-201** Independence National Historical Park; **204** (4) The Granger Collection, New York; **205** Virginia Tourism Corp; **208** The Granger Collection, New York; **211 B** Richard Hamilton Smith/CORBIS; **211 T** Raymond Bial; **212** The Granger Collection, New York; **213 R** Gary Randall/Getty Images, Inc.-Taxi; **213 L** Bob Krist/CORBIS; **214** James Wilson (1742-1798) American Revolutionary Statesman, 1792 by Jean Pierre Henri Louis. (1755-1799) Watercolor on ivory, 6.7 × 5.2 cm., detail, Smithsonian American Art Museum, Washington, D.C./Art Resource, NY; **216 BR** © CORBIS/Bettmann; **216 TL** Art Resource, NY; **216 BL** © CORBIS/Bettmann; **216 BR** Jon Feingersh/Stock, Boston; **216 TR** © CORBIS/Bettmann; **216 Bkgrnd** Jon Feingersh/Stock, Boston; **218** © CORBIS; **219** © CORBIS; **220** Courtesy of the Library of Congress; **225** Courtesy of the Library of Congress; **227 & 228** Donovan Reese/Getty Images-Photodisc-; **244** © Corbis Royalty Free; **250** Photograph by Robin Miller, 2001. Independence National Historical Park; **251** © Bettmann/CORBIS; **252** © CORBIS/Bettmann; **253 T** © CORBIS/Bettmann; **253 M** © Archivo Iconografico, S.A./CORBIS; **253 B** © CORBIS; **254** Steve Bronstein/Getty Images; **255 R** Courtesy of the Library of Congress; **255 MR** Drug Enforcement Administration; **255 ML** Tony Freeman/PhotoEdit; **255 L** California Historical Society, San Francisco; **258** © Joseph Sohm; ChromoSohm, Inc./CORBIS; **263** Collection, Supreme Court Historical Society. Steve Petteway, Photographer.; **265** Jeff Cadge/Getty Images; **266** The Granger Collection, New York; **267 L** Jeff Greenberg/Omni-Photo Communications, Inc.; **267 R** Nick Ut/AP/Wide World Photos; **269** © Michael S. Yamashita/CORBIS; **270** Paul Sakuma/AP/Wide World Photos; **271** © Paul Conklin/PhotoEdit; **272 B** © Corbis/Bettmann; **273 R** Portrait of George Washington (1732-99), 1853 (oil on canvas), Peale, Rembrandt (1778-1860)/© Collection of the New-York Historical Society, USA,/The Bridgeman Art Library; **273 B** Jim Conaty/Omni-Photo Communications, Inc.; **274** The Granger Collection, New York; **275 T** The Granger Collection, New York; **275 M** National Geographic Society; **276 BL** Thomas Sully, Andrew Jackson,

Acknowledgments

detail, Andrew W. Mellon Collection. Photograph © Board of Trustees, National Gallery of Art, Washington; **276 T** The Art Collection of the Union League of Philadelphia; **277 TL** The Granger Collection, New York; **277 TR** Copyright © North Wind/North Wind Picture Archives—All rights reserved.; **277 B** John Guthrie, Guthrie Studios; **278-279** Mr. and Mrs. John A. Harney; **282** The Granger Collection, New York; **283** The Granger Collection, New York; **285** Art Resource, NY (detail); **286 B** The Metropolitan Museum of Art, Gift of Edgar William and Bernice Chrysler Garbisch, 1963. (63.201.2) Photograph © 1983 The Metropolitan Museum of Art; **286 L** The Granger Collection, New York; **286 TL** © CORBIS; **286 TR** © Bettmann/CORBIS; **288** Library of Congress, Prints & Photographs Division, LC-USZC4-1495; **289 T** Abby Aldrich Rockefeller Folk Art Museum, Colonial Williamsburg Foundation, Williamsburg, VA; **289 B** Dave King/© Dorling Kindersley; **290** The Granger Collection, New York; **291 L** White House Historical Association (White House Collection) (55); **291 R** The Granger Collection, New York; **292 B** Joe Raedle/Newsmakers/Getty Images; **292 T** Democratic National Committee; **294 L** The Granger Collection, New York; **294 R** Kevin Fleming/CORBIS; **296** Cliche Bibliotheque nationale de France-Paris; **298** The Granger Collection, New York; **299** The Granger Collection, New York; **301** © National Portrait Gallery, Smithsonian Institution/Art Resource, NY; **304** The Metropolitan Museum of Art, Gift of Edgar William and Bernice Chrysler Garbisch, 1963. (63.201.2) Photograph © 1983 The Metropolitan Museum of Art; **305** Courtesy of the Library of Congress; **306-307** The Granger Collection, New York; **308 TL** White House Collection, copyright White House Historical Association; **308 TR** © National Portrait Gallery, Smithsonian Institution/Art Resource, NY; **309 L** Field Museum of Natural History; **309 R** From the Collection of Mac G. and Janelle Morris; **310** SuperStock, Inc.; **311** Nathan Beck/Omni-Photo Communications, Inc.; **314** The Granger Collection, New York; **315** The Granger Collection, New York; **317** NASA/Johnson Space Center; **318** O.C. Seltzer, Lewis and Clark with Sacagawea, at the Great Falls of the Missouri River, #0137.871. From the Collection of Gilcrease Museum, Tulsa in BOB. Also, ON PAGE: The Thomas Gilcrease Institute of Art Tulsa, Oklahoma; **320 B** Dick Durrance/National Geographic Society; **320 T** The Granger Collection, New York; **321 M** Independence National Historical Park; **321 TR** Smithsonian Institution, Photo no. 95-3550; **321 B** Missouri Historical Society, St. Louis; **321 TL** Independence National Historical Park; **321 M** Independence National Historical Park; **322** The Granger Collection, New York; **323** Copyright © North Wind/North Wind Picture Archives—All rights reserved.; **324** The Fotomas Index; **327** From the collection of Mac G. and Janelle C. Morris; **328 L** The Granger Collection; **330** Field Museum of Natural History; **336-337** Art Resource, NY; **340** The Bridgeman Art Library; **341 TR** Daniel Webster, c.1828., detail, National Portrait Gallery, Smithsonian Institution/Art Resource, NY; **341 TL** The Granger Collection, New York; **341 B** John Caldwell Calhoun, ca. 1818-25, detail, National Portrait Gallery, Smithsonian Institution/Art Resource, NY; **343** Copyright © V&A Images/—All rights reserved.; **344** Courtesy of the Metropolitan Museum of Art, Rogers Fund, 1942 (42.95.7). Photograph © 1995 By the Metropolitan Museum of Art, NY; **345** The Granger Collection, New York; **349 R** © CORBIS; **349 L** Rose DiBiasi/Freezepic Photography; **351 L** THE COUNTY ELECTION, 1852 (detail), George Caleb Bingham, American, 1811-1879, oil on canvas, 38 × 52", The Saint Louis Art Museum. Gift of Bank of America.; **351 R** Courtesy of the Library of Congress; **352** Thomas Sully, Andrew Jackson, detail, Andrew W. Mellon Collection. Photograph © Board of Trustees, National Gallery of Art, Washington; **353** Robert Cruikshank. "The President's Levee, or all Creation going to the White House. Courtesy of the Library of Congress; **355** Mary Evans Picture Library; **358 Inset** Trail of Tears Commission, Inc.; **358 L** John Guthrie, Guthrie Studios; **361 L** Courtesy of the Library of Congress; **361 R** Pearson Education/PH School Division; **362** SuperStock, Inc.; **363** Courtesy of the Library of Congress; **365** Courtesy of the Library of Congress; **366 BR** The Granger Collection, New York; **366 BL** Corning Museum of Glass; **366 TR** Getty Images Inc.–Hulton Archive Photos; **366 TL** © New-York Historical Society, New York, USA/Bridgeman Art Library, London/New York; **371** The Granger Collection, New York; **372** The Metropolitan Museum of Art, Gift of Edgar William and Bernice Chrysler Garbisch, 1963. (63.201.2) Photograph © 1983 The Metropolitan Museum of Art; **373** © CORBIS; **374 T** © Bettmann/CORBIS; **374 BR** Courtesy of the Library of Congress; **374 BL** Courtesy of the Library of Congress; **375** © Bettmann/CORBIS; **376 T** © CORBIS; **376 B** © CORBIS; **377 TR** © CORBIS; **377 TL** Image by courtesy of the Wedgwood Museum Trust Limited, Barlaston, Staffordshire, England.;

377 B Collection of The New-York Historical Society, negative no. 26280ON; **378-379** Clyde DeLand/SuperStock; **382** © Bettmann/CORBIS; **383** Dave King/© Dorling Kindersley; **384** The Granger Collection, New York; **385** Michael Newman/PhotoEdit Inc.; **386 L** The Granger Collection, New York; **386 Inset** American Textile History Museum, Lowell, Mass.; **389 T** Copyright © North Wind/North Wind Picture Archives—All rights reserved.; **390** © Roger-Viollet/The Image Works; **391** The Granger Collection, New York; **392** Matthew Brady/Library of Congress, Washington, D.C. USA/The Bridgeman Art Library, London/New York; **393** The Granger Collection, New York; **394** © CORBIS; **396** SuperStock, Inc.; **398 B** Hunter Museum of Art; **398 Inset** Liz McAulay (c) Dorling Kindersley; **399 L** Collection of The New-York Historical Society; **399 BR** New-York Historical Society, New York, USA/The Bridgeman Art Library, London/New York; **399 TR** Old Slave Mart; **400** The Granger Collection, New York; **401** © North Wind Picture Archives; **403** Courtesy of the Library of Congress; **410-411** Shelburne Museum, Shelburne, Vermont (cat #27.1.5-25) Photograph by Ken Burris.; **414** © CORBIS; **415** Courtesy of the Library of Congress; **416** © New Bedford Whaling Museum. †detail; **417 R** The Granger Collection, New York; **418** Brooke/Topical Press Agency/Getty Images; **420 T** © Kevin Fleming/CORBIS; **420 B** Fine Art Photographic Library/CORBIS; **421 TL** Culver Pictures, Inc., **421 TR** The Granger Collection, New York; **421 TM** © CORBIS; **421 BR** © CORBIS; **421 BL** The Metropolitan Museum of Art, The Elisha Whittelsey Collection, The Elisha Whittelsey Fund, 1951. MM 55138 Photograph, all rights reserved, The Metropolitan Museum of Art.; **422** The Granger Collection, New York; **423** Getty Images Inc.–Hulton Archive Photos; **424** Image by courtesy of the Wedgwood Museum Trust Limited, Barlaston, Staffordshire, England.; **425 BR** © CORBIS; **425 B** Smithsonian American Art Museum, Washington, DC/Art Resource; **427** Adelaide Johnson, Portrait monument to Lucretia Mott, Elizabeth Cady Stanton and Susan B. Anthony. Marble, c. 1920. Architect of the Capitol.; **428** © CORBIS; **430** Maria Mitchell Association; **431 R** The Granger Collection, New York; **431 L** 20th Century Fox/Everett Collection; **432 L** Courtesy of the Library of Congress; **432 R** Copyright © 1930 by R.R. Donnelly & Sons, Inc. and Plattsburgh College Foundation, Inc. All rights reserved.; **433** © Corbis/Bettmann; **434** Thomas Cole. Oil on Canvas 23 3/4 × 31 1/2. The Minneapolis Institute of Arts; **439** © New Bedford Whaling Museum; **440-441** 59.21 Benjamin Franklin Reinhart, The Emigrant Train Bedding Down for the Night, 1867, oil on canvas, 40 × 70 in. Corcoran Gallery of Art, Washington, D.C. Gift of Mr. and Mrs. Lansdell K. Christie; **444** North Wind/North Wind Picture Archives; **446** CLAVER CARROLL/photolibrary.com; **448** The Granger Collection, New York; **450 BR** The Granger Collection, New York; **450 T** © Michael T. Sedam/CORBIS; **450-451 T** William Henry Jackson/Scotts Bluff National Monument; **450 M** Geoff Brightling/© Dorling Kindersley; **451 BL** Courtesy of the Lane County Historical Museum. photo by John Zimmerman; **451 TR** Bruce Forster/© Dorling Kindersley; **452 B** The Art Archive/Gift of Ruth Koerner Oliver/Buffalo Bill Historical Center, Cody, Wyoming/6922.1; **452 T** The Granger Collection, New York; **453** PhotoDisc, Inc./Getty Images; **454** Center for American History/University of Texas at Austin; **455 R** The Granger Collection, New York; **455 B** John M. Roberts/CORBIS; **457** Bettmann/CORBIS; **460 B** Corel Professional Photos CD-ROM™; **460 T** © Bettmann/CORBIS; **461 M** Chicago Historical Society; **461 B** Color lithograph by unknown artist, Landing of the Troops at Vera Cruz, 1847. Anne S.K. Brown Military Collection, John Hay Library, Brown University; **462** California State Library; **463 T** Used by permission, Utah State Historical Society, all rights reserved; **463 L** "Handcart Pioneers" by CCA Christensen (c) by Intellectual Reserve, Inc. Courtesy of Museum of Church History and Art Used by Permission.; **464 T** Courtesy History Division, Los Angeles County Museum of Natural History; **464 B** Andrew McKinney/© Dorling Kindersley; **465** USC Regional History Center; **466** San Francisco, general view, ca. 1850-52; detail, engraving by S. Frank Marryat, Collection of The New-York Historical Society, negative no. 26280; **470** The Granger Collection, New York; **472 L** © North Wind/North Wind Picture Archives—All rights reserved.; **472 R** Library of Congress; **473** Robertstock; **474 TR** Abolition of Colonial Slavery Meeting, 1830 (letterpress), English School, (19th century)/Private Collection,/The Bridgeman Art Library; **474 M** The Granger Collection, New York; **474 TL** © Bettmann/CORBIS; **475** The Granger Collection, New York; **476 B** © CORBIS; **476 T** The Granger Collection, NY; **477 T** Mary Evans Picture Library; **477 B** His First Vote, 1868 (oil on canvas), Wood, Thomas Waterman (1823-1903)/Private Collection, Christie's Images/www.bridgeman.co.uk/The Bridgeman Art Library, London/New York;

478-479 The Granger Collection, New York; 482 © David J. & Janice L. Frent Collection/CORBIS; 483 Courtesy of the Library of Congress; 484 R Clemson University; 484 R The Granger Collection, New York; 486 L The Granger Collection; 486 L Picture History; 487 L Copyright © North Wind/North Wind Picture Archives—All rights reserved.; 487 R Illinois State University; 488 © Bettmann/CORBIS; 488 Inset RÈunion des MusÈes Nationaux/Art Resource, NY; 490 The Granger Collection, NY; 493 T The Granger Collection, New York; 493 B Pearson Education/PH School Division; 494 Courtesy of the Library of Congress; 495 John Henry Brown, "Abraham Lincoln" (1809-1865), Sixteenth US President. Watercolor on ivory, c. 1860. National Portrait Gallery, Smithsonian Institution/Art Resource, NY. (detail); 496 © CORBIS/Bettmann; 497 Kansas State Historical Society; 498 The Granger Collection, New York; 499 National Portrait Gallery, Smithsonian Institution/Art Resource, NY (NPG.71.29); 499 © CORBIS; 499 © CORBIS; 501 Hulton-Deutsch Collection/CORBIS; 502 B The Granger Collection, New York; 502 T United States Department of the Interior; 502 M Adoc-photos/Art Resource, NY; 506 Kansas State Historical Society; 507 The Granger Collection, New York; 508-509 Painting by Don Troiani/ historicalartprints.com; 512 © Medford Historical Society Collection/ CORBIS; 515 L Omni-Photo Communications, Inc.; 515 R Omni-Photo Communications, Inc.; 516 Courtesy Beverley R. Robinson Collection, US Naval Academy Museum; 517 Dave King/Dorling Kindersley (c) Confederate Memorial Hall, New Orleans; 518 The Granger Collection, New York; 519 L © Bettmann/CORBIS; 519 R Steve Helber/AP/Wide World Photos; 522-523 from Great Battles of the Civil War by kind permission of Marshall Editions Ltd; 523 BL Publisher's Press, Inc.; 523 BR Collection of Picture Research Consultants, Inc. Photo © Collection of David and Kevin Kyle; 524 © Bettmann/CORBIS; 525 Collection of the personal papers of General Robert H. Milroy, Courtesy of the Jasper County Public Library, Rensselaer, Indiana (detail); 526 AP/Wide World Photos; 528 The Granger Collection, New York; 529 The Granger Collection, New York; 530 R The Granger Collection, New York; 530 L Getty Images Inc.–Hulton Archive Photos; 532 AP/Wide World Photos; 533 SuperStock, Inc.; 535 Courtesy of the Library of Congress; 541 The Granger Collection, New York; 542-543 © CORBIS; 544 R Medford Historical Society Collection; 544 L The Granger Collection, New York; 545 L © Corbis/Bettmann; 545 R The Granger Collection, New York; 546 Smithsonian American Art Museum, Washington, DC/Art Resource, NY; 547 © CORBIS/Bettmann; 548 R © CORBIS/BETTMANN; 548 L Getty Images-Hulton Archive Photos; 550 M The Charleston Museum; 550 B The Granger Collection, New York; 550 T Dave King/Dorling Kindersley © Confederate Memorial Hall, New Orleans; 551 TL Copyright © North Wind/North Wind Picture Archives—All rights reserved.; 551 M Douglas Mudd, National Numismatic Collection, The Smithsonian Institution; 551 TR neg. #86-113-74, Rudolf Eickmeyer, National Museum of American History, Smithsonian Institution; 551 B The Museum of the Confederacy, Richmond, Virginia, Photography by KATHERINE WETZEL; 552 Courtesy of the Library of Congress; 553 L The Granger Collection, New York; 553 R Courtesy of the Library of Congress; 554 R Courtesy of the Library of Congress; 554 L Courtesy of the Library of Congress; 555 The Granger Collection, New York; 556 The Granger Collection, New York; 557 T Old Court House Museum, Vicksburg, Photo by Bob Pickett; 557 B Collection of Mississippi State Historical Museum/Mississippi Department of Archives and History; 558 © Bettmann/CORBIS; 560 Inset Courtesy of the Library of Congress; 560-561 © CORBIS; 562 © CORBIS/Bettmann; 563 © CORBIS; 565 © CORBIS; 566 His First Vote, 1868 (oil on canvas), Wood, Thomas Waterman (1823-1903)/ Private Collection, Christie's Images/www.bridgeman.co.uk/The Bridgeman Art Library, London/New York; 567 The Granger Collection, New York; 568 L © North Wind/North Wind Picture Archives—All rights reserved.; 568 B CORBIS; BM United States Department of the Interior; BR Dave King/Dorling Kindersley © Confederate Memorial Hall, New Orleans; 568 T Library of Congress; 569 T Library of Congress; B Bettmann/CORBIS; 570 (2) The Granger Collection, New York; 571 © CORBIS; 571 The Granger Collection, New York; 572-573 © Royalty-Free/Corbis; 574 T Solomon D. Butcher Collection, Nebraska State Historical Society; Bettmann/CORBIS AP Photo/ Hiroko Ami, Japan Pool; 575 T Getty Images; B Bettmann/CORBIS; 576 Solomon D. Butcher Collection, Nebraska State Historical Society; 578 The Granger Collection, New York; 579 Snark/Art Resource, NY; 580 © CORBIS; 581 T Getty Images Inc.–Hulton Archive Photos; 581 B Schomburg Center for Research in Black Culture/Art Resource, NY; 582 B © Bettmann/CORBIS; 582 M © Bettmann/CORBIS; 582 T © Bettmann/CORBIS; 583 T Hulton Archive/Getty Images; 583 B © Bettmann/Corbis; 584 © Bettmann/CORBIS; 585 The Granger Collection, New York; 586 © royalty-free/CORBIS; 587 © Underwood & Underwood/CORBIS; 588 B © CORBIS/Bettmann; 588 TR Popperfoto/Retrofile; 588 TL AP/Wide World Photos; 590 © Swim Ink 2, LLC/CORBIS; 591 R Courtesy of the Library of Congress; 591 L © CORBIS; 593 Getty Images; 594 © Bettmann/CORBIS; 596 Image by © David J. & Janice L. Frent Collection/CORBIS; 597 AP/Wide World Photos; 598 David Brauchli/Reuters/CORBIS; 599 R © Reuters/CORBIS; 599 L "USA TODAY (9/12/2001) Reprinted with Permission"; 600 AP/Wide World Photos; 606-607 Corel Professional Photos CD-ROM; 609 Heritage Image Partnership; 611 Copyright © North Wind/North Wind Picture Archives—All rights reserved.; 612 Jamestown-Yorktown Educational Trust/Bridgeman Art Library; 615 © Bettmann/CORBIS; 617 Jim Conaty/Omni-Photo Communications, Inc.; 618 © Bettmann/CORBIS; 621 © CORBIS/Bettmann; 625 The Granger Collection, New York; 627 Copyright © North Wind/North Wind Picture Archives—All rights reserved.; 629 The Granger Collection, New York; 631 The Granger Collection, New York; 633 The Granger Collection, New York; 635 Seaver Center for Western History Research, Natural History Museum of Los Angeles County; 636 The Granger Collection, New York; 638 Valentine Museum, Richmond, Virginia; 640 Courtesy of the Library of Congress; 643 01 © National Portrait Gallery, Smithsonian Institution/Art Resource, NY; 643 01 © National Portrait Gallery, Smithsonian Institution/Art Resource, NY; 643 02 © National Portrait Gallery, Smithsonian Institution/Art Resource, NY; 643 03 White House Collection, copyright White House Historical Association; 643 04 © National Portrait Gallery, Smithsonian Institution/Art Resource, NY; 643 05 © National Portrait Gallery, Smithsonian Institution/Art Resource, NY; 643 06 National Portrait Gallery, Smithsonian Institution/Art Resource, NY; 643 07 White House Collection, copyright White House Historical Association; 643 08 White House Collection, copyright White House Historical Association; 643 09 © National Portrait Gallery, Smithsonian Institution/Art Resource, NY; 643 10 © National Portrait Gallery, Smithsonian Institution/Art Resource, NY; 643 11 White House Collection, copyright White House Historical Association; 643 12 © National Portrait Gallery, Smithsonian Institution/Art Resource, NY; 644 13 White House Collection, copyright White House Historical Association; 644 14 © National Portrait Gallery, Smithsonian Institution/Art Resource, NY; 644 15 © National Portrait Gallery, Smithsonian Institution/Art Resource, NY; 644 16 White House Collection, copyright White House Historical Association; 644 17 White House Collection, copyright White House Historical Association; 644 18 © National Portrait Gallery, Smithsonian Institution/Art Resource, NY; 644 19 White House Collection, copyright White House Historical Association; 644 20 © National Portrait Gallery, Smithsonian Institution/Art Resource, NY; 644 21 © National Portrait Gallery, Smithsonian Institution/Art Resource, NY; 644 22 White House Collection, copyright White House Historical Association; 644 23 White House Collection, copyright White House Historical Association; 644 24 White House Collection, copyright White House Historical Association; 645 25 © National Portrait Gallery, Smithsonian Institution/Art Resource, NY; 645 26 © National Portrait Gallery, Smithsonian Institution/Art Resource, NY; 645 27 © National Portrait Gallery, Smithsonian Institution/Art Resource, NY; 645 28 White House Collection, copyright White House Historical Association; 645 29 White House Collection, copyright White House Historical Association; 645 30 White House Collection, copyright White House Historical Association; 645 31 White House Collection, copyright White House Historical Association; 645 32 White House Collection, copyright White House Historical Association; 645 33 White House Collection, copyright White House Historical Association; 645 34 White House Collection, copyright White House Historical Association; 645 35 © National Portrait Gallery, Smithsonian Institution/Art Resource, NY; 645 36 White House Collection, copyright White House Historical Association; 646 37 White House Collection, copyright White House Historical Association; 646 38 White House Collection, copyright White House Historical Association; 646 39 White House Collection, copyright White House Historical Association; 646 40 White House Collection, copyright White House Historical Association; 646 42 White House Historical Association (White House Collection) (6196) (detail); 646 43 Bob Daemmrich//PictureQuest/ Jupiter; 646 41 White House Historical Association (White House Collection) (6196) (detail); 646 B White House Photo Office; 650 Lawrence Migdale/Pix; 651 The Granger Collection, New York; 654 © Monica Graff/The Image Works; 662 © North Wind Picture Archives; 663 Getty Images

Acknowledgments

Text Credits

Grateful acknowledgment is made to the following for copyrighted material:

Alfred A. Knopf, Inc.
"I, Too" by Langston Hughes from *American Negro Poetry, Revised Edition,* copyright © 1974 by the Estate of Arna Bontemps. First edition copyright © by Arna Bontemps.

American Heritage
Excerpt from *Christopher Columbus, Hero and Villain* by Christine Gibson, from AmericanHeritage.com.

Bantam Books
Excerpt from *Dauntless: A Novel of Midway and Guadalcanal* by Barrett Tillman, copyright © 1992 by Barrett Tillman. Used by permission of Bantam Books, a division of Random House, Inc.

Bedford/St. Martin's
Excerpt from *Reading the American Past* by Michael P. Johnson, copyright © 2005 by Bedford/St Martin's.

Close Up Publishing
from "I Never Cared Much for Machinery" by Lucy Larcom, from *Ordinary Americans: U.S. History Through The Eyes Of Everyday People, Second Edition,* copyright © 2003 Close Up Foundation.

Creators Syndicate, Inc.
Excerpt from "The Importance of Voting" from *Talking it Over* by Hillary Rodham Clinton, copyright © 2000 by Creators Syndicate, Inc.

Da Capo Press
Excerpt from *Life in California During a Residence of Several Years in That Territory* by Alfred Robinson, copyright © 1969 by Da Capo Press, a Division of Plenum Publishing Corporation.

Doubleday
Excerpt from *Lone Star Nation* by H. W. Brands, copyright © 2004 by Doubleday, a division of Random House, Inc. Excerpt from "Valley Forge" by Maxwell Anderson, from *America On Stage,* copyright © 1934 by Maxwell Anderson. Copyright renewed © 1962 by Gilda Oakleaf Anderson, Alan Anderson, Terence Anderson, Quentin Anderson, and Hesper A. Levenstein.

Encyclopedia Britannica, Inc.
Excerpt from *The Annals of America, Volume 3: 1784-1796: Organizing the New Nation,* copyright © 1976 by Encyclopedia Britannica, Inc. "Criticizing Presidential Power" by Edward Livingston, from *The Annals of America, Volume 4: 1797-1820: Domestic Expansion and Foreign Entanglements,* copyright © 1976 by Encyclopedia Britannica, Inc. "We're Almost Froze" from *The Annals of America, Volume 10: 1866-1883: Reconstruction and Industrialization,* copyright © 1976, 1977, 1987, 2003 by Encyclopedia Britannica, Inc. "You Will Be Astounded by Davy Crockett, from *The Annals of America, Volume 6: 1833-1840: The Challenge of a Continent,* copyright 1976 by Encyclopedia Britannica, Inc." Drawing the Country Together by Henry Clay, from *The Annals of America, Volume 4: 1797-1820: Domestic Expansion and Foreign Entanglements,* copyright © 1976 by Encyclopedia Britannica, Inc. "Advancing Wealth and Power" by Andrew Jackson, from *The Annals of America, Volume 5: 1821-1832: Steps Toward Equalitarianism,* copyright © 1976 by Encyclopedia Britannica, Inc. "An Interfering Government" by John C. Calhoun, from *The Annals of America, Volume 5: 1821-1832: Steps Toward Equalitarianism,* copyright © 1976 by Encyclopedia Britannica, Inc. "A Burdensome Tax" by John Adams, from *The Annals of America, Vol. 2, 1755-1783,* copyright © 1976 by Encyclopedia Britannica, Inc. "A Bill of Rights" by Thomas Jefferson, from *The Annals of America, Volume 3: 1784-1796: Organizing the New Nation,* copyright © 1976 by Encyclopaedia Britannica, Inc. "Bind Him No Longer" by John Greenleaf Whittier, from *The Annals of America, Vol. 6: 1833-1840: The Challenge of A Continent,* copyright © 1976, 1977, 1987, 2003 by Encyclopedia Britannica, Inc. "Sacred Fire of Liberty" by George Washington, from *The Annals of America, Volume 3: 1784-1796: Organizing the New Nation,* copyright © 1976 by Encyclopedia Britannica, Inc. "Good Government" by Thomas Jefferson from *The Annals of America, Volume 4: 1797-1820: Domestic Expansion and Foreign Entanglements,* copyright © 1976 by Encyclopaedia Britannica, Inc. A Well-Regulated Militia from *The Annals of America, Vol. 2, 1755-1783* by Maryland Delegates, from *The Annals of America, Vol. 2, 1755-1783,* copyright © 1976 by Encyclopedia Britannica, Inc. "Four Bullets Through My Coat" from *The Annals of America, Vol. 2, 1755-1783,* copyright © 1976 by Encyclopedia Britannica, Inc.

Facts On File, Inc.
"Their Hearts Will Be Changed" by Rev. Charles Grandison Finney, from *Encyclopedia of American Historical Documents, Volume II,* copyright © 2004, Susan Rosenfeld, Ed. "The Public Good" from *Encyclopedia of American Historical Documents* by Susan Rosenfeld (Ed.), copyright © 2001 by Susan Rosenfeld.

Paul Halsall
Excerpt from *Medieval Sourcebook: Christopher Columbus: Extracts from Journal,* from Fordham.edu, copyright © Paul Halsall March 1996.

HarperCollinsCustomBooks
Excerpt from *Leo Africanus: Description of Timbuktu,* translated by Paul Brians et al.

Heidelberg College
"Vital to Its Survival" by G. Michael Pratt, from Fallen Timbers Battlefield: Archaeological Project at Heidelberg College from *The Battle of Fallen Timbers: An historical perspective.*

Holt, Rinehart and Winston, Inc.
Excerpt from *Eyewitnesses and Others: Readings in American History, Volume 1: Beginnings to 1865* by Patrick Henry, copyright © 1991 by Holt, Rinehart and Winston, Inc.

Hon. Heather Wilson
Excerpt from "H.R. 4766, Esther Martinez Native American Languages Preservation Act of 2006" from *Library of Congress* by Hon. Heather Wilson.

Hutchinson of London
Excerpt from *Passage to America: A history of emigrants from Great Britain and Ireland to America in the mid-nineteenth century,* copyright © 1972 Terry Coleman.

Coretta Scott King
Excerpt from the Statement by Mrs. Coretta Scott King against Apartheid given at the United Nations on March 21, 1988, copyright © 1988 by Coretta Scott King.

Estate of Martin Luther King
Excerpt from *I Have a Dream* by Martin Luther King, Jr., copyright © 1963 Martin Luther King Jr., copyright renewed © 1991 Coretta Scott King.

The Library of America
Excerpt from *The American Revolution: Writings from the War of Independence* by Philip Vickers Fithian, copyright © 2001 by Literary Classics of the United States, Inc., New York, NY. Excerpt from *The American Revolution: Writings from the War of Independence* by George Rogers Clark, copyright © 2001 by Literary Classics of the United States, Inc., New York, NY.

Longman
Excerpt from "Master of his own labour" from *America Past and Present* by Robert A. Divine, copyright © 2002 by Addison-Wesley Educational Publishers Inc.

Marshall Cavendish Corporation
Excerpt from "A National Hero" from *Magill's Survey of American Literature, Volume 1,* Frank N. Magill, Ed., copyright © 1991 by Salem Press, Inc.

National Geographic
Excerpt from "Ancient Pyramid Found at Mexico City Christian Site" from *National Geographic News, April 6, 2006,* copyright © 2006 National Geographic Society. All rights reserved.

Oxford University Press
Excerpt from *Early American Writings,* copyright © 2002 by Oxford University Press, Inc. Carla Mulford, General Editor.

Pearson Education, Inc.
Excerpt from *Sequoyah and the Cherokee Alphabet* by Robert Cwiklik, copyright © 1989 by Robert Cwiklik. Reprinted by permission of Pearson Education, Inc.

Pearson Prentice Hall, Inc.
Excerpt from "Election Fever" from *Jacksonian America: 1815-1840—New Society, Changing Politics* by Frank Otto Gatell and John M. McFaul., copyright 1970 by Prentice-Hall Inc.

Scott, Foresman and Company
Excerpt from "Dog-tax Dispute" from *Sources of the American Republic: A Documentary History of Politics, Society, and Thought* by Marvin Meyers, Alexander Kern & John G. Cawelti, copyright © 1960 by Scott, Foresman and Company.

St. Martin's Press
Excerpt from *America Firsthand: Volume I: From Settlement to Reconstruction* by Robert D. Marcus and David Burner, copyright © 1989 by St. Martin's Press, Inc.

Stonesong Press Book/Penguin
Excerpt from *Witnessing America: The Library of Congress Book of Firsthand Accounts of Life in America 1600-1900,* copyright © Noel Rae (Ed.) and The Stonesong Press, Inc., 1996.

University of California
Excerpt from *Chinese American Voices; From the Gold Rush to the Present* by Judy Yung, Gordon H. Chang, and Him Mark Lai (Ed.), copyright © by the Regents of the University of California

The University of Massachusetts Press
from *On the Altar of Freedom: A Black Soldier's Civil War Letters from the Front* by James Henry Gooding, copyright © 1991 by The University of Massachusetts Press

University of Nebraska Press
Excerpt from *The War for America: 1775-1783* by Piers Mackesy, copyright © 1993 by the University of Nebraska Press, renewal copyright © 1992 by Piers Mackesy. Excerpt from *Jedediah Smith* by Dale L. Morgan, copyright © 1953 by Dale L. Morgan, University of Nebraska Press

Viking Penguin
Excerpt from *American Colonies* by Alan Taylor, Copyright Alan Taylor, copyright © 2001, Viking Penguin

Note: Every effort has been made to locate the copyright owner of material reprinted in this book. Omissions brought to our attention will be corrected in subsequent editions.